United States Census Figures
Back to 1630

A Few Words About These United States Population Statistics.

All figures listed below for years before 1992 are US Census Bureau figures as per the source files. Where there were an assortment of figures for a specific year, we averaged them. 1992 was an estimate. Years after 1992 are our estimates on a predicted growth rate of 1%, as the average growth rate of all the averaged figures from 1972-1992 was exactly 1.00%.

The raw data from which we took these figures is appended as footnote #2. All dates not given are presumed to be July 1, as that is the official date given by the US Census Bureaus, over the years, except where otherwise noted. Dates are for footnoted figures only.

Why and How You Should Use These Tables

Given the rapid inflation that took place sometimes over the past few decades, you might be aware that if a report said a certain monetary figure was up 10% during one decade, it was prudent to check to see if the figures took the inflationary trends into account to tell you the actual value a figure in one year might represent would actually be less than figures which counted more value in lesser numbers of dollars in the previous decade.

Thus you would be wise to consult a table of Price Indices— such as the file "price10.txt" released in 1993, before your evaluation of such figures is complete.

The same is true of population figures, which are going up a certain amount every year, in a very similar manner to those price index figures, only not quite as fast, in most cases.

What Started This Report

Very recently, there was a report issued on education, which stated something on the order of people in the United States are receiving 10% more of a certain level of education, than they were a decade before.

The years and the exact figures have been altered to protect those responsible from embarrassment.

For example: let us presume the report stated:
Graduation From Grade School was up 5% from 1981 to 1991.

You would think from this report that the average kid had 5% greater chances of getting a Grade School Diploma in 91 than in 81. . .but. . .it turns out that it was just the opposite because the population was 1.097352 times larger in 91, than it had been in 1981. . .which is about 10% larger, thus in a "real education" sense, in the same way the monetary reports are given in "real dollars" or "constant dollars," education was actually moving in just the opposite direction, and thus was DOWN about 5% instead of UP about 5% from 1981 to 1991.

Remember, these were not from years quoted in the report and the figures were not exactly 5% or 10% respectively, nor the diploma referred to was not a Grade School Diploma, but they are pretty close to being exact, in terms of the percentages and years; much closer than you might expect.

Here is a footnote explanation of how to be more exact

To be exact, one would have to do a demographic analysis, of the specific portions of the population of the ages at which such diplomas were conferred, as it would be irrelevant from a realistic point of view to measure the population on whole bases if you were only concerned with people who were of the age to receive Kindergarten Diplomas between 1981 and 1991— or whatever ages and a whatever kind of diploma. Thus these figures are not as precise as they could be, but still given the trends of population and education, it is obvious that a trend in one is not following the direction of the other. A further look at the US Census figures averaged below will be sufficient to inform you that previous generations that were measured had even greater growth rates than 10%, so that the number of people getting any specific degrees or diplomas in the following decades should have been going up even more.
***

In the tables below, the first line shows the Base Year: or "The Year In Question" labeled "YEAR: ####" so if you want a chart based on 1980 as the base year, you simply search/find "YEAR: 1980" to find the relevant portions.

Once you have located the table for "YEAR: ####" you can see comparisons of that year to any other year by looking up the year you wish to compare to in the left column.

The SAMPLE comparison is 1991, presented below.

You will note a ten year comparison looks like:

year/1991 1991/year Growth%

1981 0.911285 1.097352 0.9031%

This means a 1991 statistic would have to be shrunk to about 91% of its size to be relevant to a comparable 1981 statistic.

On the other hand, and 1981 statistic would have to be enlarged, this time by about 10% to be useful in comparison to 1991.

1991 is the latest year for which we have "hard statistics" so a copy of that year is presented first for you immediate use, with year back to colonization following, starting with estimates for 2009 when the United States population should reach 300 million.

You may note some fluctuations in these figures, because we used all reports from the major media and almanacs of the periods our researchers could find. If you have access to any figures which do not appear in the footnoted materials, please send them to us for inclusion in the next edition.

We are also working on a database that will NOT show fluctuation patterns of this nature, which will be based on massaged figures presented at later dates by the Census Bureau. These will be an example of the difference between the figure we can expect on an entirely "here-and-now" basis, and those which we would probably not see about today's events until a decade or two have passed.

***BYEAR = BASE YEAR ***AYEAR = A YEAR IN COMPARISON TO THE BASE YEAR

BASE YEAR: 1991

YEAR BYEAR/AYEAR AYEAR/BYEAR GROWTH%

year/1991 1991/year Growth%

1991 1.000000 1.000000 1.2505% 1990 0.987649 1.012505 0.7224% 1989 0.980565 1.019820 1.1077% 1988 0.969823 1.031116 0.8834% 1987 0.961331 1.040225 0.5594% 1986 0.955983 1.046043 1.3056% 1985 0.943663 1.059701 0.7673% 1984 0.936477 1.067832 0.8149% 1983 0.928907 1.076534 0.9737% 1982 0.919949 1.087017 0.9508% 1981 0.911285 1.097352 0.9031% 1980 0.903129 1.107262 2.2701% 1979 0.883082 1.132398 1.0042% 1978 0.874303 1.143769 0.9896% 1977 0.865735 1.155088 0.9103% 1976 0.857925 1.165603 0.8394% 1975 0.850783 1.175387 0.9042% 1974 0.843160 1.186015 1.1568% 1973 0.833518 1.199735 0.9427% 1972 0.825734 1.211044 0.7426% 1971 0.819647 1.220038 1.4697% 1970 0.807774 1.237969 0.6968% 1969 0.802185 1.246596 0.8565% 1968 0.795372 1.257273 1.5090% 1967 0.783548 1.276246 0.9949% 1966 0.775829 1.288944 1.0575% 1965 0.767711 1.302574 1.1300% 1964 0.759132 1.317293 1.5537% 1963 0.747519 1.337759 1.4658% 1962 0.736720 1.357368 1.5364% 1961 0.725572 1.378224 2.1586% 1960 0.710240 1.407974 -1.6655% 1959 0.722269 1.384525 4.3080% 1958 0.692439 1.444170 2.1130% 1957 0.678111 1.474685 1.9895% 1956 0.664883 1.504024 2.1231% 1955 0.651061 1.535955 1.4496% 1954 0.641758 1.558221 2.1573% 1953 0.628206 1.591836 1.2298% 1952 0.620574 1.611411 1.6814% 1951 0.610312 1.638505 1.6233% 1950 0.600564 1.665103 1.4265% 1949 0.592117 1.688856 1.7790% 1948 0.581767 1.718901 1.8242% 1947 0.571345 1.750257 -2.6320% 1946 0.586789 1.704189 3.1768% 1945 0.568722 1.758328 6.4754% 1944 0.534135 1.872187 -0.3437% 1943 0.535977 1.865753 0.6562% 1942 0.532482 1.877996 0.6633% 1941 0.528974 1.890453 -5.6614% 1940 0.560718 1.783427 8.0381% 1939 0.519001 1.926780 0.8126% 1938 0.514817 1.942438 0.7762% 1937 0.510852 1.957516 0.6029% 1936 0.507790 1.969317 0.5244% 1935 0.505141 1.979644 -3.0364% 1934 0.520959 1.919535 4.6271% 1933 0.497920 2.008354 1.3921% 1932 0.491084 2.036313 -0.2051% 1931 0.492093 2.032137 0.8886% 1930 0.487759 2.050194 1.0126% 1929 0.482869 2.070954 1.1526% 1928 0.477367 2.094824 1.2160% 1927 0.471632 2.120297 1.4086% 1926 0.465081 2.150163 1.7667% 1925 0.457007 2.188150 1.4465% 1924 0.450491 2.219801 1.7700% 1923 0.442656 2.259091 1.6165% 1922 0.435614 2.295610 1.3736% 1921 0.429711 2.327144 2.3393% 1920 0.419889 2.381583 1.3140% 1919 0.414443 2.412877 0.7676% 1918 0.411286 2.431399 0.3870% 1917 0.409700 2.440808 1.3274% 1916 0.404333 2.473209 1.4083% 1915 0.398718

2

2.508038 1.4458% 1914 0.393035 2.544300 1.9424% 1913 0.385547 2.593720 1.9857% 1912 0.378040 2.645223 1.5634% 1911 0.372221 2.686578 1.8169% 1910 0.365578 2.735391 1.8781% 1909 0.358839 2.786763 2.0082% 1908 0.351775 2.842728 1.9603% 1907 0.345012 2.898453 1.8264% 1906 0.338824 2.951389 1.9357% 1905 0.332390 3.008518 2.0148% 1904 0.325825 3.069135 2.1335% 1903 0.319018 3.134616 1.8151% 1902 0.313331 3.191514 1.8943% 1901 0.307506 3.251972 3.0255% 1900 0.298475 3.350360 0.6278% 1899 0.296613 3.371395 1.7757% 1898 0.291438 3.431260 1.8078% 1897 0.286263 3.493288 1.8396% 1896 0.281092 3.557551 1.8755% 1895 0.275917 3.624274 1.9114% 1894 0.270742 3.693548 1.9486% 1893 0.265567 3.765522 1.9858% 1892 0.260396 3.840298 2.0276% 1891 0.255222 3.918165 2.6465% 1890 0.248641 4.021860 1.5328% 1889 0.244888 4.083507 2.0811% 1888 0.239895 4.168490 2.1599% 1887 0.234823 4.258524 2.2075% 1886 0.229751 4.352532 2.2592% 1885 0.224676 4.450863 2.3095% 1884 0.219604 4.553658 2.3641% 1883 0.214532 4.661312 2.4214% 1882 0.209460 4.774181 2.4815% 1881 0.204388 4.892651 3.7644% 1880 0.196973 5.076829 0.9432% 1879 0.195133 5.124715 2.1464% 1878 0.191032 5.234712 2.1913% 1877 0.186936 5.349420 2.2426% 1876 0.182836 5.469386 2.2941% 1875 0.178736 5.594857 2.3456% 1874 0.174639 5.726090 2.4043% 1873 0.170539 5.863763 2.4635% 1872 0.166439 6.008220 2.5258% 1871 0.162338 6.159974 5.9947% 1870 0.153157 6.529244 -1.0968% 1869 0.154856 6.457632 2.1930% 1868 0.151532 6.599246 2.2394% 1867 0.148213 6.747030 2.2935% 1866 0.144890 6.901773 2.3445% 1865 0.141571 7.063584 2.4037% 1864 0.138248 7.233371 2.4599% 1863 0.134929 7.411303 2.5250% 1862 0.131606 7.598439 2.5872% 1861 0.128287 7.795030 2.9504% 1860 0.124610 8.025015 2.4012% 1859 0.121688 8.217714 2.7627% 1858 0.118417 8.444746 2.8412% 1857 0.115145 8.684678 2.9243% 1856 0.111874 8.938643 3.0161% 1855 0.108598 9.208245 3.1061% 1854 0.105327 9.494258 3.2056% 1853 0.102055 9.798609 3.3118% 1852 0.098784 10.123118 3.4252% 1851 0.095512 10.469858 4.0106% 1850 0.091829 10.889763 2.3254% 1849 0.089743 11.142990 2.7841% 1848 0.087312 11.453220 2.8590% 1847 0.084885 11.780669 2.9432% 1846 0.082458 12.127393 3.0324% 1845 0.080031 12.495144 3.1325% 1844 0.077600 12.886555 3.2284% 1843 0.075173 13.302580 3.3361% 1842 0.072747 13.746361 3.4512% 1841 0.070320 14.220775 3.8105% 1840 0.067738 14.762656 2.3861% 1839 0.066160 15.114901 2.5824% 1838 0.064494 15.505226 2.6573% 1837 0.062825 15.917251 2.7232% 1836 0.061159 16.350710 2.7994% 1835 0.059494 16.808438 2.8871% 1834 0.057824 17.293718 2.9657% 1833 0.056159 17.806595 3.0563% 1832 0.054493 18.350822 3.1604% 1831 0.052824 18.930786 3.4660% 1830 0.051054 19.586921 2.4653% 1829 0.049826 20.069797 2.6804% 1828 0.048525 20.607747 10.3427% 1827 0.043977 22.739134 -4.2314% 1826 0.045920 21.776943 2.9150% 1825 0.044619 22.411749 3.0026% 1824 0.043319 23.084676 3.0955% 1823 0.042018 23.799264 3.1944% 1822 0.040717 24.559505 3.3102% 1821 0.039413 25.372472 3.2277% 1820 0.038180 26.191429 2.6573% 1819 0.037192 26.887408 2.6261% 1818 0.036240 27.593500 2.6969% 1817 0.035289 28.337678 2.7717% 1816 0.034337 29.123109 2.8507% 1815 0.033385 29.953320 2.9343% 1814 0.032434 30.832253 3.0231% 1813 0.031482 31.764328 3.1039% 1812 0.030534 32.750260 3.2172% 1811 0.029582 33.803887 3.0969% 1810 0.028694 34.850765 2.9144% 1809 0.027881 35.866449 2.8225% 1808 0.027116 36.878766 2.9199% 1807 0.026347 37.955599 2.9918% 1806 0.025581 39.091149 3.0841% 1805 0.024816 40.296740 3.1822% 1804 0.024051 41.579060 3.2868% 1803 0.023285 42.945674 3.3985% 1802 0.022520 44.405177 3.5180% 1801 0.021755 45.967371 3.3999% 1800 0.021039 47.530238 2.8419% 1799 0.020458 48.880985 2.7485% 1798 0.019911 50.224457 2.8261% 1797 0.019363 51.643866 3.7832% 1796 0.018658 53.597662 2.1272% 1795 0.018269 54.737790 3.0879% 1794 0.017722 56.428060 3.1625% 1793 0.017178 58.212604 3.2904% 1792 0.016631 60.128040 3.4024% 1791 0.016084 62.173817 3.2296% 1790 0.015581 64.181759 41.3145% 1780 0.011026 90.698101 29.4353% 1770 0.008518 117.395373 83.4728% 1750 0.004643 215.388623 29.2845% 1740 0.003591 278.464002 94.2514% 1720 0.001849 540.920206 85.8111% 1700 0.000995 1005.089677 19.2490% 1690 0.000834 1198.559886 88.0250% 1670 0.000444 2253.592493 122.0238% 1650 0.000200 5003.511905

3

2009 1.000000 1.000000 8.2857% 2001 0.923483 1.082857 1.0000% 2000 0.914340 1.093685 1.0000% 1999 0.905287 1.104622 1.0000% 1998 0.896324 1.115668 1.0000% 1997 0.887449 1.126825 1.0000% 1996 0.878663 1.138093 1.0000% 1995 0.869963 1.149475 1.0000% 1994 0.861356 1.160960 1.0008% 1993 0.852821 1.172579 1.0000% 1992 0.844377 1.184304 0.9295% 1991 0.836601 1.195313 1.2505% 1990 0.826269 1.210260 0.7224% 1989 0.820342 1.219004 1.1077% 1988 0.811355 1.232506 0.8834% 1987 0.804250 1.243394 0.5594% 1986 0.799777 1.250349 1.3056% 1985 0.789469 1.266674 0.7673% 1984 0.783458 1.276393 0.8149% 1983 0.777125 1.286795 0.9737% 1982 0.769631 1.299325 0.9508% 1981 0.762382 1.311679 0.9031% 1980 0.755559 1.323524 2.2701% 1979 0.738788 1.353569 1.0042% 1978 0.731443 1.367161 0.9896% 1977 0.724275 1.380691 0.9103% 1976 0.717741 1.393260 0.8394% 1975 0.711766 1.404955 0.9042% 1974 0.705388 1.417659 1.1568% 1973 0.697322 1.434058 0.9427% 1972 0.690810 1.447577 0.7426% 1971 0.685717 1.458327 1.4697% 1970 0.675785 1.479761 0.6968% 1969 0.671109 1.490072 0.8565% 1968 0.665409 1.502835 1.5090% 1967 0.655517 1.525513 0.9949% 1966 0.649060 1.540691 1.0575% 1965 0.642268 1.556983 1.1300% 1964 0.635091 1.574577 1.5537% 1963 0.625375 1.599041 1.4658% 1962 0.616341 1.622480 1.5364% 1961 0.607014 1.647408 2.1586% 1960 0.594188 1.682970 -1.6655% 1959 0.604252 1.654940 4.3080% 1958 0.579296 1.726235 2.1130% 1957 0.567309 1.762709 1.9895% 1956 0.556242 1.797778 2.1231% 1955 0.544678 1.835947 1.4496% 1954 0.536895 1.862561 2.1573% 1953 0.525558 1.902741 1.2298% 1952 0.519173 1.926140 1.6814% 1951 0.510588 1.958526 1.6233% 1950 0.502432 1.990318 1.4265% 1949 0.495366 2.018711 1.7790% 1948 0.486707 2.054624 1.8242% 1947 0.477988 2.092104 - 2.6320% 1946 0.490909 2.037039 3.1768% 1945 0.475794 2.101752 6.4754% 1944 0.446858 2.237849 -0.3437% 1943 0.448399 2.230158 0.6562% 1942 0.445475 2.244793 0.6633% 1941 0.442540 2.259683 -5.6614% 1940 0.469098 2.131752 8.0381% 1939 0.434196 2.303105 0.8126% 1938 0.430697 2.321821 0.7762% 1937 0.427379 2.339844 0.6029% 1936 0.424818 2.353950 0.5244% 1935 0.422602 2.366294 -3.0364% 1934 0.435835 2.294444 4.6271% 1933 0.416561 2.400611 1.3921% 1932 0.410841 2.434031 -0.2051% 1931 0.411685 2.429039 0.8886% 1930 0.408059 2.450623 1.0126% 1929 0.403969 2.475438 1.1526% 1928 0.399366 2.503969 1.2160% 1927 0.394568 2.534418 1.4086% 1926 0.389087 2.570117 1.7667% 1925 0.382333 2.615523 1.4465% 1924 0.376881 2.653357 1.7700% 1923 0.370326 2.700320 1.6165% 1922 0.364435 2.743972 1.3736% 1921 0.359497 2.781664 2.3393% 1920 0.351280 2.846736 1.3140% 1919 0.346724 2.884142 0.7676% 1918 0.344082 2.906282 0.3870% 1917 0.342756 2.917529 1.3274% 1916 0.338266 2.956257 1.4083% 1915 0.333568 2.997890 1.4458% 1914 0.328814 3.041234 1.9424% 1913 0.322549 3.100306 1.9857% 1912 0.316269 3.161868 1.5634% 1911 0.311400 3.211301 1.8169% 1910 0.305843 3.269647 1.8781% 1909 0.300205 3.331053 2.0082% 1908 0.294295 3.397949 1.9603% 1907 0.288637 3.464557 1.8264% 1906 0.283460 3.527832 1.9357% 1905 0.278078 3.596120 2.0148% 1904 0.272585 3.668576 2.1335% 1903 0.266891 3.746846 1.8151% 1902 0.262133 3.814857 1.8943% 1901 0.257260 3.887123 3.0255% 1900 0.249705 4.004728 0.6278% 1899 0.248147 4.029871 1.7757% 1898 0.243818 4.101428 1.8078% 1897 0.239488 4.175572 1.8396% 1896 0.235162 4.252386 1.8755% 1895 0.230833 4.332141 1.9114% 1894 0.226503 4.414945 1.9486% 1893 0.222174 4.500976 1.9858% 1892 0.217848 4.590356 2.0276% 1891 0.213519 4.683432 2.6465% 1890 0.208014 4.807380 1.5328% 1889 0.204873 4.881068 2.0811% 1888 0.200696 4.982649 2.1599% 1887 0.196453 5.090267 2.2075% 1886 0.192210 5.202636 2.2592% 1885 0.187964 5.320173 2.3095% 1884 0.183721 5.443044 2.3641% 1883 0.179478 5.571725 2.4214% 1882 0.175235 5.706638 2.4815% 1881 0.170991 5.848247 3.7644% 1880 0.164788 6.068398 0.9432% 1879 0.163248 6.125637 2.1464% 1878 0.159818 6.257117 2.1913% 1877 0.156391 6.394229 2.2426% 1876 0.152961 6.537627 2.2941% 1875 0.149530 6.687603 2.3456% 1874 0.146103 6.844468 2.4043% 1873 0.142673 7.009030 2.4635% 1872 0.139243 7.181701 2.5258% 1871 0.135812 7.363094 5.9947% 1870 0.128131 7.804488 -1.0968% 1869 0.129552 7.718889 2.1930% 1868 0.126772 7.888162 2.2394% 1867 0.123995 8.064810 2.2935% 1866 0.121215 8.249777 2.3445% 1865 0.118439 8.443191 2.4037% 1864 0.115659 8.646139 2.4599% 1863 0.112882 8.858824 2.5250% 1862 0.110102 9.082510 2.5872% 1861 0.107325 9.317497 2.9504% 1860 0.104249 9.592401 2.4012% 1859 0.101805 9.822738 2.7627% 1858 0.099068 10.094111 2.8412% 1857 0.096331 10.380905 2.9243% 1856 0.093594 10.684473 3.0161% 1855 0.090853 11.006732 3.1061% 1854

4

0.088117 11.348607 3.2056% 1853 0.085380 11.712401 3.3118% 1852 0.082643 12.100291 3.4252% 1851 0.079906 12.514753 4.0106% 1850 0.076825 13.016671 2.3254% 1849 0.075079 13.319356 2.7841% 1848 0.073045 13.690178 2.8590% 1847 0.071015 14.081582 2.9432% 1846 0.068984 14.496025 3.0324% 1845 0.066954 14.935603 3.1325% 1844 0.064920 15.403462 3.2284% 1843 0.062890 15.900741 3.3361% 1842 0.060860 16.431199 3.4512% 1841 0.058830 16.998272 3.8105% 1840 0.056670 17.645989 2.3861% 1839 0.055349 18.067031 2.5824% 1838 0.053956 18.533593 2.6573% 1837 0.052559 19.026090 2.7232% 1836 0.051166 19.544210 2.7994% 1835 0.049773 20.091338 2.8871% 1834 0.048376 20.671400 2.9657% 1833 0.046983 21.284448 3.0563% 1832 0.045589 21.934969 3.1604% 1831 0.044193 22.628207 3.4660% 1830 0.042712 23.412493 2.4653% 1829 0.041685 23.989682 2.6804% 1828 0.040596 24.632700 10.3427% 1827 0.036791 27.180374 -4.2314% 1826 0.038417 26.030255 2.9150% 1825 0.037329 26.789046 3.0026% 1824 0.036241 27.593404 3.0955% 1823 0.035152 28.447560 3.1944% 1822 0.034064 29.356286 3.3102% 1821 0.032973 30.328036 3.2277% 1820 0.031942 31.306946 2.6573% 1819 0.031115 32.138858 2.6261% 1818 0.030319 32.982859 2.6969% 1817 0.029523 33.872384 2.7717% 1816 0.028726 34.811219 2.8507% 1815 0.027930 35.803581 2.9343% 1814 0.027134 36.854181 3.0231% 1813 0.026338 37.968302 3.1039% 1812 0.025545 39.146799 3.2172% 1811 0.024749 40.406213 3.0969% 1810 0.024005 41.657559 2.9144% 1809 0.023325 42.871618 2.8225% 1808 0.022685 44.081654 2.9199% 1807 0.022042 45.368806 2.9918% 1806 0.021401 46.726143 3.0841% 1805 0.020761 48.167202 3.1822% 1804 0.020121 49.699975 3.2868% 1803 0.019480 51.333506 3.3985% 1802 0.018840 53.078068 3.5180% 1801 0.018200 54.945379 3.3999% 1800 0.017601 56.813493 2.8419% 1799 0.017115 58.428058 2.7485% 1798 0.016657 60.033927 2.8261% 1797 0.016199 61.730565 3.7832% 1796 0.015609 64.065962 2.1272% 1795 0.015284 65.428771 3.0879% 1794 0.014826 67.449172 3.1625% 1793 0.014371 69.582260 3.2904% 1792 0.013914 71.871805 3.4024% 1791 0.013456 74.317147 3.2296% 1790 0.013035 76.717267 41.3145% 1780 0.009224 108.412584 29.4353% 1770 0.007126 140.324170 83.4728% 1750 0.003884 257.456738 29.2845% 1740 0.003004 332.851534 94.2514% 1720 0.001547 646.568745 85.8111% 1700 0.000832 1201.396369 19.2490% 1690 0.000698 1432.653750 88.0250% 1670 0.000371 2693.747534

BASE YEAR: 2001

YEAR BYEAR/AYEAR AYEAR/BYEAR GROWTH%

2009 1.082857 0.923483 8.2857% 2001 1.000000 1.000000 1.0000% 2000 0.990099 1.010000 1.0000% 1999 0.980296 1.020100 1.0000% 1998 0.970590 1.030301 1.0000% 1997 0.960980 1.040604 1.0000% 1996 0.951466 1.051010 1.0000% 1995 0.942045 1.061520 0.9992% 1994 0.932725 1.072127 1.0008% 1993 0.923483 1.082857 1.0000% 1992 0.914340 1.093685 0.9295% 1991 0.905919 1.103851 1.2505% 1990 0.894730 1.117655 0.7224% 1989 0.888313 1.125730 1.1077% 1988 0.878581 1.138199 0.8834% 1987 0.870888 1.148253 0.5594% 1986 0.866044 1.154676 1.3056% 1985 0.854882 1.169752 0.7673% 1984 0.848373 1.178727 0.8149% 1983 0.841515 1.188333 0.9737% 1982 0.833399 1.199905 0.9508% 1981 0.825550 1.211314 0.9031% 1980 0.818162 1.222252 2.2701% 1979 0.800001 1.249998 1.0042% 1978 0.792047 1.262551 0.9896% 1977 0.784286 1.275045 0.9103% 1976 0.777211 1.286652 0.8394% 1975 0.770741 1.297453 0.9042% 1974 0.763835 1.309184 1.1568% 1973 0.755100 1.324328 0.9427% 1972 0.748048 1.336813 0.7426% 1971 0.742533 1.346741 1.4697% 1970 0.731778 1.366534 0.6968% 1969 0.726714 1.376056 0.8565% 1968 0.720543 1.387843 1.5090% 1967 0.709831 1.408786 0.9949% 1966 0.702838 1.422802 1.0575% 1965 0.695484 1.437848 1.1300% 1964 0.687713 1.454096 1.5537% 1963 0.677191 1.476687 1.4658% 1962 0.667408 1.498333 1.5364% 1961 0.657309 1.521354 2.1586% 1960 0.643420 1.554194 -1.6655% 1959 0.654318 1.528309 4.3080% 1958 0.627294 1.594149 2.1130% 1957 0.614314 1.627833 1.9895% 1956 0.602330 1.660218 2.1231% 1955 0.589808 1.695466 1.4496% 1954 0.581380 1.720044 2.1573% 1953 0.569103 1.757150 1.2298% 1952 0.562190 1.778758 1.6814% 1951 0.552494 1.808666 1.6233% 1950 0.544062 1.838026 1.4265% 1949 0.536410 1.864246 1.7790% 1948 0.527034 1.897411 1.8242% 1947 0.517592 1.932023 -2.6320% 1946 0.531584 1.881172 3.1768% 1945 0.515216 1.940933 6.4754% 1944 0.483883 2.066616 -0.3437% 1943 0.485552 2.059514 0.6562% 1942 0.482386 2.073029 0.6633% 1941 0.479207 2.086779 -5.6614% 1940 0.507966 1.968638 8.0381% 1939 0.470173

2.126879 0.8126% 1938 0.466383 2.144163 0.7762% 1937 0.462790 2.160807 0.6029% 1936
0.460017 2.173833 0.5244% 1935 0.457617 2.185233 -3.0364% 1934 0.471947 2.118881
4.6271% 1933 0.451075 2.216924 1.3921% 1932 0.444882 2.247787 -0.2051% 1931
0.445796 2.243177 0.8886% 1930 0.441870 2.263110 1.0126% 1929 0.437440 2.286026
1.1526% 1928 0.432456 2.312374 1.2160% 1927 0.427260 2.340493 1.4086% 1926 0.421326
2.373460 1.7667% 1925 0.414011 2.415392 1.4465% 1924 0.408108 2.450331 1.7700% 1923
0.401010 2.493701 1.6165% 1922 0.394631 2.534012 1.3736% 1921 0.389284 2.568820
2.3393% 1920 0.380385 2.628913 1.3140% 1919 0.375452 2.663457 0.7676% 1918 0.372592
2.683903 0.3870% 1917 0.371155 2.694289 1.3274% 1916 0.366293 2.730054 1.4083% 1915
0.361206 2.768501 1.4458% 1914 0.356058 2.808529 1.9424% 1913 0.349274 2.863081
1.9857% 1912 0.342474 2.919932 1.5634% 1911 0.337202 2.965583 1.8169% 1910 0.331185
3.019465 1.8781% 1909 0.325079 3.076172 2.0082% 1908 0.318679 3.137949 1.9603% 1907
0.312553 3.199461 1.8264% 1906 0.306947 3.257894 1.9357% 1905 0.301118 3.320957
2.0148% 1904 0.295171 3.387868 2.1335% 1903 0.289005 3.460149 1.8151% 1902 0.283853
3.522956 1.8943% 1901 0.278575 3.589693 3.0255% 1900 0.270395 3.698300 0.6278% 1899
0.268707 3.721519 1.7757% 1898 0.264019 3.787600 1.8078% 1897 0.259331 3.856071
1.8396% 1896 0.254647 3.927007 1.8755% 1895 0.249959 4.000660 1.9114% 1894 0.245271
4.077128 1.9486% 1893 0.240583 4.156576 1.9858% 1892 0.235898 4.239118 2.0276% 1891
0.231210 4.325071 2.6465% 1890 0.225249 4.439535 1.5328% 1889 0.221848 4.507585
2.0811% 1888 0.217325 4.601393 2.1599% 1887 0.212731 4.700777 2.2075% 1886 0.208136
4.804548 2.2592% 1885 0.203538 4.913091 2.3095% 1884 0.198943 5.026561 2.3641% 1883
0.194349 5.145396 2.4214% 1882 0.189754 5.269985 2.4815% 1881 0.185159 5.400759
3.7644% 1880 0.178442 5.604065 0.9432% 1879 0.176775 5.656924 2.1464% 1878 0.173060
5.778343 2.1913% 1877 0.169349 5.904964 2.2426% 1876 0.165635 6.037389 2.2941% 1875
0.161920 6.175890 2.3456% 1874 0.158209 6.320752 2.4043% 1873 0.154494 6.472722
2.4635% 1872 0.150780 6.632181 2.5258% 1871 0.147065 6.799695 5.9947% 1870 0.138748
7.207314 -1.0968% 1869 0.140287 7.128266 2.1930% 1868 0.137276 7.284586 2.2394%
1867 0.134269 7.447718 2.2935% 1866 0.131259 7.618531 2.3445% 1865 0.128252 7.797146
2.4037% 1864 0.125242 7.984565 2.4599% 1863 0.122235 8.180976 2.5250% 1862 0.119224
8.387547 2.5872% 1861 0.116218 8.604553 2.9504% 1860 0.112887 8.858422 2.4012% 1859
0.110240 9.071134 2.7627% 1858 0.107276 9.321743 2.8412% 1857 0.104312 9.586593
2.9243% 1856 0.101349 9.866932 3.0161% 1855 0.098381 10.164533 3.1061% 1854
0.095418 10.480249 3.2056% 1853 0.092454 10.816207 3.3118% 1852 0.089490 11.174417
3.4252% 1851 0.086526 11.557166 4.0106% 1850 0.083190 12.020678 2.3254% 1849
0.081299 12.300203 2.7841% 1848 0.079097 12.642651 2.8590% 1847 0.076899 13.004106
2.9432% 1846 0.074700 13.386838 3.0324% 1845 0.072502 13.792781 3.1325% 1844
0.070300 14.224840 3.2284% 1843 0.068101 14.684069 3.3361% 1842 0.065902 15.173938
3.4512% 1841 0.063704 15.697620 3.8105% 1840 0.061366 16.295776 2.3861% 1839
0.059936 16.684602 2.5824% 1838 0.058427 17.115464 2.6573% 1837 0.056914 17.570277
2.7232% 1836 0.055405 18.048752 2.7994% 1835 0.053897 18.554016 2.8871% 1834
0.052384 19.089693 2.9657% 1833 0.050875 19.655832 3.0563% 1832 0.049367 20.256578
3.1604% 1831 0.047854 20.896772 3.4660% 1830 0.046251 21.621047 2.4653% 1829
0.045138 22.154071 2.6804% 1828 0.043960 22.747887 10.3427% 1827 0.039840 25.100622
-4.2314% 1826 0.041600 24.038506 2.9150% 1825 0.040422 24.739237 3.0026% 1824
0.039243 25.482049 3.0955% 1823 0.038065 26.270847 3.1944% 1822 0.036887 27.110041
3.3102% 1821 0.035705 28.007435 3.2277% 1820 0.034588 28.911442 2.6573% 1819
0.033693 29.679699 2.6261% 1818 0.032831 30.459120 2.6969% 1817 0.031969 31.280582
2.7717% 1816 0.031107 32.147580 2.8507% 1815 0.030244 33.064010 2.9343% 1814
0.029382 34.034222 3.0231% 1813 0.028520 35.063093 3.1039% 1812 0.027661 36.151415
3.2172% 1811 0.026799 37.314464 3.0969% 1810 0.025994 38.470061 2.9144% 1809
0.025258 39.591224 2.8225% 1808 0.024565 40.708672 2.9199% 1807 0.023868 41.897336
2.9918% 1806 0.023175 43.150814 3.0841% 1805 0.022481 44.481607 3.1822% 1804
0.021788 45.897098 3.2868% 1803 0.021095 47.405637 3.3985% 1802 0.020401 49.016711
3.5180% 1801 0.019708 50.741141 3.3999% 1800 0.019060 52.466313 2.8419% 1799
0.018533 53.957336 2.7485% 1798 0.018037 55.440330 2.8261% 1797 0.017542 57.007147
3.7832% 1796 0.016902 59.163847 2.1272% 1795 0.016550 60.422379 3.0879% 1794

0.016054 62.288185 3.1625% 1793 0.015562 64.258056 3.2904% 1792 0.015067 66.372413 3.4024% 1791 0.014571 68.630646 3.2296% 1790 0.014115 70.847116 41.3145% 1780 0.009988 100.117213 29.4353% 1770 0.007717 129.587030 83.4728% 1750 0.004206 237.757003 29.2845% 1740 0.003253 307.382839 94.2514% 1720 0.001675 597.095450 85.8111% 1700 0.000901 1109.469506 19.2490% 1690 0.000756 1323.031839 88.0250% 1670 0.000402 2487.630912

BASE YEAR: 2000

YEAR BYEAR/AYEAR AYEAR/BYEAR GROWTH%

2009 1.093685 0.914340 8.2857% 2001 1.010000 0.990099 1.0000% 2000 1.000000 1.000000 1.0000% 1999 0.990099 1.010000 1.0000% 1998 0.980296 1.020100 1.0000% 1997 0.970590 1.030301 1.0000% 1996 0.960980 1.040604 1.0000% 1995 0.951466 1.051010 0.9992% 1994 0.942052 1.061512 1.0008% 1993 0.932718 1.072135 1.0000% 1992 0.923483 1.082857 0.9295% 1991 0.914978 1.092922 1.2505% 1990 0.903678 1.106589 0.7224% 1989 0.897196 1.114584 1.1077% 1988 0.887367 1.126930 0.8834% 1987 0.879597 1.136884 0.5594% 1986 0.874704 1.143244 1.3056% 1985 0.863431 1.158170 0.7673% 1984 0.856856 1.167057 0.8149% 1983 0.849930 1.176568 0.9737% 1982 0.841734 1.188024 0.9508% 1981 0.833806 1.199320 0.9031% 1980 0.826343 1.210151 2.2701% 1979 0.808001 1.237622 1.0042% 1978 0.799968 1.250050 0.9896% 1977 0.792129 1.262421 0.9103% 1976 0.784983 1.273913 0.8394% 1975 0.778448 1.284607 0.9042% 1974 0.771473 1.296222 1.1568% 1973 0.762651 1.311216 0.9427% 1972 0.755528 1.323577 0.7426% 1971 0.749959 1.333406 1.4697% 1970 0.739096 1.353004 0.6968% 1969 0.733982 1.362432 0.8565% 1968 0.727748 1.374102 1.5090% 1967 0.716929 1.394837 0.9949% 1966 0.709867 1.408715 1.0575% 1965 0.702439 1.423612 1.1300% 1964 0.694590 1.439699 1.5537% 1963 0.683963 1.462067 1.4658% 1962 0.674083 1.483498 1.5364% 1961 0.663882 1.506291 2.1586% 1960 0.649854 1.538806 -1.6655% 1959 0.660861 1.513178 4.3080% 1958 0.633567 1.578365 2.1130% 1957 0.620457 1.611715 1.9895% 1956 0.608354 1.643780 2.1231% 1955 0.595706 1.678679 1.4496% 1954 0.587194 1.703014 2.1573% 1953 0.574795 1.739752 1.2298% 1952 0.567812 1.761147 1.6814% 1951 0.558423 1.790758 1.6233% 1950 0.549503 1.819827 1.4265% 1949 0.541774 1.845788 1.7790% 1948 0.532304 1.878625 1.8242% 1947 0.522768 1.912894 -2.6320% 1946 0.536900 1.862546 3.1768% 1945 0.520368 1.921715 6.4754% 1944 0.488722 2.046154 -0.3437% 1943 0.490407 2.039122 0.6562% 1942 0.487210 2.052503 0.6633% 1941 0.484000 2.066118 -5.6614% 1940 0.513045 1.949146 8.0381% 1939 0.474874 2.105820 0.8126% 1938 0.471046 2.122933 0.7762% 1937 0.467418 2.139412 0.6029% 1936 0.464617 2.152310 0.5244% 1935 0.462193 2.163597 -3.0364% 1934 0.476667 2.097902 4.6271% 1933 0.455586 2.194974 1.3921% 1932 0.449331 2.225531 -0.2051% 1931 0.450254 2.220967 0.8886% 1930 0.446289 2.240702 1.0126% 1929 0.441815 2.263391 1.1526% 1928 0.436781 2.289479 1.2160% 1927 0.431533 2.317319 1.4086% 1926 0.425539 2.349960 1.7667% 1925 0.418152 2.391477 1.4465% 1924 0.412189 2.426070 1.7700% 1923 0.405021 2.469010 1.6165% 1922 0.398577 2.508922 1.3736% 1921 0.393177 2.543386 2.3393% 1920 0.384189 2.602884 1.3140% 1919 0.379206 2.637086 0.7676% 1918 0.376318 2.657329 0.3870% 1917 0.374867 2.667613 1.3274% 1916 0.369956 2.703024 1.4083% 1915 0.364818 2.741090 1.4458% 1914 0.359619 2.780721 1.9424% 1913 0.352767 2.834733 1.9857% 1912 0.345898 2.891022 1.5634% 1911 0.340574 2.936220 1.8169% 1910 0.334496 2.989569 1.8781% 1909 0.328330 3.045715 2.0082% 1908 0.321866 3.106880 1.9603% 1907 0.315678 3.167783 1.8264% 1906 0.310016 3.225638 1.9357% 1905 0.304129 3.288075 2.0148% 1904 0.298123 3.354325 2.1335% 1903 0.291895 3.425890 1.8151% 1902 0.286691 3.488075 1.8943% 1901 0.281361 3.554152 3.0255% 1900 0.273099 3.661682 0.6278% 1899 0.271395 3.684672 1.7757% 1898 0.266660 3.750099 1.8078% 1897 0.261925 3.817892 1.8396% 1896 0.257193 3.888125 1.8755% 1895 0.252458 3.961049 1.9114% 1894 0.247723 4.036760 1.9486% 1893 0.242988 4.115421 1.9858% 1892 0.238257 4.197146 2.0276% 1891 0.233522 4.282248 2.6465% 1890 0.227501 4.395579 1.5328% 1889 0.224067 4.462955 2.0811% 1888 0.219499 4.555835 2.1599% 1887 0.214858 4.654234 2.2075% 1886 0.210218 4.756978 2.2592% 1885 0.205573 4.864446 2.3095% 1884 0.200933 4.976792 2.3641% 1883 0.196292 5.094450 2.4214% 1882 0.191651 5.217807 2.4815% 1881 0.187011 5.347285 3.7644% 1880 0.180226 5.548578 0.9432% 1879 0.178542 5.600914 2.1464% 1878 0.174791 5.721131 2.1913% 1877 0.171043 5.846498 2.2426% 1876 0.167291 5.977612 2.2941% 1875

7

0.163539 6.114742 2.3456% 1874 0.159791 6.258169 2.4043% 1873 0.156039 6.408635
2.4635% 1872 0.152288 6.566515 2.5258% 1871 0.148536 6.732370 5.9947% 1870 0.140135
7.135954 -1.0968% 1869 0.141689 7.057688 2.1930% 1868 0.138649 7.212461 2.2394%
1867 0.135612 7.373977 2.2935% 1866 0.132571 7.543100 2.3445% 1865 0.129535 7.719945
2.4037% 1864 0.126494 7.905509 2.4599% 1863 0.123457 8.099976 2.5250% 1862 0.120417
8.304501 2.5872% 1861 0.117380 8.519359 2.9504% 1860 0.114016 8.770714 2.4012% 1859
0.111342 8.981320 2.7627% 1858 0.108349 9.229448 2.8412% 1857 0.105355 9.491675
2.9243% 1856 0.102362 9.769239 3.0161% 1855 0.099365 10.063893 3.1061% 1854
0.096372 10.376483 3.2056% 1853 0.093378 10.709115 3.3118% 1852 0.090385 11.063778
3.4252% 1851 0.087392 11.442737 4.0106% 1850 0.084022 11.901660 2.3254% 1849
0.082112 12.178418 2.7841% 1848 0.079888 12.517475 2.8590% 1847 0.077668 12.875351
2.9432% 1846 0.075447 13.254293 3.0324% 1845 0.073227 13.656217 3.1325% 1844
0.071003 14.083999 3.2284% 1843 0.068782 14.538681 3.3361% 1842 0.066562 15.023700
3.4512% 1841 0.064341 15.542197 3.8105% 1840 0.061979 16.134430 2.3861% 1839
0.060535 16.519406 2.5824% 1838 0.059011 16.946002 2.6573% 1837 0.057483 17.396312
2.7232% 1836 0.055960 17.870049 2.7994% 1835 0.054436 18.370311 2.8871% 1834
0.052908 18.900684 2.9657% 1833 0.051384 19.461218 3.0563% 1832 0.049860 20.056016
3.1604% 1831 0.048333 20.689871 3.4660% 1830 0.046714 21.406975 2.4653% 1829
0.045590 21.934721 2.6804% 1828 0.044400 22.522658 10.3427% 1827 0.040238 24.852098
-4.2314% 1826 0.042016 23.800498 2.9150% 1825 0.040826 24.494292 3.0026% 1824
0.039636 25.229748 3.0955% 1823 0.038446 26.010737 3.1944% 1822 0.037256 26.841622
3.3102% 1821 0.036062 27.730131 3.2277% 1820 0.034934 28.625187 2.6573% 1819
0.034030 29.385838 2.6261% 1818 0.033159 30.157542 2.6969% 1817 0.032288 30.970870
2.7717% 1816 0.031418 31.829284 2.8507% 1815 0.030547 32.736640 2.9343% 1814
0.029676 33.697246 3.0231% 1813 0.028805 34.715930 3.1039% 1812 0.027938 35.793477
3.2172% 1811 0.027067 36.945010 3.0969% 1810 0.026254 38.089165 2.9144% 1809
0.025511 39.199228 2.8225% 1808 0.024810 40.305612 2.9199% 1807 0.024107 41.482506
2.9918% 1806 0.023406 42.723573 3.0841% 1805 0.022706 44.041191 3.1822% 1804
0.022006 45.442666 3.2868% 1803 0.021305 46.936269 3.3985% 1802 0.020605 48.531391
3.5180% 1801 0.019905 50.238748 3.3999% 1800 0.019250 51.946839 2.8419% 1799
0.018718 53.423100 2.7485% 1798 0.018218 54.891410 2.8261% 1797 0.017717 56.442714
3.7832% 1796 0.017071 58.578060 2.1272% 1795 0.016716 59.824131 3.0879% 1794
0.016215 61.671464 3.1625% 1793 0.015718 63.621831 3.2904% 1792 0.015217 65.715253
3.4024% 1791 0.014716 67.951127 3.2296% 1790 0.014256 70.145652 41.3145% 1780
0.010088 99.125943 29.4353% 1770 0.007794 128.303977 83.4728% 1750 0.004248
235.402948 29.2845% 1740 0.003286 304.339413 94.2514% 1720 0.001692 591.183552
85.8111% 1700 0.000910 1098.484544 19.2490% 1690 0.000763 1309.932376 88.0250%
1670 0.000406 2463.000643

BASE YEAR: 1999
YEAR BYEAR/AYEAR AYEAR/BYEAR GROWTH%
2009 1.104622 0.905287 8.2857% 2001 1.020100 0.980296 1.0000% 2000 1.010000
0.990099 1.0000% 1999 1.000000 1.000000 1.0000% 1998 0.990099 1.010000 1.0000% 1997
0.980296 1.020100 1.0000% 1996 0.970590 1.030301 1.0000% 1995 0.960980 1.040604
0.9992% 1994 0.951473 1.051002 1.0008% 1993 0.942045 1.061520 1.0000% 1992 0.932718
1.072135 0.9295% 1991 0.924128 1.082101 1.2505% 1990 0.912715 1.095633 0.7224% 1989
0.906168 1.103548 1.1077% 1988 0.896241 1.115772 0.8834% 1987 0.888393 1.125628
0.5594% 1986 0.883451 1.131924 1.3056% 1985 0.872065 1.146703 0.7673% 1984 0.865425
1.155502 0.8149% 1983 0.858429 1.164918 0.9737% 1982 0.850151 1.176262 0.9508% 1981
0.842144 1.187446 0.9031% 1980 0.834607 1.198169 2.2701% 1979 0.816081 1.225368
1.0042% 1978 0.807968 1.237673 0.9896% 1977 0.800050 1.249921 0.9103% 1976 0.792833
1.261300 0.8394% 1975 0.786233 1.271888 0.9042% 1974 0.779188 1.283388 1.1568% 1973
0.770277 1.298234 0.9427% 1972 0.763084 1.310472 0.7426% 1971 0.757458 1.320204
1.4697% 1970 0.746487 1.339608 0.6968% 1969 0.741321 1.348943 0.8565% 1968 0.735026
1.360497 1.5090% 1967 0.724099 1.381027 0.9949% 1966 0.716966 1.394767 1.0575% 1965
0.709463 1.409516 1.1300% 1964 0.701536 1.425444 1.5537% 1963 0.690803 1.447591
1.4658% 1962 0.680823 1.468810 1.5364% 1961 0.670521 1.491377 2.1586% 1960 0.656353

8

1.523570 -1.6655% 1959 0.667470 1.498196 4.3080% 1958 0.639903 1.562738 2.1130% 1957 0.626662 1.595758 1.9895% 1956 0.614437 1.627505 2.1231% 1955 0.601663 1.662059 1.4496% 1954 0.593066 1.686152 2.1573% 1953 0.580543 1.722527 1.2298% 1952 0.573490 1.743710 1.6814% 1951 0.564007 1.773028 1.6233% 1950 0.554998 1.801809 1.4265% 1949 0.547192 1.827512 1.7790% 1948 0.537627 1.860025 1.8242% 1947 0.527996 1.893954 - 2.6320% 1946 0.542269 1.844105 3.1768% 1945 0.525572 1.902688 6.4754% 1944 0.493609 2.025895 -0.3437% 1943 0.495311 2.018933 0.6562% 1942 0.492082 2.032182 0.6633% 1941 0.488840 2.045661 -5.6614% 1940 0.518176 1.929847 8.0381% 1939 0.479623 2.084971 0.8126% 1938 0.475757 2.101914 0.7762% 1937 0.472092 2.118230 0.6029% 1936 0.469263 2.131000 0.5244% 1935 0.466815 2.142175 -3.0364% 1934 0.481433 2.077131 4.6271% 1933 0.460142 2.173242 1.3921% 1932 0.453824 2.203496 -0.2051% 1931 0.454757 2.198977 0.8886% 1930 0.450752 2.218517 1.0126% 1929 0.446233 2.240982 1.1526% 1928 0.441148 2.266811 1.2160% 1927 0.435848 2.294375 1.4086% 1926 0.429794 2.326694 1.7667% 1925 0.422333 2.367799 1.4465% 1924 0.416311 2.402049 1.7700% 1923 0.409071 2.444565 1.6165% 1922 0.402563 2.484082 1.3736% 1921 0.397108 2.518204 2.3393% 1920 0.388031 2.577113 1.3140% 1919 0.382999 2.610976 0.7676% 1918 0.380081 2.631019 0.3870% 1917 0.378616 2.641201 1.3274% 1916 0.373656 2.676261 1.4083% 1915 0.368467 2.713951 1.4458% 1914 0.363215 2.753189 1.9424% 1913 0.356295 2.806667 1.9857% 1912 0.349357 2.862398 1.5634% 1911 0.343980 2.907149 1.8169% 1910 0.337841 2.959969 1.8781% 1909 0.331613 3.015559 2.0082% 1908 0.325085 3.076119 1.9603% 1907 0.318835 3.136419 1.8264% 1906 0.313116 3.193701 1.9357% 1905 0.307171 3.255520 2.0148% 1904 0.301104 3.321114 2.1335% 1903 0.294814 3.391970 1.8151% 1902 0.289558 3.453540 1.8943% 1901 0.284175 3.518962 3.0255% 1900 0.275829 3.625428 0.6278% 1899 0.274109 3.648190 1.7757% 1898 0.269326 3.712969 1.8078% 1897 0.264544 3.780091 1.8396% 1896 0.259765 3.849629 1.8755% 1895 0.254983 3.921830 1.9114% 1894 0.250201 3.996792 1.9486% 1893 0.245418 4.074675 1.9858% 1892 0.240640 4.155590 2.0276% 1891 0.235857 4.239850 2.6465% 1890 0.229776 4.352058 1.5328% 1889 0.226307 4.418767 2.0811% 1888 0.221694 4.510727 2.1599% 1887 0.217007 4.608152 2.2075% 1886 0.212320 4.709879 2.2592% 1885 0.207629 4.816283 2.3095% 1884 0.202942 4.927517 2.3641% 1883 0.198255 5.044010 2.4214% 1882 0.193568 5.166145 2.4815% 1881 0.188881 5.294342 3.7644% 1880 0.182029 5.493642 0.9432% 1879 0.180328 5.545459 2.1464% 1878 0.176539 5.664486 2.1913% 1877 0.172753 5.788612 2.2426% 1876 0.168964 5.918428 2.2941% 1875 0.165175 6.054200 2.3456% 1874 0.161389 6.196207 2.4043% 1873 0.157600 6.345184 2.4635% 1872 0.153811 6.501500 2.5258% 1871 0.150021 6.665713 5.9947% 1870 0.141537 7.065301 -1.0968% 1869 0.143106 6.987810 2.1930% 1868 0.140035 7.141050 2.2394% 1867 0.136968 7.300968 2.2935% 1866 0.133897 7.468415 2.3445% 1865 0.130830 7.643510 2.4037% 1864 0.127759 7.827237 2.4599% 1863 0.124692 8.019778 2.5250% 1862 0.121621 8.222278 2.5872% 1861 0.118554 8.435009 2.9504% 1860 0.115156 8.683876 2.4012% 1859 0.112456 8.892396 2.7627% 1858 0.109432 9.138067 2.8412% 1857 0.106409 9.397698 2.9243% 1856 0.103386 9.672514 3.0161% 1855 0.100359 9.964250 3.1061% 1854 0.097335 10.273746 3.2056% 1853 0.094312 10.603084 3.3118% 1852 0.091289 10.954236 3.4252% 1851 0.088266 11.329443 4.0106% 1850 0.084862 11.783822 2.3254% 1849 0.082934 12.057839 2.7841% 1848 0.080687 12.393540 2.8590% 1847 0.078444 12.747873 2.9432% 1846 0.076202 13.123063 3.0324% 1845 0.073959 13.521007 3.1325% 1844 0.071713 13.944553 3.2284% 1843 0.069470 14.394733 3.3361% 1842 0.067227 14.874950 3.4512% 1841 0.064984 15.388313 3.8105% 1840 0.062599 15.974683 2.3861% 1839 0.061140 16.355848 2.5824% 1838 0.059601 16.778220 2.6573% 1837 0.058058 17.224071 2.7232% 1836 0.056519 17.693118 2.7994% 1835 0.054980 18.188426 2.8871% 1834 0.053437 18.713548 2.9657% 1833 0.051898 19.268533 3.0563% 1832 0.050359 19.857442 3.1604% 1831 0.048816 20.485021 3.4660% 1830 0.047181 21.195025 2.4653% 1829 0.046046 21.717546 2.6804% 1828 0.044844 22.299662 10.3427% 1827 0.040640 24.606038 -4.2314% 1826 0.042436 23.564850 2.9150% 1825 0.041234 24.251774 3.0026% 1824 0.040032 24.979949 3.0955% 1823 0.038830 25.753205 3.1944% 1822 0.037628 26.575863 3.3102% 1821 0.036422 27.455575 3.2277% 1820 0.035284 28.341770 2.6573% 1819 0.034370 29.094889 2.6261% 1818 0.033491 29.858952 2.6969% 1817 0.032611 30.664228 2.7717% 1816 0.031732 31.514143 2.8507% 1815 0.030852 32.412515 2.9343% 1814 0.029973

33.363609 3.0231% 1813 0.029093 34.372208 3.1039% 1812 0.028217 35.439086 3.2172%
1811 0.027338 36.579217 3.0969% 1810 0.026517 37.712045 2.9144% 1809 0.025766
38.811117 2.8225% 1808 0.025059 39.906546 2.9199% 1807 0.024348 41.071788 2.9918%
1806 0.023640 42.300568 3.0841% 1805 0.022933 43.605139 3.1822% 1804 0.022226
44.992739 3.2868% 1803 0.021519 46.471553 3.3985% 1802 0.020811 48.050883 3.5180%
1801 0.020104 49.741335 3.3999% 1800 0.019443 51.432514 2.8419% 1799 0.018906
52.894158 2.7485% 1798 0.018400 54.347931 2.8261% 1797 0.017894 55.883875 3.7832%
1796 0.017242 57.998079 2.1272% 1795 0.016883 59.231813 3.0879% 1794 0.016377
61.060855 3.1625% 1793 0.015875 62.991912 3.2904% 1792 0.015369 65.064607 3.4024%
1791 0.014864 67.278344 3.2296% 1790 0.014399 69.451140 41.3145% 1780 0.010189
98.144498 29.4353% 1770 0.007872 127.033640 83.4728% 1750 0.004291 233.072226
29.2845% 1740 0.003319 301.326151 94.2514% 1720 0.001708 585.330249 85.8111% 1700
0.000919 1087.608458 19.2490% 1690 0.000771 1296.962747 88.0250% 1670 0.000410
2438.614495

BASE YEAR: 1998

YEAR BYEAR/AYEAR AYEAR/BYEAR GROWTH%

2009 1.115668 0.896324 8.2857% 2001 1.030301 0.970590 1.0000% 2000 1.020100
0.980296 1.0000% 1999 1.010000 0.990099 1.0000% 1998 1.000000 1.000000 1.0000% 1997
0.990099 1.010000 1.0000% 1996 0.980296 1.020100 1.0000% 1995 0.970590 1.030301
0.9992% 1994 0.960988 1.040596 1.0008% 1993 0.951466 1.051010 1.0000% 1992 0.942045
1.061520 0.9295% 1991 0.933370 1.071387 1.2505% 1990 0.921842 1.084785 0.7224% 1989
0.915230 1.092622 1.1077% 1988 0.905203 1.104725 0.8834% 1987 0.897277 1.114483
0.5594% 1986 0.892286 1.120717 1.3056% 1985 0.880786 1.135350 0.7673% 1984 0.874079
1.144061 0.8149% 1983 0.867014 1.153385 0.9737% 1982 0.858652 1.164616 0.9508% 1981
0.850565 1.175689 0.9031% 1980 0.842953 1.186306 2.2701% 1979 0.824242 1.213236
1.0042% 1978 0.816047 1.225419 0.9896% 1977 0.808051 1.237546 0.9103% 1976 0.800761
1.248812 0.8394% 1975 0.794095 1.259295 0.9042% 1974 0.786980 1.270681 1.1568% 1973
0.777980 1.285380 0.9427% 1972 0.770714 1.297497 0.7426% 1971 0.765033 1.307133
1.4697% 1970 0.753952 1.326344 0.6968% 1969 0.748735 1.335587 0.8565% 1968 0.742376
1.347027 1.5090% 1967 0.731340 1.367354 0.9949% 1966 0.724135 1.380958 1.0575% 1965
0.716558 1.395561 1.1300% 1964 0.708551 1.411331 1.5537% 1963 0.697711 1.433258
1.4658% 1962 0.687632 1.454267 1.5364% 1961 0.677227 1.476611 2.1586% 1960 0.662917
1.508486 -1.6655% 1959 0.674144 1.483362 4.3080% 1958 0.646302 1.547265 2.1130%
1957 0.632928 1.579958 1.9895% 1956 0.620582 1.611391 2.1231% 1955 0.607680 1.645603
1.4496% 1954 0.598997 1.669458 2.1573% 1953 0.586348 1.705472 1.2298% 1952 0.579225
1.726445 1.6814% 1951 0.569647 1.755473 1.6233% 1950 0.560548 1.783969 1.4265% 1949
0.552664 1.809418 1.7790% 1948 0.543004 1.841609 1.8242% 1947 0.533276 1.875202 -
2.6320% 1946 0.547691 1.825846 3.1768% 1945 0.530828 1.883850 6.4754% 1944 0.498545
2.005837 -0.3437% 1943 0.500264 1.998943 0.6562% 1942 0.497003 2.012061 0.6633%
1941 0.493728 2.025407 -5.6614% 1940 0.523357 1.910740 8.0381% 1939 0.484419
2.064327 0.8126% 1938 0.480514 2.081103 0.7762% 1937 0.476813 2.097257 0.6029% 1936
0.473956 2.109901 0.5244% 1935 0.471483 2.120965 -3.0364% 1934 0.486248 2.056565
4.6271% 1933 0.464743 2.151725 1.3921% 1932 0.458363 2.181679 -0.2051% 1931
0.459304 2.177205 0.8886% 1930 0.455259 2.196552 1.0126% 1929 0.450695 2.218794
1.1526% 1928 0.445560 2.244367 1.2160% 1927 0.440207 2.271659 1.4086% 1926 0.434092
2.303657 1.7667% 1925 0.426556 2.344355 1.4465% 1924 0.420474 2.378267 1.7700% 1923
0.413161 2.420361 1.6165% 1922 0.406589 2.459487 1.3736% 1921 0.401079 2.493271
2.3393% 1920 0.391911 2.551597 1.3140% 1919 0.386828 2.585125 0.7676% 1918 0.383882
2.604970 0.3870% 1917 0.382402 2.615050 1.3274% 1916 0.377392 2.649764 1.4083% 1915
0.372151 2.687080 1.4458% 1914 0.366847 2.725930 1.9424% 1913 0.359857 2.778878
1.9857% 1912 0.352851 2.834057 1.5634% 1911 0.347419 2.878365 1.8169% 1910 0.341220
2.930662 1.8781% 1909 0.334930 2.985702 2.0082% 1908 0.328336 3.045662 1.9603% 1907
0.322023 3.105365 1.8264% 1906 0.316248 3.162080 1.9357% 1905 0.310242 3.223287
2.0148% 1904 0.304115 3.288231 2.1335% 1903 0.297762 3.358387 1.8151% 1902 0.292454
3.419346 1.8943% 1901 0.287016 3.484121 3.0255% 1900 0.278588 3.589533 0.6278% 1899
0.276850 3.612069 1.7757% 1898 0.272019 3.676207 1.8078% 1897 0.267189 3.742664

1.8396% 1896 0.262363 3.811514 1.8755% 1895 0.257533 3.883000 1.9114% 1894 0.252703
3.957220 1.9486% 1893 0.247873 4.034331 1.9858% 1892 0.243046 4.114445 2.0276% 1891
0.238216 4.197871 2.6465% 1890 0.232074 4.308968 1.5328% 1889 0.228571 4.375017
2.0811% 1888 0.223911 4.466067 2.1599% 1887 0.219177 4.562527 2.2075% 1886 0.214443
4.663246 2.2592% 1885 0.209705 4.768597 2.3095% 1884 0.204971 4.878730 2.3641% 1883
0.200237 4.994070 2.4214% 1882 0.195504 5.114995 2.4815% 1881 0.190770 5.241923
3.7644% 1880 0.183849 5.439249 0.9432% 1879 0.182131 5.490554 2.1464% 1878 0.178304
5.608402 2.1913% 1877 0.174481 5.731299 2.2426% 1876 0.170653 5.859830 2.2941% 1875
0.166826 5.994258 2.3456% 1874 0.163003 6.134859 2.4043% 1873 0.159176 6.282360
2.4635% 1872 0.155349 6.437129 2.5258% 1871 0.151522 6.599716 5.9947% 1870 0.142952
6.995347 -1.0968% 1869 0.144537 6.918624 2.1930% 1868 0.141436 7.070347 2.2394%
1867 0.138338 7.228681 2.2935% 1866 0.135236 7.394471 2.3445% 1865 0.132138 7.567832
2.4037% 1864 0.129037 7.749740 2.4599% 1863 0.125939 7.940374 2.5250% 1862 0.122837
8.140869 2.5872% 1861 0.119739 8.351494 2.9504% 1860 0.116308 8.597897 2.4012% 1859
0.113580 8.804353 2.7627% 1858 0.110527 9.047591 2.8412% 1857 0.107473 9.304652
2.9243% 1856 0.104420 9.576746 3.0161% 1855 0.101362 9.865594 3.1061% 1854 0.098309
10.172026 3.2056% 1853 0.095255 10.498103 3.3118% 1852 0.092202 10.845778 3.4252%
1851 0.089148 11.217270 4.0106% 1850 0.085711 11.667151 2.3254% 1849 0.083763
11.938455 2.7841% 1848 0.081494 12.270832 2.8590% 1847 0.079229 12.621656 2.9432%
1846 0.076964 12.993131 3.0324% 1845 0.074699 13.387136 3.1325% 1844 0.072430
13.806488 3.2284% 1843 0.070165 14.252211 3.3361% 1842 0.067899 14.727673 3.4512%
1841 0.065634 15.235954 3.8105% 1840 0.063225 15.816518 2.3861% 1839 0.061752
16.193909 2.5824% 1838 0.060197 16.612098 2.6573% 1837 0.058639 17.053536 2.7232%
1836 0.057084 17.517939 2.7994% 1835 0.055530 18.008343 2.8871% 1834 0.053972
18.528266 2.9657% 1833 0.052417 19.077755 3.0563% 1832 0.050863 19.660833 3.1604%
1831 0.049304 20.282199 3.4660% 1830 0.047653 20.985173 2.4653% 1829 0.046506
21.502520 2.6804% 1828 0.045292 22.078873 10.3427% 1827 0.041047 24.362414 -4.2314%
1826 0.042860 23.331535 2.9150% 1825 0.041646 24.011657 3.0026% 1824 0.040432
24.732623 3.0955% 1823 0.039218 25.498223 3.1944% 1822 0.038004 26.312736 3.3102%
1821 0.036787 27.183738 3.2277% 1820 0.035636 28.061158 2.6573% 1819 0.034714
28.806821 2.6261% 1818 0.033826 29.563319 2.6969% 1817 0.032937 30.360621 2.7717%
1816 0.032049 31.202121 2.8507% 1815 0.031161 32.091599 2.9343% 1814 0.030273
33.033277 3.0231% 1813 0.029384 34.031889 3.1039% 1812 0.028500 35.088204 3.2172%
1811 0.027611 36.217047 3.0969% 1810 0.026782 37.338658 2.9144% 1809 0.026023
38.426848 2.8225% 1808 0.025309 39.511432 2.9199% 1807 0.024591 40.665137 2.9918%
1806 0.023877 41.881750 3.0841% 1805 0.023162 43.173405 3.1822% 1804 0.022448
44.547266 3.2868% 1803 0.021734 46.011439 3.3985% 1802 0.021019 47.575131 3.5180%
1801 0.020305 49.248846 3.3999% 1800 0.019637 50.923281 2.8419% 1799 0.019095
52.370454 2.7485% 1798 0.018584 53.809833 2.8261% 1797 0.018073 55.330569 3.7832%
1796 0.017414 57.423841 2.1272% 1795 0.017052 58.645359 3.0879% 1794 0.016541
60.456292 3.1625% 1793 0.016034 62.368229 3.2904% 1792 0.015523 64.420403 3.4024%
1791 0.015012 66.612221 3.2296% 1790 0.014543 68.763505 41.3145% 1780 0.010291
97.172770 29.4353% 1770 0.007951 125.775881 83.4728% 1750 0.004333 230.764580
29.2845% 1740 0.003352 298.342723 94.2514% 1720 0.001726 579.534899 85.8111% 1700
0.000929 1076.840056 19.2490% 1690 0.000779 1284.121530 88.0250% 1670 0.000414
2414.469794

BASE YEAR: 1997
YEAR BYEAR/AYEAR AYEAR/BYEAR GROWTH%

2009 1.126825 0.887449 8.2857% 2001 1.040604 0.960980 1.0000% 2000 1.030301
0.970590 1.0000% 1999 1.020100 0.980296 1.0000% 1998 1.010000 0.990099 1.0000% 1997
1.000000 1.000000 1.0000% 1996 0.990099 1.010000 1.0000% 1995 0.980296 1.020100
0.9992% 1994 0.970598 1.030293 1.0008% 1993 0.960980 1.040604 1.0000% 1992 0.951466
1.051010 0.9295% 1991 0.942703 1.060779 1.2505% 1990 0.931060 1.074044 0.7224% 1989
0.924382 1.081804 1.1077% 1988 0.914255 1.093787 0.8834% 1987 0.906250 1.103449
0.5594% 1986 0.901209 1.109621 1.3056% 1985 0.889594 1.124109 0.7673% 1984 0.882820
1.132734 0.8149% 1983 0.875684 1.141965 0.9737% 1982 0.867239 1.153085 0.9508% 1981

11

0.859071 1.164048 0.9031% 1980 0.851382 1.174560 2.2701% 1979 0.832484 1.201224
1.0042% 1978 0.824208 1.213286 0.9896% 1977 0.816131 1.225293 0.9103% 1976 0.808769
1.236447 0.8394% 1975 0.802036 1.246826 0.9042% 1974 0.794849 1.258100 1.1568% 1973
0.785760 1.272653 0.9427% 1972 0.778422 1.284651 0.7426% 1971 0.772683 1.294191
1.4697% 1970 0.761491 1.313212 0.6968% 1969 0.756222 1.322363 0.8565% 1968 0.749800
1.333690 1.5090% 1967 0.738653 1.353816 0.9949% 1966 0.731377 1.367285 1.0575% 1965
0.723723 1.381743 1.1300% 1964 0.715637 1.397357 1.5537% 1963 0.704688 1.419067
1.4658% 1962 0.694508 1.439868 1.5364% 1961 0.683999 1.461991 2.1586% 1960 0.669546
1.493550 -1.6655% 1959 0.680886 1.468675 4.3080% 1958 0.652765 1.531946 2.1130%
1957 0.639257 1.564315 1.9895% 1956 0.626788 1.595437 2.1231% 1955 0.613757 1.629310
1.4496% 1954 0.604987 1.652928 2.1573% 1953 0.592211 1.688586 1.2298% 1952 0.585017
1.709352 1.6814% 1951 0.575343 1.738092 1.6233% 1950 0.566153 1.766306 1.4265% 1949
0.558190 1.791503 1.7790% 1948 0.548434 1.823375 1.8242% 1947 0.538609 1.856636 -
2.6320% 1946 0.553168 1.807769 3.1768% 1945 0.536136 1.865198 6.4754% 1944 0.503530
1.985977 -0.3437% 1943 0.505267 1.979152 0.6562% 1942 0.501973 1.992140 0.6633%
1941 0.498665 2.005353 -5.6614% 1940 0.528591 1.891822 8.0381% 1939 0.489263
2.043889 0.8126% 1938 0.485320 2.060498 0.7762% 1937 0.481581 2.076492 0.6029% 1936
0.478695 2.089011 0.5244% 1935 0.476198 2.099966 -3.0364% 1934 0.491110 2.036203
4.6271% 1933 0.469391 2.130421 1.3921% 1932 0.462946 2.160079 -0.2051% 1931
0.463898 2.155649 0.8886% 1930 0.459812 2.174804 1.0126% 1929 0.455202 2.196825
1.1526% 1928 0.450015 2.222146 1.2160% 1927 0.444609 2.249167 1.4086% 1926 0.438433
2.280848 1.7667% 1925 0.430822 2.321144 1.4465% 1924 0.424679 2.354719 1.7700% 1923
0.417293 2.396397 1.6165% 1922 0.410655 2.435135 1.3736% 1921 0.405090 2.468586
2.3393% 1920 0.395831 2.526333 1.3140% 1919 0.390697 2.559530 0.7676% 1918 0.387720
2.579178 0.3870% 1917 0.386226 2.589159 1.3274% 1916 0.381166 2.623528 1.4083% 1915
0.375873 2.660475 1.4458% 1914 0.370516 2.698940 1.9424% 1913 0.363456 2.751364
1.9857% 1912 0.356380 2.805997 1.5634% 1911 0.350894 2.849866 1.8169% 1910 0.344632
2.901646 1.8781% 1909 0.338279 2.956141 2.0082% 1908 0.331619 3.015507 1.9603% 1907
0.325244 3.074619 1.8264% 1906 0.319410 3.130772 1.9357% 1905 0.313345 3.191374
2.0148% 1904 0.307156 3.255675 2.1335% 1903 0.300740 3.325135 1.8151% 1902 0.295378
3.385491 1.8943% 1901 0.289887 3.449624 3.0255% 1900 0.281374 3.553993 0.6278% 1899
0.279618 3.576306 1.7757% 1898 0.274740 3.639809 1.8078% 1897 0.269861 3.705608
1.8396% 1896 0.264987 3.773776 1.8755% 1895 0.260108 3.844555 1.9114% 1894 0.255230
3.918039 1.9486% 1893 0.250351 3.994387 1.9858% 1892 0.245477 4.073708 2.0276% 1891
0.240598 4.156308 2.6465% 1890 0.234395 4.266305 1.5328% 1889 0.230856 4.331700
2.0811% 1888 0.226150 4.421848 2.1599% 1887 0.221369 4.517354 2.2075% 1886 0.216587
4.617076 2.2592% 1885 0.211802 4.721383 2.3095% 1884 0.207021 4.830425 2.3641% 1883
0.202240 4.944623 2.4214% 1882 0.197459 5.064352 2.4815% 1881 0.192677 5.190022
3.7644% 1880 0.185687 5.385395 0.9432% 1879 0.183952 5.436192 2.1464% 1878 0.180087
5.552874 2.1913% 1877 0.176225 5.674554 2.2426% 1876 0.172360 5.801812 2.2941% 1875
0.168495 5.934908 2.3456% 1874 0.164633 6.074117 2.4043% 1873 0.160768 6.220158
2.4635% 1872 0.156902 6.373395 2.5258% 1871 0.153037 6.534372 5.9947% 1870 0.144382
6.926087 -1.0968% 1869 0.145983 6.850122 2.1930% 1868 0.142850 7.000344 2.2394%
1867 0.139721 7.157110 2.2935% 1866 0.136589 7.321258 2.3445% 1865 0.133460 7.492903
2.4037% 1864 0.130327 7.673009 2.4599% 1863 0.127198 7.861757 2.5250% 1862 0.124065
8.060267 2.5872% 1861 0.120936 8.268806 2.9504% 1860 0.117471 8.512769 2.4012% 1859
0.114716 8.717181 2.7627% 1858 0.111632 8.958011 2.8412% 1857 0.108548 9.212526
2.9243% 1856 0.105464 9.481927 3.0161% 1855 0.102376 9.767915 3.1061% 1854 0.099292
10.071312 3.2056% 1853 0.096208 10.394161 3.3118% 1852 0.093124 10.738394 3.4252%
1851 0.090040 11.106208 4.0106% 1850 0.086568 11.551634 2.3254% 1849 0.084601
11.820252 2.7841% 1848 0.082309 12.149338 2.8590% 1847 0.080021 12.496689 2.9432%
1846 0.077733 12.864486 3.0324% 1845 0.075446 13.254590 3.1325% 1844 0.073154
13.669790 3.2284% 1843 0.070866 14.111100 3.3361% 1842 0.068578 14.581855 3.4512%
1841 0.066291 15.085103 3.8105% 1840 0.063857 15.659919 2.3861% 1839 0.062369
16.033573 2.5824% 1838 0.060799 16.447622 2.6573% 1837 0.059225 16.884689 2.7232%
1836 0.057655 17.344494 2.7994% 1835 0.056085 17.830043 2.8871% 1834 0.054511

18.344818 2.9657% 1833 0.052941 18.888867 3.0563% 1832 0.051371 19.466172 3.1604%
1831 0.049797 20.081385 3.4660% 1830 0.048129 20.777399 2.4653% 1829 0.046971
21.289624 2.6804% 1828 0.045745 21.860270 10.3427% 1827 0.041457 24.121202 -4.2314%
1826 0.043289 23.100529 2.9150% 1825 0.042063 23.773918 3.0026% 1824 0.040837
24.487745 3.0955% 1823 0.039611 25.245765 3.1944% 1822 0.038384 26.052214 3.3102%
1821 0.037155 26.914592 3.2277% 1820 0.035993 27.783325 2.6573% 1819 0.035061
28.521605 2.6261% 1818 0.034164 29.270613 2.6969% 1817 0.033267 30.060021 2.7717%
1816 0.032370 30.893190 2.8507% 1815 0.031472 31.773860 2.9343% 1814 0.030575
32.706215 3.0231% 1813 0.029678 33.694940 3.1039% 1812 0.028785 34.740796 3.2172%
1811 0.027887 35.858462 3.0969% 1810 0.027050 36.968969 2.9144% 1809 0.026284
38.046384 2.8225% 1808 0.025562 39.120229 2.9199% 1807 0.024837 40.262512 2.9918%
1806 0.024116 41.467079 3.0841% 1805 0.023394 42.745946 3.1822% 1804 0.022673
44.106204 3.2868% 1803 0.021951 45.555880 3.3985% 1802 0.021230 47.104090 3.5180%
1801 0.020508 48.761234 3.3999% 1800 0.019834 50.419090 2.8419% 1799 0.019286
51.851934 2.7485% 1798 0.018770 53.277062 2.8261% 1797 0.018254 54.782742 3.7832%
1796 0.017589 56.855288 2.1272% 1795 0.017222 58.064712 3.0879% 1794 0.016706
59.857715 3.1625% 1793 0.016194 61.750722 3.2904% 1792 0.015678 63.782577 3.4024%
1791 0.015162 65.952695 3.2296% 1790 0.014688 68.082679 41.3145% 1780 0.010394
96.210664 29.4353% 1770 0.008030 124.530575 83.4728% 1750 0.004377 228.479782
29.2845% 1740 0.003385 295.388835 94.2514% 1720 0.001743 573.796931 85.8111% 1700
0.000938 1066.178274 19.2490% 1690 0.000787 1271.407457 88.0250% 1670 0.000418
2390.564155

BASE YEAR: 1996

YEAR BYEAR/AYEAR AYEAR/BYEAR GROWTH%

2009 1.138093 0.878663 8.2857% 2001 1.051010 0.951466 1.0000% 2000 1.040604
0.960980 1.0000% 1999 1.030301 0.970590 1.0000% 1998 1.020100 0.980296 1.0000% 1997
1.010000 0.990099 1.0000% 1996 1.000000 1.000000 1.0000% 1995 0.990099 1.010000
0.9992% 1994 0.980304 1.020092 1.0008% 1993 0.970590 1.030301 1.0000% 1992 0.960980
1.040604 0.9295% 1991 0.952130 1.050276 1.2505% 1990 0.940371 1.063410 0.7224% 1989
0.933626 1.071093 1.1077% 1988 0.923398 1.082957 0.8834% 1987 0.915312 1.092524
0.5594% 1986 0.910221 1.098635 1.3056% 1985 0.898490 1.112979 0.7673% 1984 0.891648
1.121519 0.8149% 1983 0.884441 1.130658 0.9737% 1982 0.875911 1.141668 0.9508% 1981
0.867662 1.152523 0.9031% 1980 0.859896 1.162931 2.2701% 1979 0.840809 1.189330
1.0042% 1978 0.832450 1.201273 0.9896% 1977 0.824293 1.213161 0.9103% 1976 0.816857
1.224205 0.8394% 1975 0.810057 1.234482 0.9042% 1974 0.802798 1.245644 1.1568% 1973
0.793617 1.260053 0.9427% 1972 0.786206 1.271932 0.7426% 1971 0.780410 1.281377
1.4697% 1970 0.769106 1.300210 0.6968% 1969 0.763784 1.309270 0.8565% 1968 0.757298
1.320485 1.5090% 1967 0.746040 1.340411 0.9949% 1966 0.738690 1.353747 1.0575% 1965
0.730961 1.368063 1.1300% 1964 0.722793 1.383522 1.5537% 1963 0.711735 1.405017
1.4658% 1962 0.701453 1.425612 1.5364% 1961 0.690839 1.447516 2.1586% 1960 0.676241
1.478762 -1.6655% 1959 0.687695 1.454134 4.3080% 1958 0.659292 1.516778 2.1130%
1957 0.645650 1.548827 1.9895% 1956 0.633055 1.579641 2.1231% 1955 0.619894 1.613178
1.4496% 1954 0.611037 1.636563 2.1573% 1953 0.598134 1.671867 1.2298% 1952 0.590867
1.692427 1.6814% 1951 0.581097 1.720883 1.6233% 1950 0.571815 1.748818 1.4265% 1949
0.563772 1.773766 1.7790% 1948 0.553918 1.805322 1.8242% 1947 0.543995 1.838254 -
2.6320% 1946 0.558700 1.789870 3.1768% 1945 0.541497 1.846731 6.4754% 1944 0.508566
1.966314 -0.3437% 1943 0.510320 1.959556 0.6562% 1942 0.506993 1.972415 0.6633%
1941 0.503652 1.985499 -5.6614% 1940 0.533877 1.873091 8.0381% 1939 0.494156
2.023652 0.8126% 1938 0.490173 2.040097 0.7762% 1937 0.486397 2.055933 0.6029% 1936
0.483482 2.068328 0.5244% 1935 0.480960 2.079174 -3.0364% 1934 0.496021 2.016043
4.6271% 1933 0.474085 2.109327 1.3921% 1932 0.467576 2.138692 -0.2051% 1931
0.468536 2.134305 0.8886% 1930 0.464410 2.153271 1.0126% 1929 0.459754 2.175075
1.1526% 1928 0.454516 2.200144 1.2160% 1927 0.449055 2.226898 1.4086% 1926 0.442818
2.258266 1.7667% 1925 0.435130 2.298162 1.4465% 1924 0.428926 2.331405 1.7700% 1923
0.421466 2.372671 1.6165% 1922 0.414761 2.411025 1.3736% 1921 0.409141 2.444144
2.3393% 1920 0.399789 2.501320 1.3140% 1919 0.394604 2.534188 0.7676% 1918 0.391598

2.553641 0.3870% 1917 0.390088 2.563524 1.3274% 1916 0.384978 2.597553 1.4083% 1915
0.379631 2.634134 1.4458% 1914 0.374221 2.672218 1.9424% 1913 0.367091 2.724123
1.9857% 1912 0.359943 2.778215 1.5634% 1911 0.354403 2.821650 1.8169% 1910 0.348078
2.872917 1.8781% 1909 0.341662 2.926872 2.0082% 1908 0.334935 2.985651 1.9603% 1907
0.328496 3.044177 1.8264% 1906 0.322604 3.099774 1.9357% 1905 0.316478 3.159776
2.0148% 1904 0.310228 3.223440 2.1335% 1903 0.303747 3.292213 1.8151% 1902 0.298332
3.351972 1.8943% 1901 0.292785 3.415470 3.0255% 1900 0.284187 3.518805 0.6278% 1899
0.282414 3.540897 1.7757% 1898 0.277487 3.603771 1.8078% 1897 0.272560 3.668919
1.8396% 1896 0.267636 3.736412 1.8755% 1895 0.262709 3.806490 1.9114% 1894 0.257782
3.879247 1.9486% 1893 0.252855 3.954839 1.9858% 1892 0.247931 4.033375 2.0276% 1891
0.243004 4.115156 2.6465% 1890 0.236739 4.224065 1.5328% 1889 0.233165 4.288812
2.0811% 1888 0.228411 4.378068 2.1599% 1887 0.223582 4.472627 2.2075% 1886 0.218753
4.571362 2.2592% 1885 0.213920 4.674637 2.3095% 1884 0.209091 4.782599 2.3641% 1883
0.204262 4.895667 2.4214% 1882 0.199433 5.014210 2.4815% 1881 0.194604 5.138636
3.7644% 1880 0.187544 5.332075 0.9432% 1879 0.185792 5.382368 2.1464% 1878 0.181888
5.497895 2.1913% 1877 0.177988 5.618370 2.2426% 1876 0.174084 5.744368 2.2941% 1875
0.170180 5.876147 2.3456% 1874 0.166279 6.013978 2.4043% 1873 0.162375 6.158573
2.4635% 1872 0.158471 6.310292 2.5258% 1871 0.154567 6.469675 5.9947% 1870 0.145825
6.857511 -1.0968% 1869 0.147443 6.782299 2.1930% 1868 0.144279 6.931033 2.2394%
1867 0.141118 7.086247 2.2935% 1866 0.137954 7.248770 2.3445% 1865 0.134794 7.418716
2.4037% 1864 0.131630 7.597039 2.4599% 1863 0.128470 7.783917 2.5250% 1862 0.125306
7.980462 2.5872% 1861 0.122146 8.186936 2.9504% 1860 0.118645 8.428484 2.4012% 1859
0.115863 8.630872 2.7627% 1858 0.112748 8.869318 2.8412% 1857 0.109633 9.121313
2.9243% 1856 0.106518 9.388047 3.0161% 1855 0.103400 9.671203 3.1061% 1854 0.100285
9.971596 3.2056% 1853 0.097170 10.291249 3.3118% 1852 0.094055 10.632073 3.4252%
1851 0.090940 10.996246 4.0106% 1850 0.087434 11.437262 2.3254% 1849 0.085447
11.703220 2.7841% 1848 0.083132 12.029048 2.8590% 1847 0.080821 12.372960 2.9432%
1846 0.078511 12.737115 3.0324% 1845 0.076200 13.123356 3.1325% 1844 0.073886
13.534446 3.2284% 1843 0.071575 13.971386 3.3361% 1842 0.069264 14.437480 3.4512%
1841 0.066953 14.935745 3.8105% 1840 0.064496 15.504870 2.3861% 1839 0.062993
15.874825 2.5824% 1838 0.061407 16.284775 2.6573% 1837 0.059818 16.717514 2.7232%
1836 0.058232 17.172766 2.7994% 1835 0.056646 17.653507 2.8871% 1834 0.055056
18.163186 2.9657% 1833 0.053471 18.701848 3.0563% 1832 0.051885 19.273437 3.1604%
1831 0.050295 19.882559 3.4660% 1830 0.048611 20.571682 2.4653% 1829 0.047441
21.078836 2.6804% 1828 0.046203 21.643832 10.3427% 1827 0.041872 23.882378 -4.2314%
1826 0.043722 22.871811 2.9150% 1825 0.042484 23.538533 3.0026% 1824 0.041245
24.245292 3.0955% 1823 0.040007 24.995807 3.1944% 1822 0.038768 25.794271 3.3102%
1821 0.037526 26.648111 3.2277% 1820 0.036353 27.508242 2.6573% 1819 0.035412
28.239212 2.6261% 1818 0.034506 28.980805 2.6969% 1817 0.033599 29.762397 2.7717%
1816 0.032693 30.587316 2.8507% 1815 0.031787 31.459267 2.9343% 1814 0.030881
32.382391 3.0231% 1813 0.029975 33.361327 3.1039% 1812 0.029072 34.396828 3.2172%
1811 0.028166 35.503428 3.0969% 1810 0.027320 36.602939 2.9144% 1809 0.026547
37.669688 2.8225% 1808 0.025818 38.732900 2.9199% 1807 0.025085 39.863873 2.9918%
1806 0.024357 41.056514 3.0841% 1805 0.023628 42.322719 3.1822% 1804 0.022899
43.669509 3.2868% 1803 0.022171 45.104832 3.3985% 1802 0.021442 46.637713 3.5180%
1801 0.020713 48.278449 3.3999% 1800 0.020032 49.919891 2.8419% 1799 0.019479
51.338549 2.7485% 1798 0.018958 52.749566 2.8261% 1797 0.018436 54.240339 3.7832%
1796 0.017764 56.292364 2.1272% 1795 0.017394 57.489814 3.0879% 1794 0.016873
59.265064 3.1625% 1793 0.016356 61.139329 3.2904% 1792 0.015835 63.151067 3.4024%
1791 0.015314 65.299697 3.2296% 1790 0.014835 67.408593 41.3145% 1780 0.010498
95.258083 29.4353% 1770 0.008110 123.297599 83.4728% 1750 0.004421 226.217606
29.2845% 1740 0.003419 292.464193 94.2514% 1720 0.001760 568.115772 85.8111% 1700
0.000947 1055.622053 19.2490% 1690 0.000794 1258.819263 88.0250% 1670 0.000422
2366.895201

BASE YEAR: 1995
YEAR BYEAR/AYEAR AYEAR/BYEAR GROWTH%

14

2009 1.149474 0.869963 8.2857% 2001 1.061520 0.942045 1.0000% 2000 1.051010 0.951466 1.0000% 1999 1.040604 0.960980 1.0000% 1998 1.030301 0.970590 1.0000% 1997 1.020100 0.980296 1.0000% 1996 1.010000 0.990099 1.0000% 1995 1.000000 1.000000 0.9992% 1994 0.990107 1.009992 1.0008% 1993 0.980296 1.020100 1.0000% 1992 0.970590 1.030301 0.9295% 1991 0.961652 1.039878 1.2505% 1990 0.949774 1.052882 0.7224% 1989 0.942962 1.060488 1.1077% 1988 0.932632 1.072235 0.8834% 1987 0.924465 1.081707 0.5594% 1986 0.919323 1.087757 1.3056% 1985 0.907475 1.101959 0.7673% 1984 0.900565 1.110414 0.8149% 1983 0.893285 1.119464 0.9737% 1982 0.884670 1.130364 0.9508% 1981 0.876338 1.141112 0.9031% 1980 0.868495 1.151417 2.2701% 1979 0.849217 1.177555 1.0042% 1978 0.840774 1.189380 0.9896% 1977 0.832536 1.201150 0.9103% 1976 0.825025 1.212084 0.8394% 1975 0.818157 1.222259 0.9042% 1974 0.810826 1.233310 1.1568% 1973 0.801554 1.247577 0.9427% 1972 0.794068 1.259338 0.7426% 1971 0.788214 1.268690 1.4697% 1970 0.776797 1.287337 0.6968% 1969 0.771422 1.296307 0.8565% 1968 0.764871 1.307411 1.5090% 1967 0.753500 1.327140 0.9949% 1966 0.746077 1.340344 1.0575% 1965 0.738270 1.354518 1.1300% 1964 0.730021 1.369824 1.5537% 1963 0.718852 1.391106 1.4658% 1962 0.708468 1.411497 1.5364% 1961 0.697747 1.433184 2.1586% 1960 0.683004 1.464121 -1.6655% 1959 0.694572 1.439736 4.3080% 1958 0.665885 1.501760 2.1130% 1957 0.652106 1.533492 1.9895% 1956 0.639386 1.564001 2.1231% 1955 0.626093 1.597206 1.4496% 1954 0.617147 1.620359 2.1573% 1953 0.604115 1.655314 1.2298% 1952 0.596776 1.675671 1.6814% 1951 0.586908 1.703845 1.6233% 1950 0.577533 1.731503 1.4265% 1949 0.569410 1.756204 1.7790% 1948 0.559457 1.787447 1.8242% 1947 0.549435 1.820053 -2.6320% 1946 0.564287 1.772149 3.1768% 1945 0.546912 1.828446 6.4754% 1944 0.513651 1.946846 -0.3437% 1943 0.515423 1.940155 0.6562% 1942 0.512063 1.952887 0.6633% 1941 0.508688 1.965840 -5.6614% 1940 0.539216 1.854545 8.0381% 1939 0.499098 2.003616 0.8126% 1938 0.495075 2.019898 0.7762% 1937 0.491261 2.035577 0.6029% 1936 0.488317 2.047849 0.5244% 1935 0.485770 2.058588 -3.0364% 1934 0.500981 1.996082 4.6271% 1933 0.478826 2.088443 1.3921% 1932 0.472251 2.117516 -0.2051% 1931 0.473222 2.113174 0.8886% 1930 0.469054 2.131951 1.0126% 1929 0.464352 2.153539 1.1526% 1928 0.459061 2.178361 1.2160% 1927 0.453546 2.204850 1.4086% 1926 0.447246 2.235907 1.7667% 1925 0.439482 2.275408 1.4465% 1924 0.433215 2.308322 1.7700% 1923 0.425681 2.349179 1.6165% 1922 0.418909 2.387154 1.3736% 1921 0.413233 2.419945 2.3393% 1920 0.403787 2.476555 1.3140% 1919 0.398550 2.509097 0.7676% 1918 0.395514 2.528358 0.3870% 1917 0.393989 2.538142 1.3274% 1916 0.388828 2.571834 1.4083% 1915 0.383428 2.608053 1.4458% 1914 0.377963 2.645761 1.9424% 1913 0.370762 2.697151 1.9857% 1912 0.363543 2.750708 1.5634% 1911 0.357947 2.793713 1.8169% 1910 0.351559 2.844472 1.8781% 1909 0.345078 2.897893 2.0082% 1908 0.338285 2.956090 1.9603% 1907 0.331781 3.014037 1.8264% 1906 0.325830 3.069084 1.9357% 1905 0.319643 3.128491 2.0148% 1904 0.313330 3.191525 2.1335% 1903 0.306785 3.259617 1.8151% 1902 0.301315 3.318784 1.8943% 1901 0.295713 3.381653 3.0255% 1900 0.287029 3.483965 0.6278% 1899 0.285238 3.505839 1.7757% 1898 0.280262 3.568090 1.8078% 1897 0.275285 3.632593 1.8396% 1896 0.270313 3.699418 1.8755% 1895 0.265336 3.768802 1.9114% 1894 0.260360 3.840838 1.9486% 1893 0.255383 3.915682 1.9858% 1892 0.250411 3.993440 2.0276% 1891 0.245434 4.074412 2.6465% 1890 0.239106 4.182242 1.5328% 1889 0.235496 4.246348 2.0811% 1888 0.230695 4.334720 2.1599% 1887 0.225818 4.428344 2.2075% 1886 0.220941 4.526101 2.2592% 1885 0.216060 4.628353 2.3095% 1884 0.211182 4.735247 2.3641% 1883 0.206305 4.847195 2.4214% 1882 0.201428 4.964564 2.4815% 1881 0.196550 5.087758 3.7644% 1880 0.189420 5.279282 0.9432% 1879 0.187650 5.329077 2.1464% 1878 0.183707 5.443460 2.1913% 1877 0.179767 5.562742 2.2426% 1876 0.175824 5.687493 2.2941% 1875 0.171881 5.817967 2.3456% 1874 0.167942 5.954433 2.4043% 1873 0.163999 6.097597 2.4635% 1872 0.160056 6.247814 2.5258% 1871 0.156113 6.405619 5.9947% 1870 0.147284 6.789615 -1.0968% 1869 0.148917 6.715148 2.1930% 1868 0.145721 6.862409 2.2394% 1867 0.142530 7.016086 2.2935% 1866 0.139334 7.177000 2.3445% 1865 0.136142 7.345263 2.4037% 1864 0.132947 7.521821 2.4599% 1863 0.129755 7.706849 2.5250% 1862 0.126559 7.901448 2.5872% 1861 0.123367 8.105877 2.9504% 1860 0.119832 8.345034 2.4012% 1859 0.117022 8.545418 2.7627% 1858 0.113876 8.781503 2.8412% 1857 0.110730 9.031003 2.9243% 1856 0.107584 9.295096 3.0161% 1855 0.104434 9.575449 3.1061% 1854 0.101288

9.872868 3.2056% 1853 0.098142 10.189355 3.3118% 1852 0.094996 10.526805 3.4252%
1851 0.091850 10.887372 4.0106% 1850 0.088308 11.324021 2.3254% 1849 0.086301
11.587347 2.7841% 1848 0.083963 11.909948 2.8590% 1847 0.081630 12.250455 2.9432%
1846 0.079296 12.611005 3.0324% 1845 0.076962 12.993422 3.1325% 1844 0.074624
13.400442 3.2284% 1843 0.072291 13.833056 3.3361% 1842 0.069957 14.294535 3.4512%
1841 0.067623 14.787867 3.8105% 1840 0.065141 15.351357 2.3861% 1839 0.063623
15.717648 2.5824% 1838 0.062021 16.123539 2.6573% 1837 0.060416 16.551994 2.7232%
1836 0.058814 17.002739 2.7994% 1835 0.057212 17.478720 2.8871% 1834 0.055607
17.983352 2.9657% 1833 0.054005 18.516681 3.0563% 1832 0.052404 19.082611 3.1604%
1831 0.050798 19.685702 3.4660% 1830 0.049097 20.368002 2.4653% 1829 0.047915
20.870135 2.6804% 1828 0.046665 21.429537 10.3427% 1827 0.042291 23.645919 -4.2314%
1826 0.044159 22.645358 2.9150% 1825 0.042908 23.305478 3.0026% 1824 0.041658
24.005240 3.0955% 1823 0.040407 24.748324 3.1944% 1822 0.039156 25.538882 3.3102%
1821 0.037901 26.384268 3.2277% 1820 0.036716 27.235883 2.6573% 1819 0.035766
27.959616 2.6261% 1818 0.034851 28.693866 2.6969% 1817 0.033935 29.467720 2.7717%
1816 0.033020 30.284472 2.8507% 1815 0.032105 31.147790 2.9343% 1814 0.031190
32.061773 3.0231% 1813 0.030275 33.031017 3.1039% 1812 0.029363 34.056265 3.2172%
1811 0.028448 35.151909 3.0969% 1810 0.027593 36.240534 2.9144% 1809 0.026812
37.296720 2.8225% 1808 0.026076 38.349406 2.9199% 1807 0.025336 39.469181 2.9918%
1806 0.024600 40.650014 3.0841% 1805 0.023864 41.903682 3.1822% 1804 0.023128
43.237138 3.2868% 1803 0.022392 44.658249 3.3985% 1802 0.021656 46.175954 3.5180%
1801 0.020920 47.800445 3.3999% 1800 0.020232 49.425635 2.8419% 1799 0.019673
50.830246 2.7485% 1798 0.019147 52.227293 2.8261% 1797 0.018621 53.703305 3.7832%
1796 0.017942 55.735014 2.1272% 1795 0.017568 56.920608 3.0879% 1794 0.017042
58.678281 3.1625% 1793 0.016520 60.533989 3.2904% 1792 0.015993 62.525808 3.4024%
1791 0.015467 64.653166 3.2296% 1790 0.014983 66.741181 41.3145% 1780 0.010603
94.314933 29.4353% 1770 0.008192 122.076831 83.4728% 1750 0.004465 223.977827
29.2845% 1740 0.003453 289.568507 94.2514% 1720 0.001778 562.490862 85.8111% 1700
0.000957 1045.170347 19.2490% 1690 0.000802 1246.355703 88.0250% 1670 0.000427
2343.460590

BASE YEAR: 1994

YEAR BYEAR/AYEAR AYEAR/BYEAR GROWTH%

2009 1.160960 0.861356 8.2857% 2001 1.072127 0.932725 1.0000% 2000 1.061512
0.942052 1.0000% 1999 1.051002 0.951473 1.0000% 1998 1.040596 0.960988 1.0000% 1997
1.030293 0.970598 1.0000% 1996 1.020092 0.980304 1.0000% 1995 1.009992 0.990107
0.9992% 1994 1.000000 1.000000 1.0008% 1993 0.990091 1.010008 1.0000% 1992 0.980288
1.020108 0.9295% 1991 0.971261 1.029590 1.2505% 1990 0.959265 1.042465 0.7224% 1989
0.952384 1.049996 1.1077% 1988 0.941951 1.061627 0.8834% 1987 0.933703 1.071005
0.5594% 1986 0.928509 1.076996 1.3056% 1985 0.916542 1.091057 0.7673% 1984 0.909563
1.099429 0.8149% 1983 0.902211 1.108388 0.9737% 1982 0.893510 1.119181 0.9508% 1981
0.885095 1.129823 0.9031% 1980 0.877173 1.140026 2.2701% 1979 0.857703 1.165905
1.0042% 1978 0.849176 1.177613 0.9896% 1977 0.840854 1.189266 0.9103% 1976 0.833269
1.200093 0.8394% 1975 0.826332 1.210167 0.9042% 1974 0.818928 1.221109 1.1568% 1973
0.809563 1.235234 0.9427% 1972 0.802002 1.246879 0.7426% 1971 0.796090 1.256139
1.4697% 1970 0.784559 1.274601 0.6968% 1969 0.779130 1.283482 0.8565% 1968 0.772513
1.294476 1.5090% 1967 0.761029 1.314010 0.9949% 1966 0.753532 1.327083 1.0575% 1965
0.745647 1.341117 1.1300% 1964 0.737315 1.356272 1.5537% 1963 0.726035 1.377343
1.4658% 1962 0.715547 1.397533 1.5364% 1961 0.704719 1.419005 2.1586% 1960 0.689828
1.449636 -1.6655% 1959 0.701512 1.425493 4.3080% 1958 0.672539 1.486903 2.1130%
1957 0.658622 1.518320 1.9895% 1956 0.645775 1.548527 2.1231% 1955 0.632349 1.581404
1.4496% 1954 0.623314 1.604328 2.1573% 1953 0.610151 1.638938 1.2298% 1952 0.602739
1.659093 1.6814% 1951 0.592772 1.686988 1.6233% 1950 0.583304 1.714373 1.4265% 1949
0.575100 1.738829 1.7790% 1948 0.565047 1.769763 1.8242% 1947 0.554925 1.802047 -
2.6320% 1946 0.569925 1.754616 3.1768% 1945 0.552377 1.810357 6.4754% 1944 0.518784
1.927585 -0.3437% 1943 0.520573 1.920960 0.6562% 1942 0.517179 1.933566 0.6633%
1941 0.513771 1.946391 -5.6614% 1940 0.544604 1.836198 8.0381% 1939 0.504085

1.983793 0.8126% 1938 0.500021 1.999914 0.7762% 1937 0.496170 2.015439 0.6029% 1936
0.493197 2.027589 0.5244% 1935 0.490624 2.038222 -3.0364% 1934 0.505987 1.976334
4.6271% 1933 0.483610 2.067781 1.3921% 1932 0.476970 2.096567 -0.2051% 1931
0.477950 2.092267 0.8886% 1930 0.473741 2.110859 1.0126% 1929 0.468992 2.132233
1.1526% 1928 0.463648 2.156809 1.2160% 1927 0.458078 2.183036 1.4086% 1926 0.451715
2.213786 1.7667% 1925 0.443873 2.252897 1.4465% 1924 0.437544 2.285485 1.7700% 1923
0.429934 2.325937 1.6165% 1922 0.423095 2.363537 1.3736% 1921 0.417362 2.396003
2.3393% 1920 0.407821 2.452053 1.3140% 1919 0.402532 2.484273 0.7676% 1918 0.399466
2.503344 0.3870% 1917 0.397926 2.513031 1.3274% 1916 0.392713 2.546390 1.4083% 1915
0.387259 2.582251 1.4458% 1914 0.381740 2.619585 1.9424% 1913 0.374466 2.670467
1.9857% 1912 0.367175 2.723494 1.5634% 1911 0.361523 2.766073 1.8169% 1910 0.355072
2.816331 1.8781% 1909 0.348526 2.869223 2.0082% 1908 0.341665 2.926844 1.9603% 1907
0.335096 2.984218 1.8264% 1906 0.329086 3.038720 1.9357% 1905 0.322837 3.097540
2.0148% 1904 0.316461 3.159950 2.1335% 1903 0.309850 3.227368 1.8151% 1902 0.304326
3.285950 1.8943% 1901 0.298668 3.348197 3.0255% 1900 0.289807 3.449497 0.6278% 1899
0.288089 3.471154 1.7757% 1898 0.283062 3.532790 1.8078% 1897 0.278036 3.596654
1.8396% 1896 0.273014 3.662818 1.8755% 1895 0.267988 3.731516 1.9114% 1894 0.262961
3.802840 1.9486% 1893 0.257935 3.876943 1.9858% 1892 0.252913 3.953932 2.0276% 1891
0.247887 4.034103 2.6465% 1890 0.241495 4.140866 1.5328% 1889 0.237850 4.204338
2.0811% 1888 0.233001 4.291835 2.1599% 1887 0.228074 4.384533 2.2075% 1886 0.223148
4.481323 2.2592% 1885 0.218218 4.582563 2.3095% 1884 0.213292 4.688399 2.3641% 1883
0.208366 4.799240 2.4214% 1882 0.203440 4.915448 2.4815% 1881 0.198514 5.037423
3.7644% 1880 0.191312 5.227052 0.9432% 1879 0.189525 5.276355 2.1464% 1878 0.185542
5.389606 2.1913% 1877 0.181564 5.507708 2.2426% 1876 0.177581 5.631225 2.2941% 1875
0.173599 5.760408 2.3456% 1874 0.169620 5.895524 2.4043% 1873 0.165638 6.037271
2.4635% 1872 0.161655 6.186002 2.5258% 1871 0.157673 6.342246 5.9947% 1870 0.148755
6.722443 -1.0968% 1869 0.150405 6.648713 2.1930% 1868 0.147177 6.794517 2.2394%
1867 0.143954 6.946674 2.2935% 1866 0.140726 7.105996 2.3445% 1865 0.137503 7.272594
2.4037% 1864 0.134275 7.447405 2.4599% 1863 0.131051 7.630602 2.5250% 1862 0.127824
7.823276 2.5872% 1861 0.124600 8.025683 2.9504% 1860 0.121029 8.262473 2.4012% 1859
0.118191 8.460875 2.7627% 1858 0.115014 8.694624 2.8412% 1857 0.111836 8.941656
2.9243% 1856 0.108659 9.203136 3.0161% 1855 0.105477 9.480715 3.1061% 1854 0.102300
9.775192 3.2056% 1853 0.099122 10.088548 3.3118% 1852 0.095945 10.422660 3.4252%
1851 0.092767 10.779659 4.0106% 1850 0.089190 11.211989 2.3254% 1849 0.087163
11.472709 2.7841% 1848 0.084802 11.792119 2.8590% 1847 0.082445 12.129257 2.9432%
1846 0.080088 12.486240 3.0324% 1845 0.077731 12.864873 3.1325% 1844 0.075370
13.267866 3.2284% 1843 0.073013 13.696200 3.3361% 1842 0.070656 14.153114 3.4512%
1841 0.068299 14.641565 3.8105% 1840 0.065792 15.199480 2.3861% 1839 0.064258
15.562148 2.5824% 1838 0.062641 15.964023 2.6573% 1837 0.061019 16.388239 2.7232%
1836 0.059402 16.834525 2.7994% 1835 0.057784 17.305797 2.8871% 1834 0.056163
17.805436 2.9657% 1833 0.054545 18.333489 3.0563% 1832 0.052927 18.893820 3.1604%
1831 0.051306 19.490945 3.4660% 1830 0.049587 20.166494 2.4653% 1829 0.048394
20.663659 2.6804% 1828 0.047131 21.217527 10.3427% 1827 0.042713 23.411981 -4.2314%
1826 0.044600 22.421319 2.9150% 1825 0.043337 23.074909 3.0026% 1824 0.042074
23.767747 3.0955% 1823 0.040811 24.503480 3.1944% 1822 0.039547 25.286217 3.3102%
1821 0.038280 26.123239 3.2277% 1820 0.037083 26.966429 2.6573% 1819 0.036123
27.683002 2.6261% 1818 0.035199 28.409987 2.6969% 1817 0.034275 29.176185 2.7717%
1816 0.033350 29.984856 2.8507% 1815 0.032426 30.839633 2.9343% 1814 0.031501
31.744574 3.0231% 1813 0.030577 32.704229 3.1039% 1812 0.029657 33.719334 3.2172%
1811 0.028732 34.804138 3.0969% 1810 0.027869 35.881993 2.9144% 1809 0.027080
36.927730 2.8225% 1808 0.026337 37.970002 2.9199% 1807 0.025589 39.078698 2.9918%
1806 0.024846 40.247849 3.0841% 1805 0.024103 41.489113 3.1822% 1804 0.023359
42.809377 3.2868% 1803 0.022616 44.216429 3.3985% 1802 0.021873 45.719118 3.5180%
1801 0.021129 47.327538 3.3999% 1800 0.020435 48.936649 2.8419% 1799 0.019870
50.327364 2.7485% 1798 0.019338 51.710590 2.8261% 1797 0.018807 53.171999 3.7832%
1796 0.018121 55.183607 2.1272% 1795 0.017744 56.357472 3.0879% 1794 0.017212

58.097756 3.1625% 1793 0.016685 59.935104 3.2904% 1792 0.016153 61.907218 3.4024% 1791 0.015622 64.013529 3.2296% 1790 0.015133 66.080886 41.3145% 1780 0.010709 93.381841 29.4353% 1770 0.008273 120.869081 83.4728% 1750 0.004509 221.761934 29.2845% 1740 0.003488 286.703701 94.2514% 1720 0.001796 556.925937 85.8111% 1700 0.000966 1034.830100 19.2490% 1690 0.000810 1234.025057 88.0250% 1670 0.000431 2320.275889

BASE YEAR: 1993

YEAR BYEAR/AYEAR AYEAR/BYEAR GROWTH%

2009 1.172579 0.852821 8.2857% 2001 1.082857 0.923483 1.0000% 2000 1.072135 0.932718 1.0000% 1999 1.061520 0.942045 1.0000% 1998 1.051010 0.951466 1.0000% 1997 1.040604 0.960980 1.0000% 1996 1.030301 0.970590 1.0000% 1995 1.020100 0.980296 0.9992% 1994 1.010008 0.990091 1.0008% 1993 1.000000 1.000000 1.0000% 1992 0.990099 1.010000 0.9295% 1991 0.980981 1.019388 1.2505% 1990 0.968865 1.032136 0.7224% 1989 0.961916 1.039592 1.1077% 1988 0.951377 1.051108 0.8834% 1987 0.943047 1.060393 0.5594% 1986 0.937801 1.066324 1.3056% 1985 0.925715 1.080246 0.7673% 1984 0.918666 1.088535 0.8149% 1983 0.911240 1.097406 0.9737% 1982 0.902452 1.108092 0.9508% 1981 0.893953 1.118628 0.9031% 1980 0.885952 1.128730 2.2701% 1979 0.866287 1.154352 1.0042% 1978 0.857674 1.165944 0.9896% 1977 0.849270 1.177482 0.9103% 1976 0.841608 1.188202 0.8394% 1975 0.834602 1.198176 0.9042% 1974 0.827123 1.209009 1.1568% 1973 0.817665 1.222995 0.9427% 1972 0.810029 1.234524 0.7426% 1971 0.804057 1.243692 1.4697% 1970 0.792411 1.261971 0.6968% 1969 0.786928 1.270765 0.8565% 1968 0.780245 1.281650 1.5090% 1967 0.768645 1.300990 0.9949% 1966 0.761073 1.313934 1.0575% 1965 0.753109 1.327828 1.1300% 1964 0.744694 1.342833 1.5537% 1963 0.733301 1.363696 1.4658% 1962 0.722708 1.383685 1.5364% 1961 0.711772 1.404945 2.1586% 1960 0.696732 1.435272 -1.6655% 1959 0.708532 1.411368 4.3080% 1958 0.679270 1.472170 2.1130% 1957 0.665214 1.503276 1.9895% 1956 0.652238 1.533184 2.1231% 1955 0.638678 1.565735 1.4496% 1954 0.629552 1.588432 2.1573% 1953 0.616258 1.622698 1.2298% 1952 0.608771 1.642653 1.6814% 1951 0.598705 1.670272 1.6233% 1950 0.589141 1.697386 1.4265% 1949 0.580855 1.721599 1.7790% 1948 0.570702 1.752227 1.8242% 1947 0.560478 1.784191 -2.6320% 1946 0.575629 1.737230 3.1768% 1945 0.557905 1.792419 6.4754% 1944 0.523976 1.908485 -0.3437% 1943 0.525783 1.901926 0.6562% 1942 0.522355 1.914407 0.6633% 1941 0.518913 1.927105 -5.6614% 1940 0.550054 1.818004 8.0381% 1939 0.509130 1.964137 0.8126% 1938 0.505026 1.980098 0.7762% 1937 0.501135 1.995468 0.6029% 1936 0.498132 2.007499 0.5244% 1935 0.495534 2.018026 -3.0364% 1934 0.511051 1.956751 4.6271% 1933 0.488450 2.047292 1.3921% 1932 0.481744 2.075793 -0.2051% 1931 0.482734 2.071536 0.8886% 1930 0.478482 2.089944 1.0126% 1929 0.473685 2.111106 1.1526% 1928 0.468288 2.135438 1.2160% 1927 0.462662 2.161405 1.4086% 1926 0.456235 2.191851 1.7667% 1925 0.448315 2.230574 1.4465% 1924 0.441923 2.262839 1.7700% 1923 0.434237 2.302891 1.6165% 1922 0.427329 2.340117 1.3736% 1921 0.421539 2.372262 2.3393% 1920 0.411903 2.427757 1.3140% 1919 0.406561 2.459658 0.7676% 1918 0.403463 2.478539 0.3870% 1917 0.401908 2.488131 1.3274% 1916 0.396643 2.521159 1.4083% 1915 0.391135 2.556664 1.4458% 1914 0.385560 2.593629 1.9424% 1913 0.378214 2.644007 1.9857% 1912 0.370850 2.696508 1.5634% 1911 0.365141 2.738666 1.8169% 1910 0.358625 2.788425 1.8781% 1909 0.352014 2.840793 2.0082% 1908 0.345084 2.897843 1.9603% 1907 0.338450 2.954648 1.8264% 1906 0.332379 3.008610 1.9357% 1905 0.326068 3.066847 2.0148% 1904 0.319628 3.128639 2.1335% 1903 0.312951 3.195390 1.8151% 1902 0.307372 3.253391 1.8943% 1901 0.301657 3.315021 3.0255% 1900 0.292799 3.415317 0.6278% 1899 0.290972 3.436760 1.7757% 1898 0.285895 3.497785 1.8078% 1897 0.280819 3.561016 1.8396% 1896 0.275746 3.626525 1.8755% 1895 0.270670 3.694542 1.9114% 1894 0.265593 3.765159 1.9486% 1893 0.260517 3.838528 1.9858% 1892 0.255444 3.914754 2.0276% 1891 0.250367 3.994130 2.6465% 1890 0.243912 4.099835 1.5328% 1889 0.240230 4.162678 2.0811% 1888 0.235332 4.249309 2.1599% 1887 0.230357 4.341088 2.2075% 1886 0.225382 4.436919 2.2592% 1885 0.220402 4.537156 2.3095% 1884 0.215427 4.641944 2.3641% 1883 0.210452 4.751686 2.4214% 1882 0.205476 4.866743 2.4815% 1881 0.200501 4.987509 3.7644% 1880 0.193227 5.175259 0.9432% 1879 0.191422 5.224074 2.1464% 1878 0.187399 5.336202 2.1913% 1877 0.183381 5.453134 2.2426% 1876 0.179358 5.575427 2.2941% 1875

18

0.175336 5.703330 2.3456% 1874 0.171318 5.837107 2.4043% 1873 0.167295 5.977450 2.4635% 1872 0.163273 6.124707 2.5258% 1871 0.159251 6.279403 5.9947% 1870 0.150244 6.655833 -1.0968% 1869 0.151910 6.582833 2.1930% 1868 0.148650 6.727193 2.2394% 1867 0.145394 6.877842 2.2935% 1866 0.142135 7.035585 2.3445% 1865 0.138879 7.200532 2.4037% 1864 0.135619 7.373611 2.4599% 1863 0.132363 7.554994 2.5250% 1862 0.129103 7.745758 2.5872% 1861 0.125847 7.946160 2.9504% 1860 0.122240 8.180604 2.4012% 1859 0.119374 8.377039 2.7627% 1858 0.116165 8.608473 2.8412% 1857 0.112955 8.853057 2.9243% 1856 0.109746 9.111946 3.0161% 1855 0.106533 9.386775 3.1061% 1854 0.103324 9.678333 3.2056% 1853 0.100114 9.988584 3.3118% 1852 0.096905 10.319385 3.4252% 1851 0.093696 10.672848 4.0106% 1850 0.090083 11.100893 2.3254% 1849 0.088036 11.359030 2.7841% 1848 0.085651 11.675275 2.8590% 1847 0.083270 12.009073 2.9432% 1846 0.080890 12.362519 3.0324% 1845 0.078509 12.737400 3.1125% 1844 0.076124 13.136400 3.2284% 1843 0.073744 13.560490 3.3361% 1842 0.071363 14.012876 3.4512% 1841 0.068982 14.496487 3.8105% 1840 0.066450 15.048874 2.3861% 1839 0.064902 15.407948 2.5824% 1838 0.063268 15.805842 2.6573% 1837 0.061630 16.225854 2.7232% 1836 0.059996 16.667718 2.7994% 1835 0.058362 17.134320 2.8871% 1834 0.056725 17.629009 2.9657% 1833 0.055091 18.151830 3.0563% 1832 0.053457 18.706608 3.1604% 1831 0.051819 19.297816 3.4660% 1830 0.050083 19.966672 2.4653% 1829 0.048878 20.458910 2.6804% 1828 0.047603 21.007290 10.3427% 1827 0.043141 23.180001 -4.2314% 1826 0.045047 22.199155 2.9150% 1825 0.043771 22.846268 3.0026% 1824 0.042495 23.532242 3.0955% 1823 0.041219 24.260684 3.1944% 1822 0.039943 25.035665 3.3102% 1821 0.038663 25.864394 3.2277% 1820 0.037454 26.699229 2.6573% 1819 0.036485 27.408701 2.6261% 1818 0.035551 28.128483 2.6969% 1817 0.034618 28.887090 2.7717% 1816 0.033684 29.687748 2.8507% 1815 0.032750 30.534055 2.9343% 1814 0.031817 31.430029 3.0231% 1813 0.030883 32.380175 3.1039% 1812 0.029953 33.385222 3.2172% 1811 0.029020 34.459277 3.0969% 1810 0.028148 35.526452 2.9144% 1809 0.027351 36.561828 2.8225% 1808 0.026600 37.593772 2.9199% 1807 0.025845 38.691483 2.9918% 1806 0.025095 39.849048 3.0841% 1805 0.024344 41.078014 3.1822% 1804 0.023593 42.385195 3.2868% 1803 0.022842 43.778306 3.3985% 1802 0.022092 45.266105 3.5180% 1801 0.021341 46.858587 3.3999% 1800 0.020639 48.451754 2.8419% 1799 0.020069 49.828690 2.7485% 1798 0.019532 51.198210 2.8261% 1797 0.018995 52.645138 3.7832% 1796 0.018303 54.636814 2.1272% 1795 0.017921 55.799047 3.0879% 1794 0.017385 57.522088 3.1625% 1793 0.016852 59.341230 3.2904% 1792 0.016315 61.293803 3.4024% 1791 0.015778 63.379243 3.2296% 1790 0.015284 65.426116 41.3145% 1780 0.010816 92.456557 29.4353% 1770 0.008356 119.671435 83.4728% 1750 0.004554 219.564580 29.2845% 1740 0.003523 283.862864 94.2514% 1720 0.001814 551.407572 85.8111% 1700 0.000976 1024.576365 19.2490% 1690 0.000818 1221.797576 88.0250% 1670 0.000435 2297.285165

BASE YEAR: 1992
YEAR BYEAR/AYEAR AYEAR/BYEAR GROWTH%
2009 1.184304 0.844377 8.2857% 2001 1.093685 0.914340 1.0000% 2000 1.082857 0.923483 1.0000% 1999 1.072135 0.932718 1.0000% 1998 1.061520 0.942045 1.0000% 1997 1.051010 0.951466 1.0000% 1996 1.040604 0.960980 1.0000% 1995 1.030301 0.970590 0.9992% 1994 1.020108 0.980288 1.0008% 1993 1.010010 0.990099 1.0000% 1992 1.000000 1.000000 0.9295% 1991 0.990791 1.009295 1.2505% 1990 0.978554 1.021916 0.7224% 1989 0.971535 1.029299 1.1077% 1988 0.960891 1.040701 0.8834% 1987 0.952477 1.049894 0.5594% 1986 0.947179 1.055766 1.3056% 1985 0.934972 1.069551 0.7673% 1984 0.927853 1.077757 0.8149% 1983 0.920352 1.086540 0.9737% 1982 0.911477 1.097121 0.9508% 1981 0.902892 1.107552 0.9031% 1980 0.894811 1.117554 2.2701% 1979 0.874949 1.142923 1.0042% 1978 0.866251 1.154400 0.9896% 1977 0.857762 1.165824 0.9103% 1976 0.850024 1.176437 0.8394% 1975 0.842948 1.186313 0.9042% 1974 0.835395 1.197039 1.1568% 1973 0.825841 1.210886 0.9427% 1972 0.818129 1.222301 0.7426% 1971 0.812098 1.231378 1.4697% 1970 0.800335 1.249476 0.6968% 1969 0.794797 1.258183 0.8565% 1968 0.788047 1.268960 1.5090% 1967 0.776332 1.288109 0.9949% 1966 0.768684 1.300925 1.0575% 1965 0.760641 1.314681 1.1300% 1964 0.752141 1.329537 1.5537% 1963 0.740634 1.350194 1.4658% 1962 0.729935 1.369985 1.5364% 1961 0.718890 1.391034 2.1586% 1960 0.703699

1.421062 -1.6655% 1959 0.715618 1.397394 4.3080% 1958 0.686062 1.457594 2.1130% 1957 0.671866 1.488392 1.9895% 1956 0.658760 1.518004 2.1231% 1955 0.645065 1.550232 1.4496% 1954 0.635847 1.572705 2.1573% 1953 0.622420 1.606632 1.2298% 1952 0.614859 1.626389 1.6814% 1951 0.604692 1.653735 1.6233% 1950 0.595033 1.680580 1.4265% 1949 0.586664 1.704554 1.7790% 1948 0.576409 1.734879 1.8242% 1947 0.566083 1.766526 - 2.6320% 1946 0.581385 1.720030 3.1768% 1945 0.563484 1.774672 6.4754% 1944 0.529216 1.889589 -0.3437% 1943 0.531041 1.883095 0.6562% 1942 0.527579 1.895453 0.6633% 1941 0.524102 1.908025 -5.6614% 1940 0.555554 1.800004 8.0381% 1939 0.514221 1.944690 0.8126% 1938 0.510076 1.960493 0.7762% 1937 0.506147 1.975711 0.6029% 1936 0.503114 1.987622 0.5244% 1935 0.500489 1.998045 -3.0364% 1934 0.516162 1.937377 4.6271% 1933 0.493335 2.027022 1.3921% 1932 0.486561 2.055241 -0.2051% 1931 0.487561 2.051026 0.8886% 1930 0.483267 2.069251 1.0126% 1929 0.478422 2.090204 1.1526% 1928 0.472971 2.114295 1.2160% 1927 0.467289 2.140005 1.4086% 1926 0.460798 2.170149 1.7667% 1925 0.452798 2.208489 1.4465% 1924 0.446342 2.240435 1.7700% 1923 0.438579 2.280090 1.6165% 1922 0.431602 2.316948 1.3736% 1921 0.425754 2.348774 2.3393% 1920 0.416022 2.403720 1.3140% 1919 0.410626 2.435305 0.7676% 1918 0.407498 2.453999 0.3870% 1917 0.405927 2.463496 1.3274% 1916 0.400609 2.496197 1.4083% 1915 0.395046 2.531351 1.4458% 1914 0.389416 2.567949 1.9424% 1913 0.381996 2.617829 1.9857% 1912 0.374558 2.669810 1.5634% 1911 0.368793 2.711550 1.8169% 1910 0.362212 2.760817 1.8781% 1909 0.355535 2.812666 2.0082% 1908 0.348535 2.869152 1.9603% 1907 0.341834 2.925394 1.8264% 1906 0.335703 2.978822 1.9357% 1905 0.329328 3.036483 2.0148% 1904 0.322824 3.097663 2.1335% 1903 0.316080 3.163752 1.8151% 1902 0.310445 3.221179 1.8943% 1901 0.304674 3.282199 3.0255% 1900 0.295727 3.381502 0.6278% 1899 0.293881 3.402733 1.7757% 1898 0.288754 3.463153 1.8078% 1897 0.283627 3.525759 1.8396% 1896 0.278504 3.590619 1.8755% 1895 0.273376 3.657962 1.9114% 1894 0.268249 3.727880 1.9486% 1893 0.263122 3.800523 1.9858% 1892 0.257998 3.875994 2.0276% 1891 0.252871 3.954584 2.6465% 1890 0.246351 4.059243 1.5328% 1889 0.242632 4.121464 2.0811% 1888 0.237686 4.207237 2.1599% 1887 0.232661 4.298107 2.2075% 1886 0.227635 4.392989 2.2592% 1885 0.222606 4.492234 2.3095% 1884 0.217581 4.595984 2.3641% 1883 0.212556 4.704640 2.4214% 1882 0.207531 4.818557 2.4815% 1881 0.202506 4.938128 3.7644% 1880 0.195159 5.124019 0.9432% 1879 0.193336 5.172350 2.1464% 1878 0.189273 5.283369 2.1913% 1877 0.185215 5.399143 2.2426% 1876 0.181152 5.520225 2.2941% 1875 0.177090 5.646862 2.3456% 1874 0.173031 5.779314 2.4043% 1873 0.168968 5.918267 2.4635% 1872 0.164906 6.064067 2.5258% 1871 0.160843 6.217231 5.9947% 1870 0.151747 6.589934 -1.0968% 1869 0.153429 6.517656 2.1930% 1868 0.150137 6.660587 2.2394% 1867 0.146848 6.809744 2.2935% 1866 0.143556 6.965926 2.3445% 1865 0.140267 7.129240 2.4037% 1864 0.136975 7.300605 2.4599% 1863 0.133686 7.480192 2.5250% 1862 0.130394 7.669067 2.5872% 1861 0.127105 7.867485 2.9504% 1860 0.123463 8.099608 2.4012% 1859 0.120568 8.294098 2.7627% 1858 0.117326 8.523240 2.8412% 1857 0.114085 8.765403 2.9243% 1856 0.110844 9.021728 3.0161% 1855 0.107598 9.293836 3.1061% 1854 0.104357 9.582508 3.2056% 1853 0.101115 9.889688 3.3118% 1852 0.097874 10.217213 3.4252% 1851 0.094633 10.567176 4.0106% 1850 0.090984 10.990984 2.3254% 1849 0.088916 11.246564 2.7841% 1848 0.086508 11.559678 2.8590% 1847 0.084103 11.890171 2.9432% 1846 0.081699 12.240117 3.0324% 1845 0.079294 12.611287 3.1325% 1844 0.076886 13.006337 3.2284% 1843 0.074481 13.426228 3.3361% 1842 0.072077 13.874135 3.4512% 1841 0.069672 14.352958 3.8105% 1840 0.067115 14.899876 2.3861% 1839 0.065551 15.255394 2.5824% 1838 0.063900 15.649348 2.6573% 1837 0.062246 16.065202 2.7232% 1836 0.060596 16.502691 2.7994% 1835 0.058946 16.964674 2.8871% 1834 0.057292 17.454464 2.9657% 1833 0.055642 17.972108 3.0563% 1832 0.053992 18.521394 3.1604% 1831 0.052338 19.106749 3.4660% 1830 0.050584 19.768982 2.4653% 1829 0.049367 20.256347 2.6804% 1828 0.048079 20.799297 10.3427% 1827 0.043572 22.950496 -4.2314% 1826 0.045497 21.979361 2.9150% 1825 0.044209 22.620068 3.0026% 1824 0.042920 23.299249 3.0955% 1823 0.041631 24.020479 3.1944% 1822 0.040342 24.787787 3.3102% 1821 0.039050 25.608311 3.2277% 1820 0.037829 26.434880 2.6573% 1819 0.036850 27.137328 2.6261% 1818 0.035907 27.849984 2.6969% 1817 0.034964 28.601079 2.7717% 1816 0.034021 29.393810 2.8507% 1815 0.033078 30.231738 2.9343% 1814 0.032135

31.118841 3.0231% 1813 0.031192 32.059579 3.1039% 1812 0.030253 33.054675 3.2172% 1811 0.029310 34.118097 3.0969% 1810 0.028430 35.174705 2.9144% 1809 0.027624 36.199829 2.8225% 1808 0.026866 37.221556 2.9199% 1807 0.026104 38.308399 2.9918% 1806 0.025346 39.454503 3.0841% 1805 0.024587 40.671301 3.1822% 1804 0.023829 41.965540 3.2868% 1803 0.023071 43.344857 3.3985% 1802 0.022313 44.817926 3.5180% 1801 0.021554 46.394641 3.3999% 1800 0.020845 47.972034 2.8419% 1799 0.020269 49.335336 2.7485% 1798 0.019727 50.691297 2.8261% 1797 0.019185 52.123899 3.7832% 1796 0.018486 54.095855 2.1272% 1795 0.018101 55.246581 3.0879% 1794 0.017558 56.952562 3.1625% 1793 0.017020 58.753693 3.2904% 1792 0.016478 60.686934 3.4024% 1791 0.015936 62.751726 3.2296% 1790 0.015437 64.778333 41.3145% 1780 0.010924 91.541145 29.4353% 1770 0.008440 118.486570 83.4728% 1750 0.004600 217.390673 29.2845% 1740 0.003558 281.052341 94.2514% 1720 0.001832 545.948091 85.8111% 1700 0.000986 1014.432045 19.2490% 1690 0.000827 1209.700570 88.0250% 1670 0.000440 2274.539768

BASE YEAR: 1991

YEAR BYEAR/AYEAR AYEAR/BYEAR GROWTH%

2009 1.195313 0.836601 8.2857% 2001 1.103851 0.905919 1.0000% 2000 1.092922 0.914978 1.0000% 1999 1.082101 0.924128 1.0000% 1998 1.071387 0.933370 1.0000% 1997 1.060779 0.942703 1.0000% 1996 1.050276 0.952130 1.0000% 1995 1.039878 0.961652 0.9992% 1994 1.029590 0.971261 1.0008% 1993 1.019388 0.980981 1.0000% 1992 1.009295 0.990791 0.9295% 1991 1.000000 1.000000 1.2505% 1990 0.987649 1.012505 0.7224% 1989 0.980565 1.019820 1.1077% 1988 0.969823 1.031116 0.8834% 1987 0.961331 1.040225 0.5594% 1986 0.955983 1.046043 1.3056% 1985 0.943663 1.059701 0.7673% 1984 0.936477 1.067832 0.8149% 1983 0.928907 1.076534 0.9737% 1982 0.919949 1.087017 0.9508% 1981 0.911285 1.097352 0.9031% 1980 0.903129 1.107262 2.2701% 1979 0.883082 1.132398 1.0042% 1978 0.874303 1.143769 0.9896% 1977 0.865735 1.155088 0.9103% 1976 0.857925 1.165603 0.8394% 1975 0.850783 1.175387 0.9042% 1974 0.843160 1.186015 1.1568% 1973 0.833518 1.199735 0.9427% 1972 0.825734 1.211044 0.7426% 1971 0.819647 1.220038 1.4697% 1970 0.807774 1.237969 0.6968% 1969 0.802185 1.246596 0.8565% 1968 0.795372 1.257273 1.5090% 1967 0.783548 1.276246 0.9949% 1966 0.775829 1.288944 1.0575% 1965 0.767711 1.302574 1.1300% 1964 0.759132 1.317293 1.5537% 1963 0.747519 1.337759 1.4658% 1962 0.736720 1.357368 1.5364% 1961 0.725572 1.378224 2.1586% 1960 0.710240 1.407974 -1.6655% 1959 0.722269 1.384525 4.3080% 1958 0.692439 1.444170 2.1130% 1957 0.678111 1.474685 1.9895% 1956 0.664883 1.504024 2.1231% 1955 0.651061 1.535955 1.4496% 1954 0.641758 1.558221 2.1573% 1953 0.628206 1.591836 1.2298% 1952 0.620574 1.611411 1.6814% 1951 0.610312 1.638505 1.6233% 1950 0.600564 1.665103 1.4265% 1949 0.592117 1.688856 1.7790% 1948 0.581767 1.718901 1.8242% 1947 0.571345 1.750257 -2.6320% 1946 0.586789 1.704189 3.1768% 1945 0.568722 1.758328 6.4754% 1944 0.534135 1.872187 -0.3437% 1943 0.535977 1.865753 0.6562% 1942 0.532482 1.877996 0.6633% 1941 0.528974 1.890453 -5.6614% 1940 0.560718 1.783427 8.0381% 1939 0.519001 1.926780 0.8126% 1938 0.514817 1.942438 0.7762% 1937 0.510852 1.957516 0.6029% 1936 0.507790 1.969317 0.5244% 1935 0.505141 1.979644 -3.0364% 1934 0.520959 1.919535 4.6271% 1933 0.497920 2.008354 1.3921% 1932 0.491084 2.036313 -0.2051% 1931 0.492093 2.032137 0.8886% 1930 0.487759 2.050194 1.0126% 1929 0.482869 2.070954 1.1526% 1928 0.477367 2.094824 1.2160% 1927 0.471632 2.120297 1.4086% 1926 0.465081 2.150163 1.7667% 1925 0.457007 2.188150 1.4465% 1924 0.450491 2.219801 1.7700% 1923 0.442656 2.259091 1.6165% 1922 0.435614 2.295610 1.3736% 1921 0.429711 2.327144 2.3393% 1920 0.419889 2.381583 1.3140% 1919 0.414443 2.412877 0.7676% 1918 0.411286 2.431399 0.3870% 1917 0.409700 2.440808 1.3274% 1916 0.404333 2.473209 1.4083% 1915 0.398718 2.508038 1.4458% 1914 0.393035 2.544300 1.9424% 1913 0.385547 2.593720 1.9857% 1912 0.378040 2.645223 1.5634% 1911 0.372221 2.686578 1.8169% 1910 0.365578 2.735391 1.8781% 1909 0.358839 2.786763 2.0082% 1908 0.351775 2.842728 1.9603% 1907 0.345012 2.898453 1.8264% 1906 0.338824 2.951389 1.9357% 1905 0.332390 3.008518 2.0148% 1904 0.325825 3.069135 2.1335% 1903 0.319018 3.134616 1.8151% 1902 0.313331 3.191514 1.8943% 1901 0.307506 3.251972 3.0255% 1900 0.298475 3.350360 0.6278% 1899 0.296613 3.371395 1.7757% 1898 0.291438 3.431260 1.8078% 1897 0.286263 3.493288

1.8396% 1896 0.281092 3.557551 1.8755% 1895 0.275917 3.624274 1.9114% 1894 0.270742 3.693548 1.9486% 1893 0.265567 3.765522 1.9858% 1892 0.260396 3.840298 2.0276% 1891 0.255222 3.918165 2.6465% 1890 0.248641 4.021860 1.5328% 1889 0.244888 4.083507 2.0811% 1888 0.239895 4.168490 2.1599% 1887 0.234823 4.258524 2.2075% 1886 0.229751 4.352532 2.2592% 1885 0.224676 4.450863 2.3095% 1884 0.219604 4.553658 2.3641% 1883 0.214532 4.661312 2.4214% 1882 0.209460 4.774181 2.4815% 1881 0.204388 4.892651 3.7644% 1880 0.196973 5.076829 0.9432% 1879 0.195133 5.124715 2.1464% 1878 0.191032 5.234712 2.1913% 1877 0.186936 5.349420 2.2426% 1876 0.182836 5.469386 2.2941% 1875 0.178736 5.594857 2.3456% 1874 0.174639 5.726090 2.4043% 1873 0.170539 5.863763 2.4635% 1872 0.166439 6.008220 2.5258% 1871 0.162338 6.159974 5.9947% 1870 0.153157 6.529244 -1.0968% 1869 0.154856 6.457632 2.1930% 1868 0.151532 6.599246 2.2394% 1867 0.148213 6.747030 2.2935% 1866 0.144890 6.901773 2.3445% 1865 0.141571 7.063584 2.4037% 1864 0.138248 7.233371 2.4599% 1863 0.134929 7.411303 2.5250% 1862 0.131606 7.598439 2.5872% 1861 0.128287 7.795030 2.9504% 1860 0.124610 8.025015 2.4012% 1859 0.121688 8.217714 2.7627% 1858 0.118417 8.444746 2.8412% 1857 0.115145 8.684678 2.9243% 1856 0.111874 8.938643 3.0161% 1855 0.108598 9.208245 3.1061% 1854 0.105327 9.494258 3.2056% 1853 0.102055 9.798609 3.3118% 1852 0.098784 10.123118 3.4252% 1851 0.095512 10.469858 4.0106% 1850 0.091829 10.889763 2.3254% 1849 0.089743 11.142990 2.7841% 1848 0.087312 11.453220 2.8590% 1847 0.084885 11.780669 2.9432% 1846 0.082458 12.127393 3.0324% 1845 0.080031 12.495144 3.1325% 1844 0.077600 12.886555 3.2284% 1843 0.075173 13.302580 3.3361% 1842 0.072747 13.746361 3.4512% 1841 0.070320 14.220775 3.8105% 1840 0.067738 14.762656 2.3861% 1839 0.066160 15.114901 2.5824% 1838 0.064494 15.505226 2.6573% 1837 0.062825 15.917251 2.7232% 1836 0.061159 16.350710 2.7994% 1835 0.059494 16.808438 2.8871% 1834 0.057824 17.293718 2.9657% 1833 0.056159 17.806595 3.0563% 1832 0.054493 18.350822 3.1604% 1831 0.052824 18.930786 3.4660% 1830 0.051054 19.586921 2.4653% 1829 0.049826 20.069797 2.6804% 1828 0.048525 20.607747 10.3427% 1827 0.043977 22.739134 -4.2314% 1826 0.045920 21.776943 2.9150% 1825 0.044619 22.411749 3.0026% 1824 0.043319 23.084676 3.0955% 1823 0.042018 23.799264 3.1944% 1822 0.040717 24.559505 3.3102% 1821 0.039413 25.372472 3.2277% 1820 0.038180 26.191429 2.6573% 1819 0.037192 26.887408 2.6261% 1818 0.036240 27.593500 2.6969% 1817 0.035289 28.337678 2.7717% 1816 0.034337 29.123109 2.8507% 1815 0.033385 29.953320 2.9343% 1814 0.032434 30.832253 3.0231% 1813 0.031482 31.764328 3.1039% 1812 0.030534 32.750260 3.2172% 1811 0.029582 33.803887 3.0969% 1810 0.028694 34.850765 2.9144% 1809 0.027881 35.866449 2.8225% 1808 0.027116 36.878766 2.9199% 1807 0.026347 37.955599 2.9918% 1806 0.025581 39.091149 3.0841% 1805 0.024816 40.296740 3.1822% 1804 0.024051 41.579060 3.2868% 1803 0.023285 42.945674 3.3985% 1802 0.022520 44.405177 3.5180% 1801 0.021755 45.967371 3.3999% 1800 0.021039 47.530238 2.8419% 1799 0.020458 48.880985 2.7485% 1798 0.019911 50.224457 2.8261% 1797 0.019363 51.643866 3.7832% 1796 0.018658 53.597662 2.1272% 1795 0.018269 54.737790 3.0879% 1794 0.017722 56.428060 3.1625% 1793 0.017178 58.212604 3.2904% 1792 0.016631 60.128040 3.4024% 1791 0.016084 62.173817 3.2296% 1790 0.015581 64.181759 41.3145% 1780 0.011026 90.698101 29.4353% 1770 0.008518 117.395373 83.4728% 1750 0.004643 215.388623 29.2845% 1740 0.003591 278.464002 94.2514% 1720 0.001849 540.920206 85.8111% 1700 0.000995 1005.089677 19.2490% 1690 0.000834 1198.559886 88.0250% 1670 0.000444 2253.592493

BASE YEAR: 1990

YEAR BYEAR/AYEAR AYEAR/BYEAR GROWTH%

2009 1.210260 0.826269 8.2857% 2001 1.117655 0.894730 1.0000% 2000 1.106589 0.903678 1.0000% 1999 1.095633 0.912715 1.0000% 1998 1.084785 0.921842 1.0000% 1997 1.074044 0.931060 1.0000% 1996 1.063410 0.940371 1.0000% 1995 1.052882 0.949774 0.9992% 1994 1.042465 0.959265 1.0008% 1993 1.032136 0.968865 1.0000% 1992 1.021916 0.978554 0.9295% 1991 1.012505 0.987649 1.2505% 1990 1.000000 1.000000 0.7224% 1989 0.992827 1.007224 1.1077% 1988 0.981951 1.018381 0.8834% 1987 0.973352 1.027377 0.5594% 1986 0.967938 1.033124 1.3056% 1985 0.955463 1.046613 0.7673% 1984 0.948188 1.054643 0.8149% 1983 0.940523 1.063238 0.9737% 1982 0.931453 1.073591 0.9508% 1981

22

0.922680 1.083799 0.9031% 1980 0.914422 1.093586 2.2701% 1979 0.894125 1.118412 1.0042% 1978 0.885236 1.129642 0.9896% 1977 0.876561 1.140821 0.9103% 1976 0.868654 1.151207 0.8394% 1975 0.861423 1.160870 0.9042% 1974 0.853704 1.171367 1.1568% 1973 0.843941 1.184917 0.9427% 1972 0.836059 1.196087 0.7426% 1971 0.829896 1.204970 1.4697% 1970 0.817876 1.222680 0.6968% 1969 0.812216 1.231200 0.8565% 1968 0.805318 1.241745 1.5090% 1967 0.793346 1.260484 0.9949% 1966 0.785531 1.273024 1.0575% 1965 0.777311 1.286486 1.1300% 1964 0.768626 1.301024 1.5537% 1963 0.756866 1.321237 1.4658% 1962 0.745932 1.340604 1.5364% 1961 0.734645 1.361201 2.1586% 1960 0.719122 1.390585 -1.6655% 1959 0.731302 1.367425 4.3080% 1958 0.701098 1.426334 2.1130% 1957 0.686591 1.456471 1.9895% 1956 0.673198 1.485448 2.1231% 1955 0.659202 1.516985 1.4496% 1954 0.649783 1.538976 2.1573% 1953 0.636061 1.572175 1.2298% 1952 0.628334 1.591509 1.6814% 1951 0.617944 1.618268 1.6233% 1950 0.608074 1.644537 1.4265% 1949 0.599521 1.667997 1.7790% 1948 0.589042 1.697672 1.8242% 1947 0.578489 1.728640 - 2.6320% 1946 0.594127 1.683141 3.1768% 1945 0.575834 1.736612 6.4754% 1944 0.540814 1.849064 -0.3437% 1943 0.542679 1.842710 0.6562% 1942 0.539141 1.854802 0.6633% 1941 0.535589 1.867105 -5.6614% 1940 0.567730 1.761400 8.0381% 1939 0.525491 1.902983 0.8126% 1938 0.521255 1.918447 0.7762% 1937 0.517240 1.933339 0.6029% 1936 0.514140 1.944995 0.5244% 1935 0.511458 1.955194 -3.0364% 1934 0.527474 1.895827 4.6271% 1933 0.504147 1.983550 1.3921% 1932 0.497225 2.011163 -0.2051% 1931 0.498247 2.007038 0.8886% 1930 0.493858 2.024873 1.0126% 1929 0.488908 2.045377 1.1526% 1928 0.483337 2.068951 1.2160% 1927 0.477530 2.094110 1.4086% 1926 0.470897 2.123607 1.7667% 1925 0.462722 2.161125 1.4465% 1924 0.456124 2.192385 1.7700% 1923 0.448191 2.231190 1.6165% 1922 0.441061 2.267258 1.3736% 1921 0.435085 2.298402 2.3393% 1920 0.425140 2.352168 1.3140% 1919 0.419626 2.383076 0.7676% 1918 0.416429 2.401370 0.3870% 1917 0.414824 2.410663 1.3274% 1916 0.409389 2.442663 1.4083% 1915 0.403704 2.477062 1.4458% 1914 0.397950 2.512876 1.9424% 1913 0.390368 2.561686 1.9857% 1912 0.382767 2.612552 1.5634% 1911 0.376875 2.653397 1.8169% 1910 0.370150 2.701607 1.8781% 1909 0.363327 2.752345 2.0082% 1908 0.356174 2.807619 1.9603% 1907 0.349326 2.862655 1.8264% 1906 0.343061 2.914937 1.9357% 1905 0.336546 2.971361 2.0148% 1904 0.329899 3.031229 2.1335% 1903 0.323008 3.095901 1.8151% 1902 0.317249 3.152096 1.8943% 1901 0.311351 3.211808 3.0255% 1900 0.302208 3.308981 0.6278% 1899 0.300322 3.329756 1.7757% 1898 0.295083 3.388881 1.8078% 1897 0.289843 3.450144 1.8396% 1896 0.284607 3.513613 1.8755% 1895 0.279368 3.579512 1.9114% 1894 0.274128 3.647930 1.9486% 1893 0.268888 3.719015 1.9858% 1892 0.263653 3.792867 2.0276% 1891 0.258413 3.869773 2.6465% 1890 0.251750 3.972187 1.5328% 1889 0.247950 4.033073 2.0811% 1888 0.242895 4.117007 2.1599% 1887 0.237760 4.205928 2.2075% 1886 0.232624 4.298775 2.2592% 1885 0.227485 4.395892 2.3095% 1884 0.222350 4.497417 2.3641% 1883 0.217215 4.603742 2.4214% 1882 0.212079 4.715216 2.4815% 1881 0.206944 4.832223 3.7644% 1880 0.199437 5.014127 0.9432% 1879 0.197573 5.061422 2.1464% 1878 0.193421 5.170059 2.1913% 1877 0.189274 5.283351 2.2426% 1876 0.185122 5.401836 2.2941% 1875 0.180971 5.525757 2.3456% 1874 0.176823 5.655369 2.4043% 1873 0.172672 5.791342 2.4635% 1872 0.168520 5.934014 2.5258% 1871 0.164368 6.083894 5.9947% 1870 0.155072 6.448603 -1.0968% 1869 0.156792 6.377876 2.1930% 1868 0.153427 6.517741 2.2394% 1867 0.150067 6.663700 2.2935% 1866 0.146702 6.816532 2.3445% 1865 0.143342 6.976343 2.4037% 1864 0.139977 7.144033 2.4599% 1863 0.136616 7.319768 2.5250% 1862 0.133252 7.504593 2.5872% 1861 0.129891 7.698755 2.9504% 1860 0.126169 7.925900 2.4012% 1859 0.123210 8.116220 2.7627% 1858 0.119898 8.340447 2.8412% 1857 0.116585 8.577416 2.9243% 1856 0.113273 8.828245 3.0161% 1855 0.109956 9.094517 3.1061% 1854 0.106644 9.376998 3.2056% 1853 0.103332 9.677589 3.3118% 1852 0.100019 9.998091 3.4252% 1851 0.096707 10.340548 4.0106% 1850 0.092978 10.755266 3.3254% 1849 0.090865 11.005366 2.7841% 1848 0.088404 11.311765 2.8590% 1847 0.085946 11.635169 2.9432% 1846 0.083489 11.977611 3.0324% 1845 0.081032 12.340820 3.1325% 1844 0.078571 12.727397 3.2284% 1843 0.076113 13.138283 3.3361% 1842 0.073656 13.576584 3.4512% 1841 0.071199 14.045138 3.8105% 1840 0.068586 14.580327 2.3861% 1839 0.066987 14.928221 2.5824% 1838 0.065301 15.313726 2.6573% 1837 0.063611 15.720661 2.7232% 1836 0.061924 16.148767 2.7994% 1835 0.060238 16.600842 2.8871% 1834 0.058548 17.080129

2.9657% 1833 0.056861 17.586671 3.0563% 1832 0.055175 18.124177 3.1604% 1831
0.053485 18.696977 3.4660% 1830 0.051693 19.345008 2.4653% 1829 0.050449 19.821921
2.6804% 1828 0.049132 20.353227 10.3427% 1827 0.044527 22.458290 -4.2314% 1826
0.046494 21.507982 2.9150% 1825 0.045177 22.134948 3.0026% 1824 0.043860 22.799564
3.0955% 1823 0.042544 23.505326 3.1944% 1822 0.041227 24.256178 3.3102% 1821
0.039906 25.059104 3.2277% 1820 0.038658 25.867947 2.6573% 1819 0.037657 26.555330
2.6261% 1818 0.036694 27.252701 2.6969% 1817 0.035730 27.987688 2.7717% 1816
0.034766 28.763418 2.8507% 1815 0.033803 29.583375 2.9343% 1814 0.032839 30.451453
3.0231% 1813 0.031876 31.372016 3.1039% 1812 0.030916 32.345771 3.2172% 1811
0.029952 33.386386 3.0969% 1810 0.029053 34.420334 2.9144% 1809 0.028230 35.423473
2.8225% 1808 0.027455 36.423287 2.9199% 1807 0.026676 37.486821 2.9918% 1806
0.025901 38.608345 3.0841% 1805 0.025126 39.799047 3.1822% 1804 0.024351 41.065529
3.2868% 1803 0.023576 42.415265 3.3985% 1802 0.022802 43.856742 3.5180% 1801
0.022027 45.399642 3.3999% 1800 0.021302 46.943206 2.8419% 1799 0.020714 48.277270
2.7485% 1798 0.020160 49.604150 2.8261% 1797 0.019606 51.006028 3.7832% 1796
0.018891 52.935693 2.1272% 1795 0.018497 54.061740 3.0879% 1794 0.017943 55.731134
3.1625% 1793 0.017393 57.493637 3.2904% 1792 0.016839 59.385416 3.4024% 1791
0.016285 61.405926 3.2296% 1790 0.015776 63.389069 41.3145% 1780 0.011163 89.577915
29.4353% 1770 0.008625 115.945457 83.4728% 1750 0.004701 212.728422 29.2845% 1740
0.003636 275.024775 94.2514% 1720 0.001872 534.239459 85.8111% 1700 0.001007
992.676110 19.2490% 1690 0.000845 1183.756825 88.0250% 1670 0.000449 2225.759035
BASE YEAR: 1989
YEAR BYEAR/AYEAR AYEAR/BYEAR GROWTH%
2009 1.219004 0.820342 8.2857% 2001 1.125730 0.888313 1.0000% 2000 1.114584
0.897196 1.0000% 1999 1.103548 0.906168 1.0000% 1998 1.092622 0.915230 1.0000% 1997
1.081804 0.924382 1.0000% 1996 1.071093 0.933626 1.0000% 1995 1.060488 0.942962
0.9992% 1994 1.049996 0.952384 1.0008% 1993 1.039592 0.961916 1.0000% 1992 1.029299
0.971535 0.9295% 1991 1.019820 0.980565 1.2505% 1990 1.007224 0.992827 0.7224% 1989
1.000000 1.000000 1.1077% 1988 0.989045 1.011077 0.8834% 1987 0.980384 1.020008
0.5594% 1986 0.974931 1.025714 1.3056% 1985 0.962366 1.039106 0.7673% 1984 0.955038
1.047079 0.8149% 1983 0.947318 1.055612 0.9737% 1982 0.938182 1.065891 0.9508% 1981
0.929346 1.076025 0.9031% 1980 0.921029 1.085743 2.2701% 1979 0.900585 1.110390
1.0042% 1978 0.891631 1.121540 0.9896% 1977 0.882894 1.132639 0.9103% 1976 0.874929
1.142950 0.8394% 1975 0.867646 1.152544 0.9042% 1974 0.859871 1.162965 1.1568% 1973
0.850038 1.176418 0.9427% 1972 0.842100 1.187508 0.7426% 1971 0.835892 1.196327
1.4697% 1970 0.823784 1.213910 0.6968% 1969 0.818084 1.222369 0.8565% 1968 0.811136
1.232839 1.5090% 1967 0.799078 1.251443 0.9949% 1966 0.791206 1.263893 1.0575% 1965
0.782927 1.277259 1.1300% 1964 0.774178 1.291692 1.5537% 1963 0.762334 1.311760
1.4658% 1962 0.751321 1.330988 1.5364% 1961 0.739953 1.351438 2.1586% 1960 0.724317
1.380611 -1.6655% 1959 0.736585 1.357617 4.3080% 1958 0.706163 1.416103 2.1130%
1957 0.691551 1.446025 1.9895% 1956 0.678061 1.474793 2.1231% 1955 0.663965 1.506104
1.4496% 1954 0.654477 1.527937 2.1573% 1953 0.640657 1.560899 1.2298% 1952 0.632874
1.580094 1.6814% 1951 0.622409 1.606661 1.6233% 1950 0.612467 1.632742 1.4265% 1949
0.603853 1.656033 1.7790% 1948 0.593298 1.685495 1.8242% 1947 0.582669 1.716241 -
2.6320% 1946 0.598419 1.671069 3.1768% 1945 0.579994 1.724155 6.4754% 1944 0.544721
1.835802 -0.3437% 1943 0.546600 1.829492 0.6562% 1942 0.543036 1.841498 0.6633%
1941 0.539458 1.853713 -5.6614% 1940 0.571832 1.748766 8.0381% 1939 0.529287
1.889334 0.8126% 1938 0.525021 1.904687 0.7762% 1937 0.520977 1.919472 0.6029% 1936
0.517855 1.931044 0.5244% 1935 0.515153 1.941170 -3.0364% 1934 0.531285 1.882229
4.6271% 1933 0.507789 1.969322 1.3921% 1932 0.500817 1.996738 -0.2051% 1931
0.501846 1.992643 0.8886% 1930 0.497426 2.010349 1.0126% 1929 0.492440 2.030706
1.1526% 1928 0.486828 2.054112 1.2160% 1927 0.480980 2.079090 1.4086% 1926 0.474299
2.108375 1.7667% 1925 0.466065 2.145624 1.4465% 1924 0.459419 2.176660 1.7700% 1923
0.451429 2.215186 1.6165% 1922 0.444248 2.250995 1.3736% 1921 0.438228 2.281916
2.3393% 1920 0.428211 2.335297 1.3140% 1919 0.422657 2.365983 0.7676% 1918 0.419437
2.384145 0.3870% 1917 0.417821 2.393372 1.3274% 1916 0.412347 2.425142 1.4083% 1915

24

0.406621 2.459295 1.4458% 1914 0.400825 2.494852 1.9424% 1913 0.393188 2.543311 1.9857% 1912 0.385533 2.593813 1.5634% 1911 0.379598 2.634365 1.8169% 1910 0.372824 2.682229 1.8781% 1909 0.365951 2.732603 2.0082% 1908 0.358747 2.787480 1.9603% 1907 0.351850 2.842122 1.8264% 1906 0.345539 2.894029 1.9357% 1905 0.338977 2.950048 2.0148% 1904 0.332283 3.009487 2.1335% 1903 0.325341 3.073695 1.8151% 1902 0.319541 3.129487 1.8943% 1901 0.313600 3.188771 3.0255% 1900 0.304391 3.285247 0.6278% 1899 0.302492 3.305873 1.7757% 1898 0.297214 3.364574 1.8078% 1897 0.291937 3.425397 1.8396% 1896 0.286663 3.488411 1.8755% 1895 0.281386 3.553837 1.9114% 1894 0.276108 3.621765 1.9486% 1893 0.270831 3.692340 1.9858% 1892 0.265558 3.765663 2.0276% 1891 0.260280 3.842016 2.6465% 1890 0.253569 3.943696 1.5328% 1889 0.249741 4.004145 2.0811% 1888 0.244650 4.087477 2.1599% 1887 0.239477 4.175760 2.2075% 1886 0.234305 4.267942 2.2592% 1885 0.229129 4.364362 2.3095% 1884 0.223956 4.465158 2.3641% 1883 0.218784 4.570721 2.4214% 1882 0.213612 4.681396 2.4815% 1881 0.208439 4.797563 3.7644% 1880 0.200877 4.978162 0.9432% 1879 0.199000 5.025118 2.1464% 1878 0.194819 5.132976 2.1913% 1877 0.190641 5.245455 2.2426% 1876 0.186460 5.363090 2.2941% 1875 0.182278 5.486123 2.3456% 1874 0.178101 5.614805 2.4043% 1873 0.173919 5.749802 2.4635% 1872 0.169737 5.891451 2.5258% 1871 0.165556 6.040256 5.9947% 1870 0.156193 6.402350 -1.0968% 1869 0.157925 6.332130 2.1930% 1868 0.154536 6.470992 2.2394% 1867 0.151151 6.615903 2.2935% 1866 0.147762 6.767639 2.3445% 1865 0.144377 6.926305 2.4037% 1864 0.140988 7.092792 2.4599% 1863 0.137603 7.267266 2.5250% 1862 0.134214 7.450765 2.5872% 1861 0.130830 7.643535 2.9504% 1860 0.127080 7.869050 2.4012% 1859 0.124100 8.058005 2.7627% 1858 0.120764 8.280624 2.8412% 1857 0.117427 8.515894 2.9243% 1856 0.114091 8.764923 3.0161% 1855 0.110751 9.029285 3.1061% 1854 0.107414 9.309740 3.2056% 1853 0.104078 9.608175 3.3118% 1852 0.100742 9.926378 3.4252% 1851 0.097475 10.266379 4.0106% 1850 0.093649 10.678123 2.3254% 1849 0.091521 10.926428 2.7841% 1848 0.089042 11.230629 2.8590% 1847 0.086567 11.551714 2.9432% 1846 0.084092 11.891700 3.0324% 1845 0.081617 12.252304 3.1325% 1844 0.079138 12.636108 3.2284% 1843 0.076663 13.044047 3.3361% 1842 0.074188 13.479204 3.4512% 1841 0.071713 13.944397 3.8105% 1840 0.069081 14.475747 2.3861% 1839 0.067471 14.821146 2.5824% 1838 0.065773 15.203886 2.6573% 1837 0.064070 15.607903 2.7232% 1836 0.062372 16.032938 2.7994% 1835 0.060673 16.481770 2.8871% 1834 0.058971 16.957619 2.9657% 1833 0.057272 17.460528 3.0563% 1832 0.055574 17.994178 3.1604% 1831 0.053871 18.562871 3.4660% 1830 0.052066 19.206253 2.4653% 1829 0.050814 19.679745 2.6804% 1828 0.049487 20.207240 10.3427% 1827 0.044849 22.297205 -4.2314% 1826 0.046830 21.353713 2.9150% 1825 0.045504 21.976182 3.0026% 1824 0.044177 22.636031 3.0955% 1823 0.042851 23.336731 3.1944% 1822 0.041524 24.082197 3.3102% 1821 0.040194 24.879364 3.2277% 1820 0.038937 25.682405 2.6573% 1819 0.037929 26.364858 2.6261% 1818 0.036959 27.057227 2.6969% 1817 0.035988 27.786942 2.7717% 1816 0.035018 28.557108 2.8507% 1815 0.034047 29.371184 2.9343% 1814 0.033076 30.233036 3.0231% 1813 0.032106 31.146996 3.1039% 1812 0.031139 32.113766 3.2172% 1811 0.030169 33.146917 3.0969% 1810 0.029262 34.173449 2.9144% 1809 0.028434 35.169393 2.8225% 1808 0.027653 36.162036 2.9199% 1807 0.026869 37.217941 2.9918% 1806 0.026088 38.331421 3.0841% 1805 0.025308 39.513583 3.1822% 1804 0.024527 40.770981 3.2868% 1803 0.023747 42.111035 3.3985% 1802 0.022966 43.542173 3.5180% 1801 0.022186 45.074007 3.3999% 1800 0.021456 46.606499 2.8419% 1799 0.020863 47.930994 2.7485% 1798 0.020305 49.248357 2.8261% 1797 0.019747 50.640180 3.7832% 1796 0.019027 52.556004 2.1272% 1795 0.018631 53.673974 3.0879% 1794 0.018073 55.331394 3.1625% 1793 0.017519 57.081256 3.2904% 1792 0.016961 58.959466 3.4024% 1791 0.016403 60.965483 3.2296% 1790 0.015890 62.934402 41.3145% 1780 0.011244 88.935405 29.4353% 1770 0.008687 115.113822 83.4728% 1750 0.004735 211.202597 29.2845% 1740 0.003662 273.052120 94.2514% 1720 0.001885 530.407550 85.8111% 1700 0.001015 985.555998 19.2490% 1690 0.000851 1175.266160 88.0250% 1670 0.000453 2209.794459

BASE YEAR: 1988

YEAR	BYEAR/AYEAR	AYEAR/BYEAR	GROWTH%
2009	1.232506	0.811355	8.2857%
2001	1.138199	0.878581	1.0000%
2000	1.126930	0.887367	1.0000%
1999	1.115772	0.896241	1.0000%
1998	1.104725	0.905203	1.0000%
1997			

1.093787 0.914255 1.0000% 1996 1.082957 0.923398 1.0000% 1995 1.072235 0.932632
0.9992% 1994 1.061627 0.941951 1.0008% 1993 1.051108 0.951377 1.0000% 1992 1.040701
0.960891 0.9295% 1991 1.031116 0.969823 1.2505% 1990 1.018381 0.981951 0.7224% 1989
1.011077 0.989045 1.1077% 1988 1.000000 1.000000 0.8834% 1987 0.991244 1.008834
0.5594% 1986 0.985730 1.014477 1.3056% 1985 0.973026 1.027722 0.7673% 1984 0.965617
1.035608 0.8149% 1983 0.957811 1.044047 0.9737% 1982 0.948574 1.054214 0.9508% 1981
0.939640 1.064237 0.9031% 1980 0.931231 1.073848 2.2701% 1979 0.910560 1.098225
1.0042% 1978 0.901508 1.109253 0.9896% 1977 0.892674 1.120230 0.9103% 1976 0.884621
1.130428 0.8394% 1975 0.877257 1.139917 0.9042% 1974 0.869396 1.150224 1.1568% 1973
0.859454 1.163530 0.9427% 1972 0.851427 1.174499 0.7426% 1971 0.845151 1.183221
1.4697% 1970 0.832909 1.200611 0.6968% 1969 0.827146 1.208977 0.8565% 1968 0.820121
1.219332 1.5090% 1967 0.807929 1.237733 0.9949% 1966 0.799970 1.250047 1.0575% 1965
0.791599 1.263266 1.1300% 1964 0.782754 1.277541 1.5537% 1963 0.770779 1.297389
1.4658% 1962 0.759644 1.316407 1.5364% 1961 0.748149 1.336633 2.1586% 1960 0.732340
1.365486 -1.6655% 1959 0.744744 1.342744 4.3080% 1958 0.713985 1.400589 2.1130%
1957 0.699211 1.430183 1.9895% 1956 0.685572 1.458636 2.1231% 1955 0.671319 1.489605
1.4496% 1954 0.661727 1.511198 2.1573% 1953 0.647753 1.543798 1.2298% 1952 0.639884
1.562783 1.6814% 1951 0.629303 1.589060 1.6233% 1950 0.619251 1.614854 1.4265% 1949
0.610541 1.637891 1.7790% 1948 0.599869 1.667030 1.8242% 1947 0.589123 1.697439 -
2.6320% 1946 0.605048 1.652762 3.1768% 1945 0.586419 1.705267 6.4754% 1944 0.550755
1.815690 -0.3437% 1943 0.552654 1.809450 0.6562% 1942 0.549051 1.821324 0.6633%
1941 0.545433 1.833405 -5.6614% 1940 0.578166 1.729608 8.0381% 1939 0.535150
1.868635 0.8126% 1938 0.530836 1.883821 0.7762% 1937 0.526747 1.898444 0.6029% 1936
0.523591 1.909889 0.5244% 1935 0.520859 1.919904 -3.0364% 1934 0.537170 1.861609
4.6271% 1933 0.513414 1.947748 1.3921% 1932 0.506364 1.974863 -0.2051% 1931
0.507405 1.970813 0.8886% 1930 0.502936 1.988325 1.0126% 1929 0.497894 2.008459
1.1526% 1928 0.492221 2.031608 1.2160% 1927 0.486307 2.056312 1.4086% 1926 0.479553
2.085277 1.7667% 1925 0.471227 2.122118 1.4465% 1924 0.464508 2.152814 1.7700% 1923
0.456430 2.190918 1.6165% 1922 0.449169 2.226335 1.3736% 1921 0.443082 2.256917
2.3393% 1920 0.432954 2.309713 1.3140% 1919 0.427339 2.340063 0.7676% 1918 0.424083
2.358026 0.3870% 1917 0.422449 2.367152 1.3274% 1916 0.416914 2.398574 1.4083% 1915
0.411125 2.432353 1.4458% 1914 0.405265 2.467520 1.9424% 1913 0.397543 2.515449
1.9857% 1912 0.389803 2.565397 1.5634% 1911 0.383803 2.605505 1.8169% 1910 0.376954
2.652845 1.8781% 1909 0.370005 2.702667 2.0082% 1908 0.362721 2.756943 1.9603% 1907
0.355747 2.810986 1.8264% 1906 0.349366 2.862324 1.9357% 1905 0.342732 2.917729
2.0148% 1904 0.335963 2.976517 2.1335% 1903 0.328945 3.040022 1.8151% 1902 0.323081
3.095203 1.8943% 1901 0.317074 3.153837 3.0255% 1900 0.307763 3.249256 0.6278% 1899
0.305843 3.269656 1.7757% 1898 0.300507 3.327714 1.8078% 1897 0.295171 3.387871
1.8396% 1896 0.289839 3.450194 1.8755% 1895 0.284503 3.514904 1.9114% 1894 0.279167
3.582087 1.9486% 1893 0.273831 3.651889 1.9858% 1892 0.268499 3.724408 2.0276% 1891
0.263163 3.799925 2.6465% 1890 0.256378 3.900491 1.5328% 1889 0.252507 3.960279
2.0811% 1888 0.247360 4.042697 2.1599% 1887 0.242130 4.130013 2.2075% 1886 0.236900
4.221185 2.2592% 1885 0.231667 4.316548 2.3095% 1884 0.226437 4.416241 2.3641% 1883
0.221207 4.520647 2.4214% 1882 0.215978 4.630109 2.4815% 1881 0.210748 4.745004
3.7644% 1880 0.203102 4.923625 0.9432% 1879 0.201205 4.970066 2.1464% 1878 0.196977
5.076743 2.1913% 1877 0.192753 5.187989 2.2426% 1876 0.188525 5.304336 2.2941% 1875
0.184297 5.426020 2.3456% 1874 0.180073 5.553292 2.4043% 1873 0.175845 5.686811
2.4635% 1872 0.171618 5.826908 2.5258% 1871 0.167390 5.974083 5.9947% 1870 0.157923
6.332210 -1.0968% 1869 0.159674 6.262759 2.1930% 1868 0.156248 6.400099 2.2394%
1867 0.152825 6.543424 2.2935% 1866 0.149399 6.693497 2.3445% 1865 0.145976 6.850424
2.4037% 1864 0.142550 7.015088 2.4599% 1863 0.139128 7.187651 2.5250% 1862 0.135701
7.369139 2.5872% 1861 0.132279 7.559797 2.9504% 1860 0.128488 7.782842 2.4012% 1859
0.125475 7.969727 2.7627% 1858 0.122102 8.189907 2.8412% 1857 0.118728 8.422599
2.9243% 1856 0.115355 8.668900 3.0161% 1855 0.111977 8.930366 3.1061% 1854 0.108604
9.207748 3.2056% 1853 0.105231 9.502914 3.3118% 1852 0.101858 9.817631 3.4252% 1851
0.098484 10.153907 4.0106% 1850 0.094687 10.561140 2.3254% 1849 0.092535 10.806725

2.7841% 1848 0.090028 11.107594 2.8590% 1847 0.087526 11.425161 2.9432% 1846 0.085024 11.761422 3.0324% 1845 0.082521 12.118076 3.1325% 1844 0.080015 12.497675 3.2284% 1843 0.077513 12.901145 3.3361% 1842 0.075010 13.331534 3.4512% 1841 0.072508 13.791631 3.8105% 1840 0.069846 14.317160 2.3861% 1839 0.068219 14.658775 2.5824% 1838 0.066501 15.037322 2.6573% 1837 0.064780 15.436912 2.7232% 1836 0.063062 15.857291 2.7994% 1835 0.061345 16.301206 2.8871% 1834 0.059624 16.771842 2.9657% 1833 0.057906 17.269242 3.0563% 1832 0.056189 17.797046 3.1604% 1831 0.054468 18.359508 3.4660% 1830 0.052643 18.995842 2.4653% 1829 0.051377 19.464146 2.6804% 1828 0.050035 19.985863 10.3427% 1827 0.045345 22.052931 -4.2314% 1826 0.047349 21.119775 2.9150% 1825 0.046008 21.735425 3.0026% 1824 0.044667 22.388045 3.0955% 1823 0.043326 23.081068 3.1944% 1822 0.041984 23.818368 3.3102% 1821 0.040639 24.606801 3.2277% 1820 0.039368 25.401045 2.6573% 1819 0.038349 26.076021 2.6261% 1818 0.037368 26.760805 2.6969% 1817 0.036387 27.482526 2.7717% 1816 0.035405 28.244255 2.8507% 1815 0.034424 29.049412 2.9343% 1814 0.033443 29.901822 3.0231% 1813 0.032461 30.805769 3.1039% 1812 0.031484 31.761948 3.2172% 1811 0.030503 32.783780 3.0969% 1810 0.029587 33.799066 2.9144% 1809 0.028749 34.784099 2.8225% 1808 0.027960 35.765867 2.9199% 1807 0.027166 36.810205 2.9918% 1806 0.026377 37.911487 3.0841% 1805 0.025588 39.080697 3.1822% 1804 0.024799 40.324320 3.2868% 1803 0.024010 41.649693 3.3985% 1802 0.023221 43.065152 3.5180% 1801 0.022431 44.580204 3.3999% 1800 0.021694 46.095908 2.8419% 1799 0.021094 47.405893 2.7485% 1798 0.020530 48.708823 2.8261% 1797 0.019966 50.085398 3.7832% 1796 0.019238 51.980234 2.1272% 1795 0.018837 53.085956 3.0879% 1794 0.018273 54.725218 3.1625% 1793 0.017713 56.455910 3.2904% 1792 0.017149 58.313543 3.4024% 1791 0.016584 60.297584 3.2296% 1790 0.016066 62.244932 41.3145% 1780 0.011369 87.961085 29.4353% 1770 0.008783 113.852707 83.4728% 1750 0.004787 208.888794 29.2845% 1740 0.003703 270.060733 94.2514% 1720 0.001906 524.596740 85.8111% 1700 0.001026 974.758868 19.2490% 1690 0.000860 1162.390684 88.0250% 1670 0.000458 2185.585344

BASE YEAR: 1987

YEAR BYEAR/AYEAR AYEAR/BYEAR GROWTH%

2009 1.243394 0.804250 8.2857% 2001 1.148253 0.870888 1.0000% 2000 1.136884 0.879597 1.0000% 1999 1.125628 0.888393 1.0000% 1998 1.114483 0.897277 1.0000% 1997 1.103449 0.906250 1.0000% 1996 1.092524 0.915312 1.0000% 1995 1.081707 0.924465 0.9992% 1994 1.071005 0.933703 1.0008% 1993 1.060393 0.943047 1.0000% 1992 1.049894 0.952477 0.9295% 1991 1.040225 0.961331 1.2505% 1990 1.027377 0.973352 0.7224% 1989 1.020008 0.980384 1.1077% 1988 1.008834 0.991244 0.8834% 1987 1.000000 1.000000 0.5594% 1986 0.994437 1.005594 1.3056% 1985 0.981621 1.018723 0.7673% 1984 0.974147 1.026539 0.8149% 1983 0.966272 1.034905 0.9737% 1982 0.956954 1.044983 0.9508% 1981 0.947941 1.054918 0.9031% 1980 0.939457 1.064445 2.2701% 1979 0.918604 1.088609 1.0042% 1978 0.909471 1.099540 0.9896% 1977 0.900559 1.110421 0.9103% 1976 0.892435 1.120530 0.8394% 1975 0.885006 1.129936 0.9042% 1974 0.877076 1.140153 1.1568% 1973 0.867046 1.153342 0.9427% 1972 0.858948 1.164214 0.7426% 1971 0.852617 1.172860 1.4697% 1970 0.840267 1.190098 0.6968% 1969 0.834432 1.198391 0.8565% 1968 0.827366 1.208656 1.5090% 1967 0.815064 1.226895 0.9949% 1966 0.807037 1.239101 1.0575% 1965 0.798592 1.252204 1.1300% 1964 0.789668 1.266354 1.5537% 1963 0.777587 1.286029 1.4658% 1962 0.766354 1.304880 1.5364% 1961 0.754758 1.324929 2.1586% 1960 0.738809 1.353529 -1.6655% 1959 0.751323 1.330986 4.3080% 1958 0.720292 1.388325 2.1130% 1957 0.705388 1.417660 1.9895% 1956 0.691628 1.445864 2.1231% 1955 0.677249 1.476561 1.4496% 1954 0.667572 1.497966 2.1573% 1953 0.653475 1.530280 1.2298% 1952 0.645536 1.549099 1.6814% 1951 0.634862 1.575145 1.6233% 1950 0.624721 1.600714 1.4265% 1949 0.615935 1.623549 1.7790% 1948 0.605168 1.652433 1.8242% 1947 0.594327 1.682576 -2.6320% 1946 0.610393 1.638290 3.1768% 1945 0.591599 1.690335 6.4754% 1944 0.555620 1.799791 -0.3437% 1943 0.557536 1.793606 0.6562% 1942 0.553901 1.805376 0.6633% 1941 0.550252 1.817351 -5.6614% 1940 0.583273 1.714463 8.0381% 1939 0.539877 1.852273 0.8126% 1938 0.535525 1.867325 0.7762% 1937 0.531400 1.881820 0.6029% 1936 0.528216 1.893165 0.5244% 1935 0.525460 1.903093 -3.0364% 1934 0.541915 1.845308 4.6271% 1933 0.517949 1.930693 1.3921% 1932 0.510837 1.957570 -0.2051% 1931

27

0.511887 1.953556 0.8886% 1930 0.507379 1.970915 1.0126% 1929 0.502292 1.990872
1.1526% 1928 0.496569 2.013819 1.2160% 1927 0.490603 2.038307 1.4086% 1926 0.483789
2.067018 1.7667% 1925 0.475390 2.103536 1.4465% 1924 0.468612 2.133963 1.7700% 1923
0.460462 2.171734 1.6165% 1922 0.453137 2.206840 1.3736% 1921 0.446996 2.237155
2.3393% 1920 0.436779 2.289489 1.3140% 1919 0.431114 2.319573 0.7676% 1918 0.427830
2.337379 0.3870% 1917 0.426180 2.346424 1.3274% 1916 0.420597 2.377571 1.4083% 1915
0.414756 2.411054 1.4458% 1914 0.408845 2.445914 1.9424% 1913 0.401055 2.493423
1.9857% 1912 0.393247 2.542934 1.5634% 1911 0.387193 2.582690 1.8169% 1910 0.380284
2.629615 1.8781% 1909 0.373273 2.679001 2.0082% 1908 0.365925 2.732802 1.9603% 1907
0.358890 2.786372 1.8264% 1906 0.352453 2.837261 1.9357% 1905 0.345760 2.892181
2.0148% 1904 0.338931 2.950454 2.1335% 1903 0.331851 3.013402 1.8151% 1902 0.325935
3.068100 1.8943% 1901 0.319875 3.126221 3.0255% 1900 0.310481 3.220804 0.6278% 1899
0.308544 3.241026 1.7757% 1898 0.303161 3.298575 1.8078% 1897 0.297778 3.358206
1.8396% 1896 0.292399 3.419983 1.8755% 1895 0.287016 3.484126 1.9114% 1894 0.281633
3.550721 1.9486% 1893 0.276250 3.619912 1.9858% 1892 0.270871 3.691796 2.0276% 1891
0.265488 3.766652 2.6465% 1890 0.258643 3.866337 1.5328% 1889 0.254738 3.925601
2.0811% 1888 0.249545 4.007298 2.1599% 1887 0.244269 4.093850 2.2075% 1886 0.238993
4.184223 2.2592% 1885 0.233713 4.278751 2.3095% 1884 0.228437 4.377571 2.3641% 1883
0.223161 4.481063 2.4214% 1882 0.217885 4.589567 2.4815% 1881 0.212610 4.703455
3.7644% 1880 0.204897 4.880512 0.9432% 1879 0.202982 4.926546 2.1464% 1878 0.198717
5.032289 2.1913% 1877 0.194456 5.142562 2.2426% 1876 0.190190 5.257889 2.2941% 1875
0.185925 5.378508 2.3456% 1874 0.181664 5.504666 2.4043% 1873 0.177399 5.637016
2.4635% 1872 0.173134 5.775886 2.5258% 1871 0.168868 5.921772 5.9947% 1870 0.159318
6.276763 -1.0968% 1869 0.161085 6.207920 2.1930% 1868 0.157628 6.344058 2.2394%
1867 0.154175 6.486127 2.2935% 1866 0.150718 6.634887 2.3445% 1865 0.147266 6.790440
2.4037% 1864 0.143809 6.953661 2.4599% 1863 0.140357 7.124713 2.5250% 1862 0.136900
7.304613 2.5872% 1861 0.133447 7.493601 2.9504% 1860 0.129623 7.714693 2.4012% 1859
0.126583 7.899941 2.7627% 1858 0.123180 8.118194 2.8412% 1857 0.119777 8.348848
2.9243% 1856 0.116374 8.592992 3.0161% 1855 0.112967 8.852169 3.1061% 1854 0.109564
9.127122 3.2056% 1853 0.106160 9.419704 3.3118% 1852 0.102757 9.731665 3.4252% 1851
0.099354 10.064996 4.0106% 1850 0.095523 10.468664 2.3254% 1849 0.093352 10.712098
2.7841% 1848 0.090824 11.010332 2.8590% 1847 0.088299 11.325119 2.9432% 1846
0.085775 11.658435 3.0324% 1845 0.083250 12.011966 3.1325% 1844 0.080722 12.388242
3.2284% 1843 0.078197 12.788179 3.3361% 1842 0.075673 13.214800 3.4512% 1841
0.073148 13.670868 3.8105% 1840 0.070463 14.191795 2.3861% 1839 0.068821 14.530418
2.5824% 1838 0.067089 14.905651 2.6573% 1837 0.065352 15.301742 2.7232% 1836
0.063620 15.718440 2.7994% 1835 0.061887 16.158468 2.8871% 1834 0.060150 16.624983
2.9657% 1833 0.058418 17.118027 3.0563% 1832 0.056685 17.641209 3.1604% 1831
0.054949 18.198746 3.4660% 1830 0.053108 18.829509 2.4653% 1829 0.051830 19.293713
2.6804% 1828 0.050477 19.810861 10.3427% 1827 0.045746 21.859829 -4.2314% 1826
0.047767 20.934845 2.9150% 1825 0.046414 21.545103 3.0026% 1824 0.045061 22.192008
3.0955% 1823 0.043708 22.878964 3.1944% 1822 0.042355 23.609807 3.3102% 1821
0.040998 24.391337 3.2277% 1820 0.039716 25.178626 2.6573% 1819 0.038688 25.847692
2.6261% 1818 0.037698 26.526480 2.6969% 1817 0.036708 27.241881 2.7717% 1816
0.035718 27.996940 2.8507% 1815 0.034728 28.795047 2.9343% 1814 0.033738 29.639993
3.0231% 1813 0.032748 30.536025 3.1039% 1812 0.031762 31.483831 3.2172% 1811
0.030772 32.496716 3.0969% 1810 0.029848 33.503112 2.9144% 1809 0.029003 34.479519
2.8225% 1808 0.028207 35.452691 2.9199% 1807 0.027406 36.487884 2.9918% 1806
0.026610 37.579523 3.0841% 1805 0.025814 38.738495 3.1822% 1804 0.025018 39.971228
3.2868% 1803 0.024222 41.284997 3.3985% 1802 0.023426 42.688061 3.5180% 1801
0.022630 44.189847 3.3999% 1800 0.021886 45.692278 2.8419% 1799 0.021281 46.990793
2.7485% 1798 0.020712 48.282314 2.8261% 1797 0.020142 49.646836 3.7832% 1796
0.019408 51.525080 2.1272% 1795 0.019004 52.621120 3.0879% 1794 0.018435 54.246028
3.1625% 1793 0.017869 55.961565 3.2904% 1792 0.017300 57.802933 3.4024% 1791
0.016731 59.769601 3.2296% 1790 0.016207 61.699898 41.3145% 1780 0.011469 87.190872
29.4353% 1770 0.008861 112.855780 83.4728% 1750 0.004830 207.059703 29.2845% 1740

0.003736 267.696003 94.2514% 1720 0.001923 520.003218 85.8111% 1700 0.001035
966.223595 19.2490% 1690 0.000868 1152.212452 88.0250% 1670 0.000462 2166.447721

BASE YEAR: 1986

YEAR BYEAR/AYEAR AYEAR/BYEAR GROWTH%

2009 1.250349 0.799777 8.2857% 2001 1.154676 0.866044 1.0000% 2000 1.143244
0.874704 1.0000% 1999 1.131924 0.883451 1.0000% 1998 1.120717 0.892286 1.0000% 1997
1.109621 0.901209 1.0000% 1996 1.098635 0.910221 1.0000% 1995 1.087757 0.919323
0.9992% 1994 1.076996 0.928509 1.0008% 1993 1.066324 0.937801 1.0000% 1992 1.055766
0.947179 0.9295% 1991 1.046043 0.955983 1.2505% 1990 1.033124 0.967938 0.7224% 1989
1.025714 0.974931 1.1077% 1988 1.014477 0.985730 0.8834% 1987 1.005594 0.994437
0.5594% 1986 1.000000 1.000000 1.3056% 1985 0.987112 1.013056 0.7673% 1984 0.979596
1.020829 0.8149% 1983 0.971677 1.029148 0.9737% 1982 0.962307 1.039170 0.9508% 1981
0.953243 1.049050 0.9031% 1980 0.944712 1.058524 2.2701% 1979 0.923742 1.082553
1.0042% 1978 0.914558 1.093424 0.9896% 1977 0.905597 1.104244 0.9103% 1976 0.897427
1.114297 0.8394% 1975 0.889956 1.123651 0.9042% 1974 0.881982 1.133810 1.1568% 1973
0.871896 1.146926 0.9427% 1972 0.863753 1.157738 0.7426% 1971 0.857386 1.166336
1.4697% 1970 0.844967 1.183478 0.6968% 1969 0.839120 1.191725 0.8565% 1968 0.831994
1.201932 1.5090% 1967 0.819625 1.220070 0.9949% 1966 0.811551 1.232209 1.0575% 1965
0.803059 1.245239 1.1300% 1964 0.794085 1.259310 1.5537% 1963 0.781937 1.278876
1.4658% 1962 0.770641 1.297622 1.5364% 1961 0.758979 1.317559 2.1586% 1960 0.742942
1.346000 -1.6655% 1959 0.755525 1.323583 4.3080% 1958 0.724321 1.380602 2.1130%
1957 0.709334 1.409774 1.9895% 1956 0.695497 1.437821 2.1231% 1955 0.681038 1.468348
1.4496% 1954 0.671306 1.489633 2.1573% 1953 0.657130 1.521768 1.2298% 1952 0.649147
1.540482 1.6814% 1951 0.638413 1.566384 1.6233% 1950 0.628216 1.591810 1.4265% 1949
0.619380 1.614518 1.7790% 1948 0.608553 1.643241 1.8242% 1947 0.597651 1.673216 -
2.6320% 1946 0.613807 1.629177 3.1768% 1945 0.594908 1.680932 6.4754% 1944 0.558728
1.789780 -0.3437% 1943 0.560655 1.783629 0.6562% 1942 0.557000 1.795333 0.6633%
1941 0.553329 1.807242 -5.6614% 1940 0.586536 1.704926 8.0381% 1939 0.542897
1.841970 0.8126% 1938 0.538521 1.856938 0.7762% 1937 0.534373 1.871353 0.6029% 1936
0.531171 1.882635 0.5244% 1935 0.528400 1.892507 -3.0364% 1934 0.544946 1.835043
4.6271% 1933 0.520846 1.919953 1.3921% 1932 0.513695 1.946681 -0.2051% 1931
0.514750 1.942689 0.8886% 1930 0.510217 1.959952 1.0126% 1929 0.505102 1.979798
1.1526% 1928 0.499347 2.002617 1.2160% 1927 0.493348 2.026969 1.4086% 1926 0.486495
2.055520 1.7667% 1925 0.478049 2.091835 1.4465% 1924 0.471233 2.122093 1.7700% 1923
0.463037 2.159654 1.6165% 1922 0.455671 2.194565 1.3736% 1921 0.449497 2.224710
2.3393% 1920 0.439222 2.276753 1.3140% 1919 0.433525 2.306670 0.7676% 1918 0.430223
2.324377 0.3870% 1917 0.428564 2.333372 1.3274% 1916 0.422950 2.364346 1.4083% 1915
0.417076 2.397643 1.4458% 1914 0.411132 2.432308 1.9424% 1913 0.403299 2.479553
1.9857% 1912 0.395446 2.528789 1.5634% 1911 0.389359 2.568324 1.8169% 1910 0.382411
2.614988 1.8781% 1909 0.375361 2.664099 2.0082% 1908 0.367972 2.717601 1.9603% 1907
0.360897 2.770873 1.8264% 1906 0.354424 2.821479 1.9357% 1905 0.347694 2.876093
2.0148% 1904 0.340827 2.934042 2.1335% 1903 0.333670 2.996640 1.8151% 1902 0.327758
3.051034 1.8943% 1901 0.321664 3.108831 3.0255% 1900 0.312218 3.202889 0.6278% 1899
0.310270 3.222998 1.7757% 1898 0.304857 3.280227 1.8078% 1897 0.299444 3.339525
1.8396% 1896 0.294035 3.400959 1.8755% 1895 0.288621 3.464746 1.9114% 1894 0.283208
3.530970 1.9486% 1893 0.277795 3.599776 1.9858% 1892 0.272386 3.671261 2.0276% 1891
0.266973 3.745700 2.6465% 1890 0.260089 3.844831 1.5328% 1889 0.256163 3.903765
2.0811% 1888 0.250941 3.985007 2.1599% 1887 0.245635 4.071078 2.2075% 1886 0.240330
4.160948 2.2592% 1885 0.235020 4.254951 2.3095% 1884 0.229715 4.353221 2.3641% 1883
0.224410 4.456137 2.4214% 1882 0.219104 4.564037 2.4815% 1881 0.213799 4.677292
3.7644% 1880 0.206043 4.853364 0.9432% 1879 0.204117 4.899142 2.1464% 1878 0.199828
5.004297 2.1913% 1877 0.195543 5.113956 2.2426% 1876 0.191254 5.228642 2.2941% 1875
0.186965 5.348590 2.3456% 1874 0.182680 5.474046 2.4043% 1873 0.178391 5.605660
2.4635% 1872 0.174102 5.743758 2.5258% 1871 0.169813 5.888832 5.9947% 1870 0.160209
6.241848 -1.0968% 1869 0.161986 6.173389 2.1930% 1868 0.158510 6.308769 2.2394%
1867 0.155038 6.450048 2.2935% 1866 0.151562 6.597980 2.3445% 1865 0.148090 6.752668

29

2.4037% 1864 0.144614 6.914981 2.4599% 1863 0.141142 7.085082 2.5250% 1862 0.137666
7.263981 2.5872% 1861 0.134194 7.451918 2.9504% 1860 0.130348 7.671780 2.4012% 1859
0.127291 7.855998 2.7627% 1858 0.123869 8.073036 2.8412% 1857 0.120447 8.302407
2.9243% 1856 0.117025 8.545194 3.0161% 1855 0.113599 8.802929 3.1061% 1854 0.110176
9.076353 3.2056% 1853 0.106754 9.367306 3.3118% 1852 0.103332 9.677532 3.4252% 1851
0.099910 10.009009 4.0106% 1850 0.096058 10.410431 2.3254% 1849 0.093875 10.652512
2.7841% 1848 0.091332 10.949087 2.8590% 1847 0.088793 11.262123 2.9432% 1846
0.086255 11.593585 3.0324% 1845 0.083716 11.945149 3.1325% 1844 0.081173 12.319332
3.2284% 1843 0.078635 12.717044 3.3361% 1842 0.076096 13.141292 3.4512% 1841
0.073557 13.594823 3.8105% 1840 0.070857 14.112852 2.3861% 1839 0.069206 14.449592
2.5824% 1838 0.067464 14.822737 2.6573% 1837 0.065718 15.216626 2.7232% 1836
0.063975 15.631006 2.7994% 1835 0.062233 16.068586 2.8871% 1834 0.060487 16.532506
2.9657% 1833 0.058745 17.022808 3.0563% 1832 0.057003 17.543080 3.1604% 1831
0.055256 18.097515 3.4660% 1830 0.053405 18.724769 2.4653% 1829 0.052120 19.186391
2.6804% 1828 0.050760 19.700662 10.3427% 1827 0.046002 21.738233 -4.2314% 1826
0.048034 20.818394 2.9150% 1825 0.046674 21.425258 3.0026% 1824 0.045313 22.068565
3.0955% 1823 0.043953 22.751699 3.1944% 1822 0.042592 23.478477 3.3102% 1821
0.041227 24.255660 3.2277% 1820 0.039938 25.038569 2.6573% 1819 0.038905 25.703913
2.6261% 1818 0.037909 26.378925 2.6969% 1817 0.036914 27.090347 2.7717% 1816
0.035918 27.841206 2.8507% 1815 0.034922 28.634874 2.9343% 1814 0.033927 29.475119
3.0231% 1813 0.032931 30.366167 3.1039% 1812 0.031940 31.308701 3.2172% 1811
0.030944 32.315952 3.0969% 1810 0.030015 33.316749 2.9144% 1809 0.029165 34.287726
2.8225% 1808 0.028364 35.255484 2.9199% 1807 0.027560 36.284919 2.9918% 1806
0.026759 37.370485 3.0841% 1805 0.025959 38.523011 3.1822% 1804 0.025158 39.748887
3.2868% 1803 0.024357 41.055347 3.3985% 1802 0.023557 42.450608 3.5180% 1801
0.022756 43.944039 3.3999% 1800 0.022008 45.438113 2.8419% 1799 0.021400 46.729405
2.7485% 1798 0.020827 48.013742 2.8261% 1797 0.020255 49.370674 3.7832% 1796
0.019517 51.238470 2.1272% 1795 0.019110 52.328413 3.0879% 1794 0.018538 53.944283
3.1625% 1793 0.017969 55.650277 3.2904% 1792 0.017397 57.481402 3.4024% 1791
0.016825 59.437130 3.2296% 1790 0.016298 61.356690 41.3145% 1780 0.011533 86.705870
29.4353% 1770 0.008910 112.228015 83.4728% 1750 0.004857 205.907926 29.2845% 1740
0.003756 266.206935 94.2514% 1720 0.001934 517.110682 85.8111% 1700 0.001041
960.848944 19.2490% 1690 0.000873 1145.803232 88.0250% 1670 0.000464 2154.396783
BASE YEAR: 1985
YEAR BYEAR/AYEAR AYEAR/BYEAR GROWTH%
2009 1.266674 0.789469 8.2857% 2001 1.169752 0.854882 1.0000% 2000 1.158170
0.863431 1.0000% 1999 1.146703 0.872065 1.0000% 1998 1.135350 0.880786 1.0000% 1997
1.124109 0.889594 1.0000% 1996 1.112979 0.898490 1.0000% 1995 1.101959 0.907475
0.9992% 1994 1.091057 0.916542 1.0008% 1993 1.080246 0.925715 1.0000% 1992 1.069551
0.934972 0.9295% 1991 1.059701 0.943663 1.2505% 1990 1.046613 0.955463 0.7224% 1989
1.039106 0.962366 1.1077% 1988 1.027722 0.973026 0.8834% 1987 1.018723 0.981621
0.5594% 1986 1.013056 0.987112 1.3056% 1985 1.000000 1.000000 0.7673% 1984 0.992386
1.007673 0.8149% 1983 0.984364 1.015885 0.9737% 1982 0.974871 1.025777 0.9508% 1981
0.965689 1.035530 0.9031% 1980 0.957046 1.044882 2.2701% 1979 0.935803 1.068601
1.0042% 1978 0.926499 1.079332 0.9896% 1977 0.917420 1.090013 0.9103% 1976 0.909144
1.099936 0.8394% 1975 0.901576 1.109169 0.9042% 1974 0.893497 1.119198 1.1568% 1973
0.883279 1.132145 0.9427% 1972 0.875030 1.142817 0.7426% 1971 0.868580 1.151304
1.4697% 1970 0.855999 1.168225 0.6968% 1969 0.850076 1.176366 0.8565% 1968 0.842856
1.186442 1.5090% 1967 0.830326 1.204346 0.9949% 1966 0.822147 1.216328 1.0575% 1965
0.813544 1.229190 1.1300% 1964 0.804453 1.243080 1.5537% 1963 0.792146 1.262393
1.4658% 1962 0.780702 1.280898 1.5364% 1961 0.768889 1.300578 2.1586% 1960 0.752642
1.328653 -1.6655% 1959 0.765390 1.306524 4.3080% 1958 0.733778 1.362809 2.1130%
1957 0.718595 1.391605 1.9895% 1956 0.704577 1.419291 2.1231% 1955 0.689929 1.449424
1.4496% 1954 0.680071 1.470435 2.1573% 1953 0.665710 1.502156 1.2298% 1952 0.657623
1.520629 1.6814% 1951 0.646749 1.546196 1.6233% 1950 0.636418 1.571295 1.4265% 1949
0.627467 1.593710 1.7790% 1948 0.616499 1.622063 1.8242% 1947 0.605454 1.651652 -

30

2.6320% 1946 0.621821 1.608180 3.1768% 1945 0.602675 1.659268 6.4754% 1944 0.566023
1.766713 -0.3437% 1943 0.567975 1.760641 0.6562% 1942 0.564272 1.772195 0.6633%
1941 0.560554 1.783950 -5.6614% 1940 0.594194 1.682953 8.0381% 1939 0.549985
1.818230 0.8126% 1938 0.545552 1.833006 0.7762% 1937 0.541350 1.847235 0.6029% 1936
0.538106 1.858371 0.5244% 1935 0.535299 1.868116 -3.0364% 1934 0.552061 1.811393
4.6271% 1933 0.527646 1.895209 1.3921% 1932 0.520402 1.921592 -0.2051% 1931
0.521471 1.917651 0.8886% 1930 0.516878 1.934692 1.0126% 1929 0.511697 1.954282
1.1526% 1928 0.505866 1.976807 1.2160% 1927 0.499789 2.000845 1.4086% 1926 0.492847
2.029029 1.7667% 1925 0.484291 2.064875 1.4465% 1924 0.477385 2.094744 1.7700% 1923
0.469083 2.131820 1.6165% 1922 0.461621 2.166281 1.3736% 1921 0.455365 2.196038
2.3393% 1920 0.444957 2.247410 1.3140% 1919 0.439186 2.276942 0.7676% 1918 0.435840
2.294420 0.3870% 1917 0.434160 2.303300 1.3274% 1916 0.428472 2.333874 1.4083% 1915
0.422522 2.366742 1.4458% 1914 0.416500 2.400961 1.9424% 1913 0.408564 2.447596
1.9857% 1912 0.400609 2.496198 1.5634% 1911 0.394443 2.535223 1.8169% 1910 0.387404
2.581286 1.8781% 1909 0.380262 2.629764 2.0082% 1908 0.372776 2.682576 1.9603% 1907
0.365609 2.735162 1.8264% 1906 0.359052 2.785115 1.9357% 1905 0.352233 2.839026
2.0148% 1904 0.345277 2.896228 2.1335% 1903 0.338064 2.958020 1.8151% 1902 0.332037
3.011712 1.8943% 1901 0.325864 3.068764 3.0255% 1900 0.316295 3.161610 0.6278% 1899
0.314321 3.181460 1.7757% 1898 0.308837 3.237951 1.8078% 1897 0.303353 3.296486
1.8396% 1896 0.297874 3.357128 1.8755% 1895 0.292390 3.420092 1.9114% 1894 0.286906
3.485463 1.9486% 1893 0.281422 3.553382 1.9858% 1892 0.275942 3.623945 2.0276% 1891
0.270458 3.697425 2.6465% 1890 0.263485 3.795278 1.5328% 1889 0.259508 3.853453
2.0811% 1888 0.254217 3.933649 2.1599% 1887 0.248842 4.018610 2.2075% 1886 0.243468
4.107322 2.2592% 1885 0.238089 4.200113 2.3095% 1884 0.232714 4.297116 2.3641% 1883
0.227340 4.398706 2.4214% 1882 0.221965 4.505216 2.4815% 1881 0.216590 4.617011
3.7644% 1880 0.208733 4.790814 0.9432% 1879 0.206782 4.836002 2.1464% 1878 0.202437
4.939802 2.1913% 1877 0.198096 5.048047 2.2426% 1876 0.193751 5.161255 2.2941% 1875
0.189406 5.279657 2.3456% 1874 0.185065 5.403497 2.4043% 1873 0.180720 5.533414
2.4635% 1872 0.176375 5.669732 2.5258% 1871 0.172030 5.812937 5.9947% 1870 0.162301
6.161403 -1.0968% 1869 0.164101 6.093826 2.1930% 1868 0.160579 6.227462 2.2394%
1867 0.157062 6.366920 2.2935% 1866 0.153540 6.512945 2.3445% 1865 0.150023 6.665640
2.4037% 1864 0.146502 6.825861 2.4599% 1863 0.142984 6.993769 2.5250% 1862 0.139463
7.170363 2.5872% 1861 0.135946 7.355878 2.9504% 1860 0.132050 7.572906 2.4012% 1859
0.128953 7.754750 2.7627% 1858 0.125486 7.968991 2.8412% 1857 0.122020 8.195406
2.9243% 1856 0.118553 8.435063 3.0161% 1855 0.115082 8.689476 3.1061% 1854 0.111615
8.959377 3.2056% 1853 0.108148 9.246581 3.3118% 1852 0.104681 9.552808 3.4252% 1851
0.101214 9.880013 4.0106% 1850 0.097312 10.276262 2.3254% 1849 0.095100 10.515222
2.7841% 1848 0.092524 10.807975 2.8590% 1847 0.089953 11.116977 2.9432% 1846
0.087381 11.444167 3.0324% 1845 0.084809 11.791200 3.1325% 1844 0.082233 12.160560
3.2284% 1843 0.079661 12.553147 3.3361% 1842 0.077090 12.971927 3.4512% 1841
0.074518 13.419613 3.8105% 1840 0.071783 13.930966 2.3861% 1839 0.070110 14.263366
2.5824% 1838 0.068345 14.631702 2.6573% 1837 0.066576 15.020514 2.7232% 1836
0.064811 15.429553 2.7994% 1835 0.063046 15.861494 2.8871% 1834 0.061277 16.319435
2.9657% 1833 0.059512 16.803418 3.0563% 1832 0.057747 17.316984 3.1604% 1831
0.055978 17.864274 3.4660% 1830 0.054102 18.483444 2.4653% 1829 0.052801 18.939117
2.6804% 1828 0.051422 19.446760 10.3427% 1827 0.046603 21.458070 -4.2314% 1826
0.048662 20.550086 2.9150% 1825 0.047283 21.149129 3.0026% 1824 0.045905 21.784145
3.0955% 1823 0.044527 22.458475 3.1944% 1822 0.043148 23.175886 3.3102% 1821
0.041766 23.943053 3.2277% 1820 0.040460 24.715872 2.6573% 1819 0.039413 25.372641
2.6261% 1818 0.038404 26.038954 2.6969% 1817 0.037395 26.741207 2.7717% 1816
0.036387 27.482388 2.8507% 1815 0.035378 28.265827 2.9343% 1814 0.034370 29.095244
3.0231% 1813 0.033361 29.974808 3.1039% 1812 0.032357 30.905195 3.2172% 1811
0.031348 31.899464 3.0969% 1810 0.030407 32.887363 2.9144% 1809 0.029546 33.845826
2.8225% 1808 0.028735 34.801111 2.9199% 1807 0.027919 35.817279 2.9918% 1806
0.027108 36.888854 3.0841% 1805 0.026297 38.026526 3.1822% 1804 0.025486 39.236603
3.2868% 1803 0.024675 40.526226 3.3985% 1802 0.023864 41.903504 3.5180% 1801

0.023053 43.377689 3.3999% 1800 0.022295 44.852507 2.8419% 1799 0.021679 46.127156
2.7485% 1798 0.021099 47.394941 2.8261% 1797 0.020519 48.734385 3.7832% 1796
0.019771 50.578108 2.1272% 1795 0.019360 51.654005 3.0879% 1794 0.018780 53.249049
3.1625% 1793 0.018204 54.933056 3.2904% 1792 0.017624 56.740582 3.4024% 1791
0.017044 58.671105 3.2296% 1790 0.016511 60.565925 41.3145% 1780 0.011684 85.588405
29.4353% 1770 0.009027 110.781621 83.4728% 1750 0.004920 203.254185 29.2845% 1740
0.003806 262.776060 94.2514% 1720 0.001959 510.446160 85.8111% 1700 0.001054
948.465524 19.2490% 1690 0.000884 1131.036122 88.0250% 1670 0.000470 2126.630920

BASE YEAR: 1984

YEAR BYEAR/AYEAR AYEAR/BYEAR GROWTH%

2009 1.276393 0.783458 8.2857% 2001 1.178727 0.848373 1.0000% 2000 1.167057
0.856856 1.0000% 1999 1.155502 0.865425 1.0000% 1998 1.144061 0.874079 1.0000% 1997
1.132734 0.882820 1.0000% 1996 1.121519 0.891648 1.0000% 1995 1.110414 0.900565
0.9992% 1994 1.099429 0.909563 1.0008% 1993 1.088535 0.918666 1.0000% 1992 1.077757
0.927853 0.9295% 1991 1.067832 0.936477 1.2505% 1990 1.054643 0.948188 0.7224% 1989
1.047079 0.955038 1.1077% 1988 1.035608 0.965617 0.8834% 1987 1.026539 0.974147
0.5594% 1986 1.020829 0.979596 1.3056% 1985 1.007673 0.992386 0.7673% 1984 1.000000
1.000000 0.8149% 1983 0.991916 1.008149 0.9737% 1982 0.982351 1.017966 0.9508% 1981
0.973099 1.027645 0.9031% 1980 0.964389 1.036925 2.2701% 1979 0.942983 1.060464
1.0042% 1978 0.933608 1.071113 0.9896% 1977 0.924459 1.081713 0.9103% 1976 0.916120
1.091560 0.8394% 1975 0.908493 1.100723 0.9042% 1974 0.900353 1.110676 1.1568% 1973
0.890057 1.123524 0.9427% 1972 0.881744 1.134115 0.7426% 1971 0.875245 1.142538
1.4697% 1970 0.862567 1.159330 0.6968% 1969 0.856598 1.167409 0.8565% 1968 0.849323
1.177408 1.5090% 1967 0.836697 1.195175 0.9949% 1966 0.828455 1.207066 1.0575% 1965
0.819786 1.219831 1.1300% 1964 0.810626 1.233615 1.5537% 1963 0.798224 1.252781
1.4658% 1962 0.786693 1.271145 1.5364% 1961 0.774788 1.290675 2.1586% 1960 0.758417
1.318536 -1.6655% 1959 0.771262 1.296576 4.3080% 1958 0.739409 1.352432 2.1130%
1957 0.724108 1.381009 1.9895% 1956 0.709983 1.408484 2.1231% 1955 0.695223 1.438387
1.4496% 1954 0.685289 1.459238 2.1573% 1953 0.670818 1.490718 1.2298% 1952 0.662669
1.509050 1.6814% 1951 0.651711 1.534423 1.6233% 1950 0.641301 1.559330 1.4265% 1949
0.632281 1.581575 1.7790% 1948 0.621229 1.609712 1.8242% 1947 0.610100 1.639076 -
2.6320% 1946 0.626592 1.595934 3.1768% 1945 0.607299 1.646634 6.4754% 1944 0.570366
1.753261 -0.3437% 1943 0.572333 1.747235 0.6562% 1942 0.568602 1.758701 0.6633%
1941 0.564855 1.770366 -5.6614% 1940 0.598753 1.670138 8.0381% 1939 0.554205
1.804386 0.8126% 1938 0.549738 1.819049 0.7762% 1937 0.545503 1.833169 0.6029% 1936
0.542234 1.844221 0.5244% 1935 0.539406 1.853892 -3.0364% 1934 0.556297 1.797601
4.6271% 1933 0.531695 1.880778 1.3921% 1932 0.524395 1.906961 -0.2051% 1931
0.525472 1.903050 0.8886% 1930 0.520844 1.919960 1.0126% 1929 0.515623 1.939401
1.1526% 1928 0.509748 1.961755 1.2160% 1927 0.503624 1.985610 1.4086% 1926 0.496628
2.013579 1.7667% 1925 0.488007 2.049152 1.4465% 1924 0.481048 2.078793 1.7700% 1923
0.472682 2.115587 1.6165% 1922 0.465163 2.149786 1.3736% 1921 0.458859 2.179317
2.3393% 1920 0.448371 2.230298 1.3140% 1919 0.442555 2.259604 0.7676% 1918 0.439184
2.276950 0.3870% 1917 0.437491 2.285761 1.3274% 1916 0.431760 2.316103 1.4083% 1915
0.425764 2.348721 1.4458% 1914 0.419696 2.382679 1.9424% 1913 0.411699 2.428959
1.9857% 1912 0.403683 2.477190 1.5634% 1911 0.397469 2.515919 1.8169% 1910 0.390376
2.561631 1.8781% 1909 0.383180 2.609740 2.0082% 1908 0.375636 2.662150 1.9603% 1907
0.368414 2.714335 1.8264% 1906 0.361807 2.763908 1.9357% 1905 0.354936 2.817409
2.0148% 1904 0.347926 2.874175 2.1335% 1903 0.340658 2.935496 1.8151% 1902 0.334585
2.988780 1.8943% 1901 0.328364 3.045398 3.0255% 1900 0.318721 3.137536 0.6278% 1899
0.316733 3.157235 1.7757% 1898 0.312207 3.213296 1.8078% 1897 0.305681 3.271385
1.8396% 1896 0.300159 3.331565 1.8755% 1895 0.294633 3.394050 1.9114% 1894 0.289107
3.458923 1.9486% 1893 0.283581 3.526325 1.9858% 1892 0.278060 3.596351 2.0276% 1891
0.272534 3.669272 2.6465% 1890 0.265507 3.766380 1.5328% 1889 0.261499 3.824111
2.0811% 1888 0.256167 3.903696 2.1599% 1887 0.250752 3.988010 2.2075% 1886 0.245336
4.076047 2.2592% 1885 0.239916 4.168132 2.3095% 1884 0.234500 4.264396 2.3641% 1883
0.229084 4.365213 2.4214% 1882 0.223668 4.470911 2.4815% 1881 0.218252 4.581856

32

3.7644% 1880 0.210334 4.754335 0.9432% 1879 0.208369 4.799179 2.1464% 1878 0.203991
4.902188 2.1913% 1877 0.199616 5.009609 2.2426% 1876 0.195238 5.121955 2.2941% 1875
0.190860 5.239456 2.3456% 1874 0.186485 5.362352 2.4043% 1873 0.182107 5.491280
2.4635% 1872 0.177728 5.626561 2.5258% 1871 0.173350 5.768675 5.9947% 1870 0.163546
6.114488 -1.0968% 1869 0.165360 6.047425 2.1930% 1868 0.161811 6.180043 2.2394%
1867 0.158267 6.318440 2.2935% 1866 0.154718 6.463353 2.3445% 1865 0.151174 6.614885
2.4037% 1864 0.147626 6.773886 2.4599% 1863 0.144082 6.940516 2.5250% 1862 0.140533
7.115765 2.5872% 1861 0.136989 7.299867 2.9504% 1860 0.133063 7.515243 2.4012% 1859
0.129943 7.695702 2.7627% 1858 0.126449 7.908312 2.8412% 1857 0.122956 8.133003
2.9243% 1856 0.119462 8.370835 3.0161% 1855 0.115965 8.623311 3.1061% 1854 0.112471
8.891156 3.2056% 1853 0.108978 9.176173 3.3118% 1852 0.105484 9.480069 3.4252% 1851
0.101991 9.804783 4.0106% 1850 0.098058 10.198014 2.3254% 1849 0.095830 10.435155
2.7841% 1848 0.093234 10.725679 2.8590% 1847 0.090643 11.032327 2.9432% 1846
0.088051 11.357026 3.0324% 1845 0.085460 11.701417 3.1325% 1844 0.082864 12.067965
3.2284% 1843 0.080273 12.457562 3.3361% 1842 0.077681 12.873153 3.4512% 1841
0.075090 13.317431 3.8105% 1840 0.072333 13.824890 2.3861% 1839 0.070648 14.154759
2.5824% 1838 0.068869 14.520290 2.6573% 1837 0.067086 14.906142 2.7232% 1836
0.065308 15.312066 2.7994% 1835 0.063530 15.740719 2.8871% 1834 0.061747 16.195172
2.9657% 1833 0.059968 16.675470 3.0563% 1832 0.058190 17.185126 3.1604% 1831
0.056407 17.728249 3.4660% 1830 0.054518 18.342704 2.4653% 1829 0.053206 18.794906
2.6804% 1828 0.051817 19.298684 10.3427% 1827 0.046960 21.294680 -4.2314% 1826
0.049035 20.393610 2.9150% 1825 0.047646 20.988091 3.0026% 1824 0.046257 21.618272
3.0955% 1823 0.044868 22.287467 3.1944% 1822 0.043479 22.999416 3.3102% 1821
0.042086 23.760741 3.2277% 1820 0.040770 24.527675 2.6573% 1819 0.039715 25.179443
2.6261% 1818 0.038699 25.840683 2.6969% 1817 0.037682 26.537588 2.7717% 1816
0.036666 27.273126 2.8507% 1815 0.035650 28.050600 2.9343% 1814 0.034634 28.873701
3.0231% 1813 0.033617 29.746568 3.1039% 1812 0.032605 30.669870 3.2172% 1811
0.031589 31.656568 3.0969% 1810 0.030640 32.636945 2.9144% 1809 0.029772 33.588110
2.8225% 1808 0.028955 34.536122 2.9199% 1807 0.028134 35.544551 2.9918% 1806
0.027316 36.607968 3.0841% 1805 0.026499 37.736977 3.1822% 1804 0.025682 38.937840
3.2868% 1803 0.024865 40.217643 3.3985% 1802 0.024047 41.584434 3.5180% 1801
0.023230 43.047393 3.3999% 1800 0.022466 44.510982 2.8419% 1799 0.021846 45.775926
2.7485% 1798 0.021261 47.034057 2.8261% 1797 0.020677 48.363301 3.7832% 1796
0.019923 50.192986 2.1272% 1795 0.019508 51.260690 3.0879% 1794 0.018924 52.843589
3.1625% 1793 0.018344 54.514774 3.2904% 1792 0.017759 56.308536 3.4024% 1791
0.017175 58.224359 3.2296% 1790 0.016638 60.104752 41.3145% 1780 0.011773 84.936700
29.4353% 1770 0.009096 109.938085 83.4728% 1750 0.004958 201.706525 29.2845% 1740
0.003835 260.775177 94.2514% 1720 0.001974 506.559417 85.8111% 1700 0.001062
941.243523 19.2490% 1690 0.000891 1122.423954 88.0250% 1670 0.000474 2110.437891

BASE YEAR: 1983

YEAR BYEAR/AYEAR AYEAR/BYEAR GROWTH%

2009 1.286795 0.777125 8.2857% 2001 1.188333 0.841515 1.0000% 2000 1.176568
0.849930 1.0000% 1999 1.164918 0.858429 1.0000% 1998 1.153385 0.867014 1.0000% 1997
1.141965 0.875684 1.0000% 1996 1.130658 0.884441 1.0000% 1995 1.119464 0.893285
0.9992% 1994 1.108388 0.902211 1.0008% 1993 1.097406 0.911240 1.0000% 1992 1.086540
0.920352 0.9295% 1991 1.076534 0.928907 1.2505% 1990 1.063238 0.940523 0.7224% 1989
1.055612 0.947318 1.1077% 1988 1.044047 0.957811 0.8834% 1987 1.034905 0.966272
0.5594% 1986 1.029148 0.971677 1.3056% 1985 1.015885 0.984364 0.7673% 1984 1.008149
0.991916 0.8149% 1983 1.000000 1.000000 0.9737% 1982 0.990356 1.009737 0.9508% 1981
0.981029 1.019338 0.9031% 1980 0.972249 1.028543 2.2701% 1979 0.950668 1.051892
1.0042% 1978 0.941216 1.062455 0.9896% 1977 0.931993 1.072969 0.9103% 1976 0.923586
1.082737 0.8394% 1975 0.915897 1.091826 0.9042% 1974 0.907690 1.101698 1.1568% 1973
0.897310 1.114442 0.9427% 1972 0.888930 1.124948 0.7426% 1971 0.882377 1.133302
1.4697% 1970 0.869597 1.149959 0.6968% 1969 0.863579 1.157972 0.8565% 1968 0.856245
1.167890 1.5090% 1967 0.843516 1.185514 0.9949% 1966 0.835206 1.197309 1.0575% 1965
0.826467 1.209970 1.1300% 1964 0.817232 1.223643 1.5537% 1963 0.804729 1.242654

1.4658% 1962 0.793104 1.260869 1.5364% 1961 0.781103 1.280242 2.1586% 1960 0.764598
1.307877 -1.6655% 1959 0.777548 1.286095 4.3080% 1958 0.745434 1.341500 2.1130%
1957 0.730010 1.369845 1.9895% 1956 0.715769 1.397098 2.1231% 1955 0.700889 1.426760
1.4496% 1954 0.690874 1.447442 2.1573% 1953 0.676285 1.478667 1.2298% 1952 0.668069
1.496851 1.6814% 1951 0.657022 1.522019 1.6233% 1950 0.646527 1.546726 1.4265% 1949
0.637434 1.568790 1.7790% 1948 0.626292 1.596700 1.8242% 1947 0.615072 1.625826 -
2.6320% 1946 0.631699 1.583034 3.1768% 1945 0.612249 1.633323 6.4754% 1944 0.575014
1.739088 -0.3437% 1943 0.576997 1.733111 0.6562% 1942 0.573235 1.744484 0.6633%
1941 0.569458 1.756055 -5.6614% 1940 0.603632 1.656638 8.0381% 1939 0.558722
1.789800 0.8126% 1938 0.554218 1.804344 0.7762% 1937 0.549949 1.818350 0.6029% 1936
0.546653 1.829313 0.5244% 1935 0.543802 1.838906 -3.0364% 1934 0.560831 1.783070
4.6271% 1933 0.536028 1.865575 1.3921% 1932 0.528668 1.891546 -0.2051% 1931
0.529755 1.887666 0.8886% 1930 0.525089 1.904440 1.0126% 1929 0.519825 1.923724
1.1526% 1928 0.513902 1.945897 1.2160% 1927 0.507728 1.969559 1.4086% 1926 0.500675
1.997302 1.7667% 1925 0.491984 2.032588 1.4465% 1924 0.484969 2.061989 1.7700% 1923
0.476534 2.098486 1.6165% 1922 0.468953 2.132408 1.3736% 1921 0.462599 2.161700
2.3393% 1920 0.452025 2.212269 1.3140% 1919 0.446162 2.241338 0.7676% 1918 0.442763
2.258544 0.3870% 1917 0.441056 2.267284 1.3274% 1916 0.435278 2.297381 1.4083% 1915
0.429233 2.329735 1.4458% 1914 0.423116 2.363418 1.9424% 1913 0.415054 2.409325
1.9857% 1912 0.406973 2.457166 1.5634% 1911 0.400708 2.495581 1.8169% 1910 0.393558
2.540924 1.8781% 1909 0.386303 2.588644 2.0082% 1908 0.378697 2.640630 1.9603% 1907
0.371417 2.692393 1.8264% 1906 0.364755 2.741566 1.9357% 1905 0.357829 2.794634
2.0148% 1904 0.350761 2.850941 2.1335% 1903 0.343434 2.911767 1.8151% 1902 0.337311
2.964620 1.8943% 1901 0.331040 3.020780 3.0255% 1900 0.321319 3.112174 0.6278% 1899
0.319314 3.131713 1.7757% 1898 0.313743 3.187321 1.8078% 1897 0.308172 3.244940
1.8396% 1896 0.302605 3.304634 1.8755% 1895 0.297034 3.366614 1.9114% 1894 0.291463
3.430963 1.9486% 1893 0.285892 3.497820 1.9858% 1892 0.280326 3.567280 2.0276% 1891
0.274755 3.639611 2.6465% 1890 0.267671 3.735934 1.5328% 1889 0.263630 3.793199
2.0811% 1888 0.258255 3.872140 2.1599% 1887 0.252795 3.955773 2.2075% 1886 0.247335
4.043098 2.2592% 1885 0.241871 4.134438 2.3095% 1884 0.236411 4.229925 2.3641% 1883
0.230951 4.329926 2.4214% 1882 0.225491 4.434770 2.4815% 1881 0.220031 4.544818
3.7644% 1880 0.212048 4.715903 0.9432% 1879 0.210067 4.760384 2.1464% 1878 0.205653
4.862561 2.1913% 1877 0.201243 4.969114 2.2426% 1876 0.196829 5.080552 2.2941% 1875
0.192415 5.197102 2.3456% 1874 0.188005 5.319005 2.4043% 1873 0.183591 5.446891
2.4635% 1872 0.179177 5.581078 2.5258% 1871 0.174763 5.722043 5.9947% 1870 0.164879
6.065061 -1.0968% 1869 0.166707 5.998540 2.1930% 1868 0.163130 6.130087 2.2394%
1867 0.159557 6.267364 2.2935% 1866 0.155979 6.411106 2.3445% 1865 0.152406 6.561413
2.4037% 1864 0.148829 6.719129 2.4599% 1863 0.145256 6.884412 2.5250% 1862 0.141678
7.058244 2.5872% 1861 0.138105 7.240858 2.9504% 1860 0.134147 7.454493 2.4012% 1859
0.131002 7.633493 2.7627% 1858 0.127480 7.844384 2.8412% 1857 0.123958 8.067259
2.9243% 1856 0.120436 8.303169 3.0161% 1855 0.116910 8.553604 3.1061% 1854 0.113388
8.819284 3.2056% 1853 0.109866 9.101997 3.3118% 1852 0.106344 9.403436 3.4252% 1851
0.102822 9.725525 4.0106% 1850 0.098857 10.115578 3.3254% 1849 0.096611 10.350802
2.7841% 1848 0.093994 10.638977 2.8590% 1847 0.091381 10.943147 2.9432% 1846
0.088769 11.265221 3.0324% 1845 0.086156 11.606828 3.1325% 1844 0.083539 11.970412
3.2284% 1843 0.080927 12.356860 3.3361% 1842 0.078314 12.769092 3.4512% 1841
0.075701 13.209778 3.8105% 1840 0.072923 13.713135 2.3861% 1839 0.071223 14.040338
2.5824% 1838 0.069430 14.402914 2.6573% 1837 0.067633 14.785647 2.7232% 1836
0.065840 15.188290 2.7994% 1835 0.064047 15.613477 2.8871% 1834 0.062250 16.064257
2.9657% 1833 0.060457 16.540672 3.0563% 1832 0.058664 17.046209 3.1604% 1831
0.056867 17.584941 3.4660% 1830 0.054962 18.194429 2.4653% 1829 0.053640 18.642977
2.6804% 1828 0.052239 19.142682 10.3427% 1827 0.047343 21.122543 -4.2314% 1826
0.049435 20.228756 2.9150% 1825 0.048034 20.818432 3.0026% 1824 0.046634 21.443519
3.0955% 1823 0.045234 22.107305 3.1944% 1822 0.043834 22.813498 3.3102% 1821
0.042429 23.568669 3.2277% 1820 0.041103 24.329404 2.6573% 1819 0.040039 24.975904
2.6261% 1818 0.039014 25.631798 2.6969% 1817 0.037989 26.323070 2.7717% 1816

34

0.036965 27.052662 2.8507% 1815 0.035940 27.823851 2.9343% 1814 0.034916 28.640298 3.0231% 1813 0.033891 29.506109 3.1039% 1812 0.032871 30.421948 3.2172% 1811 0.031846 31.400670 3.0969% 1810 0.030890 32.373122 2.9144% 1809 0.030015 33.316598 2.8225% 1808 0.029191 34.256946 2.9199% 1807 0.028363 35.257225 2.9918% 1806 0.027539 36.312045 3.0841% 1805 0.026715 37.431927 3.1822% 1804 0.025891 38.623083 3.2868% 1803 0.025067 39.892541 3.3985% 1802 0.024243 41.248283 3.5180% 1801 0.023420 42.699417 3.3999% 1800 0.022649 44.151174 2.8419% 1799 0.022024 45.405893 2.7485% 1798 0.021434 46.653854 2.8261% 1797 0.020845 47.972353 3.7832% 1796 0.020085 49.787248 2.1272% 1795 0.019667 50.846321 3.0879% 1794 0.019078 52.416424 3.1625% 1793 0.018493 54.074100 3.2904% 1792 0.017904 55.853362 3.4024% 1791 0.017315 57.753698 3.2296% 1790 0.016773 59.618891 41.3145% 1780 0.011869 84.250108 29.4353% 1770 0.009170 109.049392 83.4728% 1750 0.004998 200.076016 29.2845% 1740 0.003866 258.667182 94.2514% 1720 0.001990 502.464607 85.8111% 1700 0.001071 933.634914 19.2490% 1690 0.000898 1113.350760 88.0250% 1670 0.000478 2093.378016

BASE YEAR: 1982

YEAR BYEAR/AYEAR AYEAR/BYEAR GROWTH%

2009 1.299325 0.769631 8.2857% 2001 1.199905 0.833399 1.0000% 2000 1.188024 0.841734 1.0000% 1999 1.176262 0.850151 1.0000% 1998 1.164616 0.858652 1.0000% 1997 1.153085 0.867239 1.0000% 1996 1.141668 0.875911 1.0000% 1995 1.130364 0.884670 0.9992% 1994 1.119181 0.893510 1.0008% 1993 1.108092 0.902452 1.0000% 1992 1.097121 0.911477 0.9295% 1991 1.087017 0.919949 1.2505% 1990 1.073591 0.931453 0.7224% 1989 1.065891 0.938182 1.1077% 1988 1.054214 0.948574 0.8834% 1987 1.044983 0.956954 0.5594% 1986 1.039170 0.962307 1.3056% 1985 1.025777 0.974871 0.7673% 1984 1.017966 0.982351 0.8149% 1983 1.009737 0.990356 0.9737% 1982 1.000000 1.000000 0.9508% 1981 0.990581 1.009508 0.9031% 1980 0.981716 1.018625 2.2701% 1979 0.959925 1.041748 1.0042% 1978 0.950381 1.052209 0.9896% 1977 0.941069 1.062622 0.9103% 1976 0.932579 1.072295 0.8394% 1975 0.924816 1.081296 0.9042% 1974 0.916529 1.091073 1.1568% 1973 0.906048 1.103695 0.9427% 1972 0.897586 1.114099 0.7426% 1971 0.890969 1.122373 1.4697% 1970 0.878064 1.138869 0.6968% 1969 0.871988 1.146805 0.8565% 1968 0.864583 1.156628 1.5090% 1967 0.851730 1.174082 0.9949% 1966 0.843339 1.185763 1.0575% 1965 0.834514 1.198302 1.1300% 1964 0.825190 1.211843 1.5537% 1963 0.812565 1.230670 1.4658% 1962 0.800827 1.248710 1.5364% 1961 0.788709 1.267895 2.1586% 1960 0.772043 1.295265 -1.6655% 1959 0.785119 1.273692 4.3080% 1958 0.752693 1.328563 2.1130% 1957 0.737118 1.356635 1.9895% 1956 0.722739 1.383625 2.1231% 1955 0.707714 1.413001 1.4496% 1954 0.697601 1.433484 2.1573% 1953 0.682870 1.464408 1.2298% 1952 0.674574 1.482416 1.6814% 1951 0.663420 1.507341 1.6233% 1950 0.652823 1.531810 1.4265% 1949 0.643641 1.553661 1.7790% 1948 0.632390 1.581302 1.8242% 1947 0.621061 1.610147 -2.6320% 1946 0.637850 1.567767 3.1768% 1945 0.618210 1.617572 6.4754% 1944 0.580613 1.722317 -0.3437% 1943 0.582616 1.716398 0.6562% 1942 0.578817 1.727661 0.6633% 1941 0.575003 1.739121 -5.6614% 1940 0.609510 1.640662 8.0381% 1939 0.564162 1.772540 0.8126% 1938 0.559615 1.786944 0.7762% 1937 0.555304 1.800815 0.6029% 1936 0.551976 1.811672 0.5244% 1935 0.549097 1.821172 -3.0364% 1934 0.566292 1.765875 4.6271% 1933 0.541247 1.847584 1.3921% 1932 0.533816 1.873304 -0.2051% 1931 0.534913 1.869462 0.8886% 1930 0.530202 1.886074 1.0126% 1929 0.524887 1.905173 1.1526% 1928 0.518906 1.927131 1.2160% 1927 0.512672 1.950565 1.4086% 1926 0.505551 1.978041 1.7667% 1925 0.496774 2.012986 1.4465% 1924 0.489691 2.042104 1.7700% 1923 0.481174 2.078249 1.6165% 1922 0.473520 2.111844 1.3736% 1921 0.467103 2.140854 2.3393% 1920 0.456426 2.190935 1.3140% 1919 0.450506 2.219724 0.7676% 1918 0.447075 2.236763 0.3870% 1917 0.445351 2.245419 1.3274% 1916 0.439517 2.275226 1.4083% 1915 0.433413 2.307268 1.4458% 1914 0.427236 2.340626 1.9424% 1913 0.419006 2.386090 1.9857% 1912 0.410936 2.433470 1.5634% 1911 0.404610 2.471515 1.8169% 1910 0.397390 2.516420 1.8781% 1909 0.390064 2.563680 2.0082% 1908 0.382385 2.615165 1.9603% 1907 0.375033 2.666429 1.8264% 1906 0.368307 2.715128 1.9357% 1905 0.361313 2.767684 2.0148% 1904 0.354177 2.823448 2.1335% 1903 0.346778 2.883687 1.8151% 1902 0.340596 2.936030 1.8943% 1901 0.334264 2.991649 3.0255% 1900 0.324448 3.082161 0.6278% 1899 0.322423 3.101512 1.7757% 1898 0.316798 3.156584 1.8078% 1897 0.311173 3.213648

1.8396% 1896 0.305552 3.272766 1.8755% 1895 0.299927 3.334148 1.9114% 1894 0.294301
3.397876 1.9486% 1893 0.288676 3.464088 1.9858% 1892 0.283055 3.532879 2.0276% 1891
0.277430 3.604512 2.6465% 1890 0.270277 3.699906 1.5328% 1889 0.266197 3.756619
2.0811% 1888 0.260770 3.834799 2.1599% 1887 0.255257 3.917625 2.2075% 1886 0.249744
4.004108 2.2592% 1885 0.244226 4.094567 2.3095% 1884 0.238713 4.189133 2.3641% 1883
0.233200 4.288170 2.4214% 1882 0.227687 4.392003 2.4815% 1881 0.222173 4.500989
3.7644% 1880 0.214113 4.670425 0.9432% 1879 0.212113 4.714477 2.1464% 1878 0.207656
4.815668 2.1913% 1877 0.203203 4.921194 2.2426% 1876 0.198746 5.031557 2.2941% 1875
0.194289 5.146984 2.3456% 1874 0.189836 5.267711 2.4043% 1873 0.185379 5.394364
2.4635% 1872 0.180922 5.527256 2.5258% 1871 0.176465 5.666862 5.9947% 1870 0.166484
6.006572 -1.0968% 1869 0.168331 5.940693 2.1930% 1868 0.164718 6.070971 2.2394%
1867 0.161110 6.206924 2.2935% 1866 0.157498 6.349280 2.3445% 1865 0.153890 6.498137
2.4037% 1864 0.150278 6.654333 2.4599% 1863 0.146670 6.818022 2.5250% 1862 0.143058
6.990177 2.5872% 1861 0.139450 7.171030 2.9504% 1860 0.135454 7.382605 2.4012% 1859
0.132277 7.559879 2.7627% 1858 0.128721 7.768736 2.8412% 1857 0.125165 7.989462
2.9243% 1856 0.121609 8.223097 3.0161% 1855 0.118048 8.471117 3.1061% 1854 0.114492
8.734234 3.2056% 1853 0.110936 9.014221 3.3118% 1852 0.107380 9.312753 3.4252% 1851
0.103823 9.631736 4.0106% 1850 0.099820 10.018027 2.3254% 1849 0.097552 10.250983
2.7841% 1848 0.094909 10.536379 2.8590% 1847 0.092271 10.837616 2.9432% 1846
0.089633 11.156584 3.0324% 1845 0.086995 11.494896 3.1325% 1844 0.084353 11.854975
3.2284% 1843 0.081715 12.237696 3.3361% 1842 0.079077 12.645953 3.4512% 1841
0.076439 13.082389 3.8105% 1840 0.073633 13.580892 2.3861% 1839 0.071917 13.904939
2.5824% 1838 0.070106 14.264019 2.6573% 1837 0.068292 14.643060 2.7232% 1836
0.066481 15.041821 2.7994% 1835 0.064671 15.462907 2.8871% 1834 0.062856 15.909340
2.9657% 1833 0.061046 16.381161 3.0563% 1832 0.059235 16.881822 3.1604% 1831
0.057421 17.415359 3.4660% 1830 0.055497 18.018970 2.4653% 1829 0.054162 18.463191
2.6804% 1828 0.052748 18.958078 10.3427% 1827 0.047804 20.918846 -4.2314% 1826
0.049916 20.033679 2.9150% 1825 0.048502 20.617668 3.0026% 1824 0.047088 21.236726
3.0955% 1823 0.045674 21.894111 3.1944% 1822 0.044261 22.593494 3.3102% 1821
0.042842 23.341382 3.2277% 1820 0.041503 24.094781 2.6573% 1819 0.040428 24.735046
2.6261% 1818 0.039394 25.384615 2.6969% 1817 0.038359 26.069221 2.7717% 1816
0.037325 26.791777 2.8507% 1815 0.036290 27.555529 2.9343% 1814 0.035256 28.364103
3.0231% 1813 0.034221 29.221564 3.1039% 1812 0.033191 30.128571 3.2172% 1811
0.032157 31.097855 3.0969% 1810 0.031191 32.060929 2.9144% 1809 0.030307 32.995306
2.8225% 1808 0.029475 33.926587 2.9199% 1807 0.028639 34.917219 2.9918% 1806
0.027807 35.961866 3.0841% 1805 0.026975 37.070949 3.1822% 1804 0.026143 38.250618
3.2868% 1803 0.025311 39.507834 3.3985% 1802 0.024480 40.850502 3.5180% 1801
0.023648 42.287641 3.3999% 1800 0.022870 43.725399 2.8419% 1799 0.022238 44.968017
2.7485% 1798 0.021643 46.203943 2.8261% 1797 0.021048 47.509728 3.7832% 1796
0.020281 49.307120 2.1272% 1795 0.019859 50.355980 3.0879% 1794 0.019264 51.910942
3.1625% 1793 0.018673 53.552632 3.2904% 1792 0.018078 55.314735 3.4024% 1791
0.017484 57.196746 3.2296% 1790 0.016937 59.043951 41.3145% 1780 0.011985 83.437635
29.4353% 1770 0.009259 107.997765 83.4728% 1750 0.005047 198.146566 29.2845% 1740
0.003904 256.172703 94.2514% 1720 0.002010 497.619048 85.8111% 1700 0.001082
924.631327 19.2490% 1690 0.000907 1102.614068 88.0250% 1670 0.000482 2073.190349

BASE YEAR: 1981

YEAR BYEAR/AYEAR AYEAR/BYEAR GROWTH%

2009 1.311679 0.762382 8.2857% 2001 1.211314 0.825550 1.0000% 2000 1.199320
0.833806 1.0000% 1999 1.187446 0.842144 1.0000% 1998 1.175689 0.850565 1.0000% 1997
1.164048 0.859071 1.0000% 1996 1.152523 0.867662 1.0000% 1995 1.141112 0.876338
0.9992% 1994 1.129823 0.885095 1.0008% 1993 1.118628 0.893953 1.0000% 1992 1.107552
0.902892 0.9295% 1991 1.097352 0.911285 1.2505% 1990 1.083799 0.922680 0.7224% 1989
1.076025 0.929346 1.1077% 1988 1.064237 0.939640 0.8834% 1987 1.054918 0.947941
0.5594% 1986 1.049050 0.953243 1.3056% 1985 1.035530 0.965689 0.7673% 1984 1.027645
0.973099 0.8149% 1983 1.019338 0.981029 0.9737% 1982 1.009508 0.990581 0.9508% 1981
1.000000 1.000000 0.9031% 1980 0.991050 1.009031 2.2701% 1979 0.969052 1.031936

36

1.0042% 1978 0.959418 1.042299 0.9896% 1977 0.950016 1.052613 0.9103% 1976 0.941446
1.062196 0.8394% 1975 0.933609 1.071112 0.9042% 1974 0.925243 1.080797 1.1568% 1973
0.914662 1.093300 0.9427% 1972 0.906120 1.103606 0.7426% 1971 0.899441 1.111802
1.4697% 1970 0.886413 1.128142 0.6968% 1969 0.880279 1.136004 0.8565% 1968 0.872803
1.145734 1.5090% 1967 0.859828 1.163023 0.9949% 1966 0.851358 1.174594 1.0575% 1965
0.842449 1.187015 1.1300% 1964 0.833036 1.200429 1.5537% 1963 0.820291 1.219079
1.4658% 1962 0.808441 1.236949 1.5364% 1961 0.796208 1.255954 2.1586% 1960 0.779384
1.283065 -1.6655% 1959 0.792584 1.261696 4.3080% 1958 0.759850 1.316050 2.1130%
1957 0.744127 1.343857 1.9895% 1956 0.729611 1.370593 2.1231% 1955 0.714443 1.399692
1.4496% 1954 0.704234 1.419983 2.1573% 1953 0.689363 1.450615 1.2298% 1952 0.680988
1.468454 1.6814% 1951 0.669728 1.493144 1.6233% 1950 0.659030 1.517382 1.4265% 1949
0.649761 1.539028 1.7790% 1948 0.638403 1.566408 1.8242% 1947 0.626966 1.594982 -
2.6320% 1946 0.643914 1.553001 3.1768% 1945 0.624088 1.602337 6.4754% 1944 0.586134
1.706095 -0.3437% 1943 0.588155 1.700232 0.6562% 1942 0.584321 1.711389 0.6633%
1941 0.580470 1.722741 -5.6614% 1940 0.615305 1.625209 8.0381% 1939 0.569526
1.755845 0.8126% 1938 0.564935 1.770114 0.7762% 1937 0.560584 1.783854 0.6029% 1936
0.557225 1.794608 0.5244% 1935 0.554318 1.804019 -3.0364% 1934 0.571676 1.749243
4.6271% 1933 0.546394 1.830182 1.3921% 1932 0.538892 1.855661 -0.2051% 1931
0.539999 1.851855 0.8886% 1930 0.535243 1.868310 1.0126% 1929 0.529878 1.887229
1.1526% 1928 0.523840 1.908981 1.2160% 1927 0.517546 1.932194 1.4086% 1926 0.510358
1.959410 1.7667% 1925 0.501948 1.994027 1.4465% 1924 0.494347 2.022871 1.7700% 1923
0.485749 2.058675 1.6165% 1922 0.478022 2.091954 1.3736% 1921 0.471545 2.120690
2.3393% 1920 0.460766 2.170299 1.3140% 1919 0.454790 2.198817 0.7676% 1918 0.451325
2.215696 0.3870% 1917 0.449586 2.224271 1.3274% 1916 0.443696 2.253797 1.4083% 1915
0.437534 2.285537 1.4458% 1914 0.431298 2.318581 1.9424% 1913 0.423080 2.363617
1.9857% 1912 0.414843 2.410550 1.5634% 1911 0.408457 2.448237 1.8169% 1910 0.401168
2.492720 1.8781% 1909 0.393773 2.539534 2.0082% 1908 0.386021 2.590534 1.9603% 1907
0.378599 2.641315 1.8264% 1906 0.371809 2.689555 1.9357% 1905 0.364748 2.741616
2.0148% 1904 0.357544 2.796855 2.1335% 1903 0.350075 2.856527 1.8151% 1902 0.343834
2.908377 1.8943% 1901 0.337442 2.963472 3.0255% 1900 0.327533 3.053132 0.6278% 1899
0.325489 3.072300 1.7757% 1898 0.319810 3.126854 1.8078% 1897 0.314132 3.183380
1.8396% 1896 0.308457 3.241941 1.8755% 1895 0.302778 3.302745 1.9114% 1894 0.297100
3.365873 1.9486% 1893 0.291421 3.431462 1.9858% 1892 0.285747 3.499604 2.0276% 1891
0.280068 3.570563 2.6465% 1890 0.272847 3.665058 1.5328% 1889 0.268728 3.721237
2.0811% 1888 0.263249 3.798681 2.1599% 1887 0.257684 3.880727 2.2075% 1886 0.252118
3.966395 2.2592% 1885 0.246548 4.056003 2.3095% 1884 0.240983 4.149678 2.3641% 1883
0.235417 4.247782 2.4214% 1882 0.229851 4.350637 2.4815% 1881 0.224286 4.458597
3.7644% 1880 0.216149 4.626436 0.9432% 1879 0.214129 4.670074 2.1464% 1878 0.209630
4.770312 2.1913% 1877 0.205135 4.874844 2.2426% 1876 0.200635 4.984167 2.2941% 1875
0.196136 5.098507 2.3456% 1874 0.191641 5.218097 2.4043% 1873 0.187141 5.343557
2.4635% 1872 0.182642 5.475198 2.5258% 1871 0.178142 5.613489 5.9947% 1870 0.168067
5.949999 -1.0968% 1869 0.169931 5.884740 2.1930% 1868 0.166284 6.013791 2.2394%
1867 0.162642 6.148464 2.2935% 1866 0.158996 6.289479 2.3445% 1865 0.155353 6.436935
2.4037% 1864 0.151707 6.591659 2.4599% 1863 0.148065 6.753806 2.5250% 1862 0.144418
6.924340 2.5872% 1861 0.140776 7.103490 2.9504% 1860 0.136741 7.313072 2.4012% 1859
0.133535 7.488676 2.7627% 1858 0.129945 7.695566 2.8412% 1857 0.126355 7.914213
2.9243% 1856 0.122765 8.145647 3.0161% 1855 0.119171 8.391331 3.1061% 1854 0.115581
8.651971 3.2056% 1853 0.111991 8.929321 3.3118% 1852 0.108401 9.225041 3.4252% 1851
0.104811 9.541020 4.0106% 1850 0.100769 9.923672 2.3254% 1849 0.098479 10.154434
2.7841% 1848 0.095812 10.437142 2.8590% 1847 0.093149 10.735541 2.9432% 1846
0.090485 11.051505 3.0324% 1845 0.087822 11.386632 3.1325% 1844 0.085155 11.743319
3.2284% 1843 0.082492 12.122435 3.3361% 1842 0.079829 12.526847 3.4512% 1841
0.077165 12.959172 3.8105% 1840 0.074333 13.452980 2.3861% 1839 0.072601 13.773975
2.5824% 1838 0.070773 14.129673 2.6573% 1837 0.068941 14.505144 2.7232% 1836
0.067113 14.900149 2.7994% 1835 0.065286 15.317270 2.8871% 1834 0.063454 15.759498
2.9657% 1833 0.061626 16.226875 3.0563% 1832 0.059799 16.722821 3.1604% 1831

0.057967 17.251332 3.4660% 1830 0.056025 17.849258 2.4653% 1829 0.054677 18.289296 2.6804% 1828 0.053249 18.779521 10.3427% 1827 0.048258 20.721821 -4.2314% 1826 0.050391 19.844991 2.9150% 1825 0.048963 20.423480 3.0026% 1824 0.047536 21.036708 3.0955% 1823 0.046109 21.687901 3.1944% 1822 0.044681 22.380697 3.3102% 1821 0.043250 23.121541 3.2277% 1820 0.041897 23.867844 2.6573% 1819 0.040813 24.502079 2.6261% 1818 0.039768 25.145530 2.6969% 1817 0.038724 25.823688 2.7717% 1816 0.037680 26.539439 2.8507% 1815 0.036635 27.295997 2.9343% 1814 0.035591 28.096956 3.0231% 1813 0.034547 28.946341 3.1039% 1812 0.033507 29.844805 3.2172% 1811 0.032462 30.804960 3.0969% 1810 0.031487 31.758963 2.9144% 1809 0.030596 32.684540 2.8225% 1808 0.029756 33.607049 2.9199% 1807 0.028911 34.588350 2.9918% 1806 0.028072 35.623159 3.0841% 1805 0.027232 36.721796 3.1822% 1804 0.026392 37.890354 3.2868% 1803 0.025552 39.135729 3.3985% 1802 0.024712 40.465751 3.5180% 1801 0.023872 41.889355 3.3999% 1800 0.023087 43.313571 2.8419% 1799 0.022449 44.544485 2.7485% 1798 0.021849 45.768771 2.8261% 1797 0.021248 47.062257 3.7832% 1796 0.020474 48.842721 2.1272% 1795 0.020047 49.881702 3.0879% 1794 0.019447 51.422018 3.1625% 1793 0.018851 53.048246 3.2904% 1792 0.018250 54.793753 3.4024% 1791 0.017650 56.658037 3.2296% 1790 0.017098 58.487845 41.3145% 1780 0.012099 82.651777 29.4353% 1770 0.009347 106.980587 83.4728% 1750 0.005095 196.280321 29.2845% 1740 0.003941 253.759938 94.2514% 1720 0.002029 492.932218 85.8111% 1700 0.001092 915.922678 19.2490% 1690 0.000916 1092.229087 88.0250% 1670 0.000487 2053.663986

BASE YEAR: 1980

YEAR BYEAR/AYEAR AYEAR/BYEAR GROWTH%

2009 1.323524 0.755559 8.2857% 2001 1.222252 0.818162 1.0000% 2000 1.210151 0.826343 1.0000% 1999 1.198169 0.834607 1.0000% 1998 1.186306 0.842953 1.0000% 1997 1.174560 0.851382 1.0000% 1996 1.162931 0.859896 1.0000% 1995 1.151417 0.868495 0.9992% 1994 1.140026 0.877173 1.0008% 1993 1.128730 0.885952 1.0000% 1992 1.117554 0.894811 0.9295% 1991 1.107262 0.903129 1.2505% 1990 1.093586 0.914422 0.7224% 1989 1.085743 0.921029 1.1077% 1988 1.073848 0.931231 0.8834% 1987 1.064445 0.939457 0.5594% 1986 1.058524 0.944712 1.3056% 1985 1.044882 0.957046 0.7673% 1984 1.036925 0.964389 0.8149% 1983 1.028543 0.972249 0.9737% 1982 1.018625 0.981716 0.9508% 1981 1.009031 0.991050 0.9031% 1980 1.000000 1.000000 2.2701% 1979 0.977803 1.022701 1.0042% 1978 0.968082 1.032970 0.9896% 1977 0.958596 1.043193 0.9103% 1976 0.949948 1.052689 0.8394% 1975 0.942040 1.061526 0.9042% 1974 0.933599 1.071124 1.1568% 1973 0.922922 1.083515 0.9427% 1972 0.914303 1.093729 0.7426% 1971 0.907563 1.101851 1.4697% 1970 0.894418 1.118046 0.6968% 1969 0.888228 1.125837 0.8565% 1968 0.880685 1.135480 1.5090% 1967 0.867593 1.152615 0.9949% 1966 0.859046 1.164082 1.0575% 1965 0.850057 1.176392 1.1300% 1964 0.840558 1.189685 1.5537% 1963 0.827699 1.208169 1.4658% 1962 0.815742 1.225878 1.5364% 1961 0.803398 1.244713 2.1586% 1960 0.786422 1.271582 -1.6655% 1959 0.799741 1.250404 4.3080% 1958 0.766712 1.304271 2.1130% 1957 0.750846 1.331830 1.9895% 1956 0.736200 1.358327 2.1231% 1955 0.720895 1.387165 1.4496% 1954 0.710594 1.407274 2.1573% 1953 0.695588 1.437632 1.2298% 1952 0.687138 1.455312 1.6814% 1951 0.675776 1.479781 1.6233% 1950 0.664981 1.503802 1.4265% 1949 0.655628 1.525254 1.7790% 1948 0.644168 1.552389 1.8242% 1947 0.632628 1.580707 -2.6320% 1946 0.649729 1.539102 3.1768% 1945 0.629724 1.587997 6.4754% 1944 0.591427 1.690826 -0.3437% 1943 0.593467 1.685015 0.6562% 1942 0.589597 1.696072 0.6633% 1941 0.585712 1.707322 -5.6614% 1940 0.620862 1.610664 8.0381% 1939 0.574670 1.740131 0.8126% 1938 0.570037 1.754271 0.7762% 1937 0.565646 1.767889 0.6029% 1936 0.562257 1.778547 0.5244% 1935 0.559324 1.787874 -3.0364% 1934 0.576839 1.733587 4.6271% 1933 0.551328 1.813802 1.3921% 1932 0.543758 1.839053 -0.2051% 1931 0.544876 1.835281 0.8886% 1930 0.540077 1.851589 1.0126% 1929 0.534663 1.870338 1.1526% 1928 0.528570 1.891896 1.2160% 1927 0.522220 1.914901 1.4086% 1926 0.514966 1.941874 1.7667% 1925 0.506027 1.976181 1.4465% 1924 0.498811 2.004766 1.7700% 1923 0.490136 2.040250 1.6165% 1922 0.482339 2.073231 1.3736% 1921 0.475803 2.101710 2.3393% 1920 0.464927 2.150876 1.3140% 1919 0.458897 2.179138 0.7676% 1918 0.455401 2.195866 0.3870% 1917 0.453646 2.204364 1.3274% 1916 0.447703 2.233626 1.4083% 1915 0.441485 2.265082 1.4458% 1914 0.435193 2.297830 1.9424% 1913 0.426901 2.342463

38

1.9857% 1912 0.418589 2.388976 1.5634% 1911 0.412146 2.426326 1.8169% 1910 0.404791
2.470410 1.8781% 1909 0.397329 2.516806 2.0082% 1908 0.389507 2.567349 1.9603% 1907
0.382018 2.617676 1.8264% 1906 0.375166 2.665484 1.9357% 1905 0.368042 2.717079
2.0148% 1904 0.360773 2.771824 2.1335% 1903 0.353237 2.830961 1.8151% 1902 0.346939
2.882348 1.8943% 1901 0.340489 2.936949 3.0255% 1900 0.330490 3.025807 0.6278% 1899
0.328428 3.044804 1.7757% 1898 0.322698 3.098869 1.8078% 1897 0.316968 3.154889
1.8396% 1896 0.311243 3.212926 1.8755% 1895 0.305513 3.273186 1.9114% 1894 0.299783
3.335749 1.9486% 1893 0.294053 3.400751 1.9858% 1892 0.288327 3.468283 2.0276% 1891
0.282597 3.538607 2.6465% 1890 0.275311 3.632257 1.5328% 1889 0.271155 3.687933
2.0811% 1888 0.265627 3.764683 2.1599% 1887 0.260011 3.845995 2.2075% 1886 0.254395
3.930897 2.2592% 1885 0.248775 4.019702 2.3095% 1884 0.243159 4.112539 2.3641% 1883
0.237543 4.209765 2.4214% 1882 0.231927 4.311700 2.4815% 1881 0.226311 4.418693
3.7644% 1880 0.218101 4.585030 0.9432% 1879 0.216063 4.628278 2.1464% 1878 0.211523
4.727618 2.1913% 1877 0.206987 4.831215 2.2426% 1876 0.202447 4.939560 2.2941% 1875
0.197907 5.052876 2.3456% 1874 0.193371 5.171396 2.4043% 1873 0.188831 5.295733
2.4635% 1872 0.184291 5.426196 2.5258% 1871 0.179751 5.563249 5.9947% 1870 0.169585
5.896748 -1.0968% 1869 0.171466 5.832073 2.1930% 1868 0.167786 5.959969 2.2394%
1867 0.164111 6.093437 2.2935% 1866 0.160432 6.233190 2.3445% 1865 0.156756 6.379325
2.4037% 1864 0.153077 6.532665 2.4599% 1863 0.149402 6.693360 2.5250% 1862 0.145722
6.862368 2.5872% 1861 0.142047 7.039915 2.9504% 1860 0.137976 7.247621 2.4012% 1859
0.134741 7.421654 2.7627% 1858 0.131118 7.626692 2.8412% 1857 0.127496 7.843382
2.9243% 1856 0.123874 8.072745 3.0161% 1855 0.120247 8.316230 3.1061% 1854 0.116624
8.574537 3.2056% 1853 0.113002 8.849405 3.3118% 1852 0.109380 9.142479 3.4252% 1851
0.105757 9.455629 4.0106% 1850 0.101679 9.834857 2.3254% 1849 0.099368 10.063554
2.7841% 1848 0.096677 10.343732 2.8590% 1847 0.093990 10.639460 2.9432% 1846
0.091303 10.952596 3.0324% 1845 0.088615 11.284723 3.1325% 1844 0.085924 11.638218
3.2284% 1843 0.083237 12.013941 3.3361% 1842 0.080549 12.414733 3.4512% 1841
0.077862 12.843190 3.8105% 1840 0.075004 13.332578 2.3861% 1839 0.073256 13.650700
2.5824% 1838 0.071412 14.003215 2.6573% 1837 0.069564 14.375326 2.7232% 1836
0.067720 14.766795 2.7994% 1835 0.065875 15.180183 2.8871% 1834 0.064027 15.618453
2.9657% 1833 0.062183 16.081647 3.0563% 1832 0.060339 16.573154 3.1604% 1831
0.058490 17.096936 3.4660% 1830 0.056531 17.689510 2.4653% 1829 0.055171 18.125609
2.6804% 1828 0.053730 18.611447 10.3427% 1827 0.048694 20.536365 -4.2314% 1826
0.050846 19.667382 2.9150% 1825 0.049405 20.240693 3.0026% 1824 0.047965 20.848433
3.0955% 1823 0.046525 21.493798 3.1944% 1822 0.045085 22.180394 3.3102% 1821
0.043640 22.914607 3.2277% 1820 0.042276 23.654231 2.6573% 1819 0.041181 24.282790
2.6261% 1818 0.040128 24.920482 2.6969% 1817 0.039074 25.592570 2.7717% 1816
0.038020 26.301915 2.8507% 1815 0.036966 27.051702 2.9343% 1814 0.035912 27.845492
3.0231% 1813 0.034859 28.687276 3.1039% 1812 0.033809 29.577699 3.2172% 1811
0.032755 30.529260 3.0969% 1810 0.031772 31.474726 2.9144% 1809 0.030872 32.392019
2.8225% 1808 0.030024 33.306271 2.9199% 1807 0.029173 34.278790 2.9918% 1806
0.028325 35.304338 3.0841% 1805 0.027478 36.393142 3.1822% 1804 0.026630 37.551242
3.2868% 1803 0.025783 38.785471 3.3985% 1802 0.024935 40.103589 3.5180% 1801
0.024088 41.514452 3.3999% 1800 0.023296 42.925921 2.8419% 1799 0.022652 44.145820
2.7485% 1798 0.022046 45.359148 2.8261% 1797 0.021440 46.641057 3.7832% 1796
0.020659 48.405586 2.1272% 1795 0.020228 49.435269 3.0879% 1794 0.019623 50.961800
3.1625% 1793 0.019021 52.573473 3.2904% 1792 0.018415 54.303358 3.4024% 1791
0.017809 56.150957 3.2296% 1790 0.017252 57.964388 41.3145% 1780 0.012208 81.912057
29.4353% 1770 0.009432 106.023129 83.4728% 1750 0.005141 194.523645 29.2845% 1740
0.003976 251.488828 94.2514% 1720 0.002047 488.520556 85.8111% 1700 0.001102
907.725321 19.2490% 1690 0.000924 1082.453817 88.0250% 1670 0.000491 2035.284030

BASE YEAR: 1979
YEAR BYEAR/AYEAR AYEAR/BYEAR GROWTH%
2009 1.353569 0.738788 8.2857% 2001 1.249998 0.800001 1.0000% 2000 1.237622
0.808001 1.0000% 1999 1.225368 0.816081 1.0000% 1998 1.213236 0.824242 1.0000% 1997
1.201224 0.832484 1.0000% 1996 1.189330 0.840809 1.0000% 1995 1.177555 0.849217

39

0.9992% 1994 1.165905 0.857703 1.0008% 1993 1.154352 0.866287 1.0000% 1992 1.142923
0.874949 0.9295% 1991 1.132398 0.883082 1.2505% 1990 1.118412 0.894125 0.7224% 1989
1.110390 0.900585 1.1077% 1988 1.098225 0.910560 0.8834% 1987 1.088609 0.918604
0.5594% 1986 1.082553 0.923742 1.3056% 1985 1.068601 0.935803 0.7673% 1984 1.060464
0.942983 0.8149% 1983 1.051892 0.950668 0.9737% 1982 1.041748 0.959925 0.9508% 1981
1.031936 0.969052 0.9031% 1980 1.022701 0.977803 2.2701% 1979 1.000000 1.000000
1.0042% 1978 0.990058 1.010042 0.9896% 1977 0.980356 1.020037 0.9103% 1976 0.971512
1.029323 0.8394% 1975 0.963425 1.037964 0.9042% 1974 0.954792 1.047349 1.1568% 1973
0.943873 1.059464 0.9427% 1972 0.935059 1.069452 0.7426% 1971 0.928166 1.077394
1.4697% 1970 0.914722 1.093229 0.6968% 1969 0.908392 1.100847 0.8565% 1968 0.900677
1.110276 1.5090% 1967 0.887288 1.127030 0.9949% 1966 0.878547 1.138243 1.0575% 1965
0.869354 1.150280 1.1300% 1964 0.859640 1.163278 1.5537% 1963 0.846488 1.181351
1.4658% 1962 0.834259 1.198668 1.5364% 1961 0.821636 1.217085 2.1586% 1960 0.804274
1.243357 -1.6655% 1959 0.817896 1.222649 4.3080% 1958 0.784116 1.275321 2.1130%
1957 0.767891 1.302268 1.9895% 1956 0.752912 1.328176 2.1231% 1955 0.737259 1.356375
1.4496% 1954 0.726725 1.376037 2.1573% 1953 0.711378 1.405722 1.2298% 1952 0.702737
1.423008 1.6814% 1951 0.691116 1.446935 1.6233% 1950 0.680077 1.470422 1.4265% 1949
0.670512 1.491398 1.7790% 1948 0.658791 1.517931 1.8242% 1947 0.646989 1.545620 -
2.6320% 1946 0.664479 1.504939 3.1768% 1945 0.644019 1.552748 6.4754% 1944 0.604853
1.653295 -0.3437% 1943 0.606939 1.647613 0.6562% 1942 0.602982 1.658425 0.6633%
1941 0.599009 1.669425 -5.6614% 1940 0.634956 1.574912 8.0381% 1939 0.587715
1.701505 0.8126% 1938 0.582977 1.715332 0.7762% 1937 0.578487 1.728647 0.6029% 1936
0.575020 1.739069 0.5244% 1935 0.572021 1.748189 -3.0364% 1934 0.589933 1.695107
4.6271% 1933 0.563843 1.773542 1.3921% 1932 0.556102 1.798232 -0.2051% 1931
0.557245 1.794544 0.8886% 1930 0.552337 1.810490 1.0126% 1929 0.546800 1.828823
1.1526% 1928 0.540569 1.849902 1.2160% 1927 0.534075 1.872396 1.4086% 1926 0.526657
1.898771 1.7667% 1925 0.517514 1.932316 1.4465% 1924 0.510135 1.960267 1.7700% 1923
0.501262 1.994963 1.6165% 1922 0.493288 2.027212 1.3736% 1921 0.486604 2.055059
2.3393% 1920 0.475481 2.103133 1.3140% 1919 0.469314 2.130768 0.7676% 1918 0.465739
2.147125 0.3870% 1917 0.463944 2.155434 1.3274% 1916 0.457866 2.184046 1.4083% 1915
0.451507 2.214804 1.4458% 1914 0.445072 2.246826 1.9424% 1913 0.436592 2.290468
1.9857% 1912 0.428092 2.335949 1.5634% 1911 0.421502 2.372469 1.8169% 1910 0.413980
2.415575 1.8781% 1909 0.406349 2.460941 2.0082% 1908 0.398349 2.510362 1.9603% 1907
0.390690 2.559572 1.8264% 1906 0.383683 2.606319 1.9357% 1905 0.376397 2.656769
2.0148% 1904 0.368963 2.710298 2.1335% 1903 0.361256 2.768123 1.8151% 1902 0.354815
2.818369 1.8943% 1901 0.348219 2.871758 3.0255% 1900 0.337993 2.958643 0.6278% 1899
0.335884 2.977219 1.7757% 1898 0.330024 3.030084 1.8078% 1897 0.324164 3.084861
1.8396% 1896 0.318308 3.141610 1.8755% 1895 0.312448 3.200532 1.9114% 1894 0.306588
3.261706 1.9486% 1893 0.300728 3.325265 1.9858% 1892 0.294872 3.391298 2.0276% 1891
0.289012 3.460061 2.6465% 1890 0.281561 3.551632 1.5328% 1889 0.277310 3.606072
2.0811% 1888 0.271656 3.681119 2.1599% 1887 0.265913 3.760626 2.2075% 1886 0.260170
3.843643 2.2592% 1885 0.254422 3.930478 2.3095% 1884 0.248679 4.021254 2.3641% 1883
0.242935 4.116322 2.4214% 1882 0.237192 4.215994 2.4815% 1881 0.231449 4.320612
3.7644% 1880 0.223052 4.483257 0.9432% 1879 0.220968 4.525545 2.1464% 1878 0.216325
4.622680 2.1913% 1877 0.211686 4.723977 2.2426% 1876 0.207043 4.829917 2.2941% 1875
0.202400 4.940718 2.3456% 1874 0.197761 5.056608 2.4043% 1873 0.193118 5.178184
2.4635% 1872 0.188475 5.305751 2.5258% 1871 0.183832 5.439763 5.9947% 1870 0.173435
5.765859 -1.0968% 1869 0.175358 5.702620 2.1930% 1868 0.171595 5.827676 2.2394%
1867 0.167836 5.958182 2.2935% 1866 0.164073 6.094833 2.3445% 1865 0.160315 6.237724
2.4037% 1864 0.156552 6.387660 2.4599% 1863 0.152793 6.544789 2.5250% 1862 0.149030
6.710046 2.5872% 1861 0.145272 6.883651 2.9504% 1860 0.141108 7.086747 2.4012% 1859
0.137800 7.256917 2.7627% 1858 0.134095 7.457404 2.8412% 1857 0.130390 7.669284
2.9243% 1856 0.126686 7.893556 3.0161% 1855 0.122976 8.131637 3.1061% 1854 0.119272
8.384210 3.2056% 1853 0.115567 8.652976 3.3118% 1852 0.111863 8.939545 3.4252% 1851
0.108158 9.245744 4.0106% 1850 0.103987 9.616555 2.3254% 1849 0.101624 9.840175
2.7841% 1848 0.098872 10.114134 2.8590% 1847 0.096123 10.403298 2.9432% 1846

40

0.093375 10.709484 3.0324% 1845 0.090627 11.034238 3.1325% 1844 0.087874 11.379887 3.2284% 1843 0.085126 11.747270 3.3361% 1842 0.082378 12.139166 3.4512% 1841 0.079630 12.558112 3.8105% 1840 0.076707 13.036637 2.3861% 1839 0.074919 13.347698 2.5824% 1838 0.073033 13.692388 2.6573% 1837 0.071143 14.056239 2.7232% 1836 0.069257 14.439020 2.7994% 1835 0.067371 14.843231 2.8871% 1834 0.065480 15.271773 2.9657% 1833 0.063594 15.724686 3.0563% 1832 0.061708 16.205283 3.1604% 1831 0.059818 16.717439 3.4660% 1830 0.057814 17.296859 2.4653% 1829 0.056423 17.723279 2.6804% 1828 0.054950 18.198333 10.3427% 1827 0.049799 20.080523 -4.2314% 1826 0.052000 19.230829 2.9150% 1825 0.050527 19.791415 3.0026% 1824 0.049054 20.385665 3.0955% 1823 0.047581 21.016704 3.1944% 1822 0.046108 21.688060 3.3102% 1821 0.044631 22.405976 3.2277% 1820 0.043235 23.129183 2.6573% 1819 0.042116 23.743789 2.6261% 1818 0.041039 24.367327 2.6969% 1817 0.039961 25.024497 2.7717% 1816 0.038883 25.718097 2.8507% 1815 0.037805 26.451241 2.9343% 1814 0.036728 27.227412 3.0231% 1813 0.035650 28.050510 3.1039% 1812 0.034577 28.921169 3.2172% 1811 0.033499 29.851609 3.0969% 1810 0.032493 30.776088 2.9144% 1809 0.031573 31.673019 2.8225% 1808 0.030706 32.566979 2.9199% 1807 0.029835 33.517911 2.9918% 1806 0.028968 34.520694 3.0841% 1805 0.028101 35.585331 3.1822% 1804 0.027235 36.717725 3.2868% 1803 0.026368 37.924557 3.3985% 1802 0.025501 39.213418 3.5180% 1801 0.024635 40.592964 3.3999% 1800 0.023825 41.973103 2.8419% 1799 0.023166 43.165924 2.7485% 1798 0.022547 44.352320 2.8261% 1797 0.021927 45.605775 3.7832% 1796 0.021128 47.331137 2.1272% 1795 0.020688 48.337964 3.0879% 1794 0.020068 49.830611 3.1625% 1793 0.019453 51.406510 3.2904% 1792 0.018833 53.097997 3.4024% 1791 0.018213 54.904586 3.2296% 1790 0.017644 56.677764 41.3145% 1780 0.012485 80.093871 29.4353% 1770 0.009646 103.669755 83.4728% 1750 0.005257 190.205842 29.2845% 1740 0.004067 245.906581 94.2514% 1720 0.002093 477.676963 85.8111% 1700 0.001127 887.576724 19.2490% 1690 0.000945 1058.426806 88.0250% 1670 0.000502 1990.107239

BASE YEAR: 1978

YEAR BYEAR/AYEAR AYEAR/BYEAR GROWTH%

2009 1.367161 0.731443 8.2857% 2001 1.262551 0.792047 1.0000% 2000 1.250050 0.799968 1.0000% 1999 1.237673 0.807968 1.0000% 1998 1.225419 0.816047 1.0000% 1997 1.213286 0.824208 1.0000% 1996 1.201273 0.832450 1.0000% 1995 1.189380 0.840774 0.9992% 1994 1.177613 0.849176 1.0008% 1993 1.165944 0.857674 1.0000% 1992 1.154400 0.866251 0.9295% 1991 1.143769 0.874303 1.2505% 1990 1.129642 0.885236 0.7224% 1989 1.121540 0.891631 1.1077% 1988 1.109253 0.901508 0.8834% 1987 1.099540 0.909471 0.5594% 1986 1.093424 0.914558 1.3056% 1985 1.079332 0.926499 0.7673% 1984 1.071113 0.933608 0.8149% 1983 1.062455 0.941216 0.9737% 1982 1.052209 0.950381 0.9508% 1981 1.042299 0.959418 0.9031% 1980 1.032970 0.968082 2.2701% 1979 1.010042 0.990058 1.0042% 1978 1.000000 1.000000 0.9896% 1977 0.990201 1.009896 0.9103% 1976 0.981268 1.019090 0.8394% 1975 0.973099 1.027644 0.9042% 1974 0.964380 1.036936 1.1568% 1973 0.953352 1.048931 0.9427% 1972 0.944448 1.058819 0.7426% 1971 0.937486 1.066682 1.4697% 1970 0.923907 1.082360 0.6968% 1969 0.917514 1.089902 0.8565% 1968 0.909722 1.099237 1.5090% 1967 0.896198 1.115825 0.9949% 1966 0.887369 1.126927 1.0575% 1965 0.878084 1.138844 1.1300% 1964 0.868272 1.151713 1.5537% 1963 0.854988 1.169606 1.4658% 1962 0.842637 1.186751 1.5364% 1961 0.829886 1.204984 2.1586% 1960 0.812351 1.230996 -1.6655% 1959 0.826109 1.210494 4.3080% 1958 0.791990 1.262642 2.1130% 1957 0.775602 1.289321 1.9895% 1956 0.760473 1.314972 2.1231% 1955 0.744663 1.342890 1.4496% 1954 0.734022 1.362356 2.1573% 1953 0.718522 1.391746 1.2298% 1952 0.709793 1.408861 1.6814% 1951 0.698056 1.432549 1.6233% 1950 0.686906 1.455803 1.4265% 1949 0.677245 1.476571 1.7790% 1948 0.665407 1.502840 1.8242% 1947 0.653486 1.530254 -2.6320% 1946 0.671151 1.489977 3.1768% 1945 0.650487 1.537311 6.4754% 1944 0.610927 1.636858 -0.3437% 1943 0.613033 1.631233 0.6562% 1942 0.609037 1.641937 0.6633% 1941 0.605024 1.652828 -5.6614% 1940 0.641332 1.559254 8.0381% 1939 0.593617 1.684589 0.8126% 1938 0.588832 1.698278 0.7762% 1937 0.584296 1.711461 0.6029% 1936 0.580795 1.721779 0.5244% 1935 0.577765 1.730808 -3.0364% 1934 0.595857 1.678254 4.6271% 1933 0.569505 1.755909 1.3921% 1932 0.561686 1.780354 -0.2051% 1931 0.562840 1.776702 0.8886% 1930 0.557883 1.792490 1.0126% 1929 0.552291 1.810641

1.1526% 1928 0.545998 1.831510 1.2160% 1927 0.539438 1.853781 1.4086% 1926 0.531945
1.879893 1.7667% 1925 0.522710 1.913105 1.4465% 1924 0.515257 1.940778 1.7700% 1923
0.506296 1.975129 1.6165% 1922 0.498242 2.007058 1.3736% 1921 0.491490 2.034628
2.3393% 1920 0.480256 2.082224 1.3140% 1919 0.474027 2.109584 0.7676% 1918 0.470416
2.125779 0.3870% 1917 0.468602 2.134005 1.3274% 1916 0.462464 2.162333 1.4083% 1915
0.456041 2.192785 1.4458% 1914 0.449542 2.224488 1.9424% 1913 0.440976 2.267696
1.9857% 1912 0.432390 2.312725 1.5634% 1911 0.425734 2.348882 1.8169% 1910 0.418137
2.391559 1.8781% 1909 0.410429 2.436474 2.0082% 1908 0.402349 2.485405 1.9603% 1907
0.394614 2.534125 1.8264% 1906 0.387536 2.580407 1.9357% 1905 0.380177 2.630355
2.0148% 1904 0.372668 2.683353 2.1335% 1903 0.364883 2.740603 1.8151% 1902 0.358378
2.790349 1.8943% 1901 0.351715 2.843208 3.0255% 1900 0.341387 2.929229 0.6278% 1899
0.339257 2.947620 1.7757% 1898 0.333338 2.999959 1.8078% 1897 0.327419 3.054191
1.8396% 1896 0.321505 3.110376 1.8755% 1895 0.315586 3.168712 1.9114% 1894 0.309667
3.229279 1.9486% 1893 0.303748 3.292205 1.9858% 1892 0.297833 3.357582 2.0276% 1891
0.291914 3.425662 2.6465% 1890 0.284388 3.516322 1.5328% 1889 0.280095 3.570221
2.0811% 1888 0.274384 3.644522 2.1599% 1887 0.268583 3.723238 2.2075% 1886 0.262782
3.805430 2.2592% 1885 0.256977 3.891401 2.3095% 1884 0.251176 3.981274 2.3641% 1883
0.245375 4.075397 2.4214% 1882 0.239574 4.174078 2.4815% 1881 0.233773 4.277657
3.7644% 1880 0.225292 4.438685 0.9432% 1879 0.223187 4.480552 2.1464% 1878 0.218497
4.576722 2.1913% 1877 0.213812 4.677012 2.2426% 1876 0.209122 4.781899 2.2941% 1875
0.204432 4.891598 2.3456% 1874 0.199747 5.006335 2.4043% 1873 0.195057 5.126703
2.4635% 1872 0.190367 5.253002 2.5258% 1871 0.185678 5.385681 5.9947% 1870 0.175176
5.708535 -1.0968% 1869 0.177119 5.645925 2.1930% 1868 0.173318 5.769738 2.2394%
1867 0.169522 5.898946 2.2935% 1866 0.165721 6.034238 2.3445% 1865 0.161925 6.175709
2.4037% 1864 0.158124 6.324155 2.4599% 1863 0.154328 6.479721 2.5250% 1862 0.150527
6.643335 2.5872% 1861 0.146731 6.815214 2.9504% 1860 0.142525 7.016291 2.4012% 1859
0.139183 7.184769 2.7627% 1858 0.135441 7.383263 2.8412% 1857 0.131700 7.593036
2.9243% 1856 0.127958 7.815079 3.0161% 1855 0.124211 8.050792 3.1061% 1854 0.120470
8.300855 3.2056% 1853 0.116728 8.566949 3.3118% 1852 0.112986 8.850668 3.4252% 1851
0.109244 9.153824 4.0106% 1850 0.105032 9.520948 3.2354% 1849 0.102645 9.742345
2.7841% 1848 0.099864 10.013580 2.8590% 1847 0.097089 10.299869 2.9432% 1846
0.094313 10.603010 3.0324% 1845 0.091537 10.924537 3.1325% 1844 0.088757 11.266748
3.2284% 1843 0.085981 11.630480 3.3361% 1842 0.083205 12.018479 3.4512% 1841
0.080429 12.433260 3.8105% 1840 0.077477 12.907028 2.3861% 1839 0.075672 13.214996
2.5824% 1838 0.073767 13.556259 2.6573% 1837 0.071857 13.916493 2.7232% 1836
0.069952 14.295468 2.7994% 1835 0.068047 14.695661 2.8871% 1834 0.066138 15.119942
2.9657% 1833 0.064233 15.568352 3.0563% 1832 0.062328 16.044171 3.1604% 1831
0.060418 16.551235 3.4660% 1830 0.058395 17.124895 2.4653% 1829 0.056990 17.547075
2.6804% 1828 0.055502 18.017406 10.3427% 1827 0.050300 19.880884 -4.2314% 1826
0.052522 19.039637 2.9150% 1825 0.051034 19.594650 3.0026% 1824 0.049547 20.182992
3.0955% 1823 0.048059 20.807758 3.1944% 1822 0.046571 21.472439 3.3102% 1821
0.045079 22.183218 3.2277% 1820 0.043670 22.899234 2.6573% 1819 0.042539 23.507730
2.6261% 1818 0.041451 24.125068 2.6969% 1817 0.040362 24.775705 2.7717% 1816
0.039274 25.462409 2.8507% 1815 0.038185 26.188265 2.9343% 1814 0.037097 26.956718
3.0231% 1813 0.036008 27.771634 3.1039% 1812 0.034924 28.633636 3.2172% 1811
0.033835 29.554826 3.0969% 1810 0.032819 30.470114 2.9144% 1809 0.031890 31.358128
2.8225% 1808 0.031014 32.243200 2.9199% 1807 0.030134 33.184678 2.9918% 1806
0.029259 34.177492 3.0841% 1805 0.028384 35.231544 3.1822% 1804 0.027508 36.352679
3.2868% 1803 0.026633 37.547514 3.3985% 1802 0.025758 38.823560 3.5180% 1801
0.024882 40.189391 3.3999% 1800 0.024064 41.555809 2.8419% 1799 0.023399 42.736771
2.7485% 1798 0.022773 43.911372 2.8261% 1797 0.022147 45.152365 3.7832% 1796
0.021340 46.860574 2.1272% 1795 0.020895 47.857391 3.0879% 1794 0.020270 49.335198
3.1625% 1793 0.019648 50.895429 3.2904% 1792 0.019022 52.570100 3.4024% 1791
0.018396 54.358728 3.2296% 1790 0.017821 56.114277 41.3145% 1780 0.012611 79.297583
29.4353% 1770 0.009743 102.639076 83.4728% 1750 0.005310 188.314827 29.2845% 1740

42

0.004107 243.461793 94.2514% 1720 0.002114 472.927928 85.8111% 1700 0.001138 878.752491 19.2490% 1690 0.000954 1047.903992 88.0250% 1670 0.000508 1970.321716

YEAR BYEAR/AYEAR AYEAR/BYEAR GROWTH%

2009 1.380691 0.724275 8.2857% 2001 1.275045 0.784286 1.0000% 2000 1.262421 0.792129 1.0000% 1999 1.249921 0.800050 1.0000% 1998 1.237546 0.808051 1.0000% 1997 1.225293 0.816131 1.0000% 1996 1.213161 0.824293 1.0000% 1995 1.201150 0.832536 0.9992% 1994 1.189266 0.840854 1.0008% 1993 1.177482 0.849270 1.0000% 1992 1.165824 0.857762 0.9295% 1991 1.155088 0.865735 1.2505% 1990 1.140821 0.876561 0.7224% 1989 1.132639 0.882894 1.1077% 1988 1.120230 0.892674 0.8834% 1987 1.110421 0.900559 0.5594% 1986 1.104244 0.905597 1.3056% 1985 1.090013 0.917420 0.7673% 1984 1.081713 0.924459 0.8149% 1983 1.072969 0.931993 0.9737% 1982 1.062622 0.941069 0.9508% 1981 1.052613 0.950016 0.9031% 1980 1.043193 0.958596 2.2701% 1979 1.020037 0.980356 1.0042% 1978 1.009896 0.990201 0.9896% 1977 1.000000 1.000000 0.9103% 1976 0.990979 1.009103 0.8394% 1975 0.982729 1.017574 0.9042% 1974 0.973923 1.026775 1.1568% 1973 0.962786 1.038652 0.9427% 1972 0.953795 1.048444 0.7426% 1971 0.946764 1.056230 1.4697% 1970 0.933050 1.071754 0.6968% 1969 0.926593 1.079222 0.8565% 1968 0.918724 1.088466 1.5090% 1967 0.905066 1.104891 0.9949% 1966 0.896151 1.115884 1.0575% 1965 0.886773 1.127684 1.1300% 1964 0.876865 1.140427 1.5537% 1963 0.863450 1.158145 1.4658% 1962 0.850976 1.175122 1.5364% 1961 0.838099 1.193177 2.1586% 1960 0.820390 1.218933 -1.6655% 1959 0.834285 1.198632 4.3080% 1958 0.799828 1.250269 2.1130% 1957 0.783278 1.276687 1.9895% 1956 0.767998 1.302086 2.1231% 1955 0.752032 1.329731 1.4496% 1954 0.741286 1.349007 2.1573% 1953 0.725633 1.378108 1.2298% 1952 0.716817 1.395055 1.6814% 1951 0.704964 1.418512 1.6233% 1950 0.693704 1.441538 1.4265% 1949 0.683947 1.462102 1.7790% 1948 0.671992 1.488113 1.8242% 1947 0.659953 1.515259 -2.6320% 1946 0.677793 1.475377 3.1768% 1945 0.656924 1.522247 6.4754% 1944 0.616972 1.620818 -0.3437% 1943 0.619100 1.615248 0.6562% 1942 0.615064 1.625848 0.6633% 1941 0.611011 1.636632 -5.6614% 1940 0.647679 1.543975 8.0381% 1939 0.599491 1.668081 0.8126% 1938 0.594659 1.681637 0.7762% 1937 0.590078 1.694690 0.6029% 1936 0.586542 1.704907 0.5244% 1935 0.583482 1.713848 -3.0364% 1934 0.601754 1.661809 4.6271% 1933 0.575141 1.738703 1.3921% 1932 0.567245 1.762908 -0.2051% 1931 0.568410 1.759292 0.8886% 1930 0.563404 1.774925 1.0126% 1929 0.557756 1.792898 1.1526% 1928 0.551401 1.813563 1.2160% 1927 0.544776 1.835616 1.4086% 1926 0.537209 1.861472 1.7667% 1925 0.527883 1.894358 1.4465% 1924 0.520356 1.921760 1.7700% 1923 0.511306 1.955775 1.6165% 1922 0.503172 1.987390 1.3736% 1921 0.496354 2.014690 2.3393% 1920 0.485008 2.061820 1.3140% 1919 0.478718 2.088912 0.7676% 1918 0.475071 2.104948 0.3870% 1917 0.473240 2.113094 1.3274% 1916 0.467040 2.141144 1.4083% 1915 0.460554 2.171297 1.4458% 1914 0.453990 2.202690 1.9424% 1913 0.445340 2.245474 1.9857% 1912 0.436669 2.290062 1.5634% 1911 0.429948 2.325865 1.8169% 1910 0.422275 2.368124 1.8781% 1909 0.414491 2.412599 2.0082% 1908 0.406331 2.461050 1.9603% 1907 0.398519 2.509293 1.8264% 1906 0.391371 2.555121 1.9357% 1905 0.383939 2.604580 2.0148% 1904 0.376356 2.657058 2.1335% 1903 0.368494 2.713747 1.8151% 1902 0.361925 2.763006 1.8943% 1901 0.355196 2.815347 3.0255% 1900 0.344765 2.900525 0.6278% 1899 0.342614 2.918736 1.7757% 1898 0.336637 2.970562 1.8078% 1897 0.330659 3.024263 1.8396% 1896 0.324686 3.079897 1.8755% 1895 0.318709 3.137662 1.9114% 1894 0.312731 3.197635 1.9486% 1893 0.306754 3.259945 1.9858% 1892 0.300781 3.324681 2.0276% 1891 0.294803 3.392093 2.6465% 1890 0.287202 3.481865 1.5328% 1889 0.282867 3.535236 2.0811% 1888 0.277100 3.608809 2.1599% 1887 0.271241 3.686754 2.2075% 1886 0.265383 3.768140 2.2592% 1885 0.259520 3.853269 2.3095% 1884 0.253662 3.942262 2.3641% 1883 0.247803 4.035462 2.4214% 1882 0.241945 4.133176 2.4815% 1881 0.236086 4.235740 3.7644% 1880 0.227521 4.395190 0.9432% 1879 0.225395 4.436646 2.1464% 1878 0.220659 4.531874 2.1913% 1877 0.215928 4.631181 2.2426% 1876 0.211191 4.735040 2.2941% 1875 0.206455 4.843665 2.3456% 1874 0.201724 4.957277 2.4043% 1873 0.196987 5.076466 2.4635% 1872 0.192251 5.201527 2.5258% 1871 0.187515 5.332906 5.9947% 1870 0.176910 5.652596 -1.0968% 1869 0.178872 5.590599 2.1930% 1868 0.175033 5.713200 2.2394% 1867 0.171199 5.841141 2.2935% 1866 0.167361 5.975108 2.3445% 1865 0.163527 6.115193

2.4037% 1864 0.159689 6.262183 2.4599% 1863 0.155855 6.416226 2.5250% 1862 0.152016
6.578236 2.5872% 1861 0.148183 6.748431 2.9504% 1860 0.143936 6.947537 2.4012% 1859
0.140561 7.114364 2.7627% 1858 0.136782 7.310914 2.8412% 1857 0.133003 7.518631
2.9243% 1856 0.129224 7.738498 3.0161% 1855 0.125441 7.971902 3.1061% 1854 0.121662
8.219514 3.2056% 1853 0.117883 8.483000 3.3118% 1852 0.114104 8.763940 3.4252% 1851
0.110325 9.064124 4.0106% 1850 0.106071 9.427651 2.3254% 1849 0.103660 9.646878
2.7841% 1848 0.100853 9.915456 2.8590% 1847 0.098049 10.198940 2.9432% 1846
0.095246 10.499110 3.0324% 1845 0.092443 10.817486 3.1325% 1844 0.089635 11.156344
3.2284% 1843 0.086832 11.516511 3.3361% 1842 0.084029 11.900709 3.4512% 1841
0.081225 12.311425 3.8105% 1840 0.078244 12.780550 2.3861% 1839 0.076420 13.085501
2.5824% 1838 0.074497 13.423420 2.6573% 1837 0.072568 13.780124 2.7232% 1836
0.070644 14.155385 2.7994% 1835 0.068721 14.551656 2.8871% 1834 0.066792 14.971780
2.9657% 1833 0.064869 15.415796 3.0563% 1832 0.062945 15.886952 3.1604% 1831
0.061016 16.389047 3.4660% 1830 0.058972 16.957086 2.4653% 1829 0.057554 17.375129
2.6804% 1828 0.056051 17.840852 10.3427% 1827 0.050797 19.686069 -4.2314% 1826
0.053042 18.853066 2.9150% 1825 0.051539 19.402640 3.0026% 1824 0.050037 19.985216
3.0955% 1823 0.048535 20.603860 3.1944% 1822 0.047032 21.262028 3.3102% 1821
0.045525 21.965842 3.2277% 1820 0.044102 22.674842 2.6573% 1819 0.042960 23.277375
2.6261% 1818 0.041861 23.888664 2.6969% 1817 0.040762 24.532925 2.7717% 1816
0.039662 25.212900 2.8507% 1815 0.038563 25.931643 2.9343% 1814 0.037464 26.692566
3.0231% 1813 0.036364 27.499496 3.1039% 1812 0.035270 28.353052 3.2172% 1811
0.034170 29.265214 3.0969% 1810 0.033144 30.171533 2.9144% 1809 0.032205 31.050846
2.8225% 1808 0.031321 31.927245 2.9199% 1807 0.030433 32.859497 2.9918% 1806
0.029549 33.842583 3.0841% 1805 0.028665 34.886306 3.1822% 1804 0.027781 35.996455
3.2868% 1803 0.026896 37.179581 3.3985% 1802 0.026012 38.443124 3.5180% 1801
0.025128 39.795571 3.3999% 1800 0.024302 41.148599 2.8419% 1799 0.023631 42.317988
2.7485% 1798 0.022999 43.481079 2.8261% 1797 0.022366 44.709912 3.7832% 1796
0.021551 46.401382 2.1272% 1795 0.021102 47.388431 3.0879% 1794 0.020470 48.851757
3.1625% 1793 0.019843 50.396699 3.2904% 1792 0.019210 52.054959 3.4024% 1791
0.018578 53.826060 3.2296% 1790 0.017997 55.564407 41.3145% 1780 0.012736 78.520537
29.4353% 1770 0.009839 101.633304 83.4728% 1750 0.005363 186.469508 29.2845% 1740
0.004148 241.076082 94.2514% 1720 0.002135 468.293651 85.8111% 1700 0.001149
870.141491 19.2490% 1690 0.000964 1037.635456 88.0250% 1670 0.000513 1951.014298

BASE YEAR: 1976

YEAR BYEAR/AYEAR AYEAR/BYEAR GROWTH%

2009 1.393260 0.717741 8.2857% 2001 1.286652 0.777211 1.0000% 2000 1.273913
0.784983 1.0000% 1999 1.261300 0.792833 1.0000% 1998 1.248812 0.800761 1.0000% 1997
1.236447 0.808769 1.0000% 1996 1.224205 0.816857 1.0000% 1995 1.212084 0.825025
0.9992% 1994 1.200093 0.833269 1.0008% 1993 1.188202 0.841608 1.0000% 1992 1.176437
0.850024 0.9295% 1991 1.165603 0.857925 1.2505% 1990 1.151207 0.868654 0.7224% 1989
1.142950 0.874929 1.1077% 1988 1.130428 0.884621 0.8834% 1987 1.120530 0.892435
0.5594% 1986 1.114297 0.897427 1.3056% 1985 1.099936 0.909144 0.7673% 1984 1.091560
0.916120 0.8149% 1983 1.082737 0.923586 0.9737% 1982 1.072295 0.932579 0.9508% 1981
1.062196 0.941446 0.9031% 1980 1.052689 0.949948 2.2701% 1979 1.029323 0.971512
1.0042% 1978 1.019090 0.981268 0.9896% 1977 1.009103 0.990979 0.9103% 1976 1.000000
1.000000 0.8394% 1975 0.991675 1.008394 0.9042% 1974 0.982789 1.017512 1.1568% 1973
0.971551 1.029282 0.9427% 1972 0.962477 1.038986 0.7426% 1971 0.955382 1.046701
1.4697% 1970 0.941544 1.062085 0.6968% 1969 0.935029 1.069486 0.8565% 1968 0.927088
1.078647 1.5090% 1967 0.913306 1.094924 0.9949% 1966 0.904309 1.105817 1.0575% 1965
0.894846 1.117511 1.1300% 1964 0.884847 1.130139 1.5537% 1963 0.871310 1.147697
1.4658% 1962 0.858722 1.164521 1.5364% 1961 0.845728 1.182413 2.1586% 1960 0.827858
1.207937 -1.6655% 1959 0.841879 1.187819 4.3080% 1958 0.807109 1.238990 2.1130%
1957 0.790408 1.265169 1.9895% 1956 0.774990 1.290340 2.1231% 1955 0.758878 1.317735
1.4496% 1954 0.748034 1.336837 2.1573% 1953 0.732238 1.365676 1.2298% 1952 0.723343
1.382470 1.6814% 1951 0.711382 1.405715 1.6233% 1950 0.700019 1.428533 1.4265% 1949
0.690173 1.448912 1.7790% 1948 0.678109 1.474689 1.8242% 1947 0.665961 1.501589 -

44

2.6320% 1946 0.683963 1.462067 3.1768% 1945 0.662904 1.508514 6.4754% 1944 0.622589 1.606197 -0.3437% 1943 0.624736 1.600676 0.6562% 1942 0.620663 1.611180 0.6633% 1941 0.616573 1.621867 -5.6614% 1940 0.653575 1.530047 8.0381% 1939 0.604948 1.653033 0.8126% 1938 0.600072 1.666466 0.7762% 1937 0.595450 1.679402 0.6029% 1936 0.591882 1.689527 0.5244% 1935 0.588794 1.698387 -3.0364% 1934 0.607232 1.646817 4.6271% 1933 0.580377 1.723018 1.3921% 1932 0.572408 1.747004 -0.2051% 1931 0.573585 1.743421 0.8886% 1930 0.568533 1.758913 1.0126% 1929 0.562834 1.776724 1.1526% 1928 0.556420 1.797202 1.2160% 1927 0.549736 1.819056 1.4086% 1926 0.542100 1.844679 1.7667% 1925 0.532689 1.877269 1.4465% 1924 0.525093 1.904424 1.7700% 1923 0.515961 1.938131 1.6165% 1922 0.507753 1.969462 1.3736% 1921 0.500873 1.996515 2.3393% 1920 0.489424 2.043220 1.3140% 1919 0.483076 2.070068 0.7676% 1918 0.479396 2.085959 0.3870% 1917 0.477548 2.094031 1.3274% 1916 0.471292 2.121828 1.4083% 1915 0.464747 2.151709 1.4458% 1914 0.458123 2.182819 1.9424% 1913 0.449394 2.225218 1.9857% 1912 0.440645 2.269403 1.5634% 1911 0.433861 2.304883 1.8169% 1910 0.426119 2.346761 1.8781% 1909 0.418264 2.390834 2.0082% 1908 0.410030 2.438848 1.9603% 1907 0.402147 2.486656 1.8264% 1906 0.394934 2.532071 1.9357% 1905 0.387434 2.581083 2.0148% 1904 0.379782 2.633088 2.1335% 1903 0.371849 2.689266 1.8151% 1902 0.365219 2.738080 1.8943% 1901 0.358430 2.789949 3.0255% 1900 0.347904 2.874359 0.6278% 1899 0.345733 2.892405 1.7757% 1898 0.339701 2.943764 1.8078% 1897 0.333669 2.996980 1.8396% 1896 0.327642 3.052113 1.8755% 1895 0.321610 3.109356 1.9114% 1894 0.315578 3.168788 1.9486% 1893 0.309546 3.230536 1.9858% 1892 0.303519 3.294688 2.0276% 1891 0.297487 3.361492 2.6465% 1890 0.289817 3.450455 1.5328% 1889 0.285442 3.503344 2.0811% 1888 0.279622 3.576253 2.1599% 1887 0.273711 3.653495 2.2075% 1886 0.267799 3.734147 2.2592% 1885 0.261882 3.818508 2.3095% 1884 0.255971 3.906697 2.3641% 1883 0.250059 3.999057 2.4214% 1882 0.244147 4.095890 2.4815% 1881 0.238235 4.197528 3.7644% 1880 0.229593 4.355540 0.9432% 1879 0.227447 4.396623 2.1464% 1878 0.222668 4.490991 2.1913% 1877 0.217893 4.589402 2.2426% 1876 0.213114 4.692324 2.2941% 1875 0.208335 4.799969 2.3456% 1874 0.203560 4.912557 2.4043% 1873 0.198781 5.030670 2.4635% 1872 0.194001 5.154603 2.5258% 1871 0.189222 5.284797 5.9947% 1870 0.178520 5.601603 -1.0968% 1869 0.180500 5.540165 2.1930% 1868 0.176627 5.661660 2.2394% 1867 0.172758 5.788447 2.2935% 1866 0.168885 5.921205 2.3445% 1865 0.165016 6.060026 2.4037% 1864 0.161142 6.205691 2.4599% 1863 0.157274 6.358344 2.5250% 1862 0.153400 6.518892 2.5872% 1861 0.149532 6.687552 2.9504% 1860 0.145246 6.884862 2.4012% 1859 0.141840 7.050184 2.7627% 1858 0.138027 7.244960 2.8412% 1857 0.134214 7.450804 2.9243% 1856 0.130400 7.668687 3.0161% 1855 0.126583 7.899985 3.1061% 1854 0.122769 8.145364 3.2056% 1853 0.118956 8.406473 3.3118% 1852 0.115143 8.684878 3.4252% 1851 0.111329 8.982355 4.0106% 1850 0.107037 9.342602 3.2254% 1849 0.104604 9.559852 2.7841% 1848 0.101771 9.826006 2.8590% 1847 0.098942 10.106933 2.9432% 1846 0.096113 10.404395 3.0324% 1845 0.093284 10.719899 3.1325% 1844 0.090451 11.055700 3.2284% 1843 0.087622 11.412618 3.3361% 1842 0.084794 11.793350 3.4512% 1841 0.081965 12.200361 3.8105% 1840 0.078956 12.665254 2.3861% 1839 0.077116 12.967454 2.5824% 1838 0.075175 13.302324 2.6573% 1837 0.073229 13.655810 2.7232% 1836 0.071288 14.027686 2.7994% 1835 0.069346 14.420383 2.8871% 1834 0.067400 14.836716 2.9657% 1833 0.065459 15.276726 3.0563% 1832 0.063518 15.743633 3.1604% 1831 0.061572 16.241198 3.4660% 1830 0.059509 16.804113 2.4653% 1829 0.058077 17.218384 2.6804% 1828 0.056561 17.679905 10.3427% 1827 0.051260 19.508476 -4.2314% 1826 0.053525 18.682988 2.9150% 1825 0.052009 19.227604 3.0026% 1824 0.050492 19.804925 3.0955% 1823 0.048976 20.417988 3.1944% 1822 0.047460 21.070218 3.3102% 1821 0.045940 21.767683 3.2277% 1820 0.044503 22.470287 2.6573% 1819 0.043351 23.067385 2.6261% 1818 0.042242 23.673159 2.6969% 1817 0.041133 24.311608 2.7717% 1816 0.040023 24.985449 2.8507% 1815 0.038914 25.697708 2.9343% 1814 0.037805 26.451767 3.0231% 1813 0.036695 27.251417 3.1039% 1812 0.035591 28.097273 3.2172% 1811 0.034481 29.001206 3.0969% 1810 0.033446 29.899349 2.9144% 1809 0.032498 30.770730 2.8225% 1808 0.031606 31.639222 2.9199% 1807 0.030710 32.563064 2.9918% 1806 0.029818 33.537281 3.0841% 1805 0.028925 34.571588 3.1822% 1804 0.028033 35.671723 3.2868% 1803 0.027141 36.844176 3.3985% 1802 0.026249 38.096320 3.5180% 1801

0.025357 39.436566 3.3999% 1800 0.024523 40.777388 2.8419% 1799 0.023846 41.936228
2.7485% 1798 0.023208 43.088827 2.8261% 1797 0.022570 44.306574 3.7832% 1796
0.021747 45.982784 2.1272% 1795 0.021294 46.960929 3.0879% 1794 0.020656 48.411054
3.1625% 1793 0.020023 49.942059 3.2904% 1792 0.019385 51.585360 3.4024% 1791
0.018747 53.340483 3.2296% 1790 0.018161 55.063148 41.3145% 1780 0.012851 77.812185
29.4353% 1770 0.009929 100.716447 83.4728% 1750 0.005412 184.787325 29.2845% 1740
0.004186 238.901281 94.2514% 1720 0.002155 464.069069 85.8111% 1700 0.001160
862.291750 19.2490% 1690 0.000973 1028.274715 88.0250% 1670 0.000517 1933.413762

BASE YEAR: 1975

YEAR BYEAR/AYEAR AYEAR/BYEAR GROWTH%

2009 1.404955 0.711766 8.2857% 2001 1.297453 0.770741 1.0000% 2000 1.284607
0.778448 1.0000% 1999 1.271888 0.786233 1.0000% 1998 1.259295 0.794095 1.0000% 1997
1.246826 0.802036 1.0000% 1996 1.234482 0.810057 1.0000% 1995 1.222259 0.818157
0.9992% 1994 1.210167 0.826332 1.0008% 1993 1.198176 0.834602 1.0000% 1992 1.186313
0.842948 0.9295% 1991 1.175387 0.850783 1.2505% 1990 1.160870 0.861423 0.7224% 1989
1.152544 0.867646 1.1077% 1988 1.139917 0.877257 0.8834% 1987 1.129936 0.885006
0.5594% 1986 1.123651 0.889956 1.3056% 1985 1.109169 0.901576 0.7673% 1984 1.100723
0.908493 0.8149% 1983 1.091826 0.915897 0.9737% 1982 1.081296 0.924816 0.9508% 1981
1.071112 0.933609 0.9031% 1980 1.061526 0.942040 2.2701% 1979 1.037964 0.963425
1.0042% 1978 1.027644 0.973099 0.9896% 1977 1.017574 0.982729 0.9103% 1976 1.008394
0.991675 0.8394% 1975 1.000000 1.000000 0.9042% 1974 0.991039 1.009042 1.1568% 1973
0.979706 1.020714 0.9427% 1972 0.970557 1.030337 0.7426% 1971 0.963402 1.037988
1.4697% 1970 0.949448 1.053244 0.6968% 1969 0.942878 1.060583 0.8565% 1968 0.934870
1.069667 1.5090% 1967 0.920972 1.085809 0.9949% 1966 0.911900 1.096612 1.0575% 1965
0.902358 1.108208 1.1300% 1964 0.892275 1.120731 1.5537% 1963 0.878624 1.138143
1.4658% 1962 0.865931 1.154827 1.5364% 1961 0.852828 1.172570 2.1586% 1960 0.834807
1.197881 -1.6655% 1959 0.848946 1.177931 4.3080% 1958 0.813884 1.228676 2.1130%
1957 0.797043 1.254637 1.9895% 1956 0.781495 1.279598 2.1231% 1955 0.765248 1.306765
1.4496% 1954 0.754314 1.325708 2.1573% 1953 0.738385 1.354307 1.2298% 1952 0.729415
1.370962 1.6814% 1951 0.717353 1.394013 1.6233% 1950 0.705895 1.416642 1.4265% 1949
0.695967 1.436850 1.7790% 1948 0.683802 1.462413 1.8242% 1947 0.671551 1.489089 -
2.6320% 1946 0.689705 1.449896 3.1768% 1945 0.668469 1.495956 6.4754% 1944 0.627815
1.592826 -0.3437% 1943 0.629980 1.587352 0.6562% 1942 0.625873 1.597768 0.6633%
1941 0.621749 1.608366 -5.6614% 1940 0.659061 1.517310 8.0381% 1939 0.610027
1.639273 0.8126% 1938 0.605109 1.652594 0.7762% 1937 0.600448 1.665422 0.6029% 1936
0.596850 1.675463 0.5244% 1935 0.593737 1.684249 -3.0364% 1934 0.612329 1.633109
4.6271% 1933 0.585249 1.708674 1.3921% 1932 0.577213 1.732461 -0.2051% 1931
0.578400 1.728908 0.8886% 1930 0.573305 1.744271 1.0126% 1929 0.567558 1.761934
1.1526% 1928 0.561091 1.782241 1.2160% 1927 0.554350 1.803913 1.4086% 1926 0.546650
1.829323 1.7667% 1925 0.537160 1.861641 1.4465% 1924 0.529501 1.888570 1.7700% 1923
0.520292 1.921997 1.6165% 1922 0.512015 1.953067 1.3736% 1921 0.505077 1.979895
2.3393% 1920 0.493532 2.026211 1.3140% 1919 0.487131 2.052836 0.7676% 1918 0.483420
2.068594 0.3870% 1917 0.481557 2.076599 1.3274% 1916 0.475248 2.104165 1.4083% 1915
0.468648 2.133797 1.4458% 1914 0.461969 2.164648 1.9424% 1913 0.453167 2.206694
1.9857% 1912 0.444343 2.250511 1.5634% 1911 0.437503 2.285696 1.8169% 1910 0.429696
2.327225 1.8781% 1909 0.421775 2.370932 2.0082% 1908 0.413472 2.418546 1.9603% 1907
0.405522 2.465956 1.8264% 1906 0.398249 2.510993 1.9357% 1905 0.390686 2.559597
2.0148% 1904 0.382970 2.611169 2.1335% 1903 0.374970 2.666879 1.8151% 1902 0.368285
2.715287 1.8943% 1901 0.361438 2.766724 3.0255% 1900 0.350824 2.850431 0.6278% 1899
0.348635 2.868327 1.7757% 1898 0.342553 2.919259 1.8078% 1897 0.336470 2.972032
1.8396% 1896 0.330392 3.026705 1.8755% 1895 0.324310 3.083472 1.9114% 1894 0.318227
3.142409 1.9486% 1893 0.312145 3.203643 1.9858% 1892 0.306067 3.267262 2.0276% 1891
0.299984 3.333509 2.6465% 1890 0.292250 3.421731 1.5328% 1889 0.287838 3.474180
2.0811% 1888 0.281970 3.546482 2.1599% 1887 0.276008 3.623081 2.2075% 1886 0.270047
3.703062 2.2592% 1885 0.264081 3.786720 2.3095% 1884 0.258119 3.874176 2.3641% 1883
0.252158 3.965767 2.4214% 1882 0.246197 4.061794 2.4815% 1881 0.240235 4.162586

46

3.7644% 1880 0.231520 4.319282 0.9432% 1879 0.229357 4.360023 2.1464% 1878 0.224537
4.453606 2.1913% 1877 0.219722 4.551197 2.2426% 1876 0.214903 4.653263 2.2941% 1875
0.210084 4.760012 2.3456% 1874 0.205269 4.871662 2.4043% 1873 0.200449 4.988792
2.4635% 1872 0.195630 5.111694 2.5258% 1871 0.190810 5.240803 5.9947% 1870 0.180019
5.554972 -1.0968% 1869 0.182015 5.494046 2.1930% 1868 0.178109 5.614529 2.2394%
1867 0.174208 5.740261 2.2935% 1866 0.170302 5.871914 2.3445% 1865 0.166401 6.009580
2.4037% 1864 0.162495 6.154031 2.4599% 1863 0.158594 6.305414 2.5250% 1862 0.154688
6.464626 2.5872% 1861 0.150787 6.631882 2.9504% 1860 0.146465 6.827549 2.4012% 1859
0.143031 6.991495 2.7627% 1858 0.139186 7.184649 2.8412% 1857 0.135340 7.388780
2.9243% 1856 0.131495 7.604849 3.0161% 1855 0.127645 7.834222 3.1061% 1854 0.123800
8.077557 3.2056% 1853 0.119955 8.336494 3.3118% 1852 0.116109 8.612581 3.4252% 1851
0.112264 8.907581 4.0106% 1850 0.107935 9.264829 2.3254% 1849 0.105482 9.480270
2.7841% 1848 0.102625 9.744209 2.8590% 1847 0.099773 10.022797 2.9432% 1846
0.096920 10.317784 3.0324% 1845 0.094068 10.630661 3.1325% 1844 0.091210 10.963667
3.2284% 1843 0.088358 11.317614 3.3361% 1842 0.085505 11.695176 3.4512% 1841
0.082653 12.098799 3.8105% 1840 0.079619 12.559822 2.3861% 1839 0.077763 12.859506
2.5824% 1838 0.075806 13.191589 2.6573% 1837 0.073844 13.542132 2.7232% 1836
0.071886 13.910912 2.7994% 1835 0.069928 14.300340 2.8871% 1834 0.067966 14.713208
2.9657% 1833 0.066009 15.149555 3.0563% 1832 0.064051 15.612575 3.1604% 1831
0.062089 16.105998 3.4660% 1830 0.060009 16.664226 2.4653% 1829 0.058565 17.075050
2.6804% 1828 0.057036 17.532729 10.3427% 1827 0.051690 19.346078 -4.2314% 1826
0.053974 18.527461 2.9150% 1825 0.052445 19.067544 3.0026% 1824 0.050916 19.640059
3.0955% 1823 0.049388 20.248018 3.1944% 1822 0.047859 20.894819 3.3102% 1821
0.046325 21.586478 3.2277% 1820 0.044877 22.283233 2.6573% 1819 0.043715 22.875360
2.6261% 1818 0.042597 23.476091 2.6969% 1817 0.041478 24.109226 2.7717% 1816
0.040359 24.777457 2.8507% 1815 0.039241 25.483787 2.9343% 1814 0.038122 26.231569
3.0231% 1813 0.037003 27.024562 3.1039% 1812 0.035889 27.863377 3.2172% 1811
0.034771 28.759786 3.0969% 1810 0.033726 29.650452 2.9144% 1809 0.032771 30.514578
2.8225% 1808 0.031872 31.375841 2.9199% 1807 0.030967 32.291993 2.9918% 1806
0.030068 33.258100 3.0841% 1805 0.029168 34.283797 3.1822% 1804 0.028269 35.374773
3.2868% 1803 0.027369 36.537466 3.3985% 1802 0.026470 37.779186 3.5180% 1801
0.025570 39.108276 3.3999% 1800 0.024729 40.437936 2.8419% 1799 0.024046 41.587129
2.7485% 1798 0.023403 42.730133 2.8261% 1797 0.022759 43.937743 3.7832% 1796
0.021930 45.600000 2.1272% 1795 0.021473 46.570002 3.0879% 1794 0.020830 48.008055
3.1625% 1793 0.020191 49.526316 3.2904% 1792 0.019548 51.155937 3.4024% 1791
0.018905 52.896450 3.2296% 1790 0.018313 54.604774 41.3145% 1780 0.012959 77.164437
29.4353% 1770 0.010012 99.878032 83.4728% 1750 0.005457 183.249060 29.2845% 1740
0.004221 236.912544 94.2514% 1720 0.002173 460.205920 85.8111% 1700 0.001169
855.113591 19.2490% 1690 0.000981 1019.714829 88.0250% 1670 0.000522 1917.319035

BASE YEAR: 1974

YEAR BYEAR/AYEAR AYEAR/BYEAR GROWTH%

2009 1.417659 0.705388 8.2857% 2001 1.309184 0.763835 1.0000% 2000 1.296222
0.771473 1.0000% 1999 1.283388 0.779188 1.0000% 1998 1.270681 0.786980 1.0000% 1997
1.258100 0.794849 1.0000% 1996 1.245644 0.802798 1.0000% 1995 1.233310 0.810826
0.9992% 1994 1.221109 0.818928 1.0008% 1993 1.209009 0.827123 1.0000% 1992 1.197039
0.835395 0.9295% 1991 1.186015 0.843160 1.2505% 1990 1.171367 0.853704 0.7224% 1989
1.162965 0.859871 1.1077% 1988 1.150224 0.869396 0.8834% 1987 1.140153 0.877076
0.5594% 1986 1.133810 0.881982 1.3056% 1985 1.119198 0.893497 0.7673% 1984 1.110676
0.900353 0.8149% 1983 1.101698 0.907690 0.9737% 1982 1.091073 0.916529 0.9508% 1981
1.080797 0.925243 0.9031% 1980 1.071124 0.933599 2.2701% 1979 1.047349 0.954792
1.0042% 1978 1.036936 0.964380 0.9896% 1977 1.026775 0.973923 0.9103% 1976 1.017512
0.982789 0.8394% 1975 1.009042 0.991039 0.9042% 1974 1.000000 1.000000 1.1568% 1973
0.988564 1.011568 0.9427% 1972 0.979332 1.021104 0.7426% 1971 0.972113 1.028687
1.4697% 1970 0.958032 1.043806 0.6968% 1969 0.951403 1.051080 0.8565% 1968 0.943323
1.060082 1.5090% 1967 0.929299 1.076079 0.9949% 1966 0.920145 1.086785 1.0575% 1965
0.910516 1.098278 1.1300% 1964 0.900342 1.110689 1.5537% 1963 0.886568 1.127945

47

1.4658% 1962 0.873760 1.144478 1.5364% 1961 0.860539 1.162063 2.1586% 1960 0.842355
1.187147 -1.6655% 1959 0.856622 1.167376 4.3080% 1958 0.821243 1.217666 2.1130%
1957 0.804250 1.243395 1.9895% 1956 0.788561 1.268132 2.1231% 1955 0.772167 1.295056
1.4496% 1954 0.761134 1.313829 2.1573% 1953 0.745061 1.342172 1.2298% 1952 0.736010
1.358677 1.6814% 1951 0.723840 1.381522 1.6233% 1950 0.712277 1.403947 1.4265% 1949
0.702259 1.423975 1.7790% 1948 0.689984 1.449308 1.8242% 1947 0.677623 1.475746 -
2.6320% 1946 0.695941 1.436904 3.1768% 1945 0.674513 1.482552 6.4754% 1944 0.633492
1.578553 -0.3437% 1943 0.635676 1.573128 0.6562% 1942 0.631532 1.583451 0.6633%
1941 0.627371 1.593954 -5.6614% 1940 0.665020 1.503713 8.0381% 1939 0.615542
1.624584 0.8126% 1938 0.610581 1.637785 0.7762% 1937 0.605877 1.650499 0.6029% 1936
0.602247 1.660449 0.5244% 1935 0.599105 1.669156 -3.0364% 1934 0.617866 1.618475
4.6271% 1933 0.590541 1.693364 1.3921% 1932 0.582432 1.716937 -0.2051% 1931
0.583629 1.713416 0.8886% 1930 0.578489 1.728641 1.0126% 1929 0.572690 1.746145
1.1526% 1928 0.566164 1.766271 1.2160% 1927 0.559363 1.787749 1.4086% 1926 0.551593
1.812931 1.7667% 1925 0.542017 1.844960 1.4465% 1924 0.534289 1.871647 1.7700% 1923
0.524996 1.904775 1.6165% 1922 0.516645 1.935566 1.3736% 1921 0.509644 1.962154
2.3393% 1920 0.497994 2.008055 1.3140% 1919 0.491536 2.034441 0.7676% 1918 0.487791
2.050058 0.3870% 1917 0.485911 2.057991 1.3274% 1916 0.479545 2.085310 1.4083% 1915
0.472885 2.114677 1.4458% 1914 0.466146 2.145251 1.9424% 1913 0.457264 2.186920
1.9857% 1912 0.448361 2.230345 1.5634% 1911 0.441459 2.265215 1.8169% 1910 0.433581
2.306372 1.8781% 1909 0.425589 2.349687 2.0082% 1908 0.417210 2.396874 1.9603% 1907
0.409189 2.443859 1.8264% 1906 0.401850 2.488492 1.9357% 1905 0.394219 2.536661
2.0148% 1904 0.386433 2.587771 2.1335% 1903 0.378361 2.642982 1.8151% 1902 0.371615
2.690956 1.8943% 1901 0.364706 2.741932 3.0255% 1900 0.353996 2.824889 0.6278% 1899
0.351788 2.842625 1.7757% 1898 0.345650 2.893100 1.8078% 1897 0.339512 2.945400
1.8396% 1896 0.333380 2.999584 1.8755% 1895 0.327242 3.055842 1.9114% 1894 0.321104
3.114251 1.9486% 1893 0.314967 3.174937 1.9858% 1892 0.308834 3.237985 2.0276% 1891
0.302697 3.303639 2.6465% 1890 0.294982 3.391070 1.5328% 1889 0.290440 3.443049
2.0811% 1888 0.284519 3.514703 2.1599% 1887 0.278504 3.590616 2.2075% 1886 0.272488
3.669880 2.2592% 1885 0.266469 3.752789 2.3095% 1884 0.260453 3.839461 2.3641% 1883
0.254438 3.930231 2.4214% 1882 0.248423 4.025397 2.4815% 1881 0.242407 4.125286
3.7644% 1880 0.233613 4.280578 0.9432% 1879 0.231430 4.320954 2.1464% 1878 0.226567
4.413698 2.1913% 1877 0.221709 4.510416 2.2426% 1876 0.216846 4.611567 2.2941% 1875
0.211983 4.717359 2.3456% 1874 0.207125 4.828009 2.4043% 1873 0.202262 4.944089
2.4635% 1872 0.197399 5.065889 2.5258% 1871 0.192536 5.193842 5.9947% 1870 0.181647
5.505196 -1.0968% 1869 0.183661 5.444816 2.1930% 1868 0.179720 5.564219 2.2394%
1867 0.175783 5.688824 2.2935% 1866 0.171842 5.819298 2.3445% 1865 0.167906 5.955730
2.4037% 1864 0.163964 6.098887 2.4599% 1863 0.160028 6.248913 2.5250% 1862 0.156087
6.406698 2.5872% 1861 0.152150 6.572455 2.9504% 1860 0.147790 6.766369 2.4012% 1859
0.144324 6.928846 2.7627% 1858 0.140444 7.120270 2.8412% 1857 0.136564 7.322571
2.9243% 1856 0.132684 7.536704 3.0161% 1855 0.128799 7.764022 3.1061% 1854 0.124919
8.005177 3.2056% 1853 0.121039 8.261793 3.3118% 1852 0.117159 8.535406 3.4252% 1851
0.113279 8.827763 4.0106% 1850 0.108911 9.181810 2.3254% 1849 0.106436 9.395321
2.7841% 1848 0.103553 9.656894 2.8590% 1847 0.100675 9.932986 2.9432% 1846 0.097796
10.225329 3.0324% 1845 0.094918 10.535403 3.1325% 1844 0.092035 10.865425 3.2284%
1843 0.089157 11.216200 3.3361% 1842 0.086278 11.590379 3.4512% 1841 0.083400
11.990385 3.8105% 1840 0.080339 12.447277 2.3861% 1839 0.078467 12.744276 2.5824%
1838 0.076491 13.073383 2.6573% 1837 0.074511 13.420785 2.7232% 1836 0.072536
13.786261 2.7994% 1835 0.070561 14.172199 2.8871% 1834 0.068581 14.581367 2.9657%
1833 0.066605 15.013805 3.0563% 1832 0.064621 15.472675 3.1604% 1831 0.062650
15.961677 3.4660% 1830 0.060551 16.514903 2.4653% 1829 0.059095 16.922045 2.6804%
1828 0.057552 17.375623 10.3427% 1827 0.052157 19.172723 -4.2314% 1826 0.054462
18.361442 2.9150% 1825 0.052919 18.896685 3.0026% 1824 0.051377 19.464070 3.0955%
1823 0.049834 20.066582 3.1944% 1822 0.048291 20.707587 3.3102% 1821 0.046744
21.393048 3.2277% 1820 0.045283 22.083559 2.6573% 1819 0.044110 22.670381 2.6261%
1818 0.042982 23.265729 2.6969% 1817 0.041853 23.893190 2.7717% 1816 0.040724

24.555434 2.8507% 1815 0.039595 25.255434 2.9343% 1814 0.038467 25.996515 3.0231% 1813 0.037338 26.782403 3.1039% 1812 0.036214 27.613701 3.2172% 1811 0.035085 28.502078 3.0969% 1810 0.034031 29.384763 2.9144% 1809 0.033068 30.241146 2.8225% 1808 0.032160 31.094691 2.9199% 1807 0.031247 32.002634 2.9918% 1806 0.030340 32.960084 3.0841% 1805 0.029432 33.976590 3.1822% 1804 0.028524 35.057791 3.2868% 1803 0.027617 36.210065 3.3985% 1802 0.026709 37.440659 3.5180% 1801 0.025801 38.757838 3.3999% 1800 0.024953 40.075584 2.8419% 1799 0.024263 41.214480 2.7485% 1798 0.023614 42.347242 2.8261% 1797 0.022965 43.544030 3.7832% 1796 0.022128 45.191392 2.1272% 1795 0.021667 46.152702 3.0879% 1794 0.021018 47.577870 3.1625% 1793 0.020374 49.082525 3.2904% 1792 0.019725 50.697544 3.4024% 1791 0.019076 52.422461 3.2296% 1790 0.018479 54.115477 41.3145% 1780 0.013077 76.472989 29.4353% 1770 0.010103 98.983055 83.4728% 1750 0.005506 181.607021 29.2845% 1740 0.004259 234.789642 94.2514% 1720 0.002193 456.082154 85.8111% 1700 0.001180 847.451176 19.2490% 1690 0.000990 1010.577471 88.0250% 1670 0.000526 1900.138517

BASE YEAR: 1973

YEAR BYEAR/AYEAR AYEAR/BYEAR GROWTH%

2009 1.434058 0.697322 8.2857% 2001 1.324328 0.755100 1.0000% 2000 1.311216 0.762651 1.0000% 1999 1.298234 0.770277 1.0000% 1998 1.285380 0.777980 1.0000% 1997 1.272653 0.785760 1.0000% 1996 1.260053 0.793617 1.0000% 1995 1.247577 0.801554 0.9992% 1994 1.235234 0.809563 1.0008% 1993 1.222995 0.817665 1.0000% 1992 1.210886 0.825841 0.9295% 1991 1.199735 0.833518 1.2505% 1990 1.184917 0.843941 0.7224% 1989 1.176418 0.850038 1.1077% 1988 1.163530 0.859454 0.8834% 1987 1.153342 0.867046 0.5594% 1986 1.146926 0.871896 1.3056% 1985 1.132145 0.883279 0.7673% 1984 1.123524 0.890057 0.8149% 1983 1.114442 0.897310 0.9737% 1982 1.103695 0.906048 0.9508% 1981 1.093300 0.914662 0.9031% 1980 1.083515 0.922922 2.2701% 1979 1.059464 0.943873 1.0042% 1978 1.048931 0.953352 0.9896% 1977 1.038652 0.962786 0.9103% 1976 1.029282 0.971551 0.8394% 1975 1.020714 0.979706 0.9042% 1974 1.011568 0.988564 1.1568% 1973 1.000000 1.000000 0.9427% 1972 0.990661 1.009427 0.7426% 1971 0.983358 1.016923 1.4697% 1970 0.969115 1.031870 0.6968% 1969 0.962409 1.039060 0.8565% 1968 0.954235 1.047960 1.5090% 1967 0.940049 1.063774 0.9949% 1966 0.930789 1.074357 1.0575% 1965 0.921049 1.085718 1.1300% 1964 0.910757 1.097987 1.5537% 1963 0.896824 1.115046 1.4658% 1962 0.883868 1.131391 1.5364% 1961 0.870493 1.148774 2.1586% 1960 0.852100 1.173572 -1.6655% 1959 0.866532 1.154026 4.3080% 1958 0.830743 1.203741 2.1130% 1957 0.813553 1.229176 1.9895% 1956 0.797683 1.253630 2.1231% 1955 0.781100 1.280246 1.4496% 1954 0.769939 1.298805 2.1573% 1953 0.753680 1.326823 1.2298% 1952 0.744524 1.343140 1.6814% 1951 0.732213 1.365723 1.6233% 1950 0.720517 1.387892 1.4265% 1949 0.710383 1.407691 1.7790% 1948 0.697966 1.432735 1.8242% 1947 0.685462 1.458870 -2.6320% 1946 0.703991 1.420472 3.1768% 1945 0.682316 1.465598 6.4754% 1944 0.640820 1.560501 -0.3437% 1943 0.643030 1.555138 0.6562% 1942 0.638837 1.565343 0.6633% 1941 0.634628 1.575726 -5.6614% 1940 0.672713 1.486518 8.0381% 1939 0.622663 1.606006 0.8126% 1938 0.617644 1.619056 0.7762% 1937 0.612886 1.631624 0.6029% 1936 0.609213 1.641461 0.5244% 1935 0.606035 1.650069 -3.0364% 1934 0.625013 1.599967 4.6271% 1933 0.597372 1.673999 1.3921% 1932 0.589170 1.697303 -0.2051% 1931 0.590381 1.693822 0.8886% 1930 0.585181 1.708873 1.0126% 1929 0.579315 1.726177 1.1526% 1928 0.572714 1.746073 1.2160% 1927 0.565833 1.767305 1.4086% 1926 0.557974 1.792199 1.7667% 1925 0.548287 1.823862 1.4465% 1924 0.540469 1.850244 1.7700% 1923 0.531070 1.882993 1.6165% 1922 0.522621 1.913432 1.3736% 1921 0.515540 1.939715 2.3393% 1920 0.503755 1.985091 1.3140% 1919 0.497222 2.011176 0.7676% 1918 0.493434 2.026614 0.3870% 1917 0.491532 2.034457 1.3274% 1916 0.485092 2.061463 1.4083% 1915 0.478356 2.090495 1.4458% 1914 0.471538 2.120719 1.9424% 1913 0.462554 2.161911 1.9857% 1912 0.453548 2.204840 1.5634% 1911 0.446566 2.239311 1.8169% 1910 0.438597 2.279997 1.8781% 1909 0.430512 2.322817 2.0082% 1908 0.422036 2.369464 1.9603% 1907 0.413922 2.415912 1.8264% 1906 0.406498 2.460035 1.9357% 1905 0.398779 2.507653 2.0148% 1904 0.390903 2.558178 2.1335% 1903 0.382737 2.612758 1.8151% 1902 0.375914 2.660183 1.8943% 1901 0.368925 2.710576 3.0255% 1900 0.358091 2.792585 0.6278% 1899 0.355857 2.810118 1.7757% 1898 0.349648 2.860016 1.8078% 1897 0.343440 2.911718

1.8396% 1896 0.337236 2.965282 1.8755% 1895 0.331028 3.020897 1.9114% 1894 0.324819
3.078638 1.9486% 1893 0.318610 3.138629 1.9858% 1892 0.312407 3.200956 2.0276% 1891
0.306198 3.265860 2.6465% 1890 0.298303 3.352291 1.5328% 1889 0.293800 3.403676
2.0811% 1888 0.287810 3.474511 2.1599% 1887 0.281725 3.549555 2.2075% 1886 0.275641
3.627913 2.2592% 1885 0.269551 3.709873 2.3095% 1884 0.263466 3.795554 2.3641% 1883
0.257381 3.885287 2.4214% 1882 0.251296 3.979364 2.4815% 1881 0.245212 4.078111
3.7644% 1880 0.236316 4.231627 0.9432% 1879 0.234108 4.271541 2.1464% 1878 0.229188
4.363225 2.1913% 1877 0.224274 4.458836 2.2426% 1876 0.219355 4.558831 2.2941% 1875
0.214435 4.663413 2.3456% 1874 0.209521 4.772797 2.4043% 1873 0.204601 4.887551
2.4635% 1872 0.199682 5.007958 2.5258% 1871 0.194763 5.134447 5.9947% 1870 0.183748
5.442241 -1.0968% 1869 0.185786 5.382551 2.1930% 1868 0.181799 5.500589 2.2394%
1867 0.177817 5.623769 2.2935% 1866 0.173830 5.752751 2.3445% 1865 0.169848 5.887622
2.4037% 1864 0.165861 6.029143 2.4599% 1863 0.161879 6.177453 2.5250% 1862 0.157892
6.333434 2.5872% 1861 0.153910 6.497295 2.9504% 1860 0.149499 6.688992 2.4012% 1859
0.145994 6.849611 2.7627% 1858 0.142069 7.038845 2.8412% 1857 0.138144 7.238833
2.9243% 1856 0.134219 7.450518 3.0161% 1855 0.130289 7.675236 3.1061% 1854 0.126364
7.913633 3.2056% 1853 0.122439 8.167314 3.3118% 1852 0.118514 8.437799 3.4252% 1851
0.114589 8.726812 4.0106% 1850 0.110171 9.076810 2.3254% 1849 0.107667 9.287879
2.7841% 1848 0.104751 9.546462 2.8590% 1847 0.101839 9.819396 2.9432% 1846 0.098928
10.108397 3.0324% 1845 0.096016 10.414924 3.1325% 1844 0.093100 10.741172 3.2284%
1843 0.090188 11.087936 3.3361% 1842 0.087277 11.457836 3.4512% 1841 0.084365
11.853268 3.8105% 1840 0.081268 12.304935 2.3861% 1839 0.079374 12.598538 2.5824%
1838 0.077376 12.923881 2.6573% 1837 0.075373 13.267310 2.7232% 1836 0.073375
13.628607 2.7994% 1835 0.071377 14.010131 2.8871% 1834 0.069374 14.414621 2.9657%
1833 0.067376 14.842113 3.0563% 1832 0.065378 15.295736 3.1604% 1831 0.063375
15.779146 3.4660% 1830 0.061252 16.326046 2.4653% 1829 0.059778 16.728532 2.6804%
1828 0.058218 17.176922 10.3427% 1827 0.052761 18.953472 -4.2314% 1826 0.055092
18.151468 2.9150% 1825 0.053531 18.680590 3.0026% 1824 0.051971 19.241487 3.0955%
1823 0.050411 19.837108 3.1944% 1822 0.048850 20.470783 3.3102% 1821 0.047285
21.148405 3.2277% 1820 0.045806 21.831021 2.6573% 1819 0.044621 22.411131 2.6261%
1818 0.043479 22.999672 2.6969% 1817 0.042337 23.619957 2.7717% 1816 0.041195
24.274628 2.8507% 1815 0.040053 24.966623 2.9343% 1814 0.038912 25.699230 3.0231%
1813 0.037770 26.476130 3.1039% 1812 0.036633 27.297922 3.2172% 1811 0.035491
28.176139 3.0969% 1810 0.034425 29.048731 2.9144% 1809 0.033450 29.895321 2.8225%
1808 0.032532 30.739105 2.9199% 1807 0.031609 31.636665 2.9918% 1806 0.030691
32.583165 3.0841% 1805 0.029772 33.588047 3.1822% 1804 0.028854 34.656884 3.2868%
1803 0.027936 35.795981 3.3985% 1802 0.027018 37.012502 3.5180% 1801 0.026100
38.314619 3.3999% 1800 0.025242 39.617296 2.8419% 1799 0.024544 40.743167 2.7485%
1798 0.023887 41.862976 2.8261% 1797 0.023231 43.046078 3.7832% 1796 0.022384
44.674601 2.1272% 1795 0.021918 45.624919 3.0879% 1794 0.021261 47.033788 3.1625%
1793 0.020610 48.521237 3.2904% 1792 0.019953 50.117787 3.4024% 1791 0.019296
51.822978 3.2296% 1790 0.018693 53.496634 41.3145% 1780 0.013228 75.598475 29.4353%
1770 0.010220 97.851124 83.4728% 1750 0.005570 179.530236 29.2845% 1740 0.004308
232.104682 94.2514% 1720 0.002218 450.866581 85.8111% 1700 0.001194 837.760064
19.2490% 1690 0.001001 999.020913 88.0250% 1670 0.000532 1878.409294

BASE YEAR: 1972

YEAR BYEAR/AYEAR AYEAR/BYEAR GROWTH%

2009 1.447577 0.690810 8.2857% 2001 1.336813 0.748048 1.0000% 2000 1.323577
0.755528 1.0000% 1999 1.310472 0.763084 1.0000% 1998 1.297497 0.770714 1.0000% 1997
1.284651 0.778422 1.0000% 1996 1.271932 0.786206 1.0000% 1995 1.259338 0.794068
0.9992% 1994 1.246879 0.802002 1.0008% 1993 1.234524 0.810029 1.0000% 1992 1.222301
0.818129 0.9295% 1991 1.211044 0.825734 1.2505% 1990 1.196087 0.836059 0.7224% 1989
1.187508 0.842100 1.1077% 1988 1.174499 0.851427 0.8834% 1987 1.164214 0.858948
0.5594% 1986 1.157738 0.863753 1.3056% 1985 1.142817 0.875030 0.7673% 1984 1.134115
0.881744 0.8149% 1983 1.124948 0.888930 0.9737% 1982 1.114099 0.897586 0.9508% 1981
1.103606 0.906120 0.9031% 1980 1.093729 0.914303 2.2701% 1979 1.069452 0.935059

50

1.0042% 1978 1.058819 0.944448 0.9896% 1977 1.048444 0.953795 0.9103% 1976 1.038986 0.962477 0.8394% 1975 1.030337 0.970557 0.9042% 1974 1.021104 0.979332 1.1568% 1973 1.009427 0.990661 0.9427% 1972 1.000000 1.000000 0.7426% 1971 0.992628 1.007426 1.4697% 1970 0.978251 1.022233 0.6968% 1969 0.971481 1.029356 0.8565% 1968 0.963231 1.038173 1.5090% 1967 0.948911 1.053839 0.9949% 1966 0.939564 1.064324 1.0575% 1965 0.929732 1.075579 1.1300% 1964 0.919343 1.087733 1.5537% 1963 0.905278 1.104633 1.4658% 1962 0.892200 1.120825 1.5364% 1961 0.878700 1.138045 2.1586% 1960 0.860132 1.162612 -1.6655% 1959 0.874700 1.143249 4.3080% 1958 0.838575 1.192500 2.1130% 1957 0.821223 1.217697 1.9895% 1956 0.805203 1.241923 2.1231% 1955 0.788463 1.268290 1.4496% 1954 0.777197 1.286675 2.1573% 1953 0.760785 1.314432 1.2298% 1952 0.751543 1.330596 1.6814% 1951 0.739115 1.352969 1.6233% 1950 0.727309 1.374931 1.4265% 1949 0.717080 1.394545 1.7790% 1948 0.704546 1.419354 1.8242% 1947 0.691924 1.445246 -2.6320% 1946 0.710628 1.407206 3.1768% 1945 0.688748 1.451910 6.4754% 1944 0.646861 1.545928 -0.3437% 1943 0.649092 1.540615 0.6562% 1942 0.644860 1.550725 0.6633% 1941 0.640611 1.561011 -5.6614% 1940 0.679055 1.472635 8.0381% 1939 0.628533 1.591007 0.8126% 1938 0.623466 1.603936 0.7762% 1937 0.618664 1.616387 0.6029% 1936 0.614956 1.626131 0.5244% 1935 0.611748 1.634659 -3.0364% 1934 0.630905 1.585024 4.6271% 1933 0.603003 1.658365 1.3921% 1932 0.594724 1.681452 -0.2051% 1931 0.595946 1.678003 0.8886% 1930 0.590697 1.692914 1.0126% 1929 0.584776 1.710056 1.1526% 1928 0.578113 1.729766 1.2160% 1927 0.571167 1.750800 1.4086% 1926 0.563234 1.775462 1.7667% 1925 0.553456 1.806829 1.4465% 1924 0.545564 1.832964 1.7700% 1923 0.536076 1.865407 1.6165% 1922 0.527548 1.895562 1.3736% 1921 0.520400 1.921600 2.3393% 1920 0.508504 1.966553 1.3140% 1919 0.501909 1.992393 0.7676% 1918 0.498085 2.007688 0.3870% 1917 0.496165 2.015457 1.3274% 1916 0.489665 2.042211 1.4083% 1915 0.482865 2.070971 1.4458% 1914 0.475983 2.100914 1.9424% 1913 0.466914 2.141721 1.9857% 1912 0.457823 2.184249 1.5634% 1911 0.450776 2.218398 1.8169% 1910 0.442732 2.258704 1.8781% 1909 0.434570 2.301124 2.0082% 1908 0.426015 2.347336 1.9603% 1907 0.417824 2.393350 1.8264% 1906 0.410330 2.437061 1.9357% 1905 0.402539 2.484234 2.0148% 1904 0.394588 2.534288 2.1335% 1903 0.386345 2.588357 1.8151% 1902 0.379458 2.635340 1.8943% 1901 0.372403 2.685262 3.0255% 1900 0.361467 2.766505 0.6278% 1899 0.359212 2.783874 1.7757% 1898 0.352945 2.833306 1.8078% 1897 0.346677 2.884525 1.8396% 1896 0.340415 2.937589 1.8755% 1895 0.334148 2.992685 1.9114% 1894 0.327881 3.049886 1.9486% 1893 0.321614 3.109318 1.9858% 1892 0.315352 3.171063 2.0276% 1891 0.309085 3.235360 2.6465% 1890 0.301116 3.320984 1.5328% 1889 0.296570 3.371889 2.0811% 1888 0.290524 3.442062 2.1599% 1887 0.284381 3.516406 2.2075% 1886 0.278239 3.594032 2.2592% 1885 0.272092 3.675227 2.3095% 1884 0.265950 3.760108 2.3641% 1883 0.259808 3.849002 2.4214% 1882 0.253665 3.942201 2.4815% 1881 0.247523 4.040026 3.7644% 1880 0.238543 4.192108 0.9432% 1879 0.236314 4.231649 2.1464% 1878 0.231349 4.322477 2.1913% 1877 0.226388 4.417195 2.2426% 1876 0.221422 4.516256 2.2941% 1875 0.216457 4.619861 2.3456% 1874 0.211496 4.728224 2.4043% 1873 0.206530 4.841906 2.4635% 1872 0.201565 4.961188 2.5258% 1871 0.196599 5.086497 5.9947% 1870 0.185480 5.391416 -1.0968% 1869 0.187537 5.332283 2.1930% 1868 0.183513 5.449219 2.2394% 1867 0.179493 5.571249 2.2935% 1866 0.175469 5.699026 2.3445% 1865 0.171449 5.832638 2.4037% 1864 0.167425 5.972837 2.4599% 1863 0.163405 6.119761 2.5250% 1862 0.159381 6.274286 2.5872% 1861 0.155361 6.436617 2.9504% 1860 0.150909 6.626524 2.4012% 1859 0.147370 6.785642 2.7627% 1858 0.143408 6.973110 2.8412% 1857 0.139446 7.171230 2.9243% 1856 0.135484 7.380937 3.0161% 1855 0.131517 7.603557 3.1061% 1854 0.127555 7.839727 3.2056% 1853 0.123594 8.091040 3.3118% 1852 0.119632 8.358998 3.4252% 1851 0.115670 8.645313 4.0106% 1850 0.111209 8.992042 2.3254% 1849 0.108682 9.201140 2.7841% 1848 0.105738 9.457308 2.8590% 1847 0.102799 9.727693 2.9432% 1846 0.099860 10.013994 3.0324% 1845 0.096921 10.317659 3.1325% 1844 0.093977 10.640861 3.2284% 1843 0.091038 10.984386 3.3361% 1842 0.088099 11.350831 3.4512% 1841 0.085160 11.742570 3.8105% 1840 0.082034 12.190020 2.3861% 1839 0.080123 12.480880 2.5824% 1838 0.078106 12.803185 2.6573% 1837 0.076084 13.143407 2.7232% 1836 0.074067 13.501329 2.7994% 1835 0.072050 13.879291 2.8871% 1834 0.070028 14.280003 2.9657% 1833 0.068011 14.703502 3.0563% 1832 0.065994 15.152889 3.1604% 1831 0.063972

15.631784 3.4660% 1830 0.061829 16.173577 2.4653% 1829 0.060342 16.572304 2.6804% 1828 0.058766 17.016507 10.3427% 1827 0.053258 18.776465 -4.2314% 1826 0.055611 17.981952 2.9150% 1825 0.054036 18.506132 3.0026% 1824 0.052461 19.061791 3.0955% 1823 0.050886 19.651850 3.1944% 1822 0.049311 20.279607 3.3102% 1821 0.047731 20.950900 3.2277% 1820 0.046238 21.627141 2.6573% 1819 0.045041 22.201834 2.6261% 1818 0.043889 22.784878 2.6969% 1817 0.042736 23.399371 2.7717% 1816 0.041584 24.047927 2.8507% 1815 0.040431 24.733460 2.9343% 1814 0.039278 25.459225 3.0231% 1813 0.038126 26.228870 3.1039% 1812 0.036978 27.042987 3.2172% 1811 0.035826 27.913003 3.0969% 1810 0.034749 28.777445 2.9144% 1809 0.033765 29.616129 2.8225% 1808 0.032839 30.452033 2.9199% 1807 0.031907 31.341210 2.9918% 1806 0.030980 32.278871 3.0841% 1805 0.030053 33.274369 3.1822% 1804 0.029126 34.333223 3.2868% 1803 0.028199 35.461683 3.3985% 1802 0.027273 36.666843 3.5180% 1801 0.026346 37.956799 3.3999% 1800 0.025479 39.247310 2.8419% 1799 0.024775 40.362667 2.7485% 1798 0.024113 41.472018 2.8261% 1797 0.023450 42.644071 3.7832% 1796 0.022595 44.257386 2.1272% 1795 0.022124 45.198828 3.0879% 1794 0.021462 46.594540 3.1625% 1793 0.020804 48.068098 3.2904% 1792 0.020141 49.649738 3.4024% 1791 0.019478 51.339004 3.2296% 1790 0.018869 52.997030 41.3145% 1780 0.013352 74.892462 29.4353% 1770 0.010316 96.937293 83.4728% 1750 0.005623 177.853604 29.2845% 1740 0.004349 229.937058 94.2514% 1720 0.002239 446.655942 85.8111% 1700 0.001205 829.936230 19.2490% 1690 0.001010 989.691065 88.0250% 1670 0.000537 1860.866845

BASE YEAR: 1971

YEAR BYEAR/AYEAR AYEAR/BYEAR GROWTH%

2009 1.458327 0.685717 8.2857% 2001 1.346741 0.742533 1.0000% 2000 1.333406 0.749959 1.0000% 1999 1.320204 0.757458 1.0000% 1998 1.307133 0.765033 1.0000% 1997 1.294191 0.772683 1.0000% 1996 1.281377 0.780410 1.0000% 1995 1.268690 0.788214 0.9992% 1994 1.256139 0.796090 1.0008% 1993 1.243692 0.804057 1.0000% 1992 1.231378 0.812098 0.9295% 1991 1.220038 0.819647 1.2505% 1990 1.204970 0.829896 0.7224% 1989 1.196327 0.835892 1.1077% 1988 1.183221 0.845151 0.8834% 1987 1.172860 0.852617 0.5594% 1986 1.166336 0.857386 1.3056% 1985 1.151304 0.868580 0.7673% 1984 1.142538 0.875245 0.8149% 1983 1.133302 0.882377 0.9737% 1982 1.122373 0.890969 0.9508% 1981 1.111802 0.899441 0.9031% 1980 1.101851 0.907563 2.2701% 1979 1.077394 0.928166 1.0042% 1978 1.066682 0.937486 0.9896% 1977 1.056230 0.946764 0.9103% 1976 1.046701 0.955382 0.8394% 1975 1.037988 0.963402 0.9042% 1974 1.028687 0.972113 1.1568% 1973 1.016923 0.983358 0.9427% 1972 1.007426 0.992628 0.7426% 1971 1.000000 1.000000 1.4697% 1970 0.985516 1.014697 0.6968% 1969 0.978694 1.021768 0.8565% 1968 0.970384 1.030520 1.5090% 1967 0.955958 1.046071 0.9949% 1966 0.946541 1.056478 1.0575% 1965 0.936636 1.067650 1.1300% 1964 0.926171 1.079715 1.5537% 1963 0.912001 1.096490 1.4658% 1962 0.898826 1.112562 1.5364% 1961 0.885225 1.129656 2.1586% 1960 0.866520 1.154041 -1.6655% 1959 0.881196 1.134821 4.3080% 1958 0.844802 1.183709 2.1130% 1957 0.827321 1.208720 1.9895% 1956 0.811183 1.232768 2.1231% 1955 0.794319 1.258941 1.4496% 1954 0.782969 1.277190 2.1573% 1953 0.766435 1.304742 1.2298% 1952 0.757124 1.320788 1.6814% 1951 0.744604 1.342995 1.6233% 1950 0.732711 1.364796 1.4265% 1949 0.722405 1.384265 1.7790% 1948 0.709778 1.408891 1.8242% 1947 0.697062 1.434592 - 2.6320% 1946 0.715905 1.396833 3.1768% 1945 0.693863 1.441208 6.4754% 1944 0.651665 1.534532 -0.3437% 1943 0.653912 1.529258 0.6562% 1942 0.649649 1.539293 0.6633% 1941 0.645368 1.549503 -5.6614% 1940 0.684098 1.461779 8.0381% 1939 0.633200 1.579279 0.8126% 1938 0.628096 1.592112 0.7762% 1937 0.623258 1.604471 0.6029% 1936 0.619523 1.614144 0.5244% 1935 0.616292 1.622609 -3.0364% 1934 0.635590 1.573340 4.6271% 1933 0.607482 1.646141 1.3921% 1932 0.599141 1.669057 -0.2051% 1931 0.600372 1.665634 0.8886% 1930 0.595084 1.680435 1.0126% 1929 0.589119 1.697450 1.1526% 1928 0.582406 1.717015 1.2160% 1927 0.575409 1.737894 1.4086% 1926 0.567417 1.762374 1.7667% 1925 0.557566 1.793509 1.4465% 1924 0.549616 1.819453 1.7700% 1923 0.540057 1.851656 1.6165% 1922 0.531466 1.881589 1.3736% 1921 0.524264 1.907435 2.3393% 1920 0.512280 1.952056 1.3140% 1919 0.505636 1.977706 0.7676% 1918 0.501784 1.992888 0.3870% 1917 0.499850 2.000600 1.3274% 1916 0.493302 2.027157 1.4083% 1915 0.486451 2.055705 1.4458% 1914 0.479518 2.085426 1.9424% 1913 0.470382 2.125933

1.9857% 1912 0.461223 2.168147 1.5634% 1911 0.454123 2.202044 1.8169% 1910 0.446020 2.242054 1.8781% 1909 0.437798 2.284161 2.0082% 1908 0.429179 2.330032 1.9603% 1907 0.420927 2.375707 1.8264% 1906 0.413378 2.419096 1.9357% 1905 0.405528 2.465921 2.0148% 1904 0.397519 2.515606 2.1335% 1903 0.389215 2.569277 1.8151% 1902 0.382276 2.615913 1.8943% 1901 0.375169 2.665468 3.0255% 1900 0.364151 2.746111 0.6278% 1899 0.361879 2.763352 1.7757% 1898 0.355566 2.812420 1.8078% 1897 0.349252 2.863262 1.8396% 1896 0.342943 2.915934 1.8755% 1895 0.336630 2.970624 1.9114% 1894 0.330316 3.027404 1.9486% 1893 0.324002 3.086397 1.9858% 1892 0.317694 3.147687 2.0276% 1891 0.311380 3.211510 2.6465% 1890 0.303352 3.296503 1.5328% 1889 0.298772 3.347033 2.0811% 1888 0.292681 3.416689 2.1599% 1887 0.286493 3.490484 2.2075% 1886 0.280305 3.567538 2.2592% 1885 0.274113 3.648134 2.3095% 1884 0.267925 3.732390 2.3641% 1883 0.261737 3.820628 2.4214% 1882 0.255549 3.913141 2.4815% 1881 0.249361 4.010244 3.7644% 1880 0.240315 4.161206 0.9432% 1879 0.238069 4.200455 2.1464% 1878 0.233067 4.290613 2.1913% 1877 0.228069 4.384633 2.2426% 1876 0.223067 4.482964 2.2941% 1875 0.218064 4.585805 2.3456% 1874 0.213067 4.693370 2.4043% 1873 0.208064 4.806213 2.4635% 1872 0.203062 4.924616 2.5258% 1871 0.198059 5.049001 5.9947% 1870 0.186857 5.351672 -1.0968% 1869 0.188930 5.292976 2.1930% 1868 0.184875 5.409049 2.2394% 1867 0.180826 5.530180 2.2935% 1866 0.176772 5.657015 2.3445% 1865 0.172722 5.789642 2.4037% 1864 0.168668 5.928807 2.4599% 1863 0.164619 6.074649 2.5250% 1862 0.160564 6.228034 2.5872% 1861 0.156515 6.389169 2.9504% 1860 0.152029 6.577675 2.4012% 1859 0.148464 6.735621 2.7627% 1858 0.144473 6.921707 2.8412% 1857 0.140482 7.118366 2.9243% 1856 0.136490 7.326528 3.0161% 1855 0.132494 7.547506 3.1061% 1854 0.128503 7.781936 3.2056% 1853 0.124511 8.031396 3.3118% 1852 0.120520 8.297379 3.4252% 1851 0.116529 8.581583 4.0106% 1850 0.112035 8.925756 2.3254% 1849 0.109489 9.133313 2.7841% 1848 0.106524 9.387592 2.8590% 1847 0.103563 9.655984 2.9432% 1846 0.100602 9.940175 3.0324% 1845 0.097641 10.241601 3.1325% 1844 0.094675 10.562420 3.2284% 1843 0.091714 10.903413 3.3361% 1842 0.088754 11.267157 3.4512% 1841 0.085793 11.656009 3.8105% 1840 0.082644 12.100159 2.3861% 1839 0.080718 12.388876 2.5824% 1838 0.078686 12.708805 2.6573% 1837 0.076649 13.046519 2.7232% 1836 0.074617 13.401803 2.7994% 1835 0.072585 13.776978 2.8871% 1834 0.070548 14.174736 2.9657% 1833 0.068516 14.595114 3.0563% 1832 0.066484 15.041188 3.1604% 1831 0.064447 15.516553 3.4660% 1830 0.062288 16.054351 2.4653% 1829 0.060790 16.450139 2.6804% 1828 0.059203 16.891068 10.3427% 1827 0.053654 18.638052 -4.2314% 1826 0.056024 17.849396 2.9150% 1825 0.054437 18.369712 3.0026% 1824 0.052851 18.921274 3.0955% 1823 0.051264 19.506984 3.1944% 1822 0.049672 20.130113 3.3102% 1821 0.048085 20.796458 3.2277% 1820 0.046582 21.467714 2.6573% 1819 0.045376 22.038170 2.6261% 1818 0.044215 22.616917 2.6969% 1817 0.043054 23.226879 2.7717% 1816 0.041892 23.870655 2.8507% 1815 0.040731 24.551134 2.9343% 1814 0.039570 25.271549 3.0231% 1813 0.038409 26.035521 3.1039% 1812 0.037253 26.843636 3.2172% 1811 0.036092 27.707239 3.0969% 1810 0.035007 28.565308 2.9144% 1809 0.034016 29.397810 2.8225% 1808 0.033082 30.227552 2.9199% 1807 0.032144 31.110175 2.9918% 1806 0.031210 32.040924 3.0841% 1805 0.030276 33.029083 3.1822% 1804 0.029343 34.080132 3.2868% 1803 0.028409 35.200272 3.3985% 1802 0.027475 36.396549 3.5180% 1801 0.026541 37.676996 3.3999% 1800 0.025669 38.957994 2.8419% 1799 0.024959 40.065129 2.7485% 1798 0.024292 41.166302 2.8261% 1797 0.023624 42.329715 3.7832% 1796 0.022763 43.931137 2.1272% 1795 0.022289 44.865639 3.0879% 1794 0.021621 46.251063 3.1625% 1793 0.020958 47.713758 3.2904% 1792 0.020291 49.283739 3.4024% 1791 0.019623 50.960552 3.2296% 1790 0.019009 52.606356 41.3145% 1780 0.013452 74.340383 29.4353% 1770 0.010393 96.222708 83.4728% 1750 0.005664 176.542535 29.2845% 1740 0.004381 228.242049 94.2514% 1720 0.002255 443.363363 85.8111% 1700 0.001214 823.818254 19.2490% 1690 0.001018 982.395437 88.0250% 1670 0.000541 1847.149240

BASE YEAR: 1970

YEAR BYEAR/AYEAR AYEAR/BYEAR GROWTH%

2009 1.479761 0.675785 8.2857% 2001 1.366534 0.731778 1.0000% 2000 1.353004 0.739096 1.0000% 1999 1.339608 0.746487 1.0000% 1998 1.326344 0.753952 1.0000% 1997 1.313212 0.761491 1.0000% 1996 1.300210 0.769106 1.0000% 1995 1.287337 0.776797

0.9992% 1994 1.274601 0.784559 1.0008% 1993 1.261971 0.792411 1.0000% 1992 1.249476
0.800335 0.9295% 1991 1.237969 0.807774 1.2505% 1990 1.222680 0.817876 0.7224% 1989
1.213910 0.823784 1.1077% 1988 1.200611 0.832909 0.8834% 1987 1.190098 0.840267
0.5594% 1986 1.183478 0.844967 1.3056% 1985 1.168225 0.855999 0.7673% 1984 1.159330
0.862567 0.8149% 1983 1.149959 0.869597 0.9737% 1982 1.138869 0.878064 0.9508% 1981
1.128142 0.886413 0.9031% 1980 1.118046 0.894418 2.2701% 1979 1.093229 0.914722
1.0042% 1978 1.082360 0.923907 0.9896% 1977 1.071754 0.933050 0.9103% 1976 1.062085
0.941544 0.8394% 1975 1.053244 0.949448 0.9042% 1974 1.043806 0.958032 1.1568% 1973
1.031870 0.969115 0.9427% 1972 1.022233 0.978251 0.7426% 1971 1.014697 0.985516
1.4697% 1970 1.000000 1.000000 0.6968% 1969 0.993080 1.006968 0.8565% 1968 0.984646
1.015593 1.5090% 1967 0.970008 1.030919 0.9949% 1966 0.960453 1.041176 1.0575% 1965
0.950403 1.052186 1.1300% 1964 0.939783 1.064076 1.5537% 1963 0.925405 1.080608
1.4658% 1962 0.912036 1.096447 1.5364% 1961 0.898236 1.113294 2.1586% 1960 0.879256
1.137326 -1.6655% 1959 0.894148 1.118384 4.3080% 1958 0.857219 1.166564 2.1130%
1957 0.839481 1.191213 1.9895% 1956 0.823105 1.214912 2.1231% 1955 0.805993 1.240705
1.4496% 1954 0.794476 1.258691 2.1573% 1953 0.777699 1.285844 1.2298% 1952 0.768252
1.301657 1.6814% 1951 0.755548 1.323542 1.6233% 1950 0.743479 1.345027 1.4265% 1949
0.733023 1.364214 1.7790% 1948 0.720210 1.388484 1.8242% 1947 0.707307 1.413813 -
2.6320% 1946 0.726427 1.376600 3.1768% 1945 0.704061 1.420332 6.4754% 1944 0.661242
1.512305 -0.3437% 1943 0.663523 1.507107 0.6562% 1942 0.659197 1.516997 0.6633%
1941 0.654853 1.527060 -5.6614% 1940 0.694152 1.440606 8.0381% 1939 0.642507
1.556404 0.8126% 1938 0.637328 1.569052 0.7762% 1937 0.632419 1.581231 0.6029% 1936
0.628629 1.590764 0.5244% 1935 0.625349 1.599106 -3.0364% 1934 0.644932 1.550551
4.6271% 1933 0.616410 1.622297 1.3921% 1932 0.607947 1.644881 -0.2051% 1931
0.609196 1.641508 0.8886% 1930 0.603830 1.656094 1.0126% 1929 0.597777 1.672864
1.1526% 1928 0.590966 1.692145 1.2160% 1927 0.583866 1.712722 1.4086% 1926 0.575756
1.736847 1.7667% 1925 0.565761 1.767531 1.4465% 1924 0.557694 1.793099 1.7700% 1923
0.547994 1.824836 1.6165% 1922 0.539277 1.854335 1.3736% 1921 0.531970 1.879807
2.3393% 1920 0.519810 1.923781 1.3140% 1919 0.513068 1.949060 0.7676% 1918 0.509159
1.964022 0.3870% 1917 0.507197 1.971622 1.3274% 1916 0.500552 1.997794 1.4083% 1915
0.493601 2.025929 1.4458% 1914 0.486566 2.055220 1.9424% 1913 0.477295 2.095140
1.9857% 1912 0.468002 2.136743 1.5634% 1911 0.460798 2.170149 1.8169% 1910 0.452575
2.209579 1.8781% 1909 0.444232 2.251076 2.0082% 1908 0.435486 2.296283 1.9603% 1907
0.427114 2.341296 1.8264% 1906 0.419453 2.384056 1.9357% 1905 0.411488 2.430204
2.0148% 1904 0.403361 2.479168 2.1335% 1903 0.394935 2.532062 1.8151% 1902 0.387894
2.578023 1.8943% 1901 0.380683 2.626860 3.0255% 1900 0.369503 2.706335 0.6278% 1899
0.367198 2.723327 1.7757% 1898 0.360792 2.771684 1.8078% 1897 0.354385 2.821789
1.8396% 1896 0.347984 2.873698 1.8755% 1895 0.341577 2.927596 1.9114% 1894 0.335171
2.983553 1.9486% 1893 0.328764 3.041692 1.9858% 1892 0.322363 3.102094 2.0276% 1891
0.315956 3.164993 2.6465% 1890 0.307810 3.248755 1.5328% 1889 0.303163 3.298553
2.0811% 1888 0.296983 3.367200 2.1599% 1887 0.290704 3.439926 2.2075% 1886 0.284425
3.515864 2.2592% 1885 0.278141 3.595293 2.3095% 1884 0.271863 3.678328 2.3641% 1883
0.265584 3.765289 2.4214% 1882 0.259305 3.856461 2.4815% 1881 0.253026 3.952158
3.7644% 1880 0.243847 4.100933 0.9432% 1879 0.241568 4.139614 2.1464% 1878 0.236492
4.228466 2.1913% 1877 0.231421 4.321124 2.2426% 1876 0.226345 4.418030 2.2941% 1875
0.221269 4.519382 2.3456% 1874 0.216198 4.625389 2.4043% 1873 0.211122 4.736598
2.4635% 1872 0.206046 4.853286 2.5258% 1871 0.200970 4.975869 5.9947% 1870 0.189604
5.274156 -1.0968% 1869 0.191706 5.216310 2.1930% 1868 0.187593 5.330702 2.2394%
1867 0.183484 5.450078 2.2935% 1866 0.179370 5.575076 2.3445% 1865 0.175261 5.705782
2.4037% 1864 0.171147 5.842931 2.4599% 1863 0.167038 5.986661 2.5250% 1862 0.162924
6.137824 2.5872% 1861 0.158815 6.296625 2.9504% 1860 0.154264 6.482401 2.4012% 1859
0.150646 6.638059 2.7627% 1858 0.146596 6.821449 2.8412% 1857 0.142546 7.015260
2.9243% 1856 0.138496 7.220407 3.0161% 1855 0.134441 7.438184 3.1061% 1854 0.130391
7.669219 3.2056% 1853 0.126341 7.915065 3.3118% 1852 0.122291 8.177195 3.4252% 1851
0.118241 8.457283 4.0106% 1850 0.113682 8.796471 2.3254% 1849 0.111099 9.001021
2.7841% 1848 0.108089 9.251617 2.8590% 1847 0.105085 9.516122 2.9432% 1846 0.102080

9.796197 3.0324% 1845 0.099076 10.093257 3.1325% 1844 0.096067 10.409429 3.2284%
1843 0.093062 10.745483 3.3361% 1842 0.090058 11.103958 3.4512% 1841 0.087054
11.487177 3.8105% 1840 0.083858 11.924895 2.3861% 1839 0.081904 12.209429 2.5824%
1838 0.079842 12.524724 2.6573% 1837 0.077775 12.857547 2.7232% 1836 0.075713
13.207684 2.7994% 1835 0.073652 13.577425 2.8871% 1834 0.071585 13.969422 2.9657%
1833 0.069523 14.383711 3.0563% 1832 0.067461 14.823324 3.1604% 1831 0.065395
15.291803 3.4660% 1830 0.063204 15.821812 2.4653% 1829 0.061683 16.211867 2.6804%
1828 0.060073 16.646410 10.3427% 1827 0.054442 18.368090 -4.2314% 1826 0.056848
17.590856 2.9150% 1825 0.055238 18.103636 3.0026% 1824 0.053627 18.647209 3.0955%
1823 0.052017 19.224435 3.1944% 1822 0.050407 19.838539 3.3102% 1821 0.048792
20.495232 3.2277% 1820 0.047266 21.156765 2.6573% 1819 0.046043 21.718959 2.6261%
1818 0.044865 22.289322 2.6969% 1817 0.043686 22.890450 2.7717% 1816 0.042508
23.524901 2.8507% 1815 0.041330 24.195524 2.9343% 1814 0.040152 24.905504 3.0231%
1813 0.038974 25.658410 3.1039% 1812 0.037800 26.454820 3.2172% 1811 0.036622
27.305913 3.0969% 1810 0.035522 28.151554 2.9144% 1809 0.034516 28.971997 2.8225%
1808 0.033569 29.789721 2.9199% 1807 0.032616 30.659560 2.9918% 1806 0.031669
31.576827 3.0841% 1805 0.030721 32.550673 3.1822% 1804 0.029774 33.586499 3.2868%
1803 0.028826 34.690415 3.3985% 1802 0.027879 35.869363 3.5180% 1801 0.026931
37.131264 3.3999% 1800 0.026046 38.393707 2.8419% 1799 0.025326 39.484806 2.7485%
1798 0.024649 40.570029 2.8261% 1797 0.023971 41.716591 3.7832% 1796 0.023097
43.294817 2.1272% 1795 0.022616 44.215783 3.0879% 1794 0.021939 45.581140 3.1625%
1793 0.021266 47.022649 3.2904% 1792 0.020589 48.569889 3.4024% 1791 0.019911
50.222415 3.2296% 1790 0.019288 51.844379 41.3145% 1780 0.013649 73.263600 29.4353%
1770 0.010545 94.828972 83.4728% 1750 0.005748 173.985407 29.2845% 1740 0.004446
224.936080 94.2514% 1720 0.002289 436.941471 85.8111% 1700 0.001232 811.885668
19.2490% 1690 0.001033 968.165941 88.0250% 1670 0.000549 1820.394227

BASE YEAR: 1969

YEAR BYEAR/AYEAR AYEAR/BYEAR GROWTH%

2009 1.490072 0.671109 8.2857% 2001 1.376056 0.726714 1.0000% 2000 1.362432
0.733982 1.0000% 1999 1.348943 0.741321 1.0000% 1998 1.335587 0.748735 1.0000% 1997
1.322363 0.756222 1.0000% 1996 1.309270 0.763784 1.0000% 1995 1.296307 0.771422
0.9992% 1994 1.283482 0.779130 1.0008% 1993 1.270765 0.786928 1.0000% 1992 1.258183
0.794797 0.9295% 1991 1.246596 0.802185 1.2505% 1990 1.231200 0.812216 0.7224% 1989
1.222369 0.818084 1.1077% 1988 1.208977 0.827146 0.8834% 1987 1.198391 0.834452
0.5594% 1986 1.191725 0.839120 1.3056% 1985 1.176366 0.850076 0.7673% 1984 1.167409
0.856598 0.8149% 1983 1.157972 0.863579 0.9737% 1982 1.146805 0.871988 0.9508% 1981
1.136004 0.880279 0.9031% 1980 1.125837 0.888228 2.2701% 1979 1.100847 0.908392
1.0042% 1978 1.089902 0.917514 0.9896% 1977 1.079222 0.926593 0.9103% 1976 1.069486
0.935029 0.8394% 1975 1.060583 0.942878 0.9042% 1974 1.051080 0.951403 1.1568% 1973
1.039060 0.962409 0.9427% 1972 1.029356 0.971481 0.7426% 1971 1.021768 0.978696
1.4697% 1970 1.006968 0.993080 0.6968% 1969 1.000000 1.000000 0.8565% 1968 0.991507
1.008565 1.5090% 1967 0.976768 1.023785 0.9949% 1966 0.967145 1.033971 1.0575% 1965
0.957025 1.044905 1.1300% 1964 0.946331 1.056712 1.5537% 1963 0.931854 1.073130
1.4658% 1962 0.918392 1.088860 1.5364% 1961 0.904495 1.105590 2.1586% 1960 0.885383
1.129455 -1.6655% 1959 0.900378 1.110644 4.3080% 1958 0.863192 1.158491 2.1130%
1957 0.845330 1.182969 1.9895% 1956 0.828841 1.206505 2.1231% 1955 0.811609 1.232120
1.4496% 1954 0.800012 1.249981 2.1573% 1953 0.783119 1.276946 1.2298% 1952 0.773605
1.292649 1.6814% 1951 0.760813 1.314384 1.6233% 1950 0.748660 1.335720 1.4265% 1949
0.738130 1.354774 1.7790% 1948 0.725228 1.378876 1.8242% 1947 0.712236 1.404029 -
2.6320% 1946 0.731489 1.367074 3.1768% 1945 0.708967 1.410504 6.4754% 1944 0.665850
1.501840 -0.3437% 1943 0.668146 1.496678 0.6562% 1942 0.663790 1.506500 0.6633%
1941 0.659416 1.516492 -5.6614% 1940 0.698989 1.430637 8.0381% 1939 0.646984
1.545633 0.8126% 1938 0.641769 1.558194 0.7762% 1937 0.636825 1.570289 0.6029% 1936
0.633009 1.579756 0.5244% 1935 0.629707 1.588040 -3.0364% 1934 0.649426 1.539821
4.6271% 1933 0.620705 1.611071 1.3921% 1932 0.612183 1.633499 -0.2051% 1931
0.613441 1.630149 0.8886% 1930 0.608038 1.644634 1.0126% 1929 0.601943 1.661288

55

1.1526% 1928 0.595084 1.680435 1.2160% 1927 0.587935 1.700870 1.4086% 1926 0.579768
1.724828 1.7667% 1925 0.569703 1.755300 1.4465% 1924 0.561580 1.780691 1.7700% 1923
0.551813 1.812208 1.6165% 1922 0.543035 1.841503 1.3736% 1921 0.535676 1.866799
2.3393% 1920 0.523432 1.910469 1.3140% 1919 0.516643 1.935573 0.7676% 1918 0.512707
1.950431 0.3870% 1917 0.510731 1.957979 1.3274% 1916 0.504040 1.983970 1.4083% 1915
0.497040 2.011910 1.4458% 1914 0.489956 2.040998 1.9424% 1913 0.480621 2.080642
1.9857% 1912 0.471263 2.121957 1.5634% 1911 0.464009 2.155132 1.8169% 1910 0.455729
2.194288 1.8781% 1909 0.447328 2.235499 2.0082% 1908 0.438521 2.280393 1.9603% 1907
0.430090 2.325094 1.8264% 1906 0.422376 2.367559 1.9357% 1905 0.414355 2.413387
2.0148% 1904 0.406172 2.462013 2.1335% 1903 0.397687 2.514540 1.8151% 1902 0.390597
2.560183 1.8943% 1901 0.383335 2.608682 3.0255% 1900 0.372078 2.687607 0.6278% 1899
0.369757 2.704481 1.7757% 1898 0.363306 2.752504 1.8078% 1897 0.356855 2.802262
1.8396% 1896 0.350408 2.853813 1.8755% 1895 0.343957 2.907337 1.9114% 1894 0.337506
2.962907 1.9486% 1893 0.331055 3.020644 1.9858% 1892 0.324609 3.080628 2.0276% 1891
0.318158 3.143091 2.6465% 1890 0.309955 3.226274 1.5328% 1889 0.305276 3.275727
2.0811% 1888 0.299052 3.343899 2.1599% 1887 0.292730 3.416122 2.2075% 1886 0.286407
3.491534 2.2592% 1885 0.280080 3.570414 2.3095% 1884 0.273757 3.652874 2.3641% 1883
0.267435 3.739233 2.4214% 1882 0.261112 3.829774 2.4815% 1881 0.254789 3.924809
3.7644% 1880 0.245546 4.072554 0.9432% 1879 0.243252 4.110968 2.1464% 1878 0.238140
4.199205 2.1913% 1877 0.233034 4.291222 2.2426% 1876 0.227922 4.387457 2.2941% 1875
0.222811 4.488108 2.3456% 1874 0.217705 4.593381 2.4043% 1873 0.212593 4.703820
2.4635% 1872 0.207482 4.819701 2.5258% 1871 0.202370 4.941436 5.9947% 1870 0.190925
5.237659 -1.0968% 1869 0.193042 5.180213 2.1930% 1868 0.188900 5.293814 2.2394%
1867 0.184762 5.412364 2.2935% 1866 0.180620 5.536496 2.3445% 1865 0.176482 5.666298
2.4037% 1864 0.172340 5.802498 2.4599% 1863 0.168202 5.945233 2.5250% 1862 0.164059
6.095351 2.5872% 1861 0.159922 6.253052 2.9504% 1860 0.155339 6.437543 2.4012% 1859
0.151696 6.592124 2.7627% 1858 0.147618 6.774245 2.8412% 1857 0.143540 6.966715
2.9243% 1856 0.139461 7.170442 3.0161% 1855 0.135378 7.386712 3.1061% 1854 0.131300
7.616148 3.2056% 1853 0.127222 7.860293 3.3118% 1852 0.123143 8.120609 3.4252% 1851
0.119065 8.398759 4.0106% 1850 0.114474 8.735600 2.3254% 1849 0.111873 8.938734
2.7841% 1848 0.108842 9.187597 2.8590% 1847 0.105817 9.450271 2.9432% 1846 0.102792
9.728407 3.0324% 1845 0.099766 10.023412 3.1325% 1844 0.096736 10.337396 3.2284%
1843 0.093711 10.671124 3.3361% 1842 0.090686 11.027119 3.4512% 1841 0.087660
11.407686 3.8105% 1840 0.084443 11.842375 2.3861% 1839 0.082475 12.124940 2.5824%
1838 0.080398 12.438053 2.6573% 1837 0.078317 12.768573 2.7232% 1836 0.076241
13.116287 2.7994% 1835 0.074165 13.483470 2.8871% 1834 0.072084 13.872754 2.9657%
1833 0.070008 14.284176 3.0563% 1832 0.067931 14.720747 3.1604% 1831 0.065850
15.185985 3.4660% 1830 0.063644 15.712326 2.4653% 1829 0.062113 16.099682 2.6804%
1828 0.060492 16.531217 10.3427% 1827 0.054822 18.240983 -4.2314% 1826 0.057244
17.469128 2.9150% 1825 0.055622 17.978359 3.0026% 1824 0.054001 18.518171 3.0955%
1823 0.052380 19.091402 3.1944% 1822 0.050758 19.701256 3.3102% 1821 0.049132
20.353406 3.2277% 1820 0.047596 21.010361 2.6573% 1819 0.046364 21.568664 2.6261%
1818 0.045177 22.135080 2.6969% 1817 0.043991 22.732049 2.7717% 1816 0.042804
23.362109 2.8507% 1815 0.041618 24.028091 2.9343% 1814 0.040432 24.733158 3.0231%
1813 0.039245 25.480854 3.1039% 1812 0.038064 26.271753 3.2172% 1811 0.036877
27.116957 3.0969% 1810 0.035770 27.956746 2.9144% 1809 0.034757 28.771512 2.8225%
1808 0.033803 29.583577 2.9199% 1807 0.032844 30.447396 2.9918% 1806 0.031889
31.358317 3.0841% 1805 0.030935 32.325423 3.1822% 1804 0.029981 33.354081 3.2868%
1803 0.029027 34.450358 3.3985% 1802 0.028073 35.621148 3.5180% 1801 0.027119
36.874316 3.3999% 1800 0.026227 38.128024 2.8419% 1799 0.025503 39.211572 2.7485%
1798 0.024820 40.289285 2.8261% 1797 0.024138 41.427913 3.7832% 1796 0.023258
42.995218 2.1272% 1795 0.022774 43.909811 3.0879% 1794 0.022092 45.265719 3.1625%
1793 0.021415 46.697253 3.2904% 1792 0.020732 48.233786 3.4024% 1791 0.020050
49.874877 3.2296% 1790 0.019423 51.485617 41.3145% 1780 0.013744 72.756618 29.4353%
1770 0.010619 94.172757 83.4728% 1750 0.005788 172.781431 29.2845% 1740 0.004477

223.379527 94.2514% 1720 0.002305 433.917846 85.8111% 1700 0.001240 806.267437 19.2490% 1690 0.001040 961.466255 88.0250% 1670 0.000553 1807.797140

BASE YEAR: 1968

YEAR BYEAR/AYEAR AYEAR/BYEAR GROWTH%

2009 1.502835 0.665409 8.2857% 2001 1.387843 0.720543 1.0000% 2000 1.374102 0.727748 1.0000% 1999 1.360497 0.735026 1.0000% 1998 1.347027 0.742376 1.0000% 1997 1.333690 0.749800 1.0000% 1996 1.320485 0.757298 1.0000% 1995 1.307411 0.764871 0.9992% 1994 1.294476 0.772513 1.0008% 1993 1.281650 0.780245 1.0000% 1992 1.268960 0.788047 0.9295% 1991 1.257273 0.795372 1.2505% 1990 1.241745 0.805318 0.7224% 1989 1.232839 0.811136 1.1077% 1988 1.219332 0.820121 0.8834% 1987 1.208656 0.827366 0.5594% 1986 1.201932 0.831994 1.3056% 1985 1.186442 0.842856 0.7673% 1984 1.177408 0.849323 0.8149% 1983 1.167890 0.856245 0.9737% 1982 1.156628 0.864583 0.9508% 1981 1.145734 0.872803 0.9031% 1980 1.135480 0.880685 2.2701% 1979 1.110276 0.900677 1.0042% 1978 1.099237 0.909722 0.9896% 1977 1.088466 0.918724 0.9103% 1976 1.078647 0.927088 0.8394% 1975 1.069667 0.934870 0.9042% 1974 1.060082 0.943323 1.1568% 1973 1.047960 0.954235 0.9427% 1972 1.038173 0.963231 0.7426% 1971 1.030520 0.970384 1.4697% 1970 1.015593 0.984646 0.6968% 1969 1.008565 0.991507 0.8565% 1968 1.000000 1.000000 1.5090% 1967 0.985134 1.015090 0.9949% 1966 0.975429 1.025190 1.0575% 1965 0.965222 1.036031 1.1300% 1964 0.954437 1.047738 1.5537% 1963 0.939835 1.064016 1.4658% 1962 0.926258 1.079613 1.5364% 1961 0.912242 1.096200 2.1586% 1960 0.892966 1.119863 -1.6655% 1959 0.908090 1.101212 4.3080% 1958 0.870585 1.148652 2.1130% 1957 0.852571 1.172923 1.9895% 1956 0.835940 1.196258 2.1231% 1955 0.818561 1.221656 1.4496% 1954 0.806865 1.239365 2.1573% 1953 0.789826 1.266101 1.2298% 1952 0.780231 1.281671 1.6814% 1951 0.767330 1.303221 1.6233% 1950 0.755073 1.324376 1.4265% 1949 0.744453 1.343268 1.7790% 1948 0.731440 1.367166 1.8242% 1947 0.718337 1.392105 -2.6320% 1946 0.737755 1.355464 3.1768% 1945 0.715039 1.398525 6.4754% 1944 0.671553 1.489085 -0.3437% 1943 0.673869 1.483967 0.6562% 1942 0.669476 1.493706 0.6633% 1941 0.665065 1.503613 -5.6614% 1940 0.704976 1.418487 8.0381% 1939 0.652526 1.532507 0.8126% 1938 0.647266 1.544961 0.7762% 1937 0.642280 1.556953 0.6029% 1936 0.638431 1.566340 0.5244% 1935 0.635101 1.574554 -3.0364% 1934 0.654989 1.526744 4.6271% 1933 0.626022 1.597389 1.3921% 1932 0.617426 1.619626 -0.2051% 1931 0.618695 1.616305 0.8886% 1930 0.613246 1.630667 1.0126% 1929 0.607099 1.647179 1.1526% 1928 0.600181 1.666164 1.2160% 1927 0.592970 1.686425 1.4086% 1926 0.584734 1.710179 1.7667% 1925 0.574583 1.740393 1.4465% 1924 0.566390 1.765568 1.7700% 1923 0.556539 1.796818 1.6165% 1922 0.547686 1.825864 1.3736% 1921 0.540265 1.850945 2.3393% 1920 0.527915 1.894244 1.3140% 1919 0.521068 1.919134 0.7676% 1918 0.517099 1.933867 0.3870% 1917 0.515105 1.941350 1.3274% 1916 0.508357 1.967121 1.4083% 1915 0.501298 1.994823 1.4458% 1914 0.494153 2.023665 1.9424% 1913 0.484738 2.062972 1.9857% 1912 0.475300 2.103936 1.5634% 1911 0.467983 2.136829 1.8169% 1910 0.459632 2.175653 1.8781% 1909 0.451159 2.216513 2.0082% 1908 0.442277 2.261026 1.9603% 1907 0.433774 2.305348 1.8264% 1906 0.425994 2.347452 1.9357% 1905 0.417905 2.392891 2.0148% 1904 0.409651 2.441104 2.1335% 1903 0.401093 2.493185 1.8151% 1902 0.393943 2.538440 1.8943% 1901 0.386619 2.586527 3.0255% 1900 0.375265 2.664783 0.6278% 1899 0.372924 2.681513 1.7757% 1898 0.366417 2.729128 1.8078% 1897 0.359911 2.778463 1.8396% 1896 0.353410 2.829576 1.8755% 1895 0.346904 2.882646 1.9114% 1894 0.340397 2.937744 1.9486% 1893 0.333891 2.994990 1.9858% 1892 0.327390 3.054465 2.0276% 1891 0.320883 3.116398 2.6465% 1890 0.312610 3.198874 1.5328% 1889 0.307891 3.247907 2.0811% 1888 0.301614 3.315500 2.1599% 1887 0.295237 3.387110 2.2075% 1886 0.288860 3.461882 2.2592% 1885 0.282479 3.540091 2.3095% 1884 0.276102 3.621851 2.3641% 1883 0.269725 3.707477 2.4214% 1882 0.263349 3.797249 2.4815% 1881 0.256972 3.891477 3.7644% 1880 0.247649 4.037967 0.9432% 1879 0.245335 4.076055 2.1464% 1878 0.240180 4.163543 2.1913% 1877 0.235030 4.254778 2.2426% 1876 0.229875 4.350196 2.2941% 1875 0.224719 4.449992 2.3456% 1874 0.219569 4.554371 2.4043% 1873 0.214414 4.663872 2.4635% 1872 0.209259 4.778769 2.5258% 1871 0.204104 4.899470 5.9947% 1870 0.192560 5.193177 -1.0968% 1869 0.194696 5.136219 2.1930% 1868 0.190518 5.248855 2.2394% 1867 0.186345 5.366398 2.2935% 1866 0.182167 5.489477 2.3445% 1865 0.177994 5.618176

2.4037% 1864 0.173816 5.753220 2.4599% 1863 0.169643 5.894742 2.5250% 1862 0.165465
6.043585 2.5872% 1861 0.161292 6.199947 2.9504% 1860 0.156669 6.382871 2.4012% 1859
0.152996 6.536139 2.7627% 1858 0.148882 6.716714 2.8412% 1857 0.144769 6.907549
2.9243% 1856 0.140656 7.109546 3.0161% 1855 0.136538 7.323979 3.1061% 1854 0.132425
7.551466 3.2056% 1853 0.128311 7.793538 3.3118% 1852 0.124198 8.051644 3.4252% 1851
0.120085 8.327431 4.0106% 1850 0.115455 8.661411 2.3254% 1849 0.112831 8.862821
2.7841% 1848 0.109775 9.109569 2.8590% 1847 0.106723 9.370013 2.9432% 1846 0.103672
9.645787 3.0324% 1845 0.100621 9.938287 3.1325% 1844 0.097565 10.249604 3.2284%
1843 0.094514 10.580498 3.3361% 1842 0.091462 10.933470 3.4512% 1841 0.088411
11.310805 3.8105% 1840 0.085166 11.741802 2.3861% 1839 0.083181 12.021967 2.5824%
1838 0.081087 12.332421 2.6573% 1837 0.078988 12.660134 2.7232% 1836 0.076894
13.004895 2.7994% 1835 0.074800 13.368960 2.8871% 1834 0.072701 13.754938 2.9657%
1833 0.070607 14.162865 3.0563% 1832 0.068513 14.595728 3.1604% 1831 0.066414
15.057015 3.4660% 1830 0.064189 15.578886 2.4653% 1829 0.062645 15.962953 2.6804%
1828 0.061010 16.390823 10.3427% 1827 0.055291 18.086069 -4.2314% 1826 0.057734
17.320769 2.9150% 1825 0.056099 17.825675 3.0026% 1824 0.054464 18.360903 3.0955%
1823 0.052828 18.929266 3.1944% 1822 0.051193 19.533940 3.3102% 1821 0.049553
20.180551 3.2277% 1820 0.048003 20.831927 2.6573% 1819 0.046761 21.385489 2.6261%
1818 0.045564 21.947095 2.6969% 1817 0.044368 22.538993 2.7717% 1816 0.043171
23.163703 2.8507% 1815 0.041974 23.824029 2.9343% 1814 0.040778 24.523108 3.0231%
1813 0.039581 25.264454 3.1039% 1812 0.038390 26.048636 3.2172% 1811 0.037193
26.886662 3.0969% 1810 0.036076 27.719319 2.9144% 1809 0.035054 28.527165 2.8225%
1808 0.034092 29.332334 2.9199% 1807 0.033125 30.188817 2.9918% 1806 0.032163
31.092001 3.0841% 1805 0.031200 32.050895 3.1822% 1804 0.030238 33.070816 3.2868%
1803 0.029276 34.157783 3.3985% 1802 0.028314 35.318630 3.5180% 1801 0.027351
36.561156 3.3999% 1800 0.026452 37.804216 2.8419% 1799 0.025721 38.878562 2.7485%
1798 0.025033 39.947122 2.8261% 1797 0.024345 41.076080 3.7832% 1796 0.023458
42.630074 2.1272% 1795 0.022969 43.536900 3.0879% 1794 0.022281 44.881293 3.1625%
1793 0.021598 46.300669 3.2904% 1792 0.020910 47.824154 3.4024% 1791 0.020222
49.451307 3.2296% 1790 0.019589 51.048368 41.3145% 1780 0.013862 72.138721 29.4353%
1770 0.010710 93.372981 83.4728% 1750 0.005837 171.314059 29.2845% 1740 0.004515
221.482443 94.2514% 1720 0.002324 430.232733 85.8111% 1700 0.001251 799.420088
19.2490% 1690 0.001049 953.300856 88.0250% 1670 0.000558 1792.444147

BASE YEAR: 1967
YEAR BYEAR/AYEAR AYEAR/BYEAR GROWTH%
2009 1.525513 0.655517 8.2857% 2001 1.408786 0.709831 1.0000% 2000 1.394837
0.716929 1.0000% 1999 1.381027 0.724099 1.0000% 1998 1.367354 0.731340 1.0000% 1997
1.353816 0.738653 1.0000% 1996 1.340411 0.746040 1.0000% 1995 1.327140 0.753500
0.9992% 1994 1.314010 0.761029 1.0008% 1993 1.300990 0.768645 1.0000% 1992 1.288109
0.776332 0.9295% 1991 1.276246 0.783548 1.2505% 1990 1.260484 0.793346 0.7224% 1989
1.251443 0.799078 1.1077% 1988 1.237733 0.807929 0.8834% 1987 1.226895 0.815066
0.5594% 1986 1.220070 0.819625 1.3056% 1985 1.204346 0.830326 0.7673% 1984 1.195175
0.836697 0.8149% 1983 1.185514 0.843516 0.9737% 1982 1.174082 0.851730 0.9508% 1981
1.163023 0.859828 0.9031% 1980 1.152615 0.867593 2.2701% 1979 1.127030 0.887288
1.0042% 1978 1.115825 0.896198 0.9896% 1977 1.104891 0.905066 0.9103% 1976 1.094924
0.913306 0.8394% 1975 1.085809 0.920972 0.9042% 1974 1.076079 0.929299 1.1568% 1973
1.063774 0.940049 0.9427% 1972 1.053839 0.948911 0.7426% 1971 1.046071 0.955958
1.4697% 1970 1.030919 0.970008 0.6968% 1969 1.023785 0.976768 0.8565% 1968 1.015090
0.985134 1.5090% 1967 1.000000 1.000000 0.9949% 1966 0.990149 1.009949 1.0575% 1965
0.979788 1.020629 1.1300% 1964 0.968840 1.032162 1.5537% 1963 0.954018 1.048198
1.4658% 1962 0.940236 1.063563 1.5364% 1961 0.926008 1.079904 2.1586% 1960 0.906441
1.103215 -1.6655% 1959 0.921794 1.084841 4.3080% 1958 0.883723 1.131576 2.1130%
1957 0.865437 1.155486 1.9895% 1956 0.848555 1.178474 2.1231% 1955 0.830914 1.203495
1.4496% 1954 0.819041 1.220941 2.1573% 1953 0.801745 1.247279 1.2298% 1952 0.792005
1.262618 1.6814% 1951 0.778909 1.283847 1.6233% 1950 0.766467 1.304688 1.4265% 1949
0.755687 1.323299 1.7790% 1948 0.742478 1.346841 1.8242% 1947 0.729177 1.371410 -

58

2.6320% 1946 0.748888 1.335314 3.1768% 1945 0.725829 1.377734 6.4754% 1944 0.681687 1.466948 -0.3437% 1943 0.684038 1.461907 0.6562% 1942 0.679579 1.471500 0.6633% 1941 0.675101 1.481261 -5.6614% 1940 0.715615 1.397400 8.0381% 1939 0.662372 1.509725 0.8126% 1938 0.657033 1.521993 0.7762% 1937 0.651972 1.533807 0.6029% 1936 0.648065 1.543054 0.5244% 1935 0.644685 1.551146 -3.0364% 1934 0.664873 1.504048 4.6271% 1933 0.635469 1.573642 1.3921% 1932 0.626744 1.595549 -0.2051% 1931 0.628032 1.592276 0.8886% 1930 0.622500 1.606425 1.0126% 1929 0.616260 1.622692 1.1526% 1928 0.609238 1.641395 1.2160% 1927 0.601919 1.661354 1.4086% 1926 0.593558 1.684756 1.7667% 1925 0.583254 1.714520 1.4465% 1924 0.574937 1.739321 1.7700% 1923 0.564938 1.770106 1.6165% 1922 0.555951 1.798720 1.3736% 1921 0.548417 1.823428 2.3393% 1920 0.535882 1.866084 1.3140% 1919 0.528931 1.890605 0.7676% 1918 0.524902 1.905118 0.3870% 1917 0.522878 1.912490 1.3274% 1916 0.516029 1.937877 1.4083% 1915 0.508862 1.965168 1.4458% 1914 0.501610 1.993581 1.9424% 1913 0.492052 2.032304 1.9857% 1912 0.482472 2.072658 1.5634% 1911 0.475045 2.105063 1.8169% 1910 0.466568 2.143310 1.8781% 1909 0.457967 2.183562 2.0082% 1908 0.448951 2.227414 1.9603% 1907 0.440320 2.271077 1.8264% 1906 0.432422 2.312554 1.9357% 1905 0.424211 2.357318 2.0148% 1904 0.415833 2.404814 2.1335% 1903 0.407146 2.456121 1.8151% 1902 0.399887 2.500704 1.8943% 1901 0.392453 2.548076 3.0255% 1900 0.380928 2.625168 0.6278% 1899 0.378551 2.641650 1.7757% 1898 0.371947 2.688556 1.8078% 1897 0.365342 2.737159 1.8396% 1896 0.358743 2.787511 1.8755% 1895 0.352138 2.839792 1.9114% 1894 0.345534 2.894072 1.9486% 1893 0.338929 2.950467 1.9858% 1892 0.332330 3.009057 2.0276% 1891 0.325726 3.070070 2.6465% 1890 0.317327 3.151320 1.5328% 1889 0.312537 3.199624 2.0811% 1888 0.306165 3.266212 2.1599% 1887 0.299692 3.336757 2.2075% 1886 0.293219 3.410417 2.2592% 1885 0.286741 3.487464 2.3095% 1884 0.280268 3.568009 2.3641% 1883 0.273795 3.652361 2.4214% 1882 0.267323 3.740799 2.4815% 1881 0.260850 3.833626 3.7644% 1880 0.251386 3.977939 0.9432% 1879 0.249037 4.015460 2.1464% 1878 0.243804 4.101647 2.1913% 1877 0.238577 4.191526 2.2426% 1876 0.233344 4.285526 2.2941% 1875 0.228111 4.383838 2.3456% 1874 0.222883 4.486666 2.4043% 1873 0.217650 4.594539 2.4635% 1872 0.212417 4.707728 2.5258% 1871 0.207184 4.826634 5.9947% 1870 0.195466 5.115975 -1.0968% 1869 0.197634 5.059864 2.1930% 1868 0.193393 5.170825 2.2394% 1867 0.189157 5.286621 2.2935% 1866 0.184916 5.407870 2.3445% 1865 0.180680 5.534656 2.4037% 1864 0.176439 5.667692 2.4599% 1863 0.172203 5.807111 2.5250% 1862 0.167962 5.953741 2.5872% 1861 0.163726 6.107779 2.9504% 1860 0.159034 6.287983 2.4012% 1859 0.155304 6.438973 2.7627% 1858 0.151129 6.616863 2.8412% 1857 0.146954 6.804861 2.9243% 1856 0.142759 7.003855 3.0161% 1855 0.138598 7.215101 3.1061% 1854 0.134423 7.439206 3.2056% 1853 0.130248 7.677679 3.3118% 1852 0.126072 7.931948 3.4252% 1851 0.121897 8.203635 4.0106% 1850 0.117197 8.532650 2.3254% 1849 0.114534 8.731066 2.7841% 1848 0.111431 8.974146 2.8590% 1847 0.108334 9.230718 2.9432% 1846 0.105237 9.502393 3.0324% 1845 0.102139 9.790544 3.1325% 1844 0.099037 10.097233 3.2284% 1843 0.095940 10.423208 3.3361% 1842 0.092842 10.770932 3.4512% 1841 0.089745 11.142658 3.8105% 1840 0.086451 11.567247 2.3861% 1839 0.084436 11.843248 2.5824% 1838 0.082311 12.149087 2.6573% 1837 0.080180 12.471928 2.7232% 1836 0.078054 12.811564 2.7994% 1835 0.075929 13.170216 2.8871% 1834 0.073798 13.550456 2.9657% 1833 0.071673 13.952320 3.0563% 1832 0.069547 14.378748 3.1604% 1831 0.067416 14.833177 3.4660% 1830 0.065158 15.347290 2.4653% 1829 0.063590 15.725647 2.6804% 1828 0.061930 16.147156 10.3427% 1827 0.056126 17.817200 -4.2314% 1826 0.058605 17.063277 2.9150% 1825 0.056945 17.560678 3.0026% 1824 0.055285 18.087949 3.0955% 1823 0.053625 18.647862 3.1944% 1822 0.051965 19.243548 3.3102% 1821 0.050300 19.880546 3.2277% 1820 0.048728 20.522238 2.6573% 1819 0.047466 21.067571 2.6261% 1818 0.046252 21.620828 2.6969% 1817 0.045037 22.203927 2.7717% 1816 0.043822 22.819350 2.8507% 1815 0.042608 23.469860 2.9343% 1814 0.041393 24.158546 3.0231% 1813 0.040179 24.888871 3.1039% 1812 0.038969 25.661396 3.2172% 1811 0.037754 26.486964 3.0969% 1810 0.036620 27.307243 2.9144% 1809 0.035583 28.103079 2.8225% 1808 0.034607 28.896278 2.9199% 1807 0.033625 29.740029 2.9918% 1806 0.032648 30.629786 3.0841% 1805 0.031671 31.574425 3.1822% 1804 0.030694 32.579184 3.2868% 1803 0.029718 33.649991 3.3985% 1802 0.028741 34.793582 3.5180% 1801 0.027764

36.017636 3.3999% 1800 0.026851 37.242216 2.8419% 1799 0.026109 38.300591 2.7485%
1798 0.025411 39.353266 2.8261% 1797 0.024712 40.465441 3.7832% 1796 0.023812
41.996334 2.1272% 1795 0.023316 42.889679 3.0879% 1794 0.022617 44.214086 3.1625%
1793 0.021924 45.612361 3.2904% 1792 0.021225 47.113197 3.4024% 1791 0.020527
48.716161 3.2296% 1790 0.019885 50.289481 41.3145% 1780 0.014071 71.066303 29.4353%
1770 0.010871 91.984894 83.4728% 1750 0.005925 168.767296 29.2845% 1740 0.004583
218.189874 94.2514% 1720 0.002359 423.836873 85.8111% 1700 0.001270 787.535871
19.2490% 1690 0.001065 939.129040 88.0250% 1670 0.000566 1765.797587

BASE YEAR: 1966

YEAR BYEAR/AYEAR AYEAR/BYEAR GROWTH%

2009 1.540691 0.649060 8.2857% 2001 1.422802 0.702838 1.0000% 2000 1.408715
0.709867 1.0000% 1999 1.394767 0.716966 1.0000% 1998 1.380958 0.724135 1.0000% 1997
1.367285 0.731377 1.0000% 1996 1.353747 0.738690 1.0000% 1995 1.340344 0.746077
0.9992% 1994 1.327083 0.753532 1.0008% 1993 1.313934 0.761073 1.0000% 1992 1.300925
0.768684 0.9295% 1991 1.288944 0.775829 1.2505% 1990 1.273024 0.785531 0.7224% 1989
1.263893 0.791206 1.1077% 1988 1.250047 0.799970 0.8834% 1987 1.239101 0.807037
0.5594% 1986 1.232209 0.811551 1.3056% 1985 1.216328 0.822147 0.7673% 1984 1.207066
0.828455 0.8149% 1983 1.197309 0.835206 0.9737% 1982 1.185763 0.843339 0.9508% 1981
1.174594 0.851358 0.9031% 1980 1.164082 0.859046 2.2701% 1979 1.138243 0.878547
1.0042% 1978 1.126927 0.887369 0.9896% 1977 1.115884 0.896151 0.9103% 1976 1.105817
0.904309 0.8394% 1975 1.096612 0.911900 0.9042% 1974 1.086785 0.920145 1.1568% 1973
1.074357 0.930789 0.9427% 1972 1.064324 0.939564 0.7426% 1971 1.056478 0.946541
1.4697% 1970 1.041176 0.960453 0.6968% 1969 1.033971 0.967145 0.8565% 1968 1.025190
0.975429 1.5090% 1967 1.009949 0.990149 0.9949% 1966 1.000000 1.000000 1.0575% 1965
0.989536 1.010575 1.1300% 1964 0.978479 1.021994 1.5537% 1963 0.963509 1.037873
1.4658% 1962 0.949590 1.053086 1.5364% 1961 0.935221 1.069266 2.1586% 1960 0.915460
1.092347 -1.6655% 1959 0.930965 1.074155 4.3080% 1958 0.892515 1.120429 2.1130%
1957 0.874047 1.144103 1.9895% 1956 0.856997 1.166865 2.1231% 1955 0.839180 1.191639
1.4496% 1954 0.827189 1.208913 2.1573% 1953 0.809722 1.234992 1.2298% 1952 0.799885
1.250180 1.6814% 1951 0.786658 1.271200 1.6233% 1950 0.774093 1.291835 1.4265% 1949
0.763205 1.310263 1.7790% 1948 0.749865 1.333574 1.8242% 1947 0.736431 1.357900 -
2.6320% 1946 0.756338 1.322160 3.1768% 1945 0.733051 1.364162 6.4754% 1944 0.688469
1.452497 -0.3437% 1943 0.690844 1.447505 0.6562% 1942 0.686340 1.457004 0.6633%
1941 0.681817 1.466669 -5.6614% 1940 0.722734 1.383634 8.0381% 1939 0.668962
1.494852 0.8126% 1938 0.663570 1.507000 0.7762% 1937 0.658459 1.518698 0.6029% 1936
0.654513 1.527854 0.5244% 1935 0.651099 1.535866 -3.0364% 1934 0.671487 1.489231
4.6271% 1933 0.641791 1.558140 1.3921% 1932 0.632979 1.579831 -0.2051% 1931
0.634280 1.576591 0.8886% 1930 0.628693 1.590600 1.0126% 1929 0.622391 1.606707
1.1526% 1928 0.615299 1.625225 1.2160% 1927 0.607907 1.644988 1.4086% 1926 0.599463
1.668159 1.7667% 1925 0.589056 1.697630 1.4465% 1924 0.580657 1.722187 1.7700% 1923
0.570558 1.752669 1.6165% 1922 0.561482 1.781001 1.3736% 1921 0.553874 1.805466
2.3393% 1920 0.541213 1.847701 1.3140% 1919 0.534194 1.871980 0.7676% 1918 0.530124
1.886350 0.3870% 1917 0.528081 1.893650 1.3274% 1916 0.521163 1.918787 1.4083% 1915
0.513925 1.945809 1.4458% 1914 0.506601 1.973942 1.9424% 1913 0.496948 2.012283
1.9857% 1912 0.487272 2.052241 1.5634% 1911 0.479772 2.084325 1.8169% 1910 0.471210
2.122196 1.8781% 1909 0.462524 2.162052 2.0082% 1908 0.453418 2.205471 1.9603% 1907
0.444701 2.248704 1.8264% 1906 0.436724 2.289773 1.9357% 1905 0.428431 2.334096
2.0148% 1904 0.419970 2.381124 2.1335% 1903 0.411197 2.431926 1.8151% 1902 0.403866
2.476069 1.8943% 1901 0.396358 2.522974 3.0255% 1900 0.384718 2.599307 0.6278% 1899
0.382318 2.615627 1.7757% 1898 0.375647 2.662071 1.8078% 1897 0.368977 2.710195
1.8396% 1896 0.362312 2.760051 1.8755% 1895 0.355642 2.811817 1.9114% 1894 0.348972
2.865562 1.9486% 1893 0.342301 2.921401 1.9858% 1892 0.335636 2.979415 2.0276% 1891
0.328966 3.039826 2.6465% 1890 0.320485 3.120276 1.5328% 1889 0.315646 3.168104
2.0811% 1888 0.309211 3.234036 2.1599% 1887 0.302674 3.303887 2.2075% 1886 0.296137
3.376821 2.2592% 1885 0.289594 3.453109 2.3095% 1884 0.283057 3.532860 2.3641% 1883
0.276519 3.616382 2.4214% 1882 0.269982 3.703948 2.4815% 1881 0.263445 3.795861

3.7644% 1880 0.253888 3.938752 0.9432% 1879 0.251515 3.975903 2.1464% 1878 0.246230
4.061242 2.1913% 1877 0.240950 4.150235 2.2426% 1876 0.235665 4.243309 2.2941% 1875
0.230380 4.340653 2.3456% 1874 0.225100 4.442467 2.4043% 1873 0.219815 4.549278
2.4635% 1872 0.214530 4.661352 2.5258% 1871 0.209245 4.779087 5.9947% 1870 0.197411
5.065577 -1.0968% 1869 0.199600 5.010019 2.1930% 1868 0.195317 5.119887 2.2394%
1867 0.191039 5.234542 2.2935% 1866 0.186755 5.354597 2.3445% 1865 0.182477 5.480134
2.4037% 1864 0.178194 5.611859 2.4599% 1863 0.173916 5.749904 2.5250% 1862 0.169633
5.895090 2.5872% 1861 0.165355 6.047611 2.9504% 1860 0.160616 6.226040 2.4012% 1859
0.156849 6.375542 2.7627% 1858 0.152633 6.551679 2.8412% 1857 0.148416 6.737826
2.9243% 1856 0.144199 6.934859 3.0161% 1855 0.139977 7.144024 3.1061% 1854 0.135760
7.365922 3.2056% 1853 0.131544 7.602046 3.3118% 1852 0.127327 7.853810 3.4252% 1851
0.123110 8.122820 4.0106% 1850 0.118363 8.448595 2.3254% 1849 0.115673 8.645055
2.7841% 1848 0.112540 8.885741 2.8590% 1847 0.109412 9.139786 2.9432% 1846 0.106284
9.408784 3.0324% 1845 0.103156 9.694096 3.1325% 1844 0.100022 9.997764 3.2284% 1843
0.096894 10.320528 3.3361% 1842 0.093766 10.664827 3.4512% 1841 0.090638 11.032891
3.8105% 1840 0.087311 11.453298 2.3861% 1839 0.085276 11.726579 2.5824% 1838
0.083130 12.029405 2.6573% 1837 0.080978 12.349066 2.7232% 1836 0.078831 12.685356
2.7994% 1835 0.076684 13.040475 2.8871% 1834 0.074532 13.416970 2.9657% 1833
0.072386 13.814874 3.0563% 1832 0.070239 14.237102 3.1604% 1831 0.068087 14.687054
3.4660% 1830 0.065806 15.196103 2.4653% 1829 0.064223 15.570732 2.6804% 1828
0.062547 15.988089 10.3427% 1827 0.056684 17.641682 -4.2314% 1826 0.059188 16.895186
2.9150% 1825 0.057512 17.387687 3.0026% 1824 0.055835 17.909763 3.0955% 1823
0.054159 18.464161 3.1944% 1822 0.052482 19.053978 3.3102% 1821 0.050801 19.684702
3.2277% 1820 0.049212 20.320072 2.6573% 1819 0.047939 20.860033 2.6261% 1818
0.046712 21.407840 2.6969% 1817 0.045485 21.985195 2.7717% 1816 0.044258 22.594555
2.8507% 1815 0.043032 23.238657 2.9343% 1814 0.041805 23.920559 3.0231% 1813
0.040578 24.643689 3.1039% 1812 0.039357 25.408604 3.2172% 1811 0.038130 26.226039
3.0969% 1810 0.036985 27.038237 2.9144% 1809 0.035937 27.826234 2.8225% 1808
0.034951 28.611619 2.9199% 1807 0.033959 29.447057 2.9918% 1806 0.032973 30.328050
3.0841% 1805 0.031986 31.263383 3.1822% 1804 0.031000 32.258244 3.2868% 1803
0.030013 33.318503 3.3985% 1802 0.029027 34.450828 3.5180% 1801 0.028040 35.662824
3.3999% 1800 0.027118 36.875341 2.8419% 1799 0.026369 37.923289 2.7485% 1798
0.025664 38.965595 2.8261% 1797 0.024958 40.066813 3.7832% 1796 0.024049 41.582625
2.1272% 1795 0.023548 42.467170 3.0879% 1794 0.022842 43.778530 3.1625% 1793
0.022142 45.163031 3.2904% 1792 0.021437 46.649082 3.4024% 1791 0.020731 48.236255
3.2296% 1790 0.020083 49.794075 41.3145% 1780 0.014211 70.366224 29.4353% 1770
0.010980 91.078744 83.4728% 1750 0.005984 167.104757 29.2845% 1740 0.004629
216.040470 94.2514% 1720 0.002383 419.661626 85.8111% 1700 0.001282 779.777800
19.2490% 1690 0.001075 929.877614 88.0250% 1670 0.000572 1748.402592

YEAR BYEAR/AYEAR AYEAR/BYEAR GROWTH%
2009 1.556983 0.642268 8.2857% 2001 1.437848 0.695484 1.0000% 2000 1.423612
0.702439 1.0000% 1999 1.409516 0.709463 1.0000% 1998 1.395561 0.716558 1.0000% 1997
1.381743 0.723723 1.0000% 1996 1.368063 0.730961 1.0000% 1995 1.354518 0.738270
0.9992% 1994 1.341117 0.745647 1.0008% 1993 1.327828 0.753109 1.0000% 1992 1.314681
0.760641 0.9295% 1991 1.302574 0.767711 1.2505% 1990 1.286486 0.777311 0.7224% 1989
1.277259 0.782927 1.1077% 1988 1.263266 0.791599 0.8834% 1987 1.252204 0.798592
0.5594% 1986 1.245239 0.803059 1.3056% 1985 1.229190 0.813544 0.7673% 1984 1.219831
0.819786 0.8149% 1983 1.209970 0.826467 0.9737% 1982 1.198302 0.834514 0.9508% 1981
1.187015 0.842449 0.9031% 1980 1.176392 0.850057 2.2701% 1979 1.150280 0.869354
1.0042% 1978 1.138844 0.878084 0.9896% 1977 1.127684 0.886773 0.9103% 1976 1.117511
0.894846 0.8394% 1975 1.108208 0.902358 0.9042% 1974 1.098278 0.910516 1.1568% 1973
1.085718 0.921049 0.9427% 1972 1.075579 0.929732 0.7426% 1971 1.067650 0.936636
1.4697% 1970 1.052186 0.950403 0.6968% 1969 1.044905 0.957025 0.8565% 1968 1.036031
0.965222 1.5090% 1967 1.020629 0.979788 0.9949% 1966 1.010575 0.989536 1.0575% 1965
1.000000 1.000000 1.1300% 1964 0.988826 1.011300 1.5537% 1963 0.973698 1.027012

1.4658% 1962 0.959632 1.042066 1.5364% 1961 0.945111 1.058077 2.1586% 1960 0.925140 1.080917 -1.6655% 1959 0.940809 1.062915 4.3080% 1958 0.901953 1.108705 2.1130% 1957 0.883290 1.132131 1.9895% 1956 0.866059 1.154655 2.1231% 1955 0.848054 1.179170 1.4496% 1954 0.835937 1.196263 2.1573% 1953 0.818284 1.222069 1.2298% 1952 0.808344 1.237098 1.6814% 1951 0.794977 1.257898 1.6233% 1950 0.782278 1.278317 1.4265% 1949 0.771276 1.296553 1.7790% 1948 0.757794 1.319619 1.8242% 1947 0.744219 1.343691 -2.6320% 1946 0.764336 1.308325 3.1768% 1945 0.740803 1.349887 6.4754% 1944 0.695750 1.437298 -0.3437% 1943 0.698149 1.432359 0.6562% 1942 0.693598 1.441758 0.6633% 1941 0.689027 1.451321 -5.6614% 1940 0.730377 1.369156 8.0381% 1939 0.676037 1.479210 0.8126% 1938 0.670587 1.491231 0.7762% 1937 0.665422 1.502806 0.6029% 1936 0.661434 1.511866 0.5244% 1935 0.657984 1.519794 -3.0364% 1934 0.678588 1.473648 4.6271% 1933 0.648578 1.541835 1.3921% 1932 0.639673 1.563299 -0.2051% 1931 0.640987 1.560093 0.8886% 1930 0.635342 1.573956 1.0126% 1929 0.628973 1.589894 1.1526% 1928 0.621806 1.608219 1.2160% 1927 0.614336 1.627775 1.4086% 1926 0.605802 1.650703 1.7667% 1925 0.595286 1.679866 1.4465% 1924 0.586797 1.704166 1.7700% 1923 0.576592 1.734329 1.6165% 1922 0.567420 1.762365 1.3736% 1921 0.559731 1.786573 2.3393% 1920 0.546936 1.828367 1.3140% 1919 0.539843 1.852392 0.7676% 1918 0.535730 1.866611 0.3870% 1917 0.533665 1.873835 1.3274% 1916 0.526674 1.898709 1.4083% 1915 0.519360 1.925448 1.4458% 1914 0.511958 1.953286 1.9424% 1913 0.502203 1.991227 1.9857% 1912 0.492425 2.030766 1.5634% 1911 0.484845 2.062515 1.8169% 1910 0.476193 2.099989 1.8781% 1909 0.467415 2.139428 2.0082% 1908 0.458213 2.182393 1.9603% 1907 0.449403 2.225174 1.8264% 1906 0.441343 2.265813 1.9357% 1905 0.432962 2.309672 2.0148% 1904 0.424411 2.356208 2.1335% 1903 0.415545 2.406478 1.8151% 1902 0.408137 2.450159 1.8943% 1901 0.400549 2.496574 3.0255% 1900 0.388786 2.572108 0.6278% 1899 0.386360 2.588257 1.7757% 1898 0.379620 2.634215 1.8078% 1897 0.372879 2.681835 1.8396% 1896 0.366143 2.731170 1.8755% 1895 0.359403 2.782394 1.9114% 1894 0.352662 2.835577 1.9486% 1893 0.345921 2.890832 1.9858% 1892 0.339186 2.948238 2.0276% 1891 0.332445 3.008017 2.6465% 1890 0.323874 3.087625 1.5328% 1889 0.318984 3.134953 2.0811% 1888 0.312481 3.200195 2.1599% 1887 0.305875 3.269315 2.2075% 1886 0.299268 3.341486 2.2592% 1885 0.292656 3.416976 2.3095% 1884 0.286050 3.495892 2.3641% 1883 0.279444 3.578540 2.4214% 1882 0.272837 3.665190 2.4815% 1881 0.266231 3.756141 3.7644% 1880 0.256572 3.897537 0.9432% 1879 0.254175 3.934299 2.1464% 1878 0.248834 4.018745 2.1913% 1877 0.243498 4.106807 2.2426% 1876 0.238157 4.198907 2.2941% 1875 0.232816 4.295232 2.3456% 1874 0.227481 4.395981 2.4043% 1873 0.222140 4.501674 2.4635% 1872 0.216799 4.612575 2.5258% 1871 0.211458 4.729078 5.9947% 1870 0.199498 5.012571 -1.0968% 1869 0.201711 4.957594 2.1930% 1868 0.197382 5.066313 2.2394% 1867 0.193059 5.179768 2.2935% 1866 0.188730 5.298566 2.3445% 1865 0.184407 5.422789 2.4037% 1864 0.180078 5.553137 2.4599% 1863 0.175755 5.689737 2.5250% 1862 0.171427 5.833404 2.5872% 1861 0.167103 5.984328 2.9504% 1860 0.162314 6.160890 2.4012% 1859 0.158508 6.308828 2.7627% 1858 0.154247 6.483122 2.8412% 1857 0.149985 6.667321 2.9243% 1856 0.145724 6.862293 3.0161% 1855 0.141457 7.069269 3.1061% 1854 0.137196 7.288845 3.2056% 1853 0.132935 7.522498 3.3118% 1852 0.128673 7.771627 3.4252% 1851 0.124412 8.037823 4.0106% 1850 0.119615 8.360188 3.2354% 1849 0.116896 8.554593 2.7841% 1848 0.113730 8.792760 2.8590% 1847 0.110569 9.044147 2.9432% 1846 0.107408 9.310330 3.0324% 1845 0.104246 9.592657 3.1325% 1844 0.101080 9.893147 3.2284% 1843 0.097919 10.212534 3.3361% 1842 0.094758 10.553230 3.4512% 1841 0.091597 10.917442 3.8105% 1840 0.088234 11.333450 2.3861% 1839 0.086178 11.603872 2.5824% 1838 0.084009 11.903529 2.6573% 1837 0.081834 12.219845 2.7232% 1836 0.079665 12.552616 2.7994% 1835 0.077495 12.904019 2.8871% 1834 0.075321 13.276574 2.9657% 1833 0.073151 13.670315 3.0563% 1832 0.070982 14.088124 3.1604% 1831 0.068807 14.533368 3.4660% 1830 0.066502 15.037090 2.4653% 1829 0.064902 15.407799 2.6804% 1828 0.063208 15.820789 10.3427% 1827 0.057283 17.457078 -4.2314% 1826 0.059814 16.718394 2.9150% 1825 0.058120 17.205741 3.0026% 1824 0.056426 17.722354 3.0955% 1823 0.054732 18.270951 3.1944% 1822 0.053037 18.854597 3.3102% 1821 0.051338 19.478720 3.2277% 1820 0.049733 20.107442 2.6573% 1819 0.048445 20.641753 2.6261% 1818 0.047206 21.183828 2.6969% 1817 0.045966 21.755141 2.7717% 1816 0.044726 22.358124

2.8507% 1815 0.043487 22.995486 2.9343% 1814 0.042247 23.670253 3.0231% 1813 0.041007 24.385817 3.1039% 1812 0.039773 25.142727 3.2172% 1811 0.038533 25.951609 3.0969% 1810 0.037376 26.755308 2.9144% 1809 0.036317 27.535059 2.8225% 1808 0.035320 28.312226 2.9199% 1807 0.034318 29.138922 2.9918% 1806 0.033321 30.010696 3.0841% 1805 0.032325 30.936242 3.1822% 1804 0.031328 31.920692 3.2868% 1803 0.030331 32.969857 3.3985% 1802 0.029334 34.090333 3.5180% 1801 0.028337 35.289646 3.3999% 1800 0.027405 36.489476 2.8419% 1799 0.026648 37.526459 2.7485% 1798 0.025935 38.557857 2.8261% 1797 0.025222 39.647553 3.7832% 1796 0.024303 41.147503 2.1272% 1795 0.023797 42.022791 3.0879% 1794 0.023084 43.320430 3.1625% 1793 0.022376 44.690443 3.2904% 1792 0.021663 46.160944 3.4024% 1791 0.020951 47.731509 3.2296% 1790 0.020295 49.273028 41.3145% 1780 0.014362 69.629909 29.4353% 1770 0.011096 90.125692 83.4728% 1750 0.006048 165.356167 29.2845% 1740 0.004678 213.779814 94.2514% 1720 0.002408 415.270270 85.8111% 1700 0.001296 771.618175 19.2490% 1690 0.001087 920.147338 88.0250% 1670 0.000578 1730.107239

BASE YEAR: 1964

YEAR BYEAR/AYEAR AYEAR/BYEAR GROWTH%

2009 1.574577 0.635091 8.2857% 2001 1.454096 0.687713 1.0000% 2000 1.439699 0.694590 1.0000% 1999 1.425444 0.701536 1.0000% 1998 1.411331 0.708551 1.0000% 1997 1.397357 0.715637 1.0000% 1996 1.383522 0.722793 1.0000% 1995 1.369824 0.730021 0.9992% 1994 1.356272 0.737315 1.0008% 1993 1.342833 0.744694 1.0000% 1992 1.329537 0.752141 0.9295% 1991 1.317293 0.759132 1.2505% 1990 1.301024 0.768626 0.7224% 1989 1.291692 0.774178 1.1077% 1988 1.277541 0.782754 0.8834% 1987 1.266354 0.789668 0.5594% 1986 1.259310 0.794085 1.3056% 1985 1.243080 0.804453 0.7673% 1984 1.233615 0.810626 0.8149% 1983 1.223643 0.817232 0.9737% 1982 1.211843 0.825190 0.9508% 1981 1.200429 0.833036 0.9031% 1980 1.189685 0.840558 2.2701% 1979 1.163278 0.859640 1.0042% 1978 1.151713 0.868272 0.9896% 1977 1.140427 0.876865 0.9103% 1976 1.130139 0.884847 0.8394% 1975 1.120731 0.892275 0.9042% 1974 1.110689 0.900342 1.1568% 1973 1.097987 0.910757 0.9427% 1972 1.087733 0.919343 0.7426% 1971 1.079715 0.926171 1.4697% 1970 1.064076 0.939783 0.6968% 1969 1.056712 0.946331 0.8565% 1968 1.047738 0.954437 1.5090% 1967 1.032162 0.968840 0.9949% 1966 1.021994 0.978479 1.0575% 1965 1.011300 0.988826 1.1300% 1964 1.000000 1.000000 1.5537% 1963 0.984701 1.015537 1.4658% 1962 0.970476 1.030422 1.5364% 1961 0.955791 1.046254 2.1586% 1960 0.935595 1.068839 -1.6655% 1959 0.951441 1.051038 4.3080% 1958 0.912145 1.096316 2.1130% 1957 0.893271 1.119481 1.9895% 1956 0.875846 1.141753 2.1231% 1955 0.857638 1.165994 1.4496% 1954 0.845531 1.182896 2.1573% 1953 0.827531 1.208414 1.2298% 1952 0.817478 1.223275 1.6814% 1951 0.803960 1.243842 1.6233% 1950 0.791118 1.264033 1.4265% 1949 0.779991 1.282065 1.7790% 1948 0.766358 1.304874 1.8242% 1947 0.752628 1.328677 -2.6320% 1946 0.772973 1.293706 3.1768% 1945 0.749174 1.334804 6.4754% 1944 0.703612 1.421238 -0.3437% 1943 0.706038 1.416354 0.6562% 1942 0.701435 1.425648 0.6633% 1941 0.696813 1.435104 -5.6614% 1940 0.738630 1.353857 8.0381% 1939 0.683676 1.462681 0.8126% 1938 0.678165 1.474568 0.7762% 1937 0.672941 1.486014 0.6029% 1936 0.668908 1.494973 0.5244% 1935 0.665419 1.502812 -3.0364% 1934 0.686256 1.457181 4.6271% 1933 0.655907 1.524607 1.3921% 1932 0.646901 1.545831 -0.2051% 1931 0.648231 1.542661 0.8886% 1930 0.642521 1.556369 1.0126% 1929 0.636080 1.572129 1.1526% 1928 0.628832 1.590249 1.2160% 1927 0.621278 1.609586 1.4086% 1926 0.612648 1.632259 1.7667% 1925 0.602012 1.661096 1.4465% 1924 0.593428 1.685123 1.7700% 1923 0.583108 1.714950 1.6165% 1922 0.573831 1.742672 1.3736% 1921 0.566056 1.766610 2.3393% 1920 0.553117 1.807937 1.3140% 1919 0.545943 1.831693 0.7676% 1918 0.541784 1.845754 0.3870% 1917 0.539695 1.852897 1.3274% 1916 0.532625 1.877493 1.4083% 1915 0.525228 1.903933 1.4458% 1914 0.517743 1.931461 1.9424% 1913 0.507878 1.968977 1.9857% 1912 0.497990 2.008074 1.5634% 1911 0.490324 2.039469 1.8169% 1910 0.481574 2.076524 1.8781% 1909 0.472696 2.115523 2.0082% 1908 0.463390 2.158007 1.9603% 1907 0.454481 2.200310 1.8264% 1906 0.446330 2.240495 1.9357% 1905 0.437854 2.283864 2.0148% 1904 0.429207 2.329880 2.1335% 1903 0.420241 2.379589 1.8151% 1902 0.412749 2.422782 1.8943% 1901 0.405075 2.468678 3.0255% 1900 0.393180 2.543367 0.6278% 1899 0.390726 2.559336 1.7757% 1898 0.383909 2.604781 1.8078% 1897 0.377093 2.651869

1.8396% 1896 0.370281 2.700652 1.8755% 1895 0.363464 2.751304 1.9114% 1894 0.356647
2.803892 1.9486% 1893 0.349830 2.858530 1.9858% 1892 0.343018 2.915295 2.0276% 1891
0.336202 2.974406 2.6465% 1890 0.327533 3.053124 1.5328% 1889 0.322589 3.099923
2.0811% 1888 0.316012 3.164436 2.1599% 1887 0.309331 3.232784 2.2075% 1886 0.302650
3.304148 2.2592% 1885 0.295964 3.378795 2.3095% 1884 0.289282 3.456829 2.3641% 1883
0.282601 3.538554 2.4214% 1882 0.275920 3.624236 2.4815% 1881 0.269239 3.714170
3.7644% 1880 0.259472 3.853986 0.9432% 1879 0.257047 3.890338 2.1464% 1878 0.251646
3.973840 2.1913% 1877 0.246250 4.060918 2.2426% 1876 0.240848 4.151989 2.2941% 1875
0.235447 4.247238 2.3456% 1874 0.230051 4.346861 2.4043% 1873 0.224650 4.451373
2.4635% 1872 0.219248 4.561035 2.5258% 1871 0.213847 4.676236 5.9947% 1870 0.201753
4.956561 -1.0968% 1869 0.203990 4.902198 2.1930% 1868 0.199613 5.009702 2.2394%
1867 0.195240 5.121890 2.2935% 1866 0.190863 5.239360 2.3445% 1865 0.186491 5.362196
2.4037% 1864 0.182113 5.491087 2.4599% 1863 0.177741 5.626161 2.5250% 1862 0.173364
5.768222 2.5872% 1861 0.168991 5.917460 2.9504% 1860 0.164148 6.092049 2.4012% 1859
0.160299 6.238334 2.7627% 1858 0.155990 6.410681 2.8412% 1857 0.151680 6.592821
2.9243% 1856 0.147371 6.785614 3.0161% 1855 0.143056 6.990278 3.1061% 1854 0.138746
7.207400 3.2056% 1853 0.134437 7.438442 3.3118% 1852 0.130127 7.684788 3.4252% 1851
0.125818 7.948009 4.0106% 1850 0.120966 8.266772 2.3254% 1849 0.118217 8.459005
2.7841% 1848 0.115015 8.694511 2.8590% 1847 0.111818 8.943088 2.9432% 1846 0.108621
9.206297 3.0324% 1845 0.105424 9.485470 3.1325% 1844 0.102222 9.782603 3.2284% 1843
0.099025 10.098420 3.3361% 1842 0.095828 10.435309 3.4512% 1841 0.092632 10.795452
3.8105% 1840 0.089231 11.206811 2.3861% 1839 0.087152 11.474212 2.5824% 1838
0.084958 11.770521 2.6573% 1837 0.082759 12.083302 2.7232% 1836 0.080565 12.412355
2.7994% 1835 0.078371 12.759831 2.8871% 1834 0.076172 13.128223 2.9657% 1833
0.073978 13.517565 3.0563% 1832 0.071784 13.930705 3.1604% 1831 0.069585 14.370974
3.4660% 1830 0.067254 14.869068 2.4653% 1829 0.065636 15.235635 2.6804% 1828
0.063922 15.644010 10.3427% 1827 0.057931 17.262015 -4.2314% 1826 0.060490 16.531585
2.9150% 1825 0.058777 17.013486 3.0026% 1824 0.057064 17.524327 3.0955% 1823
0.055350 18.066794 3.1944% 1822 0.053637 18.643918 3.3102% 1821 0.051918 19.261068
3.2277% 1820 0.050295 19.882764 2.6573% 1819 0.048993 20.411105 2.6261% 1818
0.047739 20.947122 2.6969% 1817 0.046486 21.512052 2.7717% 1816 0.045232 22.108298
2.8507% 1815 0.043978 22.738538 2.9343% 1814 0.042725 23.405765 3.0231% 1813
0.041471 24.113333 3.1039% 1812 0.040222 24.861786 3.2172% 1811 0.038969 25.661629
3.0969% 1810 0.037798 26.456348 2.9144% 1809 0.036728 27.227386 2.8225% 1808
0.035720 27.995869 2.9199% 1807 0.034706 28.813328 2.9918% 1806 0.033698 29.675360
3.0841% 1805 0.032690 30.590564 3.1822% 1804 0.031682 31.564015 3.2868% 1803
0.030673 32.601456 3.3985% 1802 0.029665 33.709412 3.5180% 1801 0.028657 34.895324
3.3999% 1800 0.027715 36.081747 2.8419% 1799 0.026949 37.107143 2.7485% 1798
0.026228 38.127017 2.8261% 1797 0.025507 39.204536 3.7832% 1796 0.024577 40.687726
2.1272% 1795 0.024066 41.553234 3.0879% 1794 0.023345 42.836373 3.1625% 1793
0.022629 44.191078 3.2904% 1792 0.021908 45.645148 3.4024% 1791 0.021187 47.198163
3.2296% 1790 0.020524 48.722458 41.3145% 1780 0.014524 68.851874 29.4353% 1770
0.011221 89.118640 83.4728% 1750 0.006116 163.508498 29.2845% 1740 0.004731
211.391067 94.2514% 1720 0.002435 410.630094 85.8111% 1700 0.001311 762.996214
19.2490% 1690 0.001099 909.865732 88.0250% 1670 0.000585 1710.775246
    BASE YEAR: 1963
    YEAR BYEAR/AYEAR AYEAR/BYEAR GROWTH%
    2009 1.599041 0.625375 8.2857% 2001 1.476687 0.677191 1.0000% 2000 1.462067
0.683963 1.0000% 1999 1.447591 0.690803 1.0000% 1998 1.433258 0.697711 1.0000% 1997
1.419067 0.704688 1.0000% 1996 1.405017 0.711735 1.0000% 1995 1.391106 0.718852
0.9992% 1994 1.377343 0.726035 1.0008% 1993 1.363696 0.733301 1.0000% 1992 1.350194
0.740634 0.9295% 1991 1.337759 0.747519 1.2505% 1990 1.321237 0.756866 0.7224% 1989
1.311760 0.762334 1.1077% 1988 1.297389 0.770779 0.8834% 1987 1.286029 0.777587
0.5594% 1986 1.278876 0.781937 1.3056% 1985 1.262393 0.792146 0.7673% 1984 1.252781
0.798224 0.8149% 1983 1.242654 0.804729 0.9737% 1982 1.230670 0.812565 0.9508% 1981
1.219079 0.820291 0.9031% 1980 1.208169 0.827699 2.2701% 1979 1.181351 0.846488

1.0042% 1978 1.169606 0.854988 0.9896% 1977 1.158145 0.863450 0.9103% 1976 1.147697 0.871310 0.8394% 1975 1.138143 0.878624 0.9042% 1974 1.127945 0.886568 1.1568% 1973 1.115046 0.896824 0.9427% 1972 1.104633 0.905278 0.7426% 1971 1.096490 0.912001 1.4697% 1970 1.080608 0.925405 0.6968% 1969 1.073130 0.931854 0.8565% 1968 1.064016 0.939835 1.5090% 1967 1.048198 0.954018 0.9949% 1966 1.037873 0.963509 1.0575% 1965 1.027012 0.973698 1.1300% 1964 1.015537 0.984701 1.5537% 1963 1.000000 1.000000 1.4658% 1962 0.985554 1.014658 1.5364% 1961 0.970640 1.030248 2.1586% 1960 0.950130 1.052487 -1.6655% 1959 0.966223 1.034958 4.3080% 1958 0.926317 1.079544 2.1130% 1957 0.907149 1.102354 1.9895% 1956 0.889454 1.124286 2.1231% 1955 0.870962 1.148155 1.4496% 1954 0.858517 1.164799 2.1573% 1953 0.840388 1.189927 1.2298% 1952 0.830179 1.204560 1.6814% 1951 0.816451 1.224813 1.6233% 1950 0.803410 1.244695 1.4265% 1949 0.792110 1.262451 1.7790% 1948 0.778264 1.284911 1.8242% 1947 0.764322 1.308350 -2.6320% 1946 0.784983 1.273913 3.1768% 1945 0.760813 1.314383 6.4754% 1944 0.714544 1.399495 -0.3437% 1943 0.717008 1.394685 0.6562% 1942 0.712333 1.403837 0.6633% 1941 0.707640 1.413149 -5.6614% 1940 0.750106 1.333145 8.0381% 1939 0.694298 1.440304 0.8126% 1938 0.688701 1.452008 0.7762% 1937 0.683396 1.463280 0.6029% 1936 0.679301 1.472101 0.5244% 1935 0.675757 1.479821 -3.0364% 1934 0.696918 1.434888 4.6271% 1933 0.666097 1.501282 1.3921% 1932 0.656952 1.522182 -0.2051% 1931 0.658302 1.519060 0.8886% 1930 0.652504 1.532558 1.0126% 1929 0.645963 1.548077 1.1526% 1928 0.638602 1.565920 1.2160% 1927 0.630930 1.584962 1.4086% 1926 0.622166 1.607287 1.7667% 1925 0.611366 1.635683 1.4465% 1924 0.602648 1.659343 1.7700% 1923 0.592167 1.688713 1.6165% 1922 0.582747 1.716011 1.3736% 1921 0.574850 1.739583 2.3393% 1920 0.561710 1.780277 1.3140% 1919 0.554425 1.803670 0.7676% 1918 0.550201 1.817516 0.3870% 1917 0.548080 1.824550 1.3274% 1916 0.540900 1.848769 1.4083% 1915 0.533389 1.874805 1.4458% 1914 0.525787 1.901911 1.9424% 1913 0.515769 1.938854 1.9857% 1912 0.505727 1.977353 1.5634% 1911 0.497942 2.008267 1.8169% 1910 0.489056 2.044756 1.8781% 1909 0.480041 2.083157 2.0082% 1908 0.470590 2.124992 1.9603% 1907 0.461543 2.166648 1.8264% 1906 0.453624 2.206218 1.9357% 1905 0.444657 2.248923 2.0148% 1904 0.435875 2.294235 2.1335% 1903 0.426770 2.343184 1.8151% 1902 0.419161 2.385716 1.8943% 1901 0.411369 2.430910 3.0255% 1900 0.399288 2.504457 0.6278% 1899 0.396797 2.520181 1.7757% 1898 0.389874 2.564930 1.8078% 1897 0.382951 2.611298 1.8396% 1896 0.376034 2.659336 1.8755% 1895 0.369111 2.709212 1.9114% 1894 0.362188 2.760996 1.9486% 1893 0.355265 2.814798 1.9858% 1892 0.348348 2.870694 2.0276% 1891 0.341425 2.928901 2.6465% 1890 0.332622 3.006415 1.5328% 1889 0.327601 3.052498 2.0811% 1888 0.320922 3.116024 2.1599% 1887 0.314137 3.183326 2.2075% 1886 0.307352 3.253599 2.2592% 1885 0.300562 3.327103 2.3095% 1884 0.293777 3.403944 2.3641% 1883 0.286992 3.484418 2.4214% 1882 0.280207 3.568789 2.4815% 1881 0.273422 3.657347 3.7644% 1880 0.263503 3.795024 0.9432% 1879 0.261041 3.830820 2.1464% 1878 0.255555 3.913044 2.1913% 1877 0.250076 3.998791 2.2426% 1876 0.244590 4.088468 2.2941% 1875 0.239105 4.182260 2.3456% 1874 0.233625 4.280359 2.4043% 1873 0.228140 4.383272 2.4635% 1872 0.222655 4.491256 2.5258% 1871 0.217170 4.604695 5.9947% 1870 0.204887 4.880731 -1.0968% 1869 0.207159 4.827200 2.1930% 1868 0.202714 4.933059 2.2394% 1867 0.198274 5.043531 2.2935% 1866 0.193828 5.159204 2.3445% 1865 0.189388 5.280160 2.4037% 1864 0.184943 5.407079 2.4599% 1863 0.180503 5.540087 2.5250% 1862 0.176057 5.679975 2.5872% 1861 0.171617 5.826930 2.9504% 1860 0.166699 5.998848 2.4012% 1859 0.162790 6.142894 2.7627% 1858 0.158413 6.312605 2.8412% 1857 0.154037 6.491959 2.9243% 1856 0.149660 6.681802 3.0161% 1855 0.145278 6.883335 3.1061% 1854 0.140902 7.097135 3.2056% 1853 0.136525 7.324643 3.3118% 1852 0.132149 7.567219 3.4252% 1851 0.127772 7.826414 4.0106% 1850 0.122846 8.140300 2.3254% 1849 0.120054 8.329592 2.7841% 1848 0.116802 8.561495 2.8590% 1847 0.113555 8.806269 2.9432% 1846 0.110309 9.065452 3.0324% 1845 0.107062 9.340353 3.1325% 1844 0.103810 9.632940 3.2284% 1843 0.100564 9.943926 3.3361% 1842 0.097317 10.275661 3.4512% 1841 0.094071 10.630294 3.8105% 1840 0.090618 11.035360 2.3861% 1839 0.088506 11.298669 2.5824% 1838 0.086278 11.590445 2.6573% 1837 0.084045 11.898441 2.7232% 1836 0.081817 12.222460 2.7994% 1835 0.079589 12.564620 2.8871% 1834 0.077355 12.927376 2.9657% 1833 0.075127 13.310761 3.0563% 1832 0.072899 13.717581 3.1604% 1831 0.070666 14.151115

3.4660% 1830 0.068299 14.641588 2.4653% 1829 0.066655 15.002547 2.6804% 1828
0.064915 15.404674 10.3427% 1827 0.058831 16.997926 -4.2314% 1826 0.061430 16.278670
2.9150% 1825 0.059690 16.753199 3.0026% 1824 0.057950 17.256225 3.0955% 1823
0.056210 17.790393 3.1944% 1822 0.054470 18.358687 3.3102% 1821 0.052725 18.966395
3.2277% 1820 0.051076 19.578581 2.6573% 1819 0.049754 20.098838 2.6261% 1818
0.048481 20.626655 2.6969% 1817 0.047208 21.182942 2.7717% 1816 0.045935 21.770066
2.8507% 1815 0.044661 22.390664 2.9343% 1814 0.043388 23.047683 3.0231% 1813
0.042115 23.744426 3.1039% 1812 0.040847 24.481429 3.2172% 1811 0.039574 25.269035
3.0969% 1810 0.038385 26.051595 2.9144% 1809 0.037298 26.810838 2.8225% 1808
0.036275 27.567564 2.9199% 1807 0.035245 28.372517 2.9918% 1806 0.034222 29.221361
3.0841% 1805 0.033198 30.122563 3.1822% 1804 0.032174 31.081121 3.2868% 1803
0.031150 32.102691 3.3985% 1802 0.030126 33.193696 3.5180% 1801 0.029102 34.361466
3.3999% 1800 0.028145 35.529737 2.8419% 1799 0.027368 36.539446 2.7485% 1798
0.026636 37.543716 2.8261% 1797 0.025904 38.604751 3.7832% 1796 0.024959 40.065250
2.1272% 1795 0.024439 40.917517 3.0879% 1794 0.023707 42.181025 3.1625% 1793
0.022981 43.515005 3.2904% 1792 0.022249 44.946829 3.4024% 1791 0.021516 46.476085
3.2296% 1790 0.020843 47.977059 41.3145% 1780 0.014750 67.798518 29.4353% 1770
0.011395 87.755226 83.4728% 1750 0.006211 161.007004 29.2845% 1740 0.004804
208.157023 94.2514% 1720 0.002473 404.347919 85.8111% 1700 0.001331 751.323236
19.2490% 1690 0.001116 895.945817 88.0250% 1670 0.000594 1684.602324
BASE YEAR: 1962
YEAR BYEAR/AYEAR AYEAR/BYEAR GROWTH%
2009 1.622480 0.616341 8.2857% 2001 1.498333 0.667408 1.0000% 2000 1.483498
0.674083 1.0000% 1999 1.468810 0.680823 1.0000% 1998 1.454267 0.687632 1.0000% 1997
1.439868 0.694508 1.0000% 1996 1.425612 0.701453 1.0000% 1995 1.411497 0.708468
0.9992% 1994 1.397533 0.715547 1.0008% 1993 1.383685 0.722708 1.0000% 1992 1.369985
0.729935 0.9295% 1991 1.357368 0.736720 1.2505% 1990 1.340604 0.745932 0.7224% 1989
1.330988 0.751321 1.1077% 1988 1.316407 0.759644 0.8834% 1987 1.304880 0.766354
0.5594% 1986 1.297622 0.770641 1.3056% 1985 1.280898 0.780702 0.7673% 1984 1.271145
0.786693 0.8149% 1983 1.260869 0.793104 0.9737% 1982 1.248710 0.800827 0.9508% 1981
1.236949 0.808441 0.9031% 1980 1.225878 0.815742 2.2701% 1979 1.198668 0.834259
1.0042% 1978 1.186751 0.842637 0.9896% 1977 1.175122 0.850976 0.9103% 1976 1.164521
0.858722 0.8394% 1975 1.154827 0.865931 0.9042% 1974 1.144478 0.873760 1.1568% 1973
1.131391 0.883868 0.9427% 1972 1.120825 0.892200 0.7426% 1971 1.112562 0.898826
1.4697% 1970 1.096447 0.912036 0.6968% 1969 1.088860 0.918392 0.8565% 1968 1.079613
0.926258 1.5090% 1967 1.063563 0.940236 0.9949% 1966 1.053086 0.949590 1.0575% 1965
1.042066 0.959632 1.1300% 1964 1.030422 0.970476 1.5537% 1963 1.014658 0.985554
1.4658% 1962 1.000000 1.000000 1.5364% 1961 0.984868 1.015364 2.1586% 1960 0.964058
1.037282 -1.6655% 1959 0.980386 1.020007 4.3080% 1958 0.939895 1.063948 2.1130%
1957 0.920446 1.086429 1.9895% 1956 0.902491 1.108044 2.1231% 1955 0.883729 1.131569
1.4496% 1954 0.871101 1.147972 2.1573% 1953 0.852706 1.172737 1.2298% 1952 0.842348
1.187158 1.6814% 1951 0.828419 1.207119 1.6233% 1950 0.815186 1.226714 1.4265% 1949
0.803721 1.244213 1.7790% 1948 0.789672 1.266348 1.8242% 1947 0.775525 1.289449 -
2.6320% 1946 0.796489 1.255510 3.1768% 1945 0.771965 1.295395 6.4754% 1944 0.725017
1.379277 -0.3437% 1943 0.727518 1.374537 0.6562% 1942 0.722775 1.383557 0.6633%
1941 0.718012 1.392734 -5.6614% 1940 0.761101 1.313885 8.0381% 1939 0.704475
1.419497 0.8126% 1938 0.698796 1.431032 0.7762% 1937 0.693414 1.442141 0.6029% 1936
0.689258 1.450835 0.5244% 1935 0.685663 1.458443 -3.0364% 1934 0.707134 1.414159
4.6271% 1933 0.675861 1.479594 1.3921% 1932 0.666581 1.500192 -0.2051% 1931
0.667951 1.497115 0.8886% 1930 0.662068 1.510418 1.0126% 1929 0.655431 1.525713
1.1526% 1928 0.647963 1.543298 1.2160% 1927 0.640178 1.562064 1.4086% 1926 0.631286
1.584067 1.7667% 1925 0.620327 1.612053 1.4465% 1924 0.611482 1.635371 1.7700% 1923
0.600847 1.664317 1.6165% 1922 0.591289 1.691221 1.3736% 1921 0.583277 1.714452
2.3393% 1920 0.569944 1.754559 1.3140% 1919 0.562552 1.777614 0.7676% 1918 0.558266
1.791260 0.3870% 1917 0.556114 1.798191 1.3274% 1916 0.548829 1.822061 1.4083% 1915
0.541207 1.847721 1.4458% 1914 0.533494 1.874436 1.9424% 1913 0.523329 1.910844

66

1.9857% 1912 0.513140 1.948787 1.5634% 1911 0.505241 1.979255 1.8169% 1910 0.496225
2.015216 1.8781% 1909 0.487077 2.053063 2.0082% 1908 0.477488 2.094294 1.9603% 1907
0.468308 2.135347 1.8264% 1906 0.459908 2.174346 1.9357% 1905 0.451175 2.216434
2.0148% 1904 0.442264 2.261092 2.1335% 1903 0.433025 2.309333 1.8151% 1902 0.425306
2.351251 1.8943% 1901 0.417399 2.395792 3.0255% 1900 0.405141 2.468276 0.6278% 1899
0.402613 2.483773 1.7757% 1898 0.395589 2.527876 1.8078% 1897 0.388565 2.573574
1.8396% 1896 0.381546 2.620918 1.8755% 1895 0.374521 2.670074 1.9114% 1894 0.367497
2.721109 1.9486% 1893 0.360473 2.774134 1.9858% 1892 0.353454 2.829223 2.0276% 1891
0.346430 2.886589 2.6465% 1890 0.337498 2.962983 1.5328% 1889 0.332403 3.008400
2.0811% 1888 0.325626 3.071009 2.1599% 1887 0.318742 3.137338 2.2075% 1886 0.311857
3.206596 2.2592% 1885 0.304967 3.279038 2.3095% 1884 0.298083 3.354769 2.3641% 1883
0.291199 3.434080 2.4214% 1882 0.284314 3.517233 2.4815% 1881 0.277430 3.604512
3.7644% 1880 0.267365 3.740200 0.9432% 1879 0.264867 3.775479 2.1464% 1878 0.259301
3.856515 2.1913% 1877 0.253741 3.941023 2.2426% 1876 0.248176 4.029404 2.2941% 1875
0.242610 4.121841 2.3456% 1874 0.237050 4.218523 2.4043% 1873 0.231484 4.319950
2.4635% 1872 0.225919 4.426374 2.5258% 1871 0.220353 4.538174 5.9947% 1870 0.207891
4.810222 -1.0968% 1869 0.210196 4.757465 2.1930% 1868 0.205685 4.861794 2.2394%
1867 0.201180 4.970670 2.2935% 1866 0.196670 5.084672 2.3445% 1865 0.192164 5.203881
2.4037% 1864 0.187654 5.328966 2.4599% 1863 0.183148 5.460053 2.5250% 1862 0.178638
5.597919 2.5872% 1861 0.174133 5.742751 2.9504% 1860 0.169142 5.912186 2.4012% 1859
0.165176 6.054152 2.7627% 1858 0.160735 6.221410 2.8412% 1857 0.156295 6.398173
2.9243% 1856 0.151854 6.585274 3.0161% 1855 0.147408 6.783895 3.1061% 1854 0.142967
6.994607 3.2056% 1853 0.138527 7.218828 3.3118% 1852 0.134086 7.457900 3.4252% 1851
0.129645 7.713350 4.0106% 1850 0.124646 8.022702 2.3254% 1849 0.121814 8.209259
2.7841% 1848 0.118514 8.437812 2.8590% 1847 0.115220 8.679050 2.9432% 1846 0.111926
8.934488 3.0324% 1845 0.108632 9.205418 3.1325% 1844 0.105332 9.493778 3.2284% 1843
0.102038 9.800272 3.3361% 1842 0.098744 10.127214 3.4512% 1841 0.095450 10.476724
3.8105% 1840 0.091946 10.875939 2.3861% 1839 0.089803 11.135444 2.5824% 1838
0.087543 11.423005 2.6573% 1837 0.085277 11.726551 2.7232% 1836 0.083016 12.045889
2.7994% 1835 0.080755 12.383107 2.8871% 1834 0.078489 12.740622 2.9657% 1833
0.076228 13.118468 3.0563% 1832 0.073968 13.519411 3.1604% 1831 0.071702 13.946682
3.4660% 1830 0.069300 14.430069 2.4653% 1829 0.067632 14.785814 2.6804% 1828
0.065867 15.182132 10.3427% 1827 0.059693 16.752367 -4.2314% 1826 0.062331 16.043502
2.9150% 1825 0.060565 16.511176 3.0026% 1824 0.058800 17.006934 3.0955% 1823
0.057034 17.533385 3.1944% 1822 0.055269 18.093470 3.3102% 1821 0.053498 18.692399
3.2277% 1820 0.051825 19.295740 2.6573% 1819 0.050483 19.808482 2.6261% 1818
0.049192 20.328674 2.6969% 1817 0.047900 20.876924 2.7717% 1816 0.046608 21.455566
2.8507% 1815 0.045316 22.067199 2.9343% 1814 0.044024 22.714727 3.0231% 1813
0.042732 23.401404 3.1039% 1812 0.041446 24.127760 3.2172% 1811 0.040154 24.903988
3.0969% 1810 0.038948 25.675243 2.9144% 1809 0.037845 26.423517 2.8225% 1808
0.036806 27.169311 2.9199% 1807 0.035762 27.962635 2.9918% 1806 0.034723 28.799217
3.0841% 1805 0.033684 29.687400 3.1822% 1804 0.032645 30.632110 3.2868% 1803
0.031607 31.638922 3.3985% 1802 0.030568 32.714166 3.5180% 1801 0.029529 33.865066
3.3999% 1800 0.028558 35.016460 2.8419% 1799 0.027769 36.011582 2.7485% 1798
0.027026 37.001344 2.8261% 1797 0.026283 38.047051 3.7832% 1796 0.025325 39.486451
2.1272% 1795 0.024798 40.326405 3.0879% 1794 0.024055 41.571660 3.1625% 1793
0.023317 42.886369 3.2904% 1792 0.022575 44.297508 3.4024% 1791 0.021832 45.804672
3.2296% 1790 0.021149 47.283963 41.3145% 1780 0.014966 66.819073 29.4353% 1770
0.011562 86.487477 83.4728% 1750 0.006302 158.681030 29.2845% 1740 0.004874
205.149901 94.2514% 1720 0.002509 398.506542 85.8111% 1700 0.001350 740.469310
19.2490% 1690 0.001132 883.002614 88.0250% 1670 0.000602 1660.265862
BASE YEAR: 1961
YEAR BYEAR/AYEAR AYEAR/BYEAR GROWTH%
2009 1.647408 0.607014 8.2857% 2001 1.521354 0.657309 1.0000% 2000 1.506291
0.663882 1.0000% 1999 1.491377 0.670521 1.0000% 1998 1.476611 0.677227 1.0000% 1997
1.461991 0.683999 1.0000% 1996 1.447516 0.690839 1.0000% 1995 1.433184 0.697747

67

0.9992% 1994 1.419005 0.704719 1.0008% 1993 1.404945 0.711772 1.0000% 1992 1.391034
0.718890 0.9295% 1991 1.378224 0.725572 1.2505% 1990 1.361201 0.734645 0.7224% 1989
1.351438 0.739953 1.1077% 1988 1.336633 0.748149 0.8834% 1987 1.324929 0.754758
0.5594% 1986 1.317559 0.758979 1.3056% 1985 1.300578 0.768889 0.7673% 1984 1.290675
0.774788 0.8149% 1983 1.280242 0.781103 0.9737% 1982 1.267895 0.788709 0.9508% 1981
1.255954 0.796208 0.9031% 1980 1.244713 0.803398 2.2701% 1979 1.217085 0.821636
1.0042% 1978 1.204984 0.829886 0.9896% 1977 1.193177 0.838099 0.9103% 1976 1.182413
0.845728 0.8394% 1975 1.172570 0.852828 0.9042% 1974 1.162063 0.860539 1.1568% 1973
1.148774 0.870493 0.9427% 1972 1.138045 0.878700 0.7426% 1971 1.129656 0.885225
1.4697% 1970 1.113294 0.898236 0.6968% 1969 1.105590 0.904495 0.8565% 1968 1.096200
0.912242 1.5090% 1967 1.079904 0.926008 0.9949% 1966 1.069266 0.935221 1.0575% 1965
1.058077 0.945111 1.1300% 1964 1.046254 0.955791 1.5537% 1963 1.030248 0.970640
1.4658% 1962 1.015364 0.984868 1.5364% 1961 1.000000 1.000000 2.1586% 1960 0.978870
1.021586 -1.6655% 1959 0.995449 1.004572 4.3080% 1958 0.954336 1.047849 2.1130%
1957 0.934589 1.069990 1.9895% 1956 0.916358 1.091277 2.1231% 1955 0.897307 1.114446
1.4496% 1954 0.884485 1.130601 2.1573% 1953 0.865808 1.154991 1.2298% 1952 0.855290
1.169194 1.6814% 1951 0.841147 1.188853 1.6233% 1950 0.827711 1.208151 1.4265% 1949
0.816069 1.225386 1.7790% 1948 0.801805 1.247186 1.8242% 1947 0.787441 1.269937 -
2.6320% 1946 0.808727 1.236512 3.1768% 1945 0.783826 1.275793 6.4754% 1944 0.736157
1.358406 -0.3437% 1943 0.738696 1.353738 0.6562% 1942 0.733880 1.362621 0.6633%
1941 0.729044 1.371659 -5.6614% 1940 0.772795 1.294004 8.0381% 1939 0.715299
1.398017 0.8126% 1938 0.709533 1.409378 0.7762% 1937 0.704068 1.420318 0.6029% 1936
0.699848 1.428881 0.5244% 1935 0.696198 1.436374 -3.0364% 1934 0.717999 1.392760
4.6271% 1933 0.686245 1.457205 1.3921% 1932 0.676823 1.477491 -0.2051% 1931
0.678214 1.474461 0.8886% 1930 0.672240 1.487563 1.0126% 1929 0.665502 1.502626
1.1526% 1928 0.657919 1.519945 1.2160% 1927 0.650014 1.538428 1.4086% 1926 0.640986
1.560098 1.7667% 1925 0.629858 1.587660 1.4465% 1924 0.620877 1.610625 1.7700% 1923
0.610079 1.639133 1.6165% 1922 0.600374 1.665630 1.3736% 1921 0.592238 1.688510
2.3393% 1920 0.578701 1.728009 1.3140% 1919 0.571195 1.750715 0.7676% 1918 0.566844
1.764154 0.3870% 1917 0.564659 1.770982 1.3274% 1916 0.557261 1.794490 1.4083% 1915
0.549522 1.819762 1.4458% 1914 0.541691 1.846072 1.9424% 1913 0.531369 1.881930
1.9857% 1912 0.521024 1.919299 1.5634% 1911 0.513003 1.949305 1.8169% 1910 0.503849
1.984722 1.8781% 1909 0.494561 2.021997 2.0082% 1908 0.484824 2.062603 1.9603% 1907
0.475503 2.103035 1.8264% 1906 0.466975 2.141444 1.9357% 1905 0.458107 2.182896
2.0148% 1904 0.449059 2.226877 2.1335% 1903 0.439679 2.274388 1.8151% 1902 0.431840
2.315672 1.8943% 1901 0.423812 2.359539 3.0255% 1900 0.411366 2.430927 0.6278% 1899
0.408799 2.446189 1.7757% 1898 0.401667 2.489625 1.8078% 1897 0.394535 2.534631
1.8396% 1896 0.387408 2.581258 1.8755% 1895 0.380276 2.629671 1.9114% 1894 0.373144
2.679934 1.9486% 1893 0.366011 2.732156 1.9858% 1892 0.358885 2.786412 2.0276% 1891
0.351752 2.842910 2.6465% 1890 0.342683 2.918148 1.5328% 1889 0.337510 2.962877
2.0811% 1888 0.330629 3.024539 2.1599% 1887 0.323639 3.089864 2.2075% 1886 0.316649
3.158074 2.2592% 1885 0.309653 3.229420 2.3095% 1884 0.302663 3.304005 2.3641% 1883
0.295673 3.382116 2.4214% 1882 0.288683 3.464011 2.4815% 1881 0.281693 3.549969
3.7644% 1880 0.271473 3.683604 0.9432% 1879 0.268937 3.718349 2.1464% 1878 0.263285
3.798159 2.1913% 1877 0.257640 3.881388 2.2426% 1876 0.251989 3.968432 2.2941% 1875
0.246338 4.059470 2.3456% 1874 0.240692 4.154689 2.4043% 1873 0.235041 4.254581
2.4635% 1872 0.229390 4.359394 2.5258% 1871 0.223739 4.469503 5.9947% 1870 0.211085
4.737435 -1.0968% 1869 0.213426 4.685475 2.1930% 1868 0.208846 4.788227 2.2394%
1867 0.204271 4.895454 2.2935% 1866 0.199691 5.007732 2.3445% 1865 0.195117 5.125137
2.4037% 1864 0.190537 5.248329 2.4599% 1863 0.185962 5.377432 2.5250% 1862 0.181382
5.513213 2.5872% 1861 0.176808 5.655853 2.9504% 1860 0.171741 5.822724 2.4012% 1859
0.167714 5.962541 2.7627% 1858 0.163205 6.127269 2.8412% 1857 0.158696 6.301357
2.9243% 1856 0.154187 6.485627 3.0161% 1855 0.149673 6.681242 3.1061% 1854 0.145164
6.888765 3.2056% 1853 0.140655 7.109594 3.3118% 1852 0.136146 7.345048 3.4252% 1851
0.131637 7.596633 4.0106% 1850 0.126561 7.901304 2.3254% 1849 0.123685 8.085038
2.7841% 1848 0.120335 8.310133 2.8590% 1847 0.116990 8.547720 2.9432% 1846 0.113645

8.799293 3.0324% 1845 0.110301 9.066123 3.1325% 1844 0.106950 9.350120 3.2284% 1843
0.103606 9.651976 3.3361% 1842 0.100261 9.973971 3.4512% 1841 0.096916 10.318192
3.8105% 1840 0.093359 10.711366 2.3861% 1839 0.091183 10.966944 2.5824% 1838
0.088888 11.250154 2.6573% 1837 0.086587 11.549107 2.7232% 1836 0.084291 11.863613
2.7994% 1835 0.081996 12.195728 2.8871% 1834 0.079695 12.547833 2.9657% 1833
0.077400 12.919962 3.0563% 1832 0.075104 13.314838 3.1604% 1831 0.072803 13.735643
3.4660% 1830 0.070364 14.211716 2.4653% 1829 0.068672 14.562077 2.6804% 1828
0.066879 14.952398 10.3427% 1827 0.060610 16.498873 -4.2314% 1826 0.063288 15.800734
2.9150% 1825 0.061496 16.261331 3.0026% 1824 0.059703 16.749588 3.0955% 1823
0.057910 17.268073 3.1944% 1822 0.056118 17.819683 3.3102% 1821 0.054320 18.409548
3.2277% 1820 0.052621 19.003760 2.6573% 1819 0.051259 19.508743 2.6261% 1818
0.049947 20.021064 2.6969% 1817 0.048636 20.561018 2.7717% 1816 0.047324 21.130904
2.8507% 1815 0.046012 21.733282 2.9343% 1814 0.044701 22.371011 3.0231% 1813
0.043389 23.047298 3.1039% 1812 0.042083 23.762662 3.2172% 1811 0.040771 24.527145
3.0969% 1810 0.039546 25.286730 2.9144% 1809 0.038427 26.023681 2.8225% 1808
0.037372 26.758190 2.9199% 1807 0.036311 27.539509 2.9918% 1806 0.035257 28.363432
3.0841% 1805 0.034202 29.238175 3.1822% 1804 0.033147 30.168590 3.2868% 1803
0.032092 31.160167 3.3985% 1802 0.031037 32.219141 3.5180% 1801 0.029983 33.352625
3.3999% 1800 0.028997 34.486596 2.8419% 1799 0.028195 35.466660 2.7485% 1798
0.027441 36.441446 2.8261% 1797 0.026687 37.471329 3.7832% 1796 0.025714 38.888948
2.1272% 1795 0.025179 39.716193 3.0879% 1794 0.024424 40.942605 3.1625% 1793
0.023676 42.237419 3.2904% 1792 0.022921 43.627206 3.4024% 1791 0.022167 45.111563
3.2296% 1790 0.021474 46.568470 41.3145% 1780 0.015196 65.807977 29.4353% 1770
0.011740 85.178763 83.4728% 1750 0.006399 156.279894 29.2845% 1740 0.004949
202.045605 94.2514% 1720 0.002548 392.476405 85.8111% 1700 0.001371 729.264647
19.2490% 1690 0.001150 869.641160 88.0250% 1670 0.000612 1635.142985

BASE YEAR: 1960
YEAR BYEAR/AYEAR AYEAR/BYEAR GROWTH%
2009 1.682970 0.594188 8.2857% 2001 1.554194 0.643420 1.0000% 2000 1.538806
0.649854 1.0000% 1999 1.523570 0.656353 1.0000% 1998 1.508486 0.662917 1.0000% 1997
1.493550 0.669546 1.0000% 1996 1.478762 0.676241 1.0000% 1995 1.464121 0.683004
0.9992% 1994 1.449636 0.689828 1.0008% 1993 1.435272 0.696732 1.0000% 1992 1.421062
0.703699 0.9295% 1991 1.407974 0.710240 1.2505% 1990 1.390585 0.719122 0.7224% 1989
1.380611 0.724317 1.1077% 1988 1.365486 0.732340 0.8834% 1987 1.353529 0.738809
0.5594% 1986 1.346000 0.742942 1.3056% 1985 1.328653 0.752642 0.7673% 1984 1.318536
0.758417 0.8149% 1983 1.307877 0.764598 0.9737% 1982 1.295265 0.772043 0.9508% 1981
1.283065 0.779384 0.9031% 1980 1.271582 0.786422 2.2701% 1979 1.243357 0.804274
1.0042% 1978 1.230996 0.812351 0.9896% 1977 1.218933 0.820390 0.9103% 1976 1.207937
0.827858 0.8394% 1975 1.197881 0.834807 0.9042% 1974 1.187147 0.842355 1.1568% 1973
1.173572 0.852100 0.9427% 1972 1.162612 0.860132 0.7426% 1971 1.154041 0.866520
1.4697% 1970 1.137326 0.879256 0.6968% 1969 1.129455 0.885383 0.8565% 1968 1.119863
0.892966 1.5090% 1967 1.103215 0.906441 0.9949% 1966 1.092347 0.915460 1.0575% 1965
1.080917 0.925140 1.1300% 1964 1.068839 0.935595 1.5537% 1963 1.052487 0.950130
1.4658% 1962 1.037282 0.964058 1.5364% 1961 1.021586 0.978870 2.1586% 1960 1.000000
1.000000 -1.6655% 1959 1.016937 0.983345 4.3080% 1958 0.974937 1.025708 2.1130%
1957 0.954763 1.047380 1.9895% 1956 0.936139 1.068218 2.1231% 1955 0.916677 1.090897
1.4496% 1954 0.903578 1.106711 2.1573% 1953 0.884497 1.130586 1.2298% 1952 0.873752
1.144489 1.6814% 1951 0.859304 1.163732 1.6233% 1950 0.845578 1.182623 1.4265% 1949
0.833685 1.199493 1.7790% 1948 0.819113 1.220833 1.8242% 1947 0.804439 1.243103 -
2.6320% 1946 0.826184 1.210384 3.1768% 1945 0.800746 1.248835 6.4754% 1944 0.752048
1.329703 -0.3437% 1943 0.754641 1.325133 0.6562% 1942 0.749722 1.333829 0.6633%
1941 0.744781 1.342676 -5.6614% 1940 0.789477 1.266661 8.0381% 1939 0.730739
1.368477 0.8126% 1938 0.724849 1.379597 0.7762% 1937 0.719266 1.390307 0.6029% 1936
0.714956 1.398688 0.5244% 1935 0.711226 1.406023 -3.0364% 1934 0.733498 1.363331
4.6271% 1933 0.701059 1.426414 1.3921% 1932 0.691433 1.446271 -0.2051% 1931
0.692854 1.443305 0.8886% 1930 0.686752 1.456130 1.0126% 1929 0.679867 1.470875

69

1.1526% 1928 0.672121 1.487828 1.2160% 1927 0.664046 1.505920 1.4086% 1926 0.654822
1.527132 1.7667% 1925 0.643454 1.554112 1.4465% 1924 0.634279 1.576592 1.7700% 1923
0.623248 1.604497 1.6165% 1922 0.613333 1.630434 1.3736% 1921 0.605023 1.652831
2.3393% 1920 0.591193 1.691496 1.3140% 1919 0.583525 1.713722 0.7676% 1918 0.579080
1.726877 0.3870% 1917 0.576848 1.733560 1.3274% 1916 0.569291 1.756572 1.4083% 1915
0.561385 1.781310 1.4458% 1914 0.553384 1.807064 1.9424% 1913 0.542840 1.842164
1.9857% 1912 0.532271 1.878743 1.5634% 1911 0.524077 1.908116 1.8169% 1910 0.514725
1.942785 1.8781% 1909 0.505236 1.979271 2.0082% 1908 0.495290 2.019020 1.9603% 1907
0.485768 2.058598 1.8264% 1906 0.477055 2.096195 1.9357% 1905 0.467996 2.136771
2.0148% 1904 0.458753 2.179823 2.1335% 1903 0.449170 2.226330 1.8151% 1902 0.441162
2.266741 1.8943% 1901 0.432960 2.309681 3.0255% 1900 0.420246 2.379561 0.6278% 1899
0.417624 2.394500 1.7757% 1898 0.410337 2.437019 1.8078% 1897 0.403051 2.481074
1.8396% 1896 0.395771 2.526716 1.8755% 1895 0.388485 2.574105 1.9114% 1894 0.381198
2.623306 1.9486% 1893 0.373912 2.674425 1.9858% 1892 0.366632 2.727534 2.0276% 1891
0.359345 2.782838 2.6465% 1890 0.350080 2.856486 1.5328% 1889 0.344795 2.900271
2.0811% 1888 0.337766 2.960629 2.1599% 1887 0.330625 3.024575 2.2075% 1886 0.323484
3.091343 2.2592% 1885 0.316337 3.161182 2.3095% 1884 0.309196 3.234191 2.3641% 1883
0.302055 3.310651 2.4214% 1882 0.294914 3.390815 2.4815% 1881 0.287773 3.474957
3.7644% 1880 0.277333 3.605768 0.9432% 1879 0.274742 3.639779 2.1464% 1878 0.268969
3.717903 2.1913% 1877 0.263201 3.799373 2.2426% 1876 0.257428 3.884578 2.2941% 1875
0.251655 3.973692 2.3456% 1874 0.245888 4.066899 2.4043% 1873 0.240114 4.164680
2.4635% 1872 0.234341 4.267279 2.5258% 1871 0.228568 4.375061 5.9947% 1870 0.215641
4.637332 -1.0968% 1869 0.218033 4.586470 2.1930% 1868 0.213354 4.687050 2.2394%
1867 0.208681 4.792012 2.2935% 1866 0.204002 4.901917 2.3445% 1865 0.199329 5.016841
2.4037% 1864 0.194650 5.137431 2.4599% 1863 0.189977 5.263805 2.5250% 1862 0.185298
5.396717 2.5872% 1861 0.180625 5.536343 2.9504% 1860 0.175448 5.699688 2.4012% 1859
0.171334 5.836551 2.7627% 1858 0.166728 5.997798 2.8412% 1857 0.162122 6.168208
2.9243% 1856 0.157515 6.348584 3.0161% 1855 0.152904 6.540066 3.1061% 1854 0.148297
6.743204 3.2056% 1853 0.143691 6.959366 3.3118% 1852 0.139085 7.189846 3.4252% 1851
0.134479 7.436114 4.0106% 1850 0.129293 7.734347 2.3254% 1849 0.126355 7.914199
2.7841% 1848 0.122933 8.134537 2.8590% 1847 0.119516 8.367105 2.9432% 1846 0.116099
8.613362 3.0324% 1845 0.112682 8.874554 3.1325% 1844 0.109259 9.152550 3.2284% 1843
0.105842 9.448027 3.3361% 1842 0.102425 9.763218 3.4512% 1841 0.099008 10.100166
3.8105% 1840 0.095374 10.485032 2.3861% 1839 0.093151 10.735210 2.5824% 1838
0.090806 11.012435 2.6573% 1837 0.088456 11.305071 2.7232% 1836 0.086111 11.612931
2.7994% 1835 0.083766 11.938029 2.8871% 1834 0.081415 12.282694 2.9657% 1833
0.079070 12.646960 3.0563% 1832 0.076725 13.033492 3.1604% 1831 0.074375 13.445405
3.4660% 1830 0.071883 13.911418 2.4653% 1829 0.070154 14.254377 2.6804% 1828
0.068323 14.636450 10.3427% 1827 0.061919 16.150247 -4.2314% 1826 0.064654 15.466860
2.9150% 1825 0.062823 15.917725 3.0026% 1824 0.060992 16.395665 3.0955% 1823
0.059160 16.903194 3.1944% 1822 0.057329 17.443148 3.3102% 1821 0.055492 18.020550
3.2277% 1820 0.053757 18.602206 2.6573% 1819 0.052366 19.096518 2.6261% 1818
0.051026 19.598013 2.6969% 1817 0.049686 20.126558 2.7717% 1816 0.048346 20.684403
2.8507% 1815 0.047006 21.274052 2.9343% 1814 0.045666 21.898306 3.0231% 1813
0.044326 22.560303 3.1039% 1812 0.042991 23.260551 3.2172% 1811 0.041651 24.008880
3.0969% 1810 0.040400 24.752414 2.9144% 1809 0.039256 25.473793 2.8225% 1808
0.038178 26.192782 2.9199% 1807 0.037095 26.957592 2.9918% 1806 0.036018 27.764105
3.0841% 1805 0.034940 28.620365 3.1822% 1804 0.033863 29.531120 3.2868% 1803
0.032785 30.501744 3.3985% 1802 0.031707 31.538342 3.5180% 1801 0.030630 32.647875
3.3999% 1800 0.029623 33.757885 2.8419% 1799 0.028804 34.717240 2.7485% 1798
0.028034 35.671428 2.8261% 1797 0.027263 36.679550 3.7832% 1796 0.026269 38.067214
2.1272% 1795 0.025722 38.876979 3.0879% 1794 0.024952 40.077476 3.1625% 1793
0.024187 41.344931 3.2904% 1792 0.023416 42.705351 3.4024% 1791 0.022646 44.158344
3.2296% 1790 0.021937 45.584465 41.3145% 1780 0.015524 64.417437 29.4353% 1770
0.011993 83.378913 83.4728% 1750 0.006537 152.977658 29.2845% 1740 0.005056

197.776327 94.2514% 1720 0.002603 384.183273 85.8111% 1700 0.001401 713.855090 19.2490% 1690 0.001175 851.265409 88.0250% 1670 0.000625 1600.591975

YEAR BYEAR/AYEAR AYEAR/BYEAR GROWTH%

2009 1.654940 0.604252 8.2857% 2001 1.528309 0.654318 1.0000% 2000 1.513178 0.660861 1.0000% 1999 1.498196 0.667470 1.0000% 1998 1.483362 0.674144 1.0000% 1997 1.468675 0.680886 1.0000% 1996 1.454134 0.687695 1.0000% 1995 1.439736 0.694572 0.9992% 1994 1.425493 0.701512 1.0008% 1993 1.411368 0.708532 1.0000% 1992 1.397394 0.715618 0.9295% 1991 1.384525 0.722269 1.2505% 1990 1.367425 0.731302 0.7224% 1989 1.357617 0.736585 1.1077% 1988 1.342744 0.744744 0.8834% 1987 1.330986 0.751323 0.5594% 1986 1.323583 0.755525 1.3056% 1985 1.306524 0.765390 0.7673% 1984 1.296576 0.771262 0.8149% 1983 1.286095 0.777548 0.9737% 1982 1.273692 0.785119 0.9508% 1981 1.261696 0.792584 0.9031% 1980 1.250404 0.799741 2.2701% 1979 1.222649 0.817896 1.0042% 1978 1.210494 0.826109 0.9896% 1977 1.198632 0.834285 0.9103% 1976 1.187819 0.841879 0.8394% 1975 1.177931 0.848946 0.9042% 1974 1.167376 0.856622 1.1568% 1973 1.154026 0.866532 0.9427% 1972 1.143249 0.874700 0.7426% 1971 1.134821 0.881196 1.4697% 1970 1.118384 0.894148 0.6968% 1969 1.110644 0.900378 0.8565% 1968 1.101212 0.908090 1.5090% 1967 1.084841 0.921794 0.9949% 1966 1.074155 0.930965 1.0575% 1965 1.062915 0.940809 1.1300% 1964 1.051038 0.951441 1.5537% 1963 1.034958 0.966223 1.4658% 1962 1.020007 0.980386 1.5364% 1961 1.004572 0.995449 2.1586% 1960 0.983345 1.016937 -1.6655% 1959 1.000000 1.000000 4.3080% 1958 0.958699 1.043080 2.1130% 1957 0.938862 1.065120 1.9895% 1956 0.920547 1.086310 2.1231% 1955 0.901409 1.109374 1.4496% 1954 0.888529 1.125455 2.1573% 1953 0.869766 1.149734 1.2298% 1952 0.859200 1.163873 1.6814% 1951 0.844993 1.183442 1.6233% 1950 0.831495 1.202653 1.4265% 1949 0.819800 1.219809 1.7790% 1948 0.805471 1.241510 1.8242% 1947 0.791041 1.264157 -2.6320% 1946 0.812424 1.230884 3.1768% 1945 0.787410 1.269987 6.4754% 1944 0.739523 1.352224 -0.3437% 1943 0.742073 1.347576 0.6562% 1942 0.737235 1.356419 0.6633% 1941 0.732377 1.365417 -5.6614% 1940 0.776328 1.288115 8.0381% 1939 0.718569 1.391655 0.8126% 1938 0.712777 1.402964 0.7762% 1937 0.707287 1.413854 0.6029% 1936 0.703048 1.422378 0.5244% 1935 0.699381 1.429837 -3.0364% 1934 0.721281 1.386422 4.6271% 1933 0.689383 1.450573 1.3921% 1932 0.679917 1.470767 -0.2051% 1931 0.681315 1.467750 0.8886% 1930 0.675314 1.480793 1.0126% 1929 0.668544 1.495787 1.1526% 1928 0.660927 1.513027 1.2160% 1927 0.652986 1.531426 1.4086% 1926 0.643916 1.552997 1.7667% 1925 0.632738 1.580434 1.4465% 1924 0.623716 1.603295 1.7700% 1923 0.612868 1.631673 1.6165% 1922 0.603118 1.658049 1.3736% 1921 0.594946 1.680825 2.3393% 1920 0.581347 1.720144 1.3140% 1919 0.573807 1.742747 0.7676% 1918 0.569435 1.756125 0.3870% 1917 0.567240 1.762921 1.3274% 1916 0.559809 1.786323 1.4083% 1915 0.552035 1.811480 1.4458% 1914 0.544167 1.837670 1.9424% 1913 0.533799 1.873365 1.9857% 1912 0.523406 1.910563 1.5634% 1911 0.515349 1.940433 1.8169% 1910 0.506152 1.975689 1.8781% 1909 0.496822 2.012794 2.0082% 1908 0.487041 2.053216 1.9603% 1907 0.477677 2.093464 1.8264% 1906 0.469110 2.131698 1.9357% 1905 0.460202 2.172961 2.0148% 1904 0.451112 2.216742 2.1335% 1903 0.441689 2.264037 1.8151% 1902 0.433814 2.305133 1.8943% 1901 0.425749 2.348800 3.0255% 1900 0.413247 2.419863 0.6278% 1899 0.410668 2.435056 1.7757% 1898 0.403503 2.478294 1.8078% 1897 0.396339 2.523096 1.8396% 1896 0.389179 2.569510 1.8755% 1895 0.382014 2.617703 1.9114% 1894 0.374850 2.667737 1.9486% 1893 0.367685 2.719722 1.9858% 1892 0.360525 2.773730 2.0276% 1891 0.353361 2.829971 2.6465% 1890 0.344250 2.904866 1.5328% 1889 0.339053 2.949393 2.0811% 1888 0.332141 3.010773 2.1599% 1887 0.325118 3.075802 2.2075% 1886 0.318096 3.143701 2.2592% 1885 0.311069 3.214723 2.3095% 1884 0.304047 3.288968 2.3641% 1883 0.297025 3.366724 2.4214% 1882 0.290003 3.448245 2.4815% 1881 0.282981 3.533812 3.7644% 1880 0.272714 3.666839 0.9432% 1879 0.270166 3.701426 2.1464% 1878 0.264489 3.780872 2.1913% 1877 0.258818 3.863723 2.2426% 1876 0.253141 3.950371 2.2941% 1875 0.247464 4.040995 2.3456% 1874 0.241792 4.135780 2.4043% 1873 0.236115 4.235217 2.4635% 1872 0.230438 4.339554 2.5258% 1871 0.224761 4.449161 5.9947% 1870 0.212050 4.715874 -1.0968% 1869 0.214401 4.664151 2.1930% 1868 0.209800 4.766434 2.2394% 1867 0.205205 4.873174 2.2935% 1866 0.200604 4.984940 2.3445% 1865 0.196009 5.101811

2.4037% 1864 0.191408 5.224443 2.4599% 1863 0.186813 5.352958 2.5250% 1862 0.182212
5.488121 2.5872% 1861 0.177616 5.630112 2.9504% 1860 0.172526 5.796223 2.4012% 1859
0.168481 5.935404 2.7627% 1858 0.163951 6.099382 2.8412% 1857 0.159422 6.272678
2.9243% 1856 0.154892 6.456109 3.0161% 1855 0.150357 6.650834 3.1061% 1854 0.145828
6.857413 3.2056% 1853 0.141298 7.077236 3.3118% 1852 0.136769 7.311619 3.4252% 1851
0.132239 7.562059 4.0106% 1850 0.127140 7.865343 2.3254% 1849 0.124251 8.048241
2.7841% 1848 0.120885 8.272311 2.8590% 1847 0.117525 8.508818 2.9432% 1846 0.114165
8.759245 3.0324% 1845 0.110805 9.024861 3.1325% 1844 0.107439 9.307566 3.2284% 1843
0.104079 9.608047 3.3361% 1842 0.100719 9.928577 3.4512% 1841 0.097359 10.271232
3.8105% 1840 0.093786 10.662616 2.3861% 1839 0.091600 10.917031 2.5824% 1838
0.089294 11.198952 2.6573% 1837 0.086983 11.496544 2.7232% 1836 0.084677 11.809619
2.7994% 1835 0.082371 12.140222 2.8871% 1834 0.080059 12.490725 2.9657% 1833
0.077753 12.861160 3.0563% 1832 0.075448 13.254239 3.1604% 1831 0.073136 13.673129
3.4660% 1830 0.070686 14.147035 2.4653% 1829 0.068985 14.495802 2.6804% 1828
0.067185 14.884347 10.3427% 1827 0.060887 16.423783 -4.2314% 1826 0.063578 15.728821
2.9150% 1825 0.061777 16.187322 3.0026% 1824 0.059976 16.673357 3.0955% 1823
0.058175 17.189482 3.1944% 1822 0.056374 17.738581 3.3102% 1821 0.054568 18.325762
3.2277% 1820 0.052862 18.917270 2.6573% 1819 0.051493 19.419954 2.6261% 1818
0.050176 19.929943 2.6969% 1817 0.048858 20.467440 2.7717% 1816 0.047540 21.034733
2.8507% 1815 0.046223 21.634369 2.9343% 1814 0.044905 22.269196 3.0231% 1813
0.043587 22.942405 3.1039% 1812 0.042275 23.654513 3.2172% 1811 0.040958 24.415516
3.0969% 1810 0.039727 25.171644 2.9144% 1809 0.038602 25.905241 2.8225% 1808
0.037543 26.636407 2.9199% 1807 0.036477 27.414171 2.9918% 1806 0.035418 28.234344
3.0841% 1805 0.034358 29.105105 3.1822% 1804 0.033299 30.031286 3.2868% 1803
0.032239 31.018350 3.3985% 1802 0.031179 32.072504 3.5180% 1801 0.030120 33.200829
3.3999% 1800 0.029129 34.329640 2.8419% 1799 0.028324 35.305243 2.7485% 1798
0.027567 36.275593 2.8261% 1797 0.026809 37.300788 3.7832% 1796 0.025832 38.711955
2.1272% 1795 0.025294 39.535435 3.0879% 1794 0.024536 40.756265 3.1625% 1793
0.023784 42.045187 3.2904% 1792 0.023026 43.428648 3.4024% 1791 0.022269 44.906250
3.2296% 1790 0.021572 46.356526 41.3145% 1780 0.015265 65.508470 29.4353% 1770
0.011794 84.791094 83.4728% 1750 0.006428 155.568628 29.2845% 1740 0.004972
201.126049 94.2514% 1720 0.002560 390.690154 85.8111% 1700 0.001378 725.945596
19.2490% 1690 0.001155 865.683222 88.0250% 1670 0.000614 1627.701072
BASE YEAR: 1958
YEAR BYEAR/AYEAR AYEAR/BYEAR GROWTH%
2009 1.726235 0.579296 8.2857% 2001 1.594149 0.627294 1.0000% 2000 1.578365
0.633567 1.0000% 1999 1.562738 0.639903 1.0000% 1998 1.547265 0.646302 1.0000% 1997
1.531946 0.652765 1.0000% 1996 1.516778 0.659292 1.0000% 1995 1.501760 0.665885
0.9992% 1994 1.486903 0.672539 1.0008% 1993 1.472170 0.679270 1.0000% 1992 1.457594
0.686062 0.9295% 1991 1.444170 0.692439 1.2505% 1990 1.426334 0.701098 0.7224% 1989
1.416103 0.706163 1.1077% 1988 1.400589 0.713985 0.8834% 1987 1.388325 0.720292
0.5594% 1986 1.380602 0.724321 1.3056% 1985 1.362809 0.733778 0.7673% 1984 1.352432
0.739409 0.8149% 1983 1.341500 0.745434 0.9737% 1982 1.328563 0.752693 0.9508% 1981
1.316050 0.759850 0.9031% 1980 1.304271 0.766712 2.2701% 1979 1.275321 0.784116
1.0042% 1978 1.262642 0.791990 0.9896% 1977 1.250269 0.799828 0.9103% 1976 1.238990
0.807109 0.8394% 1975 1.228676 0.813884 0.9042% 1974 1.217666 0.821243 1.1568% 1973
1.203741 0.830743 0.9427% 1972 1.192500 0.838575 0.7426% 1971 1.183709 0.844802
1.4697% 1970 1.166564 0.857219 0.6968% 1969 1.158491 0.863192 0.8565% 1968 1.148652
0.870585 1.5090% 1967 1.131576 0.883723 0.9949% 1966 1.120429 0.892515 1.0575% 1965
1.108705 0.901953 1.1300% 1964 1.096316 0.912145 1.5537% 1963 1.079544 0.926317
1.4658% 1962 1.063948 0.939895 1.5364% 1961 1.047849 0.954336 2.1586% 1960 1.025708
0.974937 -1.6655% 1959 1.043080 0.958699 4.3080% 1958 1.000000 1.000000 2.1130%
1957 0.979308 1.021130 1.9895% 1956 0.960204 1.041445 2.1231% 1955 0.940242 1.063556
1.4496% 1954 0.926807 1.078973 2.1573% 1953 0.907236 1.102249 1.2298% 1952 0.896214
1.115804 1.6814% 1951 0.881395 1.134565 1.6233% 1950 0.867316 1.152982 1.4265% 1949
0.855117 1.169430 1.7790% 1948 0.840170 1.190235 1.8242% 1947 0.825119 1.211946 -

72

2.6320% 1946 0.847423 1.180048 3.1768% 1945 0.821331 1.217535 6.4754% 1944 0.771381
1.296376 -0.3437% 1943 0.774041 1.291921 0.6562% 1942 0.768995 1.300398 0.6633%
1941 0.763928 1.309024 -5.6614% 1940 0.809773 1.234915 8.0381% 1939 0.749525
1.334178 0.8126% 1938 0.743483 1.345020 0.7762% 1937 0.737756 1.355461 0.6029% 1936
0.733335 1.363633 0.5244% 1935 0.729510 1.370783 -3.0364% 1934 0.752354 1.329161
4.6271% 1933 0.719081 1.390663 1.3921% 1932 0.709208 1.410023 -0.2051% 1931
0.710666 1.407131 0.8886% 1930 0.704406 1.419635 1.0126% 1929 0.697345 1.434010
1.1526% 1928 0.689399 1.450538 1.2160% 1927 0.681117 1.468177 1.4086% 1926 0.671656
1.488857 1.7667% 1925 0.659996 1.515161 1.4465% 1924 0.650585 1.537078 1.7700% 1923
0.639270 1.564283 1.6165% 1922 0.629101 1.589570 1.3736% 1921 0.620576 1.611405
2.3393% 1920 0.606391 1.649101 1.3140% 1919 0.598526 1.670771 0.7676% 1918 0.593967
1.683596 0.3870% 1917 0.591677 1.690112 1.3274% 1916 0.583926 1.712547 1.4083% 1915
0.575817 1.736664 1.4458% 1914 0.567610 1.761773 1.9424% 1913 0.556795 1.795993
1.9857% 1912 0.545954 1.831656 1.5634% 1911 0.537550 1.860292 1.8169% 1910 0.527957
1.894092 1.8781% 1909 0.518225 1.929664 2.0082% 1908 0.508023 1.968417 1.9603% 1907
0.498255 2.007003 1.8264% 1906 0.489319 2.043658 1.9357% 1905 0.480027 2.083216
2.0148% 1904 0.470546 2.125189 2.1335% 1903 0.460717 2.170531 1.8151% 1902 0.452503
2.209929 1.8943% 1901 0.444091 2.251793 3.0255% 1900 0.431049 2.319921 0.6278% 1899
0.428360 2.334486 1.7757% 1898 0.420886 2.375939 1.8078% 1897 0.413413 2.418890
1.8396% 1896 0.405945 2.463388 1.8755% 1895 0.398472 2.509590 1.9114% 1894 0.390998
2.557558 1.9486% 1893 0.383525 2.607395 1.9858% 1892 0.376057 2.659173 2.0276% 1891
0.368583 2.713091 2.6465% 1890 0.359080 2.784893 1.5328% 1889 0.353659 2.827581
2.0811% 1888 0.346449 2.886426 2.1599% 1887 0.339125 2.948769 2.2075% 1886 0.331800
3.013864 2.2592% 1885 0.324470 3.081952 2.3095% 1884 0.317145 3.153131 2.3641% 1883
0.309820 3.227676 2.4214% 1882 0.302496 3.305830 2.4815% 1881 0.295171 3.387863
3.7644% 1880 0.284463 3.515396 0.9432% 1879 0.281805 3.548554 2.1464% 1878 0.275883
3.624720 2.1913% 1877 0.269968 3.704148 2.2426% 1876 0.264046 3.787218 2.2941% 1875
0.258125 3.874099 2.3456% 1874 0.252209 3.964969 2.4043% 1873 0.246287 4.060300
2.4635% 1872 0.240366 4.160327 2.5258% 1871 0.234444 4.265407 5.9947% 1870 0.221185
4.521105 -1.0968% 1869 0.223638 4.471518 2.1930% 1868 0.218839 4.569577 2.2394%
1867 0.214045 4.671908 2.2935% 1866 0.209246 4.779059 2.3445% 1865 0.204453 4.891102
2.4037% 1864 0.199654 5.008670 2.4599% 1863 0.194860 5.131877 2.5250% 1862 0.190061
5.261457 2.5872% 1861 0.185268 5.397584 2.9504% 1860 0.179959 5.556835 2.4012% 1859
0.175739 5.690268 2.7627% 1858 0.171014 5.847473 2.8412% 1857 0.166289 6.013612
2.9243% 1856 0.161565 6.189467 3.0161% 1855 0.156834 6.376150 3.1061% 1854 0.152110
6.574197 3.2056% 1853 0.147385 6.784941 3.3118% 1852 0.142661 7.009644 3.4252% 1851
0.137936 7.249741 4.0106% 1850 0.132617 7.540499 3.2354% 1849 0.129603 7.715843
2.7841% 1848 0.126093 7.930659 2.8590% 1847 0.122588 8.157397 2.9432% 1846 0.119083
8.397482 3.0324% 1845 0.115579 8.652128 3.1325% 1844 0.112068 8.923157 3.2284% 1843
0.108563 9.211228 3.3361% 1842 0.105058 9.518520 3.4512% 1841 0.101554 9.847023
3.8105% 1840 0.097826 10.222242 2.3861% 1839 0.095546 10.466150 2.5824% 1838
0.093141 10.736427 2.6573% 1837 0.090730 11.021729 2.7232% 1836 0.088325 11.321873
2.7994% 1835 0.085919 11.638822 2.8871% 1834 0.083508 11.974849 2.9657% 1833
0.081103 12.329985 3.0563% 1832 0.078698 12.706829 3.1604% 1831 0.076287 13.108419
3.4660% 1830 0.073731 13.562752 2.4653% 1829 0.071957 13.897115 2.6804% 1828
0.070079 14.269613 10.3427% 1827 0.063510 15.745469 -4.2314% 1826 0.066316 15.079210
2.9150% 1825 0.064438 15.518774 3.0026% 1824 0.062560 15.984735 3.0955% 1823
0.060681 16.479544 3.1944% 1822 0.058803 17.005965 3.3102% 1821 0.056919 17.568895
3.2277% 1820 0.055139 18.135973 2.6573% 1819 0.053712 18.617896 2.6261% 1818
0.052337 19.106822 2.6969% 1817 0.050963 19.622120 2.7717% 1816 0.049588 20.165983
2.8507% 1815 0.048214 20.740854 2.9343% 1814 0.046840 21.349462 3.0231% 1813
0.045465 21.994867 3.1039% 1812 0.044096 22.677565 3.2172% 1811 0.042722 23.407138
3.0969% 1810 0.041439 24.132037 2.9144% 1809 0.040265 24.835336 2.8225% 1808
0.039160 25.536304 2.9199% 1807 0.038049 26.281946 2.9918% 1806 0.036944 27.068245
3.0841% 1805 0.035838 27.903044 3.1822% 1804 0.034733 28.790973 3.2868% 1803
0.033628 29.737270 3.3985% 1802 0.032523 30.747887 3.5180% 1801 0.031417 31.829612

3.3999% 1800 0.030384 32.911802 2.8419% 1799 0.029545 33.847112 2.7485% 1798
0.028754 34.777385 2.8261% 1797 0.027964 35.760240 3.7832% 1796 0.026945 37.113124
2.1272% 1795 0.026383 37.902594 3.0879% 1794 0.025593 39.073003 3.1625% 1793
0.024809 40.308691 3.2904% 1792 0.024018 41.635014 3.4024% 1791 0.023228 43.051590
3.2296% 1790 0.022501 44.441969 41.3145% 1780 0.015923 62.802924 29.4353% 1770
0.012302 81.289163 83.4728% 1750 0.006705 149.143534 29.2845% 1740 0.005186
192.819402 94.2514% 1720 0.002670 374.554376 85.8111% 1700 0.001437 695.963531
19.2490% 1690 0.001205 829.929895 88.0250% 1670 0.000641 1560.475871

BASE YEAR: 1957

YEAR BYEAR/AYEAR AYEAR/BYEAR GROWTH%

2009 1.762709 0.567309 8.2857% 2001 1.627833 0.614314 1.0000% 2000 1.611715
0.620457 1.0000% 1999 1.595758 0.626662 1.0000% 1998 1.579958 0.632928 1.0000% 1997
1.564315 0.639257 1.0000% 1996 1.548827 0.645650 1.0000% 1995 1.533492 0.652106
0.9992% 1994 1.518320 0.658622 1.0008% 1993 1.503276 0.665214 1.0000% 1992 1.488392
0.671866 0.9295% 1991 1.474685 0.678111 1.2505% 1990 1.456471 0.686591 0.7224% 1989
1.446025 0.691551 1.1077% 1988 1.430183 0.699211 0.8834% 1987 1.417660 0.705388
0.5594% 1986 1.409774 0.709334 1.3056% 1985 1.391605 0.718595 0.7673% 1984 1.381009
0.724108 0.8149% 1983 1.369845 0.730010 0.9737% 1982 1.356635 0.737118 0.9508% 1981
1.343857 0.744127 0.9031% 1980 1.331830 0.750846 2.2701% 1979 1.302268 0.767891
1.0042% 1978 1.289321 0.775602 0.9896% 1977 1.276687 0.783278 0.9103% 1976 1.265169
0.790408 0.8394% 1975 1.254637 0.797043 0.9042% 1974 1.243395 0.804250 1.1568% 1973
1.229176 0.813553 0.9427% 1972 1.217607 0.821223 0.7426% 1971 1.208720 0.827321
1.4697% 1970 1.191213 0.839481 0.6968% 1969 1.182969 0.845330 0.8565% 1968 1.172923
0.852571 1.5090% 1967 1.155486 0.865437 0.9949% 1966 1.144103 0.874047 1.0575% 1965
1.132131 0.883290 1.1300% 1964 1.119481 0.893271 1.5537% 1963 1.102354 0.907149
1.4658% 1962 1.086429 0.920446 1.5364% 1961 1.069990 0.934589 2.1586% 1960 1.047380
0.954763 -1.6655% 1959 1.065120 0.938862 4.3080% 1958 1.021130 0.979308 2.1130%
1957 1.000000 1.000000 1.9895% 1956 0.980493 1.019895 2.1231% 1955 0.960109 1.041548
1.4496% 1954 0.946390 1.056647 2.1573% 1953 0.926405 1.079441 1.2298% 1952 0.915151
1.092716 1.6814% 1951 0.900018 1.111088 1.6233% 1950 0.885642 1.129124 1.4265% 1949
0.873186 1.145232 1.7790% 1948 0.857923 1.165606 1.8242% 1947 0.842553 1.186868 -
2.6320% 1946 0.865329 1.155630 3.1768% 1945 0.838686 1.192342 6.4754% 1944 0.787680
1.269551 -0.3437% 1943 0.790397 1.265188 0.6562% 1942 0.785244 1.273490 0.6633%
1941 0.780069 1.281937 -5.6614% 1940 0.826883 1.209361 8.0381% 1939 0.765362
1.306571 0.8126% 1938 0.759193 1.317189 0.7762% 1937 0.753345 1.327413 0.6029% 1936
0.748830 1.335416 0.5244% 1935 0.744924 1.342419 -3.0364% 1934 0.768251 1.301658
4.6271% 1933 0.734275 1.361887 1.3921% 1932 0.724194 1.380846 -0.2051% 1931
0.725682 1.378014 0.8886% 1930 0.719290 1.390259 1.0126% 1929 0.712080 1.404337
1.1526% 1928 0.703966 1.420523 1.2160% 1927 0.695509 1.437797 1.4086% 1926 0.685848
1.458049 1.7667% 1925 0.673941 1.483808 1.4465% 1924 0.664332 1.505272 1.7700% 1923
0.652778 1.531915 1.6165% 1922 0.642393 1.556678 1.3736% 1921 0.633689 1.578062
2.3393% 1920 0.619204 1.614977 1.3140% 1919 0.611173 1.636198 0.7676% 1918 0.606517
1.648759 0.3870% 1917 0.604179 1.655139 1.3274% 1916 0.596264 1.677110 1.4083% 1915
0.587983 1.700729 1.4458% 1914 0.579603 1.725318 1.9424% 1913 0.568560 1.758830
1.9857% 1912 0.557490 1.793755 1.5634% 1911 0.548908 1.821798 1.8169% 1910 0.539113
1.854899 1.8781% 1909 0.529175 1.889735 2.0082% 1908 0.518757 1.927685 1.9603% 1907
0.508783 1.965473 1.8264% 1906 0.499658 2.001369 1.9357% 1905 0.490170 2.040109
2.0148% 1904 0.480489 2.081214 2.1335% 1903 0.470452 2.125617 1.8151% 1902 0.462064
2.164201 1.8943% 1901 0.453474 2.205198 3.0255% 1900 0.440157 2.271916 0.6278% 1899
0.437411 2.286180 1.7757% 1898 0.429779 2.326775 1.8078% 1897 0.422148 2.368837
1.8396% 1896 0.414522 2.412414 1.8755% 1895 0.406891 2.457660 1.9114% 1894 0.399260
2.504636 1.9486% 1893 0.391628 2.553442 1.9858% 1892 0.384003 2.604148 2.0276% 1891
0.376371 2.656951 2.6465% 1890 0.366667 2.727267 1.5328% 1889 0.361132 2.769071
2.0811% 1888 0.353770 2.826699 2.1599% 1887 0.346290 2.887752 2.2075% 1886 0.338811
2.951500 2.2592% 1885 0.331326 3.018179 2.3095% 1884 0.323846 3.087885 2.3641% 1883
0.316367 3.160887 2.4214% 1882 0.308888 3.237425 2.4815% 1881 0.301408 3.317760

74

3.7644% 1880 0.290474 3.442654 0.9432% 1879 0.287759 3.475126 2.1464% 1878 0.281713
3.549716 2.1913% 1877 0.275672 3.627500 2.2426% 1876 0.269625 3.708851 2.2941% 1875
0.263579 3.793934 2.3456% 1874 0.257538 3.882925 2.4043% 1873 0.251491 3.976282
2.4635% 1872 0.245445 4.074240 2.5258% 1871 0.239398 4.177146 5.9947% 1870 0.225858
4.427552 -1.0968% 1869 0.228363 4.378992 2.1930% 1868 0.223463 4.475022 2.2394%
1867 0.218568 4.575235 2.2935% 1866 0.213668 4.680169 2.3445% 1865 0.208773 4.789894
2.4037% 1864 0.203872 4.905028 2.4599% 1863 0.198978 5.025686 2.5250% 1862 0.194077
5.152585 2.5872% 1861 0.189183 5.285895 2.9504% 1860 0.183761 5.441851 2.4012% 1859
0.179452 5.572523 2.7627% 1858 0.174627 5.726475 2.8412% 1857 0.169803 5.889176
2.9243% 1856 0.164979 6.061392 3.0161% 1855 0.160148 6.244212 3.1061% 1854 0.155324
6.438161 3.2056% 1853 0.150499 6.644545 3.3118% 1852 0.145675 6.864598 3.4252% 1851
0.140851 7.099726 4.0106% 1850 0.135419 7.384468 2.3254% 1849 0.132342 7.556184
2.7841% 1848 0.128757 7.766555 2.8590% 1847 0.125178 7.988601 2.9432% 1846 0.121599
8.223718 3.0324% 1845 0.118021 8.473095 3.1325% 1844 0.114436 8.738515 3.2284% 1843
0.110857 9.020626 3.3361% 1842 0.107278 9.321559 3.4512% 1841 0.103699 9.643264
3.8105% 1840 0.099893 10.010719 2.3861% 1839 0.097565 10.249580 2.5824% 1838
0.095109 10.514265 2.6573% 1837 0.092647 10.793663 2.7232% 1836 0.090191 11.087596
2.7994% 1835 0.087735 11.397987 2.8871% 1834 0.085273 11.727061 2.9657% 1833
0.082817 12.074848 3.0563% 1832 0.080361 12.443895 3.1604% 1831 0.077899 12.837174
3.4660% 1830 0.075289 13.282107 2.4653% 1829 0.073478 13.609550 2.6804% 1828
0.071560 13.974340 10.3427% 1827 0.064852 15.419657 -4.2314% 1826 0.067718 14.767185
2.9150% 1825 0.065800 15.197654 3.0026% 1824 0.063882 15.653973 3.0955% 1823
0.061963 16.138543 3.1944% 1822 0.060045 16.654071 3.3102% 1821 0.058121 17.205353
3.2277% 1820 0.056304 17.760697 2.6573% 1819 0.054847 18.232647 2.6261% 1818
0.053443 18.711456 2.6969% 1817 0.052040 19.216092 2.7717% 1816 0.050636 19.748701
2.8507% 1815 0.049233 20.311676 2.9343% 1814 0.047829 20.907690 3.0231% 1813
0.046426 21.539741 3.1039% 1812 0.045028 22.208312 3.2172% 1811 0.043625 22.922788
3.0969% 1810 0.042314 23.632688 2.9144% 1809 0.041116 24.321434 2.8225% 1808
0.039987 25.007897 2.9199% 1807 0.038853 25.738110 2.9918% 1806 0.037724 26.508138
3.0841% 1805 0.036596 27.325663 3.1822% 1804 0.035467 28.195218 3.2868% 1803
0.034338 29.121935 3.3985% 1802 0.033210 30.111639 3.5180% 1801 0.032081 31.170981
3.3999% 1800 0.031026 32.230778 2.8419% 1799 0.030169 33.146734 2.7485% 1798
0.029362 34.057757 2.8261% 1797 0.028555 35.020274 3.7832% 1796 0.027514 36.345165
2.1272% 1795 0.026941 37.118298 3.0879% 1794 0.026134 38.264489 3.1625% 1793
0.025333 39.474608 3.2904% 1792 0.024526 40.773486 3.4024% 1791 0.023719 42.160750
3.2296% 1790 0.022977 43.522358 41.3145% 1780 0.016259 61.503381 29.4353% 1770
0.012562 79.607095 83.4728% 1750 0.006847 146.057397 29.2845% 1740 0.005296
188.829505 94.2514% 1720 0.002726 366.803947 85.8111% 1700 0.001467 681.562375
19.2490% 1690 0.001230 812.756654 88.0250% 1670 0.000654 1528.185880

BASE YEAR: 1956
YEAR BYEAR/AYEAR AYEAR/BYEAR GROWTH%

2009 1.797778 0.556242 8.2857% 2001 1.660218 0.602330 1.0000% 2000 1.643780
0.608354 1.0000% 1999 1.627505 0.614437 1.0000% 1998 1.611391 0.620582 1.0000% 1997
1.595437 0.626788 1.0000% 1996 1.579641 0.633055 1.0000% 1995 1.564001 0.639386
0.9992% 1994 1.548527 0.645775 1.0008% 1993 1.533184 0.652238 1.0000% 1992 1.518004
0.658760 0.9295% 1991 1.504024 0.664883 1.2505% 1990 1.485448 0.673198 0.7224% 1989
1.474793 0.678061 1.1077% 1988 1.458636 0.685572 0.8834% 1987 1.445864 0.691628
0.5594% 1986 1.437821 0.695497 1.3056% 1985 1.419291 0.704577 0.7673% 1984 1.408484
0.709983 0.8149% 1983 1.397098 0.715769 0.9737% 1982 1.383625 0.722739 0.9508% 1981
1.370593 0.729611 0.9031% 1980 1.358327 0.736202 2.2701% 1979 1.328176 0.752912
1.0042% 1978 1.314972 0.760473 0.9896% 1977 1.302086 0.767998 0.9103% 1976 1.290340
0.774990 0.8394% 1975 1.279598 0.781495 0.9042% 1974 1.268132 0.788561 1.1568% 1973
1.253630 0.797683 0.9427% 1972 1.241923 0.805203 0.7426% 1971 1.232768 0.811183
1.4697% 1970 1.214912 0.823105 0.6968% 1969 1.206505 0.828841 0.8565% 1968 1.196258
0.835940 1.5090% 1967 1.178474 0.848555 0.9949% 1966 1.166865 0.856997 1.0575% 1965
1.154655 0.866059 1.1300% 1964 1.141753 0.875846 1.5537% 1963 1.124286 0.889454

1.4658% 1962 1.108044 0.902491 1.5364% 1961 1.091277 0.916358 2.1586% 1960 1.068218
0.936139 -1.6655% 1959 1.086310 0.920547 4.3080% 1958 1.041445 0.960204 2.1130%
1957 1.019895 0.980493 1.9895% 1956 1.000000 1.000000 2.1231% 1955 0.979210 1.021231
1.4496% 1954 0.965219 1.036035 2.1573% 1953 0.944836 1.058385 1.2298% 1952 0.933358
1.071400 1.6814% 1951 0.917924 1.089415 1.6233% 1950 0.903262 1.107099 1.4265% 1949
0.890558 1.122892 1.7790% 1948 0.874991 1.142869 1.8242% 1947 0.859316 1.163716 -
2.6320% 1946 0.882545 1.133087 3.1768% 1945 0.855371 1.169083 6.4754% 1944 0.803351
1.244786 -0.3437% 1943 0.806122 1.240508 0.6562% 1942 0.800866 1.248648 0.6633%
1941 0.795589 1.256931 -5.6614% 1940 0.843334 1.185770 8.0381% 1939 0.780589
1.281084 0.8126% 1938 0.774297 1.291494 0.7762% 1937 0.768333 1.301520 0.6029% 1936
0.763728 1.309366 0.5244% 1935 0.759744 1.316232 -3.0364% 1934 0.783535 1.276267
4.6271% 1933 0.748884 1.335321 1.3921% 1932 0.738601 1.353910 -0.2051% 1931
0.740119 1.351134 0.8886% 1930 0.733600 1.363140 1.0126% 1929 0.726247 1.376943
1.1526% 1928 0.717971 1.392813 1.2160% 1927 0.709346 1.409750 1.4086% 1926 0.699493
1.429607 1.7667% 1925 0.687349 1.454864 1.4465% 1924 0.677549 1.475909 1.7700% 1923
0.665765 1.502032 1.6165% 1922 0.655174 1.526313 1.3736% 1921 0.646296 1.547279
2.3393% 1920 0.631523 1.583474 1.3140% 1919 0.623332 1.604281 0.7676% 1918 0.618584
1.616596 0.3870% 1917 0.616199 1.622852 1.3274% 1916 0.608126 1.644395 1.4083% 1915
0.599681 1.667553 1.4458% 1914 0.591135 1.691662 1.9424% 1913 0.579871 1.724521
1.9857% 1912 0.568581 1.758764 1.5634% 1911 0.559829 1.786261 1.8169% 1910 0.549839
1.818716 1.8781% 1909 0.539703 1.852872 2.0082% 1908 0.529078 1.890082 1.9603% 1907
0.518906 1.927133 1.8264% 1906 0.509599 1.962329 1.9357% 1905 0.499922 2.000313
2.0148% 1904 0.490048 2.040616 2.1335% 1903 0.479811 2.084153 1.8151% 1902 0.471257
2.121984 1.8943% 1901 0.462496 2.162182 3.0255% 1900 0.448914 2.227598 0.6278% 1899
0.446113 2.241584 1.7757% 1898 0.438330 2.281387 1.8078% 1897 0.430547 2.322629
1.8396% 1896 0.422769 2.365356 1.8755% 1895 0.414986 2.409719 1.9114% 1894 0.407203
2.455778 1.9486% 1893 0.399420 2.503632 1.9858% 1892 0.391642 2.553350 2.0276% 1891
0.383859 2.605122 2.6465% 1890 0.373962 2.674067 1.5328% 1889 0.368317 2.715055
2.0811% 1888 0.360808 2.771559 2.1599% 1887 0.353180 2.831421 2.2075% 1886 0.345551
2.893925 2.2592% 1885 0.337917 2.959304 2.3095% 1884 0.330289 3.027650 2.3641% 1883
0.322661 3.099228 2.4214% 1882 0.315033 3.174273 2.4815% 1881 0.307405 3.253041
3.7644% 1880 0.296253 3.375499 0.9432% 1879 0.293484 3.407337 2.1464% 1878 0.287317
3.480472 2.1913% 1877 0.281156 3.556739 2.2426% 1876 0.274989 3.636503 2.2941% 1875
0.268823 3.719927 2.3456% 1874 0.262662 3.807181 2.4043% 1873 0.256495 3.898718
2.4635% 1872 0.250328 3.994764 2.5258% 1871 0.244161 4.095663 5.9947% 1870 0.230352
4.341185 -1.0968% 1869 0.232906 4.293571 2.1930% 1868 0.227908 4.387728 2.2394%
1867 0.222916 4.485987 2.2935% 1866 0.217918 4.588873 2.3445% 1865 0.212926 4.696458
2.4037% 1864 0.207928 4.809347 2.4599% 1863 0.202936 4.927651 2.5250% 1862 0.197938
5.052075 2.5872% 1861 0.192946 5.182784 2.9504% 1860 0.187417 5.335697 2.4012% 1859
0.183022 5.463820 2.7627% 1858 0.178102 5.614770 2.8412% 1857 0.173181 5.774297
2.9243% 1856 0.168261 5.943154 3.0161% 1855 0.163334 6.122407 3.1061% 1854 0.158414
6.312573 3.2056% 1853 0.153494 6.514930 3.3118% 1852 0.148573 6.730691 3.4252% 1851
0.143653 6.961233 4.0106% 1850 0.138114 7.240420 2.3254% 1849 0.134975 7.408787
2.7841% 1848 0.131319 7.615054 2.8590% 1847 0.127669 7.832769 2.9432% 1846 0.124019
8.063300 3.0324% 1845 0.120369 8.307811 3.1325% 1844 0.116713 8.568054 3.2284% 1843
0.113063 8.844662 3.3361% 1842 0.109412 9.139725 3.4512% 1841 0.105762 9.455154
3.8105% 1840 0.101880 9.815442 2.3861% 1839 0.099506 10.049643 2.5824% 1838
0.097001 10.309164 2.6573% 1837 0.094490 10.583112 2.7232% 1836 0.091985 10.871312
2.7994% 1835 0.089480 11.175648 2.8871% 1834 0.086969 11.498303 2.9657% 1833
0.084464 11.839306 3.0563% 1832 0.081959 12.201153 3.1604% 1831 0.079449 12.586762
3.4660% 1830 0.076787 13.023014 2.4653% 1829 0.074940 13.344071 2.6804% 1828
0.072983 13.701745 10.3427% 1827 0.066143 15.118868 -4.2314% 1826 0.069065 14.479123
2.9150% 1825 0.067109 14.901195 3.0026% 1824 0.065152 15.348613 3.0955% 1823
0.063196 15.823731 3.1944% 1822 0.061240 16.329202 3.3102% 1821 0.059278 16.869730
3.2277% 1820 0.057424 17.414241 2.6573% 1819 0.055938 17.876986 2.6261% 1818
0.054506 18.346455 2.6969% 1817 0.053075 18.841246 2.7717% 1816 0.051644 19.363466

76

2.8507% 1815 0.050212 19.915459 2.9343% 1814 0.048781 20.499847 3.0231% 1813
0.047349 21.119568 3.1039% 1812 0.045924 21.775097 3.2172% 1811 0.044493 22.475637
3.0969% 1810 0.043156 23.171688 2.9144% 1809 0.041934 23.846999 2.8225% 1808
0.040783 24.520072 2.9199% 1807 0.039626 25.236040 2.9918% 1806 0.038475 25.991048
3.0841% 1805 0.037324 26.792625 3.1822% 1804 0.036173 27.645218 3.2868% 1803
0.035022 28.553857 3.3985% 1802 0.033870 29.524256 3.5180% 1801 0.032719 30.562933
3.3999% 1800 0.031644 31.602056 2.8419% 1799 0.030769 32.500145 2.7485% 1798
0.029946 33.393398 2.8261% 1797 0.029123 34.337139 3.7832% 1796 0.028061 35.636185
2.1272% 1795 0.027477 36.394237 3.0879% 1794 0.026654 37.518069 3.1625% 1793
0.025837 38.704582 3.2904% 1792 0.025014 39.978124 3.4024% 1791 0.024191 41.338326
3.2296% 1790 0.023434 42.673373 41.3145% 1780 0.016583 60.303643 29.4353% 1770
0.012812 78.054211 83.4728% 1750 0.006983 143.208276 29.2845% 1740 0.005401
185.146036 94.2514% 1720 0.002780 359.648756 85.8111% 1700 0.001496 668.267238
19.2490% 1690 0.001255 796.902329 88.0250% 1670 0.000667 1498.375782
BASE YEAR: 1955
YEAR BYEAR/AYEAR AYEAR/BYEAR GROWTH%
2009 1.835947 0.544678 8.2857% 2001 1.695466 0.589808 1.0000% 2000 1.678679
0.595706 1.0000% 1999 1.662059 0.601663 1.0000% 1998 1.645603 0.607680 1.0000% 1997
1.629310 0.613757 1.0000% 1996 1.613178 0.619894 1.0000% 1995 1.597206 0.626093
0.9992% 1994 1.581404 0.632349 1.0008% 1993 1.565735 0.638678 1.0000% 1992 1.550232
0.645065 0.9295% 1991 1.535955 0.651061 1.2505% 1990 1.516985 0.659202 0.7224% 1989
1.506104 0.663965 1.1077% 1988 1.489605 0.671319 0.8834% 1987 1.476561 0.677249
0.5594% 1986 1.468348 0.681038 1.3056% 1985 1.449424 0.689929 0.7673% 1984 1.438387
0.695223 0.8149% 1983 1.426760 0.700889 0.9737% 1982 1.413001 0.707714 0.9508% 1981
1.399692 0.714443 0.9031% 1980 1.387165 0.720895 2.2701% 1979 1.356375 0.737259
1.0042% 1978 1.342890 0.744663 0.9896% 1977 1.329731 0.752032 0.9103% 1976 1.317735
0.758878 0.8394% 1975 1.306765 0.765248 0.9042% 1974 1.295056 0.772167 1.1568% 1973
1.280246 0.781100 0.9427% 1972 1.268290 0.788463 0.7426% 1971 1.258941 0.794319
1.4697% 1970 1.240705 0.805993 0.6968% 1969 1.232120 0.811609 0.8565% 1968 1.221656
0.818561 1.5090% 1967 1.203495 0.830914 0.9949% 1966 1.191639 0.839180 1.0575% 1965
1.179170 0.848054 1.1300% 1964 1.165994 0.857638 1.5537% 1963 1.148155 0.870962
1.4658% 1962 1.131569 0.883729 1.5364% 1961 1.114446 0.897307 2.1586% 1960 1.090897
0.916677 -1.6655% 1959 1.109374 0.901409 4.3080% 1958 1.063556 0.940242 2.1130%
1957 1.041548 0.960109 1.9895% 1956 1.021231 0.979210 2.1231% 1955 1.000000 1.000000
1.4496% 1954 0.985711 1.014496 2.1573% 1953 0.964896 1.036381 1.2298% 1952 0.953174
1.049126 1.6814% 1951 0.937413 1.066766 1.6233% 1950 0.922439 1.084083 1.4265% 1949
0.909465 1.099547 1.7790% 1948 0.893568 1.119109 1.8242% 1947 0.877560 1.139523 -
2.6320% 1946 0.901282 1.109531 3.1768% 1945 0.873532 1.144778 6.4754% 1944 0.820407
1.218907 -0.3437% 1943 0.823236 1.214718 0.6562% 1942 0.817869 1.222689 0.6633%
1941 0.812480 1.230800 -5.6614% 1940 0.861238 1.161119 8.0381% 1939 0.797162
1.254451 0.8126% 1938 0.790736 1.264645 0.7762% 1937 0.784645 1.274461 0.6029% 1936
0.779943 1.282145 0.5244% 1935 0.775874 1.288868 -3.0364% 1934 0.800171 1.249734
4.6271% 1933 0.764783 1.307560 1.3921% 1932 0.754283 1.325763 -0.2051% 1931
0.755833 1.323044 0.8886% 1930 0.749176 1.334801 1.0126% 1929 0.741666 1.348317
1.1526% 1928 0.733215 1.363857 1.2160% 1927 0.724406 1.380442 1.4086% 1926 0.714344
1.399886 1.7667% 1925 0.701943 1.424618 1.4465% 1924 0.691934 1.445225 1.7700% 1923
0.679900 1.470805 1.6165% 1922 0.669084 1.494581 1.3736% 1921 0.660017 1.515111
2.3393% 1920 0.644931 1.550555 1.3140% 1919 0.636566 1.570929 0.7676% 1918 0.631717
1.582988 0.3870% 1917 0.629281 1.589114 1.3274% 1916 0.621038 1.610209 1.4083% 1915
0.612413 1.632885 1.4458% 1914 0.603685 1.656493 1.9424% 1913 0.592182 1.688669
1.9857% 1912 0.580653 1.722200 1.5634% 1911 0.571714 1.749125 1.8169% 1910 0.561512
1.780905 1.8781% 1909 0.551161 1.814352 2.0082% 1908 0.540310 1.850788 1.9603% 1907
0.529922 1.887068 1.8264% 1906 0.520418 1.921533 1.9357% 1905 0.510536 1.958728
2.0148% 1904 0.500452 1.998193 2.1335% 1903 0.489998 2.040825 1.8151% 1902 0.481262
2.077869 1.8943% 1901 0.472315 2.117231 3.0255% 1900 0.458445 2.181288 0.6278% 1899
0.455584 2.194983 1.7757% 1898 0.447636 2.233958 1.8078% 1897 0.439688 2.274342

1.8396% 1896 0.431745 2.316181 1.8755% 1895 0.423797 2.359622 1.9114% 1894 0.415848
2.404724 1.9486% 1893 0.407900 2.451583 1.9858% 1892 0.399957 2.500267 2.0276% 1891
0.392009 2.550963 2.6465% 1890 0.381902 2.618474 1.5328% 1889 0.376136 2.658611
2.0811% 1888 0.368468 2.713940 2.1599% 1887 0.360678 2.772557 2.2075% 1886 0.352888
2.833762 2.2592% 1885 0.345092 2.897781 2.3095% 1884 0.337301 2.964707 2.3641% 1883
0.329511 3.034797 2.4214% 1882 0.321721 3.108281 2.4815% 1881 0.313931 3.185412
3.7644% 1880 0.302542 3.305323 0.9432% 1879 0.299715 3.336500 2.1464% 1878 0.293417
3.408114 2.1913% 1877 0.287126 3.482796 2.2426% 1876 0.280828 3.560902 2.2941% 1875
0.274530 3.642591 2.3456% 1874 0.268238 3.728031 2.4043% 1873 0.261940 3.817665
2.4635% 1872 0.255642 3.911715 2.5258% 1871 0.249344 4.010516 5.9947% 1870 0.235242
4.250933 -1.0968% 1869 0.237851 4.204310 2.1930% 1868 0.232747 4.296509 2.2394%
1867 0.227649 4.392725 2.2935% 1866 0.222545 4.493473 2.3445% 1865 0.217447 4.598821
2.4037% 1864 0.212343 4.709362 2.4599% 1863 0.207245 4.825207 2.5250% 1862 0.202141
4.947044 2.5872% 1861 0.197043 5.075036 2.9504% 1860 0.191396 5.224771 2.4012% 1859
0.186908 5.350230 2.7627% 1858 0.181883 5.498041 2.8412% 1857 0.176858 5.654251
2.9243% 1856 0.171833 5.819598 3.0161% 1855 0.166802 5.995125 3.1061% 1854 0.161777
6.181337 3.2056% 1853 0.156752 6.379488 3.3118% 1852 0.151727 6.590763 3.4252% 1851
0.146703 6.816512 4.0106% 1850 0.141046 7.089895 2.3254% 1849 0.137841 7.254761
2.7841% 1848 0.134107 7.456740 2.8590% 1847 0.130379 7.669929 2.9432% 1846 0.126652
7.895667 3.0324% 1845 0.122924 8.135096 3.1325% 1844 0.119191 8.389928 3.2284% 1843
0.115463 8.660785 3.3361% 1842 0.111735 8.949714 3.4512% 1841 0.108008 9.258586
3.8105% 1840 0.104043 9.611383 2.3861% 1839 0.101619 9.840716 2.5824% 1838 0.099060
10.094841 2.6573% 1837 0.096496 10.363094 2.7232% 1836 0.093938 10.645302 2.7994%
1835 0.091380 10.943311 2.8871% 1834 0.088816 11.259258 2.9657% 1833 0.086258
11.593172 3.0563% 1832 0.083700 11.947497 3.1604% 1831 0.081135 12.325088 3.4660%
1830 0.078417 12.752272 2.4653% 1829 0.076531 13.066653 2.6804% 1828 0.074533
13.416891 10.3427% 1827 0.067547 14.804554 -4.2314% 1826 0.070531 14.178109 2.9150%
1825 0.068533 14.591406 3.0026% 1824 0.066536 15.029522 3.0955% 1823 0.064538
15.494762 3.1944% 1822 0.062540 15.989725 3.3102% 1821 0.060536 16.519016 3.2277%
1820 0.058643 17.052207 2.6573% 1819 0.057125 17.505331 2.6261% 1818 0.055664
17.965040 2.6969% 1817 0.054202 18.449545 2.7717% 1816 0.052740 18.960908 2.8507%
1815 0.051278 19.501425 2.9343% 1814 0.049817 20.073664 3.0231% 1813 0.048355
20.680501 3.1039% 1812 0.046899 21.322403 3.2172% 1811 0.045437 22.008378 3.0969%
1810 0.044072 22.689959 2.9144% 1809 0.042824 23.351230 2.8225% 1808 0.041649
24.010310 2.9199% 1807 0.040467 24.711394 2.9918% 1806 0.039292 25.450705 3.0841%
1805 0.038116 26.235618 3.1822% 1804 0.036941 27.070486 3.2868% 1803 0.035765
27.960235 3.3985% 1802 0.034590 28.910460 3.5180% 1801 0.033414 29.927543 3.3999%
1800 0.032315 30.945063 2.8419% 1799 0.031422 31.824481 2.7485% 1798 0.030582
32.699164 2.8261% 1797 0.029741 33.623285 3.7832% 1796 0.028657 34.895324 2.1272%
1795 0.028060 35.637617 3.0879% 1794 0.027220 36.738085 3.1625% 1793 0.026385
37.899931 3.2904% 1792 0.025545 39.146996 3.4024% 1791 0.024704 40.478920 3.2296%
1790 0.023931 41.786212 41.3145% 1780 0.016935 59.049957 29.4353% 1770 0.013084
76.431498 83.4728% 1750 0.007131 140.231039 29.2845% 1740 0.005516 181.296930
94.2514% 1720 0.002840 352.171815 85.8111% 1700 0.001528 654.374253 19.2490% 1690
0.001282 780.335076 88.0250% 1670 0.000682 1467.225201

BASE YEAR: 1954

YEAR BYEAR/AYEAR AYEAR/BYEAR GROWTH%

2009 1.862561 0.536895 8.2857% 2001 1.720044 0.581380 1.0000% 2000 1.703014
0.587194 1.0000% 1999 1.686152 0.593066 1.0000% 1998 1.669458 0.598997 1.0000% 1997
1.652928 0.604987 1.0000% 1996 1.636563 0.611037 1.0000% 1995 1.620359 0.617147
0.9992% 1994 1.604328 0.623314 1.0008% 1993 1.588432 0.629552 1.0000% 1992 1.572705
0.635847 0.9295% 1991 1.558221 0.641758 1.2505% 1990 1.538976 0.649783 0.7224% 1989
1.527937 0.654477 1.1077% 1988 1.511198 0.661727 0.8834% 1987 1.497966 0.667572
0.5594% 1986 1.489633 0.671306 1.3056% 1985 1.470435 0.680071 0.7673% 1984 1.459238
0.685289 0.8149% 1983 1.447442 0.690874 0.9737% 1982 1.433484 0.697601 0.9508% 1981
1.419983 0.704234 0.9031% 1980 1.407274 0.710594 2.2701% 1979 1.376037 0.726725

78

1.0042% 1978 1.362356 0.734022 0.9896% 1977 1.349007 0.741286 0.9103% 1976 1.336837
0.748034 0.8394% 1975 1.325708 0.754314 0.9042% 1974 1.313829 0.761134 1.1568% 1973
1.298805 0.769939 0.9427% 1972 1.286675 0.777197 0.7426% 1971 1.277190 0.782969
1.4697% 1970 1.258691 0.794476 0.6968% 1969 1.249981 0.800012 0.8565% 1968 1.239365
0.806865 1.5090% 1967 1.220941 0.819041 0.9949% 1966 1.208913 0.827189 1.0575% 1965
1.196263 0.835937 1.1300% 1964 1.182896 0.845383 1.5537% 1963 1.164799 0.858517
1.4658% 1962 1.147972 0.871101 1.5364% 1961 1.130601 0.884485 2.1586% 1960 1.106711
0.903578 -1.6655% 1959 1.125455 0.888529 4.3080% 1958 1.078973 0.926807 2.1130%
1957 1.056647 0.946390 1.9895% 1956 1.036035 0.965219 2.1231% 1955 1.014496 0.985711
1.4496% 1954 1.000000 1.000000 2.1573% 1953 0.978883 1.021573 1.2298% 1952 0.966991
1.034135 1.6814% 1951 0.951001 1.051523 1.6233% 1950 0.935811 1.068592 1.4265% 1949
0.922649 1.083836 1.7790% 1948 0.906521 1.103118 1.8242% 1947 0.890281 1.123241 -
2.6320% 1946 0.914347 1.093676 3.1768% 1945 0.886195 1.128420 6.4754% 1944 0.832300
1.201490 -0.3437% 1943 0.835170 1.197361 0.6562% 1942 0.829725 1.205218 0.6633%
1941 0.824258 1.213213 -5.6614% 1940 0.873723 1.144527 8.0381% 1939 0.808717
1.236526 0.8126% 1938 0.802199 1.246574 0.7762% 1937 0.796019 1.256251 0.6029% 1936
0.791249 1.263824 0.5244% 1935 0.787122 1.270452 -3.0364% 1934 0.811770 1.231876
4.6271% 1933 0.775869 1.288877 1.3921% 1932 0.765217 1.306819 -0.2051% 1931
0.766789 1.304139 0.8886% 1930 0.760036 1.315728 1.0126% 1929 0.752417 1.329051
1.1526% 1928 0.743843 1.344369 1.2160% 1927 0.734907 1.360717 1.4086% 1926 0.724699
1.379884 1.7667% 1925 0.712118 1.404262 1.4465% 1924 0.701964 1.424574 1.7700% 1923
0.689756 1.449789 1.6165% 1922 0.678783 1.473225 1.3736% 1921 0.669585 1.493462
2.3393% 1920 0.654280 1.528399 1.3140% 1919 0.645794 1.548482 0.7676% 1918 0.640874
1.560369 0.3870% 1917 0.638404 1.566407 1.3274% 1916 0.630040 1.587200 1.4083% 1915
0.621291 1.609553 1.4458% 1914 0.612436 1.632824 1.9424% 1913 0.600767 1.664539
1.9857% 1912 0.589070 1.697592 1.5634% 1911 0.580002 1.724132 1.8169% 1910 0.569652
1.755458 1.8781% 1909 0.559151 1.788426 2.0082% 1908 0.548143 1.824342 1.9603% 1907
0.537604 1.860104 1.8264% 1906 0.527962 1.894076 1.9357% 1905 0.517936 1.930739
2.0148% 1904 0.507707 1.969641 2.1335% 1903 0.497101 2.011663 1.8151% 1902 0.488239
2.048178 1.8943% 1901 0.479162 2.086978 3.0255% 1900 0.465090 2.150119 0.6278% 1899
0.462189 2.163618 1.7757% 1898 0.454125 2.202037 1.8078% 1897 0.446061 2.241844
1.8396% 1896 0.438004 2.283085 1.8755% 1895 0.429940 2.325905 1.9114% 1894 0.421876
2.370363 1.9486% 1893 0.413813 2.416552 1.9858% 1892 0.405755 2.464540 2.0276% 1891
0.397691 2.514512 2.6465% 1890 0.387438 2.581059 1.5328% 1889 0.381589 2.620622
2.0811% 1888 0.373809 2.675160 2.1599% 1887 0.365906 2.732940 2.2075% 1886 0.358003
2.793270 2.2592% 1885 0.350094 2.856375 2.3095% 1884 0.342191 2.922344 2.3641% 1883
0.334288 2.991433 2.4214% 1882 0.326385 3.063867 2.4815% 1881 0.318482 3.139896
3.7644% 1880 0.306928 3.258094 0.9432% 1879 0.304060 3.288825 2.1464% 1878 0.297671
3.359416 2.1913% 1877 0.291288 3.433031 2.2426% 1876 0.284899 3.510020 2.2941% 1875
0.278509 3.590542 2.3456% 1874 0.272126 3.674762 2.4043% 1873 0.265737 3.763114
2.4635% 1872 0.259348 3.855821 2.5258% 1871 0.252959 3.953210 5.9947% 1870 0.238653
4.190192 -1.0968% 1869 0.241299 4.144234 2.1930% 1868 0.236121 4.235116 2.2394%
1867 0.230949 4.329958 2.2935% 1866 0.225771 4.429265 2.3445% 1865 0.220599 4.533108
2.4037% 1864 0.215421 4.642070 2.4599% 1863 0.210249 4.756260 2.5250% 1862 0.205071
4.876356 2.5872% 1861 0.199899 5.002519 2.9504% 1860 0.194170 5.150114 2.4012% 1859
0.189617 5.273780 2.7627% 1858 0.184520 5.419480 2.8412% 1857 0.179422 5.573458
2.9243% 1856 0.174324 5.736442 3.0161% 1855 0.169220 5.909461 3.1061% 1854 0.164122
6.093012 3.2056% 1853 0.159025 6.288332 3.3118% 1852 0.153927 6.496588 3.4252% 1851
0.148829 6.719111 4.0106% 1850 0.143090 6.988588 2.3254% 1849 0.139839 7.151098
2.7841% 1848 0.136051 7.350191 2.8590% 1847 0.132269 7.560334 2.9432% 1846 0.128488
7.782846 3.0324% 1845 0.124706 8.018853 3.1325% 1844 0.120918 8.270044 3.2284% 1843
0.117137 8.537031 3.3361% 1842 0.113355 8.821832 3.4512% 1841 0.109574 9.126290
3.8105% 1840 0.105552 9.474046 2.3861% 1839 0.103092 9.700102 2.5824% 1838 0.100496
9.950596 2.6573% 1837 0.097895 10.215016 2.7232% 1836 0.095300 10.493192 2.7994%
1835 0.092705 10.786943 2.8871% 1834 0.090103 11.098375 2.9657% 1833 0.087508
11.427517 3.0563% 1832 0.084913 11.776779 3.1604% 1831 0.082311 12.148975 3.4660%

1830 0.079554 12.570055 2.4653% 1829 0.077640 12.879944 2.6804% 1828 0.075613
13.225178 10.3427% 1827 0.068526 14.593012 -4.2314% 1826 0.071554 13.975518 2.9150%
1825 0.069527 14.382910 3.0026% 1824 0.067500 14.814766 3.0955% 1823 0.065473
15.273358 3.1944% 1822 0.063447 15.761249 3.3102% 1821 0.061414 16.282976 3.2277%
1820 0.059494 16.808548 2.6573% 1819 0.057954 17.255198 2.6261% 1818 0.056471
17.708338 2.6969% 1817 0.054988 18.185920 2.7717% 1816 0.053505 18.689976 2.8507%
1815 0.052022 19.222770 2.9343% 1814 0.050539 19.786832 3.0231% 1813 0.049056
20.384998 3.1039% 1812 0.047579 21.017727 3.2172% 1811 0.046096 21.693901 3.0969%
1810 0.044711 22.365743 2.9144% 1809 0.043445 23.017565 2.8225% 1808 0.042253
23.667227 2.9199% 1807 0.041054 24.358293 2.9918% 1806 0.039861 25.087041 3.0841%
1805 0.038669 25.860738 3.1822% 1804 0.037476 26.683677 3.2868% 1803 0.036284
27.560712 3.3985% 1802 0.035091 28.497359 3.5180% 1801 0.033898 29.499909 3.3999%
1800 0.032784 30.502890 2.8419% 1799 0.031878 31.369742 2.7485% 1798 0.031025
32.231926 2.8261% 1797 0.030172 33.142843 3.7832% 1796 0.029073 34.396706 2.1272%
1795 0.028467 35.128392 3.0879% 1794 0.027614 36.213135 3.1625% 1793 0.026768
37.358380 3.2904% 1792 0.025915 38.587625 3.4024% 1791 0.025062 39.900518 3.2296%
1790 0.024278 41.189130 41.3145% 1780 0.017180 58.206193 29.4353% 1770 0.013273
75.339370 83.4728% 1750 0.007234 138.227280 29.2845% 1740 0.005596 178.706383
94.2514% 1720 0.002881 347.139640 85.8111% 1700 0.001550 645.023914 19.2490% 1690
0.001300 769.184886 88.0250% 1670 0.000691 1446.260054
    BASE YEAR: 1953
    YEAR BYEAR/AYEAR AYEAR/BYEAR GROWTH%
    2009 1.902741 0.525558 8.2857% 2001 1.757150 0.569103 1.0000% 2000 1.739752
0.574795 1.0000% 1999 1.722527 0.580543 1.0000% 1998 1.705472 0.586348 1.0000% 1997
1.688586 0.592211 1.0000% 1996 1.671867 0.598134 1.0000% 1995 1.655314 0.604115
0.9992% 1994 1.638938 0.610151 1.0008% 1993 1.622698 0.616258 1.0000% 1992 1.606632
0.622420 0.9295% 1991 1.591836 0.628206 1.2505% 1990 1.572175 0.636061 0.7224% 1989
1.560899 0.640657 1.1077% 1988 1.543798 0.647753 0.8834% 1987 1.530280 0.653475
0.5594% 1986 1.521768 0.657130 1.3056% 1985 1.502156 0.665710 0.7673% 1984 1.490718
0.670818 0.8149% 1983 1.478667 0.676285 0.9737% 1982 1.464408 0.682870 0.9508% 1981
1.450615 0.689363 0.9031% 1980 1.437632 0.695588 2.2701% 1979 1.405722 0.711378
1.0042% 1978 1.391746 0.718522 0.9896% 1977 1.378108 0.725633 0.9103% 1976 1.365676
0.732238 0.8394% 1975 1.354307 0.738385 0.9042% 1974 1.342172 0.745061 1.1568% 1973
1.326823 0.753680 0.9427% 1972 1.314432 0.760785 0.7426% 1971 1.304742 0.766435
1.4697% 1970 1.285844 0.777699 0.6968% 1969 1.276946 0.783119 0.8565% 1968 1.266101
0.789826 1.5090% 1967 1.247279 0.801745 0.9949% 1966 1.234992 0.809722 1.0575% 1965
1.222069 0.818284 1.1300% 1964 1.208414 0.827531 1.5537% 1963 1.189927 0.840388
1.4658% 1962 1.172737 0.852706 1.5364% 1961 1.154991 0.865808 2.1586% 1960 1.130586
0.884497 -1.6655% 1959 1.149734 0.869766 4.3080% 1958 1.102249 0.907236 2.1130%
1957 1.079441 0.926405 1.9895% 1956 1.058385 0.944836 2.1231% 1955 1.036381 0.964896
1.4496% 1954 1.021573 0.978883 2.1573% 1953 1.000000 1.000000 1.2298% 1952 0.987852
1.012298 1.6814% 1951 0.971517 1.029318 1.6233% 1950 0.955999 1.046027 1.4265% 1949
0.942553 1.060949 1.7790% 1948 0.926077 1.079823 1.8242% 1947 0.909487 1.099521 -
2.6320% 1946 0.934072 1.070581 3.1768% 1945 0.905312 1.104592 6.4754% 1944 0.850255
1.176118 -0.3437% 1943 0.853187 1.172076 0.6562% 1942 0.847624 1.179768 0.6633%
1941 0.842039 1.187593 -5.6614% 1940 0.892571 1.120359 8.0381% 1939 0.826164
1.210414 0.8126% 1938 0.819504 1.220250 0.7762% 1937 0.813192 1.229722 0.6029% 1936
0.808318 1.237136 0.5244% 1935 0.804102 1.243624 -3.0364% 1934 0.829282 1.205863
4.6271% 1933 0.792607 1.261659 1.3921% 1932 0.781724 1.279223 -0.2051% 1931
0.783331 1.276600 0.8886% 1930 0.776432 1.287944 1.0126% 1929 0.768648 1.300985
1.1526% 1928 0.759890 1.315980 1.2160% 1927 0.750761 1.331982 1.4086% 1926 0.740332
1.350745 1.7667% 1925 0.727480 1.374608 1.4465% 1924 0.717107 1.394492 1.7700% 1923
0.704635 1.419174 1.6165% 1922 0.693426 1.442115 1.3736% 1921 0.684030 1.461925
2.3393% 1920 0.668394 1.496124 1.3140% 1919 0.659725 1.515783 0.7676% 1918 0.654699
1.527419 0.3870% 1917 0.652176 1.533329 1.3274% 1916 0.643632 1.553683 1.4083% 1915
0.634693 1.575564 1.4458% 1914 0.625648 1.598343 1.9424% 1913 0.613727 1.629389

80

1.9857% 1912 0.601778 1.661744 1.5634% 1911 0.592514 1.687723 1.8169% 1910 0.581941
1.718388 1.8781% 1909 0.571213 1.750660 2.0082% 1908 0.559968 1.785818 1.9603% 1907
0.549202 1.820824 1.8264% 1906 0.539351 1.854079 1.9357% 1905 0.529110 1.889968
2.0148% 1904 0.518659 1.928048 2.1335% 1903 0.507825 1.969183 1.8151% 1902 0.498771
2.004927 1.8943% 1901 0.489499 2.042907 3.0255% 1900 0.475124 2.104715 0.6278% 1899
0.472159 2.117929 1.7757% 1898 0.463922 2.155537 1.8078% 1897 0.455684 2.194503
1.8396% 1896 0.447453 2.234873 1.8755% 1895 0.439215 2.276789 1.9114% 1894 0.430977
2.320308 1.9486% 1893 0.422740 2.365522 1.9858% 1892 0.414508 2.412497 2.0276% 1891
0.406271 2.461413 2.6465% 1890 0.395796 2.526555 1.5328% 1889 0.389821 2.565282
2.0811% 1888 0.381873 2.618669 2.1599% 1887 0.373800 2.675228 2.2075% 1886 0.365726
2.734285 2.2592% 1885 0.357646 2.796057 2.3095% 1884 0.349573 2.860633 2.3641% 1883
0.341499 2.928262 2.4214% 1882 0.333426 2.999167 2.4815% 1881 0.325352 3.073590
3.7644% 1880 0.313549 3.189293 0.9432% 1879 0.310619 3.219375 2.1464% 1878 0.304092
3.288475 2.1913% 1877 0.297572 3.360535 2.2426% 1876 0.291045 3.435899 2.2941% 1875
0.284518 3.514721 2.3456% 1874 0.277997 3.597162 2.4043% 1873 0.271470 3.683649
2.4635% 1872 0.264943 3.774397 2.5258% 1871 0.258416 3.869730 5.9947% 1870 0.243801
4.101708 -1.0968% 1869 0.246505 4.056721 2.1930% 1868 0.241215 4.145683 2.2394%
1867 0.235931 4.238522 2.2935% 1866 0.230642 4.335733 2.3445% 1865 0.225358 4.437383
2.4037% 1864 0.220068 4.544044 2.4599% 1863 0.214785 4.655822 2.5250% 1862 0.209495
4.773382 2.5872% 1861 0.204212 4.896881 2.9504% 1860 0.198359 5.041359 2.4012% 1859
0.193708 5.162414 2.7627% 1858 0.188500 5.305037 2.8412% 1857 0.183292 5.455763
2.9243% 1856 0.178085 5.615306 3.0161% 1855 0.172871 5.784671 3.1061% 1854 0.167663
5.964346 3.2056% 1853 0.162455 6.155541 3.3118% 1852 0.157248 6.359399 3.4252% 1851
0.152040 6.577223 4.0106% 1850 0.146177 6.841010 2.3254% 1849 0.142855 7.000088
2.7841% 1848 0.138986 7.194977 2.8590% 1847 0.135123 7.400682 2.9432% 1846 0.131260
7.618496 3.0324% 1845 0.127396 7.849519 3.1325% 1844 0.123527 8.095406 3.2284% 1843
0.119664 8.356755 3.3361% 1842 0.115801 8.635541 3.4512% 1841 0.111937 8.933570
3.8105% 1840 0.107829 9.273983 2.3861% 1839 0.105316 9.495265 2.5824% 1838 0.102664
9.740470 2.6573% 1837 0.100007 9.999306 2.7232% 1836 0.097356 10.271607 2.7994%
1835 0.094705 10.559155 2.8871% 1834 0.092047 10.864010 2.9657% 1833 0.089396
11.186203 3.0563% 1832 0.086745 11.528089 3.1604% 1831 0.084087 11.892425 3.4660%
1830 0.081270 12.304613 2.4653% 1829 0.079315 12.607959 2.6804% 1828 0.077245
12.945902 10.3427% 1827 0.070004 14.284851 -4.2314% 1826 0.073097 13.680397 2.9150%
1825 0.071027 14.079186 3.0026% 1824 0.068956 14.501922 3.0955% 1823 0.066886
14.950831 3.1944% 1822 0.064815 15.428418 3.3102% 1821 0.062739 15.939129 3.2277%
1820 0.060777 16.453602 2.6573% 1819 0.059204 16.890820 2.6261% 1818 0.057689
17.334391 2.6969% 1817 0.056174 17.801888 2.7717% 1816 0.054659 18.295300 2.8507%
1815 0.053144 18.816843 2.9343% 1814 0.051629 19.368994 3.0231% 1813 0.050114
19.954528 3.1039% 1812 0.048605 20.573896 3.2172% 1811 0.047090 21.235791 3.0969%
1810 0.045676 21.893445 2.9144% 1809 0.044382 22.531503 2.8225% 1808 0.043164
23.167447 2.9199% 1807 0.041939 23.843919 2.9918% 1806 0.040721 24.557278 3.0841%
1805 0.039503 25.314637 3.1822% 1804 0.038285 26.120198 3.2868% 1803 0.037066
26.978713 3.3985% 1802 0.035848 27.895580 3.5180% 1801 0.034630 28.876960 3.3999%
1800 0.033491 29.858761 2.8419% 1799 0.032566 30.707308 2.7485% 1798 0.031694
31.551285 2.8261% 1797 0.030823 32.442965 3.7832% 1796 0.029700 33.670351 2.1272%
1795 0.029081 34.386586 3.0879% 1794 0.028210 35.448422 3.1625% 1793 0.027345
36.569483 3.2904% 1792 0.026474 37.772771 3.4024% 1791 0.025603 39.057939 3.2296%
1790 0.024802 40.319340 41.3145% 1780 0.017551 56.977054 29.4353% 1770 0.013560
73.748429 83.4728% 1750 0.007391 135.308336 29.2845% 1740 0.005716 174.932641
94.2514% 1720 0.002943 339.809095 85.8111% 1700 0.001584 631.402949 19.2490% 1690
0.001328 752.942015 88.0250% 1670 0.000706 1415.719392

BASE YEAR: 1952

YEAR BYEAR/AYEAR AYEAR/BYEAR GROWTH%

2009 1.926140 0.519173 8.2857% 2001 1.778758 0.562190 1.0000% 2000 1.761147
0.567812 1.0000% 1999 1.743710 0.573490 1.0000% 1998 1.726445 0.579225 1.0000% 1997
1.709352 0.585017 1.0000% 1996 1.692427 0.590867 1.0000% 1995 1.675671 0.596776

0.9992% 1994 1.659093 0.602739 1.0008% 1993 1.642653 0.608771 1.0000% 1992 1.626389 0.614859 0.9295% 1991 1.611411 0.620574 1.2505% 1990 1.591509 0.628334 0.7224% 1989 1.580094 0.632874 1.1077% 1988 1.562783 0.639884 0.8834% 1987 1.549099 0.645536 0.5594% 1986 1.540482 0.649147 1.3056% 1985 1.520629 0.657623 0.7673% 1984 1.509050 0.662669 0.8149% 1983 1.496851 0.668069 0.9737% 1982 1.482416 0.674574 0.9508% 1981 1.468454 0.680988 0.9031% 1980 1.455312 0.687138 2.2701% 1979 1.423008 0.702737 1.0042% 1978 1.408861 0.709793 0.9896% 1977 1.395055 0.716817 0.9103% 1976 1.382470 0.723343 0.8394% 1975 1.370962 0.729415 0.9042% 1974 1.358677 0.736010 1.1568% 1973 1.343140 0.744524 0.9427% 1972 1.330596 0.751543 0.7426% 1971 1.320788 0.757124 1.4697% 1970 1.301657 0.768252 0.6968% 1969 1.292649 0.773605 0.8565% 1968 1.281671 0.780231 1.5090% 1967 1.262618 0.792005 0.9949% 1966 1.250180 0.799885 1.0575% 1965 1.237098 0.808344 1.1300% 1964 1.223275 0.817478 1.5537% 1963 1.204560 0.830179 1.4658% 1962 1.187158 0.842348 1.5364% 1961 1.169194 0.855290 2.1586% 1960 1.144489 0.873752 -1.6655% 1959 1.163873 0.859200 4.3080% 1958 1.115804 0.896214 2.1130% 1957 1.092716 0.915151 1.9895% 1956 1.071400 0.933358 2.1231% 1955 1.049126 0.953174 1.4496% 1954 1.034135 0.966991 2.1573% 1953 1.012298 0.987852 1.2298% 1952 1.000000 1.000000 1.6814% 1951 0.983464 1.016814 1.6233% 1950 0.967755 1.033319 1.4265% 1949 0.954144 1.048060 1.7790% 1948 0.937466 1.066706 1.8242% 1947 0.920671 1.086164 -2.6320% 1946 0.945559 1.057576 3.1768% 1945 0.916445 1.091173 6.4754% 1944 0.860711 1.161831 -0.3437% 1943 0.863679 1.157838 0.6562% 1942 0.858048 1.165436 0.6633% 1941 0.852394 1.173166 -5.6614% 1940 0.903548 1.106748 8.0381% 1939 0.836323 1.195710 0.8126% 1938 0.829582 1.205427 0.7762% 1937 0.823192 1.214784 0.6029% 1936 0.818259 1.222107 0.5244% 1935 0.813990 1.228516 -3.0364% 1934 0.839480 1.191214 4.6271% 1933 0.802354 1.246333 1.3921% 1932 0.791338 1.263683 -0.2051% 1931 0.792964 1.261091 0.8886% 1930 0.785980 1.272297 1.0126% 1929 0.778101 1.285180 1.1526% 1928 0.769235 1.299993 1.2160% 1927 0.759993 1.315801 1.4086% 1926 0.749437 1.334335 1.7667% 1925 0.736426 1.357909 1.4465% 1924 0.725926 1.377551 1.7700% 1923 0.713301 1.401933 1.6165% 1922 0.701953 1.424596 1.3736% 1921 0.692442 1.444165 2.3393% 1920 0.676614 1.477948 1.3140% 1919 0.667838 1.497369 0.7676% 1918 0.662751 1.508863 0.3870% 1917 0.660196 1.514702 1.3274% 1916 0.651547 1.534809 1.4083% 1915 0.642499 1.556424 1.4458% 1914 0.633342 1.578926 1.9424% 1913 0.621274 1.609595 1.9857% 1912 0.609178 1.641556 1.5634% 1911 0.599801 1.667221 1.8169% 1910 0.589097 1.697513 1.8781% 1909 0.578238 1.729393 2.0082% 1908 0.566854 1.764123 1.9603% 1907 0.555956 1.798705 1.8264% 1906 0.545984 1.831555 1.9357% 1905 0.535616 1.867008 2.0148% 1904 0.525038 1.904625 2.1335% 1903 0.514070 1.945261 1.8151% 1902 0.504905 1.980571 1.8943% 1901 0.495518 2.018089 3.0255% 1900 0.480967 2.079147 0.6278% 1899 0.477966 2.092200 1.7757% 1898 0.469627 2.129351 1.8078% 1897 0.461288 2.167844 1.8396% 1896 0.452955 2.207724 1.8755% 1895 0.444616 2.249130 1.9114% 1894 0.436277 2.292120 1.9486% 1893 0.427938 2.336785 1.9858% 1892 0.419606 2.383189 2.0276% 1891 0.411267 2.431511 2.6465% 1890 0.400663 2.495862 1.5328% 1889 0.394615 2.534119 2.0811% 1888 0.386569 2.586857 2.1599% 1887 0.378397 2.642729 2.2075% 1886 0.370224 2.701068 2.2592% 1885 0.362045 2.762090 2.3095% 1884 0.353872 2.825882 2.3641% 1883 0.345699 2.892689 2.4214% 1882 0.337526 2.962733 2.4815% 1881 0.329353 3.036252 3.7644% 1880 0.317405 3.150549 0.9432% 1879 0.314439 3.180265 2.1464% 1878 0.307832 3.248526 2.1913% 1877 0.301231 3.319711 2.2426% 1876 0.294624 3.394159 2.2941% 1875 0.288017 3.472023 2.3456% 1874 0.281416 3.553463 2.4043% 1873 0.274808 3.638899 2.4635% 1872 0.268201 3.728545 2.5258% 1871 0.261594 3.822720 5.9947% 1870 0.246799 4.051879 -1.0968% 1869 0.249536 4.007439 2.1930% 1868 0.244181 4.095321 2.2394% 1867 0.238833 4.187032 2.2935% 1866 0.233478 4.283061 2.3445% 1865 0.228129 4.383477 2.4037% 1864 0.222775 4.488842 2.4599% 1863 0.217426 4.599262 2.5250% 1862 0.212071 4.715394 2.5872% 1861 0.206723 4.837393 2.9504% 1860 0.200799 4.980116 2.4012% 1859 0.196090 5.099700 2.7627% 1858 0.190818 5.240590 2.8412% 1857 0.185546 5.389486 2.9243% 1856 0.180275 5.547090 3.0161% 1855 0.174997 5.714398 3.1061% 1854 0.169725 5.891890 3.2056% 1853 0.164453 6.080762 3.3118% 1852 0.159181 6.282144 3.4252% 1851 0.153910 6.497322 4.0106% 1850 0.147975 6.757904 2.3254% 1849 0.144612 6.915050 2.7841% 1848 0.140695 7.107571 2.8590% 1847 0.136784 7.310777 2.9432% 1846 0.132874

7.525945 3.0324% 1845 0.128963 7.754162 3.1325% 1844 0.125046 7.997062 3.2284% 1843 0.121135 8.255236 3.3361% 1842 0.117225 8.530635 3.4512% 1841 0.113314 8.825044 3.8105% 1840 0.109155 9.161321 2.3861% 1839 0.106611 9.379915 2.5824% 1838 0.103927 9.622141 2.6573% 1837 0.101237 9.877832 2.7232% 1836 0.098553 10.146826 2.7994% 1835 0.095869 10.430880 2.8871% 1834 0.093179 10.732033 2.9657% 1833 0.090495 11.050311 3.0563% 1832 0.087811 11.388044 3.1604% 1831 0.085121 11.747954 3.4660% 1830 0.082270 12.155134 2.4653% 1829 0.080290 12.454795 2.6804% 1828 0.078194 12.788633 10.3427% 1827 0.070865 14.111317 -4.2314% 1826 0.073996 13.514206 2.9150% 1825 0.071900 13.908150 3.0026% 1824 0.069804 14.325751 3.0955% 1823 0.067708 14.769205 3.1944% 1822 0.065613 15.240991 3.3102% 1821 0.063510 15.745498 3.2277% 1820 0.061524 16.253721 2.6573% 1819 0.059932 16.685627 2.6261% 1818 0.058398 17.123810 2.6969% 1817 0.056865 17.585628 2.7717% 1816 0.055331 18.073045 2.8507% 1815 0.053797 18.588253 2.9343% 1814 0.052264 19.133696 3.0231% 1813 0.050730 19.712117 3.1039% 1812 0.049203 20.323961 3.2172% 1811 0.047669 20.977815 3.0969% 1810 0.046237 21.627480 2.9144% 1809 0.044928 22.257787 2.8225% 1808 0.043695 22.886005 2.9199% 1807 0.042455 23.554259 2.9918% 1806 0.041222 24.258952 3.0841% 1805 0.039989 25.007111 3.1822% 1804 0.038755 25.802885 3.2868% 1803 0.037522 26.650971 3.3985% 1802 0.036289 27.556700 3.5180% 1801 0.035056 28.526157 3.3999% 1800 0.033903 29.496032 2.8419% 1799 0.032966 30.334270 2.7485% 1798 0.032084 31.167994 2.8261% 1797 0.031202 32.048843 3.7832% 1796 0.030065 33.261318 2.1272% 1795 0.029439 33.968852 3.0879% 1794 0.028557 35.017789 3.1625% 1793 0.027681 36.125231 3.2904% 1792 0.026800 37.313901 3.4024% 1791 0.025918 38.583457 3.2296% 1790 0.025107 39.829534 41.3145% 1780 0.017767 56.284887 29.4353% 1770 0.013726 72.852521 83.4728% 1750 0.007481 133.664588 29.2845% 1740 0.005787 172.807531 94.2514% 1720 0.002979 335.681038 85.8111% 1700 0.001603 623.732563 19.2490% 1690 0.001344 743.795152 88.0250% 1670 0.000715 1398.521001

BASE YEAR: 1951

YEAR BYEAR/AYEAR AYEAR/BYEAR GROWTH%

2009 1.958526 0.510588 8.2857% 2001 1.808666 0.552894 1.0000% 2000 1.790758 0.558423 1.0000% 1999 1.773028 0.564007 1.0000% 1998 1.755473 0.569647 1.0000% 1997 1.738092 0.575343 1.0000% 1996 1.720883 0.581097 1.0000% 1995 1.703845 0.586908 0.9992% 1994 1.686988 0.592772 1.0008% 1993 1.670272 0.598705 1.0000% 1992 1.653735 0.604692 0.9295% 1991 1.638505 0.610312 1.2505% 1990 1.618268 0.617944 0.7224% 1989 1.606661 0.622409 1.1077% 1988 1.589060 0.629303 0.8834% 1987 1.575145 0.634862 0.5594% 1986 1.566384 0.638413 1.3056% 1985 1.546196 0.646749 0.7673% 1984 1.534423 0.651711 0.8149% 1983 1.522019 0.657022 0.9737% 1982 1.507341 0.663420 0.9508% 1981 1.493144 0.669728 0.9031% 1980 1.479781 0.675776 2.2701% 1979 1.446935 0.691116 1.0042% 1978 1.432549 0.698056 0.9896% 1977 1.418512 0.704964 0.9103% 1976 1.405715 0.711382 0.8394% 1975 1.394013 0.717353 0.9042% 1974 1.381522 0.723840 1.1568% 1973 1.365723 0.732213 0.9427% 1972 1.352969 0.739115 0.7426% 1971 1.342995 0.744604 1.4697% 1970 1.323542 0.755548 0.6968% 1969 1.314384 0.760813 0.8565% 1968 1.303221 0.767330 1.5090% 1967 1.283847 0.778909 0.9949% 1966 1.271200 0.786658 1.0575% 1965 1.257898 0.794977 1.1300% 1964 1.243842 0.803960 1.5537% 1963 1.224813 0.816451 1.4658% 1962 1.207119 0.828419 1.5364% 1961 1.188853 0.841147 2.1586% 1960 1.163732 0.859304 -1.6655% 1959 1.183442 0.844993 4.3080% 1958 1.134565 0.881395 2.1130% 1957 1.111088 0.900018 1.9895% 1956 1.089415 0.917924 2.1231% 1955 1.066766 0.937413 1.4496% 1954 1.051523 0.951001 2.1573% 1953 1.029318 0.971517 1.2298% 1952 1.016814 0.983464 1.6814% 1951 1.000000 1.000000 1.6233% 1950 0.984027 1.016233 1.4265% 1949 0.970186 1.030730 1.7790% 1948 0.953228 1.049067 1.8242% 1947 0.936151 1.068203 -2.6320% 1946 0.961457 1.040088 3.1768% 1945 0.931854 1.073129 6.4754% 1944 0.875182 1.142619 -0.3437% 1943 0.878200 1.138692 0.6562% 1942 0.872475 1.146164 0.6633% 1941 0.866726 1.153767 -5.6614% 1940 0.918740 1.088447 8.0381% 1939 0.850385 1.175938 0.8126% 1938 0.843530 1.185494 0.7762% 1937 0.837033 1.194696 0.6029% 1936 0.832017 1.201899 0.5244% 1935 0.827676 1.208202 -3.0364% 1934 0.853595 1.171516 4.6271% 1933 0.815845 1.225724 1.3921% 1932 0.804643 1.242787 -0.2051% 1931 0.806297 1.240238 0.8886% 1930 0.799195 1.251259 1.0126% 1929 0.791184 1.263929

1.1526% 1928 0.782168 1.278497 1.2160% 1927 0.772771 1.294044 1.4086% 1926 0.762038
1.312271 1.7667% 1925 0.748808 1.335455 1.4465% 1924 0.738131 1.354772 1.7700% 1923
0.725294 1.378751 1.6165% 1922 0.713756 1.401039 1.3736% 1921 0.704084 1.420285
2.3393% 1920 0.687990 1.453509 1.3140% 1919 0.679067 1.472609 0.7676% 1918 0.673894
1.483913 0.3870% 1917 0.671296 1.489656 1.3274% 1916 0.662502 1.509430 1.4083% 1915
0.653301 1.530687 1.4458% 1914 0.643991 1.552818 1.9424% 1913 0.631720 1.582979
1.9857% 1912 0.619421 1.614412 1.5634% 1911 0.609886 1.639652 1.8169% 1910 0.599002
1.669443 1.8781% 1909 0.587960 1.700796 2.0082% 1908 0.576385 1.734952 1.9603% 1907
0.565303 1.768962 1.8264% 1906 0.555164 1.801269 1.9357% 1905 0.544622 1.836136
2.0148% 1904 0.533865 1.873131 2.1335% 1903 0.522713 1.913095 1.8151% 1902 0.513394
1.947820 1.8943% 1901 0.503850 1.984719 3.0255% 1900 0.489053 2.044767 0.6278% 1899
0.486002 2.057604 1.7757% 1898 0.477523 2.094140 1.8078% 1897 0.469044 2.131997
1.8396% 1896 0.460571 2.171217 1.8755% 1895 0.452092 2.211939 1.9114% 1894 0.443613
2.254218 1.9486% 1893 0.435134 2.298145 1.9858% 1892 0.426661 2.343781 2.0276% 1891
0.418182 2.391305 2.6465% 1890 0.407400 2.454591 1.5328% 1889 0.401249 2.492215
2.0811% 1888 0.393069 2.544081 2.1599% 1887 0.384759 2.599030 2.2075% 1886 0.376449
2.656404 2.2592% 1885 0.368132 2.716417 2.3095% 1884 0.359822 2.779154 2.3641% 1883
0.351512 2.844857 2.4214% 1882 0.343201 2.913742 2.4815% 1881 0.334891 2.986045
3.7644% 1880 0.322742 3.098452 0.9432% 1879 0.319726 3.127677 2.1464% 1878 0.313008
3.194809 2.1913% 1877 0.306296 3.264817 2.2426% 1876 0.299578 3.338034 2.2941% 1875
0.292859 3.414611 2.3456% 1874 0.286147 3.494704 2.4043% 1873 0.279429 3.578727
2.4635% 1872 0.272711 3.666891 2.5258% 1871 0.265992 3.759508 5.9947% 1870 0.250949
3.984879 -1.0968% 1869 0.253732 3.941173 2.1930% 1868 0.248287 4.027602 2.2394%
1867 0.242848 4.117796 2.2935% 1866 0.237403 4.212238 2.3445% 1865 0.231965 4.310993
2.4037% 1864 0.226520 4.414616 2.4599% 1863 0.221082 4.523210 2.5250% 1862 0.215637
4.637422 2.5872% 1861 0.210199 4.757403 2.9504% 1860 0.204175 4.897766 2.4012% 1859
0.199387 5.015373 2.7627% 1858 0.194027 5.153933 2.8412% 1857 0.188666 5.300367
2.9243% 1856 0.183306 5.455365 3.0161% 1855 0.177939 5.619906 3.1061% 1854 0.172579
5.794464 3.2056% 1853 0.167218 5.980213 3.3118% 1852 0.161858 6.178265 3.4252% 1851
0.156497 6.389884 4.0106% 1850 0.150463 6.646157 2.3254% 1849 0.147044 6.800705
2.7841% 1848 0.143061 6.990042 2.8590% 1847 0.139084 7.189888 2.9432% 1846 0.135108
7.401498 3.0324% 1845 0.131131 7.625941 3.1325% 1844 0.127148 7.864824 3.2284% 1843
0.123172 8.118729 3.3361% 1842 0.119196 8.389575 3.4512% 1841 0.115219 8.679115
3.8105% 1840 0.110990 9.009832 2.3861% 1839 0.108403 9.224811 2.5824% 1838 0.105674
9.463032 2.6573% 1837 0.102939 9.714495 2.7232% 1836 0.100210 9.979041 2.7994% 1835
0.097481 10.258398 2.8871% 1834 0.094746 10.554571 2.9657% 1833 0.092017 10.867586
3.0563% 1832 0.089288 11.199734 3.1604% 1831 0.086552 11.553693 3.4660% 1830
0.083653 11.954141 2.4653% 1829 0.081640 12.248846 2.6804% 1828 0.079509 12.577164
10.3427% 1827 0.072057 13.877976 -4.2314% 1826 0.075240 13.290738 2.9150% 1825
0.073109 13.678168 3.0026% 1824 0.070978 14.088864 3.0955% 1823 0.068847 14.524986
3.1944% 1822 0.066716 14.988971 3.3102% 1821 0.064578 15.485134 3.2277% 1820
0.062559 15.984954 2.6573% 1819 0.060939 16.409719 2.6261% 1818 0.059380 16.840655
2.6969% 1817 0.057821 17.294836 2.7717% 1816 0.056261 17.774194 2.8507% 1815
0.054702 18.280883 2.9343% 1814 0.053143 18.817307 3.0231% 1813 0.051583 19.386163
3.1039% 1812 0.050030 19.987890 3.2172% 1811 0.048471 20.630932 3.0969% 1810
0.047015 21.269854 2.9144% 1809 0.045684 21.889738 2.8225% 1808 0.044430 22.507568
2.9199% 1807 0.043169 23.164773 2.9918% 1806 0.041915 23.857813 3.0841% 1805
0.040661 24.593600 3.1822% 1804 0.039407 25.376216 3.2868% 1803 0.038153 26.210278
3.3985% 1802 0.036899 27.101030 3.5180% 1801 0.035645 28.054457 3.3999% 1800
0.034473 29.008293 2.8419% 1799 0.033520 29.832671 2.7485% 1798 0.032624 30.652609
2.8261% 1797 0.031727 31.518892 3.7832% 1796 0.030570 32.711318 2.1272% 1795
0.029934 33.407152 3.0879% 1794 0.029037 34.438745 3.1625% 1793 0.028147 35.527874
3.2904% 1792 0.027250 36.696888 3.4024% 1791 0.026354 37.945451 3.2296% 1790
0.025529 39.170924 41.3145% 1780 0.018065 55.354176 29.4353% 1770 0.013957
71.647852 83.4728% 1750 0.007607 131.454347 29.2845% 1740 0.005884 169.950033

94.2514% 1720 0.003029 330.130309 85.8111% 1700 0.001630 613.418693 19.2490% 1690 0.001367 731.495960 88.0250% 1670 0.000727 1375.395442

BASE YEAR: 1950

YEAR BYEAR/AYEAR AYEAR/BYEAR GROWTH%

2009 1.990318 0.502432 8.2857% 2001 1.838026 0.544062 1.0000% 2000 1.819827 0.549503 1.0000% 1999 1.801809 0.554998 1.0000% 1998 1.783969 0.560548 1.0000% 1997 1.766306 0.566153 1.0000% 1996 1.748818 0.571815 1.0000% 1995 1.731503 0.577533 0.9992% 1994 1.714373 0.583304 1.0008% 1993 1.697386 0.589141 1.0000% 1992 1.680580 0.595033 0.9295% 1991 1.665103 0.600564 1.2505% 1990 1.644537 0.608074 0.7224% 1989 1.632742 0.612467 1.1077% 1988 1.614854 0.619251 0.8834% 1987 1.600714 0.624721 0.5594% 1986 1.591810 0.628216 1.3056% 1985 1.571295 0.636418 0.7673% 1984 1.559330 0.641301 0.8149% 1983 1.546726 0.646527 0.9737% 1982 1.531810 0.652823 0.9508% 1981 1.517382 0.659030 0.9031% 1980 1.503802 0.664981 2.2701% 1979 1.470422 0.680077 1.0042% 1978 1.455803 0.686906 0.9896% 1977 1.441538 0.693704 0.9103% 1976 1.428533 0.700019 0.8394% 1975 1.416642 0.705895 0.9042% 1974 1.403947 0.712277 1.1568% 1973 1.387892 0.720517 0.9427% 1972 1.374931 0.727309 0.7426% 1971 1.364796 0.732711 1.4697% 1970 1.345027 0.743479 0.6968% 1969 1.335720 0.748660 0.8565% 1968 1.324376 0.755073 1.5090% 1967 1.304688 0.766467 0.9949% 1966 1.291835 0.774093 1.0575% 1965 1.278317 0.782278 1.1300% 1964 1.264033 0.791118 1.5537% 1963 1.244695 0.803410 1.4658% 1962 1.226714 0.815186 1.5364% 1961 1.208151 0.827711 2.1586% 1960 1.182623 0.845578 -1.6655% 1959 1.202653 0.831495 4.3080% 1958 1.152982 0.867316 2.1130% 1957 1.129124 0.885642 1.9895% 1956 1.107099 0.903262 2.1231% 1955 1.084083 0.922439 1.4496% 1954 1.068592 0.935811 2.1573% 1953 1.046027 0.955999 1.2298% 1952 1.033319 0.967755 1.6814% 1951 1.016233 0.984027 1.6233% 1950 1.000000 1.000000 1.4265% 1949 0.985935 1.014265 1.7790% 1948 0.968702 1.032310 1.8242% 1947 0.951348 1.051141 -2.6320% 1946 0.977064 1.023474 3.1768% 1945 0.946981 1.055988 6.4754% 1944 0.889389 1.124367 -0.3437% 1943 0.892456 1.120503 0.6562% 1942 0.886638 1.127856 0.6633% 1941 0.880795 1.135337 -5.6614% 1940 0.933654 1.071061 8.0381% 1939 0.864189 1.157154 0.8126% 1938 0.857223 1.166558 0.7762% 1937 0.850620 1.175613 0.6029% 1936 0.845523 1.182700 0.5244% 1935 0.841112 1.188902 -3.0364% 1934 0.867451 1.152803 4.6271% 1933 0.829088 1.206145 1.3921% 1932 0.817705 1.222935 -0.2051% 1931 0.819385 1.220427 0.8886% 1930 0.812168 1.231272 1.0126% 1929 0.804027 1.243740 1.1526% 1928 0.794865 1.258075 1.2160% 1927 0.785316 1.273373 1.4086% 1926 0.774408 1.291310 1.7667% 1925 0.760964 1.314123 1.4465% 1924 0.750113 1.333132 1.7700% 1923 0.737067 1.356728 1.6165% 1922 0.725342 1.378660 1.3736% 1921 0.715513 1.397598 2.3393% 1920 0.699158 1.430292 1.3140% 1919 0.690090 1.449086 0.7676% 1918 0.684833 1.460210 0.3870% 1917 0.682193 1.465861 1.3274% 1916 0.673256 1.485319 1.4083% 1915 0.663906 1.506237 1.4458% 1914 0.654444 1.528014 1.9424% 1913 0.641975 1.557694 1.9857% 1912 0.629475 1.588624 1.5634% 1911 0.619786 1.613461 1.8169% 1910 0.608726 1.642776 1.8781% 1909 0.597504 1.673629 2.0082% 1908 0.585741 1.707239 1.9603% 1907 0.574480 1.740705 1.8264% 1906 0.564176 1.772497 1.9357% 1905 0.553463 1.806807 2.0148% 1904 0.542532 1.843211 2.1335% 1903 0.531198 1.882536 1.8151% 1902 0.521728 1.916707 1.8943% 1901 0.512029 1.953016 3.0255% 1900 0.496992 2.012105 0.6278% 1899 0.493891 2.024737 1.7757% 1898 0.485274 2.060690 1.8078% 1897 0.476658 2.097942 1.8396% 1896 0.468047 2.136536 1.8755% 1895 0.459431 2.176607 1.9114% 1894 0.450814 2.218211 1.9486% 1893 0.442197 2.261435 1.9858% 1892 0.433587 2.306343 2.0276% 1891 0.424970 2.353107 2.6465% 1890 0.414013 2.415383 1.5328% 1889 0.407763 2.452406 2.0811% 1888 0.399450 2.503444 2.1599% 1887 0.391005 2.557514 2.2075% 1886 0.382560 2.613972 2.2592% 1885 0.374108 2.673026 2.3095% 1884 0.365663 2.734761 2.3641% 1883 0.357218 2.799415 2.4214% 1882 0.348772 2.867199 2.4815% 1881 0.340327 2.938348 3.7644% 1880 0.327981 3.048959 0.9432% 1879 0.324916 3.077718 2.1464% 1878 0.318089 3.143777 2.1913% 1877 0.311268 3.212667 2.2426% 1876 0.304440 3.284714 2.2941% 1875 0.297613 3.360068 2.3456% 1874 0.290792 3.438881 2.4043% 1873 0.283965 3.521563 2.4635% 1872 0.277137 3.608318 2.5258% 1871 0.270310 3.699456 5.9947% 1870 0.255022 3.921226 -1.0968% 1869 0.257850 3.878219 2.1930% 1868 0.252317 3.963267 2.2394% 1867 0.246790 4.052021 2.2935% 1866 0.241257 4.144954 2.3445% 1865 0.235731 4.242131

2.4037% 1864 0.230197 4.344099 2.4599% 1863 0.224671 4.450959 2.5250% 1862 0.219137 4.563346 2.5872% 1861 0.213611 4.681411 2.9504% 1860 0.207489 4.819532 2.4012% 1859 0.202624 4.935260 2.7627% 1858 0.197176 5.071607 2.8412% 1857 0.191729 5.215702 2.9243% 1856 0.186281 5.368224 3.0161% 1855 0.180827 5.530137 3.1061% 1854 0.175380 5.701906 3.2056% 1853 0.169933 5.884688 3.3118% 1852 0.164485 6.079576 3.4252% 1851 0.159038 6.287816 4.0106% 1850 0.152905 6.539995 2.3254% 1849 0.149431 6.692074 2.7841% 1848 0.145383 6.878387 2.8590% 1847 0.141342 7.075041 2.9432% 1846 0.137301 7.283271 3.0324% 1845 0.133260 7.504129 3.1325% 1844 0.129212 7.739196 3.2284% 1843 0.125171 7.989045 3.3361% 1842 0.121130 8.255564 3.4512% 1841 0.117089 8.540480 3.8105% 1840 0.112792 8.865914 2.3861% 1839 0.110163 9.077459 2.5824% 1838 0.107390 9.311875 2.6573% 1837 0.104610 9.559321 2.7232% 1836 0.101837 9.819641 2.7994% 1835 0.099063 10.094536 2.8871% 1834 0.096284 10.385978 2.9657% 1833 0.093510 10.693993 3.0563% 1832 0.090737 11.020836 3.1604% 1831 0.087957 11.369141 3.4660% 1830 0.085011 11.763192 2.4653% 1829 0.082966 12.053190 2.6804% 1828 0.080800 12.376263 10.3427% 1827 0.073226 13.656297 -4.2314% 1826 0.076462 13.078440 2.9150% 1825 0.074296 13.459681 3.0026% 1824 0.072130 13.863816 3.0955% 1823 0.069964 14.292972 3.1944% 1822 0.067799 14.749545 3.3102% 1821 0.065626 15.237783 3.2277% 1820 0.063574 15.729619 2.6573% 1819 0.061929 16.147599 2.6261% 1818 0.060344 16.571652 2.6969% 1817 0.058759 17.018578 2.7717% 1816 0.057175 17.490279 2.8507% 1815 0.055590 17.988874 2.9343% 1814 0.054005 18.516729 3.0231% 1813 0.052421 19.076500 3.1039% 1812 0.050842 19.668614 3.2172% 1811 0.049258 20.301385 3.0969% 1810 0.047778 20.930101 2.9144% 1809 0.046425 21.540084 2.8225% 1808 0.045151 22.148045 2.9199% 1807 0.043870 22.794752 2.9918% 1806 0.042595 23.476721 3.0841% 1805 0.041321 24.200756 3.1822% 1804 0.040047 24.970871 3.2868% 1803 0.038772 25.791609 3.3985% 1802 0.037498 26.668133 3.5180% 1801 0.036224 27.606331 3.3999% 1800 0.035032 28.544931 2.8419% 1799 0.034064 29.356141 2.7485% 1798 0.033153 30.162981 2.8261% 1797 0.032242 31.015427 3.7832% 1796 0.031067 32.188806 2.1272% 1795 0.030420 32.873525 3.0879% 1794 0.029508 33.888640 3.1625% 1793 0.028604 34.960372 3.2904% 1792 0.027693 36.110713 3.4024% 1791 0.026781 37.339332 3.2296% 1790 0.025944 38.545229 41.3145% 1780 0.018359 54.469979 29.4353% 1770 0.014184 70.503389 83.4728% 1750 0.007731 129.354570 29.2845% 1740 0.005980 167.235347 94.2514% 1720 0.003078 324.856993 85.8111% 1700 0.001657 603.620287 19.2490% 1690 0.001389 719.811454 88.0250% 1670 0.000739 1353.425648

BASE YEAR: 1949

YEAR BYEAR/AYEAR AYEAR/BYEAR GROWTH%

2009 2.018711 0.495366 8.2857% 2001 1.864246 0.536410 1.0000% 2000 1.845788 0.541774 1.0000% 1999 1.827512 0.547192 1.0000% 1998 1.809418 0.552664 1.0000% 1997 1.791503 0.558190 1.0000% 1996 1.773766 0.563772 1.0000% 1995 1.756204 0.569410 0.9992% 1994 1.738829 0.575100 1.0008% 1993 1.721599 0.580855 1.0000% 1992 1.704554 0.586664 0.9295% 1991 1.688856 0.592117 1.2505% 1990 1.667997 0.599521 0.7224% 1989 1.656033 0.603853 1.1077% 1988 1.637891 0.610541 0.8834% 1987 1.623549 0.615935 0.5594% 1986 1.614518 0.619380 1.3056% 1985 1.593710 0.627467 0.7673% 1984 1.581575 0.632281 0.8149% 1983 1.568790 0.637434 0.9737% 1982 1.553661 0.643641 0.9508% 1981 1.539028 0.649761 0.9031% 1980 1.525254 0.655628 2.2701% 1979 1.491398 0.670512 1.0042% 1978 1.476571 0.677245 0.9896% 1977 1.462102 0.683947 0.9103% 1976 1.448912 0.690173 0.8394% 1975 1.436850 0.695967 0.9042% 1974 1.423975 0.702259 1.1568% 1973 1.407691 0.710383 0.9427% 1972 1.394545 0.717080 0.7426% 1971 1.384265 0.722405 1.4697% 1970 1.364214 0.733023 0.6968% 1969 1.354774 0.738130 0.8565% 1968 1.343268 0.744453 1.5090% 1967 1.323299 0.755687 0.9949% 1966 1.310263 0.763205 1.0575% 1965 1.296553 0.771276 1.1300% 1964 1.282065 0.779991 1.5537% 1963 1.262451 0.792110 1.4658% 1962 1.244213 0.803721 1.5364% 1961 1.225386 0.816069 2.1586% 1960 1.199493 0.833685 -1.6655% 1959 1.219809 0.819800 4.3080% 1958 1.169430 0.855117 2.1130% 1957 1.145232 0.873186 1.9895% 1956 1.122892 0.890558 2.1231% 1955 1.099547 0.909465 1.4496% 1954 1.083836 0.922649 2.1573% 1953 1.060949 0.942553 1.2298% 1952 1.048060 0.954144 1.6814% 1951 1.030730 0.970186 1.6233% 1950 1.014265 0.985935 1.4265% 1949 1.000000 1.000000 1.7790% 1948 0.982521 1.017790 1.8242% 1947 0.964919 1.036357 -

2.6320% 1946 0.991002 1.009079 3.1768% 1945 0.960490 1.041136 6.4754% 1944 0.902076
1.108554 -0.3437% 1943 0.905187 1.104744 0.6562% 1942 0.899286 1.111993 0.6633%
1941 0.893360 1.119369 -5.6614% 1940 0.946972 1.055997 8.0381% 1939 0.876517
1.140879 0.8126% 1938 0.869452 1.150150 0.7762% 1937 0.862755 1.159078 0.6029% 1936
0.857584 1.166066 0.5244% 1935 0.853111 1.172181 -3.0364% 1934 0.879825 1.136589
4.6271% 1933 0.840915 1.189180 1.3921% 1932 0.829369 1.205735 -0.2051% 1931
0.831074 1.203262 0.8886% 1930 0.823754 1.213955 1.0126% 1929 0.815496 1.226247
1.1526% 1928 0.806204 1.240381 1.2160% 1927 0.796519 1.255464 1.4086% 1926 0.785455
1.273148 1.7667% 1925 0.771819 1.295640 1.4465% 1924 0.760814 1.314382 1.7700% 1923
0.747582 1.337646 1.6165% 1922 0.735689 1.359269 1.3736% 1921 0.725721 1.377941
2.3393% 1920 0.709132 1.410175 1.3140% 1919 0.699935 1.428705 0.7676% 1918 0.694602
1.439672 0.3870% 1917 0.691925 1.445244 1.3274% 1916 0.682860 1.464428 1.4083% 1915
0.673377 1.485052 1.4458% 1914 0.663780 1.506523 1.9424% 1913 0.651133 1.535785
1.9857% 1912 0.638455 1.566281 1.5634% 1911 0.628627 1.590768 1.8169% 1910 0.617409
1.619671 1.8781% 1909 0.606028 1.650090 2.0082% 1908 0.594097 1.683227 1.9603% 1907
0.582675 1.716223 1.8264% 1906 0.572224 1.747567 1.9357% 1905 0.561358 1.781394
2.0148% 1904 0.550271 1.817286 2.1335% 1903 0.538776 1.856059 1.8151% 1902 0.529171
1.889749 1.8943% 1901 0.519333 1.925547 3.0255% 1900 0.504082 1.983805 0.6278% 1899
0.500937 1.996260 1.7757% 1898 0.492197 2.031707 1.8078% 1897 0.483457 2.068435
1.8396% 1896 0.474724 2.106486 1.8755% 1895 0.465985 2.145994 1.9114% 1894 0.457245
2.187012 1.9486% 1893 0.448505 2.229629 1.9858% 1892 0.439772 2.273905 2.0276% 1891
0.431032 2.320011 2.6465% 1890 0.419919 2.381411 1.5328% 1889 0.413580 2.417914
2.0811% 1888 0.405148 2.468233 2.1599% 1887 0.396582 2.521544 2.2075% 1886 0.388017
2.577208 2.2592% 1885 0.379445 2.635431 2.3095% 1884 0.370879 2.696297 2.3641% 1883
0.362313 2.760042 2.4214% 1882 0.353748 2.826873 2.4815% 1881 0.345182 2.897021
3.7644% 1880 0.332660 3.006076 0.9432% 1879 0.329551 3.034430 2.1464% 1878 0.322626
3.099561 2.1913% 1877 0.315708 3.167482 2.2426% 1876 0.308783 3.238516 2.2941% 1875
0.301859 3.312809 2.3456% 1874 0.294941 3.390514 2.4043% 1873 0.288016 3.472033
2.4635% 1872 0.281091 3.557568 2.5258% 1871 0.274166 3.647424 5.9947% 1870 0.258660
3.866075 -1.0968% 1869 0.261529 3.823673 2.1930% 1868 0.255916 3.907525 2.2394%
1867 0.250311 3.995030 2.2935% 1866 0.244699 4.086656 2.3445% 1865 0.239093 4.182467
2.4037% 1864 0.233481 4.283001 2.4599% 1863 0.227876 4.388357 2.5250% 1862 0.222264
4.499164 2.5872% 1861 0.216658 4.615568 2.9504% 1860 0.210449 4.751746 2.4012% 1859
0.205514 4.865847 2.7627% 1858 0.199989 5.000276 2.8412% 1857 0.194464 5.142344
2.9243% 1856 0.188939 5.292721 3.0161% 1855 0.183407 5.452357 3.1061% 1854 0.177882
5.621710 3.2056% 1853 0.172357 5.801921 3.3118% 1852 0.166832 5.994069 3.4252% 1851
0.161306 6.199379 4.0106% 1850 0.155087 6.448012 2.3254% 1849 0.151562 6.597952
2.7841% 1848 0.147457 6.781645 2.8590% 1847 0.143358 6.975533 2.9432% 1846 0.139260
7.180833 3.0324% 1845 0.135161 7.398585 3.1325% 1844 0.131056 7.630346 3.2284% 1843
0.126957 7.876681 3.3361% 1842 0.122858 8.139452 3.4512% 1841 0.118760 8.420360
3.8105% 1840 0.114401 8.741217 2.3861% 1839 0.111734 8.949787 2.5824% 1838 0.108922
9.180906 2.6573% 1837 0.106102 9.424872 2.7232% 1836 0.103289 9.681531 2.7994% 1835
0.100477 9.952559 2.8871% 1834 0.097657 10.239902 2.9657% 1833 0.094844 10.543585
3.0563% 1832 0.092032 10.865831 3.1604% 1831 0.089212 11.209237 3.4660% 1830
0.086224 11.597746 2.4653% 1829 0.084149 11.883665 2.6804% 1828 0.081952 12.202194
10.3427% 1827 0.074271 13.464225 -4.2314% 1826 0.077552 12.894495 2.9150% 1825
0.075356 13.270374 3.0026% 1824 0.073159 13.668826 3.0955% 1823 0.070963 14.091945
3.1944% 1822 0.068766 14.542097 3.3102% 1821 0.066563 15.023468 3.2277% 1820
0.064481 15.508386 2.6573% 1819 0.062812 15.920487 2.6261% 1818 0.061205 16.338576
2.6969% 1817 0.059590 16.779217 2.7717% 1816 0.057990 17.244283 2.8507% 1815
0.056383 17.735865 2.9343% 1814 0.054776 18.256297 3.0231% 1813 0.053168 18.808194
3.1039% 1812 0.051568 19.391981 3.2172% 1811 0.049960 20.015851 3.0969% 1810
0.048460 20.635725 2.9144% 1809 0.047087 21.237128 2.8225% 1808 0.045795 21.836538
2.9199% 1807 0.044496 22.474150 2.9918% 1806 0.043203 23.146528 3.0841% 1805
0.041910 23.860379 3.1822% 1804 0.040618 24.619662 3.2868% 1803 0.039325 25.428857
3.3985% 1802 0.038033 26.293053 3.5180% 1801 0.036740 27.218055 3.3999% 1800

0.035532 28.143455 2.8419% 1799 0.034550 28.943255 2.7485% 1798 0.033626 29.738747
2.8261% 1797 0.032702 30.579203 3.7832% 1796 0.031510 31.736079 2.1272% 1795
0.030854 32.411168 3.0879% 1794 0.029929 33.412005 3.1625% 1793 0.029012 34.468663
3.2904% 1792 0.028088 35.602825 3.4024% 1791 0.027163 36.814164 3.2296% 1790
0.026314 38.003101 41.3145% 1780 0.018621 53.703874 29.4353% 1770 0.014386
69.511778 83.4728% 1750 0.007841 127.535232 29.2845% 1740 0.006065 164.883227
94.2514% 1720 0.003122 320.287967 85.8111% 1700 0.001680 595.130530 19.2490% 1690
0.001409 709.687500 88.0250% 1670 0.000749 1334.390080

BASE YEAR: 1948

YEAR BYEAR/AYEAR AYEAR/BYEAR GROWTH%

2009 2.054624 0.486707 8.2857% 2001 1.897411 0.527034 1.0000% 2000 1.878625
0.532304 1.0000% 1999 1.860025 0.537627 1.0000% 1998 1.841609 0.543004 1.0000% 1997
1.823375 0.548434 1.0000% 1996 1.805322 0.553918 1.0000% 1995 1.787447 0.559457
0.9992% 1994 1.769763 0.565047 1.0008% 1993 1.752227 0.570702 1.0000% 1992 1.734879
0.576409 0.9295% 1991 1.718901 0.581767 1.2505% 1990 1.697672 0.589042 0.7224% 1989
1.685495 0.593298 1.1077% 1988 1.667030 0.599869 0.8834% 1987 1.652433 0.605168
0.5594% 1986 1.643241 0.608553 1.3056% 1985 1.622063 0.616499 0.7673% 1984 1.609712
0.621229 0.8149% 1983 1.596700 0.626292 0.9737% 1982 1.581302 0.632390 0.9508% 1981
1.566408 0.638403 0.9031% 1980 1.552389 0.644168 2.2701% 1979 1.517931 0.658791
1.0042% 1978 1.502840 0.665407 0.9896% 1977 1.488113 0.671992 0.9103% 1976 1.474689
0.678109 0.8394% 1975 1.462413 0.683802 0.9042% 1974 1.449308 0.689984 1.1568% 1973
1.432735 0.697966 0.9427% 1972 1.419354 0.704546 0.7426% 1971 1.408891 0.709778
1.4697% 1970 1.388484 0.720210 0.6968% 1969 1.378876 0.725228 0.8565% 1968 1.367166
0.731440 1.5090% 1967 1.346841 0.742478 0.9949% 1966 1.333574 0.749865 1.0575% 1965
1.319619 0.757794 1.1300% 1964 1.304874 0.766358 1.5537% 1963 1.284911 0.778264
1.4658% 1962 1.266348 0.789672 1.5364% 1961 1.247186 0.801805 2.1586% 1960 1.220833
0.819113 -1.6655% 1959 1.241510 0.805471 4.3080% 1958 1.190235 0.840170 2.1130%
1957 1.165606 0.857923 1.9895% 1956 1.142869 0.874991 2.1231% 1955 1.119109 0.893568
1.4496% 1954 1.103118 0.906521 2.1573% 1953 1.079823 0.926077 1.2298% 1952 1.066706
0.937466 1.6814% 1951 1.049067 0.953228 1.6233% 1950 1.032310 0.968702 1.4265% 1949
1.017790 0.982521 1.7790% 1948 1.000000 1.000000 1.8242% 1947 0.982085 1.018242 -
2.6320% 1946 1.008633 0.991441 3.1768% 1945 0.977577 1.022937 6.4754% 1944 0.918125
1.089177 -0.3437% 1943 0.921291 1.085433 0.6562% 1942 0.915285 1.092556 0.6633%
1941 0.909254 1.099803 -5.6614% 1940 0.963820 1.037539 8.0381% 1939 0.892111
1.120937 0.8126% 1938 0.884920 1.130046 0.7762% 1937 0.878103 1.138818 0.6029% 1936
0.872841 1.145684 0.5244% 1935 0.868288 1.151692 -3.0364% 1934 0.895478 1.116722
4.6271% 1933 0.855876 1.168394 1.3921% 1932 0.844124 1.184660 -0.2051% 1931
0.845859 1.182230 0.8886% 1930 0.838409 1.192735 1.0126% 1929 0.830004 1.204813
1.1526% 1928 0.820547 1.218699 1.2160% 1927 0.810689 1.233519 1.4086% 1926 0.799428
1.250894 1.7667% 1925 0.785550 1.272993 1.4465% 1924 0.774349 1.291407 1.7700% 1923
0.760882 1.314265 1.6165% 1922 0.748778 1.335510 1.3736% 1921 0.738631 1.353855
2.3393% 1920 0.721747 1.385526 1.3140% 1919 0.712387 1.403732 0.7676% 1918 0.706960
1.414508 0.3870% 1917 0.704234 1.419982 1.3274% 1916 0.695009 1.438831 1.4083% 1915
0.685357 1.459094 1.4458% 1914 0.675589 1.480190 1.9424% 1913 0.662717 1.508941
1.9857% 1912 0.649813 1.538903 1.5634% 1911 0.639811 1.562962 1.8169% 1910 0.628393
1.591360 1.8781% 1909 0.616809 1.621247 2.0082% 1908 0.604666 1.653805 1.9603% 1907
0.593041 1.686224 1.8264% 1906 0.582404 1.717021 1.9357% 1905 0.571345 1.750256
2.0148% 1904 0.560061 1.785521 2.1335% 1903 0.548361 1.823616 1.8151% 1902 0.538585
1.856717 1.8943% 1901 0.528572 1.891890 3.0255% 1900 0.513050 1.949129 0.6278% 1899
0.509849 1.961366 1.7757% 1898 0.500953 1.996194 1.8078% 1897 0.492058 2.032280
1.8396% 1896 0.483170 2.069666 1.8755% 1895 0.474275 2.108483 1.9114% 1894 0.465379
2.148784 1.9486% 1893 0.456484 2.190656 1.9858% 1892 0.447596 2.234158 2.0276% 1891
0.438701 2.279459 2.6465% 1890 0.427390 2.339785 1.5328% 1889 0.420937 2.375650
2.0811% 1888 0.412356 2.425090 2.1599% 1887 0.403638 2.477468 2.2075% 1886 0.394920
2.532159 2.2592% 1885 0.386195 2.589365 2.3095% 1884 0.377477 2.649168 2.3641% 1883
0.368759 2.711798 2.4214% 1882 0.360041 2.777461 2.4815% 1881 0.351323 2.846383

3.7644% 1880 0.338578 2.953532 0.9432% 1879 0.335414 2.981390 2.1464% 1878 0.328366 3.045382 2.1913% 1877 0.321325 3.112116 2.2426% 1876 0.314277 3.181908 2.2941% 1875 0.307229 3.254903 2.3456% 1874 0.300188 3.331250 2.4043% 1873 0.293140 3.411344 2.4635% 1872 0.286092 3.495384 2.5258% 1871 0.279044 3.583669 5.9947% 1870 0.263262 3.798499 -1.0968% 1869 0.266181 3.756837 2.1930% 1868 0.260469 3.839224 2.2394% 1867 0.254764 3.925199 2.2935% 1866 0.249052 4.015224 2.3445% 1865 0.243347 4.109360 2.4037% 1864 0.237635 4.208136 2.4599% 1863 0.231930 4.311651 2.5250% 1862 0.226218 4.420521 2.5872% 1861 0.220512 4.534891 2.9504% 1860 0.214193 4.668688 2.4012% 1859 0.209170 4.780795 2.7627% 1858 0.203547 4.912874 2.8412% 1857 0.197923 5.052459 2.9243% 1856 0.192300 5.200207 3.0161% 1855 0.186670 5.357053 3.1061% 1854 0.181046 5.523446 3.2056% 1853 0.175423 5.700507 3.3118% 1852 0.169800 5.889296 3.4252% 1851 0.164176 6.091018 4.0106% 1850 0.157846 6.335304 2.3254% 1849 0.154259 6.482623 2.7841% 1848 0.150080 6.663105 2.8590% 1847 0.145909 6.853604 2.9432% 1846 0.141737 7.055316 3.0324% 1845 0.137566 7.269262 3.1325% 1844 0.133387 7.496972 3.2284% 1843 0.129216 7.739001 3.3361% 1842 0.125044 7.997179 3.4512% 1841 0.120873 8.273177 3.8105% 1840 0.116436 8.588426 2.3861% 1839 0.113722 8.793350 2.5824% 1838 0.110859 9.020429 2.6573% 1837 0.107990 9.260131 2.7232% 1836 0.105127 9.512303 2.7994% 1835 0.102264 9.778594 2.8871% 1834 0.099395 10.060914 2.9657% 1833 0.096532 10.359289 3.0563% 1832 0.093669 10.675902 3.1604% 1831 0.090799 11.013306 3.4660% 1830 0.087758 11.395024 2.4653% 1829 0.085646 11.675945 2.6804% 1828 0.083410 11.988907 10.3427% 1827 0.075592 13.228877 -4.2314% 1826 0.078932 12.669106 2.9150% 1825 0.076696 13.038415 3.0026% 1824 0.074461 13.429902 3.0955% 1823 0.072225 13.845626 3.1944% 1822 0.069989 14.287909 3.3102% 1821 0.067747 14.760866 3.2277% 1820 0.065628 15.237309 2.6573% 1819 0.063930 15.642206 2.6261% 1818 0.062294 16.052987 2.6969% 1817 0.060658 16.485925 2.7717% 1816 0.059022 16.942863 2.8507% 1815 0.057386 17.425852 2.9343% 1814 0.055750 17.937187 3.0231% 1813 0.054114 18.479437 3.1039% 1812 0.052485 19.053019 3.2172% 1811 0.050849 19.665985 3.0969% 1810 0.049322 20.275024 2.9144% 1809 0.047925 20.865915 2.8225% 1808 0.046610 21.454848 2.9199% 1807 0.045287 22.081314 2.9918% 1806 0.043972 22.741939 3.0841% 1805 0.042656 23.443313 3.1822% 1804 0.041341 24.189324 3.2868% 1803 0.040025 24.984375 3.3985% 1802 0.038709 25.833465 3.5180% 1801 0.037394 26.742299 3.3999% 1800 0.036164 27.651523 2.8419% 1799 0.035165 28.437343 2.7485% 1798 0.034224 29.218930 2.8261% 1797 0.033284 30.044696 3.7832% 1796 0.032070 31.181350 2.1272% 1795 0.031402 31.844639 3.0879% 1794 0.030462 32.827982 3.1625% 1793 0.029528 33.866170 3.2904% 1792 0.028587 34.980508 3.4024% 1791 0.027647 36.170673 3.2296% 1790 0.026782 37.338828 41.3145% 1780 0.018952 52.765160 29.4353% 1770 0.014642 68.296751 83.4728% 1750 0.007980 125.305987 29.2845% 1740 0.006173 162.001159 94.2514% 1720 0.003178 314.689511 85.8111% 1700 0.001710 584.727979 19.2490% 1690 0.001434 697.282557 88.0250% 1670 0.000763 1311.065684

BASE YEAR: 1947
YEAR BYEAR/AYEAR AYEAR/BYEAR GROWTH%

2009 2.092104 0.477988 8.2857% 2001 1.932023 0.517592 1.0000% 2000 1.912894 0.522768 1.0000% 1999 1.893954 0.527996 1.0000% 1998 1.875202 0.533276 1.0000% 1997 1.856636 0.538609 1.0000% 1996 1.838254 0.543995 1.0000% 1995 1.820053 0.549435 0.9992% 1994 1.802047 0.554925 1.0008% 1993 1.784191 0.560478 1.0000% 1992 1.766526 0.566083 0.9295% 1991 1.750257 0.571345 1.2505% 1990 1.728640 0.578489 0.7224% 1989 1.716241 0.582669 1.1077% 1988 1.697439 0.589123 0.8834% 1987 1.682576 0.594327 0.5594% 1986 1.673216 0.597651 1.3056% 1985 1.651652 0.605454 0.7673% 1984 1.639076 0.610100 0.8149% 1983 1.625826 0.615072 0.9737% 1982 1.610147 0.621061 0.9508% 1981 1.594982 0.626966 0.9031% 1980 1.580707 0.632628 2.2701% 1979 1.545620 0.646989 1.0042% 1978 1.530254 0.653486 0.9896% 1977 1.515259 0.659953 0.9103% 1976 1.501589 0.665961 0.8394% 1975 1.489089 0.671551 0.9042% 1974 1.475746 0.677623 1.1568% 1973 1.458870 0.685462 0.9427% 1972 1.445246 0.691924 0.7426% 1971 1.434592 0.697062 1.4697% 1970 1.413813 0.707307 0.6968% 1969 1.404029 0.712236 0.8565% 1968 1.392105 0.718337 1.5090% 1967 1.371410 0.729177 0.9949% 1966 1.357900 0.736431 1.0575% 1965 1.343691 0.744219 1.1300% 1964 1.328677 0.752628 1.5537% 1963 1.308350 0.764322

89

1.4658% 1962 1.289449 0.775525 1.5364% 1961 1.269937 0.787441 2.1586% 1960 1.243103
0.804439 -1.6655% 1959 1.264157 0.791041 4.3080% 1958 1.211946 0.825119 2.1130%
1957 1.186868 0.842553 1.9895% 1956 1.163716 0.859316 2.1231% 1955 1.139523 0.877560
1.4496% 1954 1.123241 0.890281 2.1573% 1953 1.099521 0.909487 1.2298% 1952 1.086164
0.920671 1.6814% 1951 1.068203 0.936151 1.6233% 1950 1.051141 0.951348 1.4265% 1949
1.036357 0.964919 1.7790% 1948 1.018242 0.982085 1.8242% 1947 1.000000 1.000000 -
2.6320% 1946 1.027032 0.973680 3.1768% 1945 0.995410 1.004612 6.4754% 1944 0.934873
1.069664 -0.3437% 1943 0.938097 1.065988 0.6562% 1942 0.931981 1.072983 0.6633%
1941 0.925840 1.080100 -5.6614% 1940 0.981401 1.018951 8.0381% 1939 0.908384
1.100856 0.8126% 1938 0.901062 1.109802 0.7762% 1937 0.894121 1.118416 0.6029% 1936
0.888763 1.125159 0.5244% 1935 0.884127 1.131059 -3.0364% 1934 0.911813 1.096716
4.6271% 1933 0.871488 1.147463 1.3921% 1932 0.859522 1.163437 -0.2051% 1931
0.861289 1.161051 0.8886% 1930 0.853703 1.171368 1.0126% 1929 0.845145 1.183229
1.1526% 1928 0.835515 1.196867 1.2160% 1927 0.825477 1.211421 1.4086% 1926 0.814011
1.228484 1.7667% 1925 0.799880 1.250188 1.4465% 1924 0.788474 1.268272 1.7700% 1923
0.774761 1.290720 1.6165% 1922 0.762436 1.311585 1.3736% 1921 0.752105 1.329601
2.3393% 1920 0.734913 1.360705 1.3140% 1919 0.725382 1.378584 0.7676% 1918 0.719856
1.389167 0.3870% 1917 0.717081 1.394543 1.3274% 1916 0.707687 1.413055 1.4083% 1915
0.697859 1.432955 1.4458% 1914 0.687913 1.453672 1.9424% 1913 0.674806 1.481908
1.9857% 1912 0.661667 1.511334 1.5634% 1911 0.651482 1.534962 1.8169% 1910 0.639856
1.562851 1.8781% 1909 0.628061 1.592203 2.0082% 1908 0.615696 1.624178 1.9603% 1907
0.603859 1.656016 1.8264% 1906 0.593028 1.686261 1.9357% 1905 0.581767 1.718901
2.0148% 1904 0.570277 1.753534 2.1335% 1903 0.558364 1.790946 1.8151% 1902 0.548410
1.823454 1.8943% 1901 0.538214 1.857997 3.0255% 1900 0.522409 1.914211 0.6278% 1899
0.519149 1.926229 1.7757% 1898 0.510092 1.960432 1.8078% 1897 0.501034 1.995872
1.8396% 1896 0.491984 2.032588 1.8755% 1895 0.482926 2.070710 1.9114% 1894 0.473869
2.110289 1.9486% 1893 0.464811 2.151411 1.9858% 1892 0.455761 2.194134 2.0276% 1891
0.446703 2.238623 2.6465% 1890 0.435186 2.297868 1.5328% 1889 0.428616 2.333090
2.0811% 1888 0.419878 2.381645 2.1599% 1887 0.411001 2.433085 2.2075% 1886 0.402124
2.486796 2.2592% 1885 0.393240 2.542977 2.3095% 1884 0.384363 2.601708 2.3641% 1883
0.375486 2.663216 2.4214% 1882 0.366609 2.727703 2.4815% 1881 0.357732 2.795390
3.7644% 1880 0.344754 2.900620 0.9432% 1879 0.341532 2.927979 2.1464% 1878 0.334356
2.990825 2.1913% 1877 0.327186 3.056363 2.2426% 1876 0.320010 3.124905 2.2941% 1875
0.312833 3.196592 2.3456% 1874 0.305664 3.271571 2.4043% 1873 0.298487 3.350230
2.4635% 1872 0.291310 3.432765 2.5258% 1871 0.284134 3.519468 5.9947% 1870 0.268064
3.730449 -1.0968% 1869 0.271037 3.689534 2.1930% 1868 0.265221 3.770445 2.2394%
1867 0.259411 3.854880 2.2935% 1866 0.253595 3.943292 2.3445% 1865 0.247786 4.035741
2.4037% 1864 0.241970 4.132748 2.4599% 1863 0.236160 4.234409 2.5250% 1862 0.230344
4.341328 2.5872% 1861 0.224535 4.453649 2.9504% 1860 0.218100 4.585050 2.4012% 1859
0.212986 4.695148 2.7627% 1858 0.207260 4.824861 2.8412% 1857 0.201534 4.961945
2.9243% 1856 0.195808 5.107047 3.0161% 1855 0.190075 5.261082 3.1061% 1854 0.184349
5.424495 3.2056% 1853 0.178623 5.598384 3.3118% 1852 0.172897 5.783790 3.4252% 1851
0.167171 5.981898 4.0106% 1850 0.160725 6.221809 2.3254% 1849 0.157072 6.366488
2.7841% 1848 0.152818 6.543737 2.8590% 1847 0.148570 6.730823 2.9432% 1846 0.144323
6.928922 3.0324% 1845 0.140075 7.139035 3.1325% 1844 0.135820 7.362665 3.2284% 1843
0.131573 7.600359 3.3361% 1842 0.127325 7.853911 3.4512% 1841 0.123077 8.124965
3.8105% 1840 0.118560 8.434566 2.3861% 1839 0.115797 8.635819 2.5824% 1838 0.112882
8.858829 2.6573% 1837 0.109960 9.094237 2.7232% 1836 0.107045 9.341892 2.7994% 1835
0.104130 9.603413 2.8871% 1834 0.101208 9.880675 2.9657% 1833 0.098293 10.173704
3.0563% 1832 0.095378 10.484646 3.1604% 1831 0.092456 10.816005 3.4660% 1830
0.089358 11.190884 2.4653% 1829 0.087208 11.466773 2.6804% 1828 0.084932 11.774128
10.3427% 1827 0.076971 12.991885 -4.2314% 1826 0.080372 12.442142 2.9150% 1825
0.078096 12.804835 3.0026% 1824 0.075819 13.189308 3.0955% 1823 0.073542 13.597584
3.1944% 1822 0.071266 14.031944 3.3102% 1821 0.068983 14.496428 3.2277% 1820
0.066826 14.964335 2.6573% 1819 0.065096 15.361979 2.6261% 1818 0.063430 15.765401
2.6969% 1817 0.061764 16.190583 2.7717% 1816 0.060099 16.639335 2.8507% 1815

0.058433 17.113671 2.9343% 1814 0.056767 17.615845 3.0231% 1813 0.055101 18.148381 3.1039% 1812 0.053443 18.711688 3.2172% 1811 0.051777 19.313673 3.0969% 1810 0.050221 19.911801 2.9144% 1809 0.048799 20.492106 2.8225% 1808 0.047460 21.070488 2.9199% 1807 0.046113 21.685731 2.9918% 1806 0.044774 22.334522 3.0841% 1805 0.043434 23.023330 3.1822% 1804 0.042095 23.755977 3.2868% 1803 0.040755 24.536785 3.3985% 1802 0.039416 25.370664 3.5180% 1801 0.038076 26.263215 3.3999% 1800 0.036824 27.156151 2.8419% 1799 0.035806 27.927893 2.7485% 1798 0.034849 28.695479 2.8261% 1797 0.033891 29.506451 3.7832% 1796 0.032655 30.622742 2.1272% 1795 0.031975 31.274148 3.0879% 1794 0.031017 32.239875 3.1625% 1793 0.030067 33.259464 3.2904% 1792 0.029109 34.353839 3.4024% 1791 0.028151 35.522682 3.2296% 1790 0.027270 36.669910 41.3145% 1780 0.019298 51.819882 29.4353% 1770 0.014909 67.073228 83.4728% 1750 0.008126 123.061155 29.2845% 1740 0.006285 159.098940 94.2514% 1720 0.003236 309.051909 85.8111% 1700 0.001741 574.252690 19.2490% 1690 0.001460 684.790875 88.0250% 1670 0.000777 1287.578195

BASE YEAR: 1946

YEAR BYEAR/AYEAR AYEAR/BYEAR GROWTH%

2009 2.037039 0.490909 8.2857% 2001 1.881172 0.531584 1.0000% 2000 1.862546 0.536900 1.0000% 1999 1.844105 0.542269 1.0000% 1998 1.825846 0.547691 1.0000% 1997 1.807769 0.553168 1.0000% 1996 1.789870 0.558700 1.0000% 1995 1.772149 0.564287 0.9992% 1994 1.754616 0.569925 1.0008% 1993 1.737230 0.575629 1.0000% 1992 1.720030 0.581385 0.9295% 1991 1.704189 0.586789 1.2505% 1990 1.683141 0.594127 0.7224% 1989 1.671069 0.598419 1.1077% 1988 1.652762 0.605048 0.8834% 1987 1.638290 0.610393 0.5594% 1986 1.629177 0.613807 1.3056% 1985 1.608180 0.621821 0.7673% 1984 1.595934 0.626592 0.8149% 1983 1.583034 0.631699 0.9737% 1982 1.567767 0.637850 0.9508% 1981 1.553001 0.643914 0.9031% 1980 1.539102 0.649729 2.2701% 1979 1.504939 0.664479 1.0042% 1978 1.489977 0.671151 0.9896% 1977 1.475377 0.677793 0.9103% 1976 1.462067 0.683963 0.8394% 1975 1.449896 0.689705 0.9042% 1974 1.436904 0.695941 1.1568% 1973 1.420472 0.703991 0.9427% 1972 1.407206 0.710628 0.7426% 1971 1.396833 0.715905 1.4697% 1970 1.376600 0.726427 0.6968% 1969 1.367074 0.731489 0.8565% 1968 1.355464 0.737755 1.5090% 1967 1.335314 0.748888 0.9949% 1966 1.322160 0.756338 1.0575% 1965 1.308325 0.764336 1.1300% 1964 1.293706 0.772973 1.5537% 1963 1.273913 0.784983 1.4658% 1962 1.255510 0.796489 1.5364% 1961 1.236512 0.808727 2.1586% 1960 1.210384 0.826184 -1.6655% 1959 1.230884 0.812424 4.3080% 1958 1.180048 0.847423 2.1130% 1957 1.155630 0.865329 1.9895% 1956 1.133087 0.882545 2.1231% 1955 1.109531 0.901282 1.4496% 1954 1.093676 0.914347 2.1573% 1953 1.070581 0.934072 1.2298% 1952 1.057576 0.945559 1.6814% 1951 1.040088 0.961457 1.6233% 1950 1.023474 0.977064 1.4265% 1949 1.009079 0.991002 1.7790% 1948 0.991441 1.008633 1.8242% 1947 0.973680 1.027032 -2.6320% 1946 1.000000 1.000000 3.1768% 1945 0.969210 1.031768 6.4754% 1944 0.910267 1.098579 -0.3437% 1943 0.913406 1.094804 0.6562% 1942 0.907451 1.101988 0.6633% 1941 0.901471 1.109298 -5.6614% 1940 0.955570 1.046495 8.0381% 1939 0.884475 1.130614 0.8126% 1938 0.877346 1.139802 0.7762% 1937 0.870588 1.148649 0.6029% 1936 0.865371 1.155574 0.5244% 1935 0.860856 1.161634 -3.0364% 1934 0.887814 1.126363 4.6271% 1933 0.848550 1.178481 1.3921% 1932 0.836900 1.194887 -0.2051% 1931 0.838619 1.192436 0.8886% 1930 0.831233 1.203032 1.0126% 1929 0.822901 1.215214 1.1526% 1928 0.813524 1.229220 1.2160% 1927 0.803750 1.244167 1.4086% 1926 0.792586 1.261693 1.7667% 1925 0.778827 1.283983 1.4465% 1924 0.767722 1.302556 1.7700% 1923 0.754369 1.325610 1.6165% 1922 0.742369 1.347039 1.3736% 1921 0.732310 1.365543 2.3393% 1920 0.715570 1.397487 1.3140% 1919 0.706289 1.415850 0.7676% 1918 0.700909 1.426719 0.3870% 1917 0.698207 1.432240 1.3274% 1916 0.689060 1.451252 1.4083% 1915 0.679491 1.471690 1.4458% 1914 0.669807 1.492968 1.9424% 1913 0.657045 1.521967 1.9857% 1912 0.644252 1.552188 1.5634% 1911 0.634335 1.576455 1.8169% 1910 0.623015 1.605098 1.8781% 1909 0.611530 1.635243 2.0082% 1908 0.599491 1.668082 1.9603% 1907 0.587965 1.700781 1.8264% 1906 0.577419 1.731843 1.9357% 1905 0.566455 1.765366 2.0148% 1904 0.555267 1.800935 2.1335% 1903 0.543668 1.839359 1.8151% 1902 0.533975 1.872746 1.8943% 1901 0.524048 1.908222 3.0255% 1900 0.508659 1.965955 0.6278% 1899 0.505485 1.978299 1.7757% 1898 0.496666 2.013426 1.8078% 1897 0.487847 2.049824

1.8396% 1896 0.479034 2.087533 1.8755% 1895 0.470215 2.126685 1.9114% 1894 0.461396
2.167334 1.9486% 1893 0.452577 2.209568 1.9858% 1892 0.443765 2.253445 2.0276% 1891
0.434946 2.299137 2.6465% 1890 0.423732 2.359984 1.5328% 1889 0.417335 2.396158
2.0811% 1888 0.408827 2.446025 2.1599% 1887 0.400183 2.498856 2.2075% 1886 0.391540
2.554019 2.2592% 1885 0.382890 2.611719 2.3095% 1884 0.374246 2.672037 2.3641% 1883
0.365603 2.735208 2.4214% 1882 0.356960 2.801438 2.4815% 1881 0.348316 2.870955
3.7644% 1880 0.335680 2.979029 0.9432% 1879 0.332543 3.007128 2.1464% 1878 0.325556
3.071672 2.1913% 1877 0.318575 3.138982 2.2426% 1876 0.311587 3.209377 2.2941% 1875
0.304599 3.283002 2.3456% 1874 0.297618 3.360008 2.4043% 1873 0.290631 3.440793
2.4635% 1872 0.283643 3.525559 2.5258% 1871 0.276655 3.614606 5.9947% 1870 0.261009
3.831290 -1.0968% 1869 0.263903 3.789269 2.1930% 1868 0.258240 3.872367 2.2394%
1867 0.252584 3.959085 2.2935% 1866 0.246921 4.049886 2.3445% 1865 0.241264 4.144835
2.4037% 1864 0.235601 4.244464 2.4599% 1863 0.229945 4.348873 2.5250% 1862 0.224282
4.458682 2.5872% 1861 0.218625 4.574039 2.9504% 1860 0.212360 4.708992 2.4012% 1859
0.207380 4.822066 2.7627% 1858 0.201805 4.955286 2.8412% 1857 0.196229 5.096076
2.9243% 1856 0.190654 5.245100 3.0161% 1855 0.185072 5.403299 3.1061% 1854 0.179497
5.571129 3.2056% 1853 0.173922 5.749718 3.3118% 1852 0.168346 5.940137 3.4252% 1851
0.162771 6.143600 4.0106% 1850 0.156495 6.389996 2.3254% 1849 0.152938 6.538586
2.7841% 1848 0.148796 6.720626 2.8590% 1847 0.144660 6.912770 2.9432% 1846 0.140524
7.116223 3.0324% 1845 0.136388 7.332016 3.1325% 1844 0.132246 7.561692 3.2284% 1843
0.128110 7.805811 3.3361% 1842 0.123974 8.066217 3.4512% 1841 0.119838 8.344598
3.8105% 1840 0.115439 8.662568 2.3861% 1839 0.112749 8.869261 2.5824% 1838 0.109911
9.098300 2.6573% 1837 0.107066 9.340071 2.7232% 1836 0.104227 9.594421 2.7994% 1835
0.101389 9.863011 2.8871% 1834 0.098544 10.147768 2.9657% 1833 0.095706 10.448718
3.0563% 1832 0.092867 10.768065 3.1604% 1831 0.090022 11.108382 3.4660% 1830
0.087006 11.493394 2.4653% 1829 0.084913 11.776741 2.6804% 1828 0.082697 12.092404
10.3427% 1827 0.074945 13.343079 -4.2314% 1826 0.078257 12.778476 2.9150% 1825
0.076040 13.150973 3.0026% 1824 0.073823 13.545839 3.0955% 1823 0.071607 13.965152
3.1944% 1822 0.069390 14.411253 3.3102% 1821 0.067167 14.888294 3.2277% 1820
0.065067 15.368849 2.6573% 1819 0.063382 15.777242 2.6261% 1818 0.061761 16.191569
2.6969% 1817 0.060139 16.628245 2.7717% 1816 0.058517 17.089127 2.8507% 1815
0.056895 17.576286 2.9343% 1814 0.055273 18.092034 3.0231% 1813 0.053651 18.638966
3.1039% 1812 0.052036 19.217500 3.2172% 1811 0.050414 19.835757 3.0969% 1810
0.048900 20.450054 2.9144% 1809 0.047515 21.046046 2.8225% 1808 0.046211 21.640063
2.9199% 1807 0.044900 22.271937 2.9918% 1806 0.043595 22.938265 3.0841% 1805
0.042291 23.645694 3.1822% 1804 0.040987 24.398145 3.2868% 1803 0.039682 25.200060
3.3985% 1802 0.038378 26.056480 3.5180% 1801 0.037074 26.973159 3.3999% 1800
0.035855 27.890232 2.8419% 1799 0.034864 28.682836 2.7485% 1798 0.033931 29.471171
2.8261% 1797 0.032999 30.304065 3.7832% 1796 0.031796 31.450531 2.1272% 1795
0.031134 32.119546 3.0879% 1794 0.030201 33.111378 3.1625% 1793 0.029275 34.158530
3.2904% 1792 0.028343 35.282487 3.4024% 1791 0.027410 36.482927 3.2296% 1790
0.026553 37.661166 41.3145% 1780 0.018790 53.220670 29.4353% 1770 0.014517
68.886341 83.4728% 1750 0.007912 126.387726 29.2845% 1740 0.006120 163.399680
94.2514% 1720 0.003151 317.406156 85.8111% 1700 0.001696 589.775807 19.2490% 1690
0.001422 703.302044 88.0250% 1670 0.000756 1322.383825

BASE YEAR: 1945

YEAR	BYEAR/AYEAR	AYEAR/BYEAR	GROWTH%

2009 2.101752 0.475794 8.2857% 2001 1.940933 0.515216 1.0000% 2000 1.921715
0.520368 1.0000% 1999 1.902688 0.525572 1.0000% 1998 1.883850 0.530828 1.0000% 1997
1.865198 0.536136 1.0000% 1996 1.846731 0.541497 1.0000% 1995 1.828446 0.546912
0.9992% 1994 1.810357 0.552377 1.0008% 1993 1.792419 0.557905 1.0000% 1992 1.774672
0.563484 0.9295% 1991 1.758328 0.568722 1.2505% 1990 1.736612 0.575834 0.7224% 1989
1.724155 0.579994 1.1077% 1988 1.705267 0.586419 0.8834% 1987 1.690335 0.591599
0.5594% 1986 1.680932 0.594908 1.3056% 1985 1.659268 0.602675 0.7673% 1984 1.646634
0.607299 0.8149% 1983 1.633323 0.612249 0.9737% 1982 1.617572 0.618210 0.9508% 1981
1.602337 0.624088 0.9031% 1980 1.587997 0.629724 2.2701% 1979 1.552748 0.644019

1.0042% 1978 1.537311 0.650487 0.9896% 1977 1.522247 0.656924 0.9103% 1976 1.508514 0.662904 0.8394% 1975 1.495956 0.668469 0.9042% 1974 1.482552 0.674513 1.1568% 1973 1.465598 0.682316 0.9427% 1972 1.451910 0.688748 0.7426% 1971 1.441208 0.693863 1.4697% 1970 1.420332 0.704061 0.6968% 1969 1.410504 0.708967 0.8565% 1968 1.398525 0.715039 1.5090% 1967 1.377734 0.725829 0.9949% 1966 1.364162 0.733051 1.0575% 1965 1.349887 0.740803 1.1300% 1964 1.334804 0.749174 1.5537% 1963 1.314383 0.760813 1.4658% 1962 1.295395 0.771965 1.5364% 1961 1.275793 0.783826 2.1586% 1960 1.248835 0.800746 -1.6655% 1959 1.269987 0.787410 4.3080% 1958 1.217535 0.821331 2.1130% 1957 1.192342 0.838686 1.9895% 1956 1.169083 0.855371 2.1231% 1955 1.144778 0.873532 1.4496% 1954 1.128420 0.886195 2.1573% 1953 1.104592 0.905312 1.2298% 1952 1.091173 0.916445 1.6814% 1951 1.073129 0.931854 1.6233% 1950 1.055988 0.946981 1.4265% 1949 1.041136 0.960490 1.7790% 1948 1.022937 0.977577 1.8242% 1947 1.004612 0.995410 -2.6320% 1946 1.031768 0.969210 3.1768% 1945 1.000000 1.000000 6.4754% 1944 0.939184 1.064754 -0.3437% 1943 0.942423 1.061095 0.6562% 1942 0.936279 1.068058 0.6633% 1941 0.930109 1.075142 -5.6614% 1940 0.985927 1.014274 8.0381% 1939 0.912573 1.095802 0.8126% 1938 0.905217 1.104707 0.7762% 1937 0.898245 1.113283 0.6029% 1936 0.892862 1.119994 0.5244% 1935 0.888204 1.125867 -3.0364% 1934 0.916018 1.091682 4.6271% 1933 0.875507 1.142195 1.3921% 1932 0.863486 1.158096 -0.2051% 1931 0.865261 1.155721 0.8886% 1930 0.857640 1.165991 1.0126% 1929 0.849042 1.177797 1.1526% 1928 0.839368 1.191373 1.2160% 1927 0.829284 1.205860 1.4086% 1926 0.817765 1.222845 1.7667% 1925 0.803568 1.244449 1.4465% 1924 0.792111 1.262450 1.7700% 1923 0.778334 1.284795 1.6165% 1922 0.765952 1.305564 1.3736% 1921 0.755574 1.323498 2.3393% 1920 0.738302 1.354459 1.3140% 1919 0.728727 1.372256 0.7676% 1918 0.723175 1.382790 0.3870% 1917 0.720388 1.388142 1.3274% 1916 0.710950 1.406568 1.4083% 1915 0.701077 1.426377 1.4458% 1914 0.691085 1.446999 1.9424% 1913 0.677918 1.475106 1.9857% 1912 0.664718 1.504396 1.5634% 1911 0.654486 1.527916 1.8169% 1910 0.642807 1.555677 1.8781% 1909 0.630957 1.584894 2.0082% 1908 0.618535 1.616722 1.9603% 1907 0.606644 1.648414 1.8264% 1906 0.595763 1.678520 1.9357% 1905 0.584450 1.711011 2.0148% 1904 0.572907 1.745485 2.1335% 1903 0.560939 1.782725 1.8151% 1902 0.550939 1.815084 1.8943% 1901 0.540696 1.849468 3.0255% 1900 0.524818 1.905424 0.6278% 1899 0.521543 1.917387 1.7757% 1898 0.512444 1.951433 1.8078% 1897 0.503345 1.986710 1.8396% 1896 0.494252 2.023258 1.8755% 1895 0.485153 2.061205 1.9114% 1894 0.476054 2.100602 1.9486% 1893 0.466955 2.141535 1.9858% 1892 0.457862 2.184062 2.0276% 1891 0.448763 2.228347 2.6465% 1890 0.437193 2.287320 1.5328% 1889 0.430593 2.322381 2.0811% 1888 0.421814 2.370713 2.1599% 1887 0.412896 2.421916 2.2075% 1886 0.403978 2.475381 2.2592% 1885 0.395053 2.531304 2.3095% 1884 0.386135 2.589766 2.3641% 1883 0.377217 2.650991 2.4214% 1882 0.368299 2.715182 2.4815% 1881 0.359381 2.782558 3.7644% 1880 0.346344 2.887305 0.9432% 1879 0.343107 2.914539 2.1464% 1878 0.335898 2.977096 2.1913% 1877 0.328695 3.042333 2.2426% 1876 0.321485 3.110561 2.2941% 1875 0.314276 3.181919 2.3456% 1874 0.307073 3.256554 2.4043% 1873 0.299863 3.334852 2.4635% 1872 0.292654 3.417007 2.5258% 1871 0.285444 3.503313 5.9947% 1870 0.269300 3.713325 -1.0968% 1869 0.272287 3.672598 2.1930% 1868 0.266444 3.753137 2.2394% 1867 0.260608 3.837181 2.2935% 1866 0.254765 3.925191 2.3445% 1865 0.248929 4.017216 2.4037% 1864 0.243086 4.113778 2.4599% 1863 0.237250 4.214972 2.5250% 1862 0.231406 4.321400 2.5872% 1861 0.225570 4.433205 2.9504% 1860 0.219106 4.564003 2.4012% 1859 0.213968 4.673595 2.7627% 1858 0.208216 4.802713 2.8412% 1857 0.202463 4.939168 2.9243% 1856 0.196711 5.083604 3.0161% 1855 0.190951 5.236932 3.1061% 1854 0.185199 5.399594 3.2056% 1853 0.179447 5.572685 3.3118% 1852 0.173694 5.757241 3.4252% 1851 0.167942 5.954439 4.0106% 1850 0.161466 6.193248 2.3254% 1849 0.157797 6.337264 2.7841% 1848 0.153523 6.513699 2.8590% 1847 0.149255 6.699926 2.9432% 1846 0.144988 6.897116 3.0324% 1845 0.140721 7.106264 3.1325% 1844 0.136447 7.328868 3.2284% 1843 0.132179 7.565471 3.3361% 1842 0.127912 7.817859 3.4512% 1841 0.123645 8.087668 3.8105% 1840 0.119106 8.395848 2.3861% 1839 0.116331 8.596177 2.5824% 1838 0.113402 8.818164 2.6573% 1837 0.110467 9.052492 2.7232% 1836 0.107538 9.299010 2.7994% 1835 0.104610 9.559330 2.8871% 1834 0.101674 9.835319 2.9657% 1833 0.098746 10.127004 3.0563% 1832 0.095817 10.436518 3.1604% 1831 0.092882 10.766356 3.4660% 1830

0.089771 11.139514 2.4653% 1829 0.087611 11.414136 2.6804% 1828 0.085324 11.720080
10.3427% 1827 0.077326 12.932248 -4.2314% 1826 0.080743 12.385028 2.9150% 1825
0.078456 12.746056 3.0026% 1824 0.076169 13.128765 3.0955% 1823 0.073882 13.535167
3.1944% 1822 0.071595 13.967533 3.3102% 1821 0.069301 14.429885 3.2277% 1820
0.067134 14.895644 2.6573% 1819 0.065396 15.291462 2.6261% 1818 0.063723 15.693033
2.6969% 1817 0.062049 16.116263 2.7717% 1816 0.060376 16.562955 2.8507% 1815
0.058702 17.035114 2.9343% 1814 0.057029 17.534983 3.0231% 1813 0.055355 18.065074
3.1039% 1812 0.053689 18.625795 3.2172% 1811 0.052016 19.225017 3.0969% 1810
0.050453 19.820399 2.9144% 1809 0.049024 20.398041 2.8225% 1808 0.047679 20.973768
2.9199% 1807 0.046326 21.586187 2.9918% 1806 0.044980 22.231999 3.0841% 1805
0.043635 22.917645 3.1822% 1804 0.042289 23.646929 3.2868% 1803 0.040943 24.424153
3.3985% 1802 0.039597 25.254204 3.5180% 1801 0.038252 26.142659 3.3999% 1800
0.036994 27.031495 2.8419% 1799 0.035972 27.799695 2.7485% 1798 0.035009 28.563757
2.8261% 1797 0.034047 29.371007 3.7832% 1796 0.032806 30.482173 2.1272% 1795
0.032123 31.130589 3.0879% 1794 0.031161 32.091883 3.1625% 1793 0.030205 33.106792
3.2904% 1792 0.029243 34.196143 3.4024% 1791 0.028281 35.359622 3.2296% 1790
0.027396 36.501583 41.3145% 1780 0.019387 51.582012 29.4353% 1770 0.014978
66.765339 83.4728% 1750 0.008164 122.496263 29.2845% 1740 0.006314 158.368623
94.2514% 1720 0.003251 307.633258 85.8111% 1700 0.001749 571.616680 19.2490% 1690
0.001467 681.647457 88.0250% 1670 0.000780 1281.667784
BASE YEAR: 1944
YEAR BYEAR/AYEAR AYEAR/BYEAR GROWTH%
2009 2.237849 0.446858 8.2857% 2001 2.066616 0.483883 1.0000% 2000 2.046154
0.488722 1.0000% 1999 2.025895 0.493609 1.0000% 1998 2.005837 0.498545 1.0000% 1997
1.985977 0.503530 1.0000% 1996 1.966314 0.508566 1.0000% 1995 1.946846 0.513651
0.9992% 1994 1.927585 0.518784 1.0008% 1993 1.908485 0.523976 1.0000% 1992 1.889589
0.529216 0.9295% 1991 1.872187 0.534135 1.2505% 1990 1.849064 0.540814 0.7224% 1989
1.835802 0.544721 1.1077% 1988 1.815690 0.550755 0.8834% 1987 1.799791 0.555620
0.5594% 1986 1.789780 0.558728 1.3056% 1985 1.766713 0.566023 0.7673% 1984 1.753261
0.570366 0.8149% 1983 1.739088 0.575014 0.9737% 1982 1.722317 0.580613 0.9508% 1981
1.706095 0.586134 0.9031% 1980 1.690826 0.591427 2.2701% 1979 1.653295 0.604853
1.0042% 1978 1.636858 0.610927 0.9896% 1977 1.620818 0.616972 0.9103% 1976 1.606197
0.622589 0.8394% 1975 1.592826 0.627815 0.9042% 1974 1.578553 0.633492 1.1568% 1973
1.560501 0.640820 0.9427% 1972 1.545928 0.646861 0.7426% 1971 1.534532 0.651665
1.4697% 1970 1.512305 0.661242 0.6968% 1969 1.501840 0.665850 0.8565% 1968 1.489085
0.671553 1.5090% 1967 1.466948 0.681687 0.9949% 1966 1.452497 0.688469 1.0575% 1965
1.437298 0.695750 1.1300% 1964 1.421238 0.703612 1.5537% 1963 1.399495 0.714544
1.4658% 1962 1.379277 0.725017 1.5364% 1961 1.358406 0.736157 2.1586% 1960 1.329703
0.752048 -1.6655% 1959 1.352224 0.739523 4.3080% 1958 1.296376 0.771381 2.1130%
1957 1.269551 0.787680 1.9895% 1956 1.244786 0.803351 2.1231% 1955 1.218907 0.820407
1.4496% 1954 1.201490 0.832300 2.1573% 1953 1.176118 0.850255 1.2298% 1952 1.161831
0.860711 1.6814% 1951 1.142619 0.875182 1.6233% 1950 1.124367 0.889389 1.4265% 1949
1.108554 0.902076 1.7790% 1948 1.089177 0.918125 1.8242% 1947 1.069664 0.934873 -
2.6320% 1946 1.098579 0.910267 3.1768% 1945 1.064754 0.939184 6.4754% 1944 1.000000
1.000000 -0.3437% 1943 1.003449 0.996563 0.6562% 1942 0.996907 1.003103 0.6633%
1941 0.990338 1.009756 -5.6614% 1940 1.049770 0.952590 8.0381% 1939 0.971666
1.029160 0.8126% 1938 0.963834 1.037523 0.7762% 1937 0.956410 1.045577 0.6029% 1936
0.950678 1.051881 0.5244% 1935 0.945719 1.057397 -3.0364% 1934 0.975334 1.025290
4.6271% 1933 0.932200 1.072732 1.3921% 1932 0.919400 1.087665 -0.2051% 1931
0.921290 1.085435 0.8886% 1930 0.913175 1.095080 1.0126% 1929 0.904021 1.106168
1.1526% 1928 0.893721 1.118918 1.2160% 1927 0.882983 1.132524 1.4086% 1926 0.870719
1.148477 1.7667% 1925 0.855603 1.168767 1.4465% 1924 0.843403 1.185673 1.7700% 1923
0.828735 1.206659 1.6165% 1922 0.815551 1.226165 1.3736% 1921 0.804500 1.243008
2.3393% 1920 0.786111 1.272086 1.3140% 1919 0.775915 1.288801 0.7676% 1918 0.770004
1.298694 0.3870% 1917 0.767036 1.303720 1.3274% 1916 0.756987 1.321026 1.4083% 1915
0.746475 1.339630 1.4458% 1914 0.735836 1.358999 1.9424% 1913 0.721816 1.385396

94

1.9857% 1912 0.707762 1.412905 1.5634% 1911 0.696867 1.434994 1.8169% 1910 0.684431
1.461067 1.8781% 1909 0.671814 1.488507 2.0082% 1908 0.658588 1.518400 1.9603% 1907
0.645926 1.548164 1.8264% 1906 0.634341 1.576439 1.9357% 1905 0.622295 1.606954
2.0148% 1904 0.610005 1.639331 2.1335% 1903 0.597262 1.674307 1.8151% 1902 0.586614
1.704698 1.8943% 1901 0.575708 1.736991 3.0255% 1900 0.558802 1.789544 0.6278% 1899
0.555315 1.800779 1.7757% 1898 0.545627 1.832755 1.8078% 1897 0.535938 1.865886
1.8396% 1896 0.526257 1.900211 1.8755% 1895 0.516569 1.935850 1.9114% 1894 0.506880
1.972852 1.9486% 1893 0.497192 2.011296 1.9858% 1892 0.487511 2.051236 2.0276% 1891
0.477822 2.092827 2.6465% 1890 0.465503 2.148214 1.5328% 1889 0.458475 2.181143
2.0811% 1888 0.449128 2.226535 2.1599% 1887 0.439633 2.274625 2.2075% 1886 0.430137
2.324838 2.2592% 1885 0.420635 2.377360 2.3095% 1884 0.411139 2.432266 2.3641% 1883
0.401644 2.489768 2.4214% 1882 0.392148 2.550055 2.4815% 1881 0.382653 2.613334
3.7644% 1880 0.368771 2.711710 0.9432% 1879 0.365325 2.737288 2.1464% 1878 0.357649
2.796041 2.1913% 1877 0.349979 2.857310 2.2426% 1876 0.342303 2.921389 2.2941% 1875
0.334626 2.988407 2.3456% 1874 0.326957 3.058503 2.4043% 1873 0.319281 3.132039
2.4635% 1872 0.311604 3.209198 2.5258% 1871 0.303928 3.290255 5.9947% 1870 0.286739
3.487495 -1.0968% 1869 0.289919 3.449245 2.1930% 1868 0.283697 3.524886 2.2394%
1867 0.277483 3.603822 2.2935% 1866 0.271262 3.686476 2.3445% 1865 0.265048 3.772905
2.4037% 1864 0.258826 3.863594 2.4599% 1863 0.252612 3.958634 2.5250% 1862 0.246391
4.058589 2.5872% 1861 0.240177 4.163595 2.9504% 1860 0.233294 4.286438 2.4012% 1859
0.227823 4.389366 2.7627% 1858 0.221698 4.510631 2.8412% 1857 0.215574 4.638787
2.9243% 1856 0.209449 4.774439 3.0161% 1855 0.203316 4.918443 3.1061% 1854 0.197192
5.071212 3.2056% 1853 0.191067 5.233776 3.3118% 1852 0.184942 5.407108 3.4252% 1851
0.178817 5.592314 4.0106% 1850 0.171922 5.816599 2.3254% 1849 0.168015 5.951857
2.7841% 1848 0.163464 6.117561 2.8590% 1847 0.158920 6.292463 2.9432% 1846 0.154377
6.477660 3.0324% 1845 0.149833 6.674089 3.1325% 1844 0.145282 6.883155 3.2284% 1843
0.140739 7.105368 3.3361% 1842 0.136195 7.342408 3.4512% 1841 0.131652 7.595808
3.8105% 1840 0.126819 7.885246 2.3861% 1839 0.123864 8.073392 2.5824% 1838 0.120746
8.281878 2.6573% 1837 0.117620 8.501955 2.7232% 1836 0.114502 8.733480 2.7994% 1835
0.111384 8.977969 2.8871% 1834 0.108258 9.237174 2.9657% 1833 0.105140 9.511119
3.0563% 1832 0.102022 9.801810 3.1604% 1831 0.098896 10.111588 3.4660% 1830
0.095584 10.462053 2.4653% 1829 0.093284 10.719974 2.6804% 1828 0.090849 11.007311
10.3427% 1827 0.082333 12.145759 -4.2314% 1826 0.085971 11.631819 2.9150% 1825
0.083536 11.970891 3.0026% 1824 0.081101 12.330325 3.0955% 1823 0.078666 12.712011
3.1944% 1822 0.076231 13.118082 3.3102% 1821 0.073788 13.552316 3.2277% 1820
0.071481 13.989749 2.6573% 1819 0.069631 14.361496 2.6261% 1818 0.067849 14.738644
2.6969% 1817 0.066067 15.136135 2.7717% 1816 0.064285 15.555661 2.8507% 1815
0.062503 15.999105 2.9343% 1814 0.060722 16.468574 3.0231% 1813 0.058940 16.966428
3.1039% 1812 0.057166 17.493048 3.2172% 1811 0.055384 18.055827 3.0969% 1810
0.053720 18.615000 2.9144% 1809 0.052199 19.157512 2.8225% 1808 0.050766 19.698226
2.9199% 1807 0.049326 20.273400 2.9918% 1806 0.047893 20.879936 3.0841% 1805
0.046460 21.523884 3.1822% 1804 0.045027 22.208816 3.2868% 1803 0.043594 22.938772
3.3985% 1802 0.042161 23.718343 3.5180% 1801 0.040729 24.552765 3.3999% 1800
0.039389 25.387546 2.8419% 1799 0.038301 26.109027 2.7485% 1798 0.037276 26.826622
2.8261% 1797 0.036252 27.584777 3.7832% 1796 0.034930 28.628367 2.1272% 1795
0.034203 29.237349 3.0879% 1794 0.033178 30.140181 3.1625% 1793 0.032161 31.093367
3.2904% 1792 0.031137 32.116468 3.4024% 1791 0.030112 33.209188 3.2296% 1790
0.029170 34.281700 41.3145% 1780 0.020642 48.444996 29.4353% 1770 0.015948
62.704934 83.4728% 1750 0.008692 115.046522 29.2845% 1740 0.006723 148.737266
94.2514% 1720 0.003461 288.924213 85.8111% 1700 0.001863 536.853200 19.2490% 1690
0.001562 640.192338 88.0250% 1670 0.000831 1203.721787

BASE YEAR: 1943

YEAR BYEAR/AYEAR AYEAR/BYEAR GROWTH%

2009 2.230158 0.448399 8.2857% 2001 2.059514 0.485552 1.0000% 2000 2.039122
0.490407 1.0000% 1999 2.018933 0.495311 1.0000% 1998 1.998943 0.500264 1.0000% 1997
1.979152 0.505267 1.0000% 1996 1.959556 0.510320 1.0000% 1995 1.940155 0.515423

95

0.9992% 1994 1.920960 0.520573 1.0008% 1993 1.901926 0.525783 1.0000% 1992 1.883095
0.531041 0.9295% 1991 1.865753 0.535977 1.2505% 1990 1.842710 0.542679 0.7224% 1989
1.829492 0.546600 1.1077% 1988 1.809450 0.552654 0.8834% 1987 1.793606 0.557536
0.5594% 1986 1.783629 0.560655 1.3056% 1985 1.760641 0.567975 0.7673% 1984 1.747235
0.572333 0.8149% 1983 1.733111 0.576997 0.9737% 1982 1.716398 0.582616 0.9508% 1981
1.700232 0.588155 0.9031% 1980 1.685015 0.593467 2.2701% 1979 1.647613 0.606939
1.0042% 1978 1.631233 0.613033 0.9896% 1977 1.615248 0.619100 0.9103% 1976 1.600676
0.624736 0.8394% 1975 1.587352 0.629980 0.9042% 1974 1.573128 0.635676 1.1568% 1973
1.555138 0.643030 0.9427% 1972 1.540615 0.649092 0.7426% 1971 1.529258 0.653912
1.4697% 1970 1.507107 0.663523 0.6968% 1969 1.496678 0.668146 0.8565% 1968 1.483967
0.673869 1.5090% 1967 1.461907 0.684038 0.9949% 1966 1.447505 0.690844 1.0575% 1965
1.432359 0.698149 1.1300% 1964 1.416354 0.706038 1.5537% 1963 1.394685 0.717008
1.4658% 1962 1.374537 0.727518 1.5364% 1961 1.353738 0.738696 2.1586% 1960 1.325133
0.754641 -1.6655% 1959 1.347576 0.742073 4.3080% 1958 1.291921 0.774041 2.1130%
1957 1.265188 0.790397 1.9895% 1956 1.240508 0.806122 2.1231% 1955 1.214718 0.823236
1.4496% 1954 1.197361 0.835170 2.1573% 1953 1.172076 0.853187 1.2298% 1952 1.157838
0.863679 1.6814% 1951 1.138692 0.878200 1.6233% 1950 1.120503 0.892456 1.4265% 1949
1.104744 0.905187 1.7790% 1948 1.085433 0.921291 1.8242% 1947 1.065988 0.938097 -
2.6320% 1946 1.094804 0.913406 3.1768% 1945 1.061095 0.942423 6.4754% 1944 0.996563
1.003449 -0.3437% 1943 1.000000 1.000000 0.6562% 1942 0.993481 1.006562 0.6633%
1941 0.986934 1.013239 -5.6614% 1940 1.046162 0.955875 8.0381% 1939 0.968327
1.032709 0.8126% 1938 0.960521 1.041101 0.7762% 1937 0.953123 1.049183 0.6029% 1936
0.947411 1.055508 0.5244% 1935 0.942469 1.061043 -3.0364% 1934 0.971982 1.028826
4.6271% 1933 0.928996 1.076431 1.3921% 1932 0.916241 1.091416 -0.2051% 1931
0.918124 1.089178 0.8886% 1930 0.910037 1.098856 1.0126% 1929 0.900915 1.109983
1.1526% 1928 0.890649 1.122777 1.2160% 1927 0.879949 1.136430 1.4086% 1926 0.867726
1.152437 1.7667% 1925 0.852662 1.172797 1.4465% 1924 0.840504 1.189762 1.7700% 1923
0.825886 1.210820 1.6165% 1922 0.812748 1.230393 1.3736% 1921 0.801735 1.247295
2.3393% 1920 0.783409 1.276473 1.3140% 1919 0.773248 1.293246 0.7676% 1918 0.767358
1.303173 0.3870% 1917 0.764400 1.308216 1.3274% 1916 0.754386 1.325582 1.4083% 1915
0.743909 1.344250 1.4458% 1914 0.733307 1.363685 1.9424% 1913 0.719335 1.390173
1.9857% 1912 0.705329 1.417778 1.5634% 1911 0.694472 1.439943 1.8169% 1910 0.682079
1.466106 1.8781% 1909 0.669505 1.493640 2.0082% 1908 0.656325 1.523636 1.9603% 1907
0.643706 1.553503 1.8264% 1906 0.632161 1.581876 1.9357% 1905 0.620157 1.612495
2.0148% 1904 0.607908 1.644985 2.1335% 1903 0.595209 1.680081 1.8151% 1902 0.584598
1.710577 1.8943% 1901 0.573730 1.742981 3.0255% 1900 0.556881 1.795715 0.6278% 1899
0.553407 1.806989 1.7757% 1898 0.543752 1.839075 1.8078% 1897 0.534096 1.872321
1.8396% 1896 0.524449 1.906764 1.8755% 1895 0.514794 1.942526 1.9114% 1894 0.505138
1.979656 1.9486% 1893 0.495483 2.018232 1.9858% 1892 0.485835 2.058310 2.0276% 1891
0.476180 2.100045 2.6465% 1890 0.463903 2.155623 1.5328% 1889 0.456900 2.188665
2.0811% 1888 0.447585 2.234214 2.1599% 1887 0.438122 2.282469 2.2075% 1886 0.428659
2.332856 2.2592% 1885 0.419189 2.385559 2.3095% 1884 0.409726 2.440654 2.3641% 1883
0.400263 2.498355 2.4214% 1882 0.390801 2.558849 2.4815% 1881 0.381338 2.622347
3.7644% 1880 0.367504 2.721062 0.9432% 1879 0.364070 2.746728 2.1464% 1878 0.356419
2.805683 2.1913% 1877 0.348777 2.867164 2.2426% 1876 0.341127 2.931463 2.2941% 1875
0.333476 2.998713 2.3456% 1874 0.325834 3.069050 2.4043% 1873 0.318184 3.142840
2.4635% 1872 0.310533 3.220266 2.5258% 1871 0.302883 3.301602 5.9947% 1870 0.285753
3.499522 -1.0968% 1869 0.288922 3.461140 2.1930% 1868 0.282722 3.537042 2.2394%
1867 0.276530 3.616251 2.2935% 1866 0.270329 3.699189 2.3445% 1865 0.264137 3.785916
2.4037% 1864 0.257937 3.876918 2.4599% 1863 0.251744 3.972285 2.5250% 1862 0.245544
4.072586 2.5872% 1861 0.239352 4.177954 2.9504% 1860 0.232492 4.301220 2.4012% 1859
0.227040 4.404503 2.7627% 1858 0.220937 4.526187 2.8412% 1857 0.214833 4.654785
2.9243% 1856 0.208729 4.790904 3.0161% 1855 0.202618 4.935404 3.1061% 1854 0.196514
5.088701 3.2056% 1853 0.190410 5.251826 3.3118% 1852 0.184306 5.425755 3.4252% 1851
0.178202 5.611599 4.0106% 1850 0.171331 5.836659 2.3254% 1849 0.167437 5.972382
2.7841% 1848 0.162902 6.138659 2.8590% 1847 0.158374 6.314164 2.9432% 1846 0.153846

6.499999 3.0324% 1845 0.149318 6.697106 3.1325% 1844 0.144783 6.906893 3.2284% 1843 0.140255 7.129872 3.3361% 1842 0.135727 7.367729 3.4512% 1841 0.131199 7.622003 3.8105% 1840 0.126383 7.912439 2.3861% 1839 0.123438 8.101234 2.5824% 1838 0.120331 8.310439 2.6573% 1837 0.117216 8.531275 2.7232% 1836 0.114108 8.763599 2.7994% 1835 0.111001 9.008930 2.8871% 1834 0.107886 9.269029 2.9657% 1833 0.104779 9.543919 3.0563% 1832 0.101671 9.835612 3.1604% 1831 0.098557 10.146459 3.4660% 1830 0.095255 10.498132 2.4653% 1829 0.092963 10.756943 2.6804% 1828 0.090536 11.045271 10.3427% 1827 0.082050 12.187645 -4.2314% 1826 0.085676 11.671933 2.9150% 1825 0.083249 12.012174 3.0026% 1824 0.080822 12.372847 3.0955% 1823 0.078395 12.755850 3.1944% 1822 0.075969 13.163321 3.3102% 1821 0.073535 13.599053 3.2277% 1820 0.071235 14.037995 2.6573% 1819 0.069391 14.411023 2.6261% 1818 0.067616 14.789472 2.6969% 1817 0.065840 15.188334 2.7717% 1816 0.064064 15.609306 2.8507% 1815 0.062289 16.054280 2.9343% 1814 0.060513 16.525368 3.0231% 1813 0.058737 17.024938 3.1039% 1812 0.056969 17.553375 3.2172% 1811 0.055193 18.118094 3.0969% 1810 0.053535 18.679196 2.9144% 1809 0.052019 19.223579 2.8225% 1808 0.050592 19.766157 2.9199% 1807 0.049156 20.343315 2.9918% 1806 0.047728 20.951943 3.0841% 1805 0.046300 21.598112 3.1822% 1804 0.044872 22.285405 3.2868% 1803 0.043444 23.017879 3.3985% 1802 0.042017 23.800138 3.5180% 1801 0.040589 24.637438 3.3999% 1800 0.039254 25.475098 2.8419% 1799 0.038169 26.199066 2.7485% 1798 0.037148 26.919136 2.8261% 1797 0.036127 27.679907 3.7832% 1796 0.034810 28.727095 2.1272% 1795 0.034085 29.338178 3.0879% 1794 0.033064 30.244123 3.1625% 1793 0.032051 31.200596 3.2904% 1792 0.031030 32.227226 3.4024% 1791 0.030009 33.323714 3.2296% 1790 0.029070 34.399924 41.3145% 1780 0.020571 48.612064 29.4353% 1770 0.015893 62.921179 83.4728% 1750 0.008662 115.443273 29.2845% 1740 0.006700 149.250203 94.2514% 1720 0.003449 289.920601 85.8111% 1700 0.001856 538.704599 19.2490% 1690 0.001557 642.400114 88.0250% 1670 0.000828 1207.872958

BASE YEAR: 1942

YEAR BYEAR/AYEAR AYEAR/BYEAR GROWTH%

2009 2.244793 0.445475 8.2857% 2001 2.073029 0.482386 1.0000% 2000 2.052503 0.487210 1.0000% 1999 2.032182 0.492082 1.0000% 1998 2.012061 0.497003 1.0000% 1997 1.992140 0.501973 1.0000% 1996 1.972415 0.506993 1.0000% 1995 1.952887 0.512063 0.9992% 1994 1.933566 0.517179 1.0008% 1993 1.914407 0.522355 1.0000% 1992 1.895453 0.527579 0.9295% 1991 1.877996 0.532482 1.2505% 1990 1.854802 0.539141 0.7224% 1989 1.841498 0.543036 1.1077% 1988 1.821324 0.549051 0.8834% 1987 1.805376 0.553901 0.5594% 1986 1.795333 0.557000 1.3056% 1985 1.772195 0.564272 0.7673% 1984 1.758701 0.568602 0.8149% 1983 1.744484 0.573235 0.9737% 1982 1.727661 0.578817 0.9508% 1981 1.711389 0.584321 0.9031% 1980 1.696072 0.589597 2.2701% 1979 1.658425 0.602982 1.0042% 1978 1.641937 0.609037 0.9896% 1977 1.625848 0.615064 0.9103% 1976 1.611180 0.620663 0.8394% 1975 1.597768 0.625873 0.9042% 1974 1.583451 0.631532 1.1568% 1973 1.565343 0.638837 0.9427% 1972 1.550725 0.644860 0.7426% 1971 1.539293 0.649649 1.4697% 1970 1.516997 0.659197 0.6968% 1969 1.506500 0.663790 0.8565% 1968 1.493706 0.669476 1.5090% 1967 1.471500 0.679579 0.9949% 1966 1.457004 0.686340 1.0575% 1965 1.441758 0.693598 1.1300% 1964 1.425648 0.701435 1.5537% 1963 1.403837 0.712333 1.4658% 1962 1.383557 0.722775 1.5364% 1961 1.362621 0.733880 2.1586% 1960 1.333829 0.749722 -1.6655% 1959 1.356419 0.737235 4.3080% 1958 1.300398 0.768995 2.1130% 1957 1.273490 0.785244 1.9895% 1956 1.248648 0.800866 2.1231% 1955 1.222689 0.817869 1.4496% 1954 1.205218 0.829725 2.1573% 1953 1.179768 0.847624 1.2298% 1952 1.165436 0.858048 1.6814% 1951 1.146164 0.872475 1.6233% 1950 1.127856 0.886638 1.4265% 1949 1.111993 0.899286 1.7790% 1948 1.092556 0.915285 1.8242% 1947 1.072983 0.931981 -2.6320% 1946 1.101988 0.907451 3.1768% 1945 1.068058 0.936279 6.4754% 1944 1.003103 0.996907 -0.3437% 1943 1.006562 0.993481 0.6562% 1942 1.000000 1.000000 0.6633% 1941 0.993411 1.006633 -5.6614% 1940 1.053027 0.949643 8.0381% 1939 0.974681 1.025977 0.8126% 1938 0.966824 1.034314 0.7762% 1937 0.959377 1.042343 0.6029% 1936 0.953628 1.048627 0.5244% 1935 0.948653 1.054126 -3.0364% 1934 0.978360 1.022119 4.6271% 1933 0.935092 1.069413 1.3921% 1932 0.922253 1.084301 -0.2051% 1931 0.924149 1.082077 0.8886% 1930 0.916009 1.091692 1.0126% 1929 0.906827 1.102747

97

1.1526% 1928 0.896494 1.115457 1.2160% 1927 0.885723 1.129021 1.4086% 1926 0.873420
1.144924 1.7667% 1925 0.858258 1.165151 1.4465% 1924 0.846020 1.182005 1.7700% 1923
0.831306 1.202926 1.6165% 1922 0.818082 1.222372 1.3736% 1921 0.806996 1.239163
2.3393% 1920 0.788550 1.268151 1.3140% 1919 0.778323 1.284814 0.7676% 1918 0.772393
1.294677 0.3870% 1917 0.769416 1.299687 1.3274% 1916 0.759336 1.316940 1.4083% 1915
0.748791 1.335486 1.4458% 1914 0.738119 1.354795 1.9424% 1913 0.724055 1.381110
1.9857% 1912 0.709958 1.408534 1.5634% 1911 0.699029 1.430556 1.8169% 1910 0.686555
1.456548 1.8781% 1909 0.673899 1.483902 2.0082% 1908 0.660632 1.513703 1.9603% 1907
0.647931 1.543375 1.8264% 1906 0.636309 1.571563 1.9357% 1905 0.624226 1.601983
2.0148% 1904 0.611898 1.634260 2.1335% 1903 0.599115 1.669128 1.8151% 1902 0.588434
1.699425 1.8943% 1901 0.577495 1.731618 3.0255% 1900 0.560536 1.784008 0.6278% 1899
0.557038 1.795209 1.7757% 1898 0.547320 1.827085 1.8078% 1897 0.537601 1.860115
1.8396% 1896 0.527890 1.894333 1.8755% 1895 0.518172 1.929862 1.9114% 1894 0.508453
1.966749 1.9486% 1893 0.498735 2.005074 1.9858% 1892 0.489024 2.044891 2.0276% 1891
0.479305 2.086354 2.6465% 1890 0.466947 2.141569 1.5328% 1889 0.459898 2.174396
2.0811% 1888 0.450522 2.219648 2.1599% 1887 0.440997 2.267589 2.2075% 1886 0.431472
2.317647 2.2592% 1885 0.421940 2.370006 2.3095% 1884 0.412415 2.424742 2.3641% 1883
0.402890 2.482067 2.4214% 1882 0.393365 2.542167 2.4815% 1881 0.383840 2.605250
3.7644% 1880 0.369915 2.703322 0.9432% 1879 0.366459 2.728821 2.1464% 1878 0.358758
2.787392 2.1913% 1877 0.351065 2.848472 2.2426% 1876 0.343365 2.912352 2.2941% 1875
0.335665 2.979163 2.3456% 1874 0.327972 3.049042 2.4043% 1873 0.320272 3.122351
2.4635% 1872 0.312571 3.199271 2.5258% 1871 0.304811 3.280077 5.9947% 1870 0.287628
3.476707 -1.0968% 1869 0.290818 3.438575 2.1930% 1868 0.284577 3.513982 2.2394%
1867 0.278344 3.592675 2.2935% 1866 0.272103 3.675073 2.3445% 1865 0.265870 3.761234
2.4037% 1864 0.259630 3.851642 2.4599% 1863 0.253396 3.946388 2.5250% 1862 0.247156
4.046035 2.5872% 1861 0.240922 4.150716 2.9504% 1860 0.234018 4.273179 2.4012% 1859
0.228530 4.375788 2.7627% 1858 0.222386 4.496678 2.8412% 1857 0.216242 4.624438
2.9243% 1856 0.210099 4.759670 3.0161% 1855 0.203947 4.903228 3.1061% 1854 0.197803
5.055525 3.2056% 1853 0.191659 5.217587 3.3118% 1852 0.185516 5.390382 3.4252% 1851
0.179372 5.575015 4.0106% 1850 0.172455 5.798607 2.3254% 1849 0.168536 5.933446
2.7841% 1848 0.163971 6.098638 2.8590% 1847 0.159413 6.272999 2.9432% 1846 0.154856
6.457623 3.0324% 1845 0.150298 6.653444 3.1325% 1844 0.145733 6.861864 3.2284% 1843
0.141175 7.083389 3.3361% 1842 0.136618 7.319695 3.4512% 1841 0.132060 7.572312
3.8105% 1840 0.127213 7.860854 2.3861% 1839 0.124248 8.048418 2.5824% 1838 0.121120
8.256260 2.6573% 1837 0.117985 8.475655 2.7232% 1836 0.114857 8.706465 2.7994% 1835
0.111729 8.950197 2.8871% 1834 0.108594 9.208600 2.9657% 1833 0.105466 9.481698
3.0563% 1832 0.102339 9.771490 3.1604% 1831 0.099203 10.080310 3.4660% 1830
0.095880 10.429690 2.4653% 1829 0.093573 10.686813 2.6804% 1828 0.091131 10.973262
10.3427% 1827 0.082589 12.108188 -4.2314% 1826 0.086238 11.595838 2.9150% 1825
0.083795 11.933861 3.0026% 1824 0.081353 12.292183 3.0955% 1823 0.078910 12.672689
3.1944% 1822 0.076467 13.077504 3.3102% 1821 0.074017 13.510394 3.2277% 1820
0.071703 13.946475 2.6573% 1819 0.069847 14.317071 2.6261% 1818 0.068059 14.693053
2.6969% 1817 0.066272 15.089314 2.7717% 1816 0.064485 15.507542 2.8507% 1815
0.062697 15.949615 2.9343% 1814 0.060910 16.417632 3.0231% 1813 0.059123 16.913945
3.1039% 1812 0.057343 17.438936 3.2172% 1811 0.055556 17.999974 3.0969% 1810
0.053887 18.557418 2.9144% 1809 0.052361 19.098252 2.8225% 1808 0.050924 19.637293
2.9199% 1807 0.049479 20.210688 2.9918% 1806 0.048041 20.815348 3.0841% 1805
0.046604 21.457304 3.1822% 1804 0.045167 22.140117 3.2868% 1803 0.043730 22.867815
3.3985% 1802 0.042292 23.644974 3.5180% 1801 0.040855 24.476815 3.3999% 1800
0.039512 25.309014 2.8419% 1799 0.038420 26.028263 2.7485% 1798 0.037392 26.743639
2.8261% 1797 0.036364 27.499449 3.7832% 1796 0.035039 28.539811 2.1272% 1795
0.034309 29.146909 3.0879% 1794 0.033281 30.046948 3.1625% 1793 0.032261 30.997186
3.2904% 1792 0.031233 32.017122 3.4024% 1791 0.030206 33.106462 3.2296% 1790
0.029261 34.175656 41.3145% 1780 0.020706 48.295141 29.4353% 1770 0.015997
62.510967 83.4728% 1750 0.008719 114.690647 29.2845% 1740 0.006744 148.277174

94.2514% 1720 0.003472 288.030478 85.8111% 1700 0.001868 535.192543 19.2490% 1690 0.001567 638.212020 88.0250% 1670 0.000833 1199.998293

YEAR BYEAR/AYEAR AYEAR/BYEAR GROWTH%

2009 2.259683 0.442540 8.2857% 2001 2.086779 0.479207 1.0000% 2000 2.066118 0.484000 1.0000% 1999 2.045661 0.488840 1.0000% 1998 2.025407 0.493728 1.0000% 1997 2.005353 0.498665 1.0000% 1996 1.985499 0.503652 1.0000% 1995 1.965840 0.508688 0.9992% 1994 1.946391 0.513771 1.0008% 1993 1.927105 0.518913 1.0000% 1992 1.908025 0.524102 0.9295% 1991 1.890453 0.528974 1.2505% 1990 1.867105 0.535589 0.7224% 1989 1.853713 0.539458 1.1077% 1988 1.833405 0.545433 0.8834% 1987 1.817351 0.550252 0.5594% 1986 1.807242 0.553329 1.3056% 1985 1.783950 0.560554 0.7673% 1984 1.770366 0.564855 0.8149% 1983 1.756055 0.569458 0.9737% 1982 1.739121 0.575003 0.9508% 1981 1.722741 0.580470 0.9031% 1980 1.707322 0.585712 2.2701% 1979 1.669425 0.599009 1.0042% 1978 1.652828 0.605024 0.9896% 1977 1.636632 0.611011 0.9103% 1976 1.621867 0.616573 0.8394% 1975 1.608366 0.621749 0.9042% 1974 1.593954 0.627371 1.1568% 1973 1.575726 0.634628 0.9427% 1972 1.561011 0.640611 0.7426% 1971 1.549503 0.645368 1.4697% 1970 1.527060 0.654853 0.6968% 1969 1.516492 0.659416 0.8565% 1968 1.503613 0.665065 1.5090% 1967 1.481261 0.675101 0.9949% 1966 1.466669 0.681817 1.0575% 1965 1.451321 0.689027 1.1300% 1964 1.435104 0.696813 1.5537% 1963 1.413149 0.707640 1.4658% 1962 1.392734 0.718012 1.5364% 1961 1.371659 0.729044 2.1586% 1960 1.342676 0.744781 -1.6655% 1959 1.365417 0.732377 4.3080% 1958 1.309024 0.763928 2.1130% 1957 1.281937 0.780069 1.9895% 1956 1.256931 0.795589 2.1231% 1955 1.230800 0.812480 1.4496% 1954 1.213213 0.824258 2.1573% 1953 1.187593 0.842039 1.2298% 1952 1.173166 0.852394 1.6814% 1951 1.153767 0.866726 1.6233% 1950 1.135337 0.880795 1.4265% 1949 1.119369 0.893360 1.7790% 1948 1.099803 0.909254 1.8242% 1947 1.080100 0.925840 -2.6320% 1946 1.109298 0.901471 3.1768% 1945 1.075142 0.930109 6.4754% 1944 1.009756 0.990338 -0.3437% 1943 1.013239 0.986934 0.6562% 1942 1.006633 0.993411 0.6633% 1941 1.000000 1.000000 -5.6614% 1940 1.060012 0.943386 8.0381% 1939 0.981146 1.019216 0.8126% 1938 0.973237 1.027499 0.7762% 1937 0.965741 1.035474 0.6029% 1936 0.959954 1.041717 0.5244% 1935 0.954946 1.047180 -3.0364% 1934 0.984850 1.015384 4.6271% 1933 0.941295 1.062367 1.3921% 1932 0.928371 1.077156 -0.2051% 1931 0.930278 1.074947 0.8886% 1930 0.922085 1.084499 1.0126% 1929 0.912842 1.095480 1.1526% 1928 0.902440 1.108107 1.2160% 1927 0.891598 1.121581 1.4086% 1926 0.879214 1.137380 1.7667% 1925 0.863951 1.157474 1.4465% 1924 0.851632 1.174217 1.7700% 1923 0.836820 1.195000 1.6165% 1922 0.823508 1.214317 1.3736% 1921 0.812349 1.230998 2.3393% 1920 0.793780 1.259795 1.3140% 1919 0.783485 1.276348 0.7676% 1918 0.777517 1.286146 0.3870% 1917 0.774519 1.291123 1.3274% 1916 0.764373 1.308262 1.4083% 1915 0.753758 1.326686 1.4458% 1914 0.743015 1.345868 1.9424% 1913 0.728858 1.372010 1.9857% 1912 0.714667 1.399253 1.5634% 1911 0.703666 1.421129 1.8169% 1910 0.691109 1.446950 1.8781% 1909 0.678369 1.474124 2.0082% 1908 0.665014 1.503728 1.9603% 1907 0.652228 1.533205 1.8264% 1906 0.640530 1.561207 1.9357% 1905 0.628367 1.591427 2.0148% 1904 0.615956 1.623492 2.1335% 1903 0.603089 1.658129 1.8151% 1902 0.592337 1.688227 1.8943% 1901 0.581325 1.720208 3.0255% 1900 0.564254 1.772253 0.6278% 1899 0.560733 1.783379 1.7757% 1898 0.550950 1.815046 1.8078% 1897 0.541167 1.847858 1.8396% 1896 0.531392 1.881851 1.8755% 1895 0.521609 1.917146 1.9114% 1894 0.511826 1.953790 1.9486% 1893 0.502043 1.991862 1.9858% 1892 0.492267 2.031417 2.0276% 1891 0.482484 2.072606 2.6465% 1890 0.470045 2.127458 1.5328% 1889 0.462948 2.160068 2.0811% 1888 0.453510 2.205022 2.1599% 1887 0.443922 2.252647 2.2075% 1886 0.434334 2.302375 2.2592% 1885 0.424739 2.354389 2.3095% 1884 0.415150 2.408765 2.3641% 1883 0.405562 2.465712 2.4214% 1882 0.395974 2.525416 2.4815% 1881 0.386386 2.588084 3.7644% 1880 0.372369 2.685509 0.9432% 1879 0.368889 2.710840 2.1464% 1878 0.361138 2.769025 2.1913% 1877 0.353394 2.829702 2.2426% 1876 0.345643 2.893162 2.2941% 1875 0.337891 2.959532 2.3456% 1874 0.330147 3.028951 2.4043% 1873 0.322396 3.101776 2.4635% 1872 0.314644 3.178190 2.5258% 1871 0.306893 3.258464 5.9947% 1870 0.289536 3.453798 -1.0968% 1869 0.292747 3.415918 2.1930% 1868 0.286465 3.490828 2.2394% 1867 0.280190 3.569001 2.2935% 1866 0.273908 3.650857 2.3445% 1865 0.267634 3.736450

99

2.4037% 1864 0.261352 3.826263 2.4599% 1863 0.255077 3.920384 2.5250% 1862 0.248795
4.019374 2.5872% 1861 0.242520 4.123366 2.9504% 1860 0.235570 4.245022 2.4012% 1859
0.230046 4.346955 2.7627% 1858 0.223861 4.467048 2.8412% 1857 0.217677 4.593966
2.9243% 1856 0.211492 4.728307 3.0161% 1855 0.205300 4.870919 3.1061% 1854 0.199115
5.022213 3.2056% 1853 0.192931 5.183206 3.3118% 1852 0.186746 5.354863 3.4252% 1851
0.180561 5.538279 4.0106% 1850 0.173599 5.760398 2.3254% 1849 0.169654 5.894348
2.7841% 1848 0.165059 6.058452 2.8590% 1847 0.160471 6.231664 2.9432% 1846 0.155883
6.415072 3.0324% 1845 0.151295 6.609603 3.1325% 1844 0.146700 6.816649 3.2284% 1843
0.142112 7.036715 3.3361% 1842 0.137524 7.271464 3.4512% 1841 0.132936 7.522416
3.8105% 1840 0.128056 7.809057 2.3861% 1839 0.125072 7.995385 2.5824% 1838 0.121924
8.201857 2.6573% 1837 0.118768 8.419807 2.7232% 1836 0.115619 8.649096 2.7994% 1835
0.112470 8.891222 2.8871% 1834 0.109314 9.147922 2.9657% 1833 0.106166 9.419220
3.0563% 1832 0.103017 9.707102 3.1604% 1831 0.099861 10.013888 3.4660% 1830
0.096516 10.360966 2.4653% 1829 0.094194 10.616395 2.6804% 1828 0.091735 10.900956
10.3427% 1827 0.083137 12.028404 -4.2314% 1826 0.086810 11.519430 2.9150% 1825
0.084351 11.855226 3.0026% 1824 0.081892 12.211186 3.0955% 1823 0.079433 12.589185
3.1944% 1822 0.076974 12.991332 3.3102% 1821 0.074508 13.421370 3.2277% 1820
0.072178 13.854577 2.6573% 1819 0.070310 14.222732 2.6261% 1818 0.068511 14.596236
2.6969% 1817 0.066712 14.989887 2.7717% 1816 0.064912 15.405359 2.8507% 1815
0.063113 15.844518 2.9343% 1814 0.061314 16.309451 3.0231% 1813 0.059515 16.802494
3.1039% 1812 0.057723 17.324026 3.2172% 1811 0.055924 17.881367 3.0969% 1810
0.054244 18.435138 2.9144% 1809 0.052708 18.972408 2.8225% 1808 0.051261 19.507897
2.9199% 1807 0.049807 20.077514 2.9918% 1806 0.048360 20.678189 3.0841% 1805
0.046913 21.315916 3.1822% 1804 0.045466 21.994229 3.2868% 1803 0.044020 22.717132
3.3985% 1802 0.042573 23.489171 3.5180% 1801 0.041126 24.315530 3.3999% 1800
0.039774 25.142246 2.8419% 1799 0.038675 25.856755 2.7485% 1798 0.037640 26.567417
2.8261% 1797 0.036606 27.318247 3.7832% 1796 0.035271 28.351753 2.1272% 1795
0.034537 28.954851 3.0879% 1794 0.033502 29.848959 3.1625% 1793 0.032475 30.792936
3.2904% 1792 0.031440 31.806152 3.4024% 1791 0.030406 32.888314 3.2296% 1790
0.029455 33.950463 41.3145% 1780 0.020843 47.976910 29.4353% 1770 0.016103
62.099064 83.4728% 1750 0.008777 113.934916 29.2845% 1740 0.006789 147.300133
94.2514% 1720 0.003495 286.132561 85.8111% 1700 0.001881 531.666002 19.2490% 1690
0.001577 634.006654 88.0250% 1670 0.000839 1192.091153
 BASE YEAR: 1940
 YEAR BYEAR/AYEAR AYEAR/BYEAR GROWTH%
 2009 2.131752 0.469098 8.2857% 2001 1.968638 0.507966 1.0000% 2000 1.949146
0.513045 1.0000% 1999 1.929847 0.518176 1.0000% 1998 1.910740 0.523357 1.0000% 1997
1.891822 0.528591 1.0000% 1996 1.873091 0.533877 1.0000% 1995 1.854545 0.539216
0.9992% 1994 1.836198 0.544604 1.0008% 1993 1.818004 0.550054 1.0000% 1992 1.800004
0.555554 0.9295% 1991 1.783427 0.560718 1.2505% 1990 1.761400 0.567730 0.7224% 1989
1.748766 0.571832 1.1077% 1988 1.729608 0.578166 0.8834% 1987 1.714463 0.583273
0.5594% 1986 1.704926 0.586536 1.3056% 1985 1.682953 0.594194 0.7673% 1984 1.670138
0.598753 0.8149% 1983 1.656638 0.603632 0.9737% 1982 1.640662 0.609510 0.9508% 1981
1.625209 0.615305 0.9031% 1980 1.610664 0.620862 2.2701% 1979 1.574912 0.634956
1.0042% 1978 1.559254 0.641332 0.9896% 1977 1.543975 0.647679 0.9103% 1976 1.530047
0.653575 0.8394% 1975 1.517310 0.659061 0.9042% 1974 1.503713 0.665020 1.1568% 1973
1.486518 0.672713 0.9427% 1972 1.472635 0.679055 0.7426% 1971 1.461779 0.684098
1.4697% 1970 1.440606 0.694152 0.6968% 1969 1.430637 0.698989 0.8565% 1968 1.418487
0.704976 1.5090% 1967 1.397400 0.715615 0.9949% 1966 1.383634 0.722734 1.0575% 1965
1.369156 0.730377 1.1300% 1964 1.353857 0.738630 1.5537% 1963 1.333145 0.750106
1.4658% 1962 1.313885 0.761101 1.5364% 1961 1.294004 0.772795 2.1586% 1960 1.266661
0.789477 -1.6655% 1959 1.288115 0.776328 4.3080% 1958 1.234915 0.809773 2.1130%
1957 1.209361 0.826883 1.9895% 1956 1.185770 0.843334 2.1231% 1955 1.161119 0.861238
1.4496% 1954 1.144527 0.873723 2.1573% 1953 1.120359 0.892571 1.2298% 1952 1.106748
0.903548 1.6814% 1951 1.088447 0.918740 1.6233% 1950 1.071061 0.933654 1.4265% 1949
1.055997 0.946972 1.7790% 1948 1.037539 0.963820 1.8242% 1947 1.018951 0.981401 -

100

2.6320% 1946 1.046495 0.955570 3.1768% 1945 1.014274 0.985927 6.4754% 1944 0.952590
1.049770 -0.3437% 1943 0.955875 1.046162 0.6562% 1942 0.949643 1.053027 0.6633%
1941 0.943386 1.060012 -5.6614% 1940 1.000000 1.000000 8.0381% 1939 0.925599
1.080381 0.8126% 1938 0.918138 1.089161 0.7762% 1937 0.911066 1.097615 0.6029% 1936
0.905606 1.104232 0.5244% 1935 0.900882 1.110023 -3.0364% 1934 0.929093 1.076319
4.6271% 1933 0.888004 1.126121 1.3921% 1932 0.875812 1.141798 -0.2051% 1931
0.877611 1.139456 0.8886% 1930 0.869882 1.149582 1.0126% 1929 0.861162 1.161222
1.1526% 1928 0.851349 1.174606 1.2160% 1927 0.841121 1.188889 1.4086% 1926 0.829438
1.205636 1.7667% 1925 0.815039 1.226936 1.4465% 1924 0.803417 1.244683 1.7700% 1923
0.789444 1.266714 1.6165% 1922 0.776886 1.287191 1.3736% 1921 0.766359 1.304872
2.3393% 1920 0.748841 1.335397 1.3140% 1919 0.739129 1.352944 0.7676% 1918 0.733498
1.363330 0.3870% 1917 0.730670 1.368606 1.3274% 1916 0.721098 1.386773 1.4083% 1915
0.711084 1.406303 1.4458% 1914 0.700950 1.426636 1.9424% 1913 0.687594 1.454346
1.9857% 1912 0.674207 1.483225 1.5634% 1911 0.663828 1.506414 1.8169% 1910 0.651982
1.533784 1.8781% 1909 0.639963 1.562589 2.0082% 1908 0.627364 1.593970 1.9603% 1907
0.615303 1.625216 1.8264% 1906 0.604267 1.654898 1.9357% 1905 0.592792 1.686931
2.0148% 1904 0.581084 1.720920 2.1335% 1903 0.568946 1.757637 1.8151% 1902 0.558803
1.789540 1.8943% 1901 0.548414 1.823440 3.0255% 1900 0.532309 1.878609 0.6278% 1899
0.528988 1.890403 1.7757% 1898 0.519759 1.923970 1.8078% 1897 0.510529 1.958751
1.8396% 1896 0.501307 1.994784 1.8755% 1895 0.492078 2.032197 1.9114% 1894 0.482849
2.071040 1.9486% 1893 0.473620 2.111397 1.9858% 1892 0.464398 2.153326 2.0276% 1891
0.455169 2.196987 2.6465% 1890 0.443433 2.255131 1.5328% 1889 0.436739 2.289698
2.0811% 1888 0.427835 2.337349 2.1599% 1887 0.418790 2.387832 2.2075% 1886 0.409745
2.440545 2.2592% 1885 0.400692 2.495681 2.3095% 1884 0.391647 2.553319 2.3641% 1883
0.382602 2.613683 2.4214% 1882 0.373557 2.676971 2.4815% 1881 0.364511 2.743399
3.7644% 1880 0.351287 2.846671 0.9432% 1879 0.348005 2.873522 2.1464% 1878 0.340692
2.935199 2.1913% 1877 0.333387 2.999518 2.2426% 1876 0.326074 3.066785 2.2941% 1875
0.318762 3.137139 2.3456% 1874 0.311456 3.210724 2.4043% 1873 0.304144 3.287920
2.4635% 1872 0.296831 3.368919 2.5258% 1871 0.289519 3.454010 5.9947% 1870 0.273144
3.661067 -1.0968% 1869 0.276173 3.620913 2.1930% 1868 0.270247 3.700319 2.2394%
1867 0.264328 3.783184 2.2935% 1866 0.258401 3.869951 2.3445% 1865 0.252482 3.960681
2.4037% 1864 0.246555 4.055884 2.4599% 1863 0.240636 4.155654 2.5250% 1862 0.234710
4.260584 2.5872% 1861 0.228790 4.370816 2.9504% 1860 0.222233 4.499773 2.4012% 1859
0.217022 4.607823 2.7627% 1858 0.211188 4.735124 2.8412% 1857 0.205353 4.869659
2.9243% 1856 0.199519 5.012061 3.0161% 1855 0.193677 5.163232 3.1061% 1854 0.187843
5.323605 3.2056% 1853 0.182008 5.494260 3.3118% 1852 0.176174 5.676218 3.4252% 1851
0.170339 5.870642 4.0106% 1850 0.163771 6.106090 2.3254% 1849 0.160049 6.248079
2.7841% 1848 0.155714 6.422031 2.8590% 1847 0.151386 6.605637 2.9432% 1846 0.147058
6.800052 3.0324% 1845 0.142730 7.006257 3.1325% 1844 0.138394 7.225728 3.2284% 1843
0.134066 7.459001 3.3361% 1842 0.129738 7.707837 3.4512% 1841 0.125410 7.973850
3.8105% 1840 0.120807 8.277692 2.3861% 1839 0.117991 8.475202 2.5824% 1838 0.115021
8.694065 2.6573% 1837 0.112044 8.925095 2.7232% 1836 0.109073 9.168143 2.7994% 1835
0.106103 9.424800 2.8871% 1834 0.103126 9.696905 2.9657% 1833 0.100155 9.984485
3.0563% 1832 0.097185 10.289643 3.1604% 1831 0.094208 10.614839 3.4660% 1830
0.091052 10.982746 2.4653% 1829 0.088861 11.253504 2.6804% 1828 0.086542 11.555142
10.3427% 1827 0.078430 12.750250 -4.2314% 1826 0.081895 12.210732 2.9150% 1825
0.079576 12.566679 3.0026% 1824 0.077256 12.944002 3.0955% 1823 0.074936 13.344684
3.1944% 1822 0.072617 13.770966 3.3102% 1821 0.070290 14.226811 3.2277% 1820
0.068092 14.686015 2.6573% 1819 0.066329 15.076263 6.2261% 1818 0.064632 15.472182
2.6969% 1817 0.062935 15.889457 2.7717% 1816 0.061238 16.329862 2.8507% 1815
0.059540 16.795376 2.9343% 1814 0.057843 17.288211 3.0231% 1813 0.056146 17.810842
3.1039% 1812 0.054455 18.363672 3.2172% 1811 0.052758 18.954460 3.0969% 1810
0.051173 19.541464 2.9144% 1809 0.049724 20.110976 2.8225% 1808 0.048359 20.678601
2.9199% 1807 0.046987 21.282401 2.9918% 1806 0.045622 21.919125 3.0841% 1805
0.044257 22.595122 3.1822% 1804 0.042892 23.314142 3.2868% 1803 0.041528 24.080428
3.3985% 1802 0.040163 24.898798 3.5180% 1801 0.038798 25.774749 3.3999% 1800

0.037522 26.651077 2.8419% 1799 0.036485 27.408466 2.7485% 1798 0.035509 28.161775
2.8261% 1797 0.034533 28.957664 3.7832% 1796 0.033274 30.053193 2.1272% 1795
0.032581 30.692484 3.0879% 1794 0.031605 31.640249 3.1625% 1793 0.030636 32.640876
3.2904% 1792 0.029660 33.714896 3.4024% 1791 0.028685 34.862000 3.2296% 1790
0.027787 35.987891 41.3145% 1780 0.019663 50.856090 29.4353% 1770 0.015192
65.825741 83.4728% 1750 0.008280 120.772356 29.2845% 1740 0.006405 156.139879
94.2514% 1720 0.003297 303.303891 85.8111% 1700 0.001774 563.572236 19.2490% 1690
0.001488 672.054534 88.0250% 1670 0.000791 1263.630688

BASE YEAR: 1939

YEAR BYEAR/AYEAR AYEAR/BYEAR GROWTH%

2009 2.303105 0.434196 8.2857% 2001 2.126879 0.470173 1.0000% 2000 2.105820
0.474874 1.0000% 1999 2.084971 0.479623 1.0000% 1998 2.064327 0.484419 1.0000% 1997
2.043889 0.489263 1.0000% 1996 2.023652 0.494156 1.0000% 1995 2.003616 0.499098
0.9992% 1994 1.983793 0.504085 1.0008% 1993 1.964137 0.509130 1.0000% 1992 1.944690
0.514221 0.9295% 1991 1.926780 0.519001 1.2505% 1990 1.902983 0.525491 0.7224% 1989
1.889334 0.529287 1.1077% 1988 1.868635 0.535150 0.8834% 1987 1.852273 0.539877
0.5594% 1986 1.841970 0.542897 1.3056% 1985 1.818230 0.549985 0.7673% 1984 1.804386
0.554205 0.8149% 1983 1.789800 0.558722 0.9737% 1982 1.772540 0.564162 0.9508% 1981
1.755845 0.569526 0.9031% 1980 1.740131 0.574670 2.2701% 1979 1.701505 0.587715
1.0042% 1978 1.684589 0.593617 0.9896% 1977 1.668081 0.599491 0.9103% 1976 1.653033
0.604948 0.8394% 1975 1.639273 0.610027 0.9042% 1974 1.624584 0.615542 1.1568% 1973
1.606006 0.622663 0.9427% 1972 1.591007 0.628533 0.7426% 1971 1.579279 0.633200
1.4697% 1970 1.556404 0.642507 0.6968% 1969 1.545633 0.646984 0.8565% 1968 1.532507
0.652526 1.5090% 1967 1.509725 0.662372 0.9949% 1966 1.494852 0.668962 1.0575% 1965
1.479210 0.676037 1.1300% 1964 1.462681 0.683676 1.5537% 1963 1.440304 0.694298
1.4658% 1962 1.419497 0.704475 1.5364% 1961 1.398017 0.715299 2.1586% 1960 1.368477
0.730739 -1.6655% 1959 1.391655 0.718569 4.3080% 1958 1.334178 0.749525 2.1130%
1957 1.306571 0.765362 1.9895% 1956 1.281084 0.780589 2.1231% 1955 1.254451 0.797162
1.4496% 1954 1.236526 0.808717 2.1573% 1953 1.210414 0.826164 1.2298% 1952 1.195710
0.836323 1.6814% 1951 1.175938 0.850385 1.6233% 1950 1.157154 0.864189 1.4265% 1949
1.140879 0.876517 1.7790% 1948 1.120937 0.892111 1.8242% 1947 1.100856 0.908384 -
2.6320% 1946 1.130614 0.884475 3.1768% 1945 1.095802 0.912573 6.4754% 1944 1.029160
0.971666 -0.3437% 1943 1.032709 0.968327 0.6562% 1942 1.025977 0.974681 0.6633%
1941 1.019216 0.981146 -5.6614% 1940 1.080381 0.925599 8.0381% 1939 1.000000
1.000000 0.8126% 1938 0.991939 1.008126 0.7762% 1937 0.984299 1.015952 0.6029% 1936
0.978400 1.022077 0.5244% 1935 0.973296 1.027437 -3.0364% 1934 1.003774 0.996240
4.6271% 1933 0.959383 1.042337 1.3921% 1932 0.946210 1.056848 -0.2051% 1931
0.948155 1.054680 0.8886% 1930 0.939804 1.064052 1.0126% 1929 0.930383 1.074826
1.1526% 1928 0.919781 1.087215 1.2160% 1927 0.908731 1.100435 1.4086% 1926 0.896109
1.115936 1.7667% 1925 0.880552 1.135651 1.4465% 1924 0.867997 1.152078 1.7700% 1923
0.852901 1.172470 1.6165% 1922 0.839333 1.191423 1.3736% 1921 0.827959 1.207789
2.3393% 1920 0.809034 1.236043 1.3140% 1919 0.798541 1.252284 0.7676% 1918 0.792457
1.261897 0.3870% 1917 0.789403 1.266781 1.3274% 1916 0.779061 1.283597 1.4083% 1915
0.768242 1.301673 1.4458% 1914 0.757293 1.320493 1.9424% 1913 0.742864 1.346142
1.9857% 1912 0.728400 1.372872 1.5634% 1911 0.717187 1.394336 1.8169% 1910 0.704389
1.419669 1.8781% 1909 0.691404 1.446332 2.0082% 1908 0.677793 1.475377 1.9603% 1907
0.664762 1.504299 1.8264% 1906 0.652838 1.531772 1.9357% 1905 0.640442 1.561423
2.0148% 1904 0.627793 1.592883 2.1335% 1903 0.614678 1.626867 1.8151% 1902 0.603720
1.656397 1.8943% 1901 0.592496 1.687775 3.0255% 1900 0.575096 1.738839 0.6278% 1899
0.571508 1.749756 1.7757% 1898 0.561537 1.780826 1.8078% 1897 0.551566 1.813019
1.8396% 1896 0.541603 1.846371 1.8755% 1895 0.531632 1.881000 1.9114% 1894 0.521661
1.916953 1.9486% 1893 0.511690 1.954308 1.9858% 1892 0.501727 1.993117 2.0276% 1891
0.491756 2.033530 2.6465% 1890 0.479077 2.087347 1.5328% 1889 0.471844 2.119343
2.0811% 1888 0.462225 2.163449 2.1599% 1887 0.452453 2.210176 2.2075% 1886 0.442680
2.258966 2.2592% 1885 0.432900 2.310000 2.3095% 1884 0.423128 2.363351 2.3641% 1883
0.413356 2.419224 2.4214% 1882 0.403583 2.477802 2.4815% 1881 0.393811 2.539288

3.7644% 1880 0.379524 2.634877 0.9432% 1879 0.375978 2.659730 2.1464% 1878 0.368078 2.716818 2.1913% 1877 0.360185 2.776352 2.2426% 1876 0.352285 2.838615 2.2941% 1875 0.344384 2.903734 2.3456% 1874 0.336491 2.971844 2.4043% 1873 0.328591 3.043296 2.4635% 1872 0.320691 3.118269 2.5258% 1871 0.312790 3.197030 5.9947% 1870 0.295100 3.388681 -1.0968% 1869 0.298373 3.351515 2.1930% 1868 0.291970 3.425012 2.2394% 1867 0.285575 3.501712 2.2935% 1866 0.279172 3.582024 2.3445% 1865 0.272777 3.666004 2.4037% 1864 0.266374 3.754123 2.4599% 1863 0.259979 3.846470 2.5250% 1862 0.253576 3.943594 2.5872% 1861 0.247181 4.045625 2.9504% 1860 0.240097 4.164987 2.4012% 1859 0.234467 4.264998 2.7627% 1858 0.228163 4.382828 2.8412% 1857 0.221860 4.507353 2.9243% 1856 0.215556 4.639161 3.0161% 1855 0.209245 4.779084 3.1061% 1854 0.202942 4.927525 3.2056% 1853 0.196638 5.085483 3.3118% 1852 0.190335 5.253904 3.4252% 1851 0.184031 5.433862 4.0106% 1850 0.176935 5.651793 2.3254% 1849 0.172914 5.783218 2.7841% 1848 0.168230 5.944227 2.8590% 1847 0.163554 6.114174 2.9432% 1846 0.158878 6.294123 3.0324% 1845 0.154202 6.484987 3.1325% 1843 0.149519 6.688129 3.2284% 1843 0.144843 6.904046 3.3361% 1842 0.140167 7.134369 3.4512% 1841 0.135491 7.380590 3.8105% 1840 0.130517 7.661826 2.3861% 1839 0.127476 7.844642 2.5824% 1838 0.124267 8.047221 2.6573% 1837 0.121050 8.261062 2.7232% 1836 0.117841 8.486027 2.7994% 1835 0.114632 8.723589 2.8871% 1834 0.111415 8.975449 2.9657% 1833 0.108206 9.241633 3.0563% 1832 0.104997 9.524087 3.1604% 1831 0.101780 9.825088 3.4660% 1830 0.098371 10.165622 2.4653% 1829 0.096004 10.416236 2.6804% 1828 0.093498 10.695432 10.3427% 1827 0.084734 11.801623 -4.2314% 1826 0.088478 11.302245 2.9150% 1825 0.085972 11.631710 3.0026% 1824 0.083466 11.980959 3.0955% 1823 0.080960 12.351831 3.1944% 1822 0.078454 12.746397 3.3102% 1821 0.075940 13.168327 3.2277% 1820 0.073565 13.593366 2.6573% 1819 0.071661 13.954579 2.6261% 1818 0.069827 14.321042 2.6969% 1817 0.067994 14.707270 2.7717% 1816 0.066160 15.114909 2.8507% 1815 0.064326 15.545789 2.9343% 1814 0.062492 16.001956 3.0231% 1813 0.060659 16.485703 3.1039% 1812 0.058833 16.997403 3.2172% 1811 0.056999 17.544236 3.0969% 1810 0.055287 18.087566 2.9144% 1809 0.053721 18.614706 2.8225% 1808 0.052246 19.140099 2.9199% 1807 0.050764 19.698977 2.9918% 1806 0.049289 20.288327 3.0841% 1805 0.047815 20.914030 3.1822% 1804 0.046340 21.579555 3.2868% 1803 0.044866 22.288828 3.3985% 1802 0.043391 23.046311 3.5180% 1801 0.041916 23.857091 3.3999% 1800 0.040538 24.668219 2.8419% 1799 0.039418 25.369258 2.7485% 1798 0.038363 26.066521 2.8261% 1797 0.037309 26.803195 3.7832% 1796 0.035949 27.817216 2.1272% 1795 0.035200 28.408943 3.0879% 1794 0.034146 29.286194 3.1625% 1793 0.033099 30.212373 3.2904% 1792 0.032045 31.206485 3.4024% 1791 0.030990 32.268245 3.2296% 1790 0.030021 33.310368 41.3145% 1780 0.021244 47.072364 29.4353% 1770 0.016413 60.928262 83.4728% 1750 0.008946 111.786812 29.2845% 1740 0.006919 144.522968 94.2514% 1720 0.003562 280.737881 85.8111% 1700 0.001917 521.642088 19.2490% 1690 0.001608 622.053232 88.0250% 1670 0.000855 1169.615728

BASE YEAR: 1938

YEAR	BYEAR/AYEAR	AYEAR/BYEAR	GROWTH%

2009 2.321821 0.430697 8.2857% 2001 2.144163 0.466383 1.0000% 2000 2.122933 0.471046 1.0000% 1999 2.101914 0.475757 1.0000% 1998 2.081103 0.480514 1.0000% 1997 2.060498 0.485320 1.0000% 1996 2.040097 0.490173 1.0000% 1995 2.019898 0.495075 0.9992% 1994 1.999914 0.500021 1.0008% 1993 1.980098 0.505026 1.0000% 1992 1.960493 0.510076 0.9295% 1991 1.942438 0.514817 1.2505% 1990 1.918447 0.521255 0.7224% 1989 1.904687 0.525021 1.1077% 1988 1.883821 0.530836 0.8834% 1987 1.867325 0.535525 0.5594% 1986 1.856938 0.538521 1.3056% 1985 1.833006 0.545552 0.7673% 1984 1.819049 0.549738 0.8149% 1983 1.804344 0.554218 0.9737% 1982 1.786944 0.559615 0.9508% 1981 1.770114 0.564935 0.9031% 1980 1.754271 0.570037 2.2701% 1979 1.715332 0.582977 1.0042% 1978 1.698278 0.588832 0.9896% 1977 1.681637 0.594659 0.9103% 1976 1.666466 0.600072 0.8394% 1975 1.652594 0.605109 0.9042% 1974 1.637785 0.610581 1.1568% 1973 1.619056 0.617644 0.9427% 1972 1.603936 0.623466 0.7426% 1971 1.592112 0.628096 1.4697% 1970 1.569052 0.637328 0.6968% 1969 1.558194 0.641769 0.8565% 1968 1.544961 0.647266 1.5090% 1967 1.521993 0.657033 0.9949% 1966 1.507000 0.663570 1.0575% 1965 1.491231 0.670587 1.1300% 1964 1.474568 0.678165 1.5537% 1963 1.452008 0.688701

1.4658% 1962 1.431032 0.698796 1.5364% 1961 1.409378 0.709533 2.1586% 1960 1.379597
0.724849 -1.6655% 1959 1.402964 0.712777 4.3080% 1958 1.345020 0.743483 2.1130%
1957 1.317189 0.759193 1.9895% 1956 1.291494 0.774297 2.1231% 1955 1.264645 0.790736
1.4496% 1954 1.246574 0.802199 2.1573% 1953 1.220250 0.819504 1.2298% 1952 1.205427
0.829582 1.6814% 1951 1.185494 0.843530 1.6233% 1950 1.166558 0.857223 1.4265% 1949
1.150150 0.869452 1.7790% 1948 1.130046 0.884920 1.8242% 1947 1.109802 0.901062 -
2.6320% 1946 1.139802 0.877346 3.1768% 1945 1.104707 0.905217 6.4754% 1944 1.037523
0.963834 -0.3437% 1943 1.041101 0.960521 0.6562% 1942 1.034314 0.966824 0.6633%
1941 1.027499 0.973237 -5.6614% 1940 1.089161 0.918138 8.0381% 1939 1.008126
0.991939 0.8126% 1938 1.000000 1.000000 0.7762% 1937 0.992297 1.007762 0.6029% 1936
0.986351 1.013838 0.5244% 1935 0.981205 1.019155 -3.0364% 1934 1.011931 0.988209
4.6271% 1933 0.967179 1.033935 1.3921% 1932 0.953899 1.048328 -0.2051% 1931
0.955860 1.046179 0.8886% 1930 0.947441 1.055475 1.0126% 1929 0.937943 1.066162
1.1526% 1928 0.927256 1.078451 1.2160% 1927 0.916116 1.091565 1.4086% 1926 0.903391
1.106940 1.7667% 1925 0.887708 1.126497 1.4465% 1924 0.875050 1.142791 1.7700% 1923
0.859832 1.163019 1.6165% 1922 0.846153 1.181819 1.3736% 1921 0.834688 1.198053
2.3393% 1920 0.815608 1.226079 1.3140% 1919 0.805030 1.242190 0.7676% 1918 0.798897
1.251726 0.3870% 1917 0.795817 1.256570 1.3274% 1916 0.785392 1.273250 1.4083% 1915
0.774485 1.291181 1.4458% 1914 0.763447 1.309849 1.9424% 1913 0.748900 1.335291
1.9857% 1912 0.734319 1.361805 1.5634% 1911 0.723016 1.383096 1.8169% 1910 0.710113
1.408226 1.8781% 1909 0.697023 1.434673 2.0082% 1908 0.683301 1.463485 1.9603% 1907
0.670164 1.492173 1.8264% 1906 0.658144 1.519425 1.9357% 1905 0.645646 1.548836
2.0148% 1904 0.632894 1.580043 2.1335% 1903 0.619673 1.613753 1.8151% 1902 0.608626
1.643045 1.8943% 1901 0.597311 1.674170 3.0255% 1900 0.579770 1.724822 0.6278% 1899
0.576153 1.735652 1.7757% 1898 0.566101 1.766471 1.8078% 1897 0.556049 1.798404
1.8396% 1896 0.546004 1.831488 1.8755% 1895 0.535952 1.865838 1.9114% 1894 0.525900
1.901501 1.9486% 1893 0.515848 1.938555 1.9858% 1892 0.505804 1.977051 2.0276% 1891
0.495752 2.017138 2.6465% 1890 0.482970 2.070522 1.5328% 1889 0.475679 2.102259
2.0811% 1888 0.465981 2.146010 2.1599% 1887 0.456129 2.192360 2.2075% 1886 0.446278
2.240757 2.2592% 1885 0.436418 2.291380 2.3095% 1884 0.426567 2.344300 2.3641% 1883
0.416715 2.399723 2.4214% 1882 0.406863 2.457829 2.4815% 1881 0.397011 2.518820
3.7644% 1880 0.382608 2.613638 0.9432% 1879 0.379033 2.638291 2.1464% 1878 0.371069
2.694918 2.1913% 1877 0.363112 2.753972 2.2426% 1876 0.355147 2.815733 2.2941% 1875
0.347183 2.880327 2.3456% 1874 0.339226 2.947888 2.4043% 1873 0.331261 3.018765
2.4635% 1872 0.323297 3.093134 2.5258% 1871 0.315332 3.171259 5.9947% 1870 0.297498
3.361366 -1.0968% 1869 0.300797 3.324499 2.1930% 1868 0.294342 3.397404 2.2394%
1867 0.287895 3.473486 2.2935% 1866 0.281440 3.553150 2.3445% 1865 0.274993 3.636453
2.4037% 1864 0.268538 3.723862 2.4599% 1863 0.262091 3.815465 2.5250% 1862 0.255636
3.911805 2.5872% 1861 0.249189 4.013014 2.9504% 1860 0.242048 4.131414 2.4012% 1859
0.236372 4.230619 2.7627% 1858 0.230017 4.347498 2.8412% 1857 0.223663 4.471020
2.9243% 1856 0.217308 4.601765 3.0161% 1855 0.210946 4.740561 3.1061% 1854 0.204591
4.887805 3.2056% 1853 0.198236 5.044490 3.3118% 1852 0.191881 5.211553 3.4252% 1851
0.185527 5.390061 4.0106% 1850 0.178373 5.606235 2.3254% 1849 0.174319 5.736600
2.7841% 1848 0.169598 5.896312 2.8590% 1847 0.164883 6.064888 2.9432% 1846 0.160169
6.243388 3.0324% 1845 0.155455 6.432712 3.1325% 1844 0.150734 6.634217 3.2284% 1843
0.146020 6.848394 3.3361% 1842 0.141306 7.076860 3.4512% 1841 0.136592 7.321096
3.8105% 1840 0.131578 7.600066 2.3861% 1839 0.128511 7.781407 2.5824% 1838 0.125276
7.982354 2.6573% 1837 0.122034 8.194471 2.7232% 1836 0.118798 8.417623 2.7994% 1835
0.115563 8.653269 2.8871% 1834 0.112320 8.903100 2.9657% 1833 0.109085 9.167137
3.0563% 1832 0.105850 9.447315 3.1604% 1831 0.102607 9.745890 3.4660% 1830 0.099170
10.083679 2.4653% 1829 0.096784 10.332272 2.6804% 1828 0.094258 10.609218 10.3427%
1827 0.085423 11.706492 -4.2314% 1826 0.089197 11.211140 2.9150% 1825 0.086671
11.537949 3.0026% 1824 0.084144 11.884383 3.0955% 1823 0.081618 12.252265 3.1944%
1822 0.079091 12.643650 3.3102% 1821 0.076557 13.062179 3.2277% 1820 0.074163
13.483792 2.6573% 1819 0.072243 13.842094 2.6261% 1818 0.070395 14.205602 2.6969%
1817 0.068546 14.588718 2.7717% 1816 0.066697 14.993071 2.8507% 1815 0.064849

15.420477 2.9343% 1814 0.063000 15.872967 3.0231% 1813 0.061152 16.352815 3.1039%
1812 0.059311 16.860390 3.2172% 1811 0.057462 17.402815 3.0969% 1810 0.055736
17.941765 2.9144% 1809 0.054158 18.464657 2.8225% 1808 0.052671 18.985815 2.9199%
1807 0.051177 19.540187 2.9918% 1806 0.049690 20.124787 3.0841% 1805 0.048203
20.745446 3.1822% 1804 0.046717 21.405606 3.2868% 1803 0.045230 22.109162 3.3985%
1802 0.043744 22.860539 3.5180% 1801 0.042257 23.664783 3.3999% 1800 0.040867
24.469373 2.8419% 1799 0.039738 25.164761 2.7485% 1798 0.038675 25.856403 2.8261%
1797 0.037612 26.587139 3.7832% 1796 0.036241 27.592986 2.1272% 1795 0.035486
28.179944 3.0879% 1794 0.034423 29.050123 3.1625% 1793 0.033368 29.968837 3.2904%
1792 0.032305 30.954936 3.4024% 1791 0.031242 32.008136 3.2296% 1790 0.030265
33.041859 41.3145% 1780 0.021417 46.692922 29.4353% 1770 0.016546 60.437130
83.4728% 1750 0.009018 110.885719 29.2845% 1740 0.006976 143.357995 94.2514% 1720
0.003591 278.474903 85.8111% 1700 0.001933 517.437226 19.2490% 1690 0.001621
617.038973 88.0250% 1670 0.000862 1160.187668

BASE YEAR: 1937

YEAR BYEAR/AYEAR AYEAR/BYEAR GROWTH%

2009 2.339844 0.427379 8.2857% 2001 2.160807 0.462790 1.0000% 2000 2.139412
0.467418 1.0000% 1999 2.118230 0.472092 1.0000% 1998 2.097257 0.476813 1.0000% 1997
2.076492 0.481581 1.0000% 1996 2.055933 0.486397 1.0000% 1995 2.035577 0.491261
0.9992% 1994 2.015439 0.496170 1.0008% 1993 1.995468 0.501135 1.0000% 1992 1.975711
0.506147 0.9295% 1991 1.957516 0.510852 1.2505% 1990 1.933339 0.517240 0.7224% 1989
1.919472 0.520977 1.1077% 1988 1.898444 0.526747 0.8834% 1987 1.881820 0.531400
0.5594% 1986 1.871353 0.534373 1.3056% 1985 1.847235 0.541350 0.7673% 1984 1.833169
0.545503 0.8149% 1983 1.818350 0.549949 0.9737% 1982 1.800815 0.555304 0.9508% 1981
1.783854 0.560584 0.9031% 1980 1.767889 0.565646 2.2701% 1979 1.728647 0.578487
1.0042% 1978 1.711461 0.584296 0.9896% 1977 1.694690 0.590078 0.9103% 1976 1.679402
0.595450 0.8394% 1975 1.665422 0.600448 0.9042% 1974 1.650499 0.605877 1.1568% 1973
1.631624 0.612886 0.9427% 1972 1.616387 0.618664 0.7426% 1971 1.604471 0.623258
1.4697% 1970 1.581231 0.632419 0.6968% 1969 1.570289 0.636825 0.8565% 1968 1.556953
0.642280 1.5090% 1967 1.533807 0.651972 0.9949% 1966 1.518698 0.658459 1.0575% 1965
1.502806 0.665422 1.1300% 1964 1.486014 0.672941 1.5537% 1963 1.463280 0.683396
1.4658% 1962 1.442141 0.693414 1.5364% 1961 1.420318 0.704068 2.1586% 1960 1.390307
0.719266 -1.6655% 1959 1.413854 0.707287 4.3080% 1958 1.355461 0.737756 2.1130%
1957 1.327413 0.753345 1.9895% 1956 1.301520 0.768333 2.1231% 1955 1.274461 0.784645
1.4496% 1954 1.256251 0.796019 2.1573% 1953 1.229722 0.813192 1.2298% 1952 1.214784
0.823192 1.6814% 1951 1.194696 0.837033 1.6233% 1950 1.175613 0.850620 1.4265% 1949
1.159078 0.862755 1.7790% 1948 1.138818 0.878103 1.8242% 1947 1.118416 0.894121 -
2.6320% 1946 1.148649 0.870588 3.1768% 1945 1.113283 0.898245 6.4754% 1944 1.045577
0.956410 -0.3437% 1943 1.049183 0.953123 0.6562% 1942 1.042343 0.959377 0.6633%
1941 1.035474 0.965741 -5.6614% 1940 1.097615 0.911066 8.0381% 1939 1.015952
0.984299 0.8126% 1938 1.007762 0.992297 0.7762% 1937 1.000000 1.000000 0.6029% 1936
0.994007 1.006029 0.5244% 1935 0.988822 1.011304 -3.0364% 1934 1.019787 0.980597
4.6271% 1933 0.974687 1.025971 1.3921% 1932 0.961304 1.040254 -0.2051% 1931
0.963280 1.038120 0.8886% 1930 0.954795 1.047345 1.0126% 1929 0.945224 1.057950
1.1526% 1928 0.934454 1.070144 1.2160% 1927 0.923227 1.083157 1.4086% 1926 0.910403
1.098414 1.7667% 1925 0.894599 1.117820 1.4465% 1924 0.881843 1.133989 1.7700% 1923
0.866506 1.154060 1.6165% 1922 0.852722 1.172716 1.3736% 1921 0.841167 1.188825
2.3393% 1920 0.821939 1.216635 1.3140% 1919 0.811279 1.232622 0.7676% 1918 0.805099
1.242084 0.3870% 1917 0.801995 1.246891 1.3274% 1916 0.791488 1.263442 1.4083% 1915
0.780497 1.281235 1.4458% 1914 0.769373 1.299759 1.9424% 1913 0.754714 1.325006
1.9857% 1912 0.740019 1.351316 1.5634% 1911 0.728628 1.372442 1.8169% 1910 0.715626
1.397379 1.8781% 1909 0.702434 1.423622 2.0082% 1908 0.688605 1.452212 1.9603% 1907
0.675366 1.480679 1.8264% 1906 0.663252 1.507721 1.9357% 1905 0.650658 1.536906
2.0148% 1904 0.637807 1.567872 2.1335% 1903 0.624484 1.601323 1.8151% 1902 0.613350
1.630390 1.8943% 1901 0.601947 1.661275 3.0255% 1900 0.584270 1.711537 0.6278% 1899
0.580625 1.722282 1.7757% 1898 0.570495 1.752864 1.8078% 1897 0.560365 1.784552

1.8396% 1896 0.550243 1.817380 1.8755% 1895 0.540113 1.851466 1.9114% 1894 0.529983
1.886855 1.9486% 1893 0.519853 1.923623 1.9858% 1892 0.509730 1.961822 2.0276% 1891
0.499600 2.001600 2.6465% 1890 0.486719 2.054573 1.5328% 1889 0.479371 2.086066
2.0811% 1888 0.469598 2.129480 2.1599% 1887 0.459670 2.175473 2.2075% 1886 0.449742
2.223498 2.2592% 1885 0.439806 2.273730 2.3095% 1884 0.429878 2.326243 2.3641% 1883
0.419950 2.381238 2.4214% 1882 0.410021 2.438897 2.4815% 1881 0.400093 2.499418
3.7644% 1880 0.385578 2.593506 0.9432% 1879 0.381976 2.617969 2.1464% 1878 0.373949
2.674160 2.1913% 1877 0.365931 2.732759 2.2426% 1876 0.357904 2.794044 2.2941% 1875
0.349878 2.858141 2.3456% 1874 0.341859 2.925182 2.4043% 1873 0.333833 2.995512
2.4635% 1872 0.325806 3.069308 2.5258% 1871 0.317780 3.146832 5.9947% 1870 0.299807
3.335474 -1.0968% 1869 0.303132 3.298891 2.1930% 1868 0.296627 3.371235 2.2394%
1867 0.290130 3.446731 2.2935% 1866 0.283625 3.525781 2.3445% 1865 0.277128 3.608442
2.4037% 1864 0.270623 3.695178 2.4599% 1863 0.264126 3.786075 2.5250% 1862 0.257621
3.881674 2.5872% 1861 0.251124 3.982103 2.9504% 1860 0.243927 4.099591 2.4012% 1859
0.238207 4.198032 2.7627% 1858 0.231803 4.314011 2.8412% 1857 0.225399 4.436581
2.9243% 1856 0.218995 4.566319 3.0161% 1855 0.212583 4.704046 3.1061% 1854 0.206179
4.850156 3.2056% 1853 0.199775 5.005634 3.3118% 1852 0.193371 5.171410 3.4252% 1851
0.186967 5.348543 4.0106% 1850 0.179757 5.563052 2.3254% 1849 0.175672 5.692413
2.7841% 1848 0.170914 5.850895 2.8590% 1847 0.166163 6.018172 2.9432% 1846 0.161413
6.195297 3.0324% 1845 0.156662 6.383163 3.1325% 1844 0.151904 6.583116 3.2284% 1843
0.147153 6.795643 3.3361% 1842 0.142402 7.022349 3.4512% 1841 0.137652 7.264704
3.8105% 1840 0.132599 7.541525 2.3861% 1839 0.129509 7.721470 2.5824% 1838 0.126249
7.920868 2.6573% 1837 0.122981 8.131351 2.7232% 1836 0.119721 8.352785 2.7994% 1835
0.116460 8.586616 2.8871% 1834 0.113192 8.834522 2.9657% 1833 0.109932 9.096526
3.0563% 1832 0.106672 9.374545 3.1604% 1831 0.103404 9.670821 3.4660% 1830 0.099940
10.006008 2.4653% 1829 0.097535 10.252686 2.6804% 1828 0.094989 10.527499 10.3427%
1827 0.086086 11.616321 -4.2314% 1826 0.089889 11.124784 2.9150% 1825 0.087343
11.449076 3.0026% 1824 0.084797 11.792841 3.0955% 1823 0.082251 12.157890 3.1944%
1822 0.079705 12.546260 3.3102% 1821 0.077151 12.961566 3.2277% 1820 0.074739
13.379931 2.6573% 1819 0.072804 13.735473 2.6261% 1818 0.070941 14.096181 2.6969%
1817 0.069078 14.476346 2.7717% 1816 0.067215 14.877584 2.8507% 1815 0.065352
15.301699 2.9343% 1814 0.063489 15.750703 3.0231% 1813 0.061626 16.226855 3.1039%
1812 0.059771 16.730519 3.2172% 1811 0.057908 17.268767 3.0969% 1810 0.056169
17.803566 2.9144% 1809 0.054578 18.322429 2.8225% 1808 0.053080 18.839573 2.9199%
1807 0.051574 19.389675 2.9918% 1806 0.050076 19.969772 3.0841% 1805 0.048578
20.585650 3.1822% 1804 0.047079 21.240725 3.2868% 1803 0.045581 21.938862 3.3985%
1802 0.044083 22.684451 3.5180% 1801 0.042585 23.482501 3.3999% 1800 0.041185
24.280894 2.8419% 1799 0.040047 24.970925 2.7485% 1798 0.038975 25.657240 2.8261%
1797 0.037904 26.382347 3.7832% 1796 0.036522 27.380446 2.1272% 1795 0.035762
27.962883 3.0879% 1794 0.034690 28.826359 3.1625% 1793 0.033627 29.737796 3.2904%
1792 0.032556 30.716500 3.4024% 1791 0.031485 31.761588 3.2296% 1790 0.030500
32.787348 41.3145% 1780 0.021583 46.333261 29.4353% 1770 0.016675 59.971603
83.4728% 1750 0.009088 110.031602 29.2845% 1740 0.007030 142.253754 94.2514% 1720
0.003619 276.329901 85.8111% 1700 0.001948 513.451574 19.2490% 1690 0.001633
612.286122 88.0250% 1670 0.000869 1151.251117

BASE YEAR: 1936
YEAR BYEAR/AYEAR AYEAR/BYEAR GROWTH%

2009 2.353950 0.424818 8.2857% 2001 2.173833 0.460017 1.0000% 2000 2.152310
0.464617 1.0000% 1999 2.131000 0.469263 1.0000% 1998 2.109901 0.473956 1.0000% 1997
2.089011 0.478695 1.0000% 1996 2.068328 0.483482 1.0000% 1995 2.047849 0.488317
0.9992% 1994 2.027589 0.493197 1.0008% 1993 2.007499 0.498132 1.0000% 1992 1.987622
0.503114 0.9295% 1991 1.969317 0.507790 1.2505% 1990 1.944995 0.514140 0.7224% 1989
1.931044 0.517855 1.1077% 1988 1.909889 0.523591 0.8834% 1987 1.893165 0.528216
0.5594% 1986 1.882635 0.531171 1.3056% 1985 1.858371 0.538106 0.7673% 1984 1.844221
0.542234 0.8149% 1983 1.829313 0.546653 0.9737% 1982 1.811672 0.551976 0.9508% 1981
1.794608 0.557225 0.9031% 1980 1.778547 0.562257 2.2701% 1979 1.739069 0.575020

106

1.0042% 1978 1.721779 0.580795 0.9896% 1977 1.704907 0.586542 0.9103% 1976 1.689527
0.591882 0.8394% 1975 1.675463 0.596850 0.9042% 1974 1.660449 0.602247 1.1568% 1973
1.641461 0.609213 0.9427% 1972 1.626131 0.614956 0.7426% 1971 1.614144 0.619523
1.4697% 1970 1.590764 0.628629 0.6968% 1969 1.579756 0.633009 0.8565% 1968 1.566340
0.638431 1.5090% 1967 1.543054 0.648065 0.9949% 1966 1.527854 0.654513 1.0575% 1965
1.511866 0.661434 1.1300% 1964 1.494973 0.668908 1.5537% 1963 1.472101 0.679301
1.4658% 1962 1.450835 0.689258 1.5364% 1961 1.428881 0.699848 2.1586% 1960 1.398688
0.714956 -1.6655% 1959 1.422378 0.703048 4.3080% 1958 1.363633 0.733335 2.1130%
1957 1.335416 0.748830 1.9895% 1956 1.309366 0.763728 2.1231% 1955 1.282145 0.779943
1.4496% 1954 1.263824 0.791249 2.1573% 1953 1.237136 0.808318 1.2298% 1952 1.222107
0.818259 1.6814% 1951 1.201899 0.832017 1.6233% 1950 1.182700 0.845523 1.4265% 1949
1.166066 0.857584 1.7790% 1948 1.145684 0.872841 1.8242% 1947 1.125159 0.888763 -
2.6320% 1946 1.155574 0.865371 3.1768% 1945 1.119994 0.892862 6.4754% 1944 1.051881
0.950678 -0.3437% 1943 1.055508 0.947411 0.6562% 1942 1.048627 0.953628 0.6633%
1941 1.041717 0.959954 -5.6614% 1940 1.104232 0.905606 8.0381% 1939 1.022077
0.978400 0.8126% 1938 1.013838 0.986351 0.7762% 1937 1.006029 0.994007 0.6029% 1936
1.000000 1.000000 0.5244% 1935 0.994783 1.005244 -3.0364% 1934 1.025935 0.974721
4.6271% 1933 0.980563 1.019823 1.3921% 1932 0.967100 1.034020 -0.2051% 1931
0.969087 1.031899 0.8886% 1930 0.960552 1.041069 1.0126% 1929 0.950923 1.051610
1.1526% 1928 0.940087 1.063731 1.2160% 1927 0.928793 1.076666 1.4086% 1926 0.915892
1.091832 1.7667% 1925 0.899992 1.111121 1.4465% 1924 0.887159 1.127193 1.7700% 1923
0.871730 1.147144 1.6165% 1922 0.857862 1.165688 1.3736% 1921 0.846238 1.181701
2.3393% 1920 0.826894 1.209344 1.3140% 1919 0.816170 1.225235 0.7676% 1918 0.809952
1.234641 0.3870% 1917 0.806830 1.239418 1.3274% 1916 0.796260 1.255871 1.4083% 1915
0.785202 1.273557 1.4458% 1914 0.774012 1.291970 1.9424% 1913 0.759264 1.317065
1.9857% 1912 0.744481 1.343218 1.5634% 1911 0.733021 1.364218 1.8169% 1910 0.719940
1.389005 1.8781% 1909 0.706668 1.415091 2.0082% 1908 0.692756 1.443509 1.9603% 1907
0.679437 1.471806 1.8264% 1906 0.667251 1.498686 1.9357% 1905 0.654581 1.527696
2.0148% 1904 0.641652 1.558476 2.1335% 1903 0.628248 1.591727 1.8151% 1902 0.617048
1.620619 1.8943% 1901 0.605576 1.651319 3.0255% 1900 0.587793 1.701280 0.6278% 1899
0.584125 1.711961 1.7757% 1898 0.573934 1.742360 1.8078% 1897 0.563743 1.773858
1.8396% 1896 0.553560 1.806489 1.8755% 1895 0.543369 1.840371 1.9114% 1894 0.533178
1.875547 1.9486% 1893 0.522987 1.912095 1.9858% 1892 0.512803 1.950065 2.0276% 1891
0.502612 1.989606 2.6465% 1890 0.489653 2.042261 1.5328% 1889 0.482261 2.073565
2.0811% 1888 0.472429 2.116718 2.1599% 1887 0.462441 2.162436 2.2075% 1886 0.452453
2.210173 2.2592% 1885 0.442457 2.260104 2.3095% 1884 0.432469 2.312302 2.3641% 1883
0.422481 2.366969 2.4214% 1882 0.412493 2.424282 2.4815% 1881 0.402505 2.484440
3.7644% 1880 0.387903 2.577964 0.9432% 1879 0.384278 2.602280 2.1464% 1878 0.376204
2.658135 2.1913% 1877 0.368137 2.716383 2.2426% 1876 0.360062 2.777301 2.2941% 1875
0.351987 2.841013 2.3456% 1874 0.343920 2.907652 2.4043% 1873 0.335845 2.977561
2.4635% 1872 0.327771 3.050915 2.5258% 1871 0.319696 3.127974 5.9947% 1870 0.301615
3.315486 -1.0968% 1869 0.304960 3.279122 2.1930% 1868 0.298415 3.351032 2.2394%
1867 0.291879 3.426076 2.2935% 1866 0.285335 3.504653 2.3445% 1865 0.278799 3.586818
2.4037% 1864 0.272254 3.673034 2.4599% 1863 0.265718 3.763387 2.5250% 1862 0.259174
3.858413 2.5872% 1861 0.252638 3.958239 2.9504% 1860 0.245397 4.075023 2.4012% 1859
0.239643 4.172875 2.7627% 1858 0.233200 4.288159 2.8412% 1857 0.226758 4.409994
2.9243% 1856 0.220315 4.538955 3.0161% 1855 0.213865 4.675856 3.1061% 1854 0.207422
4.821091 3.2056% 1853 0.200979 4.975637 3.3118% 1852 0.194537 5.140420 3.4252% 1851
0.188094 5.316491 4.0106% 1850 0.180841 5.529714 2.3254% 1849 0.176732 5.658301
2.7841% 1848 0.171944 5.815833 2.8590% 1847 0.167165 5.982108 2.9432% 1846 0.162386
6.158171 3.0324% 1845 0.157607 6.344911 3.1325% 1844 0.152820 6.543666 3.2284% 1843
0.148040 6.754919 3.3361% 1842 0.143261 6.980267 3.4512% 1841 0.138482 7.221170
3.8105% 1840 0.133399 7.496331 2.3861% 1839 0.130290 7.675198 2.5824% 1838 0.127010
7.873401 2.6573% 1837 0.123722 8.082623 2.7232% 1836 0.120442 8.302730 2.7994% 1835
0.117162 8.535160 2.8871% 1834 0.113875 8.781580 2.9657% 1833 0.110595 9.042014
3.0563% 1832 0.107315 9.318367 3.1604% 1831 0.104027 9.612867 3.4660% 1830 0.100542

107

9.946046 2.4653% 1829 0.098123 10.191246 2.6804% 1828 0.095562 10.464411 10.3427%
1827 0.086605 11.546709 -4.2314% 1826 0.090431 11.058117 2.9150% 1825 0.087870
11.380466 3.0026% 1824 0.085308 11.722171 3.0955% 1823 0.082747 12.085032 3.1944%
1822 0.080186 12.471075 3.3102% 1821 0.077616 12.883892 3.2277% 1820 0.075189
13.299750 2.6573% 1819 0.073243 13.653161 2.6261% 1818 0.071369 14.011708 2.6969%
1817 0.069495 14.389594 2.7717% 1816 0.067620 14.788428 2.8507% 1815 0.065746
15.210001 2.9343% 1814 0.063872 15.656315 3.0231% 1813 0.061998 16.129613 3.1039%
1812 0.060131 16.630260 3.2172% 1811 0.058257 17.165282 3.0969% 1810 0.056507
17.696876 2.9144% 1809 0.054907 18.212630 2.8225% 1808 0.053400 18.726674 2.9199%
1807 0.051885 19.273480 2.9918% 1806 0.050378 19.850101 3.0841% 1805 0.048870
20.462288 3.1822% 1804 0.047363 21.113438 3.2868% 1803 0.045856 21.807391 3.3985%
1802 0.044349 22.548512 3.5180% 1801 0.042842 23.341779 3.3999% 1800 0.041433
24.135387 2.8419% 1799 0.040288 24.821283 2.7485% 1798 0.039210 25.503485 2.8261%
1797 0.038133 26.224247 3.7832% 1796 0.036743 27.216366 2.1272% 1795 0.035977
27.795311 3.0879% 1794 0.034900 28.653614 3.1625% 1793 0.033830 29.559788 3.2904%
1792 0.032752 30.532427 3.4024% 1791 0.031674 31.571252 3.2296% 1790 0.030683
32.590866 41.3145% 1780 0.021713 46.055604 29.4353% 1770 0.016775 59.612215
83.4728% 1750 0.009143 109.372224 29.2845% 1740 0.007072 141.401281 94.2514% 1720
0.003641 274.673960 85.8111% 1700 0.001959 510.374651 19.2490% 1690 0.001643
608.616920 88.0250% 1670 0.000874 1144.352100
BASE YEAR: 1935
YEAR BYEAR/AYEAR AYEAR/BYEAR GROWTH%
2009 2.366294 0.422602 8.2857% 2001 2.185233 0.457617 1.0000% 2000 2.163597
0.462193 1.0000% 1999 2.142175 0.466815 1.0000% 1998 2.120965 0.471483 1.0000% 1997
2.099966 0.476198 1.0000% 1996 2.079174 0.480960 1.0000% 1995 2.058588 0.485770
0.9992% 1994 2.038222 0.490624 1.0008% 1993 2.018026 0.495534 1.0000% 1992 1.998045
0.500489 0.9295% 1991 1.979644 0.505141 1.2505% 1990 1.955194 0.511458 0.7224% 1989
1.941170 0.515153 1.1077% 1988 1.919904 0.520859 0.8834% 1987 1.903093 0.525460
0.5594% 1986 1.892507 0.528400 1.3056% 1985 1.868116 0.535299 0.7673% 1984 1.853892
0.539406 0.8149% 1983 1.838906 0.543802 0.9737% 1982 1.821172 0.549097 0.9508% 1981
1.804019 0.554318 0.9031% 1980 1.787874 0.559324 2.2701% 1979 1.748189 0.572021
1.0042% 1978 1.730808 0.577765 0.9896% 1977 1.713848 0.583482 0.9103% 1976 1.698387
0.588794 0.8394% 1975 1.684249 0.593737 0.9042% 1974 1.669156 0.599105 1.1568% 1973
1.650069 0.606035 0.9427% 1972 1.634659 0.611748 0.7426% 1971 1.622609 0.616292
1.4697% 1970 1.599106 0.625349 0.6968% 1969 1.588040 0.629707 0.8565% 1968 1.574554
0.635101 1.5090% 1967 1.551146 0.644685 0.9949% 1966 1.535866 0.651099 1.0575% 1965
1.519794 0.657984 1.1300% 1964 1.502812 0.665419 1.5537% 1963 1.479821 0.675757
1.4658% 1962 1.458443 0.685663 1.5364% 1961 1.436374 0.696198 2.1586% 1960 1.406023
0.711226 -1.6655% 1959 1.429837 0.699381 4.3080% 1958 1.370783 0.729510 2.1130%
1957 1.342419 0.744924 1.9895% 1956 1.316232 0.759744 2.1231% 1955 1.288868 0.775874
1.4496% 1954 1.270452 0.787122 2.1573% 1953 1.243624 0.804102 1.2298% 1952 1.228516
0.813990 1.6814% 1951 1.208202 0.827676 1.6233% 1950 1.188902 0.841112 1.4265% 1949
1.172181 0.853111 1.7790% 1948 1.151692 0.868288 1.8242% 1947 1.131059 0.884127 -
2.6320% 1946 1.161634 0.860856 3.1768% 1945 1.125867 0.888204 6.4754% 1944 1.057397
0.945719 -0.3437% 1943 1.061043 0.942469 0.6562% 1942 1.054126 0.948653 0.6633%
1941 1.047180 0.954946 -5.6614% 1940 1.110023 0.900882 8.0381% 1939 1.027437
0.973296 0.8126% 1938 1.019155 0.981205 0.7762% 1937 1.011304 0.988822 0.6029% 1936
1.005244 0.994783 0.5244% 1935 1.000000 1.000000 -3.0364% 1934 1.031315 0.969636
4.6271% 1933 0.985705 1.014503 1.3921% 1932 0.972171 1.028626 -0.2051% 1931
0.974169 1.026516 0.8886% 1930 0.965589 1.035638 1.0126% 1929 0.955909 1.046124
1.1526% 1928 0.945017 1.058182 1.2160% 1927 0.933664 1.071049 1.4086% 1926 0.920695
1.086136 1.7667% 1925 0.904712 1.105325 1.4465% 1924 0.891811 1.121313 1.7700% 1923
0.876301 1.141160 1.6165% 1922 0.862361 1.159607 1.3736% 1921 0.850676 1.175536
2.3393% 1920 0.831231 1.203036 1.3140% 1919 0.820450 1.218844 0.7676% 1918 0.814200
1.228200 0.3870% 1917 0.811061 1.232953 1.3274% 1916 0.800436 1.249320 1.4083% 1915
0.789320 1.266914 1.4458% 1914 0.778070 1.285231 1.9424% 1913 0.763245 1.310195

108

1.9857% 1912 0.748385 1.336211 1.5634% 1911 0.736865 1.357101 1.8169% 1910 0.723715 1.381759 1.8781% 1909 0.710374 1.407709 2.0082% 1908 0.696389 1.435979 1.9603% 1907 0.683000 1.464128 1.8264% 1906 0.670750 1.490868 1.9357% 1905 0.658013 1.519727 2.0148% 1904 0.645017 1.550347 2.1335% 1903 0.631543 1.583424 1.8151% 1902 0.620284 1.612165 1.8943% 1901 0.608752 1.642705 3.0255% 1900 0.590875 1.692405 0.6278% 1899 0.587188 1.703031 1.7757% 1898 0.576944 1.733271 1.8078% 1897 0.566699 1.764604 1.8396% 1896 0.556463 1.797066 1.8755% 1895 0.546218 1.830770 1.9114% 1894 0.535974 1.865763 1.9486% 1893 0.525729 1.902120 1.9858% 1892 0.515492 1.939893 2.0276% 1891 0.505248 1.979227 2.6465% 1890 0.492221 2.031607 1.5328% 1889 0.484790 2.062748 2.0811% 1888 0.474907 2.105676 2.1599% 1887 0.464866 2.151156 2.2075% 1886 0.454826 2.198643 2.2592% 1885 0.444778 2.248314 2.3095% 1884 0.434737 2.300240 2.3641% 1883 0.424697 2.354621 2.4214% 1882 0.414656 2.411636 2.4815% 1881 0.404616 2.471480 3.7644% 1880 0.389937 2.564516 0.9432% 1879 0.386294 2.588705 2.1464% 1878 0.378176 2.644269 2.1913% 1877 0.370067 2.702213 2.2426% 1876 0.361950 2.762813 2.2941% 1875 0.353833 2.826193 2.3456% 1874 0.345724 2.892484 2.4043% 1873 0.337606 2.962029 2.4635% 1872 0.329489 3.035000 2.5258% 1871 0.321372 3.111657 5.9947% 1870 0.303197 3.298190 -1.0968% 1869 0.306559 3.262016 2.1930% 1868 0.299980 3.333551 2.2394% 1867 0.293410 3.408203 2.2935% 1866 0.286831 3.486370 2.3445% 1865 0.280261 3.568107 2.4037% 1864 0.273682 3.653874 2.4599% 1863 0.267112 3.743755 2.5250% 1862 0.260533 3.838285 2.5872% 1861 0.253962 3.937591 2.9504% 1860 0.246684 4.053766 2.4012% 1859 0.240900 4.151106 2.7627% 1858 0.234423 4.265789 2.8412% 1857 0.227947 4.386989 2.9243% 1856 0.221470 4.515277 3.0161% 1855 0.214986 4.651464 3.1061% 1854 0.208510 4.795941 3.2056% 1853 0.202033 4.949681 3.3118% 1852 0.195557 5.113604 3.4252% 1851 0.189080 5.288757 4.0106% 1850 0.181789 5.500868 2.3254% 1849 0.177658 5.628784 2.7841% 1848 0.172846 5.785494 2.8590% 1847 0.168042 5.950902 2.9432% 1846 0.163237 6.126046 3.0324% 1845 0.158433 6.311813 3.1325% 1844 0.153621 6.509530 3.2284% 1843 0.148817 6.719681 3.3361% 1842 0.144012 6.943854 3.4512% 1841 0.139208 7.183500 3.8105% 1840 0.134098 7.457226 2.3861% 1839 0.130973 7.635159 2.5824% 1838 0.127676 7.832329 2.6573% 1837 0.124371 8.040460 2.7232% 1836 0.121074 8.259418 2.7994% 1835 0.117777 8.490635 2.8871% 1834 0.114472 8.735770 2.9657% 1833 0.111175 8.994845 3.0563% 1832 0.107878 9.269757 3.1604% 1831 0.104573 9.562721 3.4660% 1830 0.101070 9.894161 2.4653% 1829 0.098638 10.138082 2.6804% 1828 0.096063 10.409823 10.3427% 1827 0.087059 11.486474 -4.2314% 1826 0.090906 11.000432 2.9150% 1825 0.088331 11.321098 3.0026% 1824 0.085756 11.661022 3.0955% 1823 0.083181 12.021989 3.1944% 1822 0.080606 12.406019 3.3102% 1821 0.078023 12.816682 3.2277% 1820 0.075584 13.230371 2.6573% 1819 0.073627 13.581938 2.6261% 1818 0.071743 13.938615 2.6969% 1817 0.069859 14.314530 2.7717% 1816 0.067975 14.711283 2.8507% 1815 0.066091 15.130657 2.9343% 1814 0.064207 15.574642 3.0231% 1813 0.062323 16.045472 3.1039% 1812 0.060447 16.543506 3.2172% 1811 0.058563 17.075737 3.0969% 1810 0.056803 17.604558 2.9144% 1809 0.055195 18.117622 2.8225% 1808 0.053680 18.628985 2.9199% 1807 0.052157 19.172938 2.9918% 1806 0.050642 19.746551 3.0841% 1805 0.049127 20.355545 3.1822% 1804 0.047612 21.003298 3.2868% 1803 0.046096 21.693631 3.3985% 1802 0.044581 22.430886 3.5180% 1801 0.043066 23.220015 3.3999% 1800 0.041650 24.009483 2.8419% 1799 0.040499 24.691801 2.7485% 1798 0.039416 25.370444 2.8261% 1797 0.038333 26.087446 3.7832% 1796 0.036935 27.074389 2.1272% 1795 0.036166 27.650315 3.0879% 1794 0.035083 28.504140 3.1625% 1793 0.034007 29.405586 3.2904% 1792 0.032924 30.373152 3.4024% 1791 0.031840 31.406558 3.2296% 1790 0.030844 32.420853 41.3145% 1780 0.021827 45.815350 29.4353% 1770 0.016863 59.301243 83.4728% 1750 0.009191 108.801674 29.2845% 1740 0.007109 140.663648 94.2514% 1720 0.003660 273.241098 85.8111% 1700 0.001970 507.712236 19.2490% 1690 0.001652 605.442015 88.0250% 1670 0.000878 1138.382484

BASE YEAR: 1934

YEAR BYEAR/AYEAR AYEAR/BYEAR GROWTH%

2009 2.294444 0.435835 8.2857% 2001 2.118881 0.471947 1.0000% 2000 2.097902 0.476667 1.0000% 1999 2.077131 0.481433 1.0000% 1998 2.056565 0.486248 1.0000% 1997 2.036203 0.491110 1.0000% 1996 2.016043 0.496021 1.0000% 1995 1.996082 0.500981

0.9992% 1994 1.976334 0.505987 1.0008% 1993 1.956751 0.511051 1.0000% 1992 1.937377 0.516162 0.9295% 1991 1.919535 0.520959 1.2505% 1990 1.895827 0.527474 0.7224% 1989 1.882229 0.531285 1.1077% 1988 1.861609 0.537170 0.8834% 1987 1.845308 0.541915 0.5594% 1986 1.835043 0.544946 1.3056% 1985 1.811393 0.552061 0.7673% 1984 1.797601 0.556297 0.8149% 1983 1.783070 0.560831 0.9737% 1982 1.765875 0.566292 0.9508% 1981 1.749243 0.571676 0.9031% 1980 1.733587 0.576839 2.2701% 1979 1.695107 0.589933 1.0042% 1978 1.678254 0.595857 0.9896% 1977 1.661809 0.601754 0.9103% 1976 1.646817 0.607232 0.8394% 1975 1.633109 0.612329 0.9042% 1974 1.618475 0.617866 1.1568% 1973 1.599967 0.625013 0.9427% 1972 1.585024 0.630905 0.7426% 1971 1.573340 0.635590 1.4697% 1970 1.550551 0.644932 0.6968% 1969 1.539821 0.649426 0.8565% 1968 1.526744 0.654989 1.5090% 1967 1.504048 0.664873 0.9949% 1966 1.489231 0.671487 1.0575% 1965 1.473648 0.678588 1.1300% 1964 1.457181 0.686256 1.5537% 1963 1.434888 0.696918 1.4658% 1962 1.414159 0.707134 1.5364% 1961 1.392760 0.717999 2.1586% 1960 1.363331 0.733498 -1.6655% 1959 1.386422 0.721281 4.3080% 1958 1.329161 0.752354 2.1130% 1957 1.301658 0.768251 1.9895% 1956 1.276267 0.783535 2.1231% 1955 1.249734 0.800171 1.4496% 1954 1.231876 0.811770 2.1573% 1953 1.205863 0.829282 1.2298% 1952 1.191214 0.839480 1.6814% 1951 1.171516 0.853595 1.6233% 1950 1.152803 0.867451 1.4265% 1949 1.136589 0.879825 1.7790% 1948 1.116722 0.895478 1.8242% 1947 1.096716 0.911813 -2.6320% 1946 1.126363 0.887814 3.1768% 1945 1.091682 0.916018 6.4754% 1944 1.025290 0.975334 -0.3437% 1943 1.028826 0.971982 0.6562% 1942 1.022119 0.978360 0.6633% 1941 1.015384 0.984850 -5.6614% 1940 1.076319 0.929093 8.0381% 1939 0.996240 1.003774 0.8126% 1938 0.988209 1.011931 0.7762% 1937 0.980597 1.019787 0.6029% 1936 0.974721 1.025935 0.5244% 1935 0.969636 1.031315 -3.0364% 1934 1.000000 1.000000 4.6271% 1933 0.955775 1.046271 1.3921% 1932 0.942652 1.060837 -0.2051% 1931 0.944589 1.058661 0.8886% 1930 0.936270 1.068068 1.0126% 1929 0.926884 1.078883 1.1526% 1928 0.916323 1.091318 1.2160% 1927 0.905314 1.104589 1.4086% 1926 0.892739 1.120148 1.7667% 1925 0.877241 1.139937 1.4465% 1924 0.864733 1.156427 1.7700% 1923 0.849693 1.176895 1.6165% 1922 0.836176 1.195920 1.3736% 1921 0.824846 1.212347 2.3393% 1920 0.805991 1.240708 1.3140% 1919 0.795538 1.257011 0.7676% 1918 0.789478 1.266660 0.3870% 1917 0.786434 1.271562 1.3274% 1916 0.776132 1.288441 1.4083% 1915 0.765353 1.306586 1.4458% 1914 0.754445 1.325477 1.9424% 1913 0.740070 1.351223 1.9857% 1912 0.725661 1.378054 1.5634% 1911 0.714491 1.399598 1.8169% 1910 0.701741 1.425028 1.8781% 1909 0.688804 1.451791 2.0082% 1908 0.675244 1.480946 1.9603% 1907 0.662262 1.509977 1.8264% 1906 0.650384 1.537554 1.9357% 1905 0.638033 1.567316 2.0148% 1904 0.625432 1.598895 2.1335% 1903 0.612367 1.633008 1.8151% 1902 0.601450 1.662649 1.8943% 1901 0.590268 1.694146 3.0255% 1900 0.572934 1.745402 0.6278% 1899 0.569359 1.756360 1.7757% 1898 0.559426 1.787547 1.8078% 1897 0.549492 1.819862 1.8396% 1896 0.539566 1.853340 1.8755% 1895 0.529633 1.888100 1.9114% 1894 0.519699 1.924189 1.9486% 1893 0.509766 1.961684 1.9858% 1892 0.499840 2.000640 2.0276% 1891 0.489907 2.041205 2.6465% 1890 0.477276 2.095226 1.5328% 1889 0.470070 2.127342 2.0811% 1888 0.460487 2.171615 2.1599% 1887 0.450751 2.218518 2.2075% 1886 0.441016 2.267493 2.2592% 1885 0.431273 2.318719 2.3095% 1884 0.421537 2.372271 2.3641% 1883 0.411801 2.428355 2.4214% 1882 0.402066 2.487155 2.4815% 1881 0.392330 2.548873 3.7644% 1880 0.378097 2.644822 0.9432% 1879 0.374564 2.669769 2.1464% 1878 0.366694 2.727073 2.1913% 1877 0.358831 2.786831 2.2426% 1876 0.350960 2.849329 2.2941% 1875 0.343089 2.914694 2.3456% 1874 0.335226 2.983061 2.4043% 1873 0.327355 3.054783 2.4635% 1872 0.319485 3.130039 2.5258% 1871 0.311614 3.209097 5.9947% 1870 0.293990 3.401472 -1.0968% 1869 0.297251 3.364165 2.1930% 1868 0.290872 3.437940 2.2394% 1867 0.284501 3.514929 2.2935% 1866 0.278122 3.595544 2.3445% 1865 0.271751 3.679841 2.4037% 1864 0.265372 3.768293 2.4599% 1863 0.259001 3.860989 2.5250% 1862 0.252622 3.958479 2.5872% 1861 0.246251 4.060895 2.9504% 1860 0.239194 4.180707 2.4012% 1859 0.233585 4.281096 2.7627% 1858 0.227305 4.399370 2.8412% 1857 0.221025 4.524365 2.9243% 1856 0.214746 4.656671 3.0161% 1855 0.208458 4.797123 3.1061% 1854 0.202179 4.946124 3.2056% 1853 0.195899 5.104678 3.3118% 1852 0.189619 5.273734 3.4252% 1851 0.183339 5.454372 4.0106% 1850 0.176270 5.673125 2.3254% 1849 0.172264 5.805046 2.7841% 1848 0.167598 5.966664 2.8590% 1847 0.162939 6.137251 2.9432% 1846 0.158281

110

6.317880 3.0324% 1845 0.153622 6.509464 3.1325% 1844 0.148956 6.713373 3.2284% 1843 0.144298 6.930105 3.3361% 1842 0.139640 7.161297 3.4512% 1841 0.134981 7.408448 3.8105% 1840 0.130026 7.690746 2.3861% 1839 0.126996 7.874251 2.5824% 1838 0.123799 8.077595 2.6573% 1837 0.120595 8.292243 2.7232% 1836 0.117398 8.518057 2.7994% 1835 0.114201 8.756515 2.8871% 1834 0.110996 9.009327 2.9657% 1833 0.107799 9.276515 3.0563% 1832 0.104602 9.560035 3.1604% 1831 0.101398 9.862173 3.4660% 1830 0.098001 10.203992 2.4653% 1829 0.095643 10.455551 2.6804% 1828 0.093146 10.735801 10.3427% 1827 0.084415 11.846168 -4.2314% 1826 0.088145 11.344905 2.9150% 1825 0.085649 11.675613 3.0026% 1824 0.083152 12.026181 3.0955% 1823 0.080655 12.398452 3.1944% 1822 0.078159 12.794507 3.3102% 1821 0.075654 13.218030 3.2277% 1820 0.073289 13.644673 2.6573% 1819 0.071392 14.007250 2.6261% 1818 0.069565 14.375096 2.6969% 1817 0.067738 14.762782 2.7717% 1816 0.065911 15.171960 2.8507% 1815 0.064084 15.604466 2.9343% 1814 0.062257 16.062355 3.0231% 1813 0.060431 16.547928 3.1039% 1812 0.058611 17.061558 3.2172% 1811 0.056784 17.610456 3.0969% 1810 0.055079 18.155837 2.9144% 1809 0.053519 18.684967 2.8225% 1808 0.052050 19.212343 2.9199% 1807 0.050573 19.773329 2.9918% 1806 0.049104 20.364905 3.0841% 1805 0.047635 20.992969 3.1822% 1804 0.046166 21.661006 3.2868% 1803 0.044697 22.372956 3.3985% 1802 0.043228 23.133298 3.5180% 1801 0.041759 23.947138 3.3999% 1800 0.040386 24.761328 2.8419% 1799 0.039270 25.465013 2.7485% 1798 0.038219 26.164907 2.8261% 1797 0.037169 26.904362 3.7832% 1796 0.035814 27.922210 2.1272% 1795 0.035068 28.516171 3.0879% 1794 0.034017 29.396733 3.1625% 1793 0.032975 30.326408 3.2904% 1792 0.031924 31.324273 3.4024% 1791 0.030874 32.390039 3.2296% 1790 0.029908 33.436096 41.3145% 1780 0.021164 47.250036 29.4353% 1770 0.016351 61.158233 83.4728% 1750 0.008912 112.208746 29.2845% 1740 0.006893 145.068463 94.2514% 1720 0.003549 281.797512 85.8111% 1700 0.001910 523.611000 19.2490% 1690 0.001602 624.401141 88.0250% 1670 0.000852 1174.030384

BASE YEAR: 1933
YEAR BYEAR/AYEAR AYEAR/BYEAR GROWTH%

2009 2.400611 0.416561 8.2857% 2001 2.216924 0.451075 1.0000% 2000 2.194974 0.455586 1.0000% 1999 2.173242 0.460142 1.0000% 1998 2.151725 0.464743 1.0000% 1997 2.130421 0.469391 1.0000% 1996 2.109327 0.474085 1.0000% 1995 2.088443 0.478826 0.9992% 1994 2.067781 0.483610 1.0008% 1993 2.047292 0.488450 1.0000% 1992 2.027022 0.493335 0.9295% 1991 2.008354 0.497920 1.2505% 1990 1.983550 0.504147 0.7224% 1989 1.969322 0.507789 1.1077% 1988 1.947748 0.513414 0.8834% 1987 1.930693 0.517949 0.5594% 1986 1.919953 0.520846 1.3056% 1985 1.895209 0.527646 0.7673% 1984 1.880778 0.531695 0.8149% 1983 1.865575 0.536028 0.9737% 1982 1.847584 0.541247 0.9508% 1981 1.830182 0.546394 0.9031% 1980 1.813802 0.551328 2.2701% 1979 1.773542 0.563843 1.0042% 1978 1.755909 0.569505 0.9896% 1977 1.738703 0.575141 0.9103% 1976 1.723018 0.580377 0.8394% 1975 1.708674 0.585249 0.9042% 1974 1.693364 0.590541 1.1568% 1973 1.673999 0.597372 0.9427% 1972 1.658365 0.603003 0.7426% 1971 1.646141 0.607482 1.4697% 1970 1.622297 0.616410 0.6968% 1969 1.611071 0.620705 0.8565% 1968 1.597389 0.626022 1.5090% 1967 1.573642 0.635469 0.9949% 1966 1.558140 0.641791 1.0575% 1965 1.541835 0.648578 1.1300% 1964 1.524607 0.655907 1.5537% 1963 1.501282 0.666097 1.4658% 1962 1.479594 0.675861 1.5364% 1961 1.457205 0.686245 2.1586% 1960 1.426414 0.701059 -1.6655% 1959 1.450573 0.689383 4.3080% 1958 1.390663 0.719081 2.1130% 1957 1.361887 0.734275 1.9895% 1956 1.335321 0.748884 2.1231% 1955 1.307560 0.764783 1.4496% 1954 1.288877 0.775869 2.1573% 1953 1.261659 0.792607 1.2298% 1952 1.246333 0.802354 1.6814% 1951 1.225724 0.815845 1.6233% 1950 1.206145 0.829088 1.4265% 1949 1.189180 0.840915 1.7790% 1948 1.168394 0.855876 1.8242% 1947 1.147463 0.871488 -2.6320% 1946 1.178481 0.848550 3.1768% 1945 1.142195 0.875507 6.4754% 1944 1.072732 0.932200 -0.3437% 1943 1.076431 0.928996 0.6562% 1942 1.069413 0.935092 0.6633% 1941 1.062367 0.941295 -5.6614% 1940 1.126121 0.888004 8.0381% 1939 1.042337 0.959383 0.8126% 1938 1.033935 0.967179 0.7762% 1937 1.025971 0.974687 0.6029% 1936 1.019823 0.980563 0.5244% 1935 1.014503 0.985705 -3.0364% 1934 1.046271 0.955775 4.6271% 1933 1.000000 1.000000 1.3921% 1932 0.986270 1.013921 -0.2051% 1931 0.988297 1.011842 0.8886% 1930 0.979592 1.020833 1.0126% 1929 0.969772 1.031170

111

1.1526% 1928 0.958722 1.043055 1.2160% 1927 0.947204 1.055739 1.4086% 1926 0.934047
1.070609 1.7667% 1925 0.917832 1.089524 1.4465% 1924 0.904745 1.105284 1.7700% 1923
0.889010 1.124847 1.6165% 1922 0.874867 1.143030 1.3736% 1921 0.863013 1.158732
2.3393% 1920 0.843286 1.185838 1.3140% 1919 0.832348 1.201420 0.7676% 1918 0.826008
1.210643 0.3870% 1917 0.822823 1.215328 1.3274% 1916 0.812044 1.231460 1.4083% 1915
0.800767 1.248803 1.4458% 1914 0.789354 1.266858 1.9424% 1913 0.774314 1.291465
1.9857% 1912 0.759238 1.317110 1.5634% 1911 0.747551 1.337701 1.8169% 1910 0.734211
1.362006 1.8781% 1909 0.720676 1.387586 2.0082% 1908 0.706488 1.415452 1.9603% 1907
0.692906 1.443198 1.8264% 1906 0.680478 1.469556 1.9357% 1905 0.667556 1.498002
2.0148% 1904 0.654371 1.528184 2.1335% 1903 0.640702 1.560788 1.8151% 1902 0.629280
1.589119 1.8943% 1901 0.617580 1.619222 3.0255% 1900 0.599444 1.668212 0.6278% 1899
0.595704 1.678686 1.7757% 1898 0.585311 1.708493 1.8078% 1897 0.574918 1.739379
1.8396% 1896 0.564533 1.771376 1.8755% 1895 0.554140 1.804599 1.9114% 1894 0.543747
1.839092 1.9486% 1893 0.533354 1.874929 1.9858% 1892 0.522968 1.912162 2.0276% 1891
0.512575 1.950933 2.6465% 1890 0.499360 2.002565 1.5328% 1889 0.491821 2.033260
2.0811% 1888 0.481794 2.075575 2.1599% 1887 0.471608 2.120405 2.2075% 1886 0.461422
2.167213 2.2592% 1885 0.451228 2.216174 2.3095% 1884 0.441042 2.267358 2.3641% 1883
0.430856 2.320961 2.4214% 1882 0.420670 2.377161 2.4815% 1881 0.410484 2.436149
3.7644% 1880 0.395592 2.527855 0.9432% 1879 0.391896 2.551699 2.1464% 1878 0.383661
2.606468 2.1913% 1877 0.375434 2.663584 2.2426% 1876 0.367199 2.723318 2.2941% 1875
0.358964 2.785792 2.3456% 1874 0.350737 2.851135 2.4043% 1873 0.342503 2.919686
2.4635% 1872 0.334268 2.991613 2.5258% 1871 0.326033 3.067175 5.9947% 1870 0.307594
3.251042 -1.0968% 1869 0.311005 3.215385 2.1930% 1868 0.304331 3.285897 2.2394%
1867 0.297665 3.359482 2.2935% 1866 0.290991 3.436532 2.3445% 1865 0.284325 3.517100
2.4037% 1864 0.277651 3.601641 2.4599% 1863 0.270985 3.690237 2.5250% 1862 0.264311
3.783416 2.5872% 1861 0.257646 3.881302 2.9504% 1860 0.250262 3.995816 2.4012% 1859
0.244393 4.091765 2.7627% 1858 0.237823 4.204809 2.8412% 1857 0.231253 4.324276
2.9243% 1856 0.224682 4.450730 3.0161% 1855 0.218104 4.584970 3.1061% 1854 0.211534
4.727382 3.2056% 1853 0.204963 4.878924 3.3118% 1852 0.198393 5.040504 3.4252% 1851
0.191822 5.213153 4.0106% 1850 0.184426 5.422232 2.3254% 1849 0.180235 5.548319
2.7841% 1848 0.175353 5.702789 2.8590% 1847 0.170479 5.865832 2.9432% 1846 0.165605
6.038473 3.0324% 1845 0.160731 6.221584 3.1325% 1844 0.155849 6.416475 3.2284% 1843
0.150975 6.623622 3.3361% 1842 0.146101 6.844590 3.4512% 1841 0.141227 7.080810
3.8105% 1840 0.136043 7.350623 2.3861% 1839 0.132872 7.526013 2.5824% 1838 0.129528
7.720364 2.6573% 1837 0.126175 7.925519 2.7232% 1836 0.122830 8.141347 2.7994% 1835
0.119485 8.369259 2.8871% 1834 0.116132 8.610890 2.9657% 1833 0.112787 8.866202
3.0563% 1832 0.109442 9.137243 3.1604% 1831 0.106089 9.426019 3.4660% 1830 0.102535
9.752722 2.4653% 1829 0.100068 9.993156 2.6804% 1828 0.097456 10.261012 10.3427%
1827 0.088321 11.322272 -4.2314% 1826 0.092224 10.843178 2.9150% 1825 0.089612
11.159261 3.0026% 1824 0.086999 11.494324 3.0955% 1823 0.084387 11.850132 3.1944%
1822 0.081775 12.228672 3.3102% 1821 0.079155 12.633464 3.2277% 1820 0.076680
13.041239 2.6573% 1819 0.074695 13.387781 2.6261% 1818 0.072784 13.739359 2.6969%
1817 0.070872 14.109900 2.7717% 1816 0.068961 14.500982 2.8507% 1815 0.067049
14.914360 2.9343% 1814 0.065138 15.351999 3.0231% 1813 0.063227 15.816098 3.1039%
1812 0.061323 16.307013 3.2172% 1811 0.059412 16.831635 3.0969% 1810 0.057627
17.352897 2.9144% 1809 0.055995 17.858626 2.8225% 1808 0.054458 18.362679 2.9199%
1807 0.052913 18.898856 2.9918% 1806 0.051376 19.464269 3.0841% 1805 0.049839
20.064557 3.1822% 1804 0.048302 20.703050 3.2868% 1803 0.046765 21.383515 3.3985%
1802 0.045228 22.110231 3.5180% 1801 0.043691 22.888079 3.3999% 1800 0.042254
23.666261 2.8419% 1799 0.041087 24.338825 2.7485% 1798 0.039988 25.007767 2.8261%
1797 0.038889 25.714520 3.7832% 1796 0.037471 26.687354 2.1272% 1795 0.036690
27.255047 3.0879% 1794 0.035591 28.096666 3.1625% 1793 0.034500 28.985226 3.2904%
1792 0.033401 29.938960 3.4024% 1791 0.032302 30.957594 3.2296% 1790 0.031292
31.957389 41.3145% 1780 0.022143 45.160409 29.4353% 1770 0.017108 58.453517
83.4728% 1750 0.009324 107.246327 29.2845% 1740 0.007212 138.652827 94.2514% 1720

0.003713 269.335049 85.8111% 1700 0.001998 500.454364 19.2490% 1690 0.001676 596.787072 88.0250% 1670 0.000891 1122.109026

BASE YEAR: 1932

YEAR BYEAR/AYEAR AYEAR/BYEAR GROWTH%

2009 2.434031 0.410841 8.2857% 2001 2.247787 0.444882 1.0000% 2000 2.225531 0.449331 1.0000% 1999 2.203496 0.453824 1.0000% 1998 2.181679 0.458363 1.0000% 1997 2.160079 0.462946 1.0000% 1996 2.138692 0.467576 1.0000% 1995 2.117516 0.472251 0.9992% 1994 2.096567 0.476970 1.0008% 1993 2.075793 0.481744 1.0000% 1992 2.055241 0.486561 0.9295% 1991 2.036313 0.491084 1.2505% 1990 2.011163 0.497225 0.7224% 1989 1.996738 0.500817 1.1077% 1988 1.974863 0.506364 0.8834% 1987 1.957570 0.510837 0.5594% 1986 1.946681 0.513695 1.3056% 1985 1.921592 0.520402 0.7673% 1984 1.906961 0.524395 0.8149% 1983 1.891546 0.528668 0.9737% 1982 1.873304 0.533816 0.9508% 1981 1.855661 0.538892 0.9031% 1980 1.839053 0.543758 2.2701% 1979 1.798232 0.556102 1.0042% 1978 1.780354 0.561686 0.9896% 1977 1.762908 0.567245 0.9103% 1976 1.747004 0.572408 0.8394% 1975 1.732461 0.577213 0.9042% 1974 1.716937 0.582432 1.1568% 1973 1.697303 0.589170 0.9427% 1972 1.681452 0.594724 0.7426% 1971 1.669057 0.599141 1.4697% 1970 1.644881 0.607947 0.6968% 1969 1.633499 0.612183 0.8565% 1968 1.619626 0.617426 1.5090% 1967 1.595549 0.626744 0.9949% 1966 1.579831 0.632979 1.0575% 1965 1.563299 0.639673 1.1300% 1964 1.545831 0.646901 1.5537% 1963 1.522182 0.656952 1.4658% 1962 1.500192 0.666581 1.5364% 1961 1.477491 0.676823 2.1586% 1960 1.446271 0.691433 -1.6655% 1959 1.470767 0.679917 4.3080% 1958 1.410023 0.709208 2.1130% 1957 1.380846 0.724194 1.9895% 1956 1.353910 0.738601 2.1231% 1955 1.325763 0.754283 1.4496% 1954 1.306819 0.765217 2.1573% 1953 1.279223 0.781724 1.2298% 1952 1.263683 0.791338 1.6814% 1951 1.242787 0.804643 1.6233% 1950 1.222935 0.817705 1.4265% 1949 1.205735 0.829369 1.7790% 1948 1.184660 0.844124 1.8242% 1947 1.163437 0.859522 -2.6320% 1946 1.194887 0.836900 3.1768% 1945 1.158096 0.863486 6.4754% 1944 1.087665 0.919400 -0.3437% 1943 1.091416 0.916241 0.6562% 1942 1.084301 0.922253 0.6633% 1941 1.077156 0.928371 -5.6614% 1940 1.141798 0.875812 8.0381% 1939 1.056848 0.946210 0.8126% 1938 1.048328 0.953899 0.7762% 1937 1.040254 0.961304 0.6029% 1936 1.034020 0.967100 0.5244% 1935 1.028626 0.972171 -3.0364% 1934 1.060837 0.942652 4.6271% 1933 1.013921 0.986270 1.3921% 1932 1.000000 1.000000 -0.2051% 1931 1.002055 0.997949 0.8886% 1930 0.993229 1.006817 1.0126% 1929 0.983273 1.017012 1.1526% 1928 0.972069 1.028734 1.2160% 1927 0.960390 1.041243 1.4086% 1926 0.947050 1.055910 1.7667% 1925 0.930609 1.074565 1.4465% 1924 0.917340 1.090108 1.7700% 1923 0.901386 1.109403 1.6165% 1922 0.887047 1.127337 1.3736% 1921 0.875027 1.142822 2.3393% 1920 0.855025 1.169556 1.3140% 1919 0.843936 1.184924 0.7676% 1918 0.837507 1.194020 0.3870% 1917 0.834278 1.198641 1.3274% 1916 0.823349 1.214552 1.4083% 1915 0.811915 1.231657 1.4458% 1914 0.800343 1.249464 1.9424% 1913 0.785094 1.273733 1.9857% 1912 0.769808 1.299026 1.5634% 1911 0.757958 1.319335 1.8169% 1910 0.744432 1.343306 1.8781% 1909 0.730709 1.368534 2.0082% 1908 0.716323 1.396017 1.9603% 1907 0.702552 1.423383 1.8264% 1906 0.689951 1.449379 1.9357% 1905 0.676849 1.477434 2.0148% 1904 0.663481 1.507202 2.1335% 1903 0.649621 1.539358 1.8151% 1902 0.638040 1.567300 1.8943% 1901 0.626178 1.596990 3.0255% 1900 0.607789 1.645307 0.6278% 1899 0.603997 1.655637 1.7757% 1898 0.593459 1.685036 1.8078% 1897 0.582922 1.715497 1.8396% 1896 0.572392 1.747055 1.8755% 1895 0.561854 1.779822 1.9114% 1894 0.551316 1.813841 1.9486% 1893 0.540778 1.849186 1.9858% 1892 0.530249 1.885907 2.0276% 1891 0.519711 1.924147 2.6465% 1890 0.506311 1.975069 1.5328% 1889 0.498668 2.005344 2.0811% 1888 0.488501 2.047077 2.1599% 1887 0.478173 2.091291 2.2075% 1886 0.467846 2.137457 2.2592% 1885 0.457510 2.185746 2.3095% 1884 0.447182 2.236227 2.3641% 1883 0.436854 2.289094 2.4214% 1882 0.426526 2.344522 2.4815% 1881 0.416198 2.402701 3.7644% 1880 0.401099 2.493148 0.9432% 1879 0.397351 2.516664 2.1464% 1878 0.389002 2.570681 2.1913% 1877 0.380661 2.627013 2.2426% 1876 0.372311 2.685926 2.2941% 1875 0.363962 2.747543 2.3456% 1874 0.355620 2.811989 2.4043% 1873 0.347271 2.879598 2.4635% 1872 0.338921 2.950538 2.5258% 1871 0.330572 3.025062 5.9947% 1870 0.311876 3.206405 -1.0968% 1869 0.315334 3.171238 2.1930% 1868 0.308568 3.240782 2.2394% 1867 0.301809 3.313356 2.2935% 1866 0.295042 3.389348 2.3445% 1865 0.288283 3.468810

2.4037% 1864 0.281516 3.552190 2.4599% 1863 0.274758 3.639570 2.5250% 1862 0.267991
3.731469 2.5872% 1861 0.261232 3.828011 2.9504% 1860 0.253746 3.940953 2.4012% 1859
0.247796 4.035585 2.7627% 1858 0.241134 4.147077 2.8412% 1857 0.234472 4.264903
2.9243% 1856 0.227810 4.389621 3.0161% 1855 0.221140 4.522019 3.1061% 1854 0.214478
4.662475 3.2056% 1853 0.207817 4.811937 3.3118% 1852 0.201155 4.971298 3.4252% 1851
0.194493 5.141576 4.0106% 1850 0.186993 5.347784 2.3254% 1849 0.182744 5.472140
2.7841% 1848 0.177794 5.624489 2.8590% 1847 0.172852 5.785294 2.9432% 1846 0.167910
5.955564 3.0324% 1845 0.162968 6.136161 3.1325% 1844 0.158018 6.328377 3.2284% 1843
0.153077 6.532679 3.3361% 1842 0.148135 6.750613 3.4512% 1841 0.143193 6.983590
3.8105% 1840 0.137937 7.249699 2.3861% 1839 0.134722 7.422680 2.5824% 1838 0.131331
7.614363 2.6573% 1837 0.127931 7.816701 2.7232% 1836 0.124540 8.029566 2.7994% 1835
0.121148 8.254349 2.8871% 1834 0.117749 8.492662 2.9657% 1833 0.114357 8.744528
3.0563% 1832 0.110966 9.011789 3.1604% 1831 0.107566 9.296599 3.4660% 1830 0.103963
9.618816 2.4653% 1829 0.101462 9.855949 2.6804% 1828 0.098813 10.120127 10.3427% 1827
0.089551 11.166817 -4.2314% 1826 0.093508 10.694301 2.9150% 1825 0.090859
11.006043 3.0026% 1824 0.088211 11.336507 3.0955% 1823 0.085562 11.687429 3.1944% 1822 0.082913 12.060771 3.3102% 1821 0.080257 12.460006 3.2277% 1820 0.077747
12.862183 2.6573% 1819 0.075735 13.203966 2.6261% 1818 0.073797 13.550717 2.6969% 1817 0.071859 13.916170 2.7717% 1816 0.069921 14.301882 2.8507% 1815 0.067983
14.709585 2.9343% 1814 0.066045 15.141215 3.0231% 1813 0.064107 15.598942 3.1039% 1812 0.062177 16.083117 3.2172% 1811 0.060239 16.600536 3.0969% 1810 0.058430
17.114641 2.9144% 1809 0.056775 17.613426 2.8225% 1808 0.055216 18.110559 2.9199% 1807 0.053650 18.639374 2.9918% 1806 0.052091 19.197024 3.0841% 1805 0.050533
19.789070 3.1822% 1804 0.048974 20.418796 3.2868% 1803 0.047416 21.089918 3.3985% 1802 0.045858 21.806656 3.5180% 1801 0.044299 22.573824 3.3999% 1800 0.042842
23.341322 2.8419% 1799 0.041659 24.004652 2.7485% 1798 0.040544 24.664409 2.8261% 1797 0.039430 25.361458 3.7832% 1796 0.037993 26.320935 2.1272% 1795 0.037201
26.880834 3.0879% 1794 0.036050 27.710897 3.1625% 1793 0.034981 28.587258 3.2904% 1792 0.033866 29.527897 3.4024% 1791 0.032752 30.532544 3.2296% 1790 0.031727
31.518612 41.3145% 1780 0.022452 44.540354 29.4353% 1770 0.017346 57.650947
83.4728% 1750 0.009454 105.773830 29.2845% 1740 0.007313 136.749117 94.2514% 1720
0.003765 265.637066 85.8111% 1700 0.002026 493.583101 19.2490% 1690 0.001699
588.593156 88.0250% 1670 0.000904 1106.702413

BASE YEAR: 1931
YEAR BYEAR/AYEAR AYEAR/BYEAR GROWTH%
2009 2.429039 0.411685 8.2857% 2001 2.243177 0.445796 1.0000% 2000 2.220967
0.450254 1.0000% 1999 2.198977 0.454757 1.0000% 1998 2.177205 0.459304 1.0000% 1997
2.155649 0.463898 1.0000% 1996 2.134305 0.468536 1.0000% 1995 2.113174 0.473222
0.9992% 1994 2.092267 0.477950 1.0008% 1993 2.071536 0.482734 1.0000% 1992 2.051026
0.487561 0.9295% 1991 2.032137 0.492093 1.2505% 1990 2.007038 0.498247 0.7224% 1989
1.992643 0.501846 1.1077% 1988 1.970813 0.507405 0.8834% 1987 1.953556 0.511887
0.5594% 1986 1.942689 0.514750 1.3056% 1985 1.917651 0.521471 0.7673% 1984 1.903050
0.525472 0.8149% 1983 1.887666 0.529755 0.9737% 1982 1.869462 0.534913 0.9508% 1981
1.851855 0.539999 0.9031% 1980 1.835281 0.544876 2.2701% 1979 1.794544 0.557245
1.0042% 1978 1.776702 0.562840 0.9896% 1977 1.759292 0.568410 0.9103% 1976 1.743421
0.573585 0.8394% 1975 1.728908 0.578400 0.9042% 1974 1.713416 0.583629 1.1568% 1973
1.693822 0.590381 0.9427% 1972 1.678003 0.595946 0.7426% 1971 1.665634 0.600372
1.4697% 1970 1.641508 0.609196 0.6968% 1969 1.630149 0.613441 0.8565% 1968 1.616305
0.618695 1.5090% 1967 1.592276 0.628032 0.9949% 1966 1.576591 0.634280 1.0575% 1965
1.560093 0.640987 1.1300% 1964 1.542661 0.648231 1.5537% 1963 1.519060 0.658302
1.4658% 1962 1.497115 0.667951 1.5364% 1961 1.474461 0.678214 2.1586% 1960 1.443305
0.692854 -1.6655% 1959 1.467750 0.681315 4.3080% 1958 1.407131 0.710666 2.1130%
1957 1.378014 0.725682 1.9895% 1956 1.351134 0.740119 2.1231% 1955 1.323044 0.755833
1.4496% 1954 1.304139 0.766789 2.1573% 1953 1.276600 0.783331 1.2298% 1952 1.261091
0.792964 1.6814% 1951 1.240238 0.806297 1.6233% 1950 1.220427 0.819385 1.4265% 1949
1.203262 0.831074 1.7790% 1948 1.182230 0.845859 1.8242% 1947 1.161051 0.861289 -

114

2.6320% 1946 1.192436 0.838619 3.1768% 1945 1.155721 0.865261 6.4754% 1944 1.085435
0.921290 -0.3437% 1943 1.089178 0.918124 0.6562% 1942 1.082077 0.924149 0.6633%
1941 1.074947 0.930278 -5.6614% 1940 1.139456 0.877611 8.0381% 1939 1.054680
0.948155 0.8126% 1938 1.046179 0.955860 0.7762% 1937 1.038120 0.963280 0.6029% 1936
1.031899 0.969087 0.5244% 1935 1.026516 0.974169 -3.0364% 1934 1.058661 0.944589
4.6271% 1933 1.011842 0.988297 1.3921% 1932 0.997949 1.002055 -0.2051% 1931
1.000000 1.000000 0.8886% 1930 0.991192 1.008886 1.0126% 1929 0.981256 1.019102
1.1526% 1928 0.970075 1.030848 1.2160% 1927 0.958421 1.043383 1.4086% 1926 0.945108
1.058080 1.7667% 1925 0.928701 1.076773 1.4465% 1924 0.915459 1.092348 1.7700% 1923
0.899537 1.111683 1.6165% 1922 0.885227 1.129653 1.3736% 1921 0.873232 1.145171
2.3393% 1920 0.853272 1.171960 1.3140% 1919 0.842205 1.187359 0.7676% 1918 0.835789
1.196474 0.3870% 1917 0.832567 1.201104 1.3274% 1916 0.821660 1.217048 1.4083% 1915
0.810249 1.234188 1.4458% 1914 0.798702 1.252032 1.9424% 1913 0.783484 1.276351
1.9857% 1912 0.768229 1.301695 1.5634% 1911 0.756403 1.322046 1.8169% 1910 0.742905
1.346066 1.8781% 1909 0.729210 1.371346 2.0082% 1908 0.714854 1.398886 1.9603% 1907
0.701111 1.426308 1.8264% 1906 0.688536 1.452357 1.9357% 1905 0.675461 1.480470
2.0148% 1904 0.662120 1.510299 2.1335% 1903 0.648289 1.542522 1.8151% 1902 0.636731
1.570521 1.8943% 1901 0.624894 1.600272 3.0255% 1900 0.606543 1.648688 0.6278% 1899
0.602758 1.659040 1.7757% 1898 0.592242 1.688498 1.8078% 1897 0.581726 1.719022
1.8396% 1896 0.571218 1.750645 1.8755% 1895 0.560702 1.783479 1.9114% 1894 0.550186
1.817569 1.9486% 1893 0.539669 1.852986 1.9858% 1892 0.529161 1.889783 2.0276% 1891
0.518645 1.928101 2.6465% 1890 0.505273 1.979128 1.5328% 1889 0.497645 2.009465
2.0811% 1888 0.487499 2.051284 2.1599% 1887 0.477193 2.095589 2.2075% 1886 0.466886
2.141850 2.2592% 1885 0.456571 2.190238 2.3095% 1884 0.446265 2.240822 2.3641% 1883
0.435958 2.293799 2.4214% 1882 0.425651 2.349340 2.4815% 1881 0.415345 2.407638
3.7644% 1880 0.400277 2.498271 0.9432% 1879 0.396537 2.521836 2.1464% 1878 0.388204
2.575964 2.1913% 1877 0.379880 2.632411 2.2426% 1876 0.371547 2.691446 2.2941% 1875
0.363215 2.753189 2.3456% 1874 0.354891 2.817768 2.4043% 1873 0.346558 2.885516
2.4635% 1872 0.338226 2.956602 2.5258% 1871 0.329894 3.031279 5.9947% 1870 0.311236
3.212994 -1.0968% 1869 0.314688 3.177755 2.1930% 1868 0.307935 3.247442 2.2394%
1867 0.301190 3.320165 2.2935% 1866 0.294437 3.396313 2.3445% 1865 0.287692 3.475939
2.4037% 1864 0.280939 3.559490 2.4599% 1863 0.274194 3.647049 2.5250% 1862 0.267441
3.739138 2.5872% 1861 0.260696 3.835878 2.9504% 1860 0.253225 3.949052 2.4012% 1859
0.247287 4.043879 2.7627% 1858 0.240639 4.155599 2.8412% 1857 0.233991 4.273668
2.9243% 1856 0.227343 4.398642 3.0161% 1855 0.220687 4.531312 3.1061% 1854 0.214038
4.672057 3.2056% 1853 0.207390 4.821825 3.3118% 1852 0.200742 4.981514 3.4252% 1851
0.194094 5.152142 4.0106% 1850 0.186610 5.358774 3.2254% 1849 0.182369 5.483386
2.7841% 1848 0.177429 5.636048 2.8590% 1847 0.172498 5.797183 2.9432% 1846 0.167566
5.967803 3.0324% 1845 0.162634 6.148771 3.1325% 1844 0.157694 6.341382 3.2284% 1843
0.152763 6.546104 3.3361% 1842 0.147831 6.764486 3.4512% 1841 0.142899 6.997942
3.8105% 1840 0.137654 7.264597 2.3861% 1839 0.134446 7.437935 2.5824% 1838 0.131061
7.630011 2.6573% 1837 0.127669 7.832765 2.7232% 1836 0.124284 8.046068 2.7994% 1835
0.120900 8.271312 2.8871% 1834 0.117507 8.510115 2.9657% 1833 0.114123 8.762498
3.0563% 1832 0.110738 9.030309 3.1604% 1831 0.107346 9.315705 3.4660% 1830 0.103750
9.638584 2.4653% 1829 0.101253 9.876204 2.6804% 1828 0.098610 10.140925 10.3427%
1827 0.089367 11.189766 -4.2314% 1826 0.093316 10.716278 2.9150% 1825 0.090673
11.028662 3.0026% 1824 0.088030 11.359804 3.0955% 1823 0.085387 11.711448 3.1944%
1822 0.082743 12.085557 3.3102% 1821 0.080092 12.485612 3.2277% 1820 0.077588
12.888615 2.6573% 1819 0.075579 13.231101 2.6261% 1818 0.073645 13.578564 2.6969%
1817 0.071711 13.944769 2.7717% 1816 0.069777 14.331274 2.8507% 1815 0.067843
14.739815 2.9343% 1814 0.065909 15.172332 3.0231% 1813 0.063975 15.630999 3.1039%
1812 0.062049 16.116169 3.2172% 1811 0.060115 16.634651 3.0969% 1810 0.058310
17.149813 2.9144% 1809 0.056658 17.649623 2.8225% 1808 0.055103 18.147777 2.9199%
1807 0.053540 18.677679 2.9918% 1806 0.051985 19.236475 3.0841% 1805 0.050429
19.829738 3.1822% 1804 0.048874 20.460758 3.2868% 1803 0.047319 21.133260 3.3985%
1802 0.045764 21.851470 3.5180% 1801 0.044208 22.620215 3.3999% 1800 0.042755

115

23.389290 2.8419% 1799 0.041573 24.053983 2.7485% 1798 0.040461 24.715097 2.8261% 1797 0.039349 25.413578 3.7832% 1796 0.037915 26.375027 2.1272% 1795 0.037125 26.936076 3.0879% 1794 0.036013 27.767845 3.1625% 1793 0.034909 28.646006 3.2904% 1792 0.033797 29.588579 3.4024% 1791 0.032685 30.595291 3.2296% 1790 0.031662 31.583385 41.3145% 1780 0.022406 44.631887 29.4353% 1770 0.017310 57.769424 83.4728% 1750 0.009435 105.991203 29.2845% 1740 0.007298 137.030146 94.2514% 1720 0.003757 266.182969 85.8111% 1700 0.002022 494.597449 19.2490% 1690 0.001695 589.802757 88.0250% 1670 0.000902 1108.976765

BASE YEAR: 1930

YEAR BYEAR/AYEAR AYEAR/BYEAR GROWTH%

2009 2.450623 0.408059 8.2857% 2001 2.263110 0.441870 1.0000% 2000 2.240702 0.446289 1.0000% 1999 2.218517 0.450752 1.0000% 1998 2.196552 0.455259 1.0000% 1997 2.174804 0.459812 1.0000% 1996 2.153271 0.464410 1.0000% 1995 2.131951 0.469054 0.9992% 1994 2.110859 0.473741 1.0008% 1993 2.089944 0.478482 1.0000% 1992 2.069251 0.483267 0.9295% 1991 2.050194 0.487759 1.2505% 1990 2.024873 0.493858 0.7224% 1989 2.010349 0.497426 1.1077% 1988 1.988325 0.502936 0.8834% 1987 1.970915 0.507379 0.5594% 1986 1.959952 0.510217 1.3056% 1985 1.934692 0.516878 0.7673% 1984 1.919960 0.520844 0.8149% 1983 1.904440 0.525089 0.9737% 1982 1.886074 0.530202 0.9508% 1981 1.868310 0.535243 0.9031% 1980 1.851589 0.540077 2.2701% 1979 1.810490 0.552337 1.0042% 1978 1.792490 0.557883 0.9896% 1977 1.774925 0.563404 0.9103% 1976 1.758913 0.568533 0.8394% 1975 1.744271 0.573305 0.9042% 1974 1.728641 0.578489 1.1568% 1973 1.708873 0.585181 0.9427% 1972 1.692914 0.590697 0.7426% 1971 1.680435 0.595084 1.4697% 1970 1.656094 0.603830 0.6968% 1969 1.644634 0.608038 0.8565% 1968 1.630667 0.613246 1.5090% 1967 1.606425 0.622500 0.9949% 1966 1.590600 0.628693 1.0575% 1965 1.573956 0.635342 1.1300% 1964 1.556369 0.642521 1.5537% 1963 1.532558 0.652504 1.4658% 1962 1.510418 0.662068 1.5364% 1961 1.487563 0.672240 2.1586% 1960 1.456130 0.686752 -1.6655% 1959 1.480793 0.675314 4.3080% 1958 1.419635 0.704406 2.1130% 1957 1.390259 0.719290 1.9895% 1956 1.363140 0.733600 2.1231% 1955 1.334801 0.749176 1.4496% 1954 1.315728 0.760036 2.1573% 1953 1.287944 0.776432 1.2298% 1952 1.272297 0.785980 1.6814% 1951 1.251259 0.799195 1.6233% 1950 1.231272 0.812168 1.4265% 1949 1.213955 0.823754 1.7790% 1948 1.192735 0.838409 1.8242% 1947 1.171368 0.853703 -2.6320% 1946 1.203032 0.831233 3.1768% 1945 1.165991 0.857640 6.4754% 1944 1.095080 0.913175 -0.3437% 1943 1.098856 0.910037 0.6562% 1942 1.091692 0.916009 0.6633% 1941 1.084499 0.922085 -5.6614% 1940 1.149582 0.869882 8.0381% 1939 1.064052 0.939804 0.8126% 1938 1.055475 0.947441 0.7762% 1937 1.047345 0.954795 0.6029% 1936 1.041069 0.960552 0.5244% 1935 1.035638 0.965589 -3.0364% 1934 1.068068 0.936270 4.6271% 1933 1.020833 0.979592 1.3921% 1932 1.006817 0.993229 -0.2051% 1931 1.008886 0.991192 0.8886% 1930 1.000000 1.000000 1.0126% 1929 0.989976 1.010126 1.1526% 1928 0.978695 1.021768 1.2160% 1927 0.966937 1.034193 1.4086% 1926 0.953506 1.048761 1.7667% 1925 0.936953 1.067289 1.4465% 1924 0.923594 1.082727 1.7700% 1923 0.907531 1.101891 1.6165% 1922 0.893093 1.119704 1.3736% 1921 0.880992 1.135084 2.3393% 1920 0.860854 1.161638 1.3140% 1919 0.849689 1.176902 0.7676% 1918 0.843216 1.185936 0.3870% 1917 0.839965 1.190525 1.3274% 1916 0.828961 1.206329 1.4083% 1915 0.817449 1.223317 1.4458% 1914 0.805799 1.241004 1.9424% 1913 0.790446 1.265109 1.9857% 1912 0.775056 1.290230 1.5634% 1911 0.763125 1.310402 1.8169% 1910 0.749507 1.334211 1.8781% 1909 0.735690 1.359268 2.0082% 1908 0.721207 1.386565 1.9603% 1907 0.707341 1.413745 1.8264% 1906 0.694654 1.439565 1.9357% 1905 0.681463 1.467431 2.0148% 1904 0.668004 1.496997 2.1335% 1903 0.654050 1.528936 1.8151% 1902 0.642389 1.556688 1.8943% 1901 0.630446 1.586177 3.0255% 1900 0.611932 1.634167 0.6278% 1899 0.608114 1.644427 1.7757% 1898 0.597505 1.673627 1.8078% 1897 0.586895 1.703882 1.8396% 1896 0.576294 1.735226 1.8755% 1895 0.565684 1.767771 1.9114% 1894 0.555074 1.801560 1.9486% 1893 0.544465 1.836666 1.9858% 1892 0.533863 1.873138 2.0276% 1891 0.523254 1.911119 2.6465% 1890 0.509763 1.961697 1.5328% 1889 0.502067 1.991766 2.0811% 1888 0.491831 2.033217 2.1599% 1887 0.481433 2.077132 2.2075% 1886 0.471035 2.122985 2.2592% 1885 0.460628 2.170947 2.3095% 1884 0.450230 2.221086 2.3641% 1883 0.439832 2.273595 2.4214% 1882 0.429434 2.328648 2.4815% 1881 0.419036 2.386433

116

3.7644% 1880 0.403834 2.476267 0.9432% 1879 0.400060 2.499624 2.1464% 1878 0.391654
2.553276 2.1913% 1877 0.383255 2.609226 2.2426% 1876 0.374849 2.667740 2.2941% 1875
0.366443 2.728940 2.3456% 1874 0.358044 2.792950 2.4043% 1873 0.349638 2.860101
2.4635% 1872 0.341232 2.930561 2.5258% 1871 0.332825 3.004580 5.9947% 1870 0.314002
3.184695 -1.0968% 1869 0.317484 3.149766 2.1930% 1868 0.310671 3.218839 2.2394%
1867 0.303866 3.290922 2.2935% 1866 0.297053 3.366400 2.3445% 1865 0.290248 3.445324
2.4037% 1864 0.283436 3.528139 2.4599% 1863 0.276631 3.614927 2.5250% 1862 0.269818
3.706204 2.5872% 1861 0.263013 3.802093 2.9504% 1860 0.255475 3.914270 2.4012% 1859
0.249485 4.008261 2.7627% 1858 0.242778 4.118998 2.8412% 1857 0.236070 4.236027
2.9243% 1856 0.229363 4.359900 3.0161% 1855 0.222648 4.491401 3.1061% 1854 0.215940
4.630907 3.2056% 1853 0.209233 4.779356 3.3118% 1852 0.202526 4.937638 3.4252% 1851
0.195819 5.106764 4.0106% 1850 0.188268 5.311576 2.3254% 1849 0.183990 5.435090
2.7841% 1848 0.179006 5.586407 2.8590% 1847 0.174030 5.746123 2.9432% 1846 0.169055
5.915241 3.0324% 1845 0.164079 6.094615 3.1325% 1844 0.159096 6.285529 3.2284% 1843
0.154120 6.488448 3.3361% 1842 0.149145 6.704907 3.4512% 1841 0.144169 6.936306
3.8105% 1840 0.138877 7.200613 2.3861% 1839 0.135641 7.372423 2.5824% 1838 0.132226
7.562808 2.6573% 1837 0.128803 7.763776 2.7232% 1836 0.125389 7.975200 2.7994% 1835
0.121974 8.198461 2.8871% 1834 0.118551 8.435161 2.9657% 1833 0.115137 8.685321
3.0563% 1832 0.111722 8.950772 3.1604% 1831 0.108299 9.233654 3.4660% 1830 0.104672
9.553690 2.4653% 1829 0.102153 9.789217 2.6804% 1828 0.099487 10.051607 10.3427%
1827 0.090161 11.091209 -4.2314% 1826 0.094145 10.621892 2.9150% 1825 0.091479
10.931524 3.0026% 1824 0.088812 11.259750 3.0955% 1823 0.086145 11.608297 3.1944%
1822 0.083479 11.979111 3.3102% 1821 0.080804 12.375643 3.2277% 1820 0.078277
12.775096 2.6573% 1819 0.076251 13.114566 2.6261% 1818 0.074300 13.458968 2.6969%
1817 0.072349 13.821948 2.7717% 1816 0.070398 14.205048 2.8507% 1815 0.068446
14.609991 2.9343% 1814 0.066495 15.038698 3.0231% 1813 0.064544 15.493325 3.1039%
1812 0.062601 15.974222 3.2172% 1811 0.060650 16.488138 3.0969% 1810 0.058828
16.998762 2.9144% 1809 0.057162 17.494170 2.8225% 1808 0.055593 17.987937 2.9199%
1807 0.054016 18.513171 2.9918% 1806 0.052447 19.067046 3.0841% 1805 0.050877
19.655083 3.1822% 1804 0.049308 20.280546 3.2868% 1803 0.047739 20.947124 3.3985%
1802 0.046170 21.659009 3.5180% 1801 0.044601 22.420983 3.3999% 1800 0.043135
23.183284 2.8419% 1799 0.041943 23.842123 2.7485% 1798 0.040821 24.497413 2.8261%
1797 0.039699 25.189742 3.7832% 1796 0.038252 26.142723 2.1272% 1795 0.037455
26.698830 3.0879% 1794 0.036333 27.523274 3.1625% 1793 0.035219 28.393701 3.2904%
1792 0.034097 29.327971 3.4024% 1791 0.032975 30.325816 3.2296% 1790 0.031944
31.305208 41.3145% 1780 0.022605 44.238783 29.4353% 1770 0.017464 57.260608
83.4728% 1750 0.009519 105.057662 29.2845% 1740 0.007363 135.823223 94.2514% 1720
0.003790 263.838505 85.8111% 1700 0.002040 490.241176 19.2490% 1690 0.001711
584.607942 88.0250% 1670 0.000910 1099.209214

BASE YEAR: 1929
YEAR BYEAR/AYEAR AYEAR/BYEAR GROWTH%

2009 2.475438 0.403969 8.2857% 2001 2.286026 0.437440 1.0000% 2000 2.263391
0.441815 1.0000% 1999 2.240982 0.446233 1.0000% 1998 2.218794 0.450695 1.0000% 1997
2.196825 0.455202 1.0000% 1996 2.175075 0.459754 1.0000% 1995 2.153539 0.464352
0.9992% 1994 2.132233 0.468992 1.0008% 1993 2.111106 0.473685 1.0000% 1992 2.090204
0.478422 0.9295% 1991 2.070954 0.482869 1.2505% 1990 2.045377 0.488908 0.7224% 1989
2.030706 0.492440 1.1077% 1988 2.008459 0.497894 0.8834% 1987 1.990872 0.502292
0.5594% 1986 1.979798 0.505102 1.3056% 1985 1.954282 0.511697 0.7673% 1984 1.939401
0.515623 0.8149% 1983 1.923724 0.519825 0.9737% 1982 1.905173 0.524887 0.9508% 1981
1.887229 0.529878 0.9031% 1980 1.870338 0.534663 2.2701% 1979 1.828823 0.546800
1.0042% 1978 1.810641 0.552291 0.9896% 1977 1.792898 0.557756 0.9103% 1976 1.776724
0.562834 0.8394% 1975 1.761934 0.567558 0.9042% 1974 1.746145 0.572690 1.1568% 1973
1.726177 0.579315 0.9427% 1972 1.710056 0.584776 0.7426% 1971 1.697450 0.589119
1.4697% 1970 1.672864 0.597777 0.6968% 1969 1.661288 0.601943 0.8565% 1968 1.647179
0.607099 1.5090% 1967 1.622692 0.616260 0.9949% 1966 1.606707 0.622391 1.0575% 1965
1.589894 0.628973 1.1300% 1964 1.572129 0.636080 1.5537% 1963 1.548077 0.645963

117

1.4658% 1962 1.525713 0.655431 1.5364% 1961 1.502626 0.665502 2.1586% 1960 1.470875
0.679867 -1.6655% 1959 1.495787 0.668544 4.3080% 1958 1.434010 0.697345 2.1130%
1957 1.404337 0.712080 1.9895% 1956 1.376943 0.726247 2.1231% 1955 1.348317 0.741666
1.4496% 1954 1.329051 0.752417 2.1573% 1953 1.300985 0.768648 1.2298% 1952 1.285180
0.778101 1.6814% 1951 1.263929 0.791184 1.6233% 1950 1.243740 0.804027 1.4265% 1949
1.226247 0.815496 1.7790% 1948 1.204813 0.830004 1.8242% 1947 1.183229 0.845145 -
2.6320% 1946 1.215214 0.822901 3.1768% 1945 1.177797 0.849042 6.4754% 1944 1.106168
0.904021 -0.3437% 1943 1.109983 0.900915 0.6562% 1942 1.102747 0.906827 0.6633%
1941 1.095480 0.912842 -5.6614% 1940 1.161222 0.861162 8.0381% 1939 1.074826
0.930383 0.8126% 1938 1.066162 0.937943 0.7762% 1937 1.057950 0.945224 0.6029% 1936
1.051610 0.950923 0.5244% 1935 1.046124 0.955909 -3.0364% 1934 1.078883 0.926884
4.6271% 1933 1.031170 0.969772 1.3921% 1932 1.017012 0.983273 -0.2051% 1931
1.019102 0.981256 0.8886% 1930 1.010126 0.989976 1.0126% 1929 1.000000 1.000000
1.1526% 1928 0.988605 1.011526 1.2160% 1927 0.976728 1.023826 1.4086% 1926 0.963161
1.038248 1.7667% 1925 0.946441 1.056590 1.4465% 1924 0.932946 1.071874 1.7700% 1923
0.916720 1.090846 1.6165% 1922 0.902137 1.108479 1.3736% 1921 0.889913 1.123706
2.3393% 1920 0.869571 1.149993 1.3140% 1919 0.858293 1.165104 0.7676% 1918 0.851754
1.174048 0.3870% 1917 0.848471 1.178591 1.3274% 1916 0.837355 1.194236 1.4083% 1915
0.825727 1.211054 1.4458% 1914 0.813958 1.228564 1.9424% 1913 0.798450 1.252427
1.9857% 1912 0.782904 1.277296 1.5634% 1911 0.770852 1.297266 1.8169% 1910 0.757096
1.320836 1.8781% 1909 0.743140 1.345642 2.0082% 1908 0.728509 1.372666 1.9603% 1907
0.714503 1.399574 1.8264% 1906 0.701688 1.425135 1.9357% 1905 0.688364 1.452721
2.0148% 1904 0.674768 1.481991 2.1335% 1903 0.660672 1.513609 1.8151% 1902 0.648894
1.541084 1.8943% 1901 0.636830 1.570277 3.0255% 1900 0.618129 1.617786 0.6278% 1899
0.614272 1.627943 1.7757% 1898 0.603555 1.656850 1.8078% 1897 0.592838 1.686801
1.8396% 1896 0.582129 1.717832 1.8755% 1895 0.571412 1.750050 1.9114% 1894 0.560695
1.783501 1.9486% 1893 0.549978 1.818254 1.9858% 1892 0.539269 1.854361 2.0276% 1891
0.528552 1.891961 2.6465% 1890 0.514925 1.942032 1.5328% 1889 0.507151 1.971800
2.0811% 1888 0.496812 2.012836 2.1599% 1887 0.486308 2.056310 2.2075% 1886 0.475804
2.101704 2.2592% 1885 0.465293 2.149185 2.3095% 1884 0.454789 2.198821 2.3641% 1883
0.444286 2.250804 2.4214% 1882 0.433782 2.305305 2.4815% 1881 0.423279 2.362510
3.7644% 1880 0.407923 2.451444 0.9432% 1879 0.404111 2.474567 2.1464% 1878 0.395620
2.527681 2.1913% 1877 0.387136 2.583070 2.2426% 1876 0.378645 2.640998 2.2941% 1875
0.370153 2.701584 2.3456% 1874 0.361670 2.764952 2.4043% 1873 0.353178 2.831430
2.4635% 1872 0.344687 2.901184 2.5258% 1871 0.336195 2.974461 5.9947% 1870 0.317181
3.152771 -1.0968% 1869 0.320699 3.118192 2.1930% 1868 0.313817 3.186573 2.2394%
1867 0.306943 3.257933 2.2935% 1866 0.300061 3.332654 2.3445% 1865 0.293187 3.410787
2.4037% 1864 0.286306 3.492772 2.4599% 1863 0.279432 3.578690 2.5250% 1862 0.272550
3.669052 2.5872% 1861 0.265676 3.763979 2.9504% 1860 0.258062 3.875032 2.4012% 1859
0.252011 3.968081 2.7627% 1858 0.245236 4.077707 2.8412% 1857 0.238461 4.193563
2.9243% 1856 0.231686 4.316195 3.0161% 1855 0.224902 4.446378 3.1061% 1854 0.218127
4.584485 3.2056% 1853 0.211352 4.731446 3.3118% 1852 0.204577 4.888142 3.4252% 1851
0.197802 5.055572 4.0106% 1850 0.190174 5.258331 2.3254% 1849 0.185853 5.380606
2.7841% 1848 0.180819 5.530407 2.8590% 1847 0.175793 5.688522 2.9432% 1846 0.170767
5.855944 3.0324% 1845 0.165741 6.033520 3.1325% 1844 0.160707 6.222520 3.2284% 1843
0.155681 6.423406 3.3361% 1842 0.150655 6.637694 3.4512% 1841 0.145629 6.866774
3.8105% 1840 0.140283 7.128431 2.3861% 1839 0.137014 7.298520 2.5824% 1838 0.133565
7.486996 2.6573% 1837 0.130108 7.685950 2.7232% 1836 0.126658 7.895254 2.7994% 1835
0.123209 8.116277 2.8871% 1834 0.119752 8.350603 2.9657% 1833 0.116303 8.598256
3.0563% 1832 0.112853 8.861046 3.1604% 1831 0.109396 9.141093 3.4660% 1830 0.105731
9.457920 2.4653% 1829 0.103188 9.691086 2.6804% 1828 0.100494 9.950846 10.3427%
1827 0.091074 10.980027 -4.2314% 1826 0.095098 10.515415 2.9150% 1825 0.092405
10.821943 3.0026% 1824 0.089711 11.146878 3.0955% 1823 0.087018 11.491931 3.1944%
1822 0.084324 11.859028 3.3102% 1821 0.081622 12.251585 3.2277% 1820 0.079070
12.647034 2.6573% 1819 0.077023 12.983101 2.6261% 1818 0.075052 13.324051 2.6969%
1817 0.073081 13.683391 2.7717% 1816 0.071110 14.062652 2.8507% 1815 0.069139

14.463535 2.9343% 1814 0.067168 14.887945 3.0231% 1813 0.065197 15.338015 3.1039%
1812 0.063235 15.814091 3.2172% 1811 0.061264 16.322855 3.0969% 1810 0.059423
16.828360 2.9144% 1809 0.057741 17.318802 2.8225% 1808 0.056156 17.807619 2.9199%
1807 0.054563 18.327589 2.9918% 1806 0.052978 18.875911 3.0841% 1805 0.051393
19.458054 3.1822% 1804 0.049808 20.077246 3.2868% 1803 0.048223 20.737142 3.3985%
1802 0.046638 21.441891 3.5180% 1801 0.045053 22.196227 3.3999% 1800 0.043571
22.950887 2.8419% 1799 0.042367 23.603121 2.7485% 1798 0.041234 24.251842 2.8261%
1797 0.040101 24.937231 3.7832% 1796 0.038639 25.880659 2.1272% 1795 0.037834
26.431192 3.0879% 1794 0.036701 27.247371 3.1625% 1793 0.035576 28.109072 3.2904%
1792 0.034442 29.033977 3.4024% 1791 0.033309 30.021820 3.2296% 1790 0.032267
30.991393 41.3145% 1780 0.022833 43.795317 29.4353% 1770 0.017641 56.686607
83.4728% 1750 0.009615 104.004527 29.2845% 1740 0.007437 134.461683 94.2514% 1720
0.003829 261.193694 85.8111% 1700 0.002060 485.326823 19.2490% 1690 0.001728
578.747624 88.0250% 1670 0.000919 1088.190349

BASE YEAR: 1928
YEAR BYEAR/AYEAR AYEAR/BYEAR GROWTH%
2009 2.503969 0.399366 8.2857% 2001 2.312374 0.432456 1.0000% 2000 2.289479
0.436781 1.0000% 1999 2.266811 0.441148 1.0000% 1998 2.244367 0.445560 1.0000% 1997
2.222146 0.450015 1.0000% 1996 2.200144 0.454516 1.0000% 1995 2.178361 0.459061
0.9992% 1994 2.156809 0.463648 1.0008% 1993 2.135438 0.468288 1.0000% 1992 2.114295
0.472971 0.9295% 1991 2.094824 0.477367 1.2505% 1990 2.068951 0.483337 0.7224% 1989
2.054112 0.486828 1.1077% 1988 2.031608 0.492221 0.8834% 1987 2.013819 0.496569
0.5594% 1986 2.002617 0.499347 1.3056% 1985 1.976807 0.505866 0.7673% 1984 1.961755
0.509748 0.8149% 1983 1.945897 0.513902 0.9737% 1982 1.927131 0.518906 0.9508% 1981
1.908981 0.523840 0.9031% 1980 1.891896 0.528570 2.2701% 1979 1.849902 0.540569
1.0042% 1978 1.831510 0.545998 0.9896% 1977 1.813563 0.551401 0.9103% 1976 1.797202
0.556420 0.8394% 1975 1.782241 0.561091 0.9042% 1974 1.766271 0.566164 1.1568% 1973
1.746073 0.572714 0.9427% 1972 1.729766 0.578113 0.7426% 1971 1.717015 0.582406
1.4697% 1970 1.692145 0.590966 0.6968% 1969 1.680435 0.595084 0.8565% 1968 1.666164
0.600181 1.5090% 1967 1.641395 0.609238 0.9949% 1966 1.625225 0.615299 1.0575% 1965
1.608219 0.621806 1.1300% 1964 1.590249 0.628832 1.5537% 1963 1.565920 0.638602
1.4658% 1962 1.543298 0.647963 1.5364% 1961 1.519945 0.657919 2.1586% 1960 1.487828
0.672121 -1.6655% 1959 1.513027 0.660927 4.3080% 1958 1.450538 0.689399 2.1130%
1957 1.420523 0.703966 1.9895% 1956 1.392813 0.717971 2.1231% 1955 1.363857 0.733215
1.4496% 1954 1.344369 0.743843 2.1573% 1953 1.315980 0.759890 1.2298% 1952 1.299993
0.769235 1.6814% 1951 1.278497 0.782168 1.6233% 1950 1.258075 0.794865 1.4265% 1949
1.240381 0.806204 1.7790% 1948 1.218699 0.820547 1.8242% 1947 1.196867 0.835515 -
2.6320% 1946 1.229220 0.813524 3.1768% 1945 1.191373 0.839368 6.4754% 1944 1.118918
0.893721 -0.3437% 1943 1.122777 0.890649 0.6562% 1942 1.115457 0.896494 0.6633%
1941 1.108107 0.902440 -5.6614% 1940 1.174606 0.851349 8.0381% 1939 1.087215
0.919781 0.8126% 1938 1.078451 0.927256 0.7762% 1937 1.070144 0.934454 0.6029% 1936
1.063731 0.940087 0.5244% 1935 1.058182 0.945017 -3.0364% 1934 1.091318 0.916323
4.6271% 1933 1.043055 0.958722 1.3921% 1932 1.028734 0.972069 -0.2051% 1931
1.030848 0.970075 0.8886% 1930 1.021768 0.978695 1.0126% 1929 1.011526 0.988605
1.1526% 1928 1.000000 1.000000 1.2160% 1927 0.987986 1.012160 1.4086% 1926 0.974263
1.026417 1.7667% 1925 0.957349 1.044551 1.4465% 1924 0.943699 1.059660 1.7700% 1923
0.927286 1.078416 1.6165% 1922 0.912535 1.095849 1.3736% 1921 0.900170 1.110902
2.3393% 1920 0.879593 1.136889 1.3140% 1919 0.868185 1.151828 0.7676% 1918 0.861571
1.160670 0.3870% 1917 0.858250 1.165162 1.3274% 1916 0.847007 1.180628 1.4083% 1915
0.835244 1.197255 1.4458% 1914 0.823340 1.214565 1.9424% 1913 0.807652 1.238156
1.9857% 1912 0.791927 1.262742 1.5634% 1911 0.779737 1.282484 1.8169% 1910 0.765822
1.305786 1.8781% 1909 0.751705 1.330309 2.0082% 1908 0.736906 1.357025 1.9603% 1907
0.722739 1.383626 1.8264% 1906 0.709776 1.408896 1.9357% 1905 0.696298 1.436168
2.0148% 1904 0.682545 1.465104 2.1335% 1903 0.668287 1.496362 1.8151% 1902 0.656373
1.523524 1.8943% 1901 0.644170 1.552384 3.0255% 1900 0.625253 1.599352 0.6278% 1899
0.621352 1.609393 1.7757% 1898 0.610512 1.637970 1.8078% 1897 0.599671 1.667581

1.8396% 1896 0.588839 1.698258 1.8755% 1895 0.577998 1.730109 1.9114% 1894 0.567158
1.763178 1.9486% 1893 0.556317 1.797536 1.9858% 1892 0.545485 1.833232 2.0276% 1891
0.534644 1.870403 2.6465% 1890 0.520860 1.919903 1.5328% 1889 0.512996 1.949332
2.0811% 1888 0.502538 1.989900 2.1599% 1887 0.491913 2.032879 2.2075% 1886 0.481289
2.077756 2.2592% 1885 0.470656 2.124696 2.3095% 1884 0.460031 2.173766 2.3641% 1883
0.449406 2.225157 2.4214% 1882 0.438782 2.279037 2.4815% 1881 0.428157 2.335590
3.7644% 1880 0.412624 2.423511 0.9432% 1879 0.408769 2.446371 2.1464% 1878 0.400179
2.498879 2.1913% 1877 0.391598 2.553637 2.2426% 1876 0.383009 2.610905 2.2941% 1875
0.374420 2.670801 2.3456% 1874 0.365838 2.733447 2.4043% 1873 0.357249 2.799168
2.4635% 1872 0.348660 2.868126 2.5258% 1871 0.340070 2.940569 5.9947% 1870 0.320837
3.116846 -1.0968% 1869 0.324395 3.082661 2.1930% 1868 0.317434 3.150263 2.2394%
1867 0.310481 3.220810 2.2935% 1866 0.303520 3.294680 2.3445% 1865 0.296567 3.371922
2.4037% 1864 0.289606 3.452973 2.4599% 1863 0.282653 3.537912 2.5250% 1862 0.275691
3.627245 2.5872% 1861 0.268738 3.721091 2.9504% 1860 0.261037 3.830878 2.4012% 1859
0.254916 3.922866 2.7627% 1858 0.248062 4.031244 2.8412% 1857 0.241209 4.145780
2.9243% 1856 0.234356 4.267014 3.0161% 1855 0.227494 4.395713 3.1061% 1854 0.220641
4.532247 3.2056% 1853 0.213788 4.677533 3.3118% 1852 0.206935 4.832443 3.4252% 1851
0.200081 4.997966 4.0106% 1850 0.192366 5.198414 2.3254% 1849 0.187995 5.319297
2.7841% 1848 0.182903 5.467390 2.8590% 1847 0.177819 5.623704 2.9432% 1846 0.172735
5.789218 3.0324% 1845 0.167651 5.964771 3.1325% 1844 0.162559 6.151617 3.2284% 1843
0.157475 6.350214 3.3361% 1842 0.152391 6.562061 3.4512% 1841 0.147307 6.788530
3.8105% 1840 0.141900 7.047206 2.3861% 1839 0.138593 7.215356 2.5824% 1838 0.135104
7.401685 2.6573% 1837 0.131607 7.598372 2.7232% 1836 0.128118 7.805291 2.7994% 1835
0.124629 8.023795 2.8871% 1834 0.121132 8.255452 2.9657% 1833 0.117643 8.500282
3.0563% 1832 0.114154 8.760079 3.1604% 1831 0.110657 9.036934 3.4660% 1830 0.106950
9.350151 2.4653% 1829 0.104377 9.580661 2.6804% 1828 0.101652 9.837460 10.3427%
1827 0.092124 10.854914 -4.2314% 1826 0.096195 10.395596 2.9150% 1825 0.093470
10.698631 3.0026% 1824 0.090745 11.019865 3.0955% 1823 0.088021 11.360985 3.1944%
1822 0.085296 11.723899 3.3102% 1821 0.082563 12.111983 3.2277% 1820 0.079981
12.502926 2.6573% 1819 0.077911 12.835164 2.6261% 1818 0.075917 13.172229 2.6969%
1817 0.073924 13.527475 2.7717% 1816 0.071930 13.902414 2.8507% 1815 0.069936
14.298729 2.9343% 1814 0.067943 14.718303 3.0231% 1813 0.065949 15.163245 3.1039%
1812 0.063964 15.633896 3.2172% 1811 0.061970 16.136863 3.0969% 1810 0.060108
16.636608 2.9144% 1809 0.058406 17.121462 2.8225% 1808 0.056803 17.604709 2.9199%
1807 0.055191 18.118754 2.9918% 1806 0.053588 18.660828 3.0841% 1805 0.051985
19.236337 3.1822% 1804 0.050382 19.848475 3.2868% 1803 0.048778 20.500851 3.3985%
1802 0.047175 21.197570 3.5180% 1801 0.045572 21.943310 3.3999% 1800 0.044073
22.689371 2.8419% 1799 0.042856 23.334173 2.7485% 1798 0.041709 23.975503 2.8261%
1797 0.040563 24.653082 3.7832% 1796 0.039084 25.585760 2.1272% 1795 0.038270
26.130020 3.0879% 1794 0.037124 26.936899 3.1625% 1793 0.035986 27.788781 3.2904%
1792 0.034839 28.703147 3.4024% 1791 0.033693 29.679734 3.2296% 1790 0.032639
30.638260 41.3145% 1780 0.023097 43.296288 29.4353% 1770 0.017844 56.040687
83.4728% 1750 0.009726 102.819440 29.2845% 1740 0.007523 132.929549 94.2514% 1720
0.003873 258.217503 85.8111% 1700 0.002084 479.796732 19.2490% 1690 0.001748
572.153042 88.0250% 1670 0.000930 1075.790885

BASE YEAR: 1927

YEAR BYEAR/AYEAR AYEAR/BYEAR GROWTH%

2009 2.534418 0.394568 8.2857% 2001 2.340493 0.427260 1.0000% 2000 2.317319
0.431533 1.0000% 1999 2.294375 0.435848 1.0000% 1998 2.271659 0.440207 1.0000% 1997
2.249167 0.444609 1.0000% 1996 2.226898 0.449055 1.0000% 1995 2.204850 0.453546
0.9992% 1994 2.183036 0.458078 1.0008% 1993 2.161405 0.462662 1.0000% 1992 2.140005
0.467289 0.9295% 1991 2.120297 0.471632 1.2505% 1990 2.094110 0.477530 0.7224% 1989
2.079090 0.480980 1.1077% 1988 2.056312 0.486307 0.8834% 1987 2.038307 0.490603
0.5594% 1986 2.026969 0.493348 1.3056% 1985 2.000845 0.499789 0.7673% 1984 1.985610
0.503624 0.8149% 1983 1.969559 0.507728 0.9737% 1982 1.950565 0.512672 0.9508% 1981
1.932194 0.517546 0.9031% 1980 1.914901 0.522220 2.2701% 1979 1.872396 0.534075

1.0042% 1978 1.853781 0.539438 0.9896% 1977 1.835616 0.544776 0.9103% 1976 1.819056 0.549736 0.8394% 1975 1.803913 0.554350 0.9042% 1974 1.787749 0.559363 1.1568% 1973 1.767305 0.565833 0.9427% 1972 1.750800 0.571167 0.7426% 1971 1.737894 0.575409 1.4697% 1970 1.712722 0.583866 0.6968% 1969 1.700870 0.587935 0.8565% 1968 1.686425 0.592970 1.5090% 1967 1.661354 0.601919 0.9949% 1966 1.644988 0.607907 1.0575% 1965 1.627775 0.614336 1.1300% 1964 1.609586 0.621278 1.5537% 1963 1.584962 0.630930 1.4658% 1962 1.562064 0.640178 1.5364% 1961 1.538428 0.650014 2.1586% 1960 1.505920 0.664046 -1.6655% 1959 1.531426 0.652986 4.3080% 1958 1.468177 0.681117 2.1130% 1957 1.437797 0.695509 1.9895% 1956 1.409750 0.709346 2.1231% 1955 1.380442 0.724406 1.4496% 1954 1.360717 0.734907 2.1573% 1953 1.331982 0.750761 1.2298% 1952 1.315801 0.759993 1.6814% 1951 1.294044 0.772771 1.6233% 1950 1.273373 0.785316 1.4265% 1949 1.255464 0.796519 1.7790% 1948 1.233519 0.810689 1.8242% 1947 1.211421 0.825477 -2.6320% 1946 1.244167 0.803750 3.1768% 1945 1.205860 0.829284 6.4754% 1944 1.132524 0.882983 -0.3437% 1943 1.136430 0.879949 0.6562% 1942 1.129021 0.885723 0.6633% 1941 1.121581 0.891598 -5.6614% 1940 1.188889 0.841121 8.0381% 1939 1.100435 0.908731 0.8126% 1938 1.091565 0.916116 0.7762% 1937 1.083157 0.923227 0.6029% 1936 1.076666 0.928793 0.5244% 1935 1.071049 0.933664 -3.0364% 1934 1.104589 0.905314 4.6271% 1933 1.055739 0.947204 1.3921% 1932 1.041243 0.960390 -0.2051% 1931 1.043383 0.958421 0.8886% 1930 1.034193 0.966937 1.0126% 1929 1.023826 0.976728 1.1526% 1928 1.012160 0.987986 1.2160% 1927 1.000000 1.000000 1.4086% 1926 0.986110 1.014086 1.7667% 1925 0.968991 1.032002 1.4465% 1924 0.955174 1.046929 1.7700% 1923 0.938562 1.065460 1.6165% 1922 0.923631 1.082683 1.3736% 1921 0.911116 1.097555 2.3393% 1920 0.890289 1.123231 1.3140% 1919 0.878742 1.137990 0.7676% 1918 0.872048 1.146726 0.3870% 1917 0.868686 1.151163 1.3274% 1916 0.857306 1.166444 1.4083% 1915 0.845401 1.182871 1.4458% 1914 0.833352 1.199973 1.9424% 1913 0.817473 1.223281 1.9857% 1912 0.801557 1.247572 1.5634% 1911 0.789218 1.267076 1.8169% 1910 0.775135 1.290098 1.8781% 1909 0.760846 1.314327 2.0082% 1908 0.745867 1.340722 1.9603% 1907 0.731527 1.367003 1.8264% 1906 0.718407 1.391970 1.9357% 1905 0.704765 1.418914 2.0148% 1904 0.690845 1.447502 2.1335% 1903 0.676414 1.478385 1.8151% 1902 0.664355 1.505220 1.8943% 1901 0.652003 1.533734 3.0255% 1900 0.632856 1.580137 0.6278% 1899 0.628908 1.590058 1.7757% 1898 0.617935 1.618292 1.8078% 1897 0.606963 1.647547 1.8396% 1896 0.595999 1.677855 1.8755% 1895 0.585027 1.709324 1.9114% 1894 0.574054 1.741996 1.9486% 1893 0.563082 1.775941 1.9858% 1892 0.552118 1.811207 2.0276% 1891 0.541145 1.847932 2.6465% 1890 0.527193 1.896838 1.5328% 1889 0.519234 1.925913 2.0811% 1888 0.508649 1.965994 2.1599% 1887 0.497895 2.008456 2.2075% 1886 0.487141 2.052794 2.2592% 1885 0.476379 2.099170 2.3095% 1884 0.465625 2.147651 2.3641% 1883 0.454871 2.198424 2.4214% 1882 0.444117 2.251657 2.4815% 1881 0.433364 2.307531 3.7644% 1880 0.417642 2.394395 0.9432% 1879 0.413739 2.416980 2.1464% 1878 0.405046 2.468858 2.1913% 1877 0.396360 2.522958 2.2426% 1876 0.387666 2.579538 2.2941% 1875 0.378973 2.638714 2.3456% 1874 0.370287 2.700607 2.4043% 1873 0.361593 2.765539 2.4635% 1872 0.352899 2.833669 2.5258% 1871 0.344206 2.905241 5.9947% 1870 0.324739 3.079401 -1.0968% 1869 0.328340 3.045626 2.1930% 1868 0.321294 3.112416 2.2394% 1867 0.314256 3.182116 2.2935% 1866 0.307210 3.255097 2.3445% 1865 0.300173 3.331412 2.4037% 1864 0.293127 3.411489 2.4599% 1863 0.286090 3.495408 2.5250% 1862 0.279044 3.583667 2.5872% 1861 0.272006 3.676386 2.9504% 1860 0.264211 3.784854 2.4012% 1859 0.258015 3.875737 2.7627% 1858 0.251079 3.982813 2.8412% 1857 0.244142 4.095972 2.9243% 1856 0.237206 4.215750 3.0161% 1855 0.230261 4.342903 3.1061% 1854 0.223324 4.477796 3.2056% 1853 0.216388 4.621338 3.3118% 1852 0.209451 4.774387 3.4252% 1851 0.202514 4.937920 4.0106% 1850 0.194706 5.135961 2.3254% 1849 0.190281 5.255391 2.7841% 1848 0.185127 5.401705 2.8590% 1847 0.179981 5.556141 2.9432% 1846 0.174835 5.719667 3.0324% 1845 0.169690 5.893110 3.1325% 1844 0.164536 6.077712 3.2284% 1843 0.159390 6.273923 3.3361% 1842 0.154244 6.483224 3.4512% 1841 0.149099 6.706973 3.8105% 1840 0.143626 6.962541 2.3861% 1839 0.140279 7.128671 2.5824% 1838 0.136747 7.312761 2.6573% 1837 0.133207 7.507085 2.7232% 1836 0.129676 7.711519 2.7994% 1835 0.126145 7.927398 2.8871% 1834 0.122605 8.156271 2.9657% 1833 0.119074 8.398161 3.0563% 1832 0.115542 8.654836 3.1604% 1831 0.112003 8.928365 3.4660% 1830 0.108251

121

9.237819 2.4653% 1829 0.105646 9.465559 2.6804% 1828 0.102888 9.719274 10.3427%
1827 0.093244 10.724504 -4.2314% 1826 0.097364 10.270704 2.9150% 1825 0.094606
10.570099 3.0026% 1824 0.091849 10.887473 3.0955% 1823 0.089091 11.224495 3.1944%
1822 0.086333 11.583049 3.3102% 1821 0.083567 11.966470 3.2277% 1820 0.080954
12.352717 2.6573% 1819 0.078858 12.680963 2.6261% 1818 0.076840 13.013979 2.6969%
1817 0.074823 13.364957 2.7717% 1816 0.072805 13.735391 2.8507% 1815 0.070787
14.126945 2.9343% 1814 0.068769 14.541478 3.0231% 1813 0.066751 14.981074 3.1039%
1812 0.064741 15.446071 3.2172% 1811 0.062723 15.942996 3.0969% 1810 0.060839
16.436737 2.9144% 1809 0.059116 16.915766 2.8225% 1808 0.057494 17.393207 2.9199%
1807 0.055863 17.901076 2.9918% 1806 0.054240 18.436638 3.0841% 1805 0.052617
19.005233 3.1822% 1804 0.050994 19.610016 3.2868% 1803 0.049372 20.254556 3.3985%
1802 0.047749 20.942904 3.5180% 1801 0.046126 21.679685 3.3999% 1800 0.044609
22.416782 2.8419% 1799 0.043377 23.053838 2.7485% 1798 0.042216 23.687463 2.8261%
1797 0.041056 24.356901 3.7832% 1796 0.039560 25.278374 2.1272% 1795 0.038736
25.816095 3.0879% 1794 0.037575 26.613280 3.1625% 1793 0.036423 27.454928 3.2904%
1792 0.035263 28.358309 3.4024% 1791 0.034103 29.323163 3.2296% 1790 0.033036
30.270173 41.3145% 1780 0.023378 42.776129 29.4353% 1770 0.018061 55.367418
83.4728% 1750 0.009844 101.584173 29.2845% 1740 0.007614 131.332542 94.2514% 1720
0.003920 255.115294 85.8111% 1700 0.002110 474.032483 19.2490% 1690 0.001769
565.279230 88.0250% 1670 0.000941 1062.866399

BASE YEAR: 1926

YEAR BYEAR/AYEAR AYEAR/BYEAR GROWTH%

2009 2.570117 0.389087 8.2857% 2001 2.373460 0.421326 1.0000% 2000 2.349960
0.425539 1.0000% 1999 2.326694 0.429794 1.0000% 1998 2.303657 0.434092 1.0000% 1997
2.280848 0.438433 1.0000% 1996 2.258266 0.442818 1.0000% 1995 2.235907 0.447246
0.9992% 1994 2.213786 0.451715 1.0008% 1993 2.191851 0.456235 1.0000% 1992 2.170149
0.460798 0.9295% 1991 2.150163 0.465081 1.2505% 1990 2.123607 0.470897 0.7224% 1989
2.108375 0.474299 1.1077% 1988 2.085277 0.479553 0.8834% 1987 2.067018 0.483789
0.5594% 1986 2.055520 0.486495 1.3056% 1985 2.029029 0.492847 0.7673% 1984 2.013579
0.496628 0.8149% 1983 1.997302 0.500675 0.9737% 1982 1.978041 0.505551 0.9508% 1981
1.959410 0.510358 0.9031% 1980 1.941874 0.514966 2.2701% 1979 1.898771 0.526657
1.0042% 1978 1.879893 0.531945 0.9896% 1977 1.861472 0.537209 0.9103% 1976 1.844679
0.542100 0.8394% 1975 1.829323 0.546650 0.9042% 1974 1.812931 0.551593 1.1568% 1973
1.792199 0.557974 0.9427% 1972 1.775462 0.563234 0.7426% 1971 1.762374 0.567417
1.4697% 1970 1.736847 0.575756 0.6968% 1969 1.724828 0.579768 0.8565% 1968 1.710179
0.584734 1.5090% 1967 1.684756 0.593558 0.9949% 1966 1.668159 0.599463 1.0575% 1965
1.650703 0.605802 1.1300% 1964 1.632259 0.612648 1.5537% 1963 1.607287 0.622166
1.4658% 1962 1.584067 0.631286 1.5364% 1961 1.560098 0.640986 2.1586% 1960 1.527132
0.654822 -1.6655% 1959 1.552997 0.643916 4.3080% 1958 1.488857 0.671656 2.1130%
1957 1.458049 0.685848 1.9895% 1956 1.429607 0.699493 2.1231% 1955 1.399886 0.714344
1.4496% 1954 1.379884 0.724699 2.1573% 1953 1.350745 0.740332 1.2298% 1952 1.334335
0.749437 1.6814% 1951 1.312271 0.762038 1.6233% 1950 1.291310 0.774408 1.4265% 1949
1.273148 0.785455 1.7790% 1948 1.250894 0.799428 1.8242% 1947 1.228484 0.814011 -
2.6320% 1946 1.261693 0.792586 3.1768% 1945 1.222845 0.817765 6.4754% 1944 1.148477
0.870719 -0.3437% 1943 1.152437 0.867726 0.6562% 1942 1.144924 0.873420 0.6633%
1941 1.137380 0.879214 -5.6614% 1940 1.205636 0.829438 8.0381% 1939 1.115936
0.896109 0.8126% 1938 1.106940 0.903391 0.7762% 1937 1.098414 0.910403 0.6029% 1936
1.091832 0.915892 0.5244% 1935 1.086136 0.920695 -3.0364% 1934 1.120148 0.892739
4.6271% 1933 1.070609 0.934047 1.3921% 1932 1.055910 0.947050 -0.2051% 1931
1.058080 0.945108 0.8886% 1930 1.048761 0.953506 1.0126% 1929 1.038248 0.963161
1.1526% 1928 1.026417 0.974263 1.2160% 1927 1.014086 0.986110 1.4086% 1926 1.000000
1.000000 1.7667% 1925 0.982640 1.017667 1.4465% 1924 0.968629 1.032387 1.7700% 1923
0.951782 1.050660 1.6165% 1922 0.936641 1.067645 1.3736% 1921 0.923950 1.082310
2.3393% 1920 0.902830 1.107629 1.3140% 1919 0.891120 1.122183 0.7676% 1918 0.884332
1.130798 0.3870% 1917 0.880923 1.135174 1.3274% 1916 0.869382 1.150242 1.4083% 1915
0.857309 1.166441 1.4458% 1914 0.845090 1.183305 1.9424% 1913 0.828988 1.206290

122

1.9857% 1912 0.812848 1.230243 1.5634% 1911 0.800335 1.249476 1.8169% 1910 0.786053
1.272178 1.8781% 1909 0.771563 1.296071 2.0082% 1908 0.756373 1.322099 1.9603% 1907
0.741831 1.348015 1.8264% 1906 0.728526 1.372635 1.9357% 1905 0.714692 1.399205
2.0148% 1904 0.700576 1.427396 2.1335% 1903 0.685942 1.457850 1.8151% 1902 0.673713
1.484312 1.8943% 1901 0.661187 1.512430 3.0255% 1900 0.641771 1.558189 0.6278% 1899
0.637767 1.567972 1.7757% 1898 0.626640 1.595814 1.8078% 1897 0.615513 1.624662
1.8396% 1896 0.604394 1.654549 1.8755% 1895 0.593267 1.685581 1.9114% 1894 0.582140
1.717799 1.9486% 1893 0.571013 1.751273 1.9858% 1892 0.559895 1.786050 2.0276% 1891
0.548768 1.822264 2.6465% 1890 0.534619 1.870490 1.5328% 1889 0.526548 1.899162
2.0811% 1888 0.515813 1.938686 2.1599% 1887 0.504908 1.980558 2.2075% 1886 0.494003
2.024280 2.2592% 1885 0.483089 2.070012 2.3095% 1884 0.472184 2.117820 2.3641% 1883
0.461278 2.167888 2.4214% 1882 0.450373 2.220381 2.4815% 1881 0.439468 2.275479
3.7644% 1880 0.423525 2.361137 0.9432% 1879 0.419567 2.383408 2.1464% 1878 0.410751
2.434565 2.1913% 1877 0.401943 2.487913 2.2426% 1876 0.393127 2.543708 2.2941% 1875
0.384311 2.602062 2.3456% 1874 0.375503 2.663096 2.4043% 1873 0.366687 2.727125
2.4635% 1872 0.357870 2.794309 2.5258% 1871 0.349054 2.864887 5.9947% 1870 0.329313
3.036627 -1.0968% 1869 0.332965 3.003322 2.1930% 1868 0.325820 3.069184 2.2394%
1867 0.318683 3.137915 2.2935% 1866 0.311538 3.209884 2.3445% 1865 0.304401 3.285138
2.4037% 1864 0.297256 3.364103 2.4599% 1863 0.290119 3.446856 2.5250% 1862 0.282974
3.533890 2.5872% 1861 0.275838 3.625320 2.9504% 1860 0.267933 3.732282 2.4012% 1859
0.261650 3.821903 2.7627% 1858 0.254615 3.927491 2.8412% 1857 0.247581 4.039079
2.9243% 1856 0.240544 4.157193 3.0161% 1855 0.233504 4.282580 3.1061% 1854 0.226470
4.415599 3.2056% 1853 0.219436 4.557147 3.3118% 1852 0.212401 4.708070 3.4252% 1851
0.205367 4.869332 4.0106% 1850 0.197448 5.064622 2.3254% 1849 0.192961 5.182393
2.7841% 1848 0.187734 5.326675 2.8590% 1847 0.182516 5.478965 2.9432% 1846 0.177298
5.640220 3.0324% 1845 0.172080 5.811254 3.1325% 1844 0.166853 5.993292 3.2284% 1843
0.161635 6.186777 3.3361% 1842 0.156417 6.393171 3.4512% 1841 0.151199 6.613812
3.8105% 1840 0.145649 6.865830 2.3861% 1839 0.142255 7.029653 2.5824% 1838 0.138673
7.211186 2.6573% 1837 0.135084 7.402811 2.7232% 1836 0.131503 7.604404 2.7994% 1835
0.127922 7.817285 2.8871% 1834 0.124332 8.042979 2.9657% 1833 0.120751 8.281509
3.0563% 1832 0.117170 8.534618 3.1604% 1831 0.113580 8.804349 3.4660% 1830 0.109775
9.109504 2.4653% 1829 0.107134 9.334081 2.6804% 1828 0.104338 9.584271 10.3427%
1827 0.094558 10.575539 -4.2314% 1826 0.098736 10.128042 2.9150% 1825 0.095939
10.423278 3.0026% 1824 0.093142 10.736244 3.0955% 1823 0.090346 11.068585 3.1944%
1822 0.087549 11.422159 3.3102% 1821 0.084744 11.800254 3.2277% 1820 0.082094
12.181136 2.6573% 1819 0.079969 12.504822 2.6261% 1818 0.077923 12.833212 2.6969%
1817 0.075876 13.179315 2.7717% 1816 0.073830 13.544604 2.8507% 1815 0.071784
13.930719 2.9343% 1814 0.069737 14.339495 3.0231% 1813 0.067691 14.772985 3.1039%
1812 0.065653 15.231523 3.2172% 1811 0.063607 15.721545 3.0969% 1810 0.061696
16.208428 2.9144% 1809 0.059949 16.680803 2.8225% 1808 0.058304 17.151613 2.9199%
1807 0.056649 17.652427 2.9918% 1806 0.055004 18.180550 3.0841% 1805 0.053358
18.741248 3.1822% 1804 0.051713 19.337630 3.2868% 1803 0.050067 19.973216 3.3985%
1802 0.048421 20.652003 3.5180% 1801 0.046776 21.378550 3.3999% 1800 0.045238
22.105410 2.8419% 1799 0.043988 22.733616 2.7485% 1798 0.042811 23.358440 2.8261%
1797 0.041634 24.018580 3.7832% 1796 0.040117 24.927253 2.1272% 1795 0.039281
25.457505 3.0879% 1794 0.038105 26.243618 3.1625% 1793 0.036936 27.073575 3.2904%
1792 0.035760 27.964408 3.4024% 1791 0.034583 28.915860 3.2296% 1790 0.033501
29.849716 41.3145% 1780 0.023707 42.181962 29.4353% 1770 0.018316 54.598355
83.4728% 1750 0.009983 100.173153 29.2845% 1740 0.007722 129.508312 94.2514% 1720
0.003975 251.571701 85.8111% 1700 0.002139 467.448095 19.2490% 1690 0.001794
557.427410 88.0250% 1670 0.000954 1048.103012

BASE YEAR: 1925

YEAR BYEAR/AYEAR AYEAR/BYEAR GROWTH%

2009 2.615523 0.382333 8.2857% 2001 2.415392 0.414011 1.0000% 2000 2.391477
0.418152 1.0000% 1999 2.367799 0.422333 1.0000% 1998 2.344355 0.426556 1.0000% 1997
2.321144 0.430822 1.0000% 1996 2.298162 0.435130 1.0000% 1995 2.275408 0.439482

123

0.9992% 1994 2.252897 0.443873 1.0008% 1993 2.230574 0.448315 1.0000% 1992 2.208489
0.452798 0.9295% 1991 2.188150 0.457007 1.2505% 1990 2.161125 0.462722 0.7224% 1989
2.145624 0.466065 1.1077% 1988 2.122118 0.471227 0.8834% 1987 2.103536 0.475390
0.5594% 1986 2.091835 0.478049 1.3056% 1985 2.064875 0.484291 0.7673% 1984 2.049152
0.488007 0.8149% 1983 2.032588 0.491984 0.9737% 1982 2.012986 0.496774 0.9508% 1981
1.994027 0.501498 0.9031% 1980 1.976181 0.506027 2.2701% 1979 1.932316 0.517514
1.0042% 1978 1.913105 0.522710 0.9896% 1977 1.894358 0.527883 0.9103% 1976 1.877269
0.532689 0.8394% 1975 1.861641 0.537160 0.9042% 1974 1.844960 0.542017 1.1568% 1973
1.823862 0.548287 0.9427% 1972 1.806829 0.553456 0.7426% 1971 1.793509 0.557566
1.4697% 1970 1.767531 0.565761 0.6968% 1969 1.755300 0.569703 0.8565% 1968 1.740393
0.574583 1.5090% 1967 1.714520 0.583254 0.9949% 1966 1.697630 0.589056 1.0575% 1965
1.679866 0.595286 1.1300% 1964 1.661096 0.602012 1.5537% 1963 1.635683 0.611366
1.4658% 1962 1.612053 0.620327 1.5364% 1961 1.587660 0.629858 2.1586% 1960 1.554112
0.643454 -1.6655% 1959 1.580434 0.632738 4.3080% 1958 1.515161 0.659996 2.1130%
1957 1.483808 0.673941 1.9895% 1956 1.454864 0.687349 2.1231% 1955 1.424618 0.701943
1.4496% 1954 1.404262 0.712118 2.1573% 1953 1.374608 0.727480 1.2298% 1952 1.357909
0.736426 1.6814% 1951 1.335455 0.748808 1.6233% 1950 1.314123 0.760964 1.4265% 1949
1.295640 0.771819 1.7790% 1948 1.272993 0.785550 1.8242% 1947 1.250188 0.799880 -
2.6320% 1946 1.283983 0.778827 3.1768% 1945 1.244449 0.803568 6.4754% 1944 1.168767
0.855603 -0.3437% 1943 1.172797 0.852662 0.6562% 1942 1.165151 0.858258 0.6633%
1941 1.157474 0.863951 -5.6614% 1940 1.226936 0.815039 8.0381% 1939 1.135651
0.880552 0.8126% 1938 1.126497 0.887708 0.7762% 1937 1.117820 0.894599 0.6029% 1936
1.111121 0.899992 0.5244% 1935 1.105325 0.904712 -3.0364% 1934 1.139937 0.877241
4.6271% 1933 1.089524 0.917832 1.3921% 1932 1.074565 0.930609 -0.2051% 1931
1.076773 0.928701 0.8886% 1930 1.067289 0.936953 1.0126% 1929 1.056590 0.946441
1.1526% 1928 1.044551 0.957349 1.2160% 1927 1.032002 0.968991 1.4086% 1926 1.017667
0.982640 1.7667% 1925 1.000000 1.000000 1.4465% 1924 0.985741 1.014465 1.7700% 1923
0.968597 1.032421 1.6165% 1922 0.953189 1.049110 1.3736% 1921 0.940273 1.063521
2.3393% 1920 0.918780 1.088400 1.3140% 1919 0.906863 1.102702 0.7676% 1918 0.899955
1.111167 0.3870% 1917 0.896486 1.115467 1.3274% 1916 0.884741 1.130274 1.4083% 1915
0.872455 1.146191 1.4458% 1914 0.860020 1.162763 1.9424% 1913 0.843634 1.185348
1.9857% 1912 0.827208 1.208885 1.5634% 1911 0.814475 1.227785 1.8169% 1910 0.799940
1.250093 1.8781% 1909 0.785194 1.273571 2.0082% 1908 0.769736 1.299147 1.9603% 1907
0.754937 1.324614 1.8264% 1906 0.741397 1.348806 1.9357% 1905 0.727318 1.374914
2.0148% 1904 0.712953 1.402616 2.1335% 1903 0.698060 1.432542 1.8151% 1902 0.685615
1.458544 1.8943% 1901 0.672869 1.486174 3.0255% 1900 0.653109 1.531139 0.6278% 1899
0.649034 1.540752 1.7757% 1898 0.637710 1.568110 1.8078% 1897 0.626387 1.596458
1.8396% 1896 0.615072 1.625826 1.8755% 1895 0.603748 1.656319 1.9114% 1894 0.592425
1.687978 1.9486% 1893 0.581101 1.720870 1.9858% 1892 0.569786 1.755043 2.0276% 1891
0.558463 1.790629 2.6465% 1890 0.544064 1.838018 1.5328% 1889 0.535851 1.866192
2.0811% 1888 0.524926 1.905030 2.1599% 1887 0.513828 1.946176 2.2075% 1886 0.502730
1.989138 2.2592% 1885 0.491624 2.034076 2.3095% 1884 0.480526 2.081054 2.3641% 1883
0.469428 2.130253 2.4214% 1882 0.458330 2.181834 2.4815% 1881 0.447232 2.235976
3.7644% 1880 0.431007 2.320147 0.9432% 1879 0.426980 2.342031 2.1464% 1878 0.418008
2.392300 2.1913% 1877 0.409044 2.444723 2.2426% 1876 0.400072 2.499548 2.2941% 1875
0.391100 2.556889 2.3456% 1874 0.382137 2.616864 2.4043% 1873 0.373165 2.679781
2.4635% 1872 0.364193 2.745799 2.5258% 1871 0.355221 2.815152 5.9947% 1870 0.335131
2.983911 -1.0968% 1869 0.338847 2.951184 2.1930% 1868 0.331576 3.015902 2.2394%
1867 0.324313 3.083441 2.2935% 1866 0.317042 3.154160 2.3445% 1865 0.309779 3.228108
2.4037% 1864 0.302508 3.305702 2.4599% 1863 0.295245 3.387018 2.5250% 1862 0.287974
3.472541 2.5872% 1861 0.280711 3.562384 2.9504% 1860 0.272666 3.667489 2.4012% 1859
0.266272 3.755554 2.7627% 1858 0.259114 3.859309 2.8412% 1857 0.251955 3.968960
2.9243% 1856 0.244797 4.085023 3.0161% 1855 0.237629 4.208233 3.1061% 1854 0.230471
4.338944 3.2056% 1853 0.223312 4.478034 3.3118% 1852 0.216154 4.626337 3.4252% 1851
0.208995 4.784799 4.0106% 1850 0.200936 4.976699 2.3254% 1849 0.196370 5.092425
2.7841% 1848 0.191051 5.234203 2.8590% 1847 0.185741 5.383849 2.9432% 1846 0.180430

5.542305 3.0324% 1845 0.175120 5.710370 3.1325% 1844 0.169801 5.889247 3.2284% 1843 0.164491 6.079373 3.3361% 1842 0.159180 6.282185 3.4512% 1841 0.153870 6.498995 3.8105% 1840 0.148222 6.746639 2.3861% 1839 0.144768 6.907617 2.5824% 1838 0.141123 7.085999 2.6573% 1837 0.137470 7.274297 2.7232% 1836 0.133826 7.472391 2.7994% 1835 0.130182 7.681576 2.8871% 1834 0.126529 7.903352 2.9657% 1833 0.122884 8.137740 3.0563% 1832 0.119240 8.386456 3.1604% 1831 0.115587 8.651504 3.4660% 1830 0.111715 8.951362 2.4653% 1829 0.109027 9.172040 2.6804% 1828 0.106181 9.417887 10.3427% 1827 0.096228 10.391946 -4.2314% 1826 0.100480 9.952218 2.9150% 1825 0.097634 10.242328 3.0026% 1824 0.094788 10.549861 3.0955% 1823 0.091942 10.876433 3.1944% 1822 0.089096 11.223868 3.3102% 1821 0.086241 11.595400 3.2277% 1820 0.083544 11.969669 2.6573% 1819 0.081382 12.287736 2.6261% 1818 0.079299 12.610426 2.6969% 1817 0.077217 12.950520 2.7717% 1816 0.075134 13.309468 2.8507% 1815 0.073052 13.688880 2.9343% 1814 0.070970 14.090559 3.0231% 1813 0.068887 14.516523 3.1039% 1812 0.066813 14.967101 3.2172% 1811 0.064731 15.448617 3.0969% 1810 0.062786 15.927047 2.9144% 1809 0.061008 16.391222 2.8225% 1808 0.059334 16.853858 2.9199% 1807 0.057650 17.345978 2.9918% 1806 0.055976 17.864933 3.0841% 1805 0.054301 18.415896 3.1822% 1804 0.052626 19.001926 3.2868% 1803 0.050952 19.626478 3.3985% 1802 0.049277 20.293481 3.5180% 1801 0.047602 21.007415 3.3999% 1800 0.046037 21.721656 2.8419% 1799 0.044765 22.338957 2.7485% 1798 0.043567 22.952934 2.8261% 1797 0.042370 23.601614 3.7832% 1796 0.040825 24.494512 2.1272% 1795 0.039975 25.015559 3.0879% 1794 0.038778 25.788024 3.1625% 1793 0.037589 26.603573 3.2904% 1792 0.036392 27.478941 3.4024% 1791 0.035194 28.413876 3.2296% 1790 0.034093 29.331520 41.3145% 1780 0.024126 41.449676 29.4353% 1770 0.018639 53.650519 83.4728% 1750 0.010159 98.434131 29.2845% 1740 0.007858 127.260027 94.2514% 1720 0.004045 247.204376 85.8111% 1700 0.002177 459.333121 19.2490% 1690 0.001826 547.750380 88.0250% 1670 0.000971 1029.907775

BASE YEAR: 1924

YEAR BYEAR/AYEAR AYEAR/BYEAR GROWTH%

2009 2.653357 0.376881 8.2857% 2001 2.450331 0.408108 1.0000% 2000 2.426070 0.412189 1.0000% 1999 2.402049 0.416311 1.0000% 1998 2.378267 0.420474 1.0000% 1997 2.354719 0.424679 1.0000% 1996 2.331405 0.428926 1.0000% 1995 2.308322 0.433215 0.9992% 1994 2.285485 0.437544 1.0008% 1993 2.262839 0.441923 1.0000% 1992 2.240435 0.446342 0.9295% 1991 2.219801 0.450491 1.2505% 1990 2.192385 0.456124 0.7224% 1989 2.176660 0.459419 1.1077% 1988 2.152814 0.464508 0.8834% 1987 2.133963 0.468612 0.5594% 1986 2.122093 0.471233 1.3056% 1985 2.094744 0.477385 0.7673% 1984 2.078793 0.481048 0.8149% 1983 2.061989 0.484969 0.9737% 1982 2.042104 0.489691 0.9508% 1981 2.022871 0.494347 0.9031% 1980 2.004766 0.498811 2.2701% 1979 1.960267 0.510135 1.0042% 1978 1.940778 0.515257 0.9896% 1977 1.921760 0.520356 0.9103% 1976 1.904424 0.525093 0.8394% 1975 1.888570 0.529501 0.9042% 1974 1.871647 0.534289 1.1568% 1973 1.850244 0.540469 0.9427% 1972 1.832964 0.545564 0.7426% 1971 1.819453 0.549616 1.4697% 1970 1.793059 0.557694 0.6968% 1969 1.780691 0.561580 0.8565% 1968 1.765568 0.566390 1.5090% 1967 1.739321 0.574937 0.9949% 1966 1.722187 0.580657 1.0575% 1965 1.704166 0.586797 1.1300% 1964 1.685123 0.593428 1.5537% 1963 1.659343 0.602648 1.4658% 1962 1.635371 0.611482 1.5364% 1961 1.610625 0.620877 2.1586% 1960 1.576592 0.634279 -1.6655% 1959 1.603295 0.623716 4.3080% 1958 1.537078 0.650585 2.1130% 1957 1.505272 0.664332 1.9895% 1956 1.475909 0.677549 2.1231% 1955 1.445225 0.691934 1.4496% 1954 1.424574 0.701964 2.1573% 1953 1.394492 0.717107 1.2298% 1952 1.377551 0.725926 1.6814% 1951 1.354772 0.738131 1.6233% 1950 1.333132 0.750113 1.4265% 1949 1.314382 0.760814 1.7790% 1948 1.291407 0.774349 1.8242% 1947 1.268272 0.788474 -2.6320% 1946 1.302556 0.767722 3.1768% 1945 1.262560 0.792111 6.4754% 1944 1.185673 0.843403 -0.3437% 1943 1.189762 0.840504 0.6562% 1942 1.182005 0.846020 0.6633% 1941 1.174217 0.851632 -5.6614% 1940 1.244683 0.803417 8.0381% 1939 1.152078 0.867997 0.8126% 1938 1.142791 0.875050 0.7762% 1937 1.133989 0.881843 0.6029% 1936 1.127193 0.887159 0.5244% 1935 1.121313 0.891811 -3.0364% 1934 1.156427 0.864733 4.6271% 1933 1.105284 0.904745 1.3921% 1932 1.090108 0.917340 -0.2051% 1931 1.092348 0.915459 0.8886% 1930 1.082727 0.923594 1.0126% 1929 1.071874 0.932946

1.1526% 1928 1.059660 0.943699 1.2160% 1927 1.046929 0.955174 1.4086% 1926 1.032387
0.968629 1.7667% 1925 1.014465 0.985741 1.4465% 1924 1.000000 1.000000 1.7700% 1923
0.982608 1.017700 1.6165% 1922 0.966977 1.034151 1.3736% 1921 0.953874 1.048357
2.3393% 1920 0.932070 1.072881 1.3140% 1919 0.919981 1.086979 0.7676% 1918 0.912973
1.095323 0.3870% 1917 0.909453 1.099562 1.3274% 1916 0.897539 1.114158 1.4083% 1915
0.885075 1.129848 1.4458% 1914 0.872461 1.146183 1.9424% 1913 0.855837 1.168447
1.9857% 1912 0.839174 1.191648 1.5634% 1911 0.826256 1.210279 1.8169% 1910 0.811512
1.232268 1.8781% 1909 0.796552 1.255411 2.0082% 1908 0.780870 1.280623 1.9603% 1907
0.765857 1.305726 1.8264% 1906 0.752121 1.329573 1.9357% 1905 0.737839 1.355310
2.0148% 1904 0.723266 1.382617 2.1335% 1903 0.708157 1.412115 1.8151% 1902 0.695533
1.437747 1.8943% 1901 0.682602 1.464983 3.0255% 1900 0.662556 1.509306 0.6278% 1899
0.658422 1.518782 1.7757% 1898 0.646935 1.545751 1.8078% 1897 0.635448 1.573694
1.8396% 1896 0.623969 1.602644 1.8755% 1895 0.612482 1.632702 1.9114% 1894 0.600994
1.663909 1.9486% 1893 0.589507 1.696333 1.9858% 1892 0.578028 1.730019 2.0276% 1891
0.566541 1.765097 2.6465% 1890 0.551934 1.811810 1.5328% 1889 0.543602 1.839582
2.0811% 1888 0.532519 1.877866 2.1599% 1887 0.521261 1.918425 2.2075% 1886 0.510002
1.960775 2.2592% 1885 0.498735 2.005073 2.3095% 1884 0.487477 2.051381 2.3641% 1883
0.476218 2.099878 2.4214% 1882 0.464960 2.150724 2.4815% 1881 0.453701 2.204094
3.7644% 1880 0.437242 2.287065 0.9432% 1879 0.433156 2.308637 2.1464% 1878 0.424054
2.358189 2.1913% 1877 0.414961 2.409864 2.2426% 1876 0.405859 2.463908 2.2941% 1875
0.396757 2.520431 2.3456% 1874 0.387664 2.579550 2.4043% 1873 0.378563 2.641571
2.4635% 1872 0.369461 2.706647 2.5258% 1871 0.360359 2.775011 5.9947% 1870 0.339978
2.941364 -1.0968% 1869 0.343749 2.909104 2.1930% 1868 0.336372 2.972899 2.2394%
1867 0.329004 3.039475 2.2935% 1866 0.321628 3.109185 2.3445% 1865 0.314260 3.182079
2.4037% 1864 0.306883 3.258566 2.4599% 1863 0.299516 3.338723 2.5250% 1862 0.292139
3.423026 2.5872% 1861 0.284771 3.511589 2.9504% 1860 0.276610 3.615195 2.4012% 1859
0.270124 3.702004 2.7627% 1858 0.262862 3.804280 2.8412% 1857 0.255600 3.912367
2.9243% 1856 0.248338 4.026776 3.0161% 1855 0.241067 4.148229 3.1061% 1854 0.233805
4.277075 3.2056% 1853 0.226543 4.414183 3.3118% 1852 0.219280 4.560371 3.4252% 1851
0.212018 4.716574 4.0106% 1850 0.203843 4.905737 2.3254% 1849 0.199211 5.019814
2.7841% 1848 0.193815 5.159570 2.8590% 1847 0.188427 5.307082 2.9432% 1846 0.183040
5.463278 3.0324% 1845 0.177653 5.628947 3.1325% 1844 0.172257 5.805274 3.2284% 1843
0.166870 5.992689 3.3361% 1842 0.161483 6.192608 3.4512% 1841 0.156096 6.406327
3.8105% 1840 0.150366 6.650440 2.3861% 1839 0.146862 6.809123 2.5824% 1838 0.143165
6.984961 2.6573% 1837 0.139459 7.170574 2.7232% 1836 0.135762 7.365843 2.7994% 1835
0.132065 7.572046 2.8871% 1834 0.128359 7.790660 2.9657% 1833 0.124662 8.021706
3.0563% 1832 0.120965 8.266875 3.1604% 1831 0.117259 8.528144 3.4660% 1830 0.113331
8.823726 2.4653% 1829 0.110604 9.041258 2.6804% 1828 0.107717 9.283599 10.3427%
1827 0.097620 10.243769 -4.2314% 1826 0.101934 9.810311 2.9150% 1825 0.099046
10.096285 3.0026% 1824 0.096159 10.399433 3.0955% 1823 0.093272 10.721348 3.1944%
1822 0.090385 11.063830 3.3102% 1821 0.087489 11.430064 3.2277% 1820 0.084753
11.798996 2.6573% 1819 0.082559 12.112528 2.6261% 1818 0.080447 12.430616 2.6969%
1817 0.078334 12.765862 2.7717% 1816 0.076221 13.119691 2.8507% 1815 0.074109
13.493693 2.9343% 1814 0.071996 13.889644 3.0231% 1813 0.069883 14.309535 3.1039%
1812 0.067780 14.753689 3.2172% 1811 0.065667 15.228338 3.0969% 1810 0.063694
15.699947 2.9144% 1809 0.061891 16.157503 2.8225% 1808 0.060192 16.613542 2.9199%
1807 0.058484 17.098646 2.9918% 1806 0.056785 17.610200 3.0841% 1805 0.055086
18.153308 3.1822% 1804 0.053387 18.730981 3.2868% 1803 0.051689 19.346628 3.3985%
1802 0.049990 20.004121 3.5180% 1801 0.048291 20.707875 3.3999% 1800 0.046703
21.411932 2.8419% 1799 0.045412 22.020431 2.7485% 1798 0.044198 22.625653 2.8261%
1797 0.042983 23.265083 3.7832% 1796 0.041416 24.145250 2.1272% 1795 0.040553
24.658867 3.0879% 1794 0.039339 25.420318 3.1625% 1793 0.038133 26.224239 3.2904%
1792 0.036918 27.087125 3.4024% 1791 0.035703 28.008728 3.2296% 1790 0.034586
28.913288 41.3145% 1780 0.024475 40.858654 29.4353% 1770 0.018909 52.885528
83.4728% 1750 0.010306 97.030579 29.2845% 1740 0.007972 125.445453 94.2514% 1720

0.004104 243.679541 85.8111% 1700 0.002209 452.783587 19.2490% 1690 0.001852
539.940124 88.0250% 1670 0.000985 1015.222538

YEAR BYEAR/AYEAR AYEAR/BYEAR GROWTH%

2009 2.700320 0.370326 8.2857% 2001 2.493701 0.401010 1.0000% 2000 2.469010
0.405021 1.0000% 1999 2.444565 0.409071 1.0000% 1998 2.420361 0.413161 1.0000% 1997
2.396397 0.417293 1.0000% 1996 2.372671 0.421466 1.0000% 1995 2.349179 0.425681
0.9992% 1994 2.325937 0.429934 1.0008% 1993 2.302891 0.434237 1.0000% 1992 2.280090
0.438579 0.9295% 1991 2.259091 0.442656 1.2505% 1990 2.231190 0.448191 0.7224% 1989
2.215186 0.451429 1.1077% 1988 2.190918 0.456430 0.8834% 1987 2.171734 0.460462
0.5594% 1986 2.159654 0.463037 1.3056% 1985 2.131820 0.469083 0.7673% 1984 2.115587
0.472682 0.8149% 1983 2.098486 0.476534 0.9737% 1982 2.078249 0.481174 0.9508% 1981
2.058675 0.485749 0.9031% 1980 2.040250 0.490136 2.2701% 1979 1.994963 0.501262
1.0042% 1978 1.975129 0.506296 0.9896% 1977 1.955775 0.511306 0.9103% 1976 1.938131
0.515961 0.8394% 1975 1.921997 0.520292 0.9042% 1974 1.904775 0.524996 1.1568% 1973
1.882993 0.531070 0.9427% 1972 1.865407 0.536076 0.7426% 1971 1.851656 0.540057
1.4697% 1970 1.824836 0.547994 0.6968% 1969 1.812208 0.551813 0.8565% 1968 1.796818
0.556539 1.5090% 1967 1.770106 0.564938 0.9949% 1966 1.752669 0.570558 1.0575% 1965
1.734329 0.576592 1.1300% 1964 1.714950 0.583108 1.5537% 1963 1.688713 0.592167
1.4658% 1962 1.664317 0.600847 1.5364% 1961 1.639133 0.610079 2.1586% 1960 1.604497
0.623248 -1.6655% 1959 1.631673 0.612868 4.3080% 1958 1.564283 0.639270 2.1130%
1957 1.531915 0.652778 1.9895% 1956 1.502032 0.665765 2.1231% 1955 1.470805 0.679900
1.4496% 1954 1.449789 0.689756 2.1573% 1953 1.419174 0.704635 1.2298% 1952 1.401933
0.713301 1.6814% 1951 1.378751 0.725294 1.6233% 1950 1.356728 0.737067 1.4265% 1949
1.337646 0.747582 1.7790% 1948 1.314265 0.760882 1.8242% 1947 1.290720 0.774761 -
2.6320% 1946 1.325610 0.754369 3.1768% 1945 1.284795 0.778334 6.4754% 1944 1.206659
0.828735 -0.3437% 1943 1.210820 0.825886 0.6562% 1942 1.202926 0.831306 0.6633%
1941 1.195000 0.836820 -5.6614% 1940 1.266714 0.789444 8.0381% 1939 1.172470
0.852901 0.8126% 1938 1.163019 0.859832 0.7762% 1937 1.154060 0.866506 0.6029% 1936
1.147144 0.871730 0.5244% 1935 1.141160 0.876301 -3.0364% 1934 1.176895 0.849693
4.6271% 1933 1.124847 0.889010 1.3921% 1932 1.109403 0.901386 -0.2051% 1931
1.111683 0.899537 0.8886% 1930 1.101891 0.907531 1.0126% 1929 1.090846 0.916720
1.1526% 1928 1.078416 0.927286 1.2160% 1927 1.065460 0.938562 1.4086% 1926 1.050660
0.951782 1.7667% 1925 1.032421 0.968597 1.4465% 1924 1.017700 0.982608 1.7700% 1923
1.000000 1.000000 1.6165% 1922 0.984092 1.016165 1.3736% 1921 0.970757 1.030124
2.3393% 1920 0.948567 1.054222 1.3140% 1919 0.936265 1.068074 0.7676% 1918 0.929132
1.076273 0.3870% 1917 0.925550 1.080438 1.3274% 1916 0.913425 1.094780 1.4083% 1915
0.900740 1.110198 1.4458% 1914 0.887903 1.126249 1.9424% 1913 0.870985 1.148125
1.9857% 1912 0.854027 1.170923 1.5634% 1911 0.840881 1.189230 1.8169% 1910 0.825875
1.210837 1.8781% 1909 0.810651 1.233577 2.0082% 1908 0.794691 1.258350 1.9603% 1907
0.779413 1.283017 1.8264% 1906 0.765433 1.306450 1.9357% 1905 0.750898 1.331738
2.0148% 1904 0.736068 1.358571 2.1335% 1903 0.720692 1.387556 1.8151% 1902 0.707843
1.412742 1.8943% 1901 0.694684 1.439504 3.0255% 1900 0.674283 1.483057 0.6278% 1899
0.670076 1.492368 1.7757% 1898 0.658385 1.518867 1.8078% 1897 0.646695 1.546325
1.8396% 1896 0.635013 1.574771 1.8755% 1895 0.623322 1.604306 1.9114% 1894 0.611632
1.634971 1.9486% 1893 0.599941 1.666830 1.9858% 1892 0.588259 1.699930 2.0276% 1891
0.576569 1.734399 2.6465% 1890 0.561703 1.780300 1.5328% 1889 0.553223 1.807588
2.0811% 1888 0.541945 1.845207 2.1599% 1887 0.530487 1.885060 2.2075% 1886 0.519029
1.926674 2.2592% 1885 0.507563 1.970201 2.3095% 1884 0.496105 2.015703 2.3641% 1883
0.484647 2.063357 2.4214% 1882 0.473189 2.113319 2.4815% 1881 0.461732 2.165760
3.7644% 1880 0.444981 2.247288 0.9432% 1879 0.440823 2.268485 2.1464% 1878 0.431560
2.317176 2.1913% 1877 0.422306 2.367952 2.2426% 1876 0.413043 2.421056 2.2941% 1875
0.403780 2.476596 2.3456% 1874 0.394526 2.534687 2.4043% 1873 0.385263 2.595629
2.4635% 1872 0.376000 2.659574 2.5258% 1871 0.366737 2.726748 5.9947% 1870 0.345996
2.890208 -1.0968% 1869 0.349833 2.858509 2.1930% 1868 0.342326 2.921195 2.2394%
1867 0.334828 2.986612 2.2935% 1866 0.327320 3.055110 2.3445% 1865 0.319822 3.126737

2.4037% 1864 0.312315 3.201894 2.4599% 1863 0.304817 3.280657 2.5250% 1862 0.297310
3.363494 2.5872% 1861 0.289812 3.450515 2.9504% 1860 0.281506 3.552320 2.4012% 1859
0.274905 3.637619 2.7627% 1858 0.267514 3.738116 2.8412% 1857 0.260124 3.844324
2.9243% 1856 0.252733 3.956743 3.0161% 1855 0.245334 4.076084 3.1061% 1854 0.237943
4.202689 3.2056% 1853 0.230552 4.337412 3.3118% 1852 0.223162 4.481058 3.4252% 1851
0.215771 4.634544 4.0106% 1850 0.207451 4.820417 2.3254% 1849 0.202737 4.932510
2.7841% 1848 0.197245 5.069835 2.8590% 1847 0.191763 5.214782 2.9432% 1846 0.186280
5.368261 3.0324% 1845 0.180798 5.531049 3.1325% 1844 0.175306 5.704309 3.2284% 1843
0.169824 5.888465 3.3361% 1842 0.164341 6.084907 3.4512% 1841 0.158859 6.294909
3.8105% 1840 0.153027 6.534776 2.3861% 1839 0.149461 6.690699 2.5824% 1838 0.145699
6.863479 2.6573% 1837 0.141927 7.045864 2.7232% 1836 0.138165 7.237737 2.7994% 1835
0.134402 7.440354 2.8871% 1834 0.130631 7.655166 2.9657% 1833 0.126868 7.882194
3.0563% 1832 0.123106 8.123099 3.1604% 1831 0.119334 8.379823 3.4660% 1830 0.115337
8.670265 2.4653% 1829 0.112562 8.884013 2.6804% 1828 0.109623 9.122140 10.3427%
1827 0.099348 10.065611 -4.2314% 1826 0.103738 9.639691 2.9150% 1825 0.100799
9.920692 3.0026% 1824 0.097861 10.218567 3.0955% 1823 0.094923 10.534883 3.1944%
1822 0.091984 10.871409 3.3102% 1821 0.089037 11.231273 3.2277% 1820 0.086253
11.593789 2.6573% 1819 0.084020 11.901869 2.6261% 1818 0.081870 12.214424 2.6969%
1817 0.079720 12.543839 2.7717% 1816 0.077570 12.891515 2.8507% 1815 0.075420
13.259012 2.9343% 1814 0.073270 13.648077 3.0231% 1813 0.071120 14.060666 3.1039%
1812 0.068979 14.497094 3.2172% 1811 0.066829 14.963489 3.0969% 1810 0.064822
15.426895 2.9144% 1809 0.062986 15.876493 2.8225% 1808 0.061257 16.324601 2.9199%
1807 0.059519 16.801268 2.9918% 1806 0.057790 17.303926 3.0841% 1805 0.056061
17.837588 3.1822% 1804 0.054332 18.405214 3.2868% 1803 0.052603 19.010154 3.3985%
1802 0.050875 19.656211 3.5180% 1801 0.049146 20.347726 3.3999% 1800 0.047530
21.039538 2.8419% 1799 0.046216 21.637454 2.7485% 1798 0.044980 22.232150 2.8261%
1797 0.043744 22.860460 3.7832% 1796 0.042149 23.725319 2.1272% 1795 0.041271
24.230003 3.0879% 1794 0.040035 24.978211 3.1625% 1793 0.038808 25.768150 3.2904%
1792 0.037571 26.616029 3.4024% 1791 0.036335 27.521604 3.2296% 1790 0.035198
28.410431 41.3145% 1780 0.024908 40.148045 29.4353% 1770 0.019243 51.965749
83.4728% 1750 0.010488 95.343035 29.2845% 1740 0.008113 123.263720 94.2514% 1720
0.004176 239.441495 85.8111% 1700 0.002248 444.908828 19.2490% 1690 0.001885
530.549548 88.0250% 1670 0.001002 997.565907
BASE YEAR: 1922
YEAR BYEAR/AYEAR AYEAR/BYEAR GROWTH%
2009 2.743972 0.364435 8.2857% 2001 2.534012 0.394631 1.0000% 2000 2.508922
0.398577 1.0000% 1999 2.484082 0.402563 1.0000% 1998 2.459487 0.406589 1.0000% 1997
2.435135 0.410655 1.0000% 1996 2.411025 0.414761 1.0000% 1995 2.387154 0.418909
0.9992% 1994 2.363537 0.423095 1.0008% 1993 2.340117 0.427329 1.0000% 1992 2.316948
0.431602 0.9295% 1991 2.295610 0.435614 1.2505% 1990 2.267258 0.441061 0.7224% 1989
2.250995 0.444248 1.1077% 1988 2.226335 0.449169 0.8834% 1987 2.206840 0.453137
0.5594% 1986 2.194565 0.455671 1.3056% 1985 2.166281 0.461621 0.7673% 1984 2.149786
0.465163 0.8149% 1983 2.132408 0.468953 0.9737% 1982 2.111844 0.473520 0.9508% 1981
2.091954 0.478022 0.9031% 1980 2.073231 0.482339 2.2701% 1979 2.027212 0.493288
1.0042% 1978 2.007058 0.498242 0.9896% 1977 1.987390 0.503172 0.9103% 1976 1.969462
0.507753 0.8394% 1975 1.953067 0.512015 0.9042% 1974 1.935566 0.516645 1.1568% 1973
1.913432 0.522621 0.9427% 1972 1.895562 0.527548 0.7426% 1971 1.881589 0.531466
1.4697% 1970 1.854335 0.539277 0.6968% 1969 1.841503 0.543035 0.8565% 1968 1.825864
0.547686 1.5090% 1967 1.798720 0.555951 0.9949% 1966 1.781001 0.561482 1.0575% 1965
1.762365 0.567420 1.1300% 1964 1.742672 0.573831 1.5537% 1963 1.716011 0.582747
1.4658% 1962 1.691221 0.591289 1.5364% 1961 1.665630 0.600374 2.1586% 1960 1.630434
0.613333 -1.6655% 1959 1.658049 0.603118 4.3080% 1958 1.589570 0.629101 2.1130%
1957 1.556678 0.642393 1.9895% 1956 1.526313 0.655174 2.1231% 1955 1.494581 0.669084
1.4496% 1954 1.473225 0.678783 2.1573% 1953 1.442115 0.693426 1.2298% 1952 1.424596
0.701953 1.6814% 1951 1.401039 0.713756 1.6233% 1950 1.378660 0.725342 1.4265% 1949
1.359269 0.735689 1.7790% 1948 1.335510 0.748778 1.8242% 1947 1.311585 0.762436 -

128

2.6320% 1946 1.347039 0.742369 3.1768% 1945 1.305564 0.765952 6.4754% 1944 1.226165
0.815551 -0.3437% 1943 1.230393 0.812748 0.6562% 1942 1.222372 0.818082 0.6633%
1941 1.214317 0.823508 -5.6614% 1940 1.287191 0.776886 8.0381% 1939 1.191423
0.839333 0.8126% 1938 1.181819 0.846153 0.7762% 1937 1.172716 0.852722 0.6029% 1936
1.165688 0.857862 0.5244% 1935 1.159607 0.862361 -3.0364% 1934 1.195920 0.836176
4.6271% 1933 1.143030 0.874867 1.3921% 1932 1.127337 0.887047 -0.2051% 1931
1.129653 0.885227 0.8886% 1930 1.119704 0.893093 1.0126% 1929 1.108479 0.902137
1.1526% 1928 1.095849 0.912535 1.2160% 1927 1.082683 0.923631 1.4086% 1926 1.067645
0.936641 1.7667% 1925 1.049110 0.953189 1.4465% 1924 1.034151 0.966977 1.7700% 1923
1.016165 0.984092 1.6165% 1922 1.000000 1.000000 1.3736% 1921 0.986450 1.013736
2.3393% 1920 0.963901 1.037451 1.3140% 1919 0.951400 1.051083 0.7676% 1918 0.944152
1.059152 0.3870% 1917 0.940512 1.063250 1.3274% 1916 0.928191 1.077364 1.4083% 1915
0.915301 1.092537 1.4458% 1914 0.902256 1.108333 1.9424% 1913 0.885065 1.129861
1.9857% 1912 0.867832 1.152296 1.5634% 1911 0.854474 1.170311 1.8169% 1910 0.839226
1.191575 1.8781% 1909 0.823755 1.213953 2.0082% 1908 0.807538 1.238332 1.9603% 1907
0.792012 1.262607 1.8264% 1906 0.777807 1.285667 1.9357% 1905 0.763037 1.310553
2.0148% 1904 0.747966 1.336958 2.1335% 1903 0.732342 1.365483 1.8151% 1902 0.719286
1.390268 1.8943% 1901 0.705913 1.416605 3.0255% 1900 0.685183 1.459464 0.6278% 1899
0.680908 1.468627 1.7757% 1898 0.669028 1.494705 1.8078% 1897 0.657149 1.521726
1.8396% 1896 0.645278 1.549719 1.8755% 1895 0.633399 1.578785 1.9114% 1894 0.621519
1.608962 1.9486% 1893 0.609639 1.640314 1.9858% 1892 0.597769 1.672888 2.0276% 1891
0.585889 1.706808 2.6465% 1890 0.570783 1.751979 1.5328% 1889 0.562166 1.778833
2.0811% 1888 0.550705 1.815853 2.1599% 1887 0.539062 1.855073 2.2075% 1886 0.527419
1.896024 2.2592% 1885 0.515767 1.938859 2.3095% 1884 0.504124 1.983637 2.3641% 1883
0.492481 2.030533 2.4214% 1882 0.480839 2.079700 2.4815% 1881 0.469196 2.131307
3.7644% 1880 0.452174 2.211538 0.9432% 1879 0.447949 2.232398 2.1464% 1878 0.438536
2.280314 2.1913% 1877 0.429133 2.330283 2.2426% 1876 0.419720 2.382542 2.2941% 1875
0.410307 2.437199 2.3456% 1874 0.400904 2.494365 2.4043% 1873 0.391491 2.554338
2.4635% 1872 0.382078 2.617265 2.5258% 1871 0.372664 2.683371 5.9947% 1870 0.351589
2.844231 -1.0968% 1869 0.355488 2.813035 2.1930% 1868 0.347859 2.874725 2.2394%
1867 0.340240 2.939101 2.2935% 1866 0.332612 3.006510 2.3445% 1865 0.324992 3.076996
2.4037% 1864 0.317364 3.150958 2.4599% 1863 0.309744 3.228468 2.5250% 1862 0.302116
3.309987 2.5872% 1861 0.294497 3.395624 2.9504% 1860 0.286057 3.495809 2.4012% 1859
0.279349 3.579752 2.7627% 1858 0.271839 3.678650 2.8412% 1857 0.264329 3.783168
2.9243% 1856 0.256819 3.893799 3.0161% 1855 0.249299 4.011241 3.1061% 1854 0.241789
4.135833 3.2056% 1853 0.234279 4.268412 3.3118% 1852 0.226769 4.409773 3.4252% 1851
0.219259 4.560817 4.0106% 1850 0.210804 4.743734 2.3254% 1849 0.206014 4.854043
2.7841% 1848 0.200434 4.989184 2.8590% 1847 0.194862 5.131825 2.9432% 1846 0.189291
5.282863 3.0324% 1845 0.183720 5.443061 3.1325% 1844 0.178140 5.613565 3.2284% 1843
0.172569 5.794791 3.3361% 1842 0.166998 5.988108 3.4512% 1841 0.161427 6.194770
3.8105% 1840 0.155501 6.430820 2.3861% 1839 0.151877 6.584263 2.5824% 1838 0.148054
6.754295 2.6573% 1837 0.144222 6.933778 2.7232% 1836 0.140398 7.122599 2.7994% 1835
0.136575 7.321992 2.8871% 1834 0.132742 7.533387 2.9657% 1833 0.128919 7.756803
3.0563% 1832 0.125096 7.993876 3.1604% 1831 0.121263 8.246517 3.4660% 1830 0.117201
8.532338 2.4653% 1829 0.114381 8.742686 2.6804% 1828 0.111395 8.977024 10.3427% 1827
0.100954 9.905487 -4.2314% 1826 0.105415 9.486343 2.9150% 1825 0.102429
9.762873 3.0026% 1824 0.099443 10.056010 3.0955% 1823 0.096457 10.367294 3.1944%
1822 0.093471 10.698466 3.3102% 1821 0.090476 11.052606 3.2277% 1820 0.087647
11.409355 2.6573% 1819 0.085379 11.712533 2.6261% 1818 0.083194 12.020117 2.6969%
1817 0.081009 12.344291 2.7717% 1816 0.078824 12.686436 2.8507% 1815 0.076640
13.048087 2.9343% 1814 0.074455 13.430963 3.0231% 1813 0.072270 13.836988 3.1039%
1812 0.070094 14.266474 3.2172% 1811 0.067910 14.725449 3.0969% 1810 0.065870
15.181483 2.9144% 1809 0.064004 15.623929 2.8225% 1808 0.062247 16.064909 2.9199%
1807 0.060481 16.533993 2.9918% 1806 0.058725 17.028654 3.0841% 1805 0.056968
17.553827 3.1822% 1804 0.055211 18.112423 3.2868% 1803 0.053454 18.707740 3.3985%
1802 0.051697 19.343520 3.5180% 1801 0.049940 20.024034 3.3999% 1800 0.048298

20.704840 2.8419% 1799 0.046963 21.293244 2.7485% 1798 0.045707 21.878480 2.8261%
1797 0.044451 22.496795 3.7832% 1796 0.042830 23.347895 2.1272% 1795 0.041938
23.844551 3.0879% 1794 0.040682 24.580857 3.1625% 1793 0.039435 25.358229 3.2904%
1792 0.038179 26.192620 3.4024% 1791 0.036922 27.083789 3.2296% 1790 0.035767
27.958477 41.3145% 1780 0.025310 39.509368 29.4353% 1770 0.019555 51.139075
83.4728% 1750 0.010658 93.826314 29.2845% 1740 0.008244 121.302836 94.2514% 1720
0.004244 235.632450 85.8111% 1700 0.002284 437.831200 19.2490% 1690 0.001915
522.109544 88.0250% 1670 0.001019 981.696586

BASE YEAR: 1921

YEAR BYEAR/AYEAR AYEAR/BYEAR GROWTH%

2009 2.781664 0.359497 8.2857% 2001 2.568820 0.389284 1.0000% 2000 2.543386
0.393177 1.0000% 1999 2.518204 0.397108 1.0000% 1998 2.493271 0.401079 1.0000% 1997
2.468586 0.405090 1.0000% 1996 2.444144 0.409141 1.0000% 1995 2.419945 0.413233
0.9992% 1994 2.396003 0.417362 1.0008% 1993 2.372262 0.421539 1.0000% 1992 2.348774
0.425754 0.9295% 1991 2.327144 0.429711 1.2505% 1990 2.298402 0.435085 0.7224% 1989
2.281916 0.438228 1.1077% 1988 2.256917 0.443082 0.8834% 1987 2.237155 0.446996
0.5594% 1986 2.224710 0.449497 1.3056% 1985 2.196038 0.455365 0.7673% 1984 2.179317
0.458859 0.8149% 1983 2.161700 0.462599 0.9737% 1982 2.140854 0.467103 0.9508% 1981
2.120690 0.471545 0.9031% 1980 2.101710 0.475803 2.2701% 1979 2.055059 0.486604
1.0042% 1978 2.034628 0.491490 0.9896% 1977 2.014690 0.496354 0.9103% 1976 1.996515
0.500873 0.8394% 1975 1.979895 0.505077 0.9042% 1974 1.962154 0.509644 1.1568% 1973
1.939715 0.515540 0.9427% 1972 1.921600 0.520400 0.7426% 1971 1.907435 0.524264
1.4697% 1970 1.879807 0.531970 0.6968% 1969 1.866799 0.535676 0.8565% 1968 1.850945
0.540265 1.5090% 1967 1.823428 0.548417 0.9949% 1966 1.805466 0.553874 1.0575% 1965
1.786573 0.559731 1.1300% 1964 1.766610 0.566056 1.5537% 1963 1.739583 0.574850
1.4658% 1962 1.714452 0.583277 1.5364% 1961 1.688510 0.592238 2.1586% 1960 1.652831
0.605023 -1.6655% 1959 1.680825 0.594946 4.3080% 1958 1.611405 0.620576 2.1130%
1957 1.578062 0.633689 1.9895% 1956 1.547279 0.646296 2.1231% 1955 1.515111 0.660017
1.4496% 1954 1.493462 0.669585 2.1573% 1953 1.461925 0.684030 1.2298% 1952 1.444165
0.692442 1.6814% 1951 1.420285 0.704084 1.6233% 1950 1.397598 0.715513 1.4265% 1949
1.377941 0.725721 1.7790% 1948 1.353855 0.738631 1.8242% 1947 1.329601 0.752105 -
2.6320% 1946 1.365543 0.732310 3.1768% 1945 1.323498 0.755574 6.4754% 1944 1.243008
0.804500 -0.3437% 1943 1.247295 0.801735 0.6562% 1942 1.239163 0.806996 0.6633%
1941 1.230998 0.812349 -5.6614% 1940 1.304872 0.766359 8.0381% 1939 1.207789
0.827959 0.8126% 1938 1.198053 0.834688 0.7762% 1937 1.188825 0.841167 0.6029% 1936
1.181701 0.846238 0.5244% 1935 1.175536 0.850676 -3.0364% 1934 1.212347 0.824846
4.6271% 1933 1.158732 0.863013 1.3921% 1932 1.142822 0.875027 -0.2051% 1931
1.145171 0.873232 0.8886% 1930 1.135084 0.880992 1.0126% 1929 1.123706 0.889913
1.1526% 1928 1.110902 0.900170 1.2160% 1927 1.097555 0.911116 1.4086% 1926 1.082310
0.923950 1.7667% 1925 1.063521 0.940273 1.4465% 1924 1.048357 0.953874 1.7700% 1923
1.030124 0.970757 1.6165% 1922 1.013736 0.986450 1.3736% 1921 1.000000 1.000000
2.3393% 1920 0.977142 1.023393 1.3140% 1919 0.964468 1.036841 0.7676% 1918 0.957121
1.044800 0.3870% 1917 0.953431 1.048843 1.3274% 1916 0.940941 1.062766 1.4083% 1915
0.927874 1.077733 1.4458% 1914 0.914650 1.093315 1.9424% 1913 0.897222 1.114551
1.9857% 1912 0.879753 1.136682 1.5634% 1911 0.866211 1.154453 1.8169% 1910 0.850754
1.175429 1.8781% 1909 0.835070 1.197504 2.0082% 1908 0.818630 1.221553 1.9603% 1907
0.802892 1.245498 1.8264% 1906 0.788491 1.268245 1.9357% 1905 0.773518 1.292794
2.0148% 1904 0.758241 1.318842 2.1335% 1903 0.742402 1.346980 1.8151% 1902 0.729166
1.371430 1.8943% 1901 0.715610 1.397409 3.0255% 1900 0.694595 1.439688 0.6278% 1899
0.690261 1.448727 1.7757% 1898 0.678218 1.474451 1.8078% 1897 0.666176 1.501106
1.8396% 1896 0.654142 1.528720 1.8755% 1895 0.642099 1.557392 1.9114% 1894 0.630056
1.587160 1.9486% 1893 0.618014 1.618088 1.9858% 1892 0.605980 1.650220 2.0276% 1891
0.593937 1.683680 2.6465% 1890 0.578624 1.728239 1.5328% 1889 0.569888 1.754730
2.0811% 1888 0.558270 1.791248 2.1599% 1887 0.546467 1.829936 2.2075% 1886 0.534664
1.870332 2.2592% 1885 0.522852 1.912586 2.3095% 1884 0.511049 1.956758 2.3641% 1883
0.499246 2.003019 2.4214% 1882 0.487444 2.051520 2.4815% 1881 0.475641 2.102428

130

3.7644% 1880 0.458385 2.181571 0.9432% 1879 0.454102 2.202148 2.1464% 1878 0.444560
2.249415 2.1913% 1877 0.435027 2.298706 2.2426% 1876 0.425485 2.350257 2.2941% 1875
0.415943 2.404174 2.3456% 1874 0.406411 2.460566 2.4043% 1873 0.396869 2.519726
2.4635% 1872 0.387327 2.581800 2.5258% 1871 0.377785 2.647011 5.9947% 1870 0.356419
2.805690 -1.0968% 1869 0.360371 2.774918 2.1930% 1868 0.352638 2.835771 2.2394%
1867 0.344914 2.899275 2.2935% 1866 0.337181 2.965770 2.3445% 1865 0.329456 3.035302
2.4037% 1864 0.321723 3.108262 2.4599% 1863 0.313999 3.184721 2.5250% 1862 0.306266
3.265136 2.5872% 1861 0.298542 3.349613 2.9504% 1860 0.289986 3.448440 2.4012% 1859
0.283186 3.531245 2.7627% 1858 0.275573 3.628803 2.8412% 1857 0.267960 3.731905
2.9243% 1856 0.260346 3.841036 3.0161% 1855 0.252724 3.956887 3.1061% 1854 0.245111
4.079791 3.2056% 1853 0.237497 4.210574 3.3118% 1852 0.229884 4.350019 3.4252% 1851
0.222271 4.499017 4.0106% 1850 0.213700 4.679455 2.3254% 1849 0.208844 4.788269
2.7841% 1848 0.203187 4.921579 2.8590% 1847 0.197539 5.062287 2.9432% 1846 0.191891
5.211278 3.0324% 1845 0.186244 5.369305 3.1325% 1844 0.180587 5.537499 3.2284% 1843
0.174939 5.716270 3.3361% 1842 0.169292 5.906968 3.4512% 1841 0.163644 6.110828
3.8105% 1840 0.157637 6.343681 2.3861% 1839 0.153964 6.495044 2.5824% 1838 0.150088
6.662772 2.6573% 1837 0.146203 6.839823 2.7232% 1836 0.142327 7.026086 2.7994% 1835
0.138451 7.222777 2.8871% 1834 0.134566 7.431307 2.9657% 1833 0.130690 7.651696
3.0563% 1832 0.126814 7.885557 3.1604% 1831 0.122929 8.134774 3.4660% 1830 0.118811
8.416722 2.4653% 1829 0.115953 8.624220 2.6804% 1828 0.112926 8.855383 10.3427%
1827 0.102341 9.771264 -4.2314% 1826 0.106863 9.357800 2.9150% 1825 0.103836
9.630583 3.0026% 1824 0.100809 9.919747 3.0955% 1823 0.097782 10.226814 3.1944%
1822 0.094755 10.553498 3.3102% 1821 0.091719 10.902839 3.2277% 1820 0.088851
11.254755 2.6573% 1819 0.086551 11.553825 2.6261% 1818 0.084337 11.857241 2.6969%
1817 0.082122 12.177022 2.7717% 1816 0.079907 12.514531 2.8507% 1815 0.077692
12.871282 2.9343% 1814 0.075478 13.248969 3.0231% 1813 0.073263 13.649493 3.1039%
1812 0.071057 14.073159 3.2172% 1811 0.068842 14.525914 3.0969% 1810 0.066775
14.975770 2.9144% 1809 0.064884 15.412220 2.8225% 1808 0.063103 15.847224 2.9199%
1807 0.061312 16.309952 2.9918% 1806 0.059531 16.797911 3.0841% 1805 0.057750
17.315967 3.1822% 1804 0.055969 17.866994 3.2868% 1803 0.054188 18.454244 3.3985%
1802 0.052407 19.081409 3.5180% 1801 0.050626 19.752702 3.3999% 1800 0.048961
20.424283 2.8419% 1799 0.047608 21.004714 2.7485% 1798 0.046335 21.582020 2.8261%
1797 0.045061 22.191956 3.7832% 1796 0.043419 23.031524 2.1272% 1795 0.042514
23.521450 3.0879% 1794 0.041241 24.247778 3.1625% 1793 0.039977 25.014617 3.2904%
1792 0.038703 25.837704 3.4024% 1791 0.037430 26.716795 3.2296% 1790 0.036259
27.579631 41.3145% 1780 0.025658 38.974004 29.4353% 1770 0.019823 50.446125
83.4728% 1750 0.010804 92.554938 29.2845% 1740 0.008357 119.659144 94.2514% 1720
0.004302 232.439556 85.8111% 1700 0.002315 431.898450 19.2490% 1690 0.001942
515.034796 88.0250% 1670 0.001033 968.394290

BASE YEAR: 1920
YEAR BYEAR/AYEAR AYEAR/BYEAR GROWTH%

2009 2.846736 0.351280 8.2857% 2001 2.628913 0.380385 1.0000% 2000 2.602884
0.384189 1.0000% 1999 2.577113 0.388031 1.0000% 1998 2.551597 0.391911 1.0000% 1997
2.526333 0.395831 1.0000% 1996 2.501320 0.399789 1.0000% 1995 2.476555 0.403787
0.9992% 1994 2.452053 0.407821 1.0008% 1993 2.427757 0.411903 1.0000% 1992 2.403720
0.416022 0.9295% 1991 2.381583 0.419889 1.2505% 1990 2.352168 0.425140 0.7224% 1989
2.335297 0.428211 1.1077% 1988 2.309713 0.432954 0.8834% 1987 2.289489 0.436779
0.5594% 1986 2.276753 0.439222 1.3056% 1985 2.247410 0.444957 0.7673% 1984 2.230298
0.448371 0.8149% 1983 2.212269 0.452025 0.9737% 1982 2.190935 0.456426 0.9508% 1981
2.170299 0.460766 0.9031% 1980 2.150876 0.464927 2.2701% 1979 2.103133 0.475481
1.0042% 1978 2.082224 0.480256 0.9896% 1977 2.061820 0.485008 0.9103% 1976 2.043220
0.489424 0.8394% 1975 2.026211 0.493532 0.9042% 1974 2.008055 0.497994 1.1568% 1973
1.985091 0.503755 0.9427% 1972 1.966553 0.508504 0.7426% 1971 1.952056 0.512280
1.4697% 1970 1.923781 0.519810 0.6968% 1969 1.910469 0.523432 0.8565% 1968 1.894244
0.527915 1.5090% 1967 1.866084 0.535882 0.9949% 1966 1.847701 0.541213 1.0575% 1965
1.828367 0.546936 1.1300% 1964 1.807937 0.553117 1.5537% 1963 1.780277 0.561710

131

1.4658% 1962 1.754559 0.569944 1.5364% 1961 1.728009 0.578701 2.1586% 1960 1.691496
0.591193 -1.6655% 1959 1.720144 0.581347 4.3080% 1958 1.649101 0.606391 2.1130%
1957 1.614977 0.619204 1.9895% 1956 1.583474 0.631523 2.1231% 1955 1.550555 0.644931
1.4496% 1954 1.528399 0.654280 2.1573% 1953 1.496124 0.668394 1.2298% 1952 1.477948
0.676614 1.6814% 1951 1.453509 0.687990 1.6233% 1950 1.430292 0.699158 1.4265% 1949
1.410175 0.709132 1.7790% 1948 1.385526 0.721747 1.8242% 1947 1.360705 0.734913 -
2.6320% 1946 1.397487 0.715570 3.1768% 1945 1.354459 0.738302 6.4754% 1944 1.272086
0.786111 -0.3437% 1943 1.276473 0.783409 0.6562% 1942 1.268151 0.788550 0.6633%
1941 1.259795 0.793780 -5.6614% 1940 1.335397 0.748841 8.0381% 1939 1.236043
0.809034 0.8126% 1938 1.226079 0.815608 0.7762% 1937 1.216635 0.821939 0.6029% 1936
1.209344 0.826894 0.5244% 1935 1.203036 0.831231 -3.0364% 1934 1.240708 0.805991
4.6271% 1933 1.185838 0.843286 1.3921% 1932 1.169556 0.855025 -0.2051% 1931
1.171960 0.853272 0.8886% 1930 1.161638 0.860854 1.0126% 1929 1.149993 0.869571
1.1526% 1928 1.136889 0.879593 1.2160% 1927 1.123231 0.890289 1.4086% 1926 1.107629
0.902830 1.7667% 1925 1.088400 0.918780 1.4465% 1924 1.072881 0.932070 1.7700% 1923
1.054222 0.948567 1.6165% 1922 1.037451 0.963901 1.3736% 1921 1.023393 0.977142
2.3393% 1920 1.000000 1.000000 1.3140% 1919 0.987030 1.013140 0.7676% 1918 0.979511
1.020917 0.3870% 1917 0.975735 1.024868 1.3274% 1916 0.962953 1.038473 1.4083% 1915
0.949580 1.053097 1.4458% 1914 0.936046 1.068323 1.9424% 1913 0.918211 1.089074
1.9857% 1912 0.900334 1.110699 1.5634% 1911 0.886474 1.128064 1.8169% 1910 0.870655
1.148560 1.8781% 1909 0.854605 1.170131 2.0082% 1908 0.837781 1.193630 1.9603% 1907
0.821674 1.217028 1.8264% 1906 0.806936 1.239255 1.9357% 1905 0.791613 1.263243
2.0148% 1904 0.775978 1.288695 2.1335% 1903 0.759769 1.316190 1.8151% 1902 0.746224
1.340081 1.8943% 1901 0.732350 1.365467 3.0255% 1900 0.710844 1.406779 0.6278% 1899
0.706409 1.415611 1.7757% 1898 0.694084 1.440748 1.8078% 1897 0.681760 1.466793
1.8396% 1896 0.669444 1.493776 1.8755% 1895 0.657120 1.521792 1.9114% 1894 0.644795
1.550880 1.9486% 1893 0.632471 1.581101 1.9858% 1892 0.620156 1.612498 2.0276% 1891
0.607831 1.645194 2.6465% 1890 0.592160 1.688734 1.5328% 1889 0.583220 1.714619
2.0811% 1888 0.571330 1.750303 2.1599% 1887 0.559251 1.788107 2.2075% 1886 0.547172
1.827580 2.2592% 1885 0.535083 1.868868 2.3095% 1884 0.523004 1.912030 2.3641% 1883
0.510925 1.957233 2.4214% 1882 0.498846 2.004625 2.4815% 1881 0.486767 2.054369
3.7644% 1880 0.469108 2.131704 0.9432% 1879 0.464725 2.151811 2.1464% 1878 0.454960
2.197997 2.1913% 1877 0.445204 2.246162 2.2426% 1876 0.435439 2.296534 2.2941% 1875
0.425674 2.349218 2.3456% 1874 0.415918 2.404321 2.4043% 1873 0.406153 2.462129
2.4635% 1872 0.396387 2.522784 2.5258% 1871 0.386622 2.586504 5.9947% 1870 0.364756
2.741557 -1.0968% 1869 0.368801 2.711488 2.1930% 1868 0.360887 2.770950 2.2394%
1867 0.352982 2.833003 2.2935% 1866 0.345068 2.897978 2.3445% 1865 0.337164 2.965920
2.4037% 1864 0.329249 3.037212 2.4599% 1863 0.321345 3.111924 2.5250% 1862 0.313431
3.190500 2.5872% 1861 0.305526 3.273046 2.9504% 1860 0.296770 3.369614 2.4012% 1859
0.289811 3.450527 2.7627% 1858 0.282019 3.545855 2.8412% 1857 0.274228 3.646600
2.9243% 1856 0.266437 3.753237 3.0161% 1855 0.258636 3.866439 3.1061% 1854 0.250845
3.986533 3.2056% 1853 0.243053 4.114327 3.3118% 1852 0.235262 4.250584 3.4252% 1851
0.227470 4.396177 4.0106% 1850 0.218699 4.572490 2.3254% 1849 0.213729 4.678817
2.7841% 1848 0.207940 4.809079 2.8590% 1847 0.202160 4.946572 2.9432% 1846 0.196380
5.092157 3.0324% 1845 0.190601 5.246572 3.1325% 1844 0.184811 5.410921 3.2284% 1843
0.179032 5.585605 3.3361% 1842 0.173252 5.771944 3.4512% 1841 0.167472 5.971145
3.8105% 1840 0.161325 6.198675 2.3861% 1839 0.157565 6.346578 2.5824% 1838 0.153599
6.510472 2.6573% 1837 0.149623 6.683476 2.7232% 1836 0.145656 6.865481 2.7994% 1835
0.141690 7.057676 2.8871% 1834 0.137714 7.261439 2.9657% 1833 0.133747 7.476791
3.0563% 1832 0.129781 7.705306 3.1604% 1831 0.125805 7.948826 3.4660% 1830 0.121590
8.224330 2.4653% 1829 0.118665 8.427084 2.6804% 1828 0.115567 8.652963 10.3427%
1827 0.104735 9.547909 -4.2314% 1826 0.109363 9.143896 2.9150% 1825 0.106265
9.410443 3.0026% 1824 0.103167 9.692998 3.0955% 1823 0.100070 9.993045 3.1944% 1822
0.096972 10.312262 3.3102% 1821 0.093865 10.653618 3.2277% 1820 0.090930 10.997489
2.6573% 1819 0.088576 11.289723 2.6261% 1818 0.086310 11.586203 2.6969% 1817
0.084043 11.898675 2.7717% 1816 0.081776 12.228469 2.8507% 1815 0.079510 12.577065

2.9343% 1814 0.077243 12.946119 3.0231% 1813 0.074977 13.337487 3.1039% 1812
0.072720 13.751469 3.2172% 1811 0.070453 14.193875 3.0969% 1810 0.068337 14.633448
2.9144% 1809 0.066401 15.059922 2.8225% 1808 0.064579 15.484982 2.9199% 1807
0.062747 15.937133 2.9918% 1806 0.060924 16.413937 3.0841% 1805 0.059101 16.920152
3.1822% 1804 0.057278 17.458584 3.2868% 1803 0.055456 18.032410 3.3985% 1802
0.053633 18.645239 3.5180% 1801 0.051810 19.301187 3.3999% 1800 0.050107 19.957417
2.8419% 1799 0.048722 20.524580 2.7485% 1798 0.047419 21.088690 2.8261% 1797
0.046115 21.684684 3.7832% 1796 0.044434 22.505061 2.1272% 1795 0.043509 22.983788
3.0879% 1794 0.042206 23.693513 3.1625% 1793 0.040912 24.442823 3.2904% 1792
0.039609 25.247093 3.4024% 1791 0.038305 26.106092 3.2296% 1790 0.037107 26.949205
41.3145% 1780 0.026258 38.083121 29.4353% 1770 0.020287 49.293008 83.4728% 1750
0.011057 90.439281 29.2845% 1740 0.008553 116.923929 94.2514% 1720 0.004403
227.126362 85.8111% 1700 0.002370 422.025947 19.2490% 1690 0.001987 503.261930
88.0250% 1670 0.001057 946.258356
BASE YEAR: 1919
YEAR BYEAR/AYEAR AYEAR/BYEAR GROWTH%
2009 2.884142 0.346724 8.2857% 2001 2.663457 0.375452 1.0000% 2000 2.637086
0.379206 1.0000% 1999 2.610976 0.382999 1.0000% 1998 2.585125 0.386828 1.0000% 1997
2.559530 0.390697 1.0000% 1996 2.534188 0.394604 1.0000% 1995 2.509097 0.398550
0.9992% 1994 2.484273 0.402532 1.0008% 1993 2.459658 0.406561 1.0000% 1992 2.435305
0.410626 0.9295% 1991 2.412877 0.414443 1.2505% 1990 2.383076 0.419626 0.7224% 1989
2.365983 0.422657 1.1077% 1988 2.340063 0.427339 0.8834% 1987 2.319573 0.431114
0.5594% 1986 2.306670 0.433525 1.3056% 1985 2.276942 0.439186 0.7673% 1984 2.259604
0.442555 0.8149% 1983 2.241338 0.446162 0.9737% 1982 2.219724 0.450506 0.9508% 1981
2.198817 0.454790 0.9031% 1980 2.179138 0.458897 2.2701% 1979 2.130768 0.469314
1.0042% 1978 2.109584 0.474027 0.9896% 1977 2.088912 0.478718 0.9103% 1976 2.070068
0.483076 0.8394% 1975 2.052836 0.487131 0.9042% 1974 2.034441 0.491536 1.1568% 1973
2.011176 0.497222 0.9427% 1972 1.992393 0.501909 0.7426% 1971 1.977706 0.505636
1.4697% 1970 1.949060 0.513068 0.6968% 1969 1.935573 0.516643 0.8565% 1968 1.919134
0.521068 1.5090% 1967 1.890605 0.528931 0.9949% 1966 1.871980 0.534194 1.0575% 1965
1.852392 0.539843 1.1300% 1964 1.831693 0.545943 1.5537% 1963 1.803670 0.554425
1.4658% 1962 1.777614 0.562552 1.5364% 1961 1.750715 0.571195 2.1586% 1960 1.713722
0.583525 -1.6655% 1959 1.742747 0.573807 4.3080% 1958 1.670771 0.598526 2.1130%
1957 1.636198 0.611173 1.9895% 1956 1.604281 0.623332 2.1231% 1955 1.570929 0.636566
1.4496% 1954 1.548482 0.645794 2.1573% 1953 1.515783 0.659725 1.2298% 1952 1.497369
0.667838 1.6814% 1951 1.472609 0.679067 1.6233% 1950 1.449086 0.690090 1.4265% 1949
1.428705 0.699935 1.7790% 1948 1.403732 0.712387 1.8242% 1947 1.378584 0.725382 -
2.6320% 1946 1.415850 0.706289 3.1768% 1945 1.372256 0.728727 6.4754% 1944 1.288801
0.775915 -0.3437% 1943 1.293246 0.773248 0.6562% 1942 1.284814 0.778323 0.6633%
1941 1.276348 0.783485 -5.6614% 1940 1.352944 0.739129 8.0381% 1939 1.252284
0.798541 0.8126% 1938 1.242190 0.805030 0.7762% 1937 1.232622 0.811279 0.6029% 1936
1.225235 0.816170 0.5244% 1935 1.218844 0.820450 -3.0364% 1934 1.257011 0.795538
4.6271% 1933 1.201420 0.832348 1.3921% 1932 1.184924 0.843936 -0.2051% 1931
1.187359 0.842205 0.8886% 1930 1.176902 0.849689 1.0126% 1929 1.165104 0.858293
1.1526% 1928 1.151828 0.868185 1.2160% 1927 1.137990 0.878742 1.4086% 1926 1.122183
0.891120 1.7667% 1925 1.102702 0.906863 1.4465% 1924 1.086979 0.919981 1.7700% 1923
1.068074 0.936265 1.6165% 1922 1.051083 0.951400 1.3736% 1921 1.036841 0.964468
2.3393% 1920 1.013140 0.987030 1.3140% 1919 1.000000 1.000000 0.7676% 1918 0.992382
1.007676 0.3870% 1917 0.988556 1.011576 1.3274% 1916 0.975606 1.025004 1.4083% 1915
0.962057 1.039439 1.4458% 1914 0.948346 1.054467 1.9424% 1913 0.930277 1.074949
1.9857% 1912 0.912164 1.096294 1.5634% 1911 0.898123 1.113434 1.8169% 1910 0.882096
1.133664 1.8781% 1909 0.865835 1.154955 2.0082% 1908 0.848789 1.178149 1.9603% 1907
0.832471 1.201244 1.8264% 1906 0.817539 1.223183 1.9357% 1905 0.802015 1.246859
2.0148% 1904 0.786175 1.271982 2.1335% 1903 0.769752 1.299120 1.8151% 1902 0.756029
1.322701 1.8943% 1901 0.741973 1.347757 3.0255% 1900 0.720184 1.388534 0.6278% 1899
0.715691 1.397251 1.7757% 1898 0.703204 1.422062 1.8078% 1897 0.690718 1.447769

1.8396% 1896 0.678241 1.474402 1.8755% 1895 0.665754 1.502055 1.9114% 1894 0.653268 1.530765 1.9486% 1893 0.640782 1.560594 1.9858% 1892 0.628305 1.591585 2.0276% 1891 0.615818 1.623856 2.6465% 1890 0.599941 1.666832 1.5328% 1889 0.590883 1.692381 2.0811% 1888 0.578837 1.727602 2.1599% 1887 0.566599 1.764915 2.2075% 1886 0.554362 1.803877 2.2592% 1885 0.542114 1.844629 2.3095% 1884 0.529877 1.887232 2.3641% 1883 0.517639 1.931848 2.4214% 1882 0.505401 1.978626 2.4815% 1881 0.493164 2.027725 3.7644% 1880 0.475272 2.104057 0.9432% 1879 0.470831 2.123903 2.1464% 1878 0.460938 2.169490 2.1913% 1877 0.451054 2.217030 2.2426% 1876 0.441160 2.266749 2.2941% 1875 0.431267 2.318750 2.3456% 1874 0.421383 2.373138 2.4043% 1873 0.411489 2.430196 2.4635% 1872 0.401596 2.490065 2.5258% 1871 0.391702 2.552958 5.9947% 1870 0.369549 2.706000 -1.0968% 1869 0.373647 2.676321 2.1930% 1868 0.365629 2.735012 2.2394% 1867 0.357621 2.796260 2.2935% 1866 0.349602 2.860392 2.3445% 1865 0.341594 2.927453 2.4037% 1864 0.333576 2.997820 2.4599% 1863 0.325567 3.071563 2.5250% 1862 0.317549 3.149120 2.5872% 1861 0.309540 3.230596 2.9504% 1860 0.300669 3.325911 2.4012% 1859 0.293619 3.405774 2.7627% 1858 0.285725 3.499866 2.8412% 1857 0.277831 3.599304 2.9243% 1856 0.269938 3.704558 3.0161% 1855 0.262034 3.816293 3.1061% 1854 0.254141 3.934829 3.2056% 1853 0.246247 4.060965 3.3118% 1852 0.238353 4.195456 3.4252% 1851 0.230459 4.339160 4.0106% 1850 0.221573 4.513186 2.3254% 1849 0.216538 4.618134 2.7841% 1848 0.210672 4.746707 2.8590% 1847 0.204817 4.882416 2.9432% 1846 0.198961 5.026113 3.0324% 1845 0.193105 5.178525 3.1325% 1844 0.187240 5.340743 3.2284% 1843 0.181384 5.513161 3.3361% 1842 0.175528 5.697084 3.4512% 1841 0.169673 5.893701 3.8105% 1840 0.163445 6.118280 2.3861% 1839 0.159636 6.264265 2.5824% 1838 0.155617 6.426033 2.6573% 1837 0.151589 6.596794 2.7232% 1836 0.147570 6.776438 2.7994% 1835 0.143552 6.966140 2.8871% 1834 0.139523 7.167261 2.9657% 1833 0.135505 7.379819 3.0563% 1832 0.131486 7.605370 3.1604% 1831 0.127458 7.845732 3.4660% 1830 0.123188 8.117663 2.4653% 1829 0.120224 8.317788 2.6804% 1828 0.117086 8.540737 10.3427% 1827 0.106111 9.424076 -4.2314% 1826 0.110800 9.025302 2.9150% 1825 0.107661 9.288393 3.0026% 1824 0.104523 9.567283 3.0955% 1823 0.101385 9.863439 3.1944% 1822 0.098246 10.178516 3.3102% 1821 0.095098 10.515444 3.2277% 1820 0.092125 10.854855 2.6573% 1819 0.089740 11.143299 2.6261% 1818 0.087444 11.435934 2.6969% 1817 0.085147 11.744353 2.7717% 1816 0.082851 12.069869 2.8507% 1815 0.080555 12.413945 2.9343% 1814 0.078258 12.778212 3.0231% 1813 0.075962 13.164504 3.1039% 1812 0.073675 13.573117 3.2172% 1811 0.071379 14.009786 3.0969% 1810 0.069235 14.443657 2.9144% 1809 0.067274 14.864600 2.8225% 1808 0.065427 15.284147 2.9199% 1807 0.063571 15.730433 2.9918% 1806 0.061724 16.201054 3.0841% 1805 0.059878 16.700703 3.1822% 1804 0.058031 17.232152 3.2868% 1803 0.056184 17.798535 3.3985% 1802 0.054338 18.403416 3.5180% 1801 0.052491 19.050857 3.3999% 1800 0.050765 19.698576 2.8419% 1799 0.049362 20.258383 2.7485% 1798 0.048042 20.815176 2.8261% 1797 0.046721 21.403441 3.7832% 1796 0.045018 22.213177 2.1272% 1795 0.044081 22.685696 3.0879% 1794 0.042760 23.386216 3.1625% 1793 0.041449 24.125808 3.2904% 1792 0.040129 24.919647 3.4024% 1791 0.038809 25.767505 3.2296% 1790 0.037594 26.599683 41.3145% 1780 0.026603 37.589196 29.4353% 1770 0.020553 48.653694 83.4728% 1750 0.011202 89.266314 29.2845% 1740 0.008665 115.407465 94.2514% 1720 0.004461 224.180609 85.8111% 1700 0.002401 416.552411 19.2490% 1690 0.002013 496.734791 88.0250% 1670 0.001071 933.985702

BASE YEAR: 1918

YEAR BYEAR/AYEAR AYEAR/BYEAR GROWTH%

2009 2.906282 0.344082 8.2857% 2001 2.683903 0.372592 1.0000% 2000 2.657329 0.376318 1.0000% 1999 2.631019 0.380081 1.0000% 1998 2.604970 0.383882 1.0000% 1997 2.579178 0.387720 1.0000% 1996 2.553641 0.391598 1.0000% 1995 2.528358 0.395514 0.9992% 1994 2.503344 0.399466 1.0008% 1993 2.478539 0.403463 1.0000% 1992 2.453999 0.407498 0.9295% 1991 2.431399 0.411286 1.2505% 1990 2.401370 0.416429 0.7224% 1989 2.384145 0.419437 1.1077% 1988 2.358026 0.424083 0.8834% 1987 2.337379 0.427830 0.5594% 1986 2.324377 0.430223 1.3056% 1985 2.294420 0.435840 0.7673% 1984 2.276950 0.439184 0.8149% 1983 2.258544 0.442763 0.9737% 1982 2.236763 0.447075 0.9508% 1981 2.215696 0.451325 0.9031% 1980 2.195866 0.455401 2.2701% 1979 2.147125 0.465739

1.0042% 1978 2.125779 0.470416 0.9896% 1977 2.104948 0.475071 0.9103% 1976 2.085959
0.479396 0.8394% 1975 2.068594 0.483420 0.9042% 1974 2.050058 0.487791 1.1568% 1973
2.026614 0.493434 0.9427% 1972 2.007688 0.498085 0.7426% 1971 1.992888 0.501784
1.4697% 1970 1.964022 0.509159 0.6968% 1969 1.950431 0.512707 0.8565% 1968 1.933867
0.517099 1.5090% 1967 1.905118 0.524902 0.9949% 1966 1.886350 0.530124 1.0575% 1965
1.866611 0.535730 1.1300% 1964 1.845754 0.541784 1.5537% 1963 1.817516 0.550201
1.4658% 1962 1.791260 0.558266 1.5364% 1961 1.764154 0.566844 2.1586% 1960 1.726877
0.579080 -1.6655% 1959 1.756125 0.569435 4.3080% 1958 1.683596 0.593967 2.1130%
1957 1.648759 0.606517 1.9895% 1956 1.616596 0.618584 2.1231% 1955 1.582988 0.631717
1.4496% 1954 1.560369 0.640874 2.1573% 1953 1.527419 0.654699 1.2298% 1952 1.508863
0.662751 1.6814% 1951 1.483913 0.673894 1.6233% 1950 1.460210 0.684833 1.4265% 1949
1.439672 0.694602 1.7790% 1948 1.414508 0.706960 1.8242% 1947 1.389167 0.719856 -
2.6320% 1946 1.426719 0.700909 3.1768% 1945 1.382790 0.723175 6.4754% 1944 1.298694
0.770004 -0.3437% 1943 1.303173 0.767358 0.6562% 1942 1.294677 0.772393 0.6633%
1941 1.286146 0.777517 -5.6614% 1940 1.363330 0.733498 8.0381% 1939 1.261897
0.792457 0.8126% 1938 1.251726 0.798897 0.7762% 1937 1.242084 0.805099 0.6029% 1936
1.234641 0.809952 0.5244% 1935 1.228200 0.814200 -3.0364% 1934 1.266660 0.789478
4.6271% 1933 1.210643 0.826008 1.3921% 1932 1.194020 0.837507 -0.2051% 1931
1.196474 0.835789 0.8886% 1930 1.185936 0.843216 1.0126% 1929 1.174048 0.851754
1.1526% 1928 1.160670 0.861571 1.2160% 1927 1.146726 0.872048 1.4086% 1926 1.130798
0.884332 1.7667% 1925 1.111167 0.899955 1.4465% 1924 1.095323 0.912973 1.7700% 1923
1.076273 0.929132 1.6165% 1922 1.059152 0.944152 1.3736% 1921 1.044800 0.957121
2.3393% 1920 1.020917 0.979511 1.3140% 1919 1.007676 0.992382 0.7676% 1918 1.000000
1.000000 0.3870% 1917 0.996145 1.003870 1.3274% 1916 0.983095 1.017196 1.4083% 1915
0.969443 1.031521 1.4458% 1914 0.955626 1.046434 1.9424% 1913 0.937418 1.066760
1.9857% 1912 0.919166 1.087943 1.5634% 1911 0.905017 1.104951 1.8169% 1910 0.888867
1.125028 1.8781% 1909 0.872481 1.146156 2.0082% 1908 0.855305 1.169174 1.9603% 1907
0.838861 1.192093 1.8264% 1906 0.823815 1.213864 1.9357% 1905 0.808172 1.237361
2.0148% 1904 0.792210 1.262292 2.1335% 1903 0.775661 1.289223 1.8151% 1902 0.761833
1.312624 1.8943% 1901 0.747669 1.337490 3.0255% 1900 0.725713 1.377956 0.6278% 1899
0.721185 1.386607 1.7757% 1898 0.708602 1.411228 1.8078% 1897 0.696020 1.436740
1.8396% 1896 0.683447 1.463170 1.8755% 1895 0.670865 1.490613 1.9114% 1894 0.658283
1.519104 1.9486% 1893 0.645700 1.548706 1.9858% 1892 0.633128 1.579460 2.0276% 1891
0.620545 1.611486 2.6465% 1890 0.604546 1.654134 1.5328% 1889 0.595419 1.679489
2.0811% 1888 0.583280 1.714441 2.1599% 1887 0.570949 1.751470 2.2075% 1886 0.558617
1.790135 2.2592% 1885 0.546276 1.830577 2.3095% 1884 0.533944 1.872855 2.3641% 1883
0.521613 1.917132 2.4214% 1882 0.509281 1.963553 2.4815% 1881 0.496949 2.012278
3.7644% 1880 0.478921 2.088028 0.9432% 1879 0.474446 2.107723 2.1464% 1878 0.464476
2.152963 2.1913% 1877 0.454516 2.200141 2.2426% 1876 0.444547 2.249481 2.2941% 1875
0.434578 2.301085 2.3456% 1874 0.424618 2.355060 2.4043% 1873 0.414648 2.411683
2.4635% 1872 0.404679 2.471096 2.5258% 1871 0.394709 2.533510 5.9947% 1870 0.372386
2.685385 -1.0968% 1869 0.376516 2.655933 2.1930% 1868 0.368436 2.714176 2.2394%
1867 0.360366 2.774958 2.2935% 1866 0.352286 2.838602 2.3445% 1865 0.344216 2.905152
2.4037% 1864 0.336136 2.974983 2.4599% 1863 0.328066 3.048164 2.5250% 1862 0.319987
3.125130 2.5872% 1861 0.311917 3.205985 2.9504% 1860 0.302978 3.300575 2.4012% 1859
0.295873 3.379829 2.7627% 1858 0.287919 3.473204 2.8412% 1857 0.279964 3.571885
2.9243% 1856 0.272010 3.676337 3.0161% 1855 0.264046 3.787221 3.1061% 1854 0.256092
3.904854 3.2056% 1853 0.248137 4.030029 3.3118% 1852 0.240183 4.163495 3.4252% 1851
0.232228 4.306104 4.0106% 1850 0.223274 4.478805 2.3254% 1849 0.218200 4.582954
2.7841% 1848 0.212290 4.710547 2.8590% 1847 0.206389 4.845222 2.9432% 1846 0.200488
4.987825 3.0324% 1845 0.194588 5.139076 3.1325% 1844 0.188677 5.300057 3.2284% 1843
0.182777 5.471162 3.3361% 1842 0.176876 5.653684 3.4512% 1841 0.170975 5.848803
3.8105% 1840 0.164699 6.071671 2.3861% 1839 0.160861 6.216544 2.5824% 1838 0.156812
6.377080 2.6573% 1837 0.152752 6.546539 2.7232% 1836 0.148703 6.724815 2.7994% 1835
0.144653 6.913072 2.8871% 1834 0.140594 7.112661 2.9657% 1833 0.136545 7.323600
3.0563% 1832 0.132495 7.547433 3.1604% 1831 0.128436 7.785964 3.4660% 1830 0.124134

8.055823 2.4653% 1829 0.121147 8.254423 2.6804% 1828 0.117985 8.475674 10.3427%
1827 0.106926 9.352284 -4.2314% 1826 0.111650 8.956548 2.9150% 1825 0.108488
9.217635 3.0026% 1824 0.105325 9.494400 3.0955% 1823 0.102163 9.788300 3.1944% 1822
0.099000 10.100976 3.3102% 1821 0.095828 10.435338 3.2277% 1820 0.092832 10.772164
2.6573% 1819 0.090429 11.058410 2.6261% 1818 0.088115 11.348816 2.6969% 1817
0.085801 11.654885 2.7717% 1816 0.083487 11.977922 2.8507% 1815 0.081173 12.319376
2.9343% 1814 0.078859 12.680869 3.0231% 1813 0.076545 13.064218 3.1039% 1812
0.074241 13.469718 3.2172% 1811 0.071927 13.903060 3.0969% 1810 0.069766 14.333626
2.9144% 1809 0.067790 14.751362 2.8225% 1808 0.065930 15.167714 2.9199% 1807
0.064059 15.610600 2.9918% 1806 0.062198 16.077635 3.0841% 1805 0.060337 16.573478
3.1822% 1804 0.058477 17.100878 3.2868% 1803 0.056616 17.662947 3.3985% 1802
0.054755 18.263220 3.5180% 1801 0.052894 18.905728 3.3999% 1800 0.051155 19.548513
2.8419% 1799 0.049741 20.104056 2.7485% 1798 0.048411 20.656607 2.8261% 1797
0.047080 21.240390 3.7832% 1796 0.045364 22.043959 2.1272% 1795 0.044419 22.512877
3.0879% 1794 0.043088 23.208061 3.1625% 1793 0.041768 23.942019 3.2904% 1792
0.040437 24.729810 3.4024% 1791 0.039106 25.571209 3.2296% 1790 0.037883 26.397048
41.3145% 1780 0.026808 37.302843 29.4353% 1770 0.020711 48.283052 83.4728% 1750
0.011288 88.586287 29.2845% 1740 0.008731 114.528296 94.2514% 1720 0.004495
222.472812 85.8111% 1700 0.002419 413.379135 19.2490% 1690 0.002029 492.950689
88.0250% 1670 0.001079 926.870643

BASE YEAR: 1917

YEAR BYEAR/AYEAR AYEAR/BYEAR GROWTH%

2009 2.917529 0.342756 8.2857% 2001 2.694289 0.371155 1.0000% 2000 2.667613
0.374867 1.0000% 1999 2.641201 0.378616 1.0000% 1998 2.615050 0.382402 1.0000% 1997
2.589159 0.386226 1.0000% 1996 2.563524 0.390088 1.0000% 1995 2.538142 0.393989
0.9992% 1994 2.513031 0.397926 1.0008% 1993 2.488131 0.401908 1.0000% 1992 2.463496
0.405927 0.9295% 1991 2.440808 0.409700 1.2505% 1990 2.410663 0.414824 0.7224% 1989
2.393372 0.417821 1.1077% 1988 2.367152 0.422449 0.8834% 1987 2.346424 0.426180
0.5594% 1986 2.333372 0.428564 1.3056% 1985 2.303300 0.434160 0.7673% 1984 2.285761
0.437491 0.8149% 1983 2.267284 0.441056 0.9737% 1982 2.245419 0.445351 0.9508% 1981
2.224271 0.449586 0.9031% 1980 2.204364 0.453646 2.2701% 1979 2.155434 0.463944
1.0042% 1978 2.134005 0.468602 0.9896% 1977 2.113094 0.473240 0.9103% 1976 2.094031
0.477548 0.8394% 1975 2.076599 0.481557 0.9042% 1974 2.057991 0.485911 1.1568% 1973
2.034457 0.491532 0.9427% 1972 2.015457 0.496165 0.7426% 1971 2.000600 0.499850
1.4697% 1970 1.971622 0.507197 0.6968% 1969 1.957979 0.510731 0.8565% 1968 1.941350
0.515105 1.5090% 1967 1.912490 0.522878 0.9949% 1966 1.893650 0.528081 1.0575% 1965
1.873835 0.533665 1.1300% 1964 1.852897 0.539695 1.5537% 1963 1.824550 0.548080
1.4658% 1962 1.798191 0.556114 1.5364% 1961 1.770982 0.564659 2.1586% 1960 1.733560
0.576848 -1.6655% 1959 1.762921 0.567240 4.3080% 1958 1.690112 0.591677 2.1130%
1957 1.655139 0.604179 1.9895% 1956 1.622852 0.616199 2.1231% 1955 1.589114 0.629281
1.4496% 1954 1.566407 0.638404 2.1573% 1953 1.533329 0.652176 1.2298% 1952 1.514702
0.660196 1.6814% 1951 1.489656 0.671296 1.6233% 1950 1.465861 0.682193 1.4265% 1949
1.445244 0.691925 1.7790% 1948 1.419982 0.704234 1.8242% 1947 1.394543 0.717081 -
2.6320% 1946 1.432240 0.698207 3.1768% 1945 1.388142 0.720388 6.4754% 1944 1.303720
0.767036 -0.3437% 1943 1.308216 0.764400 0.6562% 1942 1.299687 0.769416 0.6633%
1941 1.291123 0.774519 -5.6614% 1940 1.368606 0.730670 8.0381% 1939 1.266781
0.789403 0.8126% 1938 1.256570 0.795817 0.7762% 1937 1.246891 0.801995 0.6029% 1936
1.239418 0.806830 0.5244% 1935 1.232953 0.811061 -3.0364% 1934 1.271562 0.786434
4.6271% 1933 1.215328 0.822823 1.3921% 1932 1.198641 0.834278 -0.2051% 1931
1.201104 0.832567 0.8886% 1930 1.190525 0.839965 1.0126% 1929 1.178591 0.848471
1.1526% 1928 1.165162 0.858250 1.2160% 1927 1.151163 0.868686 1.4086% 1926 1.135174
0.880923 1.7667% 1925 1.115467 0.896486 1.4465% 1924 1.099562 0.909453 1.7700% 1923
1.080438 0.925550 1.6165% 1922 1.063250 0.940512 1.3736% 1921 1.048843 0.953431
2.3393% 1920 1.024868 0.975735 1.3140% 1919 1.011576 0.988556 0.7676% 1918 1.003870
0.996145 0.3870% 1917 1.000000 1.000000 1.3274% 1916 0.986900 1.013274 1.4083% 1915
0.973194 1.027544 1.4458% 1914 0.959324 1.042400 1.9424% 1913 0.941046 1.062648

136

1.9857% 1912 0.922723 1.083749 1.5634% 1911 0.908519 1.100692 1.8169% 1910 0.892307
1.120691 1.8781% 1909 0.875858 1.141738 2.0082% 1908 0.858615 1.164667 1.9603% 1907
0.842107 1.187497 1.8264% 1906 0.827003 1.209185 1.9357% 1905 0.811299 1.232591
2.0148% 1904 0.795276 1.257426 2.1335% 1903 0.778663 1.284253 1.8151% 1902 0.764781
1.307564 1.8943% 1901 0.750563 1.332334 3.0255% 1900 0.728521 1.372644 0.6278% 1899
0.723976 1.381262 1.7757% 1898 0.711345 1.405788 1.8078% 1897 0.698714 1.431201
1.8396% 1896 0.686092 1.457530 1.8755% 1895 0.673461 1.484866 1.9114% 1894 0.660830
1.513248 1.9486% 1893 0.648199 1.542736 1.9858% 1892 0.635578 1.573371 2.0276% 1891
0.622947 1.605273 2.6465% 1890 0.606886 1.647757 1.5328% 1889 0.597724 1.673014
2.0811% 1888 0.585538 1.707832 2.1599% 1887 0.573158 1.744719 2.2075% 1886 0.560779
1.783234 2.2592% 1885 0.548390 1.823520 2.3095% 1884 0.536011 1.865635 2.3641% 1883
0.523631 1.909741 2.4214% 1882 0.511252 1.955983 2.4815% 1881 0.498872 2.004521
3.7644% 1880 0.480774 2.079979 0.9432% 1879 0.476282 2.099598 2.1464% 1878 0.466274
2.144663 2.1913% 1877 0.456275 2.191659 2.2426% 1876 0.446267 2.240809 2.2941% 1875
0.436259 2.292215 2.3456% 1874 0.426261 2.345981 2.4043% 1873 0.416253 2.402386
2.4635% 1872 0.406245 2.461570 2.5258% 1871 0.396237 2.523743 5.9947% 1870 0.373827
2.675033 -1.0968% 1869 0.377973 2.645694 2.1930% 1868 0.369862 2.703713 2.2394%
1867 0.361760 2.764260 2.2935% 1866 0.353649 2.827659 2.3445% 1865 0.345548 2.893953
2.4037% 1864 0.337437 2.963514 2.4599% 1863 0.329336 3.036413 2.5250% 1862 0.321225
3.113083 2.5872% 1861 0.313124 3.193626 2.9504% 1860 0.304150 3.287851 2.4012% 1859
0.297018 3.366800 2.7627% 1858 0.289033 3.459815 2.8412% 1857 0.281048 3.558116
2.9243% 1856 0.273063 3.662165 3.0161% 1855 0.265068 3.772621 3.1061% 1854 0.257083
3.889801 3.2056% 1853 0.249097 4.014493 3.3118% 1852 0.241112 4.147445 3.4252% 1851
0.233127 4.289504 4.0106% 1850 0.224138 4.461539 2.3254% 1849 0.219044 4.565287
2.7841% 1848 0.213111 4.692388 2.8590% 1847 0.207188 4.826544 2.9432% 1846 0.201264
4.968597 3.0324% 1845 0.195341 5.119265 3.1325% 1844 0.189407 5.279626 3.2284% 1843
0.183484 5.450071 3.3361% 1842 0.177560 5.631889 3.4512% 1841 0.171637 5.826256
3.8105% 1840 0.165337 6.048265 2.3861% 1839 0.161484 6.192580 2.5824% 1838 0.157418
6.352496 2.6573% 1837 0.153344 6.521303 2.7232% 1836 0.149278 6.698891 2.7994% 1835
0.145213 6.886423 2.8871% 1834 0.141138 7.085242 2.9657% 1833 0.137073 7.295368
3.0563% 1832 0.133008 7.518338 3.1604% 1831 0.128933 7.755949 3.4660% 1830 0.124614
8.024768 2.4653% 1829 0.121616 8.222602 2.6804% 1828 0.118441 8.443001 10.3427%
1827 0.107340 9.316231 -4.2314% 1826 0.112082 8.922021 2.9150% 1825 0.108908
9.182101 3.0026% 1824 0.105733 9.457799 3.0955% 1823 0.102558 9.750566 3.1944% 1822
0.099383 10.062037 3.3102% 1821 0.096199 10.395110 3.2277% 1820 0.093191 10.730637
2.6573% 1819 0.090779 11.015780 2.6261% 1818 0.088456 11.305066 2.6969% 1817
0.086133 11.609956 2.7717% 1816 0.083810 11.931747 2.8507% 1815 0.081487 12.271885
2.9343% 1814 0.079164 12.631984 3.0231% 1813 0.076841 13.013856 3.1039% 1812
0.074528 13.417792 3.2172% 1811 0.072205 13.849464 3.0969% 1810 0.070036 14.278370
2.9144% 1809 0.068053 14.694496 2.8225% 1808 0.066185 15.109242 2.9199% 1807
0.064307 15.550421 2.9918% 1806 0.062439 16.015656 3.0841% 1805 0.060571 16.509588
3.1822% 1804 0.058703 17.034955 3.2868% 1803 0.056835 17.594857 3.3985% 1802
0.054967 18.192816 3.5180% 1801 0.053099 18.832847 3.3999% 1800 0.051353 19.473154
2.8419% 1799 0.049934 20.026556 2.7485% 1798 0.048598 20.576977 2.8261% 1797
0.047262 21.158509 3.7832% 1796 0.045539 21.958980 2.1272% 1795 0.044591 22.426091
3.0879% 1794 0.043255 23.118595 3.1625% 1793 0.041929 23.849723 3.2904% 1792
0.040594 24.634478 3.4024% 1791 0.039258 25.472633 3.2296% 1790 0.038030 26.295288
41.3145% 1780 0.026911 37.159042 29.4353% 1770 0.020791 48.096923 83.4728% 1750
0.011332 88.244790 29.2845% 1740 0.008765 114.086793 94.2514% 1720 0.004512
221.615187 85.8111% 1700 0.002428 411.785572 19.2490% 1690 0.002036 491.050380
88.0250% 1670 0.001083 923.297587

BASE YEAR: 1916

YEAR BYEAR/AYEAR AYEAR/BYEAR GROWTH%

2009 2.956257 0.338266 8.2857% 2001 2.730054 0.366293 1.0000% 2000 2.703024
0.369956 1.0000% 1999 2.676261 0.373656 1.0000% 1998 2.649764 0.377392 1.0000% 1997
2.623528 0.381166 1.0000% 1996 2.597553 0.384978 1.0000% 1995 2.571834 0.388828

137

0.9992% 1994 2.546390 0.392713 1.0008% 1993 2.521159 0.396643 1.0000% 1992 2.496197
0.400609 0.9295% 1991 2.473209 0.404333 1.2505% 1990 2.442663 0.409389 0.7224% 1989
2.425142 0.412347 1.1077% 1988 2.398574 0.416914 0.8834% 1987 2.377571 0.420597
0.5594% 1986 2.364346 0.422950 1.3056% 1985 2.333874 0.428472 0.7673% 1984 2.316103
0.431760 0.8149% 1983 2.297381 0.435278 0.9737% 1982 2.275226 0.439517 0.9508% 1981
2.253797 0.443696 0.9031% 1980 2.233626 0.447703 2.2701% 1979 2.184046 0.457866
1.0042% 1978 2.162333 0.462464 0.9896% 1977 2.141144 0.467040 0.9103% 1976 2.121828
0.471292 0.8394% 1975 2.104165 0.475248 0.9042% 1974 2.085310 0.479545 1.1568% 1973
2.061463 0.485092 0.9427% 1972 2.042211 0.489665 0.7426% 1971 2.027157 0.493302
1.4697% 1970 1.997794 0.500552 0.6968% 1969 1.983970 0.504040 0.8565% 1968 1.967121
0.508357 1.5090% 1967 1.937877 0.516029 0.9949% 1966 1.918787 0.521163 1.0575% 1965
1.898709 0.526674 1.1300% 1964 1.877493 0.532625 1.5537% 1963 1.848769 0.540900
1.4658% 1962 1.822061 0.548829 1.5364% 1961 1.794490 0.557261 2.1586% 1960 1.756572
0.569291 -1.6655% 1959 1.786323 0.559809 4.3080% 1958 1.712547 0.583926 2.1130%
1957 1.677110 0.596264 1.9895% 1956 1.644395 0.608126 2.1231% 1955 1.610209 0.621038
1.4496% 1954 1.587200 0.630040 2.1573% 1953 1.553683 0.643632 1.2298% 1952 1.534809
0.651547 1.6814% 1951 1.509430 0.662502 1.6233% 1950 1.485319 0.673256 1.4265% 1949
1.464428 0.682860 1.7790% 1948 1.438831 0.695009 1.8242% 1947 1.413055 0.707687 -
2.6320% 1946 1.451252 0.689060 3.1768% 1945 1.406568 0.710950 6.4754% 1944 1.321026
0.756987 -0.3437% 1943 1.325582 0.754386 0.6562% 1942 1.316940 0.759336 0.6633%
1941 1.308262 0.764373 -5.6614% 1940 1.386773 0.721098 8.0381% 1939 1.283597
0.779061 0.8126% 1938 1.273250 0.785392 0.7762% 1937 1.263442 0.791488 0.6029% 1936
1.255871 0.796260 0.5244% 1935 1.249320 0.800436 -3.0364% 1934 1.288441 0.776132
4.6271% 1933 1.231460 0.812044 1.3921% 1932 1.214552 0.823349 -0.2051% 1931
1.217048 0.821660 0.8886% 1930 1.206329 0.828961 1.0126% 1929 1.194236 0.837355
1.1526% 1928 1.180628 0.847007 1.2160% 1927 1.166444 0.857306 1.4086% 1926 1.150242
0.869382 1.7667% 1925 1.130274 0.884741 1.4465% 1924 1.114158 0.897539 1.7700% 1923
1.094780 0.913425 1.6165% 1922 1.077364 0.928191 1.3736% 1921 1.062766 0.940941
2.3393% 1920 1.038473 0.962953 1.3140% 1919 1.025004 0.975606 0.7676% 1918 1.017196
0.983095 0.3870% 1917 1.013274 0.986900 1.3274% 1916 1.000000 1.000000 1.4083% 1915
0.986113 1.014083 1.4458% 1914 0.972059 1.028745 1.9424% 1913 0.953537 1.048727
1.9857% 1912 0.934972 1.069551 1.5634% 1911 0.920579 1.086272 1.8169% 1910 0.904152
1.106009 1.8781% 1909 0.887484 1.126781 2.0082% 1908 0.870012 1.149409 1.9603% 1907
0.853286 1.171940 1.8264% 1906 0.837981 1.193344 1.9357% 1905 0.822069 1.216443
2.0148% 1904 0.805832 1.240953 2.1335% 1903 0.788999 1.267429 1.8151% 1902 0.774933
1.290434 1.8943% 1901 0.760526 1.314880 3.0255% 1900 0.738192 1.354662 0.6278% 1899
0.733586 1.363167 1.7757% 1898 0.720787 1.387372 1.8078% 1897 0.707989 1.412452
1.8396% 1896 0.695200 1.438435 1.8755% 1895 0.682401 1.465414 1.9114% 1894 0.669602
1.493424 1.9486% 1893 0.656804 1.522525 1.9858% 1892 0.644015 1.552759 2.0276% 1891
0.631216 1.584244 2.6465% 1890 0.614942 1.626171 1.5328% 1889 0.605658 1.651097
2.0811% 1888 0.593310 1.685459 2.1599% 1887 0.580767 1.721862 2.2075% 1886 0.568223
1.759873 2.2592% 1885 0.555669 1.799631 2.3095% 1884 0.543126 1.841194 2.3641% 1883
0.530582 1.884723 2.4214% 1882 0.518038 1.930359 2.4815% 1881 0.505495 1.978260
3.7644% 1880 0.487156 2.052730 0.9432% 1879 0.482604 2.072092 2.1464% 1878 0.472463
2.116567 2.1913% 1877 0.462332 2.162947 2.2426% 1876 0.452191 2.211454 2.2941% 1875
0.442050 2.262186 2.3456% 1874 0.431919 2.315248 2.4043% 1873 0.421778 2.370913
2.4635% 1872 0.411637 2.429322 2.5258% 1871 0.401497 2.490681 5.9947% 1870 0.378789
2.639989 -1.0968% 1869 0.382990 2.611034 2.1930% 1868 0.374771 2.668294 2.2394%
1867 0.366563 2.728047 2.2935% 1866 0.358344 2.790615 2.3445% 1865 0.350135 2.856040
2.4037% 1864 0.341916 2.924691 2.4599% 1863 0.333708 2.996635 2.5250% 1862 0.325489
3.072300 2.5872% 1861 0.317280 3.151788 2.9504% 1860 0.308187 3.244779 2.4012% 1859
0.300961 3.322694 2.7627% 1858 0.292870 3.414490 2.8412% 1857 0.284778 3.511503
2.9243% 1856 0.276687 3.614189 3.0161% 1855 0.268586 3.723198 3.1061% 1854 0.260495
3.838843 3.2056% 1853 0.252404 3.961902 3.3118% 1852 0.244313 4.093111 3.4252% 1851
0.236222 4.233310 4.0106% 1850 0.227113 4.403091 2.3254% 1849 0.221952 4.505479
2.7841% 1848 0.215940 4.630916 2.8590% 1847 0.209938 4.763314 2.9432% 1846 0.203936

138

4.903506 3.0324% 1845 0.197934 5.052200 3.1325% 1844 0.191922 5.210460 3.2284% 1843 0.185919 5.378673 3.3361% 1842 0.179917 5.558108 3.4512% 1841 0.173915 5.749930 3.8105% 1840 0.167531 5.969030 2.3861% 1839 0.163627 6.111454 2.5824% 1838 0.159508 6.269276 2.6573% 1837 0.155379 6.435871 2.7232% 1836 0.151260 6.611133 2.7994% 1835 0.147141 6.796207 2.8871% 1834 0.143012 6.992422 2.9657% 1833 0.138893 7.199795 3.0563% 1832 0.134774 7.419844 3.1604% 1831 0.130645 7.654343 3.4660% 1830 0.126268 7.919640 2.4653% 1829 0.123230 8.114883 2.6804% 1828 0.120014 8.332394 10.3427% 1827 0.108764 9.194184 -4.2314% 1826 0.113570 8.805138 2.9150% 1825 0.110353 9.061811 3.0026% 1824 0.107136 9.333898 3.0955% 1823 0.103920 9.622829 3.1944% 1822 0.100703 9.930220 3.3102% 1821 0.097476 10.258929 3.2277% 1820 0.094428 10.590061 2.6573% 1819 0.091984 10.871468 2.6261% 1818 0.089630 11.156965 2.6969% 1817 0.087276 11.457860 2.7717% 1816 0.084923 11.775436 2.8507% 1815 0.082569 12.111118 2.9343% 1814 0.080215 12.466500 3.0231% 1813 0.077861 12.843368 3.1039% 1812 0.075517 13.242013 3.2172% 1811 0.073163 13.668029 3.0969% 1810 0.070966 14.091317 2.9144% 1809 0.068956 14.501991 2.8225% 1808 0.067063 14.911304 2.9199% 1807 0.065161 15.346704 2.9918% 1806 0.063268 15.805844 3.0841% 1805 0.061375 16.293305 3.1822% 1804 0.059482 16.811789 3.2868% 1803 0.057589 17.364356 3.3985% 1802 0.055696 17.954481 3.5180% 1801 0.053804 18.586128 3.3999% 1800 0.052034 19.218047 2.8419% 1799 0.050597 19.764198 2.7485% 1798 0.049243 20.307409 2.8261% 1797 0.047890 20.881323 3.7832% 1796 0.046144 21.671307 2.1272% 1795 0.045183 22.132299 3.0879% 1794 0.043829 22.815731 3.1625% 1793 0.042486 23.537281 3.2904% 1792 0.041132 24.311755 3.4024% 1791 0.039779 25.138930 3.2296% 1790 0.038534 25.950808 41.3145% 1780 0.027269 36.672241 29.4353% 1770 0.021047 47.466831 83.4728% 1750 0.011483 87.088743 29.2845% 1740 0.008882 112.592204 94.2514% 1720 0.004572 218.711926 85.8111% 1700 0.002461 406.390992 19.2490% 1690 0.002063 484.617395 88.0250% 1670 0.001097 911.201966

BASE YEAR: 1915
YEAR BYEAR/AYEAR AYEAR/BYEAR GROWTH%

2009 2.997890 0.333568 8.2857% 2001 2.768501 0.361206 1.0000% 2000 2.741090 0.364818 1.0000% 1999 2.713951 0.368467 1.0000% 1998 2.687080 0.372151 1.0000% 1997 2.660475 0.375873 1.0000% 1996 2.634134 0.379631 1.0000% 1995 2.608053 0.383428 0.9992% 1994 2.582251 0.387259 1.0008% 1993 2.556664 0.391135 1.0000% 1992 2.531351 0.395046 0.9295% 1991 2.508038 0.398718 1.2505% 1990 2.477062 0.403704 0.7224% 1989 2.459295 0.406621 1.1077% 1988 2.432353 0.411125 0.8834% 1987 2.411054 0.414756 0.5594% 1986 2.397643 0.417076 1.3056% 1985 2.366742 0.422522 0.7673% 1984 2.348721 0.425764 0.8149% 1983 2.329735 0.429233 0.9737% 1982 2.307268 0.433413 0.9508% 1981 2.285537 0.437534 0.9031% 1980 2.265082 0.441485 2.2701% 1979 2.214804 0.451507 1.0042% 1978 2.192785 0.456041 0.9896% 1977 2.171297 0.460554 0.9103% 1976 2.151709 0.464747 0.8394% 1975 2.133797 0.468648 0.9042% 1974 2.114677 0.472885 1.1568% 1973 2.090495 0.478356 0.9427% 1972 2.070971 0.482865 0.7426% 1971 2.055705 0.486451 1.4697% 1970 2.025929 0.493601 0.6968% 1969 2.011910 0.497040 0.8565% 1968 1.994823 0.501298 1.5090% 1967 1.965168 0.508862 0.9949% 1966 1.945809 0.513925 1.0575% 1965 1.925448 0.519360 1.1300% 1964 1.903933 0.525228 1.5537% 1963 1.874805 0.533389 1.4658% 1962 1.847721 0.541207 1.5364% 1961 1.819762 0.549522 2.1586% 1960 1.781310 0.561385 -1.6655% 1959 1.811480 0.552035 4.3080% 1958 1.736664 0.575817 2.1130% 1957 1.700729 0.587983 1.9895% 1956 1.667553 0.599681 2.1231% 1955 1.632885 0.612413 1.4496% 1954 1.609553 0.621291 2.1573% 1953 1.575564 0.634693 1.2298% 1952 1.556424 0.642499 1.6814% 1951 1.530687 0.653301 1.6233% 1950 1.506237 0.663906 1.4265% 1949 1.485052 0.673377 1.7790% 1948 1.459094 0.685357 1.8242% 1947 1.432955 0.697859 -2.6320% 1946 1.471690 0.679491 3.1768% 1945 1.426377 0.701077 6.4754% 1944 1.339630 0.746475 -0.3437% 1943 1.344250 0.743909 0.6562% 1942 1.335486 0.748791 0.6633% 1941 1.326686 0.753758 -5.6614% 1940 1.406303 0.711084 8.0381% 1939 1.301673 0.768242 0.8126% 1938 1.291181 0.774485 0.7762% 1937 1.281235 0.780497 0.6029% 1936 1.273557 0.785202 0.5244% 1935 1.266914 0.789320 -3.0364% 1934 1.306586 0.765353 4.6271% 1933 1.248803 0.800767 1.3921% 1932 1.231657 0.811915 -0.2051% 1931 1.234188 0.810249 0.8886% 1930 1.223317 0.817449 1.0126% 1929 1.211054 0.825727

139

1.1526% 1928 1.197255 0.835244 1.2160% 1927 1.182871 0.845401 1.4086% 1926 1.166441
0.857309 1.7667% 1925 1.146191 0.872455 1.4465% 1924 1.129848 0.885075 1.7700% 1923
1.110198 0.900740 1.6165% 1922 1.092537 0.915301 1.3736% 1921 1.077733 0.927874
2.3393% 1920 1.053097 0.949580 1.3140% 1919 1.039439 0.962057 0.7676% 1918 1.031521
0.969443 0.3870% 1917 1.027544 0.973194 1.3274% 1916 1.014083 0.986113 1.4083% 1915
1.000000 1.000000 1.4458% 1914 0.985748 1.014458 1.9424% 1913 0.966966 1.034163
1.9857% 1912 0.948139 1.054698 1.5634% 1911 0.933544 1.071187 1.8169% 1910 0.916885
1.090650 1.8781% 1909 0.899983 1.111133 2.0082% 1908 0.882265 1.133447 1.9603% 1907
0.865302 1.155665 1.8264% 1906 0.849782 1.176772 1.9357% 1905 0.833646 1.199550
2.0148% 1904 0.817181 1.223719 2.1335% 1903 0.800110 1.249828 1.8151% 1902 0.785846
1.272514 1.8943% 1901 0.771236 1.296620 3.0255% 1900 0.748588 1.335849 0.6278% 1899
0.743917 1.344236 1.7757% 1898 0.730938 1.368105 1.8078% 1897 0.717959 1.392837
1.8396% 1896 0.704990 1.418459 1.8755% 1895 0.692011 1.445063 1.9114% 1894 0.679032
1.472684 1.9486% 1893 0.666053 1.501381 1.9858% 1892 0.653084 1.531196 2.0276% 1891
0.640105 1.562243 2.6465% 1890 0.623602 1.603588 1.5328% 1889 0.614187 1.628168
2.0811% 1888 0.601666 1.662052 2.1599% 1887 0.588946 1.697950 2.2075% 1886 0.576225
1.735433 2.2592% 1885 0.563495 1.774639 2.3095% 1884 0.550775 1.815625 2.3641% 1883
0.538054 1.858549 2.4214% 1882 0.525334 1.903552 2.4815% 1881 0.512613 1.950788
3.7644% 1880 0.494017 2.024223 0.9432% 1879 0.489401 2.043316 2.1464% 1878 0.479117
2.087174 2.1913% 1877 0.468843 2.132910 2.2426% 1876 0.458559 2.180743 2.2941% 1875
0.448276 2.230770 2.3456% 1874 0.438002 2.283095 2.4043% 1873 0.427718 2.337988
2.4635% 1872 0.417435 2.395585 2.5258% 1871 0.407151 2.456092 5.9947% 1870 0.384124
2.603327 -1.0968% 1869 0.388384 2.574774 2.1930% 1868 0.380049 2.631238 2.2394%
1867 0.371725 2.690162 2.2935% 1866 0.363390 2.751861 2.3445% 1865 0.355066 2.816378
2.4037% 1864 0.346732 2.884075 2.4599% 1863 0.338407 2.955020 2.5250% 1862 0.330073
3.029634 2.5872% 1861 0.321748 3.108018 2.9504% 1860 0.312528 3.199717 2.4012% 1859
0.305199 3.276550 2.7627% 1858 0.296994 3.367072 2.8412% 1857 0.288789 3.462737
2.9243% 1856 0.280584 3.563998 3.0161% 1855 0.272369 3.671493 3.1061% 1854 0.264164
3.785531 3.2056% 1853 0.255959 3.906881 3.3118% 1852 0.247754 4.036269 3.4252% 1851
0.239548 4.174520 4.0106% 1850 0.230312 4.341944 2.3254% 1849 0.225078 4.442910
2.7841% 1848 0.218981 4.566605 2.8590% 1847 0.212894 4.697164 2.9432% 1846 0.206808
4.835409 3.0324% 1845 0.200721 4.982038 3.1325% 1844 0.194624 5.138101 3.2284% 1843
0.188538 5.303977 3.3361% 1842 0.182451 5.480921 3.4512% 1841 0.176364 5.670078
3.8105% 1840 0.169891 5.886136 2.3861% 1839 0.165932 6.026582 2.5824% 1838 0.161754
6.182212 2.6573% 1837 0.157567 6.346494 2.7232% 1836 0.153390 6.519322 2.7994% 1835
0.149213 6.701826 2.8871% 1834 0.145026 6.895316 2.9657% 1833 0.140849 7.099809
3.0563% 1832 0.136672 7.316803 3.1604% 1831 0.132485 7.548044 3.4660% 1830 0.128047
7.809657 2.4653% 1829 0.124966 8.002189 2.6804% 1828 0.121704 8.216679 10.3427%
1827 0.110296 9.066501 -4.2314% 1826 0.115169 8.682858 2.9150% 1825 0.111907
8.935967 3.0026% 1824 0.108645 9.204275 3.0955% 1823 0.105383 9.489194 3.1944% 1822
0.102121 9.792316 3.3102% 1821 0.098849 10.116460 3.2277% 1820 0.095758 10.442993
2.6573% 1819 0.093279 10.720493 2.6261% 1818 0.090892 11.002024 2.6969% 1817
0.088505 11.298741 2.7717% 1816 0.086119 11.611907 2.8507% 1815 0.083732 11.942927
2.9343% 1814 0.081345 12.293373 3.0231% 1813 0.078958 12.665008 3.1039% 1812
0.076581 13.058117 3.2172% 1811 0.074194 13.478217 3.0969% 1810 0.071965 13.895626
2.9144% 1809 0.069927 14.300597 2.8225% 1808 0.068008 14.704226 2.9199% 1807
0.066078 15.133579 2.9918% 1806 0.064159 15.586343 3.0841% 1805 0.062239 16.067034
3.1822% 1804 0.060320 16.578318 3.2868% 1803 0.058400 17.123212 3.3985% 1802
0.056481 17.705142 3.5180% 1801 0.054561 18.328017 3.3999% 1800 0.052767 18.951160
2.8419% 1799 0.051309 19.489727 2.7485% 1798 0.049937 20.025393 2.8261% 1797
0.048564 20.591337 3.7832% 1796 0.046794 21.370351 2.1272% 1795 0.045819 21.824940
3.0879% 1794 0.044447 22.498881 3.1625% 1793 0.043084 23.210411 3.2904% 1792
0.041712 23.974130 3.4024% 1791 0.040339 24.789818 3.2296% 1790 0.039077 25.590420
41.3145% 1780 0.027653 36.162962 29.4353% 1770 0.021364 46.807644 83.4728% 1750
0.011644 85.879313 29.2845% 1740 0.009007 111.028600 94.2514% 1720 0.004637

215.674603 85.8111% 1700 0.002495 400.747310 19.2490% 1690 0.002093 477.887357 88.0250% 1670 0.001113 898.547811

2009 3.041234 0.328814 8.2857% 2001 2.808529 0.356058 1.0000% 2000 2.780721 0.359619 1.0000% 1999 2.753189 0.363215 1.0000% 1998 2.725930 0.366847 1.0000% 1997 2.698940 0.370516 1.0000% 1996 2.672218 0.374221 1.0000% 1995 2.645761 0.377963 0.9992% 1994 2.619585 0.381740 1.0008% 1993 2.593629 0.385560 1.0000% 1992 2.567949 0.389416 0.9295% 1991 2.544300 0.393035 1.2505% 1990 2.512876 0.397950 0.7224% 1989 2.494852 0.400825 1.1077% 1988 2.467520 0.405265 0.8834% 1987 2.445914 0.408845 0.5594% 1986 2.432308 0.411132 1.3056% 1985 2.400961 0.416500 0.7673% 1984 2.382679 0.419696 0.8149% 1983 2.363418 0.423116 0.9737% 1982 2.340626 0.427236 0.9508% 1981 2.318581 0.431298 0.9031% 1980 2.297830 0.435193 2.2701% 1979 2.246826 0.445072 1.0042% 1978 2.224488 0.449542 0.9896% 1977 2.202690 0.453990 0.9103% 1976 2.182819 0.458123 0.8394% 1975 2.164648 0.461969 0.9042% 1974 2.145251 0.466146 1.1568% 1973 2.120719 0.471538 0.9427% 1972 2.100914 0.475983 0.7426% 1971 2.085426 0.479518 1.4697% 1970 2.055220 0.486566 0.6968% 1969 2.040998 0.489956 0.8565% 1968 2.023665 0.494153 1.5090% 1967 1.993581 0.501610 0.9949% 1966 1.973942 0.506601 1.0575% 1965 1.953286 0.511958 1.1300% 1964 1.931461 0.517743 1.5537% 1963 1.901911 0.525787 1.4658% 1962 1.874436 0.533494 1.5364% 1961 1.846072 0.541691 2.1586% 1960 1.807064 0.553384 -1.6655% 1959 1.837670 0.544167 4.3080% 1958 1.761773 0.567610 2.1130% 1957 1.725318 0.579603 1.9895% 1956 1.691662 0.591135 2.1231% 1955 1.656493 0.603685 1.4496% 1954 1.632824 0.612436 2.1573% 1953 1.598343 0.625648 1.2298% 1952 1.578926 0.633342 1.6814% 1951 1.552818 0.643991 1.6233% 1950 1.528014 0.654444 1.4265% 1949 1.506523 0.663780 1.7790% 1948 1.480190 0.675589 1.8242% 1947 1.453672 0.687913 -2.6320% 1946 1.492968 0.669807 3.1768% 1945 1.446999 0.691085 6.4754% 1944 1.358999 0.735836 -0.3437% 1943 1.363685 0.733307 0.6562% 1942 1.354795 0.738119 0.6633% 1941 1.345868 0.743015 -5.6614% 1940 1.426636 0.700950 8.0381% 1939 1.320493 0.757293 0.8126% 1938 1.309849 0.763447 0.7762% 1937 1.299759 0.769373 0.6029% 1936 1.291970 0.774012 0.5244% 1935 1.285231 0.778070 -3.0364% 1934 1.325477 0.754445 4.6271% 1933 1.266858 0.789354 1.3921% 1932 1.249464 0.800343 -0.2051% 1931 1.252032 0.798702 0.8886% 1930 1.241004 0.805799 1.0126% 1929 1.228564 0.813958 1.1526% 1928 1.214565 0.823340 1.2160% 1927 1.199973 0.833352 1.4086% 1926 1.183305 0.845090 1.7667% 1925 1.162763 0.860020 1.4465% 1924 1.146183 0.872461 1.7700% 1923 1.126249 0.887903 1.6165% 1922 1.108333 0.902256 1.3736% 1921 1.093315 0.914650 2.3393% 1920 1.068323 0.936046 1.3140% 1919 1.054467 0.948346 0.7676% 1918 1.046434 0.955626 0.3870% 1917 1.042400 0.959324 1.3274% 1916 1.028745 0.972059 1.4083% 1915 1.014458 0.985748 1.4458% 1914 1.000000 1.000000 1.9424% 1913 0.980946 1.019424 1.9857% 1912 0.961847 1.039666 1.5634% 1911 0.947041 1.055920 1.8169% 1910 0.930141 1.075106 1.8781% 1909 0.912995 1.095297 2.0082% 1908 0.895020 1.117293 1.9603% 1907 0.877813 1.139195 1.8264% 1906 0.862069 1.160000 1.9357% 1905 0.845699 1.182454 2.0148% 1904 0.828996 1.206279 2.1335% 1903 0.811678 1.232015 1.8151% 1902 0.797208 1.254378 1.8943% 1901 0.782387 1.278140 3.0255% 1900 0.759411 1.316810 0.6278% 1899 0.754673 1.325078 1.7757% 1898 0.741506 1.348607 1.8078% 1897 0.728339 1.372986 1.8396% 1896 0.715183 1.398244 1.8755% 1895 0.702016 1.424468 1.9114% 1894 0.688850 1.451695 1.9486% 1893 0.675683 1.479984 1.9858% 1892 0.662527 1.509373 2.0276% 1891 0.649360 1.539978 2.6465% 1890 0.632618 1.580733 1.5328% 1889 0.623067 1.604963 2.0811% 1888 0.610365 1.638365 2.1599% 1887 0.597461 1.673751 2.2075% 1886 0.584556 1.710699 2.2592% 1885 0.571642 1.749347 2.3095% 1884 0.558738 1.789749 2.3641% 1883 0.545833 1.832061 2.4214% 1882 0.532929 1.876422 2.4815% 1881 0.520025 1.922985 3.7644% 1880 0.501159 1.995374 0.9432% 1879 0.496476 2.014195 2.1464% 1878 0.486044 2.057427 2.1913% 1877 0.475622 2.102512 2.2426% 1876 0.465189 2.149663 2.2941% 1875 0.454757 2.198977 2.3456% 1874 0.444335 2.250556 2.4043% 1873 0.433902 2.304667 2.4635% 1872 0.423470 2.361443 2.5258% 1871 0.413037 2.421088 5.9947% 1870 0.389678 2.566224 -1.0968% 1869 0.393999 2.538078 2.1930% 1868 0.385544 2.593738 2.2394% 1867 0.377099 2.651822 2.2935% 1866 0.368644 2.712642 2.3445% 1865 0.360200 2.776239

2.4037% 1864 0.351745 2.842971 2.4599% 1863 0.343300 2.912905 2.5250% 1862 0.334845
2.986456 2.5872% 1861 0.326400 3.063723 2.9504% 1860 0.317046 3.154115 2.4012% 1859
0.309612 3.229853 2.7627% 1858 0.301288 3.319084 2.8412% 1857 0.292964 3.413386
2.9243% 1856 0.284640 3.513204 3.0161% 1855 0.276307 3.619167 3.1061% 1854 0.267983
3.731580 3.2056% 1853 0.259659 3.851201 3.3118% 1852 0.251336 3.978744 3.4252% 1851
0.243012 4.115025 4.0106% 1850 0.233641 4.280063 2.3254% 1849 0.228332 4.379590
2.7841% 1848 0.222147 4.501521 2.8590% 1847 0.215972 4.630220 2.9432% 1846 0.209798
4.766495 3.0324% 1845 0.203623 4.911035 3.1325% 1844 0.197438 5.064873 3.2284% 1843
0.191264 5.228385 3.3361% 1842 0.185089 5.402807 3.4512% 1841 0.178914 5.589269
3.8105% 1840 0.172347 5.802247 2.3861% 1839 0.168331 5.940692 2.5824% 1838 0.164093
6.094104 2.6573% 1837 0.159845 6.256044 2.7232% 1836 0.155608 6.426409 2.7994% 1835
0.151370 6.606312 2.8871% 1834 0.147123 6.797044 2.9657% 1833 0.142885 6.998623
3.0563% 1832 0.138648 7.212524 3.1604% 1831 0.134400 7.440470 3.4660% 1830 0.129898
7.698354 2.4653% 1829 0.126773 7.888142 2.6804% 1828 0.123463 8.099575 10.3427%
1827 0.111891 8.937286 -4.2314% 1826 0.116835 8.559111 2.9150% 1825 0.113525
8.808612 3.0026% 1824 0.110216 9.073096 3.0955% 1823 0.106907 9.353954 3.1944% 1822
0.103597 9.652756 3.3102% 1821 0.100278 9.972281 3.2277% 1820 0.097142 10.294160
2.6573% 1819 0.094628 10.567704 2.6261% 1818 0.092206 10.845224 2.6969% 1817
0.089785 11.137712 2.7717% 1816 0.087364 11.446414 2.8507% 1815 0.084942 11.772716
2.9343% 1814 0.082521 12.118168 3.0231% 1813 0.080099 12.484507 3.1039% 1812
0.077688 12.872013 3.2172% 1811 0.075266 13.286126 3.0969% 1810 0.073006 13.697586
2.9144% 1809 0.070938 14.096786 2.8225% 1808 0.068991 14.494662 2.9199% 1807
0.067034 14.917896 2.9918% 1806 0.065086 15.364207 3.0841% 1805 0.063139 15.838047
3.1822% 1804 0.061192 16.342045 3.2868% 1803 0.059245 16.879172 3.3985% 1802
0.057297 17.452809 3.5180% 1801 0.055350 18.066806 3.3999% 1800 0.053530 18.681068
2.8419% 1799 0.052051 19.211960 2.7485% 1798 0.050659 19.739992 2.8261% 1797
0.049266 20.297870 3.7832% 1796 0.047470 21.065781 2.1272% 1795 0.046482 21.513892
3.0879% 1794 0.045089 22.178228 3.1625% 1793 0.043707 22.879617 3.2904% 1792
0.042315 23.632451 3.4024% 1791 0.040922 24.436514 3.2296% 1790 0.039642 25.225707
41.3145% 1780 0.028052 35.647569 29.4353% 1770 0.021673 46.140543 83.4728% 1750
0.011813 84.655364 29.2845% 1740 0.009137 109.446223 94.2514% 1720 0.004704
212.600815 85.8111% 1700 0.002531 395.035871 19.2490% 1690 0.002123 471.076521
88.0250% 1670 0.001129 885.741734
BASE YEAR: 1913
YEAR BYEAR/AYEAR AYEAR/BYEAR GROWTH%
2009 3.100306 0.322549 8.2857% 2001 2.863081 0.349274 1.0000% 2000 2.834733
0.352767 1.0000% 1999 2.806667 0.356295 1.0000% 1998 2.778878 0.359857 1.0000% 1997
2.751364 0.363456 1.0000% 1996 2.724123 0.367091 1.0000% 1995 2.697151 0.370762
0.9992% 1994 2.670467 0.374466 1.0008% 1993 2.644007 0.378214 1.0000% 1992 2.617829
0.381996 0.9295% 1991 2.593720 0.385547 1.2505% 1990 2.561686 0.390368 0.7224% 1989
2.543311 0.393188 1.1077% 1988 2.515449 0.397543 0.8834% 1987 2.493423 0.401055
0.5594% 1986 2.479553 0.403299 1.3056% 1985 2.447596 0.408564 0.7673% 1984 2.428959
0.411699 0.8149% 1983 2.409325 0.415054 0.9737% 1982 2.386090 0.419096 0.9508% 1981
2.363617 0.423080 0.9031% 1980 2.342463 0.426901 2.2701% 1979 2.290468 0.436592
1.0042% 1978 2.267696 0.440976 0.9896% 1977 2.245474 0.445340 0.9103% 1976 2.225218
0.449394 0.8394% 1975 2.206694 0.453167 0.9042% 1974 2.186920 0.457264 1.1568% 1973
2.161911 0.462554 0.9427% 1972 2.141721 0.466914 0.7426% 1971 2.125933 0.470382
1.4697% 1970 2.095140 0.477295 0.6968% 1969 2.080642 0.480621 0.8565% 1968 2.062972
0.484738 1.5090% 1967 2.032304 0.492052 0.9949% 1966 2.012283 0.496948 1.0575% 1965
1.991227 0.502203 1.1300% 1964 1.968977 0.507878 1.5537% 1963 1.938854 0.515769
1.4658% 1962 1.910844 0.523329 1.5364% 1961 1.881930 0.531369 2.1586% 1960 1.842164
0.542840 -1.6655% 1959 1.873365 0.533799 4.3080% 1958 1.795993 0.556795 2.1130%
1957 1.758830 0.568560 1.9895% 1956 1.724521 0.579871 2.1231% 1955 1.688669 0.592182
1.4496% 1954 1.664539 0.600767 2.1573% 1953 1.629389 0.613727 1.2298% 1952 1.609595
0.621274 1.6814% 1951 1.582979 0.631720 1.6233% 1950 1.557694 0.641975 1.4265% 1949
1.535785 0.651133 1.7790% 1948 1.508941 0.662717 1.8242% 1947 1.481908 0.674806 -

142

2.6320% 1946 1.521967 0.657045 3.1768% 1945 1.475106 0.677918 6.4754% 1944 1.385396
0.721816 -0.3437% 1943 1.390173 0.719335 0.6562% 1942 1.381110 0.724055 0.6633%
1941 1.372010 0.728858 -5.6614% 1940 1.454346 0.687594 8.0381% 1939 1.346142
0.742864 0.8126% 1938 1.335291 0.748900 0.7762% 1937 1.325006 0.754714 0.6029% 1936
1.317065 0.759264 0.5244% 1935 1.310195 0.763245 -3.0364% 1934 1.351223 0.740070
4.6271% 1933 1.291465 0.774314 1.3921% 1932 1.273733 0.785094 -0.2051% 1931
1.276351 0.783484 0.8886% 1930 1.265109 0.790446 1.0126% 1929 1.252427 0.798450
1.1526% 1928 1.238156 0.807652 1.2160% 1927 1.223281 0.817473 1.4086% 1926 1.206290
0.828988 1.7667% 1925 1.185348 0.843634 1.4465% 1924 1.168447 0.855837 1.7700% 1923
1.148125 0.870985 1.6165% 1922 1.129861 0.885065 1.3736% 1921 1.114551 0.897222
2.3393% 1920 1.089074 0.918211 1.3140% 1919 1.074949 0.930277 0.7676% 1918 1.066760
0.937418 0.3870% 1917 1.062648 0.941046 1.3274% 1916 1.048727 0.953537 1.4083% 1915
1.034163 0.966966 1.4458% 1914 1.019424 0.980946 1.9424% 1913 1.000000 1.000000
1.9857% 1912 0.980530 1.019857 1.5634% 1911 0.965436 1.035801 1.8169% 1910 0.948208
1.054621 1.8781% 1909 0.930728 1.074427 2.0082% 1908 0.912405 1.096004 1.9603% 1907
0.894864 1.117489 1.8264% 1906 0.878813 1.137898 1.9357% 1905 0.862125 1.159924
2.0148% 1904 0.845098 1.183295 2.1335% 1903 0.827444 1.208541 1.8151% 1902 0.812693
1.230477 1.8943% 1901 0.797584 1.253787 3.0255% 1900 0.774161 1.291720 0.6278% 1899
0.769331 1.299830 1.7757% 1898 0.755909 1.322911 1.8078% 1897 0.742487 1.346826
1.8396% 1896 0.729075 1.371602 1.8755% 1895 0.715652 1.397327 1.9114% 1894 0.702230
1.424035 1.9486% 1893 0.688808 1.451784 1.9858% 1892 0.675395 1.480614 2.0276% 1891
0.661973 1.510635 2.6465% 1890 0.644906 1.550615 1.5328% 1889 0.635170 1.574383
2.0811% 1888 0.622220 1.607148 2.1599% 1887 0.609065 1.641860 2.2075% 1886 0.595911
1.678104 2.2592% 1885 0.582745 1.716015 2.3095% 1884 0.569590 1.755647 2.3641% 1883
0.556436 1.797153 2.4214% 1882 0.543281 1.840669 2.4815% 1881 0.530126 1.886345
3.7644% 1880 0.510894 1.957355 0.9432% 1879 0.506120 1.975817 2.1464% 1878 0.495485
2.018226 2.1913% 1877 0.484860 2.062451 2.2426% 1876 0.474225 2.108704 2.2941% 1875
0.463590 2.157079 2.3456% 1874 0.452965 2.207675 2.4043% 1873 0.442330 2.260754
2.4635% 1872 0.431695 2.316449 2.5258% 1871 0.421060 2.374957 5.9947% 1870 0.397247
2.517328 -1.0968% 1869 0.401652 2.489719 2.1930% 1868 0.393033 2.544317 2.2394%
1867 0.384424 2.601295 2.2935% 1866 0.375805 2.660956 2.3445% 1865 0.367196 2.723341
2.4037% 1864 0.358577 2.788802 2.4599% 1863 0.349968 2.857403 2.5250% 1862 0.341349
2.929553 2.5872% 1861 0.332740 3.005348 2.9504% 1860 0.323204 3.094018 2.4012% 1859
0.315625 3.168312 2.7627% 1858 0.307140 3.255844 2.8412% 1857 0.298655 3.348349
2.9243% 1856 0.290169 3.446264 3.0161% 1855 0.281674 3.550208 3.1061% 1854 0.273188
3.660480 3.2056% 1853 0.264703 3.777821 3.3118% 1852 0.256217 3.902934 3.4252% 1851
0.247732 4.036619 4.0106% 1850 0.238180 4.198512 2.3254% 1849 0.232767 4.296142
2.7841% 1848 0.226462 4.415751 2.8590% 1847 0.220167 4.541998 2.9432% 1846 0.213873
4.675676 3.0324% 1845 0.207578 4.817461 3.1325% 1844 0.201273 4.968368 3.2284% 1843
0.194979 5.128765 3.3361% 1842 0.188684 5.299864 3.4512% 1841 0.182389 5.482772
3.8105% 1840 0.175695 5.691693 2.3861% 1839 0.171600 5.827499 2.5824% 1838 0.167280
5.977988 2.6573% 1837 0.162950 6.136843 2.7232% 1836 0.158630 6.303962 2.7994% 1835
0.154311 6.480437 2.8871% 1834 0.149980 6.667535 2.9657% 1833 0.145661 6.865273
3.0563% 1832 0.141341 7.075098 3.1604% 1831 0.137011 7.298701 3.4660% 1830 0.132421
7.551672 2.4653% 1829 0.129235 7.737843 2.6804% 1828 0.125861 7.945248 10.3427%
1827 0.114064 8.766997 -4.2314% 1826 0.119104 8.396028 2.9150% 1825 0.115730
8.640775 3.0026% 1824 0.112357 8.900220 3.0955% 1823 0.108983 9.175727 3.1944% 1822
0.105610 9.468835 3.3102% 1821 0.102226 9.782272 3.2277% 1820 0.099029 10.098018
2.6573% 1819 0.096466 10.366350 2.6261% 1818 0.093997 10.638582 2.6969% 1817
0.091529 10.925497 2.7717% 1816 0.089061 11.228317 2.8507% 1815 0.086592 11.548402
2.9343% 1814 0.084124 11.887272 3.0231% 1813 0.081655 12.246631 3.1039% 1812
0.079197 12.626753 3.2172% 1811 0.076728 13.032976 3.0969% 1810 0.074424 13.436596
2.9144% 1809 0.072316 13.828189 2.8225% 1808 0.070331 14.218485 2.9199% 1807
0.068336 14.633654 2.9918% 1806 0.066351 15.071462 3.0841% 1805 0.064365 15.536274
3.1822% 1804 0.062380 16.030668 3.2868% 1803 0.060395 16.557561 3.3985% 1802
0.058410 17.120268 3.5180% 1801 0.056425 17.722567 3.3999% 1800 0.054570 18.325124

143

2.8419% 1799 0.053062 18.845900 2.7485% 1798 0.051643 19.363872 2.8261% 1797
0.050223 19.911120 3.7832% 1796 0.048392 20.664400 2.1272% 1795 0.047384 21.103972
3.0879% 1794 0.045965 21.755650 3.1625% 1793 0.044556 22.443675 3.2904% 1792
0.043137 23.182165 3.4024% 1791 0.041717 23.970907 3.2296% 1790 0.040412 24.745063
41.3145% 1780 0.028597 34.968350 29.4353% 1770 0.022094 45.261394 83.4728% 1750
0.012042 83.042364 29.2845% 1740 0.009314 107.360866 94.2514% 1720 0.004795
208.549979 85.8111% 1700 0.002581 387.508968 19.2490% 1690 0.002164 462.100760
88.0250% 1670 0.001151 868.865058

BASE YEAR: 1912

YEAR BYEAR/AYEAR AYEAR/BYEAR GROWTH%

2009 3.161868 0.316269 8.2857% 2001 2.919932 0.342474 1.0000% 2000 2.891022
0.345898 1.0000% 1999 2.862398 0.349357 1.0000% 1998 2.834057 0.352851 1.0000% 1997
2.805997 0.356380 1.0000% 1996 2.778215 0.359943 1.0000% 1995 2.750708 0.363543
0.9992% 1994 2.723494 0.367175 1.0008% 1993 2.696508 0.370850 1.0000% 1992 2.669810
0.374558 0.9295% 1991 2.645223 0.378040 1.2505% 1990 2.612552 0.382767 0.7224% 1989
2.593813 0.385533 1.1077% 1988 2.565397 0.389803 0.8834% 1987 2.542934 0.393247
0.5594% 1986 2.528789 0.395446 1.3056% 1985 2.496198 0.400609 0.7673% 1984 2.477190
0.403683 0.8149% 1983 2.457166 0.406973 0.9737% 1982 2.433470 0.410936 0.9508% 1981
2.410550 0.414843 0.9031% 1980 2.388976 0.418589 2.2701% 1979 2.335949 0.428092
1.0042% 1978 2.312725 0.432390 0.9896% 1977 2.290062 0.436669 0.9103% 1976 2.269403
0.440645 0.8394% 1975 2.250511 0.444343 0.9042% 1974 2.230345 0.448361 1.1568% 1973
2.204840 0.453548 0.9427% 1972 2.184249 0.457823 0.7426% 1971 2.168147 0.461223
1.4697% 1970 2.136743 0.468002 0.6968% 1969 2.121957 0.471263 0.8565% 1968 2.103936
0.475300 1.5090% 1967 2.072658 0.482472 0.9949% 1966 2.052241 0.487272 1.0575% 1965
2.030766 0.492425 1.1300% 1964 2.008074 0.497990 1.5537% 1963 1.977353 0.505727
1.4658% 1962 1.948787 0.513140 1.5364% 1961 1.919299 0.521024 2.1586% 1960 1.878743
0.532271 -1.6655% 1959 1.910563 0.523406 4.3080% 1958 1.831656 0.545954 2.1130%
1957 1.793755 0.557490 1.9895% 1956 1.758764 0.568581 2.1231% 1955 1.722200 0.580653
1.4496% 1954 1.697592 0.589070 2.1573% 1953 1.661744 0.601778 1.2298% 1952 1.641556
0.609178 1.6814% 1951 1.614412 0.619421 1.6233% 1950 1.588624 0.629475 1.4265% 1949
1.566281 0.638455 1.7790% 1948 1.538903 0.649813 1.8242% 1947 1.511334 0.661667 -
2.6320% 1946 1.552188 0.644252 3.1768% 1945 1.504396 0.664718 6.4754% 1944 1.412905
0.707762 -0.3437% 1943 1.417778 0.705329 0.6562% 1942 1.408534 0.709958 0.6633%
1941 1.399253 0.714667 -5.6614% 1940 1.483225 0.674207 8.0381% 1939 1.372872
0.728400 0.8126% 1938 1.361805 0.734319 0.7762% 1937 1.351316 0.740019 0.6029% 1936
1.343218 0.744481 0.5244% 1935 1.336211 0.748385 -3.0364% 1934 1.378054 0.725661
4.6271% 1933 1.317110 0.759238 1.3921% 1932 1.299026 0.769808 -0.2051% 1931
1.301695 0.768229 0.8886% 1930 1.290230 0.775056 1.0126% 1929 1.277296 0.782904
1.1526% 1928 1.262742 0.791927 1.2160% 1927 1.247572 0.801557 1.4086% 1926 1.230243
0.812848 1.7667% 1925 1.208885 0.827208 1.4465% 1924 1.191648 0.839174 1.7700% 1923
1.170923 0.854027 1.6165% 1922 1.152296 0.867832 1.3736% 1921 1.136682 0.879753
2.3393% 1920 1.110699 0.900334 1.3140% 1919 1.096294 0.912164 0.7676% 1918 1.087943
0.919166 0.3870% 1917 1.083749 0.922723 1.3274% 1916 1.069551 0.934972 1.4083% 1915
1.054698 0.948139 1.4458% 1914 1.039666 0.961847 1.9424% 1913 1.019857 0.980530
1.9857% 1912 1.000000 1.000000 1.5634% 1911 0.984607 1.015634 1.8169% 1910 0.967036
1.034087 1.8781% 1909 0.949210 1.053508 2.0082% 1908 0.930522 1.074665 1.9603% 1907
0.912633 1.095731 1.8264% 1906 0.896264 1.115743 1.9357% 1905 0.879244 1.137340
2.0148% 1904 0.861879 1.160256 2.1335% 1903 0.843875 1.185010 1.8151% 1902 0.828830
1.206520 1.8943% 1901 0.813421 1.229376 3.0255% 1900 0.789534 1.266570 0.6278% 1899
0.784608 1.274522 1.7757% 1898 0.770919 1.297154 1.8078% 1897 0.757230 1.320603
1.8396% 1896 0.743552 1.344897 1.8755% 1895 0.729863 1.370121 1.9114% 1894 0.716174
1.396309 1.9486% 1893 0.702485 1.423518 1.9858% 1892 0.688807 1.451786 2.0276% 1891
0.675118 1.481223 2.6465% 1890 0.657711 1.520424 1.5328% 1889 0.647782 1.543729
2.0811% 1888 0.634576 1.575856 2.1599% 1887 0.621160 1.609892 2.2075% 1886 0.607743
1.645431 2.2592% 1885 0.594317 1.682604 2.3095% 1884 0.580901 1.721465 2.3641% 1883
0.567485 1.762163 2.4214% 1882 0.554068 1.804831 2.4815% 1881 0.540652 1.849618

3.7644% 1880 0.521038 1.919245 0.9432% 1879 0.516170 1.937348 2.1464% 1878 0.505323
1.978931 2.1913% 1877 0.494488 2.022295 2.2426% 1876 0.483642 2.067647 2.2941% 1875
0.472795 2.115080 2.3456% 1874 0.461960 2.164691 2.4043% 1873 0.451113 2.216737
2.4635% 1872 0.440267 2.271348 2.5258% 1871 0.429421 2.328717 5.9947% 1870 0.405135
2.468316 -1.0968% 1869 0.409627 2.441244 2.1930% 1868 0.400837 2.494779 2.2394%
1867 0.392057 2.550647 2.2935% 1866 0.383267 2.609147 2.3445% 1865 0.374487 2.670317
2.4037% 1864 0.365697 2.734504 2.4599% 1863 0.356917 2.801769 2.5250% 1862 0.348127
2.872514 2.5872% 1861 0.339347 2.946833 2.9504% 1860 0.329622 3.033777 2.4012% 1859
0.321893 3.106625 2.7627% 1858 0.313239 3.192452 2.8412% 1857 0.304585 3.283156
2.9243% 1856 0.295931 3.379165 3.0161% 1855 0.287267 3.481085 3.1061% 1854 0.278613
3.589210 3.2056% 1853 0.269959 3.704266 3.3118% 1852 0.261305 3.826944 3.4252% 1851
0.252651 3.958025 4.0106% 1850 0.242909 4.116766 2.3254% 1849 0.237389 4.212496
2.7841% 1848 0.230959 4.329776 2.8590% 1847 0.224539 4.453564 2.9432% 1846 0.218120
4.584640 3.0324% 1845 0.211700 4.723665 3.1325% 1844 0.205270 4.871634 3.2284% 1843
0.198850 5.028908 3.3361% 1842 0.192431 5.196675 3.4512% 1841 0.186011 5.376022
3.8105% 1840 0.179183 5.580875 2.3861% 1839 0.175008 5.714037 2.5824% 1838 0.170602
5.861596 2.6573% 1837 0.166186 6.017358 2.7232% 1836 0.161780 6.181223 2.7994% 1835
0.157375 6.354262 2.8871% 1834 0.152959 6.537718 2.9657% 1833 0.148553 6.731606
3.0563% 1832 0.144147 6.937345 3.1604% 1831 0.139731 7.156595 3.4660% 1830 0.135050
7.404640 2.4653% 1829 0.131801 7.587187 2.6804% 1828 0.128361 7.790553 10.3427%
1827 0.116329 8.596303 -4.2314% 1826 0.121469 8.232556 2.9150% 1825 0.118028
8.472538 3.0026% 1824 0.114588 8.726932 3.0955% 1823 0.111147 8.997074 3.1944% 1822
0.107707 9.284476 3.3102% 1821 0.104256 9.591810 3.2277% 1820 0.100996 9.901409
2.6573% 1819 0.098381 10.164516 2.6261% 1818 0.095864 10.431448 2.6969% 1817
0.093346 10.712777 2.7717% 1816 0.090829 11.009701 2.8507% 1815 0.088311 11.323554
2.9343% 1814 0.085794 11.655826 3.0231% 1813 0.083277 12.008187 3.1039% 1812
0.080770 12.380909 3.2172% 1811 0.078252 12.779223 3.0969% 1810 0.075901 13.174984
2.9144% 1809 0.073752 13.558953 2.8225% 1808 0.071728 13.941650 2.9199% 1807
0.069693 14.348736 2.9918% 1806 0.067668 14.778019 3.0841% 1805 0.065644 15.233781
3.1822% 1804 0.063619 15.718549 3.2868% 1803 0.061595 16.235184 3.3985% 1802
0.059570 16.786934 3.5180% 1801 0.057546 17.377506 3.3999% 1800 0.055653 17.968332
2.8419% 1799 0.054116 18.478969 2.7485% 1798 0.052668 18.986855 2.8261% 1797
0.051220 19.523449 3.7832% 1796 0.049353 20.262062 2.1272% 1795 0.048325 20.693076
3.0879% 1794 0.046878 21.332065 3.1625% 1793 0.045441 22.006694 3.2904% 1792
0.043993 22.730806 3.4024% 1791 0.042546 23.504191 3.2296% 1790 0.041215 24.263274
41.3145% 1780 0.029165 34.287513 29.4353% 1770 0.022533 44.380150 83.4728% 1750
0.012281 81.425521 29.2845% 1740 0.009499 105.270539 94.2514% 1720 0.004890
204.489489 85.8111% 1700 0.002632 379.964129 19.2490% 1690 0.002207 453.103612
88.0250% 1670 0.001174 851.948168

BASE YEAR: 1911
YEAR BYEAR/AYEAR AYEAR/BYEAR GROWTH%
2009 3.211301 0.311400 8.2857% 2001 2.965583 0.337202 1.0000% 2000 2.936220
0.340574 1.0000% 1999 2.907149 0.343980 1.0000% 1998 2.878365 0.347419 1.0000% 1997
2.849866 0.350894 1.0000% 1996 2.821650 0.354403 1.0000% 1995 2.793713 0.357947
0.9992% 1994 2.766073 0.361523 1.0008% 1993 2.738666 0.365141 1.0000% 1992 2.711550
0.368793 0.9295% 1991 2.686578 0.372221 1.2505% 1990 2.653397 0.376875 0.7224% 1989
2.634365 0.379598 1.1077% 1988 2.605505 0.383803 0.8834% 1987 2.582690 0.387193
0.5594% 1986 2.568324 0.389359 1.3056% 1985 2.535223 0.394443 0.7673% 1984 2.515919
0.397469 0.8149% 1983 2.495581 0.400708 0.9737% 1982 2.471515 0.404610 0.9508% 1981
2.448237 0.408457 0.9031% 1980 2.426326 0.412146 2.2701% 1979 2.372469 0.421502
1.0042% 1978 2.348882 0.425734 0.9896% 1977 2.325865 0.429948 0.9103% 1976 2.304883
0.433861 0.8394% 1975 2.285696 0.437503 0.9042% 1974 2.265215 0.441459 1.1568% 1973
2.239311 0.446566 0.9427% 1972 2.218398 0.450776 0.7426% 1971 2.202044 0.454123
1.4697% 1970 2.170149 0.460798 0.6968% 1969 2.155132 0.464009 0.8565% 1968 2.136829
0.467983 1.5090% 1967 2.105063 0.475045 0.9949% 1966 2.084325 0.479772 1.0575% 1965
2.062515 0.484845 1.1300% 1964 2.039469 0.490324 1.5537% 1963 2.008267 0.497942

145

1.4658% 1962 1.979255 0.505241 1.5364% 1961 1.949305 0.513003 2.1586% 1960 1.908116 0.524077 -1.6655% 1959 1.940433 0.515349 4.3080% 1958 1.860292 0.537550 2.1130% 1957 1.821798 0.548908 1.9895% 1956 1.786261 0.559829 2.1231% 1955 1.749125 0.571714 1.4496% 1954 1.724132 0.580002 2.1573% 1953 1.687723 0.592514 1.2298% 1952 1.667221 0.599801 1.6814% 1951 1.639652 0.609886 1.6233% 1950 1.613461 0.619786 1.4265% 1949 1.590768 0.628627 1.7790% 1948 1.562962 0.639811 1.8242% 1947 1.534962 0.651482 -2.6320% 1946 1.576455 0.634335 3.1768% 1945 1.527916 0.654486 6.4754% 1944 1.434994 0.696867 -0.3437% 1943 1.439943 0.694472 0.6562% 1942 1.430556 0.699029 0.6633% 1941 1.421129 0.703666 -5.6614% 1940 1.506414 0.663828 8.0381% 1939 1.394336 0.717187 0.8126% 1938 1.383096 0.723016 0.7762% 1937 1.372442 0.728628 0.6029% 1936 1.364218 0.733021 0.5244% 1935 1.357101 0.736865 -3.0364% 1934 1.399598 0.714491 4.6271% 1933 1.337701 0.747551 1.3921% 1932 1.319335 0.757958 -0.2051% 1931 1.322046 0.756403 0.8886% 1930 1.310402 0.763125 1.0126% 1929 1.297266 0.770852 1.1526% 1928 1.282484 0.779737 1.2160% 1927 1.267076 0.789218 1.4086% 1926 1.249476 0.800335 1.7667% 1925 1.227785 0.814475 1.4465% 1924 1.210279 0.826256 1.7700% 1923 1.189230 0.840881 1.6165% 1922 1.170311 0.854474 1.3736% 1921 1.154453 0.866211 2.3393% 1920 1.128064 0.886474 1.3140% 1919 1.113434 0.898123 0.7676% 1918 1.104951 0.905017 0.3870% 1917 1.100692 0.908519 1.3274% 1916 1.086272 0.920579 1.4083% 1915 1.071187 0.933544 1.4458% 1914 1.055920 0.947041 1.9424% 1913 1.035801 0.965436 1.9857% 1912 1.015634 0.984607 1.5634% 1911 1.000000 1.000000 1.8169% 1910 0.982155 1.018169 1.8781% 1909 0.964050 1.037291 2.0082% 1908 0.945070 1.058122 1.9603% 1907 0.926901 1.078864 1.8264% 1906 0.910276 1.098568 1.9357% 1905 0.892991 1.119833 2.0148% 1904 0.875354 1.142396 2.1335% 1903 0.857068 1.166769 1.8151% 1902 0.841788 1.187947 1.8943% 1901 0.826138 1.210451 3.0255% 1900 0.801877 1.247074 0.6278% 1899 0.796874 1.254903 1.7757% 1898 0.782971 1.277186 1.8078% 1897 0.769069 1.300274 1.8396% 1896 0.755176 1.324194 1.8755% 1895 0.741273 1.349030 1.9114% 1894 0.727371 1.374815 1.9486% 1893 0.713468 1.401605 1.9858% 1892 0.699575 1.429438 2.0276% 1891 0.685673 1.458422 2.6465% 1890 0.667994 1.497019 1.5328% 1889 0.657909 1.519966 2.0811% 1888 0.644497 1.551598 2.1599% 1887 0.630871 1.585111 2.2075% 1886 0.617245 1.620103 2.2592% 1885 0.603608 1.656703 2.3095% 1884 0.589982 1.694966 2.3641% 1883 0.576357 1.735037 2.4214% 1882 0.562731 1.777049 2.4815% 1881 0.549105 1.821146 3.7644% 1880 0.529184 1.889701 0.9432% 1879 0.524239 1.907525 2.1464% 1878 0.513224 1.948468 2.1913% 1877 0.502219 1.991165 2.2426% 1876 0.491203 2.035819 2.2941% 1875 0.480187 2.082522 2.3456% 1874 0.469182 2.131369 2.4043% 1873 0.458166 2.182614 2.4635% 1872 0.447150 2.236384 2.5258% 1871 0.436135 2.292870 5.9947% 1870 0.411468 2.430320 -1.0968% 1869 0.416031 2.403664 2.1930% 1868 0.407104 2.456376 2.2394% 1867 0.398187 2.511384 2.2935% 1866 0.389259 2.568983 2.3445% 1865 0.380342 2.629212 2.4037% 1864 0.371414 2.692410 2.4599% 1863 0.362497 2.758640 2.5250% 1862 0.353570 2.828296 2.5872% 1861 0.344653 2.901471 2.9504% 1860 0.334775 2.987077 2.4012% 1859 0.326925 3.058803 2.7627% 1858 0.318136 3.143309 2.8412% 1857 0.309347 3.232617 2.9243% 1856 0.300558 3.327148 3.0161% 1855 0.291758 3.427499 3.1061% 1854 0.282969 3.533960 3.2056% 1853 0.274180 3.647245 3.3118% 1852 0.265390 3.768034 3.4252% 1851 0.256601 3.897098 4.0106% 1850 0.246707 4.053395 2.3254% 1849 0.241100 4.147651 2.7841% 1848 0.234570 4.263126 2.8590% 1847 0.228050 4.385009 2.9432% 1846 0.221530 4.514067 3.0324% 1845 0.215010 4.650951 3.1325% 1844 0.208479 4.796643 3.2284% 1843 0.201959 4.951495 3.3361% 1842 0.195439 5.116680 3.4512% 1841 0.188919 5.293267 3.8105% 1840 0.181985 5.494966 2.3861% 1839 0.177744 5.626079 2.5824% 1838 0.173269 5.771366 2.6573% 1837 0.168784 5.924730 2.7232% 1836 0.164310 6.086073 2.7994% 1835 0.159835 6.256449 2.8871% 1834 0.155350 6.437080 2.9657% 1833 0.150875 6.627983 3.0563% 1832 0.146401 6.830556 3.1604% 1831 0.141916 7.046430 3.4660% 1830 0.137162 7.290657 2.4653% 1829 0.133862 7.470394 2.6804% 1828 0.130367 7.670630 10.3427% 1827 0.118148 8.463977 -4.2314% 1826 0.123368 8.105829 2.9150% 1825 0.119874 8.342117 3.0026% 1824 0.116379 8.592594 3.0955% 1823 0.112885 8.858579 3.1944% 1822 0.109391 9.141556 3.3102% 1821 0.105886 9.444159 3.2277% 1820 0.102575 9.748992 2.6573% 1819 0.099920 10.008050 2.6261% 1818 0.097363 10.270872 2.6969% 1817 0.094806 10.547871 2.7717% 1816 0.092249 10.840224 2.8507% 1815 0.089692 11.149246

2.9343% 1814 0.087135 11.476403 3.0231% 1813 0.084578 11.823340 3.1039% 1812 0.082032 12.190325 3.2172% 1811 0.079475 12.582507 3.0969% 1810 0.077088 12.972176 2.9144% 1809 0.074905 13.350235 2.8225% 1808 0.072849 13.727040 2.9199% 1807 0.070782 14.127860 2.9918% 1806 0.068726 14.550535 3.0841% 1805 0.066670 14.999281 3.1822% 1804 0.064614 15.476587 3.2868% 1803 0.062558 15.985269 3.3985% 1802 0.060501 16.528526 3.5180% 1801 0.058445 17.110007 3.3999% 1800 0.056524 17.691738 2.8419% 1799 0.054962 18.194514 2.7485% 1798 0.053491 18.694583 2.8261% 1797 0.052021 19.222916 3.7832% 1796 0.050125 19.950159 2.1272% 1795 0.049081 20.374539 3.0879% 1794 0.047611 21.003692 3.1625% 1793 0.046151 21.667936 3.2904% 1792 0.044681 22.380901 3.4024% 1791 0.043211 23.142382 3.2296% 1790 0.041859 23.889780 41.3145% 1780 0.029621 33.759711 29.4353% 1770 0.022885 43.696988 83.4728% 1750 0.012473 80.172105 29.2845% 1740 0.009648 103.650066 94.2514% 1720 0.004967 201.341699 85.8111% 1700 0.002673 374.115185 19.2490% 1690 0.002242 446.128802 88.0250% 1670 0.001192 838.833780

BASE YEAR: 1910

YEAR BYEAR/AYEAR AYEAR/BYEAR GROWTH%

2009 3.269647 0.305843 8.2857% 2001 3.019465 0.331185 1.0000% 2000 2.989569 0.334496 1.0000% 1999 2.959969 0.337841 1.0000% 1998 2.930662 0.341220 1.0000% 1997 2.901646 0.344632 1.0000% 1996 2.872917 0.348078 1.0000% 1995 2.844472 0.351559 0.9992% 1994 2.816331 0.355072 1.0008% 1993 2.788425 0.358625 1.0000% 1992 2.760817 0.362212 0.9295% 1991 2.735391 0.365578 1.2505% 1990 2.701607 0.370150 0.7224% 1989 2.682229 0.372824 1.1077% 1988 2.652845 0.376954 0.8834% 1987 2.629615 0.380284 0.5594% 1986 2.614988 0.382411 1.3056% 1985 2.581286 0.387404 0.7673% 1984 2.561631 0.390376 0.8149% 1983 2.540924 0.393558 0.9737% 1982 2.516420 0.397390 0.9508% 1981 2.492720 0.401168 0.9031% 1980 2.470410 0.404791 2.2701% 1979 2.415575 0.413980 1.0042% 1978 2.391559 0.418137 0.9896% 1977 2.368124 0.422275 0.9103% 1976 2.346761 0.426119 0.8394% 1975 2.327225 0.429696 0.9042% 1974 2.306372 0.433581 1.1568% 1973 2.279997 0.438597 0.9427% 1972 2.258704 0.442732 0.7426% 1971 2.242054 0.446020 1.4697% 1970 2.209579 0.452575 0.6968% 1969 2.194288 0.455729 0.8565% 1968 2.175653 0.459632 1.5090% 1967 2.143310 0.466568 0.9949% 1966 2.122196 0.471210 1.0575% 1965 2.099989 0.476193 1.1300% 1964 2.076524 0.481574 1.5537% 1963 2.044756 0.489056 1.4658% 1962 2.015216 0.496225 1.5364% 1961 1.984722 0.503849 2.1586% 1960 1.942785 0.514725 -1.6655% 1959 1.975689 0.506152 4.3080% 1958 1.894092 0.527957 2.1130% 1957 1.854899 0.539113 1.9895% 1956 1.818716 0.549839 2.1231% 1955 1.780905 0.561512 1.4496% 1954 1.755458 0.569652 2.1573% 1953 1.718388 0.581941 1.2298% 1952 1.697513 0.589097 1.6814% 1951 1.669443 0.599002 1.6233% 1950 1.642776 0.608726 1.4265% 1949 1.619671 0.617409 1.7790% 1948 1.591360 0.628393 1.8242% 1947 1.562851 0.639856 -2.6320% 1946 1.605098 0.623015 3.1768% 1945 1.555677 0.642807 6.4754% 1944 1.461067 0.684431 -0.3437% 1943 1.466106 0.682079 0.6562% 1942 1.456548 0.686555 0.6633% 1941 1.446950 0.691109 -5.6614% 1940 1.533784 0.651982 8.0381% 1939 1.419669 0.704389 0.8126% 1938 1.408226 0.710113 0.7762% 1937 1.397379 0.715626 0.6029% 1936 1.389005 0.719940 0.5244% 1935 1.381759 0.723715 -3.0364% 1934 1.425028 0.701741 4.6271% 1933 1.362006 0.734211 1.3921% 1932 1.343306 0.744432 -0.2051% 1931 1.346066 0.742905 0.8886% 1930 1.334211 0.749507 1.0126% 1929 1.320836 0.757096 1.1526% 1928 1.305786 0.765822 1.2160% 1927 1.290098 0.775135 1.4086% 1926 1.272178 0.786053 1.7667% 1925 1.250093 0.799940 1.4465% 1924 1.232268 0.811512 1.7700% 1923 1.210837 0.825875 1.6165% 1922 1.191575 0.839226 1.3736% 1921 1.175429 0.850754 2.3393% 1920 1.148560 0.870655 1.3140% 1919 1.133664 0.882096 0.7676% 1918 1.125028 0.888867 0.3870% 1917 1.120691 0.892307 1.3274% 1916 1.106009 0.904152 1.4083% 1915 1.090650 0.916885 1.4458% 1914 1.075106 0.930141 1.9424% 1913 1.054621 0.948208 1.9857% 1912 1.034087 0.967036 1.5634% 1911 1.018169 0.982155 1.8169% 1910 1.000000 1.000000 1.8781% 1909 0.981566 1.018781 2.0082% 1908 0.962241 1.039240 1.9603% 1907 0.943742 1.059612 1.8264% 1906 0.926815 1.078964 1.9357% 1905 0.909215 1.099849 2.0148% 1904 0.891258 1.122010 2.1335% 1903 0.872640 1.145948 1.8151% 1902 0.857083 1.166749 1.8943% 1901 0.841148 1.188851 3.0255% 1900 0.816447 1.224820 0.6278% 1899 0.811353 1.232509 1.7757% 1898 0.797197 1.254395 1.8078% 1897 0.783042 1.277071

147

1.8396% 1896 0.768897 1.300564 1.8755% 1895 0.754742 1.324957 1.9114% 1894 0.740586
1.350282 1.9486% 1893 0.726431 1.376594 1.9858% 1892 0.712286 1.403930 2.0276% 1891
0.698131 1.432397 2.6465% 1890 0.680131 1.470305 1.5328% 1889 0.669863 1.492842
2.0811% 1888 0.656207 1.523910 2.1599% 1887 0.642333 1.556824 2.2075% 1886 0.628460
1.591192 2.2592% 1885 0.614575 1.627140 2.3095% 1884 0.600702 1.664719 2.3641% 1883
0.586829 1.704075 2.4214% 1882 0.572955 1.745338 2.4815% 1881 0.559082 1.788648
3.7644% 1880 0.538799 1.855979 0.9432% 1879 0.533764 1.873486 2.1464% 1878 0.522549
1.913698 2.1913% 1877 0.511343 1.955633 2.2426% 1876 0.500128 1.999490 2.2941% 1875
0.488912 2.045359 2.3456% 1874 0.477707 2.093335 2.4043% 1873 0.466491 2.143665
2.4635% 1872 0.455275 2.196476 2.5258% 1871 0.444059 2.251954 5.9947% 1870 0.418945
2.386951 -1.0968% 1869 0.423590 2.360771 2.1930% 1868 0.414501 2.412542 2.2394%
1867 0.405421 2.466569 2.2935% 1866 0.396332 2.523140 2.3445% 1865 0.387253 2.582294
2.4037% 1864 0.378163 2.644364 2.4599% 1863 0.369084 2.709413 2.5250% 1862 0.359994
2.777826 2.5872% 1861 0.350915 2.849695 2.9504% 1860 0.340858 2.933772 2.4012% 1859
0.332865 3.004219 2.7627% 1858 0.323916 3.087217 2.8412% 1857 0.314967 3.174931
2.9243% 1856 0.306019 3.267775 3.0161% 1855 0.297059 3.366336 3.1061% 1854 0.288110
3.470896 3.2056% 1853 0.279161 3.582160 3.3118% 1852 0.270212 3.700794 3.4252% 1851
0.261263 3.827554 4.0106% 1850 0.251189 3.981063 2.3254% 1849 0.245481 4.073637
2.7841% 1848 0.238832 4.187050 2.8590% 1847 0.232193 4.306759 2.9432% 1846 0.225555
4.433513 3.0324% 1845 0.218916 4.567955 3.1325% 1844 0.212267 4.711047 3.2284% 1843
0.205629 4.863136 3.3361% 1842 0.198990 5.025373 3.4512% 1841 0.192352 5.198809
3.8105% 1840 0.185291 5.396909 2.3861% 1839 0.180973 5.525682 2.5824% 1838 0.176417
5.668377 2.6573% 1837 0.171851 5.819004 2.7232% 1836 0.167295 5.977467 2.7994% 1835
0.162739 6.144803 2.8871% 1834 0.158173 6.322211 2.9657% 1833 0.153617 6.509707
3.0563% 1832 0.149061 6.708665 3.1604% 1831 0.144494 6.920687 3.4660% 1830 0.139654
7.160556 2.4653% 1829 0.136294 7.337085 2.6804% 1828 0.132736 7.533748 10.3427%
1827 0.120294 8.312937 -4.2314% 1826 0.125610 7.961181 2.9150% 1825 0.122052
8.193252 3.0026% 1824 0.118494 8.439260 3.0955% 1823 0.114936 8.700498 3.1944% 1822
0.111378 8.978426 3.3102% 1821 0.107809 9.275629 3.2277% 1820 0.104438 9.575022
2.6573% 1819 0.101735 9.829457 2.6261% 1818 0.099132 10.087589 2.6969% 1817
0.096528 10.359644 2.7717% 1816 0.093925 10.646781 2.8507% 1815 0.091322 10.950288
2.9343% 1814 0.088718 11.271607 3.0231% 1813 0.086115 11.612354 3.1039% 1812
0.083523 11.972789 3.2172% 1811 0.080919 12.357973 3.0969% 1810 0.078489 12.740689
2.9144% 1809 0.076266 13.112001 2.8225% 1808 0.074173 13.482082 2.9199% 1807
0.072068 13.875749 2.9918% 1806 0.069975 14.290881 3.0841% 1805 0.067881 14.731620
3.1822% 1804 0.065788 15.200408 3.2868% 1803 0.063694 15.700013 3.3985% 1802
0.061601 16.233576 3.5180% 1801 0.059507 16.804680 3.3999% 1800 0.057551 17.376031
2.8419% 1799 0.055960 17.869834 2.7485% 1798 0.054463 18.360979 2.8261% 1797
0.052966 18.879884 3.7832% 1796 0.051036 19.594150 2.1272% 1795 0.049973 20.010956
3.0879% 1794 0.048476 20.628883 3.1625% 1793 0.046990 21.281273 3.2904% 1792
0.045493 21.981515 3.4024% 1791 0.043996 22.729407 3.2296% 1790 0.042619 23.463468
41.3145% 1780 0.030159 33.157271 29.4353% 1770 0.023301 42.917218 83.4728% 1750
0.012700 78.741438 29.2845% 1740 0.009823 101.800437 94.2514% 1720 0.005057
197.748769 85.8111% 1700 0.002722 367.439123 19.2490% 1690 0.002282 438.167662
88.0250% 1670 0.001214 823.864844

BASE YEAR: 1909

YEAR BYEAR/AYEAR AYEAR/BYEAR GROWTH%

2009 3.331053 0.300205 8.2857% 2001 3.076172 0.325079 1.0000% 2000 3.045715
0.328330 1.0000% 1999 3.015559 0.331613 1.0000% 1998 2.985702 0.334930 1.0000% 1997
2.956141 0.338279 1.0000% 1996 2.926872 0.341662 1.0000% 1995 2.897893 0.345078
0.9992% 1994 2.869223 0.348526 1.0008% 1993 2.840793 0.352014 1.0000% 1992 2.812666
0.355535 0.9295% 1991 2.786763 0.358839 1.2505% 1990 2.752345 0.363327 0.7224% 1989
2.732603 0.365951 1.1077% 1988 2.702667 0.370005 0.8834% 1987 2.679001 0.373273
0.5594% 1986 2.664099 0.375361 1.3056% 1985 2.629764 0.380262 0.7673% 1984 2.609740
0.383180 0.8149% 1983 2.588644 0.386303 0.9737% 1982 2.563680 0.390064 0.9508% 1981
2.539534 0.393773 0.9031% 1980 2.516806 0.397329 2.2701% 1979 2.460941 0.406349

148

1.0042% 1978 2.436474 0.410429 0.9896% 1977 2.412599 0.414491 0.9103% 1976 2.390834 0.418264 0.8394% 1975 2.370932 0.421775 0.9042% 1974 2.349687 0.425589 1.1568% 1973 2.322817 0.430512 0.9427% 1972 2.301124 0.434570 0.7426% 1971 2.284161 0.437798 1.4697% 1970 2.251076 0.444232 0.6968% 1969 2.235499 0.447328 0.8565% 1968 2.216513 0.451159 1.5090% 1967 2.183562 0.457967 0.9949% 1966 2.162052 0.462524 1.0575% 1965 2.139428 0.467415 1.1300% 1964 2.115523 0.472696 1.5537% 1963 2.083157 0.480041 1.4658% 1962 2.053063 0.487077 1.5364% 1961 2.021997 0.494561 2.1586% 1960 1.979271 0.505236 -1.6655% 1959 2.012794 0.496822 4.3080% 1958 1.929664 0.518225 2.1130% 1957 1.889735 0.529175 1.9895% 1956 1.852872 0.539703 2.1231% 1955 1.814352 0.551161 1.4496% 1954 1.788426 0.559151 2.1573% 1953 1.750660 0.571213 1.2298% 1952 1.729393 0.578238 1.6814% 1951 1.700796 0.587960 1.6233% 1950 1.673629 0.597504 1.4265% 1949 1.650090 0.606028 1.7790% 1948 1.621247 0.616809 1.8242% 1947 1.592203 0.628061 -2.6320% 1946 1.635243 0.611530 3.1768% 1945 1.584894 0.630957 6.4754% 1944 1.488507 0.671814 -0.3437% 1943 1.493640 0.669505 0.6562% 1942 1.483902 0.673899 0.6633% 1941 1.474124 0.678369 -5.6614% 1940 1.562589 0.639963 8.0381% 1939 1.446332 0.691404 0.8126% 1938 1.434673 0.697023 0.7762% 1937 1.423622 0.702434 0.6029% 1936 1.415091 0.706668 0.5244% 1935 1.407709 0.710374 -3.0364% 1934 1.451791 0.688804 4.6271% 1933 1.387586 0.720676 1.3921% 1932 1.368534 0.730709 -0.2051% 1931 1.371346 0.729210 0.8886% 1930 1.359268 0.735690 1.0126% 1929 1.345642 0.743140 1.1526% 1928 1.330309 0.751705 1.2160% 1927 1.314327 0.760846 1.4086% 1926 1.296071 0.771563 1.7667% 1925 1.273571 0.785194 1.4465% 1924 1.255411 0.796552 1.7700% 1923 1.233577 0.810651 1.6165% 1922 1.213953 0.823755 1.3736% 1921 1.197504 0.835070 2.3393% 1920 1.170131 0.854605 1.3140% 1919 1.154955 0.865835 0.7676% 1918 1.146156 0.872481 0.3870% 1917 1.141738 0.875858 1.3274% 1916 1.126781 0.887484 1.4083% 1915 1.111133 0.899983 1.4458% 1914 1.095297 0.912995 1.9424% 1913 1.074427 0.930728 1.9857% 1912 1.053508 0.949210 1.5634% 1911 1.037291 0.964050 1.8169% 1910 1.018781 0.981566 1.8781% 1909 1.000000 1.000000 2.0082% 1908 0.980313 1.020082 1.9603% 1907 0.961466 1.040079 1.8264% 1906 0.944221 1.059074 1.9357% 1905 0.926291 1.079574 2.0148% 1904 0.907996 1.101326 2.1335% 1903 0.889029 1.124823 1.8151% 1902 0.873179 1.145240 1.8943% 1901 0.856946 1.166935 3.0255% 1900 0.831780 1.202241 0.6278% 1899 0.826590 1.209789 1.7757% 1898 0.812169 1.231271 1.8078% 1897 0.797748 1.253529 1.8396% 1896 0.783338 1.276589 1.8755% 1895 0.768916 1.300532 1.9114% 1894 0.754495 1.325390 1.9486% 1893 0.740074 1.351217 1.9858% 1892 0.725663 1.378050 2.0276% 1891 0.711242 1.405991 2.6465% 1890 0.692904 1.443201 1.5328% 1889 0.682444 1.465323 2.0811% 1888 0.668531 1.495818 2.1599% 1887 0.654397 1.528125 2.2075% 1886 0.640263 1.561859 2.2592% 1885 0.626118 1.597144 2.3095% 1884 0.611984 1.634031 2.3641% 1883 0.597850 1.672662 2.4214% 1882 0.583716 1.713163 2.4815% 1881 0.569582 1.755675 3.7644% 1880 0.548918 1.821766 0.9432% 1879 0.543789 1.838949 2.1464% 1878 0.532362 1.878420 2.1913% 1877 0.520947 1.919582 2.2426% 1876 0.509520 1.962630 2.2941% 1875 0.498094 2.007654 2.3456% 1874 0.486678 2.054746 2.4043% 1873 0.475252 2.104148 2.4635% 1872 0.463825 2.155985 2.5258% 1871 0.452399 2.210440 5.9947% 1870 0.426813 2.342949 -1.0968% 1869 0.431544 2.317252 2.1930% 1868 0.422285 2.368068 2.2394% 1867 0.413036 2.421099 2.2935% 1866 0.403775 2.476627 2.3445% 1865 0.394525 2.534691 2.4037% 1864 0.385265 2.595617 2.4599% 1863 0.376015 2.659466 2.5250% 1862 0.366755 2.726618 2.5872% 1861 0.357505 2.797162 2.9504% 1860 0.347260 2.879690 2.4012% 1859 0.339117 2.948838 2.7627% 1858 0.330000 3.030306 2.8412% 1857 0.320883 3.116403 2.9243% 1856 0.311766 3.207536 3.0161% 1855 0.302638 3.304280 3.1061% 1854 0.293521 3.406912 3.2056% 1853 0.284404 3.516125 3.3118% 1852 0.275287 3.632572 3.4252% 1851 0.266170 3.756996 4.0106% 1850 0.255907 3.907674 2.3254% 1849 0.250091 3.998542 2.7841% 1848 0.243317 4.109865 2.8590% 1847 0.236554 4.227366 2.9432% 1846 0.229791 4.351784 3.0324% 1845 0.223028 4.483748 3.1325% 1844 0.216254 4.624202 3.2284% 1843 0.209490 4.773487 3.3361% 1842 0.202727 4.932734 3.4512% 1841 0.195964 5.102972 3.8105% 1840 0.188771 5.297420 2.3861% 1839 0.184372 5.423819 2.5824% 1838 0.179731 5.563883 2.6573% 1837 0.175078 5.711734 2.7232% 1836 0.170437 5.867276 2.7994% 1835 0.165795 6.031527 2.8871% 1834 0.161143 6.205665 2.9657% 1833 0.156502 6.389705 3.0563% 1832 0.151860 6.584995 3.1604% 1831 0.147208 6.793109 3.4660% 1830 0.142277

7.028555 2.4653% 1829 0.138854 7.201830 2.6804% 1828 0.135229 7.394868 10.3427%
1827 0.122554 8.159693 -4.2314% 1826 0.127969 7.814421 2.9150% 1825 0.124344
8.042215 3.0026% 1824 0.120719 8.283687 3.0955% 1823 0.117095 8.540109 3.1944% 1822
0.113470 8.812914 3.3102% 1821 0.109834 9.104638 3.2277% 1820 0.106400 9.398512
2.6573% 1819 0.103646 9.648257 2.6261% 1818 0.100993 9.901630 2.6969% 1817 0.098341
10.168671 2.7717% 1816 0.095689 10.450514 2.8507% 1815 0.093037 10.748426 2.9343%
1814 0.090385 11.063822 3.0231% 1813 0.087732 11.398287 3.1039% 1812 0.085091
11.752078 3.2172% 1811 0.082439 12.130161 3.0969% 1810 0.079963 12.505822 2.9144%
1809 0.077698 12.870289 2.8225% 1808 0.075566 13.233548 2.9199% 1807 0.073422
13.619958 2.9918% 1806 0.071289 14.027438 3.0841% 1805 0.069156 14.460051 3.1822%
1804 0.067023 14.920198 3.2868% 1803 0.064890 15.410593 3.3985% 1802 0.062758
15.934319 3.5180% 1801 0.060625 16.494896 3.3999% 1800 0.058631 17.055714 2.8419%
1799 0.057011 17.540415 2.7485% 1798 0.055486 18.022505 2.8261% 1797 0.053961
18.531845 3.7832% 1796 0.051994 19.232944 2.1272% 1795 0.050911 19.642066 3.0879%
1794 0.049386 20.248601 3.1625% 1793 0.047872 20.888966 3.2904% 1792 0.046347
21.576299 3.4024% 1791 0.044822 22.310404 3.2296% 1790 0.043420 23.030933 41.3145%
1780 0.030726 32.546037 29.4353% 1770 0.023738 42.126065 83.4728% 1750 0.012938
77.289887 29.2845% 1740 0.010008 99.923807 94.2514% 1720 0.005152 194.103389
85.8111% 1700 0.002773 360.665604 19.2490% 1690 0.002325 430.090304 88.0250% 1670
0.001237 808.677391

BASE YEAR: 1908

YEAR BYEAR/AYEAR AYEAR/BYEAR GROWTH%

2009 3.397949 0.294295 8.2857% 2001 3.137949 0.318679 1.0000% 2000 3.106880
0.321866 1.0000% 1999 3.076119 0.325085 1.0000% 1998 3.045662 0.328336 1.0000% 1997
3.015507 0.331619 1.0000% 1996 2.985651 0.334935 1.0000% 1995 2.956090 0.338285
0.9992% 1994 2.926844 0.341665 1.0008% 1993 2.897843 0.345084 1.0000% 1992 2.869152
0.348535 0.9295% 1991 2.842728 0.351775 1.2505% 1990 2.807619 0.356174 0.7224% 1989
2.787480 0.358747 1.1077% 1988 2.756943 0.362721 0.8834% 1987 2.732802 0.365925
0.5594% 1986 2.717601 0.367972 1.3056% 1985 2.682576 0.372776 0.7673% 1984 2.662150
0.375636 0.8149% 1983 2.640630 0.378697 0.9737% 1982 2.615165 0.382385 0.9508% 1981
2.590534 0.386021 0.9031% 1980 2.567349 0.389507 2.2701% 1979 2.510362 0.398349
1.0042% 1978 2.485405 0.402349 0.9896% 1977 2.461050 0.406331 0.9103% 1976 2.438848
0.410030 0.8394% 1975 2.418546 0.413472 0.9042% 1974 2.396874 0.417210 1.1568% 1973
2.369464 0.422036 0.9427% 1972 2.347336 0.426015 0.7426% 1971 2.330032 0.429179
1.4697% 1970 2.296283 0.435486 0.6968% 1969 2.280393 0.438521 0.8565% 1968 2.261026
0.442277 1.5090% 1967 2.227414 0.448951 0.9949% 1966 2.205471 0.453418 1.0575% 1965
2.182393 0.458213 1.1300% 1964 2.158007 0.463390 1.5537% 1963 2.124992 0.470590
1.4658% 1962 2.094294 0.477488 1.5364% 1961 2.062603 0.484824 2.1586% 1960 2.019020
0.495290 -1.6655% 1959 2.053216 0.487041 4.3080% 1958 1.968417 0.508023 2.1130%
1957 1.927685 0.518757 1.9895% 1956 1.890082 0.529078 2.1231% 1955 1.850788 0.540310
1.4496% 1954 1.824342 0.548143 2.1573% 1953 1.785818 0.559968 1.2298% 1952 1.764123
0.566854 1.6814% 1951 1.734950 0.576385 1.6233% 1950 1.707239 0.585741 1.4265% 1949
1.683227 0.594097 1.7790% 1948 1.653805 0.604666 1.8242% 1947 1.624178 0.615696 -
2.6320% 1946 1.668082 0.599491 3.1768% 1945 1.616722 0.618535 6.4754% 1944 1.518400
0.658588 -0.3437% 1943 1.523636 0.656325 0.6562% 1942 1.513703 0.660632 0.6633%
1941 1.503728 0.665014 -5.6614% 1940 1.593970 0.627364 8.0381% 1939 1.475377
0.677793 0.8126% 1938 1.463485 0.683301 0.7762% 1937 1.452212 0.688605 0.6029% 1936
1.443509 0.692756 0.5244% 1935 1.435979 0.696389 -3.0364% 1934 1.480946 0.675244
4.6271% 1933 1.415452 0.706488 1.3921% 1932 1.396017 0.716323 -0.2051% 1931
1.398886 0.714854 0.8886% 1930 1.386565 0.721207 1.0126% 1929 1.372666 0.728509
1.1526% 1928 1.357025 0.736906 1.2160% 1927 1.340722 0.745867 1.4086% 1926 1.322099
0.756373 1.7667% 1925 1.299147 0.769736 1.4465% 1924 1.280623 0.780870 1.7700% 1923
1.258350 0.794691 1.6165% 1922 1.238332 0.807538 1.3736% 1921 1.221553 0.818630
2.3393% 1920 1.193630 0.837781 1.3140% 1919 1.178149 0.848789 0.7676% 1918 1.169174
0.855305 0.3870% 1917 1.164667 0.858615 1.3274% 1916 1.149409 0.870012 1.4083% 1915
1.133447 0.882265 1.4458% 1914 1.117293 0.895020 1.9424% 1913 1.096004 0.912405

150

1.9857% 1912 1.074665 0.930522 1.5634% 1911 1.058122 0.945070 1.8169% 1910 1.039240 0.962241 1.8781% 1909 1.020082 0.980313 2.0082% 1908 1.000000 1.000000 1.9603% 1907 0.980774 1.019603 1.8264% 1906 0.963183 1.038224 1.9357% 1905 0.944893 1.058321 2.0148% 1904 0.926231 1.079644 2.1335% 1903 0.906883 1.102679 1.8151% 1902 0.890715 1.122694 1.8943% 1901 0.874155 1.143962 3.0255% 1900 0.848484 1.178572 0.6278% 1899 0.843190 1.185972 1.7757% 1898 0.828479 1.207031 1.8078% 1897 0.813769 1.228851 1.8396% 1896 0.799069 1.251457 1.8755% 1895 0.784358 1.274928 1.9114% 1894 0.769647 1.299297 1.9486% 1893 0.754936 1.324615 1.9858% 1892 0.740236 1.350920 2.0276% 1891 0.725525 1.378311 2.6465% 1890 0.706819 1.414789 1.5328% 1889 0.696149 1.436475 2.0811% 1888 0.681956 1.466370 2.1599% 1887 0.667538 1.498041 2.2075% 1886 0.653121 1.531111 2.2592% 1885 0.638691 1.565701 2.3095% 1884 0.624274 1.601862 2.3641% 1883 0.609856 1.639732 2.4214% 1882 0.595438 1.679436 2.4815% 1881 0.581020 1.721111 3.7644% 1880 0.559942 1.785900 0.9432% 1879 0.554709 1.802745 2.1464% 1878 0.543053 1.841439 2.1913% 1877 0.531409 1.881791 2.2426% 1876 0.519753 1.923992 2.2941% 1875 0.508097 1.968129 2.3456% 1874 0.496452 2.014294 2.4043% 1873 0.484796 2.062724 2.4635% 1872 0.473140 2.113540 2.5258% 1871 0.461484 2.166923 5.9947% 1870 0.435384 2.296823 -1.0968% 1869 0.440212 2.271632 2.1930% 1868 0.430766 2.321448 2.2394% 1867 0.421330 2.373435 2.2935% 1866 0.411884 2.427870 2.3445% 1865 0.402448 2.484790 2.4037% 1864 0.393002 2.544517 2.4599% 1863 0.383567 2.607109 2.5250% 1862 0.374120 2.672939 2.5872% 1861 0.364685 2.742095 2.9504% 1860 0.354233 2.822997 2.4012% 1859 0.345927 2.890784 2.7627% 1858 0.336627 2.970648 2.8412% 1857 0.327327 3.055050 2.9243% 1856 0.318027 3.144389 3.0161% 1855 0.308716 3.239228 3.1061% 1854 0.299416 3.339840 3.2056% 1853 0.290115 3.446903 3.3118% 1852 0.280815 3.561057 3.4252% 1851 0.271515 3.683032 4.0106% 1850 0.261046 3.830743 2.3254% 1849 0.255114 3.919822 2.7841% 1848 0.248203 4.028954 2.8590% 1847 0.241304 4.144142 2.9432% 1846 0.234406 4.266110 3.0324% 1845 0.227507 4.395476 3.1325% 1844 0.220596 4.533165 3.2284% 1843 0.213698 4.679512 3.3361% 1842 0.206799 4.835623 3.4512% 1841 0.199900 5.002509 3.8105% 1840 0.192562 5.193129 2.3861% 1839 0.188075 5.317040 2.5824% 1838 0.183340 5.454347 2.6573% 1837 0.178594 5.599287 2.7232% 1836 0.173860 5.751767 2.7994% 1835 0.169125 5.912784 2.8871% 1834 0.164379 6.083493 2.9657% 1833 0.159645 6.263910 3.0563% 1832 0.154910 6.455356 3.1604% 1831 0.150164 6.659372 3.4660% 1830 0.145134 6.890184 2.4653% 1829 0.141642 7.060048 2.6804% 1828 0.137945 7.249285 10.3427% 1827 0.125015 7.999053 -4.2314% 1826 0.130538 7.660579 2.9150% 1825 0.126841 7.883887 3.0026% 1824 0.123144 8.120606 3.0955% 1823 0.119446 8.371980 3.1944% 1822 0.115749 8.639414 3.3102% 1821 0.112040 8.925395 3.2277% 1820 0.108537 9.213483 2.6573% 1819 0.105727 9.458311 2.6261% 1818 0.103022 9.706697 2.6969% 1817 0.100316 9.968480 2.7717% 1816 0.097611 10.244774 2.8507% 1815 0.094905 10.536821 2.9343% 1814 0.092200 10.846008 3.0231% 1813 0.089494 11.173888 3.1039% 1812 0.086800 11.520714 3.2172% 1811 0.084095 11.891354 3.0969% 1810 0.081569 12.259619 2.9144% 1809 0.079259 12.616911 2.8225% 1808 0.077083 12.973018 2.9199% 1807 0.074896 13.351821 2.9918% 1806 0.072721 13.751279 3.0841% 1805 0.070545 14.175376 3.1822% 1804 0.068369 14.626463 3.2868% 1803 0.066194 15.107204 3.3985% 1802 0.064018 15.620620 3.5180% 1801 0.061842 16.170160 3.3999% 1800 0.059809 16.719937 2.8419% 1799 0.058156 17.195096 2.7485% 1798 0.056600 17.667696 2.8261% 1797 0.055045 18.167008 3.7832% 1796 0.053038 18.854304 2.1272% 1795 0.051934 19.255372 3.0879% 1794 0.050378 19.849966 3.1625% 1793 0.048834 20.477724 3.2904% 1792 0.047278 21.151526 3.4024% 1791 0.045722 21.871179 3.2296% 1790 0.044292 22.577522 41.3145% 1780 0.031343 31.905301 29.4353% 1770 0.024215 41.296727 83.4728% 1750 0.013198 75.768278 29.2845% 1740 0.010209 97.956603 94.2514% 1720 0.005255 190.282068 85.8111% 1700 0.002828 353.565165 19.2490% 1690 0.002372 421.623099 88.0250% 1670 0.001261 792.756926

BASE YEAR: 1907
YEAR BYEAR/AYEAR AYEAR/BYEAR GROWTH%

2009 3.464557 0.288637 8.2857% 2001 3.199461 0.312553 1.0000% 2000 3.167783 0.315678 1.0000% 1999 3.136419 0.318835 1.0000% 1998 3.105365 0.322023 1.0000% 1997 3.074619 0.325244 1.0000% 1996 3.044177 0.328496 1.0000% 1995 3.014037 0.331781

151

0.9992% 1994 2.984218 0.335096 1.0008% 1993 2.954648 0.338450 1.0000% 1992 2.925394
0.341834 0.9295% 1991 2.898453 0.345012 1.2505% 1990 2.862655 0.349326 0.7224% 1989
2.842122 0.351850 1.1077% 1988 2.810986 0.355747 0.8834% 1987 2.786372 0.358890
0.5594% 1986 2.770873 0.360897 1.3056% 1985 2.735162 0.365609 0.7673% 1984 2.714335
0.368414 0.8149% 1983 2.692393 0.371417 0.9737% 1982 2.666429 0.375033 0.9508% 1981
2.641315 0.378599 0.9031% 1980 2.617676 0.382018 2.2701% 1979 2.559572 0.390690
1.0042% 1978 2.534125 0.394614 0.9896% 1977 2.509293 0.398519 0.9103% 1976 2.486656
0.402147 0.8394% 1975 2.465956 0.405522 0.9042% 1974 2.443859 0.409189 1.1568% 1973
2.415912 0.413922 0.9427% 1972 2.393350 0.417824 0.7426% 1971 2.375707 0.420927
1.4697% 1970 2.341296 0.427114 0.6968% 1969 2.325094 0.430090 0.8565% 1968 2.305348
0.433774 1.5090% 1967 2.271077 0.440320 0.9949% 1966 2.248704 0.444701 1.0575% 1965
2.225174 0.449403 1.1300% 1964 2.200310 0.454481 1.5537% 1963 2.166648 0.461543
1.4658% 1962 2.135347 0.468308 1.5364% 1961 2.103035 0.475503 2.1586% 1960 2.058598
0.485768 -1.6655% 1959 2.093464 0.477677 4.3080% 1958 2.007003 0.498255 2.1130%
1957 1.965473 0.508783 1.9895% 1956 1.927133 0.518906 2.1231% 1955 1.887068 0.529922
1.4496% 1954 1.860104 0.537604 2.1573% 1953 1.820824 0.549202 1.2298% 1952 1.798705
0.555956 1.6814% 1951 1.768962 0.565303 1.6233% 1950 1.740705 0.574480 1.4265% 1949
1.716223 0.582675 1.7790% 1948 1.686224 0.593041 1.8242% 1947 1.656016 0.603859 -
2.6320% 1946 1.700781 0.587965 3.1768% 1945 1.648414 0.606644 6.4754% 1944 1.548164
0.645926 -0.3437% 1943 1.553503 0.643706 0.6562% 1942 1.543375 0.647931 0.6633%
1941 1.533205 0.652228 -5.6614% 1940 1.625216 0.615303 8.0381% 1939 1.504299
0.664762 0.8126% 1938 1.492173 0.670164 0.7762% 1937 1.480679 0.675366 0.6029% 1936
1.471806 0.679437 0.5244% 1935 1.464128 0.683000 -3.0364% 1934 1.509977 0.662262
4.6271% 1933 1.443198 0.692906 1.3921% 1932 1.423383 0.702552 -0.2051% 1931
1.426308 0.701111 0.8886% 1930 1.413745 0.707341 1.0126% 1929 1.399574 0.714503
1.1526% 1928 1.383626 0.722739 1.2160% 1927 1.367003 0.731527 1.4086% 1926 1.348015
0.741831 1.7667% 1925 1.324614 0.754937 1.4465% 1924 1.305726 0.765857 1.7700% 1923
1.283017 0.779413 1.6165% 1922 1.262607 0.792012 1.3736% 1921 1.245498 0.802892
2.3393% 1920 1.217028 0.821674 1.3140% 1919 1.201244 0.832471 0.7676% 1918 1.192093
0.838861 0.3870% 1917 1.187497 0.842107 1.3274% 1916 1.171940 0.853286 1.4083% 1915
1.155665 0.865302 1.4458% 1914 1.139195 0.877813 1.9424% 1913 1.117489 0.894864
1.9857% 1912 1.095731 0.912633 1.5634% 1911 1.078864 0.926901 1.8169% 1910 1.059612
0.943742 1.8781% 1909 1.040079 0.961466 2.0082% 1908 1.019603 0.980774 1.9603% 1907
1.000000 1.000000 1.8264% 1906 0.982064 1.018264 1.9357% 1905 0.963415 1.037974
2.0148% 1904 0.944388 1.058887 2.1335% 1903 0.924660 1.081479 1.8151% 1902 0.908175
1.101109 1.8943% 1901 0.891291 1.121968 3.0255% 1900 0.865117 1.155913 0.6278% 1899
0.859719 1.163171 1.7757% 1898 0.844720 1.183825 1.8078% 1897 0.829720 1.205225
1.8396% 1896 0.814733 1.227396 1.8755% 1895 0.799733 1.250417 1.9114% 1894 0.784734
1.274317 1.9486% 1893 0.769735 1.299149 1.9858% 1892 0.754747 1.324947 2.0276% 1891
0.739748 1.351812 2.6465% 1890 0.720675 1.387588 1.5328% 1889 0.709795 1.408858
2.0811% 1888 0.695324 1.438178 2.1599% 1887 0.680624 1.469240 2.2075% 1886 0.665923
1.501674 2.2592% 1885 0.651211 1.535600 2.3095% 1884 0.636511 1.571065 2.3641% 1883
0.621810 1.608207 2.4214% 1882 0.607110 1.647148 2.4815% 1881 0.592410 1.688021
3.7644% 1880 0.570918 1.751565 0.9432% 1879 0.565583 1.768086 2.1464% 1878 0.553699
1.806036 2.1913% 1877 0.541826 1.845612 2.2426% 1876 0.529941 1.887002 2.2941% 1875
0.518057 1.930291 2.3456% 1874 0.506184 1.975568 2.4043% 1873 0.494299 2.023067
2.4635% 1872 0.482415 2.072906 2.5258% 1871 0.470530 2.125263 5.9947% 1870 0.443919
2.252665 -1.0968% 1869 0.448841 2.227958 2.1930% 1868 0.439210 2.276817 2.2394%
1867 0.429589 2.327804 2.2935% 1866 0.419958 2.381192 2.3445% 1865 0.410337 2.437019
2.4037% 1864 0.400706 2.495597 2.4599% 1863 0.391085 2.556986 2.5250% 1862 0.381454
2.621550 2.5872% 1861 0.371833 2.689376 2.9504% 1860 0.361177 2.768723 2.4012% 1859
0.352708 2.835207 2.7627% 1858 0.343226 2.913536 2.8412% 1857 0.333743 2.996315
2.9243% 1856 0.324261 3.083936 3.0161% 1855 0.314767 3.176952 3.1061% 1854 0.305285
3.275630 3.2056% 1853 0.295802 3.380634 3.3118% 1852 0.286320 3.492594 3.4252% 1851
0.276838 3.612223 4.0106% 1850 0.266163 3.757095 2.3254% 1849 0.260114 3.844461
2.7841% 1848 0.253069 3.951494 2.8590% 1847 0.246035 4.064468 2.9432% 1846 0.239001

4.184092 3.0324% 1845 0.231966 4.310970 3.1325% 1844 0.224921 4.446012 3.2284% 1843 0.217887 4.589545 3.3361% 1842 0.210852 4.742655 3.4512% 1841 0.203818 4.906333 3.8105% 1840 0.196337 5.093288 2.3861% 1839 0.191761 5.214817 2.5824% 1838 0.186934 5.349484 2.6573% 1837 0.182095 5.491637 2.7232% 1836 0.177268 5.641185 2.7994% 1835 0.172440 5.799107 2.8871% 1834 0.167601 5.966534 2.9657% 1833 0.162774 6.143483 3.0563% 1832 0.157947 6.331247 3.1604% 1831 0.153108 6.531341 3.4660% 1830 0.147979 6.757716 2.4653% 1829 0.144419 6.924314 2.6804% 1828 0.140649 7.109913 10.3427% 1827 0.127465 7.845266 -4.2314% 1826 0.133097 7.513299 2.9150% 1825 0.129327 7.732314 3.0026% 1824 0.125557 7.964482 3.0955% 1823 0.121788 8.211023 3.1944% 1822 0.118018 8.473315 3.3102% 1821 0.114236 8.753798 3.2277% 1820 0.110664 9.036348 2.6573% 1819 0.107800 9.276469 2.6261% 1818 0.105041 9.520079 2.6969% 1817 0.102283 9.776829 2.7717% 1816 0.099524 10.047812 2.8507% 1815 0.096766 10.334244 2.9343% 1814 0.094007 10.637486 3.0231% 1813 0.091249 10.959063 3.1039% 1812 0.088502 11.299221 3.2172% 1811 0.085743 11.662735 3.0969% 1810 0.083168 12.023920 2.9144% 1809 0.080812 12.374342 2.8225% 1808 0.078594 12.723603 2.9199% 1807 0.076364 13.095123 2.9918% 1806 0.074146 13.486901 3.0841% 1805 0.071928 13.902844 3.1822% 1804 0.069709 14.345260 3.2868% 1803 0.067491 14.816757 3.3985% 1802 0.065273 15.320303 3.5180% 1801 0.063055 15.859278 3.3999% 1800 0.060981 16.398485 2.8419% 1799 0.059296 16.864509 2.7485% 1798 0.057710 17.328022 2.8261% 1797 0.056124 17.817735 3.7832% 1796 0.054078 18.491817 2.1272% 1795 0.052952 18.885175 3.0879% 1794 0.051365 19.468337 3.1625% 1793 0.049791 20.084026 3.2904% 1792 0.048205 20.744874 3.4024% 1791 0.046619 21.450690 3.2296% 1790 0.045160 22.143454 41.3145% 1780 0.031957 31.291900 29.4353% 1770 0.024690 40.502770 83.4728% 1750 0.013457 74.311582 29.2845% 1740 0.010409 96.073322 94.2514% 1720 0.005358 186.623767 85.8111% 1700 0.002884 346.767637 19.2490% 1690 0.002418 413.517110 88.0250% 1670 0.001286 777.515639

BASE YEAR: 1906
YEAR BYEAR/AYEAR AYEAR/BYEAR GROWTH%

2009 3.527832 0.283460 8.2857% 2001 3.257894 0.306947 1.0000% 2000 3.225638 0.310016 1.0000% 1999 3.193701 0.313116 1.0000% 1998 3.162080 0.316248 1.0000% 1997 3.130772 0.319410 1.0000% 1996 3.099774 0.322604 1.0000% 1995 3.069084 0.325830 0.9992% 1994 3.038720 0.329086 1.0008% 1993 3.008610 0.332379 1.0000% 1992 2.978822 0.335703 0.9295% 1991 2.951389 0.338824 1.2505% 1990 2.914937 0.343061 0.7224% 1989 2.894029 0.345539 1.1077% 1988 2.862324 0.349366 0.8834% 1987 2.837261 0.352453 0.5594% 1986 2.821479 0.354424 1.3056% 1985 2.785115 0.359052 0.7673% 1984 2.763908 0.361807 0.8149% 1983 2.741566 0.364755 0.9737% 1982 2.715128 0.368307 0.9508% 1981 2.689555 0.371809 0.9031% 1980 2.665484 0.375166 2.2701% 1979 2.606319 0.383683 1.0042% 1978 2.580407 0.387536 0.9896% 1977 2.555121 0.391371 0.9103% 1976 2.532071 0.394934 0.8394% 1975 2.510993 0.398249 0.9042% 1974 2.488492 0.401850 1.1568% 1973 2.460035 0.406498 0.9427% 1972 2.437061 0.410330 0.7426% 1971 2.419096 0.413378 1.4697% 1970 2.384056 0.419453 0.6968% 1969 2.367559 0.422376 0.8565% 1968 2.347452 0.425994 1.5090% 1967 2.312554 0.432422 0.9949% 1966 2.289773 0.436724 1.0575% 1965 2.265813 0.441343 1.1300% 1964 2.240495 0.446330 1.5537% 1963 2.206218 0.453264 1.4658% 1962 2.174346 0.459908 1.5364% 1961 2.141444 0.466975 2.1586% 1960 2.096195 0.477055 -1.6655% 1959 2.131698 0.469110 4.3080% 1958 2.043658 0.489319 2.1130% 1957 2.001369 0.499658 1.9895% 1956 1.962329 0.509599 2.1231% 1955 1.921533 0.520418 1.4496% 1954 1.894076 0.527962 2.1573% 1953 1.854079 0.539351 1.2298% 1952 1.831555 0.545984 1.6814% 1951 1.801269 0.555164 1.6233% 1950 1.772497 0.564176 1.4265% 1949 1.747567 0.572224 1.7790% 1948 1.717021 0.582404 1.8242% 1947 1.686261 0.593028 -2.6320% 1946 1.731843 0.577419 3.1768% 1945 1.678520 0.595763 6.4754% 1944 1.576439 0.634341 -0.3437% 1943 1.581876 0.632161 0.6562% 1942 1.571563 0.636309 0.6633% 1941 1.561207 0.640530 -5.6614% 1940 1.654898 0.604267 8.0381% 1939 1.531772 0.652838 0.8126% 1938 1.519425 0.658144 0.7762% 1937 1.507721 0.663252 0.6029% 1936 1.498686 0.667251 0.5244% 1935 1.490868 0.670750 -3.0364% 1934 1.537554 0.650384 4.6271% 1933 1.469556 0.680478 1.3921% 1932 1.449379 0.689951 -0.2051% 1931 1.452357 0.688536 0.8886% 1930 1.439565 0.694654 1.0126% 1929 1.425135 0.701688

153

1.1526% 1928 1.408896 0.709776 1.2160% 1927 1.391970 0.718407 1.4086% 1926 1.372635
0.728526 1.7667% 1925 1.348806 0.741397 1.4465% 1924 1.329573 0.752121 1.7700% 1923
1.306450 0.765433 1.6165% 1922 1.285667 0.777807 1.3736% 1921 1.268245 0.788491
2.3393% 1920 1.239255 0.806936 1.3140% 1919 1.223183 0.817539 0.7676% 1918 1.213864
0.823815 0.3870% 1917 1.209185 0.827003 1.3274% 1916 1.193344 0.837981 1.4083% 1915
1.176772 0.849782 1.4458% 1914 1.160000 0.862069 1.9424% 1913 1.137898 0.878813
1.9857% 1912 1.115743 0.896264 1.5634% 1911 1.098568 0.910276 1.8169% 1910 1.078964
0.926815 1.8781% 1909 1.059074 0.944221 2.0082% 1908 1.038224 0.963183 1.9603% 1907
1.018264 0.982064 1.8264% 1906 1.000000 1.000000 1.9357% 1905 0.981011 1.019357
2.0148% 1904 0.961635 1.039895 2.1335% 1903 0.941547 1.062082 1.8151% 1902 0.924761
1.081360 1.8943% 1901 0.907569 1.101845 3.0255% 1900 0.880917 1.135181 0.6278% 1899
0.875421 1.142308 1.7757% 1898 0.860147 1.162592 1.8078% 1897 0.844874 1.183608
1.8396% 1896 0.829613 1.205382 1.8755% 1895 0.814339 1.227989 1.9114% 1894 0.799066
1.251461 1.9486% 1893 0.783793 1.275847 1.9858% 1892 0.768531 1.301183 2.0276% 1891
0.753258 1.327566 2.6465% 1890 0.733837 1.362701 1.5328% 1889 0.722758 1.383588
2.0811% 1888 0.708023 1.412383 2.1599% 1887 0.693054 1.442888 2.2075% 1886 0.678086
1.474740 2.2592% 1885 0.663105 1.508057 2.3095% 1884 0.648136 1.542886 2.3641% 1883
0.633167 1.579362 2.4214% 1882 0.618198 1.617605 2.4815% 1881 0.603229 1.657745
3.7644% 1880 0.581345 1.720149 0.9432% 1879 0.575913 1.736374 2.1464% 1878 0.563811
1.773643 2.1913% 1877 0.551721 1.812509 2.2426% 1876 0.539620 1.853157 2.2941% 1875
0.527518 1.895669 2.3456% 1874 0.515428 1.940134 2.4043% 1873 0.503327 1.986781
2.4635% 1872 0.491225 2.035726 2.5258% 1871 0.479124 2.087144 5.9947% 1870 0.452026
2.212261 -1.0968% 1869 0.457039 2.187998 2.1930% 1868 0.447231 2.235980 2.2394%
1867 0.437435 2.286053 2.2935% 1866 0.427628 2.338483 2.3445% 1865 0.417832 2.393308
2.4037% 1864 0.408024 2.450836 2.4599% 1863 0.398228 2.511124 2.5250% 1862 0.388420
2.574530 2.5872% 1861 0.378624 2.641139 2.9504% 1860 0.367774 2.719064 2.4012% 1859
0.359150 2.784355 2.7627% 1858 0.349494 2.861279 2.8412% 1857 0.339839 2.942573
2.9243% 1856 0.330183 3.028623 3.0161% 1855 0.320516 3.119970 3.1061% 1854 0.310860
3.216878 3.2056% 1853 0.301205 3.319999 3.3118% 1852 0.291549 3.429951 3.4252% 1851
0.281894 3.547434 4.0106% 1850 0.271024 3.689708 2.3254% 1849 0.264865 3.775507
2.7841% 1848 0.257691 3.880620 2.8590% 1847 0.250528 3.991568 2.9432% 1846 0.243365
4.109046 3.0324% 1845 0.236203 4.233649 3.1325% 1844 0.229029 4.366268 3.2284% 1843
0.221866 4.507227 3.3361% 1842 0.214703 4.657591 3.4512% 1841 0.207541 4.818333
3.8105% 1840 0.199923 5.001935 2.3861% 1839 0.195264 5.121284 2.5824% 1838 0.190348
5.253535 2.6573% 1837 0.185421 5.393139 2.7232% 1836 0.180505 5.540005 2.7994% 1835
0.175590 5.695094 2.8871% 1834 0.170662 5.859519 2.9657% 1833 0.165747 6.033293
3.0563% 1832 0.160831 6.217690 3.1604% 1831 0.155904 6.414196 3.4660% 1830 0.150682
6.636509 2.4653% 1829 0.147056 6.800119 2.6804% 1828 0.143217 6.982389 10.3427%
1827 0.129793 7.704554 -4.2314% 1826 0.135528 7.378541 2.9150% 1825 0.131689
7.593628 3.0026% 1824 0.127851 7.821631 3.0955% 1823 0.124012 8.063750 3.1944% 1822
0.120173 8.321338 3.3102% 1821 0.116322 8.596790 3.2277% 1820 0.112685 8.874272
2.6573% 1819 0.109768 9.110086 2.6261% 1818 0.106960 9.349327 2.6969% 1817 0.104151
9.601472 2.7717% 1816 0.101342 9.867594 2.8507% 1815 0.098533 10.148889 2.9343%
1814 0.095724 10.446693 3.0231% 1813 0.092915 10.762502 3.1039% 1812 0.090118
11.096558 3.2172% 1811 0.087309 11.453552 3.0969% 1810 0.084686 11.808259 2.9144%
1809 0.082288 12.152397 2.8225% 1808 0.080029 12.495393 2.9199% 1807 0.077759
12.860250 2.9918% 1806 0.075500 13.245001 3.0841% 1805 0.073241 13.653484 3.1822%
1804 0.070983 14.087964 3.2868% 1803 0.068724 14.551005 3.3985% 1802 0.066465
15.045519 3.5180% 1801 0.064206 15.574827 3.3999% 1800 0.062095 16.104363 2.8419%
1799 0.060379 16.562028 2.7485% 1798 0.058764 17.017228 8.2061% 1797 0.057149
17.498157 3.7832% 1796 0.055066 18.160149 2.1272% 1795 0.053919 18.546451 3.0879%
1794 0.052304 19.119154 3.1625% 1793 0.050700 19.723800 3.2904% 1792 0.049085
20.372794 3.4024% 1791 0.047470 21.065952 3.2296% 1790 0.045985 21.746290 41.3145%
1780 0.032541 30.730650 29.4353% 1770 0.025141 39.776314 83.4728% 1750 0.013703
72.978732 29.2845% 1740 0.010599 94.350155 94.2514% 1720 0.005456 183.276491

154

85.8111% 1700 0.002936 340.548027 19.2490% 1690 0.002462 406.100285 88.0250% 1670 0.001310 763.570152

BASE YEAR: 1905

YEAR BYEAR/AYEAR AYEAR/BYEAR GROWTH%

2009 3.596120 0.278078 8.2857% 2001 3.320957 0.301118 1.0000% 2000 3.288075 0.304129 1.0000% 1999 3.255520 0.307171 1.0000% 1998 3.223287 0.310242 1.0000% 1997 3.191374 0.313345 1.0000% 1996 3.159776 0.316478 1.0000% 1995 3.128491 0.319643 0.9992% 1994 3.097540 0.322837 1.0008% 1993 3.066841 0.326068 1.0000% 1992 3.036483 0.329328 0.9295% 1991 3.008518 0.332390 1.2505% 1990 2.971361 0.336546 0.7224% 1989 2.950048 0.338977 1.1077% 1988 2.917729 0.342732 0.8834% 1987 2.892181 0.345760 0.5594% 1986 2.876093 0.347694 1.3056% 1985 2.839026 0.352233 0.7673% 1984 2.817409 0.354936 0.8149% 1983 2.794634 0.357829 0.9737% 1982 2.767684 0.361313 0.9508% 1981 2.741616 0.364748 0.9031% 1980 2.717079 0.368042 2.2701% 1979 2.656769 0.376397 1.0042% 1978 2.630355 0.380177 0.9896% 1977 2.604580 0.383939 0.9103% 1976 2.581083 0.387434 0.8394% 1975 2.559597 0.390686 0.9042% 1974 2.536661 0.394219 1.1568% 1973 2.507653 0.398779 0.9427% 1972 2.484234 0.402539 0.7426% 1971 2.465921 0.405528 1.4697% 1970 2.430204 0.411488 0.6968% 1969 2.413387 0.414355 0.8565% 1968 2.392891 0.417905 1.5090% 1967 2.357318 0.424211 0.9949% 1966 2.334096 0.428431 1.0575% 1965 2.309672 0.432962 1.1300% 1964 2.283864 0.437854 1.5537% 1963 2.248923 0.444657 1.4658% 1962 2.216434 0.451175 1.5364% 1961 2.182896 0.458107 2.1586% 1960 2.136771 0.467996 -1.6655% 1959 2.172961 0.460202 4.3080% 1958 2.083216 0.480027 2.1130% 1957 2.040109 0.490170 1.9895% 1956 2.000313 0.499922 2.1231% 1955 1.958728 0.510536 1.4496% 1954 1.930739 0.517936 2.1573% 1953 1.889968 0.529110 1.2298% 1952 1.867008 0.535616 1.6814% 1951 1.836136 0.544622 1.6233% 1950 1.806807 0.553463 1.4265% 1949 1.781394 0.561358 1.7790% 1948 1.750256 0.571345 1.8242% 1947 1.718901 0.581767 -2.6320% 1946 1.765366 0.566455 3.1768% 1945 1.711011 0.584450 6.4754% 1944 1.606954 0.622295 -0.3437% 1943 1.612495 0.620157 0.6562% 1942 1.601983 0.624226 0.6633% 1941 1.591427 0.628367 -5.6614% 1940 1.686931 0.592792 8.0381% 1939 1.561423 0.640442 0.8126% 1938 1.548836 0.645646 0.7762% 1937 1.536906 0.650658 0.6029% 1936 1.527696 0.654581 0.5244% 1935 1.519727 0.658013 -3.0364% 1934 1.567316 0.638033 4.6271% 1933 1.498002 0.667556 1.3921% 1932 1.477434 0.676849 -0.2051% 1931 1.480470 0.675461 0.8886% 1930 1.467431 0.681463 1.0126% 1929 1.452721 0.688364 1.1526% 1928 1.436168 0.696298 1.2160% 1927 1.418914 0.704765 1.4086% 1926 1.399205 0.714692 1.7667% 1925 1.374914 0.727318 1.4465% 1924 1.355310 0.737839 1.7700% 1923 1.331738 0.750898 1.6165% 1922 1.310553 0.763037 1.3736% 1921 1.292794 0.773518 2.3393% 1920 1.263243 0.791613 1.3140% 1919 1.246859 0.802015 0.7676% 1918 1.237361 0.808172 0.3870% 1917 1.232591 0.811299 1.3274% 1916 1.216443 0.822069 1.4083% 1915 1.199550 0.833646 1.4458% 1914 1.182454 0.845699 1.9424% 1913 1.159924 0.862125 1.9857% 1912 1.137340 0.879244 1.5634% 1911 1.119833 0.892991 1.8169% 1910 1.099849 0.909215 1.8781% 1909 1.079574 0.926291 2.0082% 1908 1.058321 0.944893 1.9603% 1907 1.037974 0.963415 1.8264% 1906 1.019357 0.981011 1.9357% 1905 1.000000 1.000000 2.0148% 1904 0.980250 1.020148 2.1335% 1903 0.959773 1.041913 1.8151% 1902 0.942662 1.060826 1.8943% 1901 0.925137 1.080922 3.0255% 1900 0.897969 1.113625 0.6278% 1899 0.892366 1.120617 1.7757% 1898 0.876797 1.140515 1.8078% 1897 0.861228 1.161133 1.8396% 1896 0.845671 1.182493 1.8755% 1895 0.830102 1.204671 1.9114% 1894 0.814533 1.227697 1.9486% 1893 0.798964 1.251620 1.9858% 1892 0.783407 1.276475 2.0276% 1891 0.767839 1.302357 2.6465% 1890 0.748042 1.336824 1.5328% 1889 0.736749 1.357315 2.0811% 1888 0.721728 1.385563 2.1599% 1887 0.706470 1.415489 2.2075% 1886 0.691211 1.446736 2.2592% 1885 0.675940 1.479420 2.3095% 1884 0.660682 1.513588 2.3641% 1883 0.645423 1.549372 2.4214% 1882 0.630164 1.586888 2.4815% 1881 0.614906 1.626266 3.7644% 1880 0.592598 1.687485 0.9432% 1879 0.587061 1.703402 2.1464% 1878 0.574725 1.739963 2.1913% 1877 0.562401 1.778091 2.2426% 1876 0.550065 1.817967 2.2941% 1875 0.537729 1.859672 2.3456% 1874 0.525405 1.903292 2.4043% 1873 0.513070 1.949054 2.4635% 1872 0.500734 1.997069 2.5258% 1871 0.488398 2.047511 5.9947% 1870 0.460776 2.170252 -1.0968% 1869 0.465886 2.146450 2.1930% 1868 0.455888 2.193521 2.2394% 1867 0.445903 2.242642 2.2935% 1866 0.435905 2.294077 2.3445% 1865 0.425920 2.347861

2.4037% 1864 0.415922 2.404297 2.4599% 1863 0.405936 2.463440 2.5250% 1862 0.395939
2.525642 2.5872% 1861 0.385953 2.590986 2.9504% 1860 0.374893 2.667431 2.4012% 1859
0.366102 2.731482 2.7627% 1858 0.356259 2.806945 2.8412% 1857 0.346417 2.886696
2.9243% 1856 0.336574 2.971112 3.0161% 1855 0.326720 3.060724 3.1061% 1854 0.316878
3.155792 3.2056% 1853 0.307035 3.256955 3.3118% 1852 0.297193 3.364819 3.4252% 1851
0.287350 3.480071 4.0106% 1850 0.276270 3.619643 2.3254% 1849 0.269992 3.703813
2.7841% 1848 0.262679 3.806931 2.8590% 1847 0.255378 3.915771 2.9432% 1846 0.248076
4.031019 3.0324% 1845 0.240775 4.153255 3.1325% 1844 0.233462 4.283356 3.2284% 1843
0.226161 4.421638 3.3361% 1842 0.218859 4.569147 3.4512% 1841 0.211558 4.726837
3.8105% 1840 0.203792 4.906953 2.3861% 1839 0.199043 5.024035 2.5824% 1838 0.194033
5.153775 2.6573% 1837 0.189010 5.290728 2.7232% 1836 0.183999 5.434805 2.7994% 1835
0.178989 5.586949 2.8871% 1834 0.173966 5.748251 2.9657% 1833 0.168955 5.918726
3.0563% 1832 0.163945 6.099622 3.1604% 1831 0.158922 6.292395 3.4660% 1830 0.153598
6.510488 2.4653% 1829 0.149903 6.670991 2.6804% 1828 0.145990 6.849800 10.3427%
1827 0.132306 7.558251 -4.2314% 1826 0.138152 7.238428 2.9150% 1825 0.134238
7.449431 3.0026% 1824 0.130325 7.673105 3.0955% 1823 0.126412 7.910627 3.1944% 1822
0.122499 8.163323 3.3102% 1821 0.118574 8.433545 3.2277% 1820 0.114867 8.705757
2.6573% 1819 0.111893 8.937094 2.6261% 1818 0.109030 9.171791 2.6969% 1817 0.106167
9.419148 2.7717% 1816 0.103303 9.680217 2.8507% 1815 0.100440 9.956171 2.9343% 1814
0.097577 10.248319 3.0231% 1813 0.094714 10.558131 3.1039% 1812 0.091862 10.885844
3.2172% 1811 0.088999 11.236059 3.0969% 1810 0.086326 11.584030 2.9144% 1809
0.083881 11.921633 2.8225% 1808 0.081579 12.258116 2.9199% 1807 0.079264 12.616045
2.9918% 1806 0.076962 12.993489 3.0841% 1805 0.074659 13.394215 3.1822% 1804
0.072357 13.820445 3.2868% 1803 0.070054 14.274693 3.3985% 1802 0.067752 14.759817
3.5180% 1801 0.065449 15.279074 3.3999% 1800 0.063297 15.798554 2.8419% 1799
0.061548 16.247529 2.7485% 1798 0.059901 16.694085 2.8261% 1797 0.058255 17.165882
3.7832% 1796 0.056132 17.815303 2.1272% 1795 0.054962 18.194270 3.0879% 1794
0.053316 18.756098 3.1625% 1793 0.051682 19.349261 3.2904% 1792 0.050035 19.985932
3.4024% 1791 0.048389 20.665927 3.2296% 1790 0.046875 21.333346 41.3145% 1780
0.033171 30.147101 29.4353% 1770 0.025627 39.020995 83.4728% 1750 0.013968
71.592928 29.2845% 1740 0.010804 92.558525 94.2514% 1720 0.005562 179.796225
85.8111% 1700 0.002993 334.081307 19.2490% 1690 0.002510 398.388783 88.0250% 1670
0.001335 749.070599

BASE YEAR: 1904

YEAR BYEAR/AYEAR AYEAR/BYEAR GROWTH%

2009 3.668576 0.272585 8.2857% 2001 3.387868 0.295171 1.0000% 2000 3.354325
0.298123 1.0000% 1999 3.321114 0.301104 1.0000% 1998 3.288231 0.304115 1.0000% 1997
3.255675 0.307156 1.0000% 1996 3.223440 0.310228 1.0000% 1995 3.191525 0.313330
0.9992% 1994 3.159950 0.316461 1.0008% 1993 3.128639 0.319628 1.0000% 1992 3.097663
0.322824 0.9295% 1991 3.069135 0.325825 1.2505% 1990 3.031229 0.329899 0.7224% 1989
3.009487 0.332283 1.1077% 1988 2.976517 0.335963 0.8834% 1987 2.950454 0.338931
0.5594% 1986 2.934042 0.340827 1.3056% 1985 2.896228 0.345277 0.7673% 1984 2.874175
0.347926 0.8149% 1983 2.850941 0.350761 0.9737% 1982 2.823448 0.354177 0.9508% 1981
2.796855 0.357544 0.9031% 1980 2.771824 0.360773 2.2701% 1979 2.710298 0.368963
1.0042% 1978 2.683353 0.372668 0.9896% 1977 2.657058 0.376356 0.9103% 1976 2.633088
0.379782 0.8394% 1975 2.611169 0.382970 0.9042% 1974 2.587771 0.386433 1.1568% 1973
2.558178 0.390903 0.9427% 1972 2.534288 0.394588 0.7426% 1971 2.515606 0.397519
1.4697% 1970 2.479168 0.403361 0.6968% 1969 2.462013 0.406172 0.8565% 1968 2.441104
0.409651 1.5090% 1967 2.404814 0.415833 0.9949% 1966 2.381124 0.419970 1.0575% 1965
2.356208 0.424411 1.1300% 1964 2.329880 0.429207 1.5537% 1963 2.294235 0.435875
1.4658% 1962 2.261092 0.442264 1.5364% 1961 2.226877 0.449059 2.1586% 1960 2.179823
0.458753 -1.6655% 1959 2.216742 0.451112 4.3080% 1958 2.125189 0.470546 2.1130%
1957 2.081214 0.480489 1.9895% 1956 2.040616 0.490048 2.1231% 1955 1.998193 0.500452
1.4496% 1954 1.969641 0.507707 2.1573% 1953 1.928048 0.518659 1.2298% 1952 1.904625
0.525038 1.6814% 1951 1.873131 0.533865 1.6233% 1950 1.843211 0.542532 1.4265% 1949
1.817286 0.550271 1.7790% 1948 1.785521 0.560061 1.8242% 1947 1.753534 0.570277 -

156

2.6320% 1946 1.800935 0.555267 3.1768% 1945 1.745485 0.572907 6.4754% 1944 1.639331
0.610005 -0.3437% 1943 1.644985 0.607908 0.6562% 1942 1.634260 0.611898 0.6633%
1941 1.623492 0.615956 -5.6614% 1940 1.720920 0.581084 8.0381% 1939 1.592883
0.627793 0.8126% 1938 1.580043 0.632894 0.7762% 1937 1.567872 0.637807 0.6029% 1936
1.558476 0.641652 0.5244% 1935 1.550347 0.645017 -3.0364% 1934 1.598895 0.625432
4.6271% 1933 1.528184 0.654371 1.3921% 1932 1.507202 0.663481 -0.2051% 1931
1.510299 0.662120 0.8886% 1930 1.496997 0.668004 1.0126% 1929 1.481991 0.674768
1.1526% 1928 1.465104 0.682545 1.2160% 1927 1.447502 0.690845 1.4086% 1926 1.427396
0.700576 1.7667% 1925 1.402616 0.712953 1.4465% 1924 1.382617 0.723266 1.7700% 1923
1.358571 0.736068 1.6165% 1922 1.336958 0.747966 1.3736% 1921 1.318842 0.758241
2.3393% 1920 1.288695 0.775978 1.3140% 1919 1.271982 0.786175 0.7676% 1918 1.262292
0.792210 0.3870% 1917 1.257426 0.795276 1.3274% 1916 1.240953 0.805832 1.4083% 1915
1.223719 0.817181 1.4458% 1914 1.206279 0.828996 1.9424% 1913 1.183295 0.845098
1.9857% 1912 1.160256 0.861879 1.5634% 1911 1.142396 0.875354 1.8169% 1910 1.122010
0.891258 1.8781% 1909 1.101326 0.907996 2.0082% 1908 1.079644 0.926231 1.9603% 1907
1.058887 0.944388 1.8264% 1906 1.039895 0.961635 1.9357% 1905 1.020148 0.980250
2.0148% 1904 1.000000 1.000000 2.1335% 1903 0.979110 1.021335 1.8151% 1902 0.961655
1.039874 1.8943% 1901 0.943777 1.059573 3.0255% 1900 0.916061 1.091630 0.6278% 1899
0.910346 1.098484 1.7757% 1898 0.894463 1.117989 1.8078% 1897 0.878580 1.138200
1.8396% 1896 0.862710 1.159138 1.8755% 1895 0.846827 1.180878 1.9114% 1894 0.830945
1.203449 1.9486% 1893 0.815062 1.226900 1.9858% 1892 0.799192 1.251264 2.0276% 1891
0.783309 1.276635 2.6465% 1890 0.763113 1.310421 1.5328% 1889 0.751593 1.330508
2.0811% 1888 0.736270 1.358197 2.1599% 1887 0.720704 1.387532 2.2075% 1886 0.705138
1.418163 2.2592% 1885 0.689559 1.450201 2.3095% 1884 0.673993 1.483694 2.3641% 1883
0.658427 1.518771 2.4214% 1882 0.642861 1.555546 2.4815% 1881 0.627295 1.594147
3.7644% 1880 0.604538 1.654157 0.9432% 1879 0.598889 1.669759 2.1464% 1878 0.586304
1.705598 2.1913% 1877 0.573732 1.742973 2.2426% 1876 0.561148 1.782061 2.2941% 1875
0.548564 1.822943 2.3456% 1874 0.535991 1.865702 2.4043% 1873 0.523407 1.910559
2.4635% 1872 0.510823 1.957627 2.5258% 1871 0.498238 2.007072 5.9947% 1870 0.470060
2.127389 -1.0968% 1869 0.475272 2.104056 2.1930% 1868 0.465074 2.150198 2.2394%
1867 0.454887 2.198349 2.2935% 1866 0.444688 2.248768 2.3445% 1865 0.434501 2.301490
2.4037% 1864 0.424302 2.356811 2.4599% 1863 0.414115 2.414786 2.5250% 1862 0.403916
2.475759 2.5872% 1861 0.393730 2.539813 2.9504% 1860 0.382446 2.614748 2.4012% 1859
0.373478 2.677534 2.7627% 1858 0.363437 2.751507 2.8412% 1857 0.353396 2.829683
2.9243% 1856 0.343356 2.912431 3.0161% 1855 0.333303 3.000274 3.1061% 1854 0.323262
3.093464 3.2056% 1853 0.313221 3.192629 3.3118% 1852 0.303181 3.298362 3.4252% 1851
0.293140 3.411339 4.0106% 1850 0.281837 3.548154 2.3254% 1849 0.275432 3.630661
2.7841% 1848 0.267971 3.731742 2.8590% 1847 0.260523 3.838433 2.9432% 1846 0.253075
3.951404 3.0324% 1845 0.245626 4.071227 3.1325% 1844 0.238166 4.198758 3.2284% 1843
0.230717 4.334309 3.3361% 1842 0.223269 4.478904 3.4512% 1841 0.215821 4.633480
3.8105% 1840 0.207899 4.810038 2.3861% 1839 0.203054 4.924808 2.5824% 1838 0.197942
5.051986 2.6573% 1837 0.192818 5.186234 2.7232% 1836 0.187707 5.327465 2.7994% 1835
0.182595 5.476605 2.8871% 1834 0.177471 5.634721 2.9657% 1833 0.172359 5.801829
3.0563% 1832 0.167248 5.979152 3.1604% 1831 0.162124 6.168118 3.4660% 1830 0.156693
6.381903 2.4653% 1829 0.152923 6.539236 2.6804% 1828 0.148931 6.714513 10.3427%
1827 0.134971 7.408972 -4.2314% 1826 0.140935 7.095466 2.9150% 1825 0.136943
7.302302 3.0026% 1824 0.132951 7.521558 3.0955% 1823 0.128959 7.754388 3.1944% 1822
0.124967 8.002094 3.3102% 1821 0.120963 8.266979 3.2277% 1820 0.117181 8.533815
2.6573% 1819 0.114148 8.760582 2.6261% 1818 0.111227 8.990644 2.6969% 1817 0.108306
9.233116 2.7717% 1816 0.105385 9.489029 2.8507% 1815 0.102464 9.759532 2.9343% 1814
0.099543 10.045910 3.0231% 1813 0.096622 10.349603 3.1039% 1812 0.093713 10.670844
3.2172% 1811 0.090792 11.014142 3.0969% 1810 0.088065 11.355241 2.9144% 1809
0.085571 11.686176 2.8225% 1808 0.083222 12.016013 2.9199% 1807 0.080861 12.366872
2.9918% 1806 0.078512 12.736863 3.0841% 1805 0.076163 13.129674 3.1822% 1804
0.073814 13.547486 3.2868% 1803 0.071466 13.992762 3.3985% 1802 0.069117 14.468304
3.5180% 1801 0.066768 14.977306 3.3999% 1800 0.064572 15.486526 2.8419% 1799

157

0.062788 15.926633 2.7485% 1798 0.061108 16.364370 2.8261% 1797 0.059429 16.826848 3.7832% 1796 0.057262 17.463443 2.1272% 1795 0.056070 17.834925 3.0879% 1794 0.054390 18.385657 3.1625% 1793 0.052723 18.967105 3.2904% 1792 0.051043 19.591202 3.4024% 1791 0.049364 20.257766 3.2296% 1790 0.047819 20.912004 41.3145% 1780 0.033839 29.551683 29.4353% 1770 0.026144 38.250314 83.4728% 1750 0.014249 70.178937 29.2845% 1740 0.011022 90.730455 94.2514% 1720 0.005674 176.245174 85.8111% 1700 0.003054 327.483061 19.2490% 1690 0.002561 390.520437 88.0250% 1670 0.001362 734.276139

BASE YEAR: 1903

YEAR BYEAR/AYEAR AYEAR/BYEAR GROWTH%

2009 3.746846 0.266891 8.2857% 2001 3.460149 0.289005 1.0000% 2000 3.425890 0.291895 1.0000% 1999 3.391970 0.294814 1.0000% 1998 3.358387 0.297762 1.0000% 1997 3.325135 0.300740 1.0000% 1996 3.292213 0.303747 1.0000% 1995 3.259617 0.306785 0.9992% 1994 3.227368 0.309850 1.0008% 1993 3.195390 0.312951 1.0000% 1992 3.163752 0.316080 0.9295% 1991 3.134616 0.319018 1.2505% 1990 3.095901 0.323008 0.7224% 1989 3.073695 0.325341 1.1077% 1988 3.040022 0.328945 0.8834% 1987 3.013402 0.331851 0.5594% 1986 2.996640 0.333707 1.3056% 1985 2.958020 0.338064 0.7673% 1984 2.935496 0.340658 0.8149% 1983 2.911767 0.343434 0.9737% 1982 2.883687 0.346778 0.9508% 1981 2.856527 0.350075 0.9031% 1980 2.830961 0.353237 2.2701% 1979 2.768123 0.361256 1.0042% 1978 2.740603 0.364883 0.9896% 1977 2.713747 0.368494 0.9103% 1976 2.689266 0.371849 0.8394% 1975 2.666879 0.374970 0.9042% 1974 2.642982 0.378361 1.1568% 1973 2.612758 0.382737 0.9427% 1972 2.588357 0.386345 0.7426% 1971 2.569277 0.389215 1.4697% 1970 2.532062 0.394935 0.6968% 1969 2.514540 0.397687 0.8565% 1968 2.493185 0.401093 1.5090% 1967 2.456121 0.407146 0.9949% 1966 2.431926 0.411197 1.0575% 1965 2.406478 0.415545 1.1300% 1964 2.379589 0.420241 1.5537% 1963 2.343184 0.426770 1.4658% 1962 2.309333 0.433025 1.5364% 1961 2.274388 0.439679 2.1586% 1960 2.226330 0.449170 -1.6655% 1959 2.264037 0.441689 4.3080% 1958 2.170531 0.460717 2.1130% 1957 2.125617 0.470452 1.9895% 1956 2.084153 0.479811 2.1231% 1955 2.040825 0.489998 1.4496% 1954 2.011663 0.497101 2.1573% 1953 1.969183 0.507825 1.2298% 1952 1.945261 0.514070 1.6814% 1951 1.913095 0.522713 1.6233% 1950 1.882536 0.531198 1.4265% 1949 1.856059 0.538776 1.7790% 1948 1.823616 0.548361 1.8242% 1947 1.790946 0.558364 -2.6320% 1946 1.839359 0.543668 3.1768% 1945 1.782725 0.560939 6.4754% 1944 1.674307 0.597262 -0.3437% 1943 1.680081 0.595209 0.6562% 1942 1.669128 0.599115 0.6633% 1941 1.658129 0.603089 -5.6614% 1940 1.757637 0.568946 8.0381% 1939 1.626867 0.614678 0.8126% 1938 1.613753 0.619673 0.7762% 1937 1.601323 0.624484 0.6029% 1936 1.591727 0.628248 0.5244% 1935 1.583424 0.631543 -3.0364% 1934 1.633008 0.612367 4.6271% 1933 1.560788 0.640702 1.3921% 1932 1.539358 0.649621 -0.2051% 1931 1.542522 0.648289 0.8886% 1930 1.528936 0.654050 1.0126% 1929 1.513609 0.660672 1.1526% 1928 1.496362 0.668287 1.2160% 1927 1.478385 0.676414 1.4086% 1926 1.457850 0.685942 1.7667% 1925 1.432542 0.698060 1.4465% 1924 1.412115 0.708157 1.7700% 1923 1.387556 0.720692 1.6165% 1922 1.365483 0.732342 1.3736% 1921 1.346980 0.742402 2.3393% 1920 1.316190 0.759769 1.3140% 1919 1.299120 0.769752 0.7676% 1918 1.289223 0.775661 0.3870% 1917 1.284253 0.778663 1.3274% 1916 1.267429 0.788999 1.4083% 1915 1.249828 0.800110 1.4458% 1914 1.232015 0.811678 1.9424% 1913 1.208541 0.827444 1.9857% 1912 1.185010 0.843875 1.5634% 1911 1.166769 0.857068 1.8169% 1910 1.145948 0.872640 1.8781% 1909 1.124823 0.889029 2.0082% 1908 1.102679 0.906883 1.9603% 1907 1.081479 0.924660 1.8264% 1906 1.062082 0.941547 1.9357% 1905 1.041913 0.959773 2.0148% 1904 1.021335 0.979110 2.1335% 1903 1.000000 1.000000 1.8151% 1902 0.982172 1.018151 1.8943% 1901 0.963912 1.037439 3.0255% 1900 0.935606 1.068827 0.6278% 1899 0.929768 1.075537 1.7757% 1898 0.913547 1.094635 1.8078% 1897 0.897325 1.114423 1.8396% 1896 0.881116 1.134924 1.8755% 1895 0.864895 1.156210 1.9114% 1894 0.848673 1.178310 1.9486% 1893 0.832452 1.201271 1.9858% 1892 0.816243 1.225126 2.0276% 1891 0.800021 1.249967 2.6465% 1890 0.779395 1.283047 1.5328% 1889 0.767628 1.302714 2.0811% 1888 0.751979 1.329825 2.1599% 1887 0.736080 1.358547 2.2075% 1886 0.720182 1.388538 2.2592% 1885 0.704271 1.419907 2.3095% 1884 0.688373 1.452700 2.3641% 1883 0.672475 1.487044 2.4214% 1882 0.656577 1.523051 2.4815% 1881 0.640678 1.560845

3.7644% 1880 0.617436 1.619602 0.9432% 1879 0.611666 1.634878 2.1464% 1878 0.598813
1.669969 2.1913% 1877 0.585973 1.706563 2.2426% 1876 0.573120 1.744835 2.2941% 1875
0.560267 1.784862 2.3456% 1874 0.547427 1.826728 2.4043% 1873 0.534574 1.870648
2.4635% 1872 0.521721 1.916733 2.5258% 1871 0.508868 1.965145 5.9947% 1870 0.480089
2.082949 -1.0968% 1869 0.485413 2.060103 2.1930% 1868 0.474996 2.105281 2.2394%
1867 0.464592 2.152427 2.2935% 1866 0.454175 2.201793 2.3445% 1865 0.443771 2.253413
2.4037% 1864 0.433355 2.307578 2.4599% 1863 0.422951 2.364342 2.5250% 1862 0.412534
2.424042 2.5872% 1861 0.402130 2.486758 2.9504% 1860 0.390606 2.560127 2.4012% 1859
0.381446 2.621602 2.7627% 1858 0.371191 2.694029 2.8412% 1857 0.360936 2.770572
2.9243% 1856 0.350681 2.851591 3.0161% 1855 0.340414 2.937599 3.1061% 1854 0.330159
3.028843 3.2056% 1853 0.319904 3.125936 3.3118% 1852 0.309649 3.229461 3.4252% 1851
0.299394 3.340077 4.0106% 1850 0.287850 3.474034 2.3254% 1849 0.281308 3.554818
2.7841% 1848 0.273689 3.653788 2.8590% 1847 0.266081 3.758250 2.9432% 1846 0.258474
3.868861 3.0324% 1845 0.250867 3.986181 3.1325% 1844 0.243247 4.111048 3.2284% 1843
0.235640 4.243767 3.3361% 1842 0.228032 4.385342 3.4512% 1841 0.220425 4.536688
3.8105% 1840 0.212334 4.709558 2.3861% 1839 0.207386 4.821931 2.5824% 1838 0.202165
4.946452 2.6573% 1837 0.196932 5.077895 2.7232% 1836 0.191711 5.216177 2.7994% 1835
0.186491 5.362201 2.8871% 1834 0.181257 5.517014 2.9657% 1833 0.176037 5.680631
3.0563% 1832 0.170816 5.854250 3.1604% 1831 0.165583 6.039269 3.4660% 1830 0.160036
6.248588 2.4653% 1829 0.156186 6.402634 2.6804% 1828 0.152109 6.574250 10.3427%
1827 0.137851 7.254202 -4.2314% 1826 0.143942 6.947245 2.9150% 1825 0.139865
7.149760 3.0026% 1824 0.135788 7.364436 3.0955% 1823 0.131711 7.592403 3.1944% 1822
0.127634 7.834933 3.3102% 1821 0.123544 8.094285 3.2277% 1820 0.119681 8.355547
2.6573% 1819 0.116583 8.577577 2.6261% 1818 0.113600 8.802834 2.6969% 1817 0.110617
9.040240 2.7717% 1816 0.107633 9.290807 2.8507% 1815 0.104650 9.555659 2.9343% 1814
0.101667 9.836055 3.0231% 1813 0.098684 10.133404 3.1039% 1812 0.095713 10.447935
3.2172% 1811 0.092729 10.784061 3.0969% 1810 0.089944 11.118034 2.9144% 1809
0.087397 11.442056 2.8225% 1808 0.084998 11.765004 2.9199% 1807 0.082586 12.108534
2.9918% 1806 0.080187 12.470795 3.0841% 1805 0.077788 12.855401 3.1822% 1804
0.075389 13.264484 3.2868% 1803 0.072990 13.700459 3.3985% 1802 0.070591 14.166067
3.5180% 1801 0.068192 14.664436 3.3999% 1800 0.065950 15.163019 2.8419% 1799
0.064128 15.593932 2.7485% 1798 0.062412 16.022525 2.8261% 1797 0.060697 16.475342
3.7832% 1796 0.058484 17.098639 2.1272% 1795 0.057266 17.462361 3.0879% 1794
0.055551 18.001588 3.1625% 1793 0.053848 18.570890 3.2904% 1792 0.052132 19.181950
3.4024% 1791 0.050417 19.834590 3.2296% 1790 0.048840 20.475161 41.3145% 1780
0.034561 28.934361 29.4353% 1770 0.026701 37.451281 83.4728% 1750 0.014553
68.712929 29.2845% 1740 0.011257 88.835134 94.2514% 1720 0.005795 172.563486
85.8111% 1700 0.003119 320.642077 19.2490% 1690 0.002615 382.362628 88.0250% 1670
0.001391 718.937417

BASE YEAR: 1902
YEAR BYEAR/AYEAR AYEAR/BYEAR GROWTH%

2009 3.814857 0.262133 8.2857% 2001 3.522956 0.283853 1.0000% 2000 3.488075
0.286691 1.0000% 1999 3.453540 0.289558 1.0000% 1998 3.419346 0.292454 1.0000% 1997
3.385491 0.295378 1.0000% 1996 3.351972 0.298332 1.0000% 1995 3.318784 0.301315
0.9992% 1994 3.285950 0.304326 1.0008% 1993 3.253391 0.307372 1.0000% 1992 3.221179
0.310445 0.9295% 1991 3.191514 0.313331 1.2505% 1990 3.152096 0.317249 0.7224% 1989
3.129487 0.319541 1.1077% 1988 3.095203 0.323081 0.8834% 1987 3.068100 0.325935
0.5594% 1986 3.051034 0.327758 1.3056% 1985 3.011712 0.332037 0.7673% 1984 2.988780
0.334585 0.8149% 1983 2.964620 0.337311 0.9737% 1982 2.936030 0.340596 0.9508% 1981
2.908377 0.343834 0.9031% 1980 2.882348 0.346939 2.2701% 1979 2.818369 0.354815
1.0042% 1978 2.790349 0.358378 0.9896% 1977 2.763006 0.361925 0.9103% 1976 2.738080
0.365219 0.8394% 1975 2.715287 0.368285 0.9042% 1974 2.690956 0.371615 1.1568% 1973
2.660183 0.375914 0.9427% 1972 2.635340 0.379458 0.7426% 1971 2.615913 0.382276
1.4697% 1970 2.578023 0.387894 0.6968% 1969 2.560183 0.390597 0.8565% 1968 2.538440
0.393943 1.5090% 1967 2.500704 0.399887 0.9949% 1966 2.476069 0.403866 1.0575% 1965
2.450159 0.408137 1.1300% 1964 2.422782 0.412749 1.5537% 1963 2.385716 0.419161

159

1.4658% 1962 2.351251 0.425306 1.5364% 1961 2.315672 0.431840 2.1586% 1960 2.266741
0.441162 -1.6655% 1959 2.305133 0.433814 4.3080% 1958 2.209929 0.452503 2.1130%
1957 2.164201 0.462064 1.9895% 1956 2.121984 0.471257 2.1231% 1955 2.077869 0.481262
1.4496% 1954 2.048178 0.488239 2.1573% 1953 2.004927 0.498771 1.2298% 1952 1.980571
0.504905 1.6814% 1951 1.947820 0.513394 1.6233% 1950 1.916707 0.521728 1.4265% 1949
1.889749 0.529171 1.7790% 1948 1.856717 0.538585 1.8242% 1947 1.823454 0.548410 -
2.6320% 1946 1.872746 0.533975 3.1768% 1945 1.815084 0.550939 6.4754% 1944 1.704698
0.586614 -0.3437% 1943 1.710577 0.584598 0.6562% 1942 1.699425 0.588434 0.6633%
1941 1.688227 0.592337 -5.6614% 1940 1.789540 0.558803 8.0381% 1939 1.656397
0.603720 0.8126% 1938 1.643045 0.608626 0.7762% 1937 1.630390 0.613350 0.6029% 1936
1.620619 0.617048 0.5244% 1935 1.612165 0.620284 -3.0364% 1934 1.662649 0.601450
4.6271% 1933 1.589119 0.629280 1.3921% 1932 1.567300 0.638040 -0.2051% 1931
1.570521 0.636731 0.8886% 1930 1.556688 0.642389 1.0126% 1929 1.541084 0.648894
1.1526% 1928 1.523524 0.656373 1.2160% 1927 1.505220 0.664355 1.4086% 1926 1.484312
0.673713 1.7667% 1925 1.458544 0.685615 1.4465% 1924 1.437747 0.695533 1.7700% 1923
1.412742 0.707843 1.6165% 1922 1.390268 0.719286 1.3736% 1921 1.371430 0.729166
2.3393% 1920 1.340081 0.746224 1.3140% 1919 1.322701 0.756029 0.7676% 1918 1.312624
0.761833 0.3870% 1917 1.307564 0.764781 1.3274% 1916 1.290434 0.774933 1.4083% 1915
1.272514 0.785846 1.4458% 1914 1.254378 0.797208 1.9424% 1913 1.230477 0.812693
1.9857% 1912 1.206520 0.828830 1.5634% 1911 1.187947 0.841788 1.8169% 1910 1.166749
0.857083 1.8781% 1909 1.145240 0.873179 2.0082% 1908 1.122694 0.890715 1.9603% 1907
1.101109 0.908175 1.8264% 1906 1.081360 0.924761 1.9357% 1905 1.060826 0.942662
2.0148% 1904 1.039874 0.961655 2.1335% 1903 1.018151 0.982172 1.8151% 1902 1.000000
1.000000 1.8943% 1901 0.981409 1.018943 3.0255% 1900 0.952588 1.049772 0.6278% 1899
0.946645 1.056363 1.7757% 1898 0.930129 1.075120 1.8078% 1897 0.913613 1.094555
1.8396% 1896 0.897110 1.114691 1.8755% 1895 0.880594 1.135597 1.9114% 1894 0.864078
1.157303 1.9486% 1893 0.847562 1.179855 1.9858% 1892 0.831059 1.203284 2.0276% 1891
0.814543 1.227682 2.6465% 1890 0.793542 1.260173 1.5328% 1889 0.781562 1.279489
2.0811% 1888 0.765628 1.306117 2.1599% 1887 0.749441 1.334327 2.2075% 1886 0.733254
1.363783 2.2592% 1885 0.717055 1.394593 2.3095% 1884 0.700868 1.426802 2.3641% 1883
0.684681 1.460533 2.4214% 1882 0.668495 1.495899 2.4815% 1881 0.652308 1.533019
3.7644% 1880 0.628643 1.590728 0.9432% 1879 0.622769 1.605732 2.1464% 1878 0.609683
1.640197 2.1913% 1877 0.596609 1.676139 2.2426% 1876 0.583523 1.713728 2.2941% 1875
0.570437 1.753042 2.3456% 1874 0.557364 1.794161 2.4043% 1873 0.544277 1.837298
2.4635% 1872 0.531191 1.882561 2.5258% 1871 0.518105 1.930110 5.9947% 1870 0.488803
2.045814 -1.0968% 1869 0.494223 2.023376 2.1930% 1868 0.483618 2.067748 2.2394%
1867 0.473025 2.114053 2.2935% 1866 0.462419 2.162539 2.3445% 1865 0.451826 2.213239
2.4037% 1864 0.441221 2.266439 2.4599% 1863 0.430628 2.322191 2.5250% 1862 0.420022
2.380826 2.5872% 1861 0.409429 2.442424 2.9504% 1860 0.397696 2.514485 2.4012% 1859
0.388370 2.574864 2.7627% 1858 0.377929 2.646000 2.8412% 1857 0.367488 2.721178
2.9243% 1856 0.357047 2.800754 3.0161% 1855 0.346593 2.885228 3.1061% 1854 0.336152
2.974845 3.2056% 1853 0.325711 3.070207 3.3118% 1852 0.315270 3.171886 3.4252% 1851
0.304829 3.280531 4.0106% 1850 0.293075 3.412100 2.3254% 1849 0.286414 3.491444
2.7841% 1848 0.278656 3.588648 2.8590% 1847 0.270911 3.691248 2.9432% 1846 0.263166
3.799887 3.0324% 1845 0.255420 3.915115 3.1325% 1844 0.247662 4.037757 3.2284% 1843
0.239917 4.168110 3.3361% 1842 0.232172 4.307160 3.4512% 1841 0.224426 4.455809
3.8105% 1840 0.216188 4.625597 2.3861% 1839 0.211150 4.735966 2.5824% 1838 0.205835
4.858267 2.6573% 1837 0.200507 4.987367 2.7232% 1836 0.195191 5.123183 2.7994% 1835
0.189876 5.266604 2.8871% 1834 0.184548 5.418657 2.9657% 1833 0.179232 5.579357
3.0563% 1832 0.173917 5.749881 3.1604% 1831 0.168589 5.931601 3.4660% 1830 0.162941
6.137188 2.4653% 1829 0.159021 6.288489 2.6804% 1828 0.154870 6.457045 10.3427%
1827 0.140353 7.124875 -4.2314% 1826 0.146555 6.823390 2.9150% 1825 0.142404
7.022295 3.0026% 1824 0.138252 7.233143 3.0955% 1823 0.134101 7.457046 3.1944% 1822
0.129950 7.695253 3.3102% 1821 0.125786 7.949981 3.2277% 1820 0.121853 8.206585
2.6573% 1819 0.118699 8.424657 2.6261% 1818 0.115662 8.645898 2.6969% 1817 0.112624
8.879072 2.7717% 1816 0.109587 9.125171 2.8507% 1815 0.106550 9.385302 2.9343% 1814

0.103512 9.660699 3.0231% 1813 0.100475 9.952747 3.1039% 1812 0.097450 10.261670 3.2172% 1811 0.094413 10.591804 3.0969% 1810 0.091577 10.919823 2.9144% 1809 0.088983 11.238068 2.8225% 1808 0.086541 11.555259 2.9199% 1807 0.084085 11.892664 2.9918% 1806 0.081643 12.248467 3.0841% 1805 0.079200 12.626216 3.1822% 1804 0.076758 13.028006 3.2868% 1803 0.074315 13.456209 3.3985% 1802 0.071873 13.913516 3.5180% 1801 0.069430 14.403000 3.3999% 1800 0.067147 14.892695 2.8419% 1799 0.065292 15.315925 2.7485% 1798 0.063545 15.736877 2.8261% 1797 0.061799 16.181622 3.7832% 1796 0.059546 16.793806 2.1272% 1795 0.058305 17.151044 3.0879% 1794 0.056559 17.680658 3.1625% 1793 0.054825 18.239810 3.2904% 1792 0.053079 18.839976 3.4024% 1791 0.051332 19.480981 3.2296% 1790 0.049726 20.110132 41.3145% 1780 0.035188 28.418522 29.4353% 1770 0.027186 36.783604 83.4728% 1750 0.014817 67.487922 29.2845% 1740 0.011461 87.251390 94.2514% 1720 0.005900 169.487042 85.8111% 1700 0.003175 314.925703 19.2490% 1690 0.002663 375.545908 88.0250% 1670 0.001416 706.120277

BASE YEAR: 1901

YEAR BYEAR/AYEAR AYEAR/BYEAR GROWTH%

2009 3.887123 0.257260 8.2857% 2001 3.589693 0.278575 1.0000% 2000 3.554152 0.281361 1.0000% 1999 3.518962 0.284175 1.0000% 1998 3.484121 0.287016 1.0000% 1997 3.449624 0.289887 1.0000% 1996 3.415470 0.292785 1.0000% 1995 3.381653 0.295713 0.9992% 1994 3.348197 0.298668 1.0008% 1993 3.315021 0.301657 1.0000% 1992 3.282199 0.304674 0.9295% 1991 3.251972 0.307506 1.2505% 1990 3.211808 0.311351 0.7224% 1989 3.188771 0.313600 1.1077% 1988 3.153837 0.317074 0.8834% 1987 3.126221 0.319875 0.5594% 1986 3.108831 0.321664 1.3056% 1985 3.068764 0.325864 0.7673% 1984 3.045398 0.328364 0.8149% 1983 3.020780 0.331040 0.9737% 1982 2.991649 0.334264 0.9508% 1981 2.963472 0.337442 0.9031% 1980 2.936949 0.340489 2.2701% 1979 2.871758 0.348219 1.0042% 1978 2.843208 0.351715 0.9896% 1977 2.815347 0.355196 0.9103% 1976 2.789949 0.358430 0.8394% 1975 2.766724 0.361438 0.9042% 1974 2.741932 0.364706 1.1568% 1973 2.710576 0.368925 0.9427% 1972 2.685262 0.372403 0.7426% 1971 2.665468 0.375169 1.4697% 1970 2.626860 0.380683 0.6968% 1969 2.608682 0.383335 0.8565% 1968 2.586527 0.386619 1.5090% 1967 2.548076 0.392453 0.9949% 1966 2.522974 0.396358 1.0575% 1965 2.496574 0.400549 1.1300% 1964 2.468678 0.405075 1.5537% 1963 2.430910 0.411369 1.4658% 1962 2.395792 0.417399 1.5364% 1961 2.359539 0.423812 2.1586% 1960 2.309681 0.432960 -1.6655% 1959 2.348800 0.425749 4.3080% 1958 2.251793 0.444091 2.1130% 1957 2.205198 0.453474 1.9895% 1956 2.162182 0.462496 2.1231% 1955 2.117231 0.472315 1.4496% 1954 2.086978 0.479162 2.1573% 1953 2.042907 0.489499 1.2298% 1952 2.018089 0.495518 1.6814% 1951 1.984719 0.503850 1.6233% 1950 1.953016 0.512029 1.4265% 1949 1.925547 0.519333 1.7790% 1948 1.891890 0.528572 1.8242% 1947 1.857997 0.538214 -2.6320% 1946 1.908222 0.524048 3.1768% 1945 1.849468 0.540696 6.4754% 1944 1.736991 0.575708 -0.3437% 1943 1.742981 0.573730 0.6562% 1942 1.731618 0.577495 0.6633% 1941 1.720208 0.581325 -5.6614% 1940 1.823440 0.548414 8.0381% 1939 1.687775 0.592496 0.8126% 1938 1.674170 0.597311 0.7762% 1937 1.661275 0.601947 0.6029% 1936 1.651319 0.605576 0.5244% 1935 1.642705 0.608752 -3.0364% 1934 1.694146 0.590268 4.6271% 1933 1.619222 0.617580 1.3921% 1932 1.596990 0.626178 -0.2051% 1931 1.600272 0.624894 0.8886% 1930 1.586177 0.630446 1.0126% 1929 1.570277 0.636830 1.1526% 1928 1.552384 0.644170 1.2160% 1927 1.533734 0.652003 1.4086% 1926 1.512430 0.661187 1.7667% 1925 1.486174 0.672869 1.4465% 1924 1.464983 0.682602 1.7700% 1923 1.439504 0.694684 1.6165% 1922 1.416605 0.705913 1.3736% 1921 1.397409 0.715610 2.3393% 1920 1.365467 0.732350 1.3140% 1919 1.347757 0.741973 0.7676% 1918 1.337490 0.747669 0.3870% 1917 1.332334 0.750563 1.3274% 1916 1.314880 0.760526 1.4083% 1915 1.296620 0.771236 1.4458% 1914 1.278140 0.782387 1.9424% 1913 1.253787 0.797584 1.9857% 1912 1.229376 0.813421 1.5634% 1911 1.210451 0.826138 1.8169% 1910 1.188851 0.841148 1.8781% 1909 1.166935 0.856946 2.0082% 1908 1.143962 0.874155 1.9603% 1907 1.121968 0.891291 1.8264% 1906 1.101845 0.907569 1.9357% 1905 1.080922 0.925137 2.0148% 1904 1.059573 0.943777 2.1335% 1903 1.037439 0.963912 1.8151% 1902 1.018943 0.981409 1.8943% 1901 1.000000 1.000000 3.0255% 1900 0.970633 1.030255 0.6278% 1899 0.964577 1.036723 1.7757% 1898 0.947749 1.055132 1.8078% 1897 0.930920 1.074206

1.8396% 1896 0.914104 1.093967 1.8755% 1895 0.897275 1.114485 1.9114% 1894 0.880447
1.135787 1.9486% 1893 0.863618 1.157920 1.9858% 1892 0.846802 1.180914 2.0276% 1891
0.829973 1.204858 2.6465% 1890 0.808574 1.236745 1.5328% 1889 0.796367 1.255702
2.0811% 1888 0.780132 1.281835 2.1599% 1887 0.763638 1.309520 2.2075% 1886 0.747145
1.338428 2.2592% 1885 0.730639 1.368666 2.3095% 1884 0.714145 1.400276 2.3641% 1883
0.697652 1.433380 2.4214% 1882 0.681158 1.468088 2.4815% 1881 0.664665 1.504518
3.7644% 1880 0.640552 1.561154 0.9432% 1879 0.634566 1.575879 2.1464% 1878 0.621232
1.609704 2.1913% 1877 0.607911 1.644977 2.2426% 1876 0.594577 1.681868 2.2941% 1875
0.581243 1.720451 2.3456% 1874 0.567922 1.760805 2.4043% 1873 0.554588 1.803141
2.4635% 1872 0.541254 1.847562 2.5258% 1871 0.527920 1.894227 5.9947% 1870 0.498063
2.007780 -1.0968% 1869 0.503586 1.985759 2.1930% 1868 0.492779 2.029306 2.2394%
1867 0.481986 2.074750 2.2935% 1866 0.471179 2.122335 2.3445% 1865 0.460386 2.172092
2.4037% 1864 0.449579 2.224303 2.4599% 1863 0.438785 2.279018 2.5250% 1862 0.427979
2.336564 2.5872% 1861 0.417185 2.397016 2.9504% 1860 0.405229 2.467738 2.4012% 1859
0.395727 2.526994 2.7627% 1858 0.385088 2.596808 2.8412% 1857 0.374449 2.670588
2.9243% 1856 0.363810 2.748684 3.0161% 1855 0.353159 2.831588 3.1061% 1854 0.342520
2.919539 3.2056% 1853 0.331881 3.013128 3.3118% 1852 0.321242 3.112917 3.4252% 1851
0.310603 3.219541 4.0106% 1850 0.298627 3.348664 2.3254% 1849 0.291840 3.426533
2.7841% 1848 0.283935 3.521931 2.8590% 1847 0.276043 3.622623 2.9432% 1846 0.268151
3.729243 3.0324% 1845 0.260259 3.842328 3.1325% 1844 0.252354 3.962689 3.2284% 1843
0.244462 4.090619 3.3361% 1842 0.236570 4.227085 3.4512% 1841 0.228678 4.372970
3.8105% 1840 0.220284 4.539601 2.3861% 1839 0.215150 4.647918 2.5824% 1838 0.209734
4.767946 2.6573% 1837 0.204305 4.894646 2.7232% 1836 0.198889 5.027937 2.7994% 1835
0.193473 5.168691 2.8871% 1834 0.188044 5.317917 2.9657% 1833 0.182627 5.475630
3.0563% 1832 0.177211 5.642983 3.1604% 1831 0.171782 5.821325 3.4660% 1830 0.166028
6.023090 2.4653% 1829 0.162033 6.171577 2.6804% 1828 0.157803 6.337000 10.3427%
1827 0.143012 6.992414 -4.2314% 1826 0.149331 6.696535 2.9150% 1825 0.145101
6.891741 3.0026% 1824 0.140871 7.098670 3.0955% 1823 0.136642 7.318410 3.1944% 1822
0.132412 7.552188 3.3102% 1821 0.128169 7.802180 3.2277% 1820 0.124162 8.054014
2.6573% 1819 0.120948 8.268032 2.6261% 1818 0.117853 8.485159 2.6969% 1817 0.114758
8.713998 2.7717% 1816 0.111663 8.955523 2.8507% 1815 0.108568 9.210817 2.9343% 1814
0.105473 9.481094 3.0231% 1813 0.102378 9.767713 3.1039% 1812 0.099296 10.070892
3.2172% 1811 0.096201 10.394889 3.0969% 1810 0.093311 10.716810 2.9144% 1809
0.090669 11.029138 2.8225% 1808 0.088180 11.340431 2.9199% 1807 0.085678 11.671564
2.9918% 1806 0.083189 12.020752 3.0841% 1805 0.080701 12.391478 3.1822% 1804
0.078212 12.785799 3.2868% 1803 0.075723 13.206041 3.3985% 1802 0.073234 13.654846
3.5180% 1801 0.070745 14.135230 3.3999% 1800 0.068419 14.615820 2.8419% 1799
0.066528 15.031182 2.7485% 1798 0.064749 15.444308 2.8261% 1797 0.062969 15.880784
3.7832% 1796 0.060674 16.481588 2.1272% 1795 0.059410 16.832184 3.0879% 1794
0.057630 17.351951 3.1625% 1793 0.055864 17.900709 3.2904% 1792 0.054084 18.489716
3.4024% 1791 0.052305 19.118804 3.2296% 1790 0.050668 19.736258 41.3145% 1780
0.035855 27.890185 29.4353% 1770 0.027701 36.099749 83.4728% 1750 0.015098
66.233234 29.2845% 1740 0.011678 85.629273 94.2514% 1720 0.006012 166.336057
85.8111% 1700 0.003236 309.070825 19.2490% 1690 0.002713 368.564021 88.0250% 1670
0.001443 692.992583

BASE YEAR: 1900
YEAR BYEAR/AYEAR AYEAR/BYEAR GROWTH%

2009 4.004728 0.249705 8.2857% 2001 3.698300 0.270395 1.0000% 2000 3.661682
0.273099 1.0000% 1999 3.625428 0.275829 1.0000% 1998 3.589533 0.278588 1.0000% 1997
3.553993 0.281374 1.0000% 1996 3.518805 0.284187 1.0000% 1995 3.483965 0.287029
0.9992% 1994 3.449497 0.289897 1.0008% 1993 3.415317 0.292799 1.0000% 1992 3.381502
0.295727 0.9295% 1991 3.350360 0.298475 1.2505% 1990 3.308981 0.302208 0.7224% 1989
3.285247 0.304391 1.1077% 1988 3.249256 0.307763 0.8834% 1987 3.220804 0.310481
0.5594% 1986 3.202889 0.312218 1.3056% 1985 3.161610 0.316295 0.7673% 1984 3.137536
0.318721 0.8149% 1983 3.112174 0.321319 0.9737% 1982 3.082161 0.324448 0.9508% 1981
3.053132 0.327533 0.9031% 1980 3.025807 0.330490 2.2701% 1979 2.958643 0.337993

162

1.0042% 1978 2.929229 0.341387 0.9896% 1977 2.900525 0.344765 0.9103% 1976 2.874359 0.347904 0.8394% 1975 2.850431 0.350824 0.9042% 1974 2.824889 0.353996 1.1568% 1973 2.792585 0.358091 0.9427% 1972 2.766505 0.361467 0.7426% 1971 2.746111 0.364151 1.4697% 1970 2.706335 0.369503 0.6968% 1969 2.687607 0.372078 0.8565% 1968 2.664783 0.375265 1.5090% 1967 2.625168 0.380928 0.9949% 1966 2.599307 0.384718 1.0575% 1965 2.572108 0.388786 1.1300% 1964 2.543367 0.393180 1.5537% 1963 2.504457 0.399288 1.4658% 1962 2.468276 0.405141 1.5364% 1961 2.430927 0.411366 2.1586% 1960 2.379561 0.420246 -1.6655% 1959 2.419863 0.413247 4.3080% 1958 2.319921 0.431049 2.1130% 1957 2.271916 0.440157 1.9895% 1956 2.227598 0.448914 2.1231% 1955 2.181288 0.458445 1.4496% 1954 2.150119 0.465090 2.1573% 1953 2.104715 0.475124 1.2298% 1952 2.079147 0.480967 1.6814% 1951 2.044767 0.489053 1.6233% 1950 2.012105 0.496992 1.4265% 1949 1.983805 0.504082 1.7790% 1948 1.949129 0.513050 1.8242% 1947 1.914211 0.522409 -2.6320% 1946 1.965955 0.508659 3.1768% 1945 1.905424 0.524818 6.4754% 1944 1.789544 0.558802 -0.3437% 1943 1.795715 0.556881 0.6562% 1942 1.784008 0.560536 0.6633% 1941 1.772253 0.564254 -5.6614% 1940 1.878609 0.532309 8.0381% 1939 1.738839 0.575096 0.8126% 1938 1.724822 0.579770 0.7762% 1937 1.711537 0.584270 0.6029% 1936 1.701280 0.587793 0.5244% 1935 1.692405 0.590875 -3.0364% 1934 1.745402 0.572934 4.6271% 1933 1.668212 0.599444 1.3921% 1932 1.645307 0.607789 -0.2051% 1931 1.648688 0.606543 0.8886% 1930 1.634167 0.611932 1.0126% 1929 1.617786 0.618129 1.1526% 1928 1.599352 0.625253 1.2160% 1927 1.580137 0.632856 1.4086% 1926 1.558189 0.641771 1.7667% 1925 1.531139 0.653109 1.4465% 1924 1.509306 0.662556 1.7700% 1923 1.483057 0.674283 1.6165% 1922 1.459464 0.685183 1.3736% 1921 1.439688 0.694595 2.3393% 1920 1.406779 0.710844 1.3140% 1919 1.388534 0.720184 0.7676% 1918 1.377956 0.725713 0.3870% 1917 1.372644 0.728521 1.3274% 1916 1.354662 0.738192 1.4083% 1915 1.335849 0.748588 1.4458% 1914 1.316810 0.759411 1.9424% 1913 1.291720 0.774161 1.9857% 1912 1.266570 0.789534 1.5634% 1911 1.247074 0.801877 1.8169% 1910 1.224820 0.816447 1.8781% 1909 1.202241 0.831780 2.0082% 1908 1.178572 0.848484 1.9603% 1907 1.155913 0.865117 1.8264% 1906 1.135181 0.880917 1.9357% 1905 1.113625 0.897969 2.0148% 1904 1.091630 0.916061 2.1335% 1903 1.068827 0.935606 1.8151% 1902 1.049772 0.952588 1.8943% 1901 1.030255 0.970633 3.0255% 1900 1.000000 1.000000 0.6278% 1899 0.993761 1.006278 1.7757% 1898 0.976423 1.024146 1.8078% 1897 0.959085 1.042660 1.8396% 1896 0.941760 1.061841 1.8755% 1895 0.924422 1.081757 1.9114% 1894 0.907085 1.102433 1.9486% 1893 0.889747 1.123915 1.9858% 1892 0.872422 1.146234 2.0276% 1891 0.855084 1.169476 2.6465% 1890 0.833038 1.200426 1.5328% 1889 0.820461 1.218826 2.0811% 1888 0.803735 1.244192 2.1599% 1887 0.786742 1.271064 2.2075% 1886 0.769750 1.299124 2.2592% 1885 0.752744 1.328473 2.3095% 1884 0.735752 1.359155 2.3641% 1883 0.718759 1.391287 2.4214% 1882 0.701767 1.424975 2.4815% 1881 0.684774 1.460336 3.7644% 1880 0.659932 1.515308 0.9432% 1879 0.653765 1.529601 2.1464% 1878 0.640028 1.562432 2.1913% 1877 0.626304 1.596670 2.2426% 1876 0.612566 1.632477 2.2941% 1875 0.598829 1.669927 2.3456% 1874 0.585104 1.709097 2.4043% 1873 0.571367 1.750189 2.4635% 1872 0.557629 1.793305 2.5258% 1871 0.543892 1.838600 5.9947% 1870 0.513131 1.948818 -1.0968% 1869 0.518822 1.927444 2.1930% 1868 0.507688 1.969712 2.2394% 1867 0.496568 2.013822 2.2935% 1866 0.485435 2.060009 2.3445% 1865 0.474315 2.108306 2.4037% 1864 0.463181 2.158983 2.4599% 1863 0.452061 2.212091 2.5250% 1862 0.440927 2.267947 2.5872% 1861 0.429807 2.326624 2.9504% 1860 0.417490 2.395269 2.4012% 1859 0.407700 2.452785 2.7627% 1858 0.396739 2.520548 2.8412% 1857 0.385778 2.592162 2.9243% 1856 0.374818 2.667965 3.0161% 1855 0.363844 2.748434 3.1061% 1854 0.352883 2.833802 3.2056% 1853 0.341922 2.924643 3.3118% 1852 0.330961 3.021501 3.4252% 1851 0.320001 3.124995 4.0106% 1850 0.307661 3.250326 2.3254% 1849 0.300670 3.325908 2.7841% 1848 0.292526 3.418504 2.8590% 1847 0.284395 3.516239 2.9432% 1846 0.276264 3.619728 3.0324% 1845 0.268133 3.729493 3.1325% 1844 0.259989 3.846319 3.2284% 1843 0.251858 3.970492 3.3361% 1842 0.243727 4.102950 3.4512% 1841 0.235596 4.244551 3.8105% 1840 0.226948 4.406289 2.3861% 1839 0.221659 4.511425 2.5824% 1838 0.216079 4.627928 2.6573% 1837 0.210486 4.750907 2.7232% 1836 0.204906 4.880284 2.7994% 1835 0.199326 5.016904 2.8871% 1834 0.193733 5.161749 2.9657% 1833 0.188153 5.314830 3.0563% 1832 0.182573 5.477268 3.1604% 1831 0.176979 5.650373 3.4660% 1830 0.171051

5.846213 2.4653% 1829 0.166935 5.990340 2.6804% 1828 0.162578 6.150904 10.3427% 1827 0.147339 6.787071 -4.2314% 1826 0.153849 6.499881 2.9150% 1825 0.149491 6.689355 3.0026% 1824 0.145134 6.890207 3.0955% 1823 0.140776 7.103494 3.1944% 1822 0.136418 7.330407 3.3102% 1821 0.132047 7.573057 3.2277% 1820 0.127918 7.817496 2.6573% 1819 0.124607 8.025228 2.6261% 1818 0.121418 8.235980 2.6969% 1817 0.118230 8.458098 2.7717% 1816 0.115041 8.692530 2.8507% 1815 0.111853 8.940328 2.9343% 1814 0.108664 9.202668 3.0231% 1813 0.105476 9.480869 3.1039% 1812 0.102300 9.775145 3.2172% 1811 0.099112 10.089627 3.0969% 1810 0.096134 10.402094 2.9144% 1809 0.093412 10.705251 2.8225% 1808 0.090848 11.007402 2.9199% 1807 0.088271 11.328811 2.9918% 1806 0.085706 11.667744 3.0841% 1805 0.083142 12.027584 3.1822% 1804 0.080578 12.410324 3.2868% 1803 0.078014 12.818225 3.3985% 1802 0.075450 13.253851 3.5180% 1801 0.072886 13.720127 3.3999% 1800 0.070489 14.186604 2.8419% 1799 0.068541 14.589769 2.7485% 1798 0.066708 14.990762 2.8261% 1797 0.064874 15.414421 3.7832% 1796 0.062509 15.997581 2.1272% 1795 0.061207 16.337881 3.0879% 1794 0.059374 16.842385 3.1625% 1793 0.057554 17.375027 3.2904% 1792 0.055720 17.946738 3.4024% 1791 0.053887 18.557352 3.2296% 1790 0.052201 19.156673 41.3145% 1780 0.036940 27.071147 29.4353% 1770 0.028539 35.039625 83.4728% 1750 0.015555 64.288194 29.2845% 1740 0.012032 83.114640 94.2514% 1720 0.006194 161.451347 85.8111% 1700 0.003333 299.994492 19.2490% 1690 0.002795 357.740580 88.0250% 1670 0.001487 672.641805

BASE YEAR: 1899

YEAR BYEAR/AYEAR AYEAR/BYEAR GROWTH%

2009 4.029871 0.248147 8.2857% 2001 3.721519 0.268707 1.0000% 2000 3.684672 0.271395 1.0000% 1999 3.648190 0.274109 1.0000% 1998 3.612069 0.276850 1.0000% 1997 3.576306 0.279618 1.0000% 1996 3.540897 0.282414 1.0000% 1995 3.505839 0.285238 0.9992% 1994 3.471154 0.288089 1.0008% 1993 3.436760 0.290972 1.0000% 1992 3.402733 0.293881 0.9295% 1991 3.371395 0.296613 1.2505% 1990 3.329756 0.300322 0.7224% 1989 3.305873 0.302492 1.1077% 1988 3.269656 0.305843 0.8834% 1987 3.241026 0.308544 0.5594% 1986 3.222998 0.310270 1.3056% 1985 3.181460 0.314321 0.7673% 1984 3.157235 0.316733 0.8149% 1983 3.131713 0.319314 0.9737% 1982 3.101512 0.322423 0.9508% 1981 3.072300 0.325489 0.9031% 1980 3.044804 0.328428 2.2701% 1979 2.977219 0.335884 1.0042% 1978 2.947620 0.339257 0.9896% 1977 2.918736 0.342614 0.9103% 1976 2.892405 0.345733 0.8394% 1975 2.868327 0.348635 0.9042% 1974 2.842625 0.351788 1.1568% 1973 2.810118 0.355857 0.9427% 1972 2.783874 0.359212 0.7426% 1971 2.763352 0.361879 1.4697% 1970 2.723327 0.367198 0.6968% 1969 2.704481 0.369757 0.8565% 1968 2.681513 0.372924 1.5090% 1967 2.641650 0.378551 0.9949% 1966 2.615627 0.382318 1.0575% 1965 2.588257 0.386360 1.1300% 1964 2.559336 0.390726 1.5537% 1963 2.520181 0.396797 1.4658% 1962 2.483773 0.402613 1.5364% 1961 2.446189 0.408799 2.1586% 1960 2.394500 0.417624 -1.6655% 1959 2.435056 0.410668 4.3080% 1958 2.334486 0.428360 2.1130% 1957 2.286180 0.437411 1.9895% 1956 2.241584 0.446113 2.1231% 1955 2.194983 0.455584 1.4496% 1954 2.163618 0.462189 2.1573% 1953 2.117929 0.472159 1.2298% 1952 2.092200 0.477966 1.6814% 1951 2.057604 0.486002 1.6233% 1950 2.024737 0.493891 1.4265% 1949 1.996260 0.500937 1.7790% 1948 1.961366 0.509849 1.8242% 1947 1.926229 0.519149 -2.6320% 1946 1.978299 0.505485 3.1768% 1945 1.917387 0.521543 6.4754% 1944 1.800779 0.555315 -0.3437% 1943 1.806989 0.553407 0.6562% 1942 1.795209 0.557038 0.6633% 1941 1.783379 0.560733 -5.6614% 1940 1.890403 0.528988 8.0381% 1939 1.749756 0.571508 0.8126% 1938 1.735652 0.576153 0.7762% 1937 1.722282 0.580625 0.6029% 1936 1.711961 0.584125 0.5244% 1935 1.703031 0.587188 -3.0364% 1934 1.756360 0.569359 4.6271% 1933 1.678686 0.595704 1.3921% 1932 1.655637 0.603997 -0.2051% 1931 1.659040 0.602758 0.8886% 1930 1.644427 0.608114 1.0126% 1929 1.627943 0.614272 1.1526% 1928 1.609393 0.621352 1.2160% 1927 1.590058 0.628908 1.4086% 1926 1.567972 0.637767 1.7667% 1925 1.540752 0.649034 1.4465% 1924 1.518782 0.658422 1.7700% 1923 1.492368 0.670076 1.6165% 1922 1.468627 0.680908 1.3736% 1921 1.448727 0.690261 2.3393% 1920 1.415611 0.706409 1.3140% 1919 1.397251 0.715691 0.7676% 1918 1.386607 0.721185 0.3870% 1917 1.381262 0.723976 1.3274% 1916 1.363167 0.733586 1.4083% 1915 1.344236 0.743917 1.4458% 1914 1.325078 0.754673 1.9424% 1913 1.299830 0.769331

164

1.9857% 1912 1.274522 0.784608 1.5634% 1911 1.254903 0.796874 1.8169% 1910 1.232509
0.811353 1.8781% 1909 1.209789 0.826590 2.0082% 1908 1.185972 0.843190 1.9603% 1907
1.163171 0.859719 1.8264% 1906 1.142308 0.875421 1.9357% 1905 1.120617 0.892366
2.0148% 1904 1.098484 0.910346 2.1335% 1903 1.075537 0.929768 1.8151% 1902 1.056363
0.946645 1.8943% 1901 1.036723 0.964577 3.0255% 1900 1.006278 0.993761 0.6278% 1899
1.000000 1.000000 1.7757% 1898 0.982553 1.017757 1.8078% 1897 0.965106 1.036155
1.8396% 1896 0.947673 1.055216 1.8755% 1895 0.930226 1.075007 1.9114% 1894 0.912780
1.095555 1.9486% 1893 0.895333 1.116903 1.9858% 1892 0.877899 1.139083 2.0276% 1891
0.860453 1.162179 2.6465% 1890 0.838268 1.192936 1.5328% 1889 0.825613 1.211222
2.0811% 1888 0.808781 1.236429 2.1599% 1887 0.791682 1.263134 2.2075% 1886 0.774583
1.291018 2.2592% 1885 0.757470 1.320184 2.3095% 1884 0.740371 1.350674 2.3641% 1883
0.723272 1.382606 2.4214% 1882 0.706173 1.416085 2.4815% 1881 0.689073 1.451224
3.7644% 1880 0.664075 1.505854 0.9432% 1879 0.657870 1.520058 2.1464% 1878 0.644046
1.552684 2.1913% 1877 0.630236 1.586708 2.2426% 1876 0.616412 1.622292 2.2941% 1875
0.602588 1.659508 2.3456% 1874 0.588778 1.698433 2.4043% 1873 0.574954 1.739269
2.4635% 1872 0.561130 1.782117 2.5258% 1871 0.547307 1.827129 5.9947% 1870 0.516353
1.936659 -1.0968% 1869 0.522079 1.915418 2.1930% 1868 0.510876 1.957423 2.2394%
1867 0.499686 2.001257 2.2935% 1866 0.488482 2.047156 2.3445% 1865 0.477292 2.095151
2.4037% 1864 0.466089 2.145512 2.4599% 1863 0.454899 2.198290 2.5250% 1862 0.443696
2.253797 2.5872% 1861 0.432506 2.312108 2.9504% 1860 0.420111 2.380324 2.4012% 1859
0.410259 2.437482 2.7627% 1858 0.399230 2.504822 2.8412% 1857 0.388200 2.575989
2.9243% 1856 0.377171 2.651319 3.0161% 1855 0.366328 2.731286 3.1061% 1854 0.355098
2.816121 3.2056% 1853 0.344069 2.906396 3.3118% 1852 0.333039 3.002649 3.4252% 1851
0.322010 3.105497 4.0106% 1850 0.309593 3.230046 2.3254% 1849 0.302558 3.305157
2.7841% 1848 0.294362 3.397175 2.8590% 1847 0.286180 3.494301 2.9432% 1846 0.277998
3.597143 3.0324% 1845 0.269816 3.706223 3.1325% 1844 0.261621 3.822321 3.2284% 1843
0.253439 3.945719 3.3361% 1842 0.245257 4.077351 3.4512% 1841 0.237075 4.218068
3.8105% 1840 0.228373 4.378797 2.3861% 1839 0.223051 4.483277 2.5824% 1838 0.217436
4.599053 2.6573% 1837 0.211808 4.721265 2.7232% 1836 0.206193 4.849835 2.7994% 1835
0.200578 4.985603 2.8871% 1834 0.194949 5.129543 2.9657% 1833 0.189334 5.281669
3.0563% 1832 0.183719 5.443094 3.1604% 1831 0.178091 5.615119 3.4660% 1830 0.172125
5.809737 2.4653% 1829 0.167984 5.952965 2.6804% 1828 0.163598 6.112528 10.3427%
1827 0.148264 6.744725 -4.2314% 1826 0.154815 6.459326 2.9150% 1825 0.150430
6.647618 3.0026% 1824 0.146045 6.847217 3.0955% 1823 0.141660 7.059173 3.1944% 1822
0.137275 7.284671 3.3102% 1821 0.132876 7.525807 3.2277% 1820 0.128721 7.768721
2.6573% 1819 0.125389 7.975157 2.6261% 1818 0.122181 8.184594 2.6969% 1817 0.118972
8.405326 2.7717% 1816 0.115764 8.638295 2.8507% 1815 0.112555 8.884547 2.9343% 1814
0.109346 9.145250 3.0231% 1813 0.106138 9.421716 3.1039% 1812 0.102943 9.714156
3.2172% 1811 0.099734 10.026676 3.0969% 1810 0.096738 10.337193 2.9144% 1809
0.093999 10.638458 2.8225% 1808 0.091418 10.938725 2.9199% 1807 0.088825 11.258128
2.9918% 1806 0.086244 11.594947 3.0841% 1805 0.083664 11.952541 3.1822% 1804
0.081084 12.332894 3.2868% 1803 0.078504 12.738249 3.3985% 1802 0.075923 13.171157
3.5180% 1801 0.073343 13.634524 3.3999% 1800 0.070932 14.098091 2.8419% 1799
0.068972 14.498740 2.7485% 1798 0.067127 14.897232 2.8261% 1797 0.065282 15.318247
3.7832% 1796 0.062902 15.897768 2.1272% 1795 0.061592 16.235945 3.0879% 1794
0.059747 16.737301 3.1625% 1793 0.057915 17.266620 3.2904% 1792 0.056070 17.834764
3.4024% 1791 0.054225 18.441568 3.2296% 1790 0.052529 19.037150 41.3145% 1780
0.037172 26.902244 29.4353% 1770 0.028718 34.821005 83.4728% 1750 0.015653
63.887086 29.2845% 1740 0.012107 82.596069 94.2514% 1720 0.006233 160.444015
85.8111% 1700 0.003354 298.122758 19.2490% 1690 0.002813 355.508555 88.0250% 1670
0.001496 668.445040

BASE YEAR: 1898

YEAR BYEAR/AYEAR AYEAR/BYEAR GROWTH%

2009 4.101428 0.243818 8.2857% 2001 3.787600 0.264019 1.0000% 2000 3.750099
0.266660 1.0000% 1999 3.712969 0.269326 1.0000% 1998 3.676207 0.272019 1.0000% 1997
3.639809 0.274740 1.0000% 1996 3.603771 0.277487 1.0000% 1995 3.568090 0.280262

0.9992% 1994 3.532790 0.283062 1.0008% 1993 3.497785 0.285895 1.0000% 1992 3.463153
0.288754 0.9295% 1991 3.431260 0.291438 1.2505% 1990 3.388881 0.295083 0.7224% 1989
3.364574 0.297214 1.1077% 1988 3.327714 0.300507 0.8834% 1987 3.298575 0.303161
0.5594% 1986 3.280227 0.304857 1.3056% 1985 3.237951 0.308837 0.7673% 1984 3.213296
0.311207 0.8149% 1983 3.187321 0.313743 0.9737% 1982 3.156584 0.316798 0.9508% 1981
3.126854 0.319810 0.9031% 1980 3.098869 0.322698 2.2701% 1979 3.030084 0.330024
1.0042% 1978 2.999959 0.333338 0.9896% 1977 2.970562 0.336637 0.9103% 1976 2.943764
0.339701 0.8394% 1975 2.919259 0.342553 0.9042% 1974 2.893100 0.345650 1.1568% 1973
2.860016 0.349648 0.9427% 1972 2.833306 0.352945 0.7426% 1971 2.812420 0.355566
1.4697% 1970 2.771684 0.360792 0.6968% 1969 2.752504 0.363306 0.8565% 1968 2.729128
0.366417 1.5090% 1967 2.688556 0.371947 0.9949% 1966 2.662071 0.375647 1.0575% 1965
2.634215 0.379620 1.1300% 1964 2.604781 0.383909 1.5537% 1963 2.564930 0.389874
1.4658% 1962 2.527876 0.395589 1.5364% 1961 2.489625 0.401667 2.1586% 1960 2.437019
0.410337 -1.6655% 1959 2.478294 0.403503 4.3080% 1958 2.375939 0.420886 2.1130%
1957 2.326775 0.429779 1.9895% 1956 2.281387 0.438330 1.2231% 1955 2.233958 0.447636
1.4496% 1954 2.202037 0.454125 2.1573% 1953 2.155537 0.463922 1.2298% 1952 2.129351
0.469627 1.6814% 1951 2.094140 0.477523 1.6233% 1950 2.060690 0.485274 1.4265% 1949
2.031707 0.492197 1.7790% 1948 1.996194 0.500953 1.8242% 1947 1.960432 0.510092 -
2.6320% 1946 2.013426 0.496666 3.1768% 1945 1.951433 0.512444 6.4754% 1944 1.832755
0.545627 -0.3437% 1943 1.839075 0.543752 0.6562% 1942 1.827085 0.547320 0.6633%
1941 1.815046 0.550950 -5.6614% 1940 1.923970 0.519759 8.0381% 1939 1.780826
0.561537 0.8126% 1938 1.766471 0.566101 0.7762% 1937 1.752864 0.570495 0.6029% 1936
1.742360 0.573934 0.5244% 1935 1.733271 0.576944 -3.0364% 1934 1.787547 0.559426
4.6271% 1933 1.708493 0.585311 1.3921% 1932 1.685036 0.593459 -0.2051% 1931
1.688498 0.592242 0.8886% 1930 1.673627 0.597505 1.0126% 1929 1.656850 0.603555
1.1526% 1928 1.637970 0.610512 1.2160% 1927 1.618292 0.617935 1.4086% 1926 1.595814
0.626640 1.7667% 1925 1.568110 0.637710 1.4465% 1924 1.545751 0.646935 1.7700% 1923
1.518867 0.658385 1.6165% 1922 1.494705 0.669028 1.3736% 1921 1.474451 0.678218
2.3393% 1920 1.440748 0.694084 1.3140% 1919 1.422062 0.703204 0.7676% 1918 1.411228
0.708602 0.3870% 1917 1.405788 0.711345 1.3274% 1916 1.387372 0.720787 1.4083% 1915
1.368105 0.730938 1.4458% 1914 1.348607 0.741506 1.9424% 1913 1.322911 0.755909
1.9857% 1912 1.297154 0.770919 1.5634% 1911 1.277186 0.782971 1.8169% 1910 1.254395
0.797197 1.8781% 1909 1.231271 0.812169 2.0082% 1908 1.207031 0.828479 1.9603% 1907
1.183825 0.844720 1.8264% 1906 1.162592 0.860147 1.9357% 1905 1.140515 0.876797
2.0148% 1904 1.117989 0.894463 2.1335% 1903 1.094635 0.913547 1.8151% 1902 1.075120
0.930129 1.8943% 1901 1.055132 0.947749 3.0255% 1900 1.024146 0.976423 0.6278% 1899
1.017757 0.982553 1.7757% 1898 1.000000 1.000000 1.8078% 1897 0.982243 1.018078
1.8396% 1896 0.964501 1.036806 1.8755% 1895 0.946744 1.056252 1.9114% 1894 0.928987
1.076441 1.9486% 1893 0.911231 1.097417 1.9858% 1892 0.893488 1.119209 2.0276% 1891
0.875731 1.141903 2.6465% 1890 0.853153 1.172123 1.5328% 1889 0.840273 1.190090
2.0811% 1888 0.823142 1.214857 2.1599% 1887 0.805739 1.241096 2.2075% 1886 0.788336
1.268494 2.2592% 1885 0.770920 1.297151 2.3095% 1884 0.753517 1.327110 2.3641% 1883
0.736115 1.358484 2.4214% 1882 0.718712 1.391378 2.4815% 1881 0.701309 1.425905
3.7644% 1880 0.675867 1.479582 0.9432% 1879 0.669551 1.493538 2.1464% 1878 0.655482
1.525595 2.1913% 1877 0.641427 1.559025 2.2426% 1876 0.627357 1.593988 2.2941% 1875
0.613288 1.630555 2.3456% 1874 0.599233 1.668801 2.4043% 1873 0.585163 1.708924
2.4635% 1872 0.571094 1.751024 2.5258% 1871 0.557025 1.795251 5.9947% 1870 0.525522
1.902871 -1.0968% 1869 0.531349 1.882000 2.1930% 1868 0.519947 1.923272 2.2394%
1867 0.508559 1.966342 2.2935% 1866 0.497156 2.011440 2.3445% 1865 0.485768 2.058598
2.4037% 1864 0.474365 2.108080 2.4599% 1863 0.462977 2.159937 2.5250% 1862 0.451574
2.214475 2.5872% 1861 0.440186 2.271769 2.9504% 1860 0.427571 2.338795 2.4012% 1859
0.417544 2.394956 2.7627% 1858 0.406319 2.461121 2.8412% 1857 0.395093 2.531047
2.9243% 1856 0.383868 2.605062 3.0161% 1855 0.372629 2.683634 3.1061% 1854 0.361404
2.766989 3.2056% 1853 0.350178 2.855689 3.3118% 1852 0.338953 2.950263 3.4252% 1851
0.327727 3.051316 4.0106% 1850 0.315090 3.173692 2.3254% 1849 0.307930 3.247492
2.7841% 1848 0.299589 3.337905 2.8590% 1847 0.291262 3.433336 2.9432% 1846 0.282935

166

3.534385 3.0324% 1845 0.274607 3.641562 3.1325% 1844 0.266267 3.755634 3.2284% 1843
0.257939 3.876879 3.3361% 1842 0.249612 4.006214 3.4512% 1841 0.241285 4.144476
3.8105% 1840 0.232428 4.302401 2.3861% 1839 0.227012 4.405059 2.5824% 1838 0.221297
4.518815 2.6573% 1837 0.215569 4.638894 2.7232% 1836 0.209854 4.765221 2.7994% 1835
0.204139 4.898620 2.8871% 1834 0.198411 5.040049 2.9657% 1833 0.192696 5.189521
3.0563% 1832 0.186981 5.348130 3.1604% 1831 0.181253 5.517153 3.4660% 1830 0.175181
5.708376 2.4653% 1829 0.170966 5.849105 2.6804% 1828 0.166503 6.005884 10.3427%
1827 0.150897 6.627051 -4.2314% 1826 0.157564 6.346632 2.9150% 1825 0.153101
6.531639 3.0026% 1824 0.148638 6.727755 3.0955% 1823 0.144175 6.936014 3.1944% 1822
0.139712 7.157577 3.3102% 1821 0.135236 7.394506 3.2277% 1820 0.131007 7.633182
2.6573% 1819 0.127616 7.836017 2.6261% 1818 0.124350 8.041799 2.6969% 1817 0.121085
8.258681 2.7717% 1816 0.117819 8.487585 2.8507% 1815 0.114554 8.729540 2.9343% 1814
0.111288 8.985695 3.0231% 1813 0.108022 9.257337 3.1039% 1812 0.104770 9.544675
3.2172% 1811 0.101505 9.851743 3.0969% 1810 0.098456 10.156843 2.9144% 1809
0.095668 10.452852 2.8225% 1808 0.093042 10.747879 2.9199% 1807 0.090402 11.061710
2.9918% 1806 0.087776 11.392652 3.0841% 1805 0.085150 11.744008 3.1822% 1804
0.082524 12.117725 3.2868% 1803 0.079898 12.516008 3.3985% 1802 0.077272 12.941363
3.5180% 1801 0.074646 13.396646 3.3999% 1800 0.072191 13.852125 2.8419% 1799
0.070196 14.245784 2.7485% 1798 0.068319 14.637323 2.8261% 1797 0.066441 15.050993
3.7832% 1796 0.064019 15.620404 2.1272% 1795 0.062685 15.952681 3.0879% 1794
0.060808 16.445290 3.1625% 1793 0.058944 16.965374 3.2904% 1792 0.057066 17.523605
3.4024% 1791 0.055188 18.119822 3.2296% 1790 0.053462 18.705014 41.3145% 1780
0.037832 26.432887 29.4353% 1770 0.029228 34.213491 83.4728% 1750 0.015931
62.772463 29.2845% 1740 0.012322 81.155035 94.2514% 1720 0.006343 157.644788
85.8111% 1700 0.003414 292.921483 19.2490% 1690 0.002863 349.306084 88.0250% 1670
0.001523 656.782842

BASE YEAR: 1897
YEAR BYEAR/AYEAR AYEAR/BYEAR GROWTH%
2009 4.175572 0.239488 8.2857% 2001 3.856071 0.259331 1.0000% 2000 3.817892
0.261925 1.0000% 1999 3.780091 0.264544 1.0000% 1998 3.742664 0.267189 1.0000% 1997
3.705608 0.269861 1.0000% 1996 3.668919 0.272560 1.0000% 1995 3.632593 0.275285
0.9992% 1994 3.596654 0.278036 1.0008% 1993 3.561016 0.280819 1.0000% 1992 3.525759
0.283627 0.9295% 1991 3.493288 0.286263 1.2505% 1990 3.450144 0.289843 0.7224% 1989
3.425397 0.291937 1.1077% 1988 3.387871 0.295171 0.8834% 1987 3.358206 0.297778
0.5594% 1986 3.339525 0.299444 1.3056% 1985 3.296486 0.303353 0.7673% 1984 3.271385
0.305681 0.8149% 1983 3.244940 0.308172 0.9737% 1982 3.213648 0.311173 0.9508% 1981
3.183380 0.314132 0.9031% 1980 3.154889 0.316968 2.2701% 1979 3.084861 0.324164
1.0042% 1978 3.054191 0.327419 0.9896% 1977 3.024263 0.330659 0.9103% 1976 2.996980
0.333669 0.8394% 1975 2.972032 0.336470 0.9042% 1974 2.945400 0.339512 1.1568% 1973
2.911718 0.343440 0.9427% 1972 2.884525 0.346677 0.7426% 1971 2.863262 0.349252
1.4697% 1970 2.821789 0.354385 0.6968% 1969 2.802262 0.356855 0.8565% 1968 2.778463
0.359911 1.5090% 1967 2.737159 0.365342 0.9949% 1966 2.710195 0.368977 1.0575% 1965
2.681835 0.372879 1.1300% 1964 2.651869 0.377093 1.5537% 1963 2.611298 0.382951
1.4658% 1962 2.573574 0.388565 1.5364% 1961 2.534631 0.394535 2.1586% 1960 2.481074
0.403051 -1.6655% 1959 2.523096 0.396339 4.3080% 1958 2.418890 0.413413 2.1130%
1957 2.368837 0.422148 1.9895% 1956 2.322629 0.430547 2.1231% 1955 2.274342 0.439688
1.4496% 1954 2.241844 0.446061 2.1573% 1953 2.194503 0.455684 1.2298% 1952 2.167844
0.461288 1.6814% 1951 2.131997 0.469044 1.6233% 1950 2.097942 0.476658 1.4265% 1949
2.068435 0.483457 1.7790% 1948 2.032280 0.492058 1.8242% 1947 1.995872 0.501034 -
2.6320% 1946 2.049824 0.487847 3.1768% 1945 1.986710 0.503345 6.4754% 1944 1.865886
0.535938 -0.3437% 1943 1.872321 0.534096 0.6562% 1942 1.860115 0.537601 0.6633%
1941 1.847858 0.541167 -5.6614% 1940 1.958751 0.510529 8.0381% 1939 1.813019
0.551566 0.8126% 1938 1.798404 0.556049 0.7762% 1937 1.784552 0.560365 0.6029% 1936
1.773858 0.563743 0.5244% 1935 1.764604 0.566699 -3.0364% 1934 1.819862 0.549492
4.6271% 1933 1.739379 0.574918 1.3921% 1932 1.715497 0.582922 -0.2051% 1931
1.719022 0.581726 0.8886% 1930 1.703882 0.586895 1.0126% 1929 1.686801 0.592838

167

1.1526% 1928 1.667581 0.599671 1.2160% 1927 1.647547 0.606963 1.4086% 1926 1.624662
0.615513 1.7667% 1925 1.596458 0.626387 1.4465% 1924 1.573694 0.635448 1.7700% 1923
1.546325 0.646695 1.6165% 1922 1.521726 0.657149 1.3736% 1921 1.501106 0.666176
2.3393% 1920 1.466793 0.681760 1.3140% 1919 1.447769 0.690718 0.7676% 1918 1.436740
0.696020 0.3870% 1917 1.431201 0.698714 1.3274% 1916 1.412452 0.707989 1.4083% 1915
1.392837 0.717959 1.4458% 1914 1.372986 0.728339 1.9424% 1913 1.346826 0.742487
1.9857% 1912 1.320603 0.757230 1.5634% 1911 1.300274 0.769069 1.8169% 1910 1.277071
0.783042 1.8781% 1909 1.253529 0.797748 2.0082% 1908 1.228851 0.813769 1.9603% 1907
1.205225 0.829720 1.8264% 1906 1.183608 0.844874 1.9357% 1905 1.161133 0.861228
2.0148% 1904 1.138200 0.878580 2.1335% 1903 1.114423 0.897325 1.8151% 1902 1.094555
0.913613 1.8943% 1901 1.074206 0.930920 3.0255% 1900 1.042660 0.959085 0.6278% 1899
1.036155 0.965106 1.7757% 1898 1.018078 0.982243 1.8078% 1897 1.000000 1.000000
1.8396% 1896 0.981936 1.018396 1.8755% 1895 0.963859 1.037496 1.9114% 1894 0.945781
1.057327 1.9486% 1893 0.927704 1.077930 1.9858% 1892 0.909640 1.099336 2.0276% 1891
0.891562 1.121626 2.6465% 1890 0.868575 1.151310 1.5328% 1889 0.855463 1.168958
2.0811% 1888 0.838022 1.193286 2.1599% 1887 0.820305 1.219059 2.2075% 1886 0.802588
1.245970 2.2592% 1885 0.784856 1.274118 2.3095% 1884 0.767139 1.303545 2.3641% 1883
0.749422 1.334362 2.4214% 1882 0.731704 1.366672 2.4815% 1881 0.713987 1.400586
3.7644% 1880 0.688085 1.453310 0.9432% 1879 0.681655 1.467018 2.1464% 1878 0.667332
1.498505 2.1913% 1877 0.653022 1.531342 2.2426% 1876 0.638698 1.565684 2.2941% 1875
0.624375 1.601602 2.3456% 1874 0.610065 1.639169 2.4043% 1873 0.595742 1.678580
2.4635% 1872 0.581418 1.719932 5.5258% 1871 0.567095 1.763374 5.9947% 1870 0.535022
1.869082 -1.0968% 1869 0.540955 1.848583 2.1930% 1868 0.529347 1.889122 2.2394%
1867 0.517752 1.931427 2.2935% 1866 0.506144 1.975724 2.3445% 1865 0.494549 2.022044
2.4037% 1864 0.482941 2.070648 2.4599% 1863 0.471346 2.121583 2.5250% 1862 0.459738
2.175154 2.5872% 1861 0.448143 2.231430 2.9504% 1860 0.435300 2.297267 2.4012% 1859
0.425092 2.352429 2.7627% 1858 0.413664 2.417420 2.8412% 1857 0.402236 2.486104
2.9243% 1856 0.390807 2.558805 3.0161% 1855 0.379365 2.635982 3.1061% 1854 0.367937
2.717857 3.2056% 1853 0.356509 2.804981 3.3118% 1852 0.345080 2.897876 3.4252% 1851
0.333652 2.997135 4.0106% 1850 0.320786 3.117339 2.3254% 1849 0.313497 3.189828
2.7841% 1848 0.305005 3.278636 2.8590% 1847 0.296527 3.372372 2.9432% 1846 0.288049
3.471626 3.0324% 1845 0.279572 3.576900 3.1325% 1844 0.271080 3.688947 3.2284% 1843
0.262602 3.808039 3.3361% 1842 0.254125 3.935078 3.4512% 1841 0.245647 4.070885
3.8105% 1840 0.236630 4.226005 2.3861% 1839 0.231116 4.326840 2.5824% 1838 0.225297
4.438576 2.6573% 1837 0.219466 4.556523 2.7232% 1836 0.213648 4.680607 2.7994% 1835
0.207829 4.811638 2.8871% 1834 0.201998 4.950555 2.9657% 1833 0.196179 5.097373
3.0563% 1832 0.190361 5.253165 3.1604% 1831 0.184529 5.419188 3.4660% 1830 0.178348
5.607015 2.4653% 1829 0.174057 5.745245 2.6804% 1828 0.169513 5.899240 10.3427%
1827 0.153625 6.509378 -4.2314% 1826 0.160412 6.233938 2.9150% 1825 0.155869
6.415659 3.0026% 1824 0.151325 6.608294 3.0955% 1823 0.146781 6.812854 3.1944% 1822
0.142238 7.030483 3.3102% 1821 0.137680 7.263206 3.2277% 1820 0.133375 7.497643
2.6573% 1819 0.129923 7.696876 2.6261% 1818 0.126598 7.899004 2.6969% 1817 0.123274
8.112035 2.7717% 1816 0.119949 8.336875 2.8507% 1815 0.116624 8.574534 2.9343% 1814
0.113300 8.826140 3.0231% 1813 0.109975 9.092959 3.1039% 1812 0.106664 9.375195
3.2172% 1811 0.103340 9.676810 3.0969% 1810 0.100236 9.976492 2.9144% 1809 0.097397
10.267245 2.8225% 1808 0.094724 10.557034 2.9199% 1807 0.092036 10.865292 2.9918%
1806 0.089363 11.190358 3.0841% 1805 0.086689 11.535475 3.1822% 1804 0.084016
11.902556 3.2868% 1803 0.081342 12.293767 3.3985% 1802 0.078668 12.711569 3.5180%
1801 0.075995 13.158768 3.3999% 1800 0.073496 13.606159 2.8419% 1799 0.071465
13.992828 2.7485% 1798 0.069554 14.377415 2.8261% 1797 0.067642 14.783740 3.7832%
1796 0.065176 15.343039 2.1272% 1795 0.063819 15.669416 3.0879% 1794 0.061907
16.153278 3.1625% 1793 0.060009 16.664127 3.2904% 1792 0.058097 17.212446 3.4024%
1791 0.056186 17.798077 3.2296% 1790 0.054428 18.372877 41.3145% 1780 0.038516
25.963530 29.4353% 1770 0.029757 33.605977 83.4728% 1750 0.016219 61.657841
29.2845% 1740 0.012545 79.714002 94.2514% 1720 0.006458 154.845560 85.8111% 1700

168

0.003476 287.720207 19.2490% 1690 0.002915 343.103612 88.0250% 1670 0.001550 645.120643

YEAR BYEAR/AYEAR AYEAR/BYEAR GROWTH%

2009 4.252386 0.235162 8.2857% 2001 3.927007 0.254647 1.0000% 2000 3.888125 0.257193 1.0000% 1999 3.849629 0.259765 1.0000% 1998 3.811514 0.262363 1.0000% 1997 3.773776 0.264987 1.0000% 1996 3.736412 0.267636 1.0000% 1995 3.699418 0.270313 0.9992% 1994 3.662818 0.273014 1.0008% 1993 3.626525 0.275746 1.0000% 1992 3.590619 0.278504 0.9295% 1991 3.557551 0.281092 1.2505% 1990 3.513613 0.284607 0.7224% 1989 3.488411 0.286663 1.1077% 1988 3.450194 0.289839 0.8834% 1987 3.419983 0.292399 0.5594% 1986 3.400959 0.294035 1.3056% 1985 3.357128 0.297874 0.7673% 1984 3.331565 0.300159 0.8149% 1983 3.304634 0.302605 0.9737% 1982 3.272766 0.305552 0.9508% 1981 3.241941 0.308457 0.9031% 1980 3.212926 0.311243 2.2701% 1979 3.141610 0.318308 1.0042% 1978 3.110376 0.321505 0.9896% 1977 3.079897 0.324686 0.9103% 1976 3.052113 0.327642 0.8394% 1975 3.026705 0.330392 0.9042% 1974 2.999584 0.333380 1.1568% 1973 2.965282 0.337236 0.9427% 1972 2.937589 0.340415 0.7426% 1971 2.915934 0.342943 1.4697% 1970 2.873698 0.347984 0.6968% 1969 2.853813 0.350408 0.8565% 1968 2.829576 0.353410 1.5090% 1967 2.787511 0.358743 0.9949% 1966 2.760051 0.362312 1.0575% 1965 2.731170 0.366143 1.1300% 1964 2.700652 0.370281 1.5537% 1963 2.659336 0.376034 1.4658% 1962 2.620918 0.381546 1.5364% 1961 2.581258 0.387408 2.1586% 1960 2.526716 0.395771 -1.6655% 1959 2.569510 0.389179 4.3080% 1958 2.463388 0.405945 2.1130% 1957 2.412414 0.414522 1.9895% 1956 2.365356 0.422769 2.1231% 1955 2.316181 0.431745 1.4496% 1954 2.283085 0.438004 2.1573% 1953 2.234873 0.447453 1.2298% 1952 2.207724 0.452955 1.6814% 1951 2.171217 0.460571 1.6233% 1950 2.136536 0.468047 1.4265% 1949 2.106486 0.474724 1.7790% 1948 2.069666 0.483170 1.8242% 1947 2.032588 0.491984 -2.6320% 1946 2.087533 0.479034 3.1768% 1945 2.023258 0.494252 6.4754% 1944 1.900211 0.526257 -0.3437% 1943 1.906764 0.524449 0.6562% 1942 1.894333 0.527890 0.6633% 1941 1.881851 0.531392 -5.6614% 1940 1.994784 0.501307 8.0381% 1939 1.846371 0.541603 0.8126% 1938 1.831488 0.546004 0.7762% 1937 1.817380 0.550243 0.6029% 1936 1.806489 0.553560 0.5244% 1935 1.797066 0.556463 -3.0364% 1934 1.853340 0.539566 4.6271% 1933 1.771376 0.564533 1.3921% 1932 1.747055 0.572392 -0.2051% 1931 1.750645 0.571218 0.8886% 1930 1.735226 0.576294 1.0126% 1929 1.717832 0.582129 1.1526% 1928 1.698258 0.588839 1.2160% 1927 1.677855 0.595999 1.4086% 1926 1.654549 0.604394 1.7667% 1925 1.625826 0.615072 1.4465% 1924 1.602644 0.623969 1.7700% 1923 1.574771 0.635013 1.6165% 1922 1.549719 0.645278 1.3736% 1921 1.528720 0.654142 2.3393% 1920 1.493776 0.669444 1.3140% 1919 1.474402 0.678241 0.7676% 1918 1.463170 0.683447 0.3870% 1917 1.457530 0.686092 1.3274% 1916 1.438435 0.695200 1.4083% 1915 1.418459 0.704990 1.4458% 1914 1.398244 0.715183 1.9424% 1913 1.371602 0.729075 1.9857% 1912 1.344897 0.743552 1.5634% 1911 1.324194 0.755176 1.8169% 1910 1.300564 0.768897 1.8781% 1909 1.276589 0.783338 2.0082% 1908 1.251457 0.799069 1.9603% 1907 1.227396 0.814733 1.8264% 1906 1.205382 0.829613 1.9357% 1905 1.182493 0.845671 2.0148% 1904 1.159138 0.862710 2.1335% 1903 1.134924 0.881116 1.8151% 1902 1.114691 0.897110 1.8943% 1901 1.093967 0.914104 3.0255% 1900 1.061841 0.941760 0.6278% 1899 1.055216 0.947673 1.7757% 1898 1.036806 0.964501 1.8078% 1897 1.018396 0.981936 1.8396% 1896 1.000000 1.000000 1.8755% 1895 0.981590 1.018755 1.9114% 1894 0.963180 1.038228 1.9486% 1893 0.944770 1.058459 1.9858% 1892 0.926374 1.079478 2.0276% 1891 0.907964 1.101366 2.6465% 1890 0.884554 1.130514 1.5328% 1889 0.871200 1.147842 2.0811% 1888 0.853439 1.171730 2.1599% 1887 0.835395 1.197038 2.2075% 1886 0.817352 1.223463 2.2592% 1885 0.799295 1.251103 2.3095% 1884 0.781251 1.279998 2.3641% 1883 0.763208 1.310259 2.4214% 1882 0.745165 1.341985 2.4815% 1881 0.727121 1.375286 3.7644% 1880 0.700743 1.427057 0.9432% 1879 0.694195 1.440518 2.1464% 1878 0.679608 1.471437 2.1913% 1877 0.665035 1.503680 2.2426% 1876 0.650448 1.537402 2.2941% 1875 0.635861 1.572671 2.3456% 1874 0.621288 1.609559 2.4043% 1873 0.606701 1.648258 2.4635% 1872 0.592114 1.688864 2.5258% 1871 0.577527 1.731521 5.9947% 1870 0.544864 1.835320 -1.0968% 1869 0.550906 1.815190 2.1930% 1868 0.539084 1.854997 2.2394% 1867 0.527277 1.896538 2.2935% 1866 0.515455 1.940035 2.3445% 1865 0.503647 1.985519

2.4037% 1864 0.491825 2.033244 2.4599% 1863 0.480017 2.083260 2.5250% 1862 0.468195 2.135862 2.5872% 1861 0.456387 2.191122 2.9504% 1860 0.443308 2.255769 2.4012% 1859 0.432912 2.309936 2.7627% 1858 0.421274 2.373753 2.8412% 1857 0.409635 2.441196 2.9243% 1856 0.397997 2.512583 3.0161% 1855 0.386344 2.588366 3.1061% 1854 0.374706 2.668762 3.2056% 1853 0.363067 2.754313 3.3118% 1852 0.351428 2.845530 3.4252% 1851 0.339790 2.942996 4.0106% 1850 0.326688 3.061028 2.3254% 1849 0.319264 3.132208 2.7841% 1848 0.310616 3.219411 2.8590% 1847 0.301982 3.311455 2.9432% 1846 0.293348 3.408916 3.0324% 1845 0.284715 3.512288 3.1325% 1844 0.276067 3.622311 3.2284% 1843 0.267433 3.739252 3.3361% 1842 0.258799 3.863996 3.4512% 1841 0.250166 3.997350 3.8105% 1840 0.240983 4.149668 2.3861% 1839 0.235367 4.248681 2.5824% 1838 0.229442 4.358399 2.6573% 1837 0.223503 4.474216 2.7232% 1836 0.217578 4.596058 2.7994% 1835 0.211653 4.724722 2.8871% 1834 0.205713 4.861130 2.9657% 1833 0.199788 5.005296 3.0563% 1832 0.193863 5.158274 3.1604% 1831 0.187924 5.321297 3.4660% 1830 0.181629 5.505732 2.4653% 1829 0.177259 5.641464 2.6804% 1828 0.172632 5.792678 10.3427% 1827 0.156451 6.391794 -4.2314% 1826 0.163363 6.121330 2.9150% 1825 0.158736 6.299769 3.0026% 1824 0.154109 6.488923 3.0955% 1823 0.149482 6.689789 3.1944% 1822 0.144854 6.903487 3.3102% 1821 0.140213 7.132005 3.2277% 1820 0.135829 7.362208 2.6573% 1819 0.132313 7.557842 2.6261% 1818 0.128927 7.756319 2.6969% 1817 0.125541 7.965502 2.7717% 1816 0.122156 8.186280 2.8507% 1815 0.118770 8.419646 2.9343% 1814 0.115384 8.666707 3.0231% 1813 0.111998 8.928706 3.1039% 1812 0.108627 9.205844 3.2172% 1811 0.105241 9.502011 3.0969% 1810 0.102080 9.796280 2.9144% 1809 0.099189 10.081781 2.8225% 1808 0.096466 10.366335 2.9199% 1807 0.093729 10.669025 2.9918% 1806 0.091007 10.988219 3.0841% 1805 0.088284 11.327101 3.1822% 1804 0.085561 11.687552 3.2868% 1803 0.082838 12.071696 3.3985% 1802 0.080116 12.481951 3.5180% 1801 0.077393 12.921072 3.3999% 1800 0.074848 13.360381 2.8419% 1799 0.072780 13.740066 2.7485% 1798 0.070833 14.117706 2.8261% 1797 0.068886 14.516691 3.7832% 1796 0.066375 15.065887 2.1272% 1795 0.064993 15.386369 3.0879% 1794 0.063046 15.861490 3.1625% 1793 0.061113 16.363112 3.2904% 1792 0.059166 16.901526 3.4024% 1791 0.057219 17.476578 3.2296% 1790 0.055429 18.040995 41.3145% 1780 0.039224 25.494533 29.4353% 1770 0.030304 32.998929 83.4728% 1750 0.016517 60.544072 29.2845% 1740 0.012776 78.274072 94.2514% 1720 0.006577 152.048477 85.8111% 1700 0.003540 282.522917 19.2490% 1690 0.002968 336.905894 88.0250% 1670 0.001579 633.467382

BASE YEAR: 1895

YEAR BYEAR/AYEAR AYEAR/BYEAR GROWTH%

2009 4.332141 0.230833 8.2857% 2001 4.000660 0.249959 1.0000% 2000 3.961049 0.252458 1.0000% 1999 3.921830 0.254983 1.0000% 1998 3.883000 0.257533 1.0000% 1997 3.844555 0.260108 1.0000% 1996 3.806490 0.262709 1.0000% 1995 3.768802 0.265336 0.9992% 1994 3.731516 0.267988 1.0008% 1993 3.694542 0.270670 1.0000% 1992 3.657962 0.273376 0.9295% 1991 3.624274 0.275917 1.2505% 1990 3.579512 0.279368 0.7224% 1989 3.553837 0.281386 1.1077% 1988 3.514904 0.284503 0.8834% 1987 3.484126 0.287016 0.5594% 1986 3.464746 0.288621 1.3056% 1985 3.420092 0.292390 0.7673% 1984 3.394050 0.294633 0.8149% 1983 3.366614 0.297034 0.9737% 1982 3.334148 0.299927 0.9508% 1981 3.302745 0.302778 0.9031% 1980 3.273186 0.305513 2.2701% 1979 3.200532 0.312448 1.0042% 1978 3.168712 0.315586 0.9896% 1977 3.137662 0.318709 0.9103% 1976 3.109356 0.321610 0.8394% 1975 3.083472 0.324310 0.9042% 1974 3.055842 0.327242 1.1568% 1973 3.020897 0.331028 0.9427% 1972 2.992685 0.334148 0.7426% 1971 2.970624 0.336630 1.4697% 1970 2.927596 0.341577 0.6968% 1969 2.907337 0.343957 0.8565% 1968 2.882646 0.346904 1.5090% 1967 2.839792 0.352138 0.9949% 1966 2.811817 0.355642 1.0575% 1965 2.782394 0.359403 1.1300% 1964 2.751304 0.363464 1.5537% 1963 2.709212 0.369111 1.4658% 1962 2.670074 0.374521 1.5364% 1961 2.629671 0.380276 2.1586% 1960 2.574105 0.388485 -1.6655% 1959 2.617703 0.382014 4.3080% 1958 2.509590 0.398472 2.1130% 1957 2.457660 0.406891 1.9895% 1956 2.409719 0.414986 2.1231% 1955 2.359622 0.423797 1.4496% 1954 2.325905 0.429940 2.1573% 1953 2.276789 0.439215 1.2298% 1952 2.249130 0.444616 1.6814% 1951 2.211939 0.452092 1.6233% 1950 2.176607 0.459431 1.4265% 1949 2.145994 0.465985 1.7790% 1948 2.108483 0.474275 1.8242% 1947 2.070710 0.482926 -

170

2.6320% 1946 2.126685 0.470215 3.1768% 1945 2.061205 0.485153 6.4754% 1944 1.935850
0.516569 -0.3437% 1943 1.942526 0.514794 0.6562% 1942 1.929862 0.518172 0.6633%
1941 1.917146 0.521609 -5.6614% 1940 2.032197 0.492078 8.0381% 1939 1.881000
0.531632 0.8126% 1938 1.865838 0.535952 0.7762% 1937 1.851466 0.540113 0.6029% 1936
1.840371 0.543369 0.5244% 1935 1.830770 0.546218 -3.0364% 1934 1.888100 0.529633
4.6271% 1933 1.804599 0.554140 1.3921% 1932 1.779822 0.561854 -0.2051% 1931
1.783479 0.560702 0.8886% 1930 1.767771 0.565684 1.0126% 1929 1.750050 0.571412
1.1526% 1928 1.730109 0.577998 1.2160% 1927 1.709324 0.585027 1.4086% 1926 1.685581
0.593267 1.7667% 1925 1.656319 0.603748 1.4465% 1924 1.632702 0.612482 1.7700% 1923
1.604306 0.623322 1.6165% 1922 1.578785 0.633399 1.3736% 1921 1.557392 0.642099
2.3393% 1920 1.521792 0.657120 1.3140% 1919 1.502055 0.665754 0.7676% 1918 1.490613
0.670865 0.3870% 1917 1.484866 0.673461 1.3274% 1916 1.465414 0.682401 1.4083% 1915
1.445063 0.692011 1.4458% 1914 1.424468 0.702016 1.9424% 1913 1.397327 0.715652
1.9857% 1912 1.370121 0.729863 1.5634% 1911 1.349030 0.741273 1.8169% 1910 1.324957
0.754742 1.8781% 1909 1.300532 0.768916 2.0082% 1908 1.274928 0.784358 1.9603% 1907
1.250417 0.799733 1.8264% 1906 1.227989 0.814339 1.9357% 1905 1.204671 0.830102
2.0148% 1904 1.180878 0.846827 2.1335% 1903 1.156210 0.864895 1.8151% 1902 1.135597
0.880594 1.8943% 1901 1.114485 0.897275 3.0255% 1900 1.081757 0.924422 0.6278% 1899
1.075007 0.930226 1.7757% 1898 1.056252 0.946744 1.8078% 1897 1.037496 0.963859
1.8396% 1896 1.018755 0.981590 1.8755% 1895 1.000000 1.000000 1.9114% 1894 0.981245
1.019114 1.9486% 1893 0.962489 1.038973 1.9858% 1892 0.943748 1.059605 2.0276% 1891
0.924993 1.081089 2.6465% 1890 0.901144 1.109701 1.5328% 1889 0.887540 1.126710
2.0811% 1888 0.869445 1.150159 2.1599% 1887 0.851064 1.175000 2.2075% 1886 0.832682
1.200939 2.2592% 1885 0.814286 1.228070 2.3095% 1884 0.795904 1.256433 2.3641% 1883
0.777522 1.286137 2.4214% 1882 0.759141 1.317279 2.4815% 1881 0.740759 1.349967
3.7644% 1880 0.713885 1.400785 0.9432% 1879 0.707215 1.413998 2.1464% 1878 0.692354
1.444348 2.1913% 1877 0.677508 1.475998 2.2426% 1876 0.662647 1.509098 2.2941% 1875
0.647787 1.543718 2.3456% 1874 0.632941 1.579927 2.4043% 1873 0.618080 1.617914
2.4635% 1872 0.603219 1.657772 2.5258% 1871 0.588359 1.699643 5.9947% 1870 0.555083
1.801531 -1.0968% 1869 0.561239 1.781773 2.1930% 1868 0.549195 1.820846 2.2394%
1867 0.537166 1.861622 2.2935% 1866 0.525122 1.904319 2.3445% 1865 0.513093 1.948965
2.4037% 1864 0.501049 1.995812 2.4599% 1863 0.489020 2.044907 2.5250% 1862 0.476976
2.096541 2.5872% 1861 0.464947 2.150784 2.9504% 1860 0.451622 2.214240 2.4012% 1859
0.441032 2.267410 2.7627% 1858 0.429175 2.330052 2.8412% 1857 0.417318 2.396253
2.9243% 1856 0.405461 2.466326 3.0161% 1855 0.393590 2.540714 3.1061% 1854 0.381733
2.619630 3.2056% 1853 0.369876 2.703606 3.3118% 1852 0.358020 2.793144 3.4252% 1851
0.346163 2.888815 4.0106% 1850 0.332815 3.004674 2.3254% 1849 0.325252 3.074544
2.7841% 1848 0.316442 3.160142 2.8590% 1847 0.307646 3.250491 2.9432% 1846 0.298850
3.346158 3.0324% 1845 0.290055 3.447627 3.1325% 1844 0.281245 3.555624 3.2284% 1843
0.272449 3.670412 3.3361% 1842 0.263653 3.792859 3.4512% 1841 0.254858 3.923758
3.8105% 1840 0.245503 4.073272 2.3861% 1839 0.239782 4.170463 2.5824% 1838 0.233745
4.278160 2.6573% 1837 0.227695 4.391845 2.7232% 1836 0.221659 4.511444 2.7994% 1835
0.215622 4.637739 2.8871% 1834 0.209572 4.771636 2.9657% 1833 0.203535 4.913148
3.0563% 1832 0.197499 5.063310 3.1604% 1831 0.191449 5.223332 3.4660% 1830 0.185035
5.404370 2.4653% 1829 0.180584 5.537604 2.6804% 1828 0.175870 5.686034 10.3427%
1827 0.159385 6.274121 -4.2314% 1826 0.166427 6.008636 2.9150% 1825 0.161713
6.183790 3.0026% 1824 0.156999 6.369462 3.0955% 1823 0.152285 6.566629 3.1944% 1822
0.147571 6.776393 3.3102% 1821 0.142843 7.000704 3.2277% 1820 0.138376 7.226669
2.6573% 1819 0.134794 7.418701 2.6261% 1818 0.131345 7.613524 2.6969% 1817 0.127896
7.818856 2.7717% 1816 0.124447 8.035570 2.8507% 1815 0.120997 8.264640 2.9343% 1814
0.117548 8.507152 3.0231% 1813 0.114099 8.764328 3.1039% 1812 0.110664 9.036364
3.2172% 1811 0.107215 9.327078 3.0969% 1810 0.103994 9.615929 2.9144% 1809 0.101049
9.896174 2.8225% 1808 0.098275 10.175490 2.9199% 1807 0.095487 10.472607 2.9918%
1806 0.092713 10.785925 3.0841% 1805 0.089940 11.118568 3.1822% 1804 0.087166
11.472383 3.2868% 1803 0.084392 11.849455 3.3985% 1802 0.081618 12.252157 3.5180%
1801 0.078844 12.683194 3.3999% 1800 0.076252 13.114415 2.8419% 1799 0.074145

171

13.487110 2.7485% 1798 0.072162 13.857797 2.8261% 1797 0.070178 14.249437 3.7832%
1796 0.067620 14.788523 2.1272% 1795 0.066212 15.103104 3.0879% 1794 0.064228
15.569479 3.1625% 1793 0.062259 16.061865 3.2904% 1792 0.060276 16.590367 3.4024%
1791 0.058293 17.154832 3.2296% 1790 0.056469 17.708859 41.3145% 1780 0.039960
25.025176 29.4353% 1770 0.030872 32.391416 83.4728% 1750 0.016827 59.429450
29.2845% 1740 0.013015 76.833039 94.2514% 1720 0.006700 149.249249 85.8111% 1700
0.003606 277.321642 19.2490% 1690 0.003024 330.703422 88.0250% 1670 0.001608
621.805183

BASE YEAR: 1894

YEAR BYEAR/AYEAR AYEAR/BYEAR GROWTH%

2009 4.414945 0.226503 8.2857% 2001 4.077128 0.245271 1.0000% 2000 4.036760
0.247723 1.0000% 1999 3.996792 0.250201 1.0000% 1998 3.957220 0.252703 1.0000% 1997
3.918039 0.255230 1.0000% 1996 3.879247 0.257782 1.0000% 1995 3.840838 0.260360
0.9992% 1994 3.802840 0.262961 1.0008% 1993 3.765159 0.265593 1.0000% 1992 3.727880
0.268249 0.9295% 1991 3.693548 0.270742 1.2505% 1990 3.647930 0.274128 0.7224% 1989
3.621765 0.276108 1.1077% 1988 3.582087 0.279167 0.8834% 1987 3.550721 0.281633
0.5594% 1986 3.530970 0.283208 1.3056% 1985 3.485463 0.286906 0.7673% 1984 3.458923
0.289107 0.8149% 1983 3.430963 0.291463 0.9737% 1982 3.397876 0.294301 0.9508% 1981
3.365873 0.297100 0.9031% 1980 3.335749 0.299783 2.2701% 1979 3.261706 0.306588
1.0042% 1978 3.229279 0.309667 0.9896% 1977 3.197635 0.312731 0.9103% 1976 3.168788
0.315578 0.8394% 1975 3.142409 0.318227 0.9042% 1974 3.114251 0.321104 1.1568% 1973
3.078638 0.324819 0.9427% 1972 3.049886 0.327881 0.7426% 1971 3.027404 0.330316
1.4697% 1970 2.983553 0.335171 0.6968% 1969 2.962907 0.337506 0.8565% 1968 2.937744
0.340397 1.5090% 1967 2.894072 0.345534 0.9949% 1966 2.865562 0.348972 1.0575% 1965
2.835577 0.352662 1.1300% 1964 2.803892 0.356647 1.5537% 1963 2.760996 0.362188
1.4658% 1962 2.721109 0.367497 1.5364% 1961 2.679934 0.373144 2.1586% 1960 2.623306
0.381198 -1.6655% 1959 2.667737 0.374850 4.3080% 1958 2.557558 0.390998 2.1130%
1957 2.504636 0.399260 1.9895% 1956 2.455778 0.407203 2.1231% 1955 2.404724 0.415848
1.4496% 1954 2.370363 0.421876 2.1573% 1953 2.320308 0.430977 1.2298% 1952 2.292120
0.436277 1.6814% 1951 2.254218 0.443613 1.6233% 1950 2.218211 0.450814 1.4265% 1949
2.187012 0.457245 1.7790% 1948 2.148784 0.465379 1.8242% 1947 2.110289 0.473869 -
2.6320% 1946 2.167334 0.461396 3.1768% 1945 2.100602 0.476054 6.4754% 1944 1.972852
0.506880 -0.3437% 1943 1.979656 0.505138 0.6562% 1942 1.966749 0.508453 0.6633%
1941 1.953790 0.511826 -5.6614% 1940 2.071040 0.482849 8.0381% 1939 1.916953
0.521661 0.8126% 1938 1.901501 0.525900 0.7762% 1937 1.886855 0.529983 0.6029% 1936
1.875547 0.533178 0.5244% 1935 1.865763 0.535974 -3.0364% 1934 1.924189 0.519699
4.6271% 1933 1.839092 0.543747 1.3921% 1932 1.813841 0.551316 -0.2051% 1931
1.817569 0.550186 0.8886% 1930 1.801560 0.555074 1.0126% 1929 1.783501 0.560695
1.1526% 1928 1.763178 0.567158 1.2160% 1927 1.741996 0.574054 1.4086% 1926 1.717799
0.582140 1.7667% 1925 1.687978 0.592425 1.4465% 1924 1.663909 0.600994 1.7700% 1923
1.634971 0.611632 1.6165% 1922 1.608962 0.621519 1.3736% 1921 1.587160 0.630056
2.3393% 1920 1.550880 0.644795 1.3140% 1919 1.530765 0.653268 0.7676% 1918 1.519104
0.658283 0.3870% 1917 1.513248 0.660830 1.3274% 1916 1.493424 0.669602 1.4083% 1915
1.472684 0.679032 1.4458% 1914 1.451695 0.688850 1.9424% 1913 1.424035 0.702230
1.9857% 1912 1.396309 0.716174 1.5634% 1911 1.374815 0.727371 1.8169% 1910 1.350282
0.740586 1.8781% 1909 1.325390 0.754495 2.0082% 1908 1.299297 0.769647 1.9603% 1907
1.274317 0.784734 1.8264% 1906 1.251461 0.799066 1.9357% 1905 1.227697 0.814533
2.0148% 1904 1.203449 0.830945 2.1335% 1903 1.178310 0.848673 1.8151% 1902 1.157303
0.864078 1.8943% 1901 1.135787 0.880447 3.0255% 1900 1.102433 0.907085 0.6278% 1899
1.095555 0.912780 1.7757% 1898 1.076441 0.928987 1.8078% 1897 1.057327 0.945781
1.8396% 1896 1.038228 0.963180 1.8755% 1895 1.019114 0.981245 1.9114% 1894 1.000000
1.000000 1.9486% 1893 0.980886 1.019486 1.9858% 1892 0.961787 1.039731 2.0276% 1891
0.942673 1.060813 2.6465% 1890 0.918368 1.088888 1.5328% 1889 0.904504 1.105578
2.0811% 1888 0.886064 1.128587 2.1599% 1887 0.867331 1.152963 2.2075% 1886 0.848598
1.178415 2.2592% 1885 0.829850 1.205037 2.3095% 1884 0.811117 1.232868 2.3641% 1883
0.792384 1.262015 2.4214% 1882 0.773651 1.292573 2.4815% 1881 0.754918 1.324648

3.7644% 1880 0.727530 1.374513 0.9432% 1879 0.720732 1.387478 2.1464% 1878 0.705588
1.417258 2.1913% 1877 0.690458 1.448315 2.2426% 1876 0.675313 1.480795 2.2941% 1875
0.660168 1.514765 2.3456% 1874 0.645038 1.550295 2.4043% 1873 0.629894 1.587569
2.4635% 1872 0.614749 1.626680 2.5258% 1871 0.599605 1.667766 5.9947% 1870 0.565693
1.767743 -1.0968% 1869 0.571966 1.748355 2.1930% 1868 0.559692 1.786696 2.2394%
1867 0.547433 1.826707 2.2935% 1866 0.535159 1.868603 2.3445% 1865 0.522900 1.912411
2.4037% 1864 0.510626 1.958380 2.4599% 1863 0.498367 2.006554 2.5250% 1862 0.486093
2.057219 2.5872% 1861 0.473834 2.110445 2.9504% 1860 0.460254 2.172712 2.4012% 1859
0.449462 2.224884 2.7627% 1858 0.437378 2.286351 2.8412% 1857 0.425295 2.351310
2.9243% 1856 0.413211 2.420069 3.0161% 1855 0.401113 2.493062 3.1061% 1854 0.389030
2.570498 3.2056% 1853 0.376946 2.652899 3.3118% 1852 0.364863 2.740757 3.4252% 1851
0.352779 2.834634 4.0106% 1850 0.339176 2.948320 2.3254% 1849 0.331468 3.016880
2.7841% 1848 0.322490 3.100872 2.8590% 1847 0.313526 3.189526 2.9432% 1846 0.304562
3.283399 3.0324% 1845 0.295599 3.382965 3.1325% 1844 0.286620 3.488937 3.2284% 1843
0.277657 3.601572 3.3361% 1842 0.268693 3.721723 3.4512% 1841 0.259729 3.850166
3.8105% 1840 0.250195 3.996876 2.3861% 1839 0.244365 4.092244 2.5824% 1838 0.238213
4.197922 2.6573% 1837 0.232047 4.309474 2.7232% 1836 0.225895 4.426830 2.7994% 1835
0.219744 4.550757 2.8871% 1834 0.213577 4.682142 2.9657% 1833 0.207426 4.821000
3.0563% 1832 0.201274 4.968345 3.1604% 1831 0.195108 5.125366 3.4660% 1830 0.188572
5.303009 2.4653% 1829 0.184035 5.433745 2.6804% 1828 0.179231 5.579390 10.3427%
1827 0.162431 6.156447 -4.2314% 1826 0.169608 5.895941 2.9150% 1825 0.164804
6.067810 3.0026% 1824 0.160000 6.250000 3.0955% 1823 0.155196 6.443469 3.1944% 1822
0.150392 6.649299 3.3102% 1821 0.145573 6.869403 3.2277% 1820 0.141021 7.091130
2.6573% 1819 0.137371 7.279561 2.6261% 1818 0.133856 7.470730 2.6969% 1817 0.130341
7.672210 2.7717% 1816 0.126825 7.884860 2.8507% 1815 0.123310 8.109633 2.9343% 1814
0.119795 8.347598 3.0231% 1813 0.116280 8.599950 3.1039% 1812 0.112779 8.866883
3.2172% 1811 0.109264 9.152145 3.0969% 1810 0.105982 9.435579 2.9144% 1809 0.102981
9.710567 2.8225% 1808 0.100154 9.984645 2.9199% 1807 0.097312 10.276189 2.9918%
1806 0.094486 10.583630 3.0841% 1805 0.091659 10.910035 3.1822% 1804 0.088832
11.257214 3.2868% 1803 0.086005 11.627214 3.3985% 1802 0.083178 12.022363 3.5180%
1801 0.080352 12.445315 3.3999% 1800 0.077709 12.868449 2.8419% 1799 0.075562
13.234154 2.7485% 1798 0.073541 13.597889 2.8261% 1797 0.071520 13.982183 3.7832%
1796 0.068912 14.511158 2.1272% 1795 0.067477 14.819839 3.0879% 1794 0.065456
15.277467 3.1625% 1793 0.063449 15.760619 3.2904% 1792 0.061428 16.279208 3.4024%
1791 0.059407 16.833087 3.2296% 1790 0.057548 17.376722 41.3145% 1780 0.040724
24.555819 29.4353% 1770 0.031462 31.783902 83.4728% 1750 0.017148 58.314827
29.2845% 1740 0.013264 75.392005 94.2514% 1720 0.006828 146.450021 85.8111% 1700
0.003675 272.120367 19.2490% 1690 0.003082 324.500951 88.0250% 1670 0.001639
610.142985

BASE YEAR: 1893
YEAR BYEAR/AYEAR AYEAR/BYEAR GROWTH%

2009 4.500976 0.222174 8.2857% 2001 4.156576 0.240583 1.0000% 2000 4.115421
0.242988 1.0000% 1999 4.074675 0.245418 1.0000% 1998 4.034331 0.247873 1.0000% 1997
3.994387 0.250351 1.0000% 1996 3.954839 0.252855 1.0000% 1995 3.915682 0.255383
0.9992% 1994 3.876943 0.257935 1.0008% 1993 3.838528 0.260517 1.0000% 1992 3.800523
0.263122 0.9295% 1991 3.765522 0.265567 1.2505% 1990 3.719015 0.268888 0.7224% 1989
3.692340 0.270831 1.1077% 1988 3.651889 0.273831 0.8834% 1987 3.619912 0.276250
0.5594% 1986 3.599776 0.277795 1.3056% 1985 3.553382 0.281422 0.7673% 1984 3.526325
0.283581 0.8149% 1983 3.497820 0.285892 0.9737% 1982 3.464088 0.288676 0.9508% 1981
3.431462 0.291421 0.9031% 1980 3.400751 0.294053 2.2701% 1979 3.325265 0.300728
1.0042% 1978 3.292205 0.303748 0.9896% 1977 3.259945 0.306754 0.9103% 1976 3.230536
0.309546 0.8394% 1975 3.203643 0.312145 0.9042% 1974 3.174937 0.314967 1.1568% 1973
3.138629 0.318610 0.9427% 1972 3.109318 0.321614 0.7426% 1971 3.086397 0.324002
1.4697% 1970 3.041692 0.328764 0.6968% 1969 3.020644 0.331055 0.8565% 1968 2.994990
0.333891 1.5090% 1967 2.950467 0.338929 0.9949% 1966 2.921401 0.342301 1.0575% 1965
2.890832 0.345921 1.1300% 1964 2.858530 0.349830 1.5537% 1963 2.814798 0.355265

173

1.4658% 1962 2.774134 0.360473 1.5364% 1961 2.732156 0.366011 2.1586% 1960 2.674425
0.373912 -1.6655% 1959 2.719722 0.367685 4.3080% 1958 2.607395 0.383525 2.1130%
1957 2.553442 0.391628 1.9895% 1956 2.503632 0.399420 2.1231% 1955 2.451583 0.407900
1.4496% 1954 2.416552 0.413813 2.1573% 1953 2.365522 0.422740 1.2298% 1952 2.336785
0.427938 1.6814% 1951 2.298145 0.435134 1.6233% 1950 2.261435 0.442197 1.4265% 1949
2.229629 0.448505 1.7790% 1948 2.190656 0.456484 1.8242% 1947 2.151411 0.464811 -
2.6320% 1946 2.209568 0.452577 3.1768% 1945 2.141535 0.466955 6.4754% 1944 2.011296
0.497192 -0.3437% 1943 2.018232 0.495483 0.6562% 1942 2.005074 0.498735 0.6633%
1941 1.991862 0.502043 -5.6614% 1940 2.111397 0.473620 8.0381% 1939 1.954308
0.511690 0.8126% 1938 1.938555 0.515848 0.7762% 1937 1.923623 0.519853 0.6029% 1936
1.912095 0.522987 0.5244% 1935 1.902120 0.525729 -3.0364% 1934 1.961684 0.509766
4.6271% 1933 1.874929 0.533354 1.3921% 1932 1.849186 0.540778 -0.2051% 1931
1.852986 0.539669 0.8886% 1930 1.836666 0.544465 1.0126% 1929 1.818254 0.549978
1.1526% 1928 1.797536 0.556317 1.2160% 1927 1.775941 0.563082 1.4086% 1926 1.751273
0.571013 1.7667% 1925 1.720870 0.581101 1.4465% 1924 1.696333 0.589507 1.7700% 1923
1.666830 0.599941 1.6165% 1922 1.640314 0.609639 1.3736% 1921 1.618088 0.618014
2.3393% 1920 1.581101 0.632471 1.3140% 1919 1.560594 0.640782 0.7676% 1918 1.548706
0.645700 0.3870% 1917 1.542736 0.648199 1.3274% 1916 1.522525 0.656804 1.4083% 1915
1.501381 0.666053 1.4458% 1914 1.479984 0.675683 1.9424% 1913 1.451784 0.688808
1.9857% 1912 1.423518 0.702485 1.5634% 1911 1.401605 0.713468 1.8169% 1910 1.376594
0.726431 1.8781% 1909 1.351217 0.740074 2.0082% 1908 1.324615 0.754936 1.9603% 1907
1.299149 0.769735 1.8264% 1906 1.275847 0.783793 1.9357% 1905 1.251620 0.798964
2.0148% 1904 1.226900 0.815062 2.1335% 1903 1.201271 0.832452 1.8151% 1902 1.179855
0.847562 1.8943% 1901 1.157920 0.863618 3.0255% 1900 1.123915 0.889747 0.6278% 1899
1.116903 0.895333 1.7757% 1898 1.097417 0.911231 1.8078% 1897 1.077930 0.927704
1.8396% 1896 1.058459 0.944770 1.8755% 1895 1.038973 0.962489 1.9114% 1894 1.019486
0.980886 1.9486% 1893 1.000000 1.000000 1.9858% 1892 0.980529 1.019858 2.0276% 1891
0.961042 1.040537 2.6465% 1890 0.936264 1.068075 1.5328% 1889 0.922129 1.084447
2.0811% 1888 0.903330 1.107015 2.1599% 1887 0.884232 1.130925 2.2075% 1886 0.865134
1.155891 2.2592% 1885 0.846021 1.182004 2.3095% 1884 0.826923 1.209303 2.3641% 1883
0.807824 1.237893 2.4214% 1882 0.788726 1.267867 2.4815% 1881 0.769628 1.299329
3.7644% 1880 0.741707 1.348241 0.9432% 1879 0.734777 1.360958 2.1464% 1878 0.719337
1.390169 2.1913% 1877 0.703912 1.420632 2.2426% 1876 0.688472 1.452491 2.2941% 1875
0.673033 1.485812 2.3456% 1874 0.657608 1.520663 2.4043% 1873 0.642168 1.557225
2.4635% 1872 0.626728 1.595588 2.5258% 1871 0.611289 1.635888 5.9947% 1870 0.576716
1.733955 -1.0968% 1869 0.583112 1.714937 2.1930% 1868 0.570599 1.752545 2.2394%
1867 0.558101 1.791792 2.2935% 1866 0.545588 1.832886 2.3445% 1865 0.533089 1.875858
2.4037% 1864 0.520576 1.920948 2.4599% 1863 0.508078 1.968201 2.5250% 1862 0.495565
2.017898 2.5872% 1861 0.483067 2.070106 2.9504% 1860 0.469223 2.131183 2.4012% 1859
0.458220 2.182357 2.7627% 1858 0.445901 2.242650 2.8412% 1857 0.433582 2.306368
2.9243% 1856 0.421263 2.373813 3.0161% 1855 0.408929 2.445410 3.1061% 1854 0.396610
2.521366 3.2056% 1853 0.384291 2.602191 3.3118% 1852 0.371973 2.688371 3.4252% 1851
0.359654 2.780453 4.0106% 1850 0.345785 2.891966 3.3254% 1849 0.337927 2.959215
2.7841% 1848 0.328774 3.041602 2.8590% 1847 0.319636 3.128562 2.9432% 1846 0.310497
3.220641 3.0324% 1845 0.301359 3.318303 3.1325% 1844 0.292205 3.422249 3.2284% 1843
0.283067 3.532732 3.3361% 1842 0.273929 3.650586 3.4512% 1841 0.264790 3.776575
3.8105% 1840 0.255071 3.920481 2.3861% 1839 0.249126 4.014025 2.5824% 1838 0.242855
4.117683 2.6573% 1837 0.236569 4.227103 2.7232% 1836 0.230297 4.342216 2.7994% 1835
0.224026 4.463774 2.8871% 1834 0.217739 4.592648 2.9657% 1833 0.211468 4.728852
3.0563% 1832 0.205196 4.873381 3.1604% 1831 0.198910 5.027400 3.4660% 1830 0.192247
5.201648 2.4653% 1829 0.187621 5.329885 2.6804% 1828 0.182724 5.472747 10.3427%
1827 0.165597 6.038774 -4.2314% 1826 0.172913 5.783247 2.9150% 1825 0.168016
5.951831 3.0026% 1824 0.163118 6.130538 3.0955% 1823 0.158220 6.320310 3.1944% 1822
0.153322 6.522205 3.3102% 1821 0.148410 6.738102 3.2277% 1820 0.143769 6.955591
2.6573% 1819 0.140048 7.140420 2.6261% 1818 0.136464 7.327935 2.6969% 1817 0.132880
7.525565 2.7717% 1816 0.129297 7.734149 2.8507% 1815 0.125713 7.954626 2.9343% 1814

174

0.122129 8.188043 3.0231% 1813 0.118546 8.435571 3.1039% 1812 0.114977 8.697403 3.2172% 1811 0.111393 8.977212 3.0969% 1810 0.108047 9.255228 2.9144% 1809 0.104987 9.524961 2.8225% 1808 0.102105 9.793799 2.9199% 1807 0.099209 10.079771 2.9918% 1806 0.096327 10.381336 3.0841% 1805 0.093445 10.701502 3.1822% 1804 0.090563 11.042045 3.2868% 1803 0.087681 11.404973 3.3985% 1802 0.084799 11.792569 3.5180% 1801 0.081917 12.207437 3.3999% 1800 0.079224 12.622484 2.8419% 1799 0.077034 12.981198 2.7485% 1798 0.074974 13.337980 2.8261% 1797 0.072913 13.714929 3.7832% 1796 0.070255 14.233794 2.1272% 1795 0.068792 14.536575 3.0879% 1794 0.066731 14.985455 3.1625% 1793 0.064686 15.459372 3.2904% 1792 0.062625 15.968050 3.4024% 1791 0.060564 16.511341 3.2296% 1790 0.058670 17.044585 41.3145% 1780 0.041517 24.086462 29.4353% 1770 0.032076 31.176388 83.4728% 1750 0.017482 57.200205 29.2845% 1740 0.013522 73.950972 94.2514% 1720 0.006961 143.650794 85.8111% 1700 0.003746 266.919091 19.2490% 1690 0.003142 318.298479 88.0250% 1670 0.001671 598.480786

BASE YEAR: 1892

YEAR BYEAR/AYEAR AYEAR/BYEAR GROWTH%

2009 4.590356 0.217848 8.2857% 2001 4.239118 0.235898 1.0000% 2000 4.197146 0.238257 1.0000% 1999 4.155590 0.240640 1.0000% 1998 4.114445 0.243046 1.0000% 1997 4.073708 0.245477 1.0000% 1996 4.033375 0.247931 1.0000% 1995 3.993440 0.250411 0.9992% 1994 3.953932 0.252913 1.0008% 1993 3.914754 0.255444 1.0000% 1992 3.875994 0.257998 0.9295% 1991 3.840298 0.260396 1.2505% 1990 3.792867 0.263653 0.7224% 1989 3.765663 0.265558 1.1077% 1988 3.724408 0.268499 0.8834% 1987 3.691796 0.270871 0.5594% 1986 3.671261 0.272386 1.3056% 1985 3.623945 0.275942 0.7673% 1984 3.596351 0.278060 0.8149% 1983 3.567280 0.280326 0.9737% 1982 3.532879 0.283055 0.9508% 1981 3.499604 0.285747 0.9031% 1980 3.468283 0.288327 2.2701% 1979 3.391298 0.294872 1.0042% 1978 3.357582 0.297833 0.9896% 1977 3.324681 0.300781 0.9103% 1976 3.294688 0.303519 0.8394% 1975 3.267262 0.306067 0.9042% 1974 3.237985 0.308834 1.1568% 1973 3.200956 0.312407 0.9427% 1972 3.171063 0.315352 0.7426% 1971 3.147687 0.317694 1.4697% 1970 3.102094 0.322363 0.6968% 1969 3.080628 0.324609 0.8565% 1968 3.054465 0.327390 1.5090% 1967 3.009057 0.332330 0.9949% 1966 2.979415 0.335636 1.0575% 1965 2.948238 0.339186 1.1300% 1964 2.915295 0.343018 1.5537% 1963 2.870694 0.348348 1.4658% 1962 2.829223 0.353454 1.5364% 1961 2.786412 0.358885 2.1586% 1960 2.727534 0.366632 -1.6655% 1959 2.773730 0.360525 4.3080% 1958 2.659173 0.376057 2.1130% 1957 2.604148 0.384003 1.9895% 1956 2.553350 0.391642 2.1231% 1955 2.500267 0.399957 1.4496% 1954 2.464540 0.405755 2.1573% 1953 2.412497 0.414508 1.2298% 1952 2.383189 0.419606 1.6814% 1951 2.343781 0.426661 1.6233% 1950 2.306343 0.433587 1.4265% 1949 2.273905 0.439772 1.7790% 1948 2.234158 0.447596 1.8242% 1947 2.194134 0.455761 -2.6320% 1946 2.253445 0.443765 3.1768% 1945 2.184062 0.457862 6.4754% 1944 2.051236 0.487511 -0.3437% 1943 2.058310 0.485835 0.6562% 1942 2.044891 0.489024 0.6633% 1941 2.031417 0.492267 -5.6614% 1940 2.153326 0.464398 8.0381% 1939 1.993117 0.501727 0.8126% 1938 1.977051 0.505804 0.7762% 1937 1.961822 0.509730 0.6029% 1936 1.950065 0.512803 0.5244% 1935 1.939893 0.515492 -3.0364% 1934 2.000640 0.499840 4.6271% 1933 1.912162 0.522968 1.3921% 1932 1.885907 0.530249 -0.2051% 1931 1.889783 0.529161 0.8886% 1930 1.873138 0.533863 1.0126% 1929 1.854361 0.539269 1.1526% 1928 1.833232 0.545485 1.2160% 1927 1.811207 0.552118 1.4086% 1926 1.786050 0.559895 1.7667% 1925 1.755043 0.569786 1.4465% 1924 1.730019 0.578028 1.7700% 1923 1.699930 0.588259 1.6165% 1922 1.672888 0.597769 1.3736% 1921 1.650220 0.605980 2.3393% 1920 1.612498 0.620156 1.3140% 1919 1.591585 0.628305 0.7676% 1918 1.579460 0.633128 0.3870% 1917 1.573371 0.635578 1.3274% 1916 1.552759 0.644015 1.4083% 1915 1.531196 0.653084 1.4458% 1914 1.509373 0.662527 1.9424% 1913 1.480614 0.675395 1.9857% 1912 1.451786 0.688807 1.5634% 1911 1.429438 0.699575 1.8169% 1910 1.403930 0.712286 1.8781% 1909 1.378050 0.725663 2.0082% 1908 1.350920 0.740236 1.9603% 1907 1.324947 0.754747 1.8264% 1906 1.301183 0.768531 1.9357% 1905 1.276475 0.783407 2.0148% 1904 1.251264 0.799192 2.1335% 1903 1.225126 0.816243 1.8151% 1902 1.203284 0.831059 1.8943% 1901 1.180914 0.846802 3.0255% 1900 1.146234 0.872422 0.6278% 1899 1.139083 0.877899 1.7757% 1898 1.119209 0.893488 1.8078% 1897 1.099336 0.909640

175

1.8396% 1896 1.079478 0.926374 1.8755% 1895 1.059605 0.943748 1.9114% 1894 1.039731
0.961787 1.9486% 1893 1.019858 0.980529 1.9858% 1892 1.000000 1.000000 2.0276% 1891
0.980127 1.020276 2.6465% 1890 0.954856 1.047278 1.5328% 1889 0.940441 1.063331
2.0811% 1888 0.921268 1.085460 2.1599% 1887 0.901791 1.108905 2.2075% 1886 0.882314
1.133384 2.2592% 1885 0.862821 1.158989 2.3095% 1884 0.843344 1.185756 2.3641% 1883
0.823866 1.213789 2.4214% 1882 0.804389 1.243180 2.4815% 1881 0.784912 1.274029
3.7644% 1880 0.756436 1.321988 0.9432% 1879 0.749368 1.334458 2.1464% 1878 0.733622
1.363100 2.1913% 1877 0.717891 1.392970 2.2426% 1876 0.702144 1.424209 2.2941% 1875
0.686398 1.456881 2.3456% 1874 0.670667 1.491054 2.4043% 1873 0.654920 1.526903
2.4635% 1872 0.639174 1.564519 2.5258% 1871 0.623428 1.604035 5.9947% 1870 0.588169
1.700192 -1.0968% 1869 0.594691 1.681545 2.1930% 1868 0.581930 1.718420 2.2394%
1867 0.569183 1.756903 2.2935% 1866 0.556422 1.797197 2.3445% 1865 0.543676 1.839332
2.4037% 1864 0.530914 1.883544 2.4599% 1863 0.518168 1.929877 2.5250% 1862 0.505406
1.978607 2.5872% 1861 0.492660 2.029798 2.9504% 1860 0.478541 2.089685 2.4012% 1859
0.467319 2.139864 2.7627% 1858 0.454756 2.198982 2.8412% 1857 0.442192 2.261460
2.9243% 1856 0.429629 2.327591 3.0161% 1855 0.417050 2.397794 3.1061% 1854 0.404486
2.472271 3.2056% 1853 0.391923 2.551523 3.3118% 1852 0.379359 2.636024 3.4252% 1851
0.366796 2.726314 4.0106% 1850 0.352652 2.835656 2.3254% 1849 0.344638 2.901595
2.7841% 1848 0.335303 2.982378 2.8590% 1847 0.325983 3.067645 2.9432% 1846 0.316663
3.157930 3.0324% 1845 0.307343 3.253691 3.1325% 1844 0.298008 3.355613 3.2284% 1843
0.288688 3.463945 3.3361% 1842 0.279368 3.579504 3.4512% 1841 0.270048 3.703040
3.8105% 1840 0.260136 3.844143 2.3861% 1839 0.254074 3.935867 2.5824% 1838 0.247678
4.037506 2.6573% 1837 0.241266 4.144796 2.7232% 1836 0.234870 4.257667 2.7994% 1835
0.228474 4.376858 2.8871% 1834 0.222063 4.503223 2.9657% 1833 0.215667 4.636774
3.0563% 1832 0.209271 4.778489 3.1604% 1831 0.202860 4.929510 3.4660% 1830 0.196064
5.100365 2.4653% 1829 0.191347 5.226104 2.6804% 1828 0.186352 5.366185 10.3427%
1827 0.168885 5.921190 -4.2314% 1826 0.176347 5.670639 2.9150% 1825 0.171352
5.835940 3.0026% 1824 0.166357 6.011168 3.0955% 1823 0.161362 6.197244 3.1944% 1822
0.156367 6.395208 3.3102% 1821 0.151357 6.606902 3.2277% 1820 0.146624 6.820156
2.6573% 1819 0.142829 7.001386 2.6261% 1818 0.139174 7.185250 2.6969% 1817 0.135519
7.379031 2.7717% 1816 0.131864 7.583555 2.8507% 1815 0.128209 7.799739 2.9343% 1814
0.124555 8.028610 3.0231% 1813 0.120900 8.271319 3.1039% 1812 0.117260 8.528052
3.2172% 1811 0.113605 8.802413 3.0969% 1810 0.110193 9.075016 2.9144% 1809 0.107072
9.339497 2.8225% 1808 0.104133 9.603100 2.9199% 1807 0.101179 9.883504 2.9918% 1806
0.098240 10.179197 3.0841% 1805 0.095300 10.493129 3.1822% 1804 0.092361 10.827040
3.2868% 1803 0.089422 11.182902 3.3985% 1802 0.086483 11.562951 3.5180% 1801
0.083544 11.969741 3.3999% 1800 0.080797 12.376706 2.8419% 1799 0.078564 12.728436
2.7485% 1798 0.076463 13.078271 2.8261% 1797 0.074361 13.447880 3.7832% 1796
0.071650 13.956642 2.1272% 1795 0.070158 14.253527 3.0879% 1794 0.068057 14.693667
3.1625% 1793 0.065970 15.158356 3.2904% 1792 0.063869 15.657129 3.4024% 1791
0.061767 16.189842 3.2296% 1790 0.059835 16.712703 41.3145% 1780 0.042342 23.617465
29.4353% 1770 0.032713 30.569340 83.4728% 1750 0.017830 56.086437 29.2845% 1740
0.013791 72.511042 94.2514% 1720 0.007100 140.853711 85.8111% 1700 0.003821
261.721802 19.2490% 1690 0.003204 312.100760 88.0250% 1670 0.001704 586.827525

BASE YEAR: 1891

YEAR BYEAR/AYEAR AYEAR/BYEAR GROWTH%

2009 4.683432 0.213519 8.2857% 2001 4.325071 0.231210 1.0000% 2000 4.282248
0.233522 1.0000% 1999 4.239850 0.235857 1.0000% 1998 4.197871 0.238216 1.0000% 1997
4.156308 0.240598 1.0000% 1996 4.115156 0.243004 1.0000% 1995 4.074412 0.245434
0.9992% 1994 4.034103 0.247887 1.0008% 1993 3.994130 0.250367 1.0000% 1992 3.954584
0.252871 0.9295% 1991 3.918165 0.255222 1.2505% 1990 3.869773 0.258413 0.7224% 1989
3.842016 0.260280 1.1077% 1988 3.799925 0.263163 0.8834% 1987 3.766652 0.265488
0.5594% 1986 3.745700 0.266973 1.3056% 1985 3.697425 0.270458 0.7673% 1984 3.669272
0.272534 0.8149% 1983 3.639611 0.274755 0.9737% 1982 3.604512 0.277430 0.9508% 1981
3.570563 0.280068 0.9031% 1980 3.538607 0.282597 2.2701% 1979 3.460061 0.289012
1.0042% 1978 3.425662 0.291914 0.9896% 1977 3.392093 0.294803 0.9103% 1976 3.361492

176

0.297487 0.8394% 1975 3.333509 0.299984 0.9042% 1974 3.303639 0.302697 1.1568% 1973 3.265860 0.306198 0.9427% 1972 3.235360 0.309085 0.7426% 1971 3.211510 0.311380 1.4697% 1970 3.164993 0.315956 0.6968% 1969 3.143091 0.318158 0.8565% 1968 3.116398 0.320883 1.5090% 1967 3.070070 0.325726 0.9949% 1966 3.039826 0.328966 1.0575% 1965 3.008017 0.332445 1.1300% 1964 2.974406 0.336202 1.5537% 1963 2.928901 0.341425 1.4658% 1962 2.886589 0.346430 1.5364% 1961 2.842910 0.351752 2.1586% 1960 2.782838 0.359345 -1.6655% 1959 2.829971 0.353361 4.3080% 1958 2.713091 0.368583 2.1130% 1957 2.656951 0.376371 1.9895% 1956 2.605122 0.383859 2.1231% 1955 2.550963 0.392009 1.4496% 1954 2.514512 0.397691 2.1573% 1953 2.461413 0.406271 1.2298% 1952 2.431511 0.411267 1.6814% 1951 2.391305 0.418182 1.6233% 1950 2.353107 0.424970 1.4265% 1949 2.320011 0.431032 1.7790% 1948 2.279459 0.438701 1.8242% 1947 2.238623 0.446703 - 2.6320% 1946 2.299137 0.434946 3.1768% 1945 2.228347 0.448763 6.4754% 1944 2.092827 0.477822 -0.3437% 1943 2.100045 0.476180 0.6562% 1942 2.086354 0.479305 0.6633% 1941 2.072606 0.482484 -5.6614% 1940 2.196987 0.455169 8.0381% 1939 2.033530 0.491756 0.8126% 1938 2.017138 0.495752 0.7762% 1937 2.001600 0.499600 0.6029% 1936 1.989606 0.502612 0.5244% 1935 1.979227 0.505248 -3.0364% 1934 2.041205 0.489907 4.6271% 1933 1.950933 0.512575 1.3921% 1932 1.924147 0.519711 -0.2051% 1931 1.928101 0.518645 0.8886% 1930 1.911119 0.523254 1.0126% 1929 1.891961 0.528552 1.1526% 1928 1.870403 0.534644 1.2160% 1927 1.847932 0.541145 1.4086% 1926 1.822264 0.548768 1.7667% 1925 1.790629 0.558463 1.4465% 1924 1.765097 0.566541 1.7700% 1923 1.734399 0.576569 1.6165% 1922 1.706808 0.585889 1.3736% 1921 1.683680 0.593937 2.3393% 1920 1.645194 0.607831 1.3140% 1919 1.623856 0.615818 0.7676% 1918 1.611486 0.620545 0.3870% 1917 1.605273 0.622947 1.3274% 1916 1.584244 0.631216 1.4083% 1915 1.562243 0.640105 1.4458% 1914 1.539978 0.649360 1.9424% 1913 1.510635 0.661973 1.9857% 1912 1.481223 0.675118 1.5634% 1911 1.458422 0.685673 1.8169% 1910 1.432397 0.698131 1.8781% 1909 1.405991 0.711242 2.0082% 1908 1.378311 0.725525 1.9603% 1907 1.351812 0.739748 1.8264% 1906 1.327566 0.753258 1.9357% 1905 1.302357 0.767839 2.0148% 1904 1.276635 0.783309 2.1335% 1903 1.249967 0.800021 1.8151% 1902 1.227682 0.814543 1.8943% 1901 1.204858 0.829973 3.0255% 1900 1.169476 0.855084 0.6278% 1899 1.162179 0.860453 1.7757% 1898 1.141903 0.875731 1.8078% 1897 1.121626 0.891562 1.8396% 1896 1.101366 0.907964 1.8755% 1895 1.081089 0.924993 1.9114% 1894 1.060813 0.942673 1.9486% 1893 1.040537 0.961042 1.9858% 1892 1.020276 0.980127 2.0276% 1891 1.000000 1.000000 2.6465% 1890 0.974217 1.026465 1.5328% 1889 0.959510 1.042199 2.0811% 1888 0.939948 1.063889 2.1599% 1887 0.920076 1.086867 2.2075% 1886 0.900204 1.110860 2.2592% 1885 0.880316 1.135956 2.3095% 1884 0.860443 1.162191 2.3641% 1883 0.840571 1.189667 2.4214% 1882 0.820699 1.218474 2.4815% 1881 0.800827 1.248710 3.7644% 1880 0.771774 1.295716 0.9432% 1879 0.764562 1.307938 2.1464% 1878 0.748497 1.336011 2.1913% 1877 0.732447 1.365287 2.2426% 1876 0.716381 1.395905 2.2941% 1875 0.700315 1.427928 2.3456% 1874 0.684265 1.461421 2.4043% 1873 0.668200 1.496559 2.4635% 1872 0.652134 1.533427 2.5258% 1871 0.636068 1.572158 5.9947% 1870 0.600095 1.666404 -1.0968% 1869 0.606749 1.648127 2.1930% 1868 0.593729 1.684270 2.2394% 1867 0.580724 1.721987 2.2935% 1866 0.567704 1.761481 2.3445% 1865 0.554699 1.802779 2.4037% 1864 0.541679 1.846112 2.4599% 1863 0.528674 1.891524 2.5250% 1862 0.515654 1.939285 2.5872% 1861 0.502649 1.989459 2.9504% 1860 0.488244 2.048157 2.4012% 1859 0.476795 2.097338 2.7627% 1858 0.463977 2.155281 2.8412% 1857 0.451158 2.216517 2.9243% 1856 0.438340 2.281334 3.0161% 1855 0.425506 2.350142 3.1061% 1854 0.412688 2.423139 3.2056% 1853 0.399869 2.500816 3.3118% 1852 0.387051 2.583638 3.4252% 1851 0.374233 2.672133 4.0106% 1850 0.359803 2.779302 2.3254% 1849 0.351626 2.843931 2.7841% 1848 0.342102 2.923108 2.8590% 1847 0.332593 3.006680 2.9432% 1846 0.323084 3.095172 3.0325% 1845 0.313575 3.189030 3.1325% 1844 0.304051 3.288926 3.2284% 1843 0.294542 3.395105 3.3361% 1842 0.285033 3.508367 3.4512% 1841 0.275524 3.629448 3.8105% 1840 0.265411 3.767748 2.3861% 1839 0.259225 3.857648 2.5824% 1838 0.252700 3.957268 2.6573% 1837 0.246158 4.062425 2.7232% 1836 0.239633 4.173053 2.7994% 1835 0.233107 4.289875 2.8871% 1834 0.226566 4.413729 2.9657% 1833 0.220040 4.544626 3.0563% 1832 0.213514 4.683525 3.1604% 1831 0.206973 4.831544 3.4660% 1830 0.200040 4.999004 2.4653% 1829 0.195227 5.122244 2.6804% 1828 0.190131 5.259541 10.3427%

1827 0.172309 5.803517 -4.2314% 1826 0.179923 5.557945 2.9150% 1825 0.174826
5.719961 3.0026% 1824 0.169730 5.891706 3.0955% 1823 0.164634 6.074085 3.1944% 1822
0.159538 6.268115 3.3102% 1821 0.154426 6.475601 3.2277% 1820 0.149597 6.684617
2.6573% 1819 0.145725 6.862245 2.6261% 1818 0.141996 7.042455 2.6969% 1817 0.138267
7.232386 2.7717% 1816 0.134538 7.432844 2.8507% 1815 0.130809 7.644732 2.9343% 1814
0.127080 7.869055 3.0231% 1813 0.123351 8.106940 3.1039% 1812 0.119638 8.358571
3.2172% 1811 0.115909 8.627480 3.0969% 1810 0.112427 8.894666 2.9144% 1809 0.109243
9.153890 2.8225% 1808 0.106244 9.412255 2.9199% 1807 0.103230 9.687086 2.9918% 1806
0.100232 9.976903 3.0841% 1805 0.097233 10.284596 3.1822% 1804 0.094234 10.611871
3.2868% 1803 0.091235 10.960661 3.3985% 1802 0.088237 11.333157 3.5180% 1801
0.085238 11.731863 3.3999% 1800 0.082435 12.130740 2.8419% 1799 0.080157 12.475480
2.7485% 1798 0.078013 12.818363 2.8261% 1797 0.075869 13.180627 3.7832% 1796
0.073103 13.679277 2.1272% 1795 0.071581 13.970263 3.0879% 1794 0.069436 14.401656
3.1625% 1793 0.067308 14.857110 3.2904% 1792 0.065164 15.345970 3.4024% 1791
0.063020 15.868097 3.2296% 1790 0.061048 16.380567 41.3145% 1780 0.043200 23.148108
29.4353% 1770 0.033376 29.961827 83.4728% 1750 0.018191 54.971814 29.2845% 1740
0.014071 71.070009 94.2514% 1720 0.007244 138.054483 85.8111% 1700 0.003898
256.520526 19.2490% 1690 0.003269 305.898289 88.0250% 1670 0.001739 575.165326
BASE YEAR: 1890
YEAR BYEAR/AYEAR AYEAR/BYEAR GROWTH%
2009 4.807380 0.208014 8.2857% 2001 4.439535 0.225249 1.0000% 2000 4.395579
0.227501 1.0000% 1999 4.352058 0.229776 1.0000% 1998 4.308968 0.232074 1.0000% 1997
4.266305 0.234395 1.0000% 1996 4.224065 0.236739 1.0000% 1995 4.182242 0.239106
0.9992% 1994 4.140866 0.241495 1.0008% 1993 4.099835 0.243912 1.0000% 1992 4.059243
0.246351 0.9295% 1991 4.021860 0.248641 1.2505% 1990 3.972187 0.251750 0.7224% 1989
3.943696 0.253569 1.1077% 1988 3.900491 0.256378 0.8834% 1987 3.866337 0.258643
0.5594% 1986 3.844831 0.260089 1.3056% 1985 3.795278 0.263485 0.7673% 1984 3.766380
0.265507 0.8149% 1983 3.735934 0.267671 0.9737% 1982 3.699906 0.270277 0.9508% 1981
3.665058 0.272847 0.9031% 1980 3.632257 0.275311 2.2701% 1979 3.551632 0.281561
1.0042% 1978 3.516322 0.284388 0.9896% 1977 3.481865 0.287202 0.9103% 1976 3.450455
0.289817 0.8394% 1975 3.421731 0.292250 0.9042% 1974 3.391070 0.294892 1.1568% 1973
3.352291 0.298303 0.9427% 1972 3.320984 0.301116 0.7426% 1971 3.296503 0.303352
1.4697% 1970 3.248755 0.307810 0.6968% 1969 3.226274 0.309955 0.8565% 1968 3.198874
0.312610 1.5090% 1967 3.151320 0.317327 0.9949% 1966 3.120276 0.320485 1.0575% 1965
3.087625 0.323874 1.1300% 1964 3.053124 0.327533 1.5537% 1963 3.006415 0.332622
1.4658% 1962 2.962983 0.337498 1.5364% 1961 2.918148 0.342683 2.1586% 1960 2.856486
0.350080 -1.6655% 1959 2.904866 0.344250 4.3080% 1958 2.784893 0.359080 2.1130%
1957 2.727267 0.366667 1.9895% 1956 2.674067 0.373962 2.1231% 1955 2.618474 0.381902
1.4496% 1954 2.581059 0.387438 2.1573% 1953 2.526555 0.395796 1.2298% 1952 2.495862
0.400663 1.6814% 1951 2.454591 0.407400 1.6233% 1950 2.415383 0.414013 1.4265% 1949
2.381411 0.419919 1.7790% 1948 2.339785 0.427390 1.8242% 1947 2.297868 0.435186 -
2.6320% 1946 2.359984 0.423732 3.1768% 1945 2.287320 0.437193 6.4754% 1944 2.148214
0.465503 -0.3437% 1943 2.155623 0.463903 0.6562% 1942 2.141569 0.466947 0.6633%
1941 2.127458 0.470045 -5.6614% 1940 2.255131 0.443433 8.0381% 1939 2.087347
0.479077 0.8126% 1938 2.070522 0.482970 0.7762% 1937 2.054573 0.486719 0.6029% 1936
2.042261 0.489653 0.5244% 1935 2.031607 0.492221 -3.0364% 1934 2.095226 0.477276
4.6271% 1933 2.002565 0.499360 1.3921% 1932 1.975069 0.506311 -0.2051% 1931
1.979128 0.505273 0.8886% 1930 1.961697 0.509763 1.0126% 1929 1.942032 0.514925
1.1526% 1928 1.919903 0.520860 1.2160% 1927 1.896838 0.527193 1.4086% 1926 1.870490
0.534619 1.7667% 1925 1.838018 0.544064 1.4465% 1924 1.811810 0.551934 1.7700% 1923
1.780300 0.561703 1.6165% 1922 1.751979 0.570783 1.3736% 1921 1.728239 0.578624
2.3393% 1920 1.688734 0.592160 1.3140% 1919 1.666832 0.599941 0.7676% 1918 1.654134
0.604546 0.3870% 1917 1.647757 0.606886 1.3274% 1916 1.626171 0.614942 1.4083% 1915
1.603588 0.623602 1.4458% 1914 1.580733 0.632618 1.9424% 1913 1.550615 0.644906
1.9857% 1912 1.520424 0.657711 1.5634% 1911 1.497019 0.667994 1.8169% 1910 1.470305
0.680131 1.8781% 1909 1.443201 0.692904 2.0082% 1908 1.414789 0.706819 1.9603% 1907

178

1.387588 0.720675 1.8264% 1906 1.362701 0.733837 1.9357% 1905 1.336824 0.748042
2.0148% 1904 1.310421 0.763113 2.1335% 1903 1.283047 0.779395 1.8151% 1902 1.260173
0.793542 1.8943% 1901 1.236745 0.808574 3.0255% 1900 1.200426 0.833038 0.6278% 1899
1.192936 0.838268 1.7757% 1898 1.172123 0.853153 1.8078% 1897 1.151310 0.868575
1.8396% 1896 1.130514 0.884554 1.8755% 1895 1.109701 0.901144 1.9114% 1894 1.088888
0.918368 1.9486% 1893 1.068075 0.936264 1.9858% 1892 1.047278 0.954856 2.0276% 1891
1.026465 0.974217 2.6465% 1890 1.000000 1.000000 1.5328% 1889 0.984903 1.015328
2.0811% 1888 0.964824 1.036458 2.1599% 1887 0.944426 1.058844 2.2075% 1886 0.924028
1.082219 2.2592% 1885 0.903613 1.106668 2.3095% 1884 0.883215 1.132227 2.3641% 1883
0.862817 1.158994 2.4214% 1882 0.842419 1.187058 2.4815% 1881 0.822021 1.216515
3.7644% 1880 0.792199 1.262309 0.9432% 1879 0.784797 1.274215 2.1464% 1878 0.768306
1.301565 2.1913% 1877 0.751831 1.330086 2.2426% 1876 0.735340 1.359915 2.2941% 1875
0.718849 1.391112 2.3456% 1874 0.702375 1.423742 2.4043% 1873 0.685884 1.457973
2.4635% 1872 0.669393 1.493891 2.5258% 1871 0.652902 1.531623 5.9947% 1870 0.615976
1.623439 -1.0968% 1869 0.622807 1.605633 2.1930% 1868 0.609442 1.640845 2.2394%
1867 0.596093 1.677590 2.2935% 1866 0.582728 1.716065 2.3445% 1865 0.569379 1.756298
2.4037% 1864 0.556015 1.798514 2.4599% 1863 0.542666 1.842755 2.5250% 1862 0.529301
1.889285 2.5872% 1861 0.515952 1.938165 2.9504% 1860 0.501165 1.995349 2.4012% 1859
0.489413 2.043262 2.7627% 1858 0.476256 2.099712 2.8412% 1857 0.463098 2.159369
2.9243% 1856 0.449941 2.222515 3.0161% 1855 0.436767 2.289549 3.1061% 1854 0.423610
2.360664 3.2056% 1853 0.410452 2.436338 3.3118% 1852 0.397295 2.517024 3.4252% 1851
0.384137 2.603238 4.0106% 1850 0.369325 2.707644 3.3254% 1849 0.360932 2.770606
2.7841% 1848 0.351155 2.847742 2.8590% 1847 0.341395 2.929160 2.9432% 1846 0.331634
3.015369 3.0324% 1845 0.321874 3.106808 3.1325% 1844 0.312097 3.204129 3.2284% 1843
0.302337 3.307569 3.3361% 1842 0.292576 3.417912 3.4512% 1841 0.282816 3.535871
3.8105% 1840 0.272435 3.670604 2.3861% 1839 0.266086 3.758187 2.5824% 1838 0.259387
3.855238 2.6573% 1837 0.252673 3.957684 2.7232% 1836 0.245975 4.065460 2.7994% 1835
0.239276 4.179270 2.8871% 1834 0.232562 4.299931 2.9657% 1833 0.225863 4.427453
3.0563% 1832 0.219165 4.562770 3.1604% 1831 0.212451 4.706973 3.4660% 1830 0.205334
4.870115 2.4653% 1829 0.200394 4.990178 2.6804% 1828 0.195163 5.123935 10.3427%
1827 0.176870 5.653886 -4.2314% 1826 0.184684 5.414645 2.9150% 1825 0.179453
5.572484 3.0026% 1824 0.174222 5.739802 3.0955% 1823 0.168991 5.917478 3.1944% 1822
0.163760 6.106505 3.3102% 1821 0.158513 6.308642 3.2277% 1820 0.153556 6.512268
2.6573% 1819 0.149582 6.685317 2.6261% 1818 0.145754 6.860881 2.6969% 1817 0.141926
7.045914 2.7717% 1816 0.138099 7.241205 2.8507% 1815 0.134271 7.447629 2.9343% 1814
0.130443 7.666168 3.0231% 1813 0.126616 7.897921 3.1039% 1812 0.122804 8.143064
3.2172% 1811 0.118976 8.405039 3.0969% 1810 0.115402 8.665336 2.9144% 1809 0.112134
8.917877 2.8225% 1808 0.109056 9.169581 2.9199% 1807 0.105962 9.437326 2.9918% 1806
0.102884 9.719670 3.0841% 1805 0.099806 10.019430 3.1822% 1804 0.096728 10.338267
3.2868% 1803 0.093650 10.678064 3.3985% 1802 0.090572 11.040957 3.5180% 1801
0.087494 11.429382 3.3999% 1800 0.084617 11.817975 2.8419% 1799 0.082279 12.153827
2.7485% 1798 0.080078 12.487869 2.8261% 1797 0.077877 12.840793 3.7832% 1796
0.075038 13.326587 2.1272% 1795 0.073475 13.610070 3.0879% 1794 0.071274 14.030341
3.1625% 1793 0.069089 14.474052 3.2904% 1792 0.066888 14.950308 3.4024% 1791
0.064687 15.458972 3.2296% 1790 0.062664 15.958230 41.3145% 1780 0.044343 22.551285
29.4353% 1770 0.034259 29.189326 83.4728% 1750 0.018673 53.554486 29.2845% 1740
0.014443 69.237624 94.2514% 1720 0.007435 134.495049 85.8111% 1700 0.004001
249.906704 19.2490% 1690 0.003356 298.011369 88.0250% 1670 0.001785 560.335943
BASE YEAR: 1889
YEAR BYEAR/AYEAR AYEAR/BYEAR GROWTH%
2009 4.881068 0.204873 8.2857% 2001 4.507585 0.221848 1.0000% 2000 4.462955
0.224067 1.0000% 1999 4.418767 0.226307 1.0000% 1998 4.375017 0.228571 1.0000% 1997
4.331700 0.230856 1.0000% 1996 4.288812 0.233165 1.0000% 1995 4.246348 0.235496
0.9992% 1994 4.204338 0.237850 1.0008% 1993 4.162678 0.240230 1.0000% 1992 4.121464
0.242632 0.9295% 1991 4.083507 0.244888 1.2505% 1990 4.033073 0.247950 0.7224% 1989
4.004145 0.249741 1.1077% 1988 3.960279 0.252507 0.8834% 1987 3.925601 0.254738

179

0.5594% 1986 3.903765 0.256163 1.3056% 1985 3.853453 0.259508 0.7673% 1984 3.824111
0.261499 0.8149% 1983 3.793199 0.263630 0.9737% 1982 3.756619 0.266197 0.9508% 1981
3.721237 0.268728 0.9031% 1980 3.687933 0.271155 2.2701% 1979 3.606072 0.277310
1.0042% 1978 3.570221 0.280095 0.9896% 1977 3.535236 0.282867 0.9103% 1976 3.503344
0.285442 0.8394% 1975 3.474180 0.287838 0.9042% 1974 3.443049 0.290440 1.1568% 1973
3.403676 0.293800 0.9427% 1972 3.371889 0.296570 0.7426% 1971 3.347033 0.298772
1.4697% 1970 3.298553 0.303163 0.6968% 1969 3.275727 0.305276 0.8565% 1968 3.247907
0.307891 1.5090% 1967 3.199624 0.312537 0.9949% 1966 3.168104 0.315646 1.0575% 1965
3.134953 0.318984 1.1300% 1964 3.099923 0.322589 1.5537% 1963 3.052498 0.327601
1.4658% 1962 3.008400 0.332403 1.5364% 1961 2.962877 0.337510 2.1586% 1960 2.900271
0.344795 -1.6655% 1959 2.949393 0.339053 4.3080% 1958 2.827581 0.353659 2.1130%
1957 2.769071 0.361132 1.9895% 1956 2.715055 0.368317 2.1231% 1955 2.658611 0.376136
1.4496% 1954 2.620622 0.381589 2.1573% 1953 2.565282 0.389821 1.2298% 1952 2.534119
0.394615 1.6814% 1951 2.492215 0.401249 1.6233% 1950 2.452406 0.407763 1.4265% 1949
2.417914 0.413580 1.7790% 1948 2.375650 0.420937 1.8242% 1947 2.333090 0.428616 -
2.6320% 1946 2.396158 0.417335 3.1768% 1945 2.322381 0.430593 6.4754% 1944 2.181143
0.458475 -0.3437% 1943 2.188665 0.456900 0.6562% 1942 2.174396 0.459898 0.6633%
1941 2.160068 0.462948 -5.6614% 1940 2.289698 0.436739 8.0381% 1939 2.119343
0.471844 0.8126% 1938 2.102259 0.475679 0.7762% 1937 2.086066 0.479371 0.6029% 1936
2.073565 0.482261 0.5244% 1935 2.062748 0.484790 -3.0364% 1934 2.127342 0.470070
4.6271% 1933 2.033260 0.491821 1.3921% 1932 2.005344 0.498668 -0.2051% 1931
2.009465 0.497645 0.8886% 1930 1.991766 0.502067 1.0126% 1929 1.971800 0.507151
1.1526% 1928 1.949332 0.512996 1.2160% 1927 1.925913 0.519234 1.4086% 1926 1.899162
0.526548 1.7667% 1925 1.866192 0.535851 1.4465% 1924 1.839582 0.543602 1.7700% 1923
1.807588 0.553223 1.6165% 1922 1.778833 0.562166 1.3736% 1921 1.754730 0.569888
2.3393% 1920 1.714619 0.583220 1.3140% 1919 1.692381 0.590883 0.7676% 1918 1.679489
0.595419 0.3870% 1917 1.673014 0.597724 1.3274% 1916 1.651097 0.605658 1.4083% 1915
1.628168 0.614187 1.4458% 1914 1.604963 0.623067 1.9424% 1913 1.574383 0.635170
1.9857% 1912 1.543729 0.647782 1.5634% 1911 1.519966 0.657909 1.8169% 1910 1.492842
0.669863 1.8781% 1909 1.465323 0.682444 2.0082% 1908 1.436475 0.696149 1.9603% 1907
1.408858 0.709795 1.8264% 1906 1.383588 0.722758 1.9357% 1905 1.357315 0.736749
2.0148% 1904 1.330508 0.751593 2.1335% 1903 1.302714 0.767628 1.8151% 1902 1.279489
0.781562 1.8943% 1901 1.255702 0.796367 3.0255% 1900 1.218826 0.820461 0.6278% 1899
1.211222 0.825613 1.7757% 1898 1.190090 0.840273 1.8078% 1897 1.168958 0.855463
1.8396% 1896 1.147842 0.871200 1.8755% 1895 1.126710 0.887540 1.9114% 1894 1.105578
0.904504 1.9486% 1893 1.084447 0.922129 1.9858% 1892 1.063331 0.940441 2.0276% 1891
1.042199 0.959510 2.6465% 1890 1.015328 0.984903 1.5328% 1889 1.000000 1.000000
2.0811% 1888 0.979613 1.020811 2.1599% 1887 0.958902 1.042859 2.2075% 1886 0.938191
1.065881 2.2592% 1885 0.917464 1.089961 2.3095% 1884 0.896753 1.115134 2.3641% 1883
0.876042 1.141497 2.4214% 1882 0.855332 1.169137 2.4815% 1881 0.834621 1.198149
3.7644% 1880 0.804342 1.243252 0.9432% 1879 0.796826 1.254979 2.1464% 1878 0.780083
1.281916 2.1913% 1877 0.763355 1.310006 2.2426% 1876 0.746612 1.339384 2.2941% 1875
0.729868 1.370111 2.3456% 1874 0.713141 1.402248 2.4043% 1873 0.696397 1.435962
2.4635% 1872 0.679653 1.471338 2.5258% 1871 0.662910 1.508501 5.9947% 1870 0.625418
1.598930 -1.0968% 1869 0.632354 1.581394 2.1930% 1868 0.618784 1.616073 2.2394%
1867 0.605230 1.652263 2.2935% 1866 0.591661 1.690158 2.3445% 1865 0.578107 1.729783
2.4037% 1864 0.564537 1.771362 2.4599% 1863 0.550984 1.814936 2.5250% 1862 0.537414
1.860763 2.5872% 1861 0.523860 1.908905 2.9504% 1860 0.508847 1.965226 2.4012% 1859
0.496915 2.012416 2.7627% 1858 0.483556 2.068013 2.8412% 1857 0.470197 2.126769
2.9243% 1856 0.456838 2.188962 3.0161% 1855 0.443462 2.254984 3.1061% 1854 0.430103
2.325025 3.2056% 1853 0.416744 2.399557 3.3118% 1852 0.403384 2.479025 3.4252% 1851
0.390025 2.563938 4.0106% 1850 0.374986 2.666767 2.3254% 1849 0.366464 2.728779
2.7841% 1848 0.356538 2.804751 2.8590% 1847 0.346628 2.884939 2.9432% 1846 0.336718
2.969847 3.0324% 1845 0.326808 3.059905 3.1325% 1844 0.316881 3.155757 3.2284% 1843
0.306971 3.257636 3.3361% 1842 0.297061 3.366312 3.4512% 1841 0.287151 3.482490
3.8105% 1840 0.276611 3.615190 2.3861% 1839 0.270164 3.701450 2.5824% 1838 0.263363

3.797036 2.6573% 1837 0.256546 3.897936 2.7232% 1836 0.249745 4.004085 2.7994% 1835
0.242944 4.116177 2.8871% 1834 0.236127 4.235016 2.9657% 1833 0.229326 4.360613
3.0563% 1832 0.222524 4.493887 3.1604% 1831 0.215707 4.635913 3.4660% 1830 0.208481
4.796592 2.4653% 1829 0.203465 4.914843 2.6804% 1828 0.198154 5.046580 10.3427%
1827 0.179581 5.568530 -4.2314% 1826 0.187515 5.332902 2.9150% 1825 0.182204
5.488358 3.0026% 1824 0.176893 5.653149 3.0955% 1823 0.171581 5.828143 3.1944% 1822
0.166270 6.014316 3.3102% 1821 0.160942 6.213402 3.2277% 1820 0.155910 6.413954
2.6573% 1819 0.151874 6.584391 2.6261% 1818 0.147988 6.757304 2.6969% 1817 0.144102
6.939544 2.7717% 1816 0.140215 7.131886 2.8507% 1815 0.136329 7.335194 2.9343% 1814
0.132443 7.550434 3.0231% 1813 0.128556 7.778687 3.1039% 1812 0.124686 8.020130
3.2172% 1811 0.120800 8.278150 3.0969% 1810 0.117171 8.534517 2.9144% 1809 0.113853
8.783246 2.8225% 1808 0.110728 9.031149 2.9199% 1807 0.107586 9.294852 2.9918% 1806
0.104461 9.572934 3.0841% 1805 0.101336 9.868169 3.1822% 1804 0.098211 10.182193
3.2868% 1803 0.095085 10.516860 3.3985% 1802 0.091960 10.874274 3.5180% 1801
0.088835 11.256836 3.3999% 1800 0.085914 11.639562 2.8419% 1799 0.083540 11.970343
2.7485% 1798 0.081305 12.299343 2.8261% 1797 0.079071 12.646938 3.7832% 1796
0.076188 13.125399 2.1272% 1795 0.074601 13.404602 3.0879% 1794 0.072367 13.818528
3.1625% 1793 0.070148 14.255540 3.2904% 1792 0.067914 14.724607 3.4024% 1791
0.065679 15.225592 3.2296% 1790 0.063624 15.717312 41.3145% 1780 0.045023 22.210833
29.4353% 1770 0.034784 28.748662 83.4728% 1750 0.018959 52.745986 29.2845% 1740
0.014664 68.192359 94.2514% 1720 0.007549 132.464607 85.8111% 1700 0.004063
246.133918 19.2490% 1690 0.003407 293.512357 88.0250% 1670 0.001812 551.876676

BASE YEAR: 1888

YEAR BYEAR/AYEAR AYEAR AYEAR/BYEAR GROWTH%

2009 4.982649 0.200696 8.2857% 2001 4.601393 0.217325 1.0000% 2000 4.555835
0.219499 1.0000% 1999 4.510727 0.221694 1.0000% 1998 4.466067 0.223911 1.0000% 1997
4.421848 0.226150 1.0000% 1996 4.378068 0.228411 1.0000% 1995 4.334720 0.230695
0.9992% 1994 4.291835 0.233001 1.0008% 1993 4.249309 0.235332 1.0000% 1992 4.207237
0.237686 0.9295% 1991 4.168490 0.239895 1.2505% 1990 4.117007 0.242895 0.7224% 1989
4.087477 0.244650 1.1077% 1988 4.042697 0.247360 0.8834% 1987 4.007298 0.249545
0.5594% 1986 3.985007 0.250941 1.3056% 1985 3.933649 0.254217 0.7673% 1984 3.903696
0.256167 0.8149% 1983 3.872140 0.258255 0.9737% 1982 3.834799 0.260770 0.9508% 1981
3.798681 0.263249 0.9031% 1980 3.764683 0.265627 2.2701% 1979 3.681119 0.271656
1.0042% 1978 3.644522 0.274384 0.9896% 1977 3.608809 0.277100 0.9103% 1976 3.576253
0.279622 0.8394% 1975 3.546482 0.281970 0.9042% 1974 3.514703 0.284519 1.1568% 1973
3.474511 0.287810 0.9427% 1972 3.442062 0.290524 0.7426% 1971 3.416689 0.292681
1.4697% 1970 3.367200 0.296983 0.6968% 1969 3.343899 0.299052 0.8565% 1968 3.315500
0.301614 1.5090% 1967 3.266212 0.306165 0.9949% 1966 3.234036 0.309211 1.0575% 1965
3.200195 0.312481 1.1300% 1964 3.164436 0.316012 1.5537% 1963 3.116024 0.320922
1.4658% 1962 3.071009 0.325626 1.5364% 1961 3.024539 0.330629 2.1586% 1960 2.960629
0.337766 -1.6655% 1959 3.010773 0.332141 4.3080% 1958 2.886426 0.346449 2.1130%
1957 2.826699 0.353770 1.9895% 1956 2.771559 0.360808 2.1231% 1955 2.713940 0.368468
1.4496% 1954 2.675160 0.373809 2.1573% 1953 2.618669 0.381873 1.2298% 1952 2.586857
0.386569 1.6814% 1951 2.544081 0.393069 1.6233% 1950 2.503444 0.399450 1.4265% 1949
2.468233 0.405148 1.7790% 1948 2.425090 0.412356 1.8242% 1947 2.381645 0.419878 -
2.6320% 1946 2.446025 0.408827 3.1768% 1945 2.370713 0.421814 6.4754% 1944 2.226535
0.449128 -0.3437% 1943 2.234214 0.447585 0.6562% 1942 2.219648 0.450522 0.6633%
1941 2.205022 0.453510 -5.6614% 1940 2.337349 0.427835 8.0381% 1939 2.163449
0.462225 0.8126% 1938 2.146010 0.465981 0.7762% 1937 2.129480 0.469598 0.6029% 1936
2.116718 0.472429 0.5244% 1935 2.105676 0.474907 -3.0364% 1934 2.171615 0.460487
4.6271% 1933 2.075575 0.481794 1.3921% 1932 2.047077 0.488501 -0.2051% 1931
2.051284 0.487499 0.8886% 1930 2.033217 0.491831 1.0126% 1929 2.012836 0.496812
1.1526% 1928 1.989900 0.502538 1.2160% 1927 1.965994 0.508649 1.4086% 1926 1.938686
0.515813 1.7667% 1925 1.905030 0.524926 1.4465% 1924 1.877866 0.532519 1.7700% 1923
1.845207 0.541945 1.6165% 1922 1.815853 0.550705 1.3736% 1921 1.791248 0.558270
2.3393% 1920 1.750303 0.571330 1.3140% 1919 1.727602 0.578837 0.7676% 1918 1.714441

181

0.583280 0.3870% 1917 1.707832 0.585538 1.3274% 1916 1.685459 0.593310 1.4083% 1915
1.662052 0.601666 1.4458% 1914 1.638365 0.610365 1.9424% 1913 1.607148 0.622220
1.9857% 1912 1.575856 0.634576 1.5634% 1911 1.551598 0.644497 1.8169% 1910 1.523910
0.656207 1.8781% 1909 1.495818 0.668531 2.0082% 1908 1.466370 0.681956 1.9603% 1907
1.438178 0.695324 1.8264% 1906 1.412383 0.708023 1.9357% 1905 1.385563 0.721728
2.0148% 1904 1.358197 0.736270 2.1335% 1903 1.329825 0.751979 1.8151% 1902 1.306117
0.765628 1.8943% 1901 1.281835 0.780132 3.0255% 1900 1.244192 0.803735 6.6278% 1899
1.236429 0.808781 1.7757% 1898 1.214857 0.823142 1.8078% 1897 1.193286 0.838022
1.8396% 1896 1.171730 0.853439 1.8755% 1895 1.150159 0.869445 1.9114% 1894 1.128587
0.886064 1.9486% 1893 1.107015 0.903330 1.9858% 1892 1.085460 0.921268 2.0276% 1891
1.063889 0.939948 2.6465% 1890 1.036458 0.964824 1.5328% 1889 1.020811 0.979613
2.0811% 1888 1.000000 1.000000 2.1599% 1887 0.978858 1.021599 2.2075% 1886 0.957716
1.044151 2.2592% 1885 0.936558 1.067740 2.3095% 1884 0.915416 1.092400 2.3641% 1883
0.894274 1.118226 2.4214% 1882 0.873132 1.145302 2.4815% 1881 0.851990 1.173722
3.7644% 1880 0.821081 1.217906 0.9432% 1879 0.813409 1.229394 2.1464% 1878 0.796317
1.255781 2.1913% 1877 0.779242 1.283299 2.2426% 1876 0.762150 1.312078 2.2941% 1875
0.745058 1.342178 2.3456% 1874 0.727982 1.373660 2.4043% 1873 0.710890 1.406687
2.4635% 1872 0.693798 1.441342 2.5258% 1871 0.676706 1.477747 5.9947% 1870 0.638434
1.566333 -1.0968% 1869 0.645514 1.549154 2.1930% 1868 0.631662 1.583126 2.2394%
1867 0.617826 1.618579 2.2935% 1866 0.603974 1.655701 2.3445% 1865 0.590138 1.694518
2.4037% 1864 0.576286 1.735249 2.4599% 1863 0.562450 1.777935 2.5250% 1862 0.548598
1.822828 2.5872% 1861 0.534763 1.869989 2.9504% 1860 0.519437 1.925161 2.4012% 1859
0.507257 1.971389 2.7627% 1858 0.493619 2.025852 2.8412% 1857 0.479982 2.083411
2.9243% 1856 0.466345 2.144336 3.0161% 1855 0.452691 2.209012 3.1061% 1854 0.439054
2.277625 3.2056% 1853 0.425417 2.350637 3.3118% 1852 0.411779 2.428485 3.4252% 1851
0.398142 2.511667 4.0106% 1850 0.382790 2.612400 2.3254% 1849 0.374091 2.673147
2.7841% 1848 0.363958 2.747570 2.8590% 1847 0.353842 2.826124 2.9432% 1846 0.343725
2.909301 3.0324% 1845 0.333609 2.997523 3.1325% 1844 0.323476 3.091420 3.2284% 1843
0.313360 3.191222 3.3361% 1842 0.303243 3.297683 3.4512% 1841 0.293127 3.411493
3.8105% 1840 0.282367 3.541487 2.3861% 1839 0.275787 3.625989 2.5824% 1838 0.268844
3.719626 2.6573% 1837 0.261885 3.818469 2.7232% 1836 0.254942 3.922453 2.7994% 1835
0.248000 4.032260 2.8871% 1834 0.241041 4.148676 2.9657% 1833 0.234098 4.271713
3.0563% 1832 0.227156 4.402270 3.1604% 1831 0.220196 4.541401 3.4660% 1830 0.212820
4.698804 2.4653% 1829 0.207700 4.814644 2.6804% 1828 0.202278 4.943695 10.3427%
1827 0.183318 5.455005 -4.2314% 1826 0.191418 5.224180 2.9150% 1825 0.185996
5.376466 3.0026% 1824 0.180574 5.537898 3.0955% 1823 0.175152 5.709324 3.1944% 1822
0.169730 5.891702 3.3102% 1821 0.164292 6.086729 3.2277% 1820 0.159155 6.283193
2.6573% 1819 0.155035 6.450155 2.6261% 1818 0.151068 6.619543 2.6969% 1817 0.147101
6.798067 2.7717% 1816 0.143133 6.986488 2.8507% 1815 0.139166 7.185652 2.9343% 1814
0.135199 7.396503 3.0231% 1813 0.131232 7.620103 3.1039% 1812 0.127281 7.856623
3.2172% 1811 0.123314 8.109383 3.0969% 1810 0.119610 8.360524 2.9144% 1809 0.116223
8.604181 2.8225% 1808 0.113032 8.847031 2.9199% 1807 0.109825 9.105358 2.9918% 1806
0.106635 9.377771 3.0841% 1805 0.103445 9.666986 3.1822% 1804 0.100255 9.974608
3.2868% 1803 0.097064 10.302452 3.3985% 1802 0.093874 10.652580 3.5180% 1801
0.090684 11.027342 3.3999% 1800 0.087702 11.402266 2.8419% 1799 0.085278 11.726304
2.7485% 1798 0.082997 12.048596 2.8261% 1797 0.080716 12.389105 3.7832% 1796
0.077774 12.857811 2.1272% 1795 0.076154 13.131322 3.0879% 1794 0.073873 13.536809
3.1625% 1793 0.071608 13.964912 3.2904% 1792 0.069327 14.424416 3.4024% 1791
0.067046 14.915187 3.2296% 1790 0.064948 15.396883 41.3145% 1780 0.045960 21.758020
29.4353% 1770 0.035508 28.162562 83.4728% 1750 0.019353 51.670653 29.2845% 1740
0.014970 66.802120 94.2514% 1720 0.007706 129.764050 85.8111% 1700 0.004147
241.115982 19.2490% 1690 0.003478 287.528517 88.0250% 1670 0.001850 540.625559

    BASE YEAR: 1887
    YEAR BYEAR/AYEAR AYEAR/BYEAR GROWTH%
     2009 5.090267 0.196453 8.2857% 2001 4.700777 0.212731 1.0000% 2000 4.654234
0.214858 1.0000% 1999 4.608152 0.217007 1.0000% 1998 4.562527 0.219177 1.0000% 1997

182

4.517354 0.221369 1.0000% 1996 4.472627 0.223582 1.0000% 1995 4.428344 0.225818 0.9992% 1994 4.384533 0.228074 1.0008% 1993 4.341088 0.230357 1.0000% 1992 4.298107 0.232661 0.9295% 1991 4.258524 0.234823 1.2505% 1990 4.205928 0.237760 0.7224% 1989 4.175760 0.239477 1.1077% 1988 4.130013 0.242130 0.8834% 1987 4.093850 0.244269 0.5594% 1986 4.071078 0.245635 1.3056% 1985 4.018610 0.248842 0.7673% 1984 3.988010 0.250752 0.8149% 1983 3.955773 0.252795 0.9737% 1982 3.917625 0.255257 0.9508% 1981 3.880727 0.257684 0.9031% 1980 3.845995 0.260011 2.2701% 1979 3.760626 0.265913 1.0042% 1978 3.723238 0.268583 0.9896% 1977 3.686754 0.271241 0.9103% 1976 3.653495 0.273711 0.8394% 1975 3.623081 0.276008 0.9042% 1974 3.590616 0.278504 1.1568% 1973 3.549555 0.281725 0.9427% 1972 3.516406 0.284381 0.7426% 1971 3.490484 0.286493 1.4697% 1970 3.439926 0.290704 0.6968% 1969 3.416122 0.292730 0.8565% 1968 3.387110 0.295237 1.5090% 1967 3.336757 0.299692 0.9949% 1966 3.303887 0.302674 1.0575% 1965 3.269315 0.305875 1.1300% 1964 3.232784 0.309331 1.5537% 1963 3.183326 0.314137 1.4658% 1962 3.137338 0.318742 1.5364% 1961 3.089864 0.323639 2.1586% 1960 3.024575 0.330625 -1.6655% 1959 3.075802 0.325118 4.3080% 1958 2.948769 0.339125 2.1130% 1957 2.887752 0.346290 1.9895% 1956 2.831421 0.353180 2.1231% 1955 2.772557 0.360678 1.4496% 1954 2.732940 0.365906 2.1573% 1953 2.675228 0.373800 1.2298% 1952 2.642729 0.378397 1.6814% 1951 2.599030 0.384759 1.6233% 1950 2.557514 0.391005 1.4265% 1949 2.521544 0.396582 1.7790% 1948 2.477468 0.403638 1.8242% 1947 2.433085 0.411001 -2.6320% 1946 2.498856 0.400183 3.1768% 1945 2.421916 0.412896 6.4754% 1944 2.274625 0.439633 -0.3437% 1943 2.282469 0.438122 0.6562% 1942 2.267589 0.440997 0.6633% 1941 2.252647 0.443922 -5.6614% 1940 2.387832 0.418790 8.0381% 1939 2.210176 0.452453 0.8126% 1938 2.192360 0.456129 0.7762% 1937 2.175473 0.459670 0.6029% 1936 2.162436 0.462441 0.5244% 1935 2.151156 0.464866 -3.0364% 1934 2.218518 0.450751 4.6271% 1933 2.120405 0.471608 1.3921% 1932 2.091291 0.478173 -0.2051% 1931 2.095589 0.477193 0.8886% 1930 2.077132 0.481433 1.0126% 1929 2.056310 0.486308 1.1526% 1928 2.032879 0.491913 1.2160% 1927 2.008456 0.497895 1.4086% 1926 1.980558 0.504908 1.7667% 1925 1.946176 0.513828 1.4465% 1924 1.918425 0.521261 1.7700% 1923 1.885060 0.530487 1.6165% 1922 1.855073 0.539062 1.3736% 1921 1.829936 0.546467 2.3393% 1920 1.788107 0.559251 1.3140% 1919 1.764915 0.566599 0.7676% 1918 1.751470 0.570949 0.3870% 1917 1.744719 0.573158 1.3274% 1916 1.721862 0.580767 1.4083% 1915 1.697950 0.588946 1.4458% 1914 1.673751 0.597461 1.9424% 1913 1.641860 0.609065 1.9857% 1912 1.609892 0.621160 1.5634% 1911 1.585111 0.630871 1.8169% 1910 1.556824 0.642333 1.8781% 1909 1.528125 0.654397 2.0082% 1908 1.498041 0.667538 1.9603% 1907 1.469240 0.680624 1.8264% 1906 1.442888 0.693054 1.9357% 1905 1.415489 0.706470 2.0148% 1904 1.387532 0.720704 2.1335% 1903 1.358547 0.736080 1.8151% 1902 1.334327 0.749441 1.8943% 1901 1.309520 0.763638 3.0255% 1900 1.271064 0.786742 0.6278% 1899 1.263134 0.791682 1.7757% 1898 1.241096 0.805739 1.8078% 1897 1.219059 0.820305 1.8396% 1896 1.197038 0.835395 1.8755% 1895 1.175000 0.851064 1.9114% 1894 1.152963 0.867331 1.9486% 1893 1.130925 0.884232 1.9858% 1892 1.108905 0.901791 2.0276% 1891 1.086867 0.920076 2.6465% 1890 1.058844 0.944426 1.5328% 1889 1.042859 0.958902 2.0811% 1888 1.021599 0.978858 2.1599% 1887 1.000000 1.000000 2.2075% 1886 0.978401 1.022075 2.2592% 1885 0.956786 1.045166 2.3095% 1884 0.935188 1.069304 2.3641% 1883 0.913589 1.094584 2.4214% 1882 0.891990 1.121088 2.4815% 1881 0.870392 1.148908 3.7644% 1880 0.838816 1.192157 0.9432% 1879 0.830978 1.203402 2.1464% 1878 0.813516 1.229232 2.1913% 1877 0.796072 1.256168 2.2426% 1876 0.778611 1.284339 2.2941% 1875 0.761150 1.313802 2.3456% 1874 0.743705 1.344619 2.4043% 1873 0.726244 1.376947 2.4635% 1872 0.708783 1.410869 2.5258% 1871 0.691322 1.446504 5.9947% 1870 0.652223 1.533218 -1.0968% 1869 0.659456 1.516402 2.1930% 1868 0.645305 1.549656 2.2394% 1867 0.631170 1.584359 2.2935% 1866 0.617019 1.620696 2.3445% 1865 0.602884 1.658693 2.4037% 1864 0.588733 1.698563 2.4599% 1863 0.574599 1.740346 2.5250% 1862 0.560447 1.784290 2.5872% 1861 0.546313 1.830453 2.9504% 1860 0.530656 1.884459 2.4012% 1859 0.518213 1.929710 2.7627% 1858 0.504281 1.983022 2.8412% 1857 0.490349 2.039364 2.9243% 1856 0.476417 2.099000 3.0161% 1855 0.462469 2.162309 3.1061% 1854 0.448537 2.229472 3.2056% 1853 0.434605 2.300940 3.3118% 1852 0.420673 2.377143 3.4252% 1851 0.406741 2.458565 4.0106% 1850 0.391058 2.557168 2.3254% 1849 0.382171 2.616632

2.7841% 1848 0.371819 2.689481 2.8590% 1847 0.361484 2.766374 2.9432% 1846 0.351149
2.847793 3.0324% 1845 0.340814 2.934149 3.1325% 1844 0.330463 3.026062 3.2284% 1843
0.320128 3.123754 3.3361% 1842 0.309793 3.227964 3.4512% 1841 0.299458 3.339367
3.8105% 1840 0.288466 3.466613 2.3861% 1839 0.281743 3.549329 2.5824% 1838 0.274651
3.640986 2.6573% 1837 0.267541 3.737739 2.7232% 1836 0.260449 3.839525 2.7994% 1835
0.253356 3.947011 2.8871% 1834 0.246247 4.060966 2.9657% 1833 0.239154 4.181401
3.0563% 1832 0.232062 4.309198 3.1604% 1831 0.224952 4.445387 3.4660% 1830 0.217417
4.599463 2.4653% 1829 0.212186 4.712853 2.6804% 1828 0.206647 4.839176 10.3427%
1827 0.187277 5.339675 -4.2314% 1826 0.195552 5.113731 2.9150% 1825 0.190013
5.262798 3.0026% 1824 0.184474 5.420817 3.0955% 1823 0.178935 5.588618 3.1944% 1822
0.173396 5.767141 3.3102% 1821 0.167840 5.958044 3.2277% 1820 0.162592 6.150354
2.6573% 1819 0.158384 6.313786 2.6261% 1818 0.154331 6.479593 2.6969% 1817 0.150278
6.654343 2.7717% 1816 0.146225 6.838780 2.8507% 1815 0.142172 7.033733 2.9343% 1814
0.138119 7.240127 3.0231% 1813 0.134066 7.459000 3.1039% 1812 0.130030 7.690519
3.2172% 1811 0.125977 7.937936 3.0969% 1810 0.122193 8.183767 2.9144% 1809 0.118733
8.422273 2.8225% 1808 0.115474 8.659988 2.9199% 1807 0.112198 8.912854 2.9918% 1806
0.108938 9.179507 3.0841% 1805 0.105679 9.462608 3.1822% 1804 0.102420 9.763726
3.2868% 1803 0.099161 10.084639 3.3985% 1802 0.095902 10.427364 3.5180% 1801
0.092642 10.794203 3.3999% 1800 0.089596 11.161201 2.8419% 1799 0.087120 11.478387
2.7485% 1798 0.084790 11.793866 2.8261% 1797 0.082459 12.127176 3.7832% 1796
0.079454 12.585972 2.1272% 1795 0.077799 12.853701 3.0879% 1794 0.075468 13.250615
3.1625% 1793 0.073155 13.669668 3.2904% 1792 0.070824 14.119456 3.4024% 1791
0.068494 14.599852 3.2296% 1790 0.066351 15.071364 41.3145% 1780 0.046953 21.298015
29.4353% 1770 0.036275 27.567152 83.4728% 1750 0.019771 50.578237 29.2845% 1740
0.015293 65.389797 94.2514% 1720 0.007873 127.020592 85.8111% 1700 0.004237
236.018334 19.2490% 1690 0.003553 281.449620 88.0250% 1670 0.001890 529.195710

BASE YEAR: 1886
YEAR BYEAR/AYEAR AYEAR/BYEAR GROWTH%
2009 5.202636 0.192210 8.2857% 2001 4.804548 0.208136 1.0000% 2000 4.756978
0.210218 1.0000% 1999 4.709879 0.212320 1.0000% 1998 4.663246 0.214443 1.0000% 1997
4.617076 0.216587 1.0000% 1996 4.571362 0.218753 1.0000% 1995 4.526101 0.220941
0.9992% 1994 4.481323 0.223148 1.0008% 1993 4.436919 0.225382 1.0000% 1992 4.392989
0.227635 0.9295% 1991 4.352532 0.229751 1.2505% 1990 4.298775 0.232624 0.7224% 1989
4.267942 0.234305 1.1077% 1988 4.221185 0.236900 0.8834% 1987 4.184223 0.238993
0.5594% 1986 4.160948 0.240330 1.3056% 1985 4.107322 0.243468 0.7673% 1984 4.076047
0.245336 0.8149% 1983 4.043098 0.247335 0.9737% 1982 4.004108 0.249744 0.9508% 1981
3.966395 0.252118 0.9031% 1980 3.930897 0.254395 2.2701% 1979 3.843643 0.260170
1.0042% 1978 3.805430 0.262782 0.9896% 1977 3.768140 0.265383 0.9103% 1976 3.734147
0.267799 0.8394% 1975 3.703062 0.270047 0.9042% 1974 3.669880 0.272488 1.1568% 1973
3.627913 0.275641 0.9427% 1972 3.594032 0.278239 0.7426% 1971 3.567538 0.280305
1.4697% 1970 3.515864 0.284425 0.6968% 1969 3.491534 0.286407 0.8565% 1968 3.461882
0.288860 1.5090% 1967 3.410417 0.293219 0.9949% 1966 3.376821 0.296137 1.0575% 1965
3.341486 0.299268 1.1300% 1964 3.304148 0.302650 1.5537% 1963 3.253599 0.307352
1.4658% 1962 3.206596 0.311857 1.5364% 1961 3.158074 0.316649 2.1586% 1960 3.091343
0.323484 -1.6655% 1959 3.143701 0.318096 4.3080% 1958 3.013864 0.331800 2.1130%
1957 2.951500 0.338811 1.9895% 1956 2.893925 0.345551 2.1231% 1955 2.833762 0.352888
1.4496% 1954 2.793270 0.358003 2.1573% 1953 2.734285 0.365726 1.2298% 1952 2.701068
0.370224 1.6814% 1951 2.656404 0.376449 1.6233% 1950 2.613972 0.382560 1.4265% 1949
2.577208 0.388017 1.7790% 1948 2.532159 0.394920 1.8242% 1947 2.486796 0.402124 -
2.6320% 1946 2.554019 0.391540 3.1768% 1945 2.475381 0.403978 6.4754% 1944 2.324838
0.430137 -0.3437% 1943 2.332856 0.428659 0.6562% 1942 2.317647 0.431472 0.6633%
1941 2.302375 0.434334 -5.6614% 1940 2.440545 0.409745 8.0381% 1939 2.258966
0.442680 0.8126% 1938 2.240757 0.446278 0.7762% 1937 2.223498 0.449742 0.6029% 1936
2.210173 0.452453 0.5244% 1935 2.198643 0.454826 -3.0364% 1934 2.267493 0.441016
4.6271% 1933 2.167213 0.461422 1.3921% 1932 2.137457 0.467846 -0.2051% 1931
2.141850 0.466886 0.8886% 1930 2.122985 0.471035 1.0126% 1929 2.101704 0.475804

184

1.1526% 1928 2.077756 0.481289 1.2160% 1927 2.052794 0.487141 1.4086% 1926 2.024280 0.494003 1.7667% 1925 1.989138 0.502730 1.4465% 1924 1.960775 0.510002 1.7700% 1923 1.926674 0.519029 1.6165% 1922 1.896024 0.527419 1.3736% 1921 1.870332 0.534664 2.3393% 1920 1.827580 0.547172 1.3140% 1919 1.803877 0.554362 0.7676% 1918 1.790135 0.558617 0.3870% 1917 1.783234 0.560779 1.3274% 1916 1.759873 0.568223 1.4083% 1915 1.735433 0.576225 1.4458% 1914 1.710699 0.584556 1.9424% 1913 1.678104 0.595911 1.9857% 1912 1.645431 0.607743 1.5634% 1911 1.620103 0.617245 1.8169% 1910 1.591192 0.628460 1.8781% 1909 1.561859 0.640263 2.0082% 1908 1.531111 0.653121 1.9603% 1907 1.501674 0.665923 1.8264% 1906 1.474740 0.678086 1.9357% 1905 1.446736 0.691211 2.0148% 1904 1.418163 0.705138 2.1335% 1903 1.388538 0.720182 1.8151% 1902 1.363783 0.733254 1.8943% 1901 1.338428 0.747145 3.0255% 1900 1.299124 0.769750 0.6278% 1899 1.291018 0.774583 1.7757% 1898 1.268494 0.788336 1.8078% 1897 1.245970 0.802588 1.8396% 1896 1.223463 0.817352 1.8755% 1895 1.200939 0.832682 1.9114% 1894 1.178415 0.848598 1.9486% 1893 1.155891 0.865134 1.9858% 1892 1.133384 0.882314 2.0276% 1891 1.110860 0.900204 2.6465% 1890 1.082219 0.924028 1.5328% 1889 1.065881 0.938191 2.0811% 1888 1.044151 0.957716 2.1599% 1887 1.022075 0.978401 2.2075% 1886 1.000000 1.000000 2.2592% 1885 0.977907 1.022592 2.3095% 1884 0.955832 1.046209 2.3641% 1883 0.933757 1.070943 2.4214% 1882 0.911681 1.096874 2.4815% 1881 0.889606 1.124093 3.7644% 1880 0.857333 1.166408 0.9432% 1879 0.849322 1.177410 2.1464% 1878 0.831475 1.202682 2.1913% 1877 0.813646 1.229036 2.2426% 1876 0.795799 1.256599 2.2941% 1875 0.777952 1.285426 2.3456% 1874 0.760123 1.315577 2.4043% 1873 0.742276 1.347207 2.4635% 1872 0.724430 1.380396 2.5258% 1871 0.706583 1.415262 5.9947% 1870 0.666621 1.500102 -1.0968% 1869 0.674014 1.483650 2.1930% 1868 0.659550 1.516186 2.2394% 1867 0.645103 1.550139 2.2935% 1866 0.630640 1.585692 2.3445% 1865 0.616193 1.622868 2.4037% 1864 0.601729 1.661876 2.4599% 1863 0.587283 1.702757 2.5250% 1862 0.572819 1.745751 2.5872% 1861 0.558373 1.790918 2.9504% 1860 0.542371 1.843758 2.4012% 1859 0.529652 1.888031 2.7627% 1858 0.515413 1.940192 2.8412% 1857 0.501174 1.995316 2.9243% 1856 0.486934 2.053665 3.0161% 1855 0.472678 2.115607 3.1061% 1854 0.458438 2.181318 3.2056% 1853 0.444199 2.251243 3.3118% 1852 0.429960 2.325800 3.4252% 1851 0.415720 2.405464 4.0106% 1850 0.399690 2.501937 2.3254% 1849 0.390607 2.560117 2.7841% 1848 0.380027 2.631392 2.8590% 1847 0.369464 2.706624 2.9432% 1846 0.358901 2.786285 3.0324% 1845 0.348338 2.870776 3.1325% 1844 0.337758 2.960703 3.2284% 1843 0.327195 3.056285 3.3361% 1842 0.316632 3.158245 3.4512% 1841 0.306069 3.267242 3.8105% 1840 0.294834 3.391740 2.3861% 1839 0.287963 3.472668 2.5824% 1838 0.280714 3.562346 2.6573% 1837 0.273447 3.657009 2.7232% 1836 0.266198 3.756597 2.7994% 1835 0.258949 3.861761 2.8871% 1834 0.251683 3.973255 2.9657% 1833 0.244434 4.091089 3.0563% 1832 0.237185 4.216126 3.1604% 1831 0.229918 4.349373 3.4660% 1830 0.222216 4.500121 2.4653% 1829 0.216870 4.611062 2.6804% 1828 0.211209 4.734657 10.3427% 1827 0.191412 5.224346 -4.2314% 1826 0.199869 5.003282 2.9150% 1825 0.194208 5.149129 3.0026% 1824 0.188546 5.303735 3.0955% 1823 0.182885 5.467912 3.1944% 1822 0.177224 5.642579 3.3102% 1821 0.171545 5.829359 3.2277% 1820 0.166182 6.017516 2.6573% 1819 0.161880 6.177418 2.6261% 1818 0.157738 6.339643 2.6969% 1817 0.153595 6.510619 2.7717% 1816 0.149453 6.691073 2.8507% 1815 0.145311 6.881815 2.9343% 1814 0.141168 7.083751 3.0231% 1813 0.137026 7.297896 3.1039% 1812 0.132901 7.524416 3.2172% 1811 0.128758 7.766488 3.0969% 1810 0.124891 8.007009 2.9144% 1809 0.121354 8.240364 2.8225% 1808 0.118023 8.472945 2.9199% 1807 0.114674 8.720349 2.9918% 1806 0.111343 8.981243 3.0841% 1805 0.108012 9.258229 3.1822% 1804 0.104681 9.552844 3.2868% 1803 0.101350 9.866826 3.3985% 1802 0.098019 10.202148 3.5180% 1801 0.094687 10.561065 3.3999% 1800 0.091574 10.920135 2.8419% 1799 0.089043 11.230471 2.7485% 1798 0.086662 11.539136 2.8261% 1797 0.084280 11.865247 3.7832% 1796 0.081207 12.314134 2.1272% 1795 0.079516 12.576080 3.0879% 1794 0.077134 12.964422 3.1625% 1793 0.074770 13.374423 3.2904% 1792 0.072388 13.814497 3.4024% 1791 0.070006 14.284517 3.2296% 1790 0.067816 14.745844 41.3145% 1780 0.047989 20.838009 29.4353% 1770 0.037076 26.971742 83.4728% 1750 0.020208 49.485822 29.2845% 1740 0.015631 63.977473 94.2514% 1720 0.008047 124.277134 85.8111% 1700 0.004330 230.920686 19.2490% 1690 0.003631 275.370722 88.0250% 1670 0.001931 517.765862

185

YEAR BYEAR/AYEAR AYEAR/BYEAR GROWTH%

2009 5.320173 0.187964 8.2857% 2001 4.913091 0.203538 1.0000% 2000 4.864446 0.205573 1.0000% 1999 4.816283 0.207629 1.0000% 1998 4.768597 0.209705 1.0000% 1997 4.721383 0.211802 1.0000% 1996 4.674637 0.213920 1.0000% 1995 4.628353 0.216060 0.9992% 1994 4.582563 0.218218 1.0008% 1993 4.537156 0.220402 1.0000% 1992 4.492234 0.222606 0.9295% 1991 4.450863 0.224676 1.2505% 1990 4.395892 0.227485 0.7224% 1989 4.364362 0.229129 1.1077% 1988 4.316548 0.231667 0.8834% 1987 4.278751 0.233713 0.5594% 1986 4.254951 0.235020 1.3056% 1985 4.200113 0.238089 0.7673% 1984 4.168132 0.239916 0.8149% 1983 4.134438 0.241871 0.9737% 1982 4.094567 0.244226 0.9508% 1981 4.056003 0.246548 0.9031% 1980 4.019702 0.248775 2.2701% 1979 3.930478 0.254422 1.0042% 1978 3.891401 0.256977 0.9896% 1977 3.853269 0.259520 0.9103% 1976 3.818508 0.261882 0.8394% 1975 3.786720 0.264081 0.9042% 1974 3.752789 0.266469 1.1568% 1973 3.709873 0.269551 0.9427% 1972 3.675227 0.272092 0.7426% 1971 3.648134 0.274113 1.4697% 1970 3.595293 0.278141 0.6968% 1969 3.570414 0.280080 0.8565% 1968 3.540091 0.282479 1.5090% 1967 3.487464 0.286741 0.9949% 1966 3.453109 0.289594 1.0575% 1965 3.416976 0.292656 1.1300% 1964 3.378795 0.295964 1.5537% 1963 3.327103 0.300562 1.4658% 1962 3.279038 0.304967 1.5364% 1961 3.229420 0.309653 2.1586% 1960 3.161182 0.316337 -1.6655% 1959 3.214723 0.311069 4.3080% 1958 3.081952 0.324470 2.1130% 1957 3.018179 0.331326 1.9895% 1956 2.959304 0.337917 2.1231% 1955 2.897781 0.345092 1.4496% 1954 2.856375 0.350094 2.1573% 1953 2.796057 0.357646 1.2298% 1952 2.762090 0.362045 1.6814% 1951 2.716417 0.368132 1.6233% 1950 2.673026 0.374108 1.4265% 1949 2.635431 0.379445 1.7790% 1948 2.589365 0.386195 1.8242% 1947 2.542977 0.393240 -2.6320% 1946 2.611719 0.382890 3.1768% 1945 2.531304 0.395053 6.4754% 1944 2.377360 0.420635 -0.3437% 1943 2.385559 0.419189 0.6562% 1942 2.370006 0.421940 0.6633% 1941 2.354389 0.424739 -5.6614% 1940 2.495681 0.400692 8.0381% 1939 2.310000 0.432900 0.8126% 1938 2.291380 0.436418 0.7762% 1937 2.273730 0.439806 0.6029% 1936 2.260104 0.442457 0.5244% 1935 2.248314 0.444778 -3.0364% 1934 2.318719 0.431273 4.6271% 1933 2.216174 0.451228 1.3921% 1932 2.185746 0.457510 -0.2051% 1931 2.190238 0.456571 0.8886% 1930 2.170947 0.460628 1.0126% 1929 2.149185 0.465293 1.1526% 1928 2.124696 0.470656 1.2160% 1927 2.099170 0.476379 1.4086% 1926 2.070012 0.483089 1.7667% 1925 2.034076 0.491624 1.4465% 1924 2.005073 0.498735 1.7700% 1923 1.970201 0.507563 1.6165% 1922 1.938859 0.515767 1.3736% 1921 1.912586 0.522852 2.3393% 1920 1.868868 0.535083 1.3140% 1919 1.844629 0.542114 0.7676% 1918 1.830577 0.546276 0.3870% 1917 1.823520 0.548390 1.3274% 1916 1.799631 0.555669 1.4083% 1915 1.774639 0.563495 1.4458% 1914 1.749347 0.571642 1.9424% 1913 1.716015 0.582745 1.9857% 1912 1.682604 0.594317 1.5634% 1911 1.656703 0.603608 1.8169% 1910 1.627140 0.614575 1.8781% 1909 1.597144 0.626118 2.0082% 1908 1.565701 0.638691 1.9603% 1907 1.535600 0.651211 1.8264% 1906 1.508057 0.663105 1.9357% 1905 1.479420 0.675940 2.0148% 1904 1.450201 0.689559 2.1335% 1903 1.419907 0.704271 1.8151% 1902 1.394593 0.717055 1.8943% 1901 1.368666 0.730639 3.0255% 1900 1.328473 0.752744 0.6278% 1899 1.320184 0.757470 1.7757% 1898 1.297151 0.770920 1.8078% 1897 1.274118 0.784856 1.8396% 1896 1.251103 0.799295 1.8755% 1895 1.228070 0.814286 1.9114% 1894 1.205037 0.829850 1.9486% 1893 1.182004 0.846021 1.9858% 1892 1.158989 0.862821 2.0276% 1891 1.135956 0.880316 2.6465% 1890 1.106668 0.903613 1.5328% 1889 1.089961 0.917464 2.0811% 1888 1.067740 0.936558 2.1599% 1887 1.045166 0.956786 2.2075% 1886 1.022592 0.977907 2.2592% 1885 1.000000 1.000000 2.3095% 1884 0.977426 1.023095 2.3641% 1883 0.954852 1.047283 2.4214% 1882 0.932278 1.072642 2.4815% 1881 0.909704 1.099259 3.7644% 1880 0.876701 1.140639 0.9432% 1879 0.868509 1.151398 2.1464% 1878 0.850259 1.176112 2.1913% 1877 0.832027 1.201884 2.2426% 1876 0.813777 1.228837 2.2941% 1875 0.795528 1.257027 2.3456% 1874 0.777295 1.286512 2.4043% 1873 0.759046 1.317444 2.4635% 1872 0.740796 1.349900 2.5258% 1871 0.722546 1.383995 5.9947% 1870 0.681681 1.466961 -1.0968% 1869 0.689241 1.450872 2.1930% 1868 0.674450 1.482689 2.2394% 1867 0.659677 1.515893 2.2935% 1866 0.644887 1.550660 2.3445% 1865 0.630114 1.587014 2.4037% 1864 0.615324 1.625161 2.4599% 1863 0.600551 1.665138 2.5250% 1862 0.585760 1.707183 2.5872% 1861 0.570987 1.751352 2.9504% 1860 0.554624 1.803024 2.4012% 1859

0.541618 1.846319 2.7627% 1858 0.527057 1.897328 2.8412% 1857 0.512496 1.951235 2.9243% 1856 0.497935 2.008294 3.0161% 1855 0.483356 2.068867 3.1061% 1854 0.468795 2.133128 3.2056% 1853 0.454234 2.201508 3.3118% 1852 0.439673 2.274417 3.4252% 1851 0.425112 2.352321 4.0106% 1850 0.408720 2.446663 2.3254% 1849 0.399432 2.503557 2.7841% 1848 0.388612 2.573258 2.8590% 1847 0.377811 2.646828 2.9432% 1846 0.367009 2.724728 3.0324% 1845 0.356207 2.807353 3.1325% 1844 0.345388 2.895294 3.2284% 1843 0.334586 2.988764 3.3361% 1842 0.323785 3.088471 3.4512% 1841 0.312983 3.195060 3.8105% 1840 0.301495 3.316807 2.3861% 1839 0.294469 3.395948 2.5824% 1838 0.287056 3.483645 2.6573% 1837 0.279625 3.576217 2.7232% 1836 0.272212 3.673604 2.7994% 1835 0.264799 3.776445 2.8871% 1834 0.257369 3.885475 2.9657% 1833 0.249956 4.000706 3.0563% 1832 0.242543 4.122981 3.1604% 1831 0.235112 4.253284 3.4660% 1830 0.227236 4.400702 2.4653% 1829 0.221769 4.509192 2.6804% 1828 0.215980 4.630056 10.3427% 1827 0.195736 5.108927 -4.2314% 1826 0.204384 4.892746 2.9150% 1825 0.198595 5.035371 3.0026% 1824 0.192806 5.186562 3.0955% 1823 0.187017 5.347112 3.1944% 1822 0.181228 5.517920 3.3102% 1821 0.175421 5.700573 3.2277% 1820 0.169936 5.884573 2.6573% 1819 0.165537 6.040943 2.6261% 1818 0.161301 6.199584 2.6969% 1817 0.157065 6.366783 2.7717% 1816 0.152829 6.543250 2.8507% 1815 0.148593 6.729778 2.9343% 1814 0.144357 6.927253 3.0231% 1813 0.140121 7.136667 3.1039% 1812 0.135903 7.358182 3.2172% 1811 0.131667 7.594906 3.0969% 1810 0.127712 7.830114 2.9144% 1809 0.124095 8.058313 2.8225% 1808 0.120689 8.285756 2.9199% 1807 0.117265 8.527694 2.9918% 1806 0.113859 8.782824 3.0841% 1805 0.110452 9.053691 3.1822% 1804 0.107046 9.341797 3.2868% 1803 0.103639 9.648842 3.3985% 1802 0.100233 9.976756 3.5180% 1801 0.096827 10.327743 3.3999% 1800 0.093643 10.678881 2.8419% 1799 0.091055 10.982361 2.7485% 1798 0.088619 11.284206 2.8261% 1797 0.086184 11.603113 3.7832% 1796 0.083042 12.042083 2.1272% 1795 0.081312 12.298242 3.0879% 1794 0.078877 12.678004 3.1625% 1793 0.076459 13.078947 3.2904% 1792 0.074023 13.509299 3.4024% 1791 0.071587 13.968935 3.2296% 1790 0.069348 14.420071 41.3145% 1780 0.049073 20.377644 29.4353% 1770 0.037913 26.375867 83.4728% 1750 0.020664 48.392552 29.2845% 1740 0.015984 62.564046 94.2514% 1720 0.008228 121.531532 85.8111% 1700 0.004428 225.819051 19.2490% 1690 0.003714 269.287072 88.0250% 1670 0.001975 506.327078

BASE YEAR: 1884

YEAR BYEAR/AYEAR AYEAR/BYEAR GROWTH%

2009 5.443044 0.183721 8.2857% 2001 5.026561 0.198943 1.0000% 2000 4.976792 0.200933 1.0000% 1999 4.927517 0.202942 1.0000% 1998 4.878730 0.204971 1.0000% 1997 4.830425 0.207021 1.0000% 1996 4.782599 0.209091 1.0000% 1995 4.735247 0.211182 0.9992% 1994 4.688399 0.213292 1.0008% 1993 4.641944 0.215427 1.0000% 1992 4.595984 0.217581 0.9295% 1991 4.553658 0.219604 1.2505% 1990 4.497417 0.222350 0.7224% 1989 4.465158 0.223956 1.1077% 1988 4.416241 0.226437 0.8834% 1987 4.377571 0.228437 0.5594% 1986 4.353221 0.229715 1.3056% 1985 4.297116 0.232714 0.7673% 1984 4.264396 0.234500 0.8149% 1983 4.229925 0.236411 0.9737% 1982 4.189133 0.238713 0.9508% 1981 4.149678 0.240983 0.9031% 1980 4.112539 0.243159 2.2701% 1979 4.021254 0.248679 1.0042% 1978 3.981214 0.251176 0.9896% 1977 3.942262 0.253662 0.9103% 1976 3.906697 0.255971 0.8394% 1975 3.874176 0.258119 0.9042% 1974 3.839461 0.260453 1.1568% 1973 3.795554 0.263466 0.9427% 1972 3.760108 0.265950 0.7426% 1971 3.732390 0.267925 1.4697% 1970 3.678328 0.271863 0.6968% 1969 3.652874 0.273757 0.8565% 1968 3.621851 0.276102 1.5090% 1967 3.568009 0.280268 0.9949% 1966 3.532860 0.283057 1.0575% 1965 3.495892 0.286050 1.1300% 1964 3.456829 0.289282 1.5537% 1963 3.403944 0.293777 1.4658% 1962 3.354769 0.298083 1.5364% 1961 3.304005 0.302663 2.1586% 1960 3.234191 0.309196 -1.6655% 1959 3.288968 0.304047 4.3080% 1958 3.153131 0.317145 2.1130% 1957 3.087885 0.323846 1.9895% 1956 3.027650 0.330289 2.1231% 1955 2.964707 0.337301 1.4496% 1954 2.922344 0.342191 2.1573% 1953 2.860633 0.349573 1.2298% 1952 2.825882 0.353872 1.6814% 1951 2.779154 0.359822 1.6233% 1950 2.734761 0.365663 1.4265% 1949 2.696297 0.370879 1.7790% 1948 2.649168 0.377477 1.8242% 1947 2.601708 0.384363 -2.6320% 1946 2.672037 0.374246 3.1768% 1945 2.589766 0.386135 6.4754% 1944 2.432266 0.411139 -0.3437% 1943 2.440654 0.409726 0.6562% 1942 2.424742 0.412415 0.6633% 1941 2.408765 0.415150 -5.6614% 1940 2.553319 0.391647 8.0381% 1939 2.363351

187

0.423128 0.8126% 1938 2.344300 0.426567 0.7762% 1937 2.326243 0.429878 0.6029% 1936
2.312302 0.432469 0.5244% 1935 2.300240 0.434737 -3.0364% 1934 2.372271 0.421537
4.6271% 1933 2.267358 0.441042 1.3921% 1932 2.236227 0.447182 -0.2051% 1931
2.240822 0.446265 0.8886% 1930 2.221086 0.450230 1.0126% 1929 2.198821 0.454789
1.1526% 1928 2.173766 0.460031 1.2160% 1927 2.147651 0.465625 1.4086% 1926 2.117820
0.472184 1.7667% 1925 2.081054 0.480526 1.4465% 1924 2.051381 0.487477 1.7700% 1923
2.015703 0.496105 1.6165% 1922 1.983637 0.504124 1.3736% 1921 1.956758 0.511049
2.3393% 1920 1.912030 0.523004 1.3140% 1919 1.887232 0.529877 0.7676% 1918 1.872855
0.533944 0.3870% 1917 1.865635 0.536011 1.3274% 1916 1.841194 0.543126 1.4083% 1915
1.815625 0.550775 1.4458% 1914 1.789749 0.558738 1.9424% 1913 1.755647 0.569590
1.9857% 1912 1.721465 0.580901 1.5634% 1911 1.694966 0.589982 1.8169% 1910 1.664719
0.600702 1.8781% 1909 1.634031 0.611984 2.0082% 1908 1.601862 0.624274 1.9603% 1907
1.571065 0.636511 1.8264% 1906 1.542886 0.648136 1.9357% 1905 1.513588 0.660682
2.0148% 1904 1.483694 0.673993 2.1335% 1903 1.452700 0.688373 1.8151% 1902 1.426802
0.700868 1.8943% 1901 1.400276 0.714145 3.0255% 1900 1.359155 0.735752 0.6278% 1899
1.350674 0.740371 1.7757% 1898 1.327110 0.753517 1.8078% 1897 1.303545 0.767139
1.8396% 1896 1.279998 0.781251 1.8755% 1895 1.256433 0.795904 1.9114% 1894 1.232868
0.811117 1.9486% 1893 1.209303 0.826923 1.9858% 1892 1.185756 0.843344 2.0276% 1891
1.162191 0.860443 2.6465% 1890 1.132227 0.883215 1.5328% 1889 1.115134 0.896753
2.0811% 1888 1.092400 0.915416 2.1599% 1887 1.069304 0.935188 2.2075% 1886 1.046209
0.955832 2.2592% 1885 1.023095 0.977426 2.3095% 1884 1.000000 1.000000 2.3641% 1883
0.976905 1.023641 2.4214% 1882 0.953809 1.048428 2.4815% 1881 0.930714 1.074444
3.7644% 1880 0.896949 1.114890 0.9432% 1879 0.888568 1.125406 2.1464% 1878 0.869897
1.149562 2.1913% 1877 0.851243 1.174752 2.2426% 1876 0.832572 1.201097 2.2941% 1875
0.813901 1.228651 2.3456% 1874 0.795247 1.257470 2.4043% 1873 0.776576 1.287704
2.4635% 1872 0.757905 1.319427 2.5258% 1871 0.739233 1.352753 5.9947% 1870 0.697425
1.433846 -1.0968% 1869 0.705159 1.418120 2.1930% 1868 0.690027 1.449219 2.2394%
1867 0.674913 1.481673 2.2935% 1866 0.659781 1.515655 2.3445% 1865 0.644667 1.551189
2.4037% 1864 0.629535 1.588475 2.4599% 1863 0.614421 1.627550 2.5250% 1862 0.599289
1.668645 2.5872% 1861 0.584175 1.711817 2.9504% 1860 0.567433 1.762323 2.4012% 1859
0.554127 1.804640 2.7627% 1858 0.539230 1.854497 2.8412% 1857 0.524332 1.907187
2.9243% 1856 0.509435 1.962959 3.0161% 1855 0.494520 2.022165 3.1061% 1854 0.479622
2.084974 3.2056% 1853 0.464725 2.151811 3.3118% 1852 0.449828 2.223074 3.4252% 1851
0.434930 2.299219 4.0106% 1850 0.418159 2.391432 2.3254% 1849 0.408657 2.447042
2.7841% 1848 0.397588 2.515169 2.8590% 1847 0.386536 2.587078 2.9432% 1846 0.375485
2.663220 3.0324% 1845 0.364434 2.743980 3.1325% 1844 0.353365 2.829935 3.2284% 1843
0.342314 2.921296 3.3361% 1842 0.331263 3.018752 3.4512% 1841 0.320212 3.122935
3.8105% 1840 0.308458 3.241934 2.3861% 1839 0.301269 3.319288 2.5824% 1838 0.293685
3.405005 2.6573% 1837 0.286083 3.495487 2.7232% 1836 0.278499 3.590676 2.7994% 1835
0.270915 3.691195 2.8871% 1834 0.263313 3.797764 2.9657% 1833 0.255729 3.910394
3.0563% 1832 0.248145 4.029908 3.1604% 1831 0.240542 4.157270 3.4660% 1830 0.232485
4.301360 2.4653% 1829 0.226891 4.407402 2.6804% 1828 0.220968 4.525537 10.3427%
1827 0.200256 4.993598 -4.2314% 1826 0.209105 4.782297 2.9150% 1825 0.203182
4.921703 3.0026% 1824 0.197259 5.069480 3.0955% 1823 0.191336 5.226406 3.1944% 1822
0.185413 5.393358 3.3102% 1821 0.179472 5.571889 3.2277% 1820 0.173861 5.751735
2.6573% 1819 0.169360 5.904574 2.6261% 1818 0.165026 6.059635 2.6969% 1817 0.160693
6.223059 2.7717% 1816 0.156359 6.395542 2.8507% 1815 0.152025 6.577860 2.9343% 1814
0.147691 6.770877 3.0231% 1813 0.143358 6.975564 3.1039% 1812 0.139042 7.192078
3.2172% 1811 0.134708 7.423458 3.0969% 1810 0.130662 7.653357 2.9144% 1809 0.126961
7.876404 2.8225% 1808 0.123476 8.098713 2.9199% 1807 0.119973 8.335190 2.9918% 1806
0.116488 8.584561 3.0841% 1805 0.113003 8.849313 3.1822% 1804 0.109518 9.130915
3.2868% 1803 0.106033 9.431029 3.3985% 1802 0.102548 9.751541 3.5180% 1801 0.099063
10.094604 3.3999% 1800 0.095805 10.437816 2.8419% 1799 0.093158 10.734445 2.7485%
1798 0.090666 11.029476 2.8261% 1797 0.088174 11.341184 3.7832% 1796 0.084960
11.770244 2.1272% 1795 0.083190 12.020621 3.0879% 1794 0.080698 12.391810 3.1625%
1793 0.078225 12.783703 3.2904% 1792 0.075733 13.204340 3.4024% 1791 0.073241

188

13.653600 3.2296% 1790 0.070949 14.094551 41.3145% 1780 0.050207 19.917638 29.4353% 1770 0.038789 25.780457 83.4728% 1750 0.021142 47.300137 29.2845% 1740 0.016353 61.151723 94.2514% 1720 0.008418 118.788074 85.8111% 1700 0.004531 220.721403 19.2490% 1690 0.003799 263.208175 88.0250% 1670 0.002021 494.897230

BASE YEAR: 1883

YEAR BYEAR/AYEAR AYEAR/BYEAR GROWTH%

2009 5.571725 0.179478 8.2857% 2001 5.145396 0.194349 1.0000% 2000 5.094450 0.196292 1.0000% 1999 5.044010 0.198255 1.0000% 1998 4.994070 0.200237 1.0000% 1997 4.944623 0.202240 1.0000% 1996 4.895667 0.204262 1.0000% 1995 4.847195 0.206305 0.9992% 1994 4.799240 0.208366 1.0008% 1993 4.751686 0.210452 1.0000% 1992 4.704640 0.212556 0.9295% 1991 4.661312 0.214532 1.2505% 1990 4.603742 0.217215 0.7224% 1989 4.570721 0.218784 1.1077% 1988 4.520647 0.221207 0.8834% 1987 4.481063 0.223161 0.5594% 1986 4.456137 0.224410 1.3056% 1985 4.398706 0.227340 0.7673% 1984 4.365213 0.229084 0.8149% 1983 4.329926 0.230951 0.9737% 1982 4.288170 0.233200 0.9508% 1981 4.247782 0.235417 0.9031% 1980 4.209765 0.237543 2.2701% 1979 4.116322 0.242935 1.0042% 1978 4.075397 0.245375 0.9896% 1977 4.035462 0.247803 0.9103% 1976 3.999057 0.250059 0.8394% 1975 3.965767 0.252158 0.9042% 1974 3.930231 0.254438 1.1568% 1973 3.885287 0.257381 0.9427% 1972 3.849002 0.259808 0.7426% 1971 3.820628 0.261737 1.4697% 1970 3.765289 0.265584 0.6968% 1969 3.739233 0.267435 0.8565% 1968 3.707477 0.269725 1.5090% 1967 3.652361 0.273795 0.9949% 1966 3.616382 0.276519 1.0575% 1965 3.578540 0.279444 1.1300% 1964 3.538554 0.282601 1.5537% 1963 3.484418 0.286992 1.4658% 1962 3.434080 0.291199 1.5364% 1961 3.382116 0.295673 2.1586% 1960 3.310651 0.302055 -1.6655% 1959 3.366724 0.297025 4.3080% 1958 3.227676 0.309820 2.1130% 1957 3.160887 0.316367 1.9895% 1956 3.099228 0.322661 2.1231% 1955 3.034797 0.329511 1.4496% 1954 2.991433 0.334288 2.1573% 1953 2.928262 0.341499 1.2298% 1952 2.892689 0.345699 1.6814% 1951 2.844857 0.351512 1.6233% 1950 2.799415 0.357218 1.4265% 1949 2.760042 0.362313 1.7790% 1948 2.711798 0.368759 1.8242% 1947 2.663216 0.375486 - 2.6320% 1946 2.735208 0.365603 3.1768% 1945 2.650991 0.377217 6.4754% 1944 2.489768 0.401644 -0.3437% 1943 2.498355 0.400263 0.6562% 1942 2.482067 0.402890 0.6633% 1941 2.465712 0.405562 -5.6614% 1940 2.613683 0.382602 8.0381% 1939 2.419224 0.413356 0.8126% 1938 2.399723 0.416715 0.7762% 1937 2.381238 0.419950 0.6029% 1936 2.366969 0.422481 0.5244% 1935 2.354621 0.424697 -3.0364% 1934 2.428355 0.411801 4.6271% 1933 2.320961 0.430856 1.3921% 1932 2.289094 0.436854 -0.2051% 1931 2.293799 0.435958 0.8886% 1930 2.273595 0.439832 1.0126% 1929 2.250804 0.444286 1.1526% 1928 2.225157 0.449406 1.2160% 1927 2.198424 0.454871 1.4086% 1926 2.167888 0.461278 1.7667% 1925 2.130253 0.469428 1.4465% 1924 2.099878 0.476218 1.7700% 1923 2.063357 0.484647 1.6165% 1922 2.030533 0.492481 1.3736% 1921 2.003019 0.499246 2.3393% 1920 1.957233 0.510925 1.3140% 1919 1.931848 0.517639 0.7676% 1918 1.917132 0.521613 0.3870% 1917 1.909741 0.523631 1.3274% 1916 1.884723 0.530582 1.4083% 1915 1.858549 0.538054 1.4458% 1914 1.832061 0.545833 1.9424% 1913 1.797153 0.556436 1.9857% 1912 1.762163 0.567485 1.5634% 1911 1.735037 0.576357 1.8169% 1910 1.704075 0.586829 1.8781% 1909 1.672662 0.597850 2.0082% 1908 1.639732 0.609856 1.9603% 1907 1.608207 0.621810 1.8264% 1906 1.579362 0.633167 1.9357% 1905 1.549372 0.645423 2.0148% 1904 1.518771 0.658427 2.1335% 1903 1.487044 0.672475 1.8151% 1902 1.460533 0.684681 1.8943% 1901 1.433380 0.697652 3.0255% 1900 1.391287 0.718759 0.6278% 1899 1.382606 0.723272 1.7757% 1898 1.358484 0.736115 1.8078% 1897 1.334362 0.749422 1.8396% 1896 1.310259 0.763208 1.8755% 1895 1.286137 0.777522 1.9114% 1894 1.262015 0.792384 1.9486% 1893 1.237893 0.807824 1.9858% 1892 1.213789 0.823866 2.0276% 1891 1.189667 0.840571 2.6465% 1890 1.158994 0.862817 1.5328% 1889 1.141497 0.876042 2.0811% 1888 1.118226 0.894274 2.1599% 1887 1.094584 0.913589 2.2075% 1886 1.070943 0.933757 2.2592% 1885 1.047283 0.954852 2.3095% 1884 1.023641 0.976905 2.3641% 1883 1.000000 1.000000 2.4214% 1882 0.976359 1.024214 2.4815% 1881 0.952717 1.049629 3.7644% 1880 0.918154 1.089142 0.9432% 1879 0.909575 1.099415 2.1464% 1878 0.890462 1.123012 2.1913% 1877 0.871368 1.147621 2.2426% 1876 0.852255 1.173358 2.2941% 1875 0.833142 1.200275 2.3456% 1874 0.814048 1.228429 2.4043% 1873 0.794935 1.257964 2.4635% 1872 0.775823 1.288955 2.5258% 1871 0.756710 1.321511 5.9947% 1870 0.713913

189

1.400731 -1.0968% 1869 0.721830 1.385368 2.1930% 1868 0.706340 1.415749 2.2394%
1867 0.690869 1.447453 2.2935% 1866 0.675379 1.480650 2.3445% 1865 0.659908 1.515364
2.4037% 1864 0.644418 1.551788 2.4599% 1863 0.628946 1.589961 2.5250% 1862 0.613457
1.630107 2.5872% 1861 0.597985 1.672282 2.9504% 1860 0.580848 1.721621 2.4012% 1859
0.567227 1.762962 2.7627% 1858 0.551978 1.811667 2.8412% 1857 0.536728 1.863140
2.9243% 1856 0.521479 1.917624 3.0161% 1855 0.506211 1.975462 3.1061% 1854 0.490961
2.036821 3.2056% 1853 0.475712 2.102114 3.3118% 1852 0.460462 2.171731 3.4252% 1851
0.445213 2.246118 4.0106% 1850 0.428045 2.336201 2.3254% 1849 0.418318 2.390526
2.7841% 1848 0.406987 2.457081 2.8590% 1847 0.395675 2.527329 2.9432% 1846 0.384362
2.601712 3.0324% 1845 0.373050 2.680606 3.1325% 1844 0.361719 2.764577 3.2284% 1843
0.350407 2.853827 3.3361% 1842 0.339094 2.949032 3.4512% 1841 0.327782 3.050809
3.8105% 1840 0.315750 3.167060 2.3861% 1839 0.308392 3.242628 2.5824% 1838 0.300628
3.326365 2.6573% 1837 0.292847 3.414757 2.7232% 1836 0.285083 3.507748 2.7994% 1835
0.277320 3.605945 2.8871% 1834 0.269538 3.710053 2.9657% 1833 0.261774 3.820082
3.0563% 1832 0.254011 3.936836 3.1604% 1831 0.246229 4.061257 3.4660% 1830 0.237981
4.202018 2.4653% 1829 0.232255 4.305611 2.6804% 1828 0.226192 4.421018 10.3427%
1827 0.204991 4.878269 -4.2314% 1826 0.214048 4.671848 2.9150% 1825 0.207985
4.808034 3.0026% 1824 0.201922 4.952398 3.0955% 1823 0.195860 5.105700 3.1944% 1822
0.189797 5.268796 3.3102% 1821 0.183715 5.443204 3.2277% 1820 0.177971 5.618896
2.6573% 1819 0.173364 5.768206 2.6261% 1818 0.168928 5.919685 2.6969% 1817 0.164492
6.079335 2.7717% 1816 0.160055 6.247835 2.8507% 1815 0.155619 6.425941 2.9343% 1814
0.151183 6.614501 3.0231% 1813 0.146747 6.814460 3.1039% 1812 0.142329 7.025974
3.2172% 1811 0.137893 7.252011 3.0969% 1810 0.133751 7.476599 2.9144% 1809 0.129963
7.694496 2.8225% 1808 0.126396 7.911670 2.9199% 1807 0.122810 8.142685 2.9918% 1806
0.119242 8.386297 3.0841% 1805 0.115675 8.644934 3.1822% 1804 0.112107 8.920033
3.2868% 1803 0.108540 9.213215 3.3985% 1802 0.104972 9.526325 3.5180% 1801 0.101405
9.861466 3.3999% 1800 0.098070 10.196750 2.8419% 1799 0.095360 10.486528 2.7485%
1798 0.092810 10.774746 2.8261% 1797 0.090259 11.079255 3.7832% 1796 0.086969
11.498406 2.1272% 1795 0.085157 11.743000 3.0879% 1794 0.082606 12.105616 3.1625%
1793 0.080074 12.488458 3.2904% 1792 0.077523 12.899380 3.4024% 1791 0.074972
13.338264 3.2296% 1790 0.072627 13.769032 41.3145% 1780 0.051394 19.457632 29.4353%
1770 0.039706 25.185047 83.4728% 1750 0.021641 46.207721 29.2845% 1740 0.016739
59.739399 94.2514% 1720 0.008617 116.044616 85.8111% 1700 0.004638 215.623754
19.2490% 1690 0.003889 257.129278 88.0250% 1670 0.002068 483.467382
    BASE YEAR: 1882
    YEAR BYEAR/AYEAR AYEAR/BYEAR GROWTH%
    2009 5.706638 0.175235 8.2857% 2001 5.269985 0.189754 1.0000% 2000 5.217807
0.191651 1.0000% 1999 5.166145 0.193568 1.0000% 1998 5.114995 0.195504 1.0000% 1997
5.064352 0.197459 1.0000% 1996 5.014210 0.199433 1.0000% 1995 4.964564 0.201428
0.9992% 1994 4.915448 0.203440 1.0008% 1993 4.866743 0.205476 1.0000% 1992 4.818557
0.207531 0.9295% 1991 4.774181 0.209460 1.2505% 1990 4.715216 0.212079 0.7224% 1989
4.681396 0.213612 1.1077% 1988 4.630109 0.215978 0.8834% 1987 4.589567 0.217885
0.5594% 1986 4.564037 0.219104 1.3056% 1985 4.505216 0.221965 0.7673% 1984 4.470911
0.223668 0.8149% 1983 4.434770 0.225491 0.9737% 1982 4.392003 0.227687 0.9508% 1981
4.350637 0.229851 0.9031% 1980 4.311700 0.231927 2.2701% 1979 4.215994 0.237192
1.0042% 1978 4.174078 0.239574 0.9896% 1977 4.133176 0.241945 0.9103% 1976 4.095890
0.244147 0.8394% 1975 4.061794 0.246197 0.9042% 1974 4.025397 0.248423 1.1568% 1973
3.979364 0.251296 0.9427% 1972 3.942201 0.253665 0.7426% 1971 3.913141 0.255549
1.4697% 1970 3.856461 0.259305 0.6968% 1969 3.829774 0.261112 0.8565% 1968 3.797249
0.263349 1.5090% 1967 3.740799 0.267323 0.9949% 1966 3.703948 0.269982 1.0575% 1965
3.665190 0.272837 1.1300% 1964 3.624236 0.275920 1.5537% 1963 3.568789 0.280207
1.4658% 1962 3.517233 0.284314 1.5364% 1961 3.464011 0.288683 2.1586% 1960 3.390815
0.294914 -1.6655% 1959 3.448245 0.290003 4.3080% 1958 3.305830 0.302496 2.1130%
1957 3.237425 0.308888 1.9895% 1956 3.174273 0.315033 2.1231% 1955 3.108281 0.321721
1.4496% 1954 3.063867 0.326385 2.1573% 1953 2.999167 0.333426 1.2298% 1952 2.962733
0.337526 1.6814% 1951 2.913742 0.343201 1.6233% 1950 2.867199 0.348772 1.4265% 1949

190

2.826873 0.353748 1.7790% 1948 2.777461 0.360041 1.8242% 1947 2.727703 0.366609 -
2.6320% 1946 2.801438 0.356960 3.1768% 1945 2.715182 0.368299 6.4754% 1944 2.550055
0.392148 -0.3437% 1943 2.558849 0.390801 0.6562% 1942 2.542167 0.393365 0.6633%
1941 2.525416 0.395974 -5.6614% 1940 2.676971 0.373557 8.0381% 1939 2.477802
0.403583 0.8126% 1938 2.457829 0.406863 0.7762% 1937 2.438897 0.410021 0.6029% 1936
2.424282 0.412493 0.5244% 1935 2.411636 0.414656 -3.0364% 1934 2.487155 0.402066
4.6271% 1933 2.377161 0.420670 1.3921% 1932 2.344522 0.426526 -0.2051% 1931
2.349340 0.425651 0.8886% 1930 2.328648 0.429434 1.0126% 1929 2.305305 0.433782
1.1526% 1928 2.279037 0.438782 1.2160% 1927 2.251657 0.444117 1.4086% 1926 2.220381
0.450373 1.7667% 1925 2.181834 0.458330 1.4465% 1924 2.150724 0.464960 1.7700% 1923
2.113319 0.473189 1.6165% 1922 2.079700 0.480839 1.3736% 1921 2.051520 0.487444
2.3393% 1920 2.004625 0.498846 1.3140% 1919 1.978626 0.505401 0.7676% 1918 1.963553
0.509281 0.3870% 1917 1.955983 0.511252 1.3274% 1916 1.930359 0.518038 1.4083% 1915
1.903552 0.525334 1.4458% 1914 1.876422 0.532929 1.9424% 1913 1.840669 0.543281
1.9857% 1912 1.804831 0.554068 1.5634% 1911 1.777049 0.562731 1.8169% 1910 1.745338
0.572955 1.8781% 1909 1.713163 0.583716 2.0082% 1908 1.679436 0.595438 1.9603% 1907
1.647148 0.607110 1.8264% 1906 1.617605 0.618198 1.9357% 1905 1.586888 0.630164
2.0148% 1904 1.555546 0.642861 2.1335% 1903 1.523051 0.656577 1.8151% 1902 1.495899
0.668495 1.8943% 1901 1.468088 0.681158 3.0255% 1900 1.424975 0.701767 0.6278% 1899
1.416085 0.706173 1.7757% 1898 1.391378 0.718712 1.8078% 1897 1.366672 0.731704
1.8396% 1896 1.341985 0.745165 1.8755% 1895 1.317209 0.759141 1.9114% 1894 1.292573
0.773651 1.9486% 1893 1.267867 0.788726 1.9858% 1892 1.243180 0.804389 2.0276% 1891
1.218474 0.820699 2.6465% 1890 1.187058 0.842419 1.5328% 1889 1.169137 0.855332
2.0811% 1888 1.145302 0.873132 2.1599% 1887 1.121088 0.891990 2.2075% 1886 1.096874
0.911681 2.2592% 1885 1.072642 0.932278 2.3095% 1884 1.048428 0.953809 2.3641% 1883
1.024214 0.976359 2.4214% 1882 1.000000 1.000000 2.4815% 1881 0.975786 1.024815
3.7644% 1880 0.940386 1.063393 0.9432% 1879 0.931599 1.073423 2.1464% 1878 0.912024
1.096463 2.1913% 1877 0.892467 1.120490 2.2426% 1876 0.872891 1.145618 2.2941% 1875
0.853316 1.171899 2.3456% 1874 0.833759 1.199387 2.4043% 1873 0.814184 1.228224
2.4635% 1872 0.794608 1.258482 2.5258% 1871 0.775033 1.290268 5.9947% 1870 0.731200
1.367616 -1.0968% 1869 0.739308 1.352616 2.1930% 1868 0.723443 1.382278 2.2394%
1867 0.707597 1.413233 2.2935% 1866 0.691732 1.445646 2.3445% 1865 0.675886 1.479538
2.4037% 1864 0.660022 1.515102 2.4599% 1863 0.644176 1.552372 2.5250% 1862 0.628311
1.591569 2.5872% 1861 0.612465 1.632747 2.9504% 1860 0.594912 1.680920 2.4012% 1859
0.580962 1.721283 2.7627% 1858 0.565343 1.768837 2.8412% 1857 0.549725 1.819093
2.9243% 1856 0.534106 1.872288 3.0161% 1855 0.518468 1.928759 3.1061% 1854 0.502849
1.988668 3.2056% 1853 0.487230 2.052417 3.3118% 1852 0.471612 2.120389 3.4252% 1851
0.455993 2.193017 4.0106% 1850 0.438410 2.280970 2.3254% 1849 0.428447 2.334011
2.7841% 1848 0.416842 2.398992 2.8590% 1847 0.405255 2.467579 2.9432% 1846 0.393669
2.540204 3.0324% 1845 0.382083 2.617233 3.1325% 1844 0.370478 2.699218 3.2284% 1843
0.358891 2.786359 3.3361% 1842 0.347305 2.879313 3.4512% 1841 0.335719 2.978684
3.8105% 1840 0.323396 3.092186 2.3861% 1839 0.315859 3.165967 2.5824% 1838 0.307908
3.247725 2.6573% 1837 0.299938 3.334028 2.7232% 1836 0.291986 3.424820 2.7994% 1835
0.284035 3.520696 2.8871% 1834 0.276064 3.622343 2.9657% 1833 0.268113 3.729770
3.0563% 1832 0.260162 3.843764 3.1604% 1831 0.252191 3.965243 3.4660% 1830 0.243743
4.102677 2.4653% 1829 0.237879 4.203820 2.6804% 1828 0.231669 4.316499 10.3427%
1827 0.209954 4.762940 -4.2314% 1826 0.219231 4.561399 2.9150% 1825 0.213021
4.694365 3.0026% 1824 0.206812 4.835317 3.0955% 1823 0.200602 4.984994 3.1944% 1822
0.194392 5.144235 3.3102% 1821 0.188164 5.314519 3.2277% 1820 0.182280 5.486057
2.6573% 1819 0.177562 5.631837 2.6261% 1818 0.173018 5.779735 2.6969% 1817 0.168475
5.935611 2.7717% 1816 0.163931 6.100127 2.8507% 1815 0.159387 6.274023 2.9343% 1814
0.154844 6.458124 3.0231% 1813 0.150300 6.653357 3.1039% 1812 0.145775 6.859870
3.2172% 1811 0.141232 7.080563 3.0969% 1810 0.136989 7.299842 2.9144% 1809 0.133110
7.512587 2.8225% 1808 0.129456 7.724627 2.9199% 1807 0.125783 7.950181 2.9918% 1806
0.122129 8.188033 3.0841% 1805 0.118476 8.440556 3.1822% 1804 0.114822 8.709151
3.2868% 1803 0.111168 8.995402 3.3985% 1802 0.107514 9.301109 3.5180% 1801 0.103860

9.628327 3.3999% 1800 0.100445 9.955685 2.8419% 1799 0.097669 10.238612 2.7485%
1798 0.095057 10.520016 2.8261% 1797 0.092444 10.817325 3.7832% 1796 0.089074
11.226567 2.1272% 1795 0.087219 11.465379 3.0879% 1794 0.084607 11.819423 3.1625%
1793 0.082013 12.193213 3.2904% 1792 0.079400 12.594421 3.4024% 1791 0.076788
13.022929 3.2296% 1790 0.074385 13.443513 41.3145% 1780 0.052638 18.997626 29.4353%
1770 0.040668 24.589637 83.4728% 1750 0.022165 45.115306 29.2845% 1740 0.017145
58.327076 94.2514% 1720 0.008826 113.301158 85.8111% 1700 0.004750 210.526106
19.2490% 1690 0.003983 251.050380 88.0250% 1670 0.002118 472.037534

BASE YEAR: 1881

YEAR BYEAR/AYEAR AYEAR/BYEAR GROWTH%

2009 5.848247 0.170991 8.2857% 2001 5.400759 0.185159 1.0000% 2000 5.347285
0.187011 1.0000% 1999 5.294342 0.188881 1.0000% 1998 5.241923 0.190770 1.0000% 1997
5.190022 0.192677 1.0000% 1996 5.138636 0.194604 1.0000% 1995 5.087758 0.196550
0.9992% 1994 5.037423 0.198514 1.0008% 1993 4.987509 0.200501 1.0000% 1992 4.938128
0.202506 0.9295% 1991 4.892651 0.204388 1.2505% 1990 4.832223 0.206944 0.7224% 1989
4.797563 0.208439 1.1077% 1988 4.745004 0.210748 0.8834% 1987 4.703455 0.212610
0.5594% 1986 4.677292 0.213799 1.3056% 1985 4.617011 0.216590 0.7673% 1984 4.581856
0.218252 0.8149% 1983 4.544818 0.220031 0.9737% 1982 4.500989 0.222173 0.9508% 1981
4.458597 0.224286 0.9031% 1980 4.418693 0.226311 2.2701% 1979 4.320612 0.231449
1.0042% 1978 4.277657 0.233773 0.9896% 1977 4.235740 0.236086 0.9103% 1976 4.197528
0.238235 0.8394% 1975 4.162586 0.240235 0.9042% 1974 4.125286 0.242407 1.1568% 1973
4.078111 0.245212 0.9427% 1972 4.040026 0.247523 0.7426% 1971 4.010244 0.249361
1.4697% 1970 3.952158 0.253026 0.6968% 1969 3.924809 0.254789 0.8565% 1968 3.891477
0.256972 1.5090% 1967 3.833626 0.260850 0.9949% 1966 3.795861 0.263445 1.0575% 1965
3.756141 0.266231 1.1300% 1964 3.714170 0.269239 1.5537% 1963 3.657347 0.273422
1.4658% 1962 3.604512 0.277430 1.5364% 1961 3.549969 0.281693 2.1586% 1960 3.474957
0.287773 -1.6655% 1959 3.533812 0.282981 4.3080% 1958 3.387863 0.295171 2.1130%
1957 3.317760 0.301408 1.9895% 1956 3.253041 0.307405 2.1231% 1955 3.185412 0.313931
1.4496% 1954 3.139896 0.318482 2.1573% 1953 3.073590 0.325352 1.2298% 1952 3.036252
0.329353 1.6814% 1951 2.986045 0.334891 1.6233% 1950 2.938348 0.340327 1.4265% 1949
2.897021 0.345182 1.7790% 1948 2.846383 0.351323 1.8242% 1947 2.795390 0.357732 -
2.6320% 1946 2.870955 0.348316 3.1768% 1945 2.782558 0.359381 6.4754% 1944 2.613334
0.382653 -0.3437% 1943 2.622347 0.381338 0.6562% 1942 2.605250 0.383840 0.6633%
1941 2.588084 0.386386 -5.6614% 1940 2.743399 0.364511 8.0381% 1939 2.539288
0.393811 0.8126% 1938 2.518820 0.397011 0.7762% 1937 2.499418 0.400093 0.6029% 1936
2.484440 0.402505 0.5244% 1935 2.471480 0.404616 -3.0364% 1934 2.548873 0.392330
4.6271% 1933 2.436149 0.410484 1.3921% 1932 2.402701 0.416198 -0.2051% 1931
2.407638 0.415345 0.8886% 1930 2.386433 0.419036 1.0126% 1929 2.362510 0.423279
1.1526% 1928 2.335590 0.428157 1.2160% 1927 2.307531 0.433364 1.4086% 1926 2.275479
0.439468 1.7667% 1925 2.235976 0.447232 1.4465% 1924 2.204094 0.453701 1.7700% 1923
2.165760 0.461732 1.6165% 1922 2.131307 0.469196 1.3736% 1921 2.102428 0.475641
2.3393% 1920 2.054369 0.486767 1.3140% 1919 2.027725 0.493164 0.7676% 1918 2.012278
0.496949 0.3870% 1917 2.004521 0.498872 1.3274% 1916 1.978260 0.505495 1.4083% 1915
1.950788 0.512613 1.4458% 1914 1.922985 0.520025 1.9424% 1913 1.886345 0.530126
1.9857% 1912 1.849618 0.540652 1.5634% 1911 1.821146 0.549105 1.8169% 1910 1.788648
0.559082 1.8781% 1909 1.755675 0.569582 2.0082% 1908 1.721111 0.581020 1.9603% 1907
1.688021 0.592410 1.8264% 1906 1.657745 0.603229 1.9357% 1905 1.626266 0.614906
2.0148% 1904 1.594147 0.627295 2.1335% 1903 1.560845 0.640678 1.8151% 1902 1.533019
0.652308 1.8943% 1901 1.504518 0.664665 3.0255% 1900 1.460336 0.684774 0.6278% 1899
1.451224 0.689073 1.7757% 1898 1.425905 0.701309 1.8078% 1897 1.400586 0.713987
1.8396% 1896 1.375286 0.727121 1.8755% 1895 1.349967 0.740759 1.9114% 1894 1.324648
0.754918 1.9486% 1893 1.299329 0.769628 1.9858% 1892 1.274029 0.784912 2.0276% 1891
1.248710 0.800827 2.6465% 1890 1.216515 0.822021 1.5328% 1889 1.198149 0.834621
2.0811% 1888 1.173722 0.851990 2.1599% 1887 1.148908 0.870392 2.2075% 1886 1.124093
0.889606 2.2592% 1885 1.099259 0.909704 2.3095% 1884 1.074444 0.930714 2.3641% 1883
1.049629 0.952717 2.4214% 1882 1.024815 0.975786 2.4815% 1881 1.000000 1.000000

3.7644% 1880 0.963722 1.037644 0.9432% 1879 0.954717 1.047431 2.1464% 1878 0.934655
1.069913 2.1913% 1877 0.914613 1.093358 2.2426% 1876 0.894552 1.117878 2.2941% 1875
0.874491 1.143523 2.3456% 1874 0.854449 1.170345 2.4043% 1873 0.834387 1.198484
2.4635% 1872 0.814326 1.228009 2.5258% 1871 0.794265 1.259026 5.9947% 1870 0.749344
1.334500 -1.0968% 1869 0.757654 1.319864 2.1930% 1868 0.741395 1.348808 2.2394%
1867 0.725156 1.379013 2.2935% 1866 0.708898 1.410641 2.3445% 1865 0.692658 1.443713
2.4037% 1864 0.676400 1.478416 2.4599% 1863 0.660161 1.514783 2.5250% 1862 0.643902
1.553031 2.5872% 1861 0.627663 1.593212 2.9504% 1860 0.609675 1.640218 2.4012% 1859
0.595379 1.679604 2.7627% 1858 0.579372 1.726006 2.8412% 1857 0.563366 1.775046
2.9243% 1856 0.547359 1.826953 3.0161% 1855 0.531334 1.882057 3.1061% 1854 0.515327
1.940514 3.2056% 1853 0.499321 2.002720 3.3118% 1852 0.483315 2.069046 3.4252% 1851
0.467308 2.139915 4.0106% 1850 0.449289 2.225739 2.3254% 1849 0.439079 2.277495
2.7841% 1848 0.427186 2.340903 2.8590% 1847 0.415312 2.407830 2.9432% 1846 0.403438
2.478696 3.0324% 1845 0.391564 2.553860 3.1325% 1844 0.379671 2.633860 3.2284% 1843
0.367797 2.718890 3.3361% 1842 0.355923 2.809594 3.4512% 1841 0.344050 2.906558
3.8105% 1840 0.331421 3.017312 2.3861% 1839 0.323697 3.089307 2.5824% 1838 0.315548
3.169085 2.6573% 1837 0.307380 3.253298 2.7232% 1836 0.299232 3.341892 2.7994% 1835
0.291083 3.435446 2.8871% 1834 0.282915 3.534632 2.9657% 1833 0.274766 3.639458
3.0563% 1832 0.266618 3.750691 3.1604% 1831 0.258449 3.869229 3.4660% 1830 0.249792
4.003335 2.4653% 1829 0.243782 4.102029 2.6804% 1828 0.237418 4.211980 10.3427%
1827 0.215164 4.647610 -4.2314% 1826 0.224671 4.450950 2.9150% 1825 0.218307
4.580697 3.0026% 1824 0.211944 4.718235 3.0955% 1823 0.205580 4.864288 3.1944% 1822
0.199216 5.019673 3.3102% 1821 0.192833 5.185834 3.2277% 1820 0.186804 5.353219
2.6573% 1819 0.181968 5.495469 2.6261% 1818 0.177312 5.639786 2.6969% 1817 0.172655
5.791887 2.7717% 1816 0.167999 5.952419 2.8507% 1815 0.163343 6.122105 2.9343% 1814
0.158686 6.301748 3.0231% 1813 0.154030 6.492253 3.1039% 1812 0.149393 6.693766
3.2172% 1811 0.144736 6.909115 3.0969% 1810 0.140389 7.123085 2.9144% 1809 0.136413
7.330678 2.8225% 1808 0.132669 7.537584 2.9199% 1807 0.128905 7.757676 2.9918% 1806
0.125160 7.989769 3.0841% 1805 0.121416 8.236178 3.1822% 1804 0.117671 8.498269
3.2868% 1803 0.113927 8.777589 3.3985% 1802 0.110182 9.075894 3.5180% 1801 0.106437
9.395188 3.3999% 1800 0.102938 9.714619 2.8419% 1799 0.100093 9.990696 2.7485% 1798
0.097416 10.265286 2.8261% 1797 0.094738 10.555396 3.7832% 1796 0.091285 10.954729
2.1272% 1795 0.089383 11.187758 3.0879% 1794 0.086706 11.533229 3.1625% 1793
0.084048 11.897969 3.2904% 1792 0.081371 12.289461 3.4024% 1791 0.078693 12.707594
3.2296% 1790 0.076231 13.117993 41.3145% 1780 0.053944 18.537620 29.4353% 1770
0.041677 23.994227 83.4728% 1750 0.022715 44.022890 29.2845% 1740 0.017570
56.914753 94.2514% 1720 0.009045 110.557701 85.8111% 1700 0.004868 205.428458
19.2490% 1690 0.004082 244.971483 88.0250% 1670 0.002171 460.607685

BASE YEAR: 1880
YEAR BYEAR/AYEAR AYEAR/BYEAR GROWTH%

2009 6.068398 0.164788 8.2857% 2001 5.604065 0.178442 1.0000% 2000 5.548578
0.180226 1.0000% 1999 5.493642 0.182029 1.0000% 1998 5.439249 0.183849 1.0000% 1997
5.385395 0.185687 1.0000% 1996 5.332075 0.187544 1.0000% 1995 5.279282 0.189420
0.9992% 1994 5.227052 0.191312 1.0008% 1993 5.175259 0.193227 1.0000% 1992 5.124019
0.195159 0.9295% 1991 5.076829 0.196973 1.2505% 1990 5.014127 0.199437 0.7224% 1989
4.978162 0.200877 1.1077% 1988 4.923625 0.203102 0.8834% 1987 4.880512 0.204897
0.5594% 1986 4.853364 0.206043 1.3056% 1985 4.790814 0.208733 0.7673% 1984 4.754335
0.210334 0.8149% 1983 4.715903 0.212048 0.9737% 1982 4.670425 0.214113 0.9508% 1981
4.626436 0.216149 0.9031% 1980 4.585030 0.218101 2.2701% 1979 4.483257 0.223052
1.0042% 1978 4.438685 0.225292 0.9896% 1977 4.395190 0.227521 0.9103% 1976 4.355540
0.229593 0.8394% 1975 4.319282 0.231520 0.9042% 1974 4.280578 0.233613 1.1568% 1973
4.231627 0.236316 0.9427% 1972 4.192108 0.238543 0.7426% 1971 4.161206 0.240315
1.4697% 1970 4.100933 0.243847 0.6968% 1969 4.072554 0.245546 0.8565% 1968 4.037967
0.247649 1.5090% 1967 3.977939 0.251386 0.9949% 1966 3.938752 0.253888 1.0575% 1965
3.897537 0.256572 1.1300% 1964 3.853986 0.259472 1.5537% 1963 3.795024 0.263503
1.4658% 1962 3.740200 0.267365 1.5364% 1961 3.683604 0.271473 2.1586% 1960 3.605768

193

0.277333 -1.6655% 1959 3.666839 0.272714 4.3080% 1958 3.515396 0.284463 2.1130% 1957 3.442654 0.290474 1.9895% 1956 3.375499 0.296253 2.1231% 1955 3.305323 0.302542 1.4496% 1954 3.258094 0.306928 2.1573% 1953 3.189293 0.313549 1.2298% 1952 3.150549 0.317405 1.6814% 1951 3.098452 0.322742 1.6233% 1950 3.048959 0.327981 1.4265% 1949 3.006076 0.332660 1.7790% 1948 2.953532 0.338578 1.8242% 1947 2.900620 0.344754 - 2.6320% 1946 2.979029 0.335680 3.1768% 1945 2.887305 0.346344 6.4754% 1944 2.711710 0.368771 -0.3437% 1943 2.721062 0.367504 0.6562% 1942 2.703322 0.369915 0.6633% 1941 2.685509 0.372369 -5.6614% 1940 2.846671 0.351287 8.0381% 1939 2.634877 0.379524 0.8126% 1938 2.613638 0.382608 0.7762% 1937 2.593506 0.385578 0.6029% 1936 2.577964 0.387903 0.5244% 1935 2.564516 0.389937 -3.0364% 1934 2.644822 0.378097 4.6271% 1933 2.527855 0.395592 1.3921% 1932 2.493148 0.401099 -0.2051% 1931 2.498271 0.400277 0.8886% 1930 2.476267 0.403834 1.0126% 1929 2.451444 0.407923 1.1526% 1928 2.423511 0.412624 1.2160% 1927 2.394395 0.417642 1.4086% 1926 2.361137 0.423525 1.7667% 1925 2.320147 0.431007 1.4465% 1924 2.287065 0.437242 1.7700% 1923 2.247288 0.444981 1.6165% 1922 2.211538 0.452174 1.3736% 1921 2.181571 0.458385 2.3393% 1920 2.131704 0.469108 1.3140% 1919 2.104057 0.475272 0.7676% 1918 2.088028 0.478921 0.3870% 1917 2.079979 0.480774 1.3274% 1916 2.052730 0.487156 1.4083% 1915 2.024223 0.494017 1.4458% 1914 1.995374 0.501159 1.9424% 1913 1.957355 0.510894 1.9857% 1912 1.919245 0.521038 1.5634% 1911 1.889701 0.529184 1.8169% 1910 1.855979 0.538799 1.8781% 1909 1.821766 0.548918 2.0082% 1908 1.785900 0.559942 1.9603% 1907 1.751565 0.570918 1.8264% 1906 1.720149 0.581345 1.9357% 1905 1.687485 0.592598 2.0148% 1904 1.654157 0.604538 2.1335% 1903 1.619602 0.617436 1.8151% 1902 1.590728 0.628643 1.8943% 1901 1.561154 0.640552 3.0255% 1900 1.515308 0.659932 0.6278% 1899 1.505854 0.664075 1.7757% 1898 1.479582 0.675867 1.8078% 1897 1.453310 0.688085 1.8396% 1896 1.427057 0.700743 1.8755% 1895 1.400785 0.713885 1.9114% 1894 1.374513 0.727530 1.9486% 1893 1.348241 0.741707 1.9858% 1892 1.321988 0.756436 2.0276% 1891 1.295716 0.771774 2.6465% 1890 1.262309 0.792199 1.5328% 1889 1.243252 0.804342 2.0811% 1888 1.217906 0.821081 2.1599% 1887 1.192157 0.838816 2.2075% 1886 1.166408 0.857333 2.2592% 1885 1.140639 0.876701 2.3095% 1884 1.114890 0.896949 2.3641% 1883 1.089142 0.918154 2.4214% 1882 1.063393 0.940386 2.4815% 1881 1.037644 0.963722 3.7644% 1880 1.000000 1.000000 0.9432% 1879 0.990656 1.009432 2.1464% 1878 0.969839 1.031099 2.1913% 1877 0.949043 1.053693 2.2426% 1876 0.928226 1.077323 2.2941% 1875 0.907410 1.102038 2.3456% 1874 0.886614 1.127887 2.4043% 1873 0.865797 1.155005 2.4635% 1872 0.844981 1.183459 2.5258% 1871 0.824164 1.213351 5.9947% 1870 0.777552 1.286087 -1.0968% 1869 0.786175 1.271981 2.1930% 1868 0.769304 1.299876 2.2394% 1867 0.752454 1.328985 2.2935% 1866 0.735583 1.359465 2.3445% 1865 0.718733 1.391338 2.4037% 1864 0.701862 1.424781 2.4599% 1863 0.685012 1.459829 2.5250% 1862 0.668141 1.496690 2.5872% 1861 0.651291 1.535413 2.9504% 1860 0.632626 1.580714 2.4012% 1859 0.617791 1.618671 2.7627% 1858 0.601182 1.663390 2.8412% 1857 0.584573 1.710650 2.9243% 1856 0.567964 1.760674 3.0161% 1855 0.551335 1.813779 3.1061% 1854 0.534726 1.870116 3.2056% 1853 0.518117 1.930065 3.3118% 1852 0.501508 1.993984 3.4252% 1851 0.484900 2.062283 4.0106% 1850 0.466202 2.144993 2.3254% 1849 0.455607 2.194872 2.7841% 1848 0.443267 2.255979 2.8590% 1847 0.430946 2.320478 2.9432% 1846 0.418625 2.388773 3.0324% 1845 0.406304 2.461210 3.1325% 1844 0.393963 2.538308 3.2284% 1843 0.381642 2.620253 3.3361% 1842 0.369322 2.707667 3.4512% 1841 0.357001 2.801113 3.8105% 1840 0.343897 2.907850 2.3861% 1839 0.335882 2.977232 2.5824% 1838 0.327427 3.054116 2.6573% 1837 0.318951 3.135274 2.7232% 1836 0.310496 3.220654 2.7994% 1835 0.302041 3.310814 2.8871% 1834 0.293565 3.406401 2.9657% 1833 0.285109 3.507424 3.0563% 1832 0.276654 3.614623 3.1604% 1831 0.268178 3.728860 3.4660% 1830 0.259195 3.858101 2.4653% 1829 0.252959 3.953215 2.6804% 1828 0.246355 4.059177 10.3427% 1827 0.223264 4.479003 -4.2314% 1826 0.233129 4.289477 2.9150% 1825 0.226525 4.414517 3.0026% 1824 0.219922 4.547066 3.0955% 1823 0.213319 4.687820 3.1944% 1822 0.206715 4.837568 3.3102% 1821 0.200092 4.997700 3.2277% 1820 0.193836 5.159013 2.6573% 1819 0.188818 5.296102 2.6261% 1818 0.183986 5.435184 2.6969% 1817 0.179155 5.581767 2.7717% 1816 0.174323 5.736476 2.8507% 1815 0.169491 5.900005 2.9343% 1814 0.164660 6.073132 3.0231% 1813 0.159828 6.256726 3.1039% 1812 0.155016 6.450928

194

3.2172% 1811 0.150185 6.658464 3.0969% 1810 0.145673 6.864671 2.9144% 1809 0.141548
7.064734 2.8225% 1808 0.137663 7.264133 2.9199% 1807 0.133757 7.476241 2.9918% 1806
0.129872 7.699914 3.0841% 1805 0.125986 7.937383 3.1822% 1804 0.122101 8.189966
3.2868% 1803 0.118215 8.459153 3.3985% 1802 0.114330 8.746636 3.5180% 1801 0.110444
9.054346 3.3999% 1800 0.106813 9.362189 2.8419% 1799 0.103861 9.628250 2.7485% 1798
0.101083 9.892879 2.8261% 1797 0.098305 10.172464 3.7832% 1796 0.094721 10.557310
2.1272% 1795 0.092748 10.781885 3.0879% 1794 0.089970 11.114823 3.1625% 1793
0.087212 11.466331 3.2904% 1792 0.084434 11.843620 3.4024% 1791 0.081655 12.246584
3.2296% 1790 0.079101 12.642095 41.3145% 1780 0.055975 17.865107 29.4353% 1770
0.043246 23.123758 83.4728% 1750 0.023571 42.425815 29.2845% 1740 0.018232
54.849982 94.2514% 1720 0.009386 106.546855 85.8111% 1700 0.005051 197.975863
19.2490% 1690 0.004236 236.084335 88.0250% 1670 0.002253 443.897623

BASE YEAR: 1879

YEAR BYEAR/AYEAR AYEAR/BYEAR GROWTH%

2009 6.125637 0.163248 8.2857% 2001 5.656924 0.176775 1.0000% 2000 5.600914
0.178542 1.0000% 1999 5.545459 0.180328 1.0000% 1998 5.490554 0.182131 1.0000% 1997
5.436192 0.183952 1.0000% 1996 5.382368 0.185792 1.0000% 1995 5.329077 0.187650
0.9992% 1994 5.276355 0.189525 1.0008% 1993 5.224074 0.191422 1.0000% 1992 5.172350
0.193336 0.9295% 1991 5.124715 0.195133 1.2505% 1990 5.061422 0.197573 0.7224% 1989
5.025118 0.199000 1.1077% 1988 4.970066 0.201205 0.8834% 1987 4.926546 0.202982
0.5594% 1986 4.899142 0.204117 1.3056% 1985 4.836002 0.206782 0.7673% 1984 4.799179
0.208369 0.8149% 1983 4.760384 0.210067 0.9737% 1982 4.714477 0.212113 0.9508% 1981
4.670074 0.214129 0.9031% 1980 4.628278 0.216063 2.2701% 1979 4.525545 0.220968
1.0042% 1978 4.480552 0.223187 0.9896% 1977 4.436646 0.225395 0.9103% 1976 4.396623
0.227447 0.8394% 1975 4.360023 0.229357 0.9042% 1974 4.320954 0.231430 1.1568% 1973
4.271541 0.234108 0.9427% 1972 4.231649 0.236314 0.7426% 1971 4.200455 0.238069
1.4697% 1970 4.139614 0.241568 0.6968% 1969 4.110968 0.243252 0.8565% 1968 4.076055
0.245335 1.5090% 1967 4.015460 0.249037 0.9949% 1966 3.975903 0.251515 1.0575% 1965
3.934299 0.254175 1.1300% 1964 3.890338 0.257047 1.5537% 1963 3.830820 0.261041
1.4658% 1962 3.775479 0.264867 1.5364% 1961 3.718349 0.268937 2.1586% 1960 3.639779
0.274742 -1.6655% 1959 3.701426 0.270166 4.3080% 1958 3.548554 0.281805 2.1130%
1957 3.475126 0.287759 1.9895% 1956 3.407337 0.293484 2.1231% 1955 3.336500 0.299715
1.4496% 1954 3.288825 0.304060 2.1573% 1953 3.219375 0.310619 1.2298% 1952 3.180265
0.314439 1.6814% 1951 3.127677 0.319726 1.6233% 1950 3.077718 0.324916 1.4265% 1949
3.034430 0.329551 1.7790% 1948 2.981390 0.335414 1.8242% 1947 2.927979 0.341532 -
2.6320% 1946 3.007128 0.332543 3.1768% 1945 2.914539 0.343107 6.4754% 1944 2.737288
0.365325 -0.3437% 1943 2.746728 0.364070 0.6562% 1942 2.728821 0.366459 0.6633%
1941 2.710840 0.368889 -5.6614% 1940 2.873522 0.348005 8.0381% 1939 2.659730
0.375978 0.8126% 1938 2.638291 0.379033 0.7762% 1937 2.617969 0.381976 0.6029% 1936
2.602280 0.384278 0.5244% 1935 2.588705 0.386294 -3.0364% 1934 2.669769 0.374564
4.6271% 1933 2.551699 0.391896 1.3921% 1932 2.516664 0.397351 -0.2051% 1931
2.521836 0.396537 0.8886% 1930 2.499624 0.400060 1.0126% 1929 2.474567 0.404111
1.1526% 1928 2.446371 0.408769 1.2160% 1927 2.416980 0.413739 1.4086% 1926 2.383408
0.419567 1.7667% 1925 2.342031 0.426980 1.4465% 1924 2.308637 0.433156 1.7700% 1923
2.268485 0.440823 1.6165% 1922 2.232398 0.447949 1.3736% 1921 2.202148 0.454102
2.3393% 1920 2.151811 0.464725 1.3140% 1919 2.123903 0.470831 0.7676% 1918 2.107723
0.474446 0.3870% 1917 2.099598 0.476282 1.3274% 1916 2.072092 0.482604 1.4083% 1915
2.043316 0.489401 1.4458% 1914 2.014195 0.496476 1.9424% 1913 1.975817 0.506120
1.9857% 1912 1.937348 0.516170 1.5634% 1911 1.907525 0.524239 1.8169% 1910 1.873486
0.533764 1.8781% 1909 1.838949 0.543789 2.0082% 1908 1.802745 0.554709 1.9603% 1907
1.768086 0.565583 1.8264% 1906 1.736374 0.575913 1.9357% 1905 1.703402 0.587061
2.0148% 1904 1.669759 0.598889 2.1335% 1903 1.634878 0.611666 1.8151% 1902 1.605732
0.622769 1.8943% 1901 1.575879 0.634566 3.0255% 1900 1.529601 0.653765 0.6278% 1899
1.520058 0.657870 1.7757% 1898 1.493538 0.669551 1.8078% 1897 1.467018 0.681655
1.8396% 1896 1.440518 0.694195 1.8755% 1895 1.413998 0.707215 1.9114% 1894 1.387478
0.720732 1.9486% 1893 1.360958 0.734777 1.9858% 1892 1.334458 0.749368 2.0276% 1891

195

1.307938 0.764562 2.6465% 1890 1.274215 0.784797 1.5328% 1889 1.254979 0.796826
2.0811% 1888 1.229394 0.813409 2.1599% 1887 1.203402 0.830978 2.2075% 1886 1.177410
0.849322 2.2592% 1885 1.151398 0.868509 2.3095% 1884 1.125406 0.888568 2.3641% 1883
1.099415 0.909575 2.4214% 1882 1.073423 0.931599 2.4815% 1881 1.047431 0.954717
3.7644% 1880 1.009432 0.990656 0.9432% 1879 1.000000 1.000000 2.1464% 1878 0.978987
1.021464 2.1913% 1877 0.957995 1.043847 2.2426% 1876 0.936982 1.067257 2.2941% 1875
0.915969 1.091740 2.3456% 1874 0.894976 1.117348 2.4043% 1873 0.873964 1.144212
2.4635% 1872 0.852951 1.172401 2.5258% 1871 0.831938 1.202013 5.9947% 1870 0.784887
1.274070 -1.0968% 1869 0.793590 1.260096 2.1930% 1868 0.776561 1.287729 2.2394%
1867 0.759551 1.316567 2.2935% 1866 0.742522 1.346762 2.3445% 1865 0.725512 1.378337
2.4037% 1864 0.708482 1.411468 2.4599% 1863 0.691473 1.446188 2.5250% 1862 0.674443
1.482705 2.5872% 1861 0.657434 1.521066 2.9504% 1860 0.638593 1.565943 2.4012% 1859
0.623618 1.603545 2.7627% 1858 0.606853 1.647847 2.8412% 1857 0.590087 1.694665
2.9243% 1856 0.573321 1.744222 3.0161% 1855 0.556536 1.796830 3.1061% 1854 0.539770
1.852641 3.2056% 1853 0.523004 1.912030 3.3118% 1852 0.506239 1.975352 3.4252% 1851
0.489473 2.043013 4.0106% 1850 0.470599 2.124950 2.3254% 1849 0.459905 2.174363
2.7841% 1848 0.447448 2.234899 2.8590% 1847 0.435011 2.298795 2.9432% 1846 0.422574
2.366452 3.0324% 1845 0.410137 2.438212 3.1325% 1844 0.397679 2.514589 3.2284% 1843
0.385242 2.595769 3.3361% 1842 0.372805 2.682366 3.4512% 1841 0.360368 2.774939
3.8105% 1840 0.347140 2.880678 2.3861% 1839 0.339051 2.949413 2.5824% 1838 0.330515
3.025578 2.6573% 1837 0.321960 3.105977 2.7232% 1836 0.313425 3.190560 2.7994% 1835
0.304889 3.279877 2.8871% 1834 0.296334 3.374571 2.9657% 1833 0.287799 3.474650
3.0563% 1832 0.279264 3.580847 3.1604% 1831 0.270708 3.694017 3.4660% 1830 0.261640
3.822050 2.4653% 1829 0.255345 3.916275 2.6804% 1828 0.248679 4.021247 10.3427%
1827 0.225370 4.437151 -4.2314% 1826 0.235328 4.249396 2.9150% 1825 0.228662
4.373267 3.0026% 1824 0.221996 4.504577 3.0955% 1823 0.215331 4.644017 3.1944% 1822
0.208665 4.792365 3.3102% 1821 0.201979 4.951001 3.2277% 1820 0.195664 5.110806
2.6573% 1819 0.190599 5.246615 2.6261% 1818 0.185722 5.384397 2.6969% 1817 0.180845
5.529610 2.7717% 1816 0.175967 5.682873 2.8507% 1815 0.171090 5.844875 2.9343% 1814
0.166213 6.016383 3.0231% 1813 0.161336 6.198262 3.1039% 1812 0.156479 6.390649
3.2172% 1811 0.151601 6.596247 3.0969% 1810 0.147047 6.800527 2.9144% 1809 0.142883
6.998720 2.8225% 1808 0.138961 7.196256 2.9199% 1807 0.135019 7.406382 2.9918% 1806
0.131097 7.627965 3.0841% 1805 0.127174 7.863215 3.1822% 1804 0.123252 8.113438
3.2868% 1803 0.119330 8.380109 3.3985% 1802 0.115408 8.664906 3.5180% 1801 0.111486
8.969741 3.3999% 1800 0.107820 9.274708 2.8419% 1799 0.104841 9.538283 2.7485% 1798
0.102036 9.800438 2.8261% 1797 0.099232 10.077411 3.7832% 1796 0.095615 10.458661
2.1272% 1795 0.093623 10.681137 3.0879% 1794 0.090819 11.010964 3.1625% 1793
0.088034 11.359187 3.2904% 1792 0.085230 11.732952 3.4024% 1791 0.082426 12.132150
3.2296% 1790 0.079847 12.523965 41.3145% 1780 0.056503 17.698173 29.4353% 1770
0.043653 22.907686 83.4728% 1750 0.023793 42.029382 29.2845% 1740 0.018404
54.337456 94.2514% 1720 0.009474 105.551266 85.8111% 1700 0.005099 196.125947
19.2490% 1690 0.004276 233.878327 88.0250% 1670 0.002274 439.749777

BASE YEAR: 1878

YEAR BYEAR/AYEAR AYEAR/BYEAR GROWTH%

2009 6.257117 0.159818 8.2857% 2001 5.778343 0.173060 1.0000% 2000 5.721131
0.174791 1.0000% 1999 5.664486 0.176539 1.0000% 1998 5.608402 0.178304 1.0000% 1997
5.552874 0.180087 1.0000% 1996 5.497895 0.181888 1.0000% 1995 5.443460 0.183707
0.9992% 1994 5.389606 0.185542 1.0008% 1993 5.336202 0.187399 1.0000% 1992 5.283369
0.189273 0.9295% 1991 5.234712 0.191032 1.2505% 1990 5.170059 0.193421 0.7224% 1989
5.132976 0.194819 1.1077% 1988 5.076743 0.196977 0.8834% 1987 5.032289 0.198717
0.5594% 1986 5.004297 0.199828 1.3056% 1985 4.939802 0.202437 0.7673% 1984 4.902188
0.203991 0.8149% 1983 4.862561 0.205653 0.9737% 1982 4.815668 0.207656 0.9508% 1981
4.770312 0.209630 0.9031% 1980 4.727618 0.211523 2.2701% 1979 4.622680 0.216325
1.0042% 1978 4.576722 0.218497 0.9896% 1977 4.531874 0.220659 0.9103% 1976 4.490991
0.222668 0.8394% 1975 4.453606 0.224537 0.9042% 1974 4.413698 0.226567 1.1568% 1973
4.363225 0.229188 0.9427% 1972 4.322477 0.231349 0.7426% 1971 4.290613 0.233067

1.4697% 1970 4.228466 0.236492 0.6968% 1969 4.199205 0.238140 0.8565% 1968 4.163543 0.240180 1.5090% 1967 4.101647 0.243804 0.9949% 1966 4.061242 0.246230 1.0575% 1965 4.018745 0.248834 1.1300% 1964 3.973840 0.251646 1.5537% 1963 3.913044 0.255555 1.4658% 1962 3.856515 0.259301 1.5364% 1961 3.798159 0.263285 2.1586% 1960 3.717903 0.268969 -1.6655% 1959 3.780872 0.264489 4.3080% 1958 3.624720 0.275883 2.1130% 1957 3.549716 0.281713 1.9895% 1956 3.480472 0.287317 2.1231% 1955 3.408114 0.293417 1.4496% 1954 3.359416 0.297671 2.1573% 1953 3.288475 0.304092 1.2298% 1952 3.248526 0.307832 1.6814% 1951 3.194809 0.313008 1.6233% 1950 3.143777 0.318089 1.4265% 1949 3.099561 0.322626 1.7790% 1948 3.045382 0.328366 1.8242% 1947 2.990825 0.334356 -2.6320% 1946 3.071672 0.325556 3.1768% 1945 2.977096 0.335898 6.4754% 1944 2.796041 0.357649 -0.3437% 1943 2.805683 0.356419 0.6562% 1942 2.787392 0.358758 0.6633% 1941 2.769025 0.361138 -5.6614% 1940 2.935199 0.340692 8.0381% 1939 2.716818 0.368078 0.8126% 1938 2.694918 0.371069 0.7762% 1937 2.674160 0.373949 0.6029% 1936 2.658135 0.376204 0.5244% 1935 2.644269 0.378176 -3.0364% 1934 2.727073 0.366694 4.6271% 1933 2.606468 0.383661 1.3921% 1932 2.570681 0.389002 -0.2051% 1931 2.575964 0.388204 0.8886% 1930 2.553276 0.391654 1.0126% 1929 2.527681 0.395620 1.1526% 1928 2.498879 0.400179 1.2160% 1927 2.468858 0.405046 1.4086% 1926 2.434565 0.410751 1.7667% 1925 2.392300 0.418008 1.4465% 1924 2.358189 0.424054 1.7700% 1923 2.317176 0.431560 1.6165% 1922 2.280314 0.438536 1.3736% 1921 2.249415 0.444560 2.3393% 1920 2.197997 0.454960 1.3140% 1919 2.169490 0.460938 0.7676% 1918 2.152963 0.464476 0.3870% 1917 2.144663 0.466274 1.3274% 1916 2.116567 0.472463 1.4083% 1915 2.087174 0.479117 1.4458% 1914 2.057427 0.486044 1.9424% 1913 2.018226 0.495485 1.9857% 1912 1.978931 0.505323 1.5634% 1911 1.948468 0.513224 1.8169% 1910 1.913698 0.522549 1.8781% 1909 1.878420 0.532362 2.0082% 1908 1.841439 0.543053 1.9603% 1907 1.806036 0.553699 1.8264% 1906 1.773643 0.563811 1.9357% 1905 1.739963 0.574725 2.0148% 1904 1.705598 0.586304 2.1335% 1903 1.669969 0.598813 1.8151% 1902 1.640197 0.609683 1.8943% 1901 1.609704 0.621232 3.0255% 1900 1.562432 0.640028 0.6278% 1899 1.552684 0.644046 1.7757% 1898 1.525595 0.655482 1.8078% 1897 1.498505 0.667332 1.8396% 1896 1.471437 0.679608 1.8755% 1895 1.444348 0.692354 1.9114% 1894 1.417258 0.705588 1.9486% 1893 1.390169 0.719337 1.9858% 1892 1.363100 0.733622 2.0276% 1891 1.336011 0.748497 2.6465% 1890 1.301565 0.768306 1.5328% 1889 1.281916 0.780083 2.0811% 1888 1.255781 0.796317 2.1599% 1887 1.229232 0.813516 2.2075% 1886 1.202682 0.831475 2.2592% 1885 1.176112 0.850259 2.3095% 1884 1.149562 0.869897 2.3641% 1883 1.123012 0.890462 2.4214% 1882 1.096463 0.912024 2.4815% 1881 1.069913 0.934655 3.7644% 1880 1.031099 0.969839 0.9432% 1879 1.021464 0.978987 2.1464% 1878 1.000000 1.000000 2.1913% 1877 0.978557 1.021913 2.2426% 1876 0.957093 1.044831 2.2941% 1875 0.935629 1.068800 2.3456% 1874 0.914186 1.093869 2.4043% 1873 0.892722 1.120169 2.4635% 1872 0.871258 1.147765 2.5258% 1871 0.849794 1.176755 5.9947% 1870 0.801733 1.247298 -1.0968% 1869 0.810624 1.233618 2.1930% 1868 0.793229 1.260670 2.2394% 1867 0.775854 1.288902 2.2935% 1866 0.758459 1.318463 2.3445% 1865 0.741084 1.349374 2.4037% 1864 0.723689 1.381809 2.4599% 1863 0.706315 1.415800 2.5250% 1862 0.688919 1.451549 2.5872% 1861 0.671545 1.489104 2.9504% 1860 0.652299 1.533039 2.4012% 1859 0.637003 1.569850 2.7627% 1858 0.619878 1.613221 2.8412% 1857 0.602753 1.659056 2.9243% 1856 0.585627 1.707571 3.0161% 1855 0.568481 1.759074 3.1061% 1854 0.551356 1.813712 3.2056% 1853 0.534230 1.871853 3.3118% 1852 0.517105 1.933844 3.4252% 1851 0.499979 2.000083 4.0106% 1850 0.480700 2.080298 2.3254% 1849 0.469776 2.128673 2.7841% 1848 0.457052 2.187937 2.8590% 1847 0.444348 2.250491 2.9432% 1846 0.431644 2.316726 3.0324% 1845 0.418940 2.386978 3.1325% 1844 0.406215 2.461751 3.2284% 1843 0.393511 2.541225 3.3361% 1842 0.380807 2.626002 3.4512% 1841 0.368103 2.716630 3.8105% 1840 0.354591 2.820147 2.3861% 1839 0.346328 2.887437 2.5824% 1838 0.337609 2.962002 2.6573% 1837 0.328870 3.040712 2.7232% 1836 0.320152 3.123517 2.7994% 1835 0.311434 3.210958 2.8871% 1834 0.302694 3.303662 2.9657% 1833 0.293976 3.401638 3.0563% 1832 0.285258 3.505603 3.1604% 1831 0.276518 3.616395 3.4660% 1830 0.267255 3.741738 2.4653% 1829 0.260825 3.833983 2.6804% 1828 0.254017 3.936749 10.3427% 1827 0.230207 4.343913 -4.2314% 1826 0.240379 4.160104 2.9150% 1825 0.233570 4.281372 3.0026% 1824 0.226761 4.409923 3.0955% 1823 0.219953 4.546433 3.1944% 1822

0.213144 4.691663 3.3102% 1821 0.206315 4.846966 3.2277% 1820 0.199864 5.003414
2.6573% 1819 0.194690 5.136368 2.6261% 1818 0.189708 5.271255 2.6969% 1817 0.184726
5.413417 2.7717% 1816 0.179744 5.563460 2.8507% 1815 0.174762 5.722057 2.9343% 1814
0.169780 5.889962 3.0231% 1813 0.164798 6.068019 3.1039% 1812 0.159837 6.256364
3.2172% 1811 0.154855 6.457641 3.0969% 1810 0.150204 6.657628 2.9144% 1809 0.145950
6.851657 2.8225% 1808 0.141944 7.045042 2.9199% 1807 0.137917 7.250753 2.9918% 1806
0.133910 7.467679 3.0841% 1805 0.129904 7.697987 3.1822% 1804 0.125898 7.942951
3.2868% 1803 0.121891 8.204019 3.3985% 1802 0.117885 8.482831 3.5180% 1801 0.113879
8.781261 3.3999% 1800 0.110134 9.079820 2.8419% 1799 0.107091 9.337856 2.7485% 1798
0.104226 9.594503 2.8261% 1797 0.101362 9.865656 3.7832% 1796 0.097667 10.238895
2.1272% 1795 0.095632 10.456696 3.0879% 1794 0.092768 10.779593 3.1625% 1793
0.089924 11.120499 3.2904% 1792 0.087059 11.486409 3.4024% 1791 0.084195 11.877219
3.2296% 1790 0.081561 12.260801 41.3145% 1780 0.057716 17.326284 29.4353% 1770
0.044590 22.426330 83.4728% 1750 0.024304 41.146225 29.2845% 1740 0.018799
53.195671 94.2514% 1720 0.009677 103.333333 85.8111% 1700 0.005208 192.004783
19.2490% 1690 0.004368 228.963878 88.0250% 1670 0.002323 430.509383
BASE YEAR: 1877
YEAR BYEAR/AYEAR AYEAR/BYEAR GROWTH%
2009 6.394229 0.156391 8.2857% 2001 5.904964 0.169349 1.0000% 2000 5.846498
0.171043 1.0000% 1999 5.788612 0.172753 1.0000% 1998 5.731299 0.174481 1.0000% 1997
5.674554 0.176225 1.0000% 1996 5.618370 0.177988 1.0000% 1995 5.562742 0.179767
0.9992% 1994 5.507708 0.181564 1.0008% 1993 5.453134 0.183381 1.0000% 1992 5.399143
0.185215 0.9295% 1991 5.349420 0.186936 1.2505% 1990 5.283351 0.189274 0.7224% 1989
5.245455 0.190641 1.1077% 1988 5.187989 0.192753 0.8834% 1987 5.142562 0.194456
0.5594% 1986 5.113956 0.195543 1.3056% 1985 5.048047 0.198096 0.7673% 1984 5.009609
0.199616 0.8149% 1983 4.969114 0.201243 0.9737% 1982 4.921194 0.203203 0.9508% 1981
4.874844 0.205135 0.9031% 1980 4.831215 0.206987 2.2701% 1979 4.723977 0.211686
1.0042% 1978 4.677012 0.213812 0.9896% 1977 4.631181 0.215928 0.9103% 1976 4.589402
0.217893 0.8394% 1975 4.551197 0.219722 0.9042% 1974 4.510416 0.221709 1.1568% 1973
4.458836 0.224274 0.9427% 1972 4.417195 0.226388 0.7426% 1971 4.384633 0.228069
1.4697% 1970 4.321124 0.231421 0.6968% 1969 4.291222 0.233034 0.8565% 1968 4.254778
0.235030 1.5090% 1967 4.191526 0.238577 0.9949% 1966 4.150235 0.240950 1.0575% 1965
4.106807 0.243498 1.1300% 1964 4.060918 0.246250 1.5537% 1963 3.998791 0.250076
1.4658% 1962 3.941023 0.253741 1.5364% 1961 3.881388 0.257640 2.1586% 1960 3.799373
0.263201 -1.6655% 1959 3.863723 0.258818 4.3080% 1958 3.704148 0.269968 2.1130%
1957 3.627500 0.275672 1.9895% 1956 3.556739 0.281156 2.1231% 1955 3.482796 0.287126
1.4496% 1954 3.433031 0.291288 2.1573% 1953 3.360535 0.297572 1.2298% 1952 3.319711
0.301231 1.6814% 1951 3.264817 0.306296 1.6233% 1950 3.212667 0.311268 1.4265% 1949
3.167482 0.315708 1.7790% 1948 3.112116 0.321325 1.8242% 1947 3.056363 0.327186 -
2.6320% 1946 3.138982 0.318575 3.1768% 1945 3.042333 0.328695 6.4754% 1944 2.857310
0.349979 -0.3437% 1943 2.867164 0.348777 0.6562% 1942 2.848472 0.351065 0.6633%
1941 2.829702 0.353394 -5.6614% 1940 2.999518 0.333387 8.0381% 1939 2.776352
0.360185 0.8126% 1938 2.753972 0.363112 0.7762% 1937 2.732759 0.365931 0.6029% 1936
2.716383 0.368137 0.5244% 1935 2.702213 0.370067 -3.0364% 1934 2.786831 0.358831
4.6271% 1933 2.663584 0.375434 1.3921% 1932 2.627013 0.380661 -0.2051% 1931
2.632411 0.379880 0.8886% 1930 2.609226 0.383255 1.0126% 1929 2.583070 0.387136
1.1526% 1928 2.553637 0.391598 1.2160% 1927 2.522958 0.396360 1.4086% 1926 2.487913
0.401943 1.7667% 1925 2.444723 0.409044 1.4465% 1924 2.409864 0.414961 1.7700% 1923
2.367952 0.422306 1.6165% 1922 2.330283 0.429133 1.3736% 1921 2.298706 0.435027
2.3393% 1920 2.246162 0.445204 1.3140% 1919 2.217030 0.451054 0.7676% 1918 2.200141
0.454516 0.3870% 1917 2.191659 0.456275 1.3274% 1916 2.162947 0.462332 1.4083% 1915
2.132910 0.468843 1.4458% 1914 2.102512 0.475622 1.9424% 1913 2.062451 0.484860
1.9857% 1912 2.022295 0.494488 1.5634% 1911 1.991165 0.502219 1.8169% 1910 1.955633
0.511343 1.8781% 1909 1.919582 0.520947 2.0082% 1908 1.881791 0.531409 1.9603% 1907
1.845612 0.541826 1.8264% 1906 1.812509 0.551721 1.9357% 1905 1.778091 0.562401
2.0148% 1904 1.742973 0.573732 2.1335% 1903 1.706563 0.585973 1.8151% 1902 1.676139

0.596609 1.8943% 1901 1.644977 0.607911 3.0255% 1900 1.596670 0.626304 0.6278% 1899
1.586708 0.630236 1.7757% 1898 1.559025 0.641427 1.8078% 1897 1.531342 0.653022
1.8396% 1896 1.503680 0.665035 1.8755% 1895 1.475998 0.677508 1.9114% 1894 1.448315
0.690458 1.9486% 1893 1.420632 0.703912 1.9858% 1892 1.392970 0.717891 2.0276% 1891
1.365287 0.732447 2.6465% 1890 1.330086 0.751831 1.5328% 1889 1.310006 0.763355
2.0811% 1888 1.283299 0.779242 2.1599% 1887 1.256168 0.796072 2.2075% 1886 1.229036
0.813646 2.2592% 1885 1.201884 0.832027 2.3095% 1884 1.174752 0.851243 2.3641% 1883
1.147621 0.871368 2.4214% 1882 1.120490 0.892467 2.4815% 1881 1.093358 0.914613
3.7644% 1880 1.053693 0.949043 0.9432% 1879 1.043847 0.957995 2.1464% 1878 1.021913
0.978557 2.1913% 1877 1.000000 1.000000 2.2426% 1876 0.978066 1.022426 2.2941% 1875
0.956132 1.045881 2.3456% 1874 0.934219 1.070413 2.4043% 1873 0.912284 1.096149
2.4635% 1872 0.890350 1.123154 2.5258% 1871 0.868416 1.151522 5.9947% 1870 0.819302
1.220552 -1.0968% 1869 0.828387 1.207165 2.1930% 1868 0.810611 1.233638 2.2394%
1867 0.792855 1.261264 2.2935% 1866 0.775079 1.290191 2.3445% 1865 0.757324 1.320439
2.4037% 1864 0.739547 1.352179 2.4599% 1863 0.721792 1.385441 2.5250% 1862 0.704016
1.420423 2.5872% 1861 0.686260 1.457173 2.9504% 1860 0.666593 1.500165 2.4012% 1859
0.650962 1.536188 2.7627% 1858 0.633461 1.578628 2.8412% 1857 0.615961 1.623480
2.9243% 1856 0.598460 1.670956 3.0161% 1855 0.580938 1.721354 3.1061% 1854 0.563437
1.774820 3.2056% 1853 0.545937 1.831714 3.3118% 1852 0.528436 1.892377 3.4252% 1851
0.510935 1.957195 4.0106% 1850 0.491234 2.035690 2.3254% 1849 0.480070 2.083028
2.7841% 1848 0.467067 2.141021 2.8590% 1847 0.454085 2.202233 2.9432% 1846 0.441102
2.267048 3.0324% 1845 0.428120 2.335794 3.1325% 1844 0.415116 2.408963 3.2284% 1843
0.402134 2.486733 3.3361% 1842 0.389152 2.569692 3.4512% 1841 0.376169 2.658377
3.8105% 1840 0.362362 2.759674 2.3861% 1839 0.353917 2.825521 2.5824% 1838 0.345008
2.898487 2.6573% 1837 0.336077 2.975510 2.7232% 1836 0.327167 3.056539 2.7994% 1835
0.318258 3.142105 2.8871% 1834 0.309327 3.232821 2.9657% 1833 0.300418 3.328697
3.0563% 1832 0.291508 3.430432 3.1604% 1831 0.282578 3.538848 3.4660% 1830 0.273112
3.661504 2.4653% 1829 0.266541 3.751771 2.6804% 1828 0.259583 3.852333 10.3427%
1827 0.235252 4.250766 -4.2314% 1826 0.245646 4.070898 2.9150% 1825 0.238688
4.189566 3.0026% 1824 0.231730 4.315361 3.0955% 1823 0.224772 4.448943 3.1944% 1822
0.217815 4.591060 3.3102% 1821 0.210836 4.743032 3.2277% 1820 0.204243 4.896125
2.6573% 1819 0.198956 5.026229 2.6261% 1818 0.193865 5.158223 2.6969% 1817 0.188774
5.297337 2.7717% 1816 0.183683 5.444162 2.8507% 1815 0.178592 5.599359 2.9343% 1814
0.173501 5.763663 3.0231% 1813 0.168410 5.937901 3.1039% 1812 0.163340 6.122208
3.2172% 1811 0.158249 6.319169 3.0969% 1810 0.153495 6.514868 2.9144% 1809 0.149148
6.704736 2.8225% 1808 0.145054 6.893975 2.9199% 1807 0.140939 7.095274 2.9918% 1806
0.136845 7.307549 3.0841% 1805 0.132751 7.532918 3.1822% 1804 0.128657 7.772630
3.2868% 1803 0.124562 8.028099 3.3985% 1802 0.120468 8.300933 3.5180% 1801 0.116374
8.592964 3.3999% 1800 0.112548 8.885120 2.8419% 1799 0.109438 9.137624 2.7485% 1798
0.106510 9.388767 2.8261% 1797 0.103583 9.654106 3.7832% 1796 0.099807 10.019341
2.1272% 1795 0.097728 10.232472 3.0879% 1794 0.094801 10.548445 3.1625% 1793
0.091895 10.882041 3.2904% 1792 0.088967 11.240105 3.4024% 1791 0.086040 11.622535
3.2296% 1790 0.083348 11.997892 41.3145% 1780 0.058981 16.954755 29.4353% 1770
0.045568 21.945440 83.4728% 1750 0.024836 40.263922 29.2845% 1740 0.019210
52.054991 94.2514% 1720 0.009889 101.117546 85.8111% 1700 0.005322 187.887605
19.2490% 1690 0.004463 224.054183 88.0250% 1670 0.002374 421.277927
     BASE YEAR: 1876
     YEAR BYEAR/AYEAR AYEAR/BYEAR GROWTH%
     2009 6.537627 0.152961 8.2857% 2001 6.037389 0.165635 1.0000% 2000 5.977612
0.167291 1.0000% 1999 5.918428 0.168964 1.0000% 1998 5.859830 0.170653 1.0000% 1997
5.801812 0.172360 1.0000% 1996 5.744368 0.174084 1.0000% 1995 5.687493 0.175824
0.9992% 1994 5.631225 0.177581 1.0008% 1993 5.575427 0.179358 1.0000% 1992 5.520225
0.181152 0.9295% 1991 5.469386 0.182836 1.2505% 1990 5.401836 0.185122 0.7224% 1989
5.363090 0.186460 1.1077% 1988 5.304336 0.188525 0.8834% 1987 5.257889 0.190190
0.5594% 1986 5.228642 0.191254 1.3056% 1985 5.161255 0.193751 0.7673% 1984 5.121955
0.195238 0.8149% 1983 5.080552 0.196829 0.9737% 1982 5.031557 0.198746 0.9508% 1981

4.984167 0.200635 0.9031% 1980 4.939560 0.202447 2.2701% 1979 4.829917 0.207043
1.0042% 1978 4.781899 0.209122 0.9896% 1977 4.735040 0.211191 0.9103% 1976 4.692324
0.213114 0.8394% 1975 4.653263 0.214903 0.9042% 1974 4.611567 0.216846 1.1568% 1973
4.558831 0.219355 0.9427% 1972 4.516256 0.221422 0.7426% 1971 4.482964 0.223067
1.4697% 1970 4.418030 0.226345 0.6968% 1969 4.387457 0.227922 0.8565% 1968 4.350196
0.229875 1.5090% 1967 4.285526 0.233344 0.9949% 1966 4.243309 0.235665 1.0575% 1965
4.198907 0.238157 1.1300% 1964 4.151989 0.240848 1.5537% 1963 4.088468 0.244590
1.4658% 1962 4.029404 0.248176 1.5364% 1961 3.968432 0.251989 2.1586% 1960 3.884578
0.257428 -1.6655% 1959 3.950371 0.253141 4.3080% 1958 3.787218 0.264046 2.1130%
1957 3.708851 0.269625 1.9895% 1956 3.636503 0.274989 2.1231% 1955 3.560902 0.280828
1.4496% 1954 3.510020 0.284899 2.1573% 1953 3.435899 0.291045 1.2298% 1952 3.394159
0.294624 1.6814% 1951 3.338034 0.299578 1.6233% 1950 3.284714 0.304440 1.4265% 1949
3.238516 0.308783 1.7790% 1948 3.181908 0.314277 1.8242% 1947 3.124905 0.320010 -
2.6320% 1946 3.209377 0.311587 3.1768% 1945 3.110561 0.321485 6.4754% 1944 2.921389
0.342303 -0.3437% 1943 2.931463 0.341127 0.6562% 1942 2.912352 0.343365 0.6633%
1941 2.893162 0.345643 -5.6614% 1940 3.066785 0.326074 8.0381% 1939 2.838615
0.352285 0.8126% 1938 2.815733 0.355147 0.7762% 1937 2.794044 0.357904 0.6029% 1936
2.777301 0.360062 0.5244% 1935 2.762813 0.361950 -3.0364% 1934 2.849329 0.350960
4.6271% 1933 2.723318 0.367199 1.3921% 1932 2.685926 0.372311 -0.2051% 1931
2.691446 0.371547 0.8886% 1930 2.667740 0.374849 1.0126% 1929 2.640998 0.378645
1.1526% 1928 2.610905 0.383009 1.2160% 1927 2.579538 0.387666 1.4086% 1926 2.543708
0.393127 1.7667% 1925 2.499548 0.400072 1.4465% 1924 2.463908 0.405859 1.7700% 1923
2.421056 0.413043 1.6165% 1922 2.382542 0.419720 1.3736% 1921 2.350257 0.425485
2.3393% 1920 2.296534 0.435439 1.3140% 1919 2.266749 0.441160 0.7676% 1918 2.249481
0.444547 0.3870% 1917 2.240809 0.446267 1.3274% 1916 2.211454 0.452191 1.4083% 1915
2.180743 0.458559 1.4458% 1914 2.149663 0.465189 1.9424% 1913 2.108704 0.474225
1.9857% 1912 2.067647 0.483642 1.5634% 1911 2.035819 0.491203 1.8169% 1910 1.999490
0.500128 1.8781% 1909 1.962630 0.509520 2.0082% 1908 1.923992 0.519753 1.9603% 1907
1.887002 0.529941 1.8264% 1906 1.853157 0.539620 1.9357% 1905 1.817967 0.550065
2.0148% 1904 1.782061 0.561148 2.1335% 1903 1.744835 0.573120 1.8151% 1902 1.713728
0.583523 1.8943% 1901 1.681868 0.594577 3.0255% 1900 1.632477 0.612566 0.6278% 1899
1.622292 0.616412 1.7757% 1898 1.593988 0.627357 1.8078% 1897 1.565684 0.638698
1.8396% 1896 1.537402 0.650448 1.8755% 1895 1.509098 0.662647 1.9114% 1894 1.480795
0.675313 1.9486% 1893 1.452491 0.688472 1.9858% 1892 1.424209 0.702144 2.0276% 1891
1.395905 0.716381 2.6465% 1890 1.359915 0.735340 1.5328% 1889 1.339384 0.746612
2.0811% 1888 1.312078 0.762150 2.1599% 1887 1.284339 0.778611 2.2075% 1886 1.256599
0.795799 2.2592% 1885 1.228837 0.813777 2.3095% 1884 1.201097 0.832572 2.3641% 1883
1.173358 0.852255 2.4214% 1882 1.145618 0.872891 2.4815% 1881 1.117878 0.894552
3.7644% 1880 1.077323 0.928226 0.9432% 1879 1.067257 0.936982 2.1464% 1878 1.044831
0.957093 2.1913% 1877 1.022426 0.978066 2.2426% 1876 1.000000 1.000000 2.2941% 1875
0.977574 1.022941 2.3456% 1874 0.955169 1.046935 2.4043% 1873 0.932743 1.072106
2.4635% 1872 0.910317 1.098518 2.5258% 1871 0.887891 1.126264 5.9947% 1870 0.837675
1.193780 -1.0968% 1869 0.846965 1.180687 2.1930% 1868 0.828790 1.206579 2.2394%
1867 0.810636 1.233599 2.2935% 1866 0.792461 1.261892 2.3445% 1865 0.774308 1.291476
2.4037% 1864 0.756132 1.322520 2.4599% 1863 0.737979 1.355052 2.5250% 1862 0.719804
1.389267 2.5872% 1861 0.701651 1.425211 2.9504% 1860 0.681542 1.467260 2.4012% 1859
0.665561 1.502493 2.7627% 1858 0.647667 1.544002 2.8412% 1857 0.629774 1.587871
2.9243% 1856 0.611881 1.634305 3.0161% 1855 0.593966 1.683597 3.1061% 1854 0.576073
1.735891 3.2056% 1853 0.558180 1.791537 3.3118% 1852 0.540287 1.850869 3.4252% 1851
0.522394 1.914266 4.0106% 1850 0.502250 1.991039 2.3254% 1849 0.490837 2.037338
2.7841% 1848 0.477541 2.094059 2.8590% 1847 0.464268 2.153929 2.9432% 1846 0.450994
2.217322 3.0324% 1845 0.437721 2.284560 3.1325% 1844 0.424426 2.356124 3.2284% 1843
0.411152 2.432189 3.3361% 1842 0.397879 2.513328 3.4512% 1841 0.384605 2.600068
3.8105% 1840 0.370488 2.699143 2.3861% 1839 0.361854 2.763546 2.5824% 1838 0.352745
2.834911 2.6573% 1837 0.343614 2.910244 2.7232% 1836 0.334505 2.989496 2.7994% 1835
0.325395 3.073185 2.8871% 1834 0.316264 3.161912 2.9657% 1833 0.307155 3.255684

200

3.0563% 1832 0.298046 3.355188 3.1604% 1831 0.288915 3.461227 3.4660% 1830 0.279237
3.581192 2.4653% 1829 0.272518 3.669479 2.6804% 1828 0.265404 3.767835 10.3427%
1827 0.240527 4.157529 -4.2314% 1826 0.251155 3.981606 2.9150% 1825 0.244041
4.097672 3.0026% 1824 0.236927 4.220707 3.0955% 1823 0.229813 4.351359 3.1944% 1822
0.222699 4.490358 3.3102% 1821 0.215564 4.638998 3.2277% 1820 0.208824 4.788733
2.6573% 1819 0.203418 4.915983 2.6261% 1818 0.198213 5.045082 2.6969% 1817 0.193008
5.181144 2.7717% 1816 0.187802 5.324749 2.8507% 1815 0.182597 5.476541 2.9343% 1814
0.177392 5.637242 3.0231% 1813 0.172186 5.807658 3.1039% 1812 0.167003 5.987922
3.2172% 1811 0.161798 6.180563 3.0969% 1810 0.156937 6.371970 2.9144% 1809 0.152493
6.557673 2.8225% 1808 0.148307 6.742761 2.9199% 1807 0.144100 6.939645 2.9918% 1806
0.139914 7.147264 3.0841% 1805 0.135728 7.367689 3.1822% 1804 0.131542 7.602143
3.2868% 1803 0.127356 7.852010 3.3985% 1802 0.123170 8.118859 3.5180% 1801 0.118984
8.404484 3.3999% 1800 0.115072 8.690232 2.8419% 1799 0.111892 8.937197 2.7485% 1798
0.108899 9.182832 2.8261% 1797 0.105906 9.442351 3.7832% 1796 0.102045 9.799575
2.1272% 1795 0.099920 10.008031 3.0879% 1794 0.096927 10.317073 3.1625% 1793
0.093955 10.643352 3.2904% 1792 0.090962 10.993562 3.4024% 1791 0.087969 11.367604
3.2296% 1790 0.085217 11.734728 41.3145% 1780 0.060303 16.582866 29.4353% 1770
0.046589 21.464085 83.4728% 1750 0.025393 39.380765 29.2845% 1740 0.019641
50.913207 94.2514% 1720 0.010111 98.899614 85.8111% 1700 0.005442 183.766441
19.2490% 1690 0.004563 219.139734 88.0250% 1670 0.002427 412.037534
BASE YEAR: 1875
YEAR BYEAR/AYEAR AYEAR/BYEAR GROWTH%
2009 6.687603 0.149530 8.2857% 2001 6.175890 0.161920 1.0000% 2000 6.114742
0.163539 1.0000% 1999 6.054200 0.165175 1.0000% 1998 5.994258 0.166826 1.0000% 1997
5.934908 0.168495 1.0000% 1996 5.876147 0.170180 1.0000% 1995 5.817967 0.171881
0.9992% 1994 5.760408 0.173599 1.0008% 1993 5.703330 0.175336 1.0000% 1992 5.646862
0.177090 0.9295% 1991 5.594857 0.178736 1.2505% 1990 5.525757 0.180971 0.7224% 1989
5.486123 0.182278 1.1077% 1988 5.426020 0.184297 0.8834% 1987 5.378508 0.185925
0.5594% 1986 5.348590 0.186965 1.3056% 1985 5.279657 0.189406 0.7673% 1984 5.239456
0.190860 0.8149% 1983 5.197102 0.192415 0.9737% 1982 5.146984 0.194289 0.9508% 1981
5.098507 0.196136 0.9031% 1980 5.052876 0.197907 2.2701% 1979 4.940718 0.202400
1.0042% 1978 4.891598 0.204432 0.9896% 1977 4.843665 0.206455 0.9103% 1976 4.799969
0.208335 0.8394% 1975 4.760012 0.210084 0.9042% 1974 4.717359 0.211983 1.1568% 1973
4.663413 0.214435 0.9427% 1972 4.619861 0.216457 0.7426% 1971 4.585805 0.218064
1.4697% 1970 4.519382 0.221269 0.6968% 1969 4.488108 0.222811 0.8565% 1968 4.449992
0.224719 1.5090% 1967 4.383838 0.228111 0.9949% 1966 4.340653 0.230380 1.0575% 1965
4.295232 0.232816 1.1300% 1964 4.247238 0.235447 1.5537% 1963 4.182260 0.239105
1.4658% 1962 4.121841 0.242610 1.5364% 1961 4.059470 0.246338 2.1586% 1960 3.973692
0.251655 -1.6655% 1959 4.040995 0.247464 4.3080% 1958 3.874099 0.258125 2.1130%
1957 3.793934 0.263579 1.9895% 1956 3.719927 0.268823 2.1231% 1955 3.642591 0.274530
1.4496% 1954 3.590542 0.278509 2.1573% 1953 3.514721 0.284518 1.2298% 1952 3.472023
0.288017 1.6814% 1951 3.414611 0.292859 1.6233% 1950 3.360068 0.297613 1.4265% 1949
3.312809 0.301859 1.7790% 1948 3.254903 0.307229 1.8242% 1947 3.196592 0.312833 -
2.6320% 1946 3.283002 0.304599 3.1768% 1945 3.181919 0.314276 6.4754% 1944 2.988407
0.334626 -0.3437% 1943 2.998713 0.333476 0.6562% 1942 2.979163 0.335665 0.6633%
1941 2.959532 0.337891 -5.6614% 1940 3.137139 0.318762 8.0381% 1939 2.903734
0.344384 0.8126% 1938 2.880327 0.347183 0.7762% 1937 2.858141 0.349878 0.6029% 1936
2.841013 0.351987 0.5244% 1935 2.826193 0.353833 -3.0364% 1934 2.914694 0.343089
4.6271% 1933 2.785792 0.358964 1.3921% 1932 2.747543 0.363962 -0.2051% 1931
2.753189 0.363215 0.8886% 1930 2.728940 0.366443 1.0126% 1929 2.701584 0.370153
1.1526% 1928 2.670801 0.374420 1.2160% 1927 2.638714 0.378973 1.4086% 1926 2.602062
0.384311 1.7667% 1925 2.556889 0.391100 1.4465% 1924 2.520431 0.396757 1.7700% 1923
2.476596 0.403780 1.6165% 1922 2.437199 0.410307 1.3736% 1921 2.404174 0.415943
2.3393% 1920 2.349218 0.425674 1.3140% 1919 2.318750 0.431267 0.7676% 1918 2.301085
0.434578 0.3870% 1917 2.292215 0.436259 1.3274% 1916 2.262186 0.442050 1.4083% 1915
2.230770 0.448276 1.4458% 1914 2.198977 0.454757 1.9424% 1913 2.157079 0.463590

201

1.9857% 1912 2.115080 0.472795 1.5634% 1911 2.082522 0.480187 1.8169% 1910 2.045359
0.488912 1.8781% 1909 2.007654 0.498094 2.0082% 1908 1.968129 0.508097 1.9603% 1907
1.930291 0.518057 1.8264% 1906 1.895669 0.527518 1.9357% 1905 1.859672 0.537729
2.0148% 1904 1.822943 0.548564 2.1335% 1903 1.784862 0.560267 1.8151% 1902 1.753042
0.570437 1.8943% 1901 1.720451 0.581243 3.0255% 1900 1.669927 0.598829 0.6278% 1899
1.659508 0.602588 1.7757% 1898 1.630555 0.613288 1.8078% 1897 1.601602 0.624375
1.8396% 1896 1.572671 0.635861 1.8755% 1895 1.543718 0.647787 1.9114% 1894 1.514765
0.660168 1.9486% 1893 1.485812 0.673033 1.9858% 1892 1.456881 0.686398 2.0276% 1891
1.427928 0.700315 2.6465% 1890 1.391112 0.718849 1.5328% 1889 1.370111 0.729868
2.0811% 1888 1.342178 0.745058 2.1599% 1887 1.313802 0.761150 2.2075% 1886 1.285426
0.777952 2.2592% 1885 1.257027 0.795528 2.3095% 1884 1.228651 0.813901 2.3641% 1883
1.200275 0.833142 2.4214% 1882 1.171899 0.853316 2.4815% 1881 1.143523 0.874491
3.7644% 1880 1.102038 0.907410 0.9432% 1879 1.091740 0.915969 2.1464% 1878 1.068800
0.935629 2.1913% 1877 1.045881 0.956132 2.2426% 1876 1.022941 0.977574 2.2941% 1875
1.000000 1.000000 2.3456% 1874 0.977082 1.023456 2.4043% 1873 0.954141 1.048063
2.4635% 1872 0.931200 1.073883 2.5258% 1871 0.908260 1.101006 5.9947% 1870 0.856892
1.167008 -1.0968% 1869 0.866395 1.154209 2.1930% 1868 0.847802 1.179520 2.2394%
1867 0.829233 1.205934 2.2935% 1866 0.810641 1.233592 2.3445% 1865 0.792071 1.262514
2.4037% 1864 0.773479 1.292861 2.4599% 1863 0.754909 1.324663 2.5250% 1862 0.736317
1.358111 2.5872% 1861 0.717747 1.393249 2.9504% 1860 0.697177 1.434356 2.4012% 1859
0.680829 1.468798 2.7627% 1858 0.662525 1.509376 2.8412% 1857 0.644222 1.552261
2.9243% 1856 0.625918 1.597653 3.0161% 1855 0.607592 1.645841 3.1061% 1854 0.589288
1.696962 3.2056% 1853 0.570985 1.751360 3.3118% 1852 0.552681 1.809361 3.4252% 1851
0.534378 1.871336 4.0106% 1850 0.513772 1.946388 2.3254% 1849 0.502097 1.991649
2.7841% 1848 0.488496 2.047098 2.8590% 1847 0.474918 2.105625 2.9432% 1846 0.461340
2.167596 3.0324% 1845 0.447763 2.233327 3.1325% 1844 0.434162 2.303286 3.2284% 1843
0.420584 2.377644 3.3361% 1842 0.407006 2.456964 3.4512% 1841 0.393428 2.541758
3.8105% 1840 0.378987 2.638612 2.3861% 1839 0.370155 2.701570 2.5824% 1838 0.360837
2.771335 2.6573% 1837 0.351496 2.844979 2.7232% 1836 0.342178 2.922453 2.7994% 1835
0.332860 3.004266 2.8871% 1834 0.323520 3.091003 2.9657% 1833 0.314201 3.182672
3.0563% 1832 0.304883 3.279945 3.1604% 1831 0.295543 3.383605 3.4660% 1830 0.285643
3.500879 2.4653% 1829 0.278770 3.587187 2.6804% 1828 0.271493 3.683337 10.3427%
1827 0.246045 4.064292 -4.2314% 1826 0.256917 3.892314 2.9150% 1825 0.249639
4.005777 3.0026% 1824 0.242362 4.126053 3.0955% 1823 0.235085 4.253775 3.1944% 1822
0.227808 4.389657 3.3102% 1821 0.220509 4.534963 3.2277% 1820 0.213614 4.681340
2.6573% 1819 0.208085 4.805736 2.6261% 1818 0.202760 4.931940 2.6969% 1817 0.197435
5.064951 2.7717% 1816 0.192111 5.205335 2.8507% 1815 0.186786 5.353724 2.9343% 1814
0.181461 5.510820 3.0231% 1813 0.176136 5.677415 3.1039% 1812 0.170834 5.853636
3.2172% 1811 0.165509 6.041957 3.0969% 1810 0.160538 6.229071 2.9144% 1809 0.155991
6.410610 2.8225% 1808 0.151709 6.591547 2.9199% 1807 0.147405 6.784016 2.9918% 1806
0.143123 6.986979 3.0841% 1805 0.138841 7.202461 3.1822% 1804 0.134559 7.431657
3.2868% 1803 0.130278 7.675920 3.3985% 1802 0.125996 7.936785 3.5180% 1801 0.121714
8.216004 3.3999% 1800 0.117712 8.495344 2.8419% 1799 0.114459 8.736771 2.7485% 1798
0.111397 8.976897 2.8261% 1797 0.108335 9.230596 3.7832% 1796 0.104386 9.579809
2.1272% 1795 0.102212 9.783590 3.0879% 1794 0.099150 10.085701 3.1625% 1793
0.096111 10.404663 3.2904% 1792 0.093049 10.747020 3.4024% 1791 0.089987 11.112673
3.2296% 1790 0.087172 11.471563 41.3145% 1780 0.061687 16.210977 29.4353% 1770
0.047658 20.982729 83.4728% 1750 0.025976 38.497608 29.2845% 1740 0.020092
49.771422 94.2514% 1720 0.010343 96.681682 85.8111% 1700 0.005567 179.645277
19.2490% 1690 0.004668 214.225285 88.0250% 1670 0.002483 402.797140

BASE YEAR: 1874
YEAR BYEAR/AYEAR AYEAR/BYEAR GROWTH%
2009 6.844468 0.146103 8.2857% 2001 6.320752 0.158209 1.0000% 2000 6.258169
0.159791 1.0000% 1999 6.196207 0.161389 1.0000% 1998 6.134859 0.163003 1.0000% 1997
6.074117 0.164633 1.0000% 1996 6.013978 0.166279 1.0000% 1995 5.954433 0.167942
0.9992% 1994 5.895524 0.169620 1.0008% 1993 5.837107 0.171318 1.0000% 1992 5.779314

202

0.173031 0.9295% 1991 5.726090 0.174639 1.2505% 1990 5.655369 0.176823 0.7224% 1989 5.614805 0.178101 1.1077% 1988 5.553292 0.180073 0.8834% 1987 5.504666 0.181664 0.5594% 1986 5.474046 0.182680 1.3056% 1985 5.403497 0.185065 0.7673% 1984 5.362352 0.186485 0.8149% 1983 5.319005 0.188005 0.9737% 1982 5.267711 0.189836 0.9508% 1981 5.218097 0.191641 0.9031% 1980 5.171396 0.193371 2.2701% 1979 5.056608 0.197761 1.0042% 1978 5.006335 0.199747 0.9896% 1977 4.957277 0.201724 0.9103% 1976 4.912557 0.203560 0.8394% 1975 4.871662 0.205269 0.9042% 1974 4.828009 0.207125 1.1568% 1973 4.772797 0.209521 0.9427% 1972 4.728224 0.211496 0.7426% 1971 4.693370 0.213067 1.4697% 1970 4.625389 0.216198 0.6968% 1969 4.593381 0.217705 0.8565% 1968 4.554371 0.219569 1.5090% 1967 4.486666 0.222883 0.9949% 1966 4.442467 0.225100 1.0575% 1965 4.395981 0.227481 1.1300% 1964 4.346861 0.230051 1.5537% 1963 4.280359 0.233625 1.4658% 1962 4.218523 0.237050 1.5364% 1961 4.154689 0.240692 2.1586% 1960 4.066899 0.245888 -1.6655% 1959 4.135780 0.241792 4.3080% 1958 3.964969 0.252209 2.1130% 1957 3.882925 0.257538 1.9895% 1956 3.807181 0.262662 2.1231% 1955 3.728031 0.268238 1.4496% 1954 3.674762 0.272126 2.1573% 1953 3.597162 0.277997 1.2298% 1952 3.553463 0.281416 1.6814% 1951 3.494704 0.286147 1.6233% 1950 3.438881 0.290792 1.4265% 1949 3.390514 0.294941 1.7790% 1948 3.331250 0.300188 1.8242% 1947 3.271571 0.305664 -2.6320% 1946 3.360008 0.297618 3.1768% 1945 3.256554 0.307073 6.4754% 1944 3.058503 0.326957 -0.3437% 1943 3.069050 0.325834 0.6562% 1942 3.049042 0.327972 0.6633% 1941 3.028951 0.330147 -5.6614% 1940 3.210724 0.311456 8.0381% 1939 2.971844 0.336491 0.8126% 1938 2.947888 0.339226 0.7762% 1937 2.925182 0.341859 0.6029% 1936 2.907652 0.343920 0.5244% 1935 2.892484 0.345724 -3.0364% 1934 2.983061 0.335226 4.6271% 1933 2.851135 0.350737 1.3921% 1932 2.811989 0.355620 -0.2051% 1931 2.817768 0.354891 0.8886% 1930 2.792950 0.358044 1.0126% 1929 2.764952 0.361670 1.1526% 1928 2.733447 0.365838 1.2160% 1927 2.700607 0.370287 1.4086% 1926 2.663096 0.375503 1.7667% 1925 2.616864 0.382137 1.4465% 1924 2.579550 0.387664 1.7700% 1923 2.534687 0.394526 1.6165% 1922 2.494365 0.400904 1.3736% 1921 2.460566 0.406411 2.3393% 1920 2.404321 0.415918 1.3140% 1919 2.373138 0.421383 0.7676% 1918 2.355060 0.424618 0.3870% 1917 2.345981 0.426261 1.3274% 1916 2.315248 0.431919 1.4083% 1915 2.283095 0.438002 1.4458% 1914 2.250556 0.444335 1.9424% 1913 2.207675 0.452965 1.9857% 1912 2.164691 0.461960 1.5634% 1911 2.131369 0.469182 1.8169% 1910 2.093335 0.477707 1.8781% 1909 2.054746 0.486678 2.0082% 1908 2.014294 0.496452 1.9603% 1907 1.975568 0.506184 1.8264% 1906 1.940134 0.515428 1.9357% 1905 1.903292 0.525405 2.0148% 1904 1.865702 0.535991 2.1335% 1903 1.826728 0.547427 1.8151% 1902 1.794161 0.557364 1.8943% 1901 1.760805 0.567922 3.0255% 1900 1.709097 0.585104 0.6278% 1899 1.698433 0.588778 1.7757% 1898 1.668801 0.599233 1.8078% 1897 1.639169 0.610065 1.8396% 1896 1.609559 0.621288 1.8755% 1895 1.579927 0.632941 1.9114% 1894 1.550295 0.645038 1.9486% 1893 1.520663 0.657608 1.9858% 1892 1.491054 0.670667 2.0276% 1891 1.461421 0.684265 2.6465% 1890 1.423742 0.702375 1.5328% 1889 1.402248 0.713141 2.0811% 1888 1.373660 0.727982 2.1599% 1887 1.344619 0.743705 2.2075% 1886 1.315577 0.760123 2.2592% 1885 1.286512 0.777295 2.3095% 1884 1.257470 0.795247 2.3641% 1883 1.228429 0.814048 2.4214% 1882 1.199387 0.833759 2.4815% 1881 1.170345 0.854449 3.7644% 1880 1.127887 0.886614 0.9432% 1879 1.117348 0.894976 2.1464% 1878 1.093869 0.914186 2.1913% 1877 1.070413 0.934219 2.2426% 1876 1.046935 0.955169 2.2941% 1875 1.023456 0.977082 2.3456% 1874 1.000000 1.000000 2.4043% 1873 0.976521 1.024043 2.4635% 1872 0.953043 1.049271 2.5258% 1871 0.929564 1.075773 5.9947% 1870 0.876991 1.140262 -1.0968% 1869 0.886717 1.127756 2.1930% 1868 0.867688 1.152487 2.2394% 1867 0.848683 1.178296 2.2935% 1866 0.829655 1.205320 2.3445% 1865 0.810649 1.233579 2.4037% 1864 0.791621 1.263230 2.4599% 1863 0.772616 1.294304 2.5250% 1862 0.753588 1.326986 2.5872% 1860 0.734582 1.361318 2.9504% 1860 0.713530 1.401482 2.4012% 1859 0.696798 1.435135 2.7627% 1858 0.678065 1.474784 2.8412% 1857 0.659332 1.516686 2.9243% 1856 0.640599 1.561038 3.0161% 1855 0.621844 1.608121 3.1061% 1854 0.603111 1.658070 3.2056% 1853 0.584378 1.711222 3.3118% 1852 0.565645 1.767894 3.4252% 1851 0.546912 1.828448 4.0106% 1850 0.525823 1.901780 2.3254% 1849 0.513874 1.946003 2.7841% 1848 0.499955 2.000182 2.8590% 1847 0.486058 2.057367 2.9432% 1846 0.472162 2.117919 3.0324% 1845 0.458265 2.182143 3.1325% 1844 0.444346 2.250498 3.2284% 1843

0.430450 2.323152 3.3361% 1842 0.416553 2.400654 3.4512% 1841 0.402657 2.483505
3.8105% 1840 0.387877 2.578139 2.3861% 1839 0.378837 2.639655 2.5824% 1838 0.369301
2.707821 2.6573% 1837 0.359741 2.779777 2.7232% 1836 0.350204 2.855476 2.7994% 1835
0.340668 2.935413 2.8871% 1834 0.331108 3.020162 2.9657% 1833 0.321571 3.109730
3.0563% 1832 0.312035 3.204774 3.1604% 1831 0.302475 3.306058 3.4660% 1830 0.292343
3.420645 2.4653% 1829 0.285309 3.504974 2.6804% 1828 0.277861 3.598921 10.3427%
1827 0.251817 3.971145 -4.2314% 1826 0.262943 3.803109 2.9150% 1825 0.255495
3.913971 3.0026% 1824 0.248047 4.031490 3.0955% 1823 0.240599 4.156285 3.1944% 1822
0.233152 4.289053 3.3102% 1821 0.225681 4.431029 3.2277% 1820 0.218625 4.574051
2.6573% 1819 0.212965 4.695597 2.6261% 1818 0.207516 4.818908 2.6969% 1817 0.202066
4.948871 2.7717% 1816 0.196617 5.086038 2.8507% 1815 0.191167 5.231025 2.9343% 1814
0.185718 5.384521 3.0231% 1813 0.180268 5.547298 3.1039% 1812 0.174841 5.719481
3.2172% 1811 0.169391 5.903485 3.0969% 1810 0.164303 6.086311 2.9144% 1809 0.159650
6.263689 2.8225% 1808 0.155268 6.440480 2.9199% 1807 0.150863 6.628537 2.9918% 1806
0.146480 6.826849 3.0841% 1805 0.142098 7.037392 3.1822% 1804 0.137716 7.261336
3.2868% 1803 0.133333 7.500000 3.3985% 1802 0.128951 7.754886 3.5180% 1801 0.124569
8.027707 3.3999% 1800 0.120473 8.300645 2.8419% 1799 0.117144 8.536538 2.7485% 1798
0.114010 8.771161 2.8261% 1797 0.110876 9.019046 3.7832% 1796 0.106835 9.360255
2.1272% 1795 0.104609 9.559366 3.0879% 1794 0.101476 9.854554 3.1625% 1793 0.098365
10.166205 3.2904% 1792 0.095232 10.500715 3.4024% 1791 0.092098 10.857988 3.2296%
1790 0.089217 11.208654 41.3145% 1780 0.063134 15.839448 29.4353% 1770 0.048776
20.501839 83.4728% 1750 0.026585 37.615306 29.2845% 1740 0.020563 48.630742
94.2514% 1720 0.010586 94.465894 85.8111% 1700 0.005697 175.528099 19.2490% 1690
0.004777 209.315589 88.0250% 1670 0.002541 393.565684

BASE YEAR: 1873

YEAR BYEAR/AYEAR AYEAR/BYEAR GROWTH%

2009 7.009030 0.142673 8.2857% 2001 6.472722 0.154494 1.0000% 2000 6.408635
0.156039 1.0000% 1999 6.345184 0.157600 1.0000% 1998 6.282360 0.159176 1.0000% 1997
6.220158 0.160768 1.0000% 1996 6.158573 0.162375 1.0000% 1995 6.097597 0.163999
0.9992% 1994 6.037271 0.165638 1.0008% 1993 5.977450 0.167295 1.0000% 1992 5.918267
0.168968 0.9295% 1991 5.863763 0.170539 1.2505% 1990 5.791342 0.172672 0.7224% 1989
5.749802 0.173919 1.1077% 1988 5.686811 0.175845 0.8834% 1987 5.637016 0.177399
0.5594% 1986 5.605660 0.178391 1.3056% 1985 5.533414 0.180720 0.7673% 1984 5.491280
0.182107 0.8149% 1983 5.446891 0.183591 0.9737% 1982 5.394364 0.185379 0.9508% 1981
5.343557 0.187141 0.9031% 1980 5.295733 0.188831 2.2701% 1979 5.178184 0.193118
1.0042% 1978 5.126703 0.195057 0.9896% 1977 5.076466 0.196987 0.9103% 1976 5.030670
0.198781 0.8394% 1975 4.988792 0.200449 0.9042% 1974 4.944089 0.202262 1.1568% 1973
4.887551 0.204601 0.9427% 1972 4.841906 0.206530 0.7426% 1971 4.806213 0.208064
1.4697% 1970 4.736598 0.211122 0.6968% 1969 4.703820 0.212593 0.8565% 1968 4.663872
0.214414 1.5090% 1967 4.594539 0.217650 0.9949% 1966 4.549278 0.219815 1.0575% 1965
4.501674 0.222140 1.1300% 1964 4.451373 0.224650 1.5537% 1963 4.383272 0.228140
1.4658% 1962 4.319950 0.231484 1.5364% 1961 4.254581 0.235041 2.1586% 1960 4.164680
0.240114 -1.6655% 1959 4.235217 0.236115 4.3080% 1958 4.060300 0.246287 2.1130%
1957 3.976282 0.251491 1.9895% 1956 3.898718 0.256495 2.1231% 1955 3.817665 0.261940
1.4496% 1954 3.763114 0.265737 2.1573% 1953 3.683649 0.271470 1.2298% 1952 3.638899
0.274808 1.6814% 1951 3.578727 0.279429 1.6233% 1950 3.521563 0.283965 1.4265% 1949
3.472033 0.288016 1.7790% 1948 3.411344 0.293140 1.8242% 1947 3.350230 0.298487 -
2.6320% 1946 3.440793 0.290631 3.1768% 1945 3.334852 0.299863 6.4754% 1944 3.132039
0.319281 -0.3437% 1943 3.142840 0.318184 0.6562% 1942 3.122351 0.320272 0.6633%
1941 3.101776 0.322396 -5.6614% 1940 3.287920 0.304144 8.0381% 1939 3.043296
0.328591 0.8126% 1938 3.018765 0.331261 0.7762% 1937 2.995512 0.333833 0.6029% 1936
2.977561 0.335845 0.5244% 1935 2.962029 0.337606 -3.0364% 1934 3.054783 0.327355
4.6271% 1933 2.919686 0.342503 1.3921% 1932 2.879598 0.347271 -0.2051% 1931
2.885516 0.346558 0.8886% 1930 2.860101 0.349638 1.0126% 1929 2.831430 0.353178
1.1526% 1928 2.799168 0.357249 1.2160% 1927 2.765539 0.361593 1.4086% 1926 2.727125
0.366687 1.7667% 1925 2.679781 0.373165 1.4465% 1924 2.641571 0.378563 1.7700% 1923

2.595629 0.385263 1.6165% 1922 2.554338 0.391491 1.3736% 1921 2.519726 0.396869
2.3393% 1920 2.462129 0.406153 1.3140% 1919 2.430196 0.411489 0.7676% 1918 2.411683
0.414648 0.3870% 1917 2.402386 0.416253 1.3274% 1916 2.370913 0.421778 1.4083% 1915
2.337988 0.427718 1.4458% 1914 2.304667 0.433902 1.9424% 1913 2.260754 0.442330
1.9857% 1912 2.216737 0.451113 1.5634% 1911 2.182614 0.458166 1.8169% 1910 2.143665
0.466491 1.8781% 1909 2.104148 0.475252 2.0082% 1908 2.062724 0.484796 1.9603% 1907
2.023067 0.494299 1.8264% 1906 1.986781 0.503327 1.9357% 1905 1.949054 0.513070
2.0148% 1904 1.910559 0.523407 2.1335% 1903 1.870648 0.534574 1.8151% 1902 1.837298
0.544277 1.8943% 1901 1.803141 0.554588 3.0255% 1900 1.750189 0.571367 0.6278% 1899
1.739269 0.574954 1.7757% 1898 1.708924 0.585163 1.8078% 1897 1.678580 0.595742
1.8396% 1896 1.648258 0.606701 1.8755% 1895 1.617914 0.618080 1.9114% 1894 1.587569
0.629894 1.9486% 1893 1.557225 0.642168 1.9858% 1892 1.526903 0.654920 2.0276% 1891
1.496559 0.668200 2.6465% 1890 1.457973 0.685884 1.5328% 1889 1.435962 0.696397
2.0811% 1888 1.406687 0.710890 2.1599% 1887 1.376947 0.726244 2.2075% 1886 1.347207
0.742276 2.2592% 1885 1.317444 0.759046 2.3095% 1884 1.287704 0.776576 2.3641% 1883
1.257964 0.794935 2.4214% 1882 1.228224 0.814184 2.4815% 1881 1.198484 0.834387
3.7644% 1880 1.155005 0.865797 0.9432% 1879 1.144212 0.873964 2.1464% 1878 1.120169
0.892722 2.1913% 1877 1.096149 0.912284 2.2426% 1876 1.072106 0.932743 2.2941% 1875
1.048063 0.954141 2.3456% 1874 1.024043 0.976521 2.4043% 1873 1.000000 1.000000
2.4635% 1872 0.975957 1.024635 2.5258% 1871 0.951914 1.050515 5.9947% 1870 0.898077
1.113490 -1.0968% 1869 0.908036 1.101278 2.1930% 1868 0.888550 1.125429 2.2394%
1867 0.869088 1.150631 2.2935% 1866 0.849602 1.177021 2.3445% 1865 0.830140 1.204616
2.4037% 1864 0.810654 1.233571 2.4599% 1863 0.791192 1.263916 2.5250% 1862 0.771706
1.295830 2.5872% 1861 0.752244 1.329356 2.9504% 1860 0.730686 1.368578 2.4012% 1859
0.713552 1.401440 2.7627% 1858 0.694368 1.440158 2.8412% 1857 0.675185 1.481076
2.9243% 1856 0.656001 1.524387 3.0161% 1855 0.636795 1.570364 3.1061% 1854 0.617611
1.619141 3.2056% 1853 0.598428 1.671044 3.3118% 1852 0.579245 1.726386 3.4252% 1851
0.560061 1.785519 4.0106% 1850 0.538466 1.857129 2.3254% 1849 0.526229 1.900314
2.7841% 1848 0.511975 1.953220 2.8590% 1847 0.497745 2.009063 2.9432% 1846 0.483514
2.068193 3.0324% 1845 0.469283 2.130909 3.1325% 1844 0.455030 2.197660 3.2284% 1843
0.440799 2.268608 3.3361% 1842 0.426568 2.344290 3.4512% 1841 0.412338 2.425196
3.8105% 1840 0.397202 2.517608 2.3861% 1839 0.387946 2.577679 2.5824% 1838 0.378180
2.644245 2.6573% 1837 0.368390 2.714511 2.7232% 1836 0.358624 2.788433 2.7994% 1835
0.348858 2.866493 2.8871% 1834 0.339069 2.949253 2.9657% 1833 0.329303 3.036718
3.0563% 1832 0.319537 3.129530 3.1604% 1831 0.309747 3.228436 3.4660% 1830 0.299371
3.340333 2.4653% 1829 0.292169 3.422682 2.6804% 1828 0.284542 3.514423 10.3427%
1827 0.257871 3.877908 -4.2314% 1826 0.269265 3.713817 2.9150% 1825 0.261638
3.822076 3.0026% 1824 0.254011 3.936836 3.0955% 1823 0.246384 4.058701 3.1944% 1822
0.238757 4.188352 3.3102% 1821 0.231107 4.326995 3.2277% 1820 0.223881 4.466659
2.6573% 1819 0.218086 4.585350 2.6261% 1818 0.212505 4.705766 2.6969% 1817 0.206925
4.832678 2.7717% 1816 0.201344 4.966624 2.8507% 1815 0.195763 5.108208 2.9343% 1814
0.190183 5.258100 3.0231% 1813 0.184602 5.417055 3.1039% 1812 0.179045 5.585195
3.2172% 1811 0.173464 5.764879 3.0969% 1810 0.168253 5.943413 2.9144% 1809 0.163489
6.116626 2.8225% 1808 0.159001 6.289266 2.9199% 1807 0.154490 6.472908 2.9918% 1806
0.150002 6.666563 3.0841% 1805 0.145515 6.872164 3.1822% 1804 0.141027 7.090849
3.2868% 1803 0.136539 7.323910 3.3985% 1802 0.132051 7.572812 3.5180% 1801 0.127564
7.839227 3.3999% 1800 0.123369 8.105757 2.8419% 1799 0.119960 8.336112 2.7485% 1798
0.116751 8.565226 2.8261% 1797 0.113542 8.807291 3.7832% 1796 0.109403 9.140489
2.1272% 1795 0.107125 9.334925 3.0879% 1794 0.103916 9.623182 3.1625% 1793 0.100730
9.927516 3.2904% 1792 0.097521 10.254173 3.4024% 1791 0.094312 10.603057 3.2296%
1790 0.091362 10.945490 41.3145% 1780 0.064651 15.467559 29.4353% 1770 0.049949
20.020483 83.4728% 1750 0.027224 36.732149 29.2845% 1740 0.021058 47.488958
94.2514% 1720 0.010840 92.247962 85.8111% 1700 0.005834 171.406935 19.2490% 1690
0.004892 204.401141 88.0250% 1670 0.002602 384.325290

BASE YEAR: 1872
YEAR BYEAR/AYEAR AYEAR/BYEAR GROWTH%

2009 7.181701 0.139243 8.2857% 2001 6.632181 0.150780 1.0000% 2000 6.566515 0.152288 1.0000% 1999 6.501500 0.153811 1.0000% 1998 6.437129 0.155349 1.0000% 1997 6.373395 0.156902 1.0000% 1996 6.310292 0.158471 1.0000% 1995 6.247814 0.160056 0.9992% 1994 6.186002 0.161655 1.0008% 1993 6.124707 0.163273 1.0000% 1992 6.064067 0.164906 0.9295% 1991 6.008220 0.166439 1.2505% 1990 5.934014 0.168520 0.7224% 1989 5.891451 0.169737 1.1077% 1988 5.826908 0.171618 0.8834% 1987 5.775886 0.173134 0.5594% 1986 5.743758 0.174102 1.3056% 1985 5.669732 0.176375 0.7673% 1984 5.626561 0.177728 0.8149% 1983 5.581078 0.179177 0.9737% 1982 5.527256 0.180922 0.9508% 1981 5.475198 0.182642 0.9031% 1980 5.426196 0.184291 2.2701% 1979 5.305751 0.188475 1.0042% 1978 5.253002 0.190367 0.9896% 1977 5.201527 0.192251 0.9103% 1976 5.154603 0.194001 0.8394% 1975 5.111694 0.195630 0.9042% 1974 5.065889 0.197399 1.1568% 1973 5.007958 0.199682 0.9427% 1972 4.961188 0.201565 0.7426% 1971 4.924616 0.203062 1.4697% 1970 4.853286 0.206046 0.6968% 1969 4.819701 0.207482 0.8565% 1968 4.778769 0.209259 1.5090% 1967 4.707728 0.212417 0.9949% 1966 4.661352 0.214530 1.0575% 1965 4.612575 0.216799 1.1300% 1964 4.561035 0.219248 1.5537% 1963 4.491256 0.222655 1.4658% 1962 4.426374 0.225919 1.5364% 1961 4.359394 0.229390 2.1586% 1960 4.267279 0.234341 -1.6655% 1959 4.339554 0.230438 4.3080% 1958 4.160327 0.240366 2.1130% 1957 4.074240 0.245445 1.9895% 1956 3.994764 0.250328 2.1231% 1955 3.911715 0.255642 1.4496% 1954 3.855821 0.259348 2.1573% 1953 3.774397 0.264943 1.2298% 1952 3.728545 0.268201 1.6814% 1951 3.666891 0.272711 1.6233% 1950 3.608318 0.277137 1.4265% 1949 3.557568 0.281091 1.7790% 1948 3.495384 0.286092 1.8242% 1947 3.432765 0.291310 - 2.6320% 1946 3.525559 0.283643 3.1768% 1945 3.417007 0.292654 6.4754% 1944 3.209198 0.311604 -0.3437% 1943 3.220266 0.310533 0.6562% 1942 3.199271 0.312571 0.6633% 1941 3.178190 0.314644 -5.6614% 1940 3.368919 0.296831 8.0381% 1939 3.118269 0.320691 0.8126% 1938 3.093134 0.323297 0.7762% 1937 3.069308 0.325806 0.6029% 1936 3.050915 0.327771 0.5244% 1935 3.035000 0.329489 -3.0364% 1934 3.130039 0.319485 4.6271% 1933 2.991613 0.334268 1.3921% 1932 2.950538 0.338921 -0.2051% 1931 2.956602 0.338226 0.8886% 1930 2.930561 0.341232 1.0126% 1929 2.901184 0.344687 1.1526% 1928 2.868126 0.348660 1.2160% 1927 2.833669 0.352899 1.4086% 1926 2.794309 0.357870 1.7667% 1925 2.745799 0.364193 1.4465% 1924 2.706647 0.369461 1.7700% 1923 2.659574 0.376000 1.6165% 1922 2.617265 0.382078 1.3736% 1921 2.581800 0.387327 2.3393% 1920 2.522784 0.396387 1.3140% 1919 2.490065 0.401596 0.7676% 1918 2.471096 0.404679 0.3870% 1917 2.461570 0.406245 1.3274% 1916 2.429322 0.411637 1.4083% 1915 2.395585 0.417435 1.4458% 1914 2.361443 0.423470 1.9424% 1913 2.316449 0.431695 1.9857% 1912 2.271348 0.440267 1.5634% 1911 2.236384 0.447150 1.8169% 1910 2.196476 0.455275 1.8781% 1909 2.155985 0.463825 2.0082% 1908 2.113540 0.473140 1.9603% 1907 2.072906 0.482415 1.8264% 1906 2.035726 0.491225 1.9357% 1905 1.997069 0.500734 2.0148% 1904 1.957627 0.510823 2.1335% 1903 1.916733 0.521721 1.8151% 1902 1.882561 0.531191 1.8943% 1901 1.847562 0.541254 3.0255% 1900 1.793305 0.557629 0.6278% 1899 1.782117 0.561130 1.7757% 1898 1.751024 0.571094 1.8078% 1897 1.719932 0.581418 1.8396% 1896 1.688864 0.592114 1.8755% 1895 1.657772 0.603219 1.9114% 1894 1.626680 0.614749 1.9486% 1893 1.595588 0.626728 1.9858% 1892 1.564519 0.639174 2.0276% 1891 1.533427 0.652134 2.6465% 1890 1.493891 0.669393 1.5328% 1889 1.471338 0.679653 2.0811% 1888 1.441342 0.693798 2.1599% 1887 1.410869 0.708783 2.2075% 1886 1.380396 0.724430 2.2592% 1885 1.349900 0.740796 2.3095% 1884 1.319427 0.757905 2.3641% 1883 1.288955 0.775823 2.4214% 1882 1.258482 0.794608 2.4815% 1881 1.228009 0.814326 3.7644% 1880 1.183459 0.844981 0.9432% 1879 1.172401 0.852951 2.1464% 1878 1.147765 0.871258 2.1913% 1877 1.123154 0.890350 2.2426% 1876 1.098518 0.910317 2.2941% 1875 1.073883 0.931200 2.3456% 1874 1.049271 0.953043 2.4043% 1873 1.024635 0.975957 2.4635% 1872 1.000000 1.000000 2.5258% 1871 0.975365 1.025258 5.9947% 1870 0.920201 1.086719 -1.0968% 1869 0.930406 1.074800 2.1930% 1868 0.910440 1.098370 2.2394% 1867 0.890498 1.122967 2.2935% 1866 0.870533 1.148722 2.3445% 1865 0.850591 1.175653 2.4037% 1864 0.830625 1.203912 2.4599% 1863 0.810683 1.233527 2.5250% 1862 0.790718 1.264674 2.5872% 1861 0.770776 1.297394 2.9504% 1860 0.748686 1.335673 2.4012% 1859 0.731130 1.367745 2.7627% 1858 0.711474 1.405532 2.8412% 1857 0.691818 1.445466 2.9243% 1856 0.672162 1.487736 3.0161% 1855 0.652483 1.532608 3.1061% 1854 0.632827

1.580212 3.2056% 1853 0.613171 1.630867 3.3118% 1852 0.593515 1.684878 3.4252% 1851
0.573859 1.742589 4.0106% 1850 0.551731 1.812477 2.3254% 1849 0.539193 1.854624
2.7841% 1848 0.524588 1.906259 2.8590% 1847 0.510007 1.960759 2.9432% 1846 0.495426
2.018467 3.0324% 1845 0.480844 2.079675 3.1325% 1844 0.466239 2.144821 3.2284% 1843
0.451658 2.214063 3.3361% 1842 0.437077 2.287926 3.4512% 1841 0.422496 2.366887
3.8105% 1840 0.406988 2.457077 2.3861% 1839 0.397503 2.515704 2.5824% 1838 0.387496
2.580669 2.6573% 1837 0.377466 2.649246 2.7232% 1836 0.367459 2.721390 2.7994% 1835
0.357453 2.797574 2.8871% 1834 0.347422 2.878343 2.9657% 1833 0.337415 2.963706
3.0563% 1832 0.327409 3.054286 3.1604% 1831 0.317378 3.150815 3.4660% 1830 0.306747
3.260021 2.4653% 1829 0.299366 3.340390 2.6804% 1828 0.291552 3.429926 10.3427%
1827 0.264224 3.784671 -4.2314% 1826 0.275898 3.624525 2.9150% 1825 0.268083
3.730181 3.0026% 1824 0.260269 3.842182 3.0955% 1823 0.252454 3.961117 3.1944% 1822
0.244639 4.087651 3.3102% 1821 0.236801 4.222960 3.2277% 1820 0.229396 4.359266
2.6573% 1819 0.223458 4.475104 2.6261% 1818 0.217740 4.592625 2.6969% 1817 0.212022
4.716485 2.7717% 1816 0.206304 4.847211 2.8507% 1815 0.200586 4.985390 2.9343% 1814
0.194868 5.131679 3.0231% 1813 0.189150 5.286812 3.1039% 1812 0.183456 5.450909
3.2172% 1811 0.177738 5.626273 3.0969% 1810 0.172399 5.800514 2.9144% 1809 0.167516
5.969563 2.8225% 1808 0.162918 6.138052 2.9199% 1807 0.158296 6.317279 2.9918% 1806
0.153698 6.506278 3.0841% 1805 0.149099 6.706935 3.1822% 1804 0.144501 6.920363
3.2868% 1803 0.139903 7.147820 3.3985% 1802 0.135304 7.390738 3.5180% 1801 0.130706
7.650747 3.3999% 1800 0.126408 7.910869 2.8419% 1799 0.122915 8.135685 2.7485% 1798
0.119627 8.359291 2.8261% 1797 0.116339 8.595536 3.7832% 1796 0.112099 8.920723
2.1272% 1795 0.109764 9.110484 3.0879% 1794 0.106476 9.391810 3.1625% 1793 0.103212
9.688827 3.2904% 1792 0.099924 10.007630 3.4024% 1791 0.096636 10.348126 3.2296%
1790 0.093613 10.682326 41.3145% 1780 0.066244 15.095670 29.4353% 1770 0.051179
19.539128 83.4728% 1750 0.027895 35.848992 29.2845% 1740 0.021576 46.347173
94.2514% 1720 0.011107 90.030030 85.8111% 1700 0.005978 167.285771 19.2490% 1690
0.005013 199.486692 88.0250% 1670 0.002666 375.084897

BASE YEAR: 1871

YEAR BYEAR/AYEAR AYEAR/BYEAR GROWTH%

2009 7.363094 0.135812 8.2857% 2001 6.799695 0.147065 1.0000% 2000 6.732370
0.148536 1.0000% 1999 6.665713 0.150021 1.0000% 1998 6.599716 0.151522 1.0000% 1997
6.534372 0.153037 1.0000% 1996 6.469675 0.154567 1.0000% 1995 6.405619 0.156113
0.9992% 1994 6.342246 0.157673 1.0008% 1993 6.279403 0.159251 1.0000% 1992 6.217231
0.160843 0.9295% 1991 6.159974 0.162338 1.2505% 1990 6.083894 0.164368 0.7224% 1989
6.040256 0.165556 1.1077% 1988 5.974083 0.167390 0.8834% 1987 5.921772 0.168868
0.5594% 1986 5.888832 0.169813 1.3056% 1985 5.812937 0.172030 0.7673% 1984 5.768675
0.173350 0.8149% 1983 5.722043 0.174763 0.9737% 1982 5.666862 0.176465 0.9508% 1981
5.613489 0.178142 0.9031% 1980 5.563249 0.179751 2.2701% 1979 5.439763 0.183832
1.0042% 1978 5.385681 0.185678 0.9896% 1977 5.332906 0.187515 0.9103% 1976 5.284797
0.189222 0.8394% 1975 5.240803 0.190810 0.9042% 1974 5.193842 0.192536 1.1568% 1973
5.134447 0.194763 0.9427% 1972 5.086497 0.196599 0.7426% 1971 5.049001 0.198059
1.4697% 1970 4.975869 0.200970 0.6968% 1969 4.941436 0.202370 0.8565% 1968 4.899470
0.204104 1.5090% 1967 4.826634 0.207184 0.9949% 1966 4.779087 0.209245 1.0575% 1965
4.729078 0.211458 1.1300% 1964 4.676236 0.213847 1.5537% 1963 4.604695 0.217170
1.4658% 1962 4.538174 0.220353 1.5364% 1961 4.469503 0.223739 2.1586% 1960 4.375061
0.228568 -1.6655% 1959 4.449161 0.224761 4.3080% 1958 4.265407 0.234444 2.1130%
1957 4.177146 0.239398 1.9895% 1956 4.095663 0.244161 2.1231% 1955 4.010516 0.249344
1.4496% 1954 3.953210 0.252959 2.1573% 1953 3.869730 0.258416 1.2298% 1952 3.822720
0.261594 1.6814% 1951 3.759508 0.265992 1.6233% 1950 3.699456 0.270310 1.4265% 1949
3.647424 0.274166 1.7790% 1948 3.583669 0.279044 1.8242% 1947 3.519468 0.284134 -
2.6320% 1946 3.614606 0.276655 3.1768% 1945 3.503313 0.285444 6.4754% 1944 3.290255
0.303928 -0.3437% 1943 3.301602 0.302883 0.6562% 1942 3.280077 0.304871 0.6633%
1941 3.258464 0.306893 -5.6614% 1940 3.454010 0.289519 8.0381% 1939 3.197030
0.312790 0.8126% 1938 3.171259 0.315332 0.7762% 1937 3.146832 0.317780 0.6029% 1936
3.127974 0.319696 0.5244% 1935 3.111657 0.321372 -3.0364% 1934 3.209097 0.311614

4.6271% 1933 3.067175 0.326033 1.3921% 1932 3.025062 0.330572 -0.2051% 1931
3.031279 0.329894 0.8886% 1930 3.004580 0.332825 1.0126% 1929 2.974461 0.336195
1.1526% 1928 2.940569 0.340070 1.2160% 1927 2.905241 0.344206 1.4086% 1926 2.864887
0.349054 1.7667% 1925 2.815152 0.355221 1.4465% 1924 2.775011 0.360359 1.7700% 1923
2.726748 0.366737 1.6165% 1922 2.683371 0.372666 1.3736% 1921 2.647011 0.377785
2.3393% 1920 2.586504 0.386622 1.3140% 1919 2.552958 0.391702 0.7676% 1918 2.533510
0.394709 0.3870% 1917 2.523743 0.396237 1.3274% 1916 2.490681 0.401497 1.4083% 1915
2.456092 0.407151 1.4458% 1914 2.421088 0.413037 1.9424% 1913 2.374957 0.421060
1.9857% 1912 2.328717 0.429421 1.5634% 1911 2.292870 0.436135 1.8169% 1910 2.251954
0.444059 1.8781% 1909 2.210440 0.452399 2.0082% 1908 2.166923 0.461484 1.9603% 1907
2.125263 0.470530 1.8264% 1906 2.087144 0.479124 1.9357% 1905 2.047511 0.488398
2.0148% 1904 2.007072 0.498238 2.1335% 1903 1.965145 0.508868 1.8151% 1902 1.930110
0.518105 1.8943% 1901 1.894227 0.527920 3.0255% 1900 1.838600 0.543892 0.6278% 1899
1.827129 0.547307 1.7757% 1898 1.795251 0.557025 1.8078% 1897 1.763374 0.567095
1.8396% 1896 1.731521 0.577527 1.8755% 1895 1.699643 0.588359 1.9114% 1894 1.667766
0.599605 1.9486% 1893 1.635888 0.611289 1.9858% 1892 1.604035 0.623428 2.0276% 1891
1.572158 0.636068 2.6465% 1890 1.531623 0.652902 1.5328% 1889 1.508501 0.662910
2.0811% 1888 1.477747 0.676706 2.1599% 1887 1.446504 0.691322 2.2075% 1886 1.415262
0.706583 2.2592% 1885 1.383995 0.722546 2.3095% 1884 1.352753 0.739233 2.3641% 1883
1.321511 0.756710 2.4214% 1882 1.290268 0.775033 2.4815% 1881 1.259026 0.794265
3.7644% 1880 1.213351 0.824164 0.9432% 1879 1.202013 0.831938 2.1464% 1878 1.176755
0.849794 2.1913% 1877 1.151522 0.868416 2.2426% 1876 1.126264 0.887891 2.2941% 1875
1.101006 0.908260 2.3456% 1874 1.075773 0.929564 2.4043% 1873 1.050515 0.951914
2.4635% 1872 1.025258 0.975365 2.5258% 1871 1.000000 1.000000 5.9947% 1870 0.943444
1.059947 -1.0968% 1869 0.953906 1.048321 2.1930% 1868 0.933436 1.071311 2.2394%
1867 0.912990 1.095302 2.2935% 1866 0.892520 1.120423 2.3445% 1865 0.872075 1.146691
2.4037% 1864 0.851605 1.174254 2.4599% 1863 0.831159 1.203139 2.5250% 1862 0.810689
1.233518 2.5872% 1861 0.790244 1.265432 2.9504% 1860 0.767597 1.302768 2.4012% 1859
0.749597 1.334050 2.7627% 1858 0.729445 1.370906 2.8412% 1857 0.709292 1.409856
2.9243% 1856 0.689140 1.451085 3.0161% 1855 0.668963 1.494851 3.1061% 1854 0.648810
1.541282 3.2056% 1853 0.628658 1.590690 3.3118% 1852 0.608506 1.643370 3.4252% 1851
0.588353 1.699660 4.0106% 1850 0.565666 1.767826 2.3254% 1849 0.552812 1.808935
2.7841% 1848 0.537838 1.859297 2.8590% 1847 0.522888 1.912454 2.9432% 1846 0.507939
1.968741 3.0324% 1845 0.492989 2.028441 3.1325% 1844 0.478016 2.091982 3.2284% 1843
0.463066 2.159519 3.3361% 1842 0.448117 2.231562 3.4512% 1841 0.433167 2.308577
3.8105% 1840 0.417267 2.396545 3.2861% 1839 0.407543 2.453728 2.5824% 1838 0.397284
2.517093 2.6573% 1837 0.387000 2.583980 2.7232% 1836 0.376740 2.654347 2.7994% 1835
0.366481 2.728654 2.8871% 1834 0.356197 2.807434 2.9657% 1833 0.345938 2.890693
3.0563% 1832 0.335678 2.979042 3.1604% 1831 0.325394 3.073193 3.4660% 1830 0.314494
3.179709 2.4653% 1829 0.306928 3.258098 2.6804% 1828 0.298915 3.345428 10.3427%
1827 0.270897 3.691434 -4.2314% 1826 0.282867 3.535233 2.9150% 1825 0.274855
3.638287 3.0026% 1824 0.266843 3.747528 3.0955% 1823 0.258830 3.863533 3.1944% 1822
0.250818 3.986950 3.3102% 1821 0.242782 4.118925 3.2277% 1820 0.235190 4.251874
2.6573% 1819 0.229103 4.364858 2.6261% 1818 0.223240 4.479484 2.6969% 1817 0.217377
4.600292 2.7717% 1816 0.211515 4.727798 2.8507% 1815 0.205652 4.862573 2.9343% 1814
0.199790 5.005257 3.0231% 1813 0.193927 5.156569 3.1039% 1812 0.188089 5.316623
3.2172% 1811 0.182227 5.487668 3.0969% 1810 0.176753 5.657616 2.9144% 1809 0.171748
5.822500 2.8225% 1808 0.167033 5.986838 2.9199% 1807 0.162294 6.161650 2.9918% 1806
0.157580 6.345993 3.0841% 1805 0.152865 6.541707 3.1822% 1804 0.148151 6.749876
3.2868% 1803 0.143436 6.971730 3.3985% 1802 0.138722 7.208663 3.5180% 1801 0.134008
7.462268 3.3999% 1800 0.129601 7.715981 2.8419% 1799 0.126020 7.935259 2.7485% 1798
0.122649 8.153356 2.8261% 1797 0.119278 8.383780 3.7832% 1796 0.114930 8.700956
2.1272% 1795 0.112536 8.886043 3.0879% 1794 0.109165 9.160439 3.1625% 1793 0.105819
9.450139 3.2904% 1792 0.102448 9.761087 3.4024% 1791 0.099077 10.093195 3.2296%
1790 0.095977 10.419161 41.3145% 1780 0.067917 14.723781 29.4353% 1770 0.052472
19.057772 83.4728% 1750 0.028599 34.965835 29.2845% 1740 0.022121 45.205389

208

94.2514% 1720 0.011388 87.812098 85.8111% 1700 0.006129 163.164607 19.2490% 1690 0.005139 194.572243 88.0250% 1670 0.002733 365.844504

BASE YEAR: 1870

YEAR BYEAR/AYEAR AYEAR/BYEAR GROWTH%

2009 7.804488 0.128131 8.2857% 2001 7.207314 0.138748 1.0000% 2000 7.135954 0.140135 1.0000% 1999 7.065301 0.141537 1.0000% 1998 6.995347 0.142952 1.0000% 1997 6.926087 0.144382 1.0000% 1996 6.857511 0.145825 1.0000% 1995 6.789615 0.147284 0.9992% 1994 6.722443 0.148755 1.0008% 1993 6.655833 0.150244 1.0000% 1992 6.589934 0.151747 0.9295% 1991 6.529244 0.153157 1.2505% 1990 6.448603 0.155072 0.7224% 1989 6.402350 0.156193 1.1077% 1988 6.332210 0.157923 0.8834% 1987 6.276763 0.159318 0.5594% 1986 6.241848 0.160209 1.3056% 1985 6.161403 0.162301 0.7673% 1984 6.114488 0.163546 0.8149% 1983 6.065061 0.164879 0.9737% 1982 6.006572 0.166484 0.9508% 1981 5.949999 0.168067 0.9031% 1980 5.896748 0.169585 2.2701% 1979 5.765859 0.173435 1.0042% 1978 5.708535 0.175176 0.9896% 1977 5.652596 0.176910 0.9103% 1976 5.601603 0.178520 0.8394% 1975 5.554972 0.180019 0.9042% 1974 5.505196 0.181647 1.1568% 1973 5.442241 0.183748 0.9427% 1972 5.391416 0.185480 0.7426% 1971 5.351672 0.186857 1.4697% 1970 5.274156 0.189604 0.6968% 1969 5.237659 0.190925 0.8565% 1968 5.193177 0.192560 1.5090% 1967 5.115975 0.195466 0.9949% 1966 5.065577 0.197411 1.0575% 1965 5.012571 0.199498 1.1300% 1964 4.956561 0.201753 1.5537% 1963 4.880731 0.204887 1.4658% 1962 4.810222 0.207891 1.5364% 1961 4.737435 0.211085 2.1586% 1960 4.637332 0.215641 -1.6655% 1959 4.715874 0.212050 4.3080% 1958 4.521105 0.221185 2.1130% 1957 4.427552 0.225858 1.9895% 1956 4.341185 0.230352 2.1231% 1955 4.250933 0.235242 1.4496% 1954 4.190192 0.238653 2.1573% 1953 4.101708 0.243801 1.2298% 1952 4.051879 0.246799 1.6814% 1951 3.984879 0.250949 1.6233% 1950 3.921226 0.255022 1.4265% 1949 3.866075 0.258660 1.7790% 1948 3.798499 0.263262 1.8242% 1947 3.730449 0.268064 -2.6320% 1946 3.831290 0.261009 3.1768% 1945 3.713325 0.269300 6.4754% 1944 3.487495 0.286739 -0.3437% 1943 3.499522 0.285753 0.6562% 1942 3.476707 0.287628 0.6633% 1941 3.453798 0.289536 -5.6614% 1940 3.661067 0.273144 8.0381% 1939 3.388681 0.295100 0.8126% 1938 3.361366 0.297498 0.7762% 1937 3.335474 0.299807 0.6029% 1936 3.315486 0.301615 0.5244% 1935 3.298190 0.303197 -3.0364% 1934 3.401472 0.293990 4.6271% 1933 3.251042 0.307594 1.3921% 1932 3.206405 0.311876 -0.2051% 1931 3.212994 0.311236 0.8886% 1930 3.184695 0.314002 1.0126% 1929 3.152771 0.317181 1.1526% 1928 3.116846 0.320837 1.2160% 1927 3.079401 0.324739 1.4086% 1926 3.036627 0.329313 1.7667% 1925 2.983911 0.335131 1.4465% 1924 2.941364 0.339978 1.7700% 1923 2.890208 0.345996 1.6165% 1922 2.844231 0.351589 1.3736% 1921 2.805690 0.356419 2.3393% 1920 2.741557 0.364756 1.3140% 1919 2.706000 0.369549 0.7676% 1918 2.685385 0.372386 0.3870% 1917 2.675033 0.373827 1.3274% 1916 2.639989 0.378789 1.4083% 1915 2.603327 0.384124 1.4458% 1914 2.566224 0.389678 1.9424% 1913 2.517328 0.397247 1.9857% 1912 2.468316 0.405135 1.5634% 1911 2.430320 0.411468 1.8169% 1910 2.386951 0.418945 1.8781% 1909 2.342949 0.426813 2.0082% 1908 2.296823 0.435384 1.9603% 1907 2.252665 0.443919 1.8264% 1906 2.212261 0.452026 1.9357% 1905 2.170252 0.460776 2.0148% 1904 2.127389 0.470060 2.1335% 1903 2.082949 0.480089 1.8151% 1902 2.045814 0.488803 1.8943% 1901 2.007780 0.498063 3.0255% 1900 1.948818 0.513131 0.6278% 1899 1.936659 0.516353 1.7757% 1898 1.902871 0.525522 1.8078% 1897 1.869082 0.535022 1.8396% 1896 1.835320 0.544864 1.8755% 1895 1.801531 0.555083 1.9114% 1894 1.767743 0.565693 1.9486% 1893 1.733955 0.576716 1.9858% 1892 1.700192 0.588169 2.0276% 1891 1.666404 0.600095 2.6465% 1890 1.623439 0.615976 1.5328% 1889 1.598930 0.625418 2.0811% 1888 1.566333 0.638434 2.1599% 1887 1.533218 0.652223 2.2075% 1886 1.500102 0.666621 2.2592% 1885 1.466961 0.681681 2.3095% 1884 1.433846 0.697425 2.3641% 1883 1.400731 0.713913 2.4214% 1882 1.367616 0.731200 2.4815% 1881 1.334500 0.749344 3.7644% 1880 1.286087 0.777552 0.9432% 1879 1.274070 0.784887 2.1464% 1878 1.247298 0.801733 2.1913% 1877 1.220552 0.819302 2.2426% 1876 1.193780 0.837675 2.2941% 1875 1.167008 0.856892 2.3456% 1874 1.140262 0.876991 2.4043% 1873 1.113490 0.898077 2.4635% 1872 1.086719 0.920201 2.5258% 1871 1.059947 0.943444 5.9947% 1870 1.000000 1.000000 -1.0968% 1869 1.011089 0.989032 2.1930% 1868 0.989392 1.010721 2.2394% 1867 0.967721 1.033355 2.2935% 1866 0.946024 1.057056 2.3445% 1865 0.924353 1.081838

209

2.4037% 1864 0.902656 1.107842 2.4599% 1863 0.880985 1.135094 2.5250% 1862 0.859288
1.163755 2.5872% 1861 0.837616 1.193864 2.9504% 1860 0.813611 1.229088 2.4012% 1859
0.794533 1.258601 2.7627% 1858 0.773172 1.293373 2.8412% 1857 0.751812 1.330120
2.9243% 1856 0.730451 1.369017 3.0161% 1855 0.709065 1.410308 3.1061% 1854 0.687704
1.454113 3.2056% 1853 0.666344 1.500726 3.3118% 1852 0.644983 1.550427 3.4252% 1851
0.623623 1.603533 4.0106% 1850 0.599576 1.667844 2.3254% 1849 0.585951 1.706628
2.7841% 1848 0.570079 1.754142 2.8590% 1847 0.554234 1.804293 2.9432% 1846 0.538388
1.857396 3.0324% 1845 0.522543 1.913720 3.1325% 1844 0.506671 1.973667 3.2284% 1843
0.490825 2.037384 3.3361% 1842 0.474980 2.105353 3.4512% 1841 0.459134 2.178012
3.8105% 1840 0.442281 2.261005 2.3861% 1839 0.431974 2.314954 2.5824% 1838 0.421100
2.374735 2.6573% 1837 0.410199 2.437840 2.7232% 1836 0.399325 2.504227 2.7994% 1835
0.388450 2.574331 2.8871% 1834 0.377550 2.648656 2.9657% 1833 0.366676 2.727206
3.0563% 1832 0.355801 2.810559 3.1604% 1831 0.344901 2.899384 3.4660% 1830 0.333347
2.999876 2.4653% 1829 0.325327 3.073832 2.6804% 1828 0.316834 3.156223 10.3427%
1827 0.287137 3.482660 -4.2314% 1826 0.299824 3.335293 2.9150% 1825 0.291331
3.432518 3.0026% 1824 0.282839 3.535582 3.0955% 1823 0.274346 3.645026 3.1944% 1822
0.265854 3.761462 3.3102% 1821 0.257336 3.885974 3.2277% 1820 0.249289 4.011403
2.6573% 1819 0.242836 4.117997 2.6261% 1818 0.236623 4.226140 2.6969% 1817 0.230409
4.340116 2.7717% 1816 0.224195 4.460411 2.8507% 1815 0.217981 4.587563 2.9343% 1814
0.211767 4.722178 3.0231% 1813 0.205553 4.864932 3.1039% 1812 0.199365 5.015934
3.2172% 1811 0.193151 5.177305 3.0969% 1810 0.187349 5.337642 2.9144% 1809 0.182043
5.493201 2.8225% 1808 0.177046 5.648244 2.9199% 1807 0.172023 5.813169 2.9918% 1806
0.167026 5.987086 3.0841% 1805 0.162029 6.171731 3.1822% 1804 0.157032 6.368128
3.2868% 1803 0.152035 6.577434 3.3985% 1802 0.147038 6.800968 3.5180% 1801 0.142041
7.040229 3.3999% 1800 0.137370 7.279593 2.8419% 1799 0.133574 7.486469 2.7485% 1798
0.130001 7.692232 2.8261% 1797 0.126428 7.909624 3.7832% 1796 0.121820 8.208862
2.1272% 1795 0.119282 8.383481 3.0879% 1794 0.115709 8.642357 3.1625% 1793 0.112162
8.915673 3.2904% 1792 0.108589 9.209036 3.4024% 1791 0.105016 9.522361 3.2296% 1790
0.101731 9.829891 41.3145% 1780 0.071989 13.891057 29.4353% 1770 0.055618 17.979933
83.4728% 1750 0.030314 32.988294 29.2845% 1740 0.023447 42.648736 94.2514% 1720
0.012071 82.845764 85.8111% 1700 0.006496 153.936608 19.2490% 1690 0.005448
183.567942 88.0250% 1670 0.002897 345.153664

BASE YEAR: 1869

YEAR BYEAR/AYEAR AYEAR/BYEAR GROWTH%

2009 7.718889 0.129552 8.2857% 2001 7.128266 0.140287 1.0000% 2000 7.057688
0.141689 1.0000% 1999 6.987810 0.143106 1.0000% 1998 6.918624 0.144537 1.0000% 1997
6.850122 0.145983 1.0000% 1996 6.782299 0.147443 1.0000% 1995 6.715148 0.148917
0.9992% 1994 6.648713 0.150405 1.0008% 1993 6.582833 0.151910 1.0000% 1992 6.517656
0.153429 0.9295% 1991 6.457632 0.154856 1.2505% 1990 6.377876 0.156792 0.7224% 1989
6.332130 0.157925 1.1077% 1988 6.262759 0.159674 0.8834% 1987 6.207920 0.161085
0.5594% 1986 6.173389 0.161986 1.3056% 1985 6.093826 0.164101 0.7673% 1984 6.047425
0.165360 0.8149% 1983 5.998540 0.166707 0.9737% 1982 5.940693 0.168331 0.9508% 1981
5.884740 0.169931 0.9031% 1980 5.832073 0.171466 2.2701% 1979 5.702620 0.175358
1.0042% 1978 5.645925 0.177119 0.9896% 1977 5.590599 0.178872 0.9103% 1976 5.540165
0.180500 0.8394% 1975 5.494046 0.182015 0.9042% 1974 5.444816 0.183661 1.1568% 1973
5.382551 0.185786 0.9427% 1972 5.332283 0.187537 0.7426% 1971 5.292976 0.188930
1.4697% 1970 5.216310 0.191706 0.6968% 1969 5.180213 0.193042 0.8565% 1968 5.136219
0.194696 1.5090% 1967 5.059864 0.197634 0.9949% 1966 5.010019 0.199600 1.0575% 1965
4.957594 0.201711 1.1300% 1964 4.902198 0.203990 1.5537% 1963 4.827200 0.207159
1.4658% 1962 4.757465 0.210196 1.5364% 1961 4.685475 0.213426 2.1586% 1960 4.586470
0.218033 -1.6655% 1959 4.664151 0.214401 4.3080% 1958 4.471518 0.223638 2.1130%
1957 4.378992 0.228363 1.9895% 1956 4.293571 0.232906 2.1231% 1955 4.204310 0.237851
1.4496% 1954 4.144234 0.241299 2.1573% 1953 4.056721 0.246505 1.2298% 1952 4.007439
0.249536 1.6814% 1951 3.941173 0.253732 1.6233% 1950 3.878219 0.257850 1.4265% 1949
3.823673 0.261529 1.7790% 1948 3.756837 0.266181 1.8242% 1947 3.689534 0.271037 -
2.6320% 1946 3.789269 0.263903 3.1768% 1945 3.672598 0.272287 6.4754% 1944 3.449245

0.289919 -0.3437% 1943 3.461140 0.288922 0.6562% 1942 3.438575 0.290818 0.6633% 1941 3.415918 0.292747 -5.6614% 1940 3.620913 0.276173 8.0381% 1939 3.351515 0.298373 0.8126% 1938 3.324499 0.300797 0.7762% 1937 3.298891 0.303132 0.6029% 1936 3.279122 0.304960 0.5244% 1935 3.262016 0.306559 -3.0364% 1934 3.364165 0.297251 4.6271% 1933 3.215385 0.311005 1.3921% 1932 3.171238 0.315334 -0.2051% 1931 3.177755 0.314688 0.8886% 1930 3.149766 0.317484 1.0126% 1929 3.118192 0.320699 1.1526% 1928 3.082661 0.324395 1.2160% 1927 3.045626 0.328340 1.4086% 1926 3.003322 0.332965 1.7667% 1925 2.951184 0.338847 1.4465% 1924 2.909104 0.343749 1.7700% 1923 2.858509 0.349833 1.6165% 1922 2.813035 0.355488 1.3736% 1921 2.774918 0.360371 2.3393% 1920 2.711488 0.368801 1.3140% 1919 2.676321 0.373647 0.7676% 1918 2.655933 0.376516 0.3870% 1917 2.645694 0.377973 1.3274% 1916 2.611034 0.382990 1.4083% 1915 2.574774 0.388384 1.4458% 1914 2.538078 0.393999 1.9424% 1913 2.489719 0.401652 1.9857% 1912 2.441244 0.409627 1.5634% 1911 2.403664 0.416031 1.8169% 1910 2.360771 0.423590 1.8781% 1909 2.317252 0.431546 2.0082% 1908 2.271632 0.440212 1.9603% 1907 2.227958 0.448841 1.8264% 1906 2.187998 0.457039 1.9357% 1905 2.146450 0.465886 2.0148% 1904 2.104056 0.475272 2.1335% 1903 2.060103 0.485413 1.8151% 1902 2.023376 0.494223 1.8943% 1901 1.985759 0.503586 3.0255% 1900 1.927444 0.518822 0.6278% 1899 1.915418 0.522079 1.7757% 1898 1.882000 0.531349 1.8078% 1897 1.848583 0.540955 1.8396% 1896 1.815190 0.550906 1.8755% 1895 1.781773 0.561239 1.9114% 1894 1.748355 0.571966 1.9486% 1893 1.714937 0.583112 1.9858% 1892 1.681545 0.594691 2.0276% 1891 1.648127 0.606749 2.6465% 1890 1.605633 0.622807 1.5328% 1889 1.581394 0.632354 2.0811% 1888 1.549154 0.645514 2.1599% 1887 1.516402 0.659456 2.2075% 1886 1.483650 0.674014 2.2592% 1885 1.450872 0.689241 2.3095% 1884 1.418120 0.705159 2.3641% 1883 1.385368 0.721830 2.4214% 1882 1.352616 0.739308 2.4815% 1881 1.319864 0.757654 3.7644% 1880 1.271981 0.786175 0.9432% 1879 1.260096 0.793590 2.1464% 1878 1.233618 0.810624 2.1913% 1877 1.207165 0.828387 2.2426% 1876 1.180687 0.846965 2.2941% 1875 1.154209 0.866395 2.3456% 1874 1.127756 0.886717 2.4043% 1873 1.101278 0.908036 2.4635% 1872 1.074800 0.930406 2.5258% 1871 1.048321 0.953906 5.9947% 1870 0.989032 1.011089 -1.0968% 1869 1.000000 1.000000 2.1930% 1868 0.978541 1.021930 2.2394% 1867 0.957107 1.044815 2.2935% 1866 0.935648 1.068778 2.3445% 1865 0.914215 1.093835 2.4037% 1864 0.892756 1.120127 2.4599% 1863 0.871322 1.147681 2.5250% 1862 0.849863 1.176660 2.5872% 1861 0.828429 1.207103 2.9504% 1860 0.804688 1.242718 2.4012% 1859 0.785819 1.272558 2.7627% 1858 0.764692 1.307715 2.8412% 1857 0.743566 1.344870 2.9243% 1856 0.722440 1.384198 3.0161% 1855 0.701288 1.425948 3.1061% 1854 0.680162 1.470238 3.2056% 1853 0.659036 1.517369 3.3118% 1852 0.637909 1.567621 3.4252% 1851 0.616783 1.621315 4.0106% 1850 0.593000 1.686340 3.2254% 1849 0.579524 1.725553 2.7841% 1848 0.563827 1.773594 2.8590% 1847 0.548155 1.824302 2.9432% 1846 0.532483 1.877994 3.0324% 1845 0.516811 1.934942 3.1325% 1844 0.501114 1.995554 3.2284% 1843 0.485442 2.059978 3.3361% 1842 0.469770 2.128700 3.4512% 1841 0.454098 2.202165 3.8105% 1840 0.437430 2.286079 2.3861% 1839 0.427236 2.340626 2.5824% 1838 0.416481 2.401070 2.6573% 1837 0.405700 2.464874 2.7232% 1836 0.394945 2.531998 2.7994% 1835 0.384190 2.602879 2.8871% 1834 0.373409 2.678028 2.9657% 1833 0.362654 2.757450 3.0563% 1832 0.351809 2.841726 3.1604% 1831 0.341118 2.931537 3.4660% 1830 0.329691 3.033143 2.4653% 1829 0.321759 3.107919 2.6804% 1828 0.313359 3.191223 10.3427% 1827 0.283988 3.521280 -4.2314% 1826 0.296535 3.372280 2.9150% 1825 0.288136 3.470583 3.0026% 1824 0.279737 3.574789 3.0955% 1823 0.271337 3.685447 3.1944% 1822 0.262938 3.803175 3.3102% 1821 0.254513 3.929067 3.2277% 1820 0.246555 4.055887 2.6573% 1819 0.240173 4.163664 2.6261% 1818 0.234027 4.273006 2.6969% 1817 0.227881 4.388246 2.7717% 1816 0.221736 4.509874 2.8507% 1815 0.215590 4.638437 2.9343% 1814 0.209444 4.774545 3.0231% 1813 0.203298 4.918881 3.1039% 1812 0.197178 5.071558 3.2172% 1811 0.191032 5.234718 3.0969% 1810 0.185294 5.396833 2.9144% 1809 0.180047 5.554117 2.8225% 1808 0.175104 5.710880 2.9199% 1807 0.170136 5.877634 2.9918% 1806 0.165194 6.053480 3.0841% 1805 0.160252 6.240173 3.1822% 1804 0.155310 6.438747 3.2868% 1803 0.150367 6.650375 3.3985% 1802 0.145425 6.876387 3.5180% 1801 0.140483 7.118301 3.3999% 1800 0.135864 7.360320 2.8419% 1799 0.132109 7.569490 2.7485% 1798 0.128575 7.777534 2.8261% 1797 0.125042 7.997338 3.7832% 1796 0.120483 8.299894

2.1272% 1795 0.117974 8.476449 3.0879% 1794 0.114440 8.738196 3.1625% 1793 0.110932
9.014543 3.2904% 1792 0.107398 9.311159 3.4024% 1791 0.103864 9.627959 3.2296% 1790
0.100615 9.938900 41.3145% 1780 0.071199 14.045101 29.4353% 1770 0.055008 18.179321
83.4728% 1750 0.029981 33.354117 29.2845% 1740 0.023190 43.121687 94.2514% 1720
0.011938 83.764479 85.8111% 1700 0.006425 155.643683 19.2490% 1690 0.005388
185.603612 88.0250% 1670 0.002865 348.981233

BASE YEAR: 1868

YEAR BYEAR/AYEAR AYEAR/BYEAR GROWTH%

2009 7.888162 0.126772 8.2857% 2001 7.284586 0.137276 1.0000% 2000 7.212461
0.138649 1.0000% 1999 7.141050 0.140035 1.0000% 1998 7.070347 0.141436 1.0000% 1997
7.000344 0.142850 1.0000% 1996 6.931033 0.144279 1.0000% 1995 6.862409 0.145721
0.9992% 1994 6.794517 0.147177 1.0008% 1993 6.727193 0.148650 1.0000% 1992 6.660587
0.150137 0.9295% 1991 6.599246 0.151532 1.2505% 1990 6.517741 0.153427 0.7224% 1989
6.470992 0.154536 1.1077% 1988 6.400099 0.156248 0.8834% 1987 6.344058 0.157628
0.5594% 1986 6.308769 0.158510 1.3056% 1985 6.227462 0.160579 0.7673% 1984 6.180043
0.161811 0.8149% 1983 6.130087 0.163130 0.9737% 1982 6.070971 0.164718 0.9508% 1981
6.013791 0.166284 0.9031% 1980 5.959969 0.167786 2.2701% 1979 5.827676 0.171595
1.0042% 1978 5.769738 0.173318 0.9896% 1977 5.713200 0.175033 0.9103% 1976 5.661660
0.176627 0.8394% 1975 5.614529 0.178109 0.9042% 1974 5.564219 0.179720 1.1568% 1973
5.500589 0.181799 0.9427% 1972 5.449219 0.183513 0.7426% 1971 5.409049 0.184875
1.4697% 1970 5.330702 0.187593 0.6968% 1969 5.293814 0.188900 0.8565% 1968 5.248855
0.190518 1.5090% 1967 5.170825 0.193393 0.9949% 1966 5.119887 0.195317 1.0575% 1965
5.066313 0.197382 1.1300% 1964 5.009702 0.199613 1.5537% 1963 4.933059 0.202714
1.4658% 1962 4.861794 0.205685 1.5364% 1961 4.788227 0.208846 2.1586% 1960 4.687050
0.213354 -1.6655% 1959 4.766434 0.209800 4.3080% 1958 4.569577 0.218839 2.1130%
1957 4.475022 0.223463 1.9895% 1956 4.387728 0.227908 2.1231% 1955 4.296509 0.232747
1.4496% 1954 4.235116 0.236121 2.1573% 1953 4.145683 0.241215 1.2298% 1952 4.095321
0.244181 1.6814% 1951 4.027602 0.248287 1.6233% 1950 3.963267 0.252317 1.4265% 1949
3.907525 0.255916 1.7790% 1948 3.839224 0.260469 1.8242% 1947 3.770445 0.265221 -
2.6320% 1946 3.872367 0.258240 3.1768% 1945 3.753137 0.266444 6.4754% 1944 3.524886
0.283697 -0.3437% 1943 3.537042 0.282722 0.6562% 1942 3.513982 0.284577 0.6633%
1941 3.490828 0.286465 -5.6614% 1940 3.700319 0.270247 8.0381% 1939 3.425012
0.291970 0.8126% 1938 3.397404 0.294342 0.7762% 1937 3.371235 0.296627 0.6029% 1936
3.351032 0.298415 0.5244% 1935 3.333551 0.299980 -3.0364% 1934 3.437940 0.290872
4.6271% 1933 3.285897 0.304331 1.3921% 1932 3.240782 0.308568 -0.2051% 1931
3.247442 0.307935 0.8886% 1930 3.218839 0.310671 1.0126% 1929 3.186573 0.313817
1.1526% 1928 3.150263 0.317434 1.2160% 1927 3.112416 0.321294 1.4086% 1926 3.069184
0.325820 1.7667% 1925 3.015902 0.331576 1.4465% 1924 2.972899 0.336372 1.7700% 1923
2.921195 0.342326 1.6165% 1922 2.874725 0.347859 1.3736% 1921 2.835771 0.352638
2.3393% 1920 2.770950 0.360887 1.3140% 1919 2.735012 0.365629 0.7676% 1918 2.714176
0.368436 0.3870% 1917 2.703713 0.369862 1.3274% 1916 2.668294 0.374771 1.4083% 1915
2.631238 0.380049 1.4458% 1914 2.593738 0.385544 1.9424% 1913 2.544317 0.393033
1.9857% 1912 2.494779 0.400837 1.5634% 1911 2.456376 0.407104 1.8169% 1910 2.412542
0.414501 1.8781% 1909 2.368068 0.422285 2.0082% 1908 2.321448 0.430766 1.9603% 1907
2.276817 0.439210 1.8264% 1906 2.235980 0.447231 1.9357% 1905 2.193521 0.455888
2.0148% 1904 2.150198 0.465074 2.1335% 1903 2.105281 0.474996 1.8151% 1902 2.067748
0.483618 1.8943% 1901 2.029306 0.492779 3.0255% 1900 1.969712 0.507688 0.6278% 1899
1.957423 0.510876 1.7757% 1898 1.923272 0.519947 1.8078% 1897 1.889122 0.529347
1.8396% 1896 1.854997 0.539084 1.8755% 1895 1.820846 0.549195 1.9114% 1894 1.786696
0.559692 1.9486% 1893 1.752545 0.570599 1.9858% 1892 1.718420 0.581930 2.0276% 1891
1.684270 0.593729 2.6465% 1890 1.640845 0.609442 1.5328% 1889 1.616073 0.618784
2.0811% 1888 1.583126 0.631662 2.1599% 1887 1.549656 0.645305 2.2075% 1886 1.516186
0.659550 2.2592% 1885 1.482689 0.674450 2.3095% 1884 1.449219 0.690027 2.3641% 1883
1.415749 0.706340 2.4214% 1882 1.382278 0.723443 2.4815% 1881 1.348808 0.741395
3.7644% 1880 1.299876 0.769304 0.9432% 1879 1.287729 0.776561 2.1464% 1878 1.260670
0.793229 2.1913% 1877 1.233638 0.810611 2.2426% 1876 1.206579 0.828790 2.2941% 1875

212

1.179520 0.847802 2.3456% 1874 1.152487 0.867688 2.4043% 1873 1.125429 0.888550
2.4635% 1872 1.098370 0.910440 2.5258% 1871 1.071311 0.933436 5.9947% 1870 1.010721
0.989392 -1.0968% 1869 1.021930 0.978541 2.1930% 1868 1.000000 1.000000 2.2394%
1867 0.978096 1.022394 2.2935% 1866 0.956167 1.045843 2.3445% 1865 0.934263 1.070362
2.4037% 1864 0.912333 1.096090 2.4599% 1863 0.890430 1.123053 2.5250% 1862 0.868500
1.151410 2.5872% 1861 0.846597 1.181200 2.9504% 1860 0.822334 1.216050 2.4012% 1859
0.803051 1.245250 2.7627% 1858 0.781462 1.279653 2.8412% 1857 0.759872 1.316011
2.9243% 1856 0.738283 1.354495 3.0161% 1855 0.716667 1.395348 3.1061% 1854 0.695078
1.438688 3.2056% 1853 0.673488 1.484807 3.3118% 1852 0.651899 1.533981 3.4252% 1851
0.630309 1.586523 4.0106% 1850 0.606005 1.650152 2.3254% 1849 0.592233 1.688525
2.7841% 1848 0.576191 1.735535 2.8590% 1847 0.560176 1.785154 2.9432% 1846 0.544160
1.837694 3.0324% 1845 0.528145 1.893420 3.1325% 1844 0.512103 1.952731 3.2284% 1843
0.496088 2.015773 3.3361% 1842 0.480072 2.083020 3.4512% 1841 0.464057 2.154909
3.8105% 1840 0.447023 2.237021 2.3861% 1839 0.436605 2.290398 2.5824% 1838 0.425614
2.349545 2.6573% 1837 0.414597 2.411980 2.7232% 1836 0.403606 2.477663 2.7994% 1835
0.392615 2.547024 2.8871% 1834 0.381598 2.620560 2.9657% 1833 0.370607 2.698277
3.0563% 1832 0.359616 2.780745 3.1604% 1831 0.348599 2.868628 3.4660% 1830 0.336921
2.968054 2.4653% 1829 0.328815 3.041226 2.6804% 1828 0.320231 3.122743 10.3427%
1827 0.290215 3.445717 -4.2314% 1826 0.303038 3.299914 2.9150% 1825 0.294455
3.396107 3.0026% 1824 0.285871 3.498078 3.0955% 1823 0.277288 3.606361 3.1944% 1822
0.268704 3.721562 3.3102% 1821 0.260095 3.844753 3.2277% 1820 0.251962 3.968852
2.6573% 1819 0.245440 4.074315 2.6261% 1818 0.239159 4.181311 2.6969% 1817 0.232879
4.294078 2.7717% 1816 0.226598 4.413096 2.8507% 1815 0.220318 4.538900 2.9343% 1814
0.214037 4.672087 3.0231% 1813 0.207757 4.813327 3.1039% 1812 0.201502 4.962727
3.2172% 1811 0.195222 5.122386 3.0969% 1810 0.189357 5.281022 2.9144% 1809 0.183995
5.434931 2.8225% 1808 0.178944 5.588330 2.9199% 1807 0.173868 5.751505 2.9918% 1806
0.168817 5.923578 3.0841% 1805 0.163766 6.106264 3.1822% 1804 0.158716 6.300577
3.2868% 1803 0.153665 6.507663 3.3985% 1802 0.148614 6.728825 3.5180% 1801 0.143564
6.965549 3.3999% 1800 0.138843 7.202374 2.8419% 1799 0.135006 7.407056 2.7485% 1798
0.131395 7.610635 2.8261% 1797 0.127784 7.825722 3.7832% 1796 0.123126 8.121785
2.1272% 1795 0.120561 8.294552 3.0879% 1794 0.116950 8.550682 3.1625% 1793 0.113365
8.821099 3.2904% 1792 0.109753 9.111350 3.4024% 1791 0.106142 9.421351 3.2296% 1790
0.102821 9.725620 41.3145% 1780 0.072761 13.743706 29.4353% 1770 0.056214 17.789209
83.4728% 1750 0.030639 32.638367 29.2845% 1740 0.023699 42.196334 94.2514% 1720
0.012200 81.966967 85.8111% 1700 0.006566 152.303707 19.2490% 1690 0.005506
181.620722 88.0250% 1670 0.002928 341.492404

BASE YEAR: 1867
YEAR BYEAR/AYEAR AYEAR/BYEAR GROWTH%

2009 8.064810 0.123995 8.2857% 2001 7.447718 0.134269 1.0000% 2000 7.373977
0.135612 1.0000% 1999 7.300968 0.136968 1.0000% 1998 7.228681 0.138338 1.0000% 1997
7.157110 0.139721 1.0000% 1996 7.086247 0.141118 1.0000% 1995 7.016086 0.142530
0.9992% 1994 6.946674 0.143954 1.0008% 1993 6.877842 0.145394 1.0000% 1992 6.809744
0.146848 0.9295% 1991 6.747030 0.148213 1.2505% 1990 6.663700 0.150067 0.7224% 1989
6.615903 0.151151 1.1077% 1988 6.543424 0.152825 0.8834% 1987 6.486127 0.154175
0.5594% 1986 6.450048 0.155038 1.3056% 1985 6.366920 0.157062 0.7673% 1984 6.318440
0.158267 0.8149% 1983 6.267364 0.159557 0.9737% 1982 6.206924 0.161110 0.9508% 1981
6.148464 0.162642 0.9031% 1980 6.093437 0.164111 2.2701% 1979 5.958182 0.167836
1.0042% 1978 5.898946 0.169522 0.9896% 1977 5.841141 0.171199 0.9103% 1976 5.788447
0.172758 0.8394% 1975 5.740261 0.174208 0.9042% 1974 5.688824 0.175783 1.1568% 1973
5.623769 0.177817 0.9427% 1972 5.571249 0.179493 0.7426% 1971 5.530180 0.180826
1.4697% 1970 5.450078 0.183484 0.6968% 1969 5.412364 0.184762 0.8565% 1968 5.366398
0.186345 1.5090% 1967 5.286621 0.189157 0.9949% 1966 5.234542 0.191039 1.0575% 1965
5.179768 0.193059 1.1300% 1964 5.121890 0.195240 1.5537% 1963 5.043531 0.198274
1.4658% 1962 4.970670 0.201180 1.5364% 1961 4.895454 0.204271 2.1586% 1960 4.792012
0.208681 -1.6655% 1959 4.873174 0.205205 4.3080% 1958 4.671908 0.214045 2.1130%
1957 4.575235 0.218568 1.9895% 1956 4.485987 0.222916 2.1231% 1955 4.392725 0.227649

213

1.4496% 1954 4.329958 0.230949 2.1573% 1953 4.238522 0.235931 1.2298% 1952 4.187032 0.238833 1.6814% 1951 4.117796 0.242848 1.6233% 1950 4.052021 0.246790 1.4265% 1949 3.995030 0.250311 1.7790% 1948 3.925199 0.254764 1.8242% 1947 3.854880 0.259411 -2.6320% 1946 3.959085 0.252584 3.1768% 1945 3.837185 0.260608 6.4754% 1944 3.603822 0.277483 -0.3437% 1943 3.616251 0.276530 0.6562% 1942 3.592675 0.278344 0.6633% 1941 3.569001 0.280190 -5.6614% 1940 3.783184 0.264328 8.0381% 1939 3.501712 0.285575 0.8126% 1938 3.473486 0.287895 0.7762% 1937 3.446731 0.290130 0.6029% 1936 3.426076 0.291879 0.5244% 1935 3.408203 0.293410 -3.0364% 1934 3.514929 0.284501 4.6271% 1933 3.359482 0.297665 1.3921% 1932 3.313356 0.301809 -0.2051% 1931 3.320165 0.301190 0.8886% 1930 3.290922 0.303866 1.0126% 1929 3.257933 0.306943 1.1526% 1928 3.220810 0.310481 1.2160% 1927 3.182116 0.314256 1.4086% 1926 3.137915 0.318683 1.7667% 1925 3.083441 0.324313 1.4465% 1924 3.039475 0.329004 1.7700% 1923 2.986612 0.334828 1.6165% 1922 2.939101 0.340240 1.3736% 1921 2.899275 0.344914 2.3393% 1920 2.833003 0.352982 1.3140% 1919 2.796260 0.357621 0.7676% 1918 2.774958 0.360366 0.3870% 1917 2.764260 0.361760 1.3274% 1916 2.728047 0.366563 1.4083% 1915 2.690162 0.371725 1.4458% 1914 2.651822 0.377099 1.9424% 1913 2.601295 0.384424 1.9857% 1912 2.550647 0.392057 1.5634% 1911 2.511384 0.398187 1.8169% 1910 2.466569 0.405421 1.8781% 1909 2.421099 0.413036 2.0082% 1908 2.373435 0.421330 1.9603% 1907 2.327804 0.429589 1.8264% 1906 2.286053 0.437435 1.9357% 1905 2.242642 0.445903 2.0148% 1904 2.198349 0.454887 2.1335% 1903 2.152427 0.464592 1.8151% 1902 2.114053 0.473025 1.8943% 1901 2.074750 0.481986 3.0255% 1900 2.013822 0.496568 0.6278% 1899 2.001257 0.499686 1.7757% 1898 1.966342 0.508559 1.8078% 1897 1.931427 0.517752 1.8396% 1896 1.896538 0.527277 1.8755% 1895 1.861622 0.537166 1.9114% 1894 1.826707 0.547433 1.9486% 1893 1.791792 0.558101 1.9858% 1892 1.756903 0.569183 2.0276% 1891 1.721987 0.580724 2.6465% 1890 1.677590 0.596093 1.5328% 1889 1.652263 0.605230 2.0811% 1888 1.618579 0.617826 2.1599% 1887 1.584359 0.631170 2.2075% 1886 1.550139 0.645103 2.2592% 1885 1.515893 0.659677 2.3095% 1884 1.481673 0.674913 2.3641% 1883 1.447453 0.690869 2.4214% 1882 1.413233 0.707597 2.4815% 1881 1.379013 0.725156 3.7644% 1880 1.328985 0.752454 0.9432% 1879 1.316567 0.759551 2.1464% 1878 1.288902 0.775854 2.1913% 1877 1.261264 0.792855 2.2426% 1876 1.233599 0.810636 2.2941% 1875 1.205934 0.829233 2.3456% 1874 1.178296 0.848683 2.4043% 1873 1.150631 0.869088 2.4635% 1872 1.122967 0.890498 2.5258% 1871 1.095302 0.912990 5.9947% 1870 1.033355 0.967721 -1.0968% 1869 1.044815 0.957107 2.1930% 1868 1.022394 0.978096 2.2394% 1867 1.000000 1.000000 2.2935% 1866 0.977579 1.022935 2.3445% 1865 0.955185 1.046917 2.4037% 1864 0.932764 1.072082 2.4599% 1863 0.910370 1.098454 2.5250% 1862 0.887949 1.126190 2.5872% 1860 0.865555 1.155328 2.9504% 1860 0.840750 1.189414 2.4012% 1859 0.821035 1.217975 2.7627% 1858 0.798962 1.251624 2.8412% 1857 0.776889 1.287185 2.9243% 1856 0.754816 1.324826 3.0161% 1855 0.732716 1.364785 3.1061% 1854 0.710643 1.407176 3.2056% 1853 0.688570 1.452285 3.3118% 1852 0.666497 1.500381 3.4252% 1851 0.644424 1.551773 4.0106% 1850 0.619576 1.614008 2.3254% 1849 0.605496 1.651540 2.7841% 1848 0.589095 1.697520 2.8590% 1847 0.572720 1.746053 2.9432% 1846 0.556346 1.797442 3.0324% 1845 0.539972 1.851947 3.1325% 1844 0.523571 1.909960 3.2284% 1843 0.507197 1.971620 3.3361% 1842 0.490823 2.037394 3.4512% 1841 0.474449 2.107709 3.8105% 1840 0.457034 2.188023 2.3861% 1839 0.446383 2.240230 2.5824% 1838 0.435146 2.298082 2.6573% 1837 0.423882 2.359149 2.7232% 1836 0.412644 2.423394 2.7994% 1835 0.401407 2.491235 2.8871% 1834 0.390143 2.563160 2.9657% 1833 0.378906 2.639175 3.0563% 1832 0.367669 2.719837 3.1604% 1831 0.356405 2.805795 3.4660% 1830 0.344466 2.903043 2.4653% 1829 0.336178 2.974612 2.6804% 1828 0.327403 3.054343 10.3427% 1827 0.296714 3.370243 -4.2314% 1826 0.309824 3.227634 2.9150% 1825 0.301049 3.321721 3.0026% 1824 0.292273 3.421457 3.0955% 1823 0.283497 3.527369 3.1944% 1822 0.274722 3.640047 3.3102% 1821 0.265919 3.760539 3.2277% 1820 0.257605 3.881920 2.6573% 1819 0.250936 3.985073 2.6261% 1818 0.244515 4.089725 2.6969% 1817 0.238094 4.200022 2.7717% 1816 0.231673 4.316434 2.8507% 1815 0.225251 4.439482 2.9343% 1814 0.218830 4.569752 3.0231% 1813 0.212409 4.707898 3.1039% 1812 0.206015 4.854026 3.2172% 1811 0.199593 5.010188 3.0969% 1810 0.193598 5.165349 2.9144% 1809 0.188115 5.315887 2.8225% 1808 0.182952 5.465926 2.9199% 1807 0.177761 5.625527 2.9918% 1806

0.172597 5.793830 3.0841% 1805 0.167434 5.972515 3.1822% 1804 0.162270 6.162572
3.2868% 1803 0.157106 6.365123 3.3985% 1802 0.151942 6.581440 3.5180% 1801 0.146779
6.812978 3.3999% 1800 0.141952 7.044616 2.8419% 1799 0.138030 7.244815 2.7485% 1798
0.134338 7.443935 2.8261% 1797 0.130645 7.654311 3.7832% 1796 0.125883 7.943889
2.1272% 1795 0.123261 8.112872 3.0879% 1794 0.119569 8.363392 3.1625% 1793 0.115903
8.627886 3.2904% 1792 0.112211 8.911779 3.4024% 1791 0.108519 9.214990 3.2296% 1790
0.105124 9.512594 41.3145% 1780 0.074390 13.442670 29.4353% 1770 0.057473 17.399562
83.4728% 1750 0.031325 31.923471 29.2845% 1740 0.024229 41.272085 94.2514% 1720
0.012473 80.171600 85.8111% 1700 0.006713 148.967716 19.2490% 1690 0.005629
177.642586 88.0250% 1670 0.002994 334.012511

BASE YEAR: 1866
YEAR BYEAR/AYEAR AYEAR/BYEAR GROWTH%

2009 8.249777 0.121215 8.2857% 2001 7.618531 0.131259 1.0000% 2000 7.543100
0.132571 1.0000% 1999 7.468415 0.133897 1.0000% 1998 7.394471 0.135236 1.0000% 1997
7.321258 0.136589 1.0000% 1996 7.248770 0.137954 1.0000% 1995 7.177000 0.139334
0.9992% 1994 7.105996 0.140726 1.0008% 1993 7.035585 0.142135 1.0000% 1992 6.965926
0.143556 0.9295% 1991 6.901773 0.144890 1.2505% 1990 6.816532 0.146702 0.7224% 1989
6.767639 0.147762 1.1077% 1988 6.693497 0.149399 0.8834% 1987 6.634887 0.150718
0.5594% 1986 6.597980 0.151562 1.3056% 1985 6.512945 0.153540 0.7673% 1984 6.463353
0.154718 0.8149% 1983 6.411106 0.155979 0.9737% 1982 6.349280 0.157498 0.9508% 1981
6.289479 0.158996 0.9031% 1980 6.233190 0.160432 2.2701% 1979 6.094833 0.164073
1.0042% 1978 6.034238 0.165721 0.9896% 1977 5.975108 0.167361 0.9103% 1976 5.921205
0.168885 0.8394% 1975 5.871914 0.170302 0.9042% 1974 5.819298 0.171842 1.1568% 1973
5.752751 0.173830 0.9427% 1972 5.699026 0.175469 0.7426% 1971 5.657015 0.176772
1.4697% 1970 5.575076 0.179370 0.6968% 1969 5.536496 0.180620 0.8565% 1968 5.489477
0.182167 1.5090% 1967 5.407870 0.184916 0.9949% 1966 5.354597 0.186755 1.0575% 1965
5.298566 0.188730 1.1300% 1964 5.239360 0.190863 1.5537% 1963 5.159204 0.193828
1.4658% 1962 5.084672 0.196670 1.5364% 1961 5.007732 0.199691 2.1586% 1960 4.901917
0.204002 -1.6655% 1959 4.984940 0.200604 4.3080% 1958 4.779059 0.209246 2.1130%
1957 4.680169 0.213668 1.9895% 1956 4.588873 0.217918 2.1231% 1955 4.493473 0.222545
1.4496% 1954 4.429265 0.225771 2.1573% 1953 4.335733 0.230642 1.2298% 1952 4.283061
0.233478 1.6814% 1951 4.212238 0.237403 1.6233% 1950 4.144954 0.241257 1.4265% 1949
4.086656 0.244699 1.7790% 1948 4.015224 0.249052 1.8242% 1947 3.943292 0.253595 -
2.6320% 1946 4.049886 0.246921 3.1768% 1945 3.925191 0.254765 6.4754% 1944 3.686476
0.271262 -0.3437% 1943 3.699189 0.270329 0.6562% 1942 3.675073 0.272103 0.6633%
1941 3.650857 0.273908 -5.6614% 1940 3.869951 0.258401 8.0381% 1939 3.582024
0.279172 0.8126% 1938 3.553150 0.281440 0.7762% 1937 3.525781 0.283625 0.6029% 1936
3.504653 0.285335 0.5244% 1935 3.486370 0.286831 -3.0364% 1934 3.595544 0.278122
4.6271% 1933 3.436532 0.290991 1.3921% 1932 3.389348 0.295042 -0.2051% 1931
3.396313 0.294437 0.8886% 1930 3.366400 0.297053 1.0126% 1929 3.332654 0.300061
1.1526% 1928 3.294680 0.303520 1.2160% 1927 3.255097 0.307210 1.4086% 1926 3.209884
0.311538 1.7667% 1925 3.154160 0.317042 1.4465% 1924 3.109185 0.321628 1.7700% 1923
3.055110 0.327320 1.6165% 1922 3.006510 0.332612 1.3736% 1921 2.965770 0.337181
2.3393% 1920 2.897978 0.345068 1.3140% 1919 2.860392 0.349602 0.7676% 1918 2.838602
0.352286 0.3870% 1917 2.827659 0.353649 1.3274% 1916 2.790615 0.358344 1.4083% 1915
2.751861 0.363390 1.4458% 1914 2.712642 0.368644 1.9424% 1913 2.660956 0.375805
1.9857% 1912 2.609147 0.383267 1.5634% 1911 2.568983 0.389259 1.8169% 1910 2.523140
0.396332 1.8781% 1909 2.476627 0.403775 2.0082% 1908 2.427870 0.411884 1.9603% 1907
2.381192 0.419958 1.8264% 1906 2.338483 0.427628 1.9357% 1905 2.294077 0.435905
2.0148% 1904 2.248768 0.444688 2.1335% 1903 2.201793 0.454175 1.8151% 1902 2.162539
0.462419 1.8943% 1901 2.122335 0.471179 3.0255% 1900 2.060009 0.485435 0.6278% 1899
2.047156 0.488482 1.7757% 1898 2.011440 0.497156 1.8078% 1897 1.975724 0.506144
1.8396% 1896 1.940035 0.515455 1.8755% 1895 1.904319 0.525122 1.9114% 1894 1.868603
0.535159 1.9486% 1893 1.832886 0.545588 1.9858% 1892 1.797197 0.556422 2.0276% 1891
1.761481 0.567704 2.6465% 1890 1.716065 0.582728 1.5328% 1889 1.690158 0.591661
2.0811% 1888 1.655701 0.603974 2.1599% 1887 1.620696 0.617019 2.2075% 1886 1.585692

215

0.630640 2.2592% 1885 1.550660 0.644887 2.3095% 1884 1.515655 0.659781 2.3641% 1883
1.480650 0.675379 2.4214% 1882 1.445646 0.691732 2.4815% 1881 1.410641 0.708898
3.7644% 1880 1.359465 0.735583 0.9432% 1879 1.346762 0.742522 2.1464% 1878 1.318463
0.758459 2.1913% 1877 1.290191 0.775079 2.2426% 1876 1.261892 0.792461 2.2941% 1875
1.233592 0.810641 2.3456% 1874 1.205320 0.829655 2.4043% 1873 1.177021 0.849602
2.4635% 1872 1.148722 0.870533 2.5258% 1871 1.120423 0.892520 5.9947% 1870 1.057056
0.946024 -1.0968% 1869 1.068778 0.935648 2.1930% 1868 1.045843 0.956167 2.2394%
1867 1.022935 0.977579 2.2935% 1866 1.000000 1.000000 2.3445% 1865 0.977092 1.023445
2.4037% 1864 0.954157 1.048045 2.4599% 1863 0.931250 1.073826 2.5250% 1862 0.908315
1.100940 2.5872% 1861 0.885407 1.129424 2.9504% 1860 0.860033 1.162747 2.4012% 1859
0.839865 1.190667 2.7627% 1858 0.817286 1.223562 2.8412% 1857 0.794707 1.258326
2.9243% 1856 0.772128 1.295123 3.0161% 1855 0.749521 1.334185 3.1061% 1854 0.726942
1.375626 3.2056% 1853 0.704363 1.419723 3.3118% 1852 0.681783 1.466742 3.4252% 1851
0.659204 1.516981 4.0106% 1850 0.633785 1.577821 2.3254% 1849 0.619383 1.614511
2.7841% 1848 0.602606 1.659460 2.8590% 1847 0.585856 1.706905 2.9432% 1846 0.569106
1.757141 3.0324% 1845 0.552356 1.810425 3.1325% 1844 0.535579 1.867137 3.2284% 1843
0.518830 1.927415 3.3361% 1842 0.502080 1.991714 3.4512% 1841 0.485330 2.060452
3.8105% 1840 0.467516 2.138966 2.3861% 1839 0.456621 2.190002 2.5824% 1838 0.445126
2.246557 2.6573% 1837 0.433603 2.306255 2.7232% 1836 0.422108 2.369059 2.7994% 1835
0.410614 2.435380 2.8871% 1834 0.399091 2.505692 2.9657% 1833 0.387596 2.580003
3.0563% 1832 0.376102 2.658856 3.1604% 1831 0.364579 2.742887 3.4660% 1830 0.352366
2.837955 2.4653% 1829 0.343889 2.907919 2.6804% 1828 0.334912 2.985863 10.3427%
1827 0.303520 3.294680 -4.2314% 1826 0.316930 3.155268 2.9150% 1825 0.307953
3.247245 3.0026% 1824 0.298976 3.344746 3.0955% 1823 0.289999 3.448282 3.1944% 1822
0.281022 3.558434 3.3102% 1821 0.272018 3.676225 3.2277% 1820 0.263513 3.794884
2.6573% 1819 0.256692 3.895724 2.6261% 1818 0.250123 3.998030 2.6969% 1817 0.243555
4.105855 2.7717% 1816 0.236986 4.219656 2.8507% 1815 0.230418 4.339945 2.9343% 1814
0.223849 4.467294 3.0231% 1813 0.217281 4.602343 3.1039% 1812 0.210740 4.745195
3.2172% 1811 0.204171 4.897855 3.0969% 1810 0.198038 5.049538 2.9144% 1809 0.192430
5.196700 2.8225% 1808 0.187148 5.343375 2.9199% 1807 0.181838 5.499398 2.9918% 1806
0.176556 5.663928 3.0841% 1805 0.171274 5.838607 3.1822% 1804 0.165992 6.024402
3.2868% 1803 0.160709 6.222411 3.3985% 1802 0.155427 6.433879 3.5180% 1801 0.150145
6.660226 3.3999% 1800 0.145208 6.886670 2.8419% 1799 0.141195 7.082380 2.7485% 1798
0.137419 7.277036 2.8261% 1797 0.133642 7.482695 3.7832% 1796 0.128770 7.765781
2.1272% 1795 0.126088 7.930975 3.0879% 1794 0.122311 8.175878 3.1625% 1793 0.118561
8.434441 3.2904% 1792 0.114785 8.711969 3.4024% 1791 0.111008 9.008383 3.2296% 1790
0.107535 9.299314 41.3145% 1780 0.076096 13.141275 29.4353% 1770 0.058791 17.009450
83.4728% 1750 0.032043 31.207721 29.2845% 1740 0.024785 40.346731 94.2514% 1720
0.012759 78.374088 85.8111% 1700 0.006867 145.627740 19.2490% 1690 0.005758
173.659696 88.0250% 1670 0.003063 326.523682

BASE YEAR: 1865

YEAR BYEAR/AYEAR AYEAR/BYEAR GROWTH%

2009 8.443191 0.118439 8.2857% 2001 7.797146 0.128252 1.0000% 2000 7.719945
0.129535 1.0000% 1999 7.643510 0.130830 1.0000% 1998 7.567832 0.132138 1.0000% 1997
7.492903 0.133460 1.0000% 1996 7.418716 0.134794 1.0000% 1995 7.345263 0.136142
0.9992% 1994 7.272594 0.137503 1.0008% 1993 7.200532 0.138879 1.0000% 1992 7.129240
0.140267 0.9295% 1991 7.063584 0.141571 1.2505% 1990 6.976343 0.143342 0.7224% 1989
6.926305 0.144377 1.1077% 1988 6.850424 0.145976 0.8834% 1987 6.790440 0.147266
0.5594% 1986 6.752668 0.148090 1.3056% 1985 6.665640 0.150023 0.7673% 1984 6.614885
0.151174 0.8149% 1983 6.561413 0.152406 0.9737% 1982 6.498137 0.153890 0.9508% 1981
6.436935 0.155353 0.9031% 1980 6.379325 0.156756 2.2701% 1979 6.237724 0.160315
1.0042% 1978 6.175709 0.161925 0.9896% 1977 6.115193 0.163527 0.9103% 1976 6.060026
0.165016 0.8394% 1975 6.009580 0.166401 0.9042% 1974 5.955730 0.167906 1.1568% 1973
5.887622 0.169848 0.9427% 1972 5.832638 0.171449 0.7426% 1971 5.789642 0.172722
1.4697% 1970 5.705782 0.175261 0.6968% 1969 5.666298 0.176482 0.8565% 1968 5.618176
0.177994 1.5090% 1967 5.534656 0.180680 0.9949% 1966 5.480134 0.182477 1.0575% 1965

216

5.422789 0.184407 1.1300% 1964 5.362196 0.186491 1.5537% 1963 5.280160 0.189388 1.4658% 1962 5.203881 0.192164 1.5364% 1961 5.125137 0.195117 2.1586% 1960 5.016841 0.199329 -1.6655% 1959 5.101811 0.196009 4.3080% 1958 4.891102 0.204453 2.1130% 1957 4.789894 0.208773 1.9895% 1956 4.696458 0.212926 2.1231% 1955 4.598821 0.217447 1.4496% 1954 4.533108 0.220599 2.1573% 1953 4.437383 0.225358 1.2298% 1952 4.383477 0.228129 1.6814% 1951 4.310993 0.231965 1.6233% 1950 4.242131 0.235731 1.4265% 1949 4.182467 0.239093 1.7790% 1948 4.109360 0.243347 1.8242% 1947 4.035741 0.247786 - 2.6320% 1945 4.144835 0.241264 3.1768% 1945 4.017216 0.248929 6.4754% 1944 3.772905 0.265048 -0.3437% 1943 3.785916 0.264137 0.6562% 1942 3.761234 0.265870 0.6633% 1941 3.736450 0.267634 -5.6614% 1940 3.960681 0.252482 8.0381% 1939 3.666004 0.272777 0.8126% 1938 3.636453 0.274993 0.7762% 1937 3.608442 0.277128 0.6029% 1936 3.586818 0.278799 0.5244% 1935 3.568107 0.280261 -3.0364% 1934 3.679841 0.271751 4.6271% 1933 3.517100 0.284325 1.3921% 1932 3.468810 0.288283 -0.2051% 1931 3.475939 0.287692 0.8886% 1930 3.445324 0.290248 1.0126% 1929 3.410787 0.293187 1.1526% 1928 3.371922 0.296567 1.2160% 1927 3.331412 0.300173 1.4086% 1926 3.285138 0.304401 1.7667% 1925 3.228108 0.309779 1.4465% 1924 3.182079 0.314260 1.7700% 1923 3.126737 0.319822 1.6165% 1922 3.076996 0.324992 1.3736% 1921 3.035302 0.329456 2.3393% 1920 2.965920 0.337164 1.3140% 1919 2.927453 0.341594 0.7676% 1918 2.905152 0.344216 0.3870% 1917 2.893953 0.345548 1.3274% 1916 2.856040 0.350135 1.4083% 1915 2.816378 0.355066 1.4458% 1914 2.776239 0.360200 1.9424% 1913 2.723341 0.367196 1.9857% 1912 2.670317 0.374487 1.5634% 1911 2.629212 0.380342 1.8169% 1910 2.582294 0.387253 1.8781% 1909 2.534691 0.394525 2.0082% 1908 2.484790 0.402448 1.9603% 1907 2.437019 0.410337 1.8264% 1906 2.393308 0.417832 1.9357% 1905 2.347861 0.425920 2.0148% 1904 2.301490 0.434501 2.1335% 1903 2.253413 0.443771 1.8151% 1902 2.213239 0.451826 1.8943% 1901 2.172092 0.460386 3.0255% 1900 2.108306 0.474315 0.6278% 1899 2.095151 0.477292 1.7757% 1898 2.058598 0.485768 1.8078% 1897 2.022044 0.494549 1.8396% 1896 1.985519 0.503647 1.8755% 1895 1.948965 0.513093 1.9114% 1894 1.912411 0.522900 1.9486% 1893 1.875858 0.533089 1.9858% 1892 1.839332 0.543676 2.0276% 1891 1.802779 0.554699 2.6465% 1890 1.756298 0.569379 1.5328% 1889 1.729783 0.578107 2.0811% 1888 1.694518 0.590138 2.1599% 1887 1.658693 0.602884 2.2075% 1886 1.622868 0.616193 2.2592% 1885 1.587014 0.630114 2.3095% 1884 1.551189 0.644667 2.3641% 1883 1.515364 0.659908 2.4214% 1882 1.479538 0.675886 2.4815% 1881 1.443713 0.692658 3.7644% 1880 1.391338 0.718733 0.9432% 1879 1.378337 0.725512 2.1464% 1878 1.349374 0.741084 2.1913% 1877 1.320439 0.757324 2.2426% 1876 1.291476 0.774308 2.2941% 1875 1.262514 0.792071 2.3456% 1874 1.233579 0.810649 2.4043% 1873 1.204616 0.830140 2.4635% 1872 1.175653 0.850591 2.5258% 1871 1.146691 0.872075 5.9947% 1870 1.081838 0.924353 -1.0968% 1869 1.093835 0.914215 2.1930% 1868 1.070362 0.934263 2.2394% 1867 1.046917 0.955185 2.2935% 1866 1.023445 0.977092 2.3445% 1865 1.000000 1.000000 2.4037% 1864 0.976527 1.024037 2.4599% 1863 0.953083 1.049227 2.5250% 1862 0.929610 1.075720 2.5872% 1861 0.906165 1.103552 2.9504% 1860 0.880196 1.136111 2.4012% 1859 0.859556 1.163392 2.7627% 1858 0.836447 1.195533 2.8412% 1857 0.813339 1.229500 2.9243% 1856 0.790230 1.265454 3.0161% 1855 0.767093 1.303622 3.1061% 1854 0.743985 1.344114 3.2056% 1853 0.720876 1.387201 3.3118% 1852 0.697768 1.433142 3.4252% 1851 0.674659 1.482230 4.0106% 1850 0.648644 1.541677 2.3254% 1849 0.633904 1.577526 2.7841% 1848 0.616733 1.621446 2.8590% 1847 0.599591 1.667803 2.9432% 1846 0.582449 1.716889 3.0324% 1845 0.565306 1.768953 3.1325% 1844 0.548136 1.824365 3.2284% 1843 0.530994 1.883262 3.3361% 1842 0.513851 1.946089 3.4512% 1841 0.496709 2.013252 3.8105% 1840 0.478476 2.089967 2.3861% 1839 0.467326 2.139835 2.5824% 1838 0.455561 2.195093 2.6573% 1837 0.443769 2.253424 2.7232% 1836 0.432005 2.314790 2.7994% 1835 0.420240 2.379591 2.8871% 1834 0.408448 2.448292 2.9657% 1833 0.396684 2.520901 3.0563% 1832 0.384919 2.597948 3.1604% 1831 0.373127 2.680054 3.4660% 1830 0.360628 2.772944 2.4653% 1829 0.351951 2.841305 2.6804% 1828 0.342764 2.917463 10.3427% 1827 0.310636 3.219206 -4.2314% 1826 0.324361 3.082988 2.9150% 1825 0.315173 3.172858 3.0026% 1824 0.305986 3.268125 3.0955% 1823 0.296798 3.369290 3.1944% 1822 0.287611 3.476919 3.3102% 1821 0.278396 3.592011 3.2277% 1820 0.269691 3.707952 2.6573% 1819 0.262710 3.806483 2.6261% 1818 0.255987 3.906445 2.6969% 1817 0.249265

4.011799 2.7717% 1816 0.242542 4.122993 2.8507% 1815 0.235820 4.240527 2.9343% 1814 0.229097 4.364959 3.0231% 1813 0.222375 4.496914 3.1039% 1812 0.215680 4.636494 3.2172% 1811 0.208958 4.785657 3.0969% 1810 0.202681 4.933865 2.9144% 1809 0.196941 5.077656 2.8225% 1808 0.191535 5.220971 2.9199% 1807 0.186101 5.373420 2.9918% 1806 0.180695 5.534181 3.0841% 1805 0.175289 5.704858 3.1822% 1804 0.169883 5.886397 3.2868% 1803 0.164477 6.079871 3.3985% 1802 0.159071 6.286494 3.5180% 1801 0.153665 6.507656 3.3999% 1800 0.148612 6.728913 2.8419% 1799 0.144506 6.920140 2.7485% 1798 0.140640 7.110337 2.8261% 1797 0.136775 7.311284 3.7832% 1796 0.131789 7.587885 2.1272% 1795 0.129044 7.749295 3.0879% 1794 0.125179 7.988588 3.1625% 1793 0.121341 8.241228 3.2904% 1792 0.117476 8.512399 3.4024% 1791 0.113610 8.802022 3.2296% 1790 0.110056 9.086289 41.3145% 1780 0.077880 12.840239 29.4353% 1770 0.060169 16.619804 83.4728% 1750 0.032795 30.492825 29.2845% 1740 0.025366 39.422482 94.2514% 1720 0.013058 76.578722 85.8111% 1700 0.007028 142.291750 19.2490% 1690 0.005893 169.681559 88.0250% 1670 0.003134 319.043789

BASE YEAR: 1864

YEAR BYEAR/AYEAR AYEAR/BYEAR GROWTH%

2009 8.646139 0.115659 8.2857% 2001 7.984565 0.125242 1.0000% 2000 7.905509 0.126494 1.0000% 1999 7.827237 0.127759 1.0000% 1998 7.749740 0.129037 1.0000% 1997 7.673009 0.130327 1.0000% 1996 7.597039 0.131630 1.0000% 1995 7.521821 0.132947 0.9992% 1994 7.447405 0.134275 1.0008% 1993 7.373611 0.135619 1.0000% 1992 7.300605 0.136975 0.9295% 1991 7.233371 0.138248 1.2505% 1990 7.144033 0.139977 0.7224% 1989 7.092792 0.140988 1.1077% 1988 7.015088 0.142550 0.8834% 1987 6.953661 0.143809 0.5594% 1986 6.914981 0.144614 1.3056% 1985 6.825861 0.146502 0.7673% 1984 6.773886 0.147626 0.8149% 1983 6.719129 0.148829 0.9737% 1982 6.654333 0.150278 0.9508% 1981 6.591659 0.151707 0.9031% 1980 6.532665 0.153077 2.2701% 1979 6.387660 0.156552 1.0042% 1978 6.324155 0.158124 0.9896% 1977 6.262183 0.159689 0.9103% 1976 6.205691 0.161142 0.8394% 1975 6.154031 0.162495 0.9042% 1974 6.098887 0.163964 1.1568% 1973 6.029143 0.165861 0.9427% 1972 5.972837 0.167425 0.7426% 1971 5.928807 0.168668 1.4697% 1970 5.842931 0.171147 0.6968% 1969 5.802498 0.172340 0.8565% 1968 5.753220 0.173816 1.5090% 1967 5.667692 0.176439 0.9949% 1966 5.611859 0.178194 1.0575% 1965 5.553137 0.180078 1.1300% 1964 5.491087 0.182113 1.5537% 1963 5.407079 0.184943 1.4658% 1962 5.328966 0.187654 1.5364% 1961 5.248329 0.190537 2.1586% 1960 5.137431 0.194650 -1.6655% 1959 5.224443 0.191408 4.3080% 1958 5.008670 0.199654 2.1130% 1957 4.905028 0.203872 1.9895% 1956 4.809347 0.207928 2.1231% 1955 4.709362 0.212343 1.4496% 1954 4.642070 0.215421 2.1573% 1953 4.544044 0.220068 1.2298% 1952 4.488842 0.222775 1.6814% 1951 4.414616 0.226520 1.6233% 1950 4.344099 0.230197 1.4265% 1949 4.283001 0.233481 1.7790% 1948 4.208136 0.237635 1.8242% 1947 4.132748 0.241970 -2.6320% 1946 4.244464 0.235601 3.1768% 1945 4.113778 0.243086 6.4754% 1944 3.863594 0.258826 -0.3437% 1943 3.876918 0.257937 0.6562% 1942 3.851642 0.259630 0.6633% 1941 3.826263 0.261352 -5.6614% 1940 4.055884 0.246555 8.0381% 1939 3.754123 0.266374 0.8126% 1938 3.723862 0.268538 0.7762% 1937 3.695178 0.270623 0.6029% 1936 3.673034 0.272254 0.5244% 1935 3.653874 0.273682 -3.0364% 1934 3.768293 0.265372 4.6271% 1933 3.601641 0.277651 1.3921% 1932 3.552190 0.281516 -0.2051% 1931 3.559490 0.280939 0.8886% 1930 3.528139 0.283436 1.0126% 1929 3.492772 0.286306 1.1526% 1928 3.452973 0.289606 1.2160% 1927 3.411489 0.293127 1.4086% 1926 3.364103 0.297256 1.7667% 1925 3.305702 0.302508 1.4465% 1924 3.258566 0.306883 1.7700% 1923 3.201894 0.312315 1.6165% 1922 3.150958 0.317364 1.3736% 1921 3.108262 0.321723 2.3393% 1920 3.037212 0.329249 1.3140% 1919 2.997820 0.333576 0.7676% 1918 2.974983 0.336136 0.3870% 1917 2.963514 0.337437 1.3274% 1916 2.924691 0.341916 1.4083% 1915 2.884075 0.346732 1.4458% 1914 2.842971 0.351745 1.9424% 1913 2.788802 0.358577 1.9857% 1912 2.734504 0.365697 1.5634% 1911 2.692410 0.371414 1.8169% 1910 2.644364 0.378163 1.8781% 1909 2.595617 0.385265 2.0082% 1908 2.544517 0.393002 1.9603% 1907 2.495597 0.400706 1.8264% 1906 2.450836 0.408024 1.9357% 1905 2.404297 0.415922 2.0148% 1904 2.356811 0.424302 2.1335% 1903 2.307578 0.433355 1.8151% 1902 2.266439 0.441221 1.8943% 1901 2.224303 0.449579 3.0255% 1900 2.158983 0.463181 0.6278% 1899 2.145512 0.466089 1.7757% 1898 2.108080 0.474365 1.8078% 1897 2.070648 0.482941

218

1.8396% 1896 2.033244 0.491825 1.8755% 1895 1.995812 0.501049 1.9114% 1894 1.958380
0.510626 1.9486% 1893 1.920948 0.520576 1.9858% 1892 1.883544 0.530914 2.0276% 1891
1.846112 0.541679 2.6465% 1890 1.798514 0.556015 1.5328% 1889 1.771362 0.564537
2.0811% 1888 1.735249 0.576286 2.1599% 1887 1.698563 0.588733 2.2075% 1886 1.661876
0.601729 2.2592% 1885 1.625161 0.615324 2.3095% 1884 1.588475 0.629535 2.3641% 1883
1.551788 0.644418 2.4214% 1882 1.515102 0.660022 2.4815% 1881 1.478416 0.676400
3.7644% 1880 1.424781 0.701862 0.9432% 1879 1.411468 0.708482 2.1464% 1878 1.381809
0.723689 2.1913% 1877 1.352179 0.739547 2.2426% 1876 1.322520 0.756132 2.2941% 1875
1.292861 0.773479 2.3456% 1874 1.263230 0.791621 2.4043% 1873 1.233571 0.810654
2.4635% 1872 1.203912 0.830625 2.5258% 1871 1.174254 0.851605 5.9947% 1870 1.107842
0.902656 -1.0968% 1869 1.120127 0.892756 2.1930% 1868 1.096090 0.912333 2.2394%
1867 1.072082 0.932764 2.2935% 1866 1.048045 0.954157 2.3445% 1865 1.024037 0.976527
2.4037% 1864 1.000000 1.000000 2.4599% 1863 0.975992 1.024599 2.5250% 1862 0.951955
1.050470 2.5872% 1861 0.927947 1.077648 2.9504% 1860 0.901353 1.109443 2.4012% 1859
0.880217 1.136084 2.7627% 1858 0.856553 1.167470 2.8412% 1857 0.832889 1.200641
2.9243% 1856 0.809225 1.235751 3.0161% 1855 0.785532 1.273023 3.1061% 1854 0.761868
1.312564 3.2056% 1853 0.738204 1.354639 3.3118% 1852 0.714540 1.399502 3.4252% 1851
0.690876 1.447438 4.0106% 1850 0.664236 1.505489 2.3254% 1849 0.649141 1.540498
2.7841% 1848 0.631558 1.583386 2.8590% 1847 0.614003 1.628656 2.9432% 1846 0.596449
1.676589 3.0324% 1845 0.578895 1.727430 3.1325% 1844 0.561311 1.781542 3.2284% 1843
0.543757 1.839057 3.3361% 1842 0.526203 1.900409 3.4512% 1841 0.508648 1.965996
3.8105% 1840 0.489978 2.040910 2.3861% 1839 0.478559 2.089607 2.5824% 1838 0.466512
2.143569 2.6573% 1837 0.454436 2.200530 2.7232% 1836 0.442389 2.260455 2.7994% 1835
0.430342 2.323735 2.8871% 1834 0.418266 2.390824 2.9657% 1833 0.406219 2.461729
3.0563% 1832 0.394171 2.536967 3.1604% 1831 0.382096 2.617146 3.4660% 1830 0.369296
2.707855 2.4653% 1829 0.360411 2.774612 2.6804% 1828 0.351002 2.848983 10.3427%
1827 0.318102 3.143643 -4.2314% 1826 0.332157 3.010622 2.9150% 1825 0.322749
3.098383 3.0026% 1824 0.313341 3.191413 3.0955% 1823 0.303933 3.290204 3.1944% 1822
0.294524 3.395306 3.3102% 1821 0.285087 3.507697 3.2277% 1820 0.276173 3.620916
2.6573% 1819 0.269024 3.717134 2.6261% 1818 0.262140 3.814750 2.6969% 1817 0.255256
3.917631 2.7717% 1816 0.248372 4.026215 2.8507% 1815 0.241488 4.140991 2.9343% 1814
0.234604 4.262502 3.0231% 1813 0.227720 4.391359 3.1039% 1812 0.220865 4.527662
3.2172% 1811 0.213980 4.673324 3.0969% 1810 0.207553 4.818053 2.9144% 1809 0.201675
4.958470 2.8225% 1808 0.196139 5.098421 2.9199% 1807 0.190575 5.247291 2.9918% 1806
0.185039 5.404278 3.0841% 1805 0.179503 5.570949 3.1822% 1804 0.173967 5.748228
3.2868% 1803 0.168431 5.937159 3.3985% 1802 0.162895 6.138933 3.5180% 1801 0.157359
6.354903 3.3999% 1800 0.152185 6.570967 2.8419% 1799 0.147979 6.757705 2.7485% 1798
0.144021 6.943438 2.8261% 1797 0.140063 7.139668 3.7832% 1796 0.134957 7.409777
2.1272% 1795 0.132146 7.567397 3.0879% 1794 0.128187 7.801074 3.1625% 1793 0.124258
8.047784 3.2904% 1792 0.120299 8.312589 3.4024% 1791 0.116341 8.595414 3.2296% 1790
0.112701 8.873009 41.3145% 1780 0.079752 12.538843 29.4353% 1770 0.061615 16.229691
83.4728% 1750 0.033583 29.777076 29.2845% 1740 0.025976 38.497129 94.2514% 1720
0.013372 74.781210 85.8111% 1700 0.007197 138.951774 19.2490% 1690 0.006035
165.698669 88.0250% 1670 0.003210 311.554960

BASE YEAR: 1863
YEAR BYEAR/AYEAR AYEAR/BYEAR GROWTH%
2009 8.858824 0.112882 8.2857% 2001 8.180976 0.122235 1.0000% 2000 8.099976
0.123457 1.0000% 1999 8.019778 0.124692 1.0000% 1998 7.940374 0.125939 1.0000% 1997
7.861757 0.127198 1.0000% 1996 7.783917 0.128470 1.0000% 1995 7.706849 0.129755
0.9992% 1994 7.630602 0.131051 1.0008% 1993 7.554994 0.132363 1.0000% 1992 7.480192
0.133686 0.9295% 1991 7.411303 0.134929 1.2505% 1990 7.319768 0.136616 0.7224% 1989
7.267266 0.137603 1.1077% 1988 7.187651 0.139128 0.8834% 1987 7.124713 0.140357
0.5594% 1986 7.085082 0.141142 1.3056% 1985 6.993769 0.142984 0.7673% 1984 6.940516
0.144082 0.8149% 1983 6.884412 0.145256 0.9737% 1982 6.818022 0.146670 0.9508% 1981
6.753806 0.148065 0.9031% 1980 6.693360 0.149402 2.2701% 1979 6.544789 0.152793
1.0042% 1978 6.479721 0.154328 0.9896% 1977 6.416226 0.155855 0.9103% 1976 6.358344

0.157274 0.8394% 1975 6.305414 0.158594 0.9042% 1974 6.248913 0.160028 1.1568% 1973
6.177453 0.161879 0.9427% 1972 6.119761 0.163405 0.7426% 1971 6.074649 0.164619
1.4697% 1970 5.986661 0.167038 0.6968% 1969 5.945233 0.168202 0.8565% 1968 5.894742
0.169643 1.5090% 1967 5.807111 0.172203 0.9949% 1966 5.749904 0.173916 1.0575% 1965
5.689737 0.175755 1.1300% 1964 5.626161 0.177741 1.5537% 1963 5.540087 0.180503
1.4658% 1962 5.460053 0.183148 1.5364% 1961 5.377432 0.185962 2.1586% 1960 5.263805
0.189977 -1.6655% 1959 5.352958 0.186813 4.3080% 1958 5.131877 0.194860 2.1130%
1957 5.025686 0.198978 1.9895% 1956 4.927651 0.202936 2.1231% 1955 4.825207 0.207245
1.4496% 1954 4.756260 0.210249 2.1573% 1953 4.655822 0.214785 1.2298% 1952 4.599262
0.217426 1.6814% 1951 4.523210 0.221082 1.6233% 1950 4.450959 0.224671 1.4265% 1949
4.388357 0.227876 1.7790% 1948 4.311651 0.231930 1.8242% 1947 4.234409 0.236160 -
2.6320% 1946 4.348873 0.229945 3.1768% 1945 4.214972 0.237250 6.4754% 1944 3.958634
0.252612 -0.3437% 1943 3.972285 0.251744 0.6562% 1942 3.946388 0.253396 0.6633%
1941 3.920384 0.255077 -5.6614% 1940 4.155654 0.240636 8.0381% 1939 3.846470
0.259979 0.8126% 1938 3.815465 0.262091 0.7762% 1937 3.786075 0.264126 0.6029% 1936
3.763387 0.265718 0.5244% 1935 3.743755 0.267112 -3.0364% 1934 3.860989 0.259001
4.6271% 1933 3.690237 0.270985 1.3921% 1932 3.639570 0.274758 -0.2051% 1931
3.647049 0.274194 0.8886% 1930 3.614927 0.276631 1.0126% 1929 3.578690 0.279432
1.1526% 1928 3.537912 0.282653 1.2160% 1927 3.495408 0.286090 1.4086% 1926 3.446856
0.290119 1.7667% 1925 3.387018 0.295245 1.4465% 1924 3.338723 0.299516 1.7700% 1923
3.280657 0.304817 1.6165% 1922 3.228468 0.309744 1.3736% 1921 3.184721 0.313999
2.3393% 1920 3.111924 0.321345 1.3140% 1919 3.071563 0.325567 0.7676% 1918 3.048164
0.328066 0.3870% 1917 3.036413 0.329336 1.3274% 1916 2.996635 0.333708 1.4083% 1915
2.955020 0.338407 1.4458% 1914 2.912905 0.343300 1.9424% 1913 2.857403 0.349968
1.9857% 1912 2.801769 0.356917 1.5634% 1911 2.758640 0.362497 1.8169% 1910 2.709413
0.369084 1.8781% 1909 2.659466 0.376015 2.0082% 1908 2.607109 0.383567 1.9603% 1907
2.556986 0.391085 1.8264% 1906 2.511124 0.398228 1.9357% 1905 2.463440 0.405936
2.0148% 1904 2.414786 0.414115 2.1335% 1903 2.364342 0.422951 1.8151% 1902 2.322191
0.430628 1.8943% 1901 2.279018 0.438785 3.0255% 1900 2.212091 0.452061 0.6278% 1899
2.198290 0.454899 1.7757% 1898 2.159937 0.462977 1.8078% 1897 2.121583 0.471346
1.8396% 1896 2.083260 0.480017 1.8755% 1895 2.044907 0.489020 1.9114% 1894 2.006554
0.498367 1.9486% 1893 1.968201 0.508078 1.9858% 1892 1.929877 0.518168 2.0276% 1891
1.891524 0.528674 2.6465% 1890 1.842755 0.542666 1.5328% 1889 1.814936 0.550984
2.0811% 1888 1.777935 0.562450 2.1599% 1887 1.740346 0.574599 2.2075% 1886 1.702757
0.587283 2.2592% 1885 1.665138 0.600551 2.3095% 1884 1.627550 0.614421 2.3641% 1883
1.589961 0.628946 2.4214% 1882 1.552372 0.644176 2.4815% 1881 1.514783 0.660161
3.7644% 1880 1.459829 0.685012 0.9432% 1879 1.446188 0.691473 2.1464% 1878 1.415800
0.706315 2.1913% 1877 1.385441 0.721792 2.2426% 1876 1.355052 0.737979 2.2941% 1875
1.324663 0.754909 2.3456% 1874 1.294304 0.772616 2.4043% 1873 1.263916 0.791192
2.4635% 1872 1.233527 0.810683 2.5258% 1871 1.203139 0.831159 5.9947% 1870 1.135094
0.880985 -1.0968% 1869 1.147681 0.871322 2.1930% 1868 1.123053 0.890430 2.2394%
1867 1.098454 0.910370 2.2935% 1866 1.073826 0.931250 2.3445% 1865 1.049227 0.953083
2.4037% 1864 1.024599 0.975992 2.4599% 1863 1.000000 1.000000 2.5250% 1862 0.975372
1.025250 2.5872% 1861 0.950773 1.051776 2.9504% 1860 0.923525 1.082808 2.4012% 1859
0.901869 1.108808 2.7627% 1858 0.877623 1.139441 2.8412% 1857 0.853377 1.171815
2.9243% 1856 0.829131 1.206083 3.0161% 1855 0.804855 1.242460 3.1061% 1854 0.780609
1.281051 3.2056% 1853 0.756363 1.322117 3.3118% 1852 0.732117 1.365903 3.4252% 1851
0.707870 1.412688 4.0106% 1850 0.680575 1.469345 2.3254% 1849 0.665109 1.503513
2.7841% 1848 0.647093 1.545372 2.8590% 1847 0.629107 1.589554 2.9432% 1846 0.611121
1.636337 3.0324% 1845 0.593135 1.685958 3.1325% 1844 0.575119 1.738771 3.2284% 1843
0.557133 1.794904 3.3361% 1842 0.539147 1.854783 3.4512% 1841 0.521160 1.918795
3.8105% 1840 0.502030 1.991911 2.3861% 1839 0.490331 2.039439 2.5824% 1838 0.477987
2.092105 2.6573% 1837 0.465615 2.147699 2.7232% 1836 0.453271 2.206186 2.7994% 1835
0.440928 2.267946 2.8871% 1834 0.428555 2.333425 2.9657% 1833 0.416211 2.402627
3.0563% 1832 0.403868 2.476059 3.1604% 1831 0.391495 2.554313 3.4660% 1830 0.378380
2.642844 2.4653% 1829 0.369276 2.707998 2.6804% 1828 0.359637 2.780583 10.3427%

1827 0.325927 3.068170 -4.2314% 1826 0.340328 2.938342 2.9150% 1825 0.330688 3.023996 3.0026% 1824 0.321049 3.114793 3.0955% 1823 0.311409 3.211212 3.1944% 1822 0.301769 3.313790 3.3102% 1821 0.292100 3.423483 3.2277% 1820 0.282967 3.533984 2.6573% 1819 0.275642 3.627892 2.6261% 1818 0.268589 3.723164 2.6969% 1817 0.261535 3.823576 2.7717% 1816 0.254482 3.929553 2.8507% 1815 0.247428 4.041573 2.9343% 1814 0.240375 4.160166 3.0231% 1813 0.233322 4.285930 3.1039% 1812 0.226298 4.418961 3.2172% 1811 0.219244 4.561126 3.0969% 1810 0.212658 4.702380 2.9144% 1809 0.206636 4.839425 2.8225% 1808 0.200964 4.976016 2.9199% 1807 0.195262 5.121312 2.9918% 1806 0.189590 5.274531 3.0841% 1805 0.183918 5.437200 3.1822% 1804 0.178246 5.610223 3.2868% 1803 0.172574 5.794619 3.3985% 1802 0.166902 5.991548 3.5180% 1801 0.161230 6.202333 3.3999% 1800 0.155928 6.413209 2.8419% 1799 0.151619 6.595464 2.7485% 1798 0.147564 6.776738 2.8261% 1797 0.143508 6.968257 3.7832% 1796 0.138277 7.231881 2.1272% 1795 0.135396 7.385717 3.0879% 1794 0.131341 7.613784 3.1625% 1793 0.127314 7.854571 3.2904% 1792 0.123259 8.113019 3.4024% 1791 0.119203 8.389053 3.2296% 1790 0.115474 8.659983 41.3145% 1780 0.081714 12.237808 29.4353% 1770 0.063131 15.840045 83.4728% 1750 0.034409 29.062180 29.2845% 1740 0.026615 37.572880 94.2514% 1720 0.013701 72.985843 85.8111% 1700 0.007374 135.615783 19.2490% 1690 0.006184 161.720532 88.0250% 1670 0.003289 304.075067

BASE YEAR: 1862
YEAR BYEAR/AYEAR AYEAR/BYEAR GROWTH%

2009 9.082510 0.110102 8.2857% 2001 8.387547 0.119224 1.0000% 2000 8.304501 0.120417 1.0000% 1999 8.222278 0.121621 1.0000% 1998 8.140869 0.122837 1.0000% 1997 8.060267 0.124065 1.0000% 1996 7.980462 0.125306 1.0000% 1995 7.901448 0.126559 0.9992% 1994 7.823276 0.127824 1.0008% 1993 7.745758 0.129103 1.0000% 1992 7.669067 0.130394 0.9295% 1991 7.598439 0.131606 1.2505% 1990 7.504593 0.133252 0.7224% 1989 7.450765 0.134214 1.1077% 1988 7.369139 0.135701 0.8834% 1987 7.304613 0.136900 0.5594% 1986 7.263981 0.137666 1.3056% 1985 7.170363 0.139463 0.7673% 1984 7.115765 0.140533 0.8149% 1983 7.058244 0.141678 0.9737% 1982 6.990177 0.143058 0.9508% 1981 6.924340 0.144418 0.9031% 1980 6.862368 0.145722 2.2701% 1979 6.710046 0.149030 1.0042% 1978 6.643335 0.150527 0.9896% 1977 6.578236 0.152016 0.9103% 1976 6.518892 0.153400 0.8394% 1975 6.464626 0.154688 0.9042% 1974 6.406698 0.156087 1.1568% 1973 6.333434 0.157892 0.9427% 1972 6.274286 0.159381 0.7426% 1971 6.228034 0.160564 1.4697% 1970 6.137824 0.162924 0.6968% 1969 6.095351 0.164059 0.8565% 1968 6.043585 0.165465 1.5090% 1967 5.953741 0.167962 0.9949% 1966 5.895090 0.169633 1.0575% 1965 5.833404 0.171427 1.1300% 1964 5.768222 0.173364 1.5537% 1963 5.679975 0.176057 1.4658% 1962 5.597919 0.178638 1.5364% 1961 5.513213 0.181382 2.1586% 1960 5.396717 0.185298 -1.6655% 1959 5.488121 0.182212 4.3080% 1958 5.261457 0.190061 2.1130% 1957 5.152585 0.194077 1.9895% 1956 5.052075 0.197938 2.1231% 1955 4.947044 0.202141 1.4496% 1954 4.876356 0.205071 2.1573% 1953 4.773382 0.209495 1.2298% 1952 4.715394 0.212071 1.6814% 1951 4.637422 0.215637 1.6233% 1950 4.563346 0.219137 1.4265% 1949 4.499164 0.222264 1.7790% 1948 4.420521 0.226218 1.8242% 1947 4.341328 0.230344 -2.6320% 1946 4.458682 0.224282 3.1768% 1945 4.321400 0.231406 6.4754% 1944 4.058589 0.246391 -0.3437% 1943 4.072586 0.245544 0.6562% 1942 4.046035 0.247156 0.6633% 1941 4.019374 0.248795 -5.6614% 1940 4.260584 0.234710 8.0381% 1939 3.943594 0.253576 0.8126% 1938 3.911805 0.255636 0.7762% 1937 3.881674 0.257621 0.6029% 1936 3.858413 0.259174 0.5244% 1935 3.838285 0.260533 -3.0364% 1934 3.958479 0.252622 4.6271% 1933 3.783416 0.264311 1.3921% 1932 3.731469 0.267991 -0.2051% 1931 3.739138 0.267441 0.8886% 1930 3.706204 0.269818 1.0126% 1929 3.669052 0.272550 1.1526% 1928 3.627245 0.275691 1.2160% 1927 3.583667 0.279044 1.4086% 1926 3.533890 0.282974 1.7667% 1925 3.472541 0.287974 1.4465% 1924 3.423026 0.292139 1.7700% 1923 3.363494 0.297310 1.6165% 1922 3.309987 0.302116 1.3736% 1921 3.265136 0.306266 2.3393% 1920 3.190500 0.313431 1.3140% 1919 3.149120 0.317549 0.7676% 1918 3.125130 0.319987 0.3870% 1917 3.113083 0.321225 1.3274% 1916 3.072300 0.325489 1.4083% 1915 3.029634 0.330073 1.4458% 1914 2.986456 0.334845 1.9424% 1913 2.929553 0.341349 1.9857% 1912 2.872514 0.348127 1.5634% 1911 2.828296 0.353570 1.8169% 1910 2.777826 0.359994 1.8781% 1909 2.726618 0.366755 2.0082% 1908 2.672939 0.374120 1.9603% 1907

2.621550 0.381454 1.8264% 1906 2.574530 0.388420 1.9357% 1905 2.525642 0.395939
2.0148% 1904 2.475759 0.403916 2.1335% 1903 2.424042 0.412534 1.8151% 1902 2.380826
0.420022 1.8943% 1901 2.336564 0.427979 3.0255% 1900 2.267947 0.440927 0.6278% 1899
2.253797 0.443696 1.7757% 1898 2.214475 0.451574 1.8078% 1897 2.175154 0.459738
1.8396% 1896 2.135862 0.468195 1.8755% 1895 2.096541 0.476976 1.9114% 1894 2.057219
0.486093 1.9486% 1893 2.017898 0.495565 1.9858% 1892 1.978607 0.505406 2.0276% 1891
1.939285 0.515654 2.6465% 1890 1.889285 0.529301 1.5328% 1889 1.860763 0.537414
2.0811% 1888 1.822828 0.548598 2.1599% 1887 1.784290 0.560447 2.2075% 1886 1.745751
0.572819 2.2592% 1885 1.707183 0.585760 2.3095% 1884 1.668645 0.599289 2.3641% 1883
1.630107 0.613457 2.4214% 1882 1.591569 0.628311 2.4815% 1881 1.553031 0.643902
3.7644% 1880 1.496690 0.668141 0.9432% 1879 1.482705 0.674443 2.1464% 1878 1.451549
0.688919 2.1913% 1877 1.420423 0.704016 2.2426% 1876 1.389267 0.719804 2.2941% 1875
1.358111 0.736317 2.3456% 1874 1.326986 0.753588 2.4043% 1873 1.295830 0.771706
2.4635% 1872 1.264674 0.790718 2.5258% 1871 1.233518 0.810689 5.9947% 1870 1.163755
0.859288 -1.0968% 1869 1.176660 0.849863 2.1930% 1868 1.151410 0.868500 2.2394%
1867 1.126190 0.887949 2.2935% 1866 1.100940 0.908315 2.3445% 1865 1.075720 0.929610
2.4037% 1864 1.050470 0.951955 2.4599% 1863 1.025250 0.975372 2.5250% 1862 1.000000
1.000000 2.5872% 1861 0.974780 1.025872 2.9504% 1860 0.946844 1.056140 2.4012% 1859
0.924641 1.081500 2.7627% 1858 0.899783 1.111379 2.8412% 1857 0.874925 1.142956
2.9243% 1856 0.850066 1.176379 3.0161% 1855 0.825178 1.211860 3.1061% 1854 0.800319
1.249501 3.2056% 1853 0.775461 1.289555 3.3118% 1852 0.750603 1.332263 3.4252% 1851
0.725744 1.377896 4.0106% 1850 0.697760 1.433158 3.3254% 1849 0.681903 1.466484
2.7841% 1848 0.663433 1.507312 2.8590% 1847 0.644992 1.550406 2.9432% 1846 0.626552
1.596037 3.0324% 1845 0.608111 1.644436 3.1325% 1844 0.589641 1.695948 3.2284% 1843
0.571200 1.750699 3.3361% 1842 0.552760 1.809103 3.4512% 1841 0.534320 1.871539
3.8105% 1840 0.514707 1.942854 2.3861% 1839 0.502712 1.989211 2.5824% 1838 0.490057
2.040580 2.6573% 1837 0.477371 2.094805 2.7232% 1836 0.464716 2.151851 2.7994% 1835
0.452061 2.212091 2.8871% 1834 0.439376 2.275957 2.9657% 1833 0.426721 2.343454
3.0563% 1832 0.414065 2.415078 3.1604% 1831 0.401380 2.491405 3.4660% 1830 0.387934
2.577756 2.4653% 1829 0.378601 2.641305 2.6804% 1828 0.368718 2.712103 10.3427%
1827 0.334157 2.992606 -4.2314% 1826 0.348921 2.865976 2.9150% 1825 0.339038
2.949520 3.0026% 1824 0.329155 3.038081 3.0955% 1823 0.319272 3.132125 3.1944% 1822
0.309389 3.232178 3.3102% 1821 0.299476 3.339169 3.2277% 1820 0.290112 3.446949
2.6573% 1819 0.282602 3.538544 2.6261% 1818 0.275371 3.631470 2.6969% 1817 0.268139
3.729408 2.7717% 1816 0.260908 3.832775 2.8507% 1815 0.253676 3.942036 2.9343% 1814
0.246444 4.057709 3.0231% 1813 0.239213 4.180375 3.1039% 1812 0.232012 4.310130
3.2172% 1811 0.224780 4.448794 3.0969% 1810 0.218028 4.586569 2.9144% 1809 0.211854
4.720239 2.8225% 1808 0.206038 4.853466 2.9199% 1807 0.200193 4.995184 2.9918% 1806
0.194377 5.144629 3.0841% 1805 0.188562 5.303292 3.1822% 1804 0.182747 5.472053
3.2868% 1803 0.176931 5.651907 3.3985% 1802 0.171116 5.843987 3.5180% 1801 0.165301
6.049581 3.3999% 1800 0.159865 6.255263 2.8419% 1799 0.155448 6.433030 2.7485% 1798
0.151290 6.609839 2.8261% 1797 0.147131 6.796641 3.7832% 1796 0.141768 7.053773
2.1272% 1795 0.138815 7.203820 3.0879% 1794 0.134657 7.426270 3.1625% 1793 0.130529
7.661127 3.2904% 1792 0.126371 7.913209 3.4024% 1791 0.122213 8.182446 3.2296% 1790
0.118389 8.446703 41.3145% 1780 0.083777 11.936412 29.4353% 1770 0.064725 15.449932
83.4728% 1750 0.035278 28.346430 29.2845% 1740 0.027287 36.647527 94.2514% 1720
0.014047 71.188331 85.8111% 1700 0.007560 132.275807 19.2490% 1690 0.006340
157.737643 88.0250% 1670 0.003372 296.586238
BASE YEAR: 1861
YEAR BYEAR/AYEAR AYEAR/BYEAR GROWTH%
2009 9.317497 0.107325 8.2857% 2001 8.604533 0.116218 1.0000% 2000 8.519359
0.117380 1.0000% 1999 8.435009 0.118554 1.0000% 1998 8.351494 0.119739 1.0000% 1997
8.268806 0.120936 1.0000% 1996 8.186936 0.122146 1.0000% 1995 8.105877 0.123367
0.9992% 1994 8.025683 0.124600 1.0008% 1993 7.946160 0.125847 1.0000% 1992 7.867485
0.127105 0.9295% 1991 7.795030 0.128287 1.2505% 1990 7.698755 0.129891 0.7224% 1989
7.643535 0.130830 1.1077% 1988 7.559797 0.132279 0.8834% 1987 7.493601 0.133447

222

0.5594% 1986 7.451918 0.134194 1.3056% 1985 7.355878 0.135946 0.7673% 1984 7.299867 0.136989 0.8149% 1983 7.240858 0.138105 0.9737% 1982 7.171030 0.139450 0.9508% 1981 7.103490 0.140776 0.9031% 1980 7.039915 0.142047 2.2701% 1979 6.883651 0.145272 1.0042% 1978 6.815214 0.146731 0.9896% 1977 6.748431 0.148183 0.9103% 1976 6.687552 0.149532 0.8394% 1975 6.631882 0.150787 0.9042% 1974 6.572455 0.152150 1.1568% 1973 6.497295 0.153910 0.9427% 1972 6.436617 0.155361 0.7426% 1971 6.389169 0.156515 1.4697% 1970 6.296625 0.158815 0.6968% 1969 6.253052 0.159922 0.8565% 1968 6.199947 0.161292 1.5090% 1967 6.107779 0.163726 0.9949% 1966 6.047611 0.165355 1.0575% 1965 5.984328 0.167103 1.1300% 1964 5.917460 0.168991 1.5537% 1963 5.826930 0.171617 1.4658% 1962 5.742751 0.174133 1.5364% 1961 5.655853 0.176808 2.1586% 1960 5.536343 0.180625 -1.6655% 1959 5.630112 0.177616 4.3080% 1958 5.397584 0.185268 2.1130% 1957 5.285895 0.189183 1.9895% 1956 5.182784 0.192946 2.1231% 1955 5.075036 0.197043 1.4496% 1954 5.002519 0.199899 2.1573% 1953 4.896881 0.204212 1.2298% 1952 4.837393 0.206723 1.6814% 1951 4.757403 0.210199 1.6233% 1950 4.681411 0.213611 1.4265% 1949 4.615568 0.216658 1.7790% 1948 4.534891 0.220512 1.8242% 1947 4.453649 0.224535 - 2.6320% 1946 4.574039 0.218625 3.1768% 1945 4.433205 0.225570 6.4754% 1944 4.163595 0.240177 -0.3437% 1943 4.177954 0.239352 0.6562% 1942 4.150716 0.240922 0.6633% 1941 4.123366 0.242520 -5.6614% 1940 4.370816 0.228790 8.0381% 1939 4.045625 0.247181 0.8126% 1938 4.013014 0.249189 0.7762% 1937 3.982103 0.251124 0.6029% 1936 3.958239 0.252638 0.5244% 1935 3.937591 0.253962 -3.0364% 1934 4.060895 0.246251 4.6271% 1933 3.881302 0.257646 1.3921% 1932 3.828011 0.261232 -0.2051% 1931 3.835878 0.260696 0.8886% 1930 3.802093 0.263013 1.0126% 1929 3.763979 0.265676 1.1526% 1928 3.721091 0.268738 1.2160% 1927 3.676386 0.272006 1.4086% 1926 3.625320 0.275838 1.7667% 1925 3.562384 0.280711 1.4465% 1924 3.511589 0.284771 1.7700% 1923 3.450515 0.289812 1.6165% 1922 3.395624 0.294497 1.3736% 1921 3.349613 0.298542 2.3393% 1920 3.273046 0.305526 1.3140% 1919 3.230596 0.309540 0.7676% 1918 3.205985 0.311917 0.3870% 1917 3.193626 0.313124 1.3274% 1916 3.151788 0.317280 1.4083% 1915 3.108018 0.321748 1.4458% 1914 3.063723 0.326400 1.9424% 1913 3.005348 0.332740 1.9857% 1912 2.946833 0.339347 1.5634% 1911 2.901471 0.344653 1.8169% 1910 2.849695 0.350915 1.8781% 1909 2.797162 0.357505 2.0082% 1908 2.742095 0.364685 1.9603% 1907 2.689376 0.371833 1.8264% 1906 2.641139 0.378624 1.9357% 1905 2.590986 0.385953 2.0148% 1904 2.539813 0.393730 2.1335% 1903 2.486758 0.402130 1.8151% 1902 2.442424 0.409429 1.8943% 1901 2.397016 0.417185 3.0255% 1900 2.326624 0.429807 0.6278% 1899 2.312108 0.432506 1.7757% 1898 2.271769 0.440186 1.8078% 1897 2.231430 0.448143 1.8396% 1896 2.191122 0.456387 1.8755% 1895 2.150784 0.464947 1.9114% 1894 2.110445 0.473834 1.9486% 1893 2.070106 0.483067 1.9858% 1892 2.029798 0.492660 2.0276% 1891 1.989459 0.502649 2.6465% 1890 1.938165 0.515952 1.5328% 1889 1.908905 0.523860 2.0811% 1888 1.869989 0.534763 2.1599% 1887 1.830453 0.546313 2.2075% 1886 1.790918 0.558373 2.2592% 1885 1.751352 0.570987 2.3095% 1884 1.711817 0.584175 2.3641% 1883 1.672282 0.597985 2.4214% 1882 1.632747 0.612465 2.4815% 1881 1.593212 0.627663 3.7644% 1880 1.535413 0.651291 0.9432% 1879 1.521066 0.657434 2.1464% 1878 1.489104 0.671545 2.1913% 1877 1.457173 0.686260 2.2426% 1876 1.425211 0.701651 2.2941% 1875 1.393249 0.717747 2.3456% 1874 1.361318 0.734582 2.4043% 1873 1.329356 0.752244 2.4635% 1872 1.297394 0.770776 2.5258% 1871 1.265432 0.790244 5.9947% 1870 1.193864 0.837616 -1.0968% 1869 1.207103 0.828429 2.1930% 1868 1.181200 0.846597 2.2394% 1867 1.155328 0.865555 2.2935% 1866 1.129424 0.885407 2.3445% 1865 1.103552 0.906165 2.4037% 1864 1.077648 0.927947 2.4599% 1863 1.051776 0.950773 2.5250% 1862 1.025872 0.974780 2.5872% 1861 1.000000 1.000000 2.9504% 1860 0.971341 1.029504 2.4012% 1859 0.948564 1.054225 2.7627% 1858 0.923063 1.083350 2.8412% 1857 0.897561 1.114130 2.9243% 1856 0.872060 1.146711 3.0161% 1855 0.846527 1.181297 3.1061% 1854 0.821026 1.217989 3.2056% 1853 0.795524 1.257033 3.3118% 1852 0.770023 1.298663 3.4252% 1851 0.744521 1.343145 4.0106% 1850 0.715813 1.397014 2.3254% 1849 0.699546 1.429499 2.7841% 1848 0.680597 1.469298 2.8590% 1847 0.661680 1.511305 2.9432% 1846 0.642762 1.555785 3.0324% 1845 0.623845 1.602963 3.1325% 1844 0.604896 1.653176 3.2284% 1843 0.585979 1.706546 3.3361% 1842 0.567061 1.763478 3.4512% 1841 0.548144 1.824339 3.8105% 1840 0.528024 1.893855 2.3861% 1839 0.515718 1.939043 2.5824% 1838 0.502736

1.989117 2.6573% 1837 0.489722 2.041974 2.7232% 1836 0.476740 2.097582 2.7994% 1835 0.463757 2.156302 2.8871% 1834 0.450743 2.218557 2.9657% 1833 0.437761 2.284352 3.0563% 1832 0.424778 2.354170 3.1604% 1831 0.411765 2.428571 3.4660% 1830 0.397971 2.512745 2.4653% 1829 0.388396 2.574692 2.6804% 1828 0.378257 2.643704 10.3427% 1827 0.342802 2.917133 -4.2314% 1826 0.357949 2.793696 2.9150% 1825 0.347810 2.875133 3.0026% 1824 0.337671 2.961461 3.0955% 1823 0.327532 3.053133 3.1944% 1822 0.317394 3.150662 3.3102% 1821 0.307224 3.254955 3.2277% 1820 0.297618 3.360017 2.6573% 1819 0.289914 3.449302 2.6261% 1818 0.282495 3.539884 2.6969% 1817 0.275077 3.635352 2.7717% 1816 0.267658 3.736113 2.8507% 1815 0.260239 3.842618 2.9343% 1814 0.252821 3.955374 3.0231% 1813 0.245402 4.074946 3.1039% 1812 0.238014 4.201429 3.2172% 1811 0.230596 4.336595 3.0969% 1810 0.223669 4.470896 2.9144% 1809 0.217335 4.601195 2.8225% 1808 0.211369 4.731062 2.9199% 1807 0.205372 4.869205 2.9918% 1806 0.199407 5.014881 3.0841% 1805 0.193441 5.169543 3.1822% 1804 0.187475 5.334048 3.2868% 1803 0.181509 5.509366 3.3985% 1802 0.175543 5.696602 3.5180% 1801 0.169577 5.897011 3.3999% 1800 0.164001 6.097506 2.8419% 1799 0.159470 6.270789 2.7485% 1798 0.155204 6.443139 2.8261% 1797 0.150938 6.625230 3.7832% 1796 0.145436 6.875877 2.1272% 1795 0.142407 7.022140 3.0879% 1794 0.138141 7.238980 3.1625% 1793 0.133906 7.467913 3.2904% 1792 0.129641 7.713639 3.4024% 1791 0.125375 7.976085 3.2296% 1790 0.121452 8.233678 41.3145% 1780 0.085945 11.635376 29.4353% 1770 0.066400 15.060286 83.4728% 1750 0.036191 27.631534 29.2845% 1740 0.027993 35.723277 94.2514% 1720 0.014411 69.392964 85.8111% 1700 0.007756 128.939817 19.2490% 1690 0.006504 153.759506 88.0250% 1670 0.003459 289.106345

BASE YEAR: 1860

YEAR BYEAR/AYEAR AYEAR/BYEAR GROWTH%

2009 9.592401 0.104249 8.2857% 2001 8.858422 0.112887 1.0000% 2000 8.770714 0.114016 1.0000% 1999 8.683876 0.115156 1.0000% 1998 8.597897 0.116308 1.0000% 1997 8.512769 0.117471 1.0000% 1996 8.428484 0.118645 1.0000% 1995 8.345034 0.119832 0.9992% 1994 8.262473 0.121029 1.0008% 1993 8.180604 0.122240 1.0000% 1992 8.099608 0.123463 0.9295% 1991 8.025015 0.124610 1.2505% 1990 7.925900 0.126169 0.7224% 1989 7.869050 0.127080 1.1077% 1988 7.782842 0.128488 0.8834% 1987 7.714693 0.129623 0.5594% 1986 7.671780 0.130348 1.3056% 1985 7.572906 0.132050 0.7673% 1984 7.515243 0.133063 0.8149% 1983 7.454493 0.134147 0.9737% 1982 7.382605 0.135454 0.9508% 1981 7.313072 0.136741 0.9031% 1980 7.247621 0.137976 2.2701% 1979 7.086747 0.141108 1.0042% 1978 7.016291 0.142525 0.9896% 1977 6.947537 0.143936 0.9103% 1976 6.884862 0.145246 0.8394% 1975 6.827549 0.146465 0.9042% 1974 6.766369 0.147790 1.1568% 1973 6.688992 0.149909 0.9427% 1972 6.626524 0.150909 0.7426% 1971 6.577675 0.152029 1.4697% 1970 6.482401 0.154264 0.6968% 1969 6.437543 0.155339 0.8565% 1968 6.382871 0.156669 1.5090% 1967 6.287983 0.159034 0.9949% 1966 6.226040 0.160616 1.0575% 1965 6.160890 0.162314 1.1300% 1964 6.092049 0.164148 1.5537% 1963 5.998848 0.166699 1.4658% 1962 5.912186 0.169142 1.5364% 1961 5.822724 0.171741 2.1586% 1960 5.699688 0.175448 -1.6655% 1959 5.796223 0.172526 4.3080% 1958 5.556835 0.179959 2.1130% 1957 5.441851 0.183761 1.9895% 1956 5.335697 0.187417 2.1231% 1955 5.224771 0.191396 1.4496% 1954 5.150114 0.194170 2.1573% 1953 5.041359 0.198359 1.2298% 1952 4.980116 0.200799 1.6814% 1951 4.897766 0.204175 1.6233% 1950 4.819532 0.207489 1.4265% 1949 4.751746 0.210449 1.7790% 1948 4.668688 0.214193 1.8242% 1947 4.585050 0.218100 -2.6320% 1946 4.708992 0.212360 3.1768% 1945 4.564003 0.219106 6.4754% 1944 4.286438 0.233294 -0.3437% 1943 4.301220 0.232492 0.6562% 1942 4.273179 0.234018 0.6633% 1941 4.245022 0.235570 -5.6614% 1940 4.499773 0.222233 8.0381% 1939 4.164987 0.240097 0.8126% 1938 4.131414 0.242048 0.7762% 1937 4.099591 0.243927 0.6029% 1936 4.075023 0.245397 0.5244% 1935 4.053766 0.246684 -3.0364% 1934 4.180707 0.239194 4.6271% 1933 3.995816 0.250262 1.3921% 1932 3.940953 0.253746 -0.2051% 1931 3.949052 0.253225 0.8886% 1930 3.914270 0.255475 1.0126% 1929 3.875032 0.258062 1.1526% 1928 3.830878 0.261037 1.2160% 1927 3.784854 0.264211 1.4086% 1926 3.732282 0.267933 1.7667% 1925 3.667489 0.272666 1.4465% 1924 3.615195 0.276610 1.7700% 1923 3.552320 0.281506 1.6165% 1922 3.495809 0.286057 1.3736% 1921 3.448440 0.289986 2.3393% 1920 3.369614 0.296770 1.3140% 1919 3.325911 0.300669 0.7676% 1918 3.300575

224

0.302978 0.3870% 1917 3.287851 0.304150 1.3274% 1916 3.244779 0.308187 1.4083% 1915 3.199717 0.312528 1.4458% 1914 3.154115 0.317046 1.9424% 1913 3.094018 0.323204 1.9857% 1912 3.033777 0.329622 1.5634% 1911 2.987077 0.334775 1.8169% 1910 2.933772 0.340858 1.8781% 1909 2.879690 0.347260 2.0082% 1908 2.822997 0.354233 1.9603% 1907 2.768723 0.361177 1.8264% 1906 2.719064 0.367774 1.9357% 1905 2.667431 0.374893 2.0148% 1904 2.614748 0.382446 2.1335% 1903 2.560127 0.390606 1.8151% 1902 2.514485 0.397696 1.8943% 1901 2.467738 0.405229 3.0255% 1900 2.395269 0.417490 0.6278% 1899 2.380324 0.420111 1.7757% 1898 2.338795 0.427571 1.8078% 1897 2.297267 0.435300 1.8396% 1896 2.255769 0.443308 1.8755% 1895 2.214240 0.451622 1.9114% 1894 2.172712 0.460254 1.9486% 1893 2.131183 0.469223 1.9858% 1892 2.089685 0.478541 2.0276% 1891 2.048157 0.488244 2.6465% 1890 1.995349 0.501165 1.5328% 1889 1.965226 0.508847 2.0811% 1888 1.925161 0.519437 2.1599% 1887 1.884459 0.530656 2.2075% 1886 1.843758 0.542371 2.2592% 1885 1.803024 0.554624 2.3095% 1884 1.762323 0.567433 2.3641% 1883 1.721621 0.580848 2.4214% 1882 1.680920 0.594912 2.4815% 1881 1.640218 0.609675 3.7644% 1880 1.580714 0.632626 0.9432% 1879 1.565943 0.638593 2.1464% 1878 1.533039 0.652299 2.1913% 1877 1.500165 0.666593 2.2426% 1876 1.467260 0.681542 2.2941% 1875 1.434356 0.697177 2.3456% 1874 1.401482 0.713530 2.4043% 1873 1.368578 0.730686 2.4635% 1872 1.335673 0.748686 2.5258% 1871 1.302768 0.767597 5.9947% 1870 1.229088 0.813611 -1.0968% 1869 1.242718 0.804688 2.1930% 1868 1.216050 0.822334 2.2394% 1867 1.189414 0.840750 2.2935% 1866 1.162747 0.860033 2.3445% 1865 1.136111 0.880196 2.4037% 1864 1.109443 0.901353 2.4599% 1863 1.082808 0.923525 2.5250% 1862 1.056140 0.946844 2.5872% 1861 1.029504 0.971341 2.9504% 1860 1.000000 1.000000 2.4012% 1859 0.976551 1.024012 2.7627% 1858 0.950297 1.052303 2.8412% 1857 0.924043 1.082201 2.9243% 1856 0.897789 1.113848 3.0161% 1855 0.871503 1.147443 3.1061% 1854 0.845249 1.183083 3.2056% 1853 0.818995 1.221008 3.3118% 1852 0.792741 1.261445 3.4252% 1851 0.766487 1.304653 4.0106% 1850 0.736932 1.356977 2.3254% 1849 0.720185 1.388532 2.7841% 1848 0.700678 1.427190 2.8590% 1847 0.681202 1.467993 2.9432% 1846 0.661726 1.511199 3.0324% 1845 0.642251 1.557024 3.1325% 1844 0.622743 1.605798 3.2284% 1843 0.603268 1.657639 3.3361% 1842 0.583792 1.712939 3.4512% 1841 0.564316 1.772056 3.8105% 1840 0.543602 1.839580 2.3861% 1839 0.530934 1.883473 2.5824% 1838 0.517568 1.932112 2.6573% 1837 0.504171 1.983454 2.7232% 1836 0.490805 2.037468 2.7994% 1835 0.477440 2.094506 2.8871% 1834 0.464042 2.154977 2.9657% 1833 0.450677 2.218886 3.0563% 1832 0.437311 2.286703 3.1604% 1831 0.423913 2.358972 3.4660% 1830 0.409713 2.440733 2.4653% 1829 0.399855 2.500905 2.6804% 1828 0.389417 2.567939 10.3427% 1827 0.352916 2.833532 -4.2314% 1826 0.368510 2.713633 2.9150% 1825 0.358072 2.792736 3.0026% 1824 0.347634 2.876590 3.0955% 1823 0.337196 2.965635 3.1944% 1822 0.326758 3.060369 3.3102% 1821 0.316288 3.161673 3.2277% 1820 0.306398 3.263724 2.6573% 1819 0.298467 3.350450 2.6261% 1818 0.290830 3.438436 2.6969% 1817 0.283192 3.531168 2.7717% 1816 0.275555 3.629041 2.8507% 1815 0.267917 3.732494 2.9343% 1814 0.260280 3.842018 3.0231% 1813 0.252642 3.958165 3.1039% 1812 0.245037 4.081022 3.2172% 1811 0.237399 4.212315 3.0969% 1810 0.230268 4.342767 2.9144% 1809 0.223747 4.469331 2.8225% 1808 0.217605 4.595476 2.9199% 1807 0.211432 4.729661 2.9918% 1806 0.205290 4.871162 3.0841% 1805 0.199148 5.021391 3.1822% 1804 0.193006 5.181182 3.2868% 1803 0.186864 5.351476 3.3985% 1802 0.180723 5.533345 3.5180% 1801 0.174581 5.728011 3.3999% 1800 0.168840 5.922760 2.8419% 1799 0.164175 6.091077 2.7485% 1798 0.159783 6.258488 2.8261% 1797 0.155391 6.435361 3.7832% 1796 0.149727 6.678824 2.1272% 1795 0.146608 6.820896 3.0879% 1794 0.142217 7.031521 3.1625% 1793 0.137857 7.253894 3.2904% 1792 0.133465 7.492577 3.4024% 1791 0.129074 7.747502 3.2296% 1790 0.125036 7.997712 41.3145% 1780 0.088481 11.301923 29.4353% 1770 0.068359 14.628680 83.4728% 1750 0.037258 26.839655 29.2845% 1740 0.028819 34.699501 94.2514% 1720 0.014836 67.404264 85.8111% 1700 0.007984 125.244591 19.2490% 1690 0.006696 149.352985 88.0250% 1670 0.003561 280.820983

BASE YEAR: 1859
YEAR BYEAR/AYEAR AYEAR/BYEAR GROWTH%

2009 9.822738 0.101805 8.2857% 2001 9.071134 0.110240 1.0000% 2000 8.981320 0.111342 1.0000% 1999 8.892396 0.112456 1.0000% 1998 8.804353 0.113580 1.0000% 1997

8.717181 0.114716 1.0000% 1996 8.630872 0.115863 1.0000% 1995 8.545418 0.117022 0.9992% 1994 8.460875 0.118191 1.0008% 1993 8.377039 0.119374 1.0000% 1992 8.294098 0.120568 0.9295% 1991 8.217714 0.121688 1.2505% 1990 8.116220 0.123210 0.7224% 1989 8.058005 0.124100 1.1077% 1988 7.969727 0.125475 0.8834% 1987 7.899941 0.126583 0.5594% 1986 7.855998 0.127291 1.3056% 1985 7.754750 0.128953 0.7673% 1984 7.695702 0.129943 0.8149% 1983 7.633493 0.131002 0.9737% 1982 7.559879 0.132277 0.9508% 1981 7.488676 0.133535 0.9031% 1980 7.421654 0.134741 2.2701% 1979 7.256917 0.137800 1.0042% 1978 7.184769 0.139183 0.9896% 1977 7.114364 0.140561 0.9103% 1976 7.050184 0.141840 0.8394% 1975 6.991495 0.143031 0.9042% 1974 6.928846 0.144324 1.1568% 1973 6.849611 0.145994 0.9427% 1972 6.785642 0.147370 0.7426% 1971 6.735621 0.148464 1.4697% 1970 6.638059 0.150646 0.6968% 1969 6.592124 0.151696 0.8565% 1968 6.536139 0.152996 1.5090% 1967 6.438973 0.155304 0.9949% 1966 6.375542 0.156849 1.0575% 1965 6.308828 0.158508 1.1300% 1964 6.238334 0.160299 1.5537% 1963 6.142894 0.162790 1.4658% 1962 6.054152 0.165176 1.5364% 1961 5.962541 0.167714 2.1586% 1960 5.836551 0.171334 -1.6655% 1959 5.935404 0.168481 4.3080% 1958 5.690268 0.175739 2.1130% 1957 5.572523 0.179452 1.9895% 1956 5.463820 0.183022 2.1231% 1955 5.350230 0.186908 1.4496% 1954 5.273780 0.189617 2.1573% 1953 5.162414 0.193708 1.2298% 1952 5.099700 0.196090 1.6814% 1951 5.015373 0.199387 1.6233% 1950 4.935260 0.202624 1.4265% 1949 4.865847 0.205514 1.7790% 1948 4.780795 0.209170 1.8242% 1947 4.695148 0.212986 -2.6320% 1946 4.822066 0.207380 3.1768% 1945 4.673595 0.213968 6.4754% 1944 4.389366 0.227823 -0.3437% 1943 4.404503 0.227040 0.6562% 1942 4.375788 0.228530 0.6633% 1941 4.346955 0.230046 -5.6614% 1940 4.607823 0.217022 8.0381% 1939 4.264998 0.234467 0.8126% 1938 4.230619 0.236372 0.7762% 1937 4.198032 0.238207 0.6029% 1936 4.172875 0.239643 0.5244% 1935 4.151106 0.240900 -3.0364% 1934 4.281096 0.233585 4.6271% 1933 4.091765 0.244393 1.3921% 1932 4.035585 0.247796 -0.2051% 1931 4.043879 0.247287 0.8886% 1930 4.008261 0.249485 1.0126% 1929 3.968081 0.252011 1.1526% 1928 3.922866 0.254916 1.2160% 1927 3.875737 0.258015 1.4086% 1926 3.821903 0.261650 1.7667% 1925 3.755554 0.266272 1.4465% 1924 3.702004 0.270124 1.7700% 1923 3.637619 0.274905 1.6165% 1922 3.579752 0.279349 1.3736% 1921 3.531245 0.283186 2.3393% 1920 3.450527 0.289811 3.1140% 1919 3.405774 0.293619 0.7676% 1918 3.379829 0.295873 0.3870% 1917 3.366800 0.297018 1.3274% 1916 3.322694 0.300961 1.4083% 1915 3.276550 0.305199 1.4458% 1914 3.229853 0.309612 1.9424% 1913 3.168312 0.315625 1.9857% 1912 3.106625 0.321893 1.5634% 1911 3.058803 0.326925 1.8169% 1910 3.004219 0.332865 1.8781% 1909 2.948838 0.339117 2.0082% 1908 2.890784 0.345927 1.9603% 1907 2.835207 0.352708 1.8264% 1906 2.784355 0.359150 1.9357% 1905 2.731482 0.366102 2.0148% 1904 2.677534 0.373478 2.1335% 1903 2.621602 0.381446 1.8151% 1902 2.574864 0.388370 1.8943% 1901 2.526994 0.395727 3.0255% 1900 2.452785 0.407700 0.6278% 1899 2.437482 0.410259 1.7757% 1898 2.394956 0.417544 1.8078% 1897 2.352429 0.425092 1.8396% 1896 2.309936 0.432912 1.8755% 1895 2.267410 0.441032 1.9114% 1894 2.224884 0.449462 1.9486% 1893 2.182357 0.458220 1.9858% 1892 2.139864 0.467319 2.0276% 1891 2.097338 0.476795 2.6465% 1890 2.043262 0.489413 1.5328% 1889 2.012416 0.496915 2.0811% 1888 1.971389 0.507257 2.1599% 1887 1.929710 0.518213 2.2075% 1886 1.888031 0.529652 2.2592% 1885 1.846319 0.541618 2.3095% 1884 1.804640 0.554127 2.3641% 1883 1.762962 0.567227 2.4214% 1882 1.721283 0.580962 2.4815% 1881 1.679604 0.595379 3.7644% 1880 1.618671 0.617791 0.9432% 1879 1.603545 0.623618 2.1464% 1878 1.569850 0.637003 2.1913% 1877 1.536188 0.650962 2.2426% 1876 1.502493 0.665561 2.2941% 1875 1.468798 0.680829 2.3456% 1874 1.435135 0.696798 2.4043% 1873 1.401440 0.713552 2.4635% 1872 1.367745 0.731130 2.5258% 1871 1.334050 0.749597 5.9947% 1870 1.258601 0.794533 -1.0968% 1869 1.272558 0.785819 2.1930% 1868 1.245250 0.803051 2.2394% 1867 1.217975 0.821035 2.2935% 1866 1.190667 0.839865 2.3445% 1865 1.163392 0.859556 2.4037% 1864 1.136084 0.880217 2.4599% 1863 1.108808 0.901869 2.5250% 1862 1.081500 0.924641 2.5872% 1861 1.054225 0.948564 2.9504% 1860 1.024012 0.976551 2.4012% 1859 1.000000 1.000000 2.7627% 1858 0.973116 1.027627 2.8412% 1857 0.946231 1.056824 2.9243% 1856 0.919347 1.087729 3.0161% 1855 0.892430 1.120536 3.1061% 1854 0.865546 1.155341 3.2056% 1853 0.838661 1.192376 3.3118% 1852 0.811777 1.231865 3.4252% 1851 0.784893 1.274060 4.0106% 1850 0.754627 1.325157 2.3254% 1849 0.737478 1.355972

226

2.7841% 1848 0.717503 1.393723 2.8590% 1847 0.697559 1.433570 2.9432% 1846 0.677616 1.475762 3.0324% 1845 0.657673 1.520513 3.1325% 1844 0.637697 1.568143 3.2284% 1843 0.617753 1.618769 3.3361% 1842 0.597810 1.672772 3.4512% 1841 0.577867 1.730502 3.8105% 1840 0.556656 1.796443 2.3861% 1839 0.543683 1.839307 2.5824% 1838 0.529996 1.886805 2.6573% 1837 0.516277 1.936944 2.7232% 1836 0.502591 1.989691 2.7994% 1835 0.488904 2.045391 2.8871% 1834 0.475185 2.104444 2.9657% 1833 0.461498 2.166855 3.0563% 1832 0.447812 2.233081 3.1604% 1831 0.434093 2.303656 3.4660% 1830 0.419551 2.383500 2.4653% 1829 0.409457 2.442260 2.6804% 1828 0.398768 2.507722 10.3427% 1827 0.361391 2.767087 -4.2314% 1826 0.377358 2.650000 2.9150% 1825 0.366670 2.727248 3.0026% 1824 0.355981 2.809136 3.0955% 1823 0.345293 2.896093 3.1944% 1822 0.334604 2.988605 3.3102% 1821 0.323883 3.087534 3.2277% 1820 0.313756 3.187191 2.6573% 1819 0.305634 3.271884 2.6261% 1818 0.297813 3.357807 2.6969% 1817 0.289993 3.448365 2.7717% 1816 0.282172 3.543943 2.8507% 1815 0.274351 3.644970 2.9343% 1814 0.266530 3.751926 3.0231% 1813 0.258709 3.865348 3.1039% 1812 0.250921 3.985325 3.2172% 1811 0.243100 4.113539 3.0969% 1810 0.235797 4.240932 2.9144% 1809 0.229120 4.364529 2.8225% 1808 0.222831 4.487716 2.9199% 1807 0.216509 4.618754 2.9918% 1806 0.210219 4.756937 3.0841% 1805 0.203930 4.903643 3.1822% 1804 0.197641 5.059687 3.2868% 1803 0.191351 5.225988 3.3985% 1802 0.185062 5.403592 3.5180% 1801 0.178773 5.593693 3.3999% 1800 0.172894 5.783876 2.8419% 1799 0.168117 5.948246 2.7485% 1798 0.163620 6.111731 2.8261% 1797 0.159123 6.284456 3.7832% 1796 0.153322 6.522210 2.1272% 1795 0.150129 6.660951 3.0879% 1794 0.145632 6.866637 3.1625% 1793 0.141167 7.083795 3.2904% 1792 0.136670 7.316881 3.4024% 1791 0.132173 7.565828 3.2296% 1790 0.128038 7.810172 41.3145% 1780 0.090605 11.036901 29.4353% 1770 0.070000 14.285648 83.4728% 1750 0.038153 26.210284 29.2845% 1740 0.029511 33.885822 94.2514% 1720 0.015192 65.823681 85.8111% 1700 0.008176 122.307692 19.2490% 1690 0.006856 145.850760 88.0250% 1670 0.003646 274.235925

BASE YEAR: 1858
YEAR BYEAR/AYEAR AYEAR/BYEAR GROWTH%

2009 10.094111 0.099068 8.2857% 2001 9.321743 0.107276 1.0000% 2000 9.229448 0.108349 1.0000% 1999 9.138067 0.109432 1.0000% 1998 9.047591 0.110527 1.0000% 1997 8.958011 0.111632 1.0000% 1996 8.869318 0.112748 1.0000% 1995 8.781503 0.113876 0.9992% 1994 8.694624 0.115014 1.0008% 1993 8.608473 0.116165 1.0000% 1992 8.523240 0.117326 0.9295% 1991 8.444746 0.118417 1.2505% 1990 8.340447 0.119898 0.7224% 1989 8.280624 0.120764 1.1077% 1988 8.189907 0.122102 0.8834% 1987 8.118194 0.123180 0.5594% 1986 8.073036 0.123869 1.3056% 1985 7.968991 0.125486 0.7673% 1984 7.908312 0.126449 0.8149% 1983 7.844384 0.127480 0.9737% 1982 7.768736 0.128721 0.9508% 1981 7.695566 0.129945 0.9031% 1980 7.626692 0.131118 2.2701% 1979 7.457404 0.134095 1.0042% 1978 7.383263 0.135441 0.9896% 1977 7.310914 0.136782 0.9103% 1976 7.244960 0.138027 0.8394% 1975 7.184649 0.139186 0.9042% 1974 7.120270 0.140444 1.1568% 1973 7.038845 0.142069 0.9427% 1972 6.973110 0.143408 0.7426% 1971 6.921707 0.144473 1.4697% 1970 6.821449 0.146596 0.6968% 1969 6.774245 0.147618 0.8565% 1968 6.716714 0.148882 1.5090% 1967 6.616863 0.151129 0.9949% 1966 6.551679 0.152633 1.0575% 1965 6.483122 0.154247 1.1300% 1964 6.410681 0.155990 1.5537% 1963 6.312605 0.158413 1.4658% 1962 6.221410 0.160735 1.5364% 1961 6.127269 0.163205 2.1586% 1960 5.997798 0.166728 -1.6655% 1959 6.099382 0.163951 4.3080% 1958 5.847473 0.171014 2.1130% 1957 5.726475 0.174627 1.9895% 1956 5.614770 0.178102 2.1231% 1955 5.498041 0.181883 1.4496% 1954 5.419480 0.184520 2.1573% 1953 5.305037 0.188500 1.2298% 1952 5.240590 0.190818 1.6814% 1951 5.153933 0.194027 1.6233% 1950 5.071607 0.197176 1.4265% 1949 5.000276 0.199989 1.7790% 1948 4.912874 0.203547 1.8242% 1947 4.824861 0.207260 -2.6320% 1946 4.955286 0.201805 3.1768% 1945 4.802713 0.208216 6.4754% 1944 4.510631 0.221698 -0.3437% 1943 4.526187 0.220937 0.6562% 1942 4.496678 0.222386 0.6633% 1941 4.467048 0.223861 -5.6614% 1940 4.735124 0.211188 8.0381% 1939 4.382828 0.228163 0.8126% 1938 4.347498 0.230017 0.7762% 1937 4.314011 0.231803 0.6029% 1936 4.288159 0.233200 0.5244% 1935 4.265789 0.234423 -3.0364% 1934 4.399370 0.227305 4.6271% 1933 4.204809 0.237823 1.3921% 1932 4.147077 0.241134 -0.2051% 1931 4.155599 0.240639 0.8886% 1930 4.118998 0.242778 1.0126% 1929 4.077707 0.245236

227

1.1526% 1928 4.031244 0.248062 1.2160% 1927 3.982813 0.251079 1.4086% 1926 3.927491
0.254615 1.7667% 1925 3.859309 0.259114 1.4465% 1924 3.804280 0.262862 1.7700% 1923
3.738116 0.267514 1.6165% 1922 3.678650 0.271839 1.3736% 1921 3.628803 0.275573
2.3393% 1920 3.545855 0.282019 1.3140% 1919 3.499866 0.285725 0.7676% 1918 3.473204
0.287919 0.3870% 1917 3.459815 0.289033 1.3274% 1916 3.414490 0.292870 1.4083% 1915
3.367072 0.296994 1.4458% 1914 3.319084 0.301288 1.9424% 1913 3.255844 0.307140
1.9857% 1912 3.192452 0.313239 1.5634% 1911 3.143309 0.318136 1.8169% 1910 3.087217
0.323916 1.8781% 1909 3.030306 0.330000 2.0082% 1908 2.970648 0.336627 1.9603% 1907
2.913536 0.343226 1.8264% 1906 2.861279 0.349494 1.9357% 1905 2.806945 0.356259
2.0148% 1904 2.751507 0.363437 2.1335% 1903 2.694029 0.371191 1.8151% 1902 2.646000
0.377929 1.8943% 1901 2.596808 0.385088 3.0255% 1900 2.520548 0.396739 0.6278% 1899
2.504822 0.399230 1.7757% 1898 2.461121 0.406319 1.8078% 1897 2.417420 0.413664
1.8396% 1896 2.373753 0.421274 1.8755% 1895 2.330052 0.429175 1.9114% 1894 2.286351
0.437378 1.9486% 1893 2.242650 0.445901 1.9858% 1892 2.198982 0.454756 2.0276% 1891
2.155281 0.463977 2.6465% 1890 2.099712 0.476256 1.5328% 1889 2.068013 0.483556
2.0811% 1888 2.025852 0.493619 2.1599% 1887 1.983022 0.504281 2.2075% 1886 1.940192
0.515413 2.2592% 1885 1.897328 0.527057 2.3095% 1884 1.854497 0.539230 2.3641% 1883
1.811667 0.551978 2.4214% 1882 1.768837 0.565343 2.4815% 1881 1.726006 0.579372
3.7644% 1880 1.663390 0.601182 0.9432% 1879 1.647847 0.606853 2.1464% 1878 1.613221
0.619878 2.1913% 1877 1.578628 0.633461 2.2426% 1876 1.544002 0.647667 2.2941% 1875
1.509376 0.662525 2.3456% 1874 1.474784 0.678065 2.4043% 1873 1.440158 0.694368
2.4635% 1872 1.405532 0.711474 2.5258% 1871 1.370906 0.729445 5.9947% 1870 1.293373
0.773172 -1.0968% 1869 1.307715 0.764692 2.1930% 1868 1.279653 0.781462 2.2394%
1867 1.251624 0.798962 2.2935% 1866 1.223562 0.817286 2.3445% 1865 1.195533 0.836447
2.4037% 1864 1.167470 0.856553 2.4599% 1863 1.139441 0.877623 2.5250% 1862 1.111379
0.899783 2.5872% 1861 1.083350 0.923063 2.9504% 1860 1.052303 0.950297 2.4012% 1859
1.027627 0.973116 2.7627% 1858 1.000000 1.000000 2.8412% 1857 0.972373 1.028412
2.9243% 1856 0.944746 1.058486 3.0161% 1855 0.917085 1.090411 3.1061% 1854 0.889458
1.124280 3.2056% 1853 0.861831 1.160320 3.3118% 1852 0.834204 1.198748 3.4252% 1851
0.806577 1.239807 4.0106% 1850 0.775476 1.289531 2.3254% 1849 0.757853 1.319517
2.7841% 1848 0.737325 1.356254 2.8590% 1847 0.716831 1.395029 2.9432% 1846 0.696336
1.436087 3.0324% 1845 0.675842 1.479635 3.1325% 1844 0.655314 1.525985 3.2284% 1843
0.634820 1.575249 3.3361% 1842 0.614326 1.627800 3.4512% 1841 0.593832 1.683979
3.8105% 1840 0.572034 1.748147 2.3861% 1839 0.558703 1.789859 2.5824% 1838 0.544639
1.836080 2.6573% 1837 0.530540 1.884870 2.7232% 1836 0.516476 1.936199 2.7994% 1835
0.502411 1.990402 2.8871% 1834 0.488313 2.047867 2.9657% 1833 0.474248 2.108600
3.0563% 1832 0.460184 2.173046 3.1604% 1831 0.446085 2.241724 3.4660% 1830 0.431142
2.319421 2.4653% 1829 0.420769 2.376602 2.6804% 1828 0.409785 2.440304 10.3427%
1827 0.371375 2.692696 -4.2314% 1826 0.387784 2.578756 2.9150% 1825 0.376800
2.653928 3.0026% 1824 0.365816 2.733614 3.0955% 1823 0.354832 2.818233 3.1944% 1822
0.343848 2.908259 3.3102% 1821 0.332831 3.004528 3.2277% 1820 0.322424 3.101506
2.6573% 1819 0.314078 3.183922 2.6261% 1818 0.306041 3.267535 2.6969% 1817 0.298004
3.355658 2.7717% 1816 0.289967 3.448666 2.8507% 1815 0.281930 3.546977 2.9343% 1814
0.273893 3.651058 3.0231% 1813 0.265856 3.761431 3.1039% 1812 0.257853 3.878182
3.2172% 1811 0.249816 4.002949 3.0969% 1810 0.242312 4.126917 2.9144% 1809 0.235450
4.247191 2.8225% 1808 0.228987 4.367066 2.9199% 1807 0.222490 4.494582 2.9918% 1806
0.216027 4.629050 3.0841% 1805 0.209564 4.771812 3.1822% 1804 0.203101 4.923660
3.2868% 1803 0.196638 5.085490 3.3985% 1802 0.190175 5.258320 3.5180% 1801 0.183712
5.443310 3.3999% 1800 0.177671 5.628380 2.8419% 1799 0.172761 5.788331 2.7485% 1798
0.168140 5.947421 2.8261% 1797 0.163519 6.115503 3.7832% 1796 0.157558 6.346865
2.1272% 1795 0.154276 6.481875 3.0879% 1794 0.149655 6.682032 3.1625% 1793 0.145067
6.893352 3.2904% 1792 0.140446 7.120172 3.4024% 1791 0.135825 7.362426 3.2296% 1790
0.131575 7.600200 41.3145% 1780 0.093108 10.740181 29.4353% 1770 0.071934 13.901587
83.4728% 1750 0.039207 25.505637 29.2845% 1740 0.030326 32.974823 94.2514% 1720
0.015612 64.054054 85.8111% 1700 0.008402 119.019530 19.2490% 1690 0.007046
141.929658 88.0250% 1670 0.003747 266.863271

YEAR BYEAR/AYEAR AYEAR/BYEAR GROWTH%

2009 10.380905 0.096331 8.2857% 2001 9.586593 0.104312 1.0000% 2000 9.491675 0.105355 1.0000% 1999 9.397698 0.106409 1.0000% 1998 9.304652 0.107473 1.0000% 1997 9.212526 0.108548 1.0000% 1996 9.121313 0.109633 1.0000% 1995 9.031003 0.110730 0.9992% 1994 8.941656 0.111836 1.0008% 1993 8.853057 0.112955 1.0000% 1992 8.765403 0.114385 0.9295% 1991 8.684678 0.115145 1.2505% 1990 8.577416 0.116585 0.7224% 1989 8.515894 0.117427 1.1077% 1988 8.422599 0.118728 0.8834% 1987 8.348848 0.119777 0.5594% 1986 8.302407 0.120447 1.3056% 1985 8.195406 0.122020 0.7673% 1984 8.133003 0.122956 0.8149% 1983 8.067259 0.123958 0.9737% 1982 7.989462 0.125165 0.9508% 1981 7.914213 0.126355 0.9031% 1980 7.843382 0.127496 2.2701% 1979 7.669284 0.130390 1.0042% 1978 7.593036 0.131700 0.9896% 1977 7.518631 0.133003 0.9103% 1976 7.450804 0.134214 0.8394% 1975 7.388780 0.135340 0.9042% 1974 7.322571 0.136564 1.1568% 1973 7.238833 0.138144 0.9427% 1972 7.171230 0.139446 0.7426% 1971 7.118366 0.140482 1.4697% 1970 7.015260 0.142546 0.6968% 1969 6.966715 0.143540 0.8565% 1968 6.907549 0.144769 1.5090% 1967 6.804861 0.146954 0.9949% 1966 6.737826 0.148416 1.0575% 1965 6.667321 0.149985 1.1300% 1964 6.592821 0.151680 1.5537% 1963 6.491959 0.154037 1.4658% 1962 6.398173 0.156295 1.5364% 1961 6.301357 0.158696 2.1586% 1960 6.168208 0.162122 -1.6655% 1959 6.272678 0.159422 4.3080% 1958 6.013612 0.166289 2.1130% 1957 5.889176 0.169803 1.9895% 1956 5.774297 0.173181 2.1231% 1955 5.654251 0.176858 1.4496% 1954 5.573458 0.179422 2.1573% 1953 5.455763 0.183292 1.2298% 1952 5.389486 0.185546 1.6814% 1951 5.300367 0.188666 1.6233% 1950 5.215702 0.191729 1.4265% 1949 5.142344 0.194464 1.7790% 1948 5.052459 0.197923 1.8242% 1947 4.961945 0.201534 -2.6320% 1946 5.096076 0.196229 3.1768% 1945 4.939168 0.202463 6.4754% 1944 4.638787 0.215574 -0.3437% 1943 4.654785 0.214833 0.6562% 1942 4.624438 0.216242 0.6633% 1941 4.593966 0.217677 -5.6614% 1940 4.869659 0.205353 8.0381% 1939 4.507353 0.221860 0.8126% 1938 4.471020 0.223663 0.7762% 1937 4.436581 0.225399 0.6029% 1936 4.409994 0.226758 0.5244% 1935 4.386989 0.227947 -3.0364% 1934 4.524365 0.221025 4.6271% 1933 4.324276 0.231253 1.3921% 1932 4.264903 0.234472 -0.2051% 1931 4.273668 0.233991 0.8886% 1930 4.236027 0.236070 1.0126% 1929 4.193563 0.238461 1.1526% 1928 4.145780 0.241209 1.2160% 1927 4.095972 0.244142 1.4086% 1926 4.039079 0.247581 1.7667% 1925 3.968960 0.251955 1.4465% 1924 3.912367 0.255600 1.7700% 1923 3.844324 0.260124 1.6165% 1922 3.783168 0.264329 1.3736% 1921 3.731905 0.267960 2.3393% 1920 3.646600 0.274228 1.3140% 1919 3.599304 0.277831 0.7676% 1918 3.571885 0.279964 0.3870% 1917 3.558116 0.281048 1.3274% 1916 3.511503 0.284778 1.4083% 1915 3.462737 0.288789 1.4458% 1914 3.413386 0.292964 1.9424% 1913 3.348349 0.298655 1.9857% 1912 3.283156 0.304585 1.5634% 1911 3.232617 0.309347 1.8169% 1910 3.174931 0.314967 1.8781% 1909 3.116403 0.320883 2.0082% 1908 3.055050 0.327327 1.9603% 1907 2.996315 0.333743 1.8264% 1906 2.942573 0.339839 1.9357% 1905 2.886696 0.346417 2.0148% 1904 2.829683 0.353396 2.1335% 1903 2.770572 0.360936 1.8151% 1902 2.721178 0.367488 1.8943% 1901 2.670588 0.374449 3.0255% 1900 2.592162 0.385778 0.6278% 1899 2.575989 0.388200 1.7757% 1898 2.531047 0.395093 1.8078% 1897 2.486104 0.402236 1.8396% 1896 2.441196 0.409635 1.8755% 1895 2.396253 0.417318 1.9114% 1894 2.351310 0.425295 1.9486% 1893 2.306368 0.433582 1.9858% 1892 2.261460 0.442192 2.0276% 1891 2.216517 0.451158 2.6465% 1890 2.159369 0.463098 1.5328% 1889 2.126769 0.470197 2.0811% 1888 2.083411 0.479982 2.1599% 1887 2.039364 0.490349 2.2075% 1886 1.995316 0.501174 2.2592% 1885 1.951235 0.512496 2.3095% 1884 1.907187 0.524332 2.3641% 1883 1.863140 0.536728 2.4214% 1882 1.819093 0.549725 2.4815% 1881 1.775046 0.563366 3.7644% 1880 1.710650 0.584573 0.9432% 1879 1.694665 0.590087 2.1464% 1878 1.659056 0.602753 2.1913% 1877 1.623480 0.615961 2.2426% 1876 1.587871 0.629774 2.2941% 1875 1.552261 0.644222 2.3456% 1874 1.516686 0.659332 2.4043% 1873 1.481076 0.675185 2.4635% 1872 1.445466 0.691818 2.5258% 1871 1.409856 0.709292 5.9947% 1870 1.330120 0.751812 -1.0968% 1869 1.344870 0.743566 2.1930% 1868 1.316011 0.759872 2.2394% 1867 1.287185 0.776889 2.2935% 1866 1.258326 0.794707 2.3445% 1865 1.229500 0.813339 2.4037% 1864 1.200641 0.832889 2.4599% 1863 1.171815 0.853377 2.5250% 1862 1.142956 0.874925 2.5872% 1861 1.114130 0.897561 2.9504% 1860 1.082201 0.924043 2.4012% 1859

1.056824 0.946231 2.7627% 1858 1.028412 0.972373 2.8412% 1857 1.000000 1.000000
2.9243% 1856 0.971588 1.029243 3.0161% 1855 0.943142 1.060286 3.1061% 1854 0.914729
1.093219 3.2056% 1853 0.886317 1.128264 3.3118% 1852 0.857905 1.165630 3.4252% 1851
0.829493 1.205555 4.0106% 1850 0.797508 1.253905 2.3254% 1849 0.779385 1.283063
2.7841% 1848 0.758274 1.318785 2.8590% 1847 0.737197 1.356489 2.9432% 1846 0.716121
1.396412 3.0324% 1845 0.695044 1.438757 3.1325% 1844 0.673933 1.483826 3.2284% 1843
0.652857 1.531730 3.3361% 1842 0.631780 1.582829 3.4512% 1841 0.610704 1.637456
3.8105% 1840 0.588287 1.699851 2.3861% 1839 0.574577 1.740410 2.5824% 1838 0.560113
1.785354 2.6573% 1837 0.545614 1.832797 2.7232% 1836 0.531150 1.882708 2.7994% 1835
0.516686 1.935413 2.8871% 1834 0.502187 1.991291 2.9657% 1833 0.487723 2.050346
3.0563% 1832 0.473258 2.113011 3.1604% 1831 0.458760 2.179791 3.4660% 1830 0.443392
2.255342 2.4653% 1829 0.432724 2.310943 2.6804% 1828 0.421428 2.372886 10.3427%
1827 0.381927 2.618305 -4.2314% 1826 0.398802 2.507513 2.9150% 1825 0.387506
2.580608 3.0026% 1824 0.376210 2.658092 3.0955% 1823 0.364914 2.740374 3.1944% 1822
0.353618 2.827912 3.3102% 1821 0.342287 2.921521 3.2277% 1820 0.331585 3.015820
2.6573% 1819 0.323002 3.095959 2.6261% 1818 0.314736 3.177262 2.6969% 1817 0.306471
3.262951 2.7717% 1816 0.298206 3.353390 2.8507% 1815 0.289940 3.448984 2.9343% 1814
0.281675 3.550190 3.0231% 1813 0.273410 3.657514 3.1039% 1812 0.265179 3.771039
3.2172% 1811 0.256914 3.892359 3.0969% 1810 0.249196 4.012902 2.9144% 1809 0.242139
4.129854 2.8225% 1808 0.235493 4.246417 2.9199% 1807 0.228812 4.370409 2.9918% 1806
0.222165 4.501163 3.0841% 1805 0.215518 4.639981 3.1822% 1804 0.208871 4.787634
3.2868% 1803 0.202225 4.944993 3.3985% 1802 0.195578 5.113048 3.5180% 1801 0.188931
5.292927 3.3999% 1800 0.182719 5.472884 2.8419% 1799 0.177670 5.628416 2.7485% 1798
0.172917 5.783111 2.8261% 1797 0.168165 5.946549 3.7832% 1796 0.162035 6.171520
2.1272% 1795 0.158660 6.302800 3.0879% 1794 0.153907 6.497427 3.1625% 1793 0.149189
6.702909 3.2904% 1792 0.144436 6.923462 3.4024% 1791 0.139684 7.159024 3.2296% 1790
0.135314 7.390229 41.3145% 1780 0.095754 10.443461 29.4353% 1770 0.073978 13.517527
83.4728% 1750 0.040321 24.800991 29.2845% 1740 0.031188 32.063825 94.2514% 1720
0.016055 62.284427 85.8111% 1700 0.008641 115.731367 19.2490% 1690 0.007246
138.008555 88.0250% 1670 0.003854 259.490617

BASE YEAR: 1856

YEAR BYEAR/AYEAR AYEAR/BYEAR GROWTH%

2009 10.684473 0.093594 8.2857% 2001 9.866932 0.101349 1.0000% 2000 9.769239
0.102362 1.0000% 1999 9.672514 0.103386 1.0000% 1998 9.576746 0.104420 1.0000% 1997
9.481927 0.105464 1.0000% 1996 9.388047 0.106518 1.0000% 1995 9.295096 0.107584
0.9992% 1994 9.203136 0.108659 1.0008% 1993 9.111946 0.109746 1.0000% 1992 9.021728
0.110844 0.9295% 1991 8.938643 0.111874 1.2505% 1990 8.828245 0.113273 0.7224% 1989
8.764923 0.114091 1.1077% 1988 8.668900 0.115355 0.8834% 1987 8.592992 0.116374
0.5594% 1986 8.545194 0.117025 1.3056% 1985 8.435063 0.118553 0.7673% 1984 8.370835
0.119462 0.8149% 1983 8.303169 0.120436 0.9737% 1982 8.223097 0.121609 0.9508% 1981
8.145647 0.122765 0.9031% 1980 8.072745 0.123874 2.2701% 1979 7.893556 0.126686
1.0042% 1978 7.815079 0.127958 0.9896% 1977 7.738498 0.129224 0.9103% 1976 7.668687
0.130400 0.8394% 1975 7.604849 0.131495 0.9002% 1974 7.536704 0.132684 1.1568% 1973
7.450518 0.134219 0.9427% 1972 7.380937 0.135484 0.7426% 1971 7.326528 0.136490
1.4697% 1970 7.220407 0.138496 0.6968% 1969 7.170442 0.139461 0.8565% 1968 7.109546
0.140656 1.5090% 1967 7.003855 0.142779 0.9949% 1966 6.934859 0.144199 1.0575% 1965
6.862293 0.145724 1.1300% 1964 6.785614 0.147371 1.5537% 1963 6.681802 0.149660
1.4658% 1962 6.585274 0.151854 1.5364% 1961 6.485627 0.154187 2.1586% 1960 6.348584
0.157515 -1.6655% 1959 6.456109 0.154892 4.3080% 1958 6.189467 0.161565 2.1130%
1957 6.061392 0.164979 1.9895% 1956 5.943154 0.168261 2.1231% 1955 5.819598 0.171833
1.4496% 1954 5.736442 0.174324 2.1573% 1953 5.615306 0.178085 1.2298% 1952 5.547090
0.180275 1.6814% 1951 5.455365 0.183306 1.6233% 1950 5.368224 0.186281 1.4265% 1949
5.292721 0.188939 1.7790% 1948 5.200207 0.192300 1.8242% 1947 5.107047 0.195808 -
2.6320% 1946 5.245100 0.190654 3.1768% 1945 5.083604 0.196711 6.4754% 1944 4.774439
0.209449 -0.3437% 1943 4.790904 0.208729 0.6562% 1942 4.759670 0.210099 0.6633%
1941 4.728307 0.211492 -5.6614% 1940 5.012061 0.199519 8.0381% 1939 4.639161

0.215556 0.8126% 1938 4.601765 0.217308 0.7762% 1937 4.566319 0.218995 0.6029% 1936
4.538955 0.220315 0.5244% 1935 4.515277 0.221470 -3.0364% 1934 4.656671 0.214746
4.6271% 1933 4.450730 0.224682 1.3921% 1932 4.389621 0.227810 -0.2051% 1931
4.398642 0.227343 0.8886% 1930 4.359900 0.229363 1.0126% 1929 4.316195 0.231686
1.1526% 1928 4.267014 0.234356 1.2160% 1927 4.215750 0.237206 1.4086% 1926 4.157193
0.240547 1.7667% 1925 4.085023 0.244797 1.4465% 1924 4.026776 0.248338 1.7700% 1923
3.956743 0.252733 1.6165% 1922 3.893799 0.256819 1.3736% 1921 3.841036 0.260346
2.3393% 1920 3.753237 0.266437 1.3140% 1919 3.704558 0.269938 0.7676% 1918 3.676337
0.272010 0.3870% 1917 3.662165 0.273063 1.3274% 1916 3.614189 0.276687 1.4083% 1915
3.563998 0.280584 1.4458% 1914 3.513204 0.284640 1.9424% 1913 3.446264 0.290169
1.9857% 1912 3.379165 0.295931 1.5634% 1911 3.327148 0.300558 1.8169% 1910 3.267775
0.306019 1.8781% 1909 3.207536 0.311766 2.0082% 1908 3.144389 0.318027 1.9603% 1907
3.083936 0.324261 1.8264% 1906 3.028623 0.330183 1.9357% 1905 2.971112 0.336574
2.0148% 1904 2.912431 0.343356 2.1335% 1903 2.851591 0.350681 1.8151% 1902 2.800754
0.357047 1.8943% 1901 2.748684 0.363810 3.0255% 1900 2.667965 0.374818 0.6278% 1899
2.651319 0.377171 1.7757% 1898 2.605062 0.383868 1.8078% 1897 2.558805 0.390807
1.8396% 1896 2.512583 0.397997 1.8755% 1895 2.466326 0.405461 1.9114% 1894 2.420069
0.413211 1.9486% 1893 2.373813 0.421263 1.9858% 1892 2.327591 0.429629 2.0276% 1891
2.281334 0.438340 2.6465% 1890 2.222515 0.449941 1.5328% 1889 2.188962 0.456838
2.0811% 1888 2.144336 0.466345 2.1599% 1887 2.099000 0.476417 2.2075% 1886 2.053665
0.486934 2.2592% 1885 2.008294 0.497935 2.3095% 1884 1.962959 0.509435 2.3641% 1883
1.917624 0.521479 2.4214% 1882 1.872288 0.534106 2.4815% 1881 1.826953 0.547359
3.7644% 1880 1.760674 0.567964 0.9432% 1879 1.744222 0.573321 2.1464% 1878 1.707571
0.585627 2.1913% 1877 1.670956 0.598460 2.2426% 1876 1.634305 0.611881 2.2941% 1875
1.597653 0.625918 2.3456% 1874 1.561038 0.640599 2.4043% 1873 1.524387 0.656001
2.4635% 1872 1.487736 0.672162 2.5258% 1871 1.451085 0.689140 5.9947% 1870 1.369017
0.730451 -1.0968% 1869 1.384198 0.722440 2.1930% 1868 1.354495 0.738283 2.2394%
1867 1.324826 0.754816 2.2935% 1866 1.295123 0.772128 2.3445% 1865 1.265454 0.790230
2.4037% 1864 1.235751 0.809225 2.4599% 1863 1.206083 0.829131 2.5250% 1862 1.176379
0.850066 2.5872% 1861 1.146711 0.872060 2.9504% 1860 1.113848 0.897789 2.4012% 1859
1.087729 0.919347 2.7627% 1858 1.058486 0.944746 2.8412% 1857 1.029243 0.971588
2.9243% 1856 1.000000 1.000000 3.0161% 1855 0.970722 1.030161 3.1061% 1854 0.941479
1.062159 3.2056% 1853 0.912236 1.096208 3.3118% 1852 0.882993 1.132512 3.4252% 1851
0.853750 1.171303 4.0106% 1850 0.820830 1.218279 2.3254% 1849 0.802176 1.246609
2.7841% 1848 0.780448 1.281315 2.8590% 1847 0.758755 1.317948 2.9432% 1846 0.737062
1.356738 3.0324% 1845 0.715369 1.397879 3.1325% 1844 0.693641 1.441668 3.2284% 1843
0.671948 1.488210 3.3361% 1842 0.650255 1.537858 3.4512% 1841 0.628562 1.590932
3.8105% 1840 0.605490 1.651554 2.3861% 1839 0.591380 1.690961 2.5824% 1838 0.576492
1.734629 2.6573% 1837 0.561570 1.780723 2.7232% 1836 0.546682 1.829216 2.7994% 1835
0.531795 1.880424 2.8871% 1834 0.516872 1.934714 2.9657% 1833 0.501985 1.992092
3.0563% 1832 0.487098 2.052976 3.1604% 1831 0.472175 2.117859 3.4660% 1830 0.456358
2.191263 2.4653% 1829 0.445378 2.245285 2.6804% 1828 0.433752 2.305467 10.3427%
1827 0.393095 2.543913 -4.2314% 1826 0.410464 2.436269 2.9150% 1825 0.398837
2.507288 3.0026% 1824 0.387211 2.582570 3.0955% 1823 0.375585 2.662514 3.1944% 1822
0.363959 2.747565 3.3102% 1821 0.352297 2.838515 3.2277% 1820 0.341281 2.930135
2.6573% 1819 0.332447 3.007997 2.6261% 1818 0.323940 3.086990 2.6969% 1817 0.315433
3.170244 2.7717% 1816 0.306926 3.258113 2.8507% 1815 0.298419 3.350992 2.9343% 1814
0.289912 3.449321 3.0231% 1813 0.281405 3.553596 3.1039% 1812 0.272934 3.663896
3.2172% 1811 0.264426 3.781769 3.0969% 1810 0.256483 3.898888 2.9144% 1809 0.249220
4.012516 2.8225% 1808 0.242379 4.125768 2.9199% 1807 0.235503 4.246237 2.9918% 1806
0.228662 4.373275 3.0841% 1805 0.221821 4.508150 3.1822% 1804 0.214979 4.651608
3.2868% 1803 0.208138 4.804496 3.3985% 1802 0.201297 4.967776 3.5180% 1801 0.194456
5.142545 3.3999% 1800 0.188062 5.317388 2.8419% 1799 0.182865 5.468502 2.7485% 1798
0.177974 5.618801 2.8261% 1797 0.173082 5.777596 3.7832% 1796 0.166773 5.996174
2.1272% 1795 0.163299 6.123725 3.0879% 1794 0.158408 6.312822 3.1625% 1793 0.153552
6.512465 3.2904% 1792 0.148660 6.726753 3.4024% 1791 0.143769 6.955621 3.2296% 1790

231

0.139271 7.180257 41.3145% 1780 0.098554 10.146741 29.4353% 1770 0.076141 13.133467 83.4728% 1750 0.041500 24.096344 29.2845% 1740 0.032100 31.152827 94.2514% 1720 0.016525 60.514801 85.8111% 1700 0.008893 112.443204 19.2490% 1690 0.007458 134.087452 88.0250% 1670 0.003966 252.117962

BASE YEAR: 1855

YEAR BYEAR/AYEAR AYEAR/BYEAR GROWTH%

2009 11.006732 0.090853 8.2857% 2001 10.164533 0.098381 1.0000% 2000 10.063893 0.099365 1.0000% 1999 9.964250 0.100359 1.0000% 1998 9.865594 0.101362 1.0000% 1997 9.767915 0.102376 1.0000% 1996 9.671203 0.103400 1.0000% 1995 9.575449 0.104434 0.9992% 1994 9.480715 0.105477 1.0008% 1993 9.386775 0.106533 1.0000% 1992 9.293836 0.107598 0.9295% 1991 9.208245 0.108598 1.2505% 1990 9.094517 0.109956 0.7224% 1989 9.029285 0.110751 1.1077% 1988 8.930366 0.111977 0.8834% 1987 8.852169 0.112967 0.5594% 1986 8.802929 0.113599 1.3056% 1985 8.689476 0.115082 0.7673% 1984 8.623311 0.115965 0.8149% 1983 8.553604 0.116910 0.9737% 1982 8.471117 0.118048 0.9508% 1981 8.391331 0.119171 0.9031% 1980 8.316230 0.120247 2.2701% 1979 8.131637 0.122976 1.0042% 1978 8.050792 0.124211 0.9896% 1977 7.971902 0.125441 0.9103% 1976 7.899985 0.126583 0.8394% 1975 7.834222 0.127645 0.9042% 1974 7.764022 0.128799 1.1568% 1973 7.675236 0.130289 0.9427% 1972 7.603557 0.131517 0.7426% 1971 7.547506 0.132494 1.4697% 1970 7.438184 0.134441 0.6968% 1969 7.386712 0.135378 0.8565% 1968 7.323979 0.136538 1.5090% 1967 7.215101 0.138598 0.9949% 1966 7.144024 0.139977 1.0575% 1965 7.069269 0.141457 1.1300% 1964 6.990278 0.143056 1.5537% 1963 6.883335 0.145278 1.4658% 1962 6.783895 0.147408 1.5364% 1961 6.681242 0.149673 2.1586% 1960 6.540066 0.152904 -1.6655% 1959 6.650834 0.150357 4.3080% 1958 6.376150 0.156834 2.1130% 1957 6.244212 0.160148 1.9895% 1956 6.122407 0.163334 2.1231% 1955 5.995125 0.166802 1.4496% 1954 5.909461 0.169220 2.1573% 1953 5.784671 0.172871 1.2298% 1952 5.714398 0.174997 1.6814% 1951 5.619906 0.177939 1.6233% 1950 5.530137 0.180827 1.4265% 1949 5.452357 0.183407 1.7790% 1948 5.357053 0.186670 1.8242% 1947 5.261082 0.190075 -2.6320% 1946 5.403299 0.185072 3.1768% 1945 5.236932 0.190951 6.4754% 1944 4.918443 0.203316 -0.3437% 1943 4.935404 0.202618 0.6562% 1942 4.903228 0.203947 0.6633% 1941 4.870919 0.205300 -5.6614% 1940 5.163232 0.193677 8.0381% 1939 4.779084 0.209245 0.8126% 1938 4.740561 0.210946 0.7762% 1937 4.704046 0.212583 0.6029% 1936 4.675856 0.213865 0.5244% 1935 4.651464 0.214986 -3.0364% 1934 4.797123 0.208458 4.6271% 1933 4.584970 0.218104 1.3921% 1932 4.522019 0.221140 -0.2051% 1931 4.531312 0.220687 0.8886% 1930 4.491401 0.222648 1.0126% 1929 4.446378 0.224902 1.1526% 1928 4.395713 0.227494 1.2160% 1927 4.342903 0.230261 1.4086% 1926 4.282580 0.233504 1.7667% 1925 4.208233 0.237629 1.4465% 1924 4.148229 0.241067 1.7700% 1923 4.076084 0.245334 1.6165% 1922 4.011241 0.249299 1.3736% 1921 3.956887 0.252724 2.3393% 1920 3.866439 0.258636 1.3140% 1919 3.816293 0.262034 0.7676% 1918 3.787221 0.264046 0.3870% 1917 3.772621 0.265068 1.3274% 1916 3.723198 0.268586 1.4083% 1915 3.671493 0.272369 1.4458% 1914 3.619167 0.276307 1.9424% 1913 3.550208 0.281674 1.9857% 1912 3.481085 0.287267 1.5634% 1911 3.427499 0.291758 1.8169% 1910 3.366336 0.297059 1.8781% 1909 3.304280 0.302638 2.0082% 1908 3.239228 0.308716 1.9603% 1907 3.176952 0.314767 1.8264% 1906 3.119970 0.320516 1.9357% 1905 3.060724 0.326720 2.0148% 1904 3.000274 0.333303 2.1335% 1903 2.937599 0.340414 1.8151% 1902 2.885228 0.346593 1.8943% 1901 2.831588 0.353159 3.0255% 1900 2.748434 0.363844 0.6278% 1899 2.731286 0.366128 1.7757% 1898 2.683634 0.372629 1.8078% 1897 2.635982 0.379365 1.8396% 1896 2.588366 0.386344 1.8755% 1895 2.540714 0.393590 1.9114% 1894 2.493062 0.401113 1.9486% 1893 2.445410 0.408929 1.9858% 1892 2.397794 0.417050 2.0276% 1891 2.350142 0.425506 2.6465% 1890 2.289549 0.436767 1.5328% 1889 2.254984 0.443462 2.0811% 1888 2.209012 0.452691 2.1599% 1887 2.162309 0.462469 2.2075% 1886 2.115607 0.472678 2.2592% 1885 2.068867 0.483356 2.3095% 1884 2.022165 0.494520 2.3641% 1883 1.975462 0.506211 2.4214% 1882 1.928759 0.518468 2.4815% 1881 1.882057 0.531334 3.7644% 1880 1.813779 0.551335 0.9432% 1879 1.796830 0.556536 2.1464% 1878 1.759074 0.568481 2.1913% 1877 1.721354 0.580938 2.2426% 1876 1.683597 0.593966 2.2941% 1875 1.645841 0.607592 2.3456% 1874 1.608121 0.621844 2.4043% 1873 1.570364 0.636795 2.4635% 1872 1.532608 0.652483 2.5258% 1871 1.494851 0.668963 5.9947% 1870

232

1.410308 0.709065 -1.0968% 1869 1.425948 0.701288 2.1930% 1868 1.395348 0.716667
2.2394% 1867 1.364785 0.732716 2.2935% 1866 1.334185 0.749521 2.3445% 1865 1.303622
0.767093 2.4037% 1864 1.273023 0.785532 2.4599% 1863 1.242460 0.804855 2.5250% 1862
1.211860 0.825178 2.5872% 1861 1.181297 0.846527 2.9504% 1860 1.147443 0.871503
2.4012% 1859 1.120536 0.892430 2.7627% 1858 1.090411 0.917085 2.8412% 1857 1.060286
0.943142 2.9243% 1856 1.030161 0.970722 3.0161% 1855 1.000000 1.000000 3.1061% 1854
0.969875 1.031061 3.2056% 1853 0.939750 1.064113 3.3118% 1852 0.909625 1.099354
3.4252% 1851 0.879500 1.137009 4.0106% 1850 0.845587 1.182610 2.3254% 1849 0.826371
1.210110 2.7841% 1848 0.803987 1.243801 2.8590% 1847 0.781640 1.279361 2.9432% 1846
0.759293 1.317015 3.0324% 1845 0.736946 1.356952 3.1325% 1844 0.714562 1.399458
3.2284% 1843 0.692215 1.444638 3.3361% 1842 0.669868 1.492832 3.4512% 1841 0.647521
1.544352 3.8105% 1840 0.623753 1.603200 2.3861% 1839 0.609216 1.641453 2.5824% 1838
0.593880 1.683842 2.6573% 1837 0.578507 1.728587 2.7232% 1836 0.563171 1.775660
2.7994% 1835 0.547835 1.825368 2.8871% 1834 0.532462 1.878069 2.9657% 1833 0.517126
1.933766 3.0563% 1832 0.501789 1.992869 3.1604% 1831 0.486416 2.055852 3.4660% 1830
0.470122 2.127107 2.4653% 1829 0.458811 2.179546 2.6804% 1828 0.446834 2.237967
10.3427% 1827 0.404951 2.469432 -4.2314% 1826 0.422844 2.364940 2.9150% 1825
0.410867 2.433878 3.0026% 1824 0.398890 2.506957 3.0955% 1823 0.386913 2.584560
3.1944% 1822 0.374936 2.667121 3.3102% 1821 0.362923 2.755408 3.2277% 1820 0.351575
2.844345 2.6573% 1819 0.342474 2.919927 2.6261% 1818 0.333711 2.996608 2.6969% 1817
0.324947 3.077424 2.7717% 1816 0.316183 3.162721 2.8507% 1815 0.307420 3.252880
2.9343% 1814 0.298656 3.348331 3.0231% 1813 0.289893 3.449553 3.1039% 1812 0.281166
3.556623 3.2172% 1811 0.272402 3.671046 3.0969% 1810 0.264219 3.784735 2.9144% 1809
0.256737 3.895036 2.8225% 1808 0.249690 4.004972 2.9199% 1807 0.242606 4.121915
2.9918% 1806 0.235558 4.245233 3.0841% 1805 0.228511 4.376159 3.1822% 1804 0.221464
4.515416 3.2868% 1803 0.214416 4.663828 3.3985% 1802 0.207369 4.822328 3.5180% 1801
0.200321 4.991980 3.3999% 1800 0.193734 5.161704 2.8419% 1799 0.188381 5.308393
2.7485% 1798 0.183342 5.454292 2.8261% 1797 0.178303 5.608437 3.7832% 1796 0.171803
5.820616 2.1272% 1795 0.168225 5.944432 3.0879% 1794 0.163186 6.127993 3.1625% 1793
0.158183 6.321791 3.2904% 1792 0.153144 6.529804 3.4024% 1791 0.148105 6.751972
3.2296% 1790 0.143471 6.970032 41.3145% 1780 0.101526 9.849662 29.4353% 1770
0.078438 12.748941 83.4728% 1750 0.042752 23.390844 29.2845% 1740 0.033068
30.240724 94.2514% 1720 0.017023 58.743029 85.8111% 1700 0.009162 109.151056
19.2490% 1690 0.007683 130.161597 88.0250% 1670 0.004086 244.736372

BASE YEAR: 1854

YEAR BYEAR/AYEAR AYEAR/BYEAR GROWTH%

2009 11.348607 0.088117 8.2857% 2001 10.480249 0.095418 1.0000% 2000
10.376483 0.096372 1.0000% 1999 10.273746 0.097335 1.0000% 1998 10.172026 0.098309
1.0000% 1997 10.071312 0.099292 1.0000% 1996 9.971596 0.100285 1.0000% 1995
9.872868 0.101288 0.9992% 1994 9.775192 0.102300 1.0008% 1993 9.678333 0.103324
1.0000% 1992 9.582508 0.104357 0.9295% 1991 9.494258 0.105327 1.2505% 1990 9.376998
0.106644 0.7224% 1989 9.309740 0.107414 1.1077% 1988 9.207748 0.108604 0.8834% 1987
9.127122 0.109564 0.5594% 1986 9.076353 0.110176 1.3056% 1985 8.959377 0.111615
0.7673% 1984 8.891156 0.112471 0.8149% 1983 8.819284 0.113388 0.9737% 1982 8.734234
0.114492 0.9508% 1981 8.651971 0.115581 0.9031% 1980 8.574537 0.116624 2.2701% 1979
8.384210 0.119272 1.0042% 1978 8.300855 0.120470 0.9896% 1977 8.219514 0.121662
0.9103% 1976 8.145364 0.122769 0.8394% 1975 8.077557 0.123800 0.9042% 1974 8.005177
0.124919 1.1568% 1973 7.913633 0.126364 0.9427% 1972 7.839727 0.127555 0.7426% 1971
7.781936 0.128503 1.4697% 1970 7.669219 0.130391 0.6968% 1969 7.616148 0.131300
0.8565% 1968 7.551466 0.132425 1.5090% 1967 7.439206 0.134423 0.9949% 1966 7.365922
0.135760 1.0575% 1965 7.288845 0.137196 1.1300% 1964 7.207400 0.138746 1.5537% 1963
7.097135 0.140902 1.4658% 1962 6.994607 0.142967 1.5364% 1961 6.888765 0.145164
2.1586% 1960 6.743204 0.148297 -1.6655% 1959 6.857413 0.145828 4.3080% 1958
6.574197 0.152110 2.1130% 1957 6.438161 0.155324 1.9895% 1956 6.312573 0.158414
2.1231% 1955 6.181337 0.161777 1.4496% 1954 6.093012 0.164122 2.1573% 1953 5.964346
0.167663 1.2298% 1952 5.891890 0.169725 1.6814% 1951 5.794464 0.172579 1.6233% 1950

233

5.701906 0.175380 1.4265% 1949 5.621710 0.177882 1.7790% 1948 5.523446 0.181046
1.8242% 1947 5.424495 0.184349 -2.6320% 1946 5.571129 0.179497 3.1768% 1945
5.399594 0.185199 6.4754% 1944 5.071212 0.197192 -0.3437% 1943 5.088701 0.196514
0.6562% 1942 5.055525 0.197803 0.6633% 1941 5.022213 0.199115 -5.6614% 1940
5.323605 0.187843 8.0381% 1939 4.927525 0.202942 0.8126% 1938 4.887805 0.204591
0.7762% 1937 4.850156 0.206179 0.6029% 1936 4.821091 0.207422 0.5244% 1935 4.795941
0.208510 -3.0364% 1934 4.946124 0.202179 4.6271% 1933 4.727382 0.211534 1.3921%
1932 4.662475 0.214478 -0.2051% 1931 4.672057 0.214038 0.8886% 1930 4.630907
0.215940 1.0126% 1929 4.584485 0.218127 1.1526% 1928 4.532247 0.220641 1.2160% 1927
4.477796 0.223324 1.4086% 1926 4.415599 0.226470 1.7667% 1925 4.338944 0.230471
1.4465% 1924 4.277075 0.233805 1.7700% 1923 4.202689 0.237943 1.6165% 1922 4.135833
0.241789 1.3736% 1921 4.079791 0.245111 2.3393% 1920 3.986533 0.250845 1.3140% 1919
3.934829 0.254141 0.7676% 1918 3.904854 0.256092 0.3870% 1917 3.889801 0.257083
1.3274% 1916 3.838843 0.260495 1.4083% 1915 3.785531 0.264164 1.4458% 1914 3.731580
0.267983 1.9424% 1913 3.660480 0.273188 1.9857% 1912 3.589210 0.278613 1.5634% 1911
3.533960 0.282969 1.8169% 1910 3.470896 0.288110 1.8781% 1909 3.406912 0.293521
2.0082% 1908 3.339840 0.299416 1.9603% 1907 3.275630 0.305285 1.8264% 1906 3.216878
0.310860 1.9357% 1905 3.155792 0.316878 2.0148% 1904 3.093464 0.323262 2.1335% 1903
3.028843 0.330159 1.8151% 1902 2.974845 0.336152 1.8943% 1901 2.919539 0.342520
3.0255% 1900 2.833802 0.352883 0.6278% 1899 2.816121 0.355098 1.7757% 1898 2.766989
0.361404 1.8078% 1897 2.717857 0.367937 1.8396% 1896 2.668762 0.374706 1.8755% 1895
2.619630 0.381733 1.9114% 1894 2.570498 0.389030 1.9486% 1893 2.521366 0.396610
1.9858% 1892 2.472271 0.404486 2.0276% 1891 2.423139 0.412688 2.6465% 1890 2.360664
0.423610 1.5328% 1889 2.325025 0.430103 2.0811% 1888 2.277625 0.439054 2.1599% 1887
2.229472 0.448537 2.2075% 1886 2.181318 0.458438 2.2592% 1885 2.133128 0.468795
2.3095% 1884 2.084974 0.479622 2.3641% 1883 2.036821 0.490961 2.4214% 1882 1.988668
0.502849 2.4815% 1881 1.940514 0.515327 3.7644% 1880 1.870116 0.534726 0.9432% 1879
1.852641 0.539770 2.1464% 1878 1.813712 0.551356 2.1913% 1877 1.774820 0.563437
2.2426% 1876 1.735891 0.576073 2.2941% 1875 1.696962 0.589288 2.3456% 1874 1.658070
0.603111 2.4043% 1873 1.619141 0.617611 2.4635% 1872 1.580212 0.632827 2.5258% 1871
1.541282 0.648810 5.9947% 1870 1.454113 0.687704 -1.0968% 1869 1.470238 0.680162
2.1930% 1868 1.438688 0.695078 2.2394% 1867 1.407176 0.710643 2.2935% 1866 1.375626
0.726942 2.3445% 1865 1.344114 0.743985 2.4037% 1864 1.312564 0.761868 2.4599% 1863
1.281051 0.780609 2.5250% 1862 1.249501 0.800319 2.5872% 1861 1.217989 0.821026
2.9504% 1860 1.183083 0.845249 2.4012% 1859 1.155341 0.865546 2.7627% 1858 1.124280
0.889458 2.8412% 1857 1.093219 0.914729 2.9243% 1856 1.062159 0.941479 3.0161% 1855
1.031061 0.969875 3.1061% 1854 1.000000 1.000000 3.2056% 1853 0.968939 1.032056
3.3118% 1852 0.937879 1.066236 3.4252% 1851 0.906818 1.102757 4.0106% 1850 0.871852
1.146984 2.3254% 1849 0.852039 1.173656 2.7841% 1848 0.828960 1.206331 2.8590% 1847
0.805918 1.240820 2.9432% 1846 0.782877 1.277340 3.0324% 1845 0.759836 1.316074
3.1325% 1844 0.736757 1.357300 3.2284% 1843 0.713716 1.401118 3.3361% 1842 0.690674
1.447860 3.4512% 1841 0.667633 1.497829 3.8105% 1840 0.643127 1.554904 2.3861% 1839
0.628139 1.592004 2.5824% 1838 0.612326 1.633116 2.6573% 1837 0.596476 1.676513
2.7232% 1836 0.580663 1.722168 2.7994% 1835 0.564851 1.770379 2.8871% 1834 0.549000
1.821492 2.9657% 1833 0.533188 1.875512 3.0563% 1832 0.517375 1.932834 3.1604% 1831
0.501525 1.993919 3.4660% 1830 0.484724 2.063028 2.4653% 1829 0.473062 2.113888
2.6804% 1828 0.460713 2.170548 10.3427% 1827 0.417529 2.395041 -4.2314% 1826
0.435978 2.293696 2.9150% 1825 0.423629 2.360558 3.0026% 1824 0.411280 2.431435
3.0955% 1823 0.398931 2.506701 3.1944% 1822 0.386582 2.586774 3.3102% 1821 0.374195
2.672402 3.2277% 1820 0.362495 2.758660 2.6573% 1819 0.353112 2.831965 2.6261% 1818
0.344076 2.906335 2.6969% 1817 0.335040 2.984717 2.7717% 1816 0.326004 3.067444
2.8507% 1815 0.316968 3.154888 2.9343% 1814 0.307933 3.247463 3.0231% 1813 0.298897
3.345635 3.1039% 1812 0.289899 3.449481 3.2172% 1811 0.280863 3.560456 3.0969% 1810
0.272426 3.670720 2.9144% 1809 0.264711 3.777699 2.8225% 1808 0.257445 3.884323
2.9199% 1807 0.250141 3.997742 2.9918% 1806 0.242875 4.117346 3.0841% 1805 0.235609
4.244327 3.1822% 1804 0.228342 4.379390 3.2868% 1803 0.221076 4.523331 3.3985% 1802

0.213810 4.677056 3.5180% 1801 0.206543 4.841597 3.3999% 1800 0.199752 5.006209
2.8419% 1799 0.194232 5.148478 2.7485% 1798 0.189037 5.289982 2.8261% 1797 0.183841
5.439484 3.7832% 1796 0.177139 5.645271 2.1272% 1795 0.173450 5.765357 3.0879% 1794
0.168254 5.943388 3.1625% 1793 0.163096 6.131348 3.2904% 1792 0.157901 6.333095
3.4024% 1791 0.152705 6.548570 3.2296% 1790 0.147928 6.760060 41.3145% 1780
0.104680 9.552942 29.4353% 1770 0.080874 12.364881 83.4728% 1750 0.044080 22.686197
29.2845% 1740 0.034095 29.329726 94.2514% 1720 0.017552 56.973402 85.8111% 1700
0.009446 105.862894 19.2490% 1690 0.007921 126.240494 88.0250% 1670 0.004213
237.363718

BASE YEAR: 1853

YEAR BYEAR/AYEAR AYEAR/BYEAR GROWTH%

2009 11.712401 0.085380 8.2857% 2001 10.816207 0.092454 1.0000% 2000
10.709115 0.093378 1.0000% 1999 10.603084 0.094312 1.0000% 1998 10.498103 0.095255
1.0000% 1997 10.394161 0.096208 1.0000% 1996 10.291249 0.097170 1.0000% 1995
10.189355 0.098142 0.9992% 1994 10.088548 0.099122 1.0008% 1993 9.988584 0.100114
1.0000% 1992 9.889688 0.101115 0.9295% 1991 9.798609 0.102055 1.2505% 1990 9.677589
0.103332 0.7224% 1989 9.608175 0.104078 1.1077% 1988 9.502914 0.105231 0.8834% 1987
9.419704 0.106160 0.5594% 1986 9.367306 0.106754 1.3056% 1985 9.246581 0.108148
0.7673% 1984 9.176173 0.108978 0.8149% 1983 9.101997 0.109866 0.9737% 1982 9.014221
0.110936 0.9508% 1981 8.929321 0.111991 0.9031% 1980 8.849405 0.113002 2.2701% 1979
8.652976 0.115567 1.0042% 1978 8.566949 0.116728 0.9896% 1977 8.483000 0.117883
0.9103% 1976 8.406473 0.118956 0.8394% 1975 8.336494 0.119955 0.9042% 1974 8.261793
0.121039 1.1568% 1973 8.167314 0.122439 0.9427% 1972 8.091040 0.123594 0.7426% 1971
8.031396 0.124511 1.4697% 1970 7.915065 0.126341 0.6968% 1969 7.860293 0.127222
0.8565% 1968 7.793538 0.128311 1.5090% 1967 7.677679 0.130248 0.9949% 1966 7.602046
0.131544 1.0575% 1965 7.522498 0.132935 1.1300% 1964 7.438442 0.134437 1.5537% 1963
7.324643 0.136525 1.4658% 1962 7.218828 0.138527 1.5364% 1961 7.109594 0.140655
2.1586% 1960 6.959366 0.143691 -1.6655% 1959 7.077236 0.141298 4.3080% 1958
6.784941 0.147385 2.1130% 1957 6.644545 0.150499 1.9895% 1956 6.514930 0.153494
2.1231% 1955 6.379488 0.156752 1.4496% 1954 6.288332 0.159025 2.1573% 1953 6.155541
0.162455 1.2298% 1952 6.080762 0.164453 1.6814% 1951 5.980213 0.167218 1.6233% 1950
5.884688 0.169933 1.4265% 1949 5.801921 0.172357 1.7790% 1948 5.700507 0.175423
1.8242% 1947 5.598384 0.178623 -2.6320% 1946 5.749718 0.173922 3.1768% 1945
5.572685 0.179447 6.4754% 1944 5.233776 0.191067 -0.3437% 1943 5.251826 0.190410
0.6562% 1942 5.217587 0.191659 0.6633% 1941 5.183206 0.192931 -5.6614% 1940
5.494260 0.182008 8.0381% 1939 5.085483 0.196638 8.8126% 1938 5.044490 0.198236
0.7762% 1937 5.005634 0.199775 0.6029% 1936 4.975637 0.200979 0.5244% 1935 4.949681
0.202033 -3.0364% 1934 5.104678 0.195899 4.6271% 1933 4.878924 0.204963 1.3921%
1932 4.811937 0.207817 -0.2051% 1931 4.821825 0.207390 0.8886% 1930 4.779356
0.209233 1.0126% 1929 4.731446 0.211352 1.1526% 1928 4.677533 0.213788 1.2160% 1927
4.621338 0.216388 1.4086% 1926 4.557147 0.219436 1.7667% 1925 4.478034 0.223312
1.4465% 1924 4.414183 0.226543 1.7700% 1923 4.337412 0.230552 1.6165% 1922 4.268412
0.234279 1.3736% 1921 4.210574 0.237497 2.3393% 1920 4.114327 0.243053 1.3140% 1919
4.060965 0.246247 0.7676% 1918 4.030029 0.248137 0.3870% 1917 4.014493 0.249097
1.3274% 1916 3.961902 0.252404 1.4083% 1915 3.906881 0.255959 1.4458% 1914 3.851201
0.259659 1.9424% 1913 3.777821 0.264703 1.9857% 1912 3.704266 0.269959 1.5634% 1911
3.647245 0.274180 1.8169% 1910 3.582160 0.279161 1.8781% 1909 3.516125 0.284404
2.0082% 1908 3.446903 0.290115 1.9603% 1907 3.380634 0.295802 1.8264% 1906 3.319999
0.301205 1.9357% 1905 3.256955 0.307035 2.0148% 1904 3.192629 0.313221 2.1335% 1903
3.125936 0.319904 1.8151% 1902 3.070207 0.325711 1.8943% 1901 3.013128 0.331881
3.0255% 1900 2.924643 0.341922 0.6278% 1899 2.906396 0.344069 1.7757% 1898 2.855689
0.350178 1.8078% 1897 2.804981 0.356509 1.8396% 1896 2.754313 0.363067 1.8755% 1895
2.703606 0.369876 1.9114% 1894 2.652899 0.376946 1.9486% 1893 2.602191 0.384291
1.9858% 1892 2.551523 0.391923 2.0276% 1891 2.500816 0.399869 2.6465% 1890 2.436338
0.410452 1.5328% 1889 2.399557 0.416744 2.0811% 1888 2.350637 0.425417 2.1599% 1887
2.300940 0.434605 2.2075% 1886 2.251243 0.444199 2.2592% 1885 2.201508 0.454234

235

2.3095% 1884 2.151811 0.464725 2.3641% 1883 2.102114 0.475712 2.4214% 1882 2.052417
0.487230 2.4815% 1881 2.002720 0.499321 3.7644% 1880 1.930065 0.518117 0.9432% 1879
1.912030 0.523004 2.1464% 1878 1.871853 0.534230 2.1913% 1877 1.831714 0.545937
2.2426% 1876 1.791537 0.558180 2.2941% 1875 1.751360 0.570985 2.3456% 1874 1.711222
0.584378 2.4043% 1873 1.671044 0.598428 2.4635% 1872 1.630867 0.613171 2.5258% 1871
1.590690 0.628658 5.9947% 1870 1.500726 0.666344 -1.0968% 1869 1.517369 0.659036
2.1930% 1868 1.484807 0.673488 2.2394% 1867 1.452285 0.688570 2.2935% 1866 1.419723
0.704363 2.3445% 1865 1.387201 0.720876 2.4037% 1864 1.354639 0.738204 2.4599% 1863
1.322117 0.756363 2.5250% 1862 1.289555 0.775461 2.5872% 1861 1.257033 0.795524
2.9504% 1860 1.221008 0.818995 2.4012% 1859 1.192376 0.838661 2.7627% 1858 1.160320
0.861831 2.8412% 1857 1.128264 0.886317 2.9243% 1856 1.096208 0.912236 3.0161% 1855
1.064113 0.939750 3.1061% 1854 1.032056 0.968939 3.2056% 1853 1.000000 1.000000
3.3118% 1852 0.967944 1.033118 3.4252% 1851 0.935887 1.068505 4.0106% 1850 0.899800
1.111358 2.3254% 1849 0.879352 1.137201 2.7841% 1848 0.855533 1.168862 2.8590% 1847
0.831753 1.202280 2.9432% 1846 0.807973 1.237665 3.0324% 1845 0.784193 1.275196
3.1325% 1844 0.760375 1.315141 3.2284% 1843 0.736595 1.357599 3.3361% 1842 0.712815
1.402889 3.4512% 1841 0.689035 1.451305 3.8105% 1840 0.663743 1.506607 2.3861% 1839
0.648275 1.542556 2.5824% 1838 0.631955 1.582391 2.6573% 1837 0.615597 1.624440
2.7232% 1836 0.599277 1.668677 2.7994% 1835 0.582958 1.715390 2.8871% 1834 0.566599
1.764916 2.9657% 1833 0.550280 1.817257 3.0563% 1832 0.533960 1.872799 3.1604% 1831
0.517602 1.931987 3.4660% 1830 0.500263 1.998949 2.4653% 1829 0.488227 2.048229
2.6804% 1828 0.475482 2.103130 10.3427% 1827 0.430914 2.320649 -4.2314% 1826
0.449953 2.222453 2.9150% 1825 0.437209 2.287238 3.0026% 1824 0.424464 2.355914
3.0955% 1823 0.411719 2.428841 3.1944% 1822 0.398974 2.506428 3.3102% 1821 0.386191
2.589395 3.2277% 1820 0.374115 2.672974 2.6573% 1819 0.364431 2.744003 2.6261% 1818
0.355106 2.816063 2.6969% 1817 0.345780 2.892010 2.7717% 1816 0.336455 2.972168
2.8507% 1815 0.327129 3.056895 2.9343% 1814 0.317804 3.146595 3.0231% 1813 0.308478
3.241718 3.1039% 1812 0.299192 3.342338 3.2172% 1811 0.289866 3.449866 3.0969% 1810
0.281159 3.556705 2.9144% 1809 0.273197 3.660361 2.8225% 1808 0.265698 3.763674
2.9199% 1807 0.258160 3.873570 2.9918% 1806 0.250661 3.989459 3.0841% 1805 0.243161
4.112496 3.1822% 1804 0.235662 4.243364 3.2868% 1803 0.228163 4.382834 3.3985% 1802
0.220664 4.531784 3.5180% 1801 0.213164 4.691214 3.3999% 1800 0.206155 4.850713
2.8419% 1799 0.200459 4.988564 2.7485% 1798 0.195096 5.125672 2.8261% 1797 0.189734
5.270530 3.7832% 1796 0.182818 5.469926 2.1272% 1795 0.179010 5.586282 3.0879% 1794
0.173648 5.758783 3.1625% 1793 0.168325 5.940905 3.2904% 1792 0.162962 6.136385
3.4024% 1791 0.157600 6.345168 3.2296% 1790 0.152670 6.550089 41.3145% 1780
0.108035 9.256222 29.4353% 1770 0.083467 11.980820 83.4728% 1750 0.045493 21.981551
29.2845% 1740 0.035188 28.418728 94.2514% 1720 0.018115 55.203775 85.8111% 1700
0.009749 102.574731 19.2490% 1690 0.008175 122.319392 88.0250% 1670 0.004348
229.991063

BASE YEAR: 1852

YEAR BYEAR/AYEAR AYEAR/BYEAR GROWTH%

2009 12.100291 0.082643 8.2857% 2001 11.174417 0.089490 1.0000% 2000
11.063778 0.090385 1.0000% 1999 10.954236 0.091289 1.0000% 1998 10.845778 0.092202
1.0000% 1997 10.738394 0.093124 1.0000% 1996 10.632073 0.094055 1.0000% 1995
10.526805 0.094996 0.9992% 1994 10.422660 0.095945 1.0008% 1993 10.319385 0.096905
1.0000% 1992 10.217213 0.097874 0.9295% 1991 10.123118 0.098784 1.2505% 1990
9.998091 0.100019 0.7224% 1989 9.926378 0.100742 1.1077% 1988 9.817631 0.101858
0.8834% 1987 9.731665 0.102757 0.5594% 1986 9.677532 0.103332 1.3056% 1985 9.552808
0.104681 0.7673% 1984 9.480069 0.105484 0.8149% 1983 9.403436 0.106344 0.9737% 1982
9.312753 0.107380 0.9508% 1981 9.225041 0.108401 0.9031% 1980 9.142479 0.109380
2.2701% 1979 8.939545 0.111863 1.0042% 1978 8.850668 0.112986 0.9896% 1977 8.763940
0.114104 0.9103% 1976 8.684878 0.115143 0.8394% 1975 8.612581 0.116109 0.9042% 1974
8.535406 0.117159 1.1568% 1973 8.437799 0.118514 0.9427% 1972 8.358998 0.119632
0.7426% 1971 8.297379 0.120520 1.4697% 1970 8.177195 0.122291 0.6968% 1969 8.120609
0.123143 0.8565% 1968 8.051644 0.124198 1.5090% 1967 7.931948 0.126072 0.9949% 1966

236

7.853810 0.127327 1.0575% 1965 7.771627 0.128673 1.1300% 1964 7.684788 0.130127 1.5537% 1963 7.567219 0.132149 1.4658% 1962 7.457900 0.134086 1.5364% 1961 7.345048 0.136146 2.1586% 1960 7.189846 0.139085 -1.6655% 1959 7.311619 0.136769 4.3080% 1958 7.009644 0.142661 2.1130% 1957 6.864598 0.145675 1.9895% 1956 6.730691 0.148573 2.1231% 1955 6.590763 0.151727 1.4496% 1954 6.496588 0.153927 2.1573% 1953 6.359399 0.157248 1.2298% 1952 6.282144 0.159181 1.6814% 1951 6.178265 0.161858 1.6233% 1950 6.079576 0.164485 1.4265% 1949 5.994069 0.166832 1.7790% 1948 5.889296 0.169800 1.8242% 1947 5.783790 0.172897 -2.6320% 1946 5.940137 0.168346 3.1768% 1945 5.757241 0.173694 6.4754% 1944 5.407108 0.184942 -0.3437% 1943 5.425755 0.184306 0.6562% 1942 5.390382 0.185516 0.6633% 1941 5.354863 0.186746 -5.6614% 1940 5.676218 0.176174 8.0381% 1939 5.253904 0.190335 0.8126% 1938 5.211553 0.191881 0.7762% 1937 5.171410 0.193371 0.6029% 1936 5.140420 0.194537 0.5244% 1935 5.113604 0.195557 -3.0364% 1934 5.273734 0.189619 4.6271% 1933 5.040504 0.198393 1.3921% 1932 4.971298 0.201155 -0.2051% 1931 4.981514 0.200742 0.8886% 1930 4.937638 0.202526 1.0126% 1929 4.888142 0.204577 1.1526% 1928 4.832443 0.206935 1.2160% 1927 4.774387 0.209451 1.4086% 1926 4.708070 0.212401 1.7667% 1925 4.626337 0.216154 1.4465% 1924 4.560371 0.219280 1.7700% 1923 4.481058 0.223162 1.6165% 1922 4.409773 0.226769 1.3736% 1921 4.350019 0.229884 2.3393% 1920 4.250584 0.235262 1.3140% 1919 4.195456 0.238353 0.7676% 1918 4.163495 0.240183 0.3870% 1917 4.147445 0.241112 1.3274% 1916 4.093111 0.244313 1.4083% 1915 4.036269 0.247754 1.4458% 1914 3.978744 0.251336 1.9424% 1913 3.902934 0.256217 1.9857% 1912 3.826944 0.261305 1.5634% 1911 3.768034 0.265390 1.8169% 1910 3.700794 0.270212 1.8781% 1909 3.632572 0.275287 2.0082% 1908 3.561057 0.280815 1.9603% 1907 3.492594 0.286320 1.8264% 1906 3.429951 0.291549 1.9357% 1905 3.364819 0.297193 2.0148% 1904 3.298362 0.303181 2.1335% 1903 3.229461 0.309649 1.8151% 1902 3.171886 0.315270 1.8943% 1901 3.112917 0.321242 3.0255% 1900 3.021501 0.330961 0.6278% 1899 3.002649 0.333039 1.7757% 1898 2.950263 0.338953 1.8078% 1897 2.897876 0.345080 1.8396% 1896 2.845530 0.351428 1.8755% 1895 2.793144 0.358020 1.9114% 1894 2.740757 0.364863 1.9486% 1893 2.688371 0.371973 1.9858% 1892 2.636024 0.379359 2.0276% 1891 2.583638 0.387051 2.6465% 1890 2.517024 0.397295 1.5328% 1889 2.479025 0.403384 2.0811% 1888 2.428485 0.411779 2.1599% 1887 2.377143 0.420673 2.2075% 1886 2.325800 0.429960 2.2592% 1885 2.274417 0.439673 2.3095% 1884 2.223074 0.449828 2.3641% 1883 2.171731 0.460462 2.4214% 1882 2.120389 0.471612 2.4815% 1881 2.069046 0.483315 3.7644% 1880 1.993984 0.501508 0.9432% 1879 1.975352 0.506239 2.1464% 1878 1.933844 0.517105 2.1913% 1877 1.892377 0.528436 2.2426% 1876 1.850869 0.540287 2.2941% 1875 1.809361 0.552681 2.3456% 1874 1.767894 0.565645 2.4043% 1873 1.726586 0.579245 2.4635% 1872 1.684878 0.593515 2.5258% 1871 1.643370 0.608506 5.9947% 1870 1.550427 0.644983 -1.0968% 1869 1.567621 0.637909 2.1930% 1868 1.533981 0.651899 2.2394% 1867 1.500381 0.666497 2.2935% 1866 1.466742 0.681783 2.3445% 1865 1.433142 0.697768 2.4037% 1864 1.399502 0.714540 2.4599% 1863 1.365903 0.732117 2.5250% 1862 1.332263 0.750603 2.5872% 1861 1.298663 0.770023 2.9504% 1860 1.261445 0.792741 2.4012% 1859 1.231865 0.811777 2.7627% 1858 1.198748 0.834204 2.8412% 1857 1.165630 0.857905 2.9243% 1856 1.132512 0.882993 3.0161% 1855 1.099354 0.909625 3.1061% 1854 1.066236 0.937879 3.2056% 1853 1.033118 0.967944 3.3118% 1852 1.000000 1.000000 3.4252% 1851 0.966882 1.034252 4.0106% 1850 0.929600 1.075732 2.3254% 1849 0.908474 1.100747 2.7841% 1848 0.883867 1.131392 2.8590% 1847 0.859299 1.163739 2.9432% 1846 0.834732 1.197990 3.0324% 1845 0.810164 1.234318 3.1325% 1844 0.785557 1.272983 3.2284% 1843 0.760989 1.314079 3.3361% 1842 0.736422 1.357918 3.4512% 1841 0.711854 1.404782 3.8105% 1840 0.685725 1.458311 2.3861% 1839 0.669744 1.493107 2.5824% 1838 0.652884 1.531665 2.6573% 1837 0.635984 1.572366 2.7232% 1836 0.619124 1.615185 2.7994% 1835 0.602264 1.660401 2.8871% 1834 0.585364 1.708339 2.9657% 1833 0.568504 1.759003 3.0563% 1832 0.551644 1.812764 3.1604% 1831 0.534744 1.870055 3.4660% 1830 0.516831 1.934870 2.4653% 1829 0.504396 1.982571 2.6804% 1828 0.491229 2.035711 10.3427% 1827 0.445185 2.246258 -4.2314% 1826 0.464855 2.151209 2.9150% 1825 0.451688 2.213918 3.0026% 1824 0.438521 2.280392 3.0955% 1823 0.425354 2.350982 3.1944% 1822 0.412187 2.426081 3.3102% 1821 0.398980 2.506389 3.2277% 1820 0.386505 2.587289 2.6573% 1819 0.376500 2.656040 2.6261% 1818

237

0.366866 2.725791 2.6969% 1817 0.357232 2.799303 2.7717% 1816 0.347597 2.876891
2.8507% 1815 0.337963 2.958902 2.9343% 1814 0.328329 3.045727 3.0231% 1813 0.318695
3.137801 3.1039% 1812 0.309100 3.235195 3.2172% 1811 0.299466 3.339276 3.0969% 1810
0.290470 3.442691 2.9144% 1809 0.282245 3.543024 2.8225% 1808 0.274497 3.643024
2.9199% 1807 0.266709 3.749398 2.9918% 1806 0.258962 3.861572 3.0841% 1805 0.251214
3.980665 3.1822% 1804 0.243467 4.107337 3.2868% 1803 0.235719 4.242337 3.3985% 1802
0.227972 4.386512 3.5180% 1801 0.220224 4.540831 3.3999% 1800 0.212983 4.695217
2.8419% 1799 0.207097 4.828649 2.7485% 1798 0.201558 4.961362 2.8261% 1797 0.196018
5.101577 3.7832% 1796 0.188872 5.294580 2.1272% 1795 0.184938 5.407206 3.0879% 1794
0.179399 5.574178 3.1625% 1793 0.173899 5.750462 3.2904% 1792 0.168359 5.939676
3.4024% 1791 0.162820 6.141765 3.2296% 1790 0.157726 6.340117 41.3145% 1780
0.111613 8.959502 29.4353% 1770 0.086231 11.596760 83.4728% 1750 0.046999 21.276905
29.2845% 1740 0.036353 27.507730 94.2514% 1720 0.018715 53.434148 85.8111% 1700
0.010072 99.286568 19.2490% 1690 0.008446 118.398289 88.0250% 1670 0.004492
222.618409

BASE YEAR: 1851

YEAR BYEAR/AYEAR AYEAR/BYEAR GROWTH%

2009 12.514753 0.079906 8.2857% 2001 11.557166 0.086526 1.0000% 2000
11.442737 0.087392 1.0000% 1999 11.329443 0.088266 1.0000% 1998 11.217270 0.089148
1.0000% 1997 11.106208 0.090040 1.0000% 1996 10.996246 0.090940 1.0000% 1995
10.887372 0.091850 0.9992% 1994 10.779659 0.092767 1.0008% 1993 10.672848 0.093696
1.0000% 1992 10.567176 0.094633 0.9295% 1991 10.469858 0.095512 1.2505% 1990
10.340548 0.096707 0.7224% 1989 10.266379 0.097405 1.1077% 1988 10.153907 0.098484
0.8834% 1987 10.064996 0.099354 0.5594% 1986 10.009009 0.099910 1.3056% 1985
9.880013 0.101214 0.7673% 1984 9.804783 0.101991 0.8149% 1983 9.725525 0.102822
0.9737% 1982 9.631736 0.103823 0.9508% 1981 9.541020 0.104811 0.9031% 1980 9.455629
0.105757 2.2701% 1979 9.245744 0.108158 1.0042% 1978 9.153824 0.109244 0.9896% 1977
9.064124 0.110325 0.9103% 1976 8.982355 0.111329 0.8394% 1975 8.907581 0.112264
0.9042% 1974 8.827763 0.113279 1.1568% 1973 8.726812 0.114589 0.9427% 1972 8.645313
0.115670 0.7426% 1971 8.581583 0.116529 1.4697% 1970 8.457283 0.118241 0.6968% 1969
8.398759 0.119065 0.8565% 1968 8.327431 0.120085 1.5090% 1967 8.203635 0.121897
0.9949% 1966 8.122820 0.123110 1.0575% 1965 8.037823 0.124412 1.1300% 1964 7.948009
0.125818 1.5537% 1963 7.826414 0.127772 1.4658% 1962 7.713350 0.129645 1.5364% 1961
7.596633 0.131637 2.1586% 1960 7.436114 0.134479 -1.6655% 1959 7.562059 0.132239
4.3080% 1958 7.249741 0.137936 2.1130% 1957 7.099726 0.140851 1.9895% 1956 6.961233
0.143653 2.1231% 1955 6.816512 0.146703 1.4496% 1954 6.719111 0.148829 2.1573% 1953
6.577223 0.152040 1.2298% 1952 6.497322 0.153910 1.6814% 1951 6.389884 0.156497
1.6233% 1950 6.287816 0.159038 1.4265% 1949 6.199379 0.161306 1.7790% 1948 6.091018
0.164176 1.8242% 1947 5.981898 0.167171 -2.6320% 1946 6.143600 0.162771 3.1768%
1945 5.954439 0.167942 6.4754% 1944 5.592314 0.178817 -0.3437% 1943 5.611599
0.178202 0.6562% 1942 5.575015 0.179372 0.6633% 1941 5.538279 0.180561 -5.6614%
1940 5.870642 0.170339 8.0381% 1939 5.433862 0.184031 0.8126% 1938 5.390061 0.185527
0.7762% 1937 5.348543 0.186967 0.6029% 1936 5.316491 0.188094 0.5244% 1935 5.288757
0.189080 -3.0364% 1934 5.454372 0.183339 4.6271% 1933 5.213153 0.191822 1.3921%
1932 5.141576 0.194493 -0.2051% 1931 5.152142 0.194094 0.8886% 1930 5.106764
0.195819 1.0126% 1929 5.055572 0.197802 1.1526% 1928 4.997966 0.200081 1.2160% 1927
4.937920 0.202514 1.4086% 1926 4.869332 0.205367 1.7667% 1925 4.784799 0.208995
1.4465% 1924 4.716574 0.212018 1.7700% 1923 4.634544 0.215771 1.6165% 1922 4.560817
0.219259 1.3736% 1921 4.499017 0.222271 2.3393% 1920 4.396177 0.227470 1.3140% 1919
4.339160 0.230459 0.7676% 1918 4.306104 0.232228 0.3870% 1917 4.289504 0.233127
1.3274% 1916 4.233310 0.236222 1.4083% 1915 4.174520 0.239548 1.4458% 1914 4.115025
0.243012 1.9424% 1913 4.036619 0.247732 1.9857% 1912 3.958025 0.252651 1.5634% 1911
3.897098 0.256601 1.8169% 1910 3.827554 0.261263 1.8781% 1909 3.756996 0.266170
2.0082% 1908 3.683032 0.271515 1.9603% 1907 3.612223 0.276838 1.8264% 1906 3.547434
0.281894 1.9357% 1905 3.480071 0.287350 2.0148% 1904 3.411339 0.293140 2.1335% 1903
3.340077 0.299394 1.8151% 1902 3.280531 0.304829 1.8943% 1901 3.219541 0.310603

3.0255% 1900 3.124995 0.320001 0.6278% 1899 3.105497 0.322010 1.7757% 1898 3.051316
0.327727 1.8078% 1897 2.997135 0.333652 1.8396% 1896 2.942996 0.339790 1.8755% 1895
2.888815 0.346163 1.9114% 1894 2.834634 0.352779 1.9486% 1893 2.780453 0.359654
1.9858% 1892 2.726314 0.366796 2.0276% 1891 2.672133 0.374233 2.6465% 1890 2.603238
0.384137 1.5328% 1889 2.563938 0.390025 2.0811% 1888 2.511667 0.398142 2.1599% 1887
2.458565 0.406741 2.2075% 1886 2.405464 0.415720 2.2592% 1885 2.352321 0.425112
2.3095% 1884 2.299219 0.434930 2.3641% 1883 2.246118 0.445213 2.4214% 1882 2.193017
0.455993 2.4815% 1881 2.139915 0.467308 3.7644% 1880 2.062283 0.484900 0.9432% 1879
2.043013 0.489473 2.1464% 1878 2.000083 0.499979 2.1913% 1877 1.957195 0.510935
2.2426% 1876 1.914266 0.522394 2.2941% 1875 1.871336 0.534378 2.3456% 1874 1.828448
0.546912 2.4043% 1873 1.785519 0.560061 2.4635% 1872 1.742589 0.573859 2.5258% 1871
1.699660 0.588353 5.9947% 1870 1.603533 0.623623 -1.0968% 1869 1.621315 0.616783
2.1930% 1868 1.586523 0.630309 2.2394% 1867 1.551773 0.644424 2.2935% 1866 1.516981
0.659204 2.3445% 1865 1.482230 0.674659 2.4037% 1864 1.447438 0.690876 2.4599% 1863
1.412688 0.707870 2.5250% 1862 1.377896 0.725744 2.5872% 1861 1.343145 0.744521
2.9504% 1860 1.304653 0.766487 2.4012% 1859 1.274060 0.784893 2.7627% 1858 1.239807
0.806577 2.8412% 1857 1.205555 0.829493 2.9243% 1856 1.171303 0.853750 3.0161% 1855
1.137009 0.879500 3.1061% 1854 1.102757 0.906818 3.2056% 1853 1.068505 0.935887
3.3118% 1852 1.034252 0.966882 3.4252% 1851 1.000000 1.000000 4.0106% 1850 0.961440
1.040106 2.3254% 1849 0.939591 1.064292 2.7841% 1848 0.914141 1.093923 2.8590% 1847
0.888732 1.125199 2.9432% 1846 0.863323 1.158315 3.0324% 1845 0.837914 1.193440
3.1325% 1844 0.812464 1.230824 3.2284% 1843 0.787055 1.270560 3.3361% 1842 0.761646
1.312946 3.4512% 1841 0.736237 1.358259 3.8105% 1840 0.709212 1.410015 2.3861% 1839
0.692685 1.443659 2.5824% 1838 0.675247 1.480939 2.6573% 1837 0.657768 1.520293
2.7232% 1836 0.640330 1.561694 2.7994% 1835 0.622893 1.605412 2.8871% 1834 0.605414
1.651762 2.9657% 1833 0.587976 1.700748 3.0563% 1832 0.570539 1.752729 3.1604% 1831
0.553060 1.808123 3.4660% 1830 0.534533 1.870791 2.4653% 1829 0.521672 1.916912
2.6804% 1828 0.508054 1.968293 10.3427% 1827 0.460433 2.171867 -4.2314% 1826
0.480777 2.079965 2.9150% 1825 0.467159 2.140597 3.0026% 1824 0.453541 2.204870
3.0955% 1823 0.439924 2.273122 3.1944% 1822 0.426306 2.345734 3.3102% 1821 0.412646
2.423383 3.2277% 1820 0.399744 2.501603 2.6573% 1819 0.389396 2.568078 2.6261% 1818
0.379432 2.635518 2.6969% 1817 0.369468 2.706596 2.7717% 1816 0.359503 2.781615
2.8507% 1815 0.349539 2.860910 2.9343% 1814 0.339575 2.944859 3.0231% 1813 0.329611
3.033883 3.1039% 1812 0.319688 3.128052 3.2172% 1811 0.309723 3.228686 3.0969% 1810
0.300420 3.328676 2.9144% 1809 0.291912 3.425686 2.8225% 1808 0.283899 3.522375
2.9199% 1807 0.275845 3.625226 2.9918% 1806 0.267832 3.733685 3.0841% 1805 0.259819
3.848833 3.1822% 1804 0.251806 3.971311 3.2868% 1803 0.243793 4.101839 3.3985% 1802
0.235780 4.241240 3.5180% 1801 0.227767 4.390448 3.3999% 1800 0.220278 4.539721
2.8419% 1799 0.214191 4.668734 2.7485% 1798 0.208461 4.797052 2.8261% 1797 0.202732
4.932623 3.7832% 1796 0.195342 5.119235 2.1272% 1795 0.191273 5.228131 3.0879% 1794
0.185543 5.389573 3.1625% 1793 0.179856 5.560018 3.2904% 1792 0.174126 5.742966
3.4024% 1791 0.168397 5.938363 3.2296% 1790 0.163128 6.130146 41.3145% 1780
0.115436 8.662782 29.4353% 1770 0.089185 11.212700 83.4728% 1750 0.048609 20.572258
29.2845% 1740 0.037599 26.596731 94.2514% 1720 0.019356 51.664522 85.8111% 1700
0.010417 95.998406 19.2490% 1690 0.008735 114.477186 88.0250% 1670 0.004646
215.245755

BASE YEAR: 1850

YEAR BYEAR/AYEAR AYEAR/BYEAR GROWTH%

2009 13.016671 0.076825 8.2857% 2001 12.020678 0.083190 1.0000% 2000
11.901660 0.084022 1.0000% 1999 11.783822 0.084862 1.0000% 1998 11.667151 0.085711
1.0000% 1997 11.551634 0.086568 1.0000% 1996 11.437262 0.087434 1.0000% 1995
11.324021 0.088308 0.9992% 1994 11.211989 0.089190 1.0008% 1993 11.100893 0.090083
1.0000% 1992 10.990984 0.090984 0.9295% 1991 10.889763 0.091829 1.2505% 1990
10.755266 0.092978 0.7224% 1989 10.678123 0.093649 1.1077% 1988 10.561140 0.094687
0.8834% 1987 10.468664 0.095523 0.5594% 1986 10.410431 0.096058 1.3056% 1985
10.276262 0.097312 0.7673% 1984 10.198014 0.098058 0.8149% 1983 10.115578 0.098857

239

0.9737% 1982 10.018027 0.099820 0.9508% 1981 9.923672 0.100769 0.9031% 1980
9.834857 0.101679 2.2701% 1979 9.616555 0.103987 1.0042% 1978 9.520948 0.105032
0.9896% 1977 9.427651 0.106071 0.9103% 1976 9.342602 0.107037 0.8394% 1975 9.264829
0.107935 0.9042% 1974 9.181810 0.108911 1.1568% 1973 9.076810 0.110171 0.9427% 1972
8.992042 0.111209 0.7426% 1971 8.925756 0.112035 1.4697% 1970 8.796471 0.113682
0.6968% 1969 8.735600 0.114474 0.8565% 1968 8.661411 0.115455 1.5090% 1967 8.532650
0.117197 0.9949% 1966 8.448595 0.118363 1.0575% 1965 8.360188 0.119615 1.1300% 1964
8.266772 0.120966 1.5537% 1963 8.140300 0.122846 1.4658% 1962 8.022702 0.124646
1.5364% 1961 7.901304 0.126561 2.1586% 1960 7.734347 0.129293 -1.6655% 1959
7.865343 0.127140 4.3080% 1958 7.540499 0.132617 2.1130% 1957 7.384468 0.135419
1.9895% 1956 7.240420 0.138114 2.1231% 1955 7.089895 0.141046 1.4496% 1954 6.988588
0.143090 2.1573% 1953 6.841010 0.146177 1.2298% 1952 6.757904 0.147975 1.6814% 1951
6.646157 0.150463 1.6233% 1950 6.539995 0.152905 1.4265% 1949 6.448012 0.155087
1.7790% 1948 6.335304 0.157846 1.8242% 1947 6.221809 0.160725 -2.6320% 1946
6.389996 0.156495 3.1768% 1945 6.193248 0.161466 6.4754% 1944 5.816599 0.171922 -
0.3437% 1943 5.836659 0.171331 0.6562% 1942 5.798607 0.172455 0.6633% 1941 5.760398
0.173599 -5.6614% 1940 6.106090 0.163771 8.0381% 1939 5.651793 0.176935 0.8126%
1938 5.606235 0.178373 0.7762% 1937 5.563052 0.179757 0.6029% 1936 5.529714 0.180841
0.5244% 1935 5.500868 0.181789 -3.0364% 1934 5.673125 0.176270 4.6271% 1933
5.422232 0.184426 1.3921% 1932 5.347784 0.186993 -0.2051% 1931 5.358774 0.186610
0.8886% 1930 5.311576 0.188268 1.0126% 1929 5.258331 0.190174 1.1526% 1928 5.198414
0.192366 1.2160% 1927 5.135961 0.194706 1.4086% 1926 5.064622 0.197448 1.7667% 1925
4.976699 0.200936 1.4465% 1924 4.905737 0.203843 1.7700% 1923 4.820417 0.207451
1.6165% 1922 4.743734 0.210804 1.3736% 1921 4.679455 0.213700 2.3393% 1920 4.572490
0.218699 1.3140% 1919 4.513186 0.221573 0.7676% 1918 4.478805 0.223274 0.3870% 1917
4.461539 0.224138 1.3274% 1916 4.403091 0.227113 1.4083% 1915 4.341944 0.230312
1.4458% 1914 4.280063 0.233641 1.9424% 1913 4.198512 0.238180 1.9857% 1912 4.116766
0.242909 1.5634% 1911 4.053395 0.246707 1.8169% 1910 3.981063 0.251189 1.8781% 1909
3.907674 0.255907 2.0082% 1908 3.830743 0.261046 1.9603% 1907 3.757095 0.266163
1.8264% 1906 3.689708 0.271024 1.9357% 1905 3.619643 0.276270 2.0148% 1904 3.548154
0.281837 2.1335% 1903 3.474034 0.287850 1.8151% 1902 3.412100 0.293075 1.8943% 1901
3.348664 0.298627 3.0255% 1900 3.250326 0.307661 0.6278% 1899 3.230046 0.309593
1.7757% 1898 3.173692 0.315090 1.8078% 1897 3.117339 0.320786 1.8396% 1896 3.061028
0.326688 1.8755% 1895 3.004674 0.332815 1.9114% 1894 2.948320 0.339176 1.9486% 1893
2.891966 0.345785 1.9858% 1892 2.835656 0.352652 2.0276% 1891 2.779302 0.359803
2.6465% 1890 2.707644 0.369325 1.5328% 1889 2.666707 0.374986 2.0811% 1888 2.612400
0.382790 2.1599% 1887 2.557168 0.391058 2.2075% 1886 2.501937 0.399690 2.2592% 1885
2.446663 0.408720 2.3095% 1884 2.391432 0.418159 2.3641% 1883 2.336201 0.428045
2.4214% 1882 2.280970 0.438410 2.4815% 1881 2.225739 0.449289 3.7644% 1880 2.144993
0.466202 0.9432% 1879 2.124950 0.470599 2.1464% 1878 2.080298 0.480700 2.1913% 1877
2.035690 0.491234 2.2426% 1876 1.991039 0.502250 2.2941% 1875 1.946388 0.513772
2.3456% 1874 1.901780 0.525823 2.4043% 1873 1.857129 0.538466 2.4635% 1872 1.812477
0.551731 2.5258% 1871 1.767826 0.565666 5.9947% 1870 1.667844 0.599576 -1.0968%
1869 1.686340 0.593000 2.1930% 1868 1.650152 0.606005 2.2394% 1867 1.614008 0.619576
2.2935% 1866 1.577821 0.633785 2.3445% 1865 1.541677 0.648644 2.4037% 1864 1.505489
0.664236 2.4599% 1863 1.469345 0.680575 2.5250% 1862 1.433158 0.697760 2.5872% 1861
1.397014 0.715813 2.9504% 1860 1.356977 0.736932 2.4012% 1859 1.325157 0.754627
2.7627% 1858 1.289531 0.775476 2.8412% 1857 1.253905 0.797508 2.9243% 1856 1.218279
0.820830 3.0161% 1855 1.182610 0.845587 3.1061% 1854 1.146984 0.871852 3.2056% 1853
1.111358 0.899800 3.3118% 1852 1.075732 0.929600 3.4252% 1851 1.040106 0.961440
4.0106% 1850 1.000000 1.000000 2.3254% 1849 0.977275 1.023254 2.7841% 1848 0.950804
1.051742 2.8590% 1847 0.924376 1.081811 2.9432% 1846 0.897948 1.113651 3.0324% 1845
0.871520 1.147421 3.1325% 1844 0.845048 1.183364 3.2284% 1843 0.818620 1.221567
3.3361% 1842 0.792192 1.262320 3.4512% 1841 0.765764 1.305885 3.8105% 1840 0.737656
1.355645 2.3861% 1839 0.720465 1.387992 2.5824% 1838 0.702329 1.423835 2.6573% 1837
0.684148 1.461671 2.7232% 1836 0.666012 1.501475 2.7994% 1835 0.647875 1.543508

240

2.8871% 1834 0.629695 1.588071 2.9657% 1833 0.611558 1.635168 3.0563% 1832 0.593421
1.685144 3.1604% 1831 0.575241 1.738402 3.4660% 1830 0.555971 1.798654 2.4653% 1829
0.542595 1.842997 2.6804% 1828 0.528431 1.892396 10.3427% 1827 0.478900 2.088120 -
4.2314% 1826 0.500059 1.999763 2.9150% 1825 0.485895 2.058057 3.0026% 1824 0.471731
2.119851 3.0955% 1823 0.457567 2.185471 3.1944% 1822 0.443403 2.255284 3.3102% 1821
0.429196 2.329938 3.2277% 1820 0.415776 2.405142 2.6573% 1819 0.405013 2.469054
2.6261% 1818 0.394650 2.533894 2.6969% 1817 0.384286 2.602231 2.7717% 1816 0.373922
2.674357 2.8507% 1815 0.363558 2.750594 2.9343% 1814 0.353194 2.831306 3.0231% 1813
0.342830 2.916898 3.1039% 1812 0.332509 3.007436 3.2172% 1811 0.322145 3.104190
3.0969% 1810 0.312468 3.200324 2.9144% 1809 0.303620 3.293593 2.8225% 1808 0.295285
3.386554 2.9199% 1807 0.286908 3.485439 2.9918% 1806 0.278574 3.589715 3.0841% 1805
0.270239 3.700424 3.1822% 1804 0.261905 3.818179 3.2868% 1803 0.253571 3.943674
3.3985% 1802 0.245236 4.077699 3.5180% 1801 0.236902 4.221155 3.3999% 1800 0.229112
4.364672 2.8419% 1799 0.222781 4.488710 2.7485% 1798 0.216822 4.612080 2.8261% 1797
0.210863 4.742424 3.7832% 1796 0.203176 4.921839 2.1272% 1795 0.198944 5.026537
3.0879% 1794 0.192985 5.181753 3.1625% 1793 0.187069 5.345627 3.2904% 1792 0.181110
5.521520 3.4024% 1791 0.175150 5.709382 3.2296% 1790 0.169671 5.893770 41.3145%
1780 0.120066 8.328749 29.4353% 1770 0.092761 10.780343 83.4728% 1750 0.050559
19.779001 29.2845% 1740 0.039107 25.571173 94.2514% 1720 0.020132 49.672360
85.8111% 1700 0.010835 92.296748 19.2490% 1690 0.009086 110.062994 88.0250% 1670
0.004832 206.945970

BASE YEAR: 1849

YEAR BYEAR/AYEAR AYEAR/BYEAR GROWTH%

2009 13.319356 0.075079 8.2857% 2001 12.300203 0.081299 1.0000% 2000
12.178418 0.082112 1.0000% 1999 12.057839 0.082934 1.0000% 1998 11.938455 0.083763
1.0000% 1997 11.820252 0.084601 1.0000% 1996 11.703220 0.085447 1.0000% 1995
11.587347 0.086301 0.9992% 1994 11.472709 0.087163 1.0008% 1993 11.359030 0.088036
1.0000% 1992 11.246564 0.088916 0.9295% 1991 11.142990 0.089743 1.2505% 1990
11.005366 0.090865 0.7224% 1989 10.926428 0.091521 1.1077% 1988 10.806725 0.092535
0.8834% 1987 10.712098 0.093352 0.5594% 1986 10.652512 0.093875 1.3056% 1985
10.515222 0.095100 0.7673% 1984 10.435155 0.095830 0.8149% 1983 10.350802 0.096611
0.9737% 1982 10.250983 0.097552 0.9508% 1981 10.154434 0.098479 0.9031% 1980
10.063554 0.099368 2.2701% 1979 9.840175 0.101624 1.0042% 1978 9.742345 0.102645
0.9896% 1977 9.646878 0.103660 0.9103% 1976 9.559852 0.104604 0.8394% 1975 9.480270
0.105482 0.9042% 1974 9.395321 0.106436 1.1568% 1973 9.287879 0.107667 0.9427% 1972
9.201140 0.108682 0.7426% 1971 9.133313 0.109489 1.4697% 1970 9.001021 0.111099
0.6968% 1969 8.938734 0.111873 0.8565% 1968 8.862821 0.112831 1.5090% 1967 8.731066
0.114534 0.9949% 1966 8.645055 0.115673 1.0575% 1965 8.554593 0.116896 1.1300% 1964
8.459005 0.118217 1.5537% 1963 8.329592 0.120054 1.4658% 1962 8.209259 0.121814
1.5364% 1961 8.085038 0.123685 2.1586% 1960 7.914199 0.126355 -1.6655% 1959
8.048241 0.124251 4.3080% 1958 7.715843 0.129603 2.1130% 1957 7.556184 0.132342
1.9895% 1956 7.408787 0.134975 2.1231% 1955 7.254761 0.137841 1.4496% 1954 7.151098
0.139839 2.1573% 1953 7.000088 0.142855 1.2298% 1952 6.915050 0.144612 1.6814% 1951
6.800705 0.147044 1.6233% 1950 6.692074 0.149431 1.4265% 1949 6.597952 0.151562
1.7790% 1948 6.482623 0.154259 1.8242% 1947 6.366488 0.157072 -2.6320% 1946
6.538586 0.152938 3.1768% 1945 6.337264 0.157797 6.4754% 1944 5.951857 0.168015 -
0.3437% 1943 5.972382 0.167437 0.6562% 1942 5.933446 0.168536 0.6633% 1941 5.894348
0.169654 -5.6614% 1940 6.248079 0.160049 8.0381% 1939 5.783218 0.172914 0.8126%
1938 5.736600 0.174319 0.7762% 1937 5.692413 0.175672 0.6029% 1936 5.658301 0.176732
0.5244% 1935 5.628784 0.177658 -3.0364% 1934 5.805046 0.172264 4.6271% 1933
5.548319 0.180235 1.3921% 1932 5.472140 0.182744 -0.2051% 1931 5.483386 0.182369
0.8886% 1930 5.435090 0.183990 1.0126% 1929 5.380606 0.185853 1.1526% 1928 5.319297
0.187995 1.2160% 1927 5.255391 0.190281 1.4086% 1926 5.182393 0.192961 1.7667% 1925
5.092425 0.196370 1.4465% 1924 5.019814 0.199211 1.7700% 1923 4.932510 0.202737
1.6165% 1922 4.854043 0.206014 1.3736% 1921 4.788269 0.208844 2.3393% 1920 4.678817
0.213729 1.3140% 1919 4.618134 0.216538 0.7676% 1918 4.582954 0.218200 0.3870% 1917

4.565287 0.219044 1.3274% 1916 4.505479 0.221952 1.4083% 1915 4.442910 0.225078
1.4458% 1914 4.379590 0.228332 1.9424% 1913 4.296142 0.232767 1.9857% 1912 4.212496
0.237389 1.5634% 1911 4.147651 0.241100 1.8169% 1910 4.073637 0.245481 1.8781% 1909
3.998542 0.250091 2.0082% 1908 3.919822 0.255114 1.9603% 1907 3.844461 0.260114
1.8264% 1906 3.775507 0.264865 1.9357% 1905 3.703813 0.269992 2.0148% 1904 3.630661
0.275432 2.1335% 1903 3.554818 0.281308 1.8151% 1902 3.491444 0.286414 1.8943% 1901
3.426533 0.291840 3.0255% 1900 3.325908 0.300670 0.6278% 1899 3.305157 0.302558
1.7757% 1898 3.247492 0.307930 1.8078% 1897 3.189828 0.313497 1.8396% 1896 3.132208
0.319264 1.8755% 1895 3.074544 0.325252 1.9114% 1894 3.016880 0.331468 1.9486% 1893
2.959215 0.337927 1.9858% 1892 2.901595 0.344638 2.0276% 1891 2.843931 0.351626
2.6465% 1890 2.770606 0.360932 1.5328% 1889 2.728779 0.366464 2.0811% 1888 2.673147
0.374091 2.1599% 1887 2.616632 0.382171 2.2075% 1886 2.560117 0.390607 2.2592% 1885
2.503557 0.399432 2.3095% 1884 2.447042 0.408657 2.3641% 1883 2.390526 0.418318
2.4214% 1882 2.334011 0.428447 2.4815% 1881 2.277495 0.439079 3.7644% 1880 2.194872
0.455607 0.9432% 1879 2.174363 0.459905 2.1464% 1878 2.128673 0.469776 2.1913% 1877
2.083028 0.480070 2.2426% 1876 2.037338 0.490837 2.2941% 1875 1.991649 0.502097
2.3456% 1874 1.946003 0.513874 2.4043% 1873 1.900314 0.526229 2.4635% 1872 1.854624
0.539193 2.5258% 1871 1.808935 0.552812 5.9947% 1870 1.706628 0.585951 -1.0968%
1869 1.725553 0.579524 2.1930% 1868 1.688525 0.592233 2.2394% 1867 1.651540 0.605496
2.2935% 1866 1.614511 0.619383 2.3445% 1865 1.577526 0.633904 2.4037% 1864 1.540498
0.649141 2.4599% 1863 1.503513 0.665109 2.5250% 1862 1.466484 0.681903 2.5872% 1861
1.429499 0.699546 2.9504% 1860 1.388532 0.720185 2.4012% 1859 1.355972 0.737478
2.7627% 1858 1.319517 0.757853 2.8412% 1857 1.283063 0.779385 2.9243% 1856 1.246609
0.802176 3.0161% 1855 1.210110 0.826371 3.1061% 1854 1.173656 0.852039 3.2056% 1853
1.137201 0.879352 3.3118% 1852 1.100747 0.908474 3.4252% 1851 1.064292 0.939591
4.0106% 1850 1.023254 0.977275 2.3254% 1849 1.000000 1.000000 2.7841% 1848 0.972913
1.027841 2.8590% 1847 0.945871 1.057227 2.9432% 1846 0.918828 1.088343 3.0324% 1845
0.891786 1.121346 3.1325% 1844 0.864699 1.156472 3.2284% 1843 0.837656 1.193807
3.3361% 1842 0.810614 1.233633 3.4512% 1841 0.783571 1.276208 3.8105% 1840 0.754809
1.324838 2.3861% 1839 0.737219 1.356449 2.5824% 1838 0.718660 1.391478 2.6573% 1837
0.700057 1.428454 2.7232% 1836 0.681499 1.467354 2.7994% 1835 0.662940 1.508432
2.8871% 1834 0.644337 1.551982 2.9657% 1833 0.625779 1.598009 3.0563% 1832 0.607220
1.646849 3.1604% 1831 0.588617 1.698896 3.4660% 1830 0.568900 1.757780 2.4653% 1829
0.555212 1.801114 2.6804% 1828 0.540718 1.849391 10.3427% 1827 0.490036 2.040667 -
4.2314% 1826 0.511688 1.954318 2.9150% 1825 0.497194 2.011287 3.0026% 1824 0.482701
2.071677 3.0955% 1823 0.468207 2.135806 3.1944% 1822 0.453714 2.204032 3.3102% 1821
0.439176 2.276990 3.2277% 1820 0.425444 2.350485 2.6573% 1819 0.414432 2.412944
2.6261% 1818 0.403827 2.476310 2.6969% 1817 0.393222 2.543095 2.7717% 1816 0.382617
2.613581 2.8507% 1815 0.372012 2.688086 2.9343% 1814 0.361407 2.766964 3.0231% 1813
0.350802 2.850611 3.1039% 1812 0.340241 2.939091 3.2172% 1811 0.329636 3.033646
3.0969% 1810 0.319734 3.127596 2.9144% 1809 0.310680 3.218746 2.8225% 1808 0.302152
3.309593 2.9199% 1807 0.293580 3.406231 2.9918% 1806 0.285051 3.508138 3.0841% 1805
0.276523 3.616331 3.1822% 1804 0.267995 3.731410 3.2868% 1803 0.259467 3.854053
3.3985% 1802 0.250939 3.985033 3.5180% 1801 0.242411 4.125228 3.3999% 1800 0.234440
4.265483 2.8419% 1799 0.227962 4.386703 2.7485% 1798 0.221864 4.507269 2.8261% 1797
0.215766 4.634651 3.7832% 1796 0.207901 4.809989 2.1272% 1795 0.203570 4.912307
3.0879% 1794 0.197472 5.063996 3.1625% 1793 0.191419 5.224146 3.2904% 1792 0.185321
5.396042 3.4024% 1791 0.179223 5.579635 3.2296% 1790 0.173616 5.759833 41.3145%
1780 0.122858 8.139476 29.4353% 1770 0.094918 10.535357 83.4728% 1750 0.051734
19.329518 29.2845% 1740 0.040016 24.990062 94.2514% 1720 0.020600 48.543544
85.8111% 1700 0.011087 90.199283 19.2490% 1690 0.009297 107.561787 88.0250% 1670
0.004945 202.243074

BASE YEAR: 1848

YEAR BYEAR/AYEAR AYEAR/BYEAR GROWTH%

2009 13.690178 0.073045 8.2857% 2001 12.642651 0.079097 1.0000% 2000
12.517475 0.079888 1.0000% 1999 12.393540 0.080687 1.0000% 1998 12.270832 0.081494

242

1.0000% 1997 12.149338 0.082309 1.0000% 1996 12.029048 0.083132 1.0000% 1995
11.909948 0.083963 0.9992% 1994 11.792119 0.084802 1.0008% 1993 11.675275 0.085651
1.0000% 1992 11.559678 0.086508 0.9295% 1991 11.453220 0.087312 1.2505% 1990
11.311765 0.088404 0.7224% 1989 11.230629 0.089042 1.1077% 1988 11.107594 0.090028
0.8834% 1987 11.010332 0.090824 0.5594% 1986 10.949087 0.091332 1.3056% 1985
10.807975 0.092524 0.7673% 1984 10.725679 0.093234 0.8149% 1983 10.638977 0.093994
0.9737% 1982 10.536379 0.094909 0.9508% 1981 10.437142 0.095812 0.9031% 1980
10.343732 0.096677 2.2701% 1979 10.114134 0.098872 1.0042% 1978 10.013580 0.099864
0.9896% 1977 9.915456 0.100853 0.9103% 1976 9.826006 0.101771 0.8394% 1975 9.744209
0.102625 0.9042% 1974 9.656894 0.103553 1.1568% 1973 9.546462 0.104751 0.9427% 1972
9.457308 0.105738 0.7426% 1971 9.387592 0.106524 1.4697% 1970 9.251617 0.108089
0.6968% 1969 9.187597 0.108842 0.8565% 1968 9.109569 0.109775 1.5090% 1967 8.974146
0.111431 0.9949% 1966 8.885741 0.112540 1.0575% 1965 8.792760 0.113730 1.1300% 1964
8.694511 0.115015 1.5537% 1963 8.561495 0.116802 1.4658% 1962 8.437812 0.118514
1.5364% 1961 8.310133 0.120335 2.1586% 1960 8.134537 0.122933 -1.6655% 1959
8.272311 0.120885 4.3080% 1958 7.930659 0.126093 2.1130% 1957 7.766555 0.128757
1.9895% 1956 7.615054 0.131319 2.1231% 1955 7.456740 0.134107 1.4496% 1954 7.350191
0.136051 2.1573% 1953 7.194977 0.138986 1.2298% 1952 7.107571 0.140695 1.6814% 1951
6.990042 0.143061 1.6233% 1950 6.878387 0.145383 1.4265% 1949 6.781645 0.147457
1.7790% 1948 6.663105 0.150080 1.8242% 1947 6.543737 0.152818 -2.6320% 1946
6.720626 0.148796 3.1768% 1945 6.513699 0.153523 6.4754% 1944 6.117561 0.163464 -
0.3437% 1943 6.138659 0.162902 0.6562% 1942 6.098638 0.163971 0.6633% 1941 6.058452
0.165059 -5.6614% 1940 6.422031 0.155714 8.0381% 1939 5.944227 0.168230 0.8126%
1938 5.896312 0.169598 0.7762% 1937 5.850895 0.170914 0.6029% 1936 5.815833 0.171944
0.5244% 1935 5.785494 0.172846 -3.0364% 1934 5.966664 0.167598 4.6271% 1933
5.702789 0.175353 1.3921% 1932 5.624489 0.177794 -0.2051% 1931 5.636048 0.177429
0.8886% 1930 5.586407 0.179006 1.0126% 1929 5.530407 0.180819 1.1526% 1928 5.467390
0.182903 1.2160% 1927 5.401705 0.185127 1.4086% 1926 5.326675 0.187734 1.7667% 1925
5.234203 0.191051 1.4465% 1924 5.159570 0.193815 1.7700% 1923 5.069835 0.197245
1.6165% 1922 4.989184 0.200434 1.3736% 1921 4.921579 0.203187 2.3393% 1920 4.809079
0.207940 1.3140% 1919 4.746707 0.210672 0.7676% 1918 4.710547 0.212290 0.3870% 1917
4.692388 0.213111 1.3274% 1916 4.630916 0.215940 1.4083% 1915 4.566605 0.218981
1.4458% 1914 4.501521 0.222147 1.9424% 1913 4.415751 0.226462 1.9857% 1912 4.329776
0.230959 1.5634% 1911 4.263126 0.234570 1.8169% 1910 4.187050 0.238832 1.8781% 1909
4.109865 0.243317 2.0082% 1908 4.028954 0.248203 1.9603% 1907 3.951494 0.253069
1.8264% 1906 3.880620 0.257691 1.9357% 1905 3.806931 0.262679 2.0148% 1904 3.731742
0.267971 2.1335% 1903 3.653788 0.273689 1.8151% 1902 3.588648 0.278656 1.8943% 1901
3.521931 0.283935 3.0255% 1900 3.418504 0.292526 0.6278% 1899 3.397175 0.294362
1.7757% 1898 3.337905 0.299589 1.8078% 1897 3.278636 0.305005 1.8396% 1896 3.219411
0.310616 1.8755% 1895 3.160142 0.316442 1.9114% 1894 3.100872 0.322490 1.9486% 1893
3.041602 0.328774 1.9858% 1892 2.982378 0.335303 2.0276% 1891 2.923108 0.342102
2.6465% 1890 2.847742 0.351155 1.5328% 1889 2.804751 0.356538 2.0811% 1888 2.747570
0.363958 2.1599% 1887 2.689481 0.371819 2.2075% 1886 2.631392 0.380027 2.2592% 1885
2.573258 0.388612 2.3095% 1884 2.515169 0.397588 2.3641% 1883 2.457081 0.406987
2.4214% 1882 2.398992 0.416842 2.4815% 1881 2.340903 0.427186 3.7644% 1880 2.255979
0.443267 0.9432% 1879 2.234899 0.447448 2.1464% 1878 2.187937 0.457052 2.1913% 1877
2.141021 0.467067 2.2426% 1876 2.094059 0.477541 2.2941% 1875 2.047098 0.488496
2.3456% 1874 2.000182 0.499955 2.4043% 1873 1.953220 0.511975 2.4635% 1872 1.906259
0.524588 2.5258% 1871 1.859297 0.537838 5.9947% 1870 1.754142 0.570079 -1.0968%
1869 1.773594 0.563827 2.1930% 1868 1.735535 0.576191 2.2394% 1867 1.697520 0.589095
2.2935% 1866 1.659460 0.602606 2.3445% 1865 1.621446 0.616733 2.4037% 1864 1.583386
0.631558 2.4599% 1863 1.545372 0.647093 2.5250% 1862 1.507312 0.663433 2.5872% 1861
1.469298 0.680597 2.9504% 1860 1.427190 0.700678 2.4012% 1859 1.393723 0.717503
2.7627% 1858 1.356254 0.737325 2.8412% 1857 1.318785 0.758274 2.9243% 1856 1.281315
0.780448 3.0161% 1855 1.243801 0.803987 3.1061% 1854 1.206331 0.828960 3.2056% 1853
1.168862 0.855533 3.3118% 1852 1.131392 0.883867 3.4252% 1851 1.093923 0.914141

4.0106% 1850 1.051742 0.950804 2.3254% 1849 1.027841 0.972913 2.7841% 1848 1.000000
1.000000 2.8590% 1847 0.972205 1.028590 2.9432% 1846 0.944409 1.058863 3.0324% 1845
0.916614 1.090972 3.1325% 1844 0.888773 1.125147 3.2284% 1843 0.860977 1.161471
3.3361% 1842 0.833182 1.200218 3.4512% 1841 0.805387 1.241640 3.8105% 1840 0.775824
1.288952 2.3861% 1839 0.757744 1.319708 2.5824% 1838 0.738668 1.353788 2.6573% 1837
0.719548 1.389762 2.7232% 1836 0.700472 1.427608 2.7994% 1835 0.681397 1.467573
2.8871% 1834 0.662276 1.509944 2.9657% 1833 0.643201 1.554724 3.0563% 1832 0.624126
1.602241 3.1604% 1831 0.605005 1.652879 3.4660% 1830 0.584738 1.710167 2.4653% 1829
0.570669 1.752328 2.6804% 1828 0.555773 1.799297 10.3427% 1827 0.503679 1.985392 -
4.2314% 1826 0.525933 1.901382 2.9150% 1825 0.511036 1.956808 3.0026% 1824 0.496140
2.015562 3.0955% 1823 0.481243 2.077954 3.1944% 1822 0.466346 2.144332 3.3102% 1821
0.451403 2.215313 3.2277% 1820 0.437289 2.286818 2.6573% 1819 0.425970 2.347585
2.6261% 1818 0.415069 2.409235 2.6969% 1817 0.404169 2.474211 2.7717% 1816 0.393269
2.542788 2.8507% 1815 0.382369 2.615275 2.9343% 1814 0.371469 2.692016 3.0231% 1813
0.360569 2.773397 3.1039% 1812 0.349714 2.859481 3.2172% 1811 0.338814 2.951475
3.0969% 1810 0.328636 3.042879 2.9144% 1809 0.319330 3.131560 2.8225% 1808 0.310564
3.219947 2.9199% 1807 0.301753 3.313967 2.9918% 1806 0.292988 3.413114 3.0841% 1805
0.284222 3.518376 3.1822% 1804 0.275456 3.630338 3.2868% 1803 0.266691 3.749659
3.3985% 1802 0.257925 3.877091 3.5180% 1801 0.249160 4.013489 3.3999% 1800 0.240967
4.149945 2.8419% 1799 0.234308 4.267881 2.7485% 1798 0.228041 4.385182 2.8261% 1797
0.221773 4.509113 3.7832% 1796 0.213689 4.679702 2.1272% 1795 0.209238 4.779249
3.0879% 1794 0.202970 4.926829 3.1625% 1793 0.196748 5.082641 3.2904% 1792 0.190481
5.249881 3.4024% 1791 0.184213 5.428501 3.2296% 1790 0.178450 5.603818 41.3145%
1780 0.126278 7.919004 29.4353% 1770 0.097561 10.249988 83.4728% 1750 0.053175
18.805945 29.2845% 1740 0.041130 24.313163 94.2514% 1720 0.021174 47.228657
85.8111% 1700 0.011395 87.756078 19.2490% 1690 0.009556 104.648289 88.0250% 1670
0.005082 196.764969
  BASE YEAR: 1847
  YEAR BYEAR/AYEAR AYEAR/BYEAR GROWTH%
  2009 14.081582 0.071015 8.2857% 2001 13.004106 0.076899 1.0000% 2000
12.875351 0.077668 1.0000% 1999 12.747873 0.078444 1.0000% 1998 12.621656 0.079229
1.0000% 1997 12.496689 0.080021 1.0000% 1996 12.372960 0.080821 1.0000% 1995
12.250455 0.081630 0.9992% 1994 12.129257 0.082445 1.0008% 1993 12.009073 0.083270
1.0000% 1992 11.890171 0.084103 0.9295% 1991 11.780669 0.084885 1.2505% 1990
11.635169 0.085946 0.7224% 1989 11.551714 0.086567 1.1077% 1988 11.425161 0.087526
0.8834% 1987 11.325119 0.088299 0.5594% 1986 11.262123 0.088793 1.3056% 1985
11.116977 0.089953 0.7673% 1984 11.032327 0.090643 0.8149% 1983 10.943147 0.091381
0.9737% 1982 10.837616 0.092271 0.9508% 1981 10.735541 0.093149 0.9031% 1980
10.639460 0.093990 2.2701% 1979 10.403298 0.096123 1.0042% 1978 10.299869 0.097089
0.9896% 1977 10.198940 0.098049 0.9103% 1976 10.106933 0.098942 0.8394% 1975
10.022797 0.099773 0.9042% 1974 9.932986 0.100675 1.1568% 1973 9.819396 0.101839
0.9427% 1972 9.727693 0.102799 0.7426% 1971 9.655984 0.103563 1.4697% 1970 9.516122
0.105085 0.6968% 1969 9.450271 0.105817 0.8565% 1968 9.370013 0.106723 1.5090% 1967
9.230718 0.108334 0.9949% 1966 9.139786 0.109412 1.0575% 1965 9.044147 0.110569
1.1300% 1964 8.943088 0.111818 1.5537% 1963 8.806269 0.113555 1.4658% 1962 8.679050
0.115220 1.5364% 1961 8.547720 0.116990 2.1586% 1960 8.367105 0.119516 -1.6655%
1959 8.508818 0.117525 4.3080% 1958 8.157397 0.122588 2.1130% 1957 7.988601 0.125178
1.9895% 1956 7.832769 0.127669 2.1231% 1955 7.669929 0.130379 1.4496% 1954 7.560334
0.132269 2.1573% 1953 7.400682 0.135123 1.2298% 1952 7.310777 0.136784 1.6814% 1951
7.189888 0.139084 1.6233% 1950 7.075041 0.141342 1.4265% 1949 6.975533 0.143358
1.7790% 1948 6.853604 0.145909 1.8242% 1947 6.730823 0.148570 -2.6320% 1946
6.912770 0.144660 3.1768% 1945 6.699926 0.149255 6.4754% 1944 6.292463 0.158920 -
0.3437% 1943 6.314164 0.158374 0.6562% 1942 6.272999 0.159413 0.6633% 1941 6.231664
0.160471 -5.6614% 1940 6.605637 0.151386 8.0381% 1939 6.114174 0.163554 0.8126%
1938 6.064888 0.164883 0.7762% 1937 6.018172 0.166163 0.6029% 1936 5.982108 0.167165
0.5244% 1935 5.950902 0.168042 -3.0364% 1934 6.137251 0.162939 4.6271% 1933

244

5.865832 0.170479 1.3921% 1932 5.785294 0.172852 -0.2051% 1931 5.797183 0.172498
0.8886% 1930 5.746123 0.174030 1.0126% 1929 5.688522 0.175793 1.1526% 1928 5.623704
0.177819 1.2160% 1927 5.556141 0.179981 1.4086% 1926 5.478965 0.182516 1.7667% 1925
5.383849 0.185741 1.4465% 1924 5.307082 0.188427 1.7700% 1923 5.214782 0.191763
1.6165% 1922 5.131825 0.194862 1.3736% 1921 5.062287 0.197539 2.3393% 1920 4.946572
0.202160 1.3140% 1919 4.882416 0.204817 0.7676% 1918 4.845222 0.206389 0.3870% 1917
4.826544 0.207188 1.3274% 1916 4.763314 0.209938 1.4083% 1915 4.697164 0.212894
1.4458% 1914 4.630220 0.215972 1.9424% 1913 4.541998 0.220167 1.9857% 1912 4.453564
0.224539 1.5634% 1911 4.385009 0.228050 1.8169% 1910 4.306759 0.232193 1.8781% 1909
4.227366 0.236554 2.0082% 1908 4.144142 0.241304 1.9603% 1907 4.064468 0.246035
1.8264% 1906 3.991568 0.250528 1.9357% 1905 3.915771 0.255378 2.0148% 1904 3.838433
0.260523 2.1335% 1903 3.758250 0.266081 1.8151% 1902 3.691248 0.270911 1.8943% 1901
3.622623 0.276043 3.0255% 1900 3.516239 0.284395 0.6278% 1899 3.494301 0.286180
1.7757% 1898 3.433336 0.291262 1.8078% 1897 3.372372 0.296527 1.8396% 1896 3.311455
0.301982 1.8755% 1895 3.250491 0.307646 1.9114% 1894 3.189526 0.313526 1.9486% 1893
3.128562 0.319636 1.9858% 1892 3.067645 0.325983 2.0276% 1891 3.006680 0.332593
2.6465% 1890 2.929160 0.341395 1.5328% 1889 2.884939 0.346628 2.0811% 1888 2.826124
0.353842 2.1599% 1887 2.766374 0.361484 2.2075% 1886 2.706624 0.369464 2.2592% 1885
2.646828 0.377811 2.3095% 1884 2.587078 0.386536 2.3641% 1883 2.527329 0.395675
2.4214% 1882 2.467579 0.405255 2.4815% 1881 2.407830 0.415312 3.7644% 1880 2.320478
0.430946 0.9432% 1879 2.298795 0.435011 2.1464% 1878 2.250491 0.444348 2.1913% 1877
2.202233 0.454085 2.2426% 1876 2.153929 0.464268 2.2941% 1875 2.105625 0.474918
2.3456% 1874 2.057367 0.486058 2.4043% 1873 2.009063 0.497745 2.4635% 1872 1.960759
0.510007 2.5258% 1871 1.912454 0.522888 5.9947% 1870 1.804293 0.554234 -1.0968%
1869 1.824302 0.548155 2.1930% 1868 1.785154 0.560176 2.2394% 1867 1.746053 0.572720
2.2935% 1866 1.706905 0.585856 2.3445% 1865 1.667803 0.599591 2.4037% 1864 1.628656
0.614003 2.4599% 1863 1.589554 0.629107 2.5250% 1862 1.550406 0.644992 2.5872% 1861
1.511305 0.661680 2.9504% 1860 1.467993 0.681202 2.4012% 1859 1.433570 0.697559
2.7627% 1858 1.395029 0.716831 2.8412% 1857 1.356489 0.737197 2.9243% 1856 1.317948
0.758755 3.0161% 1855 1.279361 0.781640 3.1061% 1854 1.240820 0.805918 3.2056% 1853
1.202280 0.831753 3.3118% 1852 1.163739 0.859299 3.4252% 1851 1.125199 0.888732
4.0106% 1850 1.081811 0.924376 2.3254% 1849 1.057227 0.945871 2.7841% 1848 1.028590
0.972205 2.8590% 1847 1.000000 1.000000 2.9432% 1846 0.971410 1.029432 3.0324% 1845
0.942820 1.060648 3.1325% 1844 0.914183 1.093873 3.2284% 1843 0.885593 1.129187
3.3361% 1842 0.857003 1.166857 3.4512% 1841 0.828413 1.207128 3.8105% 1840 0.798005
1.253125 2.3861% 1839 0.779408 1.283026 2.5824% 1838 0.759787 1.316158 2.6573% 1837
0.740120 1.351133 2.7232% 1836 0.720499 1.387927 2.7994% 1835 0.700878 1.426781
2.8871% 1834 0.681211 1.467974 2.9657% 1833 0.661590 1.511510 3.0563% 1832 0.641970
1.557706 3.1604% 1831 0.622302 1.606936 3.4660% 1830 0.601456 1.662632 2.4653% 1829
0.586985 1.703621 2.6804% 1828 0.571662 1.749285 10.3427% 1827 0.518079 1.930207 -
4.2314% 1826 0.540970 1.848532 2.9150% 1825 0.525647 1.902417 3.0026% 1824 0.510324
1.959539 3.0955% 1823 0.495001 2.020196 3.1944% 1822 0.479679 2.084729 3.3102% 1821
0.464309 2.153738 3.2277% 1820 0.449791 2.223255 2.6573% 1819 0.438148 2.282333
2.6261% 1818 0.426936 2.342269 2.6969% 1817 0.415725 2.405439 2.7717% 1816 0.404513
2.472110 2.8507% 1815 0.393301 2.542582 2.9343% 1814 0.382089 2.617190 3.0231% 1813
0.370877 2.696309 3.1039% 1812 0.359712 2.780000 3.2172% 1811 0.348500 2.869437
3.0969% 1810 0.338032 2.958301 2.9144% 1809 0.328459 3.044517 2.8225% 1808 0.319443
3.130447 2.9199% 1807 0.310380 3.221854 2.9918% 1806 0.301364 3.318245 3.0841% 1805
0.292348 3.420582 3.1822% 1804 0.283332 3.529431 3.2868% 1803 0.274316 3.645436
3.3985% 1802 0.265299 3.769326 3.5180% 1801 0.256283 3.901932 3.3999% 1800 0.247856
4.034596 2.8419% 1799 0.241007 4.149254 2.7485% 1798 0.234560 4.263294 2.8261% 1797
0.228114 4.383780 3.7832% 1796 0.219798 4.549628 2.1272% 1795 0.215220 4.646408
3.0879% 1794 0.208773 4.789886 3.1625% 1793 0.202373 4.941367 3.2904% 1792 0.195926
5.103958 3.4024% 1791 0.189480 5.277613 3.2296% 1790 0.183552 5.448057 41.3145%
1780 0.129889 7.698892 29.4353% 1770 0.100350 9.965085 83.4728% 1750 0.054695
18.283225 29.2845% 1740 0.042306 23.637367 94.2514% 1720 0.021779 45.915916

85.8111% 1700 0.011721 85.316859 19.2490% 1690 0.009829 101.739544 88.0250% 1670 0.005228 191.295800

BASE YEAR: 1846

YEAR BYEAR/AYEAR AYEAR/BYEAR GROWTH%

2009 14.496025 0.068984 8.2857% 2001 13.386838 0.074700 1.0000% 2000 13.254293 0.075447 1.0000% 1999 13.123063 0.076202 1.0000% 1998 12.993131 0.076964 1.0000% 1997 12.864486 0.077733 1.0000% 1996 12.737115 0.078511 1.0000% 1995 12.611005 0.079296 0.9992% 1994 12.486240 0.080088 1.0008% 1993 12.362519 0.080890 1.0000% 1992 12.240117 0.081699 0.9295% 1991 12.127393 0.082458 1.2505% 1990 11.977611 0.083489 0.7224% 1989 11.891700 0.084092 1.1077% 1988 11.761422 0.085024 0.8834% 1987 11.658435 0.085775 0.5594% 1986 11.593585 0.086255 1.3056% 1985 11.444167 0.087381 0.7673% 1984 11.357026 0.088051 0.8149% 1983 11.265221 0.088769 0.9737% 1982 11.156584 0.089633 0.9508% 1981 11.051505 0.090485 0.9031% 1980 10.952596 0.091303 2.2701% 1979 10.709484 0.093375 1.0042% 1978 10.603010 0.094313 0.9896% 1977 10.499110 0.095246 0.9103% 1976 10.404395 0.096113 0.8394% 1975 10.317784 0.096920 0.9042% 1974 10.225329 0.097796 1.1568% 1973 10.108397 0.098928 0.9427% 1972 10.013994 0.099860 0.7426% 1971 9.940175 0.100602 1.4697% 1970 9.796197 0.102080 0.6968% 1969 9.728407 0.102792 0.8565% 1968 9.645787 0.103672 1.5090% 1967 9.502393 0.105237 0.9949% 1966 9.408784 0.106284 1.0575% 1965 9.310330 0.107408 1.1300% 1964 9.206297 0.108621 1.5537% 1963 9.065452 0.110309 1.4658% 1962 8.934488 0.111926 1.5364% 1961 8.799293 0.113645 2.1586% 1960 8.613362 0.116099 - 1.6655% 1959 8.759245 0.114165 4.3080% 1958 8.397482 0.119083 2.1130% 1957 8.223718 0.121599 1.9895% 1956 8.063300 0.124019 2.1231% 1955 7.895667 0.126652 1.4496% 1954 7.782846 0.128488 2.1573% 1953 7.618496 0.131260 1.2298% 1952 7.525945 0.132874 1.6814% 1951 7.401498 0.135108 1.6233% 1950 7.283271 0.137301 1.4265% 1949 7.180833 0.139260 1.7790% 1948 7.055316 0.141737 1.8242% 1947 6.928922 0.144323 -2.6320% 1946 7.116223 0.140524 3.1768% 1945 6.897116 0.144988 6.4754% 1944 6.477660 0.154377 -0.3437% 1943 6.499999 0.153846 0.6562% 1942 6.457623 0.154856 0.6633% 1941 6.415072 0.155883 -5.6614% 1940 6.800052 0.147058 8.0381% 1939 6.294123 0.158878 0.8126% 1938 6.243388 0.160169 0.7762% 1937 6.195297 0.161413 0.6029% 1936 6.158171 0.162386 0.5244% 1935 6.126046 0.163237 -3.0364% 1934 6.317880 0.158281 4.6271% 1933 6.038473 0.165605 1.3921% 1932 5.955564 0.167910 -0.2051% 1931 5.967803 0.167566 0.8886% 1930 5.915241 0.169055 1.0126% 1929 5.855944 0.170767 1.1526% 1928 5.789218 0.172735 1.2160% 1927 5.719667 0.174835 1.4086% 1926 5.640220 0.177298 1.7667% 1925 5.542305 0.180430 1.4465% 1924 5.463278 0.183040 1.7700% 1923 5.368261 0.186280 1.6165% 1922 5.282863 0.189291 1.3736% 1921 5.211278 0.191891 2.3393% 1920 5.092157 0.196380 1.3140% 1919 5.026113 0.198961 0.7676% 1918 4.987825 0.200488 0.3870% 1917 4.968597 0.201264 1.3274% 1916 4.903506 0.203936 1.4083% 1915 4.835409 0.206808 1.4458% 1914 4.766495 0.209798 1.9424% 1913 4.675676 0.213873 1.9857% 1912 4.584640 0.218120 1.5634% 1911 4.514067 0.221530 1.8169% 1910 4.433513 0.225555 1.8781% 1909 4.351784 0.229791 2.0082% 1908 4.266110 0.234406 1.9603% 1907 4.184092 0.239001 1.8264% 1906 4.109046 0.243365 1.9357% 1905 4.031019 0.248076 2.0148% 1904 3.951404 0.253075 2.1335% 1903 3.868861 0.258474 1.8151% 1902 3.799887 0.263166 1.8943% 1901 3.729243 0.268151 3.0255% 1900 3.619728 0.276264 0.6278% 1899 3.597143 0.277998 1.7757% 1898 3.534385 0.282935 1.8078% 1897 3.471626 0.288049 1.8396% 1896 3.408916 0.293348 1.8755% 1895 3.346158 0.298850 1.9114% 1894 3.283399 0.304562 1.9486% 1893 3.220641 0.310497 1.9858% 1892 3.157930 0.316663 2.0276% 1891 3.095172 0.323084 2.6465% 1890 3.015369 0.331634 1.5328% 1889 2.969847 0.336718 2.0811% 1888 2.909301 0.343725 2.1599% 1887 2.847793 0.351149 2.2075% 1886 2.786285 0.358901 2.2592% 1885 2.724728 0.367009 2.3095% 1884 2.663220 0.375485 2.3641% 1883 2.601712 0.384362 2.4214% 1882 2.540204 0.393669 2.4815% 1881 2.478696 0.403438 3.7644% 1880 2.388773 0.418625 0.9432% 1879 2.366452 0.422574 2.1464% 1878 2.316726 0.431644 2.1913% 1877 2.267048 0.441102 2.2426% 1876 2.217322 0.450994 2.2941% 1875 2.167596 0.461340 2.3456% 1874 2.117919 0.472162 2.4043% 1873 2.068193 0.483514 2.4635% 1872 2.018467 0.495426 2.5258% 1871 1.968741 0.507939 5.9947% 1870 1.857396 0.538388 - 1.0968% 1869 1.877994 0.532483 2.1930% 1868 1.837694 0.544160 2.2394% 1867 1.797442

246

0.556346 2.2935% 1866 1.757141 0.569106 2.3445% 1865 1.716889 0.582449 2.4037% 1864 1.676589 0.596449 2.4599% 1863 1.636337 0.611121 2.5250% 1862 1.596037 0.626552 2.5872% 1861 1.555785 0.642762 2.9504% 1860 1.511199 0.661726 2.4012% 1859 1.475762 0.677616 2.7627% 1858 1.436087 0.696336 2.8412% 1857 1.396412 0.716121 2.9243% 1856 1.356738 0.737062 3.0161% 1855 1.317015 0.759293 3.1061% 1854 1.277340 0.782877 3.2056% 1853 1.237665 0.807973 3.3118% 1852 1.197990 0.834732 3.4252% 1851 1.158315 0.863323 4.0106% 1850 1.113651 0.897948 2.3254% 1849 1.088343 0.918828 2.7841% 1848 1.058863 0.944409 2.8590% 1847 1.029432 0.971410 2.9432% 1846 1.000000 1.000000 3.0324% 1845 0.970568 1.030324 3.1325% 1844 0.941089 1.062599 3.2284% 1843 0.911657 1.096904 3.3361% 1842 0.882226 1.133497 3.4512% 1841 0.852794 1.172616 3.8105% 1840 0.821491 1.217298 2.3861% 1839 0.802347 1.246344 2.5824% 1838 0.782149 1.278529 2.6573% 1837 0.761902 1.312504 2.7232% 1836 0.741704 1.348246 2.7994% 1835 0.721506 1.385989 2.8871% 1834 0.701260 1.426005 2.9657% 1833 0.681062 1.468295 3.0563% 1832 0.660864 1.513171 3.1604% 1831 0.640617 1.560994 3.4660% 1830 0.619158 1.615097 2.4653% 1829 0.604261 1.654914 2.6804% 1828 0.588487 1.699273 10.3427% 1827 0.533327 1.875023 -4.2314% 1826 0.556891 1.795682 2.9150% 1825 0.541118 1.848027 3.0026% 1824 0.525344 1.903515 3.0955% 1823 0.509570 1.962439 3.1944% 1822 0.493796 2.025127 3.3102% 1821 0.477974 2.092162 3.2277% 1820 0.463029 2.159692 2.6573% 1819 0.451044 2.217081 2.6261% 1818 0.439502 2.275304 2.6969% 1817 0.427960 2.336667 2.7717% 1816 0.416418 2.401432 2.8507% 1815 0.404876 2.469890 2.9343% 1814 0.393335 2.542365 3.0231% 1813 0.381793 2.619222 3.1039% 1812 0.370299 2.700519 3.2172% 1811 0.358757 2.787399 3.0969% 1810 0.347981 2.873723 2.9144% 1809 0.338126 2.957474 2.8225% 1808 0.328845 3.040684 2.9199% 1807 0.319515 3.129741 2.9918% 1806 0.310234 3.223376 3.0841% 1805 0.300952 3.322787 3.1822% 1804 0.291671 3.428524 3.2868% 1803 0.282389 3.541213 3.3985% 1802 0.273108 3.661560 3.5180% 1801 0.263826 3.790376 3.3999% 1800 0.255151 3.919246 2.8419% 1799 0.248100 4.030626 2.7485% 1798 0.241464 4.141406 2.8261% 1797 0.234827 4.258448 3.7832% 1796 0.226267 4.419554 2.1272% 1795 0.221554 4.513566 3.0879% 1794 0.214918 4.652942 3.1625% 1793 0.208329 4.800092 3.2904% 1792 0.201693 4.958035 3.4024% 1791 0.195056 5.126726 3.2296% 1790 0.188954 5.292297 41.3145% 1780 0.133712 7.478780 29.4353% 1770 0.103304 9.680182 83.4728% 1750 0.056305 17.760506 29.2845% 1740 0.043551 22.961572 94.2514% 1720 0.022420 44.603175 85.8111% 1700 0.012066 82.877640 19.2490% 1690 0.010118 98.830798 88.0250% 1670 0.005381 185.826631

BASE YEAR: 1845

YEAR BYEAR/AYEAR AYEAR/BYEAR GROWTH%

2009 14.935603 0.066954 8.2857% 2001 13.792781 0.072502 1.0000% 2000 13.656217 0.073227 1.0000% 1999 13.521007 0.073959 1.0000% 1998 13.387136 0.074699 1.0000% 1997 13.254590 0.075446 1.0000% 1996 13.123356 0.076200 1.0000% 1995 12.993422 0.076962 0.9992% 1994 12.864873 0.077731 1.0008% 1993 12.737400 0.078509 1.0000% 1992 12.611287 0.079294 0.9295% 1991 12.495144 0.080031 1.2505% 1990 12.340820 0.081032 0.7224% 1989 12.252304 0.081617 1.1077% 1988 12.118076 0.082521 0.8834% 1987 12.011506 0.083250 0.5594% 1986 11.945149 0.083716 1.3056% 1985 11.791200 0.084809 0.7673% 1984 11.701417 0.085460 0.8149% 1983 11.606828 0.086156 0.9737% 1982 11.494896 0.086995 0.9508% 1981 11.386632 0.087822 0.9031% 1980 11.284723 0.088615 2.2701% 1979 11.034238 0.090627 1.0042% 1978 10.924537 0.091537 0.9896% 1977 10.817486 0.092443 0.9103% 1976 10.719899 0.093284 0.8394% 1975 10.630661 0.094068 0.9042% 1974 10.535403 0.094918 1.1568% 1973 10.414924 0.096016 0.9427% 1972 10.317659 0.096921 0.7426% 1971 10.241601 0.097641 1.4697% 1970 10.093257 0.099076 0.6968% 1969 10.023412 0.099766 0.8565% 1968 9.938287 0.100621 1.5090% 1967 9.790544 0.102139 0.9949% 1966 9.694096 0.103156 1.0575% 1965 9.592657 0.104246 1.1300% 1964 9.485470 0.105424 1.5537% 1963 9.340353 0.107062 1.4658% 1962 9.205418 0.108632 1.5364% 1961 9.066123 0.110301 2.1586% 1960 8.874554 0.112682 -1.6655% 1959 9.024861 0.110805 4.3080% 1958 8.652128 0.115579 2.1130% 1957 8.473095 0.118021 1.9895% 1956 8.307811 0.120369 2.1231% 1955 8.135096 0.122924 1.4496% 1954 8.018853 0.124706 2.1573% 1953 7.849519 0.127396 1.2298% 1952 7.754162 0.128963 1.6814% 1951 7.625941 0.131131 1.6233% 1950 7.504129 0.133260 1.4265% 1949 7.398585

0.135161 1.7790% 1948 7.269262 0.137566 1.8242% 1947 7.139035 0.140075 -2.6320%
1946 7.332016 0.136388 3.1768% 1945 7.106264 0.140721 6.4754% 1944 6.674089 0.149833
-0.3437% 1943 6.697106 0.149318 0.6562% 1942 6.653444 0.150298 0.6633% 1941
6.609603 0.151295 -5.6614% 1940 7.006257 0.142730 8.0381% 1939 6.484987 0.154202
0.8126% 1938 6.432712 0.155455 0.7762% 1937 6.383163 0.156662 0.6029% 1936 6.344911
0.157607 0.5244% 1935 6.311813 0.158433 -3.0364% 1934 6.509464 0.153622 4.6271%
1933 6.221584 0.160731 1.3921% 1932 6.136161 0.162968 -0.2051% 1931 6.148771
0.162634 0.8886% 1930 6.094615 0.164079 1.0126% 1929 6.033520 0.165741 1.1526% 1928
5.964771 0.167651 1.2160% 1927 5.893110 0.169690 1.4086% 1926 5.811254 0.172080
1.7667% 1925 5.710370 0.175120 1.4465% 1924 5.628947 0.177653 1.7700% 1923 5.531049
0.180798 1.6165% 1922 5.443061 0.183720 1.3736% 1921 5.369305 0.186244 2.3393% 1920
5.246572 0.190601 1.3140% 1919 5.178525 0.193105 0.7676% 1918 5.139076 0.194588
0.3870% 1917 5.119265 0.195341 1.3274% 1916 5.052200 0.197934 1.4083% 1915 4.982038
0.200721 1.4458% 1914 4.911035 0.203623 1.9424% 1913 4.817461 0.207578 1.9857% 1912
4.723665 0.211700 1.5634% 1911 4.650951 0.215010 1.8169% 1910 4.567955 0.218916
1.8781% 1909 4.483748 0.223028 2.0082% 1908 4.395476 0.227507 1.9603% 1907 4.310970
0.231966 1.8264% 1906 4.233649 0.236203 1.9357% 1905 4.153255 0.240775 2.0148% 1904
4.071227 0.245626 2.1335% 1903 3.986181 0.250867 1.8151% 1902 3.915115 0.255420
1.8943% 1901 3.842328 0.260259 3.0255% 1900 3.729493 0.268133 0.6278% 1899 3.706223
0.269816 1.7757% 1898 3.641562 0.274607 1.8078% 1897 3.576900 0.279572 1.8396% 1896
3.512288 0.284715 1.8755% 1895 3.447627 0.290055 1.9114% 1894 3.382965 0.295599
1.9486% 1893 3.318303 0.301359 1.9858% 1892 3.253691 0.307343 2.0276% 1891 3.189030
0.313575 2.6465% 1890 3.106808 0.321874 1.5328% 1889 3.059905 0.326808 2.0811% 1888
2.997523 0.333609 2.1599% 1887 2.934149 0.340814 2.2075% 1886 2.870776 0.348338
2.2592% 1885 2.807353 0.356207 2.3095% 1884 2.743980 0.364434 2.3641% 1883 2.680606
0.373050 2.4214% 1882 2.617233 0.382083 2.4815% 1881 2.553860 0.391564 3.7644% 1880
2.461210 0.406304 0.9432% 1879 2.438212 0.410137 2.1464% 1878 2.386978 0.418940
2.1913% 1877 2.335794 0.428120 2.2426% 1876 2.284560 0.437721 2.2941% 1875 2.233327
0.447763 2.3456% 1874 2.182143 0.458265 2.4043% 1873 2.130909 0.469283 2.4635% 1872
2.079675 0.480844 2.5258% 1871 2.028441 0.492989 5.9947% 1870 1.913720 0.522543 -
1.0968% 1869 1.934942 0.516811 2.1930% 1868 1.893420 0.528145 2.2394% 1867 1.851947
0.539972 2.2935% 1866 1.810425 0.552356 2.3445% 1865 1.768953 0.565306 2.4037% 1864
1.727430 0.578895 2.4599% 1863 1.685958 0.593135 2.5250% 1862 1.644436 0.608111
2.5872% 1861 1.602963 0.623845 2.9504% 1860 1.557024 0.642251 2.4012% 1859 1.520513
0.657673 2.7627% 1858 1.479635 0.675842 2.8412% 1857 1.438757 0.695044 2.9243% 1856
1.397879 0.715369 3.0161% 1855 1.356952 0.736946 3.1061% 1854 1.316074 0.759836
3.2056% 1853 1.275196 0.784193 3.3118% 1852 1.234318 0.810164 3.4252% 1851 1.193440
0.837914 4.0106% 1850 1.147421 0.871520 2.3254% 1849 1.121346 0.891786 2.7841% 1848
1.090972 0.916614 2.8590% 1847 1.060648 0.942820 2.9432% 1846 1.030324 0.970568
3.0324% 1845 1.000000 1.000000 3.1325% 1844 0.969626 1.031325 3.2284% 1843 0.939302
1.064620 3.3361% 1842 0.908978 1.100136 3.4512% 1841 0.878654 1.138104 3.8105% 1840
0.846402 1.181471 2.3861% 1839 0.826677 1.209662 2.5824% 1838 0.805867 1.240900
2.6573% 1837 0.785006 1.273875 2.7232% 1836 0.764196 1.308565 2.7994% 1835 0.743385
1.345198 2.8871% 1834 0.722525 1.384035 2.9657% 1833 0.701714 1.425081 3.0563% 1832
0.680904 1.468636 3.1604% 1831 0.660044 1.515051 3.4660% 1830 0.637933 1.567563
2.4653% 1829 0.622584 1.606208 2.6804% 1828 0.606332 1.649260 10.3427% 1827
0.549500 1.819838 -4.2314% 1826 0.573779 1.742832 2.9150% 1825 0.557527 1.793637
3.0026% 1824 0.541274 1.847492 3.0955% 1823 0.525022 1.904681 3.1944% 1822 0.508770
1.965524 3.3102% 1821 0.492469 2.030587 3.2277% 1820 0.477070 2.096129 2.6573% 1819
0.464721 2.151829 2.6261% 1818 0.452829 2.208338 2.6969% 1817 0.440937 2.267895
2.7717% 1816 0.429046 2.330754 2.8507% 1815 0.417154 2.397197 2.9343% 1814 0.405262
2.467539 3.0231% 1813 0.393370 2.542134 3.1039% 1812 0.381528 2.621039 3.2172% 1811
0.369636 2.705362 3.0969% 1810 0.358533 2.789145 2.9144% 1809 0.348380 2.870431
2.8225% 1808 0.338817 2.951448 2.9199% 1807 0.329204 3.037628 2.9918% 1806 0.319641
3.128507 3.0841% 1805 0.310078 3.224992 3.1822% 1804 0.300515 3.327617 3.2868% 1803
0.290952 3.436989 3.3985% 1802 0.281389 3.553795 3.5180% 1801 0.271826 3.678819

3.3999% 1800 0.262888 3.803897 2.8419% 1799 0.255624 3.911998 2.7485% 1798 0.248786 4.019518 2.8261% 1797 0.241948 4.133115 3.7832% 1796 0.233129 4.289479 2.1272% 1795 0.228273 4.380725 3.0879% 1794 0.221435 4.515999 3.1625% 1793 0.214647 4.658818 3.2904% 1792 0.207809 4.812113 3.4024% 1791 0.200971 4.975838 3.2296% 1790 0.194684 5.136536 41.3145% 1780 0.137766 7.258668 29.4353% 1770 0.106436 9.395280 83.4728% 1750 0.058012 17.237786 29.2845% 1740 0.044872 22.285777 94.2514% 1720 0.023100 43.290433 85.8111% 1700 0.012432 80.438422 19.2490% 1690 0.010425 95.922053 88.0250% 1670 0.005545 180.357462

BASE YEAR: 1844

YEAR BYEAR/AYEAR AYEAR/BYEAR GROWTH%

2009 15.403462 0.064920 8.2857% 2001 14.224840 0.070300 1.0000% 2000 14.083999 0.071003 1.0000% 1999 13.944553 0.071713 1.0000% 1998 13.806488 0.072430 1.0000% 1997 13.669790 0.073154 1.0000% 1996 13.534446 0.073886 1.0000% 1995 13.400442 0.074624 0.9992% 1994 13.267866 0.075370 1.0008% 1993 13.136400 0.076124 1.0000% 1992 13.006337 0.076886 0.9295% 1991 12.886555 0.077600 1.2505% 1990 12.727397 0.078571 0.7224% 1989 12.636108 0.079138 1.1077% 1988 12.497675 0.080015 0.8834% 1987 12.388242 0.080722 0.5594% 1986 12.319332 0.081173 1.3056% 1985 12.160560 0.082233 0.7673% 1984 12.067965 0.082864 0.8149% 1983 11.970412 0.083539 0.9737% 1982 11.854975 0.084353 0.9508% 1981 11.743319 0.085155 0.9031% 1980 11.638218 0.085924 2.2701% 1979 11.379887 0.087874 1.0042% 1978 11.266748 0.088757 0.9896% 1977 11.156344 0.089635 0.9103% 1976 11.055700 0.090451 0.8394% 1975 10.963667 0.091210 0.9042% 1974 10.865425 0.092035 1.1568% 1973 10.741172 0.093100 0.9427% 1972 10.640861 0.093977 0.7426% 1971 10.562420 0.094675 1.4697% 1970 10.409429 0.096067 0.6968% 1969 10.337396 0.096736 0.8565% 1968 10.249604 0.097565 1.5090% 1967 10.097233 0.099037 0.9949% 1966 9.997764 0.100022 1.0575% 1965 9.893147 0.101080 1.1300% 1964 9.782603 0.102222 1.5537% 1963 9.632940 0.103810 1.4658% 1962 9.493778 0.105332 1.5364% 1961 9.350120 0.106950 2.1586% 1960 9.152550 0.109259 -1.6655% 1959 9.307566 0.107439 4.3080% 1958 8.923157 0.112068 2.1130% 1957 8.738515 0.114436 1.9895% 1956 8.568054 0.116713 2.1231% 1955 8.389928 0.119191 1.4496% 1954 8.270044 0.120918 2.1573% 1953 8.095406 0.123527 1.2298% 1952 7.997062 0.125046 1.6814% 1951 7.864824 0.127148 1.6233% 1950 7.739196 0.129212 1.4265% 1949 7.630346 0.131056 1.7790% 1948 7.496972 0.133387 1.8242% 1947 7.362665 0.135820 -2.6320% 1946 7.561692 0.132246 3.1768% 1945 7.328868 0.136447 6.4754% 1944 6.883155 0.145282 -0.3437% 1943 6.906893 0.144783 0.6562% 1942 6.861864 0.145733 0.6633% 1941 6.816649 0.146700 -5.6614% 1940 7.225728 0.138394 8.0381% 1939 6.688129 0.149519 0.8126% 1938 6.634217 0.150734 0.7762% 1937 6.583116 0.151904 0.6029% 1936 6.543666 0.152820 0.5244% 1935 6.509530 0.153621 -3.0364% 1934 6.713373 0.148956 4.6271% 1933 6.416475 0.155849 1.3921% 1932 6.328377 0.158018 -0.2051% 1931 6.341382 0.157694 0.8886% 1930 6.285529 0.159096 1.0126% 1929 6.222520 0.160707 1.1526% 1928 6.151617 0.162559 1.2160% 1927 6.077712 0.164536 1.4086% 1926 5.993292 0.166853 1.7667% 1925 5.889247 0.169801 1.4465% 1924 5.805274 0.172257 1.7700% 1923 5.704309 0.175306 1.6165% 1922 5.613565 0.178140 1.3736% 1921 5.537499 0.180587 2.3393% 1920 5.410921 0.184811 1.3140% 1919 5.340743 0.187240 0.7676% 1918 5.300057 0.188677 0.3870% 1917 5.279626 0.189407 1.3274% 1916 5.210460 0.191922 1.4083% 1915 5.138101 0.194624 1.4458% 1914 5.064873 0.197438 1.9424% 1913 4.968368 0.201273 1.9857% 1912 4.871634 0.205270 1.5634% 1911 4.796643 0.208479 1.8169% 1910 4.711047 0.212267 1.8781% 1909 4.624202 0.216254 2.0082% 1908 4.533165 0.220596 1.9603% 1907 4.446012 0.224921 1.8264% 1906 4.366268 0.229029 1.9357% 1905 4.283356 0.233462 2.0148% 1904 4.198758 0.238166 2.1335% 1903 4.111048 0.243247 1.8151% 1902 4.037757 0.247662 1.8943% 1901 3.962689 0.252354 3.0255% 1900 3.846319 0.259989 0.6278% 1899 3.822321 0.261621 1.7757% 1898 3.755634 0.266267 1.8078% 1897 3.688947 0.271080 1.8396% 1896 3.622311 0.276067 1.8755% 1895 3.555624 0.281245 1.9114% 1894 3.488937 0.286620 1.9486% 1893 3.422249 0.292205 1.9858% 1892 3.355613 0.298008 2.0276% 1891 3.288926 0.304051 2.6465% 1890 3.204129 0.312097 1.5328% 1889 3.155757 0.316881 2.0811% 1888 3.091420 0.323476 2.1599% 1887 3.026062 0.330463 2.2075% 1886 2.960703 0.337758 2.2592% 1885 2.895294 0.345388 2.3095% 1884 2.829935 0.353365 2.3641% 1883

2.764577 0.361719 2.4214% 1882 2.699218 0.370478 2.4815% 1881 2.633860 0.379671
3.7644% 1880 2.538308 0.393963 0.9432% 1879 2.514589 0.397679 2.1464% 1878 2.461751
0.406215 2.1913% 1877 2.408963 0.415116 2.2426% 1876 2.356124 0.424426 2.2941% 1875
2.303286 0.434162 2.3456% 1874 2.250498 0.444346 2.4043% 1873 2.197660 0.455030
2.4635% 1872 2.144821 0.466239 2.5258% 1871 2.091982 0.478016 5.9947% 1870 1.973667
0.506671 -1.0968% 1869 1.995554 0.501114 2.1930% 1868 1.952731 0.512103 2.2394%
1867 1.909960 0.523571 2.2935% 1866 1.867137 0.535579 2.3445% 1865 1.824365 0.548136
2.4037% 1864 1.781542 0.561311 2.4599% 1863 1.738771 0.575119 2.5250% 1862 1.695948
0.589641 2.5872% 1861 1.653176 0.604896 2.9504% 1860 1.605798 0.622743 2.4012% 1859
1.568143 0.637697 2.7627% 1858 1.525985 0.655314 2.8412% 1857 1.483826 0.673933
2.9243% 1856 1.441668 0.693641 3.0161% 1855 1.399458 0.714562 3.1061% 1854 1.357300
0.736757 3.2056% 1853 1.315141 0.760375 3.3118% 1852 1.272983 0.785557 3.4252% 1851
1.230824 0.812464 4.0106% 1850 1.183364 0.845048 2.3254% 1849 1.156472 0.864699
2.7841% 1848 1.125147 0.888773 2.8590% 1847 1.093873 0.914183 2.9432% 1846 1.062599
0.941089 3.0324% 1845 1.031325 0.969626 3.1325% 1844 1.000000 1.000000 3.2284% 1843
0.968726 1.032284 3.3361% 1842 0.937452 1.066721 3.4512% 1841 0.906178 1.103536
3.8105% 1840 0.872916 1.145586 2.3861% 1839 0.852573 1.172920 2.5824% 1838 0.831110
1.203210 2.6573% 1837 0.809597 1.235183 2.7232% 1836 0.788134 1.268819 2.7994% 1835
0.766672 1.304339 2.8871% 1834 0.745158 1.341997 2.9657% 1833 0.723696 1.381796
3.0563% 1832 0.702233 1.424029 3.1604% 1831 0.680720 1.469034 3.4660% 1830 0.657916
1.519950 2.4653% 1829 0.642087 1.557421 2.6804% 1828 0.625326 1.599166 10.3427%
1827 0.566713 1.764563 -4.2314% 1826 0.591752 1.689896 2.9150% 1825 0.574991
1.739157 3.0026% 1824 0.558230 1.791377 3.0955% 1823 0.541469 1.846829 3.1944% 1822
0.524707 1.905824 3.3102% 1821 0.507895 1.968910 3.2277% 1820 0.492014 2.032462
2.6573% 1819 0.479278 2.086470 2.6261% 1818 0.467014 2.141263 2.6969% 1817 0.454750
2.199011 2.7717% 1816 0.442486 2.259961 2.8507% 1815 0.430221 2.324385 2.9343% 1814
0.417957 2.392591 3.0231% 1813 0.405693 2.464920 3.1039% 1812 0.393479 2.541429
3.2172% 1811 0.381215 2.623190 3.0969% 1810 0.369764 2.704428 2.9144% 1809 0.359293
2.783246 2.8225% 1808 0.349430 2.861802 2.9199% 1807 0.339517 2.945364 2.9918% 1806
0.329654 3.033483 3.0841% 1805 0.319792 3.127037 3.1822% 1804 0.309929 3.226546
3.2868% 1803 0.300066 3.332595 3.3985% 1802 0.290204 3.445853 3.5180% 1801 0.280341
3.567080 3.3999% 1800 0.271123 3.688359 2.8419% 1799 0.263631 3.793177 2.7485% 1798
0.256579 3.897431 2.8261% 1797 0.249527 4.007577 3.7832% 1796 0.240431 4.159192
2.1272% 1795 0.235423 4.247667 3.0879% 1794 0.228371 4.378832 3.1625% 1793 0.221371
4.517313 3.2904% 1792 0.214319 4.665951 3.4024% 1791 0.207267 4.824704 3.2296% 1790
0.200782 4.980521 41.3145% 1780 0.142082 7.038196 29.4353% 1770 0.109771 9.109911
83.4728% 1750 0.059829 16.714213 29.2845% 1740 0.046277 21.608878 94.2514% 1720
0.023823 41.975547 85.8111% 1700 0.012821 77.995217 19.2490% 1690 0.010752
93.008555 88.0250% 1670 0.005718 174.879357

BASE YEAR: 1843
YEAR BYEAR/AYEAR AYEAR/BYEAR GROWTH%

2009 15.900741 0.062890 8.2857% 2001 14.684069 0.068101 1.0000% 2000
14.538681 0.068782 1.0000% 1999 14.394733 0.069470 1.0000% 1998 14.252211 0.070165
1.0000% 1997 14.111100 0.070866 1.0000% 1996 13.971386 0.071575 1.0000% 1995
13.833056 0.072291 0.9992% 1994 13.696200 0.073013 1.0008% 1993 13.560490 0.073744
1.0000% 1992 13.426228 0.074481 0.9295% 1991 13.302580 0.075173 1.2505% 1990
13.138283 0.076113 0.7224% 1989 13.044047 0.076663 1.1077% 1988 12.901145 0.077513
0.8834% 1987 12.788179 0.078197 0.5594% 1986 12.717044 0.078635 1.3056% 1985
12.553147 0.079661 0.7673% 1984 12.457562 0.080273 0.8149% 1983 12.356860 0.080927
0.9737% 1982 12.237696 0.081715 0.9508% 1981 12.122435 0.082492 0.9031% 1980
12.013941 0.083237 2.2701% 1979 11.747270 0.085126 1.0042% 1978 11.630480 0.085981
0.9896% 1977 11.516511 0.086832 0.9103% 1976 11.412618 0.087622 0.8394% 1975
11.317614 0.088358 0.9042% 1974 11.216200 0.089157 1.1568% 1973 11.087936 0.090188
0.9427% 1972 10.984386 0.091038 0.7426% 1971 10.903413 0.091714 1.4697% 1970
10.745483 0.093062 0.6968% 1969 10.671124 0.093711 0.8565% 1968 10.580498 0.094514
1.5090% 1967 10.423208 0.095940 0.9949% 1966 10.320528 0.096894 1.0575% 1965

250

10.212534 0.097919 1.1300% 1964 10.098420 0.099025 1.5537% 1963 9.943926 0.100564 1.4658% 1962 9.800272 0.102038 1.5364% 1961 9.651976 0.103606 2.1586% 1960 9.448027 0.105842 -1.6655% 1959 9.608047 0.104079 4.3080% 1958 9.211228 0.108563 2.1130% 1957 9.020626 0.110857 1.9895% 1956 8.844662 0.113063 2.1231% 1955 8.660785 0.115463 1.4496% 1954 8.537031 0.117137 2.1573% 1953 8.356755 0.119664 1.2298% 1952 8.255236 0.121135 1.6814% 1951 8.118729 0.123172 1.6233% 1950 7.989045 0.125171 1.4265% 1949 7.876681 0.126957 1.7790% 1948 7.739001 0.129216 1.8242% 1947 7.600359 0.131573 -2.6320% 1946 7.805811 0.128110 3.1768% 1945 7.565471 0.132179 6.4754% 1944 7.105368 0.140739 -0.3437% 1943 7.129872 0.140255 0.6562% 1942 7.083389 0.141175 0.6633% 1941 7.036715 0.142112 -5.6614% 1940 7.459001 0.134066 8.0381% 1939 6.904046 0.144843 0.8126% 1938 6.848394 0.146020 0.7762% 1937 6.795643 0.147153 0.6029% 1936 6.754919 0.148040 0.5244% 1935 6.719681 0.148817 -3.0364% 1934 6.930105 0.144298 4.6271% 1933 6.623622 0.150975 1.3921% 1932 6.532679 0.153077 -0.2051% 1931 6.546104 0.152763 0.8886% 1930 6.488448 0.154120 1.0126% 1929 6.423406 0.155681 1.1526% 1928 6.350214 0.157475 1.2160% 1927 6.273923 0.159390 1.4086% 1926 6.186777 0.161635 1.7667% 1925 6.079373 0.164491 1.4465% 1924 5.992689 0.166870 1.7700% 1923 5.888465 0.169824 1.6165% 1922 5.794791 0.172569 1.3736% 1921 5.716270 0.174939 2.3393% 1920 5.585605 0.179032 1.3140% 1919 5.513161 0.181384 0.7676% 1918 5.471162 0.182777 0.3870% 1917 5.450071 0.183484 1.3274% 1916 5.378673 0.185919 1.4083% 1915 5.303977 0.188538 1.4458% 1914 5.228385 0.191264 1.9424% 1913 5.128765 0.194979 1.9857% 1912 5.028908 0.198850 1.5634% 1911 4.951495 0.201959 1.8169% 1910 4.863136 0.205629 1.8781% 1909 4.773487 0.209490 2.0082% 1908 4.679512 0.213698 1.9603% 1907 4.589545 0.217887 1.8264% 1906 4.507227 0.221866 1.9357% 1905 4.421638 0.226161 2.0148% 1904 4.334309 0.230717 2.1335% 1903 4.243767 0.235640 1.8151% 1902 4.168110 0.239917 1.8943% 1901 4.090619 0.244462 3.0255% 1900 3.970492 0.251858 0.6278% 1899 3.945719 0.253439 1.7757% 1898 3.876879 0.257939 1.8078% 1897 3.808039 0.262602 1.8396% 1896 3.739252 0.267433 1.8755% 1895 3.670412 0.272449 1.9114% 1894 3.601572 0.277657 1.9486% 1893 3.532732 0.283067 1.9858% 1892 3.463945 0.288688 2.0276% 1891 3.395105 0.294542 2.6465% 1890 3.307569 0.302337 1.5328% 1889 3.257636 0.306971 2.0811% 1888 3.191222 0.313360 2.1599% 1887 3.123754 0.320128 2.2075% 1886 3.056285 0.327195 2.2592% 1885 2.988764 0.334586 2.3095% 1884 2.921296 0.342314 2.3641% 1883 2.853827 0.350407 2.4214% 1882 2.786359 0.358891 2.4815% 1881 2.718890 0.367797 3.7644% 1880 2.620253 0.381642 0.9432% 1879 2.595769 0.385242 2.1464% 1878 2.541225 0.393511 2.1913% 1877 2.486733 0.402134 2.2426% 1876 2.432189 0.411152 2.2941% 1875 2.377644 0.420584 2.3456% 1874 2.323152 0.430450 2.4043% 1873 2.268608 0.440759 2.4635% 1872 2.214063 0.451658 2.5258% 1871 2.159519 0.463066 5.9947% 1870 2.037384 0.490825 -1.0968% 1869 2.059978 0.485442 2.1930% 1868 2.015773 0.496088 2.2394% 1867 1.971620 0.507197 2.2935% 1866 1.927415 0.518830 2.3445% 1865 1.883262 0.530994 2.4037% 1864 1.839057 0.543757 2.4599% 1863 1.794904 0.557133 2.5250% 1862 1.750699 0.571200 2.5872% 1861 1.706546 0.585979 2.9504% 1860 1.657639 0.603268 2.4012% 1859 1.618769 0.617753 2.7627% 1858 1.575249 0.634820 2.8412% 1857 1.531730 0.652857 2.9243% 1856 1.488210 0.671948 3.0161% 1855 1.444638 0.692215 3.1061% 1854 1.401118 0.713716 3.2056% 1853 1.357599 0.736595 3.3118% 1852 1.314079 0.760989 3.4252% 1851 1.270560 0.787055 4.0106% 1850 1.221567 0.818620 2.3254% 1849 1.193807 0.837656 2.7841% 1848 1.161471 0.860977 2.8590% 1847 1.129187 0.885593 2.9432% 1846 1.096904 0.911657 3.0324% 1845 1.064620 0.939302 3.1325% 1844 1.032284 0.968726 3.2284% 1843 1.000000 1.000000 3.3361% 1842 0.967716 1.033361 3.4512% 1841 0.935433 1.069024 3.8105% 1840 0.901097 1.109759 2.3861% 1839 0.880097 1.136238 2.5824% 1838 0.857942 1.165580 2.6573% 1837 0.835734 1.196554 2.7232% 1836 0.813578 1.229138 2.7994% 1835 0.791423 1.263547 2.8871% 1834 0.769215 1.300027 2.9657% 1833 0.747059 1.338582 3.0563% 1832 0.724904 1.379494 3.1604% 1831 0.702696 1.423091 3.4660% 1830 0.679156 1.472415 2.4653% 1829 0.662816 1.508715 2.6804% 1828 0.645514 1.549154 10.3427% 1827 0.585008 1.709378 -4.2314% 1826 0.610856 1.637047 2.9150% 1825 0.593554 1.684767 3.0026% 1824 0.576252 1.735353 3.0955% 1823 0.558949 1.789071 3.1944% 1822 0.541647 1.846221 3.3102% 1821 0.524292 1.907335 3.2277% 1820 0.507898 1.968899 2.6573% 1819 0.494751 2.021218 2.6261% 1818 0.482091 2.074297 2.6969% 1817 0.469431

251

2.130239 2.7717% 1816 0.456771 2.189283 2.8507% 1815 0.444110 2.251693 2.9343% 1814 0.431450 2.317765 3.0231% 1813 0.418790 2.387832 3.1039% 1812 0.406182 2.461948 3.2172% 1811 0.393522 2.541153 3.0969% 1810 0.381701 2.619850 2.9144% 1809 0.370892 2.696203 2.8225% 1808 0.360711 2.772302 2.9199% 1807 0.350477 2.853251 2.9918% 1806 0.340296 2.938614 3.0841% 1805 0.330116 3.029243 3.1822% 1804 0.319935 3.125639 3.2868% 1803 0.309754 3.228372 3.3985% 1802 0.299573 3.338088 3.5180% 1801 0.289392 3.455523 3.3999% 1800 0.279876 3.573009 2.8419% 1799 0.272142 3.674549 2.7485% 1798 0.264863 3.775543 2.8261% 1797 0.257583 3.882245 3.7832% 1796 0.248193 4.029118 2.1272% 1795 0.243024 4.114825 3.0879% 1794 0.235744 4.241889 3.1625% 1793 0.228517 4.376039 3.2904% 1792 0.221238 4.520029 3.4024% 1791 0.213958 4.673817 3.2296% 1790 0.207264 4.824760 41.3145% 1780 0.146669 6.818084 29.4353% 1770 0.113314 8.825008 83.4728% 1750 0.061761 16.191493 29.2845% 1740 0.047771 20.933083 94.2514% 1720 0.024592 40.662806 85.8111% 1700 0.013235 75.555998 19.2490% 1690 0.011099 90.099810 88.0250% 1670 0.005903 169.410188

BASE YEAR: 1842

YEAR BYEAR/AYEAR AYEAR/BYEAR GROWTH%

2009 16.431199 0.060860 8.2857% 2001 15.173938 0.065902 1.0000% 2000 15.023700 0.066562 1.0000% 1999 14.874950 0.067227 1.0000% 1998 14.727673 0.067899 1.0000% 1997 14.581855 0.068578 1.0000% 1996 14.437480 0.069264 1.0000% 1995 14.294535 0.069957 0.9992% 1994 14.153114 0.070656 1.0008% 1993 14.012876 0.071363 1.0000% 1992 13.874135 0.072077 0.9295% 1991 13.746361 0.072747 1.2505% 1990 13.576584 0.073656 0.7224% 1989 13.479204 0.074188 1.1077% 1988 13.331534 0.075010 0.8834% 1987 13.214800 0.075673 0.5594% 1986 13.141292 0.076096 1.3056% 1985 12.971927 0.077090 0.7673% 1984 12.873153 0.077681 0.8149% 1983 12.769092 0.078314 0.9737% 1982 12.645953 0.079077 0.9508% 1981 12.526847 0.079829 0.9031% 1980 12.414733 0.080549 2.2701% 1979 12.139166 0.082378 1.0042% 1978 12.018479 0.083205 0.9896% 1977 11.900709 0.084029 0.9103% 1976 11.793350 0.084794 0.8394% 1975 11.695176 0.085505 0.9042% 1974 11.590379 0.086278 1.1568% 1973 11.457836 0.087277 0.9427% 1972 11.350831 0.088099 0.7426% 1971 11.267157 0.088754 1.4697% 1970 11.103958 0.090058 0.6968% 1969 11.027119 0.090686 0.8565% 1968 10.933470 0.091462 1.5090% 1967 10.770932 0.092842 0.9949% 1966 10.664827 0.093766 1.0575% 1965 10.553230 0.094758 1.1300% 1964 10.435309 0.095828 1.5537% 1963 10.275661 0.097317 1.4658% 1962 10.127214 0.098744 1.5364% 1961 9.973971 0.100261 2.1586% 1960 9.763218 0.102425 -1.6655% 1959 9.928577 0.100719 4.3080% 1958 9.518520 0.105058 2.1130% 1957 9.321559 0.107278 1.9895% 1956 9.139725 0.109412 2.1231% 1955 8.949714 0.111735 1.4496% 1954 8.821832 0.113355 2.1573% 1953 8.635541 0.115801 1.2298% 1952 8.530635 0.117225 1.6814% 1951 8.389575 0.119196 1.6233% 1950 8.255564 0.121130 1.4265% 1949 8.139452 0.122858 1.7790% 1948 7.997179 0.125044 1.8242% 1947 7.853911 0.127325 -2.6320% 1946 8.066217 0.123974 3.1768% 1945 7.817859 0.127912 6.4754% 1944 7.342408 0.136195 -0.3437% 1943 7.367729 0.135727 0.6562% 1942 7.319695 0.136618 0.6633% 1941 7.271464 0.137524 -5.6614% 1940 7.707837 0.129738 8.0381% 1939 7.134369 0.140167 0.8126% 1938 7.076860 0.141306 0.7762% 1937 7.022349 0.142402 0.6029% 1936 6.980267 0.143261 0.5244% 1935 6.943854 0.144012 -3.0364% 1934 7.161297 0.139640 4.6271% 1933 6.844590 0.146101 1.3921% 1932 6.750613 0.148135 -0.2051% 1931 6.764486 0.147831 0.8886% 1930 6.704907 0.149145 1.0126% 1929 6.637694 0.150655 1.1526% 1928 6.562061 0.152391 1.2160% 1927 6.483224 0.154244 1.4086% 1926 6.393171 0.156417 1.7667% 1925 6.282185 0.159180 1.4465% 1924 6.192608 0.161483 1.7700% 1923 6.084907 0.164341 1.6165% 1922 5.988108 0.166998 1.3736% 1921 5.906968 0.169292 2.3393% 1920 5.771944 0.173252 1.3140% 1919 5.697084 0.175528 0.7676% 1918 5.653684 0.176876 0.3870% 1917 5.631889 0.177560 1.3274% 1916 5.558108 0.179917 1.4083% 1915 5.480921 0.182451 1.4458% 1914 5.402807 0.185089 1.9424% 1913 5.299864 0.188684 1.9857% 1912 5.196675 0.192431 1.5634% 1911 5.116680 0.195439 1.8169% 1910 5.025373 0.198990 1.8781% 1909 4.932734 0.202727 2.0082% 1908 4.835623 0.206799 1.9603% 1907 4.742655 0.210852 1.8264% 1906 4.657591 0.214703 1.9357% 1905 4.569147 0.218859 2.0148% 1904 4.478904 0.223269 2.1335% 1903 4.385342 0.228032 1.8151% 1902 4.307160 0.232172 1.8943% 1901 4.227085 0.236570 3.0255% 1900 4.102950 0.243727

252

0.6278% 1899 4.077351 0.245257 1.7757% 1898 4.006214 0.249612 1.8078% 1897 3.935078 0.254125 1.8396% 1896 3.863996 0.258799 1.8755% 1895 3.792859 0.263653 1.9114% 1894 3.721723 0.268693 1.9486% 1893 3.650586 0.273929 1.9858% 1892 3.579504 0.279368 2.0276% 1891 3.508367 0.285033 2.6465% 1890 3.417912 0.292576 1.5328% 1889 3.366312 0.297061 2.0811% 1888 3.297683 0.303243 2.1599% 1887 3.227964 0.309793 2.2075% 1886 3.158245 0.316632 2.2592% 1885 3.088471 0.323785 2.3095% 1884 3.018752 0.331263 2.3641% 1883 2.949032 0.339094 2.4214% 1882 2.879313 0.347305 2.4815% 1881 2.809594 0.355923 3.7644% 1880 2.707667 0.369322 0.9432% 1879 2.682366 0.372805 2.1464% 1878 2.626002 0.380807 2.1913% 1877 2.569692 0.389152 2.2426% 1876 2.513328 0.397879 2.2941% 1875 2.456964 0.407006 2.3456% 1874 2.400654 0.416553 2.4043% 1873 2.344290 0.426568 2.4635% 1872 2.287926 0.437077 2.5258% 1871 2.231562 0.448117 5.9947% 1870 2.105353 0.474980 -1.0968% 1869 2.128700 0.469770 2.1930% 1868 2.083020 0.480072 2.2394% 1867 2.037394 0.490823 2.2935% 1866 1.991714 0.502080 2.3445% 1865 1.946089 0.513851 2.4037% 1864 1.900409 0.526203 2.4599% 1863 1.854783 0.539147 2.5250% 1862 1.809103 0.552760 2.5872% 1861 1.763478 0.567061 2.9504% 1860 1.712939 0.583792 2.4012% 1859 1.672772 0.597810 2.7627% 1858 1.627800 0.614326 2.8412% 1857 1.582829 0.631780 2.9243% 1856 1.537858 0.650255 3.0161% 1855 1.492832 0.669868 3.1061% 1854 1.447860 0.690674 3.2056% 1853 1.402889 0.712815 3.3118% 1852 1.357918 0.736422 3.4252% 1851 1.312946 0.761646 4.0106% 1850 1.262320 0.792192 2.3254% 1849 1.233633 0.810614 2.7841% 1848 1.200218 0.833182 2.8590% 1847 1.166857 0.857003 2.9432% 1846 1.133497 0.882226 3.0324% 1845 1.100136 0.908978 3.1325% 1844 1.066721 0.937452 3.2284% 1843 1.033361 0.967716 3.3361% 1842 1.000000 1.000000 3.4512% 1841 0.966639 1.034512 3.8105% 1840 0.931158 1.073932 2.3861% 1839 0.909458 1.099556 2.5824% 1838 0.886563 1.127951 2.6573% 1837 0.863614 1.157925 2.7232% 1836 0.840720 1.189457 2.7994% 1835 0.817825 1.222755 2.8871% 1834 0.794876 1.258058 2.9657% 1833 0.771981 1.295368 3.0563% 1832 0.749087 1.334959 3.1604% 1831 0.726138 1.377149 3.4660% 1830 0.701813 1.424880 2.4653% 1829 0.684928 1.460008 2.6804% 1828 0.667048 1.499142 10.3427% 1827 0.604524 1.654193 -4.2314% 1826 0.631235 1.584197 2.9150% 1825 0.613355 1.630377 3.0026% 1824 0.595476 1.679330 3.0955% 1823 0.577596 1.731314 3.1944% 1822 0.559717 1.786619 3.3102% 1821 0.541783 1.845759 3.2277% 1820 0.524842 1.905335 2.6573% 1819 0.511256 1.955965 2.6261% 1818 0.498174 2.007331 2.6969% 1817 0.485091 2.061468 2.7717% 1816 0.472009 2.118605 2.8507% 1815 0.458926 2.179000 2.9343% 1814 0.445844 2.242939 3.0231% 1813 0.432761 2.310744 3.1039% 1812 0.419733 2.382468 3.2172% 1811 0.406650 2.459115 3.0969% 1810 0.394435 2.535272 2.9144% 1809 0.383265 2.609159 2.8225% 1808 0.372745 2.682802 2.9199% 1807 0.362170 2.761138 2.9918% 1806 0.351649 2.843745 3.0841% 1805 0.341128 2.931448 3.1822% 1804 0.330608 3.024732 3.2868% 1803 0.320087 3.124149 3.3985% 1802 0.309567 3.230322 3.5180% 1801 0.299046 3.343966 3.3999% 1800 0.289213 3.457660 2.8419% 1799 0.281221 3.555922 2.7485% 1798 0.273699 3.653655 2.8261% 1797 0.266176 3.756912 3.7832% 1796 0.256473 3.899044 2.1272% 1795 0.251131 3.981984 3.0879% 1794 0.243609 4.104945 3.1625% 1793 0.236141 4.234765 3.2904% 1792 0.228618 4.374106 3.4024% 1791 0.221096 4.522929 3.2296% 1790 0.214179 4.669000 41.3145% 1780 0.151562 6.597972 29.4353% 1770 0.117095 8.540105 83.4728% 1750 0.063821 15.668773 29.2845% 1740 0.049365 20.257288 94.2514% 1720 0.025413 39.350064 85.8111% 1700 0.013677 73.116780 19.2490% 1690 0.011469 87.191065 88.0250% 1670 0.006100 163.941019

BASE YEAR: 1841

YEAR BYEAR/AYEAR AYEAR/BYEAR GROWTH%

2009 16.998272 0.058830 8.2857% 2001 15.697620 0.063704 1.0000% 2000 15.542197 0.064341 1.0000% 1999 15.388313 0.064984 1.0000% 1998 15.235954 0.065634 1.0000% 1997 15.085103 0.066291 1.0000% 1996 14.935745 0.066953 1.0000% 1995 14.787867 0.067623 0.9992% 1994 14.641565 0.068299 1.0008% 1993 14.496487 0.068982 1.0000% 1992 14.352958 0.069672 0.9295% 1991 14.220775 0.070320 1.2505% 1990 14.045138 0.071199 0.7224% 1989 13.944397 0.071713 1.1077% 1988 13.791631 0.072508 0.8834% 1987 13.670868 0.073148 0.5594% 1986 13.594823 0.073557 1.3056% 1985 13.419613 0.074518 0.7673% 1984 13.317431 0.075090 0.8149% 1983 13.209778 0.075701 0.9737% 1982 13.082389 0.076439 0.9508% 1981 12.959172 0.077165 0.9031% 1980

12.843190 0.077862 2.2701% 1979 12.558112 0.079630 1.0042% 1978 12.433260 0.080429 0.9896% 1977 12.311425 0.081225 0.9103% 1976 12.200361 0.081965 0.8394% 1975 12.098799 0.082653 0.9042% 1974 11.990385 0.083400 1.1568% 1973 11.853268 0.084365 0.9427% 1972 11.742570 0.085160 0.7426% 1971 11.656009 0.085793 1.4697% 1970 11.487177 0.087054 0.6968% 1969 11.407686 0.087660 0.8565% 1968 11.310805 0.088411 1.5090% 1967 11.142658 0.089745 0.9949% 1966 11.032891 0.090638 1.0575% 1965 10.917442 0.091597 1.1300% 1964 10.795452 0.092632 1.5537% 1963 10.630294 0.094071 1.4658% 1962 10.476724 0.095450 1.5364% 1961 10.318192 0.096916 2.1586% 1960 10.100166 0.099008 -1.6655% 1959 10.271232 0.097359 4.3080% 1958 9.847023 0.101554 2.1130% 1957 9.643264 0.103699 1.9895% 1956 9.455154 0.105762 2.1231% 1955 9.258586 0.108008 1.4496% 1954 9.126290 0.109574 2.1573% 1953 8.933570 0.111937 1.2298% 1952 8.825044 0.113314 1.6814% 1951 8.679115 0.115219 1.6233% 1950 8.540480 0.117089 1.4265% 1949 8.420360 0.118760 1.7790% 1948 8.273177 0.120873 1.8242% 1947 8.124965 0.123077 -2.6320% 1946 8.344598 0.119838 3.1768% 1945 8.087668 0.123645 6.4754% 1944 7.595808 0.131652 -0.3437% 1943 7.622003 0.131199 0.6562% 1942 7.572312 0.132060 0.6633% 1941 7.522416 0.132936 -5.6614% 1940 7.973850 0.125410 8.0381% 1939 7.380590 0.135491 0.8126% 1938 7.321096 0.136592 0.7762% 1937 7.264704 0.137652 0.6029% 1936 7.221170 0.138482 0.5244% 1935 7.183500 0.139208 -3.0364% 1934 7.408448 0.134981 4.6271% 1933 7.080810 0.141227 1.3921% 1932 6.983590 0.143193 - 0.2051% 1931 6.997942 0.142899 0.8886% 1930 6.936306 0.144169 1.0126% 1929 6.866774 0.145629 1.1526% 1928 6.788530 0.147307 1.2160% 1927 6.706973 0.149099 1.4086% 1926 6.613812 0.151190 1.7667% 1925 6.498995 0.153870 1.4465% 1924 6.406327 0.156096 1.7700% 1923 6.294909 0.158859 1.6165% 1922 6.194770 0.161427 1.3736% 1921 6.110828 0.163644 2.3393% 1920 5.971145 0.167472 1.3140% 1919 5.893701 0.169673 0.7676% 1918 5.848803 0.170975 0.3870% 1917 5.826256 0.171637 1.3274% 1916 5.749930 0.173915 1.4083% 1915 5.670078 0.176364 1.4458% 1914 5.589269 0.178914 1.9424% 1913 5.482772 0.182389 1.9857% 1912 5.376022 0.186011 1.5634% 1911 5.293267 0.188919 1.8169% 1910 5.198809 0.192352 1.8781% 1909 5.102972 0.195964 2.0082% 1908 5.002509 0.199900 1.9603% 1907 4.906333 0.203818 1.8264% 1906 4.818333 0.207541 1.9357% 1905 4.726837 0.211558 2.0148% 1904 4.633480 0.215821 2.1335% 1903 4.536688 0.220425 1.8151% 1902 4.455809 0.224426 1.8943% 1901 4.372970 0.228678 3.0255% 1900 4.244551 0.235596 0.6278% 1899 4.218068 0.237075 1.7757% 1898 4.144476 0.241285 1.8078% 1897 4.070885 0.245647 1.8396% 1896 3.997350 0.250166 1.8755% 1895 3.923758 0.254858 1.9114% 1894 3.850166 0.259729 1.9486% 1893 3.776575 0.264790 1.9858% 1892 3.703040 0.270048 2.0276% 1891 3.629448 0.275524 2.6465% 1890 3.535871 0.282816 1.5328% 1889 3.482490 0.287151 2.0811% 1888 3.411493 0.293127 2.1599% 1887 3.339367 0.299458 2.2075% 1886 3.267242 0.306069 2.2592% 1885 3.195060 0.312983 2.3095% 1884 3.122935 0.320212 2.3641% 1883 3.050809 0.327782 2.4214% 1882 2.978684 0.335719 2.4815% 1881 2.906558 0.344050 3.7644% 1880 2.801113 0.357001 0.9432% 1879 2.774939 0.360368 2.1464% 1878 2.716630 0.368103 2.1913% 1877 2.658377 0.376169 2.2426% 1876 2.600068 0.384605 2.2941% 1875 2.541758 0.393428 2.3456% 1874 2.483505 0.402657 2.4043% 1873 2.425196 0.412338 2.4635% 1872 2.366887 0.422496 2.5258% 1871 2.308577 0.433167 5.9947% 1870 2.178012 0.459134 -1.0968% 1869 2.202165 0.454098 2.1930% 1868 2.154909 0.464057 2.2394% 1867 2.107709 0.474449 2.2935% 1866 2.060452 0.485330 2.3445% 1865 2.013252 0.496709 2.4037% 1864 1.965996 0.508648 2.4599% 1863 1.918795 0.521160 2.5250% 1862 1.871539 0.534320 2.5872% 1861 1.824339 0.548144 2.9504% 1860 1.772056 0.564316 2.4012% 1859 1.730502 0.577867 2.7627% 1858 1.683979 0.593832 2.8412% 1857 1.637456 0.610704 2.9243% 1856 1.590932 0.628562 3.0161% 1855 1.544352 0.647521 3.1061% 1854 1.497829 0.667633 3.2056% 1853 1.451305 0.689035 3.3118% 1852 1.404782 0.711854 3.4252% 1851 1.358259 0.736237 4.0106% 1850 1.305885 0.765764 3.3254% 1849 1.276208 0.783571 2.7841% 1848 1.241640 0.805387 2.8590% 1847 1.207128 0.828413 2.9432% 1846 1.172616 0.852794 3.0324% 1845 1.138104 0.878654 3.1325% 1844 1.103536 0.906178 3.2284% 1843 1.069024 0.935433 3.3361% 1842 1.034512 0.966639 3.4512% 1841 1.000000 1.000000 3.8105% 1840 0.963294 1.038105 2.3861% 1839 0.940845 1.062875 2.5824% 1838 0.917160 1.090322 2.6573% 1837 0.893419 1.119296 2.7232% 1836 0.869734 1.149776 2.7994% 1835 0.846050 1.181964 2.8871% 1834 0.822309 1.216088 2.9657% 1833 0.798624

254

1.252154 3.0563% 1832 0.774939 1.290424 3.1604% 1831 0.751198 1.331206 3.4660% 1830
0.726034 1.377346 2.4653% 1829 0.708566 1.411301 2.6804% 1828 0.690069 1.449130
10.3427% 1827 0.625388 1.599008 -4.2314% 1826 0.653020 1.531347 2.9150% 1825
0.634523 1.575986 3.0026% 1824 0.616027 1.623306 3.0955% 1823 0.597530 1.673556
3.1944% 1822 0.579033 1.727016 3.3102% 1821 0.560480 1.784184 3.2277% 1820 0.542955
1.841772 2.6573% 1819 0.528901 1.890713 2.6261% 1818 0.515367 1.940365 2.6969% 1817
0.501833 1.992696 2.7717% 1816 0.488299 2.047927 2.8507% 1815 0.474765 2.106307
2.9343% 1814 0.461230 2.168113 3.0231% 1813 0.447696 2.233657 3.1039% 1812 0.434219
2.302987 3.2172% 1811 0.420685 2.377078 3.0969% 1810 0.408048 2.450694 2.9144% 1809
0.396492 2.522116 2.8225% 1808 0.385609 2.593302 2.9199% 1807 0.374669 2.669025
2.9918% 1806 0.363785 2.748876 3.0841% 1805 0.352901 2.833653 3.1822% 1804 0.342018
2.923825 3.2868% 1803 0.331134 3.019925 3.3985% 1802 0.320250 3.122557 3.5180% 1801
0.309367 3.232410 3.3999% 1800 0.299194 3.342310 2.8419% 1799 0.290927 3.437294
2.7485% 1798 0.283144 3.531767 2.8261% 1797 0.275342 3.631579 3.7832% 1796 0.265325
3.768969 2.1272% 1795 0.259798 3.849143 3.0879% 1794 0.252016 3.968002 3.1625% 1793
0.244290 4.093490 3.2904% 1792 0.236508 4.228183 3.4024% 1791 0.228726 4.372041
3.2296% 1790 0.221570 4.513239 41.3145% 1780 0.156792 6.377859 29.4353% 1770
0.121136 8.255202 83.4728% 1750 0.066024 15.146054 29.2845% 1740 0.051069 19.581493
94.2514% 1720 0.026290 38.037323 85.8111% 1700 0.014149 70.677561 19.2490% 1690
0.011865 84.282319 88.0250% 1670 0.006310 158.471850

BASE YEAR: 1840

YEAR BYEAR/AYEAR AYEAR/BYEAR GROWTH%

2009 17.645989 0.056670 8.2857% 2001 16.295776 0.061366 1.0000% 2000
16.134430 0.061979 1.0000% 1999 15.974683 0.062599 1.0000% 1998 15.816518 0.063225
1.0000% 1997 15.659919 0.063857 1.0000% 1996 15.504870 0.064496 1.0000% 1995
15.351357 0.065141 0.9992% 1994 15.199480 0.065792 1.0008% 1993 15.048874 0.066450
1.0000% 1992 14.899876 0.067115 0.9295% 1991 14.762656 0.067738 1.2505% 1990
14.580327 0.068586 0.7224% 1989 14.475747 0.069081 1.1077% 1988 14.317160 0.069846
0.8834% 1987 14.191795 0.070463 0.5594% 1986 14.112852 0.070857 1.3056% 1985
13.930966 0.071783 0.7673% 1984 13.824890 0.072333 0.8149% 1983 13.713135 0.072923
0.9737% 1982 13.580892 0.073633 0.9508% 1981 13.452980 0.074333 0.9031% 1980
13.332578 0.075004 2.2701% 1979 13.036637 0.076707 1.0042% 1978 12.907028 0.077477
0.9896% 1977 12.780550 0.078244 0.9103% 1976 12.665254 0.078956 0.8394% 1975
12.559822 0.079619 0.9042% 1974 12.447277 0.080339 1.1568% 1973 12.304935 0.081268
0.9427% 1972 12.190020 0.082034 0.7426% 1971 12.100159 0.082644 1.4697% 1970
11.924895 0.083858 0.6968% 1969 11.842375 0.084443 0.8565% 1968 11.741802 0.085166
1.5090% 1967 11.567247 0.086451 0.9949% 1966 11.453298 0.087311 1.0575% 1965
11.333450 0.088234 1.1300% 1964 11.206811 0.089231 1.5537% 1963 11.035360 0.090618
1.4658% 1962 10.875939 0.091946 1.5364% 1961 10.711366 0.093359 2.1586% 1960
10.485032 0.095374 -1.6655% 1959 10.662616 0.093786 4.3080% 1958 10.222242 0.097826
2.1130% 1957 10.010719 0.099893 1.9895% 1956 9.815442 0.101880 2.1231% 1955
9.611383 0.104043 1.4496% 1954 9.474046 0.105552 2.1573% 1953 9.273983 0.107829
1.2298% 1952 9.161321 0.109155 1.6814% 1951 9.009832 0.110990 1.6233% 1950 8.865914
0.112792 1.4265% 1949 8.741217 0.114401 1.7790% 1948 8.588426 0.116436 1.8242% 1947
8.434566 0.118560 -2.6320% 1946 8.662568 0.115439 3.1768% 1945 8.395848 0.119106
6.4754% 1944 7.885246 0.126819 -0.3437% 1943 7.912439 0.126383 0.6562% 1942
7.860854 0.127213 0.6633% 1941 7.809057 0.128056 -5.6614% 1940 8.277692 0.120807
8.0381% 1939 7.661826 0.130517 0.8126% 1938 7.600066 0.131578 0.7762% 1937 7.541525
0.132599 0.6029% 1936 7.496331 0.133399 0.5244% 1935 7.457226 0.134098 -3.0364%
1934 7.690740 0.130026 4.6271% 1933 7.350623 0.136043 1.3921% 1932 7.249699 0.137937
-0.2051% 1931 7.264597 0.137654 0.8886% 1930 7.200613 0.138877 1.0126% 1929
7.128431 0.140283 1.1526% 1928 7.047206 0.141900 1.2160% 1927 6.962541 0.143626
1.4086% 1926 6.865830 0.145649 1.7667% 1925 6.746639 0.148222 1.4465% 1924 6.650440
0.150366 1.7700% 1923 6.534776 0.153027 1.6165% 1922 6.430820 0.155501 1.3736% 1921
6.343681 0.157637 2.3393% 1920 6.198675 0.161325 1.3140% 1919 6.118280 0.163445
0.7676% 1918 6.071671 0.164699 0.3870% 1917 6.048265 0.165337 1.3274% 1916 5.969030

255

0.167531 1.4083% 1915 5.886136 0.169891 1.4458% 1914 5.802247 0.172347 1.9424% 1913
5.691693 0.175695 1.9857% 1912 5.580875 0.179183 1.5634% 1911 5.494966 0.181985
1.8169% 1910 5.396909 0.185291 1.8781% 1909 5.297420 0.188771 2.0082% 1908 5.193129
0.192562 1.9603% 1907 5.093288 0.196337 1.8264% 1906 5.001935 0.199923 1.9357% 1905
4.906953 0.203792 2.0148% 1904 4.810038 0.207899 2.1335% 1903 4.709558 0.212334
1.8151% 1902 4.625597 0.216188 1.8943% 1901 4.539601 0.220284 3.0255% 1900 4.406289
0.226948 0.6278% 1899 4.378797 0.228373 1.7757% 1898 4.302401 0.232428 1.8078% 1897
4.226005 0.236630 1.8396% 1896 4.149668 0.240983 1.8755% 1895 4.073272 0.245503
1.9114% 1894 3.996876 0.250195 1.9486% 1893 3.920481 0.255071 1.9858% 1892 3.844143
0.260136 2.0276% 1891 3.767748 0.265411 2.6465% 1890 3.670604 0.272435 1.5328% 1889
3.615190 0.276611 2.0811% 1888 3.541487 0.282367 2.1599% 1887 3.466613 0.288466
2.2075% 1886 3.391740 0.294834 2.2592% 1885 3.316807 0.301495 2.3095% 1884 3.241934
0.308458 2.3641% 1883 3.167060 0.315750 2.4214% 1882 3.092186 0.323396 2.4815% 1881
3.017312 0.331421 3.7644% 1880 2.907850 0.343897 0.9432% 1879 2.880678 0.347140
2.1464% 1878 2.820147 0.354591 2.1913% 1877 2.759674 0.362362 2.2426% 1876 2.699143
0.370488 2.2941% 1875 2.638612 0.378987 2.3456% 1874 2.578139 0.387877 2.4043% 1873
2.517608 0.397202 2.4635% 1872 2.457077 0.406988 2.5258% 1871 2.396545 0.417267
5.9947% 1870 2.261005 0.442281 -1.0968% 1869 2.286079 0.437430 2.1930% 1868
2.237021 0.447023 2.2394% 1867 2.188023 0.457034 2.2935% 1866 2.138966 0.467516
2.3445% 1865 2.089967 0.478476 2.4037% 1864 2.040910 0.489978 2.4599% 1863 1.991911
0.502030 2.5250% 1862 1.942854 0.514707 2.5872% 1861 1.893855 0.528024 2.9504% 1860
1.839580 0.543602 2.4012% 1859 1.796443 0.556656 2.7627% 1858 1.748147 0.572034
2.8412% 1857 1.699851 0.588287 2.9243% 1856 1.651554 0.605490 3.0161% 1855 1.603200
0.623753 3.1061% 1854 1.554904 0.643127 3.2056% 1853 1.506607 0.663743 3.3118% 1852
1.458311 0.685725 3.4252% 1851 1.410015 0.709212 4.0106% 1850 1.355645 0.737656
2.3254% 1849 1.324838 0.754809 2.7841% 1848 1.288952 0.775824 2.8590% 1847 1.253125
0.798005 2.9432% 1846 1.217298 0.821491 3.0324% 1845 1.181471 0.846402 3.1325% 1844
1.145586 0.872916 3.2284% 1843 1.109759 0.901097 3.3361% 1842 1.073932 0.931158
3.4512% 1841 1.038105 0.963294 3.8105% 1840 1.000000 1.000000 2.3861% 1839 0.976696
1.023861 2.5824% 1838 0.952108 1.050301 2.6573% 1837 0.927463 1.078211 2.7232% 1836
0.902876 1.107572 2.7994% 1835 0.878288 1.138578 2.8871% 1834 0.853643 1.171450
2.9657% 1833 0.829056 1.206192 3.0563% 1832 0.804468 1.243057 3.1604% 1831 0.779823
1.282343 3.4660% 1830 0.753700 1.326788 2.4653% 1829 0.735566 1.359498 2.6804% 1828
0.716364 1.395938 10.3427% 1827 0.649218 1.540315 -4.2314% 1826 0.677903 1.475137
2.9150% 1825 0.658702 1.518138 3.0026% 1824 0.639500 1.563721 3.0955% 1823 0.620299
1.612126 3.1944% 1822 0.601097 1.663624 3.3102% 1821 0.581838 1.718693 3.2277% 1820
0.563645 1.774168 2.6573% 1819 0.549055 1.821312 2.6261% 1818 0.535005 1.869142
2.6969% 1817 0.520955 1.919552 2.7717% 1816 0.506905 1.972755 2.8507% 1815 0.492855
2.028993 2.9343% 1814 0.478806 2.088530 3.0231% 1813 0.464756 2.151668 3.1039% 1812
0.450765 2.218453 3.2172% 1811 0.436715 2.289824 3.0969% 1810 0.423596 2.360738
2.9144% 1809 0.411601 2.429539 2.8225% 1808 0.400302 2.498112 2.9199% 1807 0.388945
2.571055 2.9918% 1806 0.377647 2.647975 3.0841% 1805 0.366349 2.729640 3.1822% 1804
0.355050 2.816503 3.2868% 1803 0.343752 2.909075 3.3985% 1802 0.332453 3.007940
3.5180% 1801 0.321155 3.113760 3.3999% 1800 0.310595 3.219627 2.8419% 1799 0.302012
3.311124 2.7485% 1798 0.293934 3.402129 2.8261% 1797 0.285855 3.498277 3.7832% 1796
0.275435 3.630625 2.1272% 1795 0.269698 3.707855 3.0879% 1794 0.261619 3.822352
3.1625% 1793 0.253599 3.943234 3.2904% 1792 0.245520 4.072983 3.4024% 1791 0.237442
4.211560 3.2296% 1790 0.230013 4.347575 41.3145% 1780 0.162767 6.143752 29.4353%
1770 0.125752 7.952185 83.4728% 1750 0.068540 14.590100 29.2845% 1740 0.053015
18.862731 94.2514% 1720 0.027292 36.641118 85.8111% 1700 0.014688 68.083256
19.2490% 1690 0.012317 81.188636 88.0250% 1670 0.006551 152.654951

BASE YEAR: 1839

YEAR BYEAR/AYEAR AYEAR/BYEAR GROWTH%

2009 18.067031 0.055349 8.2857% 2001 16.684602 0.059936 1.0000% 2000
16.519406 0.060535 1.0000% 1999 16.355848 0.061140 1.0000% 1998 16.193909 0.061752
1.0000% 1997 16.033573 0.062369 1.0000% 1996 15.874825 0.062993 1.0000% 1995

256

15.717648 0.063623 0.9992% 1994 15.562148 0.064258 1.0008% 1993 15.407948 0.064902 1.0000% 1992 15.255394 0.065551 0.9295% 1991 15.114901 0.066160 1.2505% 1990 14.928221 0.066987 0.7224% 1989 14.821146 0.067471 1.1077% 1988 14.658775 0.068219 0.8834% 1987 14.530418 0.068821 0.5594% 1986 14.449592 0.069206 1.3056% 1985 14.263366 0.070110 0.7673% 1984 14.154759 0.070648 0.8149% 1983 14.040338 0.071223 0.9737% 1982 13.904939 0.071917 0.9508% 1981 13.773975 0.072601 0.9031% 1980 13.650700 0.073256 2.2701% 1979 13.347698 0.074919 1.0042% 1978 13.214996 0.075672 0.9896% 1977 13.085501 0.076420 0.9103% 1976 12.967454 0.077116 0.8394% 1975 12.859506 0.077763 0.9042% 1974 12.744276 0.078467 1.1568% 1973 12.598538 0.079374 0.9427% 1972 12.480880 0.080123 0.7426% 1971 12.388876 0.080718 1.4697% 1970 12.209429 0.081904 0.6968% 1969 12.124940 0.082475 0.8565% 1968 12.021967 0.083181 1.5090% 1967 11.843248 0.084436 0.9949% 1966 11.726579 0.085276 1.0575% 1965 11.603872 0.086178 1.1300% 1964 11.474212 0.087152 1.5537% 1963 11.298669 0.088506 1.4658% 1962 11.135444 0.089803 1.5364% 1961 10.966944 0.091183 2.1586% 1960 10.735210 0.093151 -1.6655% 1959 10.917031 0.091600 4.3080% 1958 10.466150 0.095546 2.1130% 1957 10.249580 0.097565 1.9895% 1956 10.049643 0.099506 2.1231% 1955 9.840716 0.101619 1.4496% 1954 9.700102 0.103092 2.1573% 1953 9.495265 0.105316 1.2298% 1952 9.379915 0.106611 1.6814% 1951 9.224811 0.108403 1.6233% 1950 9.077459 0.110163 1.4265% 1949 8.949787 0.111734 1.7790% 1948 8.793350 0.113722 1.8242% 1947 8.635819 0.115797 -2.6320% 1946 8.869261 0.112749 3.1768% 1945 8.596177 0.116331 6.4754% 1944 8.073392 0.123864 -0.3437% 1943 8.101234 0.123438 0.6562% 1942 8.048418 0.124248 0.6633% 1941 7.995385 0.125072 -5.6614% 1940 8.475202 0.117991 8.0381% 1939 7.844642 0.127476 0.8126% 1938 7.781407 0.128511 0.7762% 1937 7.721470 0.129509 0.6029% 1936 7.675198 0.130290 0.5244% 1935 7.635159 0.130973 -3.0364% 1934 7.874251 0.126996 4.6271% 1933 7.526013 0.132872 1.3921% 1932 7.422680 0.134722 -0.2051% 1931 7.437935 0.134446 0.8886% 1930 7.372423 0.135641 1.0126% 1929 7.298520 0.137014 1.1526% 1928 7.215356 0.138593 1.2160% 1927 7.128671 0.140279 1.4086% 1926 7.029653 0.142255 1.7667% 1925 6.907617 0.144768 1.4465% 1924 6.809123 0.146862 1.7700% 1923 6.690699 0.149461 1.6165% 1922 6.584263 0.151877 1.3736% 1921 6.495044 0.153964 2.3393% 1920 6.346578 0.157565 1.3140% 1919 6.264265 0.159636 0.7676% 1918 6.216544 0.160861 0.3870% 1917 6.192580 0.161484 1.3274% 1916 6.111454 0.163627 1.4083% 1915 6.026582 0.165932 1.4458% 1914 5.940692 0.168331 1.9424% 1913 5.827499 0.171600 1.9857% 1912 5.714037 0.175008 1.5634% 1911 5.626079 0.177744 1.8169% 1910 5.525682 0.180973 1.8781% 1909 5.423819 0.184372 2.0082% 1908 5.317040 0.188075 1.9603% 1907 5.214817 0.191761 1.8264% 1906 5.121284 0.195264 1.9357% 1905 5.024035 0.199043 2.0148% 1904 4.924808 0.203054 2.1335% 1903 4.821931 0.207386 1.8151% 1902 4.735966 0.211150 1.8943% 1901 4.647918 0.215150 3.0255% 1900 4.511425 0.221659 0.6278% 1899 4.483277 0.223051 1.7757% 1898 4.405059 0.227012 1.8078% 1897 4.326840 0.231116 1.8396% 1896 4.248681 0.235367 1.8755% 1895 4.170463 0.239782 1.9114% 1894 4.092244 0.244365 1.9486% 1893 4.014025 0.249126 1.9858% 1892 3.935867 0.254074 2.0276% 1891 3.857648 0.259225 2.6465% 1890 3.758187 0.266086 1.5328% 1889 3.701450 0.270164 2.0811% 1888 3.625989 0.275787 2.1599% 1887 3.549329 0.281743 2.2075% 1886 3.472668 0.287963 2.2592% 1885 3.395948 0.294469 2.3095% 1884 3.319288 0.301269 2.3641% 1883 3.242628 0.308392 2.4214% 1882 3.165967 0.315859 2.4815% 1881 3.089307 0.323697 3.7644% 1880 2.977232 0.335882 0.9432% 1879 2.949413 0.339051 2.1464% 1878 2.887437 0.346328 2.1913% 1877 2.825521 0.353917 2.2426% 1876 2.763546 0.361854 2.2941% 1875 2.701570 0.370155 2.3456% 1874 2.639655 0.378837 2.4043% 1873 2.577679 0.387946 2.4635% 1872 2.515704 0.397503 2.5258% 1871 2.453728 0.407543 5.9947% 1870 2.314954 0.431974 -1.0968% 1869 2.340626 0.427236 2.1930% 1868 2.290398 0.436605 2.2394% 1867 2.240230 0.446383 2.2935% 1866 2.190002 0.456621 2.3445% 1865 2.139835 0.467326 2.4037% 1864 2.089607 0.478559 2.4599% 1863 2.039439 0.490331 2.5250% 1862 1.989211 0.502712 2.5872% 1861 1.939043 0.515718 2.9504% 1860 1.883473 0.530934 2.4012% 1859 1.839307 0.543683 2.7627% 1858 1.789859 0.558703 2.8412% 1857 1.740410 0.574577 2.9243% 1856 1.690961 0.591380 3.0161% 1855 1.641453 0.609216 3.1061% 1854 1.592004 0.628139 3.2056% 1853 1.542556 0.648275 3.3118% 1852 1.493107 0.669744 3.4252% 1851 1.443659 0.692685 4.0106% 1850 1.387992 0.720465

2.3254% 1849 1.356449 0.737219 2.7841% 1848 1.319708 0.757744 2.8590% 1847 1.283026
0.779408 2.9432% 1846 1.246344 0.802347 3.0324% 1845 1.209662 0.826677 3.1325% 1844
1.172920 0.852573 3.2284% 1843 1.136238 0.880097 3.3361% 1842 1.099556 0.909458
3.4512% 1841 1.062875 0.940845 3.8105% 1840 1.023861 0.976696 2.3861% 1839 1.000000
1.000000 2.5824% 1838 0.974826 1.025824 2.6573% 1837 0.949592 1.053083 2.7232% 1836
0.924419 1.081761 2.7994% 1835 0.899245 1.112044 2.8871% 1834 0.874011 1.144150
2.9657% 1833 0.848837 1.178082 3.0563% 1832 0.823663 1.214088 3.1604% 1831 0.798430
1.252459 3.4660% 1830 0.771683 1.295868 2.4653% 1829 0.753117 1.327815 2.6804% 1828
0.733457 1.363406 10.3427% 1827 0.664709 1.504418 -4.2314% 1826 0.694078 1.440760
2.9150% 1825 0.674419 1.482759 3.0026% 1824 0.654759 1.527279 3.0955% 1823 0.635099
1.574556 3.1944% 1822 0.615440 1.624854 3.3102% 1821 0.595720 1.678640 3.2277% 1820
0.577093 1.732822 2.6573% 1819 0.562155 1.778868 2.6261% 1818 0.547770 1.825583
2.6969% 1817 0.533385 1.874817 2.7717% 1816 0.519000 1.926781 2.8507% 1815 0.504615
1.981708 2.9343% 1814 0.490230 2.039858 3.0231% 1813 0.475845 2.101524 3.1039% 1812
0.461520 2.166753 3.2172% 1811 0.447135 2.236461 3.0969% 1810 0.433704 2.305722
2.9144% 1809 0.421422 2.372920 2.8225% 1808 0.409854 2.439895 2.9199% 1807 0.398226
2.511138 2.9918% 1806 0.386658 2.586266 3.0841% 1805 0.375090 2.666027 3.1822% 1804
0.363522 2.750866 3.2868% 1803 0.351954 2.841281 3.3985% 1802 0.340386 2.937841
3.5180% 1801 0.328818 3.041196 3.3999% 1800 0.318006 3.144595 2.8419% 1799 0.309218
3.233960 2.7485% 1798 0.300947 3.322844 2.8261% 1797 0.292676 3.416752 3.7832% 1796
0.282007 3.546015 2.1272% 1795 0.276133 3.621446 3.0879% 1794 0.267861 3.733274
3.1625% 1793 0.259650 3.851339 3.2904% 1792 0.251379 3.978064 3.4024% 1791 0.243107
4.113412 3.2296% 1790 0.235501 4.246257 41.3145% 1780 0.166651 6.000575 29.4353%
1770 0.128752 7.766864 83.4728% 1750 0.070175 14.250085 29.2845% 1740 0.054280
18.423145 94.2514% 1720 0.027943 35.787216 85.8111% 1700 0.015038 66.496612
19.2490% 1690 0.012611 79.296578 88.0250% 1670 0.006707 149.097408

BASE YEAR: 1838

YEAR BYEAR/AYEAR AYEAR/BYEAR GROWTH%

2009 18.533593 0.053956 8.2857% 2001 17.115464 0.058427 1.0000% 2000
16.946002 0.059011 1.0000% 1999 16.778220 0.059601 1.0000% 1998 16.612098 0.060197
1.0000% 1997 16.447622 0.060799 1.0000% 1996 16.284775 0.061407 1.0000% 1995
16.123539 0.062021 0.9992% 1994 15.964023 0.062641 1.0008% 1993 15.805842 0.063268
1.0000% 1992 15.649348 0.063900 0.9295% 1991 15.505226 0.064494 1.2505% 1990
15.313726 0.065301 0.7224% 1989 15.203886 0.065773 1.1077% 1988 15.037322 0.066501
0.8834% 1987 14.905651 0.067089 0.5594% 1986 14.822737 0.067464 1.3056% 1985
14.631702 0.068345 0.7673% 1984 14.520290 0.068869 0.8149% 1983 14.402914 0.069430
0.9737% 1982 14.264019 0.070106 0.9508% 1981 14.129673 0.070773 0.9031% 1980
14.003215 0.071412 2.2701% 1979 13.692388 0.073033 1.0042% 1978 13.556259 0.073767
0.9896% 1977 13.423420 0.074497 0.9103% 1976 13.302324 0.075175 0.8394% 1975
13.191589 0.075806 0.9042% 1974 13.073383 0.076491 1.1568% 1973 12.923881 0.077376
0.9427% 1972 12.803185 0.078106 0.7426% 1971 12.708805 0.078686 1.4697% 1970
12.524724 0.079842 0.6968% 1969 12.438053 0.080398 0.8565% 1968 12.332421 0.081087
1.5090% 1967 12.149087 0.082311 0.9949% 1966 12.029405 0.083130 1.0575% 1965
11.903529 0.084009 1.1300% 1964 11.770521 0.084958 1.5537% 1963 11.590445 0.086278
1.4658% 1962 11.423005 0.087543 1.5364% 1961 11.250154 0.088888 2.1586% 1960
11.012435 0.090806 -1.6655% 1959 11.198952 0.089294 4.3080% 1958 10.736427 0.093141
2.1130% 1957 10.514265 0.095109 1.9895% 1956 10.309164 0.097001 2.1231% 1955
10.094841 0.099060 1.4496% 1954 9.950596 0.100496 2.1573% 1953 9.740470 0.102664
1.2298% 1952 9.622141 0.103927 1.6814% 1951 9.463032 0.105674 1.6233% 1950 9.311875
0.107390 1.4265% 1949 9.180906 0.108922 1.7790% 1948 9.020429 0.110859 1.8242% 1947
8.858829 0.112882 -2.6320% 1946 9.098300 0.109911 3.1768% 1945 8.818164 0.113402
6.4754% 1944 8.281878 0.120746 -0.3437% 1943 8.310439 0.120331 0.6562% 1942
8.256260 0.121120 0.6633% 1941 8.201857 0.121924 -5.6614% 1940 8.694065 0.115021
8.0381% 1939 8.047221 0.124267 0.8126% 1938 7.982354 0.125276 0.7762% 1937 7.920868
0.126249 0.6029% 1936 7.873401 0.127010 0.5244% 1935 7.832329 0.127676 -3.0364%
1934 8.077595 0.123799 4.6271% 1933 7.720364 0.129528 1.3921% 1932 7.614363 0.131331

258

-0.2051% 1931 7.630011 0.131061 0.8886% 1930 7.562808 0.132226 1.0126% 1929
7.486996 0.133565 1.1526% 1928 7.401685 0.135104 1.2160% 1927 7.312761 0.136747
1.4086% 1926 7.211186 0.138673 1.7667% 1925 7.085999 0.141123 1.4465% 1924 6.984961
0.143165 1.7700% 1923 6.863479 0.145699 1.6165% 1922 6.754295 0.148054 1.3736% 1921
6.662772 0.150088 2.3393% 1920 6.510472 0.153599 1.3140% 1919 6.426033 0.155617
0.7676% 1918 6.377080 0.156812 0.3870% 1917 6.352496 0.157418 1.3274% 1916 6.269276
0.159508 1.4083% 1915 6.182212 0.161754 1.4458% 1914 6.094104 0.164093 1.9424% 1913
5.977988 0.167280 1.9857% 1912 5.861596 0.170602 1.5634% 1911 5.771366 0.173269
1.8169% 1910 5.668377 0.176417 1.8781% 1909 5.563883 0.179731 2.0082% 1908 5.454347
0.183340 1.9603% 1907 5.349484 0.186934 1.8264% 1906 5.253535 0.190348 1.9357% 1905
5.153775 0.194033 2.0148% 1904 5.051986 0.197942 2.1335% 1903 4.946452 0.202165
1.8151% 1902 4.858267 0.205835 1.8943% 1901 4.767946 0.209734 3.0255% 1900 4.627928
0.216079 0.6278% 1899 4.599053 0.217436 1.7757% 1898 4.518815 0.221297 1.8078% 1897
4.438576 0.225297 1.8396% 1896 4.358399 0.229442 1.8755% 1895 4.278160 0.233745
1.9114% 1894 4.197922 0.238213 1.9486% 1893 4.117683 0.242855 1.9858% 1892 4.037506
0.247678 2.0276% 1891 3.957268 0.252700 2.6465% 1890 3.855238 0.259387 1.5328% 1889
3.797036 0.263363 2.0811% 1888 3.719626 0.268844 2.1599% 1887 3.640986 0.274651
2.2075% 1886 3.562346 0.280714 2.2592% 1885 3.483645 0.287056 2.3095% 1884 3.405005
0.293685 2.3641% 1883 3.326365 0.300628 2.4214% 1882 3.247725 0.307908 2.4815% 1881
3.169085 0.315548 3.7644% 1880 3.054116 0.327427 0.9432% 1879 3.025578 0.330515
2.1464% 1878 2.962002 0.337609 2.1913% 1877 2.898487 0.345008 2.2426% 1876 2.834911
0.352745 2.2941% 1875 2.771335 0.360837 2.3456% 1874 2.707821 0.369301 2.4043% 1873
2.644245 0.378180 2.4635% 1872 2.580669 0.387496 2.5258% 1871 2.517093 0.397284
5.9947% 1870 2.374735 0.421100 -1.0968% 1869 2.401070 0.416481 2.1930% 1868
2.349545 0.425614 2.2394% 1867 2.298082 0.435146 2.2935% 1866 2.246557 0.445126
2.3445% 1865 2.195093 0.455561 2.4037% 1864 2.143569 0.466512 2.4599% 1863 2.092105
0.477987 2.5250% 1862 2.040580 0.490057 2.5872% 1861 1.989117 0.502736 2.9504% 1860
1.932112 0.517568 2.4012% 1859 1.886805 0.529996 2.7627% 1858 1.836080 0.544639
2.8412% 1857 1.785354 0.560113 2.9243% 1856 1.734629 0.576492 3.0161% 1855 1.683842
0.593880 3.1061% 1854 1.633116 0.612326 3.2056% 1853 1.582391 0.631955 3.3118% 1852
1.531665 0.652884 3.4252% 1851 1.480939 0.675247 4.0106% 1850 1.423835 0.702329
2.3254% 1849 1.391478 0.718660 2.7841% 1848 1.353788 0.738668 2.8590% 1847 1.316158
0.759787 2.9432% 1846 1.278529 0.782149 3.0324% 1845 1.240900 0.805867 3.1325% 1844
1.203210 0.831110 3.2284% 1843 1.165580 0.857942 3.3361% 1842 1.127951 0.886563
3.4512% 1841 1.090322 0.917160 3.8105% 1840 1.050301 0.952108 2.3861% 1839 1.025824
0.974826 2.5824% 1838 1.000000 1.000000 2.6573% 1837 0.974115 1.026573 2.7232% 1836
0.948291 1.054529 2.7994% 1835 0.922467 1.084050 2.8871% 1834 0.896581 1.115348
2.9657% 1833 0.870758 1.148425 3.0563% 1832 0.844934 1.183525 3.1604% 1831 0.819048
1.220929 3.4660% 1830 0.791611 1.263246 2.4653% 1829 0.772565 1.294389 2.6804% 1828
0.752398 1.329084 10.3427% 1827 0.681874 1.466546 -4.2314% 1826 0.712002 1.404491
2.9150% 1825 0.691835 1.445432 3.0026% 1824 0.671667 1.488832 3.0955% 1823 0.651500
1.534919 3.1944% 1822 0.631333 1.583950 3.3102% 1821 0.611104 1.636382 3.2277% 1820
0.591996 1.689200 2.6573% 1819 0.576672 1.734087 2.6261% 1818 0.561916 1.779626
2.6969% 1817 0.547159 1.827621 2.7717% 1816 0.532403 1.878277 2.8507% 1815 0.517646
1.931821 2.9343% 1814 0.502890 1.988507 3.0231% 1813 0.488133 2.048621 3.1039% 1812
0.473438 2.112208 3.2172% 1811 0.458682 2.180161 3.0969% 1810 0.444903 2.247679
2.9144% 1809 0.432304 2.313184 2.8225% 1808 0.420438 2.378473 2.9199% 1807 0.408510
2.447923 2.9918% 1806 0.396643 2.521160 3.0841% 1805 0.384776 2.598913 3.1822% 1804
0.372909 2.681616 3.2868% 1803 0.361043 2.769755 3.3985% 1802 0.349176 2.863884
3.5180% 1801 0.337309 2.964637 3.3999% 1800 0.326218 3.065433 2.8419% 1799 0.317204
3.152549 2.7485% 1798 0.308719 3.239195 2.8261% 1797 0.300234 3.330739 3.7832% 1796
0.289289 3.456748 2.1272% 1795 0.283264 3.530280 3.0879% 1794 0.274779 3.639293
3.1625% 1793 0.266355 3.754386 3.2904% 1792 0.257870 3.877921 3.4024% 1791 0.249385
4.009862 3.2296% 1790 0.241583 4.139363 41.3145% 1780 0.170954 5.849518 29.4353%
1770 0.132077 7.571342 83.4728% 1750 0.071987 13.891356 29.2845% 1740 0.055681

17.959364 94.2514% 1720 0.028665 34.886315 85.8111% 1700 0.015427 64.822639
19.2490% 1690 0.012937 77.300380 88.0250% 1670 0.006880 145.344057

BASE YEAR: 1837

YEAR BYEAR/AYEAR AYEAR/BYEAR GROWTH%

2009 19.026090 0.052559 8.2857% 2001 17.570277 0.056914 1.0000% 2000
17.396312 0.057483 1.0000% 1999 17.224071 0.058058 1.0000% 1998 17.053536 0.058639
1.0000% 1997 16.884689 0.059225 1.0000% 1996 16.717514 0.059818 1.0000% 1995
16.551994 0.060416 0.9992% 1994 16.388239 0.061019 1.0008% 1993 16.225854 0.061630
1.0000% 1992 16.065202 0.062246 0.9295% 1991 15.917251 0.062825 1.2505% 1990
15.720661 0.063611 0.7224% 1989 15.607903 0.064070 1.1077% 1988 15.436912 0.064780
0.8834% 1987 15.301742 0.065352 0.5594% 1986 15.216626 0.065718 1.3056% 1985
15.020514 0.066576 0.7673% 1984 14.906142 0.067086 0.8149% 1983 14.785647 0.067633
0.9737% 1982 14.643060 0.068292 0.9508% 1981 14.505144 0.068941 0.9031% 1980
14.375326 0.069564 2.2701% 1979 14.056239 0.071143 1.0042% 1978 13.916493 0.071857
0.9896% 1977 13.780124 0.072568 0.9103% 1976 13.655810 0.073229 0.8394% 1975
13.542132 0.073844 0.9042% 1974 13.420785 0.074511 1.1568% 1973 13.267310 0.075373
0.9427% 1972 13.143407 0.076084 0.7426% 1971 13.046519 0.076649 1.4697% 1970
12.857547 0.077775 0.6968% 1969 12.768573 0.078317 0.8565% 1968 12.660134 0.078988
1.5090% 1967 12.471928 0.080180 0.9949% 1966 12.349066 0.080978 1.0575% 1965
12.219845 0.081834 1.1300% 1964 12.083302 0.082759 1.5537% 1963 11.898441 0.084045
1.4658% 1962 11.726551 0.085277 1.5364% 1961 11.549107 0.086587 2.1586% 1960
11.305071 0.088456 -1.6655% 1959 11.496544 0.086983 4.3080% 1958 11.021729 0.090730
2.1130% 1957 10.793663 0.092647 1.9895% 1956 10.583112 0.094490 2.1231% 1955
10.363094 0.096496 1.4496% 1954 10.215016 0.097895 2.1573% 1953 9.999306 0.100007
1.2298% 1952 9.877832 0.101237 1.6814% 1951 9.714495 0.102939 1.6233% 1950 9.559321
0.104610 1.4265% 1949 9.424872 0.106102 1.7790% 1948 9.260131 0.107990 1.8242% 1947
9.094237 0.109960 -2.6320% 1946 9.340071 0.107066 3.1768% 1945 9.052492 0.110467
6.4754% 1944 8.501955 0.117620 -0.3437% 1943 8.531275 0.117216 0.6562% 1942
8.475655 0.117985 0.6633% 1941 8.419807 0.118768 -5.6614% 1940 8.925095 0.112044
8.0381% 1939 8.261062 0.121050 0.8126% 1938 8.194471 0.122034 0.7762% 1937 8.131351
0.122981 0.6029% 1936 8.082623 0.123722 0.5244% 1935 8.040460 0.124371 -3.0364%
1934 8.292243 0.120595 4.6271% 1933 7.925519 0.126175 1.3921% 1932 7.816701 0.127931
-0.2051% 1931 7.832765 0.127669 0.8886% 1930 7.763776 0.128803 1.0126% 1929
7.685950 0.130108 1.1526% 1928 7.598372 0.131607 1.2160% 1927 7.507085 0.133207
1.4086% 1926 7.402811 0.135084 1.7667% 1925 7.274297 0.137470 1.4465% 1924 7.170574
0.139459 1.7700% 1923 7.045864 0.141927 1.6165% 1922 6.933778 0.144222 1.3736% 1921
6.839823 0.146203 2.3393% 1920 6.683476 0.149623 1.3140% 1919 6.596794 0.151589
0.7676% 1918 6.546539 0.152752 0.3870% 1917 6.521303 0.153344 1.3274% 1916 6.435871
0.155379 1.4083% 1915 6.346494 0.157567 1.4458% 1914 6.256044 0.159845 1.9424% 1913
6.136843 0.162950 1.9857% 1912 6.017358 0.166186 1.5634% 1911 5.924730 0.168784
1.8169% 1910 5.819004 0.171851 1.8781% 1909 5.711734 0.175078 2.0082% 1908 5.599287
0.178594 1.9603% 1907 5.491637 0.182095 1.8264% 1906 5.393139 0.185421 1.9357% 1905
5.290728 0.189010 2.0148% 1904 5.186234 0.192818 2.1335% 1903 5.077895 0.196932
1.8151% 1902 4.987367 0.200507 1.8943% 1901 4.894646 0.204305 3.0255% 1900 4.750907
0.210486 0.6278% 1899 4.721265 0.211808 1.7757% 1898 4.638894 0.215569 1.8078% 1897
4.556523 0.219466 1.8396% 1896 4.474216 0.223503 1.8755% 1895 4.391845 0.227695
1.9114% 1894 4.309474 0.232047 1.9486% 1893 4.227103 0.236569 1.9858% 1892 4.144796
0.241266 2.0276% 1891 4.062425 0.246158 2.6465% 1890 3.957684 0.252673 1.5328% 1889
3.897936 0.256546 2.0811% 1888 3.818469 0.261885 2.1599% 1887 3.737739 0.267541
2.2075% 1886 3.657009 0.273447 2.2592% 1885 3.576217 0.279625 2.3095% 1884 3.495487
0.286083 2.3641% 1883 3.414757 0.292847 2.4214% 1882 3.334028 0.299938 2.4815% 1881
3.253298 0.307380 3.7644% 1880 3.135274 0.318951 0.9432% 1879 3.105977 0.321960
2.1464% 1878 3.040712 0.328870 2.1913% 1877 2.975510 0.336077 2.2426% 1876 2.910244
0.343614 2.2941% 1875 2.844979 0.351496 2.3456% 1874 2.779777 0.359741 2.4043% 1873
2.714511 0.368390 2.4635% 1872 2.649246 0.377466 2.5258% 1871 2.583980 0.387000
5.9947% 1870 2.437840 0.410199 -1.0968% 1869 2.464874 0.405700 2.1930% 1868

260

2.411980 0.414597 2.2394% 1867 2.359149 0.423882 2.2935% 1866 2.306255 0.433603
2.3445% 1865 2.253424 0.443769 2.4037% 1864 2.200530 0.454436 2.4599% 1863 2.147699
0.465615 2.5250% 1862 2.094805 0.477371 2.5872% 1861 2.041974 0.489722 2.9504% 1860
1.983454 0.504171 2.4012% 1859 1.936944 0.516277 2.7627% 1858 1.884870 0.530540
2.8412% 1857 1.832797 0.545614 2.9243% 1856 1.780723 0.561570 3.0161% 1855 1.728587
0.578507 3.1061% 1854 1.676513 0.596476 3.2056% 1853 1.624440 0.615597 3.3118% 1852
1.572366 0.635984 3.4252% 1851 1.520293 0.657768 4.0106% 1850 1.461671 0.684148
2.3254% 1849 1.428454 0.700057 2.7841% 1848 1.389762 0.719548 2.8590% 1847 1.351133
0.740120 2.9432% 1846 1.312504 0.761902 3.0324% 1845 1.273875 0.785006 3.1325% 1844
1.235183 0.809597 3.2284% 1843 1.196554 0.835734 3.3361% 1842 1.157925 0.863614
3.4512% 1841 1.119296 0.893419 3.8105% 1840 1.078211 0.927463 2.3861% 1839 1.053083
0.949592 2.5824% 1838 1.026573 0.974115 2.6573% 1837 1.000000 1.000000 2.7232% 1836
0.973490 1.027232 2.7994% 1835 0.946980 1.055989 2.8871% 1834 0.920406 1.086476
2.9657% 1833 0.893896 1.118698 3.0563% 1832 0.867386 1.152889 3.1604% 1831 0.840813
1.189325 3.4660% 1830 0.812647 1.230547 2.4653% 1829 0.793095 1.260883 2.6804% 1828
0.772392 1.294680 10.3427% 1827 0.699994 1.428584 -4.2314% 1826 0.730922 1.368135
2.9150% 1825 0.710219 1.408016 3.0026% 1824 0.689516 1.450293 3.0955% 1823 0.668813
1.495187 3.1944% 1822 0.648110 1.542949 3.3102% 1821 0.627343 1.594024 3.2277% 1820
0.607727 1.645474 2.6573% 1819 0.591996 1.689199 2.6261% 1818 0.576848 1.733559
2.6969% 1817 0.561699 1.780312 2.7717% 1816 0.546551 1.829657 2.8507% 1815 0.531402
1.881815 2.9343% 1814 0.516253 1.937034 3.0231% 1813 0.501105 1.995591 3.1039% 1812
0.486019 2.057532 3.2172% 1811 0.470870 2.123727 3.0969% 1810 0.456726 2.189497
2.9144% 1809 0.443792 2.253307 2.8225% 1808 0.431610 2.316906 2.9199% 1807 0.419365
2.384557 2.9918% 1806 0.407183 2.455898 3.0841% 1805 0.395001 2.531640 3.1822% 1804
0.382819 2.612201 3.2868% 1803 0.370637 2.698059 3.3985% 1802 0.358455 2.789752
3.5180% 1801 0.346273 2.887896 3.3999% 1800 0.334887 2.986083 2.8419% 1799 0.325633
3.070944 2.7485% 1798 0.316922 3.155348 2.8261% 1797 0.308212 3.244522 3.7832% 1796
0.296977 3.367269 2.1272% 1795 0.290791 3.438897 3.0879% 1794 0.282080 3.545088
3.1625% 1793 0.273423 3.657202 3.2904% 1792 0.264723 3.777539 3.4024% 1791 0.256012
3.906065 3.2296% 1790 0.248003 4.032214 41.3145% 1780 0.175497 5.698101 29.4353%
1770 0.135587 7.375355 83.4728% 1750 0.073900 13.531773 29.2845% 1740 0.057161
17.494479 94.2514% 1720 0.029426 33.983269 85.8111% 1700 0.015837 63.144679
19.2490% 1690 0.013280 75.299430 88.0250% 1670 0.007063 141.581769

BASE YEAR: 1836
YEAR BYEAR/AYEAR AYEAR/BYEAR GROWTH%
2009 19.544210 0.051166 8.2857% 2001 18.048752 0.055405 1.0000% 2000
17.870049 0.055960 1.0000% 1999 17.693118 0.056519 1.0000% 1998 17.517939 0.057084
1.0000% 1997 17.344494 0.057655 1.0000% 1996 17.172766 0.058232 1.0000% 1995
17.002739 0.058814 0.9992% 1994 16.834525 0.059402 1.0008% 1993 16.667718 0.059996
1.0000% 1992 16.502691 0.060596 0.9295% 1991 16.350710 0.061159 1.2505% 1990
16.148767 0.061924 0.7224% 1989 16.032938 0.062372 1.1077% 1988 15.857291 0.063062
0.8834% 1987 15.718440 0.063620 0.5594% 1986 15.631006 0.063975 1.3056% 1985
15.429553 0.064811 0.7673% 1984 15.312066 0.065308 0.8149% 1983 15.188290 0.065840
0.9737% 1982 15.041821 0.066481 0.9508% 1981 14.900149 0.067113 0.9031% 1980
14.766795 0.067720 2.2701% 1979 14.439020 0.069257 1.0042% 1978 14.295468 0.069952
0.9896% 1977 14.155385 0.070644 0.9103% 1976 14.027686 0.071288 0.8394% 1975
13.910912 0.071886 0.9042% 1974 13.786261 0.072536 1.1568% 1973 13.628607 0.073375
0.9427% 1972 13.501329 0.074067 0.7426% 1971 13.401803 0.074617 1.4697% 1970
13.207684 0.075713 0.6968% 1969 13.116287 0.076241 0.8565% 1968 13.004895 0.076894
1.5090% 1967 12.811564 0.078054 0.9949% 1966 12.685356 0.078831 1.0575% 1965
12.552616 0.079665 1.1300% 1964 12.412355 0.080565 1.5537% 1963 12.222460 0.081817
1.4658% 1962 12.045889 0.083016 1.5364% 1961 11.863613 0.084291 2.1586% 1960
11.612931 0.086111 -1.6655% 1959 11.809619 0.084677 4.3080% 1958 11.321873 0.088325
2.1130% 1957 11.087596 0.090191 1.9895% 1956 10.871312 0.091985 2.1231% 1955
10.645302 0.093938 1.4496% 1954 10.493192 0.095300 2.1573% 1953 10.271607 0.097356
1.2298% 1952 10.146826 0.098553 1.6814% 1951 9.979041 0.100210 1.6233% 1950

261

9.819641 0.101837 1.4265% 1949 9.681531 0.103289 1.7790% 1948 9.512303 0.105127
1.8242% 1947 9.341892 0.107045 -2.6320% 1946 9.594421 0.104227 3.1768% 1945
9.299010 0.107538 6.4754% 1944 8.733480 0.114502 -0.3437% 1943 8.763599 0.114108
0.6562% 1942 8.706465 0.114857 0.6633% 1941 8.649096 0.115619 -5.6614% 1940
9.168143 0.109073 8.0381% 1939 8.486027 0.117841 0.8126% 1938 8.417623 0.118798
0.7762% 1937 8.352785 0.119721 0.6029% 1936 8.302730 0.120442 0.5244% 1935 8.259418
0.121074 -3.0364% 1934 8.518057 0.117398 4.6271% 1933 8.141347 0.122830 1.3921%
1932 8.029566 0.124540 -0.2051% 1931 8.046068 0.124284 0.8886% 1930 7.975200
0.125389 1.0126% 1929 7.895254 0.126658 1.1526% 1928 7.805291 0.128118 1.2160% 1927
7.711519 0.129676 1.4086% 1926 7.604404 0.131503 1.7667% 1925 7.472391 0.133826
1.4465% 1924 7.365843 0.135762 1.7700% 1923 7.237737 0.138165 1.6165% 1922 7.122599
0.140398 1.3736% 1921 7.026086 0.142327 2.3393% 1920 6.865481 0.145656 1.3140% 1919
6.776438 0.147570 0.7676% 1918 6.724815 0.148703 0.3870% 1917 6.698891 0.149278
1.3274% 1916 6.611133 0.151260 1.4083% 1915 6.519322 0.153390 1.4458% 1914 6.426409
0.155608 1.9424% 1913 6.303962 0.158630 1.9857% 1912 6.181223 0.161780 1.5634% 1911
6.086073 0.164310 1.8169% 1910 5.977467 0.167295 1.8781% 1909 5.867276 0.170437
2.0082% 1908 5.751767 0.173860 1.9603% 1907 5.641185 0.177268 1.8264% 1906 5.540005
0.180505 1.9357% 1905 5.434805 0.183999 2.0148% 1904 5.327465 0.187707 2.1335% 1903
5.216177 0.191711 1.8151% 1902 5.123183 0.195191 1.8943% 1901 5.027937 0.198889
3.0255% 1900 4.880284 0.204906 0.6278% 1899 4.849835 0.206193 1.7757% 1898 4.765221
0.209854 1.8078% 1897 4.680607 0.213648 1.8396% 1896 4.596058 0.217578 1.8755% 1895
4.511444 0.221659 1.9114% 1894 4.426830 0.225895 1.9486% 1893 4.342216 0.230297
1.9858% 1892 4.257667 0.234870 2.0276% 1891 4.173053 0.239633 2.6465% 1890 4.065460
0.245975 1.5328% 1889 4.004085 0.249745 2.0811% 1888 3.922453 0.254942 2.1599% 1887
3.839525 0.260449 2.2075% 1886 3.756597 0.266198 2.2592% 1885 3.673604 0.272212
2.3095% 1884 3.590676 0.278499 2.3641% 1883 3.507748 0.285083 2.4214% 1882 3.424820
0.291986 2.4815% 1881 3.341892 0.299232 3.7644% 1880 3.220654 0.310496 0.9432% 1879
3.190560 0.313425 2.1464% 1878 3.123517 0.320152 2.1913% 1877 3.056539 0.327167
2.2426% 1876 2.989496 0.334505 2.2941% 1875 2.922453 0.342178 2.3456% 1874 2.855476
0.350204 2.4043% 1873 2.788433 0.358624 2.4635% 1872 2.721390 0.367459 2.5258% 1871
2.654347 0.376740 5.9947% 1870 2.504227 0.399325 -1.0968% 1869 2.531998 0.394945
2.1930% 1868 2.477663 0.403606 2.2394% 1867 2.423394 0.412644 2.2935% 1866 2.369059
0.422108 2.3445% 1865 2.314790 0.432005 2.4037% 1864 2.260455 0.442389 2.4599% 1863
2.206186 0.453271 2.5250% 1862 2.151851 0.464716 2.5872% 1861 2.097582 0.476740
2.9504% 1860 2.037468 0.490805 2.4012% 1859 1.989691 0.502591 2.7627% 1858 1.936199
0.516476 2.8412% 1857 1.882708 0.531150 2.9243% 1856 1.829216 0.546682 3.0161% 1855
1.775660 0.563171 3.1061% 1854 1.722168 0.580663 3.2056% 1853 1.668677 0.599277
3.3118% 1852 1.615185 0.619124 3.4252% 1851 1.561694 0.640330 4.0106% 1850 1.501475
0.666012 2.3254% 1849 1.467354 0.681499 2.7841% 1848 1.427608 0.700472 2.8590% 1847
1.387927 0.720499 2.9432% 1846 1.348246 0.741704 3.0324% 1845 1.308565 0.764196
3.1325% 1844 1.268819 0.788134 3.2284% 1843 1.229138 0.813578 3.3361% 1842 1.189457
0.840720 3.4512% 1841 1.149776 0.869734 3.8105% 1840 1.107572 0.902876 2.3861% 1839
1.081761 0.924419 2.5824% 1838 1.054529 0.948291 2.6573% 1837 1.027232 0.973490
2.7232% 1836 1.000000 1.000000 2.7994% 1835 0.972768 1.027994 2.8871% 1834 0.945471
1.057674 2.9657% 1833 0.918239 1.089041 3.0563% 1832 0.891007 1.122326 3.1604% 1831
0.863710 1.157796 3.4660% 1830 0.834777 1.197925 2.4653% 1829 0.814692 1.227457
2.6804% 1828 0.793425 1.260358 10.3427% 1827 0.719056 1.390712 -4.2314% 1826
0.750827 1.331865 2.9150% 1825 0.729560 1.370690 3.0026% 1824 0.708293 1.411845
3.0955% 1823 0.687026 1.455549 3.1944% 1822 0.665759 1.502045 3.3102% 1821 0.644427
1.551766 3.2277% 1820 0.624277 1.601853 2.6573% 1819 0.608118 1.644418 2.6261% 1818
0.592557 1.687603 2.6969% 1817 0.576995 1.733116 2.7717% 1816 0.561434 1.781153
2.8507% 1815 0.545873 1.831928 2.9343% 1814 0.530312 1.885683 3.0231% 1813 0.514751
1.942688 3.1039% 1812 0.499254 2.002987 3.2172% 1811 0.483693 2.067426 3.0969% 1810
0.469164 2.131453 2.9144% 1809 0.455878 2.193571 2.8225% 1808 0.443364 2.255484
2.9199% 1807 0.430785 2.321343 2.9918% 1806 0.418271 2.390792 3.0841% 1805 0.405758
2.464525 3.1822% 1804 0.393244 2.542951 3.2868% 1803 0.380730 2.626533 3.3985% 1802

0.368216 2.715795 3.5180% 1801 0.355703 2.811338 3.3999% 1800 0.344006 2.906922 2.8419% 1799 0.334500 2.989533 2.7485% 1798 0.325553 3.071699 2.8261% 1797 0.316605 3.158509 3.7832% 1796 0.305064 3.278002 2.1272% 1795 0.298710 3.347732 3.0879% 1794 0.289762 3.451108 3.1625% 1793 0.280879 3.560249 3.2904% 1792 0.271932 3.677396 3.4024% 1791 0.262984 3.802515 3.2296% 1790 0.254756 3.925319 41.3145% 1780 0.180276 5.547044 29.4353% 1770 0.139279 7.179833 83.4728% 1750 0.075913 13.173044 29.2845% 1740 0.058717 17.030698 94.2514% 1720 0.030228 33.082368 85.8111% 1700 0.016268 61.470705 19.2490% 1690 0.013642 73.303232 88.0250% 1670 0.007255 137.828418

BASE YEAR: 1835
YEAR BYEAR/AYEAR AYEAR/BYEAR GROWTH%

2009 20.091338 0.049773 8.2857% 2001 18.554016 0.053897 1.0000% 2000 18.370311 0.054436 1.0000% 1999 18.188426 0.054980 1.0000% 1998 18.008343 0.055530 1.0000% 1997 17.830043 0.056085 1.0000% 1996 17.653507 0.056646 1.0000% 1995 17.478720 0.057212 0.9992% 1994 17.305797 0.057784 1.0008% 1993 17.134320 0.058362 1.0000% 1992 16.964674 0.058946 0.9295% 1991 16.808438 0.059494 1.2505% 1990 16.600842 0.060238 0.7224% 1989 16.481770 0.060673 1.1077% 1988 16.301206 0.061345 0.8834% 1987 16.158468 0.061887 0.5594% 1986 16.068586 0.062233 1.3056% 1985 15.861494 0.063046 0.7673% 1984 15.740719 0.063530 0.8149% 1983 15.613477 0.064047 0.9737% 1982 15.462907 0.064671 0.9508% 1981 15.317270 0.065286 0.9031% 1980 15.180183 0.065875 2.2701% 1979 14.843231 0.067371 1.0042% 1978 14.695661 0.068047 0.9896% 1977 14.551656 0.068721 0.9103% 1976 14.420383 0.069346 0.8394% 1975 14.300340 0.069928 0.9042% 1974 14.172199 0.070561 1.1568% 1973 14.010131 0.071377 0.9427% 1972 13.879291 0.072050 0.7426% 1971 13.776978 0.072585 1.4697% 1970 13.577425 0.073652 0.6968% 1969 13.483470 0.074165 0.8565% 1968 13.368960 0.074800 1.5090% 1967 13.170216 0.075929 0.9949% 1966 13.040475 0.076684 1.0575% 1965 12.904019 0.077495 1.1300% 1964 12.759831 0.078371 1.5537% 1963 12.564620 0.079589 1.4658% 1962 12.383107 0.080755 1.5364% 1961 12.195728 0.081996 2.1586% 1960 11.938029 0.083766 -1.6655% 1959 12.140222 0.082371 4.3080% 1958 11.638822 0.085919 2.1130% 1957 11.397987 0.087735 1.9895% 1956 11.175648 0.089480 2.1231% 1955 10.943311 0.091380 1.4496% 1954 10.786943 0.092705 2.1573% 1953 10.559155 0.094705 1.2298% 1952 10.430880 0.095869 1.6814% 1951 10.258398 0.097481 1.6233% 1950 10.094536 0.099063 1.4265% 1949 9.952559 0.100477 1.7790% 1948 9.778594 0.102264 1.8242% 1947 9.603413 0.104130 -2.6320% 1946 9.863011 0.101389 3.1768% 1945 9.559330 0.104610 6.4754% 1944 8.977969 0.111384 -0.3437% 1943 9.008930 0.111001 0.6562% 1942 8.950197 0.111729 0.6633% 1941 8.891222 0.112470 -5.6614% 1940 9.424800 0.106103 8.0381% 1939 8.723589 0.114632 0.8126% 1938 8.653269 0.115563 0.7762% 1937 8.586616 0.116460 0.6029% 1936 8.535160 0.117162 0.5244% 1935 8.490635 0.117777 -3.0364% 1934 8.756515 0.114201 4.6271% 1933 8.369259 0.119485 1.3921% 1932 8.254349 0.121148 -0.2051% 1931 8.271312 0.120900 0.8886% 1930 8.198461 0.121974 1.0126% 1929 8.116277 0.123209 1.1526% 1928 8.023795 0.124629 1.2160% 1927 7.927398 0.126145 1.4086% 1926 7.817285 0.127922 1.7667% 1925 7.681576 0.130182 1.4465% 1924 7.572046 0.132065 1.7700% 1923 7.440534 0.134402 1.6165% 1922 7.321992 0.136575 1.3736% 1921 7.222777 0.138451 2.3393% 1920 7.057676 0.141690 1.3140% 1919 6.966140 0.143552 0.7676% 1918 6.913072 0.144653 0.3870% 1917 6.886423 0.145213 1.3274% 1916 6.796207 0.147141 1.4083% 1915 6.701826 0.149213 1.4458% 1914 6.606312 0.151370 1.9424% 1913 6.480437 0.154311 1.9857% 1912 6.354262 0.157375 1.5634% 1911 6.256449 0.159835 1.8169% 1910 6.144803 0.162739 1.8781% 1909 6.031527 0.165795 2.0082% 1908 5.912784 0.169125 1.9603% 1907 5.799107 0.172440 1.8264% 1906 5.695094 0.175590 1.9357% 1905 5.586949 0.178989 2.0148% 1904 5.476605 0.182595 2.1335% 1903 5.362201 0.186491 1.8151% 1902 5.266604 0.189876 1.8943% 1901 5.168691 0.193473 3.0255% 1900 5.016904 0.199326 0.6278% 1899 4.985603 0.200578 1.7757% 1898 4.898620 0.204139 1.8078% 1897 4.811638 0.207829 1.8396% 1896 4.724722 0.211653 1.8755% 1895 4.637739 0.215622 1.9114% 1894 4.550757 0.219744 1.9486% 1893 4.463774 0.224026 1.9858% 1892 4.376858 0.228474 2.0276% 1891 4.289875 0.233107 2.6465% 1890 4.179270 0.239276 1.5328% 1889 4.116177 0.242944 2.0811% 1888 4.032260 0.248000 2.1599% 1887

3.947011 0.253356 2.2075% 1886 3.861761 0.258949 2.2592% 1885 3.776445 0.264799
2.3095% 1884 3.691195 0.270915 2.3641% 1883 3.605945 0.277320 2.4214% 1882 3.520696
0.284035 2.4815% 1881 3.435446 0.291083 3.7644% 1880 3.310814 0.302041 0.9432% 1879
3.279877 0.304889 2.1464% 1878 3.210958 0.311434 2.1913% 1877 3.142105 0.318258
2.2426% 1876 3.073185 0.325395 2.2941% 1875 3.004266 0.332860 2.3456% 1874 2.935413
0.340668 2.4043% 1873 2.866493 0.348858 2.4635% 1872 2.797574 0.357453 2.5258% 1871
2.728654 0.366481 5.9947% 1870 2.574331 0.388450 -1.0968% 1869 2.602879 0.384190
2.1930% 1868 2.547024 0.392615 2.2394% 1867 2.491235 0.401407 2.2935% 1866 2.435380
0.410614 2.3445% 1865 2.379591 0.420240 2.4037% 1864 2.323735 0.430342 2.4599% 1863
2.267946 0.440928 2.5250% 1862 2.212091 0.452061 2.5872% 1861 2.156302 0.463757
2.9504% 1860 2.094506 0.477440 2.4012% 1859 2.045391 0.488904 2.7627% 1858 1.990402
0.502411 2.8412% 1857 1.935413 0.516686 2.9243% 1856 1.880424 0.531795 3.0161% 1855
1.825368 0.547835 3.1061% 1854 1.770379 0.564851 3.2056% 1853 1.715390 0.582958
3.3118% 1852 1.660401 0.602264 3.4252% 1851 1.605412 0.622893 4.0106% 1850 1.543508
0.647875 2.3254% 1849 1.508432 0.662940 2.7841% 1848 1.467573 0.681397 2.8590% 1847
1.426781 0.700878 2.9432% 1846 1.385989 0.721506 3.0324% 1845 1.345198 0.743385
3.1325% 1844 1.304339 0.766672 3.2284% 1843 1.263547 0.791423 3.3361% 1842 1.222755
0.817825 3.4512% 1841 1.181964 0.846050 3.8105% 1840 1.138578 0.878288 2.3861% 1839
1.112044 0.899245 2.5824% 1838 1.084050 0.922467 2.6573% 1837 1.055989 0.946980
2.7232% 1836 1.027994 0.972768 2.7994% 1835 1.000000 1.000000 2.8871% 1834 0.971939
1.028871 2.9657% 1833 0.943945 1.059384 3.0563% 1832 0.915950 1.091762 3.1604% 1831
0.887889 1.126267 3.4660% 1830 0.858146 1.165303 2.4653% 1829 0.837499 1.194031
2.6804% 1828 0.815637 1.226036 10.3427% 1827 0.739185 1.352840 -4.2314% 1826
0.771846 1.295596 2.9150% 1825 0.749983 1.333363 3.0026% 1824 0.728121 1.373398
3.0955% 1823 0.706259 1.415912 3.1944% 1822 0.684396 1.461141 3.3102% 1821 0.662468
1.509508 3.2277% 1820 0.641753 1.558231 2.6573% 1819 0.625142 1.599637 2.6261% 1818
0.609145 1.641646 2.6969% 1817 0.593148 1.685920 2.7717% 1816 0.577151 1.732648
2.8507% 1815 0.561154 1.782041 2.9343% 1814 0.545158 1.834332 3.0231% 1813 0.529161
1.889785 3.1039% 1812 0.513231 1.948442 3.2172% 1811 0.497234 2.011126 3.0969% 1810
0.482298 2.073409 2.9144% 1809 0.468640 2.133836 2.8225% 1808 0.455776 2.194063
2.9199% 1807 0.442845 2.258128 2.9918% 1806 0.429981 2.325686 3.0841% 1805 0.417117
2.397411 3.1822% 1804 0.404252 2.473702 3.2868% 1803 0.391388 2.555007 3.3985% 1802
0.378524 2.641838 3.5180% 1801 0.365660 2.734779 3.3999% 1800 0.353637 2.827760
2.8419% 1799 0.343865 2.908122 2.7485% 1798 0.334666 2.988050 2.8261% 1797 0.325468
3.072496 3.7832% 1796 0.313604 3.188735 2.1272% 1795 0.307072 3.256566 3.0879% 1794
0.297874 3.357127 3.1625% 1793 0.288742 3.463296 3.2904% 1792 0.279544 3.577253
3.4024% 1791 0.270346 3.698964 3.2296% 1790 0.261888 3.818425 41.3145% 1780
0.185323 5.395986 29.4353% 1770 0.143178 6.984312 83.4728% 1750 0.078038 12.814315
29.2845% 1740 0.060361 16.566917 94.2514% 1720 0.031074 32.181467 85.8111% 1700
0.016723 59.796732 19.2490% 1690 0.014024 71.307034 88.0250% 1670 0.007459
134.075067
    BASE YEAR: 1834
    YEAR BYEAR/AYEAR AYEAR/BYEAR GROWTH%
    2009 20.671400 0.048376 8.2857% 2001 19.089693 0.052384 1.0000% 2000
18.900684 0.052908 1.0000% 1999 18.713548 0.053437 1.0000% 1998 18.528266 0.053972
1.0000% 1997 18.344818 0.054511 1.0000% 1996 18.163186 0.055056 1.0000% 1995
17.983352 0.055607 0.9992% 1994 17.805436 0.056163 1.0008% 1993 17.629009 0.056725
1.0000% 1992 17.454464 0.057292 0.9295% 1991 17.293718 0.057824 1.2505% 1990
17.080129 0.058548 0.7224% 1989 16.957619 0.058971 1.1077% 1988 16.771842 0.059624
0.8834% 1987 16.624983 0.060150 0.5594% 1986 16.532506 0.060487 1.3056% 1985
16.319435 0.061277 0.7673% 1984 16.195172 0.061747 0.8149% 1983 16.064257 0.062250
0.9737% 1982 15.909340 0.062856 0.9508% 1981 15.759498 0.063454 0.9031% 1980
15.618453 0.064027 2.2701% 1979 15.271773 0.065480 1.0042% 1978 15.119942 0.066138
0.9896% 1977 14.971780 0.066792 0.9103% 1976 14.836716 0.067400 0.8394% 1975
14.713208 0.067966 0.9042% 1974 14.581367 0.068581 1.1568% 1973 14.414621 0.069374
0.9427% 1972 14.280003 0.070028 0.7426% 1971 14.174736 0.070548 1.4697% 1970

13.969422 0.071585 0.6968% 1969 13.872754 0.072084 0.8565% 1968 13.754938 0.072701 1.5090% 1967 13.550456 0.073798 0.9949% 1966 13.416970 0.074532 1.0575% 1965 13.276574 0.075321 1.1300% 1964 13.128223 0.076172 1.5537% 1963 12.927376 0.077355 1.4658% 1962 12.740622 0.078489 1.5364% 1961 12.547833 0.079695 2.1586% 1960 12.282694 0.081415 -1.6655% 1959 12.490725 0.080059 4.3080% 1958 11.974849 0.083508 2.1130% 1957 11.727061 0.085273 1.9895% 1956 11.498303 0.086969 2.1231% 1955 11.259258 0.088816 1.4496% 1954 11.098375 0.090103 2.1573% 1953 10.864010 0.092047 1.2298% 1952 10.732033 0.093179 1.6814% 1951 10.554571 0.094746 1.6233% 1950 10.385978 0.096284 1.4265% 1949 10.239902 0.097657 1.7790% 1948 10.060914 0.099395 1.8242% 1947 9.880675 0.101208 -2.6320% 1946 10.147768 0.098544 3.1768% 1945 9.835319 0.101674 6.4754% 1944 9.237174 0.108258 -0.3437% 1943 9.269029 0.107886 0.6562% 1942 9.208600 0.108594 0.6633% 1941 9.147922 0.109314 -5.6614% 1940 9.696905 0.103126 8.0381% 1939 8.975449 0.111415 0.8126% 1938 8.903100 0.112320 0.7762% 1937 8.834522 0.113192 0.6029% 1936 8.781580 0.113875 0.5244% 1935 8.735770 0.114472 -3.0364% 1934 9.009327 0.110996 4.6271% 1933 8.610890 0.116132 1.3921% 1932 8.492662 0.117749 -0.2051% 1931 8.510115 0.117507 0.8886% 1930 8.435161 0.118551 1.0126% 1929 8.350603 0.119752 1.1526% 1928 8.255452 0.121132 1.2160% 1927 8.156271 0.122605 1.4086% 1926 8.042979 0.124332 1.7667% 1925 7.903352 0.126529 1.4465% 1924 7.790660 0.128359 1.7700% 1923 7.655166 0.130631 1.6165% 1922 7.533387 0.132742 1.3736% 1921 7.431307 0.134566 2.3393% 1920 7.261439 0.137714 1.3140% 1919 7.167261 0.139523 0.7676% 1918 7.112661 0.140594 0.3870% 1917 7.085242 0.141138 1.3274% 1916 6.992422 0.143012 1.4083% 1915 6.895316 0.145026 1.4458% 1914 6.797044 0.147123 1.9424% 1913 6.667535 0.149980 1.9857% 1912 6.537718 0.152959 1.5634% 1911 6.437080 0.155350 1.8169% 1910 6.322211 0.158173 1.8781% 1909 6.205665 0.161143 2.0082% 1908 6.083493 0.164379 1.9603% 1907 5.966534 0.167601 1.8264% 1906 5.859519 0.170662 1.9357% 1905 5.748251 0.173966 2.0148% 1904 5.634721 0.177471 2.1335% 1903 5.517014 0.181257 1.8151% 1902 5.418657 0.184548 1.8943% 1901 5.317917 0.188044 3.0255% 1900 5.161749 0.193733 0.6278% 1899 5.129543 0.194949 1.7757% 1898 5.040049 0.198411 1.8078% 1897 4.950555 0.201998 1.8396% 1896 4.861130 0.205713 1.8755% 1895 4.771636 0.209572 1.9114% 1894 4.682142 0.213577 1.9486% 1893 4.592648 0.217739 1.9858% 1892 4.503223 0.222063 2.0276% 1891 4.413729 0.226566 2.6465% 1890 4.299931 0.232562 1.5328% 1889 4.235016 0.236127 2.0811% 1888 4.148676 0.241041 2.1599% 1887 4.060966 0.246247 2.2075% 1886 3.973255 0.251683 2.2592% 1885 3.885475 0.257369 2.3095% 1884 3.797764 0.263313 2.3641% 1883 3.710053 0.269538 2.4214% 1882 3.622343 0.276064 2.4815% 1881 3.534632 0.282915 3.7644% 1880 3.406401 0.293565 0.9432% 1879 3.374571 0.296334 2.1464% 1878 3.303662 0.302694 2.1913% 1877 3.232821 0.309327 2.2426% 1876 3.161912 0.316264 2.2941% 1875 3.091003 0.323520 2.3456% 1874 3.020162 0.331108 2.4043% 1873 2.949253 0.339069 2.4635% 1872 2.878343 0.347422 2.5258% 1871 2.807434 0.356197 5.9947% 1870 2.648656 0.377550 -1.0968% 1869 2.678028 0.373409 2.1930% 1868 2.620560 0.381598 2.2394% 1867 2.563160 0.390143 2.2935% 1866 2.505692 0.399091 2.3445% 1865 2.448292 0.408448 2.4037% 1864 2.390824 0.418266 2.4599% 1863 2.333425 0.428555 2.5250% 1862 2.275957 0.439376 2.5872% 1861 2.218557 0.450743 2.9504% 1860 2.154977 0.464042 2.4012% 1859 2.104444 0.475185 2.7627% 1858 2.047867 0.488313 2.8412% 1857 1.991291 0.502187 2.9243% 1856 1.934714 0.516872 3.0161% 1855 1.878069 0.532462 3.1061% 1854 1.821492 0.549000 3.2056% 1853 1.764916 0.566599 3.3118% 1852 1.708339 0.585364 3.4252% 1851 1.651762 0.605414 4.0106% 1850 1.588071 0.629695 2.3254% 1849 1.551982 0.644337 2.7841% 1848 1.509944 0.662276 2.8590% 1847 1.467974 0.681211 2.9432% 1846 1.426005 0.701260 3.0324% 1845 1.384035 0.722525 3.1325% 1844 1.341997 0.745158 3.2284% 1843 1.300027 0.769215 3.3361% 1842 1.258058 0.794876 3.4512% 1841 1.216088 0.822309 3.8105% 1840 1.171450 0.853643 2.3861% 1839 1.144150 0.874011 2.5824% 1838 1.115348 0.896581 2.6573% 1837 1.086476 0.920406 2.7232% 1836 1.057674 0.945471 2.7994% 1835 1.028871 0.971939 2.8871% 1834 1.000000 1.000000 2.9657% 1833 0.971197 1.029657 3.0563% 1832 0.942395 1.061126 3.1604% 1831 0.913524 1.094663 3.4660% 1830 0.882922 1.132603 2.4653% 1829 0.861679 1.160525 2.6804% 1828 0.839185 1.191632 10.3427% 1827 0.760527 1.314878 -4.2314% 1826 0.794130 1.259240 2.9150% 1825 0.771636 1.295947 3.0026% 1824 0.749143 1.334859

3.0955% 1823 0.726649 1.376180 3.1944% 1822 0.704156 1.420140 3.3102% 1821 0.681594
1.467150 3.2277% 1820 0.660282 1.514505 2.6573% 1819 0.643190 1.554750 2.6261% 1818
0.626732 1.595579 2.6969% 1817 0.610273 1.638611 2.7717% 1816 0.593814 1.684028
2.8507% 1815 0.577356 1.732035 2.9343% 1814 0.560897 1.782859 3.0231% 1813 0.544438
1.836755 3.1039% 1812 0.528048 1.893766 3.2172% 1811 0.511590 1.954692 3.0969% 1810
0.496222 2.015227 2.9144% 1809 0.482170 2.073958 2.8225% 1808 0.468934 2.132495
2.9199% 1807 0.455630 2.194762 2.9918% 1806 0.442395 2.260425 3.0841% 1805 0.429159
2.330137 3.1822% 1804 0.415924 2.404287 3.2868% 1803 0.402688 2.483311 3.3985% 1802
0.389453 2.567706 3.5180% 1801 0.376217 2.658039 3.3999% 1800 0.363847 2.748411
2.8419% 1799 0.353792 2.826517 2.7485% 1798 0.344329 2.904202 2.8261% 1797 0.334865
2.986279 3.7832% 1796 0.322658 3.099256 2.1272% 1795 0.315937 3.165183 3.0879% 1794
0.306474 3.262922 3.1625% 1793 0.297079 3.366113 3.2904% 1792 0.287615 3.476872
3.4024% 1791 0.278151 3.595168 3.2296% 1790 0.269449 3.711276 41.3145% 1780
0.190673 5.244569 29.4353% 1770 0.147312 6.788325 83.4728% 1750 0.080291 12.454732
29.2845% 1740 0.062104 16.102032 94.2514% 1720 0.031971 31.278421 85.8111% 1700
0.017206 58.118772 19.2490% 1690 0.014429 69.306084 88.0250% 1670 0.007674
130.312779

BASE YEAR: 1833

YEAR BYEAR/AYEAR AYEAR/BYEAR GROWTH%

2009 21.284448 0.046983 8.2857% 2001 19.655832 0.050875 1.0000% 2000
19.461218 0.051384 1.0000% 1999 19.268533 0.051898 1.0000% 1998 19.077755 0.052417
1.0000% 1997 18.888867 0.052941 1.0000% 1996 18.701848 0.053471 1.0000% 1995
18.516681 0.054005 0.9992% 1994 18.333489 0.054545 1.0008% 1993 18.151830 0.055091
1.0000% 1992 17.972108 0.055642 0.9295% 1991 17.806595 0.056159 1.2505% 1990
17.586671 0.056861 0.7224% 1989 17.460528 0.057272 1.1077% 1988 17.269242 0.057906
0.8834% 1987 17.118027 0.058418 0.5594% 1986 17.022808 0.058745 1.3056% 1985
16.803418 0.059512 0.7673% 1984 16.675470 0.059968 0.8149% 1983 16.540672 0.060457
0.9737% 1982 16.381161 0.061046 0.9508% 1981 16.226875 0.061626 0.9031% 1980
16.081647 0.062183 2.2701% 1979 15.724686 0.063594 1.0042% 1978 15.568352 0.064233
0.9896% 1977 15.415796 0.064869 0.9103% 1976 15.276726 0.065459 0.8394% 1975
15.149555 0.066009 0.9042% 1974 15.013805 0.066605 1.1568% 1973 14.842113 0.067376
0.9427% 1972 14.703502 0.068011 0.7426% 1971 14.595114 0.068516 1.4697% 1970
14.383711 0.069523 0.6968% 1969 14.284176 0.070008 0.8565% 1968 14.162865 0.070607
1.5090% 1967 13.952320 0.071673 0.9949% 1966 13.814874 0.072386 1.0575% 1965
13.670315 0.073151 1.1300% 1964 13.517565 0.073978 1.5537% 1963 13.310761 0.075127
1.4658% 1962 13.118468 0.076228 1.5364% 1961 12.919962 0.077400 2.1586% 1960
12.646960 0.079070 -1.6655% 1959 12.861160 0.077753 4.3080% 1958 12.329985 0.081103
2.1130% 1957 12.074848 0.082817 1.9895% 1956 11.839306 0.084464 2.1231% 1955
11.593172 0.086258 1.4496% 1954 11.427517 0.087508 2.1573% 1953 11.186203 0.089396
1.2298% 1952 11.050311 0.090495 1.6814% 1951 10.867586 0.092017 1.6233% 1950
10.693993 0.093510 1.4265% 1949 10.543585 0.094844 1.7790% 1948 10.359289 0.096532
1.8242% 1947 10.173704 0.098293 -2.6320% 1946 10.448718 0.095706 3.1768% 1945
10.127004 0.098746 6.4754% 1944 9.511119 0.105140 -0.3437% 1943 9.543919 0.104779
0.6562% 1942 9.481698 0.105466 0.6633% 1941 9.419220 0.106166 -5.6614% 1940
9.984485 0.100155 8.0381% 1939 9.241633 0.108206 0.8126% 1938 9.167137 0.109085
0.7762% 1937 9.096526 0.109932 0.6029% 1936 9.042014 0.110595 0.5244% 1935 8.994845
0.111175 -3.0364% 1934 9.276515 0.107799 4.6271% 1933 8.866262 0.112787 1.3921%
1932 8.744528 0.114357 -0.2051% 1931 8.762498 0.114123 0.8886% 1930 8.685321
0.115137 1.0126% 1929 8.598256 0.116303 1.1526% 1928 8.500282 0.117643 1.2160% 1927
8.398161 0.119074 1.4086% 1926 8.281509 0.120751 1.7667% 1925 8.137740 0.122884
1.4465% 1924 8.021706 0.124662 1.7700% 1923 7.882194 0.126868 1.6165% 1922 7.756803
0.128919 1.3736% 1921 7.651696 0.130690 2.3393% 1920 7.476791 0.133747 1.3140% 1919
7.379819 0.135505 0.7676% 1918 7.323600 0.136545 0.3870% 1917 7.295368 0.137073
1.3274% 1916 7.199795 0.138893 1.4083% 1915 7.099809 0.140849 1.4458% 1914 6.998623
0.142885 1.9424% 1913 6.865273 0.145661 1.9857% 1912 6.731606 0.148553 1.5634% 1911
6.627983 0.150875 1.8169% 1910 6.509707 0.153617 1.8781% 1909 6.389705 0.156502

2.0082% 1908 6.263910 0.159645 1.9603% 1907 6.143483 0.162774 1.8264% 1906 6.033293 0.165747 1.9357% 1905 5.918726 0.168955 2.0148% 1904 5.801829 0.172359 2.1335% 1903 5.680631 0.176037 1.8151% 1902 5.579357 0.179232 1.8943% 1901 5.475630 0.182627 3.0255% 1900 5.314830 0.188153 0.6278% 1899 5.281669 0.189334 1.7757% 1898 5.189521 0.192696 1.8078% 1897 5.097373 0.196179 1.8396% 1896 5.005296 0.199788 1.8755% 1895 4.913148 0.203535 1.9114% 1894 4.821000 0.207426 1.9486% 1893 4.728852 0.211468 1.9858% 1892 4.636774 0.215667 2.0276% 1891 4.544626 0.220040 2.6465% 1890 4.427453 0.225863 1.5328% 1889 4.360613 0.229326 2.0811% 1888 4.271713 0.234098 2.1599% 1887 4.181401 0.239154 2.2075% 1886 4.091089 0.244434 2.2592% 1885 4.000706 0.249956 2.3095% 1884 3.910394 0.255729 2.3641% 1883 3.820082 0.261774 2.4214% 1882 3.729770 0.268113 2.4815% 1881 3.639458 0.274766 3.7644% 1880 3.507424 0.285109 0.9432% 1879 3.474650 0.287799 2.1464% 1878 3.401638 0.293976 2.1913% 1877 3.328697 0.300418 2.2426% 1876 3.255684 0.307155 2.2941% 1875 3.182672 0.314201 2.3456% 1874 3.109730 0.321571 2.4043% 1873 3.036718 0.329303 2.4635% 1872 2.963706 0.337415 2.5258% 1871 2.890693 0.345938 5.9947% 1870 2.727206 0.366676 -1.0968% 1869 2.757450 0.362654 2.1930% 1868 2.698277 0.370607 2.2394% 1867 2.639175 0.378906 2.2935% 1866 2.580003 0.387596 2.3445% 1865 2.520901 0.396684 2.4037% 1864 2.461729 0.406219 2.4599% 1863 2.402627 0.416211 2.5250% 1862 2.343454 0.426721 2.5872% 1861 2.284352 0.437761 2.9504% 1860 2.218886 0.450677 2.4012% 1859 2.166855 0.461498 2.7627% 1858 2.108600 0.474248 2.8412% 1857 2.050346 0.487723 2.9243% 1856 1.992092 0.501985 3.0161% 1855 1.933766 0.517126 3.1061% 1854 1.875512 0.533188 3.2056% 1853 1.817257 0.550280 3.3118% 1852 1.759003 0.568504 3.4252% 1851 1.700748 0.587976 4.0106% 1850 1.635168 0.611558 2.3254% 1849 1.598009 0.625779 2.7841% 1848 1.554724 0.643201 2.8590% 1847 1.511510 0.661590 2.9432% 1846 1.468295 0.681062 3.0324% 1845 1.425081 0.701714 3.1325% 1844 1.381796 0.723696 3.2284% 1843 1.338582 0.747059 3.3361% 1842 1.295368 0.771981 3.4512% 1841 1.252154 0.798624 3.8105% 1840 1.206192 0.829056 2.3861% 1839 1.178082 0.848837 2.5824% 1838 1.148425 0.870758 2.6573% 1837 1.118698 0.893896 2.7232% 1836 1.089041 0.918239 2.7994% 1835 1.059384 0.943945 2.8871% 1834 1.029657 0.971197 2.9657% 1833 1.000000 1.000000 3.0563% 1832 0.970343 1.030563 3.1604% 1831 0.940616 1.063133 3.4660% 1830 0.909106 1.099981 2.4653% 1829 0.887233 1.127099 2.6804% 1828 0.864073 1.157310 10.3427% 1827 0.783081 1.277006 -4.2314% 1826 0.817681 1.222971 2.9150% 1825 0.794521 1.258621 3.0026% 1824 0.771360 1.296412 3.0955% 1823 0.748199 1.336542 3.1944% 1822 0.725039 1.379236 3.3102% 1821 0.701808 1.424892 3.2277% 1820 0.679863 1.470884 2.6573% 1819 0.662265 1.509969 2.6261% 1818 0.645318 1.549622 2.6969% 1817 0.628372 1.591415 2.7717% 1816 0.611425 1.635524 2.8507% 1815 0.594478 1.682148 2.9343% 1814 0.577531 1.731508 3.0231% 1813 0.560585 1.783852 3.1039% 1812 0.543709 1.839221 3.2172% 1811 0.526762 1.898391 3.0969% 1810 0.510938 1.957183 2.9144% 1809 0.496469 2.014223 2.8225% 1808 0.482841 2.071073 2.9199% 1807 0.469143 2.131547 2.9918% 1806 0.455515 2.195319 3.0841% 1805 0.441887 2.263023 3.1822% 1804 0.428259 2.335037 3.2868% 1803 0.414631 2.411785 3.3985% 1802 0.401003 2.493749 3.5180% 1801 0.387375 2.581480 3.3999% 1800 0.374637 2.669249 2.8419% 1799 0.364285 2.745106 2.7485% 1798 0.354540 2.820554 2.8261% 1797 0.344796 2.900266 3.7832% 1796 0.332227 3.009989 2.1272% 1795 0.325307 3.074018 3.0879% 1794 0.315563 3.168942 3.1625% 1793 0.305889 3.269160 3.2904% 1792 0.296145 3.376729 3.4024% 1791 0.286400 3.491617 3.2296% 1790 0.277440 3.604381 41.3145% 1780 0.196328 5.093512 29.4353% 1770 0.151681 6.592803 83.4728% 1750 0.082672 12.096003 29.2845% 1740 0.063946 15.638251 94.2514% 1720 0.032919 30.377520 85.8111% 1700 0.017716 56.444799 19.2490% 1690 0.014857 67.309886 88.0250% 1670 0.007901 126.559428

BASE YEAR: 1832

YEAR BYEAR/AYEAR AYEAR/BYEAR GROWTH%

2009 21.934969 0.045589 8.2857% 2001 20.256578 0.049367 1.0000% 2000 20.056016 0.049860 1.0000% 1999 19.857442 0.050359 1.0000% 1998 19.660833 0.050863 1.0000% 1997 19.466172 0.051371 1.0000% 1996 19.273437 0.051885 1.0000% 1995 19.082611 0.052404 0.9992% 1994 18.893820 0.052927 1.0008% 1993 18.706608 0.053457 1.0000% 1992 18.521394 0.053992 0.9295% 1991 18.350822 0.054493 1.2505% 1990

267

18.124177 0.055175 0.7224% 1989 17.994178 0.055574 1.1077% 1988 17.797046 0.056189 0.8834% 1987 17.641209 0.056685 0.5594% 1986 17.543080 0.057003 1.3056% 1985 17.316984 0.057747 0.7673% 1984 17.185126 0.058190 0.8149% 1983 17.046209 0.058664 0.9737% 1982 16.881822 0.059235 0.9508% 1981 16.722821 0.059799 0.9031% 1980 16.573154 0.060339 2.2701% 1979 16.205283 0.061708 1.0042% 1978 16.044171 0.062328 0.9896% 1977 15.886952 0.062945 0.9103% 1976 15.743633 0.063518 0.8394% 1975 15.612575 0.064051 0.9042% 1974 15.472675 0.064630 1.1568% 1973 15.295736 0.065378 0.9427% 1972 15.152889 0.065994 0.7426% 1971 15.041188 0.066484 1.4697% 1970 14.823324 0.067461 0.6968% 1969 14.720747 0.067931 0.8565% 1968 14.595728 0.068513 1.5090% 1967 14.378748 0.069547 0.9949% 1966 14.237102 0.070239 1.0575% 1965 14.088124 0.070982 1.1300% 1964 13.930705 0.071784 1.5537% 1963 13.717581 0.072899 1.4658% 1962 13.519411 0.073968 1.5364% 1961 13.314838 0.075104 2.1586% 1960 13.033492 0.076725 -1.6655% 1959 13.254239 0.075448 4.3080% 1958 12.706829 0.078698 2.1130% 1957 12.443895 0.080361 1.9895% 1956 12.201153 0.081959 2.1231% 1955 11.947497 0.083700 1.4496% 1954 11.776779 0.084913 2.1573% 1953 11.528089 0.086745 1.2298% 1952 11.388044 0.087811 1.6814% 1951 11.199734 0.089288 1.6233% 1950 11.020836 0.090737 1.4265% 1949 10.865831 0.092032 1.7790% 1948 10.675902 0.093669 1.8242% 1947 10.484646 0.095378 -2.6320% 1946 10.768065 0.092867 3.1768% 1945 10.436518 0.095817 6.4754% 1944 9.801810 0.102022 -0.3437% 1943 9.835612 0.101671 0.6562% 1942 9.771490 0.102339 0.6633% 1941 9.707102 0.103017 -5.6614% 1940 10.289643 0.097185 8.0381% 1939 9.524087 0.104997 0.8126% 1938 9.447315 0.105850 0.7762% 1937 9.374545 0.106672 0.6029% 1936 9.318367 0.107315 0.5244% 1935 9.269757 0.107878 -3.0364% 1934 9.560035 0.104602 4.6271% 1933 9.137243 0.109442 1.3921% 1932 9.011789 0.110966 -0.2051% 1931 9.030309 0.110738 0.8886% 1930 8.950772 0.111722 1.0126% 1929 8.861046 0.112853 1.1526% 1928 8.760079 0.114154 1.2160% 1927 8.654836 0.115542 1.4086% 1926 8.534618 0.117170 1.7667% 1925 8.386456 0.119240 1.4465% 1924 8.266875 0.120965 1.7700% 1923 8.123099 0.123106 1.6165% 1922 7.993876 0.125096 1.3736% 1921 7.885557 0.126814 2.3393% 1920 7.705306 0.129781 1.3140% 1919 7.605370 0.131486 0.7676% 1918 7.547433 0.132495 0.3870% 1917 7.518338 0.133008 1.3274% 1916 7.419844 0.134774 1.4083% 1915 7.316803 0.136672 1.4458% 1914 7.212524 0.138648 1.9424% 1913 7.075098 0.141341 1.9857% 1912 6.937345 0.144147 1.5634% 1911 6.830556 0.146401 1.8169% 1910 6.708665 0.149061 1.8781% 1909 6.584995 0.151860 2.0082% 1908 6.455356 0.154910 1.9603% 1907 6.331247 0.157947 1.8264% 1906 6.217690 0.160831 1.9357% 1905 6.099622 0.163945 2.0148% 1904 5.979152 0.167248 2.1335% 1903 5.854250 0.170816 1.8151% 1902 5.749881 0.173917 1.8943% 1901 5.642983 0.177211 3.0255% 1900 5.477268 0.182573 0.6278% 1899 5.443094 0.183719 1.7757% 1898 5.348130 0.186981 1.8078% 1897 5.253165 0.190361 1.8396% 1896 5.158274 0.193863 1.8755% 1895 5.063310 0.197499 1.9114% 1894 4.968345 0.201274 1.9486% 1893 4.873381 0.205196 1.9858% 1892 4.778489 0.209271 2.0276% 1891 4.683525 0.213514 2.6465% 1890 4.562770 0.219165 1.5328% 1889 4.493887 0.222524 2.0811% 1888 4.402270 0.227156 2.1599% 1887 4.309198 0.232062 2.2075% 1886 4.216126 0.237185 2.2592% 1885 4.122981 0.242543 2.3095% 1884 4.029908 0.248145 2.3641% 1883 3.936836 0.254011 2.4214% 1882 3.843764 0.260162 2.4815% 1881 3.750691 0.266618 3.7644% 1880 3.614623 0.276654 0.9432% 1879 3.580847 0.279264 2.1464% 1878 3.505603 0.285258 2.1913% 1877 3.430432 0.291508 2.2426% 1876 3.355188 0.298046 2.2941% 1875 3.279945 0.304883 2.3456% 1874 3.204774 0.312035 2.4043% 1873 3.129530 0.319537 2.4635% 1872 3.054286 0.327409 2.5258% 1871 2.979042 0.335678 5.9947% 1870 2.810559 0.355801 -1.0968% 1869 2.841726 0.351899 2.1930% 1868 2.780745 0.359616 2.2394% 1867 2.719837 0.367669 2.2935% 1866 2.658856 0.376102 2.3445% 1865 2.597948 0.384919 2.4037% 1864 2.536967 0.394171 2.4599% 1863 2.476059 0.403868 2.5250% 1862 2.415078 0.414065 2.5872% 1861 2.354170 0.424778 2.9504% 1860 2.286703 0.437311 2.4012% 1859 2.233081 0.447812 2.7627% 1858 2.173046 0.460184 2.8412% 1857 2.113011 0.473258 2.9243% 1856 2.052976 0.487098 3.0161% 1855 1.992869 0.501789 3.1061% 1854 1.932834 0.517375 3.2056% 1853 1.872799 0.533960 3.3118% 1852 1.812764 0.551644 3.4252% 1851 1.752729 0.570539 4.0106% 1850 1.685144 0.593421 2.3254% 1849 1.646849 0.607220 2.7841% 1848 1.602241 0.624126 2.8590% 1847 1.557706 0.641970 2.9432% 1846 1.513171 0.660864 3.0324% 1845 1.468636 0.680904

3.1325% 1844 1.424029 0.702233 3.2284% 1843 1.379494 0.724904 3.3361% 1842 1.334959
0.749087 3.4512% 1841 1.290424 0.774939 3.8105% 1840 1.243057 0.804468 2.3861% 1839
1.214088 0.823663 2.5824% 1838 1.183525 0.844934 2.6573% 1837 1.152889 0.867386
2.7232% 1836 1.122326 0.891007 2.7994% 1835 1.091762 0.915950 2.8871% 1834 1.061126
0.942395 2.9657% 1833 1.030563 0.970343 3.0563% 1832 1.000000 1.000000 3.1604% 1831
0.969364 1.031604 3.4660% 1830 0.936892 1.067359 2.4653% 1829 0.914350 1.093673
2.6804% 1828 0.890482 1.122988 10.3427% 1827 0.807015 1.239134 -4.2314% 1826
0.842672 1.186701 2.9150% 1825 0.818804 1.221294 3.0026% 1824 0.794935 1.257964
3.0955% 1823 0.771067 1.296904 3.1944% 1822 0.747198 1.338333 3.3102% 1821 0.723257
1.382634 3.2277% 1820 0.700642 1.427262 2.6573% 1819 0.682506 1.465188 2.6261% 1818
0.665041 1.503666 2.6969% 1817 0.647577 1.544218 2.7717% 1816 0.630112 1.587019
2.8507% 1815 0.612647 1.632260 2.9343% 1814 0.595183 1.680156 3.0231% 1813 0.577718
1.730948 3.1039% 1812 0.560326 1.784675 3.2172% 1811 0.542861 1.842091 3.0969% 1810
0.526554 1.899139 2.9144% 1809 0.511643 1.954487 2.8225% 1808 0.497599 2.009652
2.9199% 1807 0.483481 2.068332 2.9918% 1806 0.469437 2.130212 3.0841% 1805 0.455392
2.195909 3.1822% 1804 0.441348 2.265787 3.2868% 1803 0.427303 2.340259 3.3985% 1802
0.413259 2.419792 3.5180% 1801 0.399214 2.504922 3.3999% 1800 0.386087 2.590088
2.8419% 1799 0.375418 2.663695 2.7485% 1798 0.365376 2.736905 2.8261% 1797 0.355334
2.814254 3.7832% 1796 0.342381 2.920723 2.1272% 1795 0.335250 2.982852 3.0879% 1794
0.325207 3.074961 3.1625% 1793 0.315238 3.172207 3.2904% 1792 0.305196 3.276586
3.4024% 1791 0.295154 3.388067 3.2296% 1790 0.285920 3.497487 41.3145% 1780
0.202329 4.942454 29.4353% 1770 0.156316 6.397281 83.4728% 1750 0.085199 11.737274
29.2845% 1740 0.065900 15.174470 94.2514% 1720 0.033925 29.476619 85.8111% 1700
0.018258 54.770825 19.2490% 1690 0.015311 65.313688 88.0250% 1670 0.008143
122.806077

BASE YEAR: 1831

YEAR BYEAR/AYEAR AYEAR/BYEAR GROWTH%

2009 22.628207 0.044193 8.2857% 2001 20.896772 0.047854 1.0000% 2000
20.689871 0.048333 1.0000% 1999 20.485021 0.048816 1.0000% 1998 20.282199 0.049304
1.0000% 1997 20.081385 0.049797 1.0000% 1996 19.882559 0.050295 1.0000% 1995
19.685702 0.050798 0.9992% 1994 19.490945 0.051306 1.0008% 1993 19.297816 0.051819
1.0000% 1992 19.106749 0.052338 0.9295% 1991 18.930786 0.052824 1.2505% 1990
18.696977 0.053485 0.7224% 1989 18.562871 0.053871 1.1077% 1988 18.359508 0.054468
0.8834% 1987 18.198746 0.054949 0.5594% 1986 18.097515 0.055256 1.3056% 1985
17.864274 0.055978 0.7673% 1984 17.728249 0.056407 0.8149% 1983 17.584941 0.056867
0.9737% 1982 17.415359 0.057421 0.9508% 1981 17.251332 0.057967 0.9031% 1980
17.096936 0.058490 2.2701% 1979 16.717439 0.059818 1.0042% 1978 16.551235 0.060418
0.9896% 1977 16.389047 0.061016 0.9103% 1976 16.241198 0.061572 0.8394% 1975
16.105998 0.062089 0.9042% 1974 15.961677 0.062650 1.1568% 1973 15.779146 0.063375
0.9427% 1972 15.631784 0.063972 0.7426% 1971 15.516553 0.064447 1.4697% 1970
15.291803 0.065395 0.6968% 1969 15.185985 0.065850 0.8565% 1968 15.057015 0.066414
1.5090% 1967 14.833177 0.067416 0.9949% 1966 14.687054 0.068087 1.0575% 1965
14.533368 0.068807 1.1300% 1964 14.370974 0.069585 1.5537% 1963 14.151115 0.070666
1.4658% 1962 13.946682 0.071702 1.5364% 1961 13.735643 0.072803 2.1586% 1960
13.445405 0.074375 -1.6655% 1959 13.673129 0.073136 4.3080% 1958 13.108419 0.076287
2.1130% 1957 12.837174 0.077899 1.9895% 1956 12.586762 0.079449 2.1231% 1955
12.325088 0.081135 1.4496% 1954 12.148975 0.082311 2.1573% 1953 11.892425 0.084087
1.2298% 1952 11.747954 0.085121 1.6814% 1951 11.553693 0.086552 1.6233% 1950
11.369141 0.087957 1.4265% 1949 11.209237 0.089212 1.7790% 1948 11.013306 0.090799
1.8242% 1947 10.816005 0.092456 -2.6320% 1946 11.108382 0.090022 3.1768% 1945
10.766356 0.092882 6.4754% 1944 10.111588 0.098896 -0.3437% 1943 10.146459 0.098557
0.6562% 1942 10.080310 0.099203 0.6633% 1941 10.013888 0.099861 -5.6614% 1940
10.614839 0.094208 8.0381% 1939 9.825088 0.101780 0.8126% 1938 9.745890 0.102607
0.7762% 1937 9.670821 0.103404 0.6029% 1936 9.612867 0.104027 0.5244% 1935 9.562721
0.104573 -3.0364% 1934 9.862173 0.101398 4.6271% 1933 9.426019 0.106089 1.3921%
1932 9.296599 0.107566 -0.2051% 1931 9.315705 0.107346 0.8886% 1930 9.233654

269

0.108299 1.0126% 1929 9.141093 0.109396 1.1526% 1928 9.036934 0.110657 1.2160% 1927 8.928365 0.112003 1.4086% 1926 8.804349 0.113580 1.7667% 1925 8.651504 0.115587 1.4465% 1924 8.528144 0.117259 1.7700% 1923 8.379823 0.119334 1.6165% 1922 8.246517 0.121263 1.3736% 1921 8.134774 0.122929 2.3393% 1920 7.948826 0.125805 1.3140% 1919 7.845732 0.127458 0.7676% 1918 7.785964 0.128436 0.3870% 1917 7.755949 0.128933 1.3274% 1916 7.654343 0.130645 1.4083% 1915 7.548044 0.132485 1.4458% 1914 7.440470 0.134400 1.9424% 1913 7.298701 0.137011 1.9857% 1912 7.156595 0.139731 1.5634% 1911 7.046430 0.141916 1.8169% 1910 6.920687 0.144494 1.8781% 1909 6.793109 0.147208 2.0082% 1908 6.659372 0.150164 1.9603% 1907 6.531341 0.153108 1.8264% 1906 6.414196 0.155904 1.9357% 1905 6.292395 0.158922 2.0148% 1904 6.168118 0.162124 2.1335% 1903 6.039269 0.165583 1.8151% 1902 5.931601 0.168589 1.8943% 1901 5.821325 0.171782 3.0255% 1900 5.650373 0.176979 0.6278% 1899 5.615119 0.178091 1.7757% 1898 5.517153 0.181253 1.8078% 1897 5.419188 0.184529 1.8396% 1896 5.321297 0.187924 1.8755% 1895 5.223332 0.191449 1.9114% 1894 5.125366 0.195108 1.9486% 1893 5.027400 0.198910 1.9858% 1892 4.929510 0.202860 2.0276% 1891 4.831544 0.206973 2.6465% 1890 4.706973 0.212451 1.5328% 1889 4.635913 0.215707 2.0811% 1888 4.541401 0.220196 2.1599% 1887 4.445387 0.224952 2.2075% 1886 4.349373 0.229918 2.2592% 1885 4.253284 0.235112 2.3095% 1884 4.157270 0.240542 2.3641% 1883 4.061257 0.246229 2.4214% 1882 3.965243 0.252191 2.4815% 1881 3.869229 0.258449 3.7644% 1880 3.728860 0.268178 0.9432% 1879 3.694017 0.270708 2.1464% 1878 3.616395 0.276518 2.1913% 1877 3.538848 0.282578 2.2426% 1876 3.461227 0.288915 2.2941% 1875 3.383605 0.295543 2.3456% 1874 3.306058 0.302475 2.4043% 1873 3.228436 0.309747 2.4635% 1872 3.150815 0.317378 2.5258% 1871 3.073193 0.325394 5.9947% 1870 2.899384 0.344901 -1.0968% 1869 2.931537 0.341118 2.1930% 1868 2.868628 0.348599 2.2394% 1867 2.805795 0.356405 2.2935% 1866 2.742887 0.364579 2.3445% 1865 2.680054 0.373127 2.4037% 1864 2.617146 0.382096 2.4599% 1863 2.554313 0.391495 2.5250% 1862 2.491405 0.401380 2.5872% 1861 2.428571 0.411765 2.9504% 1860 2.358972 0.423913 2.4012% 1859 2.303656 0.434093 2.7627% 1858 2.241724 0.446085 2.8412% 1857 2.179791 0.458760 2.9243% 1856 2.117859 0.472175 3.0161% 1855 2.055852 0.486416 3.1061% 1854 1.993919 0.501525 3.2056% 1853 1.931987 0.517602 3.3118% 1852 1.870055 0.534744 3.4252% 1851 1.808123 0.553060 4.0106% 1850 1.738402 0.575241 2.3254% 1849 1.698896 0.588617 2.7841% 1848 1.652879 0.605005 2.8590% 1847 1.606936 0.622302 2.9432% 1846 1.560994 0.640617 3.0324% 1845 1.515051 0.660044 3.1325% 1844 1.469034 0.680720 3.2284% 1843 1.423091 0.702696 3.3361% 1842 1.377149 0.726138 3.4512% 1841 1.331206 0.751198 3.8105% 1840 1.282343 0.779823 2.3861% 1839 1.252459 0.798430 2.5824% 1838 1.220929 0.819048 2.6573% 1837 1.189325 0.840813 2.7232% 1836 1.157796 0.863710 2.7994% 1835 1.126267 0.887889 2.8871% 1834 1.094663 0.913524 2.9657% 1833 1.063133 0.940616 3.0563% 1832 1.031604 0.969364 3.1604% 1831 1.000000 1.000000 3.4660% 1830 0.966501 1.034660 2.4653% 1829 0.943248 1.060167 2.6804% 1828 0.918625 1.088584 10.3427% 1827 0.832520 1.201172 -4.2314% 1826 0.869304 1.150345 2.9150% 1825 0.844681 1.183878 3.0026% 1824 0.820059 1.219425 3.0955% 1823 0.795436 1.257173 3.1944% 1822 0.770813 1.297332 3.3102% 1821 0.746115 1.340276 3.2277% 1820 0.722786 1.383536 2.6573% 1819 0.704076 1.420301 2.6261% 1818 0.686060 1.457599 2.6969% 1817 0.668043 1.496910 2.7717% 1816 0.650026 1.538399 2.8507% 1815 0.632010 1.582254 2.9343% 1814 0.613993 1.628683 3.0231% 1813 0.595976 1.677919 3.1039% 1812 0.578035 1.730000 3.2172% 1811 0.560018 1.785657 3.0969% 1810 0.543196 1.840957 2.9144% 1809 0.527813 1.894610 2.8225% 1808 0.513345 1.948084 2.9199% 1807 0.498761 2.004967 2.9918% 1806 0.484273 2.064951 3.0841% 1805 0.469785 2.128635 3.1822% 1804 0.455296 2.196373 3.2868% 1803 0.440808 2.268563 3.3985% 1802 0.426319 2.345659 3.5180% 1801 0.411831 2.428181 3.3999% 1800 0.398289 2.510738 2.8419% 1799 0.387283 2.582090 2.7485% 1798 0.376924 2.653057 2.8261% 1797 0.366564 2.728036 3.7832% 1796 0.353202 2.831243 2.1272% 1795 0.345845 2.891470 3.0879% 1794 0.335485 2.980756 3.1625% 1793 0.325201 3.075023 3.2904% 1792 0.314841 3.176204 3.4024% 1791 0.304482 3.284270 3.2296% 1790 0.294956 3.390338 41.3145% 1780 0.208723 4.791037 29.4353% 1770 0.161257 6.201294 83.4728% 1750 0.087891 11.377690 29.2845% 1740 0.067983 14.709585 94.2514% 1720 0.034997 28.573574 85.8111% 1700

0.018835 53.092866 19.2490% 1690 0.015795 63.312738 88.0250% 1670 0.008400 119.043789

BASE YEAR: 1830

YEAR BYEAR/AYEAR AYEAR/BYEAR GROWTH%

2009 23.412493 0.042712 8.2857% 2001 21.621047 0.046251 1.0000% 2000 21.406975 0.046714 1.0000% 1999 21.195025 0.047181 1.0000% 1998 20.985173 0.047653 1.0000% 1997 20.777399 0.048129 1.0000% 1996 20.571682 0.048611 1.0000% 1995 20.368002 0.049097 0.9992% 1994 20.166494 0.049587 1.0008% 1993 19.966672 0.050083 1.0000% 1992 19.768982 0.050584 0.9295% 1991 19.586921 0.051054 1.2505% 1990 19.345008 0.051693 0.7224% 1989 19.206253 0.052066 1.1077% 1988 18.995842 0.052643 0.8834% 1987 18.829509 0.053108 0.5594% 1986 18.724769 0.053405 1.3056% 1985 18.483444 0.054102 0.7673% 1984 18.342704 0.054518 0.8149% 1983 18.194429 0.054962 0.9737% 1982 18.018970 0.055497 0.9508% 1981 17.849258 0.056025 0.9031% 1980 17.689510 0.056531 2.2701% 1979 17.296859 0.057814 1.0042% 1978 17.124895 0.058395 0.9896% 1977 16.957086 0.058972 0.9103% 1976 16.804113 0.059509 0.8394% 1975 16.664226 0.060009 0.9042% 1974 16.514903 0.060551 1.1568% 1973 16.326046 0.061252 0.9427% 1972 16.173577 0.061829 0.7426% 1971 16.054351 0.062288 1.4697% 1970 15.821812 0.063204 0.6968% 1969 15.712326 0.063644 0.8565% 1968 15.578886 0.064189 1.5090% 1967 15.347290 0.065158 0.9949% 1966 15.196103 0.065806 1.0575% 1965 15.037090 0.066502 1.1300% 1964 14.869068 0.067254 1.5537% 1963 14.641588 0.068299 1.4658% 1962 14.430069 0.069300 1.5364% 1961 14.211716 0.070364 2.1586% 1960 13.911418 0.071883 -1.6655% 1959 14.147035 0.070686 4.3080% 1958 13.562752 0.073731 2.1130% 1957 13.282107 0.075289 1.9895% 1956 13.023014 0.076787 2.1231% 1955 12.752272 0.078417 1.4496% 1954 12.570055 0.079554 2.1573% 1953 12.304613 0.081270 1.2298% 1952 12.155134 0.082270 1.6814% 1951 11.954141 0.083653 1.6233% 1950 11.763192 0.085011 1.4265% 1949 11.597746 0.086224 1.7790% 1948 11.395024 0.087758 1.8242% 1947 11.190884 0.089358 -2.6320% 1946 11.493394 0.087006 3.1768% 1945 11.139514 0.089771 6.4754% 1944 10.462053 0.095584 -0.3437% 1943 10.498132 0.095255 0.6562% 1942 10.429690 0.095880 0.6633% 1941 10.360966 0.096516 -5.6614% 1940 10.982746 0.091052 8.0381% 1939 10.165622 0.098371 0.8126% 1938 10.083679 0.099170 0.7762% 1937 10.006008 0.099940 0.6029% 1936 9.946046 0.100542 0.5244% 1935 9.894161 0.101070 -3.0364% 1934 10.203992 0.098001 4.6271% 1933 9.752722 0.102535 1.3921% 1932 9.618816 0.103963 -0.2051% 1931 9.638584 0.103750 0.8886% 1930 9.553690 0.104672 1.0126% 1929 9.457920 0.105731 1.1526% 1928 9.350151 0.106950 1.2160% 1927 9.237819 0.108251 1.4086% 1926 9.109504 0.109775 1.7667% 1925 8.951362 0.111715 1.4465% 1924 8.823726 0.113331 1.7700% 1923 8.670265 0.115337 1.6165% 1922 8.532338 0.117201 1.3736% 1921 8.416722 0.118811 2.3393% 1920 8.224330 0.121590 1.3140% 1919 8.117663 0.123188 0.7676% 1918 8.055823 0.124134 0.3870% 1917 8.024768 0.124614 1.3274% 1916 7.919640 0.126268 1.4083% 1915 7.809657 0.128047 1.4458% 1914 7.698354 0.129898 1.9424% 1913 7.551672 0.132421 1.9857% 1912 7.404640 0.135050 1.5634% 1911 7.290657 0.137162 1.8169% 1910 7.160556 0.139654 1.8781% 1909 7.028555 0.142277 2.0082% 1908 6.890184 0.145134 1.9603% 1907 6.757716 0.147979 1.8264% 1906 6.636509 0.150682 1.9357% 1905 6.510488 0.153598 2.0148% 1904 6.381903 0.156693 2.1335% 1903 6.248588 0.160036 1.8151% 1902 6.137188 0.162941 1.8943% 1901 6.023090 0.166028 3.0255% 1900 5.846213 0.171051 0.6278% 1899 5.809737 0.172125 1.7757% 1898 5.708376 0.175181 1.8078% 1897 5.607015 0.178348 1.8396% 1896 5.505732 0.181629 1.8755% 1895 5.404370 0.185035 1.9114% 1894 5.303009 0.188572 1.9486% 1893 5.201648 0.192247 1.9858% 1892 5.100365 0.196064 2.0276% 1891 4.999004 0.200040 2.6465% 1890 4.870115 0.205334 1.5328% 1889 4.796592 0.208481 2.0811% 1888 4.698804 0.212820 2.1599% 1887 4.599463 0.217417 2.2075% 1886 4.500121 0.222216 2.2592% 1885 4.400702 0.227236 2.3095% 1884 4.301360 0.232485 2.3641% 1883 4.202018 0.237981 2.4214% 1882 4.102677 0.243743 2.4815% 1881 4.003335 0.249792 3.7644% 1880 3.858101 0.259195 0.9432% 1879 3.822050 0.261640 2.1464% 1878 3.741738 0.267255 2.1913% 1877 3.661504 0.273112 2.2426% 1876 3.581192 0.279237 2.2941% 1875 3.500879 0.285643 2.3456% 1874 3.420645 0.292343 2.4043% 1873 3.340333 0.299371 2.4635% 1872 3.260021 0.306747 2.5258% 1871 3.179709 0.314494 5.9947% 1870 2.999876 0.333347 -1.0968% 1869

271

3.033143 0.329691 2.1930% 1868 2.968054 0.336921 2.2394% 1867 2.903043 0.344466
2.2935% 1866 2.837955 0.352366 2.3445% 1865 2.772944 0.360628 2.4037% 1864 2.707855
0.369296 2.4599% 1863 2.642844 0.378380 2.5250% 1862 2.577756 0.387934 2.5872% 1861
2.512745 0.397971 2.9504% 1860 2.440733 0.409713 2.4012% 1859 2.383500 0.419551
2.7627% 1858 2.319421 0.431142 2.8412% 1857 2.255342 0.443392 2.9243% 1856 2.191263
0.456358 3.0161% 1855 2.127107 0.470122 3.1061% 1854 2.063028 0.484724 3.2056% 1853
1.998949 0.500263 3.3118% 1852 1.934870 0.516831 3.4252% 1851 1.870791 0.534533
4.0106% 1850 1.798654 0.555971 2.3254% 1849 1.757780 0.568900 2.7841% 1848 1.710167
0.584738 2.8590% 1847 1.662632 0.601456 2.9432% 1846 1.615097 0.619158 3.0324% 1845
1.567563 0.637933 3.1325% 1844 1.519950 0.657916 3.2284% 1843 1.472415 0.679156
3.3361% 1842 1.424880 0.701813 3.4512% 1841 1.377346 0.726034 3.8105% 1840 1.326788
0.753700 2.3861% 1839 1.295868 0.771683 2.5824% 1838 1.263246 0.791611 2.6573% 1837
1.230547 0.812647 2.7232% 1836 1.197925 0.834777 2.7994% 1835 1.165303 0.858146
2.8871% 1834 1.132603 0.882922 2.9657% 1833 1.099981 0.909106 3.0563% 1832 1.067359
0.936892 3.1604% 1831 1.034660 0.966501 3.4660% 1830 1.000000 1.000000 2.4653% 1829
0.975940 1.024653 2.6804% 1828 0.950464 1.052118 10.3427% 1827 0.861375 1.160935 -
4.2314% 1826 0.899434 1.111810 2.9150% 1825 0.873958 1.144220 3.0026% 1824 0.848482
1.178576 3.0955% 1823 0.823005 1.215059 3.1944% 1822 0.797529 1.253873 3.3102% 1821
0.771975 1.295378 3.2277% 1820 0.747837 1.337190 2.6573% 1819 0.728479 1.372723
2.6261% 1818 0.709838 1.408772 2.6969% 1817 0.691197 1.446765 2.7717% 1816 0.672556
1.486865 2.8507% 1815 0.653915 1.529251 2.9343% 1814 0.635274 1.574125 3.0231% 1813
0.616633 1.621711 3.1039% 1812 0.598069 1.672047 3.2172% 1811 0.579428 1.725840
3.0969% 1810 0.562023 1.779288 2.9144% 1809 0.546107 1.831143 2.8225% 1808 0.531116
1.882826 2.9199% 1807 0.516048 1.937803 2.9918% 1806 0.501058 1.995778 3.0841% 1805
0.486067 2.057329 3.1822% 1804 0.471077 2.122797 3.2868% 1803 0.456086 2.192569
3.3985% 1802 0.441095 2.267083 3.5180% 1801 0.426105 2.346840 3.3999% 1800 0.412094
2.426631 2.8419% 1799 0.400706 2.495593 2.7485% 1798 0.389988 2.564183 2.8261% 1797
0.379269 2.636651 3.7832% 1796 0.365444 2.736401 2.1272% 1795 0.357832 2.794609
3.0879% 1794 0.347113 2.880905 3.1625% 1793 0.336472 2.972014 3.2904% 1792 0.325754
3.069806 3.4024% 1791 0.315035 3.174252 3.2296% 1790 0.305179 3.276766 41.3145%
1780 0.215957 4.630544 29.4353% 1770 0.166846 5.993559 83.4728% 1750 0.090938
10.996554 29.2845% 1740 0.070339 14.216834 94.2514% 1720 0.036210 27.616399
85.8111% 1700 0.019488 51.314328 19.2490% 1690 0.016342 61.191849 88.0250% 1670
0.008691 115.055987

BASE YEAR: 1829

YEAR BYEAR/AYEAR AYEAR/BYEAR GROWTH%

2009 23.989682 0.041685 8.2857% 2001 22.154071 0.045138 1.0000% 2000
21.934721 0.045590 1.0000% 1999 21.717546 0.046046 1.0000% 1998 21.502520 0.046506
1.0000% 1997 21.289624 0.046971 1.0000% 1996 21.078836 0.047441 1.0000% 1995
20.870135 0.047915 0.9992% 1994 20.663659 0.048394 1.0008% 1993 20.458910 0.048878
1.0000% 1992 20.256347 0.049367 0.9295% 1991 20.069797 0.049826 1.2505% 1990
19.821921 0.050449 0.7224% 1989 19.679745 0.050814 1.1077% 1988 19.464146 0.051377
0.8834% 1987 19.293713 0.051830 0.5594% 1986 19.186391 0.052120 1.3056% 1985
18.939117 0.052801 0.7673% 1984 18.794906 0.053206 0.8149% 1983 18.642977 0.053640
0.9737% 1982 18.463191 0.054162 0.9508% 1981 18.289296 0.054677 0.9031% 1980
18.125609 0.055171 2.2701% 1979 17.723279 0.056423 1.0042% 1978 17.547075 0.056990
0.9896% 1977 17.375129 0.057554 0.9103% 1976 17.218384 0.058077 0.8394% 1975
17.075050 0.058565 0.9042% 1974 16.922045 0.059095 1.1568% 1973 16.728532 0.059778
0.9427% 1972 16.572304 0.060342 0.7426% 1971 16.450139 0.060790 1.4697% 1970
16.211867 0.061683 0.6968% 1969 16.099682 0.062113 0.8565% 1968 15.962953 0.062645
1.5090% 1967 15.725647 0.063590 0.9949% 1966 15.570732 0.064223 1.0575% 1965
15.407799 0.064902 1.1300% 1964 15.235635 0.065636 1.5537% 1963 15.002547 0.066655
1.4658% 1962 14.785814 0.067632 1.5364% 1961 14.562077 0.068672 2.1586% 1960
14.254377 0.070154 -1.6655% 1959 14.495802 0.068985 4.3080% 1958 13.897115 0.071957
2.1130% 1957 13.609550 0.073478 1.9895% 1956 13.344071 0.074940 2.1231% 1955
13.066653 0.076531 1.4496% 1954 12.879944 0.077640 2.1573% 1953 12.607959 0.079315

272

1.2298% 1952 12.454795 0.080290 1.6814% 1951 12.248846 0.081640 1.6233% 1950
12.053190 0.082966 1.4265% 1949 11.883665 0.084149 1.7790% 1948 11.675945 0.085646
1.8242% 1947 11.466773 0.087208 -2.6320% 1946 11.776741 0.084913 3.1768% 1945
11.414136 0.087611 6.4754% 1944 10.719974 0.093284 -0.3437% 1943 10.756943 0.092963
0.6562% 1942 10.686813 0.093573 0.6633% 1941 10.616395 0.094194 -5.6614% 1940
11.253504 0.088861 8.0381% 1939 10.416236 0.096004 0.8126% 1938 10.332272 0.096784
0.7762% 1937 10.252686 0.097535 0.6029% 1936 10.191246 0.098123 0.5244% 1935
10.138082 0.098638 -3.0364% 1934 10.455551 0.095643 4.6271% 1933 9.993156 0.100068
1.3921% 1932 9.855949 0.101462 -0.2051% 1931 9.876204 0.101253 0.8886% 1930
9.789217 0.102153 1.0126% 1929 9.691086 0.103188 1.1526% 1928 9.580661 0.104377
1.2160% 1927 9.465559 0.105646 1.4086% 1926 9.334081 0.107134 1.7667% 1925 9.172040
0.109027 1.4465% 1924 9.041258 0.110604 1.7700% 1923 8.884013 0.112562 1.6165% 1922
8.742686 0.114381 1.3736% 1921 8.624220 0.115953 2.3393% 1920 8.427084 0.118665
1.3140% 1919 8.317788 0.120224 0.7676% 1918 8.254423 0.121147 0.3870% 1917 8.222602
0.121616 1.3274% 1916 8.114883 0.123230 1.4083% 1915 8.002189 0.124966 1.4458% 1914
7.888142 0.126773 1.9424% 1913 7.737843 0.129235 1.9857% 1912 7.587187 0.131801
1.5634% 1911 7.470394 0.133862 1.8169% 1910 7.337085 0.136294 1.8781% 1909 7.201830
0.138854 2.0082% 1908 7.060048 0.141642 1.9603% 1907 6.924314 0.144419 1.8264% 1906
6.800119 0.147056 1.9357% 1905 6.670991 0.149903 2.0148% 1904 6.539236 0.152923
2.1335% 1903 6.402634 0.156186 1.8151% 1902 6.288489 0.159021 1.8943% 1901 6.171577
0.162033 3.0255% 1900 5.990340 0.166935 0.6278% 1899 5.952965 0.167984 1.7757% 1898
5.849105 0.170966 1.8078% 1897 5.745245 0.174057 1.8396% 1896 5.641464 0.177259
1.8755% 1895 5.537604 0.180584 1.9114% 1894 5.433745 0.184035 1.9486% 1893 5.329885
0.187621 1.9858% 1892 5.226104 0.191347 2.0276% 1891 5.122244 0.195227 2.6465% 1890
4.990178 0.200394 1.5328% 1889 4.914843 0.203465 2.0811% 1888 4.814644 0.207700
2.1599% 1887 4.712853 0.212186 2.2075% 1886 4.611062 0.216870 2.2592% 1885 4.509192
0.221769 2.3095% 1884 4.407402 0.226891 2.3641% 1883 4.305611 0.232255 2.4214% 1882
4.203820 0.237879 2.4815% 1881 4.102029 0.243782 3.7644% 1880 3.953215 0.252959
0.9432% 1879 3.916275 0.255345 2.1464% 1878 3.833983 0.260825 2.1913% 1877 3.751771
0.266541 2.2426% 1876 3.669479 0.272518 2.2941% 1875 3.587187 0.278770 2.3456% 1874
3.504974 0.285309 2.4043% 1873 3.422682 0.292169 2.4635% 1872 3.340390 0.299366
2.5258% 1871 3.258098 0.306928 5.9947% 1870 3.073832 0.325327 -1.0968% 1869
3.107919 0.321759 2.1930% 1868 3.041226 0.328815 2.2394% 1867 2.974612 0.336178
2.2935% 1866 2.907919 0.343889 2.3445% 1865 2.841305 0.351951 2.4037% 1864 2.774612
0.360411 2.4599% 1863 2.707998 0.369276 2.5250% 1862 2.641305 0.378601 2.5872% 1861
2.574692 0.388396 2.9504% 1860 2.500905 0.399855 2.4012% 1859 2.442260 0.409457
2.7627% 1858 2.376602 0.420769 2.8412% 1857 2.310943 0.432724 2.9243% 1856 2.245285
0.445378 3.0161% 1855 2.179546 0.458811 3.1061% 1854 2.113888 0.473062 3.2056% 1853
2.048229 0.488227 3.3118% 1852 1.982571 0.504396 3.4252% 1851 1.916912 0.521672
4.0106% 1850 1.842997 0.542595 2.3254% 1849 1.801114 0.555212 2.7841% 1848 1.752328
0.570669 2.8590% 1847 1.703621 0.586985 2.9432% 1846 1.654914 0.604261 3.0324% 1845
1.606208 0.622584 3.1325% 1844 1.557421 0.642087 3.2284% 1843 1.508715 0.662816
3.3361% 1842 1.460008 0.684928 3.4512% 1841 1.411301 0.708566 3.8105% 1840 1.359498
0.735566 2.3861% 1839 1.327815 0.753117 2.5824% 1838 1.294389 0.772565 2.6573% 1837
1.260883 0.793095 2.7232% 1836 1.227457 0.814692 2.7994% 1835 1.194031 0.837499
2.8871% 1834 1.160525 0.861679 2.9657% 1833 1.127099 0.887233 3.0563% 1832 1.093673
0.914350 3.1604% 1831 1.060167 0.943248 3.4660% 1830 1.024653 0.975940 2.4653% 1829
1.000000 1.000000 2.6804% 1828 0.973896 1.026804 10.3427% 1827 0.882610 1.133003 -
4.2314% 1826 0.921608 1.085060 2.9150% 1825 0.895503 1.116690 3.0026% 1824 0.869399
1.150220 3.0955% 1823 0.843295 1.185825 3.1944% 1822 0.817191 1.223705 3.3102% 1821
0.791007 1.264212 3.2277% 1820 0.766273 1.305017 2.6573% 1819 0.746439 1.339695
2.6261% 1818 0.727338 1.374877 2.6969% 1817 0.708237 1.411956 2.7717% 1816 0.689136
1.451091 2.8507% 1815 0.670036 1.492458 2.9343% 1814 0.650935 1.536251 3.0231% 1813
0.631834 1.582693 3.1039% 1812 0.612813 1.631818 3.2172% 1811 0.593713 1.684316
3.0969% 1810 0.575878 1.736478 2.9144% 1809 0.559570 1.787086 2.8225% 1808 0.544210
1.837526 2.9199% 1807 0.528770 1.891180 2.9918% 1806 0.513410 1.947760 3.0841% 1805

0.498050 2.007830 3.1822% 1804 0.482690 2.071723 3.2868% 1803 0.467330 2.139816
3.3985% 1802 0.451970 2.212537 3.5180% 1801 0.436610 2.290376 3.3999% 1800 0.422253
2.368247 2.8419% 1799 0.410585 2.435550 2.7485% 1798 0.399602 2.502490 2.8261% 1797
0.388619 2.573213 3.7832% 1796 0.374453 2.670563 2.1272% 1795 0.366653 2.727371
3.0879% 1794 0.355671 2.811591 3.1625% 1793 0.344767 2.900508 3.2904% 1792 0.333784
2.995947 3.4024% 1791 0.322801 3.097880 3.2296% 1790 0.312703 3.197928 41.3145%
1780 0.221281 4.519134 29.4353% 1770 0.170959 5.849355 83.4728% 1750 0.093179
10.731978 29.2845% 1740 0.072073 13.874779 94.2514% 1720 0.037103 26.951952
85.8111% 1700 0.019968 50.079713 19.2490% 1690 0.016745 59.719582 88.0250% 1670
0.008906 112.287757

BASE YEAR: 1828

YEAR BYEAR/AYEAR AYEAR/BYEAR GROWTH%

2009 24.632700 0.040596 8.2857% 2001 22.747887 0.043960 1.0000% 2000
22.522658 0.044400 1.0000% 1999 22.299662 0.044844 1.0000% 1998 22.078873 0.045292
1.0000% 1997 21.860270 0.045745 1.0000% 1996 21.643832 0.046203 1.0000% 1995
21.429537 0.046665 0.9992% 1994 21.217527 0.047131 1.0008% 1993 21.007290 0.047603
1.0000% 1992 20.799297 0.048079 0.9295% 1991 20.607747 0.048525 1.2505% 1990
20.353227 0.049132 0.7224% 1989 20.207240 0.049487 1.1077% 1988 19.985863 0.050035
0.8834% 1987 19.810861 0.050477 0.5594% 1986 19.700662 0.050760 1.3056% 1985
19.446760 0.051422 0.7673% 1984 19.298684 0.051817 0.8149% 1983 19.142682 0.052239
0.9737% 1982 18.958078 0.052748 0.9508% 1981 18.779521 0.053249 0.9031% 1980
18.611447 0.053730 2.2701% 1979 18.198333 0.054950 1.0042% 1978 18.017406 0.055502
0.9896% 1977 17.840852 0.056051 0.9103% 1976 17.679905 0.056561 0.8394% 1975
17.532729 0.057036 0.9042% 1974 17.375623 0.057552 1.1568% 1973 17.176922 0.058218
0.9427% 1972 17.016507 0.058766 0.7426% 1971 16.891068 0.059203 1.4697% 1970
16.646410 0.060073 0.6968% 1969 16.531217 0.060492 0.8565% 1968 16.390823 0.061010
1.5090% 1967 16.147156 0.061930 0.9949% 1966 15.988089 0.062547 1.0575% 1965
15.820789 0.063208 1.1300% 1964 15.644010 0.063922 1.5537% 1963 15.404674 0.064915
1.4658% 1962 15.182132 0.065867 1.5364% 1961 14.952398 0.066879 2.1586% 1960
14.636450 0.068323 -1.6655% 1959 14.884347 0.067185 4.3080% 1958 14.269613 0.070079
2.1130% 1957 13.974340 0.071560 1.9895% 1956 13.701745 0.072983 2.1231% 1955
13.416891 0.074533 1.4496% 1954 13.225178 0.075613 2.1573% 1953 12.945902 0.077245
1.2298% 1952 12.788633 0.078194 1.6814% 1951 12.577164 0.079509 1.6233% 1950
12.376263 0.080800 1.4265% 1949 12.202194 0.081952 1.7790% 1948 11.988907 0.083410
1.8242% 1947 11.774128 0.084932 -2.6320% 1946 12.092404 0.082697 3.1768% 1945
11.720080 0.085324 6.4754% 1944 11.007311 0.090849 -0.3437% 1943 11.045271 0.090536
0.6562% 1942 10.973262 0.091131 0.6633% 1941 10.900956 0.091735 -5.6614% 1940
11.555142 0.086542 8.0381% 1939 10.695432 0.093498 0.8126% 1938 10.609218 0.094258
0.7762% 1937 10.527499 0.094989 0.6029% 1936 10.464411 0.095562 0.5244% 1935
10.409823 0.096063 -3.0364% 1934 10.735801 0.093146 4.6271% 1933 10.261012 0.097456
1.3921% 1932 10.120127 0.098813 -0.2051% 1931 10.140925 0.098610 0.8886% 1930
10.051607 0.099487 1.0126% 1929 9.950846 0.100494 1.1526% 1928 9.837460 0.101652
1.2160% 1927 9.719274 0.102888 1.4086% 1926 9.584271 0.104338 1.7667% 1925 9.417887
0.106181 1.4465% 1924 9.283599 0.107717 1.7700% 1923 9.122140 0.109623 1.6165% 1922
8.977024 0.111395 1.3736% 1921 8.855383 0.112926 2.3393% 1920 8.652963 0.115567
1.3140% 1919 8.540737 0.117086 0.7676% 1918 8.475674 0.117985 0.3870% 1917 8.443001
0.118441 1.3274% 1916 8.332394 0.120014 1.4083% 1915 8.216679 0.121704 1.4458% 1914
8.099575 0.123463 1.9424% 1913 7.945248 0.125861 1.9857% 1912 7.790553 0.128361
1.5634% 1911 7.670630 0.130367 1.8169% 1910 7.533748 0.132736 1.8781% 1909 7.394868
0.135229 2.0082% 1908 7.249285 0.137945 1.9603% 1907 7.109913 0.140649 1.8264% 1906
6.982389 0.143217 1.9357% 1905 6.849800 0.145990 2.0148% 1904 6.714513 0.148931
2.1335% 1903 6.574250 0.152109 1.8151% 1902 6.457045 0.154870 1.8943% 1901 6.337000
0.157803 3.0255% 1900 6.150904 0.162578 0.6278% 1899 6.112528 0.163598 1.7757% 1898
6.005884 0.166503 1.8078% 1897 5.899240 0.169513 1.8396% 1896 5.792678 0.172632
1.8755% 1895 5.686034 0.175870 1.9114% 1894 5.579390 0.179231 1.9486% 1893 5.472747
0.182724 1.9858% 1892 5.366185 0.186352 2.0276% 1891 5.259541 0.190131 2.6465% 1890

274

5.123935 0.195163 1.5328% 1889 5.046580 0.198154 2.0811% 1888 4.943695 0.202278
2.1599% 1887 4.839176 0.206647 2.2075% 1886 4.734657 0.211209 2.2592% 1885 4.630056
0.215980 2.3095% 1884 4.525537 0.220968 2.3641% 1883 4.421018 0.226192 2.4214% 1882
4.316499 0.231669 2.4815% 1881 4.211980 0.237418 3.7644% 1880 4.059177 0.246355
0.9432% 1879 4.021247 0.248679 2.1464% 1878 3.936749 0.254017 2.1913% 1877 3.852333
0.259583 2.2426% 1876 3.767835 0.265404 2.2941% 1875 3.683337 0.271493 2.3456% 1874
3.598921 0.277861 2.4043% 1873 3.514423 0.284542 2.4635% 1872 3.429926 0.291552
2.5258% 1871 3.345428 0.298915 5.9947% 1870 3.156223 0.316834 -1.0968% 1869
3.191223 0.313359 2.1930% 1868 3.122743 0.320231 2.2394% 1867 3.054343 0.327403
2.2935% 1866 2.985863 0.334912 2.3445% 1865 2.917463 0.342764 2.4037% 1864 2.848983
0.351002 2.4599% 1863 2.780583 0.359637 2.5250% 1862 2.712103 0.368718 2.5872% 1861
2.643704 0.378257 2.9504% 1860 2.567939 0.389417 2.4012% 1859 2.507722 0.398768
2.7627% 1858 2.440304 0.409785 2.8412% 1857 2.372886 0.421428 2.9243% 1856 2.305467
0.433752 3.0161% 1855 2.237967 0.446834 3.1061% 1854 2.170548 0.460713 3.2056% 1853
2.103130 0.475482 3.3118% 1852 2.035711 0.491229 3.4252% 1851 1.968293 0.508054
4.0106% 1850 1.892396 0.528431 2.3254% 1849 1.849391 0.540718 2.7841% 1848 1.799297
0.555773 2.8590% 1847 1.749285 0.571662 2.9432% 1846 1.699273 0.588487 3.0324% 1845
1.649260 0.606332 3.1325% 1844 1.599166 0.625326 3.2284% 1843 1.549154 0.645514
3.3361% 1842 1.499142 0.667048 3.4512% 1841 1.449130 0.690069 3.8105% 1840 1.395938
0.716364 2.3861% 1839 1.363406 0.733457 2.5824% 1838 1.329084 0.752398 2.6573% 1837
1.294680 0.772392 2.7232% 1836 1.260358 0.793425 2.7994% 1835 1.226036 0.815637
2.8871% 1834 1.191632 0.839185 2.9657% 1833 1.157310 0.864073 3.0563% 1832 1.122988
0.890482 3.1604% 1831 1.088584 0.918625 3.4660% 1830 1.052118 0.950464 2.4653% 1829
1.026804 0.973896 2.6804% 1828 1.000000 1.000000 10.3427% 1827 0.906268 1.103427 -
4.2314% 1826 0.946310 1.056736 2.9150% 1825 0.919506 1.087540 3.0026% 1824 0.892702
1.120194 3.0955% 1823 0.865899 1.154870 3.1944% 1822 0.839095 1.191761 3.3102% 1821
0.812209 1.231210 3.2277% 1820 0.786813 1.270951 2.6573% 1819 0.766446 1.304723
2.6261% 1818 0.746833 1.338987 2.6969% 1817 0.727221 1.375098 2.7717% 1816 0.707608
1.413212 2.8507% 1815 0.687995 1.453498 2.9343% 1814 0.668383 1.496149 3.0231% 1813
0.648770 1.541378 3.1039% 1812 0.629239 1.589221 3.2172% 1811 0.609627 1.640349
3.0969% 1810 0.591314 1.691149 2.9144% 1809 0.574569 1.740435 2.8225% 1808 0.558797
1.789558 2.9199% 1807 0.542944 1.841812 2.9918% 1806 0.527172 1.896915 3.0841% 1805
0.511400 1.955417 3.1822% 1804 0.495628 2.017642 3.2868% 1803 0.479856 2.083958
3.3985% 1802 0.464084 2.154781 3.5180% 1801 0.448312 2.230587 3.3999% 1800 0.433571
2.306426 2.8419% 1799 0.421590 2.371971 2.7485% 1798 0.410313 2.437164 2.8261% 1797
0.399036 2.506041 3.7832% 1796 0.384490 2.600850 2.1272% 1795 0.376481 2.656175
3.0879% 1794 0.365204 2.738196 3.1625% 1793 0.354008 2.824792 3.2904% 1792 0.342731
2.917740 3.4024% 1791 0.331454 3.017012 3.2296% 1790 0.321084 3.114448 41.3145%
1780 0.227213 4.401165 29.4353% 1770 0.175541 5.696662 83.4728% 1750 0.095677
10.451828 29.2845% 1740 0.074005 13.512588 94.2514% 1720 0.038098 26.248391
85.8111% 1700 0.020503 48.772419 19.2490% 1690 0.017194 58.160646 88.0250% 1670
0.009144 109.356568

BASE YEAR: 1827
YEAR BYEAR/AYEAR AYEAR/BYEAR GROWTH%

2009 27.180374 0.036791 8.2857% 2001 25.100622 0.039840 1.0000% 2000
24.852098 0.040238 1.0000% 1999 24.606038 0.040640 1.0000% 1998 24.362414 0.041047
1.0000% 1997 24.121202 0.041457 1.0000% 1996 23.882378 0.041872 1.0000% 1995
23.645919 0.042291 0.9992% 1994 23.411981 0.042713 1.0008% 1993 23.180001 0.043141
1.0000% 1992 22.950496 0.043572 0.9295% 1991 22.739134 0.043977 1.2505% 1990
22.458290 0.044527 0.7224% 1989 22.297205 0.044849 1.1077% 1988 22.052931 0.045345
0.8834% 1987 21.859829 0.045746 0.5594% 1986 21.738233 0.046002 1.3056% 1985
21.458070 0.046603 0.7673% 1984 21.294680 0.046960 0.8149% 1983 21.122543 0.047343
0.9737% 1982 20.918846 0.047804 0.9508% 1981 20.721821 0.048258 0.9031% 1980
20.536365 0.048694 2.2701% 1979 20.080523 0.049799 1.0042% 1978 19.880884 0.050300
0.9896% 1977 19.686069 0.050797 0.9103% 1976 19.508476 0.051260 0.8394% 1975
19.346078 0.051690 0.9042% 1974 19.172723 0.052157 1.1568% 1973 18.953472 0.052761

275

0.9427% 1972 18.776465 0.053258 0.7426% 1971 18.638052 0.053654 1.4697% 1970
18.368090 0.054442 0.6968% 1969 18.240983 0.054822 0.8565% 1968 18.086069 0.055291
1.5090% 1967 17.817200 0.056126 0.9949% 1966 17.641682 0.056684 1.0575% 1965
17.457078 0.057283 1.1300% 1964 17.262015 0.057931 1.5537% 1963 16.997926 0.058831
1.4658% 1962 16.752367 0.059693 1.5364% 1961 16.498873 0.060610 2.1586% 1960
16.150247 0.061919 -1.6655% 1959 16.423783 0.060887 4.3080% 1958 15.745469 0.063510
2.1130% 1957 15.419657 0.064852 1.9895% 1956 15.118868 0.066143 2.1231% 1955
14.804554 0.067547 1.4496% 1954 14.593012 0.068526 2.1573% 1953 14.284851 0.070004
1.2298% 1952 14.111317 0.070865 1.6814% 1951 13.877976 0.072057 1.6233% 1950
13.656297 0.073226 1.4265% 1949 13.464225 0.074271 1.7790% 1948 13.228877 0.075592
1.8242% 1947 12.991885 0.076971 -2.6320% 1946 13.343079 0.074945 3.1768% 1945
12.932248 0.077326 6.4754% 1944 12.145759 0.082333 -0.3437% 1943 12.187645 0.082050
0.6562% 1942 12.108188 0.082589 0.6633% 1941 12.028404 0.083137 -5.6614% 1940
12.750250 0.078430 8.0381% 1939 11.801623 0.084734 0.8126% 1938 11.706492 0.085423
0.7762% 1937 11.616321 0.086086 0.6029% 1936 11.546709 0.086605 0.5244% 1935
11.486474 0.087059 -3.0364% 1934 11.846168 0.084415 4.6271% 1933 11.322272 0.088321
1.3921% 1932 11.166817 0.089551 -0.2051% 1931 11.189766 0.089367 0.8886% 1930
11.091209 0.090161 1.0126% 1929 10.980027 0.091074 1.1526% 1928 10.854914 0.092124
1.2160% 1927 10.724504 0.093244 1.4086% 1926 10.575539 0.094558 1.7667% 1925
10.391946 0.096228 1.4465% 1924 10.243769 0.097620 1.7700% 1923 10.065611 0.099348
1.6165% 1922 9.905487 0.100954 1.3736% 1921 9.771264 0.102341 2.3393% 1920 9.547909
0.104735 1.3140% 1919 9.424076 0.106111 0.7676% 1918 9.352284 0.106926 0.3870% 1917
9.316231 0.107340 1.3274% 1916 9.194184 0.108764 1.4083% 1915 9.066501 0.110296
1.4458% 1914 8.937286 0.111891 1.9424% 1913 8.766997 0.114064 1.9857% 1912 8.596303
0.116329 1.5634% 1911 8.463977 0.118148 1.8169% 1910 8.312937 0.120294 1.8781% 1909
8.159693 0.122554 2.0082% 1908 7.999053 0.125015 1.9603% 1907 7.845266 0.127465
1.8264% 1906 7.704554 0.129793 1.9357% 1905 7.558251 0.132306 2.0148% 1904 7.408972
0.134971 2.1335% 1903 7.254202 0.137851 1.8151% 1902 7.124875 0.140353 1.8943% 1901
6.992414 0.143012 3.0255% 1900 6.787071 0.147339 0.6278% 1899 6.744725 0.148264
1.7757% 1898 6.627051 0.150897 1.8078% 1897 6.509378 0.153625 1.8396% 1896 6.391794
0.156451 1.8755% 1895 6.274121 0.159385 1.9114% 1894 6.156447 0.162431 1.9486% 1893
6.038774 0.165597 1.9858% 1892 5.921190 0.168885 2.0276% 1891 5.803517 0.172309
2.6465% 1890 5.653886 0.176870 1.5328% 1889 5.568530 0.179581 2.0811% 1888 5.455005
0.183318 2.1599% 1887 5.339675 0.187277 2.2075% 1886 5.224346 0.191412 2.2592% 1885
5.108927 0.195736 2.3095% 1884 4.993598 0.200256 2.3641% 1883 4.878269 0.204991
2.4214% 1882 4.762940 0.209954 2.4815% 1881 4.647610 0.215164 3.7644% 1880 4.479003
0.223264 0.9432% 1879 4.437151 0.225370 2.1464% 1878 4.343913 0.230207 2.1913% 1877
4.250766 0.235252 2.2426% 1876 4.157529 0.240527 2.2941% 1875 4.064292 0.246045
2.3456% 1874 3.971145 0.251817 2.4043% 1873 3.877908 0.257871 2.4635% 1872 3.784671
0.264224 2.5258% 1871 3.691434 0.270897 5.9947% 1870 3.482660 0.287137 -1.0968%
1869 3.521280 0.283988 2.1930% 1868 3.445717 0.290215 2.2394% 1867 3.370243 0.296714
2.2935% 1866 3.294680 0.303520 2.3445% 1865 3.219206 0.310636 2.4037% 1864 3.143643
0.318102 2.4599% 1863 3.068170 0.325927 2.5250% 1862 2.992606 0.334157 2.5872% 1861
2.917133 0.342802 2.9504% 1860 2.833532 0.352916 2.4012% 1859 2.767087 0.361391
2.7627% 1858 2.692696 0.371375 2.8412% 1857 2.618305 0.381927 2.9243% 1856 2.543913
0.393095 3.0161% 1855 2.469432 0.404951 3.1061% 1854 2.395041 0.417529 3.2056% 1853
2.320649 0.430914 3.3118% 1852 2.246258 0.445185 3.4252% 1851 2.171867 0.460433
4.0106% 1850 2.088120 0.478900 2.3254% 1849 2.040667 0.490036 2.7841% 1848 1.985392
0.503679 2.8590% 1847 1.930207 0.518079 2.9432% 1846 1.875023 0.533327 3.0324% 1845
1.819838 0.549500 3.1325% 1844 1.764563 0.566713 3.2284% 1843 1.709378 0.585008
3.3361% 1842 1.654193 0.604524 3.4512% 1841 1.599008 0.625388 3.8105% 1840 1.540315
0.649218 2.3861% 1839 1.504418 0.664709 2.5824% 1838 1.466546 0.681874 2.6573% 1837
1.428584 0.699994 2.7232% 1836 1.390712 0.719056 2.7994% 1835 1.352840 0.739185
2.8871% 1834 1.314878 0.760527 2.9657% 1833 1.277006 0.783081 3.0563% 1832 1.239134
0.807015 3.1604% 1831 1.201172 0.832520 3.4660% 1830 1.160935 0.861375 2.4653% 1829
1.133003 0.882610 2.6804% 1828 1.103427 0.906268 10.3427% 1827 1.000000 1.000000 -

276

4.2314% 1826 1.044184 0.957686 2.9150% 1825 1.014608 0.985603 3.0026% 1824 0.985032
1.015196 3.0955% 1823 0.955455 1.046621 3.1944% 1822 0.925879 1.080055 3.3102% 1821
0.896213 1.115806 3.2277% 1820 0.868190 1.151822 2.6573% 1819 0.845717 1.182429
2.6261% 1818 0.824076 1.213481 2.6969% 1817 0.802435 1.246207 2.7717% 1816 0.780794
1.280748 2.8507% 1815 0.759152 1.317259 2.9343% 1814 0.737511 1.355911 3.0231% 1813
0.715870 1.396901 3.1039% 1812 0.694319 1.440260 3.2172% 1811 0.672678 1.486595
3.0969% 1810 0.652472 1.532634 2.9144% 1809 0.633995 1.577301 2.8225% 1808 0.616592
1.621819 2.9199% 1807 0.599098 1.669175 2.9918% 1806 0.581695 1.719113 3.0841% 1805
0.564292 1.772132 3.1822% 1804 0.546889 1.828524 3.2868% 1803 0.529486 1.888624
3.3985% 1802 0.512083 1.952809 3.5180% 1801 0.494680 2.021509 3.3999% 1800 0.478414
2.090240 2.8419% 1799 0.465194 2.149641 2.7485% 1798 0.452750 2.208723 2.8261% 1797
0.440307 2.271145 3.7832% 1796 0.424256 2.357067 2.1272% 1795 0.415419 2.407206
3.0879% 1794 0.402976 2.481539 3.1625% 1793 0.390622 2.560018 3.2904% 1792 0.378179
2.644254 3.4024% 1791 0.365735 2.734221 3.2296% 1790 0.354293 2.822524 41.3145%
1780 0.250712 3.988635 29.4353% 1770 0.193697 5.162702 83.4728% 1750 0.105573
9.472156 29.2845% 1740 0.081659 12.246025 94.2514% 1720 0.042038 23.788074 85.8111%
1700 0.022624 44.200877 19.2490% 1690 0.018972 52.709125 88.0250% 1670 0.010090
99.106345

BASE YEAR: 1826
YEAR BYEAR/AYEAR AYEAR/BYEAR GROWTH%
2009 26.030255 0.038417 8.2857% 2001 24.038506 0.041600 1.0000% 2000
23.800498 0.042016 1.0000% 1999 23.564850 0.042436 1.0000% 1998 23.331535 0.042860
1.0000% 1997 23.100529 0.043289 1.0000% 1996 22.871811 0.043722 1.0000% 1995
22.645358 0.044159 0.9992% 1994 22.421319 0.044600 1.0008% 1993 22.199155 0.045047
1.0000% 1992 21.979361 0.045497 0.9295% 1991 21.776943 0.045920 1.2505% 1990
21.507982 0.046494 0.7224% 1989 21.353713 0.046830 1.1077% 1988 21.119775 0.047349
0.8834% 1987 20.934845 0.047767 0.5594% 1986 20.818394 0.048034 1.3056% 1985
20.550086 0.048662 0.7673% 1984 20.393610 0.049035 0.8149% 1983 20.228756 0.049435
0.9737% 1982 20.033679 0.049916 0.9508% 1981 19.844991 0.050391 0.9031% 1980
19.667382 0.050846 2.2701% 1979 19.230829 0.052000 1.0042% 1978 19.039637 0.052522
0.9896% 1977 18.853066 0.053042 0.9103% 1976 18.682988 0.053525 0.8394% 1975
18.527461 0.053974 0.9042% 1974 18.361442 0.054462 1.1568% 1973 18.151468 0.055092
0.9427% 1972 17.981952 0.055611 0.7426% 1971 17.849396 0.056024 1.4697% 1970
17.590856 0.056848 0.6968% 1969 17.469128 0.057244 0.8565% 1968 17.320769 0.057734
1.5090% 1967 17.063277 0.058605 0.9949% 1966 16.895186 0.059188 1.0575% 1965
16.718394 0.059814 1.1300% 1964 16.531585 0.060490 1.5537% 1963 16.278670 0.061430
1.4658% 1962 16.043502 0.062331 1.5364% 1961 15.800734 0.063288 2.1586% 1960
15.466860 0.064654 -1.6655% 1959 15.728821 0.063578 4.3080% 1958 15.079210 0.066316
2.1130% 1957 14.767185 0.067718 1.9895% 1956 14.479123 0.069065 2.1231% 1955
14.178109 0.070531 1.4496% 1954 13.975518 0.071554 2.1573% 1953 13.680397 0.073097
1.2298% 1952 13.514206 0.073996 1.6814% 1951 13.290738 0.075240 1.6233% 1950
13.078440 0.076462 1.4265% 1949 12.894495 0.077552 1.7790% 1948 12.669106 0.078932
1.8242% 1947 12.442142 0.080372 -2.6320% 1946 12.778476 0.078257 3.1768% 1945
12.385028 0.080743 6.4754% 1944 11.631819 0.085971 -0.3437% 1943 11.671933 0.085676
0.6562% 1942 11.595838 0.086238 0.6633% 1941 11.519430 0.086810 -5.6614% 1940
12.210732 0.081895 8.0381% 1939 11.302245 0.088478 0.8126% 1938 11.211140 0.089197
0.7762% 1937 11.124784 0.089889 0.6029% 1936 11.058117 0.090431 0.5244% 1935
11.000432 0.090906 -3.0364% 1934 11.344905 0.088145 4.6271% 1933 10.843178 0.092224
1.3921% 1932 10.694301 0.093508 -0.2051% 1931 10.716278 0.093316 0.8886% 1930
10.621892 0.094145 1.0126% 1929 10.515415 0.095098 1.1526% 1928 10.395596 0.096195
1.2160% 1927 10.270704 0.097364 1.4086% 1926 10.128042 0.098736 1.7667% 1925
9.952218 0.100480 1.4465% 1924 9.810311 0.101934 1.7700% 1923 9.639691 0.103738
1.6165% 1922 9.486343 0.105415 1.3736% 1921 9.357800 0.106863 2.3393% 1920 9.143896
0.109363 1.3140% 1919 9.025302 0.110800 0.7676% 1918 8.956548 0.111650 0.3870% 1917
8.922021 0.112082 1.3274% 1916 8.805138 0.113570 1.4083% 1915 8.682858 0.115169
1.4458% 1914 8.559111 0.116835 1.9424% 1913 8.396028 0.119104 1.9857% 1912 8.232556

`

0.121469 1.5634% 1911 8.105829 0.123368 1.8169% 1910 7.961181 0.125610 1.8781% 1909
7.814421 0.127969 2.0082% 1908 7.660579 0.130538 1.9603% 1907 7.513299 0.133097
1.8264% 1906 7.378541 0.135528 1.9357% 1905 7.238428 0.138152 2.0148% 1904 7.095466
0.140935 2.1335% 1903 6.947245 0.143942 1.8151% 1902 6.823390 0.146555 1.8943% 1901
6.696535 0.149331 3.0255% 1900 6.499881 0.153849 0.6278% 1899 6.459326 0.154815
1.7757% 1898 6.346632 0.157564 1.8078% 1897 6.233938 0.160412 1.8396% 1896 6.121330
0.163363 1.8755% 1895 6.008636 0.166427 1.9114% 1894 5.895941 0.169608 1.9486% 1893
5.783247 0.172913 1.9858% 1892 5.670639 0.176347 2.0276% 1891 5.557945 0.179923
2.6465% 1890 5.414645 0.184684 1.5328% 1889 5.332902 0.187515 2.0811% 1888 5.224180
0.191418 2.1599% 1887 5.113731 0.195552 2.2075% 1886 5.003282 0.199869 2.2592% 1885
4.892746 0.204384 2.3095% 1884 4.782297 0.209105 2.3641% 1883 4.671848 0.214048
2.4214% 1882 4.561399 0.219231 2.4815% 1881 4.450950 0.224671 3.7644% 1880 4.289477
0.233129 0.9432% 1879 4.249396 0.235328 2.1464% 1878 4.160104 0.240379 2.1913% 1877
4.070898 0.245646 2.2426% 1876 3.981606 0.251155 2.2941% 1875 3.892314 0.256917
2.3456% 1874 3.803109 0.262943 2.4043% 1873 3.713817 0.269265 2.4635% 1872 3.624525
0.275898 2.5258% 1871 3.535233 0.282867 5.9947% 1870 3.335293 0.299824 -1.0968%
1869 3.372280 0.296535 2.1930% 1868 3.299914 0.303038 2.2394% 1867 3.227634 0.309824
2.2935% 1866 3.155268 0.316930 2.3445% 1865 3.082988 0.324361 2.4037% 1864 3.010622
0.332157 2.4599% 1863 2.938342 0.340328 2.5250% 1862 2.865976 0.348921 2.5872% 1861
2.793696 0.357949 2.9504% 1860 2.713633 0.368510 2.4012% 1859 2.650000 0.377358
2.7627% 1858 2.578756 0.387784 2.8412% 1857 2.507513 0.398802 2.9243% 1856 2.436269
0.410464 3.0161% 1855 2.364940 0.422844 3.1061% 1854 2.293696 0.435978 3.2056% 1853
2.222453 0.449953 3.3118% 1852 2.151209 0.464855 3.4252% 1851 2.079965 0.480777
4.0106% 1850 1.999763 0.500059 2.3254% 1849 1.954318 0.511688 2.7841% 1848 1.901382
0.525933 2.8590% 1847 1.848532 0.540970 2.9432% 1846 1.795682 0.556891 3.0324% 1845
1.742832 0.573779 3.1325% 1844 1.689896 0.591752 3.2284% 1843 1.637047 0.610856
3.3361% 1842 1.584197 0.631235 3.4512% 1841 1.531347 0.653020 3.8105% 1840 1.475137
0.677903 2.3861% 1839 1.440760 0.694078 2.5824% 1838 1.404491 0.712002 2.6573% 1837
1.368135 0.730922 2.7232% 1836 1.331865 0.750827 2.7994% 1835 1.295596 0.771846
2.8871% 1834 1.259240 0.794130 2.9657% 1833 1.222971 0.817681 3.0563% 1832 1.186701
0.842672 3.1604% 1831 1.150345 0.869304 3.4660% 1830 1.111810 0.899434 2.4653% 1829
1.085060 0.921608 2.6804% 1828 1.056736 0.946310 10.3427% 1827 0.957686 1.044184 -
4.2314% 1826 1.000000 1.000000 2.9150% 1825 0.971675 1.029150 3.0026% 1824 0.943351
1.060051 3.0955% 1823 0.915026 1.092865 3.1944% 1822 0.886701 1.127776 3.3102% 1821
0.858290 1.165107 3.2277% 1820 0.831453 1.202714 2.6573% 1819 0.809931 1.234673
2.6261% 1818 0.789206 1.267097 2.6969% 1817 0.768480 1.301270 2.7717% 1816 0.747755
1.337337 2.8507% 1815 0.727029 1.375460 2.9343% 1814 0.706304 1.415821 3.0231% 1813
0.685579 1.458622 3.1039% 1812 0.664940 1.503896 3.2172% 1811 0.644214 1.552279
3.0969% 1810 0.624863 1.600352 2.9144% 1809 0.607168 1.646992 2.8225% 1808 0.590501
1.693478 2.9199% 1807 0.573748 1.742926 2.9918% 1806 0.557081 1.795071 3.0841% 1805
0.540415 1.850431 3.1822% 1804 0.523748 1.909316 3.2868% 1803 0.507081 1.972071
3.3985% 1802 0.490415 2.039091 3.5180% 1801 0.473748 2.110828 3.3999% 1800 0.458170
2.182595 2.8419% 1799 0.445509 2.244621 2.7485% 1798 0.433592 2.306313 2.8261% 1797
0.421675 2.371493 3.7832% 1796 0.406304 2.461211 2.1272% 1795 0.397841 2.513566
3.0879% 1794 0.385924 2.591184 3.1625% 1793 0.374093 2.673130 3.2904% 1792 0.362176
2.761087 3.4024% 1791 0.350259 2.855030 3.2296% 1790 0.339301 2.947235 41.3145%
1780 0.240104 4.164868 29.4353% 1770 0.185501 5.390810 83.4728% 1750 0.101105
9.890673 29.2845% 1740 0.078204 12.787102 94.2514% 1720 0.040259 24.839125 85.8111%
1700 0.021667 46.153846 19.2490% 1690 0.018169 55.038023 88.0250% 1670 0.009663
103.485255

BASE YEAR: 1825
YEAR BYEAR/AYEAR AYEAR/BYEAR GROWTH%
2009 26.789046 0.037329 8.2857% 2001 24.739237 0.040422 1.0000% 2000
24.494292 0.040826 1.0000% 1999 24.251774 0.041234 1.0000% 1998 24.011657 0.041646
1.0000% 1997 23.773918 0.042063 1.0000% 1996 23.538533 0.042484 1.0000% 1995
23.305478 0.042908 0.9992% 1994 23.074909 0.043337 1.0008% 1993 22.846268 0.043771

278

1.0000% 1992 22.620068 0.044209 0.9295% 1991 22.411749 0.044619 1.2505% 1990
22.134948 0.045177 0.7224% 1989 21.976182 0.045504 1.1077% 1988 21.735425 0.046008
0.8834% 1987 21.545103 0.046414 0.5594% 1986 21.425258 0.046674 1.3056% 1985
21.149129 0.047283 0.7673% 1984 20.988091 0.047646 0.8149% 1983 20.818432 0.048034
0.9737% 1982 20.617668 0.048502 0.9508% 1981 20.423480 0.048963 0.9031% 1980
20.240693 0.049405 2.2701% 1979 19.791415 0.050527 1.0042% 1978 19.594650 0.051034
0.9896% 1977 19.402640 0.051539 0.9103% 1976 19.227604 0.052009 0.8394% 1975
19.067544 0.052445 0.9042% 1974 18.896685 0.052919 1.1568% 1973 18.680590 0.053531
0.9427% 1972 18.506132 0.054036 0.7426% 1971 18.369712 0.054437 1.4697% 1970
18.103636 0.055238 0.6968% 1969 17.978359 0.055622 0.8565% 1968 17.825675 0.056099
1.5090% 1967 17.560678 0.056945 0.9949% 1966 17.387687 0.057512 1.0575% 1965
17.205741 0.058120 1.1300% 1964 17.013486 0.058777 1.5537% 1963 16.753199 0.059690
1.4658% 1962 16.511176 0.060565 1.5364% 1961 16.261331 0.061496 2.1586% 1960
15.917725 0.062823 -1.6655% 1959 16.187322 0.061777 4.3080% 1958 15.518774 0.064438
2.1130% 1957 15.197654 0.065800 1.9895% 1956 14.901195 0.067109 2.1231% 1955
14.591406 0.068533 1.4496% 1954 14.382910 0.069527 2.1573% 1953 14.079186 0.071027
1.2298% 1952 13.908150 0.071900 1.6814% 1951 13.678168 0.073109 1.6233% 1950
13.459681 0.074296 1.4265% 1949 13.270374 0.075356 1.7790% 1948 13.038415 0.076696
1.8242% 1947 12.804835 0.078096 -2.6320% 1946 13.150973 0.076040 3.1768% 1945
12.746056 0.078456 6.4754% 1944 11.970891 0.083536 -0.3437% 1943 12.012174 0.083249
0.6562% 1942 11.933861 0.083795 0.6633% 1941 11.855226 0.084351 -5.6614% 1940
12.566679 0.079576 8.0381% 1939 11.631710 0.085972 0.8126% 1938 11.537949 0.086671
0.7762% 1937 11.449076 0.087343 0.6029% 1936 11.380466 0.087870 0.5244% 1935
11.321098 0.088331 -3.0364% 1934 11.675613 0.085649 4.6271% 1933 11.159261 0.089612
1.3921% 1932 11.006043 0.090859 -0.2051% 1931 11.028662 0.090673 0.8886% 1930
10.931524 0.091479 1.0126% 1929 10.821943 0.092405 1.1526% 1928 10.698631 0.093470
1.2160% 1927 10.570099 0.094606 1.4086% 1926 10.423278 0.095939 1.7667% 1925
10.242328 0.097634 1.4465% 1924 10.096285 0.099046 1.7700% 1923 9.920692 0.100799
1.6165% 1922 9.762873 0.102429 1.3736% 1921 9.630583 0.103836 2.3393% 1920 9.410443
0.106265 1.3140% 1919 9.288393 0.107661 0.7676% 1918 9.217635 0.108488 0.3870% 1917
9.182101 0.108908 1.3274% 1916 9.061811 0.110353 1.4083% 1915 8.935967 0.111907
1.4458% 1914 8.808612 0.113525 1.9424% 1913 8.640775 0.115730 1.9857% 1912 8.472538
0.118028 1.5634% 1911 8.342117 0.119874 1.8169% 1910 8.193252 0.122052 1.8781% 1909
8.042215 0.124344 2.0082% 1908 7.883887 0.126841 1.9603% 1907 7.732314 0.129327
1.8264% 1906 7.593628 0.131689 1.9357% 1905 7.449431 0.134238 2.0148% 1904 7.302302
0.136943 2.1335% 1903 7.149760 0.139865 1.8151% 1902 7.022295 0.142404 1.8943% 1901
6.891741 0.145101 3.0255% 1900 6.689355 0.149491 0.6278% 1899 6.647618 0.150430
1.7757% 1898 6.531639 0.153101 1.8078% 1897 6.415659 0.155869 1.8396% 1896 6.299769
0.158736 1.8755% 1895 6.183790 0.161713 1.9114% 1894 6.067810 0.164804 1.9486% 1893
5.951831 0.168016 1.9858% 1892 5.835940 0.171352 2.0276% 1891 5.719961 0.174826
2.6465% 1890 5.572484 0.179453 1.5328% 1889 5.488358 0.182204 2.0811% 1888 5.376466
0.185996 2.1599% 1887 5.262798 0.190013 2.2075% 1886 5.149129 0.194208 2.2592% 1885
5.035371 0.198595 2.3095% 1884 4.921703 0.203182 2.3641% 1883 4.808034 0.207985
2.4214% 1882 4.694365 0.213021 2.4815% 1881 4.580697 0.218307 3.7644% 1880 4.414517
0.226525 0.9432% 1879 4.373267 0.228662 2.1464% 1878 4.281372 0.233570 2.1913% 1877
4.189566 0.238688 2.2426% 1876 4.097672 0.244041 2.2941% 1875 4.005777 0.249639
2.3456% 1874 3.913971 0.255495 2.4043% 1873 3.822076 0.261638 2.4635% 1872 3.730181
0.268083 2.5258% 1871 3.638287 0.274855 5.9947% 1870 3.432518 0.291331 -1.0968%
1869 3.470583 0.288136 2.1930% 1868 3.396107 0.294455 2.2394% 1867 3.321721 0.301049
2.2935% 1866 3.247245 0.307953 2.3445% 1865 3.172858 0.315173 2.4037% 1864 3.098383
0.322749 2.4599% 1863 3.023996 0.330688 2.5250% 1862 2.949520 0.339038 2.5872% 1861
2.875133 0.347810 2.9504% 1860 2.792736 0.358072 2.4012% 1859 2.727248 0.366670
2.7627% 1858 2.653928 0.376800 2.8412% 1857 2.580608 0.387506 2.9243% 1856 2.507288
0.398837 3.0161% 1855 2.433878 0.410867 3.1061% 1854 2.360558 0.423629 3.2056% 1853
2.287238 0.437209 3.3118% 1852 2.213918 0.451688 3.4252% 1851 2.140597 0.467159
4.0106% 1850 2.058057 0.485895 2.3254% 1849 2.011287 0.497194 2.7841% 1848 1.956808

0.511036 2.8590% 1847 1.902417 0.525647 2.9432% 1846 1.848027 0.541118 3.0324% 1845
1.793637 0.557527 3.1325% 1844 1.739157 0.574991 3.2284% 1843 1.684767 0.593554
3.3361% 1842 1.630377 0.613355 3.4512% 1841 1.575986 0.634523 3.8105% 1840 1.518138
0.658702 2.3861% 1839 1.482759 0.674419 2.5824% 1838 1.445432 0.691835 2.6573% 1837
1.408016 0.710219 2.7232% 1836 1.370690 0.729560 2.7994% 1835 1.333363 0.749983
2.8871% 1834 1.295947 0.771636 2.9657% 1833 1.258621 0.794521 3.0563% 1832 1.221294
0.818804 3.1604% 1831 1.183878 0.844681 3.4660% 1830 1.144220 0.873958 2.4653% 1829
1.116690 0.895503 2.6804% 1828 1.087540 0.919506 10.3427% 1827 0.985603 1.014608 -
4.2314% 1826 1.029150 0.971675 2.9150% 1825 1.000000 1.000000 3.0026% 1824 0.970850
1.030026 3.0955% 1823 0.941699 1.061910 3.1944% 1822 0.912549 1.095832 3.3102% 1821
0.883310 1.132106 3.2277% 1820 0.855690 1.168647 2.6573% 1819 0.833541 1.199701
2.6261% 1818 0.812211 1.231207 2.6969% 1817 0.790882 1.264412 2.7717% 1816 0.769552
1.299457 2.8507% 1815 0.748223 1.336501 2.9343% 1814 0.726893 1.375718 3.0231% 1813
0.705563 1.417307 3.1039% 1812 0.684323 1.461299 3.2172% 1811 0.662993 1.508311
3.0969% 1810 0.643078 1.555022 2.9144% 1809 0.624867 1.600341 2.8225% 1808 0.607714
1.645510 2.9199% 1807 0.590473 1.693558 2.9918% 1806 0.573320 1.744226 3.0841% 1805
0.556168 1.798019 3.1822% 1804 0.539015 1.855235 3.2868% 1803 0.521863 1.916213
3.3985% 1802 0.504710 1.981335 3.5180% 1801 0.487558 2.051039 3.3999% 1800 0.471526
2.120773 2.8419% 1799 0.458496 2.181043 2.7485% 1798 0.446232 2.240988 2.8261% 1797
0.433967 2.304321 3.7832% 1796 0.418148 2.391498 2.1272% 1795 0.409438 2.442370
3.0879% 1794 0.397174 2.517789 3.1625% 1793 0.384998 2.597415 3.2904% 1792 0.372734
2.682880 3.4024% 1791 0.360469 2.774162 3.2296% 1790 0.349192 2.863755 41.3145%
1780 0.247103 4.046900 29.4353% 1770 0.190908 5.238117 83.4728% 1750 0.104053
9.610523 29.2845% 1740 0.080483 12.424912 94.2514% 1720 0.041433 24.135564 85.8111%
1700 0.022298 44.846552 19.2490% 1690 0.018699 53.479087 88.0250% 1670 0.009945
100.554066
BASE YEAR: 1824
YEAR BYEAR/AYEAR AYEAR/BYEAR GROWTH%
2009 27.593404 0.036241 8.2857% 2001 25.482049 0.039243 1.0000% 2000
25.229748 0.039636 1.0000% 1999 24.979949 0.040032 1.0000% 1998 24.732623 0.040432
1.0000% 1997 24.487745 0.040837 1.0000% 1996 24.245292 0.041245 1.0000% 1995
24.005240 0.041658 0.9992% 1994 23.767747 0.042074 1.0008% 1993 23.532242 0.042495
1.0000% 1992 23.299249 0.042920 0.9295% 1991 23.084676 0.043319 1.2505% 1990
22.799564 0.043860 0.7224% 1989 22.636031 0.044177 1.1077% 1988 22.388045 0.044667
0.8834% 1987 22.192008 0.045061 0.5594% 1986 22.068565 0.045313 1.3056% 1985
21.784145 0.045905 0.7673% 1984 21.618272 0.046257 0.8149% 1983 21.443519 0.046634
0.9737% 1982 21.236726 0.047088 0.9508% 1981 21.036708 0.047536 0.9031% 1980
20.848433 0.047965 2.2701% 1979 20.385665 0.049054 1.0042% 1978 20.182992 0.049547
0.9896% 1977 19.985216 0.050037 0.9103% 1976 19.804925 0.050492 0.8394% 1975
19.640059 0.050916 0.9042% 1974 19.464070 0.051377 1.1568% 1973 19.241487 0.051971
0.9427% 1972 19.061791 0.052461 0.7426% 1971 18.921274 0.052851 1.4697% 1970
18.647209 0.053627 0.6968% 1969 18.518171 0.054001 0.8565% 1968 18.360903 0.054464
1.5090% 1967 18.087949 0.055285 0.9949% 1966 17.909763 0.055835 1.0575% 1965
17.722354 0.056426 1.1300% 1964 17.524327 0.057064 1.5537% 1963 17.256225 0.057950
1.4658% 1962 17.006934 0.058800 1.5364% 1961 16.749588 0.059703 2.1586% 1960
16.395665 0.060992 -1.6655% 1959 16.673357 0.059976 4.3080% 1958 15.984735 0.062560
2.1130% 1957 15.653973 0.063882 1.9895% 1956 15.348613 0.065152 2.1231% 1955
15.029522 0.066536 1.4496% 1954 14.814766 0.067500 2.1573% 1953 14.501922 0.068956
1.2298% 1952 14.325751 0.069804 1.6814% 1951 14.088864 0.070978 1.6233% 1950
13.863816 0.072130 1.4265% 1949 13.668826 0.073159 1.7790% 1948 13.429902 0.074461
1.8242% 1947 13.189308 0.075819 -2.6320% 1946 13.545839 0.073823 3.1768% 1945
13.128765 0.076169 6.4754% 1944 12.330325 0.081101 -0.3437% 1943 12.372847 0.080822
0.6562% 1942 12.292183 0.081353 0.6633% 1941 12.211186 0.081892 -5.6614% 1940
12.944002 0.077256 8.0381% 1939 11.980959 0.083466 0.8126% 1938 11.884383 0.084144
0.7762% 1937 11.792841 0.084797 0.6029% 1936 11.722171 0.085308 0.5244% 1935
11.661022 0.085756 -3.0364% 1934 12.026181 0.083152 4.6271% 1933 11.494324 0.086999

280

1.3921% 1932 11.336507 0.088211 -0.2051% 1931 11.359804 0.088030 0.8886% 1930
11.259750 0.088812 1.0126% 1929 11.146878 0.089711 1.1526% 1928 11.019865 0.090745
1.2160% 1927 10.887473 0.091849 1.4086% 1926 10.736244 0.093142 1.7667% 1925
10.549861 0.094788 1.4465% 1924 10.399433 0.096159 1.7700% 1923 10.218567 0.097861
1.6165% 1922 10.056010 0.099443 1.3736% 1921 9.919747 0.100809 2.3393% 1920
9.692998 0.103167 1.3140% 1919 9.567283 0.104523 0.7676% 1918 9.494400 0.105325
0.3870% 1917 9.457799 0.105733 1.3274% 1916 9.333898 0.107136 1.4083% 1915 9.204275
0.108645 1.4458% 1914 9.073096 0.110216 1.9424% 1913 8.900220 0.112357 1.9857% 1912
8.726932 0.114588 1.5634% 1911 8.592594 0.116379 1.8169% 1910 8.439260 0.118494
1.8781% 1909 8.283687 0.120719 2.0082% 1908 8.120606 0.123144 1.9603% 1907 7.964482
0.125557 1.8264% 1906 7.821631 0.127851 1.9357% 1905 7.673105 0.130325 2.0148% 1904
7.521558 0.132951 2.1335% 1903 7.364436 0.135788 1.8151% 1902 7.233143 0.138252
1.8943% 1901 7.098670 0.140871 3.0255% 1900 6.890207 0.145134 0.6278% 1899 6.847217
0.146045 1.7757% 1898 6.727755 0.148638 1.8078% 1897 6.608294 0.151325 1.8396% 1896
6.488923 0.154109 1.8755% 1895 6.369462 0.156999 1.9114% 1894 6.250000 0.160000
1.9486% 1893 6.130538 0.163118 1.9858% 1892 6.011168 0.166357 2.0276% 1891 5.891706
0.169730 2.6465% 1890 5.739802 0.174222 1.5328% 1889 5.653149 0.176893 2.0811% 1888
5.537898 0.180574 2.1599% 1887 5.420817 0.184474 2.2075% 1886 5.303735 0.188546
2.2592% 1885 5.186562 0.192806 2.3095% 1884 5.069480 0.197259 2.3641% 1883 4.952398
0.201922 2.4214% 1882 4.835317 0.206812 2.4815% 1881 4.718235 0.211944 3.7644% 1880
4.547066 0.219922 0.9432% 1879 4.504577 0.221996 2.1464% 1878 4.409923 0.226761
2.1913% 1877 4.315361 0.231730 2.2426% 1876 4.220707 0.236927 2.2941% 1875 4.126053
0.242362 2.3456% 1874 4.031490 0.248047 2.4043% 1873 3.936836 0.254011 2.4635% 1872
3.842182 0.260269 2.5258% 1871 3.747528 0.266843 5.9947% 1870 3.535582 0.282839 -
1.0968% 1869 3.574789 0.279737 2.1930% 1868 3.498078 0.285871 2.2394% 1867 3.421457
0.292273 2.2935% 1866 3.344746 0.298976 2.3445% 1865 3.268125 0.305986 2.4037% 1864
3.191413 0.313341 2.4599% 1863 3.114793 0.321049 2.5250% 1862 3.038081 0.329155
2.5872% 1861 2.961461 0.337671 2.9504% 1860 2.876590 0.347634 2.4012% 1859 2.809136
0.355981 2.7627% 1858 2.733614 0.365816 2.8412% 1857 2.658092 0.376210 2.9243% 1856
2.582570 0.387211 3.0161% 1855 2.506957 0.398890 3.1061% 1854 2.431435 0.411280
3.2056% 1853 2.355914 0.424464 3.3118% 1852 2.280392 0.438521 3.4252% 1851 2.204870
0.453541 4.0106% 1850 2.119851 0.471731 2.3254% 1849 2.071677 0.482701 2.7841% 1848
2.015562 0.496140 2.8590% 1847 1.959539 0.510324 2.9432% 1846 1.903515 0.525344
3.0324% 1845 1.847492 0.541274 3.1325% 1844 1.791377 0.558230 3.2284% 1843 1.735353
0.576252 3.3361% 1842 1.679330 0.595476 3.4512% 1841 1.623306 0.616027 3.8105% 1840
1.563721 0.639500 2.3861% 1839 1.527279 0.654759 2.5824% 1838 1.488832 0.671667
2.6573% 1837 1.450293 0.689516 2.7232% 1836 1.411845 0.708293 2.7994% 1835 1.373398
0.728121 2.8871% 1834 1.334859 0.749143 2.9657% 1833 1.296412 0.771360 3.0563% 1832
1.257964 0.794935 3.1604% 1831 1.219425 0.820059 3.4660% 1830 1.178576 0.848482
2.4653% 1829 1.150220 0.869399 2.6804% 1828 1.120194 0.892702 10.3427% 1827
1.015196 0.985032 -4.2314% 1826 1.060051 0.943351 2.9150% 1825 1.030026 0.970850
3.0026% 1824 1.000000 1.000000 3.0955% 1823 0.969974 1.030955 3.1944% 1822 0.939949
1.063888 3.3102% 1821 0.909832 1.099105 3.2277% 1820 0.881383 1.134581 2.6573% 1819
0.858568 1.164730 2.6261% 1818 0.836598 1.195317 2.6969% 1817 0.814628 1.227554
2.7717% 1816 0.792658 1.261578 2.8507% 1815 0.770688 1.297541 2.9343% 1814 0.748718
1.335616 3.0231% 1813 0.726748 1.375992 3.1039% 1812 0.704870 1.418701 3.2172% 1811
0.682900 1.464343 3.0969% 1810 0.662386 1.509693 2.9144% 1809 0.643629 1.553691
2.8225% 1808 0.625961 1.597543 2.9199% 1807 0.608202 1.644190 2.9918% 1806 0.590535
1.693381 3.0841% 1805 0.572867 1.745606 3.1822% 1804 0.555200 1.801154 3.2868% 1803
0.537532 1.860354 3.3985% 1802 0.519865 1.923578 3.5180% 1801 0.502197 1.991250
3.3999% 1800 0.485684 2.058952 2.8419% 1799 0.472263 2.117465 2.7485% 1798 0.459630
2.175662 2.8261% 1797 0.446997 2.237149 3.7832% 1796 0.430703 2.321785 2.1272% 1795
0.421732 2.371174 3.0879% 1794 0.409099 2.444395 3.1625% 1793 0.396558 2.521699
3.2904% 1792 0.383925 2.604673 3.4024% 1791 0.371293 2.693294 3.2296% 1790 0.359677
2.780276 41.3145% 1780 0.254522 3.928931 29.4353% 1770 0.196640 5.085424 83.4728%
1750 0.107177 9.330372 29.2845% 1740 0.082900 12.062721 94.2514% 1720 0.042677

281

23.432003 85.8111% 1700 0.022968 43.539259 19.2490% 1690 0.019260 51.920152 88.0250% 1670 0.010244 97.622878

BASE YEAR: 1823

YEAR BYEAR/AYEAR AYEAR/BYEAR GROWTH%

2009 28.447560 0.035152 8.2857% 2001 26.270847 0.038065 1.0000% 2000 26.010737 0.038446 1.0000% 1999 25.753205 0.038830 1.0000% 1998 25.498223 0.039218 1.0000% 1997 25.245765 0.039611 1.0000% 1996 24.995807 0.040007 1.0000% 1995 24.748324 0.040407 0.9992% 1994 24.503480 0.040811 1.0008% 1993 24.260684 0.041219 1.0000% 1992 24.020479 0.041631 0.9295% 1991 23.799264 0.042018 1.2505% 1990 23.505326 0.042544 0.7224% 1989 23.336731 0.042851 1.1077% 1988 23.081068 0.043326 0.8834% 1987 22.878964 0.043708 0.5594% 1986 22.751699 0.043953 1.3056% 1985 22.458475 0.044527 0.7673% 1984 22.287467 0.044868 0.8149% 1983 22.107305 0.045234 0.9737% 1982 21.894111 0.045674 0.9508% 1981 21.687901 0.046109 0.9031% 1980 21.493798 0.046525 2.2701% 1979 21.016704 0.047581 1.0042% 1978 20.807758 0.048059 0.9896% 1977 20.603860 0.048535 0.9103% 1976 20.417988 0.048976 0.8394% 1975 20.248018 0.049388 0.9042% 1974 20.066582 0.049834 1.1568% 1973 19.837108 0.050411 0.9427% 1972 19.651850 0.050886 0.7426% 1971 19.506984 0.051264 1.4697% 1970 19.224435 0.052017 0.6968% 1969 19.091402 0.052380 0.8565% 1968 18.929266 0.052828 1.5090% 1967 18.647862 0.053625 0.9949% 1966 18.464161 0.054159 1.0575% 1965 18.270951 0.054732 1.1300% 1964 18.066794 0.055350 1.5537% 1963 17.790393 0.056210 1.4658% 1962 17.533385 0.057034 1.5364% 1961 17.268073 0.057910 2.1586% 1960 16.903194 0.059160 -1.6655% 1959 17.189482 0.058175 4.3080% 1958 16.479544 0.060681 2.1130% 1957 16.138543 0.061963 1.9895% 1956 15.823731 0.063196 2.1231% 1955 15.494762 0.064538 1.4496% 1954 15.273358 0.065473 2.1573% 1953 14.950831 0.066886 1.2298% 1952 14.769205 0.067708 1.6814% 1951 14.524986 0.068847 1.6233% 1950 14.292972 0.069964 1.4265% 1949 14.091945 0.070963 1.7790% 1948 13.845626 0.072225 1.8242% 1947 13.597584 0.073542 -2.6320% 1946 13.965152 0.071607 3.1768% 1945 13.535167 0.073882 6.4754% 1944 12.712011 0.078666 -0.3437% 1943 12.755850 0.078395 0.6562% 1942 12.672689 0.078910 0.6633% 1941 12.589185 0.079433 -5.6614% 1940 13.344684 0.074936 8.0381% 1939 12.351831 0.080960 0.8126% 1938 12.252265 0.081618 0.7762% 1937 12.157890 0.082251 0.6029% 1936 12.085032 0.082747 0.5244% 1935 12.021989 0.083181 -3.0364% 1934 12.398452 0.080655 4.6271% 1933 11.850132 0.084387 1.3921% 1932 11.687429 0.085562 -0.2051% 1931 11.711448 0.085387 0.8886% 1930 11.608297 0.086145 1.0126% 1929 11.491931 0.087018 1.1526% 1928 11.360985 0.088021 1.2160% 1927 11.224495 0.089091 1.4086% 1926 11.068585 0.090346 1.7667% 1925 10.876433 0.091942 1.4465% 1924 10.721348 0.093272 1.7700% 1923 10.534883 0.094923 1.6165% 1922 10.367294 0.096457 1.3736% 1921 10.226814 0.097782 2.3393% 1920 9.993045 0.100070 1.3140% 1919 9.863439 0.101385 0.7676% 1918 9.788300 0.102163 0.3870% 1917 9.750566 0.102558 1.3274% 1916 9.622829 0.103920 1.4083% 1915 9.489194 0.105383 1.4458% 1914 9.353954 0.106907 1.9424% 1913 9.175727 0.108983 1.9857% 1912 8.997074 0.111147 1.5634% 1911 8.858579 0.112885 1.8169% 1910 8.700498 0.114936 1.8781% 1909 8.540109 0.117095 2.0082% 1908 8.371980 0.119446 1.9603% 1907 8.211023 0.121788 1.8264% 1906 8.063750 0.124012 1.9357% 1905 7.910627 0.126412 2.0148% 1904 7.754388 0.128959 2.1335% 1903 7.592403 0.131711 1.8151% 1902 7.457046 0.134101 1.8943% 1901 7.318410 0.136642 3.0255% 1900 7.103494 0.140776 0.6278% 1899 7.059173 0.141660 1.7757% 1898 6.936014 0.144175 1.8078% 1897 6.812854 0.146781 1.8396% 1896 6.689789 0.149482 1.8755% 1895 6.566629 0.152285 1.9114% 1894 6.443469 0.155196 1.9486% 1893 6.320310 0.158220 1.9858% 1892 6.197244 0.161362 2.0276% 1891 6.074085 0.164634 2.6465% 1890 5.917478 0.168991 1.5328% 1889 5.828143 0.171581 2.0811% 1888 5.709324 0.175152 2.1599% 1887 5.588618 0.178935 2.2075% 1886 5.467912 0.182885 2.2592% 1885 5.347112 0.187017 2.3095% 1884 5.226406 0.191336 2.3641% 1883 5.105700 0.195860 2.4214% 1882 4.984994 0.200602 2.4815% 1881 4.864288 0.205580 3.7644% 1880 4.687820 0.213319 0.9432% 1879 4.644017 0.215331 2.1464% 1878 4.546433 0.219953 2.1913% 1877 4.448943 0.224772 2.2426% 1876 4.351359 0.229813 2.2941% 1875 4.253775 0.235085 2.3456% 1874 4.156285 0.240599 2.4043% 1873 4.058701 0.246384 2.4635% 1872 3.961117 0.252454 2.5258% 1871 3.863533 0.258830 5.9947% 1870 3.645026 0.274346 -

1.0968% 1869 3.685447 0.271337 2.1930% 1868 3.606361 0.277288 2.2394% 1867 3.527369 0.283497 2.2935% 1866 3.448282 0.289999 2.3445% 1865 3.369290 0.296798 2.4037% 1864 3.290204 0.303933 2.4599% 1863 3.211212 0.311409 2.5250% 1862 3.132125 0.319272 2.5872% 1861 3.053133 0.327532 2.9504% 1860 2.965635 0.337196 2.4012% 1859 2.896093 0.345293 2.7627% 1858 2.818233 0.354832 2.8412% 1857 2.740374 0.364914 2.9243% 1856 2.662514 0.375585 3.0161% 1855 2.584560 0.386913 3.1061% 1854 2.506701 0.398931 3.2056% 1853 2.428841 0.411719 3.3118% 1852 2.350982 0.425354 3.4252% 1851 2.273122 0.439924 4.0106% 1850 2.185471 0.457567 2.3254% 1849 2.135806 0.468207 2.7841% 1848 2.077954 0.481243 2.8590% 1847 2.020196 0.495001 2.9432% 1846 1.962439 0.509570 3.0324% 1845 1.904681 0.525022 3.1325% 1844 1.846829 0.541469 3.2284% 1843 1.789071 0.558949 3.3361% 1842 1.731314 0.577596 3.4512% 1841 1.673556 0.597530 3.8105% 1840 1.612126 0.620299 2.3861% 1839 1.574556 0.635099 2.5824% 1838 1.534919 0.651500 2.6573% 1837 1.495187 0.668813 2.7232% 1836 1.455549 0.687026 2.7994% 1835 1.415912 0.706259 2.8871% 1834 1.376180 0.726649 2.9657% 1833 1.336542 0.748199 3.0563% 1832 1.296904 0.771067 3.1604% 1831 1.257173 0.795436 3.4660% 1830 1.215059 0.823005 2.4653% 1829 1.185825 0.843295 2.6804% 1828 1.154870 0.865899 10.3427% 1827 1.046621 0.955455 -4.2314% 1826 1.092865 0.915026 2.9150% 1825 1.061910 0.941699 3.0026% 1824 1.030955 0.969974 3.0955% 1823 1.000000 1.000000 3.1944% 1822 0.969045 1.031944 3.3102% 1821 0.937995 1.066103 3.2277% 1820 0.908666 1.100514 2.6573% 1819 0.885145 1.129758 2.6261% 1818 0.862495 1.159427 2.6969% 1817 0.839845 1.190696 2.7717% 1816 0.817195 1.223698 2.8507% 1815 0.794545 1.258582 2.9343% 1814 0.771895 1.295513 3.0231% 1813 0.749245 1.334677 3.1039% 1812 0.726689 1.376104 3.2172% 1811 0.704039 1.420375 3.0969% 1810 0.682891 1.464363 2.9144% 1809 0.663552 1.507040 2.8225% 1808 0.645338 1.549576 2.9199% 1807 0.627029 1.594822 2.9918% 1806 0.608815 1.642536 3.0841% 1805 0.590600 1.693193 3.1822% 1804 0.572386 1.747073 3.2868% 1803 0.554171 1.804496 3.3985% 1802 0.535957 1.865821 3.5180% 1801 0.517743 1.931462 3.3999% 1800 0.500718 1.997131 2.8419% 1799 0.486882 2.053886 2.7485% 1798 0.473858 2.110337 2.8261% 1797 0.460834 2.169977 3.7832% 1796 0.444035 2.252072 2.1272% 1795 0.434787 2.299978 3.0879% 1794 0.421763 2.371000 3.1625% 1793 0.408834 2.445983 3.2904% 1792 0.395810 2.526466 3.4024% 1791 0.382786 2.612426 3.2296% 1790 0.370810 2.696796 41.3145% 1780 0.262401 3.810962 29.4353% 1770 0.202727 4.932731 83.4728% 1750 0.110495 9.050222 29.2845% 1740 0.085466 11.700530 94.2514% 1720 0.043998 22.728443 85.8111% 1700 0.023679 42.231965 19.2490% 1690 0.019857 50.361217 88.0250% 1670 0.010561 94.691689

BASE YEAR: 1822

YEAR BYEAR/AYEAR AYEAR/BYEAR GROWTH%

2009 29.356286 0.034064 8.2857% 2001 27.110041 0.036887 1.0000% 2000 26.841622 0.037256 1.0000% 1999 26.575863 0.037628 1.0000% 1998 26.312736 0.038004 1.0000% 1997 26.052214 0.038384 1.0000% 1996 25.794271 0.038768 1.0000% 1995 25.538882 0.039156 0.9992% 1994 25.286217 0.039547 1.0008% 1993 25.035665 0.039943 1.0000% 1992 24.787787 0.040342 0.9295% 1991 24.559505 0.040717 1.2505% 1990 24.256178 0.041227 0.7224% 1989 24.082197 0.041524 1.1077% 1988 23.818368 0.041984 0.8834% 1987 23.609807 0.042355 0.5594% 1986 23.478477 0.042592 1.3056% 1985 23.175886 0.043148 0.7673% 1984 22.999416 0.043479 0.8149% 1983 22.813498 0.043834 0.9737% 1982 22.593494 0.044261 0.9508% 1981 22.380697 0.044681 0.9031% 1980 22.180394 0.045085 2.2701% 1979 21.688060 0.046108 1.0042% 1978 21.472439 0.046571 0.9896% 1977 21.262028 0.047032 0.9103% 1976 21.070218 0.047460 0.8394% 1975 20.894819 0.047859 0.9042% 1974 20.707587 0.048291 1.1568% 1973 20.470783 0.048850 0.9427% 1972 20.279607 0.049311 0.7426% 1971 20.130113 0.049677 1.4697% 1970 19.838539 0.050407 0.6968% 1969 19.701256 0.050758 0.8565% 1968 19.533940 0.051193 1.5090% 1967 19.243548 0.051965 0.9949% 1966 19.053978 0.052482 1.0575% 1965 18.854597 0.053037 1.1300% 1964 18.643918 0.053637 1.5537% 1963 18.358687 0.054470 1.4658% 1962 18.093470 0.055269 1.5364% 1961 17.819683 0.056118 2.1586% 1960 17.443148 0.057329 -1.6655% 1959 17.738581 0.056374 4.3080% 1958 17.005965 0.058803 2.1130% 1957 16.654071 0.060045 1.9895% 1956 16.329202 0.061240 2.1231% 1955 15.989725 0.062540 1.4496% 1954 15.761249 0.063447 2.1573% 1953 15.428418 0.064815

283

1.2298% 1952 15.240991 0.065613 1.6814% 1951 14.988971 0.066716 1.6233% 1950
14.749545 0.067799 1.4265% 1949 14.542097 0.068766 1.7790% 1948 14.287909 0.069989
1.8242% 1947 14.031944 0.071266 -2.6320% 1946 14.411253 0.069390 3.1768% 1945
13.967533 0.071595 6.4754% 1944 13.118082 0.076231 -0.3437% 1943 13.163321 0.075969
0.6562% 1942 13.077504 0.076467 0.6633% 1941 12.991332 0.076974 -5.6614% 1940
13.770966 0.072617 8.0381% 1939 12.746397 0.078454 0.8126% 1938 12.643650 0.079091
0.7762% 1937 12.546260 0.079705 0.6029% 1936 12.471075 0.080186 0.5244% 1935
12.406019 0.080606 -3.0364% 1934 12.794507 0.078159 4.6271% 1933 12.228672 0.081775
1.3921% 1932 12.060771 0.082913 -0.2051% 1931 12.085557 0.082743 0.8886% 1930
11.979111 0.083479 1.0126% 1929 11.859028 0.084324 1.1526% 1928 11.723899 0.085296
1.2160% 1927 11.583049 0.086333 1.4086% 1926 11.422159 0.087549 1.7667% 1925
11.223868 0.089096 1.4465% 1924 11.063830 0.090385 1.7700% 1923 10.871409 0.091984
1.6165% 1922 10.698466 0.093471 1.3736% 1921 10.553498 0.094755 2.3393% 1920
10.312262 0.096972 1.3140% 1919 10.178516 0.098246 0.7676% 1918 10.100976 0.099000
0.3870% 1917 10.062037 0.099383 1.3274% 1916 9.930220 0.100703 1.4083% 1915
9.792316 0.102121 1.4458% 1914 9.652756 0.103597 1.9424% 1913 9.468835 0.105610
1.9857% 1912 9.284476 0.107707 1.5634% 1911 9.141556 0.109391 1.8169% 1910 8.978426
0.111378 1.8781% 1909 8.812914 0.113470 2.0082% 1908 8.639414 0.115749 1.9603% 1907
8.473315 0.118018 1.8264% 1906 8.321338 0.120173 1.9357% 1905 8.163323 0.122499
2.0148% 1904 8.002094 0.124967 2.1335% 1903 7.834933 0.127634 1.8151% 1902 7.695253
0.129950 1.8943% 1901 7.552188 0.132412 3.0255% 1900 7.330407 0.136418 0.6278% 1899
7.284671 0.137275 1.7757% 1898 7.157577 0.139712 1.8078% 1897 7.030483 0.142238
1.8396% 1896 6.903487 0.144854 1.8755% 1895 6.776393 0.147571 1.9114% 1894 6.649299
0.150392 1.9486% 1893 6.522205 0.153322 1.9858% 1892 6.395208 0.156367 2.0276% 1891
6.268115 0.159538 2.6465% 1890 6.106505 0.163760 1.5328% 1889 6.014316 0.166270
2.0811% 1888 5.891702 0.169730 2.1599% 1887 5.767141 0.173396 2.2075% 1886 5.642579
0.177224 2.2592% 1885 5.517920 0.181228 2.3095% 1884 5.393358 0.185413 2.3641% 1883
5.268796 0.189797 2.4214% 1882 5.144235 0.194392 2.4815% 1881 5.019673 0.199216
3.7644% 1880 4.837568 0.206715 0.9432% 1879 4.792365 0.208665 2.1464% 1878 4.691663
0.213144 2.1913% 1877 4.591060 0.217815 2.2426% 1876 4.490358 0.222699 2.2941% 1875
4.389657 0.227808 2.3456% 1874 4.289053 0.233152 2.4043% 1873 4.188352 0.238757
2.4635% 1872 4.087651 0.244639 2.5258% 1871 3.986950 0.250818 5.9947% 1870 3.761462
0.265854 -1.0968% 1869 3.803175 0.262938 2.1930% 1868 3.721562 0.268704 2.2394%
1867 3.640047 0.274722 2.2935% 1866 3.558434 0.281022 2.3445% 1865 3.476919 0.287611
2.4037% 1864 3.395306 0.294524 2.4599% 1863 3.313790 0.301769 2.5250% 1862 3.232178
0.309389 2.5872% 1861 3.150662 0.317394 2.9504% 1860 3.060369 0.326758 2.4012% 1859
2.988605 0.334604 2.7627% 1858 2.908259 0.343848 2.8412% 1857 2.827912 0.353618
2.9243% 1856 2.747565 0.363959 3.0161% 1855 2.667121 0.374936 3.1061% 1854 2.586774
0.386582 3.2056% 1853 2.506428 0.398974 3.3118% 1852 2.426081 0.412187 3.4252% 1851
2.345734 0.426306 4.0106% 1850 2.255284 0.443403 2.3254% 1849 2.204032 0.453714
2.7841% 1848 2.144332 0.466346 2.8590% 1847 2.084729 0.479679 2.9432% 1846 2.025127
0.493796 3.0324% 1845 1.965524 0.508770 3.1325% 1844 1.905824 0.524707 3.2284% 1843
1.846221 0.541647 3.3361% 1842 1.786619 0.559717 3.4512% 1841 1.727016 0.579033
3.8105% 1840 1.663624 0.601097 2.3861% 1839 1.624854 0.615440 2.5824% 1838 1.583950
0.631333 2.6573% 1837 1.542949 0.648110 2.7232% 1836 1.502045 0.665759 2.7994% 1835
1.461141 0.684396 2.8871% 1834 1.420140 0.704156 2.9657% 1833 1.379236 0.725039
3.0563% 1832 1.338333 0.747198 3.1604% 1831 1.297332 0.770813 3.4660% 1830 1.253873
0.797529 2.4653% 1829 1.223705 0.817191 2.6804% 1828 1.191761 0.839095 10.3427%
1827 1.080055 0.925879 -4.2314% 1826 1.127776 0.886701 2.9150% 1825 1.095832
0.912549 3.0026% 1824 1.063888 0.939949 3.0955% 1823 1.031944 0.969045 3.1944% 1822
1.000000 1.000000 3.3102% 1821 0.967959 1.033102 3.2277% 1820 0.937692 1.066448
2.6573% 1819 0.913420 1.094786 2.6261% 1818 0.890047 1.123536 2.6969% 1817 0.866673
1.153838 2.7717% 1816 0.843300 1.185818 2.8507% 1815 0.819926 1.219622 2.9343% 1814
0.796552 1.255410 3.0231% 1813 0.773179 1.293362 3.1039% 1812 0.749903 1.333506
3.2172% 1811 0.726529 1.376408 3.0969% 1810 0.704705 1.419034 2.9144% 1809 0.684749
1.460390 2.8225% 1808 0.665952 1.501609 2.9199% 1807 0.647059 1.545455 2.9918% 1806

284

0.628263 1.591691 3.0841% 1805 0.609466 1.640780 3.1822% 1804 0.590670 1.692993 3.2868% 1803 0.571874 1.748638 3.3985% 1802 0.553078 1.808065 3.5180% 1801 0.534281 1.871673 3.3999% 1800 0.516713 1.935309 2.8419% 1799 0.502435 1.990308 2.7485% 1798 0.488995 2.045011 2.8261% 1797 0.475555 2.102806 3.7832% 1796 0.458220 2.182359 2.1272% 1795 0.448675 2.228782 3.0879% 1794 0.435236 2.297606 3.1625% 1793 0.421893 2.370268 3.2904% 1792 0.408453 2.448259 3.4024% 1791 0.395014 2.531558 3.2296% 1790 0.382656 2.613316 41.3145% 1780 0.270783 3.692994 29.4353% 1770 0.209203 4.780038 83.4728% 1750 0.114024 8.770072 29.2845% 1740 0.088196 11.338339 94.2514% 1720 0.045403 22.024882 85.8111% 1700 0.024435 40.924671 19.2490% 1690 0.020491 48.802281 88.0250% 1670 0.010898 91.760500

BASE YEAR: 1821

YEAR BYEAR/AYEAR AYEAR/BYEAR GROWTH%

2009 30.328036 0.032973 8.2857% 2001 28.007435 0.035705 1.0000% 2000 27.730131 0.036062 1.0000% 1999 27.455575 0.036422 1.0000% 1998 27.183738 0.036787 1.0000% 1997 26.914592 0.037155 1.0000% 1996 26.648111 0.037526 1.0000% 1995 26.384268 0.037901 0.9992% 1994 26.123239 0.038280 1.0008% 1993 25.864394 0.038663 1.0000% 1992 25.608311 0.039050 0.9295% 1991 25.372472 0.039413 1.2505% 1990 25.059104 0.039906 0.7224% 1989 24.879364 0.040194 1.1077% 1988 24.606801 0.040639 0.8834% 1987 24.391337 0.040998 0.5594% 1986 24.255660 0.041227 1.3056% 1985 23.943053 0.041766 0.7673% 1984 23.760741 0.042086 0.8149% 1983 23.568669 0.042429 0.9737% 1982 23.341382 0.042842 0.9508% 1981 23.121541 0.043250 0.9031% 1980 22.914607 0.043640 2.2701% 1979 22.405976 0.044631 1.0042% 1978 22.183218 0.045079 0.9896% 1977 21.965842 0.045525 0.9103% 1976 21.767683 0.045940 0.8394% 1975 21.586478 0.046325 0.9042% 1974 21.393048 0.046744 1.1568% 1973 21.148405 0.047285 0.9427% 1972 20.950900 0.047731 0.7426% 1971 20.796458 0.048085 1.4697% 1970 20.495232 0.048792 0.6968% 1969 20.353406 0.049132 0.8565% 1968 20.180551 0.049553 1.5090% 1967 19.880546 0.050300 0.9949% 1966 19.684702 0.050801 1.0575% 1965 19.478720 0.051338 1.1300% 1964 19.261068 0.051918 1.5537% 1963 18.966395 0.052725 1.4658% 1962 18.692399 0.053498 1.5364% 1961 18.409548 0.054320 2.1586% 1960 18.020550 0.055492 -1.6655% 1959 18.325762 0.054568 4.3080% 1958 17.568895 0.056919 2.1130% 1957 17.205353 0.058121 1.9895% 1956 16.869730 0.059278 2.1231% 1955 16.519016 0.060536 1.4496% 1954 16.282976 0.061414 2.1573% 1953 15.939129 0.062739 1.2298% 1952 15.745498 0.063510 1.6814% 1951 15.485134 0.064578 1.6233% 1950 15.237783 0.065626 1.4265% 1949 15.023468 0.066563 1.7790% 1948 14.760866 0.067747 1.8242% 1947 14.496428 0.068983 -2.6320% 1946 14.888294 0.067167 3.1768% 1945 14.429885 0.069301 6.4754% 1944 13.552316 0.073788 -0.3437% 1943 13.599053 0.073535 0.6562% 1942 13.510394 0.074017 0.6633% 1941 13.421370 0.074508 -5.6614% 1940 14.226811 0.070290 8.0381% 1939 13.168327 0.075940 0.8126% 1938 13.062179 0.076557 0.7762% 1937 12.961566 0.077151 0.6029% 1936 12.883892 0.077616 0.5244% 1935 12.816682 0.078023 -3.0364% 1934 13.218030 0.075654 4.6271% 1933 12.633464 0.079155 1.3921% 1932 12.460006 0.080257 -0.2051% 1931 12.485612 0.080092 0.8886% 1930 12.375643 0.080804 1.0126% 1929 12.251585 0.081622 1.1526% 1928 12.111983 0.082563 1.2160% 1927 11.966470 0.083567 1.4086% 1926 11.800254 0.084744 1.7667% 1925 11.595400 0.086241 1.4465% 1924 11.430064 0.087489 1.7700% 1923 11.231273 0.089037 1.6165% 1922 11.052606 0.090476 1.3736% 1921 10.902839 0.091719 2.3393% 1920 10.653618 0.093865 1.3140% 1919 10.515444 0.095098 0.7676% 1918 10.435338 0.095828 0.3870% 1917 10.395110 0.096199 1.3274% 1916 10.258929 0.097476 1.4083% 1915 10.116460 0.098849 1.4458% 1914 9.972281 0.100278 1.9424% 1913 9.782272 0.102226 1.9857% 1912 9.591810 0.104256 1.5634% 1911 9.444159 0.105886 1.8169% 1910 9.275629 0.107809 1.8781% 1909 9.104638 0.109834 2.0082% 1908 8.925395 0.112040 1.9603% 1907 8.753798 0.114236 1.8264% 1906 8.596790 0.116322 1.9357% 1905 8.433545 0.118574 2.0148% 1904 8.266979 0.120963 2.1335% 1903 8.094285 0.123544 1.8151% 1902 7.949981 0.125786 1.8943% 1901 7.802180 0.128169 3.0255% 1900 7.573057 0.132047 0.6278% 1899 7.525807 0.132876 1.7757% 1898 7.394506 0.135236 1.8078% 1897 7.263206 0.137680 1.8396% 1896 7.132005 0.140213 1.8755% 1895 7.000704 0.142843 1.9114% 1894 6.869403 0.145573 1.9486% 1893 6.738102 0.148410 1.9858% 1892 6.606902 0.151357 2.0276% 1891

6.475601 0.154426 2.6465% 1890 6.308642 0.158513 1.5328% 1889 6.213402 0.160942
2.0811% 1888 6.086729 0.164292 2.1599% 1887 5.958044 0.167840 2.2075% 1886 5.829359
0.171545 2.2592% 1885 5.700573 0.175421 2.3095% 1884 5.571889 0.179472 2.3641% 1883
5.443204 0.183715 2.4214% 1882 5.314519 0.188164 2.4815% 1881 5.185834 0.192833
3.7644% 1880 4.997700 0.200092 0.9432% 1879 4.951001 0.201979 2.1464% 1878 4.846966
0.206315 2.1913% 1877 4.743032 0.210836 2.2426% 1876 4.638998 0.215564 2.2941% 1875
4.534963 0.220509 2.3456% 1874 4.431029 0.225681 2.4043% 1873 4.326995 0.231107
2.4635% 1872 4.222960 0.236801 2.5258% 1871 4.118925 0.242782 5.9947% 1870 3.885974
0.257336 -1.0968% 1869 3.929067 0.254513 2.1930% 1868 3.844753 0.260095 2.2394%
1867 3.760539 0.265919 2.2935% 1866 3.676225 0.272018 2.3445% 1865 3.592011 0.278396
2.4037% 1864 3.507697 0.285087 2.4599% 1863 3.423483 0.292100 2.5250% 1862 3.339169
0.299476 2.5872% 1861 3.254955 0.307224 2.9504% 1860 3.161673 0.316288 2.4012% 1859
3.087534 0.323883 2.7627% 1858 3.004528 0.332831 2.8412% 1857 2.921521 0.342287
2.9243% 1856 2.838515 0.352297 3.0161% 1855 2.755408 0.362923 3.1061% 1854 2.672402
0.374195 3.2056% 1853 2.589395 0.386191 3.3118% 1852 2.506389 0.398980 3.4252% 1851
2.423383 0.412646 4.0106% 1850 2.329938 0.429196 2.3254% 1849 2.276990 0.439176
2.7841% 1848 2.215313 0.451403 2.8590% 1847 2.153738 0.464309 2.9432% 1846 2.092162
0.477974 3.0324% 1845 2.030587 0.492469 3.1325% 1844 1.968910 0.507895 3.2284% 1843
1.907335 0.524292 3.3361% 1842 1.845759 0.541783 3.4512% 1841 1.784184 0.560480
3.8105% 1840 1.718693 0.581838 2.3861% 1839 1.678640 0.595720 2.5824% 1838 1.636382
0.611104 2.6573% 1837 1.594024 0.627343 2.7232% 1836 1.551766 0.644427 2.7994% 1835
1.509508 0.662468 2.8871% 1834 1.467150 0.681594 2.9657% 1833 1.424892 0.701808
3.0563% 1832 1.382634 0.723257 3.1604% 1831 1.340276 0.746115 3.4660% 1830 1.295378
0.771975 2.4653% 1829 1.264212 0.791007 2.6804% 1828 1.231210 0.812209 10.3427%
1827 1.115806 0.896213 -4.2314% 1826 1.165107 0.858290 2.9150% 1825 1.132106
0.883310 3.0026% 1824 1.099105 0.909832 3.0955% 1823 1.066103 0.937995 3.1944% 1822
1.033102 0.967959 3.3102% 1821 1.000000 1.000000 3.2277% 1820 0.968732 1.032277
2.6573% 1819 0.943656 1.059708 2.6261% 1818 0.919509 1.087537 2.6969% 1817 0.895362
1.116867 2.7717% 1816 0.871214 1.147823 2.8507% 1815 0.847067 1.180544 2.9343% 1814
0.822920 1.215185 3.0231% 1813 0.798773 1.251921 3.1039% 1812 0.774726 1.290779
3.2172% 1811 0.750579 1.332306 3.0969% 1810 0.728032 1.373566 2.9144% 1809 0.707415
1.413597 2.8225% 1808 0.687997 1.453495 2.9199% 1807 0.668478 1.495936 2.9918% 1806
0.649059 1.540691 3.0841% 1805 0.629641 1.588207 3.1822% 1804 0.610222 1.638747
3.2868% 1803 0.590804 1.692609 3.3985% 1802 0.571385 1.750132 3.5180% 1801 0.551967
1.811703 3.3999% 1800 0.533817 1.873299 2.8419% 1799 0.519066 1.926536 2.7485% 1798
0.505182 1.979486 2.8261% 1797 0.491297 2.035429 3.7832% 1796 0.473388 2.112434
2.1272% 1795 0.463528 2.157369 3.0879% 1794 0.449643 2.223987 3.1625% 1793 0.435859
2.294321 3.2904% 1792 0.421974 2.369814 3.4024% 1791 0.408089 2.450444 3.2296% 1790
0.395322 2.529582 41.3145% 1780 0.279746 3.574666 29.4353% 1770 0.216128 4.626880
83.4728% 1750 0.117799 8.489067 29.2845% 1740 0.091116 10.975044 94.2514% 1720
0.046906 21.319176 85.8111% 1700 0.025244 39.613392 19.2490% 1690 0.021169
47.238593 88.0250% 1670 0.011259 88.820375

BASE YEAR: 1820

YEAR BYEAR/AYEAR AYEAR/BYEAR GROWTH%

2009 31.306946 0.031942 8.2857% 2001 28.911442 0.034588 1.0000% 2000
28.625187 0.034934 1.0000% 1999 28.341770 0.035284 1.0000% 1998 28.061158 0.035636
1.0000% 1997 27.783325 0.035993 1.0000% 1996 27.508242 0.036353 1.0000% 1995
27.235883 0.036716 0.9992% 1994 26.966429 0.037083 1.0008% 1993 26.699229 0.037454
1.0000% 1992 26.434880 0.037829 0.9295% 1991 26.191429 0.038180 1.2505% 1990
25.867947 0.038658 0.7224% 1989 25.682405 0.038937 1.1077% 1988 25.401045 0.039368
0.8834% 1987 25.178626 0.039716 0.5594% 1986 25.038569 0.039938 1.3056% 1985
24.715872 0.040460 0.7673% 1984 24.527675 0.040770 0.8149% 1983 24.329404 0.041103
0.9737% 1982 24.094781 0.041503 0.9508% 1981 23.867844 0.041897 0.9031% 1980
23.654231 0.042276 2.2701% 1979 23.129183 0.043235 1.0042% 1978 22.899234 0.043670
0.9896% 1977 22.674842 0.044102 0.9103% 1976 22.470287 0.044503 0.8394% 1975
22.283233 0.044877 0.9042% 1974 22.083559 0.045283 1.1568% 1973 21.831021 0.045806

0.9427% 1972 21.627141 0.046238 0.7426% 1971 21.467714 0.046582 1.4697% 1970
21.156765 0.047266 0.6968% 1969 21.010361 0.047596 0.8565% 1968 20.831927 0.048003
1.5090% 1967 20.522238 0.048728 0.9949% 1966 20.320072 0.049212 1.0575% 1965
20.107442 0.049733 1.1300% 1964 19.882764 0.050295 1.5537% 1963 19.578581 0.051076
1.4658% 1962 19.295740 0.051825 1.5364% 1961 19.003760 0.052621 2.1586% 1960
18.602206 0.053757 -1.6655% 1959 18.917270 0.052862 4.3080% 1958 18.135973 0.055139
2.1130% 1957 17.760697 0.056304 1.9895% 1956 17.414241 0.057424 2.1231% 1955
17.052207 0.058643 1.4496% 1954 16.808548 0.059494 2.1573% 1953 16.453602 0.060777
1.2298% 1952 16.253721 0.061524 1.6814% 1951 15.984954 0.062559 1.6233% 1950
15.729619 0.063574 1.4265% 1949 15.508386 0.064481 1.7790% 1948 15.237309 0.065628
1.8242% 1947 14.964335 0.066826 -2.6320% 1946 15.368849 0.065067 3.1768% 1945
14.895644 0.067134 6.4754% 1944 13.989749 0.071481 -0.3437% 1943 14.037995 0.071235
0.6562% 1942 13.946475 0.071703 0.6633% 1941 13.854577 0.072178 -5.6614% 1940
14.686015 0.068092 8.0381% 1939 13.593366 0.073565 0.8126% 1938 13.483792 0.074163
0.7762% 1937 13.379931 0.074739 0.6029% 1936 13.299750 0.075189 0.5244% 1935
13.230371 0.075584 -3.0364% 1934 13.644673 0.073289 4.6271% 1933 13.041239 0.076680
1.3921% 1932 12.862183 0.077747 -0.2051% 1931 12.888615 0.077588 0.8886% 1930
12.775096 0.078277 1.0126% 1929 12.647034 0.079070 1.1526% 1928 12.502926 0.079981
1.2160% 1927 12.352717 0.080954 1.4086% 1926 12.181136 0.082094 1.7667% 1925
11.969669 0.083544 1.4465% 1924 11.798996 0.084753 1.7700% 1923 11.593789 0.086253
1.6165% 1922 11.409355 0.087647 1.3736% 1921 11.254755 0.088851 2.3393% 1920
10.997489 0.090930 1.3140% 1919 10.854855 0.092125 0.7676% 1918 10.772164 0.092832
0.3870% 1917 10.730637 0.093191 1.3274% 1916 10.590061 0.094428 1.4083% 1915
10.442993 0.095758 1.4458% 1914 10.294160 0.097142 1.9424% 1913 10.098018 0.099029
1.9857% 1912 9.901409 0.100996 1.5634% 1911 9.748992 0.102575 1.8169% 1910 9.575022
0.104438 1.8781% 1909 9.398512 0.106400 2.0082% 1908 9.213483 0.108537 1.9603% 1907
9.036348 0.110664 1.8264% 1906 8.874272 0.112685 1.9357% 1905 8.705757 0.114867
2.0148% 1904 8.533815 0.117181 2.1335% 1903 8.355547 0.119681 1.8151% 1902 8.206585
0.121853 1.8943% 1901 8.054014 0.124162 3.0255% 1900 7.817496 0.127918 0.6278% 1899
7.768721 0.128721 1.7757% 1898 7.633182 0.131007 1.8078% 1897 7.497643 0.133375
1.8396% 1896 7.362208 0.135829 1.8755% 1895 7.226669 0.138376 1.9114% 1894 7.091130
0.141021 1.9486% 1893 6.955591 0.143769 1.9858% 1892 6.820156 0.146624 2.0276% 1891
6.684617 0.149597 2.6465% 1890 6.512268 0.153556 1.5328% 1889 6.413954 0.155910
2.0811% 1888 6.283193 0.159155 2.1599% 1887 6.150354 0.162592 2.2075% 1886 6.017516
0.166182 2.2592% 1885 5.884573 0.169936 2.3095% 1884 5.751735 0.173861 2.3641% 1883
5.618896 0.177971 2.4214% 1882 5.486057 0.182280 2.4815% 1881 5.353219 0.186804
3.7644% 1880 5.159013 0.193836 0.9432% 1879 5.110806 0.195664 2.1464% 1878 5.003414
0.199864 2.1913% 1877 4.896125 0.204243 2.2426% 1876 4.788733 0.208824 2.2941% 1875
4.681340 0.213614 2.3456% 1874 4.574051 0.218625 2.4043% 1873 4.466659 0.223881
2.4635% 1872 4.359266 0.229396 2.5258% 1871 4.251874 0.235190 5.9947% 1870 4.011403
0.249289 -1.0968% 1869 4.055887 0.246555 2.1930% 1868 3.968852 0.251962 2.2394%
1867 3.881920 0.257605 2.2935% 1866 3.794884 0.263513 2.3445% 1865 3.707952 0.269691
2.4037% 1864 3.620916 0.276173 2.4599% 1863 3.533984 0.282967 2.5250% 1862 3.446949
0.290112 2.5872% 1861 3.360017 0.297618 2.9504% 1860 3.263724 0.306398 2.4012% 1859
3.187191 0.313756 2.7627% 1858 3.101506 0.322424 2.8412% 1857 3.015820 0.331585
2.9243% 1856 2.930135 0.341281 3.0161% 1855 2.844345 0.351575 3.1061% 1854 2.758660
0.362495 3.2056% 1853 2.672974 0.374115 3.3118% 1852 2.587289 0.386505 3.4252% 1851
2.501603 0.399744 4.0106% 1850 2.405142 0.415776 2.3254% 1849 2.350485 0.425444
2.7841% 1848 2.286818 0.437289 2.8590% 1847 2.223255 0.449791 2.9432% 1846 2.159692
0.463029 3.0324% 1845 2.096129 0.477070 3.1325% 1844 2.032462 0.492014 3.2284% 1843
1.968899 0.507898 3.3361% 1842 1.905335 0.524842 3.4512% 1841 1.841772 0.542955
3.8105% 1840 1.774168 0.563645 2.3861% 1839 1.732822 0.577093 2.5824% 1838 1.689200
0.591996 2.6573% 1837 1.645474 0.607727 2.7232% 1836 1.601853 0.624277 2.7994% 1835
1.558231 0.641753 2.8871% 1834 1.514505 0.660282 2.9657% 1833 1.470884 0.679863
3.0563% 1832 1.427262 0.700642 3.1604% 1831 1.383536 0.722786 3.4660% 1830 1.337190
0.747837 2.4653% 1829 1.305017 0.766273 2.6804% 1828 1.270951 0.786813 10.3427%

1827 1.151822 0.868190 -4.2314% 1826 1.202714 0.831453 2.9150% 1825 1.168647
0.855690 3.0026% 1824 1.134581 0.881383 3.0955% 1823 1.100514 0.908666 3.1944% 1822
1.066448 0.937692 3.3102% 1821 1.032277 0.968732 3.2277% 1820 1.000000 1.000000
2.6573% 1819 0.974115 1.026573 2.6261% 1818 0.949188 1.053532 2.6969% 1817 0.924262
1.081945 2.7717% 1816 0.899335 1.111933 2.8507% 1815 0.874408 1.143631 2.9343% 1814
0.849482 1.177189 3.0231% 1813 0.824555 1.212776 3.1039% 1812 0.799732 1.250419
3.2172% 1811 0.774805 1.290647 3.0969% 1810 0.751531 1.330617 2.9144% 1809 0.730249
1.369396 2.8225% 1808 0.710204 1.408047 2.9199% 1807 0.690054 1.449161 2.9918% 1806
0.670009 1.492517 3.0841% 1805 0.649964 1.538547 3.1822% 1804 0.629919 1.587506
3.2868% 1803 0.609874 1.639684 3.3985% 1802 0.589828 1.695409 3.5180% 1801 0.569783
1.755054 3.3999% 1800 0.551048 1.814725 2.8419% 1799 0.535820 1.866297 2.7485% 1798
0.521488 1.917591 2.8261% 1797 0.507155 1.971785 3.7832% 1796 0.488667 2.046382
2.1272% 1795 0.478489 2.089912 3.0879% 1794 0.464156 2.154448 3.1625% 1793 0.449927
2.222582 3.2904% 1792 0.435594 2.295714 3.4024% 1791 0.421261 2.373823 3.2296% 1790
0.408082 2.450487 41.3145% 1780 0.288776 3.462892 29.4353% 1770 0.223104 4.482206
83.4728% 1750 0.121601 8.223630 29.2845% 1740 0.094057 10.631875 94.2514% 1720
0.048420 20.652565 85.8111% 1700 0.026059 38.374755 19.2490% 1690 0.021852
45.761530 88.0250% 1670 0.011622 86.043128
BASE YEAR: 1819
YEAR BYEAR/AYEAR AYEAR/BYEAR GROWTH%
2009 32.138858 0.031115 8.2857% 2001 29.679699 0.033693 1.0000% 2000
29.385838 0.034030 1.0000% 1999 29.094889 0.034370 1.0000% 1998 28.806821 0.034714
1.0000% 1997 28.521605 0.035061 1.0000% 1996 28.239212 0.035412 1.0000% 1995
27.959616 0.035766 0.9992% 1994 27.683002 0.036123 1.0008% 1993 27.408701 0.036485
1.0000% 1992 27.137328 0.036850 0.9295% 1991 26.887408 0.037192 1.2505% 1990
26.555330 0.037657 0.7224% 1989 26.364858 0.037929 1.1077% 1988 26.076021 0.038349
0.8834% 1987 25.847692 0.038688 0.5594% 1986 25.703913 0.038905 1.3056% 1985
25.372641 0.039413 0.7673% 1984 25.179443 0.039715 0.8149% 1983 24.975904 0.040039
0.9737% 1982 24.735046 0.040428 0.9508% 1981 24.502079 0.040813 0.9031% 1980
24.282790 0.041181 2.2701% 1979 23.743789 0.042116 1.0042% 1978 23.507730 0.042539
0.9896% 1977 23.277375 0.042960 0.9103% 1976 23.067385 0.043351 0.8394% 1975
22.875360 0.043715 0.9042% 1974 22.670381 0.044110 1.1568% 1973 22.411131 0.044621
0.9427% 1972 22.201834 0.045041 0.7426% 1971 22.038170 0.045376 1.4697% 1970
21.718959 0.046043 0.6968% 1969 21.568664 0.046364 0.8565% 1968 21.385489 0.046761
1.5090% 1967 21.067571 0.047466 0.9949% 1966 20.860033 0.047939 1.0575% 1965
20.641753 0.048445 1.1300% 1964 20.411105 0.048993 1.5537% 1963 20.098838 0.049754
1.4658% 1962 19.808482 0.050483 1.5364% 1961 19.508743 0.051259 2.1586% 1960
19.096518 0.052366 -1.6655% 1959 19.419954 0.051493 4.3080% 1958 18.617896 0.053712
2.1130% 1957 18.232647 0.054847 1.9895% 1956 17.876986 0.055938 2.1231% 1955
17.505331 0.057125 1.4496% 1954 17.255198 0.057954 2.1573% 1953 16.890820 0.059204
1.2298% 1952 16.685627 0.059932 1.6814% 1951 16.409719 0.060939 1.6233% 1950
16.147599 0.061929 1.4265% 1949 15.920487 0.062812 1.7790% 1948 15.642206 0.063930
1.8242% 1947 15.361979 0.065096 -2.6320% 1946 15.777242 0.063382 3.1768% 1945
15.291462 0.065396 6.4754% 1944 14.361496 0.069631 -0.3437% 1943 14.411023 0.069391
0.6562% 1942 14.317071 0.069847 0.6633% 1941 14.222732 0.070310 -5.6614% 1940
15.076263 0.066329 8.0381% 1939 13.954579 0.071661 0.8126% 1938 13.842094 0.072243
0.7762% 1937 13.735473 0.072804 0.6029% 1936 13.653161 0.073243 0.5244% 1935
13.581938 0.073627 -3.0364% 1934 14.007250 0.071392 4.6271% 1933 13.387781 0.074695
1.3921% 1932 13.203966 0.075735 -0.2051% 1931 13.231101 0.075579 0.8886% 1930
13.114566 0.076251 1.0126% 1929 12.983101 0.077023 1.1526% 1928 12.835164 0.077911
1.2160% 1927 12.680963 0.078858 1.4086% 1926 12.504822 0.079969 1.7667% 1925
12.287736 0.081382 1.4465% 1924 12.112528 0.082559 1.7700% 1923 11.901869 0.084020
1.6165% 1922 11.712533 0.085379 1.3736% 1921 11.553825 0.086551 2.3393% 1920
11.289723 0.088576 1.3140% 1919 11.143299 0.089740 0.7676% 1918 11.058410 0.090429
0.3870% 1917 11.015780 0.090779 1.3274% 1916 10.871468 0.091984 1.4083% 1915
10.720493 0.093279 1.4458% 1914 10.567704 0.094628 1.9424% 1913 10.366350 0.096466

1.9857% 1912 10.164516 0.098381 1.5634% 1911 10.008050 0.099920 1.8169% 1910
9.829457 0.101735 1.8781% 1909 9.648257 0.103646 2.0082% 1908 9.458311 0.105727
1.9603% 1907 9.276469 0.107800 1.8264% 1906 9.110086 0.109768 1.9357% 1905 8.937094
0.111893 2.0148% 1904 8.760582 0.114148 2.1335% 1903 8.577577 0.116583 1.8151% 1902
8.424657 0.118699 1.8943% 1901 8.268032 0.120948 3.0255% 1900 8.025228 0.124607
0.6278% 1899 7.975157 0.125389 1.7757% 1898 7.836017 0.127616 1.8078% 1897 7.696876
0.129923 1.8396% 1896 7.557842 0.132313 1.8755% 1895 7.418701 0.134794 1.9114% 1894
7.279561 0.137371 1.9486% 1893 7.140420 0.140048 1.9858% 1892 7.001386 0.142829
2.0276% 1891 6.862245 0.145725 2.6465% 1890 6.685317 0.149582 1.5328% 1889 6.584391
0.151874 2.0811% 1888 6.450155 0.155035 2.1599% 1887 6.313786 0.158384 2.2075% 1886
6.177418 0.161880 2.2592% 1885 6.040943 0.165537 2.3095% 1884 5.904574 0.169360
2.3641% 1883 5.768206 0.173364 2.4214% 1882 5.631837 0.177562 2.4815% 1881 5.495469
0.181968 3.7644% 1880 5.296102 0.188818 0.9432% 1879 5.246615 0.190599 2.1464% 1878
5.136368 0.194690 2.1913% 1877 5.026229 0.198956 2.2426% 1876 4.915983 0.203418
2.2941% 1875 4.805736 0.208085 2.3456% 1874 4.695597 0.212965 2.4043% 1873 4.585350
0.218086 2.4635% 1872 4.475104 0.223458 2.5258% 1871 4.364858 0.229103 5.9947% 1870
4.117997 0.242836 -1.0968% 1869 4.163664 0.240173 2.1930% 1868 4.074315 0.245440
2.2394% 1867 3.985073 0.250936 2.2935% 1866 3.895724 0.256692 2.3445% 1865 3.806483
0.262710 2.4037% 1864 3.717134 0.269024 2.4599% 1863 3.627892 0.275642 2.5250% 1862
3.538544 0.282602 2.5872% 1861 3.449302 0.289914 2.9504% 1860 3.350450 0.298467
2.4012% 1859 3.271884 0.305634 2.7627% 1858 3.183922 0.314078 2.8412% 1857 3.095959
0.323002 2.9243% 1856 3.007997 0.332447 3.0161% 1855 2.919927 0.342474 3.1061% 1854
2.831965 0.353112 3.2056% 1853 2.744003 0.364431 3.3118% 1852 2.656040 0.376500
3.4252% 1851 2.568078 0.389396 4.0106% 1850 2.469054 0.405013 2.3254% 1849 2.412944
0.414432 2.7841% 1848 2.347585 0.425970 2.8590% 1847 2.282333 0.438148 2.9432% 1846
2.217081 0.451044 3.0324% 1845 2.151829 0.464721 3.1325% 1844 2.086470 0.479278
3.2284% 1843 2.021218 0.494751 3.3361% 1842 1.955965 0.511256 3.4512% 1841 1.890713
0.528901 3.8105% 1840 1.821312 0.549055 2.3861% 1839 1.778868 0.562155 2.5824% 1838
1.734087 0.576672 2.6573% 1837 1.689199 0.591996 2.7232% 1836 1.644418 0.608118
2.7994% 1835 1.599637 0.625142 2.8871% 1834 1.554750 0.643190 2.9657% 1833 1.509969
0.662265 3.0563% 1832 1.465188 0.682506 3.1604% 1831 1.420301 0.704076 3.4660% 1830
1.372723 0.728479 2.4653% 1829 1.339695 0.746439 2.6804% 1828 1.304723 0.766446
10.3427% 1827 1.182429 0.845717 -4.2314% 1826 1.234673 0.809931 2.9150% 1825
1.199701 0.833541 3.0026% 1824 1.164730 0.858568 3.0955% 1823 1.129758 0.885145
3.1944% 1822 1.094786 0.913420 3.3102% 1821 1.059708 0.943656 3.2277% 1820 1.026573
0.974115 2.6573% 1819 1.000000 1.000000 2.6261% 1818 0.974411 1.026261 2.6969% 1817
0.948822 1.053939 2.7717% 1816 0.923233 1.083150 2.8507% 1815 0.897644 1.114028
2.9343% 1814 0.872055 1.146717 3.0231% 1813 0.846466 1.181383 3.1039% 1812 0.820983
1.218052 3.2172% 1811 0.795394 1.257239 3.0969% 1810 0.771501 1.296174 2.9144% 1809
0.749653 1.333950 2.8225% 1808 0.729076 1.371600 2.9199% 1807 0.708391 1.411650
2.9918% 1806 0.687813 1.453883 3.0841% 1805 0.667235 1.498722 3.1822% 1804 0.646657
1.546414 3.2868% 1803 0.626080 1.597241 3.3985% 1802 0.605502 1.651523 3.5180% 1801
0.584924 1.709624 3.3999% 1800 0.565691 1.767751 2.8419% 1799 0.550059 1.817988
2.7485% 1798 0.535345 1.867955 2.8261% 1797 0.520631 1.920745 3.7832% 1796 0.501653
1.993411 2.1272% 1795 0.491204 2.035815 3.0879% 1794 0.476490 2.098680 3.1625% 1793
0.461883 2.165051 3.2904% 1792 0.447169 2.236290 3.4024% 1791 0.432455 2.312377
3.2296% 1790 0.418926 2.387056 41.3145% 1780 0.296450 3.373256 29.4353% 1770
0.229033 4.366184 83.4728% 1750 0.124832 8.010762 29.2845% 1740 0.096556 10.356670
94.2514% 1720 0.049707 20.117975 85.8111% 1700 0.026751 37.381427 19.2490% 1690
0.022433 44.576996 88.0250% 1670 0.011931 83.815907

BASE YEAR: 1818

YEAR BYEAR/AYEAR AYEAR/BYEAR GROWTH%

2009 32.982859 0.030319 8.2857% 2001 30.459120 0.032831 1.0000% 2000
30.157542 0.033159 1.0000% 1999 29.858952 0.033491 1.0000% 1998 29.563319 0.033826
1.0000% 1997 29.270613 0.034164 1.0000% 1996 28.980805 0.034506 1.0000% 1995
28.693866 0.034851 0.9992% 1994 28.409987 0.035199 1.0008% 1993 28.128483 0.035551

289

1.0000% 1992 27.849984 0.035907 0.9295% 1991 27.593500 0.036240 1.2505% 1990
27.252701 0.036694 0.7224% 1989 27.057227 0.036959 1.1077% 1988 26.760805 0.037368
0.8834% 1987 26.526480 0.037698 0.5594% 1986 26.378925 0.037909 1.3056% 1985
26.038954 0.038404 0.7673% 1984 25.840683 0.038699 0.8149% 1983 25.631798 0.039014
0.9737% 1982 25.384615 0.039394 0.9508% 1981 25.145530 0.039768 0.9031% 1980
24.920482 0.040128 2.2701% 1979 24.367327 0.041039 1.0042% 1978 24.125068 0.041451
0.9896% 1977 23.888664 0.041861 0.9103% 1976 23.673159 0.042242 0.8394% 1975
23.476091 0.042597 0.9042% 1974 23.265729 0.042982 1.1568% 1973 22.999672 0.043479
0.9427% 1972 22.784878 0.043889 0.7426% 1971 22.616917 0.044215 1.4697% 1970
22.289322 0.044865 0.6968% 1969 22.135080 0.045177 0.8565% 1968 21.947095 0.045564
1.5090% 1967 21.620828 0.046252 0.9949% 1966 21.407840 0.046712 1.0575% 1965
21.183828 0.047206 1.1300% 1964 20.947122 0.047739 1.5537% 1963 20.626655 0.048481
1.4658% 1962 20.328674 0.049192 1.5364% 1961 20.021064 0.049947 2.1586% 1960
19.598013 0.051026 -1.6655% 1959 19.929943 0.050176 4.3080% 1958 19.106822 0.052337
2.1130% 1957 18.711456 0.053443 1.9895% 1956 18.346455 0.054506 2.1231% 1955
17.965040 0.055664 1.4496% 1954 17.708338 0.056471 2.1573% 1953 17.334391 0.057689
1.2298% 1952 17.123810 0.058398 1.6814% 1951 16.840655 0.059380 1.6233% 1950
16.571652 0.060344 1.4265% 1949 16.338576 0.061205 1.7790% 1948 16.052987 0.062294
1.8242% 1947 15.765401 0.063430 -2.6320% 1946 16.191569 0.061761 3.1768% 1945
15.693033 0.063723 6.4754% 1944 14.738644 0.067849 -0.3437% 1943 14.789472 0.067616
0.6562% 1942 14.693053 0.068059 0.6633% 1941 14.596236 0.068511 -5.6614% 1940
15.472182 0.064632 8.0381% 1939 14.321042 0.069827 0.8126% 1938 14.205602 0.070395
0.7762% 1937 14.096181 0.070941 0.6029% 1936 14.011708 0.071369 0.5244% 1935
13.938615 0.071743 -3.0364% 1934 14.375096 0.069565 4.6271% 1933 13.739359 0.072784
1.3921% 1932 13.550717 0.073797 -0.2051% 1931 13.578564 0.073645 0.8886% 1930
13.458968 0.074300 1.0126% 1929 13.324051 0.075052 1.1526% 1928 13.172229 0.075917
1.2160% 1927 13.013979 0.076840 1.4086% 1926 12.833212 0.077923 1.7667% 1925
12.610426 0.079299 1.4465% 1924 12.430616 0.080447 1.7700% 1923 12.214424 0.081870
1.6165% 1922 12.020117 0.083194 1.3736% 1921 11.857241 0.084337 2.3393% 1920
11.586203 0.086310 1.3140% 1919 11.435934 0.087444 0.7676% 1918 11.348816 0.088115
0.3870% 1917 11.305066 0.088456 1.3274% 1916 11.156965 0.089630 1.4083% 1915
11.002024 0.090892 1.4458% 1914 10.845224 0.092206 1.9424% 1913 10.638582 0.093997
1.9857% 1912 10.431448 0.095864 1.5634% 1911 10.270872 0.097363 1.8169% 1910
10.087589 0.099132 1.8781% 1909 9.901630 0.100993 2.0082% 1908 9.706697 0.103022
1.9603% 1907 9.520079 0.105041 1.8264% 1906 9.349327 0.106960 1.9357% 1905 9.171791
0.109030 2.0148% 1904 8.990644 0.111227 2.1335% 1903 8.802834 0.113600 1.8151% 1902
8.645898 0.115662 1.8943% 1901 8.485159 0.117853 3.0255% 1900 8.235980 0.121418
0.6278% 1899 8.184594 0.122181 1.7757% 1898 8.041799 0.124350 1.8078% 1897 7.899004
0.126598 1.8396% 1896 7.756319 0.128927 1.8755% 1895 7.613524 0.131345 1.9114% 1894
7.470730 0.133856 1.9486% 1893 7.327935 0.136464 1.9858% 1892 7.185250 0.139174
2.0276% 1891 7.042455 0.141996 2.6465% 1890 6.860881 0.145754 1.5328% 1889 6.757304
0.147988 2.0811% 1888 6.619543 0.151068 2.1599% 1887 6.479593 0.154331 2.2075% 1886
6.339643 0.157738 2.2592% 1885 6.199584 0.161301 2.3095% 1884 6.059635 0.165026
2.3641% 1883 5.919685 0.168928 2.4214% 1882 5.779735 0.173018 2.4815% 1881 5.639786
0.177312 3.7644% 1880 5.435184 0.183986 0.9432% 1879 5.384397 0.185722 2.1464% 1878
5.271255 0.189708 2.1913% 1877 5.158223 0.193865 2.2426% 1876 5.045082 0.198213
2.2941% 1875 4.931940 0.202760 2.3456% 1874 4.818908 0.207516 2.4043% 1873 4.705766
0.212505 2.4635% 1872 4.592625 0.217740 2.5258% 1871 4.479484 0.223240 5.9947% 1870
4.226140 0.236623 -1.0968% 1869 4.273006 0.234027 2.1930% 1868 4.181311 0.239159
2.2394% 1867 4.089725 0.244515 2.2935% 1866 3.998030 0.250123 2.3445% 1865 3.906445
0.255987 2.4037% 1864 3.814750 0.262140 2.4599% 1863 3.723164 0.268589 2.5250% 1862
3.631470 0.275371 2.5872% 1861 3.539884 0.282495 2.9504% 1860 3.438436 0.290830
2.4012% 1859 3.357807 0.297813 2.7627% 1858 3.267535 0.306041 2.8412% 1857 3.177262
0.314736 2.9243% 1856 3.086990 0.323940 3.0161% 1855 2.996608 0.333711 3.1061% 1854
2.906335 0.344076 3.2056% 1853 2.816063 0.355106 3.3118% 1852 2.725791 0.366866
3.4252% 1851 2.635518 0.379432 4.0106% 1850 2.533894 0.394650 2.3254% 1849 2.476310

0.403827 2.7841% 1848 2.409235 0.415069 2.8590% 1847 2.342269 0.426936 2.9432% 1846
2.275304 0.439502 3.0324% 1845 2.208338 0.452829 3.1325% 1844 2.141263 0.467014
3.2284% 1843 2.074297 0.482091 3.3361% 1842 2.007331 0.498174 3.4512% 1841 1.940365
0.515367 3.8105% 1840 1.869142 0.535005 2.3861% 1839 1.825583 0.547770 2.5824% 1838
1.779626 0.561916 2.6573% 1837 1.733559 0.576848 2.7232% 1836 1.687603 0.592557
2.7994% 1835 1.641646 0.609145 2.8871% 1834 1.595579 0.626732 2.9657% 1833 1.549622
0.645318 3.0563% 1832 1.503666 0.665041 3.1604% 1831 1.457599 0.686060 3.4660% 1830
1.408772 0.709838 2.4653% 1829 1.374877 0.727338 2.6804% 1828 1.338987 0.746833
10.3427% 1827 1.213481 0.824076 -4.2314% 1826 1.267097 0.789206 2.9150% 1825
1.231207 0.812211 3.0026% 1824 1.195317 0.836598 3.0955% 1823 1.159427 0.862495
3.1944% 1822 1.123536 0.890047 3.3102% 1821 1.087537 0.919509 3.2277% 1820 1.053532
0.949188 2.6573% 1819 1.026261 0.974411 2.6261% 1818 1.000000 1.000000 2.6969% 1817
0.973739 1.026969 2.7717% 1816 0.947478 1.055434 2.8507% 1815 0.921217 1.085521
2.9343% 1814 0.894956 1.117374 3.0231% 1813 0.868695 1.151153 3.1039% 1812 0.842543
1.186883 3.2172% 1811 0.816282 1.225067 3.0969% 1810 0.791762 1.263006 2.9144% 1809
0.769340 1.299815 2.8225% 1808 0.748222 1.336502 2.9199% 1807 0.726994 1.375527
2.9918% 1806 0.705876 1.416680 3.0841% 1805 0.684758 1.460371 3.1822% 1804 0.663639
1.506843 3.2868% 1803 0.642521 1.556369 3.3985% 1802 0.621403 1.609262 3.5180% 1801
0.600284 1.665877 3.3999% 1800 0.580546 1.722516 2.8419% 1799 0.564504 1.771467
2.7485% 1798 0.549404 1.820155 2.8261% 1797 0.534304 1.871595 3.7832% 1796 0.514827
1.942402 2.1272% 1795 0.504103 1.983720 3.0879% 1794 0.489003 2.044977 3.1625% 1793
0.474012 2.109649 3.2904% 1792 0.458912 2.179065 3.4024% 1791 0.443812 2.253205
3.2296% 1790 0.429927 2.325974 41.3145% 1780 0.304235 3.286937 29.4353% 1770
0.235048 4.254457 83.4728% 1750 0.128110 7.805774 29.2845% 1740 0.099092 10.091652
94.2514% 1720 0.051012 19.603175 85.8111% 1700 0.027454 36.424870 19.2490% 1690
0.023022 43.436312 88.0250% 1670 0.012244 81.671135
    BASE YEAR: 1817
    YEAR BYEAR/AYEAR AYEAR/BYEAR GROWTH%
    2009 33.872384 0.029523 8.2857% 2001 31.280582 0.031969 1.0000% 2000
30.970870 0.032288 1.0000% 1999 30.664228 0.032611 1.0000% 1998 30.360621 0.032937
1.0000% 1997 30.060021 0.033267 1.0000% 1996 29.762397 0.033599 1.0000% 1995
29.467720 0.033935 0.9992% 1994 29.176185 0.034275 1.0008% 1993 28.887090 0.034618
1.0000% 1992 28.601079 0.034964 0.9295% 1991 28.337678 0.035289 1.2505% 1990
27.987688 0.035730 0.7224% 1989 27.786942 0.035988 1.1077% 1988 27.482526 0.036387
0.8834% 1987 27.241881 0.036708 0.5594% 1986 27.090347 0.036914 1.3056% 1985
26.741207 0.037395 0.7673% 1984 26.537588 0.037682 0.8149% 1983 26.323070 0.037989
0.9737% 1982 26.069221 0.038359 0.9508% 1981 25.823688 0.038724 0.9031% 1980
25.592570 0.039074 2.2701% 1979 25.024497 0.039961 1.0042% 1978 24.775705 0.040362
0.9896% 1977 24.532925 0.040762 0.9103% 1976 24.311608 0.041133 0.8394% 1975
24.109226 0.041478 0.9042% 1974 23.893190 0.041853 1.1568% 1973 23.619957 0.042337
0.9427% 1972 23.399371 0.042736 0.7426% 1971 23.226879 0.043054 1.4697% 1970
22.890450 0.043686 0.6968% 1969 22.732049 0.043991 0.8565% 1968 22.538993 0.044368
1.5090% 1967 22.203927 0.045037 0.9949% 1966 21.985195 0.045485 1.0575% 1965
21.755141 0.045966 1.1300% 1964 21.512052 0.046486 1.5537% 1963 21.182942 0.047208
1.4658% 1962 20.876924 0.047900 1.5364% 1961 20.561018 0.048636 2.1586% 1960
20.126558 0.049686 -1.6655% 1959 20.467440 0.048858 4.3080% 1958 19.622120 0.050963
2.1130% 1957 19.216092 0.052040 1.9895% 1956 18.841246 0.053075 2.1231% 1955
18.449545 0.054202 1.4496% 1954 18.185920 0.054988 2.1573% 1953 17.801888 0.056174
1.2298% 1952 17.585628 0.056865 1.6814% 1951 17.294836 0.057821 1.6233% 1950
17.018578 0.058759 1.4265% 1949 16.779217 0.059598 1.7790% 1948 16.485925 0.060658
1.8242% 1947 16.190583 0.061764 -2.6320% 1946 16.628245 0.060139 3.1768% 1945
16.116263 0.062049 6.4754% 1944 15.136135 0.066067 -0.3437% 1943 15.188334 0.065840
0.6562% 1942 15.089314 0.066272 0.6633% 1941 14.989887 0.066712 -5.6614% 1940
15.889457 0.062935 8.0381% 1939 14.707270 0.067994 0.8126% 1938 14.588718 0.068546
0.7762% 1937 14.476346 0.069078 0.6029% 1936 14.389594 0.069495 0.5244% 1935
14.314530 0.069859 -3.0364% 1934 14.762782 0.067738 4.6271% 1933 14.109900 0.070872

291

1.3921% 1932 13.916170 0.071859 -0.2051% 1931 13.944769 0.071711 0.8886% 1930
13.821948 0.072349 1.0126% 1929 13.683391 0.073081 1.1526% 1928 13.527475 0.073924
1.2160% 1927 13.364957 0.074823 1.4086% 1926 13.179315 0.075876 1.7667% 1925
12.950520 0.077217 1.4465% 1924 12.765862 0.078334 1.7700% 1923 12.543839 0.079720
1.6165% 1922 12.344291 0.081009 1.3736% 1921 12.177022 0.082122 2.3393% 1920
11.898675 0.084043 1.3140% 1919 11.744353 0.085147 0.7676% 1918 11.654885 0.085801
0.3870% 1917 11.609956 0.086133 1.3274% 1916 11.457860 0.087276 1.4083% 1915
11.298741 0.088505 1.4458% 1914 11.137712 0.089785 1.9424% 1913 10.925497 0.091529
1.9857% 1912 10.712777 0.093346 1.5634% 1911 10.547871 0.094806 1.8169% 1910
10.359644 0.096528 1.8781% 1909 10.168671 0.098341 2.0082% 1908 9.968480 0.100316
1.9603% 1907 9.776829 0.102283 1.8264% 1906 9.601472 0.104151 1.9357% 1905 9.419148
0.106167 2.0148% 1904 9.233116 0.108306 2.1335% 1903 9.040240 0.110617 1.8151% 1902
8.879072 0.112624 1.8943% 1901 8.713998 0.114758 3.0255% 1900 8.458098 0.118230
0.6278% 1899 8.405326 0.118972 1.7757% 1898 8.258681 0.121085 1.8078% 1897 8.112035
0.123274 1.8396% 1896 7.965502 0.125541 1.8755% 1895 7.818856 0.127896 1.9114% 1894
7.672210 0.130341 1.9486% 1893 7.525565 0.132880 1.9858% 1892 7.379031 0.135519
2.0276% 1891 7.232386 0.138267 2.6465% 1890 7.045914 0.141926 1.5328% 1889 6.939544
0.144102 2.0811% 1888 6.798067 0.147101 2.1599% 1887 6.654343 0.150278 2.2075% 1886
6.510619 0.153595 2.2592% 1885 6.366783 0.157065 2.3095% 1884 6.223059 0.160693
2.3641% 1883 6.079335 0.164492 2.4214% 1882 5.935611 0.168475 2.4815% 1881 5.791887
0.172655 3.7644% 1880 5.581767 0.179155 0.9432% 1879 5.529610 0.180845 2.1464% 1878
5.413417 0.184726 2.1913% 1877 5.297337 0.188774 2.2426% 1876 5.181144 0.193008
2.2941% 1875 5.064951 0.197435 2.3456% 1874 4.948871 0.202066 2.4043% 1873 4.832678
0.206925 2.4635% 1872 4.716485 0.212022 2.5258% 1871 4.600292 0.217377 5.9947% 1870
4.340116 0.230409 -1.0968% 1869 4.388246 0.227881 2.1930% 1868 4.294078 0.232879
2.2394% 1867 4.200022 0.238094 2.2935% 1866 4.105855 0.243555 2.3445% 1865 4.011799
0.249265 2.4037% 1864 3.917631 0.255256 2.4599% 1863 3.823576 0.261535 2.5250% 1862
3.729408 0.268139 2.5872% 1861 3.635352 0.275077 2.9504% 1860 3.531168 0.283192
2.4012% 1859 3.448365 0.289993 2.7627% 1858 3.355658 0.298004 2.8412% 1857 3.262951
0.306471 2.9243% 1856 3.170244 0.315433 3.0161% 1855 3.077424 0.324947 3.1061% 1854
2.984717 0.335040 3.2056% 1853 2.892010 0.345780 3.3118% 1852 2.799303 0.357232
3.4252% 1851 2.706596 0.369468 4.0106% 1850 2.602231 0.384286 2.3254% 1849 2.543095
0.393222 2.7841% 1848 2.474211 0.404169 2.8590% 1847 2.405439 0.415725 2.9432% 1846
2.336667 0.427960 3.0324% 1845 2.267895 0.440937 3.1325% 1844 2.199011 0.454750
3.2284% 1843 2.130239 0.469431 3.3361% 1842 2.061468 0.485091 3.4512% 1841 1.992696
0.501833 3.8105% 1840 1.919552 0.520955 2.3861% 1839 1.874817 0.533385 2.5824% 1838
1.827621 0.547159 2.6573% 1837 1.780312 0.561699 2.7232% 1836 1.733116 0.576995
2.7994% 1835 1.685920 0.593148 2.8871% 1834 1.638611 0.610273 2.9657% 1833 1.591415
0.628372 3.0563% 1832 1.544218 0.647577 3.1604% 1831 1.496910 0.668043 3.4660% 1830
1.446765 0.691197 2.4653% 1829 1.411956 0.708237 2.6804% 1828 1.375098 0.727221
10.3427% 1827 1.246207 0.802435 -4.2314% 1826 1.301270 0.768480 2.9150% 1825
1.264412 0.790882 3.0026% 1824 1.227554 0.814628 3.0955% 1823 1.190696 0.839845
3.1944% 1822 1.153838 0.866673 3.3102% 1821 1.116867 0.895362 3.2277% 1820 1.081945
0.924262 2.6573% 1819 1.053939 0.948822 2.6261% 1818 1.026969 0.973739 2.6969% 1817
1.000000 1.000000 2.7717% 1816 0.973031 1.027717 2.8507% 1815 0.946061 1.057014
2.9343% 1814 0.919092 1.088030 3.0231% 1813 0.892123 1.120922 3.1039% 1812 0.865266
1.155714 3.2172% 1811 0.838296 1.192895 3.0969% 1810 0.813115 1.229838 2.9144% 1809
0.790089 1.265681 2.8225% 1808 0.768401 1.301404 2.9199% 1807 0.746601 1.339404
2.9918% 1806 0.724913 1.379476 3.0841% 1805 0.703225 1.422020 3.1822% 1804 0.681537
1.467271 3.2868% 1803 0.659849 1.515497 3.3985% 1802 0.638162 1.567001 3.5180% 1801
0.616474 1.622129 3.3999% 1800 0.596203 1.677281 2.8419% 1799 0.579728 1.724947
2.7485% 1798 0.564221 1.772356 2.8261% 1797 0.548713 1.822445 3.7832% 1796 0.528711
1.891392 2.1272% 1795 0.517699 1.931626 3.0879% 1794 0.502191 1.991273 3.1625% 1793
0.486796 2.054247 3.2904% 1792 0.471289 2.121841 3.4024% 1791 0.455782 2.194034
3.2296% 1790 0.441522 2.264891 41.3145% 1780 0.312440 3.200619 29.4353% 1770
0.241387 4.142731 83.4728% 1750 0.131565 7.600786 29.2845% 1740 0.101764 9.826634

94.2514% 1720 0.052388 19.088374 85.8111% 1700 0.028194 35.468314 19.2490% 1690 0.023643 42.295627 88.0250% 1670 0.012574 79.526363

BASE YEAR: 1816

YEAR BYEAR/AYEAR AYEAR/BYEAR GROWTH%

2009 34.811219 0.028726 8.2857% 2001 32.147580 0.031107 1.0000% 2000 31.829284 0.031418 1.0000% 1999 31.514143 0.031732 1.0000% 1998 31.202121 0.032049 1.0000% 1997 30.893190 0.032370 1.0000% 1996 30.587316 0.032693 1.0000% 1995 30.284472 0.033020 0.9992% 1994 29.984856 0.033350 1.0008% 1993 29.687748 0.033684 1.0000% 1992 29.393810 0.034021 0.9295% 1991 29.123109 0.034337 1.2505% 1990 28.763418 0.034766 0.7224% 1989 28.557108 0.035018 1.1077% 1988 28.244255 0.035405 0.8834% 1987 27.996940 0.035718 0.5594% 1986 27.841206 0.035918 1.3056% 1985 27.482388 0.036387 0.7673% 1984 27.273126 0.036666 0.8149% 1983 27.052662 0.036965 0.9737% 1982 26.791777 0.037325 0.9508% 1981 26.539439 0.037680 0.9031% 1980 26.301915 0.038020 2.2701% 1979 25.718097 0.038883 1.0042% 1978 25.462409 0.039274 0.9896% 1977 25.212900 0.039662 0.9103% 1976 24.985449 0.040023 0.8394% 1975 24.777457 0.040359 0.9042% 1974 24.555434 0.040724 1.1568% 1973 24.274628 0.041195 0.9427% 1972 24.047927 0.041584 0.7426% 1971 23.870655 0.041892 1.4697% 1970 23.524901 0.042508 0.6968% 1969 23.362109 0.042804 0.8565% 1968 23.163703 0.043171 1.5090% 1967 22.819350 0.043822 0.9949% 1966 22.594555 0.044258 1.0575% 1965 22.358124 0.044726 1.1300% 1964 22.108298 0.045232 1.5537% 1963 21.770066 0.045935 1.4658% 1962 21.455566 0.046608 1.5364% 1961 21.130904 0.047324 2.1586% 1960 20.684403 0.048346 -1.6655% 1959 21.034733 0.047540 4.3080% 1958 20.165983 0.049588 2.1130% 1957 19.748701 0.050636 1.9895% 1956 19.363466 0.051644 1.2231% 1955 18.960908 0.052740 1.4496% 1954 18.689976 0.053505 2.1573% 1953 18.295300 0.054659 1.2298% 1952 18.073045 0.055331 1.6814% 1951 17.774194 0.056261 1.6233% 1950 17.490279 0.057175 1.4265% 1949 17.244283 0.057990 1.7790% 1948 16.942863 0.059022 1.8242% 1947 16.639335 0.060099 -2.6320% 1946 17.089127 0.058517 3.1768% 1945 16.562955 0.060376 6.4754% 1944 15.555661 0.064285 -0.3437% 1943 15.609306 0.064064 0.6562% 1942 15.507542 0.064485 0.6633% 1941 15.405359 0.064912 -5.6614% 1940 16.329862 0.061238 8.0381% 1939 15.114909 0.066160 0.8126% 1938 14.993071 0.066697 0.7762% 1937 14.877584 0.067215 0.6029% 1936 14.788428 0.067620 0.5244% 1935 14.711283 0.067975 -3.0364% 1934 15.171960 0.065911 4.6271% 1933 14.500982 0.068961 1.3921% 1932 14.301882 0.069921 -0.2051% 1931 14.331274 0.069777 0.8886% 1930 14.205048 0.070398 1.0126% 1929 14.062652 0.071110 1.1526% 1928 13.902414 0.071930 1.2160% 1927 13.735391 0.072805 1.4086% 1926 13.544604 0.073830 1.7667% 1925 13.309468 0.075134 1.4465% 1924 13.119691 0.076221 1.7700% 1923 12.891515 0.077570 1.6165% 1922 12.686436 0.078824 1.3736% 1921 12.514531 0.079907 2.3393% 1920 12.228469 0.081776 1.3140% 1919 12.069869 0.082851 0.7676% 1918 11.977922 0.083487 0.3870% 1917 11.931747 0.083810 1.3274% 1916 11.775436 0.084923 1.4083% 1915 11.611907 0.086119 1.4458% 1914 11.446414 0.087364 1.9424% 1913 11.228317 0.089061 1.9857% 1912 11.009701 0.090829 1.5634% 1911 10.840224 0.092249 1.8169% 1910 10.646781 0.093925 1.8781% 1909 10.450514 0.095689 2.0082% 1908 10.244774 0.097611 1.9603% 1907 10.047812 0.099524 1.8264% 1906 9.867594 0.101342 1.9357% 1905 9.680217 0.103303 2.0148% 1904 9.489029 0.105385 2.1335% 1903 9.290807 0.107633 1.8151% 1902 9.125171 0.109587 1.8943% 1901 8.955523 0.111663 3.0255% 1900 8.692530 0.115041 0.6278% 1899 8.638295 0.115764 1.7757% 1898 8.487585 0.117819 1.8078% 1897 8.336875 0.119949 1.8396% 1896 8.186280 0.122156 1.8755% 1895 8.035570 0.124447 1.9114% 1894 7.884860 0.126825 1.9486% 1893 7.734149 0.129297 1.9858% 1892 7.583555 0.131864 2.0276% 1891 7.432844 0.134538 2.6465% 1890 7.241205 0.138099 1.5328% 1889 7.131886 0.140215 2.0811% 1888 6.986488 0.143133 2.1599% 1887 6.838780 0.146225 2.2075% 1886 6.691073 0.149453 2.2592% 1885 6.543250 0.152829 2.3095% 1884 6.395542 0.156359 2.3641% 1883 6.247835 0.160055 2.4214% 1882 6.100127 0.163931 2.4815% 1881 5.952419 0.167999 3.7644% 1880 5.736476 0.174323 0.9432% 1879 5.682873 0.175967 2.1464% 1878 5.563460 0.179744 2.1913% 1877 5.444162 0.183683 2.2426% 1876 5.324749 0.187802 2.2941% 1875 5.205335 0.192111 2.3456% 1874 5.086038 0.196617 2.4043% 1873 4.966624 0.201344 2.4635% 1872 4.847211 0.206304 2.5258% 1871 4.727798 0.211515

5.9947% 1870 4.460411 0.224195 -1.0968% 1869 4.509874 0.221736 2.1930% 1868
4.413096 0.226598 2.2394% 1867 4.316434 0.231673 2.2935% 1866 4.219656 0.236986
2.3445% 1865 4.122993 0.242542 2.4037% 1864 4.026215 0.248372 2.4599% 1863 3.929553
0.254482 2.5250% 1862 3.832775 0.260908 2.5872% 1861 3.736113 0.267658 2.9504% 1860
3.629041 0.275555 2.4012% 1859 3.543943 0.282172 2.7627% 1858 3.448666 0.289967
2.8412% 1857 3.353390 0.298206 2.9243% 1856 3.258113 0.306926 3.0161% 1855 3.162721
0.316183 3.1061% 1854 3.067444 0.326004 3.2056% 1853 2.972168 0.336455 3.3118% 1852
2.876891 0.347597 3.4252% 1851 2.781615 0.359503 4.0106% 1850 2.674357 0.373922
2.3254% 1849 2.613581 0.382617 2.7841% 1848 2.542788 0.393269 2.8590% 1847 2.472110
0.404513 2.9432% 1846 2.401432 0.416418 3.0324% 1845 2.330754 0.429046 3.1325% 1844
2.259961 0.442486 3.2284% 1843 2.189283 0.456771 3.3361% 1842 2.118605 0.472009
3.4512% 1841 2.047927 0.488299 3.8105% 1840 1.972755 0.506905 2.3861% 1839 1.926781
0.519000 2.5824% 1838 1.878277 0.532403 2.6573% 1837 1.829657 0.546551 2.7232% 1836
1.781153 0.561434 2.7994% 1835 1.732648 0.577151 2.8871% 1834 1.684028 0.593814
2.9657% 1833 1.635524 0.611425 3.0563% 1832 1.587019 0.630112 3.1604% 1831 1.538399
0.650026 3.4660% 1830 1.486865 0.672556 2.4653% 1829 1.451091 0.689136 2.6804% 1828
1.413212 0.707608 10.3427% 1827 1.280748 0.780794 -4.2314% 1826 1.337337 0.747755
2.9150% 1825 1.299457 0.769552 3.0026% 1824 1.261578 0.792658 3.0955% 1823 1.223698
0.817195 3.1944% 1822 1.185818 0.843300 3.3102% 1821 1.147823 0.871214 3.2277% 1820
1.111933 0.899335 2.6573% 1819 1.083150 0.923233 2.6261% 1818 1.055434 0.947478
2.6969% 1817 1.027717 0.973031 2.7717% 1816 1.000000 1.000000 2.8507% 1815 0.972283
1.028507 2.9343% 1814 0.944566 1.058687 3.0231% 1813 0.916850 1.090692 3.1039% 1812
0.889248 1.124545 3.2172% 1811 0.861531 1.160724 3.0969% 1810 0.835652 1.196670
2.9144% 1809 0.811988 1.231546 2.8225% 1808 0.789699 1.266306 2.9199% 1807 0.767294
1.303281 2.9918% 1806 0.745005 1.342273 3.0841% 1805 0.722716 1.383669 3.1822% 1804
0.700427 1.427700 3.2868% 1803 0.678138 1.474625 3.3985% 1802 0.655849 1.524740
3.5180% 1801 0.633560 1.578381 3.3999% 1800 0.612728 1.632045 2.8419% 1799 0.595796
1.678426 2.7485% 1798 0.579859 1.724557 2.8261% 1797 0.563922 1.773295 3.7832% 1796
0.543365 1.840383 2.1272% 1795 0.532048 1.879531 3.0879% 1794 0.516110 1.937570
3.1625% 1793 0.500289 1.998846 3.2904% 1792 0.484352 2.064616 3.4024% 1791 0.468414
2.134862 3.2296% 1790 0.453760 2.203809 41.3145% 1780 0.321099 3.114300 29.4353%
1770 0.248077 4.031004 83.4728% 1750 0.135212 7.395798 29.2845% 1740 0.104585
9.561617 94.2514% 1720 0.053840 18.573574 85.8111% 1700 0.028976 34.511758 19.2490%
1690 0.024298 41.154943 88.0250% 1670 0.012923 77.381591
BASE YEAR: 1815
YEAR BYEAR/AYEAR AYEAR/BYEAR GROWTH%
2009 35.803581 0.027930 8.2857% 2001 33.064010 0.030244 1.0000% 2000
32.736640 0.030547 1.0000% 1999 32.412515 0.030852 1.0000% 1998 32.091599 0.031161
1.0000% 1997 31.773860 0.031472 1.0000% 1996 31.459267 0.031787 1.0000% 1995
31.147790 0.032105 0.9992% 1994 30.839633 0.032426 1.0008% 1993 30.534055 0.032750
1.0000% 1992 30.231738 0.033078 0.9295% 1991 29.953320 0.033385 1.2505% 1990
29.583375 0.033803 0.7224% 1989 29.371184 0.034047 1.1077% 1988 29.049412 0.034424
0.8834% 1987 28.795047 0.034728 0.5594% 1986 28.634874 0.034922 1.3056% 1985
28.265827 0.035378 0.7673% 1984 28.050600 0.035650 0.8149% 1983 27.823851 0.035940
0.9737% 1982 27.555529 0.036290 0.9508% 1981 27.295997 0.036635 0.9031% 1980
27.051702 0.036966 2.2701% 1979 26.451241 0.037805 1.0042% 1978 26.188265 0.038185
0.9896% 1977 25.931643 0.038563 0.9103% 1976 25.697708 0.038914 0.8394% 1975
25.483787 0.039241 0.9042% 1974 25.255434 0.039595 1.1568% 1973 24.966623 0.040053
0.9427% 1972 24.733460 0.040431 0.7426% 1971 24.551134 0.040731 1.4697% 1970
24.195524 0.041330 0.6968% 1969 24.028091 0.041618 0.8565% 1968 23.824029 0.041974
1.5090% 1967 23.469860 0.042608 0.9949% 1966 23.238657 0.043032 1.0575% 1965
22.995486 0.043487 1.1300% 1964 22.738538 0.043978 1.5537% 1963 22.390664 0.044661
1.4658% 1962 22.067199 0.045316 1.5364% 1961 21.733282 0.046012 2.1586% 1960
21.274052 0.047006 -1.6655% 1959 21.634369 0.046223 4.3080% 1958 20.740854 0.048214
2.1130% 1957 20.311676 0.049233 1.9895% 1956 19.915459 0.050212 2.1231% 1955
19.501425 0.051278 1.4496% 1954 19.222770 0.052022 2.1573% 1953 18.816843 0.053144

294

1.2298% 1952 18.588253 0.053797 1.6814% 1951 18.280883 0.054702 1.6233% 1950 17.988874 0.055590 1.4265% 1949 17.735865 0.056383 1.7790% 1948 17.425852 0.057386 1.8242% 1947 17.113671 0.058433 -2.6320% 1946 17.576286 0.056895 3.1768% 1945 17.035114 0.058702 6.4754% 1944 15.999105 0.062503 -0.3437% 1943 16.054280 0.062289 0.6562% 1942 15.949615 0.062697 0.6633% 1941 15.844518 0.063113 -5.6614% 1940 16.795376 0.059540 8.0381% 1939 15.545789 0.064326 0.8126% 1938 15.420477 0.064849 0.7762% 1937 15.301699 0.065352 0.6029% 1936 15.210001 0.065746 0.5244% 1935 15.130657 0.066091 -3.0364% 1934 15.604466 0.064084 4.6271% 1933 14.914360 0.067049 1.3921% 1932 14.709585 0.067983 -0.2051% 1931 14.739815 0.067843 0.8886% 1930 14.609991 0.068446 1.0126% 1929 14.463535 0.069139 1.1526% 1928 14.298729 0.069936 1.2160% 1927 14.126945 0.070787 1.4086% 1926 13.930719 0.071784 1.7667% 1925 13.688880 0.073052 1.4465% 1924 13.493693 0.074109 1.7700% 1923 13.259012 0.075420 1.6165% 1922 13.048087 0.076640 1.3736% 1921 12.871282 0.077692 2.3393% 1920 12.577065 0.079510 1.3140% 1919 12.413945 0.080555 0.7676% 1918 12.319376 0.081173 0.3870% 1917 12.271885 0.081487 1.3274% 1916 12.111118 0.082569 1.4083% 1915 11.942927 0.083732 1.4458% 1914 11.772716 0.084942 1.9424% 1913 11.548402 0.086592 1.9857% 1912 11.323554 0.088311 1.5634% 1911 11.149246 0.089692 1.8169% 1910 10.950288 0.091322 1.8781% 1909 10.748426 0.093037 2.0082% 1908 10.536821 0.094905 1.9603% 1907 10.334244 0.096766 1.8264% 1906 10.148889 0.098533 1.9357% 1905 9.956171 0.100440 2.0148% 1904 9.759532 0.102464 2.1335% 1903 9.555659 0.104650 1.8151% 1902 9.385302 0.106550 1.8943% 1901 9.210817 0.108568 3.0255% 1900 8.940328 0.111853 0.6278% 1899 8.884547 0.112555 1.7757% 1898 8.729540 0.114554 1.8078% 1897 8.574534 0.116624 1.8396% 1896 8.419646 0.118770 1.8755% 1895 8.264640 0.120997 1.9114% 1894 8.109633 0.123310 1.9486% 1893 7.954626 0.125713 1.9858% 1892 7.799739 0.128209 2.0276% 1891 7.644732 0.130809 2.6465% 1890 7.447629 0.134271 1.5328% 1889 7.335194 0.136329 2.0811% 1888 7.185652 0.139166 2.1599% 1887 7.033733 0.142172 2.2075% 1886 6.881815 0.145311 2.2592% 1885 6.729778 0.148593 2.3095% 1884 6.577860 0.152025 2.3641% 1883 6.425941 0.155619 2.4214% 1882 6.274023 0.159387 2.4815% 1881 6.122105 0.163343 3.7644% 1880 5.900005 0.169491 0.9432% 1879 5.844875 0.171090 2.1464% 1878 5.722057 0.174762 2.1913% 1877 5.599359 0.178592 2.2426% 1876 5.476541 0.182597 2.2941% 1875 5.353724 0.186786 2.3456% 1874 5.231025 0.191167 2.4043% 1873 5.108208 0.195763 2.4635% 1872 4.985390 0.200586 2.5258% 1871 4.862573 0.205652 5.9947% 1870 4.587563 0.217981 -1.0968% 1869 4.638437 0.215590 2.1930% 1868 4.538900 0.220318 2.2394% 1867 4.439482 0.225251 2.2935% 1866 4.339945 0.230418 2.3445% 1865 4.240527 0.235820 2.4037% 1864 4.140991 0.241488 2.4599% 1863 4.041573 0.247428 2.5250% 1862 3.942036 0.253676 2.5872% 1861 3.842618 0.260239 2.9504% 1860 3.732494 0.267917 2.4012% 1859 3.644970 0.274351 2.7627% 1858 3.546977 0.281930 2.8412% 1857 3.448984 0.289940 2.9243% 1856 3.350992 0.298419 3.0161% 1855 3.252880 0.307420 3.1061% 1854 3.154888 0.316968 3.2056% 1853 3.056895 0.327129 3.3118% 1852 2.958902 0.337963 3.4252% 1851 2.860910 0.349539 4.0106% 1850 2.750594 0.363558 2.3254% 1849 2.688086 0.372012 2.7841% 1848 2.615275 0.382369 2.8590% 1847 2.542582 0.393301 2.9432% 1846 2.469890 0.404876 3.0324% 1845 2.397197 0.417154 3.1325% 1844 2.324385 0.430221 3.2284% 1843 2.251693 0.444110 3.3361% 1842 2.179000 0.458926 3.4512% 1841 2.106307 0.474765 3.8105% 1840 2.028993 0.492855 2.3861% 1839 1.981708 0.504615 2.5824% 1838 1.931821 0.517646 2.6573% 1837 1.881815 0.531402 2.7232% 1836 1.831928 0.545873 2.7994% 1835 1.782041 0.561154 2.8871% 1834 1.732035 0.577356 2.9657% 1833 1.682148 0.594478 3.0563% 1832 1.632260 0.612647 3.1604% 1831 1.582254 0.632010 3.4660% 1830 1.529251 0.653915 2.4653% 1829 1.492458 0.670036 2.6804% 1828 1.453498 0.687995 10.3427% 1827 1.317259 0.759152 -4.2314% 1826 1.375460 0.727029 2.9150% 1825 1.336501 0.748223 3.0026% 1824 1.297541 0.770688 3.0955% 1823 1.258582 0.794545 3.1944% 1822 1.219622 0.819926 3.3102% 1821 1.180544 0.847067 3.2277% 1820 1.143631 0.874408 2.6573% 1819 1.114028 0.897644 2.6261% 1818 1.085521 0.921217 2.6969% 1817 1.057014 0.946061 2.7717% 1816 1.028507 0.972283 2.8507% 1815 1.000000 1.000000 2.9343% 1814 0.971493 1.029343 3.0231% 1813 0.942986 1.060461 3.1039% 1812 0.914598 1.093377 3.2172% 1811 0.886091 1.128552 3.0969% 1810 0.859474 1.163503 2.9144% 1809 0.835135 1.197411 2.8225% 1808 0.812210 1.231208 2.9199% 1807 0.789167

1.267158 2.9918% 1806 0.766243 1.305069 3.0841% 1805 0.743319 1.345318 3.1822% 1804 0.720394 1.388129 3.2868% 1803 0.697470 1.433753 3.3985% 1802 0.674546 1.482479 3.5180% 1801 0.651621 1.534634 3.3999% 1800 0.630195 1.586810 2.8419% 1799 0.612781 1.631905 2.7485% 1798 0.596389 1.676758 2.8261% 1797 0.579998 1.724145 3.7832% 1796 0.558855 1.789373 2.1272% 1795 0.547215 1.827437 3.0879% 1794 0.530823 1.883867 3.1625% 1793 0.514550 1.943444 3.2904% 1792 0.498159 2.007392 3.4024% 1791 0.481767 2.075690 3.2296% 1790 0.466695 2.142726 41.3145% 1780 0.330253 3.027982 29.4353% 1770 0.255149 3.919278 83.4728% 1750 0.139066 7.190810 29.2845% 1740 0.107566 9.296599 94.2514% 1720 0.055375 18.058773 85.8111% 1700 0.029802 33.555201 19.2490% 1690 0.024991 40.014259 88.0250% 1670 0.013291 75.236819

BASE YEAR: 1814

YEAR BYEAR/AYEAR AYEAR/BYEAR GROWTH%

2009 36.854181 0.027134 8.2857% 2001 34.034222 0.029382 1.0000% 2000 33.697246 0.029676 1.0000% 1999 33.363609 0.029973 1.0000% 1998 33.033277 0.030273 1.0000% 1997 32.706215 0.030575 1.0000% 1996 32.382391 0.030881 1.0000% 1995 32.061773 0.031190 0.9992% 1994 31.744574 0.031501 1.0008% 1993 31.430029 0.031817 1.0000% 1992 31.118841 0.032135 0.9295% 1991 30.832253 0.032434 1.2505% 1990 30.451453 0.032839 0.7224% 1989 30.233036 0.033076 1.1077% 1988 29.901822 0.033443 0.8834% 1987 29.639993 0.033738 0.5594% 1986 29.475119 0.033927 1.3056% 1985 29.095244 0.034370 0.7673% 1984 28.873701 0.034634 0.8149% 1983 28.640298 0.034916 0.9737% 1982 28.364103 0.035256 0.9508% 1981 28.096956 0.035591 0.9031% 1980 27.845492 0.035912 2.2701% 1979 27.227412 0.036728 1.0042% 1978 26.956718 0.037097 0.9896% 1977 26.692566 0.037464 0.9103% 1976 26.451767 0.037805 0.8394% 1975 26.231569 0.038122 0.9042% 1974 25.996515 0.038467 1.1568% 1973 25.699230 0.038912 0.9427% 1972 25.459225 0.039278 0.7426% 1971 25.271549 0.039570 1.4697% 1970 24.905504 0.040152 0.6968% 1969 24.733158 0.040432 0.8565% 1968 24.523108 0.040778 1.5090% 1967 24.158546 0.041393 0.9949% 1966 23.920559 0.041805 1.0575% 1965 23.670253 0.042247 1.1300% 1964 23.405765 0.042725 1.5537% 1963 23.047683 0.043388 1.4658% 1962 22.714727 0.044024 1.5364% 1961 22.371011 0.044701 2.1586% 1960 21.898306 0.045666 -1.6655% 1959 22.269196 0.044905 4.3080% 1958 21.349462 0.046840 2.1130% 1957 20.907690 0.047829 1.9895% 1956 20.499847 0.048781 2.1231% 1955 20.073664 0.049817 1.4496% 1954 19.786832 0.050539 2.1573% 1953 19.368994 0.051629 1.2298% 1952 19.133696 0.052264 1.6814% 1951 18.817307 0.053143 1.6233% 1950 18.516729 0.054005 1.4265% 1949 18.256297 0.054776 1.7790% 1948 17.937187 0.055750 1.8242% 1947 17.615845 0.056767 -2.6320% 1946 18.092034 0.055273 3.1768% 1945 17.534983 0.057029 6.4754% 1944 16.468574 0.060722 -0.3437% 1943 16.525368 0.060513 0.6562% 1942 16.417632 0.060910 0.6633% 1941 16.309451 0.061314 -5.6614% 1940 17.288211 0.057843 8.0381% 1939 16.001956 0.062492 0.8126% 1938 15.872967 0.063000 0.7762% 1937 15.750703 0.063489 0.6029% 1936 15.656315 0.063872 0.5244% 1935 15.574642 0.064207 -3.0364% 1934 16.062355 0.062257 4.6271% 1933 15.351999 0.065138 1.3921% 1932 15.141215 0.066045 -0.2051% 1931 15.172332 0.065909 0.8886% 1930 15.038698 0.066495 1.0126% 1929 14.887945 0.067168 1.1526% 1928 14.718303 0.067943 1.2160% 1927 14.541478 0.068769 1.4086% 1926 14.339495 0.069737 1.7667% 1925 14.090559 0.070970 1.4465% 1924 13.889644 0.071996 1.7700% 1923 13.648077 0.073270 1.6165% 1922 13.430963 0.074455 1.3736% 1921 13.248969 0.075478 2.3393% 1920 12.946119 0.077243 1.3140% 1919 12.778212 0.078258 0.7676% 1918 12.680869 0.078859 0.3870% 1917 12.631984 0.079164 1.3274% 1916 12.466500 0.080215 1.4083% 1915 12.293373 0.081345 1.4458% 1914 12.118168 0.082521 1.9424% 1913 11.887272 0.084124 1.9857% 1912 11.655826 0.085794 1.5634% 1911 11.476403 0.087135 1.8169% 1910 11.271607 0.088718 1.8781% 1909 11.063822 0.090385 2.0082% 1908 10.846008 0.092200 1.9603% 1907 10.637486 0.094007 1.8264% 1906 10.446693 0.095724 1.9357% 1905 10.248319 0.097577 2.0148% 1904 10.045910 0.099543 2.1335% 1903 9.836055 0.101667 1.8151% 1902 9.660699 0.103512 1.8943% 1901 9.481094 0.105473 3.0255% 1900 9.202668 0.108664 0.6278% 1899 9.145250 0.109346 1.7757% 1898 8.985695 0.111288 1.8078% 1897 8.826140 0.113300 1.8396% 1896 8.666707 0.115384 1.8755% 1895 8.507152 0.117548 1.9114% 1894 8.347598 0.119795 1.9486% 1893 8.188043 0.122129 1.9858% 1892 8.028610

0.124555 2.0276% 1891 7.869055 0.127080 2.6465% 1890 7.666168 0.130443 1.5328% 1889 7.550434 0.132443 2.0811% 1888 7.396503 0.135199 2.1599% 1887 7.240127 0.138119 2.2075% 1886 7.083751 0.141168 2.2592% 1885 6.927253 0.144357 2.3095% 1884 6.770877 0.147691 2.3641% 1883 6.614501 0.151183 2.4214% 1882 6.458124 0.154844 2.4815% 1881 6.301748 0.158686 3.7644% 1880 6.073132 0.164660 0.9432% 1879 6.016383 0.166213 2.1464% 1878 5.889962 0.169780 2.1913% 1877 5.763663 0.173501 2.2426% 1876 5.637242 0.177392 2.2941% 1875 5.510820 0.181461 2.3456% 1874 5.384521 0.185718 2.4043% 1873 5.258100 0.190183 2.4635% 1872 5.131679 0.194868 2.5258% 1871 5.005257 0.199790 5.9947% 1870 4.722178 0.211767 -1.0968% 1869 4.774545 0.209444 2.1930% 1868 4.672087 0.214037 2.2394% 1867 4.569752 0.218830 2.2935% 1866 4.467294 0.223849 2.3445% 1865 4.364959 0.229097 2.4037% 1864 4.262502 0.234604 2.4599% 1863 4.160166 0.240375 2.5250% 1862 4.057709 0.246444 2.5872% 1861 3.955374 0.252821 2.9504% 1860 3.842018 0.260280 2.4012% 1859 3.751926 0.266530 2.7627% 1858 3.651058 0.273893 2.8412% 1857 3.550190 0.281675 2.9243% 1856 3.449321 0.289912 3.0161% 1855 3.348331 0.298656 3.1061% 1854 3.247463 0.307933 3.2056% 1853 3.146595 0.317804 3.3118% 1852 3.045727 0.328329 3.4252% 1851 2.944859 0.339575 4.0106% 1850 2.831306 0.353194 2.3254% 1849 2.766964 0.361407 2.7841% 1848 2.692016 0.371469 2.8590% 1847 2.617190 0.382089 2.9432% 1846 2.542365 0.393335 3.0324% 1845 2.467539 0.405262 3.1325% 1844 2.392591 0.417957 3.2284% 1843 2.317765 0.431450 3.3361% 1842 2.242939 0.445844 3.4512% 1841 2.168113 0.461230 3.8105% 1840 2.088530 0.478806 2.3861% 1839 2.039858 0.490230 2.5824% 1838 1.988507 0.502890 2.6573% 1837 1.937034 0.516253 2.7232% 1836 1.885683 0.530312 2.7994% 1835 1.834332 0.545158 2.8871% 1834 1.782859 0.560897 2.9657% 1833 1.731508 0.577531 3.0563% 1832 1.680156 0.595183 3.1604% 1831 1.628683 0.613993 3.4660% 1830 1.574125 0.635274 2.4653% 1829 1.536251 0.650935 2.6804% 1828 1.496149 0.668383 10.3427% 1827 1.355911 0.737511 -4.2314% 1826 1.415821 0.706304 2.9150% 1825 1.375718 0.726893 3.0026% 1824 1.335616 0.748718 3.0955% 1823 1.295513 0.771895 3.1944% 1822 1.255410 0.796552 3.3102% 1821 1.215185 0.822920 3.2277% 1820 1.177189 0.849482 2.6573% 1819 1.146717 0.872055 2.6261% 1818 1.117374 0.894956 2.6969% 1817 1.088030 0.919092 2.7717% 1816 1.058687 0.944566 2.8507% 1815 1.029343 0.971493 2.9343% 1814 1.000000 1.000000 3.0231% 1813 0.970657 1.030231 3.1039% 1812 0.941435 1.062208 3.2172% 1811 0.912092 1.096381 3.0969% 1810 0.884694 1.130335 2.9144% 1809 0.859641 1.163277 2.8225% 1808 0.836044 1.196110 2.9199% 1807 0.812324 1.231036 2.9918% 1806 0.788727 1.267865 3.0841% 1805 0.765130 1.306967 3.1822% 1804 0.741533 1.348557 3.2868% 1803 0.717936 1.392881 3.3985% 1802 0.694339 1.440218 3.5180% 1801 0.670742 1.490886 3.3999% 1800 0.648687 1.541575 2.8419% 1799 0.630762 1.585385 2.7485% 1798 0.613889 1.628958 2.8261% 1797 0.597017 1.674995 3.7832% 1796 0.575254 1.738363 2.1272% 1795 0.563272 1.775342 3.0879% 1794 0.546399 1.830163 3.1625% 1793 0.529649 1.888042 3.2904% 1792 0.512777 1.950167 3.4024% 1791 0.495904 2.016519 3.2296% 1790 0.480390 2.081643 41.3145% 1780 0.339944 2.941663 29.4353% 1770 0.262636 3.807551 83.4728% 1750 0.143147 6.985822 29.2845% 1740 0.110723 9.031581 94.2514% 1720 0.057000 17.543973 85.8111% 1700 0.030676 32.598645 19.2490% 1690 0.025724 38.873574 88.0250% 1670 0.013681 73.092046

BASE YEAR: 1813

YEAR BYEAR/AYEAR AYEAR/BYEAR GROWTH%

2009 37.968302 0.026338 8.2857% 2001 35.063093 0.028520 1.0000% 2000 34.715930 0.028805 1.0000% 1999 34.372208 0.029093 1.0000% 1998 34.031889 0.029384 1.0000% 1997 33.694940 0.029678 1.0000% 1996 33.361327 0.029975 1.0000% 1995 33.031017 0.030275 0.9992% 1994 32.704229 0.030577 1.0008% 1993 32.380175 0.030883 1.0000% 1992 32.059579 0.031192 0.9295% 1991 31.764328 0.031482 1.2505% 1990 31.372016 0.031876 0.7224% 1989 31.146996 0.032106 1.1077% 1988 30.805769 0.032461 0.8834% 1987 30.536025 0.032748 0.5594% 1986 30.366167 0.032931 1.3056% 1985 29.974808 0.033361 0.7673% 1984 29.746568 0.033617 0.8149% 1983 29.506109 0.033891 0.9737% 1982 29.221564 0.034221 0.9508% 1981 28.946341 0.034547 0.9031% 1980 28.687276 0.034859 2.2701% 1979 28.050510 0.035650 1.0042% 1978 27.771634 0.036008 0.9896% 1977 27.499496 0.036364 0.9103% 1976 27.251417 0.036695 0.8394% 1975 27.024562 0.037003 0.9042% 1974 26.782403 0.037338 1.1568% 1973 26.476130 0.037770

297

0.9427% 1972 26.228870 0.038126 0.7426% 1971 26.035521 0.038409 1.4697% 1970
25.658410 0.038974 0.6968% 1969 25.480854 0.039245 0.8565% 1968 25.264454 0.039581
1.5090% 1967 24.888871 0.040179 0.9949% 1966 24.643689 0.040578 1.0575% 1965
24.385817 0.041007 1.1300% 1964 24.113333 0.041471 1.5537% 1963 23.744426 0.042115
1.4658% 1962 23.401404 0.042732 1.5364% 1961 23.047298 0.043389 2.1586% 1960
22.560303 0.044326 -1.6655% 1959 22.942405 0.043587 4.3080% 1958 21.994867 0.045465
2.1130% 1957 21.539741 0.046426 1.9895% 1956 21.119568 0.047349 2.1231% 1955
20.680501 0.048355 1.4496% 1954 20.384998 0.049056 2.1573% 1953 19.954528 0.050114
1.2298% 1952 19.712117 0.050730 1.6814% 1951 19.386163 0.051583 1.6233% 1950
19.076500 0.052421 1.4265% 1949 18.808194 0.053168 1.7790% 1948 18.479437 0.054114
1.8242% 1947 18.148381 0.055101 -2.6320% 1946 18.638966 0.053651 3.1768% 1945
18.065074 0.055355 6.4754% 1944 16.966428 0.058940 -0.3437% 1943 17.024938 0.058737
0.6562% 1942 16.913945 0.059123 0.6633% 1941 16.802494 0.059515 -5.6614% 1940
17.810842 0.056146 8.0381% 1939 16.485703 0.060659 0.8126% 1938 16.352815 0.061152
0.7762% 1937 16.226855 0.061626 0.6029% 1936 16.129613 0.061998 0.5244% 1935
16.045472 0.062323 -3.0364% 1934 16.547928 0.060431 4.6271% 1933 15.816098 0.063227
1.3921% 1932 15.598942 0.064107 -0.2051% 1931 15.630999 0.063975 0.8886% 1930
15.493325 0.064544 1.0126% 1929 15.338015 0.065197 1.1526% 1928 15.163245 0.065949
1.2160% 1927 14.981074 0.066751 1.4086% 1926 14.772985 0.067691 1.7667% 1925
14.516523 0.068887 1.4465% 1924 14.309535 0.069883 1.7700% 1923 14.060666 0.071120
1.6165% 1922 13.836988 0.072270 1.3736% 1921 13.649493 0.073263 2.3393% 1920
13.337487 0.074977 1.3140% 1919 13.164504 0.075962 0.7676% 1918 13.064218 0.076545
0.3870% 1917 13.013856 0.076841 1.3274% 1916 12.843368 0.077861 1.4083% 1915
12.665008 0.078958 1.4458% 1914 12.484507 0.080099 1.9424% 1913 12.246631 0.081655
1.9857% 1912 12.008187 0.083277 1.5634% 1911 11.823340 0.084578 1.8169% 1910
11.612354 0.086115 1.8781% 1909 11.398287 0.087732 2.0082% 1908 11.173888 0.089494
1.9603% 1907 10.959063 0.091249 1.8264% 1906 10.762502 0.092915 1.9357% 1905
10.558131 0.094714 2.0148% 1904 10.349603 0.096622 2.1335% 1903 10.133404 0.098684
1.8151% 1902 9.952747 0.100475 1.8943% 1901 9.767713 0.102378 3.0255% 1900 9.480869
0.105476 0.6278% 1899 9.421716 0.106138 1.7757% 1898 9.257337 0.108022 1.8078% 1897
9.092959 0.109975 1.8396% 1896 8.928706 0.111998 1.8755% 1895 8.764328 0.114099
1.9114% 1894 8.599950 0.116280 1.9486% 1893 8.435571 0.118546 1.9858% 1892 8.271319
0.120900 2.0276% 1891 8.106940 0.123351 2.6465% 1890 7.897921 0.126616 1.5328% 1889
7.778687 0.128556 2.0811% 1888 7.620103 0.131232 2.1599% 1887 7.459000 0.134066
2.2075% 1886 7.297896 0.137026 2.2592% 1885 7.136667 0.140121 2.3095% 1884 6.975564
0.143358 2.3641% 1883 6.814460 0.146747 2.4214% 1882 6.653357 0.150300 2.4815% 1881
6.492253 0.154030 3.7644% 1880 6.256726 0.159828 0.9432% 1879 6.198262 0.161336
2.1464% 1878 6.068019 0.164798 2.1913% 1877 5.937901 0.168410 2.2426% 1876 5.807658
0.172186 2.2941% 1875 5.677415 0.176136 2.3456% 1874 5.547298 0.180268 2.4043% 1873
5.417055 0.184602 2.4635% 1872 5.286812 0.189150 2.5258% 1871 5.156569 0.193927
5.9947% 1870 4.864932 0.205553 -1.0968% 1869 4.918881 0.203298 2.1930% 1868
4.813327 0.207757 2.2394% 1867 4.707898 0.212409 2.2935% 1866 4.602343 0.217281
2.3445% 1865 4.496914 0.222375 2.4037% 1864 4.391359 0.227720 2.4599% 1863 4.285930
0.233322 2.5250% 1862 4.180375 0.239213 2.5872% 1861 4.074946 0.245402 2.9504% 1860
3.958165 0.252642 2.4012% 1859 3.865348 0.258709 2.7627% 1858 3.761431 0.265856
2.8412% 1857 3.657514 0.273410 2.9243% 1856 3.553596 0.281405 3.0161% 1855 3.449553
0.289893 3.1061% 1854 3.345635 0.298897 3.2056% 1853 3.241718 0.308478 3.3118% 1852
3.137801 0.318695 3.4252% 1851 3.033883 0.329611 4.0106% 1850 2.916898 0.342830
2.3254% 1849 2.850611 0.350802 2.7841% 1848 2.773397 0.360569 2.8590% 1847 2.696309
0.370877 2.9432% 1846 2.619222 0.381793 3.0324% 1845 2.542134 0.393370 3.1325% 1844
2.464920 0.405693 3.2284% 1843 2.387832 0.418790 3.3361% 1842 2.310744 0.432761
3.4512% 1841 2.233657 0.447696 3.8105% 1840 2.151668 0.464756 2.3861% 1839 2.101524
0.475845 2.5824% 1838 2.048621 0.488133 2.6573% 1837 1.995591 0.501105 2.7232% 1836
1.942688 0.514751 2.7994% 1835 1.889785 0.529161 2.8871% 1834 1.836755 0.544438
2.9657% 1833 1.783852 0.560585 3.0563% 1832 1.730948 0.577718 3.1604% 1831 1.677919
0.595976 3.4660% 1830 1.621711 0.616633 2.4653% 1829 1.582693 0.631834 2.6804% 1828

298

1.541378 0.648770 10.3427% 1827 1.396901 0.715870 -4.2314% 1826 1.458622 0.685579
2.9150% 1825 1.417307 0.705563 3.0026% 1824 1.375992 0.726748 3.0955% 1823 1.334677
0.749245 3.1944% 1822 1.293362 0.773179 3.3102% 1821 1.251921 0.798773 3.2277% 1820
1.212776 0.824555 2.6573% 1819 1.181383 0.846466 2.6261% 1818 1.151153 0.868695
2.6969% 1817 1.120922 0.892123 2.7717% 1816 1.090692 0.916850 2.8507% 1815 1.060461
0.942986 2.9343% 1814 1.030231 0.970657 3.0231% 1813 1.000000 1.000000 3.1039% 1812
0.969895 1.031039 3.2172% 1811 0.939665 1.064209 3.0969% 1810 0.911438 1.097167
2.9144% 1809 0.885628 1.129142 2.8225% 1808 0.861318 1.161012 2.9199% 1807 0.836881
1.194913 2.9918% 1806 0.812571 1.230662 3.0841% 1805 0.788260 1.268616 3.1822% 1804
0.763950 1.308986 3.2868% 1803 0.739640 1.352010 3.3985% 1802 0.715329 1.397957
3.5180% 1801 0.691019 1.447138 3.3999% 1800 0.668297 1.496340 2.8419% 1799 0.649830
1.538864 2.7485% 1798 0.632447 1.581159 2.8261% 1797 0.615065 1.625845 3.7832% 1796
0.592644 1.687354 2.1272% 1795 0.580300 1.723247 3.0879% 1794 0.562917 1.776460
3.1625% 1793 0.545661 1.832641 3.2904% 1792 0.528278 1.892942 3.4024% 1791 0.510896
1.957347 3.2296% 1790 0.494912 2.020561 41.3145% 1780 0.350220 2.855345 29.4353%
1770 0.270576 3.695824 83.4728% 1750 0.147474 6.780834 29.2845% 1740 0.114070
8.766564 94.2514% 1720 0.058723 17.029172 85.8111% 1700 0.031603 31.642088 19.2490%
1690 0.026502 37.732890 88.0250% 1670 0.014095 70.947274
BASE YEAR: 1812
YEAR BYEAR/AYEAR AYEAR/BYEAR GROWTH%
2009 39.146799 0.025545 8.2857% 2001 36.151415 0.027661 1.0000% 2000
35.793477 0.027938 1.0000% 1999 35.439086 0.028217 1.0000% 1998 35.088204 0.028500
1.0000% 1997 34.740796 0.028785 1.0000% 1996 34.396828 0.029072 1.0000% 1995
34.056265 0.029363 0.9992% 1994 33.719334 0.029657 1.0008% 1993 33.385222 0.029953
1.0000% 1992 33.054675 0.030253 0.9295% 1991 32.750260 0.030534 1.2505% 1990
32.345771 0.030916 0.7224% 1989 32.113766 0.031139 1.1077% 1988 31.761948 0.031484
0.8834% 1987 31.483831 0.031762 0.5594% 1986 31.308701 0.031940 1.3056% 1985
30.905195 0.032357 0.7673% 1984 30.669870 0.032605 0.8149% 1983 30.421948 0.032871
0.9737% 1982 30.128571 0.033191 0.9508% 1981 29.844805 0.033507 0.9031% 1980
29.577699 0.033809 2.2701% 1979 28.921169 0.034577 1.0042% 1978 28.633636 0.034924
0.9896% 1977 28.353052 0.035270 0.9103% 1976 28.097273 0.035591 0.8394% 1975
27.863377 0.035889 0.9042% 1974 27.613701 0.036214 1.1568% 1973 27.297922 0.036633
0.9427% 1972 27.042987 0.036978 0.7426% 1971 26.843636 0.037253 1.4697% 1970
26.454820 0.037800 0.6968% 1969 26.271753 0.038064 0.8565% 1968 26.048636 0.038390
1.5090% 1967 25.661396 0.038969 0.9949% 1966 25.408604 0.039357 1.0575% 1965
25.142727 0.039773 1.1300% 1964 24.861786 0.040222 1.5537% 1963 24.481429 0.040847
1.4658% 1962 24.127760 0.041446 1.5364% 1961 23.762662 0.042083 2.1586% 1960
23.260551 0.042991 -1.6655% 1959 23.654513 0.042275 4.3080% 1958 22.677565 0.044096
2.1130% 1957 22.208312 0.045028 1.9895% 1956 21.775097 0.045924 2.1231% 1955
21.322403 0.046899 1.4496% 1954 21.017727 0.047579 2.1573% 1953 20.573896 0.048605
1.2298% 1952 20.323961 0.049203 1.6814% 1951 19.987890 0.050030 1.6233% 1950
19.668614 0.050842 1.4265% 1949 19.391981 0.051568 1.7790% 1948 19.053019 0.052485
1.8242% 1947 18.711688 0.053443 -2.6320% 1946 19.217500 0.052036 3.1768% 1945
18.625795 0.053689 6.4754% 1944 17.493048 0.057166 -0.3437% 1943 17.553375 0.056969
0.6562% 1942 17.438936 0.057343 0.6633% 1941 17.324026 0.057723 -5.6614% 1940
18.363672 0.054455 8.0381% 1939 16.997403 0.058833 0.8126% 1938 16.860390 0.059311
0.7762% 1937 16.730519 0.059771 0.6029% 1936 16.630260 0.060131 0.5244% 1935
16.543506 0.060447 -3.0364% 1934 17.061558 0.058611 4.6271% 1933 16.307013 0.061323
1.3921% 1932 16.083117 0.062177 -0.2051% 1931 16.116169 0.062049 0.8886% 1930
15.974222 0.062601 1.0126% 1929 15.814091 0.063235 1.1526% 1928 15.633896 0.063964
1.2160% 1927 15.446071 0.064741 1.4086% 1926 15.231523 0.065653 1.7667% 1925
14.967101 0.066813 1.4465% 1924 14.753689 0.067780 1.7700% 1923 14.497094 0.068979
1.6165% 1922 14.266474 0.070094 1.3736% 1921 14.073159 0.071057 2.3393% 1920
13.751469 0.072720 1.3140% 1919 13.573117 0.073675 0.7676% 1918 13.469718 0.074241
0.3870% 1917 13.417792 0.074528 1.3274% 1916 13.242013 0.075517 1.4083% 1915
13.058117 0.076581 1.4458% 1914 12.872013 0.077688 1.9424% 1913 12.626753 0.079197

1.9857% 1912 12.380909 0.080770 1.5634% 1911 12.190325 0.082032 1.8169% 1910
11.972789 0.083523 1.8781% 1909 11.752078 0.085091 2.0082% 1908 11.520714 0.086800
1.9603% 1907 11.299221 0.088502 1.8264% 1906 11.096558 0.090118 1.9357% 1905
10.885844 0.091862 2.0148% 1904 10.670844 0.093713 2.1335% 1903 10.447935 0.095713
1.8151% 1902 10.261670 0.097450 1.8943% 1901 10.070892 0.099296 3.0255% 1900
9.775145 0.102300 0.6278% 1899 9.714156 0.102943 1.7757% 1898 9.544675 0.104770
1.8078% 1897 9.375195 0.106664 1.8396% 1896 9.205844 0.108627 1.8755% 1895 9.036364
0.110664 1.9114% 1894 8.866883 0.112779 1.9486% 1893 8.697403 0.114977 1.9858% 1892
8.528052 0.117260 2.0276% 1891 8.358571 0.119638 2.6465% 1890 8.143064 0.122804
1.5328% 1889 8.020130 0.124686 2.0811% 1888 7.856623 0.127281 2.1599% 1887 7.690519
0.130030 2.2075% 1886 7.524416 0.132901 2.2592% 1885 7.358182 0.135903 2.3095% 1884
7.192078 0.139042 2.3641% 1883 7.025974 0.142329 2.4214% 1882 6.859870 0.145775
2.4815% 1881 6.693766 0.149393 3.7644% 1880 6.450928 0.155016 0.9432% 1879 6.390649
0.156479 2.1464% 1878 6.256364 0.159837 2.1913% 1877 6.122208 0.163340 2.2426% 1876
5.987922 0.167003 2.2941% 1875 5.853636 0.170834 2.3456% 1874 5.719481 0.174841
2.4043% 1873 5.585195 0.179045 2.4635% 1872 5.450909 0.183456 2.5258% 1871 5.316623
0.188089 5.9947% 1870 5.015934 0.199365 -1.0968% 1869 5.071558 0.197178 2.1930%
1868 4.962727 0.201502 2.2394% 1867 4.854026 0.206015 2.2935% 1866 4.745195 0.210740
2.3445% 1865 4.636494 0.215680 2.4037% 1864 4.527662 0.220865 2.4599% 1863 4.418961
0.226298 2.5250% 1862 4.310130 0.232012 2.5872% 1861 4.201429 0.238014 2.9504% 1860
4.081022 0.245037 2.4012% 1859 3.985325 0.250921 2.7627% 1858 3.878182 0.257853
2.8412% 1857 3.771039 0.265179 2.9243% 1856 3.663896 0.272934 3.0161% 1855 3.556623
0.281166 3.1061% 1854 3.449481 0.289899 3.2056% 1853 3.342338 0.299192 3.3118% 1852
3.235195 0.309100 3.4252% 1851 3.128052 0.319688 4.0106% 1850 3.007436 0.332509
2.3254% 1849 2.939091 0.340241 2.7841% 1848 2.859481 0.349714 2.8590% 1847 2.780000
0.359712 2.9432% 1846 2.700519 0.370299 3.0324% 1845 2.621039 0.381528 3.1325% 1844
2.541429 0.393479 3.2284% 1843 2.461948 0.406182 3.3361% 1842 2.382468 0.419733
3.4512% 1841 2.302987 0.434219 3.8105% 1840 2.218453 0.450765 2.3861% 1839 2.166753
0.461520 2.5824% 1838 2.112208 0.473438 2.6573% 1837 2.057532 0.486019 2.7232% 1836
2.002987 0.499254 2.7994% 1835 1.948442 0.513231 2.8871% 1834 1.893766 0.528048
2.9657% 1833 1.839221 0.543709 3.0563% 1832 1.784675 0.560326 3.1604% 1831 1.730000
0.578035 3.4660% 1830 1.672047 0.598069 2.4653% 1829 1.631818 0.612813 2.6804% 1828
1.589221 0.629239 10.3427% 1827 1.440260 0.694319 -4.2314% 1826 1.503896 0.664940
2.9150% 1825 1.461299 0.684323 3.0026% 1824 1.418701 0.704870 3.0955% 1823 1.376104
0.726689 3.1944% 1822 1.333506 0.749903 3.3102% 1821 1.290779 0.774726 3.2277% 1820
1.250419 0.799732 2.6573% 1819 1.218052 0.820983 2.6261% 1818 1.186883 0.842543
2.6969% 1817 1.155714 0.865266 2.7717% 1816 1.124545 0.889248 2.8507% 1815 1.093377
0.914598 2.9343% 1814 1.062208 0.941435 3.0231% 1813 1.031039 0.969895 3.1039% 1812
1.000000 1.000000 3.2172% 1811 0.968831 1.032172 3.0969% 1810 0.939729 1.064137
2.9144% 1809 0.913117 1.095150 2.8225% 1808 0.888052 1.126060 2.9199% 1807 0.862857
1.158940 2.9918% 1806 0.837792 1.193613 3.0841% 1805 0.812727 1.230425 3.1822% 1804
0.787662 1.269580 3.2868% 1803 0.762597 1.311308 3.3985% 1802 0.737532 1.355873
3.5180% 1801 0.712468 1.403573 3.3999% 1800 0.689041 1.451293 2.8419% 1799 0.670000
1.492537 2.7485% 1798 0.652078 1.533559 2.8261% 1797 0.634156 1.576899 3.7832% 1796
0.611039 1.636557 2.1272% 1795 0.598312 1.671370 3.0879% 1794 0.580390 1.722981
3.1625% 1793 0.562597 1.777470 3.2904% 1792 0.544675 1.835956 3.4024% 1791 0.526753
1.898422 3.2296% 1790 0.510274 1.959733 41.3145% 1780 0.361091 2.769386 29.4353%
1770 0.278974 3.584563 83.4728% 1750 0.152052 6.576700 29.2845% 1740 0.117610
8.502650 94.2514% 1720 0.060545 16.516517 85.8111% 1700 0.032584 30.689518 19.2490%
1690 0.027325 36.596958 88.0250% 1670 0.014532 68.811439

BASE YEAR: 1811
YEAR BYEAR/AYEAR AYEAR/BYEAR GROWTH%
2009 40.406213 0.024749 8.2857% 2001 37.314464 0.026799 1.0000% 2000
36.945010 0.027067 1.0000% 1999 36.579217 0.027338 1.0000% 1998 36.217047 0.027611
1.0000% 1997 35.858462 0.027887 1.0000% 1996 35.503428 0.028166 1.0000% 1995
35.151909 0.028448 0.9992% 1994 34.804138 0.028732 1.0008% 1993 34.459277 0.029020

300

1.0000% 1992 34.118097 0.029310 0.9295% 1991 33.803887 0.029582 1.2505% 1990
33.386386 0.029952 0.7224% 1989 33.146917 0.030169 1.1077% 1988 32.783780 0.030503
0.8834% 1987 32.496716 0.030772 0.5594% 1986 32.315952 0.030944 1.3056% 1985
31.899464 0.031348 0.7673% 1984 31.656568 0.031589 0.8149% 1983 31.400670 0.031846
0.9737% 1982 31.097855 0.032157 0.9508% 1981 30.804960 0.032462 0.9031% 1980
30.529260 0.032755 2.2701% 1979 29.851609 0.033499 1.0042% 1978 29.554826 0.033835
0.9896% 1977 29.265214 0.034170 0.9103% 1976 29.001206 0.034481 0.8394% 1975
28.759786 0.034771 0.9042% 1974 28.502078 0.035085 1.1568% 1973 28.176139 0.035491
0.9427% 1972 27.913003 0.035826 0.7426% 1971 27.707239 0.036092 1.4697% 1970
27.305913 0.036622 0.6968% 1969 27.116957 0.036877 0.8565% 1968 26.886662 0.037193
1.5090% 1967 26.486964 0.037754 0.9949% 1966 26.226039 0.038130 1.0575% 1965
25.951609 0.038533 1.1300% 1964 25.661629 0.038969 1.5537% 1963 25.269035 0.039574
1.4658% 1962 24.903988 0.040154 1.5364% 1961 24.527145 0.040771 2.1586% 1960
24.008880 0.041651 -1.6655% 1959 24.415516 0.040958 4.3080% 1958 23.407138 0.042722
2.1130% 1957 22.922788 0.043625 1.9895% 1956 22.475637 0.044493 2.1231% 1955
22.008378 0.045437 1.4496% 1954 21.693901 0.046096 2.1573% 1953 21.235791 0.047090
1.2298% 1952 20.977815 0.047669 1.6814% 1951 20.630932 0.048471 1.6233% 1950
20.301385 0.049258 1.4265% 1949 20.015851 0.049960 1.7790% 1948 19.665985 0.050849
1.8242% 1947 19.313673 0.051777 -2.6320% 1946 19.835757 0.050414 3.1768% 1945
19.225017 0.052016 6.4754% 1944 18.055827 0.055384 -0.3437% 1943 18.118094 0.055193
0.6562% 1942 17.999974 0.055556 0.6633% 1941 17.881367 0.055924 -5.6614% 1940
18.954460 0.052758 8.0381% 1939 17.544236 0.056999 0.8126% 1938 17.402815 0.057462
0.7762% 1937 17.268767 0.057908 0.6029% 1936 17.165282 0.058257 0.5244% 1935
17.075737 0.058563 -3.0364% 1934 17.610456 0.056784 4.6271% 1933 16.831635 0.059412
1.3921% 1932 16.600536 0.060239 -0.2051% 1931 16.634651 0.060115 0.8886% 1930
16.488138 0.060650 1.0126% 1929 16.322855 0.061264 1.1526% 1928 16.136863 0.061970
1.2160% 1927 15.942996 0.062723 1.4086% 1926 15.721545 0.063607 1.7667% 1925
15.448617 0.064731 1.4465% 1924 15.228338 0.065667 1.7700% 1923 14.963489 0.066829
1.6165% 1922 14.725449 0.067910 1.3736% 1921 14.525914 0.068842 2.3393% 1920
14.193875 0.070453 1.3140% 1919 14.009786 0.071379 0.7676% 1918 13.903060 0.071927
0.3870% 1917 13.849464 0.072205 1.3274% 1916 13.668029 0.073163 1.4083% 1915
13.478217 0.074194 1.4458% 1914 13.286126 0.075266 1.9424% 1913 13.032976 0.076728
1.9857% 1912 12.779223 0.078252 1.5634% 1911 12.582507 0.079475 1.8169% 1910
12.357973 0.080919 1.8781% 1909 12.130161 0.082439 2.0082% 1908 11.891354 0.084095
1.9603% 1907 11.662735 0.085743 1.8264% 1906 11.453552 0.087309 1.9357% 1905
11.236059 0.088999 2.0148% 1904 11.014142 0.090792 2.1335% 1903 10.784061 0.092729
1.8151% 1902 10.591804 0.094413 1.8943% 1901 10.394889 0.096201 3.0255% 1900
10.089627 0.099112 0.6278% 1899 10.026676 0.099734 1.7757% 1898 9.851743 0.101505
1.8078% 1897 9.676810 0.103340 1.8396% 1896 9.502011 0.105241 1.8755% 1895 9.327078
0.107215 1.9114% 1894 9.152145 0.109264 1.9486% 1893 8.977212 0.111393 1.9858% 1892
8.802413 0.113605 2.0276% 1891 8.627480 0.115909 2.6465% 1890 8.405039 0.118976
1.5328% 1889 8.278150 0.120800 2.0811% 1888 8.109383 0.123314 2.1599% 1887 7.937936
0.125977 2.2075% 1886 7.766488 0.128758 2.2592% 1885 7.594906 0.131667 2.3095% 1884
7.423458 0.134708 2.3641% 1883 7.252011 0.137893 2.4214% 1882 7.080563 0.141232
2.4815% 1881 6.909115 0.144736 3.7644% 1880 6.658464 0.150185 0.9432% 1879 6.596247
0.151601 2.1464% 1878 6.457641 0.154855 2.1913% 1877 6.319169 0.158249 2.2426% 1876
6.180563 0.161798 2.2941% 1875 6.041957 0.165509 2.3456% 1874 5.903485 0.169391
2.4043% 1873 5.764879 0.173464 2.4635% 1872 5.626273 0.177738 2.5258% 1871 5.487668
0.182227 5.9947% 1870 5.177305 0.193151 -1.0968% 1869 5.234718 0.191032 2.1930%
1868 5.122386 0.195222 2.2394% 1867 5.010186 0.199593 2.2935% 1866 4.897855 0.204171
2.3445% 1865 4.785657 0.208958 2.4037% 1864 4.673324 0.213980 2.4599% 1863 4.561126
0.219244 2.5250% 1862 4.448794 0.224780 2.5872% 1861 4.336595 0.230596 2.9504% 1860
4.212315 0.237399 2.4012% 1859 4.113539 0.243100 2.7627% 1858 4.002949 0.249816
2.8412% 1857 3.892359 0.256914 2.9243% 1856 3.781769 0.264426 3.0161% 1855 3.671046
0.272402 3.1061% 1854 3.560456 0.280863 3.2056% 1853 3.449866 0.289866 3.3118% 1852
3.339276 0.299466 3.4252% 1851 3.228686 0.309723 4.0106% 1850 3.104190 0.322145

2.3254% 1849 3.033646 0.329636 2.7841% 1848 2.951475 0.338814 2.8590% 1847 2.869437
0.348500 2.9432% 1846 2.787399 0.358757 3.0324% 1845 2.705362 0.369636 3.1325% 1844
2.623190 0.381215 3.2284% 1843 2.541153 0.393522 3.3361% 1842 2.459115 0.406650
3.4512% 1841 2.377078 0.420685 3.8105% 1840 2.289824 0.436715 2.3861% 1839 2.236461
0.447135 2.5824% 1838 2.180161 0.458682 2.6573% 1837 2.123727 0.470870 2.7232% 1836
2.067426 0.483693 2.7994% 1835 2.011126 0.497234 2.8871% 1834 1.954692 0.511590
2.9657% 1833 1.898391 0.526762 3.0563% 1832 1.842091 0.542861 3.1604% 1831 1.785657
0.560018 3.4660% 1830 1.725840 0.579428 2.4653% 1829 1.684316 0.593713 2.6804% 1828
1.640349 0.609627 10.3427% 1827 1.486595 0.672678 -4.2314% 1826 1.552279 0.644214
2.91150% 1825 1.508311 0.662993 3.0026% 1824 1.464343 0.682900 3.0955% 1823 1.420375
0.704039 3.1944% 1822 1.376408 0.726529 3.3102% 1821 1.332306 0.750579 3.2277% 1820
1.290647 0.774805 2.6573% 1819 1.257239 0.795394 2.6261% 1818 1.225067 0.816282
2.6969% 1817 1.192895 0.838296 2.7717% 1816 1.160724 0.861531 2.8507% 1815 1.128552
0.886091 2.9343% 1814 1.096381 0.912092 3.0231% 1813 1.064209 0.939665 3.1039% 1812
1.032172 0.968831 3.2172% 1811 1.000000 1.000000 3.0969% 1810 0.969961 1.030969
2.9144% 1809 0.942493 1.061016 2.8225% 1808 0.916622 1.090962 2.9199% 1807 0.890617
1.122818 2.9918% 1806 0.864745 1.156410 3.0841% 1805 0.838874 1.192074 3.1822% 1804
0.813003 1.230008 3.2868% 1803 0.787131 1.270436 3.3985% 1802 0.761260 1.313612
3.5180% 1801 0.735389 1.359825 3.3999% 1800 0.711208 1.406058 2.8419% 1799 0.691555
1.446017 2.7485% 1798 0.673056 1.485760 2.8261% 1797 0.654558 1.527749 3.7832% 1796
0.630697 1.585547 2.1272% 1795 0.617560 1.619275 3.0879% 1794 0.599062 1.669277
3.1625% 1793 0.580697 1.722068 3.2904% 1792 0.562198 1.778732 3.4024% 1791 0.543700
1.839250 3.2296% 1790 0.526690 1.898650 41.3145% 1780 0.372708 2.683067 29.4353%
1770 0.287949 3.472836 83.4728% 1750 0.156944 6.371712 29.2845% 1740 0.121394
8.237633 94.2514% 1720 0.062493 16.001716 85.8111% 1700 0.033633 29.732961 19.2490%
1690 0.028204 35.456274 88.0250% 1670 0.015000 66.666667

BASE YEAR: 1810

YEAR BYEAR/AYEAR AYEAR/BYEAR GROWTH%

2009 41.657559 0.024005 8.2857% 2001 38.470061 0.025994 1.0000% 2000
38.089165 0.026254 1.0000% 1999 37.712045 0.026517 1.0000% 1998 37.338658 0.026782
1.0000% 1997 36.968969 0.027050 1.0000% 1996 36.602939 0.027320 1.0000% 1995
36.240534 0.027593 0.9992% 1994 35.881993 0.027869 1.0008% 1993 35.526452 0.028148
1.0000% 1992 35.174705 0.028430 0.9295% 1991 34.850765 0.028694 1.2505% 1990
34.420334 0.029053 0.7224% 1989 34.173449 0.029262 1.1077% 1988 33.799066 0.029587
0.8834% 1987 33.503112 0.029848 0.5594% 1986 33.316749 0.030015 1.3056% 1985
32.887363 0.030407 0.7673% 1984 32.636945 0.030640 0.8149% 1983 32.373122 0.030890
0.9737% 1982 32.060929 0.031191 0.9508% 1981 31.758963 0.031487 0.9031% 1980
31.474726 0.031772 2.2701% 1979 30.776088 0.032493 1.0042% 1978 30.470114 0.032819
0.9896% 1977 30.171533 0.033144 0.9103% 1976 29.899349 0.033446 0.8394% 1975
29.650452 0.033726 0.9042% 1974 29.384763 0.034031 1.1568% 1973 29.048731 0.034425
0.9427% 1972 28.777445 0.034749 0.7426% 1971 28.565308 0.035007 1.4697% 1970
28.151554 0.035522 0.6968% 1969 27.956746 0.035770 0.8565% 1968 27.719319 0.036076
1.5090% 1967 27.307243 0.036620 0.9949% 1966 27.038237 0.036985 1.0575% 1965
26.755308 0.037376 1.1300% 1964 26.456348 0.037798 1.5537% 1963 26.051595 0.038385
1.4658% 1962 25.675243 0.038948 1.5364% 1961 25.286730 0.039546 2.1586% 1960
24.752414 0.040400 -1.6655% 1959 25.171644 0.039727 4.3080% 1958 24.132037 0.041439
2.1130% 1957 23.632688 0.042314 1.9895% 1956 23.171688 0.043156 2.1231% 1955
22.689959 0.044072 1.4496% 1954 22.365743 0.044711 2.1573% 1953 21.893445 0.045676
1.2298% 1952 21.627480 0.046237 1.6814% 1951 21.269854 0.047015 1.6233% 1950
20.930101 0.047778 1.4265% 1949 20.635725 0.048460 1.7790% 1948 20.275024 0.049322
1.8242% 1947 19.911801 0.050221 -2.6320% 1946 20.450054 0.048900 3.1768% 1945
19.820399 0.050453 6.4754% 1944 18.615000 0.053720 -0.3437% 1943 18.679196 0.053535
0.6562% 1942 18.557418 0.053887 0.6633% 1941 18.435138 0.054244 -5.6614% 1940
19.541464 0.051173 8.0381% 1939 18.087566 0.055287 0.8126% 1938 17.941765 0.055736
0.7762% 1937 17.803566 0.056169 0.6029% 1936 17.696876 0.056507 0.5244% 1935
17.604558 0.056803 -3.0364% 1934 18.155837 0.055079 4.6271% 1933 17.352897 0.057627

302

1.3921% 1932 17.114641 0.058430 -0.2051% 1931 17.149813 0.058310 0.8886% 1930
16.998762 0.058828 1.0126% 1929 16.828360 0.059423 1.1526% 1928 16.636608 0.060108
1.2160% 1927 16.436737 0.060839 1.4086% 1926 16.208428 0.061696 1.7667% 1925
15.927047 0.062786 1.4465% 1924 15.699947 0.063694 1.7700% 1923 15.426895 0.064822
1.6165% 1922 15.181483 0.065870 1.3736% 1921 14.975770 0.066775 2.3393% 1920
14.633448 0.068337 1.3140% 1919 14.443657 0.069235 0.7676% 1918 14.333626 0.069766
0.3870% 1917 14.278370 0.070036 1.3274% 1916 14.091317 0.070966 1.4083% 1915
13.895626 0.071965 1.4458% 1914 13.697586 0.073006 1.9424% 1913 13.436596 0.074424
1.9857% 1912 13.174984 0.075901 1.5634% 1911 12.972176 0.077088 1.8169% 1910
12.740689 0.078489 1.8781% 1909 12.505822 0.079963 2.0082% 1908 12.259619 0.081569
1.9603% 1907 12.023920 0.083168 1.8264% 1906 11.808259 0.084686 1.9357% 1905
11.584030 0.086326 2.0148% 1904 11.355241 0.088065 2.1335% 1903 11.118034 0.089944
1.8151% 1902 10.919823 0.091577 1.8943% 1901 10.716810 0.093311 3.0255% 1900
10.402094 0.096134 0.6278% 1899 10.337193 0.096738 1.7757% 1898 10.156843 0.098456
1.8078% 1897 9.976492 0.100236 1.8396% 1896 9.796280 0.102080 1.8755% 1895 9.615929
0.103994 1.9114% 1894 9.435579 0.105982 1.9486% 1893 9.255228 0.108047 1.9858% 1892
9.075016 0.110193 2.0276% 1891 8.894666 0.112427 2.6465% 1890 8.665336 0.115402
1.5328% 1889 8.534517 0.117171 2.0811% 1888 8.360524 0.119610 2.1599% 1887 8.183767
0.122193 2.2075% 1886 8.007009 0.124891 2.2592% 1885 7.830114 0.127712 2.3095% 1884
7.653357 0.130662 2.3641% 1883 7.476599 0.133751 2.4214% 1882 7.299842 0.136989
2.4815% 1881 7.123085 0.140389 3.7644% 1880 6.864671 0.145673 0.9432% 1879 6.800527
0.147047 2.1464% 1878 6.657628 0.150204 2.1913% 1877 6.514868 0.153495 2.2426% 1876
6.371970 0.156937 2.2941% 1875 6.229071 0.160538 2.3456% 1874 6.086311 0.164303
2.4043% 1873 5.943413 0.168253 2.4635% 1872 5.800514 0.172399 2.5258% 1871 5.657616
0.176753 5.9947% 1870 5.337642 0.187349 -1.0968% 1869 5.396833 0.185294 2.1930%
1868 5.281022 0.189357 2.2394% 1867 5.165349 0.193598 2.2935% 1866 5.049538 0.198038
2.3445% 1865 4.933865 0.202681 2.4037% 1864 4.818053 0.207553 2.4599% 1863 4.702380
0.212658 2.5250% 1862 4.586569 0.218028 2.5872% 1861 4.470896 0.223669 2.9504% 1860
4.342767 0.230268 2.4012% 1859 4.240932 0.235797 2.7627% 1858 4.126917 0.242312
2.8412% 1857 4.012902 0.249196 2.9243% 1856 3.898888 0.256483 3.0161% 1855 3.784735
0.264219 3.1061% 1854 3.670720 0.272426 3.2056% 1853 3.556705 0.281159 3.3118% 1852
3.442691 0.290470 3.4252% 1851 3.328676 0.300420 4.0106% 1850 3.200324 0.312468
2.3254% 1849 3.127596 0.319734 2.7841% 1848 3.042879 0.328636 2.8590% 1847 2.958301
0.338032 2.9432% 1846 2.873723 0.347981 3.0324% 1845 2.789145 0.358533 3.1325% 1844
2.704428 0.369764 3.2284% 1843 2.619850 0.381701 3.3361% 1842 2.535272 0.394435
3.4512% 1841 2.450694 0.408048 3.8105% 1840 2.360738 0.423596 2.3861% 1839 2.305722
0.433704 2.5824% 1838 2.247679 0.444903 2.6573% 1837 2.189497 0.456726 2.7232% 1836
2.131453 0.469164 2.7994% 1835 2.073409 0.482298 2.8871% 1834 2.015227 0.496222
2.9657% 1833 1.957183 0.510938 3.0563% 1832 1.899139 0.526554 3.1604% 1831 1.840957
0.543196 3.4660% 1830 1.779288 0.562023 2.4653% 1829 1.736478 0.575878 2.6804% 1828
1.691149 0.591314 10.3427% 1827 1.532634 0.652472 -4.2314% 1826 1.600352 0.624863
2.9150% 1825 1.555022 0.643078 3.0026% 1824 1.509693 0.662386 3.0955% 1823 1.464363
0.682891 3.1944% 1822 1.419034 0.704705 3.3102% 1821 1.373566 0.728032 3.2277% 1820
1.330617 0.751531 2.6573% 1819 1.296174 0.771501 2.6261% 1818 1.263006 0.791762
2.6969% 1817 1.229838 0.813115 2.7717% 1816 1.196670 0.835652 2.8507% 1815 1.163503
0.859474 2.9343% 1814 1.130335 0.884694 3.0231% 1813 1.097167 0.911438 3.1039% 1812
1.064137 0.939729 3.2172% 1811 1.030969 0.969961 3.0969% 1810 1.000000 1.000000
2.9144% 1809 0.971682 1.029144 2.8225% 1808 0.945009 1.058191 2.9199% 1807 0.918198
1.089089 2.9918% 1806 0.891526 1.121673 3.0841% 1805 0.864853 1.156266 3.1822% 1804
0.838181 1.193060 3.2868% 1803 0.811508 1.232274 3.3985% 1802 0.784836 1.274152
3.5180% 1801 0.758163 1.318977 3.3999% 1800 0.733234 1.363822 2.8419% 1799 0.712972
1.402580 2.7485% 1798 0.693900 1.441129 2.8261% 1797 0.674829 1.481857 3.7832% 1796
0.650229 1.537919 2.1272% 1795 0.636686 1.570634 3.0879% 1794 0.617614 1.619134
3.1625% 1793 0.598681 1.670339 3.2904% 1792 0.579609 1.725300 3.4024% 1791 0.560538
1.784001 3.2296% 1790 0.543001 1.841617 41.3145% 1780 0.384250 2.602471 29.4353%
1770 0.296867 3.368516 83.4728% 1750 0.161804 6.180313 29.2845% 1740 0.125154

303

7.990183 94.2514% 1720 0.064429 15.521042 85.8111% 1700 0.034674 28.839817 19.2490% 1690 0.029077 34.391207 88.0250% 1670 0.015465 64.664075

2009 42.871618 0.023325 8.2857% 2001 39.591224 0.025258 1.0000% 2000 39.199228 0.025511 1.0000% 1999 38.811117 0.025766 1.0000% 1998 38.426848 0.026023 1.0000% 1997 38.046384 0.026284 1.0000% 1996 37.669688 0.026547 1.0000% 1995 37.296720 0.026812 0.9992% 1994 36.927730 0.027080 1.0008% 1993 36.561828 0.027351 1.0000% 1992 36.199829 0.027624 0.9295% 1991 35.866449 0.027881 1.2505% 1990 35.423473 0.028230 0.7224% 1989 35.169393 0.028434 1.1077% 1988 34.784099 0.028749 0.8834% 1987 34.479519 0.029003 0.5594% 1986 34.287726 0.029165 1.3056% 1985 33.845826 0.029546 0.7673% 1984 33.588110 0.029772 0.8149% 1983 33.316598 0.030015 0.9737% 1982 32.995306 0.030307 0.9508% 1981 32.684540 0.030596 0.9031% 1980 32.392019 0.030872 2.2701% 1979 31.673019 0.031573 1.0042% 1978 31.358128 0.031890 0.9896% 1977 31.050846 0.032205 0.9103% 1976 30.770730 0.032498 0.8394% 1975 30.514578 0.032771 0.9042% 1974 30.241146 0.033068 1.1568% 1973 29.895321 0.033450 0.9427% 1972 29.616129 0.033765 0.7426% 1971 29.397810 0.034016 1.4697% 1970 28.971997 0.034516 0.6968% 1969 28.771512 0.034757 0.8565% 1968 28.527165 0.035054 1.5090% 1967 28.103079 0.035583 0.9949% 1966 27.826234 0.035937 1.0575% 1965 27.535059 0.036317 1.1300% 1964 27.227386 0.036728 1.5537% 1963 26.810838 0.037298 1.4658% 1962 26.423517 0.037845 1.5364% 1961 26.023681 0.038427 2.1586% 1960 25.473793 0.039256 -1.6655% 1959 25.905241 0.038602 4.3080% 1958 24.835336 0.040265 2.1130% 1957 24.321434 0.041116 1.9895% 1956 23.846999 0.041934 2.1231% 1955 23.351230 0.042824 1.4496% 1954 23.017565 0.043445 2.1573% 1953 22.531503 0.044382 1.2298% 1952 22.257787 0.044928 1.6814% 1951 21.889738 0.045684 1.6233% 1950 21.540084 0.046425 1.4265% 1949 21.237128 0.047087 1.7790% 1948 20.865915 0.047925 1.8242% 1947 20.492106 0.048799 -2.6320% 1946 21.046046 0.047515 3.1768% 1945 20.398041 0.049024 6.4754% 1944 19.157512 0.052199 -0.3437% 1943 19.223579 0.052019 0.6562% 1942 19.098252 0.052361 0.6633% 1941 18.972408 0.052708 -5.6614% 1940 20.110976 0.049724 8.0381% 1939 18.614706 0.053721 0.8126% 1938 18.464657 0.054158 0.7762% 1937 18.322429 0.054578 0.6029% 1936 18.212630 0.054907 0.5244% 1935 18.117622 0.055195 -3.0364% 1934 18.684967 0.053519 4.6271% 1933 17.858626 0.055995 1.3921% 1932 17.613426 0.056775 -0.2051% 1931 17.649623 0.056658 0.8886% 1930 17.494170 0.057162 1.0126% 1929 17.318802 0.057741 1.1526% 1928 17.121462 0.058406 1.2160% 1927 16.915766 0.059116 1.4086% 1926 16.680803 0.059949 1.7667% 1925 16.391222 0.061008 1.4465% 1924 16.157503 0.061891 1.7700% 1923 15.876493 0.062986 1.6165% 1922 15.623929 0.064004 1.3736% 1921 15.412220 0.064884 2.3393% 1920 15.059922 0.066401 1.3140% 1919 14.864600 0.067274 0.7676% 1918 14.751362 0.067790 0.3870% 1917 14.694496 0.068053 1.3274% 1916 14.501991 0.068956 1.4083% 1915 14.300597 0.069927 1.4458% 1914 14.096786 0.070938 1.9424% 1913 13.828189 0.072316 1.9857% 1912 13.558953 0.073752 1.5634% 1911 13.350235 0.074905 1.8169% 1910 13.112001 0.076266 1.8781% 1909 12.870289 0.077698 2.0082% 1908 12.616911 0.079259 1.9603% 1907 12.374342 0.080812 1.8264% 1906 12.152397 0.082288 1.9357% 1905 11.921633 0.083881 2.0148% 1904 11.686176 0.085571 2.1335% 1903 11.442056 0.087397 1.8151% 1902 11.238068 0.088983 1.8943% 1901 11.029138 0.090669 3.0255% 1900 10.705251 0.093412 0.6278% 1899 10.638458 0.093999 1.7757% 1898 10.452852 0.095668 1.8078% 1897 10.267245 0.097397 1.8396% 1896 10.081781 0.099189 1.8755% 1895 9.896174 0.101049 1.9114% 1894 9.710567 0.102981 1.9486% 1893 9.524961 0.104987 1.9858% 1892 9.339497 0.107072 2.0276% 1891 9.153890 0.109243 2.6465% 1890 8.917877 0.112134 1.5328% 1889 8.783246 0.113853 2.0811% 1888 8.604181 0.116223 2.1599% 1887 8.422273 0.118733 2.2075% 1886 8.240364 0.121354 2.2592% 1885 8.058313 0.124095 2.3095% 1884 7.876404 0.126961 2.3641% 1883 7.694496 0.129963 2.4214% 1882 7.512587 0.133110 2.4815% 1881 7.330678 0.136413 3.7644% 1880 7.064734 0.141548 0.9432% 1879 6.998720 0.142883 2.1464% 1878 6.851657 0.145950 2.1913% 1877 6.704736 0.149148 2.2426% 1876 6.557673 0.152493 2.2941% 1875 6.410610 0.155991 2.3456% 1874 6.263689 0.159650 2.4043% 1873 6.116626 0.163489 2.4635% 1872 5.969563 0.167516 2.5258% 1871

304

5.822500 0.171748 5.9947% 1870 5.493201 0.182043 -1.0968% 1869 5.554117 0.180047
2.1930% 1868 5.434931 0.183995 2.2394% 1867 5.315887 0.188115 2.2935% 1866 5.196700
0.192430 2.3445% 1865 5.077656 0.196941 2.4037% 1864 4.958470 0.201675 2.4599% 1863
4.839425 0.206636 2.5250% 1862 4.720239 0.211854 2.5872% 1861 4.601195 0.217335
2.9504% 1860 4.469331 0.223747 2.4012% 1859 4.364529 0.229120 2.7627% 1858 4.247191
0.235450 2.8412% 1857 4.129854 0.242139 2.9243% 1856 4.012516 0.249220 3.0161% 1855
3.895036 0.256737 3.1061% 1854 3.777699 0.264711 3.2056% 1853 3.660361 0.273197
3.3118% 1852 3.543024 0.282245 3.4252% 1851 3.425686 0.291912 4.0106% 1850 3.293593
0.303620 2.3254% 1849 3.218746 0.310680 2.7841% 1848 3.131560 0.319330 2.8590% 1847
3.044517 0.328459 2.9432% 1846 2.957474 0.338126 3.0324% 1845 2.870431 0.348380
3.1325% 1844 2.783246 0.359293 3.2284% 1843 2.696203 0.370892 3.3361% 1842 2.609159
0.383265 3.4512% 1841 2.522116 0.396492 3.8105% 1840 2.429539 0.411601 2.3861% 1839
2.372920 0.421422 2.5824% 1838 2.313184 0.432304 2.6573% 1837 2.253307 0.443792
2.7232% 1836 2.193571 0.455878 2.7994% 1835 2.133836 0.468640 2.8871% 1834 2.073958
0.482170 2.9657% 1833 2.014223 0.496469 3.0563% 1832 1.954487 0.511643 3.1604% 1831
1.894610 0.527813 3.4660% 1830 1.831143 0.546107 2.4653% 1829 1.787086 0.559570
2.6804% 1828 1.740435 0.574569 10.3427% 1827 1.577301 0.633995 -4.2314% 1826
1.646992 0.607168 2.9150% 1825 1.600341 0.624867 3.0026% 1824 1.553691 0.643629
3.0955% 1823 1.507040 0.663552 3.1944% 1822 1.460390 0.684749 3.3102% 1821 1.413597
0.707415 3.2277% 1820 1.369396 0.730249 2.6573% 1819 1.333950 0.749653 2.6261% 1818
1.299815 0.769340 2.6969% 1817 1.265681 0.790089 2.7717% 1816 1.231546 0.811988
2.8507% 1815 1.197411 0.835135 2.9343% 1814 1.163277 0.859641 3.0231% 1813 1.129142
0.885628 3.1039% 1812 1.095150 0.913117 3.2172% 1811 1.061016 0.942493 3.0969% 1810
1.029144 0.971682 2.9144% 1809 1.000000 1.000000 2.8225% 1808 0.972550 1.028225
2.9199% 1807 0.944958 1.058248 2.9918% 1806 0.917508 1.089909 3.0841% 1805 0.890058
1.123522 3.1822% 1804 0.862608 1.159275 3.2868% 1803 0.835159 1.197377 3.3985% 1802
0.807709 1.238070 3.5180% 1801 0.780259 1.281626 3.3999% 1800 0.754603 1.325201
2.8419% 1799 0.733751 1.362861 2.7485% 1798 0.714123 1.400319 2.8261% 1797 0.694496
1.439894 3.7832% 1796 0.669179 1.494368 2.1272% 1795 0.655241 1.526156 3.0879% 1794
0.635614 1.573283 3.1625% 1793 0.616129 1.623038 3.2904% 1792 0.596501 1.676443
3.4024% 1791 0.576874 1.733481 3.2296% 1790 0.558826 1.789465 41.3145% 1780
0.395449 2.528773 29.4353% 1770 0.305518 3.273125 83.4728% 1750 0.166520 6.005296
29.2845% 1740 0.128801 7.763913 94.2514% 1720 0.066306 15.081510 85.8111% 1700
0.035685 28.023117 19.2490% 1690 0.029925 33.417300 88.0250% 1670 0.015915
62.832887

BASE YEAR: 1808

YEAR BYEAR/AYEAR AYEAR/BYEAR GROWTH%

2009 44.081654 0.022685 8.2857% 2001 40.708672 0.024565 1.0000% 2000
40.305612 0.024810 1.0000% 1999 39.906546 0.025059 1.0000% 1998 39.511432 0.025309
1.0000% 1997 39.120229 0.025562 1.0000% 1996 38.732900 0.025818 1.0000% 1995
38.349406 0.026076 0.9992% 1994 37.970002 0.026337 1.0008% 1993 37.593772 0.026600
1.0000% 1992 37.221556 0.026866 0.9295% 1991 36.878766 0.027116 1.2505% 1990
36.423287 0.027455 0.7224% 1989 36.162036 0.027653 1.1077% 1988 35.765867 0.027960
0.8834% 1987 35.452691 0.028207 0.5594% 1986 35.255484 0.028364 1.3056% 1985
34.801111 0.028735 0.7673% 1984 34.536122 0.028955 0.8149% 1983 34.256946 0.029191
0.9737% 1982 33.926587 0.029475 0.9508% 1981 33.607049 0.029756 0.9031% 1980
33.306271 0.030024 2.2701% 1979 32.566979 0.030706 1.0042% 1978 32.243200 0.031014
0.9896% 1977 31.927245 0.031321 0.9103% 1976 31.639222 0.031606 0.8394% 1975
31.375841 0.031872 0.9042% 1974 31.094691 0.032160 1.1568% 1973 30.739105 0.032532
0.9427% 1972 30.452033 0.032839 0.7426% 1971 30.227552 0.033082 1.4697% 1970
29.789721 0.033569 0.6968% 1969 29.583577 0.033803 0.8565% 1968 29.332334 0.034092
1.5090% 1967 28.896278 0.034607 0.9949% 1966 28.611619 0.034951 1.0575% 1965
28.312226 0.035320 1.1300% 1964 27.995869 0.035720 1.5537% 1963 27.567564 0.036275
1.4658% 1962 27.169311 0.036806 1.5364% 1961 26.758190 0.037372 2.1586% 1960
26.192782 0.038178 -1.6655% 1959 26.636407 0.037543 4.3080% 1958 25.536304 0.039160
2.1130% 1957 25.007897 0.039987 1.9895% 1956 24.520072 0.040783 2.1231% 1955

305

24.010310 0.041649 1.4496% 1954 23.667227 0.042253 2.1573% 1953 23.167447 0.043164 1.2298% 1952 22.886005 0.043695 1.6814% 1951 22.507568 0.044430 1.6233% 1950 22.148045 0.045151 1.4265% 1949 21.836538 0.045795 1.7790% 1948 21.454848 0.046610 1.8242% 1947 21.070488 0.047460 -2.6320% 1946 21.640063 0.046211 3.1768% 1945 20.973768 0.047679 6.4754% 1944 19.698226 0.050766 -0.3437% 1943 19.766157 0.050592 0.6562% 1942 19.637293 0.050924 0.6633% 1941 19.507897 0.051261 -5.6614% 1940 20.678601 0.048359 8.0381% 1939 19.140099 0.052246 0.8126% 1938 18.985815 0.052671 0.7762% 1937 18.839573 0.053080 0.6029% 1936 18.726674 0.053400 0.5244% 1935 18.628985 0.053680 -3.0364% 1934 19.212343 0.052050 4.6271% 1933 18.362679 0.054458 1.3921% 1932 18.110559 0.055216 -0.2051% 1931 18.147777 0.055103 0.8886% 1930 17.987937 0.055593 1.0126% 1929 17.807619 0.056156 1.1526% 1928 17.604709 0.056803 1.2160% 1927 17.393207 0.057494 1.4086% 1926 17.151613 0.058304 1.7667% 1925 16.853858 0.059334 1.4465% 1924 16.613542 0.060192 1.7700% 1923 16.324601 0.061257 1.6165% 1922 16.064909 0.062247 1.3736% 1921 15.847224 0.063103 2.3393% 1920 15.484982 0.064579 1.3140% 1919 15.284147 0.065427 0.7676% 1918 15.167714 0.065930 0.3870% 1917 15.109242 0.066185 1.3274% 1916 14.911304 0.067063 1.4083% 1915 14.704226 0.068008 1.4458% 1914 14.494662 0.068991 1.9424% 1913 14.218485 0.070331 1.9857% 1912 13.941650 0.071728 1.5634% 1911 13.727040 0.072849 1.8169% 1910 13.482082 0.074173 1.8781% 1909 13.233548 0.075566 2.0082% 1908 12.973018 0.077083 1.9603% 1907 12.723603 0.078594 1.8264% 1906 12.495393 0.080029 1.9357% 1905 12.258116 0.081579 2.0148% 1904 12.016013 0.083222 2.1335% 1903 11.765004 0.084998 1.8151% 1902 11.555259 0.086541 1.8943% 1901 11.340431 0.088180 3.0255% 1900 11.007402 0.090848 0.6278% 1899 10.938725 0.091418 1.7757% 1898 10.747879 0.093042 1.8078% 1897 10.557034 0.094724 1.8396% 1896 10.366335 0.096466 1.8755% 1895 10.175490 0.098275 1.9114% 1894 9.984645 0.100154 1.9486% 1893 9.793799 0.102105 1.9858% 1892 9.603100 0.104133 2.0276% 1891 9.412255 0.106244 2.6465% 1890 9.169581 0.109056 1.5328% 1889 9.031149 0.110728 2.0811% 1888 8.847031 0.113032 2.1599% 1887 8.659988 0.115474 2.2075% 1886 8.472945 0.118023 2.2592% 1885 8.285756 0.120689 2.3095% 1884 8.098713 0.123476 2.3641% 1883 7.911670 0.126396 2.4214% 1882 7.724627 0.129456 2.4815% 1881 7.537584 0.132669 3.7644% 1880 7.264133 0.137663 0.9432% 1879 7.196256 0.138961 2.1464% 1878 7.045042 0.141944 2.1913% 1877 6.893975 0.145054 2.2426% 1876 6.742761 0.148307 2.2941% 1875 6.591547 0.151709 2.3456% 1874 6.440480 0.155268 2.4043% 1873 6.289266 0.159001 2.4635% 1872 6.138052 0.162918 2.5258% 1871 5.986838 0.167033 5.9947% 1870 5.648244 0.177046 -1.0968% 1869 5.710880 0.175104 2.1930% 1868 5.588330 0.178944 2.2394% 1867 5.465926 0.182952 2.2935% 1866 5.343375 0.187148 2.3445% 1865 5.220971 0.191535 2.4037% 1864 5.098421 0.196139 2.4599% 1863 4.976016 0.200964 2.5250% 1862 4.853466 0.206038 2.5872% 1861 4.731062 0.211369 2.9504% 1860 4.595476 0.217605 2.4012% 1859 4.487716 0.222831 2.7627% 1858 4.367066 0.228987 2.8412% 1857 4.246417 0.235493 2.9243% 1856 4.125768 0.242379 3.0161% 1855 4.004972 0.249690 3.1061% 1854 3.884323 0.257445 3.2056% 1853 3.763674 0.265698 3.3118% 1852 3.643024 0.274497 3.4252% 1851 3.522375 0.283899 4.0106% 1850 3.386554 0.295285 2.3254% 1849 3.309593 0.302152 2.7841% 1848 3.219947 0.310564 2.8590% 1847 3.130447 0.319443 2.9432% 1846 3.040948 0.328845 3.0324% 1845 2.951448 0.338817 3.1325% 1844 2.861802 0.349430 3.2284% 1843 2.772302 0.360711 3.3361% 1842 2.682802 0.372745 3.4512% 1841 2.593302 0.385609 3.8105% 1840 2.498112 0.400302 2.3861% 1839 2.439895 0.409854 2.5824% 1838 2.378473 0.420438 2.6573% 1837 2.316906 0.431610 2.7232% 1836 2.255484 0.443364 2.7994% 1835 2.194063 0.455776 2.8871% 1834 2.132495 0.468934 2.9657% 1833 2.071073 0.482841 3.0563% 1832 2.009652 0.497599 3.1604% 1831 1.948084 0.513325 3.4660% 1830 1.882826 0.531116 2.4653% 1829 1.837526 0.544210 2.6804% 1828 1.789558 0.558797 10.3427% 1827 1.621819 0.616592 -4.2314% 1826 1.693478 0.590501 2.9150% 1825 1.645510 0.607714 3.0026% 1824 1.597543 0.625961 3.0955% 1823 1.549576 0.645338 3.1944% 1822 1.501609 0.665952 3.3102% 1821 1.453495 0.687997 3.2277% 1820 1.408047 0.710204 2.6573% 1819 1.371600 0.729076 2.6261% 1818 1.336502 0.748222 2.6969% 1817 1.301404 0.768401 2.7717% 1816 1.266306 0.789699 2.8507% 1815 1.231208 0.812210 2.9343% 1814 1.196110 0.836044 3.0231% 1813 1.161012 0.861318 3.1039% 1812 1.126060 0.888052 3.2172% 1811 1.090962 0.916622 3.0969% 1810

1.058191 0.945009 2.9144% 1809 1.028225 0.972550 2.8225% 1808 1.000000 1.000000
2.9199% 1807 0.971629 1.029199 2.9918% 1806 0.943405 1.059991 3.0841% 1805 0.915180
1.092681 3.1822% 1804 0.886955 1.127453 3.2868% 1803 0.858731 1.164510 3.3985% 1802
0.830506 1.204085 3.5180% 1801 0.802281 1.246445 3.3999% 1800 0.775901 1.288824
2.8419% 1799 0.754460 1.325451 2.7485% 1798 0.734279 1.361880 2.8261% 1797 0.714098
1.400369 3.7832% 1796 0.688067 1.453348 2.1272% 1795 0.673735 1.484263 3.0879% 1794
0.653554 1.530096 3.1625% 1793 0.633519 1.578486 3.2904% 1792 0.613337 1.630424
3.4024% 1791 0.593156 1.685897 3.2296% 1790 0.574599 1.740345 41.3145% 1780
0.406610 2.459358 29.4353% 1770 0.314142 3.183278 83.4728% 1750 0.171220 5.840451
29.2845% 1740 0.132436 7.550795 94.2514% 1720 0.068178 14.667525 85.8111% 1700
0.036692 27.253886 19.2490% 1690 0.030769 32.500000 88.0250% 1670 0.016364
61.108132

BASE YEAR: 1807

YEAR BYEAR/AYEAR AYEAR/BYEAR GROWTH%

2009 45.368806 0.022042 8.2857% 2001 41.897336 0.023868 1.0000% 2000
41.482506 0.024107 1.0000% 1999 41.071788 0.024348 1.0000% 1998 40.665137 0.024591
1.0000% 1997 40.262512 0.024837 1.0000% 1996 39.863873 0.025085 1.0000% 1995
39.469181 0.025336 0.9992% 1994 39.078698 0.025589 1.0008% 1993 38.691483 0.025845
1.0000% 1992 38.308399 0.026104 0.9295% 1991 37.955599 0.026347 1.2505% 1990
37.486821 0.026676 0.7224% 1989 37.217941 0.026869 1.1077% 1988 36.810205 0.027166
0.8834% 1987 36.487884 0.027406 0.5594% 1986 36.284919 0.027560 1.3056% 1985
35.817279 0.027919 0.7673% 1984 35.544551 0.028134 0.8149% 1983 35.257225 0.028363
0.9737% 1982 34.917219 0.028639 0.9508% 1981 34.588350 0.028911 0.9031% 1980
34.278790 0.029173 2.2701% 1979 33.517911 0.029835 1.0042% 1978 33.184678 0.030134
0.9896% 1977 32.859497 0.030433 0.9103% 1976 32.563064 0.030710 0.8394% 1975
32.291993 0.030967 0.9042% 1974 32.002634 0.031247 1.1568% 1973 31.636665 0.031609
0.9427% 1972 31.341210 0.031907 0.7426% 1971 31.110175 0.032144 1.4697% 1970
30.659560 0.032616 0.6968% 1969 30.447396 0.032844 0.8565% 1968 30.188817 0.033125
1.5090% 1967 29.740029 0.033625 0.9949% 1966 29.447057 0.033959 1.0575% 1965
29.138922 0.034318 1.1300% 1964 28.813328 0.034706 1.5537% 1963 28.372517 0.035245
1.4658% 1962 27.962635 0.035762 1.5364% 1961 27.539509 0.036311 2.1586% 1960
26.957592 0.037095 -1.6655% 1959 27.414171 0.036477 4.3080% 1958 26.281946 0.038049
2.1130% 1957 25.738110 0.038853 1.9895% 1956 25.236040 0.039626 2.1231% 1955
24.711394 0.040467 1.4496% 1954 24.358293 0.041054 2.1573% 1953 23.843919 0.041939
1.2298% 1952 23.554259 0.042455 1.6814% 1951 23.164773 0.043169 1.6233% 1950
22.794752 0.043870 1.4265% 1949 22.474150 0.044496 1.7790% 1948 22.081314 0.045287
1.8242% 1947 21.685731 0.046113 -2.6320% 1946 22.271937 0.044900 3.1768% 1945
21.586187 0.046326 6.4754% 1944 20.273400 0.049326 -0.3437% 1943 20.343315 0.049156
0.6562% 1942 20.210688 0.049479 0.6633% 1941 20.077514 0.049807 -5.6614% 1940
21.282401 0.046987 8.0381% 1939 19.698977 0.050764 0.8126% 1938 19.540187 0.051177
0.7762% 1937 19.389675 0.051574 0.6029% 1936 19.273480 0.051885 0.5244% 1935
19.172938 0.052157 -3.0364% 1934 19.773329 0.050573 4.6271% 1933 18.898856 0.052913
1.3921% 1932 18.639374 0.053650 -0.2051% 1931 18.677679 0.053540 0.8886% 1930
18.513171 0.054016 1.0126% 1929 18.327589 0.054563 1.1526% 1928 18.118754 0.055191
1.2160% 1927 17.901076 0.055863 1.4086% 1926 17.652427 0.056649 1.7667% 1925
17.345978 0.057650 1.4465% 1924 17.098646 0.058484 1.7700% 1923 16.801268 0.059519
1.6165% 1922 16.533993 0.060481 1.3736% 1921 16.309952 0.061312 2.3393% 1920
15.937133 0.062747 1.3140% 1919 15.730433 0.063571 0.7676% 1918 15.610600 0.064059
0.3870% 1917 15.550421 0.064307 1.3274% 1916 15.346704 0.065161 1.4083% 1915
15.133579 0.066078 1.4458% 1914 14.917896 0.067034 1.9424% 1913 14.633654 0.068336
1.9857% 1912 14.348736 0.069693 1.5634% 1911 14.127860 0.070782 1.8169% 1910
13.875749 0.072068 1.8781% 1909 13.619958 0.073422 2.0082% 1908 13.351821 0.074896
1.9603% 1907 13.095123 0.076364 1.8264% 1906 12.860250 0.077759 1.9357% 1905
12.616045 0.079264 2.0148% 1904 12.366872 0.080861 2.1335% 1903 12.108534 0.082586
1.8151% 1902 11.892664 0.084085 1.8943% 1901 11.671564 0.085678 3.0255% 1900
11.328811 0.088271 0.6278% 1899 11.258128 0.088825 1.7757% 1898 11.061710 0.090402

307

1.8078% 1897 10.865292 0.092036 1.8396% 1896 10.669025 0.093729 1.8755% 1895
10.472607 0.095487 1.9114% 1894 10.276189 0.097312 1.9486% 1893 10.079771 0.099209
1.9858% 1892 9.883504 0.101179 2.0276% 1891 9.687086 0.103230 2.6465% 1890 9.437326
0.105962 1.5328% 1889 9.294852 0.107586 2.0811% 1888 9.105358 0.109825 2.1599% 1887
8.912854 0.112198 2.2075% 1886 8.720349 0.114674 2.2592% 1885 8.527694 0.117265
2.3095% 1884 8.335190 0.119973 2.3641% 1883 8.142685 0.122810 2.4214% 1882 7.950181
0.125783 2.4815% 1881 7.757676 0.128905 3.7644% 1880 7.476241 0.133757 0.9432% 1879
7.406382 0.135019 2.1464% 1878 7.250753 0.137917 2.1913% 1877 7.095274 0.140939
2.2426% 1876 6.939645 0.144100 2.2941% 1875 6.784016 0.147405 2.3456% 1874 6.628537
0.150863 2.4043% 1873 6.472908 0.154490 2.4635% 1872 6.317279 0.158296 2.5258% 1871
6.161650 0.162294 5.9947% 1870 5.813169 0.172023 -1.0968% 1869 5.877634 0.170136
2.1930% 1868 5.751505 0.173868 2.2394% 1867 5.625527 0.177761 2.2935% 1866 5.499398
0.181838 2.3445% 1865 5.373420 0.186101 2.4037% 1864 5.247291 0.190575 2.4599% 1863
5.121312 0.195262 2.5250% 1862 4.995184 0.200193 2.5872% 1861 4.869205 0.205372
2.9504% 1860 4.729661 0.211432 2.4012% 1859 4.618754 0.216509 2.7627% 1858 4.494582
0.222490 2.8412% 1857 4.370409 0.228812 2.9243% 1856 4.246237 0.235503 3.0161% 1855
4.121915 0.242606 3.1061% 1854 3.997742 0.250141 3.2056% 1853 3.873570 0.258160
3.3118% 1852 3.749398 0.266709 3.4252% 1851 3.625226 0.275845 4.0106% 1850 3.485439
0.286908 2.3254% 1849 3.406231 0.293580 2.7841% 1848 3.313967 0.301753 2.8590% 1847
3.221854 0.310380 2.9432% 1846 3.129741 0.319515 3.0324% 1845 3.037628 0.329204
3.1325% 1844 2.945364 0.339517 3.2284% 1843 2.853251 0.350477 3.3361% 1842 2.761138
0.362170 3.4512% 1841 2.669025 0.374669 3.8105% 1840 2.571055 0.388945 2.3861% 1839
2.511138 0.398226 2.5824% 1838 2.447923 0.408510 2.6573% 1837 2.384557 0.419365
2.7232% 1836 2.321343 0.430785 2.7994% 1835 2.258128 0.442845 2.8871% 1834 2.194762
0.455630 2.9657% 1833 2.131547 0.469143 3.0563% 1832 2.068332 0.483481 3.1604% 1831
2.004967 0.498761 3.4660% 1830 1.937803 0.516048 2.4653% 1829 1.891180 0.528770
2.6804% 1828 1.841812 0.542944 10.3427% 1827 1.669175 0.599098 -4.2314% 1826
1.742926 0.573748 2.9150% 1825 1.693558 0.590473 3.0026% 1824 1.644190 0.608202
3.0955% 1823 1.594822 0.627029 3.1944% 1822 1.545455 0.647059 3.3102% 1821 1.495936
0.668478 3.2277% 1820 1.449161 0.690054 2.6573% 1819 1.411650 0.708391 2.6261% 1818
1.375527 0.726994 2.6969% 1817 1.339404 0.746601 2.7717% 1816 1.303281 0.767294
2.8507% 1815 1.267158 0.789167 2.9343% 1814 1.231036 0.812324 3.0231% 1813 1.194913
0.836881 3.1039% 1812 1.158940 0.862857 3.2172% 1811 1.122818 0.890617 3.0969% 1810
1.089089 0.918198 2.9144% 1809 1.058248 0.944958 2.8225% 1808 1.029199 0.971629
2.9199% 1807 1.000000 1.000000 2.9918% 1806 0.970951 1.029918 3.0841% 1805 0.941902
1.061681 3.1822% 1804 0.912854 1.095466 3.2868% 1803 0.883805 1.131471 3.3985% 1802
0.854756 1.169924 3.5180% 1801 0.825707 1.211083 3.3999% 1800 0.798557 1.252259
2.8419% 1799 0.776490 1.287846 2.7485% 1798 0.755719 1.323242 2.8261% 1797 0.734949
1.360639 3.7832% 1796 0.708158 1.412115 2.1272% 1795 0.693408 1.442153 3.0879% 1794
0.672637 1.486686 3.1625% 1793 0.652017 1.533703 3.2904% 1792 0.631246 1.584168
3.4024% 1791 0.610476 1.638067 3.2296% 1790 0.591377 1.690969 41.3145% 1780
0.418483 2.389584 29.4353% 1770 0.323314 3.092966 83.4728% 1750 0.176219 5.674752
29.2845% 1740 0.136303 7.336572 94.2514% 1720 0.070169 14.251394 85.8111% 1700
0.037763 26.480670 19.2490% 1690 0.031668 31.577947 88.0250% 1670 0.016842
59.374441

BASE YEAR: 1806
YEAR BYEAR/AYEAR AYEAR/BYEAR GROWTH%

2009 46.726143 0.021401 8.2857% 2001 43.150814 0.023175 1.0000% 2000
42.723573 0.023406 1.0000% 1999 42.300568 0.023640 1.0000% 1998 41.881750 0.023877
1.0000% 1997 41.467079 0.024116 1.0000% 1996 41.056514 0.024357 1.0000% 1995
40.650014 0.024600 0.9992% 1994 40.247849 0.024846 1.0008% 1993 39.849048 0.025095
1.0000% 1992 39.454503 0.025346 0.9295% 1991 39.091149 0.025581 1.2505% 1990
38.608345 0.025901 0.7224% 1989 38.331421 0.026088 1.1077% 1988 37.911487 0.026377
0.8834% 1987 37.579523 0.026610 0.5594% 1986 37.370485 0.026759 1.3056% 1985
36.888854 0.027108 0.7673% 1984 36.607968 0.027316 0.8149% 1983 36.312045 0.027539
0.9737% 1982 35.961866 0.027807 0.9508% 1981 35.623159 0.028072 0.9031% 1980

308

35.304338 0.028325 2.2701% 1979 34.520694 0.028968 1.0042% 1978 34.177492 0.029259 0.9896% 1977 33.842583 0.029549 0.9103% 1976 33.537281 0.029818 0.8394% 1975 33.258100 0.030068 0.9042% 1974 32.960084 0.030340 1.1568% 1973 32.583165 0.030691 0.9427% 1972 32.278871 0.030980 0.7426% 1971 32.040924 0.031210 1.4697% 1970 31.576827 0.031669 0.6968% 1969 31.358317 0.031889 0.8565% 1968 31.092001 0.032163 1.5090% 1967 30.629786 0.032648 0.9949% 1966 30.328050 0.032973 1.0575% 1965 30.010696 0.033321 1.1300% 1964 29.675360 0.033698 1.5537% 1963 29.221361 0.034222 1.4658% 1962 28.799217 0.034723 1.5364% 1961 28.363432 0.035257 2.1586% 1960 27.764105 0.036018 -1.6655% 1959 28.234344 0.035418 4.3080% 1958 27.068245 0.036944 2.1130% 1957 26.508138 0.037724 1.9895% 1956 25.991048 0.038475 2.1231% 1955 25.450705 0.039292 1.4496% 1954 25.087041 0.039861 2.1573% 1953 24.557278 0.040721 1.2298% 1952 24.258952 0.041222 1.6814% 1951 23.857813 0.041915 1.6233% 1950 23.476721 0.042595 1.4265% 1949 23.146528 0.043203 1.7790% 1948 22.741939 0.043972 1.8242% 1947 22.334522 0.044774 -2.6320% 1946 22.938265 0.043595 3.1768% 1945 22.231999 0.044980 6.4754% 1944 20.879936 0.047893 -0.3437% 1943 20.951943 0.047728 0.6562% 1942 20.815348 0.048041 0.6633% 1941 20.678189 0.048360 -5.6614% 1940 21.919125 0.045622 8.0381% 1939 20.288327 0.049289 0.8126% 1938 20.124787 0.049690 0.7762% 1937 19.969772 0.050076 0.6029% 1936 19.850101 0.050378 0.5244% 1935 19.746551 0.050642 -3.0364% 1934 20.364905 0.049104 4.6271% 1933 19.464269 0.051376 1.3921% 1932 19.197024 0.052091 -0.2051% 1931 19.236475 0.051985 0.8886% 1930 19.067046 0.052447 1.0126% 1929 18.875911 0.052978 1.1526% 1928 18.660828 0.053588 1.2160% 1927 18.436638 0.054240 1.4086% 1926 18.180550 0.055004 1.7667% 1925 17.864933 0.055976 1.4465% 1924 17.610200 0.056785 1.7700% 1923 17.303926 0.057790 1.6165% 1922 17.028654 0.058725 1.3736% 1921 16.797911 0.059531 2.3393% 1920 16.413937 0.060924 1.3140% 1919 16.201054 0.061724 0.7676% 1918 16.077635 0.062198 0.3870% 1917 16.015656 0.062439 1.3274% 1916 15.805844 0.063268 1.4083% 1915 15.586343 0.064159 1.4458% 1914 15.364207 0.065086 1.9424% 1913 15.071462 0.066351 1.9857% 1912 14.778019 0.067668 1.5634% 1911 14.550535 0.068726 1.8169% 1910 14.290881 0.069975 1.8781% 1909 14.027438 0.071289 2.0082% 1908 13.751279 0.072721 1.9603% 1907 13.486901 0.074146 1.8264% 1906 13.245001 0.075500 1.9357% 1905 12.993489 0.076962 2.0148% 1904 12.736863 0.078512 2.1335% 1903 12.470795 0.080187 1.8151% 1902 12.248467 0.081643 1.8943% 1901 12.020752 0.083189 3.0255% 1900 11.667744 0.085706 0.6278% 1899 11.594947 0.086244 1.7757% 1898 11.392652 0.087776 1.8078% 1897 11.190358 0.089363 1.8396% 1896 10.988219 0.091007 1.8755% 1895 10.785925 0.092713 1.9114% 1894 10.583630 0.094486 1.9486% 1893 10.381336 0.096327 1.9858% 1892 10.179197 0.098240 2.0276% 1891 9.976903 0.100232 2.6465% 1890 9.719670 0.102884 1.5328% 1889 9.572934 0.104461 2.0811% 1888 9.377771 0.106635 2.1599% 1887 9.179507 0.108938 2.2075% 1886 8.981243 0.111343 2.2592% 1885 8.782824 0.113859 2.3095% 1884 8.584561 0.116488 2.3641% 1883 8.386297 0.119242 2.4214% 1882 8.188033 0.122129 2.4815% 1881 7.989769 0.125160 3.7644% 1880 7.699914 0.129872 0.9432% 1879 7.627965 0.131097 2.1464% 1878 7.467679 0.133910 2.1913% 1877 7.307549 0.136845 2.2426% 1876 7.147264 0.139914 2.2941% 1875 6.986979 0.143123 2.3456% 1874 6.826849 0.146480 2.4043% 1873 6.666563 0.150002 2.4635% 1872 6.506278 0.153698 2.5258% 1871 6.345993 0.157580 5.9947% 1870 5.987086 0.167026 -1.0968% 1869 6.053480 0.165194 2.1930% 1868 5.923578 0.168817 2.2394% 1867 5.793830 0.172597 2.2935% 1866 5.663928 0.176556 2.3445% 1865 5.534181 0.180695 2.4037% 1864 5.404278 0.185039 2.4599% 1863 5.274531 0.189590 2.5250% 1862 5.144629 0.194377 2.5872% 1861 5.014881 0.199407 2.9504% 1860 4.871162 0.205290 2.4012% 1859 4.756937 0.210219 2.7627% 1858 4.629050 0.216027 2.8412% 1857 4.501163 0.222165 2.9243% 1856 4.373275 0.228662 3.0161% 1855 4.245233 0.235558 3.1061% 1854 4.117346 0.242875 3.2056% 1853 3.989459 0.250661 3.3118% 1852 3.861572 0.258962 3.4252% 1851 3.733685 0.267832 4.0106% 1850 3.589715 0.278574 2.3254% 1849 3.508138 0.285051 2.7841% 1848 3.413114 0.292988 2.8590% 1847 3.318245 0.301364 2.9432% 1846 3.223376 0.310234 3.0324% 1845 3.128507 0.319641 3.1325% 1844 3.033483 0.329654 3.2284% 1843 2.938614 0.340296 3.3361% 1842 2.843745 0.351649 3.4512% 1841 2.748876 0.363785 3.8105% 1840 2.647975 0.377647 2.3861% 1839 2.586266 0.386658 2.5824% 1838 2.521160 0.396643 2.6573% 1837

2.455898 0.407183 2.7232% 1836 2.390792 0.418271 2.7994% 1835 2.325686 0.429981
2.8871% 1834 2.260425 0.442395 2.9657% 1833 2.195319 0.455515 3.0563% 1832 2.130212
0.469437 3.1604% 1831 2.064951 0.484273 3.4660% 1830 1.995778 0.501058 2.4653% 1829
1.947760 0.513410 2.6804% 1828 1.896915 0.527172 10.3427% 1827 1.719113 0.581695 -
4.2314% 1826 1.795071 0.557081 2.9150% 1825 1.744226 0.573320 3.0026% 1824 1.693381
0.590535 3.0955% 1823 1.642536 0.608815 3.1944% 1822 1.591691 0.628263 3.3102% 1821
1.540691 0.649059 3.2277% 1820 1.492517 0.670009 2.6573% 1819 1.453883 0.687813
2.6261% 1818 1.416680 0.705876 2.6969% 1817 1.379476 0.724913 2.7717% 1816 1.342273
0.745005 2.8507% 1815 1.305069 0.766243 2.9343% 1814 1.267865 0.788727 3.0231% 1813
1.230662 0.812571 3.1039% 1812 1.193613 0.837792 3.2172% 1811 1.156410 0.864745
3.0969% 1810 1.121673 0.891526 2.9144% 1809 1.089909 0.917508 2.8225% 1808 1.059991
0.943405 2.9199% 1807 1.029918 0.970951 2.9918% 1806 1.000000 1.000000 3.0841% 1805
0.970082 1.030841 3.1822% 1804 0.940164 1.063644 3.2868% 1803 0.910246 1.098604
3.3985% 1802 0.880329 1.135939 3.5180% 1801 0.850411 1.175902 3.3999% 1800 0.822448
1.215882 2.8419% 1799 0.799721 1.250436 2.7485% 1798 0.778329 1.284804 2.8261% 1797
0.756937 1.321114 3.7832% 1796 0.729344 1.371095 2.1272% 1795 0.714153 1.400260
3.0879% 1794 0.692761 1.443500 3.1625% 1793 0.671524 1.489151 3.2904% 1792 0.650132
1.538150 3.4024% 1791 0.628740 1.590483 3.2296% 1790 0.609069 1.641849 41.3145%
1780 0.431003 2.320170 29.4353% 1770 0.332987 3.003119 83.4728% 1750 0.181491
5.509908 29.2845% 1740 0.140381 7.123454 94.2514% 1720 0.072268 13.837409 85.8111%
1700 0.038893 25.711439 19.2490% 1690 0.032615 30.660646 88.0250% 1670 0.017346
57.649687

BASE YEAR: 1805

YEAR BYEAR/AYEAR AYEAR/BYEAR GROWTH%

2009 48.167202 0.020761 8.2857% 2001 44.481607 0.022481 1.0000% 2000
44.041191 0.022706 1.0000% 1999 43.605139 0.022933 1.0000% 1998 43.173405 0.023162
1.0000% 1997 42.745946 0.023394 1.0000% 1996 42.322719 0.023628 1.0000% 1995
41.903682 0.023864 0.9992% 1994 41.489113 0.024103 1.0008% 1993 41.078014 0.024344
1.0000% 1992 40.671301 0.024587 0.9295% 1991 40.296740 0.024816 1.2505% 1990
39.799047 0.025126 0.7224% 1989 39.513583 0.025308 1.1077% 1988 39.080697 0.025588
0.8834% 1987 38.738495 0.025814 0.5594% 1986 38.523011 0.025959 1.3056% 1985
38.026526 0.026297 0.7673% 1984 37.736977 0.026499 0.8149% 1983 37.431927 0.026715
0.9737% 1982 37.070949 0.026975 0.9508% 1981 36.721796 0.027232 0.9031% 1980
36.393142 0.027478 2.2701% 1979 35.585331 0.028101 1.0042% 1978 35.231544 0.028384
0.9896% 1977 34.886306 0.028665 0.9103% 1976 34.571588 0.028925 0.8394% 1975
34.283797 0.029168 0.9042% 1974 33.976590 0.029432 1.1568% 1973 33.588047 0.029772
0.9427% 1972 33.274369 0.030053 0.7426% 1971 33.029083 0.030276 1.4697% 1970
32.550673 0.030721 0.6968% 1969 32.325423 0.030935 0.8565% 1968 32.050895 0.031200
1.5090% 1967 31.574425 0.031671 0.9949% 1966 31.263383 0.031986 1.0575% 1965
30.936242 0.032325 1.1300% 1964 30.590564 0.032690 1.5537% 1963 30.122563 0.033198
1.4658% 1962 29.687400 0.033684 1.5364% 1961 29.238175 0.034202 2.1586% 1960
28.620365 0.034940 -1.6655% 1959 29.105105 0.034358 4.3080% 1958 27.903044 0.035838
2.1130% 1957 27.325663 0.036596 1.9895% 1956 26.792625 0.037324 2.1231% 1955
26.235618 0.038116 1.4496% 1954 25.860738 0.038669 2.1573% 1953 25.314637 0.039503
1.2298% 1952 25.007111 0.039989 1.6814% 1951 24.593600 0.040661 1.6233% 1950
24.200756 0.041321 1.4265% 1949 23.860379 0.041910 1.7790% 1948 23.443313 0.042656
1.8242% 1947 23.023330 0.043434 -2.6320% 1946 23.645694 0.042291 3.1768% 1945
22.917645 0.043635 6.4754% 1944 21.523884 0.046460 -0.3437% 1943 21.598112 0.046300
0.6562% 1942 21.457304 0.046604 0.6633% 1941 21.315916 0.046913 -5.6614% 1940
22.595122 0.044257 8.0381% 1939 20.914030 0.047815 0.8126% 1938 20.745446 0.048203
0.7762% 1937 20.585650 0.048578 0.6029% 1936 20.462288 0.048870 0.5244% 1935
20.355545 0.049127 -3.0364% 1934 20.992969 0.047635 4.6271% 1933 20.064557 0.049839
1.3921% 1932 19.789070 0.050533 -0.2051% 1931 19.829738 0.050429 0.8886% 1930
19.655083 0.050877 1.0126% 1929 19.458054 0.051393 1.1526% 1928 19.236337 0.051985
1.2160% 1927 19.005233 0.052617 1.4086% 1926 18.741248 0.053358 1.7667% 1925
18.415896 0.054301 1.4465% 1924 18.153308 0.055086 1.7700% 1923 17.837588 0.056061

310

1.6165% 1922 17.553827 0.056968 1.3736% 1921 17.315967 0.057750 2.3393% 1920
16.920152 0.059101 1.3140% 1919 16.700703 0.059878 0.7676% 1918 16.573478 0.060337
0.3870% 1917 16.509588 0.060571 1.3274% 1916 16.293305 0.061375 1.4083% 1915
16.067034 0.062239 1.4458% 1914 15.838047 0.063139 1.9424% 1913 15.536274 0.064365
1.9857% 1912 15.233781 0.065644 1.5634% 1911 14.999281 0.066670 1.8169% 1910
14.731620 0.067881 1.8781% 1909 14.460051 0.069156 2.0082% 1908 14.175376 0.070545
1.9603% 1907 13.902844 0.071928 1.8264% 1906 13.653484 0.073241 1.9357% 1905
13.394215 0.074659 2.0148% 1904 13.129674 0.076163 2.1335% 1903 12.855401 0.077788
1.8151% 1902 12.626216 0.079200 1.8943% 1901 12.391478 0.080701 3.0255% 1900
12.027584 0.083142 0.6278% 1899 11.952541 0.083664 1.7757% 1898 11.744008 0.085150
1.8078% 1897 11.535475 0.086689 1.8396% 1896 11.327101 0.088284 1.8755% 1895
11.118568 0.089940 1.9114% 1894 10.910035 0.091659 1.9486% 1893 10.701502 0.093445
1.9858% 1892 10.493129 0.095300 2.0276% 1891 10.284596 0.097233 2.6465% 1890
10.019430 0.099806 1.5328% 1889 9.868169 0.101336 2.0811% 1888 9.666986 0.103445
2.1599% 1887 9.462608 0.105679 2.2075% 1886 9.258229 0.108012 2.2592% 1885 9.053691
0.110452 2.3095% 1884 8.849313 0.113003 2.3641% 1883 8.644934 0.115675 2.4214% 1882
8.440556 0.118476 2.4815% 1881 8.236178 0.121416 3.7644% 1880 7.937383 0.125986
0.9432% 1879 7.863215 0.127174 2.1464% 1878 7.697987 0.129904 2.1913% 1877 7.532918
0.132751 2.2426% 1876 7.367689 0.135728 2.2941% 1875 7.202461 0.138841 2.3456% 1874
7.037392 0.142098 2.4043% 1873 6.872164 0.145515 2.4635% 1872 6.706935 0.149099
2.5258% 1871 6.541707 0.152865 5.9947% 1870 6.171731 0.162029 -1.0968% 1869
6.240173 0.160252 2.1930% 1868 6.106264 0.163766 2.2394% 1867 5.972515 0.167434
2.2935% 1866 5.838607 0.171274 2.3445% 1865 5.704858 0.175289 2.4037% 1864 5.570949
0.179503 2.4599% 1863 5.437200 0.183918 2.5250% 1862 5.303292 0.188562 2.5872% 1861
5.169543 0.193441 2.9504% 1860 5.021391 0.199148 2.4012% 1859 4.903643 0.203930
2.7627% 1858 4.771812 0.209564 2.8412% 1857 4.639981 0.215518 2.9243% 1856 4.508150
0.221821 3.0161% 1855 4.376159 0.228511 3.1061% 1854 4.244327 0.235609 3.2056% 1853
4.112496 0.243161 3.3118% 1852 3.980665 0.251214 3.4252% 1851 3.848833 0.259819
4.0106% 1850 3.700424 0.270239 2.3254% 1849 3.616331 0.276523 2.7841% 1848 3.518376
0.284222 2.8590% 1847 3.420582 0.292348 2.9432% 1846 3.322787 0.300952 3.0324% 1845
3.224992 0.310078 3.1325% 1844 3.127037 0.319792 3.2284% 1843 3.029243 0.330116
3.3361% 1842 2.931448 0.341128 3.4512% 1841 2.833653 0.352901 3.8105% 1840 2.729640
0.366349 2.3861% 1839 2.666027 0.375090 2.5824% 1838 2.598913 0.384776 2.6573% 1837
2.531640 0.395001 2.7232% 1836 2.464525 0.405758 2.7994% 1835 2.397411 0.417117
2.8871% 1834 2.330137 0.429159 2.9657% 1833 2.263023 0.441887 3.0563% 1832 2.195909
0.455392 3.1604% 1831 2.128635 0.469785 3.4660% 1830 2.057329 0.486067 2.4653% 1829
2.007830 0.498050 2.6804% 1828 1.955417 0.511400 10.3427% 1827 1.772132 0.564292 -
4.2314% 1826 1.850431 0.540415 2.9150% 1825 1.798019 0.556168 3.0026% 1824 1.745606
0.572867 3.0955% 1823 1.693193 0.590600 3.1944% 1822 1.640780 0.609466 3.3102% 1821
1.588207 0.629641 3.2277% 1820 1.538547 0.649964 2.6573% 1819 1.498722 0.667235
2.6261% 1818 1.460371 0.684758 2.6969% 1817 1.422020 0.703225 2.7717% 1816 1.383669
0.722716 2.8507% 1815 1.345318 0.743319 2.9343% 1814 1.306967 0.765130 3.0231% 1813
1.268616 0.788260 3.1039% 1812 1.230425 0.812727 3.2172% 1811 1.192074 0.838874
3.0969% 1810 1.156266 0.864853 2.9144% 1809 1.123522 0.890058 2.8225% 1808 1.092681
0.915180 2.9199% 1807 1.061681 0.941902 2.9918% 1806 1.030841 0.970082 3.0841% 1805
1.000000 1.000000 3.1822% 1804 0.969159 1.031822 3.2868% 1803 0.938319 1.065736
3.3985% 1802 0.907478 1.101955 3.5180% 1801 0.876638 1.140722 3.3999% 1800 0.847813
1.179506 2.8419% 1799 0.824385 1.213026 2.7485% 1798 0.802333 1.246365 2.8261% 1797
0.780281 1.281589 3.7832% 1796 0.751838 1.330074 2.1272% 1795 0.736178 1.358368
3.0879% 1794 0.714126 1.400313 3.1625% 1793 0.692234 1.444598 3.2904% 1792 0.670182
1.492132 3.4024% 1791 0.648130 1.542899 3.2296% 1790 0.627853 1.592728 41.3145%
1780 0.444295 2.250755 29.4353% 1770 0.343257 2.913272 83.4728% 1750 0.187089
5.345063 29.2845% 1740 0.144711 6.910336 94.2514% 1720 0.074497 13.423423 85.8111%
1700 0.040093 24.942208 19.2490% 1690 0.033621 29.743346 88.0250% 1670 0.017881
55.924933

BASE YEAR: 1804

311

YEAR BYEAR/AYEAR AYEAR/BYEAR GROWTH%

2009 49.699975 0.020121 8.2857% 2001 45.897098 0.021788 1.0000% 2000 45.442666 0.022006 1.0000% 1999 44.992739 0.022226 1.0000% 1998 44.547266 0.022448 1.0000% 1997 44.106204 0.022673 1.0000% 1996 43.669509 0.022899 1.0000% 1995 43.237138 0.023128 0.9992% 1994 42.809377 0.023359 1.0008% 1993 42.385195 0.023593 1.0000% 1992 41.965540 0.023829 0.9295% 1991 41.579060 0.024051 1.2505% 1990 41.065529 0.024351 0.7224% 1989 40.770981 0.024527 1.1077% 1988 40.324320 0.024799 0.8834% 1987 39.971228 0.025018 0.5594% 1986 39.748887 0.025158 1.3056% 1985 39.236603 0.025486 0.7673% 1984 38.937840 0.025682 0.8149% 1983 38.623083 0.025891 0.9737% 1982 38.250618 0.026143 0.9508% 1981 37.890354 0.026392 0.9031% 1980 37.551242 0.026630 2.2701% 1979 36.717725 0.027235 1.0042% 1978 36.352679 0.027508 0.9896% 1977 35.996455 0.027781 0.9103% 1976 35.671723 0.028033 0.8394% 1975 35.374773 0.028269 0.9042% 1974 35.057791 0.028524 1.1568% 1973 34.656884 0.028854 0.9427% 1972 34.333223 0.029126 0.7426% 1971 34.080132 0.029343 1.4697% 1970 33.586499 0.029774 0.6968% 1969 33.354081 0.029981 0.8565% 1968 33.070816 0.030238 1.5090% 1967 32.579184 0.030694 0.9949% 1966 32.258244 0.031000 1.0575% 1965 31.920692 0.031328 1.1300% 1964 31.564015 0.031682 1.5537% 1963 31.081121 0.032174 1.4658% 1962 30.632110 0.032645 1.5364% 1961 30.168590 0.033147 2.1586% 1960 29.531120 0.033863 -1.6655% 1959 30.031286 0.033299 4.3080% 1958 28.790973 0.034733 2.1130% 1957 28.195218 0.035467 1.9895% 1956 27.645218 0.036173 2.1231% 1955 27.070486 0.036941 1.4496% 1954 26.683677 0.037476 2.1573% 1953 26.120198 0.038285 1.2298% 1952 25.802885 0.038755 1.6814% 1951 25.376216 0.039407 1.6233% 1950 24.970871 0.040047 1.4265% 1949 24.619662 0.040618 1.7790% 1948 24.189324 0.041341 1.8242% 1947 23.755977 0.042095 -2.6320% 1946 24.398145 0.040987 3.1768% 1945 23.646929 0.042289 6.4754% 1944 22.208816 0.045027 -0.3437% 1943 22.285405 0.044872 0.6562% 1942 22.140117 0.045167 0.6633% 1941 21.994229 0.045466 -5.6614% 1940 23.314142 0.042892 8.0381% 1939 21.579555 0.046340 0.8126% 1938 21.405606 0.046717 0.7762% 1937 21.240725 0.047079 0.6029% 1936 21.113438 0.047363 0.5244% 1935 21.003298 0.047612 -3.0364% 1934 21.661006 0.046166 4.6271% 1933 20.703050 0.048302 1.3921% 1932 20.418796 0.048974 -0.2051% 1931 20.460758 0.048874 0.8886% 1930 20.280546 0.049308 1.0126% 1929 20.077246 0.049808 1.1526% 1928 19.848475 0.050382 1.2160% 1927 19.610016 0.050994 1.4086% 1926 19.337630 0.051713 1.7667% 1925 19.001926 0.052626 1.4465% 1924 18.730981 0.053387 1.7700% 1923 18.405214 0.054332 1.6165% 1922 18.112423 0.055211 1.3736% 1921 17.866994 0.055969 2.3393% 1920 17.458584 0.057278 1.3140% 1919 17.232152 0.058031 0.7676% 1918 17.100878 0.058477 0.3870% 1917 17.034955 0.058703 1.3274% 1916 16.811789 0.059482 1.4083% 1915 16.578318 0.060320 1.4458% 1914 16.342045 0.061192 1.9424% 1913 16.030668 0.062380 1.9857% 1912 15.718549 0.063619 1.5634% 1911 15.476587 0.064614 1.8169% 1910 15.200408 0.065788 1.8781% 1909 14.920198 0.067023 2.0082% 1908 14.626463 0.068369 1.9603% 1907 14.345260 0.069709 1.8264% 1906 14.087964 0.070983 1.9357% 1905 13.820445 0.072357 2.0148% 1904 13.547486 0.073814 2.1335% 1903 13.264484 0.075389 1.8151% 1902 13.028006 0.076758 1.8943% 1901 12.785799 0.078212 3.0255% 1900 12.410324 0.080578 0.6278% 1899 12.332894 0.081084 1.7757% 1898 12.117725 0.082524 1.8078% 1897 11.902556 0.084016 1.8396% 1896 11.687552 0.085561 1.8755% 1895 11.472383 0.087166 1.9114% 1894 11.257214 0.088832 1.9486% 1893 11.042045 0.090563 1.9858% 1892 10.827040 0.092361 2.0276% 1891 10.611871 0.094234 2.6465% 1890 10.338267 0.096728 1.5328% 1889 10.182193 0.098211 2.0811% 1888 9.974608 0.100255 2.1599% 1887 9.763726 0.102420 2.2075% 1886 9.552844 0.104681 2.2592% 1885 9.341797 0.107046 2.3095% 1884 9.130915 0.109518 2.3641% 1883 8.920033 0.112107 2.4214% 1882 8.709151 0.114822 2.4815% 1881 8.498269 0.117671 3.7644% 1880 8.189966 0.122101 0.9432% 1879 8.113438 0.123252 2.1464% 1878 7.942951 0.125898 2.1913% 1877 7.772630 0.128657 2.2426% 1876 7.602143 0.131542 2.2941% 1875 7.431657 0.134559 2.3456% 1874 7.261336 0.137716 2.4043% 1873 7.090849 0.141027 2.4635% 1872 6.920363 0.144501 2.5258% 1871 6.749876 0.148151 5.9947% 1870 6.368128 0.157032 -1.0968% 1869 6.438747 0.155310 2.1930% 1868 6.300577 0.158716 2.2394% 1867 6.162572 0.162270 2.2935% 1866 6.024402 0.165992 2.3445% 1865 5.886397 0.169883 2.4037% 1864 5.748228

312

0.173967 2.4599% 1863 5.610223 0.178246 2.5250% 1862 5.472053 0.182747 2.5872% 1861
5.334048 0.187475 2.9504% 1860 5.181182 0.193006 2.4012% 1859 5.059687 0.197641
2.7627% 1858 4.923660 0.203101 2.8412% 1857 4.787634 0.208871 2.9243% 1856 4.651608
0.214979 3.0161% 1855 4.515416 0.221464 3.1061% 1854 4.379390 0.228342 3.2056% 1853
4.243364 0.235662 3.3118% 1852 4.107337 0.243467 3.4252% 1851 3.971311 0.251806
4.0106% 1850 3.818179 0.261905 2.3254% 1849 3.731410 0.267995 2.7841% 1848 3.630338
0.275456 2.8590% 1847 3.529431 0.283332 2.9432% 1846 3.428524 0.291671 3.0324% 1845
3.327617 0.300515 3.1325% 1844 3.226546 0.309929 3.2284% 1843 3.125639 0.319935
3.3361% 1842 3.024732 0.330608 3.4512% 1841 2.923825 0.342018 3.8105% 1840 2.816503
0.355050 2.3861% 1839 2.750866 0.363522 2.5824% 1838 2.681616 0.372909 2.6573% 1837
2.612201 0.382819 2.7232% 1836 2.542951 0.393244 2.7994% 1835 2.473702 0.404252
2.8871% 1834 2.404287 0.415924 2.9657% 1833 2.335037 0.428259 3.0563% 1832 2.265787
0.441348 3.1604% 1831 2.196373 0.455296 3.4660% 1830 2.122797 0.471077 2.4653% 1829
2.071723 0.482690 2.6804% 1828 2.017642 0.495628 10.3427% 1827 1.828524 0.546889 -
4.2314% 1826 1.909316 0.523748 2.9150% 1825 1.855235 0.539015 3.0026% 1824 1.801154
0.555200 3.0955% 1823 1.747073 0.572386 3.1944% 1822 1.692993 0.590670 3.3102% 1821
1.638747 0.610222 3.2277% 1820 1.587506 0.629919 2.6573% 1819 1.546414 0.646657
2.6261% 1818 1.506843 0.663639 2.6969% 1817 1.467271 0.681537 2.7717% 1816 1.427700
0.700427 2.8507% 1815 1.388129 0.720394 2.9343% 1814 1.348557 0.741533 3.0231% 1813
1.308986 0.763950 3.1039% 1812 1.269580 0.787662 3.2172% 1811 1.230008 0.813003
3.0969% 1810 1.193060 0.838181 2.9144% 1809 1.159275 0.862608 2.8225% 1808 1.127453
0.886955 2.9199% 1807 1.095466 0.912854 2.9918% 1806 1.063644 0.940164 3.0841% 1805
1.031822 0.969159 3.1822% 1804 1.000000 1.000000 3.2868% 1803 0.968178 1.032868
3.3985% 1802 0.936356 1.067970 3.5180% 1801 0.904534 1.105541 3.3999% 1800 0.874792
1.143129 2.8419% 1799 0.850618 1.175615 2.7485% 1798 0.827865 1.207927 2.8261% 1797
0.805111 1.242064 3.7832% 1796 0.775763 1.289054 2.1272% 1795 0.759604 1.316475
3.0879% 1794 0.736851 1.357127 3.1625% 1793 0.714262 1.400046 3.2904% 1792 0.691509
1.446113 3.4024% 1791 0.668755 1.495316 3.2296% 1790 0.647833 1.543608 41.3145%
1780 0.458434 2.181341 29.4353% 1770 0.354180 2.823425 83.4728% 1750 0.193042
5.180219 29.2845% 1740 0.149316 6.697217 94.2514% 1720 0.076867 13.009438 85.8111%
1700 0.041369 24.172977 19.2490% 1690 0.034691 28.826046 88.0250% 1670 0.018450
54.200179

BASE YEAR: 1803
YEAR BYEAR/AYEAR AYEAR/BYEAR GROWTH%
2009 51.333506 0.019480 8.2857% 2001 47.405637 0.021095 1.0000% 2000
46.936269 0.021305 1.0000% 1999 46.471553 0.021519 1.0000% 1998 46.011439 0.021734
1.0000% 1997 45.555880 0.021951 1.0000% 1996 45.104832 0.022171 1.0000% 1995
44.658249 0.022392 0.9992% 1994 44.216429 0.022616 1.0008% 1993 43.778306 0.022842
1.0000% 1992 43.344857 0.023071 0.9295% 1991 42.945674 0.023285 1.2505% 1990
42.415265 0.023576 0.7224% 1989 42.111035 0.023747 1.1077% 1988 41.649693 0.024010
0.8834% 1987 41.284997 0.024222 0.5594% 1986 41.055347 0.024357 1.3056% 1985
40.526226 0.024675 0.7673% 1984 40.217643 0.024865 0.8149% 1983 39.892541 0.025067
0.9737% 1982 39.507834 0.025311 0.9508% 1981 39.135729 0.025552 0.9031% 1980
38.785471 0.025783 2.2701% 1979 37.924557 0.026368 1.0042% 1978 37.547514 0.026633
0.9896% 1977 37.179581 0.026896 0.9103% 1976 36.844176 0.027141 0.8394% 1975
36.537466 0.027369 0.9042% 1974 36.210065 0.027617 1.1568% 1973 35.795981 0.027936
0.9427% 1972 35.461683 0.028199 0.7426% 1971 35.200272 0.028409 1.4697% 1970
34.690415 0.028826 0.6968% 1969 34.450358 0.029027 0.8565% 1968 34.157783 0.029276
1.5090% 1967 33.649991 0.029718 0.9949% 1966 33.318503 0.030013 1.0575% 1965
32.969857 0.030331 1.1300% 1964 32.601456 0.030673 1.5537% 1963 32.102691 0.031150
1.4658% 1962 31.638922 0.031607 1.5364% 1961 31.160167 0.032092 2.1586% 1960
30.501744 0.032785 -1.6655% 1959 31.018350 0.032239 4.3080% 1958 29.737270 0.033628
2.1130% 1957 29.121935 0.034338 1.9895% 1956 28.553857 0.035022 2.1231% 1955
27.960235 0.035765 1.4496% 1954 27.560712 0.036284 2.1573% 1953 26.978713 0.037066
1.2298% 1952 26.650971 0.037522 1.6814% 1951 26.210278 0.038153 1.6233% 1950
25.791609 0.038772 1.4265% 1949 25.428857 0.039325 1.7790% 1948 24.984375 0.040025

313

1.8242% 1947 24.536785 0.040755 -2.6320% 1946 25.200060 0.039682 3.1768% 1945
24.424153 0.040943 6.4754% 1944 22.938772 0.043594 -0.3437% 1943 23.017879 0.043444
0.6562% 1942 22.867815 0.043730 0.6633% 1941 22.717132 0.044020 -5.6614% 1940
24.080428 0.041528 8.0381% 1939 22.288828 0.044866 0.8126% 1938 22.109162 0.045230
0.7762% 1937 21.938862 0.045581 0.6029% 1936 21.807391 0.045856 0.5244% 1935
21.693631 0.046096 -3.0364% 1934 22.372956 0.044697 4.6271% 1933 21.383515 0.046765
1.3921% 1932 21.089918 0.047416 -0.2051% 1931 21.133260 0.047319 0.8886% 1930
20.947124 0.047739 1.0126% 1929 20.737142 0.048223 1.1526% 1928 20.500851 0.048778
1.2160% 1927 20.254556 0.049372 1.4086% 1926 19.973216 0.050067 1.7667% 1925
19.626478 0.050952 1.4465% 1924 19.346628 0.051689 1.7700% 1923 19.010154 0.052603
1.6165% 1922 18.707740 0.053454 1.3736% 1921 18.454244 0.054188 2.3393% 1920
18.032410 0.055456 1.3140% 1919 17.798535 0.056184 0.7676% 1918 17.662947 0.056616
0.3870% 1917 17.594857 0.056835 1.3274% 1916 17.364356 0.057589 1.4083% 1915
17.123212 0.058400 1.4458% 1914 16.879172 0.059245 1.9424% 1913 16.557561 0.060395
1.9857% 1912 16.235184 0.061595 1.5634% 1911 15.985269 0.062558 1.8169% 1910
15.700013 0.063694 1.8781% 1909 15.410593 0.064890 2.0082% 1908 15.107204 0.066194
1.9603% 1907 14.816757 0.067491 1.8264% 1906 14.551005 0.068724 1.9357% 1905
14.274693 0.070054 2.0148% 1904 13.992762 0.071466 2.1335% 1903 13.700459 0.072990
1.8151% 1902 13.456209 0.074315 1.8943% 1901 13.206041 0.075723 3.0255% 1900
12.818225 0.078014 0.6278% 1899 12.738249 0.078504 1.7757% 1898 12.516008 0.079898
1.8078% 1897 12.293767 0.081342 1.8396% 1896 12.071696 0.082838 1.8755% 1895
11.849455 0.084392 1.9114% 1894 11.627214 0.086005 1.9486% 1893 11.404973 0.087681
1.9858% 1892 11.182902 0.089422 2.0276% 1891 10.960661 0.091235 2.6465% 1890
10.678064 0.093650 1.5328% 1889 10.516860 0.095085 2.0811% 1888 10.302452 0.097064
2.1599% 1887 10.084639 0.099161 2.2075% 1886 9.866826 0.101350 2.2592% 1885
9.648842 0.103639 2.3095% 1884 9.431029 0.106033 2.3641% 1883 9.213215 0.108540
2.4214% 1882 8.995402 0.111168 2.4815% 1881 8.777589 0.113927 3.7644% 1880 8.459153
0.118215 0.9432% 1879 8.380109 0.119330 2.1464% 1878 8.204019 0.121891 2.1913% 1877
8.028099 0.124562 2.2426% 1876 7.852010 0.127356 2.2941% 1875 7.675920 0.130278
2.3456% 1874 7.500000 0.133333 2.4043% 1873 7.323910 0.136539 2.4635% 1872 7.147820
0.139903 2.5258% 1871 6.971730 0.143436 5.9947% 1870 6.577434 0.152035 -1.0968%
1869 6.650375 0.150367 2.1930% 1868 6.507663 0.153665 2.2394% 1867 6.365123 0.157106
2.2935% 1866 6.222411 0.160709 2.3445% 1865 6.079871 0.164477 2.4037% 1864 5.937159
0.168431 2.4599% 1863 5.794619 0.172574 2.5250% 1862 5.651907 0.176931 2.5872% 1861
5.509366 0.181509 2.9504% 1860 5.351476 0.186864 2.4012% 1859 5.225988 0.191351
2.7627% 1858 5.085490 0.196638 2.8412% 1857 4.944993 0.202225 2.9243% 1856 4.804496
0.208138 3.0161% 1855 4.663828 0.214416 3.1061% 1854 4.523331 0.221076 3.2056% 1853
4.382834 0.228163 3.3118% 1852 4.242337 0.235719 3.4252% 1851 4.101839 0.243793
4.0106% 1850 3.943674 0.253571 2.3254% 1849 3.854053 0.259467 2.7841% 1848 3.749659
0.266691 2.8590% 1847 3.645436 0.274316 2.9432% 1846 3.541213 0.282389 3.0324% 1845
3.436989 0.290952 3.1325% 1844 3.332595 0.300066 3.2284% 1843 3.228372 0.309754
3.3361% 1842 3.124149 0.320087 3.4512% 1841 3.019925 0.331134 3.8105% 1840 2.909075
0.343752 2.3861% 1839 2.841281 0.351954 2.5824% 1838 2.769755 0.361043 2.6573% 1837
2.698059 0.370637 2.7232% 1836 2.626533 0.380730 2.7994% 1835 2.555007 0.391388
2.8871% 1834 2.483311 0.402688 2.9657% 1833 2.411785 0.414631 3.0563% 1832 2.340259
0.427303 3.1604% 1831 2.268563 0.440808 3.4660% 1830 2.192569 0.456086 2.4653% 1829
2.139816 0.467330 2.6804% 1828 2.083958 0.479856 10.3427% 1827 1.888624 0.529486 -
4.2314% 1826 1.972071 0.507081 2.9150% 1825 1.916213 0.521863 3.0026% 1824 1.860354
0.537532 3.0955% 1823 1.804496 0.554171 3.1944% 1822 1.748638 0.571874 3.3102% 1821
1.692609 0.590804 3.2277% 1820 1.639684 0.609874 2.6573% 1819 1.597241 0.626080
2.6261% 1818 1.556369 0.642521 2.6969% 1817 1.515497 0.659849 2.7717% 1816 1.474625
0.678138 2.8507% 1815 1.433753 0.697470 2.9343% 1814 1.392881 0.717936 3.0231% 1813
1.352010 0.739640 3.1039% 1812 1.311308 0.762597 3.2172% 1811 1.270436 0.787131
3.0969% 1810 1.232274 0.811508 2.9144% 1809 1.197377 0.835159 2.8225% 1808 1.164510
0.858731 2.9199% 1807 1.131471 0.883805 2.9918% 1806 1.098604 0.910246 3.0841% 1805
1.065736 0.938319 3.1822% 1804 1.032868 0.968178 3.2868% 1803 1.000000 1.000000

3.3985% 1802 0.967132 1.033985 3.5180% 1801 0.934264 1.070361 3.3999% 1800 0.903544
1.106753 2.8419% 1799 0.878576 1.138205 2.7485% 1798 0.855075 1.169488 2.8261% 1797
0.831574 1.202539 3.7832% 1796 0.801260 1.248034 2.1272% 1795 0.784571 1.274582
3.0879% 1794 0.761069 1.313940 3.1625% 1793 0.737738 1.355494 3.2904% 1792 0.714237
1.400095 3.4024% 1791 0.690736 1.447732 3.2296% 1790 0.669126 1.494487 41.3145%
1780 0.473501 2.111926 29.4353% 1770 0.365821 2.733579 83.4728% 1750 0.199387
5.015374 29.2845% 1740 0.154223 6.484099 94.2514% 1720 0.079394 12.595453 85.8111%
1700 0.042728 23.403747 19.2490% 1690 0.035831 27.908745 88.0250% 1670 0.019057
52.475424

BASE YEAR: 1802

YEAR BYEAR/AYEAR AYEAR/BYEAR GROWTH%

2009 53.078068 0.018840 8.2857% 2001 49.016711 0.020401 1.0000% 2000
48.531391 0.020605 1.0000% 1999 48.050883 0.020811 1.0000% 1998 47.575131 0.021019
1.0000% 1997 47.104090 0.021230 1.0000% 1996 46.637713 0.021442 1.0000% 1995
46.175954 0.021656 0.9992% 1994 45.719118 0.021873 1.0008% 1993 45.266105 0.022092
1.0000% 1992 44.817926 0.022313 0.9295% 1991 44.405177 0.022520 1.2505% 1990
43.856742 0.022802 0.7224% 1989 43.542173 0.022966 1.1077% 1988 43.065152 0.023221
0.8834% 1987 42.688061 0.023426 0.5594% 1986 42.450608 0.023557 1.3056% 1985
41.903504 0.023864 0.7673% 1984 41.584434 0.024047 0.8149% 1983 41.248283 0.024243
0.9737% 1982 40.850502 0.024480 0.9508% 1981 40.465751 0.024712 0.9031% 1980
40.103589 0.024935 2.2701% 1979 39.213418 0.025501 1.0042% 1978 38.823560 0.025758
0.9896% 1977 38.443124 0.026012 0.9103% 1976 38.096320 0.026249 0.8394% 1975
37.779186 0.026470 0.9042% 1974 37.440659 0.026709 1.1568% 1973 37.012502 0.027018
0.9427% 1972 36.666843 0.027273 0.7426% 1971 36.396549 0.027475 1.4697% 1970
35.869363 0.027879 0.6968% 1969 35.621148 0.028073 0.8565% 1968 35.318630 0.028314
1.5090% 1967 34.793582 0.028741 0.9949% 1966 34.450828 0.029027 1.0575% 1965
34.090333 0.029334 1.1300% 1964 33.709412 0.029665 1.5537% 1963 33.193696 0.030126
1.4658% 1962 32.714166 0.030568 1.5364% 1961 32.219141 0.031037 2.1586% 1960
31.538342 0.031707 -1.6655% 1959 32.072504 0.031179 4.3080% 1958 30.747887 0.032523
2.1130% 1957 30.111639 0.033210 1.9895% 1956 29.524256 0.033870 2.1231% 1955
28.910460 0.034590 1.4496% 1954 28.497359 0.035091 2.1573% 1953 27.895580 0.035848
1.2298% 1952 27.556700 0.036289 1.6814% 1951 27.101030 0.036899 1.6233% 1950
26.668133 0.037498 1.4265% 1949 26.293053 0.038033 1.7790% 1948 25.833465 0.038709
1.8242% 1947 25.370664 0.039416 -2.6320% 1946 26.056480 0.038378 3.1768% 1945
25.254204 0.039597 6.4754% 1944 23.718343 0.042161 -0.3437% 1943 23.800138 0.042017
0.6562% 1942 23.644974 0.042292 0.6633% 1941 23.489171 0.042573 -5.6614% 1940
24.898798 0.040163 8.0381% 1939 23.046311 0.043391 0.8126% 1938 22.860539 0.043744
0.7762% 1937 22.684451 0.044083 0.6029% 1936 22.548512 0.044349 0.5244% 1935
22.430886 0.044581 -3.0364% 1934 23.133298 0.043228 4.6271% 1933 22.110231 0.045228
1.3921% 1932 21.806656 0.045858 -0.2051% 1931 21.851470 0.045764 0.8886% 1930
21.659009 0.046170 1.0126% 1929 21.441891 0.046638 1.1526% 1928 21.197570 0.047175
1.2160% 1927 20.942904 0.047749 1.4086% 1926 20.652003 0.048421 1.7667% 1925
20.293481 0.049277 1.4465% 1924 20.004121 0.049990 1.7700% 1923 19.656211 0.050875
1.6165% 1922 19.343520 0.051697 1.3736% 1921 19.081409 0.052407 2.3393% 1920
18.645239 0.053633 1.3140% 1919 18.403416 0.054338 0.7676% 1918 18.263220 0.054755
0.3870% 1917 18.192816 0.054967 1.3274% 1916 17.954481 0.055696 1.4083% 1915
17.705142 0.056481 1.4458% 1914 17.452809 0.057297 1.9424% 1913 17.120268 0.058410
1.9857% 1912 16.786934 0.059570 1.5634% 1911 16.528526 0.060501 1.8169% 1910
16.233576 0.061601 1.8781% 1909 15.934319 0.062758 2.0082% 1908 15.620620 0.064018
1.9603% 1907 15.320303 0.065273 1.8264% 1906 15.045519 0.066465 1.9357% 1905
14.759817 0.067752 2.0148% 1904 14.468304 0.069117 2.1335% 1903 14.166067 0.070591
1.8151% 1902 13.913516 0.071873 1.8943% 1901 13.654846 0.073234 3.0255% 1900
13.253851 0.075450 0.6278% 1899 13.171157 0.075923 1.7757% 1898 12.941363 0.077272
1.8078% 1897 12.711569 0.078668 1.8396% 1896 12.481951 0.080116 1.8755% 1895
12.252157 0.081618 1.9114% 1894 12.022363 0.083178 1.9486% 1893 11.792569 0.084799
1.9858% 1892 11.562951 0.086483 2.0276% 1891 11.333157 0.088237 2.6465% 1890

315

11.040957 0.090572 1.5328% 1889 10.874274 0.091960 2.0811% 1888 10.652580 0.093874
2.1599% 1887 10.427364 0.095902 2.2075% 1886 10.202148 0.098019 2.2592% 1885
9.976756 0.100233 2.3095% 1884 9.751541 0.102548 2.3641% 1883 9.526325 0.104972
2.4214% 1882 9.301109 0.107514 2.4815% 1881 9.075894 0.110182 3.7644% 1880 8.746636
0.114330 0.9432% 1879 8.664906 0.115408 2.1464% 1878 8.482831 0.117885 2.1913% 1877
8.300933 0.120468 2.2426% 1876 8.118859 0.123170 2.2941% 1875 7.936785 0.125996
2.3456% 1874 7.754886 0.128951 2.4043% 1873 7.572812 0.132051 2.4635% 1872 7.390738
0.135304 2.5258% 1871 7.208663 0.138722 5.9947% 1870 6.800968 0.147038 -1.0968%
1869 6.876387 0.145425 2.1930% 1868 6.728825 0.148614 2.2394% 1867 6.581440 0.151942
2.2935% 1866 6.433879 0.155427 2.3445% 1865 6.286494 0.159071 2.4037% 1864 6.138933
0.162895 2.4599% 1863 5.991548 0.166902 2.5250% 1862 5.843987 0.171116 2.5872% 1861
5.696602 0.175543 2.9504% 1860 5.533345 0.180723 2.4012% 1859 5.403592 0.185062
2.7627% 1858 5.258320 0.190175 2.8412% 1857 5.113048 0.195578 2.9243% 1856 4.967776
0.201297 3.0161% 1855 4.822328 0.207369 3.1061% 1854 4.677056 0.213810 3.2056% 1853
4.531784 0.220664 3.3118% 1852 4.386512 0.227972 3.4252% 1851 4.241240 0.235780
4.0106% 1850 4.077699 0.245236 3.2254% 1849 3.985033 0.250939 2.7841% 1848 3.877091
0.257925 2.8590% 1847 3.769326 0.265299 2.9432% 1846 3.661560 0.273108 3.0324% 1845
3.553795 0.281389 3.1325% 1844 3.445853 0.290204 3.2284% 1843 3.338088 0.299573
3.3361% 1842 3.230322 0.309567 3.4512% 1841 3.122557 0.320250 3.8105% 1840 3.007940
0.332453 2.3861% 1839 2.937841 0.340386 2.5824% 1838 2.863884 0.349176 2.6573% 1837
2.789752 0.358455 2.7232% 1836 2.715795 0.368216 2.7994% 1835 2.641838 0.378524
2.8871% 1834 2.567706 0.389453 2.9657% 1833 2.493749 0.401003 3.0563% 1832 2.419792
0.413259 3.1604% 1831 2.345659 0.426319 3.4660% 1830 2.267083 0.441095 2.4653% 1829
2.212537 0.451970 2.6804% 1828 2.154781 0.464084 10.3427% 1827 1.952809 0.512083 -
4.2314% 1826 2.039091 0.490415 2.9150% 1825 1.981335 0.504710 3.0026% 1824 1.923578
0.519865 3.0955% 1823 1.865821 0.535957 3.1944% 1822 1.808065 0.553078 3.3102% 1821
1.750132 0.571385 3.2277% 1820 1.695409 0.589828 2.6573% 1819 1.651523 0.605502
2.6261% 1818 1.609262 0.621403 2.6969% 1817 1.567001 0.638162 2.7717% 1816 1.524740
0.655849 2.8507% 1815 1.482479 0.674546 2.9343% 1814 1.440218 0.694339 3.0231% 1813
1.397957 0.715329 3.1039% 1812 1.355873 0.737532 3.2172% 1811 1.313612 0.761260
3.0969% 1810 1.274152 0.784836 2.9144% 1809 1.238070 0.807709 2.8225% 1808 1.204085
0.830506 2.9199% 1807 1.169924 0.854756 2.9918% 1806 1.135939 0.880329 3.0841% 1805
1.101955 0.907478 3.1822% 1804 1.067970 0.936356 3.2868% 1803 1.033985 0.967132
3.3985% 1802 1.000000 1.000000 3.5180% 1801 0.966015 1.035180 3.3999% 1800 0.934251
1.070376 2.8419% 1799 0.908435 1.100795 2.7485% 1798 0.884135 1.131050 2.8261% 1797
0.859834 1.163015 3.7832% 1796 0.828491 1.207014 2.1272% 1795 0.811234 1.232689
3.0879% 1794 0.786934 1.270754 3.1625% 1793 0.762810 1.310942 3.2904% 1792 0.738510
1.354077 3.4024% 1791 0.714210 1.400148 3.2296% 1790 0.691866 1.445367 41.3145%
1780 0.489593 2.042512 29.4353% 1770 0.378253 2.643732 83.4728% 1750 0.206163
4.850530 29.2845% 1740 0.159465 6.270981 94.2514% 1720 0.082092 12.181467 85.8111%
1700 0.044180 22.634516 19.2490% 1690 0.037049 26.991445 88.0250% 1670 0.019704
50.750670

BASE YEAR: 1801
YEAR BYEAR/AYEAR AYEAR/BYEAR GROWTH%
2009 54.945379 0.018200 8.2857% 2001 50.741141 0.019708 1.0000% 2000
50.238748 0.019905 1.0000% 1999 49.741335 0.020104 1.0000% 1998 49.248846 0.020305
1.0000% 1997 48.761234 0.020508 1.0000% 1996 48.278449 0.020713 1.0000% 1995
47.800445 0.020920 0.9992% 1994 47.327538 0.021129 1.0008% 1993 46.858587 0.021341
1.0000% 1992 46.394641 0.021554 0.9295% 1991 45.967371 0.021755 1.2505% 1990
45.399642 0.022027 0.7224% 1989 45.074007 0.022186 1.1077% 1988 44.580204 0.022431
0.8834% 1987 44.189847 0.022630 0.5594% 1986 43.944039 0.022756 1.3056% 1985
43.377689 0.023053 0.7673% 1984 43.047393 0.023230 0.8149% 1983 42.699417 0.023420
0.9737% 1982 42.287641 0.023648 0.9508% 1981 41.889355 0.023872 0.9031% 1980
41.514452 0.024088 2.2701% 1979 40.592964 0.024635 1.0042% 1978 40.189391 0.024882
0.9896% 1977 39.795571 0.025128 0.9103% 1976 39.436566 0.025357 0.8394% 1975
39.108276 0.025570 0.9042% 1974 38.757838 0.025801 1.1568% 1973 38.314619 0.026100

316

0.9427% 1972 37.956799 0.026346 0.7426% 1971 37.676996 0.026541 1.4697% 1970
37.131264 0.026931 0.6968% 1969 36.874316 0.027119 0.8565% 1968 36.561156 0.027351
1.5090% 1967 36.017636 0.027764 0.9949% 1966 35.662824 0.028040 1.0575% 1965
35.289646 0.028337 1.1300% 1964 34.895324 0.028657 1.5537% 1963 34.361466 0.029102
1.4658% 1962 33.865066 0.029529 1.5364% 1961 33.352625 0.029983 2.1586% 1960
32.647875 0.030630 -1.6655% 1959 33.200829 0.030120 4.3080% 1958 31.829612 0.031417
2.1130% 1957 31.170981 0.032081 1.9895% 1956 30.562933 0.032719 2.1231% 1955
29.927543 0.033414 1.4496% 1954 29.499909 0.033898 2.1573% 1953 28.876960 0.034630
1.2298% 1952 28.526157 0.035056 1.6814% 1951 28.054457 0.035645 1.6233% 1950
27.606331 0.036224 1.4265% 1949 27.218055 0.036740 1.7790% 1948 26.742299 0.037394
1.8242% 1947 26.263215 0.038076 -2.6320% 1946 26.973159 0.037074 3.1768% 1945
26.142659 0.038252 6.4754% 1944 24.552765 0.040729 -0.3437% 1943 24.637438 0.040589
0.6562% 1942 24.476815 0.040855 0.6633% 1941 24.315530 0.041126 -5.6614% 1940
25.774749 0.038798 8.0381% 1939 23.857091 0.041916 0.8126% 1938 23.664783 0.042257
0.7762% 1937 23.482501 0.042585 0.6029% 1936 23.341779 0.042842 0.5244% 1935
23.220015 0.043066 -3.0364% 1934 23.947138 0.041759 4.6271% 1933 22.888079 0.043691
1.3921% 1932 22.573824 0.044299 -0.2051% 1931 22.620215 0.044208 0.8886% 1930
22.420983 0.044601 1.0126% 1929 22.196227 0.045053 1.1526% 1928 21.943310 0.045572
1.2160% 1927 21.679685 0.046126 1.4086% 1926 21.378550 0.046776 1.7667% 1925
21.007415 0.047602 1.4465% 1924 20.707875 0.048291 1.7700% 1923 20.347726 0.049146
1.6165% 1922 20.024034 0.049940 1.3736% 1921 19.752702 0.050626 2.3393% 1920
19.301187 0.051810 1.3140% 1919 19.050857 0.052491 0.7676% 1918 18.905728 0.052894
0.3870% 1917 18.832847 0.053099 1.3274% 1916 18.586128 0.053804 1.4083% 1915
18.328017 0.054561 1.4458% 1914 18.066806 0.055350 1.9424% 1913 17.722567 0.056425
1.9857% 1912 17.377506 0.057546 1.5634% 1911 17.110007 0.058445 1.8169% 1910
16.804680 0.059507 1.8781% 1909 16.494896 0.060625 2.0082% 1908 16.170160 0.061842
1.9603% 1907 15.859278 0.063055 1.8264% 1906 15.574827 0.064206 1.9357% 1905
15.279074 0.065449 2.0148% 1904 14.977306 0.066768 2.1335% 1903 14.664436 0.068192
1.8151% 1902 14.403000 0.069430 1.8943% 1901 14.135230 0.070745 3.0255% 1900
13.720127 0.072886 0.6278% 1899 13.634524 0.073343 1.7757% 1898 13.396646 0.074646
1.8078% 1897 13.158768 0.075995 1.8396% 1896 12.921072 0.077393 1.8755% 1895
12.683194 0.078844 1.9114% 1894 12.445315 0.080352 1.9486% 1893 12.207437 0.081917
1.9858% 1892 11.969741 0.083544 2.0276% 1891 11.731863 0.085238 2.6465% 1890
11.429382 0.087494 1.5328% 1889 11.256836 0.088835 2.0811% 1888 11.027342 0.090684
2.1599% 1887 10.794203 0.092642 2.2075% 1886 10.561065 0.094687 2.2592% 1885
10.327743 0.096827 2.3095% 1884 10.094604 0.099063 2.3641% 1883 9.861466 0.101405
2.4214% 1882 9.628327 0.103860 2.4815% 1881 9.395188 0.106437 3.7644% 1880 9.054346
0.110444 0.9432% 1879 8.969741 0.111486 2.1464% 1878 8.781261 0.113879 2.1913% 1877
8.592964 0.116374 2.2426% 1876 8.404484 0.118984 2.2941% 1875 8.216004 0.121714
2.3456% 1874 8.027707 0.124569 2.4043% 1873 7.839227 0.127564 2.4635% 1872 7.650747
0.130706 2.5258% 1871 7.462268 0.134008 5.9947% 1870 7.040229 0.142041 -1.0968%
1869 7.118301 0.140483 2.1930% 1868 6.965549 0.143564 2.2394% 1867 6.812978 0.146779
2.2935% 1866 6.660226 0.150145 2.3445% 1865 6.507656 0.153665 2.4037% 1864 6.354903
0.157359 2.4599% 1863 6.202333 0.161230 2.5250% 1862 6.049581 0.165301 2.5872% 1861
5.897011 0.169577 2.9504% 1860 5.728011 0.174581 2.4012% 1859 5.593693 0.178773
2.7627% 1858 5.443310 0.183712 2.8412% 1857 5.292927 0.188931 2.9243% 1856 5.142545
0.194456 3.0161% 1855 4.991980 0.200321 3.1061% 1854 4.841597 0.206543 3.2056% 1853
4.691214 0.213164 3.3118% 1852 4.540831 0.220224 3.4252% 1851 4.390448 0.227767
4.0106% 1850 4.221155 0.236902 2.3254% 1849 4.125228 0.242411 2.7841% 1848 4.013489
0.249160 2.8590% 1847 3.901932 0.256283 2.9432% 1846 3.790376 0.263826 3.0324% 1845
3.678819 0.271826 3.1325% 1844 3.567080 0.280341 3.2284% 1843 3.455523 0.289392
3.3361% 1842 3.343966 0.299046 3.4512% 1841 3.232410 0.309367 3.8105% 1840 3.113760
0.321155 2.3861% 1839 3.041196 0.328818 2.5824% 1838 2.964637 0.337309 2.6573% 1837
2.887896 0.346273 2.7232% 1836 2.811338 0.355703 2.7994% 1835 2.734779 0.365660
2.8871% 1834 2.658039 0.376217 2.9657% 1833 2.581480 0.387375 3.0563% 1832 2.504922
0.399214 3.1604% 1831 2.428181 0.411831 3.4660% 1830 2.346840 0.426105 2.4653% 1829

2.290376 0.436610 2.6804% 1828 2.230587 0.448312 10.3427% 1827 2.021509 0.494680 -
4.2314% 1826 2.110828 0.473748 2.9150% 1825 2.051039 0.487558 3.0026% 1824 1.991250
0.502197 3.0955% 1823 1.931462 0.517743 3.1944% 1822 1.871673 0.534281 3.3102% 1821
1.811703 0.551967 3.2277% 1820 1.755054 0.569783 2.6573% 1819 1.709624 0.584924
2.6261% 1818 1.665877 0.600284 2.6969% 1817 1.622129 0.616474 2.7717% 1816 1.578381
0.633560 2.8507% 1815 1.534634 0.651621 2.9343% 1814 1.490886 0.670742 3.0231% 1813
1.447138 0.691019 3.1039% 1812 1.403573 0.712468 3.2172% 1811 1.359825 0.735389
3.0969% 1810 1.318977 0.758163 2.9144% 1809 1.281626 0.780259 2.8225% 1808 1.246445
0.802281 2.9199% 1807 1.211083 0.825707 2.9918% 1806 1.175902 0.850411 3.0841% 1805
1.140722 0.876638 3.1822% 1804 1.105541 0.904534 3.2868% 1803 1.070361 0.934264
3.3985% 1802 1.035180 0.966015 3.5180% 1801 1.000000 1.000000 3.3999% 1800 0.967118
1.033999 2.8419% 1799 0.940394 1.063384 2.7485% 1798 0.915239 1.092611 2.8261% 1797
0.890084 1.123490 3.7832% 1796 0.857638 1.165994 2.1272% 1795 0.839774 1.190797
3.0879% 1794 0.814619 1.227568 3.1625% 1793 0.789646 1.266390 3.2904% 1792 0.764491
1.308059 3.4024% 1791 0.739336 1.352564 3.2296% 1790 0.716206 1.396246 41.3145%
1780 0.506817 1.973097 29.4353% 1770 0.391560 2.553885 83.4728% 1750 0.213416
4.685685 29.2845% 1740 0.165075 6.057862 94.2514% 1720 0.084980 11.767482 85.8111%
1700 0.045735 21.865285 19.2490% 1690 0.038352 26.074144 88.0250% 1670 0.020397
49.025916

BASE YEAR: 1800

YEAR BYEAR/AYEAR AYEAR/BYEAR GROWTH%

2009 56.813493 0.017601 8.2857% 2001 52.466313 0.019060 1.0000% 2000
51.946839 0.019250 1.0000% 1999 51.432514 0.019443 1.0000% 1998 50.923281 0.019637
1.0000% 1997 50.419090 0.019834 1.0000% 1996 49.919891 0.020032 1.0000% 1995
49.425635 0.020232 0.9992% 1994 48.936649 0.020435 1.0008% 1993 48.451754 0.020639
1.0000% 1992 47.972034 0.020845 0.9295% 1991 47.530238 0.021039 1.2505% 1990
46.943206 0.021302 0.7224% 1989 46.606499 0.021456 1.1077% 1988 46.095908 0.021694
0.8834% 1987 45.692278 0.021886 0.5594% 1986 45.438113 0.022008 1.3056% 1985
44.852507 0.022295 0.7673% 1984 44.510982 0.022466 0.8149% 1983 44.151174 0.022649
0.9737% 1982 43.725399 0.022870 0.9508% 1981 43.313571 0.023087 0.9031% 1980
42.925921 0.023296 2.2701% 1979 41.973103 0.023825 1.0042% 1978 41.555809 0.024064
0.9896% 1977 41.148599 0.024302 0.9103% 1976 40.777388 0.024523 0.8394% 1975
40.437936 0.024729 0.9042% 1974 40.075584 0.024953 1.1568% 1973 39.617296 0.025242
0.9427% 1972 39.247310 0.025479 0.7426% 1971 38.957994 0.025669 1.4697% 1970
38.393707 0.026046 0.6968% 1969 38.128024 0.026227 0.8565% 1968 37.804216 0.026452
1.5090% 1967 37.242216 0.026851 0.9949% 1966 36.875341 0.027118 1.0575% 1965
36.489476 0.027405 1.1300% 1964 36.081747 0.027715 1.5537% 1963 35.529737 0.028145
1.4658% 1962 35.016460 0.028558 1.5364% 1961 34.486596 0.028997 2.1586% 1960
33.757885 0.029623 -1.6655% 1959 34.329640 0.029129 4.3080% 1958 32.911802 0.030384
2.1130% 1957 32.230778 0.031026 1.9895% 1956 31.602056 0.031644 2.1231% 1955
30.945063 0.032315 1.4496% 1954 30.502890 0.032784 2.1573% 1953 29.858761 0.033491
1.2298% 1952 29.496032 0.033903 1.6814% 1951 29.008293 0.034473 1.6233% 1950
28.544931 0.035032 1.4265% 1949 28.143455 0.035532 1.7790% 1948 27.651523 0.036164
1.8242% 1947 27.156151 0.036824 -2.6320% 1946 27.890232 0.035855 3.1768% 1945
27.031495 0.036994 6.4754% 1944 25.387546 0.039389 -0.3437% 1943 25.475098 0.039254
0.6562% 1942 25.309014 0.039512 0.6633% 1941 25.142246 0.039774 -5.6614% 1940
26.651077 0.037522 8.0381% 1939 24.668219 0.040538 0.8126% 1938 24.469373 0.040867
0.7762% 1937 24.280894 0.041185 0.6029% 1936 24.135387 0.041433 0.5244% 1935
24.009483 0.041650 -3.0364% 1934 24.761328 0.040386 4.6271% 1933 23.666261 0.042254
1.3921% 1932 23.341322 0.042842 -0.2051% 1931 23.389290 0.042755 0.8886% 1930
23.183284 0.043135 1.0126% 1929 22.950887 0.043571 1.1526% 1928 22.689371 0.044073
1.2160% 1927 22.416782 0.044609 1.4086% 1926 22.105410 0.045238 1.7667% 1925
21.721656 0.046037 1.4465% 1924 21.411932 0.046703 1.7700% 1923 21.039538 0.047530
1.6165% 1922 20.704840 0.048298 1.3736% 1921 20.424283 0.048961 2.3393% 1920
19.957417 0.050107 1.3140% 1919 19.698576 0.050765 0.7676% 1918 19.548513 0.051155
0.3870% 1917 19.473154 0.051353 1.3274% 1916 19.218047 0.052034 1.4083% 1915

318

18.951160 0.052767 1.4458% 1914 18.681068 0.053530 1.9424% 1913 18.325124 0.054570
1.9857% 1912 17.968332 0.055653 1.5634% 1911 17.691738 0.056524 1.8169% 1910
17.376031 0.057551 1.8781% 1909 17.055714 0.058631 2.0082% 1908 16.719937 0.059809
1.9603% 1907 16.398485 0.060981 1.8264% 1906 16.104363 0.062095 1.9357% 1905
15.798554 0.063297 2.0148% 1904 15.486526 0.064572 2.1335% 1903 15.163019 0.065950
1.8151% 1902 14.892695 0.067147 1.8943% 1901 14.615820 0.068419 3.0255% 1900
14.186604 0.070489 0.6278% 1899 14.098091 0.070932 1.7757% 1898 13.852125 0.072191
1.8078% 1897 13.606159 0.073496 1.8396% 1896 13.360381 0.074848 1.8755% 1895
13.114415 0.076252 1.9114% 1894 12.868449 0.077709 1.9486% 1893 12.622484 0.079224
1.9858% 1892 12.376706 0.080797 2.0276% 1891 12.130740 0.082435 2.6465% 1890
11.817975 0.084617 1.5328% 1889 11.639562 0.085914 2.0811% 1888 11.402266 0.087702
2.1599% 1887 11.161201 0.089596 2.2075% 1886 10.920135 0.091574 2.2592% 1885
10.678881 0.093643 2.3095% 1884 10.437816 0.095805 2.3641% 1883 10.196750 0.098070
2.4214% 1882 9.955685 0.100445 2.4815% 1881 9.714619 0.102938 3.7644% 1880 9.362189
0.106813 0.9432% 1879 9.274708 0.107820 2.1464% 1878 9.079820 0.110134 2.1913% 1877
8.885120 0.112548 2.2426% 1876 8.690232 0.115072 2.2941% 1875 8.495344 0.117712
2.3456% 1874 8.300645 0.120473 2.4043% 1873 8.105757 0.123369 2.4635% 1872 7.910869
0.126408 2.5258% 1871 7.715981 0.129601 5.9947% 1870 7.279593 0.137370 -1.0968%
1869 7.360320 0.135864 2.1930% 1868 7.202374 0.138843 2.2394% 1867 7.044616 0.141952
2.2935% 1866 6.886670 0.145208 2.3445% 1865 6.728913 0.148612 2.4037% 1864 6.570967
0.152185 2.4599% 1863 6.413209 0.155928 2.5250% 1862 6.255263 0.159865 2.5872% 1861
6.097506 0.164001 2.9504% 1860 5.922760 0.168840 2.4012% 1859 5.783876 0.172894
2.7627% 1858 5.628380 0.177671 2.8412% 1857 5.472884 0.182719 2.9243% 1856 5.317388
0.188062 3.0161% 1855 5.161704 0.193734 3.1061% 1854 5.006209 0.199752 3.2056% 1853
4.850713 0.206155 3.3118% 1852 4.695217 0.212983 3.4252% 1851 4.539721 0.220278
4.0106% 1850 4.364672 0.229112 2.3254% 1849 4.265483 0.234440 2.7841% 1848 4.149945
0.240967 2.8590% 1847 4.034596 0.247856 2.9432% 1846 3.919246 0.255151 3.0324% 1845
3.803897 0.262888 3.1325% 1844 3.688359 0.271123 3.2284% 1843 3.573009 0.279876
3.3361% 1842 3.457660 0.289213 3.4512% 1841 3.342310 0.299194 3.8105% 1840 3.219627
0.310595 2.3861% 1839 3.144595 0.318006 2.5824% 1838 3.065433 0.326218 2.6573% 1837
2.986083 0.334887 2.7232% 1836 2.906922 0.344006 2.7994% 1835 2.827760 0.353637
2.8871% 1834 2.748411 0.363847 2.9657% 1833 2.669249 0.374637 3.0563% 1832 2.590088
0.386087 3.1604% 1831 2.510738 0.398289 3.4660% 1830 2.426631 0.412094 2.4653% 1829
2.368247 0.422253 2.6804% 1828 2.306426 0.433571 10.3427% 1827 2.090240 0.478414 -
4.2314% 1826 2.182595 0.458170 2.9150% 1825 2.120773 0.471526 3.0026% 1824 2.058952
0.485684 3.0955% 1823 1.997131 0.500718 3.1944% 1822 1.935309 0.516713 3.3102% 1821
1.873299 0.533817 3.2277% 1820 1.814725 0.551048 2.6573% 1819 1.767751 0.565691
2.6261% 1818 1.722516 0.580546 2.6969% 1817 1.677281 0.596203 2.7717% 1816 1.632045
0.612728 2.85507% 1815 1.586810 0.630195 2.9343% 1814 1.541575 0.648687 3.0231% 1813
1.496340 0.668297 3.1039% 1812 1.451293 0.689041 3.2172% 1811 1.406058 0.711208
3.0969% 1810 1.363822 0.733234 2.9144% 1809 1.325201 0.754603 2.8225% 1808 1.288824
0.775901 2.9199% 1807 1.252259 0.798557 2.9918% 1806 1.215882 0.822448 3.0841% 1805
1.179506 0.847813 3.1822% 1804 1.143129 0.874792 3.2868% 1803 1.106753 0.903544
3.3985% 1802 1.070376 0.934251 3.5180% 1801 1.033999 0.967118 3.3999% 1800 1.000000
1.000000 2.8419% 1799 0.972367 1.028419 2.7485% 1798 0.946356 1.056684 2.8261% 1797
0.920346 1.086548 3.7832% 1796 0.886797 1.127654 2.1272% 1795 0.868326 1.151641
3.0879% 1794 0.842316 1.187203 3.1625% 1793 0.816494 1.224749 3.2904% 1792 0.790484
1.265048 3.4024% 1791 0.764474 1.308090 3.2296% 1790 0.740557 1.350335 41.3145%
1780 0.524049 1.908219 29.4353% 1770 0.404873 2.469909 83.4728% 1750 0.220672
4.531613 29.2845% 1740 0.170687 5.858670 94.2514% 1720 0.087869 11.380549 85.8111%
1700 0.047290 21.146321 19.2490% 1690 0.039656 25.216787 88.0250% 1670 0.021091
47.413870

BASE YEAR: 1799
YEAR BYEAR/AYEAR AYEAR/BYEAR GROWTH%
2009 58.428058 0.017115 8.2857% 2001 53.957336 0.018533 1.0000% 2000
53.423100 0.018718 1.0000% 1999 52.894158 0.018906 1.0000% 1998 52.370454 0.019095

319

1.0000% 1997 51.851934 0.019286 1.0000% 1996 51.338549 0.019479 1.0000% 1995
50.830246 0.019673 0.9992% 1994 50.327364 0.019870 1.0008% 1993 49.828690 0.020069
1.0000% 1992 49.335336 0.020269 0.9295% 1991 48.880985 0.020458 1.2505% 1990
48.277270 0.020714 0.7224% 1989 47.930994 0.020863 1.1077% 1988 47.405893 0.021094
0.8834% 1987 46.990793 0.021281 0.5594% 1986 46.729405 0.021400 1.3056% 1985
46.127156 0.021679 0.7673% 1984 45.775926 0.021846 0.8149% 1983 45.405893 0.022024
0.9737% 1982 44.968017 0.022238 0.9508% 1981 44.544485 0.022449 0.9031% 1980
44.145820 0.022652 2.2701% 1979 43.165924 0.023166 1.0042% 1978 42.736771 0.023399
0.9896% 1977 42.317988 0.023631 0.9103% 1976 41.936228 0.023846 0.8394% 1975
41.587129 0.024046 0.9042% 1974 41.214480 0.024263 1.1568% 1973 40.743167 0.024544
0.9427% 1972 40.362667 0.024775 0.7426% 1971 40.065129 0.024959 1.4697% 1970
39.484806 0.025326 0.6968% 1969 39.211572 0.025503 0.8565% 1968 38.878562 0.025721
1.5090% 1967 38.300591 0.026109 0.9949% 1966 37.923289 0.026369 1.0575% 1965
37.526459 0.026648 1.1300% 1964 37.107143 0.026949 1.5537% 1963 36.539446 0.027368
1.4658% 1962 36.011582 0.027769 1.5364% 1961 35.466660 0.028195 2.1586% 1960
34.717240 0.028804 -1.6655% 1959 35.305243 0.028324 4.3080% 1958 33.847112 0.029545
2.1130% 1957 33.146734 0.030169 1.9895% 1956 32.500145 0.030769 2.1231% 1955
31.824481 0.031422 1.4496% 1954 31.369742 0.031878 2.1573% 1953 30.707308 0.032566
1.2298% 1952 30.334270 0.032966 1.6814% 1951 29.832671 0.033520 1.6233% 1950
29.356141 0.034064 1.4265% 1949 28.943255 0.034550 1.7790% 1948 28.437343 0.035165
1.8242% 1947 27.927893 0.035806 -2.6320% 1946 28.682836 0.034864 3.1768% 1945
27.799695 0.035972 6.4754% 1944 26.109027 0.038301 -0.3437% 1943 26.199066 0.038169
0.6562% 1942 26.028263 0.038420 0.6633% 1941 25.856755 0.038675 -5.6614% 1940
27.408466 0.036485 8.0381% 1939 25.369258 0.039418 0.8126% 1938 25.164761 0.039738
0.7762% 1937 24.970925 0.040047 0.6029% 1936 24.821283 0.040288 0.5244% 1935
24.691801 0.040499 -3.0364% 1934 25.465013 0.039270 4.6271% 1933 24.338825 0.041087
1.3921% 1932 24.004652 0.041659 -0.2051% 1931 24.053983 0.041573 0.8886% 1930
23.842123 0.041943 1.0126% 1929 23.603121 0.042367 1.1526% 1928 23.334173 0.042856
1.2160% 1927 23.053838 0.043377 1.4086% 1926 22.733616 0.043988 1.7667% 1925
22.338957 0.044765 1.4465% 1924 22.020431 0.045412 1.7700% 1923 21.637454 0.046216
1.6165% 1922 21.293244 0.046963 1.3736% 1921 21.004714 0.047608 2.3393% 1920
20.524580 0.048722 1.3140% 1919 20.258383 0.049362 0.7676% 1918 20.104056 0.049741
0.3870% 1917 20.026556 0.049934 1.3274% 1916 19.764198 0.050597 1.4083% 1915
19.489727 0.051309 1.4458% 1914 19.211960 0.052051 1.9424% 1913 18.845900 0.053062
1.9857% 1912 18.478969 0.054116 1.5634% 1911 18.194514 0.054962 1.8169% 1910
17.869834 0.055960 1.8781% 1909 17.540415 0.057011 2.0082% 1908 17.195096 0.058156
1.9603% 1907 16.864509 0.059296 1.8264% 1906 16.562028 0.060379 1.9357% 1905
16.247529 0.061548 2.0148% 1904 15.926633 0.062788 2.1335% 1903 15.593932 0.064128
1.8151% 1902 15.315925 0.065292 1.8943% 1901 15.031182 0.066528 3.0255% 1900
14.589769 0.068541 0.6278% 1899 14.498740 0.068972 1.7757% 1898 14.245784 0.070196
1.8078% 1897 13.992828 0.071465 1.8396% 1896 13.740066 0.072780 1.8755% 1895
13.487110 0.074145 1.9114% 1894 13.234154 0.075562 1.9486% 1893 12.981198 0.077034
1.9858% 1892 12.728436 0.078564 2.0276% 1891 12.475480 0.080157 2.6465% 1890
12.153827 0.082279 1.5328% 1889 11.970343 0.083540 2.0811% 1888 11.726304 0.085278
2.1599% 1887 11.478387 0.087120 2.2075% 1886 11.230471 0.089043 2.2592% 1885
10.982361 0.091055 2.3095% 1884 10.734445 0.093158 2.3641% 1883 10.486528 0.095360
2.4214% 1882 10.238612 0.097669 2.4815% 1881 9.990696 0.100093 3.7644% 1880
9.628250 0.103861 0.9432% 1879 9.538283 0.104841 2.1464% 1878 9.337856 0.107091
2.1913% 1877 9.137624 0.109438 2.2426% 1876 8.937197 0.111892 2.2941% 1875 8.736771
0.114459 2.3456% 1874 8.536538 0.117144 2.4043% 1873 8.336112 0.119960 2.4635% 1872
8.135685 0.122915 2.5258% 1871 7.935259 0.126020 5.9947% 1870 7.486469 0.133574 -
1.0968% 1869 7.569490 0.132109 2.1930% 1868 7.407056 0.135006 2.2394% 1867 7.244815
0.138030 2.2935% 1866 7.082380 0.141195 2.3445% 1865 6.920140 0.144506 2.4037% 1864
6.757705 0.147979 2.4599% 1863 6.595464 0.151619 2.5250% 1862 6.433030 0.155448
2.5872% 1861 6.270789 0.159470 2.9504% 1860 6.091077 0.164175 2.4012% 1859 5.948246
0.168117 2.7627% 1858 5.788331 0.172761 2.8412% 1857 5.628416 0.177670 2.9243% 1856

320

5.468502 0.182865 3.0161% 1855 5.308393 0.188381 3.1061% 1854 5.148478 0.194232
3.2056% 1853 4.988564 0.200459 3.3118% 1852 4.828649 0.207097 3.4252% 1851 4.668734
0.214191 4.0106% 1850 4.488710 0.222781 2.3254% 1849 4.386703 0.227962 2.7841% 1848
4.267881 0.234308 2.8590% 1847 4.149254 0.241007 2.9432% 1846 4.030626 0.248100
3.0324% 1845 3.911998 0.255624 3.1325% 1844 3.793177 0.263631 3.2284% 1843 3.674549
0.272142 3.3361% 1842 3.555922 0.281221 3.4512% 1841 3.437294 0.290927 3.8105% 1840
3.311124 0.302012 2.3861% 1839 3.233960 0.309218 2.5824% 1838 3.152549 0.317204
2.6573% 1837 3.070944 0.325633 2.7232% 1836 2.989533 0.334500 2.7994% 1835 2.908122
0.343865 2.8871% 1834 2.826517 0.353792 2.9657% 1833 2.745106 0.364285 3.0563% 1832
2.663695 0.375418 3.1604% 1831 2.582090 0.387283 3.4660% 1830 2.495593 0.400706
2.4653% 1829 2.435550 0.410585 2.6804% 1828 2.371971 0.421590 10.3427% 1827
2.149641 0.465194 -4.2314% 1826 2.244621 0.445509 2.9150% 1825 2.181043 0.458496
3.0026% 1824 2.117465 0.472263 3.0955% 1823 2.053886 0.486882 3.1944% 1822 1.990308
0.502435 3.3102% 1821 1.926536 0.519066 3.2277% 1820 1.866297 0.535820 2.6573% 1819
1.817988 0.550059 2.6261% 1818 1.771467 0.564504 2.6969% 1817 1.724947 0.579728
2.7717% 1816 1.678426 0.595796 2.8507% 1815 1.631905 0.612781 2.9343% 1814 1.585385
0.630762 3.0231% 1813 1.538864 0.649830 3.1039% 1812 1.492537 0.670000 3.2172% 1811
1.446017 0.691555 3.0969% 1810 1.402580 0.712972 2.9144% 1809 1.362861 0.733751
2.8225% 1808 1.325451 0.754460 2.9199% 1807 1.287846 0.776490 2.9918% 1806 1.250436
0.799721 3.0841% 1805 1.213026 0.824385 3.1822% 1804 1.175615 0.850618 3.2868% 1803
1.138205 0.878576 3.3985% 1802 1.100795 0.908435 3.5180% 1801 1.063384 0.940394
3.3999% 1800 1.028419 0.972367 2.8419% 1799 1.000000 1.000000 2.7485% 1798 0.973251
1.027485 2.8261% 1797 0.946501 1.056523 3.7832% 1796 0.911998 1.096493 2.1272% 1795
0.893003 1.119818 3.0879% 1794 0.866253 1.154397 3.1625% 1793 0.839698 1.190905
3.2904% 1792 0.812948 1.230091 3.4024% 1791 0.786199 1.271943 3.2296% 1790 0.761602
1.313021 41.3145% 1780 0.538942 1.855488 29.4353% 1770 0.416379 2.401657 83.4728%
1750 0.226943 4.406389 29.2845% 1740 0.175538 5.696776 94.2514% 1720 0.090366
11.066066 85.8111% 1700 0.048633 20.561977 19.2490% 1690 0.040783 24.519962
88.0250% 1670 0.021690 46.103664

BASE YEAR: 1798

YEAR BYEAR/AYEAR AYEAR/BYEAR GROWTH%

2009 60.033927 0.016657 8.2857% 2001 55.440330 0.018037 1.0000% 2000
54.891410 0.018218 1.0000% 1999 54.347931 0.018400 1.0000% 1998 53.809833 0.018584
1.0000% 1997 53.277062 0.018770 1.0000% 1996 52.749566 0.018958 1.0000% 1995
52.227293 0.019147 0.9992% 1994 51.710590 0.019338 1.0008% 1993 51.198210 0.019532
1.0000% 1992 50.691297 0.019727 0.9295% 1991 50.224457 0.019911 1.2505% 1990
49.604150 0.020160 0.7224% 1989 49.248357 0.020305 1.1077% 1988 48.708823 0.020530
0.8834% 1987 48.282314 0.020712 0.5594% 1986 48.013742 0.020827 1.3056% 1985
47.394941 0.021099 0.7673% 1984 47.034057 0.021261 0.8149% 1983 46.653854 0.021434
0.9737% 1982 46.203943 0.021643 0.9508% 1981 45.768771 0.021849 0.9031% 1980
45.359148 0.022046 2.2701% 1979 44.352320 0.022547 1.0042% 1978 43.911372 0.022773
0.9896% 1977 43.481079 0.022999 0.9103% 1976 43.088827 0.023208 0.8394% 1975
42.730133 0.023403 0.9042% 1974 42.347242 0.023614 1.1568% 1973 41.862976 0.023887
0.9427% 1972 41.472018 0.024113 0.7426% 1971 41.166302 0.024292 1.4697% 1970
40.570029 0.024649 0.6968% 1969 40.289285 0.024820 0.8565% 1968 39.947122 0.025033
1.5090% 1967 39.353266 0.025411 0.9949% 1966 38.965595 0.025664 1.0575% 1965
38.557857 0.025935 1.1300% 1964 38.127017 0.026228 1.5537% 1963 37.543716 0.026636
1.4658% 1962 37.001344 0.027026 1.5364% 1961 36.441446 0.027441 2.1586% 1960
35.671428 0.028034 -1.6655% 1959 36.275593 0.027567 4.3080% 1958 34.777385 0.028754
2.1130% 1957 34.057757 0.029362 1.9895% 1956 33.393398 0.029946 2.1231% 1955
32.699164 0.030582 1.4496% 1954 32.231926 0.031025 2.1573% 1953 31.551285 0.031694
1.2298% 1952 31.167994 0.032084 1.6814% 1951 30.652609 0.032624 1.6233% 1950
30.162981 0.033153 1.4265% 1949 29.738747 0.033626 1.7790% 1948 29.218930 0.034224
1.8242% 1947 28.695479 0.034849 -2.6320% 1946 29.471171 0.033931 3.1768% 1945
28.563757 0.035009 6.4754% 1944 26.826622 0.037276 -0.3437% 1943 26.919136 0.037148
0.6562% 1942 26.743639 0.037392 0.6633% 1941 26.567417 0.037640 -5.6614% 1940

28.161775 0.035509 8.0381% 1939 26.066521 0.038363 0.8126% 1938 25.856403 0.038675
0.7762% 1937 25.657240 0.038975 0.6029% 1936 25.503485 0.039210 0.5244% 1935
25.370444 0.039416 -3.0364% 1934 26.164907 0.038219 4.6271% 1933 25.007767 0.039988
1.3921% 1932 24.664409 0.040544 -0.2051% 1931 24.715097 0.040461 0.8886% 1930
24.497413 0.040821 1.0126% 1929 24.251842 0.041234 1.1526% 1928 23.975503 0.041709
1.2160% 1927 23.687463 0.042216 1.4086% 1926 23.358440 0.042811 1.7667% 1925
22.952934 0.043567 1.4465% 1924 22.625653 0.044198 1.7700% 1923 22.232150 0.044980
1.6165% 1922 21.878480 0.045707 1.3736% 1921 21.582020 0.046335 2.3393% 1920
21.088690 0.047419 1.3140% 1919 20.815176 0.048042 0.7676% 1918 20.656607 0.048411
0.3870% 1917 20.576977 0.048598 1.3274% 1916 20.307409 0.049243 1.4083% 1915
20.025393 0.049937 1.4458% 1914 19.739992 0.050659 1.9424% 1913 19.363872 0.051643
1.9857% 1912 18.986855 0.052668 1.5634% 1911 18.694583 0.053491 1.8169% 1910
18.360979 0.054463 1.8781% 1909 18.022505 0.055486 2.0082% 1908 17.667696 0.056600
1.9603% 1907 17.328022 0.057710 1.8264% 1906 17.017228 0.058764 1.9357% 1905
16.694085 0.059901 2.0148% 1904 16.364370 0.061108 2.1335% 1903 16.022525 0.062412
1.8151% 1902 15.736877 0.063545 1.8943% 1901 15.444308 0.064749 3.0255% 1900
14.990762 0.066708 0.6278% 1899 14.897232 0.067127 1.7757% 1898 14.637323 0.068319
1.8078% 1897 14.377415 0.069554 1.8396% 1896 14.117706 0.070833 1.8755% 1895
13.857797 0.072162 1.9114% 1894 13.597889 0.073541 1.9486% 1893 13.337980 0.074974
1.9858% 1892 13.078271 0.076463 2.0276% 1891 12.818363 0.078013 2.6465% 1890
12.487869 0.080078 1.5328% 1889 12.299343 0.081305 2.0811% 1888 12.048596 0.082997
2.1599% 1887 11.793866 0.084790 2.2075% 1886 11.539136 0.086662 2.2592% 1885
11.284206 0.088619 2.3095% 1884 11.029476 0.090666 2.3641% 1883 10.774746 0.092810
2.4214% 1882 10.520016 0.095057 2.4815% 1881 10.265286 0.097416 3.7644% 1880
9.892879 0.101083 0.9432% 1879 9.800438 0.102036 2.1464% 1878 9.594503 0.104226
2.1913% 1877 9.388767 0.106510 2.2426% 1876 9.182832 0.108899 2.2941% 1875 8.976897
0.111397 2.3456% 1874 8.771161 0.114010 2.4043% 1873 8.565226 0.116751 2.4635% 1872
8.359291 0.119627 2.5258% 1871 8.153356 0.122649 5.9947% 1870 7.692232 0.130001 -
1.0968% 1869 7.777534 0.128575 2.1930% 1868 7.610635 0.131395 2.2394% 1867 7.443935
0.134338 2.2935% 1866 7.277036 0.137419 2.3445% 1865 7.110337 0.140640 2.4037% 1864
6.943438 0.144021 2.4599% 1863 6.776738 0.147564 2.5250% 1862 6.609839 0.151290
2.5872% 1861 6.443139 0.155204 2.9504% 1860 6.258488 0.159783 2.4012% 1859 6.111731
0.163620 2.7627% 1858 5.947421 0.168140 2.8412% 1857 5.783111 0.172917 2.9243% 1856
5.618801 0.177974 3.0161% 1855 5.454292 0.183342 3.1061% 1854 5.289982 0.189037
3.2056% 1853 5.125672 0.195096 3.3118% 1852 4.961362 0.201558 3.4252% 1851 4.797052
0.208461 4.0106% 1850 4.612080 0.216822 3.3254% 1849 4.507269 0.221864 2.7841% 1848
4.385182 0.228041 2.8590% 1847 4.263294 0.234560 2.9432% 1846 4.141406 0.241464
3.0324% 1845 4.019518 0.248786 3.1325% 1844 3.897431 0.256579 3.2284% 1843 3.775543
0.264863 3.3361% 1842 3.653655 0.273699 3.4512% 1841 3.531767 0.283144 3.8105% 1840
3.402129 0.293934 2.3861% 1839 3.322844 0.300947 2.5824% 1838 3.239195 0.308719
2.6573% 1837 3.155348 0.316922 2.7232% 1836 3.071699 0.325553 2.7994% 1835 2.988050
0.334666 2.8871% 1834 2.904202 0.344329 2.9657% 1833 2.820554 0.354540 3.0563% 1832
2.736905 0.365376 3.1604% 1831 2.653057 0.376924 3.4660% 1830 2.564183 0.389988
2.4653% 1829 2.502490 0.399602 2.6804% 1828 2.437164 0.410313 10.3427% 1827
2.208723 0.452750 -4.2314% 1826 2.306313 0.433592 2.9150% 1825 2.240988 0.446232
3.0026% 1824 2.175662 0.459630 3.0955% 1823 2.110337 0.473858 3.1944% 1822 2.045011
0.488995 3.3102% 1821 1.979486 0.505182 3.2277% 1820 1.917591 0.521488 2.6573% 1819
1.867955 0.535345 2.6261% 1818 1.820155 0.549404 2.6969% 1817 1.772356 0.564221
2.7717% 1816 1.724557 0.579859 2.8507% 1815 1.676758 0.596389 2.9343% 1814 1.628958
0.613889 3.0231% 1813 1.581159 0.632447 3.1039% 1812 1.533559 0.652078 3.2172% 1811
1.485760 0.673056 3.0969% 1810 1.441129 0.693900 2.9144% 1809 1.400319 0.714123
2.8225% 1808 1.361880 0.734279 2.9199% 1807 1.323242 0.755719 2.9918% 1806 1.284804
0.778329 3.0841% 1805 1.246365 0.802333 3.1822% 1804 1.207927 0.827865 3.2868% 1803
1.169488 0.855075 3.3985% 1802 1.131050 0.884135 3.5180% 1801 1.092611 0.915239
3.3999% 1800 1.056684 0.946356 2.8419% 1799 1.027485 0.973251 2.7485% 1798 1.000000
1.000000 2.8261% 1797 0.972515 1.028261 3.7832% 1796 0.937064 1.067163 2.1272% 1795

0.917546 1.089863 3.0879% 1794 0.890062 1.123518 3.1625% 1793 0.862776 1.159049
3.2904% 1792 0.835292 1.197186 3.4024% 1791 0.807807 1.237919 3.2296% 1790 0.782535
1.277899 41.3145% 1780 0.553754 1.805855 29.4353% 1770 0.427823 2.337414 83.4728%
1750 0.233181 4.288521 29.2845% 1740 0.180362 5.544390 94.2514% 1720 0.092850
10.770056 85.8111% 1700 0.049970 20.011957 19.2490% 1690 0.041904 23.864068
88.0250% 1670 0.022286 44.870420

BASE YEAR: 1797

YEAR BYEAR/AYEAR AYEAR/BYEAR GROWTH%

2009 61.730565 0.016199 8.2857% 2001 57.007147 0.017542 1.0000% 2000
56.442714 0.017717 1.0000% 1999 55.883875 0.017894 1.0000% 1998 55.330569 0.018073
1.0000% 1997 54.782742 0.018254 1.0000% 1996 54.240339 0.018436 1.0000% 1995
53.703305 0.018621 0.9992% 1994 53.171999 0.018807 1.0008% 1993 52.645138 0.018995
1.0000% 1992 52.123899 0.019185 0.9295% 1991 51.643866 0.019363 1.2505% 1990
51.006028 0.019606 0.7224% 1989 50.640180 0.019747 1.1077% 1988 50.085398 0.019966
0.8834% 1987 49.646836 0.020142 0.5594% 1986 49.370674 0.020255 1.3056% 1985
48.734385 0.020519 0.7673% 1984 48.363301 0.020677 0.8149% 1983 47.972353 0.020845
0.9737% 1982 47.509728 0.021048 0.9508% 1981 47.062257 0.021248 0.9031% 1980
46.641057 0.021440 2.2701% 1979 45.605775 0.021927 1.0042% 1978 45.152365 0.022147
0.9896% 1977 44.709912 0.022366 0.9103% 1976 44.306574 0.022570 0.8394% 1975
43.937743 0.022759 0.9042% 1974 43.544030 0.022965 1.1568% 1973 43.046078 0.023231
0.9427% 1972 42.644071 0.023450 0.7426% 1971 42.329715 0.023624 1.4697% 1970
41.716591 0.023971 0.6968% 1969 41.427913 0.024138 0.8565% 1968 41.076080 0.024345
1.5090% 1967 40.465441 0.024712 0.9949% 1966 40.066813 0.024958 1.0575% 1965
39.647553 0.025222 1.1300% 1964 39.204536 0.025507 1.5537% 1963 38.604751 0.025904
1.4658% 1962 38.047051 0.026283 1.5364% 1961 37.471329 0.026687 2.1586% 1960
36.679550 0.027263 -1.6655% 1959 37.300788 0.026809 4.3080% 1958 35.760240 0.027964
2.1130% 1957 35.020274 0.028555 1.9895% 1956 34.337139 0.029123 2.1231% 1955
33.623285 0.029741 1.4496% 1954 33.142843 0.030172 2.1573% 1953 32.442965 0.030823
1.2298% 1952 32.048843 0.031202 1.6814% 1951 31.518892 0.031727 1.6233% 1950
31.015427 0.032242 1.4265% 1949 30.579203 0.032702 1.7790% 1948 30.044696 0.033284
1.8242% 1947 29.506451 0.033891 -2.6320% 1946 30.304065 0.032999 3.1768% 1945
29.371007 0.034047 6.4754% 1944 27.584777 0.036252 -0.3437% 1943 27.679907 0.036127
0.6562% 1942 27.499449 0.036364 0.6633% 1941 27.318247 0.036606 -5.6614% 1940
28.957664 0.034533 8.0381% 1939 26.803195 0.037309 0.8126% 1938 26.587139 0.037612
0.7762% 1937 26.382347 0.037904 0.6029% 1936 26.224247 0.038133 0.5244% 1935
26.087446 0.038333 -3.0364% 1934 26.904362 0.037169 4.6271% 1933 25.714520 0.038889
1.3921% 1932 25.361458 0.039430 -0.2051% 1931 25.413578 0.039349 0.8886% 1930
25.189742 0.039699 1.0126% 1929 24.937231 0.040101 1.1526% 1928 24.653082 0.040563
1.2160% 1927 24.356901 0.041056 1.4086% 1926 24.018580 0.041634 1.7667% 1925
23.601614 0.042370 1.4465% 1924 23.265083 0.042983 1.7700% 1923 22.860460 0.043744
1.6165% 1922 22.496795 0.044451 1.3736% 1921 22.191956 0.045061 2.3393% 1920
21.684684 0.046115 1.3140% 1919 21.403441 0.046721 0.7676% 1918 21.240390 0.047080
0.3870% 1917 21.158509 0.047262 1.3274% 1916 20.881323 0.047890 1.4083% 1915
20.591337 0.048564 1.4458% 1914 20.297870 0.049266 1.9424% 1913 19.911120 0.050223
1.9857% 1912 19.523449 0.051220 1.5634% 1911 19.222916 0.052021 1.8169% 1910
18.879884 0.052966 1.8781% 1909 18.531845 0.053961 2.0082% 1908 18.167008 0.055045
1.9603% 1907 17.817735 0.056124 1.8264% 1906 17.498157 0.057149 1.9357% 1905
17.165882 0.058255 2.0148% 1904 16.826848 0.059429 2.1335% 1903 16.475342 0.060697
1.8151% 1902 16.181622 0.061799 1.8943% 1901 15.880784 0.062969 3.0255% 1900
15.414421 0.064874 0.6209% 1899 15.318247 0.065282 1.7757% 1898 15.050993 0.066441
1.8078% 1897 14.783740 0.067642 1.8396% 1896 14.516691 0.068886 1.8755% 1895
14.249437 0.070178 1.9114% 1894 13.982183 0.071520 1.9486% 1893 13.714929 0.072913
1.9858% 1892 13.447880 0.074361 2.0276% 1891 13.180627 0.075869 2.6465% 1890
12.840793 0.077877 1.5328% 1889 12.646938 0.079071 2.0811% 1888 12.389105 0.080716
2.1599% 1887 12.127176 0.082459 2.2075% 1886 11.865247 0.084280 2.2592% 1885
11.603113 0.086184 2.3095% 1884 11.341184 0.088174 2.3641% 1883 11.079255 0.090259

2.4214% 1882 10.817325 0.092444 2.4815% 1881 10.555396 0.094738 3.7644% 1880
10.172464 0.098305 0.9432% 1879 10.077411 0.099232 2.1464% 1878 9.865656 0.101362
2.1913% 1877 9.654106 0.103583 2.2426% 1876 9.442351 0.105906 2.2941% 1875 9.230596
0.108335 2.3456% 1874 9.019046 0.110876 2.4043% 1873 8.807291 0.113542 2.4635% 1872
8.595536 0.116339 2.5258% 1871 8.383780 0.119278 5.9947% 1870 7.909624 0.126428 -
1.0968% 1869 7.997338 0.125042 2.1930% 1868 7.825722 0.127784 2.2394% 1867 7.654311
0.130645 2.2935% 1866 7.482695 0.133642 2.3445% 1865 7.311284 0.136775 2.4037% 1864
7.139668 0.140063 2.4599% 1863 6.968257 0.143508 2.5250% 1862 6.796641 0.147131
2.5872% 1861 6.625230 0.150938 2.9504% 1860 6.435361 0.155391 2.4012% 1859 6.284456
0.159123 2.7627% 1858 6.115503 0.163519 2.8412% 1857 5.946549 0.168165 2.9243% 1856
5.777596 0.173082 3.0161% 1855 5.608437 0.178303 3.1061% 1854 5.439484 0.183841
3.2056% 1853 5.270530 0.189734 3.3118% 1852 5.101577 0.196018 3.4252% 1851 4.932623
0.202732 4.0106% 1850 4.742424 0.210863 2.3254% 1849 4.634651 0.215766 2.7841% 1848
4.509113 0.221773 2.8590% 1847 4.383780 0.228114 2.9432% 1846 4.258448 0.234827
3.0324% 1845 4.133115 0.241948 3.1325% 1844 4.007577 0.249527 3.2284% 1843 3.882245
0.257583 3.3361% 1842 3.756912 0.266176 3.4512% 1841 3.631579 0.275362 3.8105% 1840
3.498277 0.285855 2.3861% 1839 3.416752 0.292676 2.5824% 1838 3.330739 0.300234
2.6573% 1837 3.244522 0.308212 2.7232% 1836 3.158509 0.316605 2.7994% 1835 3.072496
0.325468 2.8871% 1834 2.986279 0.334865 2.9657% 1833 2.900266 0.344796 3.0563% 1832
2.814254 0.355334 3.1604% 1831 2.728036 0.366564 3.4660% 1830 2.636651 0.379269
2.4653% 1829 2.573213 0.388619 2.6804% 1828 2.506041 0.399036 10.3427% 1827
2.271145 0.440307 -4.2314% 1826 2.371493 0.421675 2.9150% 1825 2.304321 0.433967
3.0026% 1824 2.237149 0.446997 3.0955% 1823 2.169977 0.460834 3.1944% 1822 2.102806
0.475555 3.3102% 1821 2.035429 0.491297 3.2277% 1820 1.971785 0.507155 2.6573% 1819
1.920745 0.520631 2.6261% 1818 1.871595 0.534304 2.6969% 1817 1.822445 0.548713
2.7717% 1816 1.773295 0.563922 2.8507% 1815 1.724145 0.579998 2.9343% 1814 1.674995
0.597017 3.0231% 1813 1.625845 0.615065 3.1039% 1812 1.576899 0.634156 3.2172% 1811
1.527749 0.654558 3.0969% 1810 1.481857 0.674829 2.9144% 1809 1.439894 0.694496
2.8225% 1808 1.400369 0.714098 2.9199% 1807 1.360639 0.734949 2.9918% 1806 1.321114
0.756937 3.0841% 1805 1.281589 0.780281 3.1822% 1804 1.242064 0.805111 3.2868% 1803
1.202539 0.831574 3.3985% 1802 1.163015 0.859834 3.5180% 1801 1.123490 0.890084
3.3999% 1800 1.086548 0.920346 2.8419% 1799 1.056523 0.946501 2.7485% 1798 1.028261
0.972515 2.8261% 1797 1.000000 1.000000 3.7832% 1796 0.963547 1.037832 2.1272% 1795
0.943477 1.059909 3.0879% 1794 0.915216 1.092638 3.1625% 1793 0.887160 1.127193
3.2904% 1792 0.858898 1.164282 3.4024% 1791 0.830637 1.203895 3.2296% 1790 0.804650
1.242776 41.3145% 1780 0.569404 1.756222 29.4353% 1770 0.439914 2.273172 83.4728%
1750 0.239771 4.170653 29.2845% 1740 0.185460 5.392005 94.2514% 1720 0.095474
10.474045 85.8111% 1700 0.051382 19.461937 19.2490% 1690 0.043088 23.208175
88.0250% 1670 0.022916 43.637176

BASE YEAR: 1796
YEAR BYEAR/AYEAR AYEAR/BYEAR GROWTH%

2009 64.065962 0.015609 8.2857% 2001 59.163847 0.016902 1.0000% 2000
58.578060 0.017071 1.0000% 1999 57.998079 0.017242 1.0000% 1998 57.423841 0.017414
1.0000% 1997 56.855288 0.017589 1.0000% 1996 56.292364 0.017764 1.0000% 1995
55.735014 0.017942 0.9992% 1994 55.183607 0.018121 1.0008% 1993 54.636814 0.018303
1.0000% 1992 54.095855 0.018486 0.9295% 1991 53.597662 0.018658 1.2505% 1990
52.935693 0.018891 0.7224% 1989 52.556004 0.019027 1.1077% 1988 51.980234 0.019238
0.8834% 1987 51.525080 0.019408 0.5594% 1986 51.238470 0.019517 1.3056% 1985
50.578108 0.019771 0.7673% 1984 50.192986 0.019923 0.8149% 1983 49.787248 0.020085
0.9737% 1982 49.307120 0.020281 0.9508% 1981 48.842721 0.020474 0.9031% 1980
48.405586 0.020659 2.2701% 1979 47.331137 0.021128 1.0042% 1978 46.860574 0.021340
0.9896% 1977 46.401382 0.021551 0.9103% 1976 45.982784 0.021747 0.8394% 1975
45.600000 0.021930 0.9042% 1974 45.191392 0.022128 1.1568% 1973 44.674601 0.022384
0.9427% 1972 44.257386 0.022595 0.7426% 1971 43.931137 0.022763 1.4697% 1970
43.294817 0.023097 0.6968% 1969 42.995218 0.023258 0.8565% 1968 42.630074 0.023458
1.5090% 1967 41.996334 0.023812 0.9949% 1966 41.582625 0.024049 1.0575% 1965

41.147503 0.024303 1.1300% 1964 40.687726 0.024577 1.5537% 1963 40.065250 0.024959 1.4658% 1962 39.486451 0.025325 1.5364% 1961 38.888948 0.025714 2.1586% 1960 38.067214 0.026269 -1.6655% 1959 38.711955 0.025832 4.3080% 1958 37.113124 0.026945 2.1130% 1957 36.345165 0.027514 1.9895% 1956 35.636185 0.028061 2.1231% 1955 34.895324 0.028657 1.4496% 1954 34.396706 0.029073 2.1573% 1953 33.670351 0.029700 1.2298% 1952 33.261318 0.030065 1.6814% 1951 32.711318 0.030570 1.6233% 1950 32.188806 0.031067 1.4265% 1949 31.736079 0.031510 1.7790% 1948 31.181350 0.032070 1.8242% 1947 30.622742 0.032655 -2.6320% 1946 31.450531 0.031796 3.1768% 1945 30.482173 0.032806 6.4754% 1944 28.628367 0.034930 -0.3437% 1943 28.727095 0.034810 0.6562% 1942 28.539811 0.035039 0.6633% 1941 28.351753 0.035271 -5.6614% 1940 30.053193 0.033274 8.0381% 1939 27.817216 0.035949 0.8126% 1938 27.592986 0.036241 0.7762% 1937 27.380446 0.036522 0.6029% 1936 27.216366 0.036743 0.5244% 1935 27.074389 0.036935 -3.0364% 1934 27.922210 0.035814 4.6271% 1933 26.687354 0.037471 1.3921% 1932 26.320935 0.037993 -0.2051% 1931 26.375027 0.037915 0.8886% 1930 26.142723 0.038252 1.0126% 1929 25.880659 0.038639 1.1526% 1928 25.585760 0.039084 1.2160% 1927 25.278374 0.039560 1.4086% 1926 24.927253 0.040117 1.7667% 1925 24.494512 0.040825 1.4465% 1924 24.145250 0.041416 1.7700% 1923 23.725319 0.042149 1.6165% 1922 23.347895 0.042830 1.3736% 1921 23.031524 0.043419 2.3393% 1920 22.505061 0.044434 1.3140% 1919 22.213177 0.045018 0.7676% 1918 22.043959 0.045364 0.3870% 1917 21.958980 0.045539 1.3274% 1916 21.671307 0.046144 1.4083% 1915 21.370351 0.046794 1.4458% 1914 21.065781 0.047470 1.9424% 1913 20.664400 0.048392 1.9857% 1912 20.262062 0.049353 1.5634% 1911 19.950159 0.050125 1.8169% 1910 19.594150 0.051036 1.8781% 1909 19.232944 0.051994 2.0082% 1908 18.854304 0.053038 1.9603% 1907 18.491817 0.054078 1.8264% 1906 18.160149 0.055066 1.9357% 1905 17.815303 0.056132 2.0148% 1904 17.463443 0.057262 2.1335% 1903 17.098639 0.058484 1.8151% 1902 16.793806 0.059546 1.8943% 1901 16.481588 0.060674 3.0255% 1900 15.997581 0.062509 0.6278% 1899 15.897768 0.062902 1.7757% 1898 15.620404 0.064019 1.8078% 1897 15.343039 0.065176 1.8396% 1896 15.065887 0.066375 1.8755% 1895 14.788523 0.067620 1.9114% 1894 14.511158 0.068912 1.9486% 1893 14.233794 0.070255 1.9858% 1892 13.956642 0.071650 2.0276% 1891 13.679277 0.073103 2.6465% 1890 13.326587 0.075038 1.5328% 1889 13.125399 0.076188 2.0811% 1888 12.857811 0.077774 2.1599% 1887 12.585972 0.079454 2.2075% 1886 12.314134 0.081207 2.2592% 1885 12.042083 0.083042 2.3095% 1884 11.770244 0.084960 2.3641% 1883 11.498406 0.086969 2.4214% 1882 11.226567 0.089074 2.4815% 1881 10.954729 0.091285 3.7644% 1880 10.557310 0.094721 0.9432% 1879 10.458661 0.095615 2.1464% 1878 10.238895 0.097667 2.1913% 1877 10.019341 0.099807 2.2426% 1876 9.799575 0.102045 2.2941% 1875 9.579809 0.104386 2.3456% 1874 9.360255 0.106835 2.4043% 1873 9.140489 0.109403 2.4635% 1872 8.920723 0.112099 2.5258% 1871 8.700956 0.114930 5.9947% 1870 8.208862 0.121820 -1.0968% 1869 8.299894 0.120483 2.1930% 1868 8.121785 0.123126 2.2394% 1867 7.943889 0.125883 2.2935% 1866 7.765781 0.128770 2.3445% 1865 7.587885 0.131789 2.4037% 1864 7.409777 0.134957 2.4599% 1863 7.231881 0.138277 2.5250% 1862 7.053773 0.141768 2.5872% 1861 6.875877 0.145436 2.9504% 1860 6.678824 0.149727 2.4012% 1859 6.522210 0.153522 2.7627% 1858 6.346865 0.157558 2.8412% 1857 6.171520 0.162035 2.9243% 1856 5.996174 0.166773 3.0161% 1855 5.820616 0.171803 3.1061% 1854 5.645271 0.177139 3.2056% 1853 5.469926 0.182818 3.3118% 1852 5.294580 0.188872 3.4252% 1851 5.119235 0.195342 4.0106% 1850 4.921839 0.203176 2.3254% 1849 4.809989 0.207901 2.7841% 1848 4.679702 0.213689 2.8590% 1847 4.549628 0.219798 2.9432% 1846 4.419554 0.226267 3.0324% 1845 4.289479 0.233129 3.1325% 1844 4.159192 0.240431 3.2284% 1843 4.029118 0.248193 3.3361% 1842 3.899044 0.256473 3.4512% 1841 3.768969 0.265325 3.8105% 1840 3.630625 0.275435 2.3861% 1839 3.546015 0.282007 2.5824% 1838 3.456748 0.289289 2.6573% 1837 3.367269 0.296977 2.7232% 1836 3.278002 0.305064 2.7994% 1835 3.188735 0.313604 2.8871% 1834 3.099256 0.322658 2.9657% 1833 3.009989 0.332227 3.0563% 1832 2.920723 0.342381 3.1604% 1831 2.831243 0.353202 3.4660% 1830 2.736401 0.365444 2.4653% 1829 2.670563 0.374453 2.6804% 1828 2.600850 0.384490 10.3427% 1827 2.357067 0.424256 -4.2314% 1826 2.461211 0.406304 2.9150% 1825 2.391498 0.418148 3.0026% 1824 2.321785 0.430703 3.0955% 1823 2.252072 0.444035 3.1944% 1822

325

2.182359 0.458220 3.3102% 1821 2.112434 0.473388 3.2277% 1820 2.046382 0.488667
2.6573% 1819 1.993411 0.501653 2.6261% 1818 1.942402 0.514827 2.6969% 1817 1.891392
0.528711 2.7717% 1816 1.840383 0.543365 2.8507% 1815 1.789373 0.558855 2.9343% 1814
1.738363 0.575254 3.0231% 1813 1.687354 0.592644 3.1039% 1812 1.636557 0.611039
3.2172% 1811 1.585547 0.630697 3.0969% 1810 1.537919 0.650229 2.9144% 1809 1.494368
0.669179 2.8225% 1808 1.453348 0.688067 2.9199% 1807 1.412115 0.708158 2.9918% 1806
1.371095 0.729344 3.0841% 1805 1.330074 0.751838 3.1822% 1804 1.289054 0.775763
3.2868% 1803 1.248034 0.801260 3.3985% 1802 1.207014 0.828491 3.5180% 1801 1.165994
0.857638 3.3999% 1800 1.127654 0.886797 2.8419% 1799 1.096493 0.911998 2.7485% 1798
1.067163 0.937064 2.8261% 1797 1.037832 0.963547 3.7832% 1796 1.000000 1.000000
2.1272% 1795 0.979171 1.021272 3.0879% 1794 0.949841 1.052808 3.1625% 1793 0.920723
1.086103 3.2904% 1792 0.891392 1.121841 3.4024% 1791 0.862062 1.160010 3.2296% 1790
0.835092 1.197473 41.3145% 1780 0.590946 1.692203 29.4353% 1770 0.456557 2.190308
83.4728% 1750 0.248842 4.018620 29.2845% 1740 0.192476 5.195451 94.2514% 1720
0.099086 10.092235 85.8111% 1700 0.053326 18.752491 19.2490% 1690 0.044718
22.362167 88.0250% 1670 0.023783 42.046470

BASE YEAR: 1795

YEAR BYEAR/AYEAR AYEAR/BYEAR GROWTH%

2009 65.428771 0.015284 8.2857% 2001 60.422379 0.016550 1.0000% 2000
59.824131 0.016716 1.0000% 1999 59.231813 0.016883 1.0000% 1998 58.645359 0.017052
1.0000% 1997 58.064712 0.017222 1.0000% 1996 57.489814 0.017394 1.0000% 1995
56.920608 0.017568 0.9992% 1994 56.357472 0.017744 1.0008% 1993 55.799047 0.017921
1.0000% 1992 55.246581 0.018101 0.9295% 1991 54.737790 0.018269 1.2505% 1990
54.061740 0.018497 0.7224% 1989 53.673974 0.018631 1.1077% 1988 53.085956 0.018837
0.8834% 1987 52.621120 0.019004 0.5594% 1986 52.328413 0.019110 1.3056% 1985
51.654005 0.019360 0.7673% 1984 51.260690 0.019508 0.8149% 1983 50.846321 0.019667
0.9737% 1982 50.355980 0.019859 0.9508% 1981 49.881702 0.020047 0.9031% 1980
49.435269 0.020228 2.2701% 1979 48.337964 0.020688 1.0042% 1978 47.857391 0.020895
0.9896% 1977 47.388431 0.021102 0.9103% 1976 46.960929 0.021294 0.8394% 1975
46.570002 0.021473 0.9042% 1974 46.152702 0.021667 1.1568% 1973 45.624919 0.021918
0.9427% 1972 45.198828 0.022124 0.7426% 1971 44.865639 0.022289 1.4697% 1970
44.215783 0.022616 0.6968% 1969 43.909811 0.022774 0.8565% 1968 43.536900 0.022969
1.5090% 1967 42.889679 0.023316 0.9949% 1966 42.467170 0.023548 1.0575% 1965
42.022791 0.023797 1.1300% 1964 41.553234 0.024066 1.5537% 1963 40.917517 0.024439
1.4658% 1962 40.326405 0.024798 1.5364% 1961 39.716193 0.025179 2.1586% 1960
38.876979 0.025722 -1.6655% 1959 39.535435 0.025294 4.3080% 1958 37.902594 0.026383
2.1130% 1957 37.118298 0.026941 1.9895% 1956 36.394237 0.027477 2.1231% 1955
35.637617 0.028060 1.4496% 1954 35.128392 0.028467 2.1573% 1953 34.386586 0.029081
1.2298% 1952 33.968852 0.029439 1.6814% 1951 33.407152 0.029934 1.6233% 1950
32.873525 0.030420 1.4265% 1949 32.411168 0.030854 1.7790% 1948 31.844639 0.031402
1.8242% 1947 31.274148 0.031975 -2.6320% 1946 32.119546 0.031134 3.1768% 1945
31.130589 0.032123 6.4754% 1944 29.237349 0.034203 -0.3437% 1943 29.338178 0.034085
0.6562% 1942 29.146909 0.034309 0.6633% 1941 28.954851 0.034537 -5.6614% 1940
30.692484 0.032581 8.0381% 1939 28.408943 0.035200 0.8126% 1938 28.179944 0.035486
0.7762% 1937 27.962883 0.035762 0.6029% 1936 27.795311 0.035977 0.5244% 1935
27.650315 0.036166 -3.0364% 1934 28.516171 0.035068 4.6271% 1933 27.255047 0.036690
1.3921% 1932 26.880834 0.037201 -0.2051% 1931 26.936076 0.037125 0.8886% 1930
26.698830 0.037455 1.0126% 1929 26.431192 0.037834 1.1526% 1928 26.130020 0.038270
1.2160% 1927 25.816095 0.038736 1.4086% 1926 25.457505 0.039281 1.7667% 1925
25.015559 0.039975 1.4465% 1924 24.658867 0.040553 1.7700% 1923 24.230003 0.041271
1.6165% 1922 23.844551 0.041938 1.3736% 1921 23.521450 0.042514 2.3393% 1920
22.983788 0.043509 1.3140% 1919 22.685696 0.044081 0.7676% 1918 22.512877 0.044419
0.3870% 1917 22.426091 0.044591 1.3274% 1916 22.132299 0.045183 1.4083% 1915
21.824940 0.045819 1.4458% 1914 21.513892 0.046482 1.9424% 1913 21.103972 0.047384
1.9857% 1912 20.693076 0.048325 1.5634% 1911 20.374539 0.049081 1.8169% 1910
20.010956 0.049973 1.8781% 1909 19.642066 0.050911 2.0082% 1908 19.255372 0.051934

326

1.9603% 1907 18.885175 0.052952 1.8264% 1906 18.546451 0.053919 1.9357% 1905
18.194270 0.054962 2.0148% 1904 17.834925 0.056070 2.1335% 1903 17.462361 0.057266
1.8151% 1902 17.151044 0.058305 1.8943% 1901 16.832184 0.059410 3.0255% 1900
16.337881 0.061207 0.6278% 1899 16.235945 0.061592 1.7757% 1898 15.952681 0.062685
1.8078% 1897 15.669416 0.063819 1.8396% 1896 15.386369 0.064993 1.8755% 1895
15.103104 0.066212 1.9114% 1894 14.819839 0.067477 1.9486% 1893 14.536575 0.068792
1.9858% 1892 14.253527 0.070158 2.0276% 1891 13.970263 0.071581 2.6465% 1890
13.610070 0.073475 1.5328% 1889 13.404602 0.074601 2.0811% 1888 13.131322 0.076154
2.1599% 1887 12.853701 0.077799 2.2075% 1886 12.576080 0.079516 2.2592% 1885
12.298242 0.081312 2.3095% 1884 12.020621 0.083190 2.3641% 1883 11.743000 0.085157
2.4214% 1882 11.465379 0.087219 2.4815% 1881 11.187758 0.089383 3.7644% 1880
10.781885 0.092748 0.9432% 1879 10.681137 0.093623 2.1464% 1878 10.456696 0.095632
2.1913% 1877 10.232472 0.097728 2.2426% 1876 10.008031 0.099920 2.2941% 1875
9.783590 0.102212 2.3456% 1874 9.559366 0.104609 2.4043% 1873 9.334925 0.107125
2.4635% 1872 9.110484 0.109764 2.5258% 1871 8.886043 0.112536 5.9947% 1870 8.383481
0.119282 -1.0968% 1869 8.476449 0.117974 2.1930% 1868 8.294552 0.120561 2.2394%
1867 8.112872 0.123261 2.2935% 1866 7.930975 0.126088 2.3445% 1865 7.749295 0.129044
2.4037% 1864 7.567397 0.132146 2.4599% 1863 7.385717 0.135396 2.5250% 1862 7.203820
0.138815 2.5872% 1861 7.022140 0.142407 2.9504% 1860 6.820896 0.146608 2.4012% 1859
6.660951 0.150129 2.7627% 1858 6.481875 0.154276 2.8412% 1857 6.302800 0.158660
2.9243% 1856 6.123725 0.163299 3.0161% 1855 5.944432 0.168225 3.1061% 1854 5.765357
0.173450 3.2056% 1853 5.586282 0.173910 3.3118% 1852 5.407206 0.184938 3.4252% 1851
5.228131 0.191273 4.0106% 1850 5.026537 0.198944 2.3254% 1849 4.912307 0.203570
2.7841% 1848 4.779249 0.209238 2.8590% 1847 4.646408 0.215220 2.9432% 1846 4.513566
0.221554 3.0324% 1845 4.380725 0.228273 3.1325% 1844 4.247667 0.235423 3.2284% 1843
4.114825 0.243024 3.3361% 1842 3.981984 0.251131 3.4512% 1841 3.849143 0.259798
3.8105% 1840 3.707855 0.269698 2.3861% 1839 3.621446 0.276133 2.5824% 1838 3.530280
0.283264 2.6573% 1837 3.438897 0.290791 2.7232% 1836 3.347732 0.298710 2.7994% 1835
3.256566 0.307072 2.8871% 1834 3.165183 0.315937 2.9657% 1833 3.074018 0.325307
3.0563% 1832 2.982852 0.335250 3.1604% 1831 2.891470 0.345845 3.4660% 1830 2.794609
0.357832 2.4653% 1829 2.727371 0.366653 2.6804% 1828 2.656175 0.376481 10.3427%
1827 2.407206 0.415419 -4.2314% 1826 2.513566 0.397841 2.9150% 1825 2.442370
0.409438 3.0026% 1824 2.371174 0.421732 3.0955% 1823 2.299978 0.434787 3.1944% 1822
2.228782 0.448675 3.3102% 1821 2.157369 0.463528 3.2277% 1820 2.089912 0.478489
2.6573% 1819 2.035815 0.491204 2.6261% 1818 1.983720 0.504103 2.6969% 1817 1.931626
0.517699 2.7717% 1816 1.879531 0.532048 2.8507% 1815 1.827437 0.547215 2.9343% 1814
1.775342 0.563272 3.0231% 1813 1.723247 0.580300 3.1039% 1812 1.671370 0.598312
3.2172% 1811 1.619275 0.617560 3.0969% 1810 1.570634 0.636686 2.9144% 1809 1.526156
0.655241 2.8225% 1808 1.484263 0.673735 2.9199% 1807 1.442153 0.693408 2.9918% 1806
1.400260 0.714153 3.0841% 1805 1.358368 0.736178 3.1822% 1804 1.316475 0.759604
3.2868% 1803 1.274582 0.784571 3.3985% 1802 1.232689 0.811234 3.5180% 1801 1.190797
0.839774 3.3999% 1800 1.151641 0.868326 2.8419% 1799 1.119818 0.893003 2.7485% 1798
1.089863 0.917546 2.8261% 1797 1.059909 0.943477 3.7832% 1796 1.021272 0.979171
2.1272% 1795 1.000000 1.000000 3.0879% 1794 0.970046 1.030879 3.1625% 1793 0.940308
1.063481 3.2904% 1792 0.910354 1.098474 3.4024% 1791 0.880399 1.135848 3.2296% 1790
0.852856 1.172531 41.3145% 1780 0.603516 1.656956 29.4353% 1770 0.466269 2.144686
83.4728% 1750 0.254135 3.934916 29.2845% 1740 0.196570 5.087235 94.2514% 1720
0.101194 9.882025 85.8111% 1700 0.054461 18.361897 19.2490% 1690 0.045670 21.896388
88.0250% 1670 0.024289 41.170688
BASE YEAR: 1794
YEAR BYEAR/AYEAR AYEAR/BYEAR GROWTH%
2009 67.449172 0.014826 8.2857% 2001 62.288185 0.016054 1.0000% 2000
61.671464 0.016215 1.0000% 1999 61.060855 0.016377 1.0000% 1998 60.456292 0.016541
1.0000% 1997 59.857715 0.016706 1.0000% 1996 59.265064 0.016873 1.0000% 1995
58.678281 0.017042 0.9992% 1994 58.097756 0.017212 1.0008% 1993 57.522088 0.017385
1.0000% 1992 56.952562 0.017558 0.9295% 1991 56.428060 0.017722 1.2505% 1990

55.731134 0.017943 0.7224% 1989 55.331394 0.018073 1.1077% 1988 54.725218 0.018273
0.8834% 1987 54.246028 0.018435 0.5594% 1986 53.944283 0.018538 1.3056% 1985
53.249049 0.018780 0.7673% 1984 52.843589 0.018924 0.8149% 1983 52.416424 0.019078
0.9737% 1982 51.910942 0.019264 0.9508% 1981 51.422018 0.019447 0.9031% 1980
50.961800 0.019623 2.2701% 1979 49.830611 0.020068 1.0042% 1978 49.335198 0.020270
0.9896% 1977 48.851757 0.020470 0.9103% 1976 48.411054 0.020656 0.8394% 1975
48.008055 0.020830 0.9042% 1974 47.577870 0.021018 1.1568% 1973 47.033788 0.021261
0.9427% 1972 46.594540 0.021462 0.7426% 1971 46.251063 0.021621 1.4697% 1970
45.581140 0.021939 0.6968% 1969 45.265719 0.022092 0.8565% 1968 44.881293 0.022281
1.5090% 1967 44.214086 0.022617 0.9949% 1966 43.778530 0.022842 1.0575% 1965
43.320430 0.023084 1.1300% 1964 42.836373 0.023345 1.5537% 1963 42.181025 0.023707
1.4658% 1962 41.571660 0.024055 1.5364% 1961 40.942605 0.024424 2.1586% 1960
40.077476 0.024952 -1.6655% 1959 40.756265 0.024536 4.3080% 1958 39.073003 0.025593
2.1130% 1957 38.264489 0.026134 1.9895% 1956 37.518069 0.026654 2.1231% 1955
36.738085 0.027220 1.4496% 1954 36.213135 0.027614 2.1573% 1953 35.448422 0.028210
1.2298% 1952 35.017789 0.028557 1.6814% 1951 34.438745 0.029037 1.6233% 1950
33.888640 0.029508 1.4265% 1949 33.412005 0.029929 1.7790% 1948 32.827982 0.030462
1.8242% 1947 32.239875 0.031017 -2.6320% 1946 33.111378 0.030201 3.1768% 1945
32.091883 0.031161 6.4754% 1944 30.140181 0.033178 -0.3437% 1943 30.244123 0.033064
0.6562% 1942 30.046948 0.033281 0.6633% 1941 29.848959 0.033502 -5.6614% 1940
31.640249 0.031605 8.0381% 1939 29.286194 0.034146 0.8126% 1938 29.050123 0.034423
0.7762% 1937 28.826359 0.034690 0.6029% 1936 28.653614 0.034900 0.5244% 1935
28.504140 0.035083 -3.0364% 1934 29.396733 0.034017 4.6271% 1933 28.096666 0.035591
1.3921% 1932 27.710897 0.036087 -0.2051% 1931 27.767845 0.036013 0.8886% 1930
27.523274 0.036333 1.0126% 1929 27.247371 0.036701 1.1526% 1928 26.936899 0.037124
1.2160% 1927 26.613280 0.037575 1.4086% 1926 26.243618 0.038105 1.7667% 1925
25.788024 0.038778 1.4465% 1924 25.420318 0.039339 1.7700% 1923 24.978211 0.040035
1.6165% 1922 24.580857 0.040682 1.3736% 1921 24.247778 0.041241 2.3393% 1920
23.693513 0.042206 1.3140% 1919 23.386216 0.042760 0.7676% 1918 23.208061 0.043088
0.3870% 1917 23.118595 0.043255 1.3274% 1916 22.815731 0.043829 1.4083% 1915
22.498881 0.044447 1.4458% 1914 22.178228 0.045089 1.9424% 1913 21.755650 0.045965
1.9857% 1912 21.332065 0.046878 1.5634% 1911 21.003692 0.047611 1.8169% 1910
20.628883 0.048476 1.8781% 1909 20.248601 0.049386 2.0082% 1908 19.849966 0.050378
1.9603% 1907 19.468337 0.051365 1.8264% 1906 19.119154 0.052304 1.9357% 1905
18.756098 0.053316 2.0148% 1904 18.385657 0.054390 2.1335% 1903 18.001588 0.055551
1.8151% 1902 17.680568 0.056559 1.8943% 1901 17.351951 0.057630 3.0255% 1900
16.842385 0.059374 0.6278% 1899 16.737301 0.059747 1.7757% 1898 16.445290 0.060808
1.8078% 1897 16.153278 0.061907 1.8396% 1896 15.861490 0.063046 1.8755% 1895
15.569479 0.064228 1.9114% 1894 15.277467 0.065456 1.9486% 1893 14.985455 0.066731
1.9858% 1892 14.693667 0.068057 2.0276% 1891 14.401656 0.069436 2.6465% 1890
14.030341 0.071274 1.5328% 1889 13.818528 0.072367 2.0811% 1888 13.536809 0.073873
2.1599% 1887 13.250615 0.075468 2.2075% 1886 12.964422 0.077134 2.2592% 1885
12.678004 0.078877 2.3095% 1884 12.391810 0.080698 2.3641% 1883 12.105616 0.082606
2.4214% 1882 11.819423 0.084607 2.4815% 1881 11.533229 0.086706 3.7644% 1880
11.114823 0.089970 0.9432% 1879 11.010964 0.090819 2.1464% 1878 10.779593 0.092768
2.1913% 1877 10.548445 0.094801 2.2426% 1876 10.317073 0.096927 2.2941% 1875
10.085701 0.099150 2.3456% 1874 9.854554 0.101476 2.4043% 1873 9.623182 0.103916
2.4635% 1872 9.391810 0.106476 2.5258% 1871 9.160439 0.109165 5.9947% 1870 8.642357
0.115709 -1.0968% 1869 8.738196 0.114440 2.1930% 1868 8.550682 0.116950 2.2394%
1867 8.363392 0.119569 2.2935% 1866 8.175878 0.122311 2.3445% 1865 7.988588 0.125179
2.4037% 1864 7.801074 0.128187 2.4599% 1863 7.613784 0.131341 2.5250% 1862 7.426270
0.134657 2.5872% 1861 7.238980 0.138141 2.9504% 1860 7.031521 0.142217 2.4012% 1859
6.866637 0.145632 2.7627% 1858 6.682032 0.149655 2.8412% 1857 6.497427 0.153907
2.9243% 1856 6.312822 0.158408 3.0161% 1855 6.127993 0.163186 3.1061% 1854 5.943388
0.168254 3.2056% 1853 5.758783 0.173648 3.3118% 1852 5.574178 0.179399 3.4252% 1851
5.389573 0.185543 4.0106% 1850 5.181753 0.192985 2.3254% 1849 5.063996 0.197472

2.7841% 1848 4.926829 0.202970 2.8590% 1847 4.789886 0.208773 2.9432% 1846 4.652942
0.214918 3.0324% 1845 4.515999 0.221435 3.1325% 1844 4.378832 0.228371 3.2284% 1843
4.241889 0.235744 3.3361% 1842 4.104945 0.243609 3.4512% 1841 3.968002 0.252016
3.8105% 1840 3.822352 0.261619 2.3861% 1839 3.733274 0.267861 2.5824% 1838 3.639293
0.274779 2.6573% 1837 3.545088 0.282080 2.7232% 1836 3.451108 0.289762 2.7994% 1835
3.357127 0.297874 2.8871% 1834 3.262922 0.306474 2.9657% 1833 3.168942 0.315563
3.0563% 1832 3.074961 0.325207 3.1604% 1831 2.980756 0.335485 3.4660% 1830 2.880905
0.347113 2.4653% 1829 2.811591 0.355671 2.6804% 1828 2.738196 0.365204 10.3427%
1827 2.481539 0.402976 -4.2314% 1826 2.591184 0.385924 2.9150% 1825 2.517789
0.397174 3.0026% 1824 2.444395 0.409099 3.0955% 1823 2.371000 0.421763 3.1944% 1822
2.297606 0.435236 3.3102% 1821 2.223987 0.449643 3.2277% 1820 2.154448 0.464156
2.6573% 1819 2.098680 0.476490 2.6261% 1818 2.044977 0.489003 2.6969% 1817 1.991273
0.502191 2.7717% 1816 1.937570 0.516110 2.8507% 1815 1.883867 0.530823 2.9343% 1814
1.830163 0.546399 3.0231% 1813 1.776460 0.562917 3.1039% 1812 1.722981 0.580390
3.2172% 1811 1.669277 0.599062 3.0969% 1810 1.619134 0.617614 2.9144% 1809 1.573283
0.635614 2.8225% 1808 1.530096 0.653554 2.9199% 1807 1.486686 0.672637 2.9918% 1806
1.443500 0.692761 3.0841% 1805 1.400313 0.714126 3.1822% 1804 1.357127 0.736851
3.2868% 1803 1.313940 0.761069 3.3985% 1802 1.270754 0.786934 3.5180% 1801 1.227568
0.814619 3.3999% 1800 1.187203 0.842316 2.8419% 1799 1.154397 0.866253 2.7485% 1798
1.123518 0.890062 2.8261% 1797 1.092638 0.915216 3.7832% 1796 1.052808 0.949841
2.1272% 1795 1.030879 0.970046 3.0879% 1794 1.000000 1.000000 3.1625% 1793 0.969344
1.031625 3.2904% 1792 0.938465 1.065570 3.4024% 1791 0.907586 1.101824 3.2296% 1790
0.879192 1.137409 41.3145% 1780 0.622153 1.607323 29.4353% 1770 0.480667 2.080443
83.4728% 1750 0.261983 3.817048 29.2845% 1740 0.202640 4.934850 94.2514% 1720
0.104319 9.586015 85.8111% 1700 0.056142 17.811877 19.2490% 1690 0.047080 21.240494
88.0250% 1670 0.025039 39.937444

BASE YEAR: 1793
YEAR BYEAR/AYEAR AYEAR/BYEAR GROWTH%
2009 69.582260 0.014371 8.2857% 2001 64.258056 0.015562 1.0000% 2000
63.621831 0.015718 1.0000% 1999 62.991912 0.015875 1.0000% 1998 62.368229 0.016034
1.0000% 1997 61.750722 0.016194 1.0000% 1996 61.139329 0.016356 1.0000% 1995
60.533989 0.016520 0.9992% 1994 59.935104 0.016685 1.0008% 1993 59.341230 0.016852
1.0000% 1992 58.753693 0.017020 0.9295% 1991 58.212604 0.017178 1.2505% 1990
57.493637 0.017393 0.7224% 1989 57.081256 0.017519 1.1077% 1988 56.455910 0.017713
0.8834% 1987 55.961565 0.017869 0.5594% 1986 55.650277 0.017969 1.3056% 1985
54.933056 0.018204 0.7673% 1984 54.514774 0.018344 0.8149% 1983 54.074100 0.018493
0.9737% 1982 53.552632 0.018673 0.9508% 1981 53.048246 0.018851 0.9031% 1980
52.573473 0.019021 2.2701% 1979 51.406510 0.019453 1.0042% 1978 50.895429 0.019648
0.9896% 1977 50.396699 0.019843 0.9103% 1976 49.942059 0.020023 0.8394% 1975
49.526316 0.020191 0.9042% 1974 49.082525 0.020374 1.1568% 1973 48.521237 0.020610
0.9427% 1972 48.068098 0.020804 0.7426% 1971 47.713758 0.020958 1.4697% 1970
47.022649 0.021266 0.6968% 1969 46.697253 0.021415 0.8565% 1968 46.300669 0.021598
1.5090% 1967 45.612361 0.021924 0.9949% 1966 45.163031 0.022142 1.0575% 1965
44.690443 0.022376 1.1300% 1964 44.191078 0.022629 1.5537% 1963 43.515005 0.022981
1.4658% 1962 42.886369 0.023317 1.5364% 1961 42.237419 0.023676 2.1586% 1960
41.344931 0.024187 -1.6655% 1959 42.045187 0.023784 4.3080% 1958 40.308691 0.024809
2.1130% 1957 39.474608 0.025333 1.9895% 1956 38.704582 0.025837 2.1231% 1955
37.899931 0.026385 1.4496% 1954 37.358380 0.026768 2.1573% 1953 36.569483 0.027345
1.2298% 1952 36.125231 0.027681 1.6814% 1951 35.527874 0.028147 1.6233% 1950
34.960372 0.028604 1.4265% 1949 34.468663 0.029012 1.7790% 1948 33.866170 0.029528
1.8242% 1947 33.259464 0.030067 -2.6320% 1946 34.158530 0.029275 3.1768% 1945
33.106792 0.030205 6.4754% 1944 31.093367 0.032161 -0.3437% 1943 31.200596 0.032051
0.6562% 1942 30.997186 0.032261 0.6633% 1941 30.792936 0.032475 -5.6614% 1940
32.640876 0.030636 8.0381% 1939 30.212373 0.033099 0.8126% 1938 29.968837 0.033368
0.7762% 1937 29.737996 0.033627 0.6029% 1936 29.559788 0.033830 0.5244% 1935
29.405586 0.034007 -3.0364% 1934 30.326408 0.032975 4.6271% 1933 28.985226 0.034500

1.3921% 1932 28.587258 0.034981 -0.2051% 1931 28.646006 0.034909 0.8886% 1930
28.393701 0.035219 1.0126% 1929 28.109072 0.035576 1.1526% 1928 27.788781 0.035986
1.2160% 1927 27.454928 0.036423 1.4086% 1926 27.073575 0.036936 1.7667% 1925
26.603573 0.037589 1.4465% 1924 26.224239 0.038133 1.7700% 1923 25.768150 0.038808
1.6165% 1922 25.358229 0.039435 1.3736% 1921 25.014617 0.039977 2.3393% 1920
24.442823 0.040912 1.3140% 1919 24.125808 0.041449 0.7676% 1918 23.942019 0.041768
0.3870% 1917 23.849723 0.041929 1.3274% 1916 23.537281 0.042486 1.4083% 1915
23.210411 0.043084 1.4458% 1914 22.879617 0.043707 1.9424% 1913 22.443675 0.044556
1.9857% 1912 22.006694 0.045441 1.5634% 1911 21.667936 0.046151 1.8169% 1910
21.281273 0.046990 1.8781% 1909 20.888966 0.047872 2.0082% 1908 20.477724 0.048834
1.9603% 1907 20.084026 0.049791 1.8264% 1906 19.723800 0.050700 1.9357% 1905
19.349261 0.051682 2.0148% 1904 18.967105 0.052723 2.1335% 1903 18.570890 0.053848
1.8151% 1902 18.239810 0.054825 1.8943% 1901 17.900709 0.055864 3.0255% 1900
17.375027 0.057554 0.6278% 1899 17.266620 0.057915 1.7757% 1898 16.965374 0.058944
1.8078% 1897 16.664127 0.060009 1.8396% 1896 16.363112 0.061113 1.8755% 1895
16.061865 0.062259 1.9114% 1894 15.760619 0.063449 1.9486% 1893 15.459372 0.064686
1.9858% 1892 15.158356 0.065970 2.0276% 1891 14.857110 0.067308 2.6465% 1890
14.474052 0.069089 1.5328% 1889 14.255540 0.070148 2.0811% 1888 13.964912 0.071608
2.1599% 1887 13.669668 0.073155 2.2075% 1886 13.374423 0.074770 2.2592% 1885
13.078947 0.076459 2.3095% 1884 12.783703 0.078225 2.3641% 1883 12.488458 0.080074
2.4214% 1882 12.193213 0.082013 2.4815% 1881 11.897969 0.084048 3.7644% 1880
11.466331 0.087212 0.9432% 1879 11.359187 0.088034 2.1464% 1878 11.120499 0.089924
2.1913% 1877 10.882041 0.091895 2.2426% 1876 10.643352 0.093955 2.2941% 1875
10.404663 0.096111 2.3456% 1874 10.166205 0.098365 2.4043% 1873 9.927516 0.100730
2.4635% 1872 9.688827 0.103212 2.5258% 1871 9.450139 0.105819 5.9947% 1870 8.915673
0.112162 -1.0968% 1869 9.014543 0.110932 2.1930% 1868 8.821099 0.113365 2.2394%
1867 8.627886 0.115903 2.2935% 1866 8.434441 0.118561 2.3445% 1865 8.241228 0.121341
2.4037% 1864 8.047784 0.124258 2.4599% 1863 7.854571 0.127314 2.5250% 1862 7.661127
0.130529 2.5872% 1861 7.467913 0.133906 2.9504% 1860 7.253894 0.137857 2.4012% 1859
7.083795 0.141167 2.7627% 1858 6.893352 0.145067 2.8412% 1857 6.702909 0.149189
2.9243% 1856 6.512465 0.153552 3.0161% 1855 6.321791 0.158183 3.1061% 1854 6.131348
0.163096 3.2056% 1853 5.940905 0.168325 3.3118% 1852 5.750462 0.173899 3.4252% 1851
5.560018 0.179856 4.0106% 1850 5.345627 0.187069 2.3254% 1849 5.224146 0.191419
2.7841% 1848 5.082641 0.196748 2.8590% 1847 4.941367 0.202373 2.9432% 1846 4.800092
0.208329 3.0324% 1845 4.658818 0.214647 3.1325% 1844 4.517313 0.221371 3.2284% 1843
4.376039 0.228517 3.3361% 1842 4.234765 0.236141 3.4512% 1841 4.093490 0.244290
3.8105% 1840 3.943234 0.253599 2.3861% 1839 3.851339 0.259650 2.5824% 1838 3.754386
0.266355 2.6573% 1837 3.657202 0.273433 2.7232% 1836 3.560249 0.280879 2.7994% 1835
3.463296 0.288742 2.8871% 1834 3.366113 0.297079 2.9657% 1833 3.269160 0.305889
3.0563% 1832 3.172207 0.315238 3.1604% 1831 3.075023 0.325201 3.4660% 1830 2.972014
0.336472 2.4653% 1829 2.900508 0.344767 2.6804% 1828 2.824792 0.354008 10.3427%
1827 2.560018 0.390622 -4.2314% 1826 2.673130 0.374093 2.9150% 1825 2.597415
0.384998 3.0026% 1824 2.521699 0.396558 3.0955% 1823 2.445983 0.408834 3.1944% 1822
2.370268 0.421893 3.3102% 1821 2.294321 0.435859 3.2277% 1820 2.222582 0.449927
2.6573% 1819 2.165051 0.461883 2.6261% 1818 2.109649 0.474012 2.6969% 1817 2.054247
0.486796 2.7717% 1816 1.998846 0.500289 2.8507% 1815 1.943444 0.514550 2.9343% 1814
1.888042 0.529649 3.0231% 1813 1.832641 0.545661 3.1039% 1812 1.777470 0.562597
3.2172% 1811 1.722068 0.580697 3.0969% 1810 1.670339 0.598681 2.9144% 1809 1.623038
0.616129 2.8225% 1808 1.578486 0.633519 2.9199% 1807 1.533703 0.652017 2.9918% 1806
1.489151 0.671524 3.0841% 1805 1.444598 0.692234 3.1822% 1804 1.400046 0.714262
3.2868% 1803 1.355494 0.737738 3.3985% 1802 1.310942 0.762810 3.5180% 1801 1.266390
0.789646 3.3999% 1800 1.224749 0.816494 2.8419% 1799 1.190905 0.839698 2.7485% 1798
1.159049 0.862776 2.8261% 1797 1.127193 0.887160 3.7832% 1796 1.086103 0.920723
2.1272% 1795 1.063481 0.940308 3.0879% 1794 1.031625 0.969344 3.1625% 1793 1.000000
1.000000 3.2904% 1792 0.968144 1.032904 3.4024% 1791 0.936288 1.068047 3.2296% 1790
0.906996 1.102541 41.3145% 1780 0.641828 1.558049 29.4353% 1770 0.495868 2.016666

330

83.4728% 1750 0.270268 3.700034 29.2845% 1740 0.209049 4.783569 94.2514% 1720
0.107618 9.292149 85.8111% 1700 0.057918 17.265843 19.2490% 1690 0.048569 20.589354
88.0250% 1670 0.025831 38.713137

BASE YEAR: 1792

YEAR BYEAR/AYEAR AYEAR/BYEAR GROWTH%

2009 71.871805 0.013914 8.2857% 2001 66.372413 0.015067 1.0000% 2000
65.715253 0.015217 1.0000% 1999 65.064607 0.015369 1.0000% 1998 64.420403 0.015523
1.0000% 1997 63.782577 0.015678 1.0000% 1996 63.151067 0.015835 1.0000% 1995
62.525808 0.015993 0.9992% 1994 61.907218 0.016153 1.0008% 1993 61.293803 0.016315
1.0000% 1992 60.686934 0.016478 0.9295% 1991 60.128040 0.016631 1.2505% 1990
59.385416 0.016839 0.7224% 1989 58.959466 0.016961 1.1077% 1988 58.313543 0.017149
0.8834% 1987 57.802933 0.017300 0.5594% 1986 57.481402 0.017397 1.3056% 1985
56.740582 0.017624 0.7673% 1984 56.308536 0.017759 0.8149% 1983 55.853362 0.017904
0.9737% 1982 55.314735 0.018078 0.9508% 1981 54.793753 0.018250 0.9031% 1980
54.303358 0.018415 2.2701% 1979 53.097997 0.018833 1.0042% 1978 52.570100 0.019022
0.9896% 1977 52.054959 0.019210 0.9103% 1976 51.585360 0.019385 0.8394% 1975
51.155937 0.019548 0.9042% 1974 50.697544 0.019725 1.1568% 1973 50.117787 0.019953
0.9427% 1972 49.649738 0.020141 0.7426% 1971 49.283739 0.020291 1.4697% 1970
48.569889 0.020589 0.6968% 1969 48.233786 0.020732 0.8565% 1968 47.824154 0.020910
1.5090% 1967 47.113197 0.021225 0.9949% 1966 46.649082 0.021437 1.0575% 1965
46.160944 0.021663 1.1300% 1964 45.645148 0.021908 1.5537% 1963 44.946829 0.022249
1.4658% 1962 44.297508 0.022575 1.5364% 1961 43.627206 0.022921 2.1586% 1960
42.705351 0.023416 -1.6655% 1959 43.428648 0.023026 4.3080% 1958 41.635014 0.024018
2.1130% 1957 40.773486 0.024526 1.9895% 1956 39.978124 0.025014 2.1231% 1955
39.146996 0.025545 1.4496% 1954 38.587625 0.025915 2.1573% 1953 37.772771 0.026474
1.2298% 1952 37.313901 0.026800 1.6814% 1951 36.696888 0.027250 1.6233% 1950
36.110713 0.027693 1.4265% 1949 35.602825 0.028088 1.7790% 1948 34.980508 0.028587
1.8242% 1947 34.353839 0.029109 -2.6320% 1946 35.282487 0.028343 3.1768% 1945
34.196143 0.029243 6.4754% 1944 32.116468 0.031137 -0.3437% 1943 32.227226 0.031030
0.6562% 1942 32.017122 0.031233 0.6633% 1941 31.806152 0.031440 -5.6614% 1940
33.714896 0.029660 8.0381% 1939 31.206485 0.032045 0.8126% 1938 30.954936 0.032305
0.7762% 1937 30.716500 0.032556 0.6029% 1936 30.532427 0.032752 0.5244% 1935
30.373152 0.032924 -3.0364% 1934 31.324273 0.031924 4.6271% 1933 29.938960 0.033401
1.3921% 1932 29.527897 0.033866 -0.2051% 1931 29.588579 0.033797 0.8886% 1930
29.327971 0.034097 1.0126% 1929 29.033977 0.034442 1.1526% 1928 28.703147 0.034839
1.2160% 1927 28.358309 0.035263 1.4086% 1926 27.964408 0.035760 1.7667% 1925
27.478941 0.036392 1.4465% 1924 27.087125 0.036918 1.7700% 1923 26.616029 0.037571
1.6165% 1922 26.192620 0.038179 1.3736% 1921 25.837702 0.038703 2.3393% 1920
25.247093 0.039609 1.3140% 1919 24.919647 0.040129 0.7676% 1918 24.729810 0.040437
0.3870% 1917 24.634478 0.040594 1.3274% 1916 24.311755 0.041132 1.4083% 1915
23.974130 0.041712 1.4458% 1914 23.632451 0.042315 1.9424% 1913 23.182165 0.043137
1.9857% 1912 22.730806 0.043993 1.5634% 1911 22.380901 0.044681 1.8169% 1910
21.981515 0.045493 1.8781% 1909 21.576299 0.046347 2.0082% 1908 21.151526 0.047278
1.9603% 1907 20.744874 0.048205 1.8264% 1906 20.372794 0.049085 1.9357% 1905
19.985932 0.050035 2.0148% 1904 19.591202 0.051043 2.1335% 1903 19.181950 0.052132
1.8151% 1902 18.839976 0.053079 1.8943% 1901 18.489716 0.054084 3.0255% 1900
17.946738 0.055720 0.6278% 1899 17.834764 0.056070 1.7757% 1898 17.523605 0.057066
1.8078% 1897 17.212446 0.058097 1.8396% 1896 16.901526 0.059166 1.8755% 1895
16.590367 0.060276 1.9114% 1894 16.279208 0.061428 1.9486% 1893 15.968050 0.062625
1.9858% 1892 15.657129 0.063869 2.0276% 1891 15.345970 0.065164 2.6465% 1890
14.950308 0.066888 1.5328% 1889 14.724607 0.067914 2.0811% 1888 14.424416 0.069327
2.1599% 1887 14.119456 0.070824 2.2075% 1886 13.814497 0.072388 2.2592% 1885
13.509299 0.074023 2.3095% 1884 13.204340 0.075733 2.3641% 1883 12.899380 0.077523
2.4214% 1882 12.594421 0.079400 2.4815% 1881 12.289461 0.081371 3.7644% 1880
11.843620 0.084434 0.9432% 1879 11.732952 0.085230 2.1464% 1878 11.486409 0.087059
2.1913% 1877 11.240105 0.088967 2.2426% 1876 10.993562 0.090962 2.2941% 1875

10.747020 0.093049 2.3456% 1874 10.500715 0.095232 2.4043% 1873 10.254173 0.097521 2.4635% 1872 10.007630 0.099924 2.5258% 1871 9.761087 0.102448 5.9947% 1870 9.209036 0.108589 -1.0968% 1869 9.311159 0.107398 2.1930% 1868 9.111350 0.109753 2.2394% 1867 8.911779 0.112211 2.2935% 1866 8.711969 0.114785 2.3445% 1865 8.512399 0.117476 2.4037% 1864 8.312589 0.120299 2.4599% 1863 8.113019 0.123259 2.5250% 1862 7.913209 0.126371 2.5872% 1861 7.713639 0.129641 2.9504% 1860 7.492577 0.133465 2.4012% 1859 7.316881 0.136670 2.7627% 1858 7.120172 0.140446 2.8412% 1857 6.923462 0.144436 2.9243% 1856 6.726753 0.148660 3.0161% 1855 6.529804 0.153144 3.1061% 1854 6.333095 0.157901 3.2056% 1853 6.136385 0.162962 3.3118% 1852 5.939676 0.168359 3.4252% 1851 5.742966 0.174126 4.0106% 1850 5.521520 0.181110 2.3254% 1849 5.396042 0.185321 2.7841% 1848 5.249881 0.190481 2.8590% 1847 5.103958 0.195926 2.9432% 1846 4.958035 0.201693 3.0324% 1845 4.812113 0.207809 3.1325% 1844 4.665951 0.214319 3.2284% 1843 4.520029 0.221238 3.3361% 1842 4.374106 0.228618 3.4512% 1841 4.228183 0.236508 3.8105% 1840 4.072983 0.245520 2.3861% 1839 3.978064 0.251379 2.5824% 1838 3.877921 0.257870 2.6573% 1837 3.777539 0.264723 2.7232% 1836 3.677396 0.271932 2.7994% 1835 3.577253 0.279544 2.8871% 1834 3.476872 0.287615 2.9657% 1833 3.376729 0.296145 3.0563% 1832 3.276586 0.305196 3.1604% 1831 3.176204 0.314841 3.4660% 1830 3.069806 0.325754 2.4653% 1829 2.995947 0.333784 2.6804% 1828 2.917740 0.342731 10.3427% 1827 2.644254 0.378179 -4.2314% 1826 2.761087 0.362176 2.9150% 1825 2.682880 0.372734 3.0026% 1824 2.604673 0.383925 3.0955% 1823 2.526466 0.395810 3.1944% 1822 2.448259 0.408453 3.3102% 1821 2.369814 0.421974 3.2277% 1820 2.295714 0.435594 2.6573% 1819 2.236290 0.447169 2.6261% 1818 2.179065 0.458912 2.6969% 1817 2.121841 0.471289 2.7717% 1816 2.064616 0.484352 2.8507% 1815 2.007392 0.498159 2.9343% 1814 1.950167 0.512777 3.0231% 1813 1.892942 0.528278 3.1039% 1812 1.835956 0.544675 3.2172% 1811 1.778732 0.562198 3.0969% 1810 1.725300 0.579609 2.9144% 1809 1.676443 0.596501 2.8225% 1808 1.630424 0.613337 2.9199% 1807 1.584168 0.631246 2.9918% 1806 1.538150 0.650132 3.0841% 1805 1.492132 0.670182 3.1822% 1804 1.446113 0.691509 3.2868% 1803 1.400095 0.714237 3.3985% 1802 1.354077 0.738510 3.5180% 1801 1.308059 0.764491 3.3999% 1800 1.265048 0.790484 2.8419% 1799 1.230091 0.812948 2.7485% 1798 1.197186 0.835292 2.8261% 1797 1.164282 0.858898 3.7832% 1796 1.121841 0.891392 2.1272% 1795 1.098474 0.910354 3.0879% 1794 1.065570 0.938465 3.1625% 1793 1.032904 0.968144 3.2904% 1792 1.000000 1.000000 3.4024% 1791 0.967096 1.034024 3.2296% 1790 0.936840 1.067418 41.3145% 1780 0.662947 1.508416 29.4353% 1770 0.512184 1.952423 83.4728% 1750 0.279161 3.582166 29.2845% 1740 0.215928 4.631184 94.2514% 1720 0.111159 8.996139 85.8111% 1700 0.059824 16.715823 19.2490% 1690 0.050167 19.933460 88.0250% 1670 0.026681 37.479893

BASE YEAR: 1791

YEAR BYEAR/AYEAR AYEAR/BYEAR GROWTH%

2009 74.317147 0.013456 8.2857% 2001 68.630646 0.014571 1.0000% 2000 67.951127 0.014716 1.0000% 1999 67.278344 0.014864 1.0000% 1998 66.612221 0.015012 1.0000% 1997 65.952695 0.015162 1.0000% 1996 65.299697 0.015314 1.0000% 1995 64.653166 0.015467 0.9992% 1994 64.013529 0.015622 1.0008% 1993 63.379243 0.015778 1.0000% 1992 62.751726 0.015936 0.9295% 1991 62.173817 0.016084 1.2505% 1990 61.405926 0.016285 0.7224% 1989 60.965483 0.016403 1.1077% 1988 60.297584 0.016584 0.8834% 1987 59.769601 0.016731 0.5594% 1986 59.437130 0.016825 1.3056% 1985 58.671105 0.017044 0.7673% 1984 58.224359 0.017175 0.8149% 1983 57.753698 0.017315 0.9737% 1982 57.196746 0.017484 0.9508% 1981 56.658037 0.017650 0.9031% 1980 56.150957 0.017809 2.2701% 1979 54.904586 0.018213 1.0042% 1978 54.358728 0.018396 0.9896% 1977 53.826060 0.018578 0.9103% 1976 53.340483 0.018747 0.8394% 1975 52.896450 0.018905 0.9042% 1974 52.422461 0.019076 1.1568% 1973 51.822978 0.019296 0.9427% 1972 51.339004 0.019478 0.7426% 1971 50.960552 0.019623 1.4697% 1970 50.222415 0.019911 0.6968% 1969 49.874877 0.020050 0.8565% 1968 49.451307 0.020222 1.5090% 1967 48.716161 0.020527 0.9949% 1966 48.236255 0.020731 1.0575% 1965 47.731509 0.020951 1.1300% 1964 47.198163 0.021187 1.5537% 1963 46.476085 0.021516 1.4658% 1962 45.804672 0.021832 1.5364% 1961 45.111563 0.022167 2.1586% 1960 44.158344 0.022646 -1.6655% 1959 44.906250 0.022269 4.3080% 1958 43.051590 0.023228

332

2.1130% 1957 42.160750 0.023719 1.9895% 1956 41.338326 0.024191 2.1231% 1955
40.478920 0.024704 1.4496% 1954 39.900518 0.025062 2.1573% 1953 39.057939 0.025603
1.2298% 1952 38.583457 0.025918 1.6814% 1951 37.945451 0.026354 1.6233% 1950
37.339332 0.026781 1.4265% 1949 36.814164 0.027163 1.7790% 1948 36.170673 0.027647
1.8242% 1947 35.522682 0.028151 -2.6320% 1946 36.482927 0.027410 3.1768% 1945
35.359622 0.028281 6.4754% 1944 33.209188 0.030112 -0.3437% 1943 33.323714 0.030009
0.6562% 1942 33.106462 0.030206 0.6633% 1941 32.888314 0.030406 -5.6614% 1940
34.862000 0.028685 8.0381% 1939 32.268245 0.030990 0.8126% 1938 32.008136 0.031242
0.7762% 1937 31.761588 0.031485 0.6029% 1936 31.571252 0.031674 0.5244% 1935
31.406558 0.031840 -3.0364% 1934 32.390039 0.030874 4.6271% 1933 30.957594 0.032302
1.3921% 1932 30.532544 0.032752 -0.2051% 1931 30.595291 0.032685 0.8886% 1930
30.325816 0.032975 1.0126% 1929 30.021820 0.033309 1.1526% 1928 29.679734 0.033693
1.2160% 1927 29.323163 0.034103 1.4086% 1926 28.915860 0.034583 1.7667% 1925
28.413876 0.035194 1.4465% 1924 28.008728 0.035703 1.7700% 1923 27.521604 0.036335
1.6165% 1922 27.083789 0.036922 1.3736% 1921 26.716795 0.037430 2.3393% 1920
26.106092 0.038305 1.3140% 1919 25.767505 0.038809 0.7676% 1918 25.571209 0.039106
0.3870% 1917 25.472633 0.039258 1.3274% 1916 25.138930 0.039779 1.4083% 1915
24.789818 0.040339 1.4458% 1914 24.436514 0.040922 1.9424% 1913 23.970907 0.041717
1.9857% 1912 23.504191 0.042546 1.5634% 1911 23.142382 0.043211 1.8169% 1910
22.729407 0.043996 1.8781% 1909 22.310404 0.044822 2.0082% 1908 21.871179 0.045722
1.9603% 1907 21.450690 0.046619 1.8264% 1906 21.065952 0.047470 1.9357% 1905
20.665927 0.048389 2.0148% 1904 20.257766 0.049364 2.1335% 1903 19.834590 0.050417
1.8151% 1902 19.480981 0.051332 1.8943% 1901 19.118804 0.052305 3.0255% 1900
18.557352 0.053887 0.6278% 1899 18.441568 0.054225 1.7757% 1898 18.119822 0.055188
1.8078% 1897 17.798077 0.056186 1.8396% 1896 17.476578 0.057219 1.8755% 1895
17.154832 0.058293 1.9114% 1894 16.833087 0.059407 1.9486% 1893 16.511341 0.060564
1.9858% 1892 16.189842 0.061767 2.0276% 1891 15.868097 0.063020 2.6465% 1890
15.458972 0.064687 1.5328% 1889 15.225592 0.065679 2.0811% 1888 14.915187 0.067046
2.1599% 1887 14.599852 0.068494 2.2075% 1886 14.284517 0.070006 2.2592% 1885
13.968935 0.071587 2.3095% 1884 13.653600 0.073241 2.3641% 1883 13.338264 0.074972
2.4214% 1882 13.022929 0.076788 2.4815% 1881 12.707594 0.078693 3.7644% 1880
12.246584 0.081655 0.9432% 1879 12.132150 0.082426 2.1464% 1878 11.877219 0.084195
2.1913% 1877 11.622535 0.086040 2.2426% 1876 11.367604 0.087969 2.2941% 1875
11.112673 0.089987 2.3456% 1874 10.857988 0.092098 2.4043% 1873 10.603057 0.094312
2.4635% 1872 10.348126 0.096636 2.5258% 1871 10.093195 0.099077 5.9947% 1870
9.522361 0.105016 -1.0968% 1869 9.627959 0.103864 2.1930% 1868 9.421351 0.106142
2.2394% 1867 9.214990 0.108519 2.2935% 1866 9.008383 0.111008 2.3445% 1865 8.802022
0.113610 2.4037% 1864 8.595414 0.116341 2.4599% 1863 8.389053 0.119203 2.5250% 1862
8.182446 0.122213 2.5872% 1861 7.976085 0.125375 2.9504% 1860 7.747502 0.129074
2.4012% 1859 7.565828 0.132173 2.7627% 1858 7.362426 0.135825 2.8412% 1857 7.159024
0.139684 2.9243% 1856 6.955621 0.143769 3.0161% 1855 6.751972 0.148105 3.1061% 1854
6.548570 0.152705 3.2056% 1853 6.345168 0.157600 3.3118% 1852 6.141765 0.162820
3.4252% 1851 5.938363 0.168397 4.0106% 1850 5.709382 0.175150 2.3254% 1849 5.579635
0.179223 2.7841% 1848 5.428501 0.184213 2.8590% 1847 5.277613 0.189480 2.9432% 1846
5.126726 0.195056 3.0324% 1845 4.975838 0.200971 3.1325% 1844 4.824704 0.207267
3.2284% 1843 4.673817 0.213958 3.3361% 1842 4.522929 0.221096 3.4512% 1841 4.372041
0.228726 3.8105% 1840 4.211560 0.237442 2.3861% 1839 4.113412 0.243107 2.5824% 1838
4.009862 0.249385 2.6573% 1837 3.906065 0.256012 2.7232% 1836 3.802515 0.262984
2.7994% 1835 3.698964 0.270346 2.8871% 1834 3.595168 0.278151 2.9657% 1833 3.491617
0.286400 3.0563% 1832 3.388067 0.295154 3.1604% 1831 3.284270 0.304482 3.4660% 1830
3.174252 0.315035 2.4653% 1829 3.097880 0.322801 2.6804% 1828 3.017012 0.331454
10.3427% 1827 2.734221 0.365735 -4.2314% 1826 2.855030 0.350259 2.9150% 1825
2.774162 0.360469 3.0026% 1824 2.693294 0.371293 3.0955% 1823 2.612426 0.382786
3.1944% 1822 2.531558 0.395014 3.3102% 1821 2.450444 0.408089 3.2277% 1820 2.373823
0.421261 2.6573% 1819 2.312377 0.432455 2.6261% 1818 2.253205 0.443812 2.6969% 1817
2.194034 0.455782 2.7717% 1816 2.134862 0.468414 2.8507% 1815 2.075690 0.481767

2.9343% 1814 2.016519 0.495904 3.0231% 1813 1.957347 0.510896 3.1039% 1812 1.898422
0.526753 3.2172% 1811 1.839250 0.543700 3.0969% 1810 1.784001 0.560538 2.9144% 1809
1.733481 0.576874 2.8225% 1808 1.685897 0.593156 2.9199% 1807 1.638067 0.610476
2.9918% 1806 1.590483 0.628740 3.0841% 1805 1.542899 0.648130 3.1822% 1804 1.495316
0.668755 3.2868% 1803 1.447732 0.690736 3.3985% 1802 1.400148 0.714210 3.5180% 1801
1.352564 0.739336 3.3999% 1800 1.308090 0.764474 2.8419% 1799 1.271943 0.786199
2.7485% 1798 1.237919 0.807807 2.8261% 1797 1.203895 0.830637 3.7832% 1796 1.160010
0.862062 2.1272% 1795 1.135848 0.880399 3.0879% 1794 1.101824 0.907586 3.1625% 1793
1.068047 0.936288 3.2904% 1792 1.034024 0.967096 3.4024% 1791 1.000000 1.000000
3.2296% 1790 0.968715 1.032296 41.3145% 1780 0.685503 1.458783 29.4353% 1770
0.529610 1.888180 83.4728% 1750 0.288659 3.464298 29.2845% 1740 0.223274 4.478799
94.2514% 1720 0.114941 8.700129 85.8111% 1700 0.061859 16.165803 19.2490% 1690
0.051874 19.277567 88.0250% 1670 0.027589 36.246649
    BASE YEAR: 1790
    YEAR BYEAR/AYEAR AYEAR/BYEAR GROWTH%
    2009 76.717267 0.013035 8.2857% 2001 70.847116 0.014115 1.0000% 2000
70.145652 0.014256 1.0000% 1999 69.451140 0.014399 1.0000% 1998 68.763505 0.014543
1.0000% 1997 68.082679 0.014688 1.0000% 1996 67.408593 0.014835 1.0000% 1995
66.741181 0.014983 0.9992% 1994 66.080886 0.015133 1.0008% 1993 65.426116 0.015284
1.0000% 1992 64.778333 0.015437 0.9295% 1991 64.181759 0.015581 1.2505% 1990
63.389069 0.015776 0.7224% 1989 62.934402 0.015890 1.1077% 1988 62.244932 0.016066
0.8834% 1987 61.699898 0.016207 0.5594% 1986 61.356690 0.016298 1.3056% 1985
60.565925 0.016511 0.7673% 1984 60.104752 0.016638 0.8149% 1983 59.618891 0.016773
0.9737% 1982 59.043951 0.016937 0.9508% 1981 58.487845 0.017098 0.9031% 1980
57.964388 0.017252 2.2701% 1979 56.677764 0.017644 1.0042% 1978 56.114277 0.017821
0.9896% 1977 55.564407 0.017997 0.9103% 1976 55.063148 0.018161 0.8394% 1975
54.604774 0.018313 0.9042% 1974 54.115477 0.018479 1.1568% 1973 53.496634 0.018693
0.9427% 1972 52.997030 0.018869 0.7426% 1971 52.606356 0.019009 1.4697% 1970
51.844379 0.019288 0.6968% 1969 51.485617 0.019423 0.8565% 1968 51.048368 0.019589
1.5090% 1967 50.289481 0.019885 0.9949% 1966 49.794075 0.020083 1.0575% 1965
49.273028 0.020295 1.1300% 1964 48.722458 0.020524 1.5537% 1963 47.977059 0.020843
1.4658% 1962 47.283963 0.021149 1.5364% 1961 46.568470 0.021474 2.1586% 1960
45.584465 0.021937 -1.6655% 1959 46.356526 0.021572 4.3080% 1958 44.441969 0.022501
2.1130% 1957 43.522358 0.022977 1.9895% 1956 42.673373 0.023434 2.1231% 1955
41.786212 0.023931 1.4496% 1954 41.189130 0.024278 2.1573% 1953 40.319340 0.024802
1.2298% 1952 39.829534 0.025107 1.6814% 1951 39.170924 0.025529 1.6233% 1950
38.545229 0.025944 1.4265% 1949 38.003101 0.026314 1.7790% 1948 37.338828 0.026782
1.8242% 1947 36.669910 0.027270 -2.6320% 1946 37.661166 0.026553 3.1768% 1945
36.501583 0.027396 6.4754% 1944 34.281700 0.029170 -0.3437% 1943 34.399924 0.029070
0.6562% 1942 34.175656 0.029261 0.6633% 1941 33.950463 0.029455 -5.6614% 1940
35.987891 0.027787 8.0381% 1939 33.310368 0.030021 0.8126% 1938 33.041859 0.030265
0.7762% 1937 32.787348 0.030500 0.6029% 1936 32.590866 0.030683 0.5244% 1935
32.420853 0.030844 -3.0364% 1934 33.436096 0.029908 4.6271% 1933 31.957389 0.031292
1.3921% 1932 31.518612 0.031727 -0.2051% 1931 31.583385 0.031662 0.8886% 1930
31.305208 0.031944 1.0126% 1929 30.991393 0.032267 1.1526% 1928 30.638260 0.032639
1.2160% 1927 30.270173 0.033036 1.4086% 1926 29.849716 0.033501 1.7667% 1925
29.331520 0.034093 1.4465% 1924 28.913288 0.034586 1.7700% 1923 28.410431 0.035198
1.6165% 1922 27.958477 0.035767 1.3736% 1921 27.579631 0.036259 2.3393% 1920
26.949205 0.037107 1.3140% 1919 26.599683 0.037594 0.7676% 1918 26.397048 0.037883
0.3870% 1917 26.295288 0.038030 1.3274% 1916 25.950808 0.038534 1.4083% 1915
25.590420 0.039077 1.4458% 1914 25.225707 0.039642 1.9424% 1913 24.745063 0.040412
1.9857% 1912 24.263274 0.041215 1.5634% 1911 23.889780 0.041859 1.8169% 1910
23.463468 0.042619 1.8781% 1909 23.030933 0.043420 2.0082% 1908 22.577522 0.044292
1.9603% 1907 22.143454 0.045160 1.8264% 1906 21.746290 0.045985 1.9357% 1905
21.333346 0.046875 2.0148% 1904 20.912004 0.047819 2.1335% 1903 20.475161 0.048840
1.8151% 1902 20.110132 0.049726 1.8943% 1901 19.736258 0.050668 3.0255% 1900

19.156673 0.052201 0.6278% 1899 19.037150 0.052529 1.7757% 1898 18.705014 0.053462
1.8078% 1897 18.372877 0.054428 1.8396% 1896 18.040995 0.055429 1.8755% 1895
17.708859 0.056469 1.9114% 1894 17.376722 0.057548 1.9486% 1893 17.044585 0.058670
1.9858% 1892 16.712703 0.059835 2.0276% 1891 16.380567 0.061048 2.6465% 1890
15.958230 0.062664 1.5328% 1889 15.717312 0.063624 2.0811% 1888 15.396883 0.064948
2.1599% 1887 15.071364 0.066351 2.2075% 1886 14.745844 0.067816 2.2592% 1885
14.420071 0.069348 2.3095% 1884 14.094551 0.070949 2.3641% 1883 13.769032 0.072627
2.4214% 1882 13.443513 0.074385 2.4815% 1881 13.117993 0.076231 3.7644% 1880
12.642095 0.079101 0.9432% 1879 12.523965 0.079847 2.1464% 1878 12.260801 0.081561
2.1913% 1877 11.997892 0.083348 2.2426% 1876 11.734728 0.085217 2.2941% 1875
11.471563 0.087172 2.3456% 1874 11.208654 0.089217 2.4043% 1873 10.945490 0.091362
2.4635% 1872 10.682326 0.093613 2.5258% 1871 10.419161 0.095977 5.9947% 1870
9.829891 0.101731 -1.0968% 1869 9.938900 0.100615 2.1930% 1868 9.725620 0.102821
2.2394% 1867 9.512594 0.105124 2.2935% 1866 9.299314 0.107535 2.3445% 1865 9.086289
0.110056 2.4037% 1864 8.873009 0.112701 2.4599% 1863 8.659983 0.115474 2.5250% 1862
8.446703 0.118389 2.5872% 1861 8.233678 0.121452 2.9504% 1860 7.997712 0.125036
2.4012% 1859 7.810172 0.128038 2.7627% 1858 7.600200 0.131575 2.8412% 1857 7.390229
0.135314 2.9243% 1856 7.180257 0.139271 3.0161% 1855 6.970032 0.143471 3.1061% 1854
6.760060 0.147928 3.2056% 1853 6.550089 0.152670 3.3118% 1852 6.340117 0.157726
3.4252% 1851 6.130146 0.163128 4.0106% 1850 5.893770 0.169671 2.3254% 1849 5.759833
0.173616 2.7841% 1848 5.603818 0.178450 2.8590% 1847 5.448057 0.183552 2.9432% 1846
5.292297 0.188954 3.0324% 1845 5.136536 0.194684 3.1325% 1844 4.980521 0.200782
3.2284% 1843 4.824760 0.207264 3.3361% 1842 4.669000 0.214179 3.4512% 1841 4.513239
0.221570 3.8105% 1840 4.347575 0.230013 2.3861% 1839 4.246257 0.235501 2.5824% 1838
4.139363 0.241583 2.6573% 1837 4.032214 0.248003 2.7232% 1836 3.925319 0.254756
2.7994% 1835 3.818425 0.261888 2.8871% 1834 3.711276 0.269449 2.9657% 1833 3.604381
0.277440 3.0563% 1832 3.497487 0.285920 3.1604% 1831 3.390338 0.294956 3.4660% 1830
3.276766 0.305179 2.4653% 1829 3.197928 0.312703 2.6804% 1828 3.114448 0.321084
10.3427% 1827 2.822524 0.354293 -4.2314% 1826 2.947235 0.339301 2.9150% 1825
2.863755 0.349192 3.0026% 1824 2.780276 0.359677 3.0955% 1823 2.696796 0.370810
3.1944% 1822 2.613316 0.382656 3.3102% 1821 2.529582 0.395322 3.2277% 1820 2.450487
0.408082 2.6573% 1819 2.387056 0.418926 2.6261% 1818 2.325974 0.429927 2.6969% 1817
2.264891 0.441522 2.7717% 1816 2.203809 0.453760 2.8507% 1815 2.142726 0.466695
2.9343% 1814 2.081643 0.480390 3.0231% 1813 2.020561 0.494912 3.1039% 1812 1.959733
0.510274 3.2172% 1811 1.898650 0.526690 3.0969% 1810 1.841617 0.543001 2.9144% 1809
1.789465 0.558826 2.8225% 1808 1.740345 0.574599 2.9199% 1807 1.690969 0.591377
2.9918% 1806 1.641849 0.609069 3.0841% 1805 1.592728 0.627853 3.1822% 1804 1.543608
0.647833 3.2868% 1803 1.494487 0.669126 3.3985% 1802 1.445367 0.691866 3.5180% 1801
1.396246 0.716206 3.3999% 1800 1.350335 0.740557 2.8419% 1799 1.313021 0.761602
2.7485% 1798 1.277899 0.782535 2.8261% 1797 1.242776 0.804650 3.7832% 1796 1.197473
0.835092 2.1272% 1795 1.172531 0.852856 3.0879% 1794 1.137409 0.879192 3.1625% 1793
1.102541 0.906996 3.2904% 1792 1.067418 0.936840 3.4024% 1791 1.032296 0.968715
3.2296% 1790 1.000000 1.000000 41.3145% 1780 0.707642 1.413145 29.4353% 1770
0.546715 1.829108 83.4728% 1750 0.297981 3.355916 29.2845% 1740 0.230485 4.338678
94.2514% 1720 0.118653 8.427943 85.8111% 1700 0.063857 15.660052 19.2490% 1690
0.053549 18.674463 88.0250% 1670 0.028480 35.112663

BASE YEAR: 1780

YEAR BYEAR/AYEAR AYEAR/BYEAR GROWTH%

2009 108.412584 0.009224 8.2857% 2001 100.117213 0.009988 1.0000% 2000
99.125943 0.010088 1.0000% 1999 98.144498 0.010189 1.0000% 1998 97.172770 0.010291
1.0000% 1997 96.210664 0.010394 1.0000% 1996 95.258083 0.010498 1.0000% 1995
94.314933 0.010603 0.9992% 1994 93.381841 0.010709 1.0008% 1993 92.456557 0.010816
1.0000% 1992 91.541145 0.010924 0.9295% 1991 90.698101 0.011026 1.2505% 1990
89.577915 0.011163 0.7224% 1989 88.935405 0.011244 1.1077% 1988 87.961085 0.011369
0.8834% 1987 87.190872 0.011469 0.5594% 1986 86.705870 0.011533 1.3056% 1985
85.588405 0.011684 0.7673% 1984 84.936700 0.011773 0.8149% 1983 84.250108 0.011869

335

0.9737% 1982 83.437635 0.011985 0.9508% 1981 82.651777 0.012099 0.9031% 1980
81.912057 0.012208 2.2701% 1979 80.093871 0.012485 1.0042% 1978 79.297583 0.012611
0.9896% 1977 78.520537 0.012736 0.9103% 1976 77.812185 0.012851 0.8394% 1975
77.164437 0.012959 0.9042% 1974 76.472989 0.013077 1.1568% 1973 75.598475 0.013228
0.9427% 1972 74.892462 0.013352 0.7426% 1971 74.340383 0.013452 1.4697% 1970
73.263600 0.013649 0.6968% 1969 72.756618 0.013744 0.8565% 1968 72.138721 0.013862
1.5090% 1967 71.066303 0.014071 0.9949% 1966 70.366224 0.014211 1.0575% 1965
69.629909 0.014362 1.1300% 1964 68.851874 0.014524 1.5537% 1963 67.798518 0.014750
1.4658% 1962 66.819073 0.014966 1.5364% 1961 65.807977 0.015196 2.1586% 1960
64.417437 0.015524 -1.6655% 1959 65.508470 0.015265 4.3080% 1958 62.802924 0.015923
2.1130% 1957 61.503381 0.016259 1.9895% 1956 60.303643 0.016583 2.1231% 1955
59.049957 0.016935 1.4496% 1954 58.206193 0.017180 2.1573% 1953 56.977054 0.017551
1.2298% 1952 56.284887 0.017767 1.6814% 1951 55.354176 0.018065 1.6233% 1950
54.469979 0.018359 1.4265% 1949 53.703874 0.018621 1.7790% 1948 52.765160 0.018952
1.8242% 1947 51.819882 0.019298 -2.6320% 1946 53.220670 0.018790 3.1768% 1945
51.582012 0.019387 6.4754% 1944 48.444996 0.020642 -0.3437% 1943 48.612064 0.020571
0.6562% 1942 48.295141 0.020706 0.6633% 1941 47.976910 0.020843 -5.6614% 1940
50.856090 0.019663 8.0381% 1939 47.072364 0.021244 0.8126% 1938 46.692922 0.021417
0.7762% 1937 46.333261 0.021583 0.6029% 1936 46.055604 0.021713 0.5244% 1935
45.815350 0.021827 -3.0364% 1934 47.250036 0.021164 4.6271% 1933 45.160409 0.022143
1.3921% 1932 44.540354 0.022452 -0.2051% 1931 44.631887 0.022406 0.8886% 1930
44.238783 0.022605 1.0126% 1929 43.795317 0.022833 1.1526% 1928 43.296288 0.023097
1.2160% 1927 42.776129 0.023378 1.4086% 1926 42.181962 0.023707 1.7667% 1925
41.449676 0.024126 1.4465% 1924 40.858654 0.024475 1.7700% 1923 40.148045 0.024908
1.6165% 1922 39.509368 0.025310 1.3736% 1921 38.974004 0.025658 2.3393% 1920
38.083121 0.026258 1.3140% 1919 37.589196 0.026603 0.7676% 1918 37.302843 0.026808
0.3870% 1917 37.159042 0.026911 1.3274% 1916 36.672241 0.027269 1.4083% 1915
36.162962 0.027653 1.4458% 1914 35.647569 0.028052 1.9424% 1913 34.968350 0.028597
1.9857% 1912 34.287513 0.029165 1.5634% 1911 33.759711 0.029621 1.8169% 1910
33.157271 0.030159 1.8781% 1909 32.546037 0.030726 2.0082% 1908 31.905301 0.031343
1.9603% 1907 31.291900 0.031957 1.8264% 1906 30.730650 0.032541 1.9357% 1905
30.147101 0.033171 2.0148% 1904 29.551683 0.033839 2.1335% 1903 28.934361 0.034561
1.8151% 1902 28.418522 0.035188 1.8943% 1901 27.890185 0.035855 3.0255% 1900
27.071147 0.036940 0.6278% 1899 26.902244 0.037172 1.7757% 1898 26.432887 0.037832
1.8078% 1897 25.963530 0.038516 1.8396% 1896 25.494533 0.039224 1.8755% 1895
25.025176 0.039960 1.9114% 1894 24.555819 0.040724 1.9486% 1893 24.086462 0.041517
1.9858% 1892 23.617465 0.042342 2.0276% 1891 23.148108 0.043200 2.6465% 1890
22.551285 0.044343 1.5328% 1889 22.210833 0.045023 2.0811% 1888 21.758020 0.045960
2.1599% 1887 21.298015 0.046953 2.2075% 1886 20.838009 0.047989 2.2592% 1885
20.377644 0.049073 2.3095% 1884 19.917638 0.050207 2.3641% 1883 19.457632 0.051394
2.4214% 1882 18.997626 0.052638 2.4815% 1881 18.537620 0.053944 3.7644% 1880
17.865107 0.055975 0.9432% 1879 17.698173 0.056503 2.1464% 1878 17.326284 0.057716
2.1913% 1877 16.954755 0.058981 2.2426% 1876 16.582866 0.060303 2.2941% 1875
16.210977 0.061687 2.3456% 1874 15.839448 0.063134 2.4043% 1873 15.467559 0.064651
2.4635% 1872 15.095670 0.066244 2.5258% 1871 14.723781 0.067917 5.9947% 1870
13.891057 0.071989 -1.0968% 1869 14.045101 0.071199 2.1930% 1868 13.743706 0.072761
2.2394% 1867 13.442670 0.074390 2.2935% 1866 13.141275 0.076096 2.3445% 1865
12.840239 0.077880 2.4037% 1864 12.538843 0.079752 2.4599% 1863 12.237808 0.081714
2.5250% 1862 11.936412 0.083777 2.5872% 1861 11.635376 0.085945 2.9504% 1860
11.301923 0.088481 2.4012% 1859 11.036901 0.090605 2.7627% 1858 10.740181 0.093108
2.8412% 1857 10.443461 0.095754 2.9243% 1856 10.146741 0.098554 3.0161% 1855
9.849662 0.101526 3.1061% 1854 9.552942 0.104680 3.2056% 1853 9.256222 0.108035
3.3118% 1852 8.959502 0.111613 3.4252% 1851 8.662782 0.115436 4.0106% 1850 8.328749
0.120066 2.3254% 1849 8.139476 0.122858 2.7841% 1848 7.919004 0.126278 2.8590% 1847
7.698892 0.129889 2.9432% 1846 7.478780 0.133712 3.0324% 1845 7.258668 0.137766
3.1325% 1844 7.038196 0.142082 3.2284% 1843 6.818084 0.146669 3.3361% 1842 6.597972

336

0.151562 3.4512% 1841 6.377859 0.156792 3.8105% 1840 6.143752 0.162767 2.3861% 1839 6.000575 0.166651 2.5824% 1838 5.849518 0.170954 2.6573% 1837 5.698101 0.175497 2.7232% 1836 5.547044 0.180276 2.7994% 1835 5.395986 0.185323 2.8871% 1834 5.244569 0.190673 2.9657% 1833 5.093512 0.196328 3.0563% 1832 4.942454 0.202329 3.1604% 1831 4.791037 0.208723 3.4660% 1830 4.630544 0.215957 2.4653% 1829 4.519134 0.221281 2.6804% 1828 4.401165 0.227213 10.3427% 1827 3.988635 0.250712 -4.2314% 1826 4.164868 0.240104 2.9150% 1825 4.046900 0.247103 3.0026% 1824 3.928931 0.254522 3.0955% 1823 3.810962 0.262401 3.1944% 1822 3.692994 0.270783 3.3102% 1821 3.574666 0.279746 3.2277% 1820 3.462892 0.288776 2.6573% 1819 3.373256 0.296450 2.6261% 1818 3.286937 0.304235 2.6969% 1817 3.200619 0.312440 2.7717% 1816 3.114300 0.321099 2.8507% 1815 3.027982 0.330253 2.9343% 1814 2.941663 0.339944 3.0231% 1813 2.855345 0.350220 3.1039% 1812 2.769386 0.361091 3.2172% 1811 2.683067 0.372708 3.0969% 1810 2.602471 0.384250 2.9144% 1809 2.528773 0.395449 2.8225% 1808 2.459358 0.406610 2.9199% 1807 2.389584 0.418483 2.9918% 1806 2.320170 0.431003 3.0841% 1805 2.250755 0.444295 3.1822% 1804 2.181341 0.458434 3.2868% 1803 2.111926 0.473501 3.3985% 1802 2.042512 0.489593 3.5180% 1801 1.973097 0.506817 3.3999% 1800 1.908219 0.524049 2.8419% 1799 1.855488 0.538942 2.7485% 1798 1.805855 0.553754 2.8261% 1797 1.756222 0.569404 3.7832% 1796 1.692203 0.590946 2.1272% 1795 1.656956 0.603516 3.0879% 1794 1.607323 0.622153 3.1625% 1793 1.558049 0.641828 3.2904% 1792 1.508416 0.662947 3.4024% 1791 1.458783 0.685503 3.2296% 1790 1.413145 0.707642 41.3145% 1780 1.000000 1.000000 29.4353% 1770 0.772587 1.294353 83.4728% 1750 0.421090 2.374786 29.2845% 1740 0.325709 3.070230 94.2514% 1720 0.167674 5.963964 85.8111% 1700 0.090239 11.081706 19.2490% 1690 0.075673 13.214829 88.0250% 1670 0.040246 24.847185

YEAR BYEAR/AYEAR AYEAR/BYEAR GROWTH%

2009 140.324170 0.007126 8.2857% 2001 129.587030 0.007717 1.0000% 2000 128.303977 0.007794 1.0000% 1999 127.033640 0.007872 1.0000% 1998 125.775881 0.007951 1.0000% 1997 124.530575 0.008030 1.0000% 1996 123.297599 0.008110 1.0000% 1995 122.076831 0.008192 0.9992% 1994 120.869081 0.008273 1.0008% 1993 119.671435 0.008356 1.0000% 1992 118.486570 0.008440 0.9295% 1991 117.395373 0.008518 1.2505% 1990 115.945457 0.008625 0.7224% 1989 115.113822 0.008687 1.1077% 1988 113.852707 0.008783 0.8834% 1987 112.855780 0.008861 0.5594% 1986 112.228015 0.008910 1.3056% 1985 110.781621 0.009027 0.7673% 1984 109.938085 0.009096 0.8149% 1983 109.049392 0.009170 0.9737% 1982 107.997765 0.009259 0.9508% 1981 106.980587 0.009347 0.9031% 1980 106.023129 0.009432 2.2701% 1979 103.669755 0.009646 1.0042% 1978 102.639076 0.009743 0.9896% 1977 101.633304 0.009839 0.9103% 1976 100.716447 0.009929 0.8394% 1975 99.878032 0.010012 0.9042% 1974 98.983055 0.010103 1.1568% 1973 97.851124 0.010220 0.9427% 1972 96.937293 0.010316 0.7426% 1971 96.222708 0.010393 1.4697% 1970 94.828972 0.010545 0.6968% 1969 94.172757 0.010619 0.8565% 1968 93.372981 0.010710 1.5090% 1967 91.984894 0.010871 0.9949% 1966 91.078744 0.010980 1.0575% 1965 90.125692 0.011096 1.1300% 1964 89.118640 0.011221 1.5537% 1963 87.755226 0.011395 1.4658% 1962 86.487477 0.011562 1.5364% 1961 85.178763 0.011740 2.1586% 1960 83.378913 0.011993 -1.6655% 1959 84.791094 0.011794 4.3080% 1958 81.289163 0.012302 2.1130% 1957 79.607095 0.012562 1.9895% 1956 78.054211 0.012812 2.1231% 1955 76.431498 0.013084 1.4496% 1954 75.339370 0.013273 2.1573% 1953 73.748429 0.013560 1.2298% 1952 72.852521 0.013726 1.6814% 1951 71.647852 0.013957 1.6233% 1950 70.503389 0.014184 1.4265% 1949 69.511778 0.014386 1.7790% 1948 68.296751 0.014642 1.8242% 1947 67.073228 0.014909 -2.6320% 1946 68.886341 0.014517 3.1768% 1945 66.765339 0.014978 6.4754% 1944 62.704934 0.015948 -0.3437% 1943 62.921179 0.015893 0.6562% 1942 62.510967 0.015997 0.6633% 1941 62.099064 0.016103 -5.6614% 1940 65.825741 0.015192 8.0381% 1939 60.928262 0.016413 0.8126% 1938 60.437130 0.016546 0.7762% 1937 59.971603 0.016675 0.6029% 1936 59.612215 0.016775 0.5244% 1935 59.301243 0.016863 -3.0364% 1934 61.158233 0.016351 4.6271% 1933 58.453517 0.017108 1.3921% 1932 57.650947 0.017346 -0.2051% 1931 57.769424 0.017310 0.8886% 1930 57.260608 0.017464 1.0126% 1929 56.686607 0.017641 1.1526% 1928 56.040687

0.017844 1.2160% 1927 55.367418 0.018061 1.4086% 1926 54.598355 0.018316 1.7667%
1925 53.650519 0.018639 1.4465% 1924 52.885528 0.018909 1.7700% 1923 51.965749
0.019243 1.6165% 1922 51.139075 0.019555 1.3736% 1921 50.446125 0.019823 2.3393%
1920 49.293008 0.020287 1.3140% 1919 48.653694 0.020553 0.7676% 1918 48.283052
0.020711 0.3870% 1917 48.096923 0.020791 1.3274% 1916 47.466831 0.021067 1.4083%
1915 46.807644 0.021364 1.4458% 1914 46.140543 0.021673 1.9424% 1913 45.261394
0.022094 1.9857% 1912 44.380150 0.022533 1.5634% 1911 43.696988 0.022885 1.8169%
1910 42.917218 0.023301 1.8781% 1909 42.126065 0.023738 2.0082% 1908 41.296727
0.024215 1.9603% 1907 40.502770 0.024690 1.8264% 1906 39.776314 0.025141 1.9357%
1905 39.020995 0.025627 2.0148% 1904 38.250314 0.026144 2.1335% 1903 37.451281
0.026701 1.8151% 1902 36.783604 0.027186 1.8943% 1901 36.099749 0.027701 3.0255%
1900 35.039625 0.028539 0.6278% 1899 34.821005 0.028718 1.7757% 1898 34.213491
0.029228 1.8078% 1897 33.605977 0.029757 1.8396% 1896 32.998929 0.030304 1.8755%
1895 32.391416 0.030872 1.9114% 1894 31.783902 0.031462 1.9486% 1893 31.176388
0.032076 1.9858% 1892 30.569340 0.032713 2.0276% 1891 29.961827 0.033376 2.6465%
1890 29.189326 0.034259 1.5328% 1889 28.748662 0.034784 2.0811% 1888 28.162562
0.035508 2.1599% 1887 27.567152 0.036275 2.2075% 1886 26.971742 0.037076 2.2592%
1885 26.375867 0.037913 2.3095% 1884 25.780457 0.038789 2.3641% 1883 25.185047
0.039706 2.4214% 1882 24.589637 0.040668 2.4815% 1881 23.994227 0.041677 3.7644%
1880 23.123758 0.043246 0.9432% 1879 22.907686 0.043653 2.1464% 1878 22.426330
0.044590 2.1913% 1877 21.945440 0.045568 2.2426% 1876 21.464085 0.046589 2.2941%
1875 20.982729 0.047658 2.3456% 1874 20.501839 0.048776 2.4043% 1873 20.020483
0.049949 2.4635% 1872 19.539128 0.051179 2.5258% 1871 19.057772 0.052472 5.9947%
1870 17.979933 0.055618 -1.0968% 1869 18.179321 0.055008 2.1930% 1868 17.789209
0.056214 2.2394% 1867 17.399562 0.057473 2.2935% 1866 17.009450 0.058791 2.3445%
1865 16.619804 0.060169 2.4037% 1864 16.229691 0.061615 2.4599% 1863 15.840045
0.063131 2.5250% 1862 15.449932 0.064725 2.5872% 1861 15.060286 0.066400 2.9504%
1860 14.628680 0.068359 2.4012% 1859 14.285648 0.070000 2.7627% 1858 13.901587
0.071934 2.8412% 1857 13.517527 0.073978 2.9243% 1856 13.133467 0.076141 3.0161%
1855 12.748941 0.078438 3.1061% 1854 12.364881 0.080874 3.2056% 1853 11.980820
0.083467 3.3118% 1852 11.596760 0.086231 3.4252% 1851 11.212700 0.089185 4.0106%
1850 10.780343 0.092761 2.3254% 1849 10.535357 0.094918 2.7841% 1848 10.249988
0.097561 2.8590% 1847 9.965085 0.100350 2.9432% 1846 9.680182 0.103304 3.0324% 1845
9.395280 0.106436 3.1325% 1844 9.109911 0.109771 3.2284% 1843 8.825008 0.113314
3.3361% 1842 8.540105 0.117095 3.4512% 1841 8.255202 0.121136 3.8105% 1840 7.952185
0.125752 2.3861% 1839 7.766864 0.128752 2.5824% 1838 7.571342 0.132077 2.6573% 1837
7.375355 0.135587 2.7232% 1836 7.179833 0.139279 2.7994% 1835 6.984312 0.143178
2.8871% 1834 6.788325 0.147312 2.9657% 1833 6.592803 0.151681 3.0563% 1832 6.397281
0.156316 3.1604% 1831 6.201294 0.161257 3.4660% 1830 5.993559 0.166846 2.4653% 1829
5.849355 0.170959 2.6804% 1828 5.696662 0.175541 10.3427% 1827 5.162702 0.193697 -
4.2314% 1826 5.390810 0.185501 2.9150% 1825 5.238117 0.190908 3.0026% 1824 5.085424
0.196640 3.0955% 1823 4.932731 0.202727 3.1944% 1822 4.780038 0.209203 3.3102% 1821
4.626880 0.216128 3.2277% 1820 4.482206 0.223104 2.6573% 1819 4.366184 0.229033
2.6261% 1818 4.254457 0.235048 2.6969% 1817 4.142731 0.241387 2.7717% 1816 4.031004
0.248077 2.8507% 1815 3.919278 0.255149 2.9343% 1814 3.807551 0.262636 3.0231% 1813
3.695824 0.270576 3.1039% 1812 3.584563 0.278974 3.2172% 1811 3.472836 0.287949
3.0969% 1810 3.368516 0.296867 2.9144% 1809 3.273125 0.305518 2.8225% 1808 3.183278
0.314142 2.9199% 1807 3.092966 0.323314 2.9918% 1806 3.003119 0.332987 3.0841% 1805
2.913272 0.343257 3.1822% 1804 2.823425 0.354180 3.2868% 1803 2.733579 0.365821
3.3985% 1802 2.643732 0.378253 3.5180% 1801 2.553885 0.391560 3.3999% 1800 2.469909
0.404873 2.8419% 1799 2.401657 0.416379 2.7485% 1798 2.337414 0.427823 2.8261% 1797
2.273172 0.439914 3.7832% 1796 2.190308 0.456557 2.1272% 1795 2.144686 0.466269
3.0879% 1794 2.080443 0.480667 3.1625% 1793 2.016666 0.495868 3.2904% 1792 1.952423
0.512184 3.4024% 1791 1.888180 0.529610 3.2296% 1790 1.829108 0.546715 41.3145%
1780 1.294353 0.772587 29.4353% 1770 1.000000 1.000000 83.4728% 1750 0.545040
1.834728 29.2845% 1740 0.421582 2.372019 94.2514% 1720 0.217029 4.607679 85.8111%

1700 0.116801 8.561578 19.2490% 1690 0.097947 10.209601 88.0250% 1670 0.052093
19.196604

YEAR BYEAR/AYEAR AYEAR/BYEAR GROWTH%

2009 257.456738 0.003884 8.2857% 2001 237.757003 0.004206 1.0000% 2000
235.402948 0.004248 1.0000% 1999 233.072226 0.004291 1.0000% 1998 230.764580
0.004333 1.0000% 1997 228.479782 0.004377 1.0000% 1996 226.217606 0.004421 1.0000%
1995 223.977827 0.004465 0.9992% 1994 221.761934 0.004509 1.0008% 1993 219.564580
0.004554 1.0000% 1992 217.390673 0.004600 0.9295% 1991 215.388623 0.004643 1.2505%
1990 212.728422 0.004701 0.7224% 1989 211.202597 0.004735 1.1077% 1988 208.888794
0.004787 0.8834% 1987 207.059703 0.004830 0.5594% 1986 205.907926 0.004857 1.3056%
1985 203.254185 0.004920 0.7673% 1984 201.706525 0.004958 0.8149% 1983 200.076016
0.004998 0.9737% 1982 198.146566 0.005047 0.9508% 1981 196.280321 0.005095 0.9031%
1980 194.523645 0.005141 2.2701% 1979 190.205842 0.005257 1.0042% 1978 188.314827
0.005310 0.9896% 1977 186.469508 0.005363 0.9103% 1976 184.787325 0.005412 0.8394%
1975 183.249060 0.005457 0.9042% 1974 181.607021 0.005506 1.1568% 1973 179.530236
0.005570 0.9427% 1972 177.853604 0.005623 0.7426% 1971 176.542535 0.005664 1.4697%
1970 173.985407 0.005748 0.6968% 1969 172.781431 0.005788 0.8565% 1968 171.314059
0.005837 1.5090% 1967 168.767296 0.005925 0.9949% 1966 167.104757 0.005984 1.0575%
1965 165.356167 0.006048 1.1300% 1964 163.508498 0.006116 1.5537% 1963 161.007004
0.006211 1.4658% 1962 158.681030 0.006302 1.5364% 1961 156.279894 0.006399 2.1586%
1960 152.977658 0.006537 -1.6655% 1959 155.568628 0.006428 4.3080% 1958 149.143534
0.006705 2.1130% 1957 146.057397 0.006847 1.9895% 1956 143.208276 0.006983 2.1231%
1955 140.231039 0.007131 1.4496% 1954 138.227280 0.007234 2.1573% 1953 135.308336
0.007391 1.2298% 1952 133.664588 0.007481 1.6814% 1951 131.454347 0.007607 1.6233%
1950 129.354570 0.007731 1.4265% 1949 127.535232 0.007841 1.7790% 1948 125.305987
0.007980 1.8242% 1947 123.061155 0.008126 -2.6320% 1946 126.387726 0.007912 3.1768%
1945 122.496263 0.008164 6.4754% 1944 115.046522 0.008692 -0.3437% 1943 115.443273
0.008662 0.6562% 1942 114.690647 0.008719 0.6633% 1941 113.934916 0.008777 -5.6614%
1940 120.772356 0.008280 8.0381% 1939 111.786812 0.008946 0.8126% 1938 110.885719
0.009018 0.7762% 1937 110.031602 0.009088 0.6029% 1936 109.372224 0.009143 0.5244%
1935 108.801674 0.009191 -3.0364% 1934 112.208746 0.008912 4.6271% 1933 107.246327
0.009324 1.3921% 1932 105.773830 0.009454 -0.2051% 1931 105.991203 0.009435 0.8886%
1930 105.057662 0.009519 1.0126% 1929 104.004527 0.009615 1.1526% 1928 102.819440
0.009726 1.2160% 1927 101.584173 0.009844 1.4086% 1926 100.173153 0.009983 1.7667%
1925 98.434131 0.010159 1.4465% 1924 97.030579 0.010306 1.7700% 1923 95.343035
0.010488 1.6165% 1922 93.826314 0.010658 1.3736% 1921 92.554938 0.010804 2.3393%
1920 90.439281 0.011057 1.3140% 1919 89.266314 0.011202 0.7676% 1918 88.586287
0.011288 0.3870% 1917 88.244790 0.011332 1.3274% 1916 87.088743 0.011483 1.4083%
1915 85.879313 0.011644 1.4458% 1914 84.655364 0.011813 1.9424% 1913 83.042364
0.012042 1.9857% 1912 81.425521 0.012281 1.5634% 1911 80.172105 0.012473 1.8169%
1910 78.741438 0.012700 1.8781% 1909 77.289887 0.012938 2.0082% 1908 75.768278
0.013198 1.9603% 1907 74.311582 0.013457 1.8264% 1906 72.978732 0.013703 1.9357%
1905 71.592928 0.013968 2.0148% 1904 70.178937 0.014249 2.1335% 1903 68.712929
0.014553 1.8151% 1902 67.487922 0.014817 1.8943% 1901 66.233234 0.015098 3.0255%
1900 64.288194 0.015555 0.6278% 1899 63.887086 0.015653 1.7757% 1898 62.772463
0.015931 1.8078% 1897 61.657841 0.016219 1.8396% 1896 60.544072 0.016517 1.8755%
1895 59.429450 0.016827 1.9114% 1894 58.314827 0.017148 1.9486% 1893 57.200205
0.017482 1.9858% 1892 56.086437 0.017830 2.0276% 1891 54.971814 0.018191 2.6465%
1890 53.554486 0.018673 1.5328% 1889 52.745986 0.018959 2.0811% 1888 51.670653
0.019353 2.1599% 1887 50.578237 0.019771 2.2075% 1886 49.485822 0.020208 2.2592%
1885 48.392552 0.020664 2.3095% 1884 47.300137 0.021142 2.3641% 1883 46.207721
0.021641 2.4214% 1882 45.115306 0.022165 2.4815% 1881 44.022890 0.022715 3.7644%
1880 42.425815 0.023571 0.9432% 1879 42.029382 0.023793 2.1464% 1878 41.146225
0.024304 2.1913% 1877 40.263922 0.024836 2.2426% 1876 39.380765 0.025393 2.2941%
1875 38.497608 0.025976 2.3456% 1874 37.615306 0.026585 2.4043% 1873 36.732149

0.027224 2.4635% 1872 35.848992 0.027895 2.5258% 1871 34.965835 0.028599 5.9947%
1870 32.988294 0.030314 -1.0968% 1869 33.354117 0.029981 2.1930% 1868 32.638367
0.030639 2.2394% 1867 31.923471 0.031325 2.2935% 1866 31.207721 0.032043 2.3445%
1865 30.492825 0.032795 2.4037% 1864 29.777076 0.033583 2.4599% 1863 29.062180
0.034409 2.5250% 1862 28.346430 0.035278 2.5872% 1861 27.631534 0.036191 2.9504%
1860 26.839655 0.037258 2.4012% 1859 26.210284 0.038153 2.7627% 1858 25.505637
0.039207 2.8412% 1857 24.800991 0.040321 2.9243% 1856 24.096344 0.041500 3.0161%
1855 23.390844 0.042752 3.1061% 1854 22.686197 0.044080 3.2056% 1853 21.981551
0.045493 3.3118% 1852 21.276905 0.046999 3.4252% 1851 20.572258 0.048609 4.0106%
1850 19.779001 0.050559 2.3254% 1849 19.329518 0.051734 2.7841% 1848 18.805945
0.053175 2.8590% 1847 18.283225 0.054695 2.9432% 1846 17.760506 0.056305 3.0324%
1845 17.237786 0.058012 3.1325% 1844 16.714213 0.059829 3.2284% 1843 16.191493
0.061761 3.3361% 1842 15.668773 0.063821 3.4512% 1841 15.146054 0.066024 3.8105%
1840 14.590100 0.068540 2.3861% 1839 14.250085 0.070175 2.5824% 1838 13.891356
0.071987 2.6573% 1837 13.531773 0.073900 2.7232% 1836 13.173044 0.075913 2.7994%
1835 12.814315 0.078038 2.8871% 1834 12.454732 0.080291 2.9657% 1833 12.096003
0.082672 3.0563% 1832 11.737274 0.085199 3.1604% 1831 11.377690 0.087891 3.4660%
1830 10.996554 0.090938 2.4653% 1829 10.731978 0.093179 2.6804% 1828 10.451828
0.095677 10.3427% 1827 9.472156 0.105573 -4.2314% 1826 9.890673 0.101105 2.9150%
1825 9.610523 0.104053 3.0026% 1824 9.330372 0.107177 3.0955% 1823 9.050222 0.110495
3.1944% 1822 8.770072 0.114024 3.3102% 1821 8.489067 0.117799 3.2277% 1820 8.223630
0.121601 2.6573% 1819 8.010762 0.124832 2.6261% 1818 7.805774 0.128110 2.6969% 1817
7.600786 0.131565 2.7717% 1816 7.395798 0.135212 2.8507% 1815 7.190810 0.139066
2.9343% 1814 6.985822 0.143147 3.0231% 1813 6.780834 0.147474 3.1039% 1812 6.576700
0.152052 3.2172% 1811 6.371712 0.156944 3.0969% 1810 6.180313 0.161804 2.9144% 1809
6.005296 0.166520 2.8225% 1808 5.840451 0.171220 2.9199% 1807 5.674752 0.176219
2.9918% 1806 5.509908 0.181491 3.0841% 1805 5.345063 0.187089 3.1822% 1804 5.180219
0.193042 3.2868% 1803 5.015374 0.199387 3.3985% 1802 4.850530 0.206163 3.5180% 1801
4.685685 0.213416 3.3999% 1800 4.531613 0.220672 2.8419% 1799 4.406389 0.226943
2.7485% 1798 4.288521 0.233181 2.8261% 1797 4.170653 0.239771 3.7832% 1796 4.018620
0.248842 2.1272% 1795 3.934916 0.254135 3.0879% 1794 3.817048 0.261983 3.1625% 1793
3.700034 0.270268 3.2904% 1792 3.582166 0.279161 3.4024% 1791 3.464298 0.288659
3.2296% 1790 3.355916 0.297981 41.3145% 1780 2.374786 0.421090 29.4353% 1770
1.834728 0.545040 83.4728% 1750 1.000000 1.000000 29.2845% 1740 0.773488 1.292845
94.2514% 1720 0.398189 2.511369 85.8111% 1700 0.214298 4.666401 19.2490% 1690
0.179706 5.564639 88.0250% 1670 0.095576 10.462913

BASE YEAR: 1740

YEAR BYEAR/AYEAR AYEAR/BYEAR GROWTH%

2009 332.851534 0.003004 8.2857% 2001 307.382839 0.003253 1.0000% 2000
304.339413 0.003286 1.0000% 1999 301.326151 0.003319 1.0000% 1998 298.342723
0.003352 1.0000% 1997 295.388835 0.003385 1.0000% 1996 292.464193 0.003419 1.0000%
1995 289.568507 0.003453 0.9992% 1994 286.703701 0.003488 1.0008% 1993 283.862864
0.003523 1.0000% 1992 281.052341 0.003558 0.9295% 1991 278.464002 0.003591 1.2505%
1990 275.024775 0.003636 0.7224% 1989 273.052120 0.003662 1.1077% 1988 270.060733
0.003703 0.8834% 1987 267.696003 0.003736 0.5594% 1986 266.206935 0.003756 1.3056%
1985 262.776060 0.003806 0.7673% 1984 260.775177 0.003835 0.8149% 1983 258.667182
0.003866 0.9737% 1982 256.172703 0.003904 0.9508% 1981 253.759938 0.003941 0.9031%
1980 251.488828 0.003976 2.2701% 1979 245.906581 0.004067 1.0042% 1978 243.461793
0.004107 0.9896% 1977 241.076082 0.004148 0.9103% 1976 238.901281 0.004186 0.8394%
1975 236.912544 0.004221 0.9042% 1974 234.789642 0.004259 1.1568% 1973 232.104682
0.004308 0.9427% 1972 229.937058 0.004349 0.7426% 1971 228.242049 0.004381 1.4697%
1970 224.936080 0.004446 0.6968% 1969 223.379527 0.004477 0.8565% 1968 221.482443
0.004515 1.5090% 1967 218.189874 0.004583 0.9949% 1966 216.040470 0.004629 1.0575%
1965 213.779814 0.004678 1.1300% 1964 211.391067 0.004731 1.5537% 1963 208.157023
0.004804 1.4658% 1962 205.149901 0.004874 1.5364% 1961 202.045605 0.004949 2.1586%
1960 197.776327 0.005056 -1.6655% 1959 201.126049 0.004972 4.3080% 1958 192.819402

340

0.005186 2.1130% 1957 188.829505 0.005296 1.9895% 1956 185.146036 0.005401 2.1231% 1955 181.296930 0.005516 1.4496% 1954 178.706383 0.005596 2.1573% 1953 174.932641 0.005716 1.2298% 1952 172.807531 0.005787 1.6814% 1951 169.950033 0.005884 1.6233% 1950 167.235347 0.005980 1.4265% 1949 164.883227 0.006065 1.7790% 1948 162.001159 0.006173 1.8242% 1947 159.098940 0.006285 -2.6320% 1946 163.399680 0.006120 3.1768% 1945 158.368623 0.006314 6.4754% 1944 148.737266 0.006723 -0.3437% 1943 149.250203 0.006700 0.6562% 1942 148.277174 0.006744 0.6633% 1941 147.300133 0.006789 -5.6614% 1940 156.139879 0.006405 8.0381% 1939 144.522968 0.006919 0.8126% 1938 143.357995 0.006976 0.7762% 1937 142.253754 0.007030 0.6029% 1936 141.401281 0.007072 0.5244% 1935 140.663648 0.007109 -3.0364% 1934 145.068463 0.006893 4.6271% 1933 138.652827 0.007212 1.3921% 1932 136.749117 0.007313 -0.2051% 1931 137.030146 0.007298 0.8886% 1930 135.823223 0.007363 1.0126% 1929 134.461683 0.007437 1.1526% 1928 132.929549 0.007523 1.2160% 1927 131.332542 0.007614 1.4086% 1926 129.508312 0.007722 1.7667% 1925 127.260027 0.007858 1.4465% 1924 125.445453 0.007972 1.7700% 1923 123.263720 0.008113 1.6165% 1922 121.302836 0.008244 1.3736% 1921 119.659144 0.008357 2.3393% 1920 116.923929 0.008553 1.3140% 1919 115.407465 0.008665 0.7676% 1918 114.528296 0.008731 0.3870% 1917 114.086793 0.008765 1.3274% 1916 112.592204 0.008882 1.4083% 1915 111.028600 0.009007 1.4458% 1914 109.446223 0.009137 1.9424% 1913 107.360866 0.009314 1.9857% 1912 105.270539 0.009499 1.5634% 1911 103.650066 0.009648 1.8169% 1910 101.800437 0.009823 1.8781% 1909 99.923807 0.010008 2.0082% 1908 97.956603 0.010209 1.9603% 1907 96.073322 0.010409 1.8264% 1906 94.350155 0.010599 1.9357% 1905 92.558525 0.010804 2.0148% 1904 90.730455 0.011022 2.1335% 1903 88.835134 0.011257 1.8151% 1902 87.251390 0.011461 1.8943% 1901 85.629273 0.011678 3.0255% 1900 83.114640 0.012032 0.6278% 1899 82.596069 0.012107 1.7757% 1898 81.155035 0.012322 1.8078% 1897 79.714002 0.012545 1.8396% 1896 78.274072 0.012776 1.8755% 1895 76.833039 0.013015 1.9114% 1894 75.392005 0.013264 1.9486% 1893 73.950972 0.013522 1.9858% 1892 72.511042 0.013791 2.0276% 1891 71.070009 0.014071 2.6465% 1890 69.237624 0.014443 1.5328% 1889 68.192359 0.014664 2.0811% 1888 66.802120 0.014970 2.1599% 1887 65.389797 0.015293 2.2075% 1886 63.977473 0.015631 2.2592% 1885 62.564046 0.015984 2.3095% 1884 61.151723 0.016353 2.3641% 1883 59.739399 0.016739 2.4214% 1882 58.327076 0.017145 2.4815% 1881 56.914753 0.017570 3.7644% 1880 54.849982 0.018232 0.9432% 1879 54.337456 0.018404 2.1464% 1878 53.195671 0.018799 2.1913% 1877 52.054991 0.019210 2.2426% 1876 50.913207 0.019641 2.2941% 1875 49.771422 0.020092 2.3456% 1874 48.630742 0.020563 2.4043% 1873 47.488958 0.021058 2.4635% 1872 46.347173 0.021576 2.5258% 1871 45.205389 0.022121 5.9947% 1870 42.648736 0.023447 -1.0968% 1869 43.121687 0.023190 2.1930% 1868 42.196334 0.023699 2.2394% 1867 41.272085 0.024229 2.2935% 1866 40.346731 0.024785 2.3445% 1865 39.422482 0.025366 2.4037% 1864 38.497129 0.025976 2.4599% 1863 37.572880 0.026615 2.5250% 1862 36.647527 0.027287 2.5872% 1861 35.723277 0.027993 2.9504% 1860 34.699501 0.028819 2.4012% 1859 33.885822 0.029511 2.7627% 1858 32.974823 0.030326 2.8412% 1857 32.063825 0.031188 2.9243% 1856 31.152827 0.032100 3.0161% 1855 30.240724 0.033068 3.1061% 1854 29.329726 0.034095 3.2056% 1853 28.418728 0.035188 3.3118% 1852 27.507730 0.036353 3.4252% 1851 26.596731 0.037599 4.0106% 1850 25.571173 0.039107 3.2254% 1849 24.990062 0.040016 2.7841% 1848 24.313163 0.041130 2.8590% 1847 23.637367 0.042306 2.9432% 1846 22.961572 0.043551 3.0324% 1845 22.285777 0.044872 3.1325% 1844 21.608878 0.046277 3.2284% 1843 20.933083 0.047771 3.3361% 1842 20.257288 0.049365 3.4512% 1841 19.581493 0.051069 3.8105% 1840 18.862731 0.053015 2.3861% 1839 18.423145 0.054280 2.5824% 1838 17.959364 0.055681 2.6573% 1837 17.494479 0.057161 2.7232% 1836 17.030698 0.058717 2.7994% 1835 16.566917 0.060361 2.8871% 1834 16.102032 0.062104 2.9657% 1833 15.638251 0.063946 3.0563% 1832 15.174470 0.065900 3.1604% 1831 14.709585 0.067983 3.4660% 1830 14.216834 0.070339 2.4653% 1829 13.874779 0.072073 2.6804% 1828 13.512588 0.074005 10.3427% 1827 12.246025 0.081659 -4.2314% 1826 12.787102 0.078204 2.9150% 1825 12.424912 0.080483 3.0026% 1824 12.062721 0.082900 3.0955% 1823 11.700530 0.085466 3.1944% 1822 11.338339 0.088196 3.3102% 1821 10.975044 0.091116 3.2277% 1820 10.631875 0.094057 2.6573% 1819 10.356670 0.096556 2.6261% 1818 10.091652

0.099092 2.6969% 1817 9.826634 0.101764 2.7717% 1816 9.561617 0.104585 2.8507% 1815
9.296599 0.107566 2.9343% 1814 9.031581 0.110723 3.0231% 1813 8.766564 0.114070
3.1039% 1812 8.502650 0.117610 3.2172% 1811 8.237633 0.121394 3.0969% 1810 7.990183
0.125154 2.9144% 1809 7.763913 0.128801 2.8225% 1808 7.550795 0.132436 2.9199% 1807
7.336572 0.136303 2.9918% 1806 7.123454 0.140381 3.0841% 1805 6.910336 0.144711
3.1822% 1804 6.697217 0.149316 3.2868% 1803 6.484099 0.154223 3.3985% 1802 6.270981
0.159465 3.5180% 1801 6.057862 0.165075 3.3999% 1800 5.858670 0.170687 2.8419% 1799
5.696776 0.175538 2.7485% 1798 5.544390 0.180362 2.8261% 1797 5.392005 0.185460
3.7832% 1796 5.195451 0.192476 2.1272% 1795 5.087235 0.196570 3.0879% 1794 4.934850
0.202640 3.1625% 1793 4.783569 0.209049 3.2904% 1792 4.631184 0.215928 3.4024% 1791
4.478799 0.223274 3.2296% 1790 4.338678 0.230485 41.3145% 1780 3.070230 0.325709
29.4353% 1770 2.372019 0.421582 83.4728% 1750 1.292845 0.773488 29.2845% 1740
1.000000 1.000000 94.2514% 1720 0.514797 1.942514 85.8111% 1700 0.277054 3.609406
19.2490% 1690 0.232332 4.304183 88.0250% 1670 0.123564 8.092940

BASE YEAR: 1720

YEAR BYEAR/AYEAR AYEAR/BYEAR GROWTH%

2009 646.568745 0.001547 8.2857% 2001 597.095450 0.001675 1.0000% 2000
591.183552 0.001692 1.0000% 1999 585.330249 0.001708 1.0000% 1998 579.534899
0.001726 1.0000% 1997 573.796931 0.001743 1.0000% 1996 568.115772 0.001760 1.0000%
1995 562.490862 0.001778 0.9992% 1994 556.925937 0.001796 1.0008% 1993 551.407572
0.001814 1.0000% 1992 545.948091 0.001832 0.9295% 1991 540.920206 0.001849 1.2505%
1990 534.239459 0.001872 0.7224% 1989 530.407550 0.001885 1.1077% 1988 524.596740
0.001906 0.8834% 1987 520.003218 0.001923 0.5594% 1986 517.110682 0.001934 1.3056%
1985 510.446160 0.001959 0.7673% 1984 506.559417 0.001974 0.8149% 1983 502.464607
0.001990 0.9737% 1982 497.619048 0.002010 0.9508% 1981 492.932218 0.002029 0.9031%
1980 488.520556 0.002047 2.2701% 1979 477.676963 0.002093 1.0042% 1978 472.927928
0.002114 0.9896% 1977 468.293651 0.002135 0.9103% 1976 464.069069 0.002155 0.8394%
1975 460.205920 0.002173 0.9042% 1974 456.082154 0.002193 1.1568% 1973 450.866581
0.002218 0.9427% 1972 446.655942 0.002239 0.7426% 1971 443.363363 0.002255 1.4697%
1970 436.941471 0.002289 0.6968% 1969 433.917846 0.002305 0.8565% 1968 430.232733
0.002324 1.5090% 1967 423.836873 0.002359 0.9949% 1966 419.661626 0.002383 1.0575%
1965 415.270270 0.002408 1.1300% 1964 410.630094 0.002435 1.5537% 1963 404.347919
0.002473 1.4658% 1962 398.506542 0.002509 1.5364% 1961 392.476405 0.002548 2.1586%
1960 384.183273 0.002603 -1.6655% 1959 390.690154 0.002560 4.3080% 1958 374.554376
0.002670 2.1130% 1957 366.803947 0.002726 1.9895% 1956 359.648756 0.002780 2.1231%
1955 352.171815 0.002840 1.4496% 1954 347.139640 0.002881 2.1573% 1953 339.809095
0.002943 1.2298% 1952 335.681038 0.002979 1.6814% 1951 330.130309 0.003029 1.6233%
1950 324.856993 0.003078 1.4265% 1949 320.287967 0.003122 1.7790% 1948 314.689511
0.003178 1.8242% 1947 309.051909 0.003236 -2.6320% 1946 317.406156 0.003151 3.1768%
1945 307.633258 0.003251 6.4754% 1944 288.924213 0.003461 -0.3437% 1943 289.920601
0.003449 0.6562% 1942 288.030478 0.003472 0.6633% 1941 286.132561 0.003495 -5.6614%
1940 303.303891 0.003297 8.0381% 1939 280.737881 0.003562 0.8126% 1938 278.474903
0.003591 0.7762% 1937 276.329901 0.003619 0.6029% 1936 274.673960 0.003641 0.5244%
1935 273.241098 0.003660 -3.0364% 1934 281.797512 0.003549 4.6271% 1933 269.335049
0.003713 1.3921% 1932 265.637066 0.003765 -0.2051% 1931 266.182969 0.003757 0.8886%
1930 263.838505 0.003790 1.0126% 1929 261.193694 0.003829 1.1526% 1928 258.217503
0.003873 1.2160% 1927 255.115294 0.003920 1.4086% 1926 251.571701 0.003975 1.7667%
1925 247.204376 0.004045 1.4465% 1924 243.679541 0.004104 1.7700% 1923 239.441495
0.004176 1.6165% 1922 235.632450 0.004244 1.3736% 1921 232.439556 0.004302 2.3393%
1920 227.126362 0.004403 1.3140% 1919 224.180609 0.004461 0.7676% 1918 222.472812
0.004495 0.3870% 1917 221.615187 0.004512 1.3274% 1916 218.711926 0.004572 1.4083%
1915 215.674603 0.004637 1.4458% 1914 212.600815 0.004704 1.9424% 1913 208.549979
0.004795 1.9857% 1912 204.489489 0.004890 1.5634% 1911 201.341699 0.004967 1.8169%
1910 197.748769 0.005057 1.8781% 1909 194.103389 0.005152 2.0082% 1908 190.282068
0.005255 1.9603% 1907 186.623767 0.005358 1.8264% 1906 183.276491 0.005456 1.9357%
1905 179.796225 0.005562 2.0148% 1904 176.245174 0.005674 2.1335% 1903 172.563486

0.005795 1.8151% 1902 169.487042 0.005900 1.8943% 1901 166.336057 0.006012 3.0255%
1900 161.451347 0.006194 0.6278% 1899 160.444015 0.006233 1.7757% 1898 157.644788
0.006343 1.8078% 1897 154.845560 0.006458 1.8396% 1896 152.048477 0.006577 1.8755%
1895 149.249249 0.006700 1.9114% 1894 146.450021 0.006828 1.9486% 1893 143.650794
0.006961 1.9858% 1892 140.853711 0.007100 2.0276% 1891 138.054483 0.007244 2.6465%
1890 134.495049 0.007435 1.5328% 1889 132.464607 0.007549 2.0811% 1888 129.764050
0.007706 2.1599% 1887 127.020592 0.007873 2.2075% 1886 124.277134 0.008047 2.2592%
1885 121.531532 0.008228 2.3095% 1884 118.788074 0.008418 2.3641% 1883 116.044616
0.008617 2.4214% 1882 113.301158 0.008826 2.4815% 1881 110.557701 0.009045 3.7644%
1880 106.546855 0.009386 0.9432% 1879 105.551266 0.009474 2.1464% 1878 103.333333
0.009677 2.1913% 1877 101.117546 0.009889 2.2426% 1876 98.899614 0.010111 2.2941%
1875 96.681682 0.010343 2.3456% 1874 94.465894 0.010586 2.4043% 1873 92.247962
0.010840 2.4635% 1872 90.030030 0.011107 2.5258% 1871 87.812098 0.011388 5.9947%
1870 82.845764 0.012071 -1.0968% 1869 83.764479 0.011938 2.1930% 1868 81.966967
0.012200 2.2394% 1867 80.171600 0.012473 2.2935% 1866 78.374088 0.012759 2.3445%
1865 76.578722 0.013058 2.4037% 1864 74.781210 0.013372 2.4599% 1863 72.985843
0.013701 2.5250% 1862 71.188331 0.014047 2.5872% 1861 69.392964 0.014411 2.9504%
1860 67.404264 0.014836 2.4012% 1859 65.823681 0.015192 2.7627% 1858 64.054054
0.015612 2.8412% 1857 62.284427 0.016055 2.9243% 1856 60.514801 0.016525 3.0161%
1855 58.743029 0.017023 3.1061% 1854 56.973402 0.017552 3.2056% 1853 55.203775
0.018115 3.3118% 1852 53.434148 0.018715 3.4252% 1851 51.664522 0.019356 4.0106%
1850 49.672360 0.020132 2.3254% 1849 48.543544 0.020600 2.7841% 1848 47.228657
0.021174 2.8590% 1847 45.915916 0.021779 2.9432% 1846 44.603175 0.022420 3.0324%
1845 43.290433 0.023100 3.1325% 1844 41.975547 0.023823 3.2284% 1843 40.662806
0.024592 3.3361% 1842 39.350064 0.025413 3.4512% 1841 38.037323 0.026290 3.8105%
1840 36.641118 0.027292 2.3861% 1839 35.787216 0.027943 2.5824% 1838 34.886315
0.028665 2.6573% 1837 33.983269 0.029426 2.7232% 1836 33.082368 0.030228 2.7994%
1835 32.181467 0.031074 2.8871% 1834 31.278421 0.031971 2.9657% 1833 30.377520
0.032919 3.0563% 1832 29.476619 0.033925 3.1604% 1831 28.573574 0.034997 3.4660%
1830 27.616399 0.036210 2.4653% 1829 26.951952 0.037103 2.6804% 1828 26.248391
0.038098 10.3427% 1827 23.788074 0.042038 -4.2314% 1826 24.839125 0.040259 2.9150%
1825 24.135564 0.041433 3.0026% 1824 23.432003 0.042677 3.0955% 1823 22.728443
0.043998 3.1944% 1822 22.024882 0.045403 3.3102% 1821 21.319176 0.046906 3.2277%
1820 20.652565 0.048420 2.6573% 1819 20.117975 0.049707 2.6261% 1818 19.603175
0.051012 2.6969% 1817 19.088374 0.052388 2.7717% 1816 18.573574 0.053840 2.8507%
1815 18.058773 0.055375 2.9343% 1814 17.543973 0.057000 3.0231% 1813 17.029172
0.058723 3.1039% 1812 16.516517 0.060545 3.2172% 1811 16.001716 0.062493 3.0969%
1810 15.521042 0.064429 2.9144% 1809 15.081510 0.066306 2.8225% 1808 14.667525
0.068178 2.9199% 1807 14.251394 0.070169 2.9918% 1806 13.837409 0.072268 3.0841%
1805 13.423423 0.074497 3.1822% 1804 13.009438 0.076867 3.2868% 1803 12.595453
0.079394 3.3985% 1802 12.181467 0.082092 3.5180% 1801 11.767482 0.084980 3.3999%
1800 11.380549 0.087869 2.8419% 1799 11.066066 0.090366 2.7485% 1798 10.770056
0.092850 2.8261% 1797 10.474045 0.095474 3.7832% 1796 10.092235 0.099086 2.1272%
1795 9.882025 0.101194 3.0879% 1794 9.586015 0.104319 3.1625% 1793 9.292149 0.107618
3.2904% 1792 8.996139 0.111159 3.4024% 1791 8.700129 0.114941 3.2296% 1790 8.427943
0.118653 41.3145% 1780 5.963964 0.167674 29.4353% 1770 4.607679 0.217029 83.4728%
1750 2.511369 0.398189 29.2845% 1740 1.942514 0.514797 94.2514% 1720 1.000000
1.000000 85.8111% 1700 0.538181 1.858111 19.2490% 1690 0.451308 2.215779 88.0250%
1670 0.240026 4.166220

BASE YEAR: 1700

YEAR BYEAR/AYEAR AYEAR/BYEAR GROWTH%

2009 1201.396369 0.000832 8.2857% 2001 1109.469506 0.000901 1.0000% 2000
1098.484544 0.000910 1.0000% 1999 1087.608458 0.000919 1.0000% 1998 1076.840056
0.000929 1.0000% 1997 1066.178274 0.000938 1.0000% 1996 1055.622053 0.000947
1.0000% 1995 1045.170347 0.000957 0.9992% 1994 1034.830100 0.000966 1.0008% 1993
1024.576365 0.000976 1.0000% 1992 1014.432045 0.000986 0.9295% 1991 1005.089677

343

0.000995 1.2505% 1990 992.676110 0.001007 0.7224% 1989 985.555998 0.001015 1.1077%
1988 974.758868 0.001026 0.8834% 1987 966.223595 0.001035 0.5594% 1986 960.848944
0.001041 1.3056% 1985 948.465524 0.001054 0.7673% 1984 941.243523 0.001062 0.8149%
1983 933.634914 0.001071 0.9737% 1982 924.631327 0.001082 0.9508% 1981 915.922678
0.001092 0.9031% 1980 907.725321 0.001102 2.2701% 1979 887.576724 0.001127 1.0042%
1978 878.752491 0.001138 0.9896% 1977 870.141491 0.001149 0.9103% 1976 862.291750
0.001160 0.8394% 1975 855.113591 0.001169 0.9042% 1974 847.451176 0.001180 1.1568%
1973 837.760064 0.001194 0.9427% 1972 829.936230 0.001205 0.7426% 1971 823.818254
0.001214 1.4697% 1970 811.885668 0.001232 0.6968% 1969 806.267437 0.001240 0.8565%
1968 799.420088 0.001251 1.5090% 1967 787.535871 0.001270 0.9949% 1966 779.777800
0.001282 1.0575% 1965 771.618175 0.001296 1.1300% 1964 762.996214 0.001311 1.5537%
1963 751.323236 0.001331 1.4658% 1962 740.469310 0.001350 1.5364% 1961 729.264647
0.001371 2.1586% 1960 713.855090 0.001401 -1.6655% 1959 725.945596 0.001378 4.3080%
1958 695.963531 0.001437 2.1130% 1957 681.562375 0.001467 1.9895% 1956 668.267238
0.001496 2.1231% 1955 654.374253 0.001528 1.4496% 1954 645.023914 0.001550 2.1573%
1953 631.402949 0.001584 1.2298% 1952 623.732563 0.001603 1.6814% 1951 613.418693
0.001630 1.6233% 1950 603.620287 0.001657 1.4265% 1949 595.130530 0.001680 1.7790%
1948 584.727979 0.001710 1.8242% 1947 574.252690 0.001741 -2.6320% 1946 589.775807
0.001696 3.1768% 1945 571.616680 0.001749 6.4754% 1944 536.853200 0.001863 -0.3437%
1943 538.704599 0.001856 0.6562% 1942 535.192543 0.001868 0.6633% 1941 531.666002
0.001881 -5.6614% 1940 563.572236 0.001774 8.0381% 1939 521.642088 0.001917 0.8126%
1938 517.437226 0.001933 0.7762% 1937 513.451574 0.001948 0.6029% 1936 510.374651
0.001959 0.5244% 1935 507.712236 0.001970 -3.0364% 1934 523.611000 0.001910 4.6271%
1933 500.454364 0.001998 1.3921% 1932 493.583101 0.002026 -0.2051% 1931 494.597449
0.002022 0.8886% 1930 490.241176 0.002040 1.0126% 1929 485.326823 0.002060 1.1526%
1928 479.796732 0.002084 1.2160% 1927 474.032483 0.002110 1.4086% 1926 467.448095
0.002139 1.7667% 1925 459.333121 0.002177 1.4465% 1924 452.783587 0.002209 1.7700%
1923 444.908828 0.002248 1.6165% 1922 437.831200 0.002284 1.3736% 1921 431.898450
0.002315 2.3393% 1920 422.025947 0.002370 1.3140% 1919 416.552411 0.002401 0.7676%
1918 413.379135 0.002419 0.3870% 1917 411.785572 0.002428 1.3274% 1916 406.390992
0.002461 1.4083% 1915 400.747310 0.002495 1.4458% 1914 395.035871 0.002531 1.9424%
1913 387.508968 0.002581 1.9857% 1912 379.964129 0.002632 1.5634% 1911 374.115185
0.002673 1.8169% 1910 367.439123 0.002722 1.8781% 1909 360.665604 0.002773 2.0082%
1908 353.565165 0.002828 1.9603% 1907 346.767637 0.002884 1.8264% 1906 340.548027
0.002936 1.9357% 1905 334.081307 0.002993 2.0148% 1904 327.483061 0.003054 2.1335%
1903 320.642077 0.003119 1.8151% 1902 314.925703 0.003175 1.8943% 1901 309.070825
0.003236 3.0255% 1900 299.994492 0.003333 0.6278% 1899 298.122758 0.003354 1.7757%
1898 292.921483 0.003414 1.8078% 1897 287.720207 0.003476 1.8396% 1896 282.522917
0.003540 1.8755% 1895 277.321642 0.003606 1.9114% 1894 272.120367 0.003675 1.9486%
1893 266.919091 0.003746 1.9858% 1892 261.721802 0.003821 2.0276% 1891 256.520526
0.003898 2.6465% 1890 249.906704 0.004001 1.5328% 1889 246.133918 0.004063 2.0811%
1888 241.115982 0.004147 2.1599% 1887 236.018334 0.004237 2.2075% 1886 230.920686
0.004330 2.2592% 1885 225.819051 0.004428 2.3095% 1884 220.721403 0.004531 2.3641%
1883 215.623754 0.004638 2.4214% 1882 210.526106 0.004750 2.4815% 1881 205.428458
0.004868 3.7644% 1880 197.975863 0.005051 0.9432% 1879 196.125947 0.005099 2.1464%
1878 192.004783 0.005208 2.1913% 1877 187.887605 0.005322 2.2426% 1876 183.766441
0.005442 2.2941% 1875 179.645277 0.005567 2.3456% 1874 175.528099 0.005697 2.4043%
1873 171.406935 0.005834 2.4635% 1872 167.285771 0.005978 2.5258% 1871 163.164607
0.006129 5.9947% 1870 153.936608 0.006496 -1.0968% 1869 155.643683 0.006425 2.1930%
1868 152.303707 0.006566 2.2394% 1867 148.967716 0.006713 2.2935% 1866 145.627740
0.006867 2.3445% 1865 142.291750 0.007028 2.4037% 1864 138.951774 0.007197 2.4599%
1863 135.615783 0.007374 2.5250% 1862 132.275807 0.007560 2.5872% 1861 128.939817
0.007756 2.9504% 1860 125.244591 0.007984 2.4012% 1859 122.307692 0.008176 2.7627%
1858 119.019530 0.008402 2.8412% 1857 115.731367 0.008641 2.9243% 1856 112.443204
0.008893 3.0161% 1855 109.151056 0.009162 3.1061% 1854 105.862894 0.009446 3.2056%
1853 102.574731 0.009749 3.3118% 1852 99.286568 0.010072 3.4252% 1851 95.998406

0.010417 4.0106% 1850 92.296748 0.010835 2.3254% 1849 90.199283 0.011087 2.7841%
1848 87.756078 0.011395 2.8590% 1847 85.316859 0.011721 2.9432% 1846 82.877640
0.012066 3.0324% 1845 80.438422 0.012432 3.1325% 1844 77.995217 0.012821 3.2284%
1843 75.555998 0.013235 3.3361% 1842 73.116780 0.013677 3.4512% 1841 70.677561
0.014149 3.8105% 1840 68.083256 0.014688 2.3861% 1839 66.496612 0.015038 2.5824%
1838 64.822639 0.015427 2.6573% 1837 63.144679 0.015837 2.7232% 1836 61.470705
0.016268 2.7994% 1835 59.796732 0.016723 2.8871% 1834 58.118772 0.017206 2.9657%
1833 56.444799 0.017716 3.0563% 1832 54.770825 0.018258 3.1604% 1831 53.092866
0.018835 3.4660% 1830 51.314328 0.019488 2.4653% 1829 50.079713 0.019968 2.6804%
1828 48.772419 0.020503 10.3427% 1827 44.200877 0.022624 -4.2314% 1826 46.153846
0.021667 2.9150% 1825 44.846552 0.022298 3.0026% 1824 43.539259 0.022968 3.0955%
1823 42.231965 0.023679 3.1944% 1822 40.924671 0.024435 3.3102% 1821 39.613392
0.025244 3.2277% 1820 38.374755 0.026059 2.6573% 1819 37.381427 0.026751 2.6261%
1818 36.424870 0.027454 2.6969% 1817 35.468314 0.028194 2.7717% 1816 34.511758
0.028976 2.8507% 1815 33.555201 0.029802 2.9343% 1814 32.598645 0.030676 3.0231%
1813 31.642088 0.031603 3.1039% 1812 30.689518 0.032584 3.2172% 1811 29.732961
0.033633 3.0969% 1810 28.839817 0.034674 2.9144% 1809 28.023117 0.035685 2.8225%
1808 27.253886 0.036692 2.9199% 1807 26.480670 0.037763 2.9918% 1806 25.711439
0.038893 3.0841% 1805 24.942208 0.040093 3.1822% 1804 24.172977 0.041369 3.2868%
1803 23.403747 0.042728 3.3985% 1802 22.634516 0.044180 3.5180% 1801 21.865285
0.045735 3.3999% 1800 21.146321 0.047290 2.8419% 1799 20.561977 0.048633 2.7485%
1798 20.011957 0.049970 2.8261% 1797 19.461937 0.051382 3.7832% 1796 18.752491
0.053326 2.1272% 1795 18.361897 0.054461 3.0879% 1794 17.811877 0.056142 3.1625%
1793 17.265843 0.057918 3.2904% 1792 16.715823 0.059824 3.4024% 1791 16.165803
0.061859 3.2296% 1790 15.660052 0.063857 41.3145% 1780 11.081706 0.090239 29.4353%
1770 8.561578 0.116801 83.4728% 1750 4.666401 0.214298 29.2845% 1740 3.609406
0.277054 94.2514% 1720 1.858111 0.538181 85.8111% 1700 1.000000 1.000000 19.2490%
1690 0.838581 1.192490 88.0250% 1670 0.445994 2.242181

BASE YEAR: 1690

YEAR BYEAR/AYEAR AYEAR/BYEAR GROWTH%

2009 1432.653750 0.000698 8.2857% 2001 1323.031839 0.000756 1.0000% 2000
1309.932376 0.000763 1.0000% 1999 1296.962747 0.000771 1.0000% 1998 1284.121530
0.000779 1.0000% 1997 1271.407457 0.000787 1.0000% 1996 1258.819263 0.000794
1.0000% 1995 1246.355703 0.000802 0.9992% 1994 1234.025057 0.000810 1.0008% 1993
1221.797576 0.000818 1.0000% 1992 1209.700570 0.000827 0.9295% 1991 1198.559886
0.000834 1.2505% 1990 1183.756825 0.000845 0.7224% 1989 1175.266160 0.000851
1.1077% 1988 1162.390684 0.000860 0.8834% 1987 1152.212452 0.000868 0.5594% 1986
1145.803232 0.000873 1.3056% 1985 1131.036122 0.000884 0.7673% 1984 1122.423954
0.000891 0.8149% 1983 1113.350760 0.000898 0.9737% 1982 1102.614068 0.000907
0.9508% 1981 1092.229087 0.000916 0.9031% 1980 1082.453817 0.000924 2.2701% 1979
1058.426806 0.000945 1.0042% 1978 1047.903992 0.000954 0.9896% 1977 1037.635456
0.000964 0.9103% 1976 1028.274715 0.000973 0.8394% 1975 1019.714829 0.000981
0.9042% 1974 1010.577471 0.000990 1.1568% 1973 999.020913 0.001001 0.9427% 1972
989.691065 0.001010 0.7426% 1971 982.395437 0.001018 1.4697% 1970 968.165941
0.001033 0.6968% 1969 961.466255 0.001040 0.8565% 1968 953.300856 0.001049 1.5090%
1967 939.129040 0.001065 0.9949% 1966 929.877614 0.001075 1.0575% 1965 920.147338
0.001087 1.1300% 1964 909.865732 0.001099 1.5537% 1963 895.945817 0.001116 1.4658%
1962 883.002614 0.001132 1.5364% 1961 869.641160 0.001150 2.1586% 1960 851.265409
0.001175 -1.6655% 1959 865.683222 0.001155 4.3080% 1958 829.929895 0.001205 2.1130%
1957 812.756654 0.001230 1.9895% 1956 796.902329 0.001255 2.1231% 1955 780.335076
0.001282 1.4496% 1954 769.184886 0.001300 2.1573% 1953 752.942015 0.001328 1.2298%
1952 743.795152 0.001344 1.6814% 1951 731.495960 0.001367 1.6233% 1950 719.811454
0.001389 1.4265% 1949 709.687500 0.001409 1.7790% 1948 697.282557 0.001434 1.8242%
1947 684.790875 0.001460 -2.6320% 1946 703.302044 0.001422 3.1768% 1945 681.647457
0.001467 6.4754% 1944 640.192338 0.001562 -0.3437% 1943 642.400114 0.001557 0.6562%
1942 638.212020 0.001567 0.6633% 1941 634.006654 0.001577 -5.6614% 1940 672.054534

0.001488 8.0381% 1939 622.053232 0.001608 0.8126% 1938 617.038973 0.001621 0.7762%
1937 612.286122 0.001633 0.6029% 1936 608.616920 0.001643 0.5244% 1935 605.442015
0.001652 -3.0364% 1934 624.401141 0.001602 4.6271% 1933 596.787072 0.001676 1.3921%
1932 588.593156 0.001699 -0.2051% 1931 589.802757 0.001695 0.8886% 1930 584.607942
0.001711 1.0126% 1929 578.747624 0.001728 1.1526% 1928 572.153042 0.001748 1.2160%
1927 565.279230 0.001769 1.4086% 1926 557.427410 0.001794 1.7667% 1925 547.750380
0.001826 1.4465% 1924 539.940124 0.001852 1.7700% 1923 530.549548 0.001885 1.6165%
1922 522.109544 0.001915 1.3736% 1921 515.034796 0.001942 2.3393% 1920 503.261930
0.001987 1.3140% 1919 496.734791 0.002013 0.7676% 1918 492.950689 0.002029 0.3870%
1917 491.050380 0.002036 1.3274% 1916 484.617395 0.002063 1.4083% 1915 477.887357
0.002093 1.4458% 1914 471.076521 0.002123 1.9424% 1913 462.100760 0.002164 1.9857%
1912 453.103612 0.002207 1.5634% 1911 446.128802 0.002242 1.8169% 1910 438.167662
0.002282 1.8781% 1909 430.090304 0.002325 2.0082% 1908 421.623099 0.002372 1.9603%
1907 413.517110 0.002418 1.8264% 1906 406.100285 0.002462 1.9357% 1905 398.388783
0.002510 2.0148% 1904 390.520437 0.002561 2.1335% 1903 382.362628 0.002615 1.8151%
1902 375.545908 0.002663 1.8943% 1901 368.564021 0.002713 3.0255% 1900 357.740580
0.002795 0.6278% 1899 355.508555 0.002813 1.7757% 1898 349.306084 0.002863 1.8078%
1897 343.103612 0.002915 1.8396% 1896 336.905894 0.002968 1.8755% 1895 330.703422
0.003024 1.9114% 1894 324.500951 0.003082 1.9486% 1893 318.298479 0.003142 1.9858%
1892 312.100760 0.003204 2.0276% 1891 305.898289 0.003269 2.6465% 1890 298.011369
0.003356 1.5328% 1889 293.512357 0.003407 2.0811% 1888 287.528517 0.003478 2.1599%
1887 281.449620 0.003553 2.2075% 1886 275.370722 0.003631 2.2592% 1885 269.287072
0.003714 2.3095% 1884 263.208175 0.003799 2.3641% 1883 257.129278 0.003889 2.4214%
1882 251.050380 0.003983 2.4815% 1881 244.971483 0.004082 3.7644% 1880 236.084335
0.004236 0.9432% 1879 233.878327 0.004276 2.1464% 1878 228.963878 0.004368 2.1913%
1877 224.054183 0.004463 2.2426% 1876 219.139734 0.004563 2.2941% 1875 214.225285
0.004668 2.3456% 1874 209.315589 0.004777 2.4043% 1873 204.401141 0.004892 2.4635%
1872 199.486692 0.005013 2.5258% 1871 194.572243 0.005139 5.9947% 1870 183.567942
0.005448 -1.0968% 1869 185.603612 0.005388 2.1930% 1868 181.620722 0.005506 2.2394%
1867 177.642586 0.005629 2.2935% 1866 173.659696 0.005758 2.3445% 1865 169.681559
0.005893 2.4037% 1864 165.698669 0.006035 2.4599% 1863 161.720532 0.006184 2.5250%
1862 157.737643 0.006340 2.5872% 1861 153.759506 0.006504 2.9504% 1860 149.352985
0.006696 2.4012% 1859 145.850760 0.006856 2.7627% 1858 141.929658 0.007046 2.8412%
1857 138.008555 0.007246 2.9243% 1856 134.087452 0.007458 3.0161% 1855 130.161597
0.007683 3.1061% 1854 126.240494 0.007921 3.2056% 1853 122.319392 0.008175 3.3118%
1852 118.398289 0.008446 3.4252% 1851 114.477186 0.008735 4.0106% 1850 110.062994
0.009086 2.3254% 1849 107.561787 0.009297 2.7841% 1848 104.648289 0.009556 2.8590%
1847 101.739544 0.009829 2.9432% 1846 98.830798 0.010118 3.0324% 1845 95.922053
0.010425 3.1325% 1844 93.008555 0.010752 3.2284% 1843 90.099810 0.011099 3.3361%
1842 87.191065 0.011469 3.4512% 1841 84.282319 0.011865 3.8105% 1840 81.188636
0.012317 2.3861% 1839 79.296578 0.012611 2.5824% 1838 77.300380 0.012937 2.6573%
1837 75.299430 0.013280 2.7232% 1836 73.303232 0.013642 2.7994% 1835 71.307034
0.014024 2.8871% 1834 69.306084 0.014429 2.9657% 1833 67.309886 0.014857 3.0563%
1832 65.313688 0.015311 3.1604% 1831 63.312738 0.015795 3.4660% 1830 61.191849
0.016342 2.4653% 1829 59.719582 0.016745 2.6804% 1828 58.160646 0.017194 10.3427%
1827 52.709125 0.018972 -4.2314% 1826 55.038023 0.018169 2.9150% 1825 53.479087
0.018699 3.0026% 1824 51.920152 0.019260 3.0955% 1823 50.361217 0.019857 3.1944%
1822 48.802281 0.020491 3.3102% 1821 47.238593 0.021169 3.2277% 1820 45.761530
0.021852 2.6573% 1819 44.576996 0.022433 2.6261% 1818 43.436312 0.023022 2.6969%
1817 42.295627 0.023643 2.7717% 1816 41.154943 0.024298 2.8507% 1815 40.014259
0.024991 2.9343% 1814 38.873574 0.025724 3.0231% 1813 37.732890 0.026502 3.1039%
1812 36.596958 0.027325 3.2172% 1811 35.456274 0.028204 3.0969% 1810 34.391207
0.029077 2.9144% 1809 33.417300 0.029925 2.8225% 1808 32.500000 0.030769 2.9199%
1807 31.577947 0.031668 2.9918% 1806 30.660646 0.032615 3.0841% 1805 29.743346
0.033621 3.1822% 1804 28.826046 0.034691 3.2868% 1803 27.908745 0.035831 3.3985%
1802 26.991445 0.037049 3.5180% 1801 26.074144 0.038352 3.3999% 1800 25.216787

346

0.039656 2.8419% 1799 24.519962 0.040783 2.7485% 1798 23.864068 0.041904 2.8261% 1797 23.208175 0.043088 3.7832% 1796 22.362167 0.044718 2.1272% 1795 21.896388 0.045670 3.0879% 1794 21.240494 0.047080 3.1625% 1793 20.589354 0.048569 3.2904% 1792 19.933460 0.050167 3.4024% 1791 19.277567 0.051874 3.2296% 1790 18.674463 0.053549 41.3145% 1780 13.214829 0.075673 29.4353% 1770 10.209601 0.097947 83.4728% 1750 5.564639 0.179706 29.2845% 1740 4.304183 0.232332 94.2514% 1720 2.215779 0.451308 85.8111% 1700 1.192490 0.838581 19.2490% 1690 1.000000 1.000000 88.0250% 1670 0.531844 1.880250

BASE YEAR: 1670

YEAR BYEAR/AYEAR AYEAR/BYEAR GROWTH%

2009 2693.747534 0.000371 8.2857% 2001 2487.630912 0.000402 1.0000% 2000 2463.000643 0.000406 1.0000% 1999 2438.614495 0.000410 1.0000% 1998 2414.469794 0.000414 1.0000% 1997 2390.564155 0.000418 1.0000% 1996 2366.895201 0.000422 1.0000% 1995 2343.460590 0.000427 0.9992% 1994 2320.275889 0.000431 1.0008% 1993 2297.285165 0.000435 1.0000% 1992 2274.539768 0.000440 0.9295% 1991 2253.592493 0.000444 1.2505% 1990 2225.759035 0.000449 0.7224% 1989 2209.794459 0.000453 1.1077% 1988 2185.585344 0.000458 0.8834% 1987 2166.447721 0.000462 0.5594% 1986 2154.396783 0.000464 1.3056% 1985 2126.630920 0.000470 0.7673% 1984 2110.437891 0.000474 0.8149% 1983 2093.378016 0.000478 0.9737% 1982 2073.190349 0.000482 0.9508% 1981 2053.663986 0.000487 0.9031% 1980 2035.284030 0.000491 2.2701% 1979 1990.107239 0.000502 1.0042% 1978 1970.321716 0.000508 0.9896% 1977 1951.014298 0.000513 0.9103% 1976 1933.413762 0.000517 0.8394% 1975 1917.319035 0.000522 0.9042% 1974 1900.138517 0.000526 1.1568% 1973 1878.409294 0.000532 0.9427% 1972 1860.866845 0.000537 0.7426% 1971 1847.149240 0.000541 1.4697% 1970 1820.394227 0.000549 0.6968% 1969 1807.797140 0.000553 0.8565% 1968 1792.444147 0.000558 1.5090% 1967 1765.797587 0.000566 0.9949% 1966 1748.402592 0.000572 1.0575% 1965 1730.107239 0.000578 1.1300% 1964 1710.775246 0.000585 1.5537% 1963 1684.602324 0.000594 1.4658% 1962 1660.265862 0.000602 1.5364% 1961 1635.142985 0.000612 2.1586% 1960 1600.591975 0.000625 -1.6655% 1959 1627.701072 0.000614 4.3080% 1958 1560.475871 0.000641 2.1130% 1957 1528.185880 0.000654 1.9895% 1956 1498.375782 0.000667 2.1231% 1955 1467.225201 0.000682 1.4496% 1954 1446.260054 0.000691 2.1573% 1953 1415.719392 0.000706 1.2298% 1952 1398.521001 0.000715 1.6814% 1951 1375.395442 0.000727 1.6233% 1950 1353.425648 0.000739 1.4265% 1949 1334.390080 0.000749 1.7790% 1948 1311.065684 0.000763 1.8242% 1947 1287.578195 0.000777 -2.6320% 1946 1322.383825 0.000756 3.1768% 1945 1281.667784 0.000780 6.4754% 1944 1203.721787 0.000831 -0.3437% 1943 1207.872958 0.000828 0.6562% 1942 1199.998293 0.000833 0.6633% 1941 1192.091153 0.000839 -5.6614% 1940 1263.630688 0.000791 8.0381% 1939 1169.615728 0.000855 0.8126% 1938 1160.187668 0.000862 0.7762% 1937 1151.251117 0.000869 0.6029% 1936 1144.352100 0.000874 0.5244% 1935 1138.382484 0.000878 -3.0364% 1934 1174.030384 0.000852 4.6271% 1933 1122.109026 0.000891 1.3921% 1932 1106.702413 0.000904 -0.2051% 1931 1108.976765 0.000902 0.8886% 1930 1099.209214 0.000910 1.0126% 1929 1088.190349 0.000919 1.1526% 1928 1075.790885 0.000930 1.2160% 1927 1062.866399 0.000941 1.4086% 1926 1048.103012 0.000954 1.7667% 1925 1029.907775 0.000971 1.4465% 1924 1015.222538 0.000985 1.7700% 1923 997.565907 0.001002 1.6165% 1922 981.696586 0.001019 1.3736% 1921 968.394290 0.001033 2.3393% 1920 946.258356 0.001057 1.3140% 1919 933.985702 0.001071 0.7676% 1918 926.870643 0.001079 0.3870% 1917 923.297587 0.001083 1.3274% 1916 911.201966 0.001097 1.4083% 1915 898.547811 0.001113 1.4458% 1914 885.741734 0.001129 1.9424% 1913 868.865058 0.001151 1.9857% 1912 851.948168 0.001174 1.5634% 1911 838.833780 0.001192 1.8169% 1910 823.864844 0.001214 1.8781% 1909 808.677391 0.001237 2.0082% 1908 792.756926 0.001261 1.9603% 1907 777.515639 0.001286 1.8264% 1906 763.570152 0.001310 1.9357% 1905 749.070599 0.001335 2.0148% 1904 734.276139 0.001362 2.1335% 1903 718.937417 0.001391 1.8151% 1902 706.120277 0.001416 1.8943% 1901 692.992583 0.001443 3.0255% 1900 672.641805 0.001487 0.6278% 1899 668.445040 0.001496 1.7757% 1898 656.782842 0.001523 1.8078% 1897 645.120643 0.001550 1.8396% 1896 633.467382 0.001579 1.8755% 1895 621.805183 0.001608 1.9114% 1894 610.142985 0.001639 1.9486%

1893 598.480786 0.001671 1.9858% 1892 586.827525 0.001704 2.0276% 1891 575.165326
0.001739 2.6465% 1890 560.335943 0.001785 1.5328% 1889 551.876676 0.001812 2.0811%
1888 540.625559 0.001850 2.1599% 1887 529.195710 0.001890 2.2075% 1886 517.765862
0.001931 2.2592% 1885 506.327078 0.001975 2.3095% 1884 494.897230 0.002021 2.3641%
1883 483.467382 0.002068 2.4214% 1882 472.037534 0.002118 2.4815% 1881 460.607685
0.002171 3.7644% 1880 443.897623 0.002253 0.9432% 1879 439.749777 0.002274 2.1464%
1878 430.509383 0.002323 2.1913% 1877 421.277927 0.002374 2.2426% 1876 412.037534
0.002427 2.2941% 1875 402.797140 0.002483 2.3456% 1874 393.565684 0.002541 2.4043%
1873 384.325290 0.002602 2.4635% 1872 375.084897 0.002666 2.5258% 1871 365.844504
0.002733 5.9947% 1870 345.153664 0.002897 -1.0968% 1869 348.981233 0.002865 2.1930%
1868 341.492404 0.002928 2.2394% 1867 334.012511 0.002994 2.2935% 1866 326.523682
0.003063 2.3445% 1865 319.043789 0.003134 2.4037% 1864 311.554960 0.003210 2.4599%
1863 304.075067 0.003289 2.5250% 1862 296.586238 0.003372 2.5872% 1861 289.106345
0.003459 2.9504% 1860 280.820983 0.003561 2.4012% 1859 274.235925 0.003646 2.7627%
1858 266.863271 0.003747 2.8412% 1857 259.490617 0.003854 2.9243% 1856 252.117962
0.003966 3.0161% 1855 244.736372 0.004086 3.1061% 1854 237.363718 0.004213 3.2056%
1853 229.991063 0.004348 3.3118% 1852 222.618409 0.004492 3.4252% 1851 215.245755
0.004646 4.0106% 1850 206.945970 0.004832 2.3254% 1849 202.243074 0.004945 2.7841%
1848 196.764969 0.005082 2.8590% 1847 191.295800 0.005228 2.9432% 1846 185.826631
0.005381 3.0324% 1845 180.357462 0.005545 3.1325% 1844 174.879357 0.005718 3.2284%
1843 169.410188 0.005903 3.3361% 1842 163.941019 0.006100 3.4512% 1841 158.471850
0.006310 3.8105% 1840 152.654951 0.006551 2.3861% 1839 149.097408 0.006707 2.5824%
1838 145.344057 0.006880 2.6573% 1837 141.581769 0.007063 2.7232% 1836 137.828418
0.007255 2.7994% 1835 134.075067 0.007459 2.8871% 1834 130.312779 0.007674 2.9657%
1833 126.559428 0.007901 3.0563% 1832 122.806077 0.008143 3.1604% 1831 119.043789
0.008400 3.4660% 1830 115.055987 0.008691 2.4653% 1829 112.287757 0.008906 2.6804%
1828 109.356568 0.009144 10.3427% 1827 99.106345 0.010090 -4.2314% 1826 103.485255
0.009663 2.9150% 1825 100.554066 0.009945 3.0026% 1824 97.622878 0.010244 3.0955%
1823 94.691689 0.010561 3.1944% 1822 91.760500 0.010898 3.3102% 1821 88.820375
0.011259 3.2277% 1820 86.043128 0.011622 2.6573% 1819 83.815907 0.011931 2.6261%
1818 81.671135 0.012244 2.6969% 1817 79.526363 0.012574 2.7717% 1816 77.381591
0.012923 2.8507% 1815 75.236819 0.013291 2.9343% 1814 73.092046 0.013681 3.0231%
1813 70.947274 0.014095 3.1039% 1812 68.811439 0.014532 3.2172% 1811 66.666667
0.015000 3.0969% 1810 64.664075 0.015465 2.9144% 1809 62.832887 0.015915 2.8225%
1808 61.108132 0.016364 2.9199% 1807 59.374441 0.016842 2.9918% 1806 57.649687
0.017346 3.0841% 1805 55.924933 0.017881 3.1822% 1804 54.200179 0.018450 3.2868%
1803 52.475424 0.019057 3.3985% 1802 50.750670 0.019704 3.5180% 1801 49.025916
0.020397 3.3999% 1800 47.413870 0.021091 2.8419% 1799 46.103664 0.021690 2.7485%
1798 44.870420 0.022286 2.8261% 1797 43.637176 0.022916 3.7832% 1796 42.046470
0.023783 2.1272% 1795 41.170688 0.024289 3.0879% 1794 39.937444 0.025039 3.1625%
1793 38.713137 0.025831 3.2904% 1792 37.479893 0.026681 3.4024% 1791 36.246649
0.027589 3.2296% 1790 35.112663 0.028480 41.3145% 1780 24.847185 0.040246 29.4353%
1770 19.196604 0.052093 83.4728% 1750 10.462913 0.095576 29.2845% 1740 8.092940
0.123564 94.2514% 1720 4.166220 0.240026 85.8111% 1700 2.242181 0.445994 19.2490%
1690 1.880250 0.531844 88.0250% 1670 1.000000 1.000000

***Footnote #2

All dates other than multiples of 10 [census years] are official estimates

1991 7/1 252,177,000* 1991 252,688,000A 1990 249,415,000 1990 249,924,000A
1990 248,709,873 1989 246,820,000 1989 247,343,000A 1989 247,732,000 1988 244,534,000
1988 245,057,000A 1988 244,600,000 1987 242,651,000 1987 242,200,000 1986 241,077,000
1985 237,200,000 1985 238,740,000 1984 236,158,000 1983 234,249,000 1982 231,990,000
1981 229,805,000 1980 242,321,000 1980 240,162,000 1980 237,950,000 1980 235,847,000
1980 223,239,000 1980 233,806,000 1980 231,669,000 1980 229,457,000 1980 227,220,000
1980 242,836,000A 1980 240,680,000A 1980 238,492,000A 1980 236,370,000A 1980
234,321,000A 1980 232,192,000A 1980 229,958,000A 1980 227,722,000A 1980 226,545,805
1979 7/1 224,567,000 1979 7/1 225,055,000A 1979 220,819,000 1978 7/1 222,095,000 1978

348

7/1 222,585,000A 1978 218,863,000 1977 7/1 219,760,000 1977 7/1 220,239,000A 1977
216,877,000 1976 7/1 217,563,000 1976 7/1 218,035,000A 1976 215,135,000 1975 7/1
215,465,000 1975 7/1 215,973,000A 1975 213,631,000 1974 7/1 213,342,000 1974 7/1
213,854,000A 1974 211,909,000 1973 7/1 209,844,000 1973 7/1 210,396,000A 1973
210,544,000 1972 7/1 208,230,000 1972 7/1 208,842,000A 1972 208,232,000 1971 7/1
206,212,000 1971 7/1 207,045,000A 1971 207,180,000 1970 revised 203,235,298 1970 7/1
203,806,000 1970 7/1 204,875,000A 1970 203,810,000 1970 4/1 203,211,926 1970 4/1
204,765,770 1970 203,302,031 1969 201,385,000 1969 202,677,000A 1969 7/1 201,385,000
1969 7/1 202,677,000A 1969 203,200,000* 1968 199,399,000 1968 7/1 199,399,000 1968
7/1 200,706,000A 1968 200,706,000A 1968 201,750,000 1967 200,000,000* 1967 7/1
195,457,000 1967 7/1 198,712,000A 1967 198,712,000A 1967 197,457,000 1966 195,857,000
1966 7/1 195,576,000 1966 7/1 196,560,000A 1966 196,560,000A 1966 195,576,000 1965
7/1 193,526,000 1965 7/1 194,303,000A 1965 193,818,000 1965 194,303,000A 1965
193,526,000 1964 191,889,000A 1964 191,141,000 1964 192,320,000 1964 7/1 191,141,000
1964 7/1 191,889,000A 1963 189,242,000A 1963 188,483,000 1963 7/1 188,483,000 1963
7/1 189,242,000A 1963 188,531,000 1962 186,538,000A 1962 185,771,000 1962 185,822,000
1962 7/1 185,771,000 1962 7/1 186,538,000A 1961 182,992,000 1961 183,691,000A 1961
7/1 182,992,000 1961 7/1 183,691,000A 1961 182,953,000 7/1/61 est 1960 180,671,000A
1960 177,135,000 1960 4/1 178,464,236 1960 7/1 179,979,000 1960 7/1 180,671,000A 1960
4/1 179,323,175* 1959 177,830,000A 1959 177,073,000A 1959 196,289,000 1959
178,000,000* 1959 7/1 177,135,000 1959 7/1 177,830,000A 1958 174,171,000A 1958
173,320,000 1958 7/1 174,149,000 1958 7/1 174,882,000A 1958 175,500,000* 12/58 +
Alaska 1957 171,274,000A 1957 170,371,000 1957 7/1 171,187,000 1957 7/1 171,984,000A
1957 171,229,000 7/1/57 1956 167,191,000 7/1/56 1956 186,221,000A 1956 167,306,000
1956 7/1 168,088,000 1956 7/1 168,903,000A 1955 162,284,000 7/1/55 1955 165,275,000A
1955 164,308,000 1955 7/1 165,069,000 1955 7/1 165,931,000A 1954 162,414,000 7/1/54
1954 162,391,000A 1954 161,164,000 1954 7/1 161,884,000 1954 7/1 163,026,000A 1953
159,565,000A 1953 158,242,000 1953 ****below 1953 7/1 158,596,000 1953 7/1
160,184,000A 1952 157,505,000 9/1/52 1952 156,954,000A 1952 155,687,000 1952 7/1
156,393,000 1952 7/1 157,553,000A 1951 154,353,000 7/1/51 1951 154,287,000A 1951
153,310,000 1951 7/1 153,982,000 1951 7/1 154,878,000A 1950 154,233,000* 4/1/50
revised 1952 1950 4/1 150,697,361 1950 151,684,000A 1950 151,235,000 1950 150,697,361*
4/1/50 est* non est 1950 7/1 151,868,000 1950 7/1 152,271,000A 1950 4/1 151,325,798*
AL & HA 1949 149,188,000A 1949 148,665,000 1949 150,000,000 7/1/49+ 1949 7/1
149,767,000A 1949 7/1 149,304,000 1948 146,631,000A 1948 146,093,000 1948 147,280,000
10/1/48 rel on 12/9/48 1948 7/1 147,208,000A 1948 7/1 146,730,000 1947 144,708,000
1947 144,126,000A 1947 143,446,000 1947 7/1 144,698,000A 1947 7/1 144,083,000 1946
141,000,000 8/46 * 1946 141,389,000A 1946 140,054,000 1946 170,000,000 1946 7/1
141,936,000A 1946 7/1 140,686,000 1945 139,928,000A 1945 132,481,000 1945 140,000,000
11/20/45 1945 7/1 140,468,000A 1945 7/1 133,434,000 1945 152,000,000 inc possessions
1944 138,100,874 1/1/44 est 1944 138,397,000A 1944 132,855,000 1944 7/1 138,916,000A
1944 7/1 133,915,000 1943 136,739,000A 1943 134,245,000 1943 7/1 137,250,000A 1943
7/1 135,107,000 1943 135,645,969 1/1/43 est 1942 133,965,237 1/1/42 est 1942
134,860,000A 1942 133,920,000 1942 7/1 135,361,000A 1942 7/1 134,617,000 1941
133,403,000A 1941 133,121,000 1941 7/1 133,894,000A 1941 7/1 133,669,000 1940 7/1
132,594,000A 1940 4/1 131,669,275* 1940 132,122,000A 1940 131,954,000 1940 7/1
132,547,000 1940 4/1 150,621,231 inc possessions 1939 131,128,000A 1939 130,880,000
1939 7/1 130,880,000* 1938 129,969,000A 1938 129,825,000 1938 7/1 129,825,000* 1937
128,961,000A 1937 128,825,000 1937 7/1 128,825,000* 1936 128,181,000A 1936
128,053,000 1936 7/1 128,053,000* 1935 127,362,000A 1935 127,250,000 1935 7/1
127,520,000* 1934 126,485,000A 1934 126,374,000 1934 7/1 136,374,000* 1933 7/1
125,579,000* 1933 125,690,000A 1933 125,549,000 1932 7/1 122,840,000* 1932
124,949,000A 1932 124,840,000 1931 124,149,000A 1931 124,149,000 1931 7/1
124,040,000* 1930 4/1 122,775,046* 1930 123,188,000A 1930 123,077,000 1930 7/1
123,077,000* 1929 121,767,000 1929 7/1 121,770,000 1928 120,013,000 7/1/28 est 1928
120,509,000 1928 7/1 120,501,000 1927 118,628,000 7/1/27 est 1927 119,035,000 1927 7/1

119,038,000 1926 117,135,817 7/1/26 est 1926 117,136,000 7/1/26 est 1926 117,197,000 1926 7/1 117,399,000 1925 115,829,000 1925 113,493,720* 7/1/25 est 1925 7/1 115,832,000 1924 114,109,000 1924 112,078,611 7/1/24 est 1924 7/1 114,113,000 1923 110,663,502 7/1/23 est 1923 111,947,000 1923 7/1 111,950,000 1922 109,248,393 7/1/22 est 1922 110,049,000 1922 7/1 110,055,000 1921 107,833,284 7/1/21 est 1921 108,538,000 1921 7/1 108,541,000 1920 106,461,000 1920 7/1 106,466,000 1920 106,418,284 7/1/20 est 1920 105,683,108 10/7/20 Dir of Census Bureau 1920 1/1 105,710,620* 1919 104,514,000 1919 7/1 104,512,000* 1918 105,253,300 7/1/18 1918 103,208,000 1918 7/1 103,203,000* [WWI, * years exclude armed forces abroad] 1917 103,368,000 1917 7/1 103,266,000* 1916 7/1 101,966,000 1916 101,961,000 1915 100,546,000 1915 7/1 100,549,000 1914 99,111,000 1914 7/1 99,118,000 1913 97,225,000 1913 7/1 97,227,000 1912 95,335,000 1912 7/1 95,331,000 1911 93,863,000 1911 7/1 93,868,000 1910 4/15 91,109,542 4/15/10 1910 4/15 91,972,266* 1910 92,407,000 1910 add ~1.5M outside Continental US 1910 7/1 92,407,000 1909 90,490,000 1909 7/1 90,492,000 1908 7/1 88,709,000 1908 88,710,000 1907 87,008,000 1907 7/1 87,000,000 1906 85,450,000 1906 7/1 85,450,000*** 1906 7/1 85,437,000 1905 83,822,000 1905 7/1 83,822,000 1905 7/1 83,820,000 1904 82,166,000 1904 7/1 82,166,000 1904 7/1 82,165,000 1903* 79,900,389 est 1903 7/1 80,632,000* 1903 80,632,000 1902* 78,576,436 est 1902 79,163,000 1902 7/1 79,160,000 1901* 77,274,967 est 1901 77,584,000 1901 7/1 77,584,000 1901 7/1 77,585,000 1900 76,094,000 1900 7/1 76,094,000* 1900 4/15 74,610,523 1900 7/1 76,094,000* 1900 6/1 75,994,575* 1900 6/1 75,994,575* 1900 4/15 74,610,523 1899 74,799,000 1898 73,494,000 1897 72,189,000 1896 70,885,000 1895 69,580,000 1894 68,275,000 1893 66,970,000 1892 65,666,000 1891 64,361,000 1890 6/1 62,947,714* 1890 6/1 62,116,811 1890 63,056,000 1890 6/1 62,116,811 1890 6/1 62,947,714* 1889 61,755,000 1888 60,496,000 1887 59,217,000 1886 57,938,000 1885 56,658,000 1884 55,379,000 1883 54,100,000 1882 52,821,000 1881 51,542,000 1880 50,262,000 1880 6/1 50,155,783* 1880 6/1 49,371,340 1880 6/1 50,155,783* 1880 6/1 49,371,340 1879 49,208,000 1878 48,174,000 1877 47,141,000 1876 46,107,000 1875 45,073,000 1874 44,040,000 1873 43,006,000 1872 41,972,000 1871 40,938,000 1870 39,905,000 1870 6/1 38,155,505 1870 6/1 39,818,449 1870 6/1 39,818,449 1870 6/1 38,558,371* 1870 6/1 38,155,505 1869 39,051,000 1868 38,213,000 1867 37,376,000 1866 36,538,000 1865 35,701,000 1864 34,863,000 1863 34,026,000 1862 33,188,000 1861 32,351,000 1860 6/1 31,218,021 1860 6/1 31,218,021 1860 31,513,000 1860 6/1 31,443,321* 1860 6/1 31,443,321* 1859 30,687,000 1858 29,862,000 1857 29,037,000 1856 28,212,000 1855 27,386,000 1854 26,561,000 1853 25,736,000 1852 24,911,000 1851 24,086,000 1850 6/1 23,067,262 1850 23,261,000 1850 6/1 23,191,876* 1850 6/1 23,067,262 1850 6/1 23,191,876* 1849 22,631,000 1848 22,018,000 1847 21,406,000 1846 20,794,000 1845 20,182,000 1844 19,569,000 1843 18,957,000 1842 18,345,000 1841 17,733,000 1840 17,120,000 1840 6/1 17,069,453* 1840 6/1 17,069,453* 1839 16,684,000 1838 16,264,000 1837 15,843,000 1836 15,423,000 1835 15,003,000 1834 14,582,000 1833 14,162,000 1832 13,742,000 1831 13,321,000 1830 6/1 12,866,020* 1830 12,901,000 1830 6/1 12,866,020* 1829 12,565,000 1828 12,237,000 1827 11,090,000 1826 11,580,000 1825 11,252,000 1824 10,924,000 1823 10,596,000 1822 10,268,000 1821 9,939,000 1820 8/7 9,638,453* 1820 8/7 9,638,453* 1820 9,618,000 1819 9,379,000 1818 9,139,000 1817 8,899,000 1816 8,659,000 1815 8,419,000 1814 8,179,000 1813 7,939,000 1812 7,700,000 1811 7,460,000 1810 8/6 7,239,881* 1810 7,224,000 1810 8/6 7,239,881* 1809 7,031,000 1808 6,838,000 1807 6,644,000 1806 6,451,000 1805 6,258,000 1804 6,065,000 1803 5,872,000 1802 5,679,000 1801 5,486,000 1800 8/4 5,308,483* 1800 5,297,000 1800 8/4 5,308,483* 1799 5,159,000 1798 5,021,000 1797 4,883,000 1796 4,705,000 1795 4,607,000 1794 4,469,000 1793 4,332,000 1792 4,194,000 1791 4,056,000 1790 3,929,000 1790 8/2 3,929,214* 1780 2,780,400 1770 2,148,100 1750 1,170,800 1740 905,600 1720 466,200 1700 250,900 1690 210,400 1670 111,900 1650 50,400 1630 4,600

* indicates a figure has been found in multiple sources.

www.ingramcontent.com/pod-product-compliance
Lightning Source LLC
Chambersburg PA
CBHW070103290526
45789CB00005B/1910